Union Calendar No. 205

109th Congress
2nd Session

Report
109-377

A FAILURE OF INITIATIVE

Final Report of the Select Bipartisan Committee to Investigate the Preparation for and Response to Hurricane Katrina

Report by the
Select Bipartisan Committee
to Investigate the Preparation
for and Response
to Hurricane Katrina

Available via the World Wide Web: http://www.gpoaccess.gov/congress/index.html

February 15, 2006. — Committed to the Committee of the Whole House on the State of the Union and ordered to be printed

U.S. GOVERNMENT PRINTING OFFICE
Keeping America Informed I www.gpo.gov
WASHINGTON 2006

23950 PDF

For sale by the Superintendent of Documents, U.S. Government Printing Office
Internet: bookstore.gpo.gov Phone: toll free (866) 512-1800; DC area (202) 512-1800
Fax: (202) 512-2250 Mail: Stop SSOP, Washington, DC 20402-0001

COVER PHOTO: FEMA, BACKGROUND PHOTO: NASA

SELECT BIPARTISAN COMMITTEE
TO INVESTIGATE THE PREPARATION FOR AND RESPONSE
TO HURRICANE KATRINA

TOM DAVIS, (VA) Chairman

HAROLD ROGERS (KY)

CHRISTOPHER SHAYS (CT)

HENRY BONILLA (TX)

STEVE BUYER (IN)

SUE MYRICK (NC)

MAC THORNBERRY (TX)

KAY GRANGER (TX)

CHARLES W. "CHIP" PICKERING (MS)

BILL SHUSTER (PA)

JEFF MILLER (FL)

Members who participated at the invitation of the Select Committee

CHARLIE MELANCON (LA)

GENE TAYLOR (MS)

WILLIAM J. JEFFERSON (LA)

CYNTHIA MCKINNEY (GA)

SHELIA JACKSON-LEE (TX)

STAFF DESIGNATIONS

David L. Marin	Staff Director	Wimberly Fair	Professional Staff
J. Keith Ausbrook	Special Counsel	Chuck Turner	Special Investigator
Michael Geffroy	Deputy Special Counsel	Robert White	Press Secretary
Lawrence J. Halloran	Deputy Special Counsel	Drew Crockett	Art Editor
Robert Borden	Senior Associate Special Counsel	Teresa Austin	Chief Clerk
Daniel Mathews	Senior Professional Staff	Amy Laudeman	Deputy Clerk
Arthur Wu	Senior Professional Staff	Robin Butler	Administrative Officer/Financial Administrator
Thomas E. Hawley	Senior Professional Staff	Michael Sazonov	Staff Assistant
Grace A. Washbourne	Senior Professional Staff	Pat DeQuattro	Coast Guard Fellow
Kim Kotlar	Senior Professional Staff	Justin Swick	Law Clerk
Anne Marie Turner	Associate Special Counsel	Elizabeth Ryan	Law Clerk
Charles M. Phillips	Associate Special Counsel	Stephen L. Caldwell	GAO Detailee
Steve Castor	Assistant Special Counsel	Bill MacBlane	GAO Detailee
Kim Baronof	Professional Staff	Brooke Bennett	Research Assistant
Risa Salsburg	Professional Staff	Jay O'Callahan	Research Assistant
Susie Schulte	Professional Staff	Michael Arkush	Editorial Assistant
Shalley Kim	Professional Staff	Margaret Peterlin	Speaker's Designee

HOUSE OF REPRESENTATIVES,
Washington, DC, February 15, 2006.

Hon. J. Dennis Hastert,
Speaker of the House of Representatives,
Washington, DC.

DEAR MR. SPEAKER: By direction of the Select Bipartisan Committee to Investigate the Preparation for and Response to Hurricane Katrina, I submit herewith the committee's report to the 109th Congress.

Tom Davis,
Chairman.

"Pandemonium did not reign. It poured."

JOHN KENDRICK BANGS
American author and satirist

"Five frogs are sitting on a log. Four decide to jump off.
How many are left?
Answer: five.
Why? Because there's a difference between deciding and doing."

MARK L. FELDMAN and MICHAEL F. SPRATT
American businessmen
Five Frogs on a Log

"Don't find a fault. Find a remedy."

HENRY FORD
American automobile manufacturer

"Hurricane Katrina was a force of Nature.
What we've done after it is an Act of God."

Banner hanging in Harrison County, MS, Emergency Operations Center

In-i-tia-tive, *n.*
The power or ability to begin or follow through energetically with a plan or task;
enterprise and determination.

TABLE OF CONTENTS

109th Congress	House of Representatives	Report No.
2nd Session		109-377

February 15, 2006 — Comitted to the Committee of the Whole House on the state of the Union and ordered to be printed

———————————————

Mr. Tom Davis of Virginia, from the Select Bipartisan Committee to Investigate the Preparation for the Response to Hurricane Katrina submitted the following report:

Final Report of the Select Bipartisan Committee to Investigate the Preparation for and Response to Hurricane Katrina

PREFACE

On September 15, 2005, the House of Representatives approved H. Res. 437, which created the Select Bipartisan Committee to Investigate the Preparation for and Response to Hurricane Katrina ("the Select Committee").

According to the resolution, the Committee was charged with conducting "a full and complete investigation and study and to report its findings to the House not later than February 15, 2006, regarding— (1) the development, coordination, and execution by local, State, and Federal authorities of emergency response plans and other activities in preparation for Hurricane Katrina; and (2) the local, State, and Federal government response to Hurricane Katrina."

The Committee presents the report narrative and the findings that stem from it to the U.S. House of Representatives and the American people for their consideration. Members of the Select Committee agree unanimously with the report and its findings. Other Members of Congress who participated in the Select Committee's hearings and investigation but were not official members of the Select Committee, while concurring with a majority of the report's findings, have presented additional views as well, which we offer herein on their behalf.

First and foremost, this report is issued with our continued thoughts and prayers for Katrina's victims. Their families. Their friends. The loss of life, of property, of livelihoods and dreams has been enormous. And we salute all Americans who have stepped up to the plate to help in any way they can.

It has been said civilization is a race between education and catastrophe. With Katrina, we have had the catastrophe, and we are racing inexorably toward the next. Americans want to know: what have we learned?

Two months before the Committee was established, former Speaker of the House Newt Gingrich testified before a Government Reform subcommittee about the need to move the government to an "entrepreneurial" model and away from its current "bureaucratic" model, so that we can get government to move with Information Age speed and effectiveness.

"*Implementing* policy effectively," Speaker Gingrich said, "is ultimately as important as *making* the right policy."

The Select Committee first convened on September 22, 2005, understanding, like Speaker Gingrich, that a policy that cannot be implemented effectively is no policy at all.

The Select Committee was created because, in the tragic aftermath of Katrina, America was again confronted with the vast divide between policy creation and policy implementation. With the life-and-death difference between theory and practice.

The Select Committee has spent much of the past five months examining the aftermath of this catastrophic disaster. It has become increasingly clear that local, state, and federal government agencies failed to meet the needs of the residents of Louisiana, Mississippi, and Alabama. It has been our job to figure out why, and to make sure we are better prepared for the future.

Our mandate was clear: gather facts about the preparation for and response to Katrina, at all levels of government.

Investigate aggressively, follow the facts wherever they may lead, and find out what went right and what went wrong. Ask why coordination and information sharing between local, state, and federal governments was so dismal.

- Why situational awareness was so foggy, for so long.
- Why *all* residents, especially the most helpless, were not evacuated more quickly.
- Why supplies and equipment and support were so slow in arriving.
- Why so much taxpayer money aimed at better preparing and protecting the Gulf coast was left on the table, unspent or, in some cases, misspent.
- Why the adequacy of preparation and response seemed to vary significantly from state to state, county to county, town to town.
- Why unsubstantiated rumors and uncritically repeated press reports – at times fueled by top officials – were able to delay, disrupt, and diminish the response.
- And why government at all levels failed to react more effectively to a storm that was predicted with unprecedented timeliness and accuracy.

We agreed early on that the task before us was too important for carping. This was not about politics. Katrina did not distinguish between Republicans and Democrats.

This was about getting the information we need to chart a new and better course for emergency preparation and response. The American people want the facts, and they've been watching. They alone will judge whether our review has been thorough and fair. Our final exam is this report.

Our report marks the culmination of 9 public hearings, scores of interviews and briefings, and the review of more than 500,000 pages of documents.

Our investigation revealed that Katrina was a national failure, an abdication of the most solemn obligation to provide for the common welfare. At every level – individual, corporate, philanthropic, and governmental – we failed to meet the challenge that was Katrina. In this cautionary tale, all the little pigs built houses of straw.

Of all we found along the timeline running from the fictional Hurricane Pam to the tragically real devastation along the Gulf coast, this conclusion stands out: A National Response Plan is not enough.

What's needed is a National Action Plan. Not a plan that says Washington will do everything, but one that says, when all else fails, the federal government must do something, whether it's formally requested or not. Not even the perfect bureaucratic storm of flaws and failures can wash away the fundamental governmental responsibility to protect public health and safety.

Still, no political storm surge from Katrina should be allowed to breach the sovereign boundaries between localities, states, and the federal government. Our system of federalism wisely relies on those closest to the people to meet immediate needs. But faith in federalism alone cannot sanctify a dysfunctional system in which DHS and FEMA simply wait for requests for aid that state and local officials may be unable or unwilling to convey. In this instance, blinding lack of situational awareness and disjointed decision making needlessly compounded and prolonged Katrina's horror.

In many respects, our report is a litany of mistakes, misjudgments, lapses, and absurdities all cascading together, blinding us to what was coming and hobbling any collective effort to respond.

This is not to say there were not many, many heroes, or that some aspects of the preparation and response were not, by any standard, successful. We found many examples of astounding individual initiative that saved lives and stand in stark contrast to the larger institutional failures. Nor do we mean to focus on assigning individual blame. Obtaining a full accounting and identifying lessons learned does not require finger pointing, instinctively tempting as that may be.

There was also an element of simple bad luck with Katrina that aggravated the inadequate response. The hurricane arrived over a weekend, at the end of the month. People on fixed incomes had little money for gas or food or lodging, making them more likely to remain in place and wait for their next check. Communicating via television or radio with families enmeshed in their weekend routines was difficult at best, as was finding drivers and other needed volunteers.

Over the past several months, we have become more than familiar with the disaster declaration process outlined in the Stafford Act. We understand the goals, structure and mechanisms of the National Response Plan. We've digested the alphabet soup of "coordinating elements" established by the Plan: the HSOC (Homeland Security Operations Center) and RRCC (Regional Response Coordination Center); JFOs (Joint Field Offices) and PFOs (Principal Federal Officials); the IIMG (Interagency Incident Management Group); and much more.

But the American people don't care about acronyms or organizational charts. They want to know who was supposed to do what, when, and whether the job got done. And if it didn't get done, they want to know how we are going to make sure it does the next time.

This report is a story about the National Response Plan, and how its 15 Emergency Support Functions (ESFs) were implemented with Katrina. We offer details on how well the ESFs were followed. Where there were problems, we've asked why. Where even flawless execution led to unacceptable results, we've returned to questioning the underlying plan.

We should be clear about the limitations of our investigation and the parameters of this report. We focused on the preparation for and response to Katrina, for the most part paring down the timeline to one week before and two weeks after the storm. We did not, at least intentionally, delve into important, longer-term rebuilding and recovery issues that will continue to have a central place on the congressional agenda for months and years to come. In many areas — housing, education, health, contracting — "response" bleeds into "recovery," and the distinctions we've made are admittedly difficult and somewhat arbitrary.

Further, this report is only a summary of our work. We are hopeful that – indeed, certain that – more information will arise. The Select Committee has constrained its narrative and findings to those that can shed the most light, make the biggest difference, and trigger the most obvious near-term actions. Readers will note that we focus considerable attention on a handful of "key events" – evacuation plans and the execution of them; conditions and events at the Superdome, Convention Center, and highways; nursing homes and hospitals – as a means of illustrating what went right and wrong in countless other locales.

What this Select Committee has done is not rocket science.

We've gathered facts and established timelines based on some fairly rudimentary but important questions posed to the right people in both the public and private sectors.

- What did you need and what did you get?
- Where were you in the days and hours right before, during, and after the storm?
- Who were you talking to?
- What were you doing?
- Does that match what you were *supposed* to be doing? Why or why not?

In other words, the Select Committee has matched what was *supposed* to happen under federal, state, and local plans against what *actually* happened.

Our findings emerged from this process of matching.

Too often there were too many cooks in the kitchen, and because of that the response to Katrina was at times overdone, at times underdone. Too often, because everybody was in charge, nobody was in charge.

Many government officials continue to stubbornly resist recognizing that fundamental changes in disaster management are needed. This report illustrates that we have to stop waiting for the disaster that fits our response plan and instead design a scalable capacity to meet whatever Mother Nature throws at us. It's not enough to say, "We wouldn't be here if the levees had not failed." The levees *did* fail, and government and other organizations failed in turn – in many, many ways.

It remains difficult to understand how government could respond so ineffectively to a disaster that was anticipated for years, and for which specific dire warnings had been issued for days. This crisis was not only predictable, it was predicted.

If this is what happens when we have advance warning, we shudder to imagine the consequences when we do not. Four and a half years after 9/11, America is still not ready for prime time.

This is particularly distressing because we know we remain at risk for terrorist attacks, and because the 2006 hurricane season is right around the corner. With this report we hope to do our part to enhance preparation and response.

With Katrina, there was no shortage of plans. There were plans, but there was not enough plan-*ning*.

Government failed because it did not learn from past experiences, or because lessons thought to be learned were somehow not implemented. **If 9/11 was a failure of imagination, then Katrina was a failure of initiative. It was a failure of leadership.**

Tom Davis
Harold Rogers
Christopher Shays
Henry Bonilla
Steve Buyer
Sue Myrick
Mac Thornberry
Kay Granger
Charles W. "Chip" Pickering
Bill Shuster
Jeff Miller

FEMA

EXECUTIVE SUMMARY
OF FINDINGS

The Select Committee identified failures at all levels of government that significantly undermined and detracted from the heroic efforts of first responders, private individuals and organizations, faith-based groups, and others.

The institutional and individual failures we have identified became all the more clear when compared to the heroic efforts of those who acted decisively. Those who didn't flinch, who took matters into their own hands when bureaucratic inertia was causing death, injury, and suffering. Those whose exceptional initiative saved time and money and lives.

We salute the exceptions to the rule, or, more accurately, the exceptions that proved the rule. People like Mike Ford, the owner of three nursing homes who wisely chose to evacuate his patients in Plaquemines Parish before Katrina hit, due in large part to his close and long-standing working relationship with Jesse St. Amant, Director of the Plaquemines Office of Emergency Preparedness.

People like Dr. Gregory Henderson, a pathologist who showed that not all looting represented lawlessness when, with the aid of New Orleans police officers, he raided pharmacies for needed medication and supplies and set up ad hoc clinics in downtown hotels before moving on to the Convention Center.

But these acts of leadership were too few and far between. And no one heard about or learned from them until it was too late.

The preparation for and response to Hurricane Katrina show we are still an analog government in a digital age. We must recognize that we are woefully incapable of storing, moving, and accessing information – especially in times of crisis.

Many of the problems we have identified can be categorized as "information gaps" – or at least problems with information-related implications, or failures to act decisively because information was sketchy at best. Better information would have been an optimal weapon against Katrina. Information sent to the right people at the right place at the right time. Information moved within agencies, across departments, and between jurisdictions of

government as well. Seamlessly. Securely. Efficiently.

Unfortunately, no government does these things well, especially big governments.

The federal government is the largest purchaser of information technology in the world, by far. One would think we could share information by now. But Katrina again proved we cannot.

We reflect on the 9/11 Commission's finding that "the most important failure was one of imagination." The Select Committee believes Katrina was primarily a failure of initiative. But there is, of course, a nexus between the two. Both imagination and initiative – in other words, *leadership* – require good information. And a coordinated process for sharing it. And a willingness to use information – however imperfect or incomplete – to fuel action.

With Katrina, the reasons reliable information did not reach more people more quickly are many, and these reasons provide the foundation for our findings.

In essence, we found that while a national emergency management system that relies on state and local governments to identify needs and request resources is adequate for most disasters, a catastrophic disaster like Katrina can and did overwhelm most aspects of the system for an initial period of time. No one anticipated the degree and scope of the destruction the storm would cause, even though many could and should have.

The failure of local, state, and federal governments to respond more effectively to Katrina — which had been predicted in theory for many years, and forecast with startling accuracy for five days — demonstrates that whatever improvements have been made to our capacity to respond to natural or man-made disasters, four and half years after 9/11, we are still not fully prepared. Local first responders were largely overwhelmed and unable to perform their duties, and the National Response Plan did not adequately provide a way for federal assets to quickly supplement or, if necessary, supplant first responders.

The failure of initiative was also a failure of agility. Response plans at all levels of government lacked flexibility and adaptability. Inflexible procedures often delayed the response. Officials at all levels seemed to be waiting for the disaster that fit their plans, rather than planning and building scalable capacities to meet whatever Mother Nature threw at them. We again encountered the risk-averse culture that pervades big government, and again recognized the need for organizations as agile and responsive as the 21st century world in which we live.

One-size-fits-all plans proved impervious to clear warnings of extraordinary peril. Category 5 needs elicited a Category 1 response. Ours was a response that could not adequately accept civilian and international generosity, and one for which the Congress, through inadequate oversight and accounting of state and local use of federal funds, must accept some blame.

In crafting our findings, we did not guide the facts. We let the facts guide us. The Select Committee's report elaborates on the following findings, which are summarized in part here, in the order in which they appear:

The accuracy and timeliness of National Weather Service and National Hurricane Center forecasts prevented further loss of life

The Hurricane Pam exercise reflected recognition by all levels of government of the dangers of a catastrophic hurricane striking New Orleans

- Implementation of lessons learned from Hurricane Pam was incomplete.

Levees protecting New Orleans were not built for the most severe hurricanes

- Responsibilities for levee operations and maintenance were diffuse.

- The lack of a warning system for breaches and other factors delayed repairs to the levees.

- The ultimate cause of the levee failures is under investigation, and results to be determined.

The failure of complete evacuations led to preventable deaths, great suffering, and further delays in relief

- Evacuations of general populations went relatively well in all three states.

- Despite adequate warning 56 hours before landfall, Governor Blanco and Mayor Nagin delayed ordering a mandatory evacuation in New Orleans until 19 hours before landfall.

- The failure to order timely mandatory evacuations, Mayor Nagin's decision to shelter but not evacuate the remaining population, and decisions of individuals led to an incomplete evacuation.

- The incomplete pre-landfall evacuation led to deaths, thousands of dangerous rescues, and horrible conditions for those who remained.

- Federal, state, and local officials' failure to anticipate the post-landfall conditions delayed post-landfall evacuation and support.

Critical elements of the National Response Plan were executed late, ineffectively, or not at all

- It does not appear the President received adequate advice and counsel from a senior disaster professional.

- Given the well-known consequences of a major hurricane striking New Orleans, the Secretary should have designated an Incident of National Significance no later than Saturday, two days prior to landfall, when the National Weather Service predicted New Orleans would be struck by a Category 4 or 5 hurricane and President Bush declared a federal emergency.

- The Secretary should have convened the Interagency Incident Management Group on Saturday, two days prior to landfall, or earlier to analyze Katrina's potential consequences and anticipate what the federal response would need to accomplish.

- The Secretary should have designated the Principal Federal Official on Saturday, two days prior to landfall, from the roster of PFOs who had successfully completed the required training, unlike then-FEMA Director Michael Brown. Considerable confusion was caused by the Secretary's PFO decisions.

- A proactive federal response, or push system, is not a new concept, but it is rarely utilized.

- The Secretary should have invoked the Catastrophic Incident Annex to direct the federal response posture to fully switch from a reactive to proactive mode of operations.

- Absent the Secretary's invocation of the Catastrophic Incident Annex, the federal response evolved into a push system over several days.

- The Homeland Security Operations Center failed to provide valuable situational information to the White House and key operational officials during the disaster.

- The White House failed to de-conflict varying damage assessments and discounted information that ultimately proved accurate.

- Federal agencies, including DHS, had varying degrees of unfamiliarity with their roles and responsibilities under the National Response Plan and National Incident Management System.

- Once activated, the Emergency Management Assistance Compact enabled an unprecedented level of mutual aid assistance to reach the disaster area in a timely and effective manner.

- Earlier presidential involvement might have resulted in a more effective response.

DHS and the states were not prepared for this catastrophic event

- While a majority of state and local preparedness grants are required to have a terrorism purpose, this does not preclude a dual use application.

- Despite extensive preparedness initiatives, DHS was not prepared to respond to the catastrophic effects of Hurricane Katrina.

- DHS and FEMA lacked adequate trained and experienced staff for the Katrina response.

- The readiness of FEMA's national emergency response teams was inadequate and reduced the effectiveness of the federal response.

Massive communications damage and a failure to adequately plan for alternatives impaired response efforts, command and control, and situational awareness

- Massive inoperability had the biggest effect on communications, limiting command and control, situational awareness, and federal, state, and local officials' ability to address unsubstantiated media reports.

- Some local and state responders prepared for communications losses but still experienced problems, while others were caught unprepared.

- The National Communication System met many of the challenges posed by Hurricane Katrina, enabling critical communication during the response, but gaps in the system did result in delayed response and inadequate delivery of relief supplies.

Command and control was impaired at all levels, delaying relief

- Lack of communications and situational awareness paralyzed command and control.

- A lack of personnel, training, and funding also weakened command and control.

- Ineffective command and control delayed many relief efforts.

The military played an invaluable role, but coordination was lacking

- The National Response Plan's Catastrophic Incident Annex as written would have delayed the active duty military response, even if it had been implemented.

- DOD/DHS coordination was not effective during Hurricane Katrina.

- DOD, FEMA, and the state of Louisiana had difficulty coordinating with each other, which slowed the response.

- National Guard and DOD response operations were comprehensive, but perceived as slow.

- The Coast Guard's response saved many lives, but coordination with other responders could improve.

- The Army Corps of Engineers provided critical resources to Katrina victims, but pre-landfall contracts were not adequate.

- DOD has not yet incorporated or implemented lessons learned from joint exercises in military assistance to civil authorities that would have allowed for a more effective response to Katrina.

- The lack of integration of National Guard and active duty forces hampered the military response.

- Northern Command does not have adequate insight into state response capabilities or adequate interface with governors, which contributed to a lack of mutual understanding and trust during the Katrina response.

- Even DOD lacked situational awareness of post-landfall conditions, which contributed to a slower response.

- DOD lacked an information sharing protocol that would have enhanced joint situational awareness and communications between all military components.

- Joint Task Force Katrina command staff lacked joint training, which contributed to the lack of coordination between active duty components.

- Joint Task Force Katrina, the National Guard, Louisiana, and Mississippi lacked needed communications equipment and the interoperability required for seamless on-the-ground coordination.

- EMAC processing, pre-arranged state compacts, and Guard equipment packages need improvement.

- Equipment, personnel, and training shortfalls affected the National Guard response.

- Search and rescue operations were a tremendous success, but coordination and integration between the military services, the National Guard, the Coast Guard, and other rescue organizations was lacking.

The collapse of local law enforcement and lack of effective public communications led to civil unrest and further delayed relief

- A variety of conditions led to lawlessness and violence in hurricane stricken areas.

- The New Orleans Police Department was ill-prepared for continuity of operations and lost almost all effectiveness.

- The lack of a government public communications strategy and media hype of violence exacerbated public concerns and further delayed relief.

- EMAC and military assistance were critical for restoring law and order.

- Federal law enforcement agencies were also critical to restoring law and order and coordinating activities.

Medical care and evacuations suffered from a lack of advance preparations, inadequate communications, and difficulties coordinating efforts

- Deployment of medical personnel was reactive, not proactive.

- Poor planning and pre-positioning of medical supplies and equipment led to delays and shortages.

- New Orleans was unprepared to provide evacuations and medical care for its special needs population and dialysis patients, and Louisiana officials lacked a common definition of "special needs."

- Most hospital and Veterans Affairs Medical Center emergency plans did not offer concrete guidance about if or when evacuations should take place.

- New Orleans hospitals, Veterans Affairs Medical Center, and medical first responders were not adequately prepared for a full evacuation of medical facilities.

- The government did not effectively coordinate private air transport capabilities for the evacuation of medical patients.

- Hospital and Veterans Affairs Medical Center emergency plans did not adequately prepare for communication needs.

- Following Hurricane Katrina, New Orleans Veterans Affairs Medical Center and hospitals' inability to communicate impeded their ability to ask for help.

- Medical responders did not have adequate communications equipment or operability.

- Evacuation decisions for New Orleans nursing homes were subjective and, in one case, led to preventable deaths.

- Lack of electronic patient medical records contributed to difficulties and delays in medical treatment of evacuees.

- Top officials at the Department at Health and Human Services and the National Disaster Medical System do not share a common understanding of who controls the National Disaster Medical System under Emergency Support Function-8.

- Lack of coordination led to delays in recovering dead bodies.

- Deployment confusion, uncertainty about mission assignments, and government red tape delayed medical care.

Long-standing weaknesses and the magnitude of the disaster overwhelmed FEMA's ability to provide emergency shelter and temporary housing

- Relocation plans did not adequately provide for shelter. Housing plans were haphazard and inadequate.

- State and local governments made inappropriate selections of shelters of last resort. The lack of a regional database of shelters contributed to an inefficient and ineffective evacuation and sheltering process.

- There was inappropriate delay in getting people out of shelters and into temporary housing – delays that officials should have foreseen due to manufacturing limitations.

- FEMA failed to take advantage of the Department of Housing and Urban Development's expertise in large-scale housing challenges.

FEMA logistics and contracting systems did not support a targeted, massive, and sustained provision of commodities

- FEMA management lacked situational awareness of existing requirements and of resources in the supply chain. An overwhelmed logistics system made it challenging to get supplies, equipment, and personnel where and when needed.

- Procedures for requesting federal assistance raised numerous concerns.

- The failure at all levels to enter into advance contracts led to chaos and the potential for waste and fraud as acquisitions were made in haste.

- Before Katrina, FEMA suffered from a lack of sufficiently trained procurement professionals. DHS procurement continues to be decentralized and lacking a uniform approach, and its procurement office was understaffed given the volume and dollar value of work.

- Ambiguous statutory guidance regarding local contractor participation led to ongoing disputes over procuring debris removal and other services.

- Attracting emergency contractors and corporate support could prove challenging given the scrutiny that companies have endured.

Contributions by charitable organizations assisted many in need, but the American Red Cross and others faced challenges due to the size of the mission, inadequate logistics capacity, and a disorganized shelter process

"We were abandoned. City officials did nothing to protect us. We were told to go to the Superdome, the Convention Center, the interstate bridge for safety. We did this more than once. In fact, we tried them all for every day over a week. We saw buses, helicopters and FEMA trucks, but no one stopped to help us. We never felt so cut off in all our lives. When you feel like this you do one of two things, you either give up or go into survival mode. We chose the latter. This is how we made it. We slept next to dead bodies, we slept on streets at least four times next to human feces and urine. There was garbage everywhere in the city. Panic and fear had taken over."

Patricia Thompson
New Orleans Citizen and Evacuee
Select Committee Hearing, December 6, 2005[1]

When Hurricane Katrina made landfall near the Louisiana-Mississippi border on the morning of August 29, 2005, it set in motion a series of events that exposed vast numbers of Americans to extraordinary suffering. Not only would Katrina become the most expensive natural disaster in U.S. history, it would also prove to be one of the deadliest.

From the marshes of Louisiana's Plaquemines Parish to the urban center of New Orleans to the coastal communities of Mississippi and Alabama, Katrina cut an enormous swath of physical destruction, environmental devastation, and human suffering.

With the overtopping and breaching of the New Orleans levees, the vast majority of the city became submerged, requiring the emergency evacuation of tens of thousands of residents who had not left prior to the storm. Lifted off roofs by helicopters or carried to safety in boats, they were taken to the Superdome, the Convention Center, a piece of high ground known as the Cloverleaf, or any other dry spot in the city.

At these locations, they were subjected to unbearable conditions: limited light, air, and sewage facilities in the Superdome, the blistering heat of the sun, and in many cases limited food and water. They feared for their safety

and survival — and the survival of their city.

"You had people living where people aren't supposed to live," said Dr. Juliette Saussy, Director of New Orleans Emergency Medical Services, referring to the dire situations in the Superdome and Convention Center. "In general, people were just trying to survive. Some people acted badly. But most just wanted something to eat and drink, and wanted to feel safe."[2]

At least 1,100 Louisianans died as a result of Katrina.

Mississippians have understandably felt slighted that the devastation to their state has received less national public attention than New Orleans. Mississippi experienced a different storm than Louisiana — in essence, a massive, blender-like storm surge versus the New Orleans flooding caused by breached and overtopped levees.

By the end of the day on August 29, due largely to a storm surge that reached 34 feet in the western parts of the state — and extended inland as far as 10 miles — more than half of Mississippi was without power and had suffered serious wind and water damage. In addition to the surge, high winds and tornadoes left thousands of homes damaged and destroyed, and as many as 66,000 Mississippians were displaced from their homes.

FEMA

STAFF PHOTO

"It was the in and out of the surge that killed us. The out, in particular. It carried everything away."

Katrina completely flattened entire neighborhoods in communities such as Waveland, Bay St. Louis, and Pass Christian, but its damage was not limited to those who lived closest to the Gulf of Mexico. Even well inland, there is no debate over whether homes may be habitable or not. They just aren't there anymore. In these towns, brick walkways and front porches lead up to . . . nothing. Just a concrete slab where a house used to stand.

The storm careened upwards through the entire state with hurricane force winds and tornados, reaching Jackson, the state capital, and its northern most counties, and transforming 28,000 square miles — or 60 percent of the state — into a catastrophic disaster area. By the time the storm had passed, at least 230 people were dead and nearly 200,000 people were displaced from their homes. Agricultural, forestry, gaming, and poultry industries were severely damaged. Department of Homeland Security (DHS) reports estimate Veterinary Medical Assistant Teams disposed of over three million chickens that were destroyed by the storm.

STAFF PHOTO

While winds upon landfall were not as powerful as those of Hurricane Camille in 1969, Katrina was in many ways the "perfect storm" for coastal Mississippi. The combination of high winds, extraordinarily low barometric pressure, and arrival during a high tide resulted in a storm surge nearly twice that of Camille's. Wind-whipped water flooded towns not only from the south, but from the north — not just from the Gulf, but from the bayous.

This was not a tsunami-like, single wave of destruction. This was a sustained, ever-growing high tide, one that kept coming for hours. And when the water did roar back toward the Gulf, it took everything with it — furniture, pool tables, refrigerators, 30-foot boats, countless household items. Everything that was once inside was suddenly outside.

"Even the very accurate forecasts didn't capture the magnitude and devastation," said Eddie Favre, Mayor of Bay St. Louis. "It was the in and out of the surge that killed us. The out, in particular. It carried everything away."[3]

"Our infrastructure was devastated," Gulfport Mayor Brent Warr said. "The water came in, blew off manhole covers, then receded and caused a vacuum, sucking gators and DVD players and lots and lots of sand into water and sewer pipes. You couldn't have backed a truck up to a manhole cover and dumped it in more effectively."[4]

Out on his converted shrimp boat on the evening following Katrina's landfall, Rep. Gene Taylor, whose home was destroyed, recalls seeing complete and utter devastation on the ground and a telling sight in the air. "Birds were so tired all they could do was hold their wings out and soar on the wind," he said. "Our seagulls, if I had to guess, ended up in Arkansas."[5]

Very little wildlife remains evident in the storm-ravaged areas. National Guardsman stationed in Louisiana said they rarely see any pelicans or alligators any more. There are few shrimp boats working the Gulf, and elected officials in Mississippi guess it will take two years for the state's oyster industry to begin to recover.

Areas presumed to be flood-proof, like the Diamondhead community — built after Hurricane Camille miles north Bay of St. Louis — suffered flood damage.

Wind shifts "caused a lot of areas considered safe to be flooded, like the town of DeLisle, where my district director's brother lives," Taylor said on a tour bus with Select Committee Members in January. "His house was pancaked. When he came home and tried to crawl in to see what he could salvage, he ended up face to face with an alligator. He ended up shooting the thing. People got mad because they were hungry and he let the alligator rot in his front yard."[6]

While only two hurricane-related deaths were reported in Alabama, Katrina caused significant damage along its coast with a wave surge of 13.5 feet, exceeding the 100-year flood level of 12 feet, despite the fact that the state did not suffer a direct hit from the hurricane. Bayou La Batre and Dauphin Island received the brunt of the storm in Alabama, losing 800 and 200 homes, respectively. The storm caused wind damage as far north as Tuscaloosa County. Mobile Bay spilled into downtown and flooded large sections of the city, destroying hundreds of homes. The sheer power of the storm dislodged a nearby oil drilling platform, which became caught under the U.S. Highway 98 bridge.

The overall toll from the devastation is still being tallied. At the time this report was issued, more than ,000 people from storm-affected states remained unaccounted for.

During the most recent fact-finding trip to the Gulf Coast in late January 2006, Members and staff of the Select Committee were shocked by the level of devastation and slow pace of cleanup. So many towns, cities, and parishes remain almost entirely empty.

A throbbing metropolis of 470,000 before the storm, New Orleans had become at the time of our writing a struggling city that is home to barely 100,000 people—although officials say that figure almost doubles for now during the daytime, when contractors and employees come into the city to work.

Significant portions of the city and region remain uninhabitable. In St. Bernard Parish, a few miles east of downtown New Orleans, only four houses did not suffer catastrophic damage from wind, rain, or the sudden flood that resulted from the breaking of the levees of the Mississippi River-Gulf Outlet Canal (MR-GO). The parish, once home to nearly 0,000 people, has seen its population dip to about 7,000, with nearly all of those people living in temporary housing.

In all of the affected communities, the local economies remain on the brink of disaster, fearful of another punch that would surely be the knockout blow. In Mississippi, Hancock County lost 64 percent of its real property value. In Bay St. Louis and Waveland, the figure is estimated to be closer to 90 percent.

Investigative context: an overview

It's been said that experience is the best teacher. The unfortunate thing is that the learning process is sometimes such a painful one.

This report is the result of a five-month journey by the Select Committee to gather information from all those who learned painful lessons during Katrina. It examines how well local, state, and federal officials worked with each other and with private entities to alleviate the suffering of so many of our fellow citizens.

In crafting an investigative plan, the Select Committee faced and overcame several challenges. We had to appoint Members quickly and rely on other committees to detail staff to the Select Committee. We had to move quickly, while memories and evidence were fresh. We had to gather as much information as we could while leaving time to write and design a consensus report before our February 15, 2006 deadline. We had to remain focused on our prescribed "right-before-and-right-after-the-storm" timeframe, despite significant interest in longer-term issues and challenges. Like juggling with knives, we had to keep multiple investigative elements in play simultaneously — preparing for and holding high-profile public hearings; requesting, receiving, and reviewing documents; and conducting interviews and briefings.

And all this had to be done in a less-than-ideal political atmosphere.

The Select Committee remains grateful to those Democrats who chose to participate in our investigation in defiance of their leadership's decision not to appoint Members officially to the panel. The refusal by the Minority Leader was self-defeating, given that the Select Committee's composition and minority subpoena authority would have given the Democrats more clout than they enjoy on any standing committee of the House.

Despite this strategy, the Select Committee's review and the creation of this report have been bipartisan endeavors in spirit and in fact.

On September 15, before the Select Committee was established by a bipartisan House vote, the Government Reform Committee held a hearing on the early lessons learned from Katrina. At that hearing, the Committee's Ranking Member, Rep. Henry Waxman, said there were "two steps we should take right away."[7]

First, he said, we should request basic documents from the agencies. And second, he said, "We need to hear from Michael Brown and Michael Chertoff. These are the two government officials most responsible for the inadequate response, and the Committee should call them to testify without delay."[8]

The Select Committee did not delay. We met and exceeded those goals. While many who so urgently called on Congress to swiftly investigate refused to participate and instead prejudged our efforts, we investigated aggressively what went wrong and what went right.

The Select Committee continuously invited any and all interested Democrats to join our hearings, giving them full and equal opportunity to make statements and question witnesses and help guide the direction of our inquiry, including identifying and inviting witnesses. Five Democratic members did just that: Representative Charlie Melancon, Representative Gene Taylor, Representative Bill Jefferson, Representative Cynthia McKinney, and Representative Sheila Jackson Lee. Document requests submitted to federal, state, and local agencies were signed by both Chairman Davis and Rep. Melancon.

In addition to direct member participation, Democratic Members and staff were assigned to travel with Republican Members and staff to the affected locales, and Rep. Waxman's top Government Reform Committee investigative staff assisted Democratic participants. Finally, Democratic members were repeatedly invited to offer narrative text and findings for inclusion in this report.

The Select Committee, beyond extending these courtesies, remained focused on the job of Congress. In our system of checks and balances, the Congress has both the duty and the obligation to ask tough questions. We did not believe it was appropriate to outsource our congressional oversight responsibility. The American people did not want us to punt. They wanted answers, and they wanted them quickly. If there is a consensus down the road to establish an outside commission, which some purportedly wanted, so be it. The two were not and are not mutually exclusive. However, a commission will take months to set up, and an eternity to finish its work. We needed to begin immediately, while evidence and memories were fresh.

News reports and other statements suggested many Democrats felt the same. For example, Bloomberg News reported in November that "Some House Democrats Want [a] Larger Role in Katrina Investigation."[9] In that report, ep. Gene Taylor said, "It's really important that we're here. I certainly wish more of my colleagues who are interested in this would participate . . . . Mr. Davis, to his credit, has been extremely fair."

Rep. Maxine Waters, who had told Chairman Davis she wanted to participate but later said she could not, told Bloomberg, "I feel a certain void and a great absence from these discussions. I was hoping that our leaders could a find a way . . . so we could participate."[10]

Rep. Neil Abercrombie said he unsuccessfully expressed interest in serving on the committee. "The position of Ms. Pelosi and the leadership is pretty clear," he said. "I have a different view."[11]

Democrats who did buck their leadership have acknowledged both the value of their participation and the eagerness of the Select Committee to have them participate. Rep. Cynthia McKinney expressed her regret about the Democrats' failure to officially appoint Members to the Committee while thanking Chairman Davis for convening a hearing

STAFF PHOTO

on December 6th featuring testimony from African-American residents and evacuees:

I would like to thank you, Mr. Chairman, for allowing us to have this day. Because were it left up to — I will get in trouble now. But were it left up to the Democratic leadership, we would not have had this day, because we wouldn't be here. The Democratic leadership has instructed us to boycott this panel…. So I would like to thank my Chairman for giving us the opportunity to invite people who don't have the opportunity to come and testify before Congress…. We are here to serve all of the people of this country, and too rarely do we hear from all of the people.[12]

Regardless of who did or did not participate in our investigation, the Select Committee had a job to do, and we were determined to do it right.

Hearing chronology: an overview

The Select Committee held nine hearings over the course of approximately three months. Select Committee Members and staff simultaneously conducted scores of interviews and received dozens of briefings from local, state, and federal officials; non-governmental organizations; private companies and individuals who provided or offered external support after Katrina; and hurricane victims. Select Committee Members and staff traveled numerous times to the Gulf Coast. The Select Committee also requested and received more than 500,000 pages of documents from a wide array of sources.

The information gleaned from our investigation is provided in detailed, narrative form in subsequent chapters. What follows here is a brief synopsis of the topics, questions, and themes raised at each of our hearings:

"Predicting Hurricanes:
What We Knew About Katrina and When"
September 22, 2005 Select Committee hearing

The Select Committee began at a logical place: a hearing to establish a record of who was told what, and when, about the nature of the hurricane in the days immediately before the storm. We explored the timeline of Katrina progressing from a tropical depression to a major hurricane, and asked when warnings were issued to the public and to federal, state, and local officials. We reaffirmed what we already suspected — at least two federal agencies passed Katrina's test with flying colors: the National Weather Service (NWS) and the National Hurricane Center.

Many who escaped the storm's wrath owe their lives to these agencies' accuracy. This hearing provided a backdrop for the remainder of our inquiry. We repeatedly tried to determine how government could respond so ineffectively to a disaster that was so accurately forecast.

How accurately?

■ Storm-track projections released to the public **56 hours** before Katrina came ashore were off by **only 15 miles.** The average 48-hour error is 160 miles, and the average 24-hour error is 85 miles.

■ The Hurricane Center's predicted strength for Katrina at landfall, **two days before** the storm hit, was off the mark by only 10 miles per hour.

We repeatedly tried to determine how government could respond so ineffectively to a disaster that was so accurately forecast.

■ NWS Director Max Mayfield personally spoke by telephone with the governors of Mississippi and Louisiana and the mayor of New Orleans two days prior to landfall to warn them of what was coming. He also gave daily pre-storm video briefings to federal officials in Washington, including top Federal Emergency Management Agency (FEMA) and DHS brass.

■ The day before Katrina hit, the NWS office in Slidell, Louisiana issued a warning saying, "MOST OF THE AREA WILL BE UNINHABITABLE FOR WEEKS...PERHAPS LONGER...HUMAN SUFFERING INCREDIBLE BY MODERN STANDARDS."

The Select Committee determined — despite more recently revised reports that Katrina was actually a strong Category 3 storm at landfall, not a Category 4 — that Katrina's strength and the potential disaster it could bring were made clear well in advance through briefings and formal advisories. Inadequate response could not be blamed on lack of advance warning.

AP PHOTO/ANDY NEWMAN

"Hurricane Katrina: The Role of the Federal Emergency Management Agency"
September 27, 2005 Select Committee hearing

This hearing featuring former FEMA Director Michael Brown attempted to construct a timeline of what FEMA did and did not do before, during, and after Katrina mad landfall.

Fair or not, by the time of this hearing, FEMA in genera and Brown in particular had become the symbol of all tha went wrong with the government's response to Katrina.

By the September 27 hearing date, with the emergence of Hurricane Rita, the Select Committee had the ability to compare and contrast disaster response actions after the two storms. While Rita was predicted to be a very different

AP PHOTO/DENNIS COOK

storm from Katrina — a mere size Large compared to a siz XXXL, and a storm that struck a far less densely populated area — it was immediately clear that governments at all levels did things differently this time around.

More supplies were stockpiled on the ground *prior* to Rita's arrival. The federal government declared Rita an "incident of national significance" *two days before* landfall triggering our most thorough response, and named a federal officer in charge. These steps occurred *two days aft* Katrina. Ten thousand National Guardsmen were called to Texas in advance of Rita; Louisiana summoned 1,500

before Katrina. Search and Rescue operations were far better coordinated.

Even if a little rough around the edges, the massive pre-storm evacuation of Houston and surrounding locales showed improved foresight from state and local officials — and how lives can be saved when people pay attention to a coordinated message from their government.

We also attempted to clarify FEMA's role in disaster response. We were faced with the problematic reality that many Americans — and perhaps even some state and local officials — falsely viewed FEMA as some sort of national fire and rescue team. An important task for the Select Committee moving forward was defining what FEMA is — what it can and cannot do based on what it is actually charged with doing by statute.

We noted that FEMA is **not** a first responder agency with the resources to assume principal responsibility for overwhelmed state and local governments during a disaster. This is the real world, not the reel world. There is no Tommy Lee Jones character that comes in and takes charge of…well…*everything*.

But we also attempted to contextualize that discussion. In other words, before getting to what FEMA cannot do, we wanted to understand what they simply did not do. Just because they are not "first responders" does not mean they should be a second thought.

We explored the possible causes of FEMA's inadequate response, which are covered exhaustively in subsequent chapters. Among those discussed at the hearing: Inadequacies in the Stafford Act. Organizational or budgetary or grant-making shortcomings. State and local governments that didn't know how to ask for help, or simply didn't. A bureaucratic mindset that now emphasizes terrorism to the exclusion of natural disaster planning. We looked at these possibilities, and more.

We also examined why FEMA seemed unable to implement lessons that should have been learned well in advance of Katrina. There were the lessons of previous hurricanes. Further, FEMA officials participated in the now-widely-known exercise called Hurricane Pam in July 2004, an exercise that predicted with eerie similarity Katrina's impact on New Orleans, including an evacuation of a million people, overflowing levees, and the destruction of hundreds of thousands of buildings.

"Hurricane Katrina: The Role of the Department of Homeland Security"
October 19, 2005 Select Committee hearing

Although by this date FEMA and Michael Brown had received the most attention from Members of Congress, state and local officials, and the news media in Katrina's wake, the Select Committee sought to recognize that DHS and Secretary Michael Chertoff have primary responsibility for managing the national response to a catastrophic disaster, according to the National Response Plan (NRP).

Therefore, three weeks after hearing from Michael Brown, we turned to his boss, the man who ultimately fired him.

We needed to find out if Michael Brown had it right when he testified that FEMA had been under-funded and under-staffed, that it had become "emaciated," and that Congress had undermined FEMA's effectiveness when the agency was folded into DHS.

Michael Brown testified that he asked the Department for funding to implement the lessons learned from the Hurricane Pam exercise and that those funds were denied. He also testified about brain drain, diminished financial resources, and "assessments" of $70 to $80 million by DHS for department-wide programs. He said he had written memos to Secretary Ridge and Secretary Chertoff regarding the inadequacy of FEMA's resources. We asked Secretary Chertoff about those assertions.

We also sought to establish the Department's role and responsibilities in a disaster. What resources can the Secretary bring to bear? What triggers the decision to deploy those resources? During Katrina, how personally involved was Secretary Chertoff in seeking, authorizing, or deploying specific resources?

Under the National Response Plan, the DHS Secretary is the federal official charged with declaring an Incident of National Significance. Part of that declaration entails naming a Principal Federal Official (PFO), to manage the response.

The government's pre-landfall decision to declare an Incident of National Significance with Rita suggested awareness that the call came too late with Katrina. And, based on some of Brown's emails, we knew that he *resented* being named the PFO by the Secretary. We needed to ask Secretary Chertoff what he thought about that, and what those comments said about the underlying NRP.

Finally, we asked Secretary Chertoff what we asked all officials during our investigation: Where were you in the days and hours right before, during, and after the hurricane? What were you doing? Who were you talking to?

New York University Professor Paul Light wrote shortly after Katrina that, "Mr. Chertoff is just about the only official in Washington who can say 'I told you so' about FEMA," based on some of the reforms he outlined in July 2005 in his Second Stage Review. We asked Secretary Chertoff if he believed FEMA's response to Katrina would have been better if the reforms had been in place on August 29.

"Hurricane Katrina: Preparedness and Response by the Department of Defense, the Coast Guard, and the National Guard of Louisiana, Mississippi, and Alabama"
October 27, 2005 Select Committee hearing

STAFF PHOTO

At this hearing we examined Department of Defense responsibilities, procedures, and coordination with the Department of Homeland Security in the event of a catastrophic disaster.

We looked at the roles of the National Guard and U.S. Northern Command in disaster response as the operational arms of DOD and the states, and we reviewed the role of the Coast Guard, a unique national asset with both military capabilities and domestic law enforcement authorities.

We sought to establish a timeline of the military's actions — what they were asked to do, when they were asked, and whether the jobs actually got done.

We acknowledged the heroic efforts that DOD, National Guard, and Coast Guard personnel made, efforts that saved many, many lives. The mobilization was massive and, at least once the call went out, swift and effective.

But we also discussed problems with the military response. The Select Committee believed even some of the successes occurred despite less-than-optimal planning, and too often officers were planning in a crisis environment.

There were problems: With situational awareness and damage assessments. With coordinating search and rescue operations. With the effective use of Defense Coordinating Officers by FEMA. With an early and persistent disconnect between DOD and state and local authorities. With inadequate telecommunications that prevented effective coordination. And, once again, with failing to learn as much as possible from previous disasters.

While we continued to emphasize that local first responders are best suited for handling local emergencies, the recurring question was: What happens when first responders are overwhelmed, as they clearly were in Katrina?

As a result, we asked whether DOD anticipated these circumstances, what preparations were made, and what actions were taken with regard to the National Response Plan's "Catastrophic Incident Annex" — the annex that authorizes federal agencies to act when state and local capacity even to know what they need is compromised by the sheer size of the calamity.

Our hearing came amid growing debate over an expanded military role in future disasters. President Bush prompted the discussion in a nationally televised address from New Orleans on September 15, saying, "It is now clear that a challenge on this scale requires greater federal authority and a broader role for the armed forces — the institution of our government most capable of massive logistical operations on a moment's notice."

Two witnesses — Paul McHale, Assistant Secretary of Defense for Homeland Defense, and Admiral Timothy J. Keating, Commander, North American Aerospace Defense Command and U.S. Northern Command — had indicated prior to the hearing that DOD was considering training and equipping an active duty force specifically for disaster response.

Those remarks led to some confusion over specifics, and even to some outright opposition.

On October 13, the National Governors Association issued a statement reasserting their authority. "Governors are responsible for the safety and welfare of their citizens and are in the best position to coordinate all resources to prepare for, respond to, and recover from disasters," the association wrote.

An October 21 statement by Assistant to the President for Homeland Security Advisor Frances Townsend, who is leading President Bush's examination of the federal response to Katrina, also spawned negative reactions from state officials. Townsend reportedly said she was considering whether there is "a narrow band of cases" in which the President should seize control when a disaster strikes.[13] A spokesperson for Louisiana Gov. Kathleen Babineaux Blanco responded by saying she could not think of an instance in which the President should be able to unilaterally take control. "We don't believe Katrina was the time, and I don't know what another time would be," Denise Bottcher told the Times-Picayune.[14]

The Select Committee, therefore, began addressing this basic tension. On the one hand, we heard understandable caution from our Members and witnesses against over-reacting to Katrina with sweeping changes to laws or processes, caution against deviating too wildly from the locals-as-first-responders paradigm. None of us believed the best lesson to be learned from Katrina was that all answers can be found in Washington.

On the other hand, the call for increasing the military's role in domestic affairs is easy to grasp. Who else can respond the way the military can? Who else can stand up when others have fallen?

This tension was reflected in the National Response Plan *before* Katrina. The Catastrophic Incident Annex assumes that local response capabilities may be "insufficient," as they will be "quickly overwhelmed." But the NRP plan states federal resources will only be integrated into the response effort *upon a request by state and local authorities* and assumes state and local officials will be able to do the integrating themselves.

The Select Committee was left wondering if the plan as written tried to have its cake and eat it too. How can we rely on the overwhelmed to acknowledge they are

overwhelmed, and then expect them to direct and manage the process of coming to their rescue?

We agreed we needed a closer evaluation of existing procedures for DOD under the National Response Plan, paying particular attention to DOD's role when first responders are wiped out or otherwise incapable of providing the initial response.

We agreed that Incidents of National Significance require a response on a national scale. But we also agreed the devil is in the details. We cannot expect the Marines to swoop in with MREs every time a storm hits. We train soldiers to fight wars. You can't kill a storm.

So what is the threshold? When can or should the Stafford Act's assumption that states will be able to "pull" needed federal resources to meet their needs give way to the operational imperative that federal agencies "push" assets to those who need them? What would spur the kind of enhanced or heightened military role that some have been promoting in the aftermath of Katrina? When would we pull that trigger? And finally, would it have made a difference in the response to Katrina?

The fact is, military resources are not infinite. It seems the kind of standing humanitarian force that would be needed to provide this sort of immediate assistance at a moment's notice would either threaten readiness or require an expansion of the active force and a significant boost in how well they are equipped.

Legal questions also arose. Were we talking about statutory changes? Should we revisit Posse Comitatus, the 127-year-old law that bars federal troops from

Do we need a larger DOD role — or just a smarter one?

assuming domestic law enforcement duties? Did Katrina demonstrate a need for a new exception to Posse Comitatus, one to be utilized after major disasters?

The Select Committee ultimately refocused the discussion by simplifying the question: Do we need a larger DOD role — *or just a smarter one?*

The Select Committee tried hard to acknowledge at this hearing what an incredible job the Coast Guard did, and recognize the National Guard's clear sense of urgency. We noted for the record that Northern Command had prepared for this storm, deploying Defense Coordinating Officers to the three states before landfall and placing units on alert.

But we also had to recognize that it was unclear how much "real" support was in place before the storm arrived, and that Secretary McHale himself had acknowledged prior to our hearing the DOD response was too slow.[15]

"Hurricane Katrina: The Federal Government's Use of Contractors to Prepare and Respond"
November 2, 2005 Select Committee hearing

Local, state, and federal governments rely heavily on contractor support to prepare for and response to disasters. This hearing examined the contracts in place prior to Katrina's landfall, and procurement planning efforts that took place in anticipation of a large-scale catastrophic event. We also reviewed the rationale and process for awarding disaster relief and recovery contracts in the immediate aftermath of Katrina.

The Select Committee asked about the internal controls in place to ensure that federal acquisition laws were followed; the terms and performance of Katrina relief contracts; and the ways in which the management and oversight of disaster-related contracting can be strengthened.

A great deal of taxpayer money went out the door to private firms to help prepare for and respond to Katrina. Part of our job was to ask whether it's been money well spent. And part of that inquiry was asking what contracts should have been in place **before** the storm arrived, based on what everyone knew — or should have known — would be needed.

STAFF PHOTO

Was the contracting system up to the task? Were we able to get what we needed, when and where we needed it? By any measure, this was an enormous storm, described as one of "Biblical" proportions. In the face of the massive destruction caused by Katrina, acquisition personnel acted to meet pressing humanitarian needs, contacting firms in an effort to provide immediate relief to survivors and to protect life and property. And thankfully, many firms responded.

FEMA

It is true that several companies were called into action on a sole-source basis under acquisition provisions that allow the government to acquire urgently needed goods and services in emergency situations. It's also true that, contrary to many media reports, some of the immediate response efforts were provided through *existing* contracts that had been previously awarded through full and open competition.

Nevertheless, concerns were raised with respect to how FEMA awarded contracts in Katrina's immediate aftermath and regarding what contract vehicles were in place before landfall. These were legitimate concerns that affect not only our findings relative to the preparation for and response to Katrina, but also how well prepared we'll be the next time — and how willing contractors will be to step up to the plate the next time they're called.

The indirect result of inefficient contracting and misdirected, even baseless charges against contractors could be a government left with more than it can manage in-house.

In the weeks following Katrina, more than 80 percent of the $1.5 billion in initial contracts awarded by FEMA were awarded on a sole-source basis or pursuant to limited competition. Many of the contracts awarded were incomplete and included open-ended or vague terms. In addition, numerous news reports questioned the terms of disaster relief agreements made in haste.

Under the Stafford Act, prime contractors are to give preference to local subcontractors, but reports indicated that not enough local businesses were being hired. Questions were also raised about the Corps of Engineers' use of a limited competition to award contracts for debris removal and clean up.

Undoubtedly, FEMA before Katrina suffered from something Congress has grappled with government-wide for many years: a lack of sufficiently trained procurement professionals.

Prior to Hurricane Katrina, the DHS Office of Inspector General (IG) had repeatedly cited the lack of consistent contract management for large, complex, high-cost procurement programs. DHS procurement continues to be decentralized and lacking a uniform approach. DHS has seven legacy procurement offices that continue to serve DHS components, including FEMA. Notably, FEMA was not reporting or tracking procurements undertaken by disaster field offices, and the procurement office remains to this day understaffed given the volume and dollar value of its work.

The Chief Procurement Officer (CPO) had established an eighth office called the Office of Procurement Operations to meet the procurement needs of the rest of DHS. After Katrina, however, the CPO reassigned its staff to assist FEMA's procurement office.

At this hearing, we learned errors were made in the contracting process before and after Katrina. The contract oversight process is not always pretty, and decisions made under life-and-death pressure are not always as lucid as those made under less complicated conditions. But there are lessons to be learned about efficient and effective contracting, even from this, hopefully, once in a lifetime event.

That there were and will be disagreements with contractors over pricing and payment schedules should come as no surprise to anyone familiar with the administration of complex contracts in difficult circumstances.

The good news is, DHS has begun establishing a rigorous oversight process for each and every federal contract related to Katrina. Now the process needs to be fully implemented.

Shortly after the emergency needs arose, DHS's Chief Procurement Officer asked the DHS Inspector General's Office to begin overseeing the acquisition process. The DHS IG assigned 60 auditors, investigators, and inspectors and planned to hire thirty additional oversight personnel. The staff is reviewing the award and administration of all major contracts, including those awarded in the initial efforts, and will monitor all contracting activities as the government develops its requirements and as the selection and award process continues to unfold.

Undoubtedly, FEMA before Katrina suffered from something Congress has grappled with government-wide for many years: a lack of sufficiently trained procurement professionals.

To further ensure that any payments made to contractors are proper and reasonable, FEMA engaged the Defense Contract Audit Agency to help monitor and oversee any payments made — and pledged not to pay on **any** vouchers until each one is audited and cleared.

The Select Committee has no patience with waste, fraud, or abuse. We expect that any such instances that are proven will result in harsh punishment for the perpetrators. We also expect that, as the conditions on the ground have improved, the next generation of contracts have been and will be awarded and administered in accordance with standard acquisition procedures.

Emergency procedures are for emergencies only.

FEMA said it continues to revisit non-competitive arrangements made immediately after the storm.

"Hurricane Katrina: Preparedness and Response by the State of Alabama"
November 9, 2005 Select Committee hearing
"Hurricane Katrina: Preparedness and Response by the State of Mississippi"
December 7, 2005 Select Committee hearing
"Hurricane Katrina: Preparation and Response by the State of Louisiana"
December 14, 2005 Select Committee hearing

The three state-focused hearings we held were arguably the most important in terms of fact-gathering. After all, we understood that in the event of an emergency, state and local government officials bear primary responsibilities under both the National Response Plan and their own laws and directives. Throughout federal, state and local planning documents the general principle is for all incidents to be handled at the lowest possible organizational and

jurisdictional level. Police, fire, public health and medical, emergency management, and other personnel are responsible for incident management at the local level. For federally declared emergencies or major disasters, DHS provides operational and/or resource coordination for federal support to on-scene incident command structures.

Our goal was to better understand the responsibilities and actions of state and local officials before, during, and after Hurricane Katrina made landfall. We explored state laws, policies, procedures, and how state and local officials interfaced with DHS and FEMA when they confronted Katrina — and how DHS interfaced with them.

The National Response Plan and the National Incident Management System were crafted to provide the framework and template, respectively, for the federal government to work with state and local authorities to prepare for and respond to crises. In turn, states, localities, tribal governments, and nongovernmental organizations are asked to align their plans and procedures with federal guidelines and procedures.

Did this coordinated alignment occur? By the time of these hearings, we knew in large part it had not. We sought to understand, from a state and local perspective, why.

"Hurricane Katrina: Voices from Inside the Storm"
December 6, 2005 Select Committee hearing

In mid-November, Rep. Cynthia McKinney asked Select Committee Chairman Tom Davis to focus a hearing on the "African-American voice" related to Hurricane Katrina.

With that request in mind, and having already planned a hearing featuring testimony from storm victims, the Select Committee sought to better understand the experiences of Gulf coast residents, including those forced

AP PHOTO/SUSAN WALSH

AP PHOTO/HARAZ N. GHANBARI

AP PHOTO/SUSAN WALSH

this very carefully," aide Johnny Anderson wrote in an e-mail. "We are getting enough bad national press on race relations."[16] E-mails from aides to former FEMA Director Michael Brown reflected similar concerns about public relations and racial politics. And Alabama officials discussed similar sensitivities about a proposal to conduct background checks on out-of-state evacuees being housed in state parks.

A CNN-Gallup poll from September 8 to 11 reported 60 percent of African-Americans, but only 12 percent of whites, believed race was a factor in the slow response to Katrina. Another poll by the Pew Research Center found that 7 in 10 blacks believed the disaster showed that racial inequality remains a major problem in America. A majority of whites disagreed.

A November survey of 46 Katrina evacuees published by the Natural Hazards Center at the University of Colorado-Boulder concluded that "issues of race and class were central to evacuation experiences."[17] For many, the evacuation process was complicated by age, mental or physical disability, the need to care for dependents, or material possessions they were trying to take with them.

The *Washington Post*, the Kaiser Family Foundation, and Harvard University also conducted face-to-face interviews with 680 randomly selected adult evacuees residing in Houston.[18] When asked, "Has your experience made you feel like the government cares about people like you, or has it made you feel like the government doesn't care?" 61 percent reported they felt the government doesn't care. Additionally, the evacuees suggested an intersection between race and class: 68 percent of respondents thought the federal government would have responded more quickly if more people trapped in the floodwaters were "wealthier and white rather than poorer and black."

At an early November forum at Emerson College, Louis Elisa — a former regional director for the Federal Emergency Management Agency under President Clinton — reportedly suggested that race *had to be* a factor in the

to evacuate, during the catastrophe. Only by hearing from those most directly affected by Katrina could we determine where, how, and why the government response at all levels was so terribly inadequate.

There was little question that Katrina had sparked renewed debate about race, class, and institutional approaches toward vulnerable population groups in the United States. In the aftermath of the storm, a wide array of media reports, public statements, and polls underscored this reality.

In his September 15 speech to the nation, President Bush touched on the issue. "As all of us saw on television, there is also some deep, persistent poverty in this region as well. And that poverty has roots in a history of racial discrimination, which cut off generations from the opportunity of America," the President said.

Since then the debate had become increasingly heated. In media interviews, Jesse Jackson compared New Orleans' shelters to the hold of a slave ship, and Louis Farrakhan suggested New Orleans' levees were intentionally blown up to destroy primarily African-American neighborhoods.

While not all the commentary has necessarily been constructive, substantiated, or fair, the Select Committee believed the issue warranted further discussion, especially within the context of understanding the experiences of those caught inside the storm, and in hopes of making sure the governmental response is more effective the next time.

We knew from government e-mails and other documents that officials were almost immediately sensitive to public perceptions of race as a factor in the inadequate response. An aide to Louisiana Governor Blanco cautioned colleagues about how to respond to a request from Rep. Maxine Waters, an African-American, for security escorts in New Orleans shortly after the storm. "Please handle

"If you get conflicting informatio from people you're not sure of, then inaction may be, from your perspective, the most prudent form of action."

inadequate response. "I am telling you, as a professional, that you could not have had a mistake of this nature…if something else was not afoot," the Boston Globe quoted Elisa.[19]

Whether or not one believed racist charges were well-founded (and clearly a majority of our members did not), the Select Committee agreed it should recognize and discuss the socioeconomic and racial backdrop against which Katrina unfolded.

As the Brookings Institution reported in October, New Orleans, which once had economically and demographically diverse neighborhoods, had grown extremely segregated by both race and income by the time of the storm. "As a result," Brookings concluded, "blacks and whites were living in quite literally different worlds before the storm hit." [20]

At the very least, the Select Committee determined it should further explore at this hearing how socioeconomic factors contributed to the experiences of those directly affected by the storm. The UC-Boulder survey found that "almost all interviewees described the evacuation process as disorderly and disorganized, with minimal communication about where evacuees were heading and when the next transportation would arrive. This created a state of uncertainty and insecurity…. [P]redominantly working-class African-Americans did not evacuate because they did not have the financial resources to do so."[21]

The Select Committee sought to learn more about whether government messages to Gulf coast residents regarding the dangers of the coming hurricane could have been presented in a more effective manner, a question which also carried racial and socioeconomic implications.

"If you don't hear the message from someone you trust, you tend to be skeptical," Margaret Sims, vice president of the Joint Center for Political and Economic Studies, told Public Relations Strategist magazine. "If you get conflicting information from people you're not sure

of, then inaction may be, from your perspective, the most prudent form of action." [22]

The same magazine article noted that disaster response may have been hampered by not taking the "circumstances" of area residents fully into account. "The people creating the verbal or image measures don't take into account access or physical barriers to opportunities in certain communities," said Linda Aldoory, director of the Center for Risk Communication Research at the University of Maryland. "With Katrina, people knew the importance of storm warnings and the need to evacuate, but didn't have the physical access to do so."[23]

In other words, the Select Committee agreed it should examine to what extent response inadequacies stemmed from the messengers — and the message. We wanted to further explore the possibility that different people may hear different things when their elected officials are telling them to evacuate.

Document request, production, and review: an overview

Within a week of its September 15, 2005 creation, the Select Committee held its first hearing. By the end of the month, Chairman Davis and Rep. Charlie Melancon, on behalf of the Select Committee and in cooperation with the Senate Committee on Homeland Security and Governmental Affairs, had submitted 19 official and comprehensive requests for documents to relevant federal agencies and state governments.

By the beginning of January 2006, 67 formal requests for documents had been issued by the Select Committee and the Senate Committee to 29 federal agencies as well as the governments of Alabama, Mississippi, and Louisiana and their subdivisions.

In response to those formal requests and numerous other staff requests, the Select Committee received hundreds of thousands of documents.

The responses by the federal agencies and state governments inundated the Select Committee. A constant stream of boxes containing responsive documents arrived daily at the Select Committee's door. Select Committee staff worked around the clock to organize and review this stream of documents. Aggressive follow-up by the Select Committee, detailed below, ensured the document production was responsive to the Select Committee's requests.

To fulfill its mission, the Select Committee needed to do more than hold hearings. We requested and received more than half a million pages of documents from governmental organizations at all levels: federal, state, and local. The information gleaned from these documents played a critical role in helping the Select Committee paint a picture of what happened and why.

STAFF PHOTO

Below is a brief overview of what was requested and what was received. Most of the governmental organizations complied with our requests in a timely and complete fashion. Efforts by others to comply unfortunately were either timely nor complete. This is discussed below as well.

In September 2005, the Senate Committee, chaired by Senator Susan Collins, began its Katrina investigation. In many cases, the two committees desired the same or similar information. To facilitate both investigations, and to eliminate waste and unnecessary duplication of efforts, the Select Committee simply asked to receive all documents requested by the Senate.

Federal

The Select Committee sent request letters to all 15 cabinet-level departments as well as many independent federal departments including: the Environmental Protection Agency (EPA), the United States Postal Service (USPS), the Agency for International Development (AID), the Tennessee Valley Authority (TVA), the Small Business Administration (SBA), the Social Security Administration (SSA), the Federal Communications Commission (FCC), the Nuclear Regulatory Commission (NRC), the Office of Personnel Management (OPM), and the National Aeronautics and Space Administration (NASA). We also requested information from the White House and the Office of the Vice President.

In particular, the Select Committee requested extensive information from the Department of Homeland Security, particularly from two of its constituent agencies, FEMA and the U.S. Coast Guard. We requested documents and communications from before August 23 related to the threat posed by a hurricane striking New Orleans or the Gulf Coast, mitigation measures or projects, emergency preparations, or emergency responses. We also sought documents and communications from between August 23 and August 29 related to the threat posed by Hurricane Katrina, mitigation measures or projects, emergency preparations, or emergency responses. And we requested documents and communications from between August 29 and September 15 related to the impact of Hurricane Katrina, mitigation measures or projects, emergency preparations, or emergency responses.

In addition, we requested information about the different elements of DHS and individuals holding key positions. We wanted to know the different roles and responsibilities of those components, as well as the actions they took before, during, and after Katrina. We asked for information regarding the activation of the National Response Plan and National Incident Management System, and any discussions about the use of the armed forces. We also requested relevant communications, specifically any requests for assistance, communications with local and state authorities, and communications that revealed any plans to prepare for the hurricane, or communications that demonstrated possible vulnerabilities to a hurricane. We also wanted any documents containing authorities, regulations, plans, and procedures of the agency, weather reports, information about medical response assets, and information about DHS and FEMA funding and budgeting.

We requested an employee directory and organization chart for FEMA, as well as the individuals in key position during the hurricane in the affected regions. We asked for documents referring to risks posed by hurricanes or flooding of New Orleans, and documents indicating whether officials knew of those risks. We also requested documents and communications regarding the levee system in New Orleans, including plans, risk assessments, and knowledge of the levees' failure, particularly documents and communications with the Army Corps of Engineers.

We sought documents and names of key individuals related to the Hurricane Pam exercise, and information about FEMA's chain of command during the storm and FEMA's authorities, plans, and policies relevant to Hurricane Katrina. In addition, we requested after-action reports for past hurricanes; information about the activation of the National Response Plan; qualifications of key FEMA personnel; and contributions of contractors and subcontractors.

Finally, we requested a description of the Coast Guard's role with respect to the National Response Plan and other domestic emergencies, specifically Hurricane Katrina. We wanted to know what components will act, who they will cooperate with, and in what capacity. We also requested information about search and rescue, such as command structures, regulations, and assets available. We also requested details about when the Coast Guard learned of certain key information before, during, and after Katrina.

DHS responded to most of these requests from the Select Committee, including requests addressed to Secretary Chertoff, Acting Undersecretary Paulison, and Assistant Secretary Robert Stephan. The Department produced in total well over 200,000 pages of documents including: (1) Briefing books, reports and communication from the Secretary's office; (2) Communications from the Deputy Secretary's office; (3) E-mails from Undersecretary Brown's office; (4) E-mails from FEMA personnel involved in planning and response efforts; (5) the National Response Plan, Hurricane plans, New Orleans and Mobile area plans, Incident Action Plans, Operation Manuals and planning worksheets, and Katrina specific plans; (6) Mission assignments, task requests and logs, action requests, tracking reports, and situation reports; (7) tasking logs and requests; (8) briefings; (9) grant program documents; (10) planned shipments; resource tracking reports, commodity maps, and staging areas; (11) audits; (12) Katrina maps and graphics; and (13) organizational charts.

The Select Committee sent specific requests to the Department of Defense as well. We sent request letters to the Office of the Secretary of Defense, the National Guard Bureau, the U.S. Army Corps of Engineers, North American Air Defense Command (NORAD), and Northern Command (NORTHCOM).

Specifically, we requested documents and communications from before August 23 by officials of the Department of Defense or any constituent agencies related to the threat posed by a hurricane striking New Orleans or the Gulf coast, mitigation measures or projects, emergency preparations, or emergency responses. We requested documents and communications from between August 2 and August 29, by officials of the Department of Defense or any constituent elements related to the threat posed by Hurricane Katrina, mitigation measures or projects, emergency preparations, or emergency responses. And, we requested documents and communications, including internal communications from between August 29 and September 15 by officials of the Department of Defense or any DOD elements related to the impact of Hurricane Katrina, mitigation measures or projects, emergency preparations, or emergency responses.

We also requested information about DOD's role and legal authority with respect to domestic emergencies and Hurricane Katrina. We wanted organizational charts, after-action reports, and plans with respect to national catastrophes. We requested information about DOD and the events of Hurricane Katrina, such as any guidance provided by the Secretary of Defense before landfall, the preparations made, specific actions taken, and personnel involved. We asked for information about Joint Task Force Katrina and on actions taken during Hurricane Katrina, specifically those of active duty troops and National Guard units; requests for assistance; and information on DOD's chain of command during the incident.

The Select Committee initially received responses from the Department of Defense on behalf of Secretary Rumsfeld that only partially complied with the various requests. On November 18, the Select Committee received a production from the Department containing: execution orders; requests for forces; correspondence regarding National Guard authorization; daily update briefings; and

FEMA

aily executive summaries. On December 14, the Select Committee received further production containing the oint Staff Director of Operations' (J-3) Redacted Timeline, utlining the Department's response actions to Hurricane atrina and the Joint Task Force Katrina Commander's ssessment Briefings.

In further response to the letter requests, on December 2 the Select Committee received: the Assistant Secretary or Defense for Homeland Defense's Smart Book; esponses to Senate interrogatories of September 28; ational Guard and Northcom timelines; Execute and eployment orders; NORTHCOM teleconference minutes; aptain Rick Snyder's, XO USS Bataan, Lessons Learned ackage; Vice Admiral Fitzgerald's e-mails, timelines, nd notes; 2nd Fleet Lessons Learned; Records of Annual lurricane exercises; memo to Admiral Starling regarding aval assets in the region; information regarding elicopter assets; Rear Admiral Kilkenny's Lessons Learned rief to the Chief of Naval Operations; Northcom requests or forces; Northcom deployment orders; Northcom meline; and twice-daily Joint Operations Center emails.

In addition the Department produced: Joint Forces ommand (JFCOM) timeline and logs of verbal rders; JFCOM Standard Operating Procedures; nified Command Plan; TOPOFF exercise paperwork;

Commander Fleet Forces command general requirement for Humanitarian Response/Disaster Relief; National Guard Bureau Readiness Documents; National Guard Bureau Senior Leadership Questions; and Katrina effects on National Guard Bureau readiness.

Despite these significant productions, Chairman Davis was concerned that the communications of senior Defense Department officials — a priority in the first request to the Department — had not been produced. Consequently, after discussions with Rep. Melancon, he issued a subpoena to the Department of Defense on December 14. The subpoena required the production of the correspondence of senior DOD officials related to Hurricane Katrina.

On December 22, the Select Committee received documents responsive to the subpoena, including official correspondence from Assistant Secretary Paul McHale, Principal Deputy Assistant Secretary Peter Verga, Admiral Keating, Lieutenant General Honoré, Lieutenant General Blum, and Colonel John Jordan. On December 30, the Select Committee received more documents responsive to the subpoena, including DOD official correspondence from Secretary Rumsfeld, Acting Deputy Secretary England, Colonel Daskevich, Brigadier General Scherling, Colonel Roberson, Colonel Chavez, Colonel Young,

Admiral Keating, and Principal Deputy Assistant Secretary Verga. On January 13, the Select Committee received further submissions of correspondence from Department officials including, Brigadier General Graham, Major General Young. And on January 17, the Select Committee received the emails of Major General Grass and Lieutenant General Vaughn.

The Select Committee also requested information from the White House. Specifically, the Select Committee requested documents and communications from before August 23 related to the threat posed by a hurricane striking New Orleans or the Gulf coast, mitigation measures or projects, emergency preparations, or emergency responses. We requested documents and communications from between August 23 and August 29 related to the threat posed by Hurricane Katrina, mitigation measures or projects, emergency preparations, or emergency responses. And we requested documents and communications from between August 29 and September 15 related to the impact of Hurricane Katrina, mitigation measures or projects, emergency preparations, or emergency responses. Initially, the White House produced more than 4,000 documents in response to these requests; however, the Select Committee was not satisfied with this initial production of documents.

In a December 6 letter, William Kelly, White House Deputy Counsel, said the September 30 and December 1 requests were too broad and asked the Select Committee to narrow the request. In response, the Select Committee insisted on briefings by senior administration officials and the production of certain items, including e-mails and documents from the White House Situation Room. As a result of our demands, a briefing was provided and more than 12,000 pages of documents from the Executive Office of the President on the response to Hurricane Katrina were delivered on December 16. The Select Committee made similar requests to the Vice President's office, which responded with almost 6,000 pages of documents.

While the Select Committee was disappointed and frustrated by the slow pace and general resistance to producing the requested documents by the White House and the Department of Defense, at the end of the day, the Select Committee believes it received enough information through documents, briefings, and interviews to understand the actions and decisions of those entities, and reach sound findings on them, without implicating executive privilege.

That's what this was about: obtaining sufficient information. Getting the documents and testimony we needed to make sure Americans are better prepared the next time. Ultimately, our public criticism of the Administration's slow pace did the job. At our insistence, the White House provided Deputy Assistant to the President for Homeland Security Ken Rapuano for a briefing with staff and Members. With the President in Texas, Homeland Security Advisor Frances Townsend out of the country, and Chief of Staff Andrew Card in Maine at the time of the storm, Rapuano offered the best view of White House knowledge and actions right before and right after Katrina. In fact, his briefing included more acknowledgements of institutional failure than any we had received previously.

The agreement with the White House gave us an opportunity to understand the White House role in Katrina while keeping the Select Committee on a parallel track with the Senate, which had not pursued White House subpoenas, and had not even subpoenaed DOD. A subpoena for White House documents would have simply derailed and delayed our inquiry, with the likelihood of a lengthy and unproductive court battle over executive privilege to follow.

State

The Select Committee sent request letters to governmenta components in the three states hit hardest by Hurricane Katrina: Alabama, Louisiana, and Mississippi. In each state, we requested information from both the office of the governor and the state's respective agency in charge of homeland security or emergency management.

Specifically, the Select Committee asked each state's governor's office for documents or communications, including internal communications, received, prepared, or sent up to the date of September 15 by state officials related to the threat posed by a hurricane, mitigation measures or projects, emergency preparations, or emergency responses. Also, for each state's office in charge of homeland security or emergency management, the Select Committee requested: information about that organization, including organization charts; the agency's responsibilities with respect to emergencies; regulations and procedures; after action reports for past hurricanes; past requests for federal grants; budgets for the agencies;

ontractors and subcontractors that assisted with Katrina; detailed chronology of events and actions taken during, before, and after the hurricane; key state personnel involved with Katrina; and all communications to and from the agencies relevant to the disaster.

The Select Committee also requested any state, county, and local emergency plans, and the identity of state and local agencies involved in those plans. Finally, the Select Committee asked for documents from the past five years that evaluate the threats posed by hurricanes and any information about exercises to prepare for hurricanes.

The Select Committee sent request letters to the Alabama Department of Homeland Security (ADHS), as well as the office of Governor Bob Riley. The State of Alabama answered all questions and replied to all requests. The state provided the Alabama Emergency Management Plan, 26 different situation reports, the Governor's proclamations, a timeline, and four Incident Action Plans. The state also provided communications such as a MOU with Mississippi, Alabama county emergency management standards, and state emergency procedures. In answering the Select Committee's questions, the state provided organization charts, key personnel, the roles and responsibilities of ADHS and the Alabama Emergency Management Agency (AEMA), state and county emergency plans and the state and local agencies involved in the response to Katrina. The state also provided risk assessments and after action reports and information on exercises to prepare for disasters. Alabama also provided information on budgets for the past five years. The state also provided timelines, a list of actions taken by state agencies in response to Katrina and a complete set of AEMA internal communications and action tracking system (EM 2000) messages.

The Select Committee sent requests to both the Louisiana Office of Homeland Security and Emergency Preparedness (LOHSEP) and to the office of Governor Kathleen Blanco. After asking for a 90 day extension on October 26 due to the need to address immediate hurricane relief, the Governor fully responded on December 1 with tens of thousands of documents on their response and preparation for Hurricane Katrina including: an overview of the Governor's actions, Executive Orders and declarations, emergency preparedness plans, the LA Citizen Awareness and Disaster Evacuation Guide, official correspondence, organization charts, notes and internal

communications. Included was the response of the Acting Deputy Director of LOHSEP based on "the best available information" in that agency's possession at that time, including specific responses to the committee's questions in the original Senate Committee letter.

The Louisiana Attorney General's Office responded with additional information on January 11 and also informed us there would be a slight delay in sending two CDs containing e-mails of the Louisiana National Guard due to technical problems. Those CDs arrived February 2.

The Select Committee sent request letters to both the Mississippi Emergency Management Agency (MEMA) and the Office of Governor Haley Barber. MEMA provided organization charts, and a listing of key personnel. MEMA produced state plans including the MS Comprehensive Emergency Management Plan (CEMP Vol. II), Contra-Flow Plan of August 2005, as well as many inter-agency state plans such as plans from Louisiana, transportation evacuation plans, and parish/city plans. MEMA provided risk assessments for hurricanes, floods, surges, and economic impacts. MEMA also included all Emergency Operations Center (EOC) maps of the state and local jurisdictions. MEMA provided information on plans and training exercises such as Hurricane Pam and Lifesaver 2004. Other items provided: timeline of events and communications such as director briefs, news releases, media advisories, MEMA situation reports, Incident Action Plans, EM 2000 messages, and mission assignments.

The documents produced by all three states and the federal government allowed the Select Committee to gain important insights into the workings of government entities stressed to the breaking point by a terrible disaster. They helped reveal the true nature of the relationship of state emergency management operations to the system of federal emergency management support. These documents allowed the Select Committee to reach conclusions about what worked well and what did not. Those conclusions will help improve preparation and response for the next disaster, protect the public, save lives, and reduce suffering. We don't pretend to have the entire universe of information related to the preparation for and response to Katrina. But we had more than enough to do our job. ∎

1 *Hearing on Hurricane Katrina: Voices from inside the Storm Before Select Comm.*, (Dec. 6, 2005) at 28 (statement of Patricia Thompson) [hereinafter *Dec. 6, 2005 Select Comm. Hearing*].

2 Interview by Select Comm. Staff with Juliette Saussy, Director, New Orleans Emergency Medical Services, in New Orleans, LA (Jan. 19, 2006).

3 Interview by Select Comm. Staff with Eddie Favre, Mayor of Bay St. Louis, in Waveland, MS (Jan. 20, 2006).

4 Interview by Select Comm. Staff with Brent Warr, Mayor of Gulfport, in Waveland, MS (Jan. 20, 2006).

5 Rep. Gene Taylor, comments to Select Comm. Members and Staff during bus tour of coastal MS (Jan. 20, 2006).

6 Rep. Gene Taylor, comments to Select Comm. Members and Staff during bus tour of coastal MS (Jan. 20, 2006).

7 *Hearing on Back to the Drawing Board: A First Look at Lessons Learned from Katrina Before House Gov't Reform Committee,* 109th Cong. (Sept. 15, 2005) at 11 (statement of Rep. Henry A. Waxman) [hereinafter *Sept. 15, 2005 Gov't Reform Hearing*].

8 *Sept. 15, 2005 Gov't Reform Hearing* at 12 (statement of Rep. Henry A. Waxman).

9 Nicholas Johnston, *Some House Democrats Want Larger Role in Katrina Investigation*, BLOOMBERG, Nov. 2, 2005.

10 *Id.*

11 *Id.*

12 *Hearing on Hurricane Katrina: Voice from Inside the Storm Before the Select Comm.*, 109th Cong. (Dec. 6, 2005).

13 Bill Walsh, *Plan would let president take control in disasters; Proposal may be seen as slap at Blanco*, TIMES-PICAYUNE (New Orleans), Oct. 22, 200. [hereinafter *Plan Article*].

14 *Plan Article*.

15 *See, e.g.*, George C. Wilson, *Suiting Up for the Next Katrina*, CONGRESS DAILY, Oct. 17, 2005 at 5.

16 E-mail correspondence from Johnny Anderson, aide to Gov. of LA, to other aides (Sept. 2, 2005) (11:56 p.m.).

17 John Barnshaw, *Continuing Significance of Race and Class among Houston Hurricane Katrina Evacuees,* NATURAL HAZARDS OBSERVER (Natural Hazards Center), Nov. 2005 at 2.

18 Wash. Post Kaiser Family Foundation, and Harvard University, *Survey of Hurricane Katrina evacuees* (2005).

19 Christine MacDonald, *Months After Katrina, a Local Storm Surge on Race and Class*, BOSTON GLOBE, Nov. 6, 2005 at 4.

20 Brookings Institution Metropolitan Policy Program, *New Orleans after the Storm: Lessons Learned from the Past, a Plan for the Future,* (Oct. 2005) at 6.

21 John Barnshaw, *Continuing Significance of Race and Class among Houston Hurricane Katrina Evacuees,* NATURAL HAZARDS OBSERVER (Natural Hazards Center), Nov. 2005 at 3.

22 Alison Stateman, *Time for a Change? What Hurricane Katrina Revealed About Race and Class in America*, PUBLIC RELATIONS STRATEGIST, Oct. 2005 at 8 (hereinafter *Strategist Article*).

23 *Strategist Article*.

FEMA

"The devastation along the Gulf Coast from Hurricane Katrina is like nothing I have witnessed before. It is catastrophic. Words cannot convey the physical destruction and personal suffering in that part of the nation."

Dr. Max Mayfield
Director, National Hurricane Center
Select Committee hearing, September 22, 2005

This report is a story about federal, state, and local emergency response plans, and how they were or were not implemented before and after Katrina. Where there were problems, we asked why. Where even flawless execution led to unacceptable results, we returned to questioning the underlying plans.

What this Select Committee has done is not rocket science. We've gathered facts and established timelines based on some fairly rudimentary but important questions posed to the right people in both the public and private sectors. What did you need and what did you get? Where were you in the days and hours right before, during, and after the storm? Who were you talking to? What were you doing? Does that match what you were *supposed* to be doing? Why or why not?

In other words, the Select Committee has matched what was *supposed to happen* under federal, state, and local plans against what *actually happened*. Our findings emerged from this process of matching. In this lengthy Background chapter, we beg your indulgence. We know that most readers do not care about acronyms or organizational charts, about authorities and capabilities or the concepts of "push" versus "pull." We know you simply want to know who was supposed to do what, when, and whether the job got done. And if it didn't get done, you want to know how we are going to make sure it does the next time.

We provide this background on the framework for emergency management to set the stage for the story we will tell. To understand the *failure of initiative*, we need to first explain the tools that were available to so many.

National framework for emergency management

General role of FEMA, creation of DHS, and FEMA's absorption into the department

The Federal Emergency Management Agency (FEMA) was established in 1979 in an effort to consolidate many of the federal policies related to the management of emergencies, including **preparedness, mitigation, disaster response, and recovery**.[1] Prior to FEMA's creation, through a mix of legislation and executive decisions, responsibility for federal emergency assistance as well as the types of assistance and eligibility underwent numerous changes. For example, administrative responsibility for assistance was shifted among a variety of federal departments, agencies, and the White House. In addition, the kinds of assistance the federal government provided and the types of organizations eligible were increased a number of times by, for example, adding provisions for disaster relief to small businesses and agricultural producers. By the late 1970s, these authorities and administrative changes had "developed into a complex mix of federal emergency management missions" with which state, local, and federal officials were dissatisfied, characterizing the situation as an inefficient maze of federal policies and responsible administrative entities.[2]

In 1978, following the incident at Three Mile Island, President Carter proposed reorganizing many of the emergency operational and coordination functions that had become dispersed throughout the federal government. In a reorganization plan submitted to Congress, the President proposed creating FEMA to administer many of the federal policies related to disasters, doing so based on a number of key principles:[3]

- Federal authorities to anticipate, prepare for, and respond to major civil emergencies should be supervised by one official responsible to the President and given attention by other federal officials at the highest levels;
- An effective civil defense system requires the most efficient use of all available resources (later embodied in the "all hazards" approach, through which civil defense capabilities would be available for any disaster, regardless of cause);
- Whenever possible, emergency responsibilities should be extensions of the regular missions of federal, state, and local agencies (later embodied in federal response plans through which FEMA coordinates and plans the assistance other federal agencies provide rather than providing the assistance directly);
- Federal intervention should be minimized by emphasizing hazard mitigation and state and local preparedness; and,

■ Federal hazard mitigation activities should be closely linked with emergency preparedness and response functions.

The President's reorganization plan took effect in April 1979 through two executive orders which created FEMA and assigned the various responsibilities previously dispersed throughout a number of other agencies.[4] These included, among others, the coordination of civil defense, civil emergency planning, and federal disaster relief;

FEMA

federal disaster preparedness; federal flood insurance authorities; dam safety; natural and nuclear disaster warning systems; and, coordination of preparedness and planning to reduce the consequences of major terrorist incidents.[5] To meet these responsibilities, FEMA focused on (1) enhancing the capability of state and local governments to respond to disasters; (2) coordinating with other federal agencies that provide resources to respond to disasters; (3) giving federal assistance directly to citizens recovering from disasters; (4) granting financial assistance to state and local governments; and, (5) providing leadership for hazard mitigation through grants, flood plain management, and other activities.[6]

FEMA's transfer to the Department of Homeland Security and role in disaster response

In 2002, Congress created the Department of Homeland Security (DHS) and placed FEMA within the new department. Specifically, the Homeland Security Act of 2002 (HSA) established in DHS the Emergency Preparedness and Response (EPR) Directorate, placing FEMA (except for its terrorism preparedness functions) into EPR along with a number of additional entities and functions.[7] For example, EPR also assumed responsibility for the Department of Health and Human Services' Office of Emergency Preparedness, which manages the National Disaster Medical System, a network of federal, state, local, private sector, and civilian volunteer medical and support personnel who augment local medical providers during disasters.[8] In addition to these functional responsibilities, the HSA assigned to EPR responsibility for:[9]

Providing federal assistance in response to requests of the states (or local governments via the states) is often referred to as a "pull" system.

■ promoting the effectiveness of emergency responders;
■ supporting the Nuclear Incident Response Team (NIRT) through standards, training exercises, and funding;
■ managing, overseeing, and coordinating federal response resources;
■ aiding disaster recovery;
■ creating an intergovernmental national incident management system;
■ consolidating existing federal response plans into one plan;
■ ensuring emergency responders have interoperative communications technology;
■ developing a coordinated strategy for public health-related activities; and
■ using private sector resources.

Federal vs. state and local roles

Pull vs. push system

The federal government responds to most natural disasters when the affected state(s) requests help because the disaster is of such severity and magnitude that an effective response is beyond the capabilities of the state and local governments.[10] This system in use for most disasters — providing federal assistance in response to requests of the states (or local governments via the states) — is often referred to as a "pull" system in that it relies on states to know what they need and to be able to request it from the federal government.[11]

In practice, states may make these requests before disasters strike because of the near certainty that federal assistance will be necessary after such an event (e.g., with hurricanes) or, afterwards, once they have conducted preliminary damage assessments and determined that their response capabilities are overwhelmed. In either case, the resources the federal government provides in any disaster response are intended to supplement state nd local government resources devoted to the ongoing disaster relief and recovery effort.[12]

In certain instances, however, the federal response may also be considered a "push" system, in which federal assistance is provided and/or moved into the affected area prior to a disaster or without waiting for specific requests from the state or local governments.[13] As discussed below, DHS's National Response Plan includes a component — the Catastrophic Incident Annex — that outlines the kinds of events that can cause damage so massive that first responders, local governments, and state governments are unable to request — or "pull" — federal assistance in the immediate aftermath of the incident, creating a situation in which "pushing" the federal resources might be necessary.

EMAC system to supplement state and local capabilities

Prior, or in addition, to seeking assistance from the federal governments, states are set up to help each other when disasters or emergencies overwhelm their capacity. States do so through participation in the Emergency Management Assistance Compact (EMAC), an interstate mutual aid agreement among member states to provide assistance after disasters overwhelm the affected state's capacity. Congress approved the creation of EMAC in 1996, building on the earlier efforts of the Southern Regional Emergency Compact that Florida and 16 other states created in 1993 after experiencing dissatisfaction with the state and federal response to Hurricane Andrew in 1992.[14] EMAC provides the legal structure for states to request assistance from one another as well as a menu of resources, such as temporary shelters and cargo aircraft, which may be available from other member states. Importantly, this assistance can, and often does, come from participating states' National Guards.[15] The National Emergency Management Association, the professional association of state emergency managers, administers the compact.[16]

Federal authorities and capabilities

When an incident overwhelms, or is likely to overwhelm, state and local resources, the Stafford Act authorizes the President, in response to a request from the governor of the affected state, to issue two types of declarations— emergency or major disaster.

Emergency declaration

The Stafford Act defines an emergency as "any occasion or instance for which, in the determination of the President, federal assistance is needed to supplement state and local efforts and capabilities to save lives and to protect property and public health and safety, or to lessen or avert the threat of a catastrophe in any part of the United States."[17] An emergency declaration is more limited in scope than a major disaster declaration; generally, federal assistance and funding for emergencies are provided to meet a specific need or to help prevent a major disaster from occurring.[18] Emergency assistance under such a declaration may include: grants to state and local governments for debris removal; direct assistance (grants) to individuals and households for temporary housing and other needs; and, assistance to states in distributing medicine and food.[19]

Major disaster declaration

A major disaster can result from a hurricane, earthquake, flood, tornado or other incident that clearly overwhelms the ability of state or local governments to respond on their own. A presidential declaration of a major disaster usually occurs after local and state governments have responded with their own resources (such as the National Guard), conducted damage assessments to determine losses and recovery needs, and determined that the disaster is of such severity and magnitude that an effective response is beyond

In certain instances, the federal response may be considered a "push" system, in which federal assistance is provided into the affected area prior to a disaster or without waiting for specific requests from the state or local governments.

the capabilities of the state and local governments.[20] Such a declaration sets into motion federal assistance to and support of state and local response efforts as well as long-term federal recovery programs.[21]

Principles of the National Response Plan and the National Incident Management System

Broadly speaking, the overall structure for the federal response to most disasters consists of the National Response Plan and National Incident Management System. The President issued Homeland Security Presidential Directive (HSPD)-5 in February 2003, directing DHS to develop a new plan for responding to emergencies (regardless of cause). Specifically, HSPD-5 required DHS to establish a single, comprehensive approach to the management of emergency events, whether the result of terrorist attacks or large-scale natural or accidental disasters.[22] According to DHS, the intent of this plan is to align federal coordination structures, capabilities, and resources into a unified, all-discipline, and all-hazards approach to domestic incident management.[23]

To implement HSPD-5, DHS developed the National Incident Management System (NIMS) and the National Response Plan (NRP). In short, the NRP defines what needs to be done in a large-scale emergency event and the NIMS defines how to manage it:

■ The NRP describes the structure and mechanisms for coordinating federal support during emergencies (or exercising direct federal authority).[24] It uses the framework of the NIMS to integrate federal government domestic prevention, protection, response, and recovery plans into a single operational plan for all hazards and all emergency response disciplines. The NRP describes operational procedures for federal support to state, local, and tribal emergency managers and defines situations in which federal authorities are to provide support and when federal authorities are to assume control. The NRP organizes capabilities, staffing, and equipment resources in terms of functions that are most likely to be needed during emergencies, such as communications or urban search and rescue, and spells out common processes and administrative requirements for executing the plan. DHS issued the NRP in December 2004 and used it for the first time in the preparation for and response to Hurricane Katrina.

■ NIMS consists of six major components of a systems approach to domestic incident management: command and management, preparedness, resource management, communications and information management, supporting technologies, and ongoing management and maintenance. According to DHS, NIMS "aligns the patchwork of federal special-purpose incident management and emergency response plans into an effective and efficient structure."[25] To do so, it defines the roles and responsibilities of federal, state, and local first responders during emergencies and establishes a core set of concepts, principles, terminology, and organizational processes to enable effective, efficient, and collaborative emergency event management at all levels. The concepts, principles, and processes underlying the NIMS are intended to improve the ability of different jurisdictions and first-responder disciplines to work together in various areas, such as command and communications.[26] NIMS, according to DHS, is based on an "appropriate balance of flexibility and standardization." It allows government and private entities to use an adjustable national framework to work together managing domestic incidents, no matter their cause, size, location, or complexity and, while doing so, provides a set of standardized organizational structures to improve interoperability among jurisdictions.[27] Beginning in federal fiscal year 2005, state and local governments were required to adopt NIMS in order to receive federal (DHS) preparedness grants or contracts.[28]

The NRP consists of 5 components: [29]

1. The *base plan* describes the overall structure and processes of a national approach to domestic incident management that integrates the efforts and resources of federal, state, local, tribal, private-sector, and non-governmental organizations. It includes planning assumptions (e.g., state and local capabilities may be overwhelmed), roles and responsibilities, a concept of operations, incident management actions, and instructions for maintaining and periodically updating the plan.

2. *Appendices* provide relevant, detailed supporting information, such as statutory authorities and a compendium of national interagency plans.

. *Support Annexes* provide guidance and describe the functional processes and administrative requirements for meeting various plan objectives, such as logistics management and coordination with the private sector (including representatives of critical infrastructure resources).

. *Emergency Support Annexes* spell out in detail the missions, policies, structures, and responsibilities of federal agencies for coordinating resource and programmatic support to state, local, and tribal governments as well as other federal agencies. Each Emergency Support Function (ESF) has a coordinator with ongoing responsibilities throughout the incident as well as one or more primary agencies responsible for accomplishing the ESF mission. Most ESFs also have support agencies responsible for assisting the primary agency or agencies.

Incident Annexes address contingency or hazard situations requiring specialized application of the NRP for seven different types of incidents: biological; catastrophic; cyber; food and agriculture; nuclear/ radiological; oil and hazardous materials; and, terrorism.

Emergency Support Functions

The ESFs are the primary vehicle through which DHS directly responds to disasters and coordinates the direct responses of other federal agencies as well as groups like the American Red Cross (Red Cross).[30] For each of the 15 ESFs, DHS identifies a primary federal agency (or, in one case, a lead organization, the Red Cross. For most ESFs, DHS also identifies one or more support agencies. Primary agencies' responsibilities include orchestrating federal support for their ESF, managing mission assignments and coordinating with state agencies, and executing contracts and procuring goods and services as needed. Support agencies' responsibilities include conducting operations at the request of DHS or the ESF primary agency, assisting with situation (or damage) assessments, and participating in training or other exercises having to do with their prevention, response, and recovery activities.[31]

The 15 ESFs, their overall purpose, primary and support agencies are as follows:

Emergency Support Function	Purpose	Primary Agency	Support Agencies
1—transportation[32]	To support DHS, other federal agencies, state, and local responders requiring transportation.	U.S. Department of Transportation	Agriculture (Forest Service); DOD; U.S. Army Corps of Engineers; DHS; Interior
2—communications[33]	To ensure the provision of federal communications support to federal, state, local, private sector response efforts during an Incident of National Significance; supplement the National Plan for Telecommunications Support in Non-wartime Emergencies (NTSP).	DHS/Information Analysis and Infrastructure Protection/National Communications System	Agriculture (Forest Service); Interior; FEMA
3—public works and engineering[34]	To coordinate and organize the capabilities and resources of the federal government to facilitate the delivery of services, technical assistance, engineering expertise, construction management, and other support relative to the condition of (or damage to) public works infrastructure and facilities.	DOD/U.S. Army Corps of Engineers (during response); FEMA (during recovery)	USDA; HHS; Interior; EPA; American Red Cross
4—firefighting[35]	To detect and suppress fires resulting from an Incident of National Significance by providing personnel, equipment, and supplies in support of state, local, and tribal agencies involved in firefighting operations.	Department of Agriculture/ Forest Service	Commerce; DOD; U.S. Army Corps of Engineers; DHS
5—emergency management[36]	To support the overall activities of the federal government for domestic incident management by providing the core management and administrative support functions in support of the NRCC, RRCC, and JFO[37] operations; ESF 5 is the "support ESF for all federal departments and agencies…from prevention to response and recovery."	FEMA	None
6—mass care, housing, and human services[38]	To support the state, regional, local and tribal government and non-governmental efforts to address the nonmedical mass care, housing, and human services needs of individuals affected by Incidents of National Significance. Mass care includes organizing feeding operations and coordinating bulk distribution of emergency relief items; housing involves providing short- and long-term assistance with housing needs; and, human services includes counseling and identifying support for special needs populations.	FEMA American Red Cross	Agriculture (Food and Nutrition Service; Forest Service); U.S. Army Corps of Engineers; DHS/National Disaster Medical System; Interior
7—resource support[39]	To assist DHS and supporting federal, state, and local agencies prior to, during, and after incidents of national significance with emergency relief supplies, facility space, office equipment, office supplies, telecommunications and others services.	GSA	DHS
8—public health and medical services[40]	To provide coordinated federal assistance to supplement state and local resources in response to public health and medical care needs for incidents of national significance. Federal support can consist of assessment of public health needs, public health surveillance, medical care personnel, and medical equipment and supplies.	HHS	DOD; U.S. Army Corps of Engineers; DHS; DOT; American Red Cross

Emergency Support Function	Purpose	Primary Agency	Support Agencies
—urban search and rescue[41]	To rapidly deploy the National Urban Search and Rescue (US&R) response system to provide specialized life-saving assistance to state and local authorities during an incident of national significance. US&R activities include locating and extracting victims and providing onsite medical assistance.	FEMA	Agriculture (Forest Service); DOD; U.S. Army Corps of Engineers; DHS/ U.S. Coast Guard; DHS/ Border and Transportation Security Directorate; DOT; U.S. AID
0—oil and hazardous materials response[42]	To provide a coordinated response to actual or potential oil and hazardous materials discharges or releases during incidents of national significance. ESF 10 operates by placing the mechanisms of the National Oil and Hazardous Substances Pollution Contingency Plan (NCP) within the broader NRP coordination structure. The NCP describes the National Response System—an organized network of agencies, programs, and resources with authorities and responsibilities in oil and hazardous materials response.	EPA DHS/U.S. Coast Guard[43]	Commerce/NOAA
1—agriculture and natural resources[44]	To support state, local tribal and other federal agencies' efforts to (1) address the provision of nutrition assistance, including determining needs, obtaining appropriate food supplies, and arranging for delivery of the supplies; (2) control and eradication of disease outbreaks and plant infestations; (3) assurance of food safety and security; and (4) protection of natural and cultural resources and historic (NCH) properties.	Department of Agriculture Department of the Interior (NCH properties)	DOD; American Red Cross
2—energy[45]	To restore damaged energy systems and components during a potential or actual Incident of National Significance; collect, evaluate, and share information on energy system damage and estimations on the impact of energy system outages within affected areas.	Department of Energy	Agriculture/Rural Utilities Service; Commerce/NOAA; U.S. Army Corps of Engineers; DHS; Interior; Department of Labor; Department of State; EPA; Nuclear Regulatory Commission; Tennessee Valley Authority (TVA)
3—public safety and security[46]	To provide via federal to federal support or federal support to state and local authorities a mechanism for coordinating and providing non-investigative/ non-criminal law enforcement, public safety, and security capabilities and resources.	DHS Department of Justice	Agriculture (Forest Service); DHS/Border and Transportation Security Directorate; DHS/Customs and Border Protection; DHS/ Immigration and Customs Enforcement; Interior
4—long-term community recovery and mitigation[47]	To provide a framework for federal support to enable community recovery from the long-term consequences of an Incident of National Significance.	Agriculture Commerce DHS/FEMA HUD Treasury SBA	Commerce; U.S. Army Corps of Engineers; Department of Energy; HHS; DHS; Interior; Department of Labor; DOT; EPA; TVA; American Red Cross
5—external affairs[48]	To provide accurate, coordinated, and timely information to affected audiences, including governments, media, the private sector, and the local populace.	FEMA	Commerce/NOAA; Department of Justice; Corporation for National and Community Service

Catastrophic disasters and incidents of National Significance (INS)

Recognizing that certain disasters are so different in terms of size, scope, and damage that they require a response above and beyond the normal procedures for "emergencies" and "major disasters," DHS defines and has distinct plans for the federal response to "catastrophic" disasters.[49] Specifically, DHS defines a catastrophic event as:

> Any natural or manmade incident, including terrorism, that results in extraordinary levels of mass casualties, damage, or disruption severely affecting the population, infrastructure, environment, economy, national morale, and/or government functions. A catastrophic event could result in sustained national impacts over a prolonged period of time; almost immediately exceeds resources normally available to state, local, tribal and private-sector authorities in the impacted area; and significantly interrupts governmental operations and emergency services to such an extent that national security could be threatened.[50]

Using this definition, DHS makes a number of assumptions about the scenarios that will unfold before, during, and after a catastrophic disaster and attempts to structure the federal response to address those assumptions (and their ramifications). DHS assumes:[51]

- A catastrophic incident results in large numbers of casualties and/or displaced persons;
- The incident may cause significant disruption of the area's critical infrastructure, including transportation, telecommunications, and public health and medical systems;
- Response activities may have to begin without the benefit of a detailed or complete situation and needs assessment because a detailed, credible operating picture may not be possible for 24 to 48 hours or longer after the incident;

- The federal government may have to mobilize and deploy assets before local and state governments request them via normal protocols because timely federal support may be necessary to save lives, prevent suffering, and mitigate severe damage; and,
- Large numbers of people may be left temporarily or permanently homeless and require temporary or longer-term interim housing.

Consequently, in anticipation of or soon after a catastrophic incident, DHS is expected to rapidly — and proactively — provide critical resources to assist and augment the ongoing state and local responses. To do so, when the Secretary of DHS declares a disaster to be "catastrophic," the department also implements the Catastrophic Incident Annex of the National Response Plan.[52] DHS characterizes this annex as establishing the context and overarching strategy for implementing and coordinating an accelerated, proactive national response to certain catastrophic disasters. When this annex is implemented, all federal agencies and others with responsibilities under the Emergency Support Functions (ESFs) of the National Response Plan are supposed to immediately begin operations. Specifically, DHS expects the federal government and others will need to provide expedited help in one or more of the following areas:[53]

- Mass care (shelter, food, emergency first aid, etc.), housing, and human services;
- Urban search and rescue, such as locating, extricating, and providing onsite medical treatment;
- Decontamination in incidents involving weapons of mass destruction;
- Public health and medical support;
- Medical equipment and supplies;
- Casualty and fatality management and transportation for deceased, injured, or exposed victims; and,
- Public information when state and local public communications channels are overwhelmed.

When the Secretary of DHS declares a disaster to be "catastrophic," the Department implements the Catastrophic Incident Annex of the National Response Plan.

All catastrophic incidents are "incidents of national significance."

Because of fundamental and time-critical differences in catastrophic disasters, FEMA has established protocols to pre-identify and rapidly deploy essential resources. Among other things, FEMA assumes the demands of responding to a catastrophic disaster may mean it has to expedite or even temporarily suspend normal operating procedures for state and local governments to request assistance, doing so proactively rather than in response to things like specific requests based on detailed damage assessments.[54] For catastrophic incidents, DHS is supposed to activate and deploy DHS-managed teams, equipment caches, and other resources in order to accelerate the timely provision of critically skilled resources and capabilities.[55] These can include medical and search and rescue teams, transportable shelters, and preventive and therapeutic pharmaceutical caches that may be necessary to save lives and contain damage.

Incidents of National Significance

DHS defines incidents of national significance (INS) as those high-impact events that require a coordinated and effective response by an appropriate combination of federal, state, local, tribal, private-sector, and nongovernmental entities in order to save lives, minimize damage, and provide the basis for long-term community recovery and mitigation activities." All catastrophic incidents are also "incidents of national significance."[56] DHS bases this definition of an INS on criteria drawn from HSPD-5:[57]

A federal department or agency acting under its own authority has requested the assistance of the Secretary of Homeland Security;

The resources of state and local authorities are overwhelmed and federal assistance has been requested by the appropriate state and local authorities in response to major disaster declarations under the Stafford Act or catastrophic incidents (as defined by DHS, above);

More than one federal department or agency has become substantially involved in responding to an incident, for example, in response to credible threats or warnings of imminent terrorist attacks; and,

The President directs the Secretary of Homeland Security to assume responsibility for managing a domestic incident.

Managing the federal response to emergencies and disasters and implementing the National Response Plan

To respond to a disaster or a potential situation that is likely to require a federal response, DHS (on its own or acting via FEMA) uses existing homeland security monitoring operations; creates or activates operational components to manage the federal response; and, designates one or more officials to coordinate. The operational components DHS uses or which can be activated (or take on situation-specific duties) include the Homeland Security Operations Center (HSOC), the Interagency Incident Management Group (IIMG), a National or Regional Coordination Center (NRCC or RRCC), Emergency Response Teams (an Advance Element, ERT-A; and a National team, ERT-N), and, the Joint Field Office (JFO), which can have one or two high-level officials directing and coordinating the federal response.

Homeland Security Operations Center

The Homeland Security Operations Center, which represents over 35 agencies, including state and local law enforcement as well as federal intelligence agencies, is always in operation. It provides situational awareness, and monitors conditions in the United States, and, in conjunction with the DHS Office of Information Analysis, issues advisories and bulletins concerning specific threats to the nation.[58] The HSOC continually monitors potential major disasters and emergencies and, when such an event occurs (or is likely) provides primary situational awareness to the Secretary and the White House. Depending on the nature of the incident and the response it demands, the HSOC may activate the Interagency Incident Management Group (IIMG).[59]

Interagency Incident Management Group

DHS is supposed to convene the IIMG when it declares a situation to be an Incident of National Significance. In addition, DHS should convene the IIMG when it determines there is a need to do so in response to incidents such as major disasters, a heightened threat situation, or, high-profile, large-scale events that present high-risk targets, such as National Special Security Events (NSSEs).[60] The IIMG is comprised of senior representatives from other DHS agencies, other federal departments and agencies, and non-governmental organizations, such as the American Red Cross, as needed. When activated, the IIMG (1) maintains strategic situational awareness of threat assessments and ongoing incident-related operations and activities; (2) provides decision-making support for incident-related prevention, preparedness, response, and recovery efforts; (3) synthesizes key intelligence, frames issues, and makes recommendations with respect to policy, operational courses of action, and resource allocation; (4) anticipates evolving federal resource and operational requirements; and, (5) maintains ongoing coordination with the Principal Federal Official (PFO) and the Joint Field Office (JFO) Coordination Group.[61]

Regional Response Coordination Center, National Response Coordination Center

For most major disasters, incidents, or emergencies, DHS (via FEMA) establishes a Regional Response Coordination Center (RRCC) using staff from regional offices. The RRCC coordinates the initial regional and field activities, such as deployment of advance teams of FEMA and other agencies' staff, and implements local federal program support until a multi-agency coordination center can be established. Depending on the scope and impact of the event, DHS (via FEMA) may also establish a National Response Coordination Center (NRCC) comprised of ESF representatives and FEMA support staff to carry out initial activation and mission assignment operations from FEMA headquarters. The NRCC supports the operations of the RRCC.[62]

Emergency Response Team-Advance Element, National Emergency Response Team

FEMA's Emergency Response Team (ERT) is the principal interagency group that staffs the multi-agency coordination center where federal, state, and local officials coordinate and direct response and recovery operations.[63] Each FEMA region maintains an ERT ready to deploy in response to threats or incidents. Before a disaster or incident (when there is warning) or soon thereafter,

the RRCC typically deploys an Emergency Response Team-Advance Element (ERT-A) to the affected area(s). The ERT-A conducts preliminary damage and needs assessments and begins coordinating with the state as well as any federal resources that may be part of the initial deployment. For large-scale, high-impact events or when FEMA otherwise determines it is needed, FEMA also deploys a National Emergency Response Team (ERT-N), which is a national-level field response team. FEMA currently has 2 ERT-Ns.

Joint Field Office

The Joint Field Office (JFO) is a multiagency coordination center that FEMA establishes locally to serve as the central point for coordinating and directing the efforts of the federal, state, and local officials involved in the response effort.[64] Often, FEMA establishes the JFO at the state's emergency operations center or other locations from which the affected state is directing response efforts. For a Stafford Act emergency or major disaster declaration, the President must designate a Federal Coordinating Officer (FCO) to direct all federal assistance in the disaster area.[65]

The Joint Field Office (JFO) is a multiagency coordination center that FEMA establishes locally to serve as the central point for coordinating and directing the efforts of the federal, state, and local officials involved in the response effort.

During an incident of national significance, which may or may not involve a Stafford Act declaration,[66] the Secretary of DHS may designate a Principal Federal Official (PFO) to act as the secretary's representative in overseeing and executing incident management responsibilities.

The FCO is responsible for managing and coordinating federal assistance in response to declared disasters and emergencies. The FCO has the authority under the Stafford Act to request and direct federal agencies to use their authorities and resources to support or conduct response and recovery operations. The FCO provides overall coordination for the federal components of the PFO and works in partnership and support of the state officials to determine and meet state and local needs for assistance.[67]

The PFO is the primary point of contact and source of situational awareness for the Secretary of DHS for incidents of national significance. The PFO is expected to facilitate federal support to the unified command structure that is set up in conjunction with state and local officials. Also, PFOs coordinate the overall federal incident management and assistance activities throughout all of the phases of emergency management—prevention, preparedness, response, and recovery. In carrying out this coordination role, the PFO does not have direct authority over the FCO or other federal and state officials.[68]

The Role of DOD, the National Guard, and the U.S. Coast Guard

The Department of Defense (DOD) makes a distinction between "homeland security" and "homeland defense" in defining mission responsibilities. Whereas homeland security refers to a concerted *national* effort to secure the homeland from threats and violence, including terrorism, homeland defense refers to *military* protection of United States territory, domestic population, and critical defense infrastructure against external threats and aggression. In the context of homeland security, DOD operates only in support of a civilian-led federal agency, referred to as Civil Support (CS). In the area of homeland defense (HD), however, DOD is the lead agency. The Assistant Secretary of Defense for Homeland Defense (ASDHD) is charged with leading the Department's activities in homeland defense, and serves as DOD's interagency liaison.[69]

Military Support to Civil Authorities

Natural Disasters	Special Events	Manmade Disaster
Severe Weather	Olympics	CBRNE-CM
Firefighting	Summits	Terrorist Incident
Earthquakes	World Fair	Oil Spill

CBRNE-CM chemical, biological, radiological, nuclear, and high-yield explosives-consequence management

JOINT PUBLICATIONS 3-26 HOMELAND SECURITY

Under the National Response Plan (NRP)[70] and the recently released DOD Joint Doctrine on Homeland Security[71] Military Support to Civil Authorities (MSCA) is normally provided only when local, state and other federal resources are overwhelmed and the Lead Federal Agency (LFA) responding to an incident or natural disaster requests assistance. This is a fundamental principle of DOD's approach to civil support: "[I]t is generally a resource of last resort."[72]

An exception is in cases of *immediate response authority*, a scenario entailing imminently serious conditions resulting from any civil emergency or attack requiring immediate action, where local military commanders may take such actions as necessary to save lives, prevent human suffering, and mitigate great property damage.[73]

The federal military role described in the NRP and the MSCA is apart from National Guard resources available to governors of affected states. Governors may utilize their own National Guard units, as well as other National Guard units made available by state EMAC compacts. In most circumstances, National Guard troops fall under the command of the Governor and the state Adjutant General, and they follow state emergency procedures.

When in state active duty status, the National Guard remains under the command of the governor, not DOD. The National Guard can also be "federalized" by the President to be placed under the command of DOD. As discussed below, a governor may also seek "Title 32 status" for the National Guard, which leaves the governor and the state Adjutant General in command, but provides federal funding and benefits.[74]

Natural disasters and man-made disasters

In the event of a natural disaster or emergency the NRP stipulates that DOD may be asked to provide assistance to DHS and FEMA in an attempt to save lives, protect property, and lessen the threat of catastrophe in the United States. When disasters occur and a military response is anticipated, DHS/FEMA will request a Defense Coordinating Officer (DCO) to serve as the single DOD point of contact within the disaster area. The DCO will be the operational contact to the designated combatant commander and designated Joint Task Force (JTF) commander.[75]

In situations when a disaster is anticipated and DOD wants to be forward leaning, Northern Command has designated a DCO prior to a DHS/FEMA request. This is done informally and is intended to allow the DCO to integrate into the state emergency operations center (EOC) as early as possible to begin assessing the needs of the affected area. This has been done in the absence of a Presidential directive and before state authorities have made specific requests for DOD support via FEMA. Additionally, the doctrine of immediate response is a DOD directive which allows deployment of some DOD resources prior to receiving formal requests from the lead federal agency.[76]

Northern Command

Within the DOD Joint Staff, civil support responsibilities reside with the Joint Director of Military Support. Northern Command (NORTHCOM) is the DOD coordinating command for domestic terrorist and natural disaster incidents. Northern Command carries out civil support missions with forces assigned as required from all the armed services, typically through the creation of a joint task force.[77] NORTHCOM has a permanently assigned Joint Interagency Coordination Group, comprised of liaison officers from other DOD components and other federal agencies, including the Department of Homeland Security.

As discussed above, unless there is specific direction from the President, requests for military assistance must originate from a lead federal agency. Typically, this falls to FEMA in natural disasters. Requests are submitted to the Office of the Secretary of Defense (OSD), where they are evaluated by the Assistant Secretary of Defense for Homeland Defense (ASDHD) according to the following criteria: legality, readiness, lethality, risk, cost, and appropriateness.[78]

Once the requests are approved by OSD, they are forwarded to the Joint Director of Military Support within the Joint Staff, who in turn provides the appropriate orders to Northern Command. A Defense Coordinating Officer is designated and deployed to the area of incident.

When the size of the response is of a greater scale, a joint task force will be created, with the DCO normally serving as task force commander. The DCO then serves as the single point of contact for DOD resources, but does not have operational control of the U.S. Army Corps of Engineers or National Guard personnel operating in state active duty or Title 32 status.[79]

The process for requesting DOD active duty forces has several layers of review. Requests for DOD assistance are to be generated at the state level. These go from the state to FEMA's Federal Coordinating Officer, who in turn requests assistance from the DCO. The DCO passes these requests on to the joint task force, which routes it through NORTHCOM to the Office of the Secretary of Defense Executive Secretariat, to the Joint Directorate of Military Support.[80]

At each stage, the requirement is validated to ensure that the request can be met and that it is legal to provide the requested assests. Once vetted, the request is tasked to the services and coordinated with Joint Forces Command and forces or resources are then allocated to the joint task force, which in turn gets the support down to the user level by way of the DCO. This process is in place not only to satisfy DOD internal requirements, but to ensure maximum coordination with both FEMA and state governments.

National Guard Bureau

The National Guard is the nation's first military responder to events within the United States. Governors historically rely on the Guard to assist civilian authorities during times of natural or manmade disasters. In particular, the National Guard is a major asset in responding to any catastrophic incident within the United States. The National Guard is a reserve component of the Departments of the Army and the Air Force, at times, called in to support federal operations. The National Guard is also a force for each state, deploying for state duty status under the control of the governor. Only the National Guard has the unique dual mission of providing forces at both the state and federal levels and is the only service that abides by two oaths-of-office, one to the governor and one to the President of the United States.[81]

The governor has command and control of the National Guard, either in state active duty or Title 32 status, unless units are federalized.[82] If federalized under Title 10, the Guard falls under the command and control of the President. While on state active duty status, the Guard's mission is to serve its state or territory during times of crisis, disaster, civil disturbance or other threats to life and property as directed by the governor. They are funded by state dollars and are entitled to state benefits and compensation. Under Title 32 status, the National Guard is trained and resourced to support federal war-fighting operations, yet remains under control of the governor, while supported by federal funds with Secretary of Defense approval.[83]

During Hurricane Katrina, the governors of Alabama, Mississippi, and Louisiana requested that all National Guard forces deployed to their states operate under Title 32 status. This request was granted retroactively to August 29 by the Secretary of Defense. Under Title 32, the governors were in command of all National Guard assets and actions during Hurricane Katrina.[84]

The National Guard may also be called up by a governor at his or her own initiative, paid by the state, to respond to a state emergency or protect state facilities. Many states do not have the fiscal resources to use the National Guard extensively in this manner.

The National Guard Bureau (NGB) is the home of the leadership of the National Guard, headed by a Chief, who is supported by the Director of Army National Guard and the Director of the Air National Guard.[85] These positions, filled by military Guard personnel, are Title 10 positions. The current chief of the National Guard Bureau is Lieutenant General H Steven Blum, and although he is

the senior Guard officer, he does not command National Guard forces. Lieutenant General Daniel James, III is the Director of the Air National Guard and Lieutenant General Clyde A. Vaughn is Director of the Army National Guard.

Under the National Response Plan, the role of the National Guard Bureau is not defined. However, in roughly 50 percent of the states and territories, the Adjutant General also serves as the state's senior emergency management official, responsible for coordinating and integrating all response agencies.[86] The National Guard Bureau and the National Guard of the individual states and territories work on a daily basis with local, state, and federal civilian agencies in various communities in all of the states and territories.

United States Coast Guard

The Coast Guard is a military, multi-mission, maritime service within the Department of Homeland Security and one of the nation's five armed services. Since its founding as the Revenue Cutter Service in 1790, the Coast Guard has provided maritime safety and security capabilities, and is renowned worldwide for it search and rescue (SAR) capabilities, whether near the shore or hundreds of miles at sea. Title 14 of the United States Code requires the Coast Guard to develop, establish, maintain and operate rescue facilities for the promotion of safety on, under and over the high seas and waters subject to the jurisdiction of the United States.

Additionally, with the passage of the Maritime Transportation Security Act (MTSA) in 2002, the Coast Guard was given added responsibilities for the enforcement of port safety, security, and marine environmental regulations including the protection and security of vessels, harbors, and waterfront facilities, deepwater ports and waterways safety.[87]

The Coast Guard has a longstanding history in the Gulf of Mexico region. The current Eighth Coast Guard District, headquartered in New Orleans, covers all or part of 26 states throughout the Gulf coast and heartland of America. It stretches from the Appalachian Mountains and Chattahoochee River in the east to the Rocky Mountains in the west, and from the U.S.-Mexico border and the Gulf of Mexico to the Canadian border in North Dakota, which includes 15,490 miles of coastline and 10,300 miles of inland navigable waterways.[88]

Within the Coast Guard's District boundaries, the operational Coast Guard is organized into Sectors which oversee response, prevention, and logistics units, and coordinate Coast Guard operations within the Sector's geographic boundaries. The areas most affected by Hurricane Katrina are those that fall within the boundaries of Sector New Orleans and Sector Mobile, Alabama.

Private authorities and capabilities — role of the American Red Cross

The American Red Cross (Red Cross) is the only nongovernmental organization with lead agency responsibilities under the NRP. The Red Cross is an independent, non-governmental organization (NGO)[89] that operates as a nonprofit, tax-exempt, charitable institution pursuant to a charter granted by the United States Congress.[90] It has the legal status of a "federal instrumentality" due to its charter requirements to carry out responsibilities delegated by the federal government. Among those responsibilities are:

> to perform all duties incumbent upon a national society in accordance with the spirit and conditions of the Geneva Conventions to which the United States is a signatory, to provide family communications and other forms of assistance to members of the U.S. military, and to maintain a system of domestic and international disaster relief, including mandated responsibilities under the Federal Response Plan coordinated by the Federal Emergency Management Agency (FEMA).[91]

The Red Cross is not a federal agency, nor does it receive federal funding on a regular basis to carry out its services and programs.[92] It receives financial support from voluntary public contributions and from cost-recovery charges for some services.[93] Its stated mission is to "provide relief to victims of disasters and help people prevent, prepare for, and respond to emergencies."[94]

To meet its mandated responsibilities under the NRP, the Red Cross functions as an ESF primary organization in coordinating the use of mass care resources in a presidentially declared disaster or emergency.[95] As the lead agency for ESF #6, dealing with Mass Care, Housing and Human Services, the Red Cross assumes the role of providing food, shelter, emergency first aid, disaster welfare information and bulk distribution of emergency relief items.[96] ESF #6 includes three primary functions: Mass Care, Housing, and Human Services:[97]

■ Mass Care involves the coordination of nonmedical care services to include sheltering of victims, organizing feeding operations, providing emergency first aid at designated sites, collecting and providing information on victims to family members, and coordinating bulk distribution of emergency relief items.

■ Housing involves the provision of assistance for short- and long-term housing needs of victims.

■ Human Services include providing victim-related recovery efforts such as counseling, identifying support for persons with special needs, expediting processing of new Federal benefits claims, assisting in collecting crime victim compensation for acts of terrorism, and expediting mail services in affected areas.

Function 1: Mass Care

■ The NRP describes the Mass Care function as comprised of six elements: coordination, shelter, feeding, emergency first aid, Disaster Welfare Information ("DWI"), and bulk distribution.[98]

■ The coordination element relates to assisting victims obtain various forms of available federal assistance, as well as gathering information about shelters and food kitchens for victims.

■ The shelter element includes the use of pre-identified shelters, creating temporary facilities capable of housing victims, and coordination of obtaining shelters outside of the immediate incident area.

■ The feeding element includes a variety of food distribution sites, from mobile food carts, to kitchens, to bulk distribution of food.

■ The emergency first-aid element consists of assisting victims with the most basic first-aid needs, as well as, coordinating the referral of victims to local hospitals, if needed, and other appropriate medical treatment options.

■ The Disaster Welfare Information ("DWI") element provides for family connectedness services. It aims to re-connect families displaced or separated by the incident, as well as assist victims of the incident to connect with family or friends located outside the area of the incident.

■ The bulk distribution element provides emergency relief items, principally ice, water and food, at specific sites to meet the urgent needs of victims within the affected area.

Function 2: Housing

The housing function addresses both the short and long-term housing needs of victims affected by an incident.[99] It is effectuated through programs designed to meet the individualized needs of victims and includes a variety of options, including provision of temporary housing, rental assistance, or financial assistance for the repair or replacement of original residences.

Function 3: Human Services

The human services function implements programs and services to assist victims restore their livelihoods.[100] It acts as a broad-based, multipurpose effort to support divergent needs such as re-routing of mail, assistance with processing federal benefits-related paperwork, assuring the provision of necessary mental health services, and providing other important, sometimes victim-specific services. The wide range of services may include support for victims with disabilities and victims who do not speak English.

With its shelters, feeding kitchens, and blood distribution capabilities, the Red Cross has long played an important role in assisting those affected by natural disasters — especially hurricanes. Due to the frequency of hurricanes in the United States, the Red Cross has developed an expertise in deploying its resources and operational capabilities to help those affected by hurricanes. In its 23-page *Tropical Storm and Hurricane Action Plan*, ("Hurricane Plan") the Red Cross outlines its systematic approach to preparing for and responding to tropical storms and hurricanes.[101] "The objective of this plan is to enable the Red Cross to be ready to deliver immediate services and assistance needed by those threatened and affected by such storms at an appropriate scope and scale," the report says.[102]

Additionally, as the NRP-model to disaster planning takes shape, the Red Cross' preparation regime is being bolstered with a Standard Operating Procedure Document for ESF #6.[103] Although not formally adopted and still in the draft stage, the document identifies the procedures, protocols, information flows and organizational relationships for the activation, implementation and operation of the Red Cross' responsibilities under ESF #6. There is also an interim Shelter Operations Management Tool Kit, which provides Red Cross chapters and shelter managers with resources to plan, open, operate, and close shelters.[104]

Adhering to the concept of all disasters being local, the Red Cross relies on its field chapters to act as first responders in opening shelters and providing for the feeding of those in need.[105] The first 48 hours of a disaster are usually handled by the local Red Cross chapters, and thereafter by national-level support, as both the federal government (FEMA), and the Red Cross National Headquarters, begin to reach the affected area.[106] The national Red Cross is structured to provide relief (mostly shelter and feeding) from days two through 30 of a disaster.[107] The local chapter ultimately is supported by its service area, of which there are eight in the United States, followed by support from the National Headquarters in Washington, D.C.[108]

For disasters such as hurricanes, the Red Cross' actions prior to landfall typically begin with activating the chapter response plans in all of the areas threatened by the storm.[109] Simultaneously, the jurisdictional service areas move into the Service Area Major Disaster Response Structure ("Disaster Response Structure"). At this time the service areas establish their contacts with the affected state's emergency operations center ("EOC"). This often involves positioning a Red Cross official at the state EOC. The service area then begins deploying resources to the threatened areas as called for under the chapters' planning requirements. Also, at this pre-landfall time, a disaster relief operations headquarters is established.[110]

During the pre-landfall stage, the local chapter is to focus on several key activities: sheltering, feeding, public information, fundraising and maintaining contact with government officials, specifically emergency management officials.[111] While the chapter response operation is arming itself with the necessary resources, the service areas shift into their Disaster Response Structure. The service area personnel are responsible for implementing the necessary facility arrangements so that storm victims can be sheltered and fed. The service area also deploys additional personnel to the chapter regions. Once the Disaster Response Structure is opened, the national headquarters shifts its Disaster Operations Center into hurricane response mode.[112] At this point, personnel from Headquarters' Preparedness and Response division are able to monitor developments and deploy additional resources as necessary.

Following landfall of a hurricane, the affected chapters continue their focus on the key activities of sheltering, feeding, disaster assessment, providing public information and liaising with government officials.[113] After the shelters and feeding kitchens are opened, the chapters expand their role to include bulk distribution of supplies. Supplies include toiletries packages, clothing and blankets, and as the storm passes, clean-up supply packs, including mops, rakes, trash bags, and cleaning supplies to assist storm victims clean their residences and neighborhoods.[114]

As the impact of the disaster becomes better understood, a Disaster Relief Operation Headquarters is established in the region. The operations headquarters is activated, meaning operational oversight and direction of Red Cross relief activities is transferred to the on-site

headquarters.[115] As the disaster headquarters staffs up, the service area's role decreases.

Outside of the affected region, other service areas and the national headquarters remain poised to assist as necessary. The main opportunities for other service areas involve shifting resources, such as cots, blankets, and other warehoused supplies, to the affected region. Personnel at national headquarters monitor events in the field and leverage relationships with national agreements with suppliers, partner groups and agencies.[116]

Service area major Disaster Response Structure

Upon the approach of a threatening hurricane, "the service area reconfigures its structure, priorities and action to provide support, guidance and resource assistance to its threatened chapters."[117] The Disaster Response Structure, led by a response manager, is comprised of four departments or cells. These are the planning cell, forward headquarters cell, information and resource management cell, and the service area response operations.[118]

Planning cell

The planning cell is focused on ensuring adequate services and logistics support. "The planning cell develops an anticipated service delivery plan and deploys the forward headquarters cell, which enables the relief operation to begin service delivery immediately after the storm makes landfall."[119] The planning cell is tasked with determining the necessary scope of Red Cross service delivery, an estimated budget and the estimated length of time needed to serve the affected area.[120] The planning cell is the heart of decision making as it relates to what people need, where they need it, and, based on a damage assessment, how long will services be necessary.

Response manager

The response manager oversees the disaster response. The manager's responsibilities include ensuring adequate levels of staffing throughout the response organization, conducting staff meetings with the Disaster Response team, leading conference calls with the affected chapters, ensuring that adequate reports are compiled for coordination with state and federal emergency

In most situations, emergency management in the U.S. envisions a process of escalation up from the local level as incidents grow or as it becomes known that an incident has overwhelmed local and state capabilities.

management officials, and assuring the sufficient movement of assets, both human and material, to the affected region.[121]

Forward headquarters cell

The forward headquarters cell is "the deployed unit of the planning cell."[122] Its most important task is to establish a relief operation headquarters and to receive Red Cross personnel, both paid Red Cross employees and volunteers, and material resources.[123] Essentially this group serves as the advance team prior to the opening of a headquarters operation near the affected area.

Information and resource management cell

The information and resource management cell is a tactical team that concentrates on gathering information and supporting the local chapters in the evacuation of people.[124] While the Red Cross does not physically transport evacuees, it is often the recipient of a large percentage of evacuees, as shelters are established. This group establishes reporting requirements, coordinates data gathering (such as shelter tallies), monitors the inbound flow of resources to shelters, helps acquire vehicles, and handles all issues related to the immediate deployment of resources, including maintaining computer systems, managing supply warehouses, and ensuring all invoices are properly processed.[125]

Service area response operations

The day-to-day paid operations staff of the service area coordinate fundraising and communications and provide the institutional knowledge of the affected area.[126] Armed with the right data, and knowledge of the area, the information and resources management cell can help provide essential services to those in need.[127]

State, local, and private authorities and capabilities

Typical local and state emergency management responsibilities

Whether the response is coming from local or state officials—or both—most emergency management agencies and government plans assume it may take 24 to 72 hours to get assistance to individuals, particularly those who remain in affected areas. Consequently, successful emergency management can, in part, depend on individuals' willingness to evacuate to places where more immediate assistance may be available (when time and circumstances permit) and/or their preparedness to survive independently for the 24 to 72 hours that responders expect it will take to first deliver assistance.

Nonetheless, as discussed elsewhere in this report, primary responsibility for the first response to any potential or imminent incident or disaster begins — and often stays — at the local and state levels. In most situations, emergency management in the U.S. envisions a process of escalation up from the local level as incidents grow or as it becomes known that an incident has overwhelmed local and state capabilities.[128]

Local emergency management

First responders — local fire, police, and emergency medical personnel who respond to all manner of incidents such as earthquakes, storms, and floods — have the lead responsibility for carrying out emergency management efforts. Their role is to prevent, protect against, respond to, and assist in the recovery from emergencies, including natural disasters. Typically, first responders are trained and equipped to arrive first at the scene of an incident and take action immediately, including entering the scene, setting up a command center, evacuating those at the scene, tending to the injured, redirecting traffic, and removing debris.[129]

Local governments — cities, towns, counties or parishes — and the officials who lead them are responsible for developing the emergency operations and response plans by which their communities respond to disasters and other emergencies, including terrorist attacks. Local emergency management directors are also generally responsible for providing training to prepare for disaster response and they seek assistance from their state emergency management agencies when the situation exceeds or exhausts local capabilities.[130] In many states, they may also negotiate and enter into mutual aid agreements with other jurisdictions to share resources when, for example, nearby jurisdictions are unaffected by the emergency and are able to provide some assistance.[131]

Particularly relevant to the preparation for Hurricane Katrina, local officials have significant responsibilities for either setting evacuation laws and policies or working with their state government to enforce state laws pertaining to evacuations.[132] According to the National Response Plan, depending on the terms of the state or local laws, local officials have "extraordinary powers" to, among other things, order evacuations. In addition, local officials may suspend local laws and order curfews.[133]

State emergency management

As the state's chief executive, the governor is responsible for the public safety and welfare of the state's citizens and generally has wide-ranging emergency management responsibilities, including requesting federal assistance when it becomes clear the state's capabilities will be insufficient or have been exhausted. Governors are responsible for coordinating state resources to address the full range of actions necessary to prevent, prepare for, and respond to incidents such as natural disasters.

Upon their declaration of an emergency or disaster, governors typically assume a variety of emergency powers, including authority to control access to an affected area and provide temporary shelter. Also, in most cases, states generally authorize their governors to order and enforce the evacuation of residents in disaster and emergency situations. The federal government generally defers to the states to enact laws dealing with evacuation, with local officials—as mentioned earlier—typically responsible for working with state officials to enforce those laws.[134]

Governors also serve as the commanders-in-chief of their state military forces,[135] specifically, the National Guard

Governors are responsible for coordinating state resources to address the full range of actions necessary to prevent, prepare for, and respond to incidents such as natural disasters.

when in state active duty or Title 32 status.[136] In state active duty — to which governors can call the Guard in response to disasters and other emergencies — National Guard personnel operate under the control of the governor, are paid according to state law, and can perform typical disaster relief tasks, such as search and rescue, debris removal, and law enforcement. Most governors have the authority to implement mutual aid agreements with other states to share resources with one another during disasters or emergencies when, for example, others (particularly nearby states) are unaffected by the emergency and able to provide assistance.[137] Most states request and provide this assistance through the EMAC.

State emergency management agencies —reporting to their respective governors — have primary responsibility for their states' disaster mitigation, preparedness, response, and recovery activities. These agencies typically coordinate with other state agencies as well as local emergency response departments to plan for and respond to potential or imminent disasters or emergencies. Among other things, state emergency management agencies are responsible for developing state emergency response plans, administering federal grant funding, and, coordinating with local and federal agencies to provide training and other emergency response-related activities.[138] Some states, such as Louisiana and Mississippi, spell out specific tasks or preparatory steps emergency management agencies must take to meet their responsibilities.

For example, Louisiana requires that its Office of Homeland Security and Emergency Preparedness determine requirements for food, clothing, and other necessities and procure and pre-position these supplies in the event of an emergency.[139] Similarly, Mississippi requires its emergency management agency to determine needs for equipment and supplies and plan and procure those items as well.[140]

pecific state and local emergency management and homeland ecurity laws and roles and esponsibilities—Alabama, Mississippi, Louisiana, and the ity of New Orleans

labama

overing statutes

wo Alabama statutes address how the state prepares for nd responds to emergencies and disasters: the Alabama mergency Management Act of 1955 (EMA) and the labama Homeland Security Act of 2003 (HSA). The EMA uthorizes the state to prepare for and manage disasters nd emergencies. It also authorizes the state to make rants to local governments to assist their emergency anagement activities and improve preparedness. The SA established a state Department of Homeland Security nd other entities) to coordinate and undertake state omeland security preparedness, planning, and response tivities.[141]

oles and responsibilities

ate documents detail the specific options and steps vailable to the chief executive, including an analysis of bernatorial prerogatives, including:[142]

STATE OF ALABAMA

First and foremost, the governor must understand and accept the fact that he/she is the primary person responsible for response and crisis management within his/her state. All citizens look to their governor as the person ultimately responsible. That is not to take away from the local responsibility of mayors, city councils, and county commissions, but, in truth and fact, "the buck stops at the governor." Secondly, although the governor must be the leader of his/her state, the governor must also be prepared to delegate.

This statement may seem rather simplistic since every governor in the United States is confronted with so many governmental and administrative decisions, on a daily basis, that they obviously need to be able to delegate. On the other hand, in the case of an emergency catastrophe situation, the number of issues that arise are exponentially greater than ordinary day-to-day issues of government, they are unusual, sometimes technical in nature, they require instantaneous decisions, as opposed to general governmental issues which commonly allow for consideration and even collaboration among advisors and affected entities. In these regards, in order to delegate, it is extremely important that the governor has surrounded himself/herself with an outstanding group of cabinet officials who are not only qualified but who are both qualified and capable of responding in emergency situations. This is most particularly true of the adjutant general of the state's National Guard, the director of the state's Department of Homeland Security, and the office of the director of the state's office of Emergency Management. Obviously each of these positions is a key appointment for every governor, but when confronted with a catastrophic emergency, the importance of the quality and qualifications of the persons holding these positions becomes extraordinarily important. Thirdly, an emergency operations center and a communications system which are capable of and designed to operate under emergency conditions become a key element of the governor's ability to communicate, manage, and lead through the crisis. Finally, there must be pre-planning ("emergency operations plan") that sets out clearly policies, procedures, and responsibilities that will be required to meet all known emergency catastrophe situations. These must be coordinated with local emergency management officials and local government officials.[143]

Consistent with the National Response Plan and the practices of other states, in Alabama responsibility for emergency preparedness and response begins at the local level and escalates as the emergency exceeds the capabilities of each level of government. The state's Emergency Operations Plan (EOP) spells this out, specifying that, "When a disaster is imminent or has occurred, local governments have the primary responsibility and will respond to preserve life and property. . . . When disaster conditions appear likely to exceed the combined capabilities of a local jurisdiction and mutual aid compact signatories, local governments will request the support of the state.... If the capabilities (financial or operational) of state government are exceeded, the governor can request federal disaster emergency assistance."[144]

Alabama's statutes authorize and direct local governments to establish emergency management organizations (agencies), appoint directors for these organizations, and confer police officer powers on their officials. In addition, local directors of emergency management may develop mutual aid agreements with public or private agencies (such as nearby counties) for emergency aid and assistance during disasters and emergencies.[145] These local directors and some of their personnel must, if they choose to receive state funding, meet state-set performance and competence standards for their positions.[146]

Alabama's statutes outline specific responsibilities of the state's Emergency Management Agency as well as its Department of Homeland Security. The state EMA has overall responsibility for preparing for and managing disasters and emergencies. Its director is appointed by the governor and also serves as an assistant director for the state's Department of Homeland Security.[147] To meet its obligations, the state EMA promulgates a statewide Emergency Operations Plan with policy and guidance for state and local disaster mitigation, preparedness, response, and recovery operations.[148] The plan also outlines state and local government responsibilities in relation to federal disaster assistance programs under the Stafford Act.[149]

Alabama's Director of Homeland Security, also appointed by the governor, heads the state's Department of Homeland Security and has overall responsibility for the state's homeland security preparedness and response activities. Specific state Department of Homeland Security responsibilities include: receiving and disseminating federal intelligence; planning and executing simulations; ensuring cooperation among public officials and the private sector; coordinating receipt and distribution of homeland security funding; and coordinating state strategy and standards for homeland security efforts.[150]

Mississippi

Governing statutes

The Mississippi Emergency Management Law outlines the specific responsibilities of key state entities and emergency responders and provides for the coordination of emergency preparedness, response, recovery and mitigation activities among state agencies, local and federal governments, and the private sector.[151] The law establishes the Mississippi Emergency Management Agency (MEMA); confers emergency powers on the governor, MEMA, municipal and county governments; and, authorizes the establishment of the Mississippi Emergency Operations Plan (MEOP).[152]

Roles and responsibilities

Consistent with the National Response Plan and the practices of other states, in Mississippi responsibility for emergency preparedness and response begins at the local level and escalates as the emergency exceeds the capabilities of each level of government. Among other things, Mississippi's governing statute spells out that "state policy for responding to disasters is to support local emergency response efforts," but it also recognizes that catastrophic disasters can overwhelm local resources and that, as a result, the state "must be capable of providing effective, coordinated, and timely support to communities and the public."[153]

The state's statute authorizes (but does not direct) counties and municipalities to create emergency management organizations, which are in turn authorized to do the various things necessary to handle emergency management functions in a disaster.[154] Local governments are also authorized to enter into mutual aid agreements within the state (for example, with nearby counties) for emergency aid and assistance during disasters and emergencies.[155] If a disaster or emergency "exceeds the capability of local resources and personnel, state resources may be made available through coordination" with MEMA. Local authorities are mandated to "recognize the severity and magnitude" of the emergency by (1) declaring a local emergency, (2) utilizing the localities own resources and (3) designating one capable person to make requests to MEMA for additional resources.[156]

The governor of Mississippi is granted broad powers to deal with a natural disaster and may assume direct operational control over all state emergency management functions.[157] For example, the governor is authorized to "determine needs for food, clothing or other necessities in the event of attack, natural, man-made or technological disasters and to procure supplies, medicines, materials, and equipment." As commander-in-chief of the state militia, the governor may order the Mississippi National Guard into active state service.[158]

The MEMA director, appointed by the governor, is responsible for, among other things: working with the governor to prepare and implement an emergency management plan that is coordinated with federal and state plans to the fullest extent possible; adopting standards and requirements for local emergency management plans; determining needs for equipment and supplies; planning for and procuring supplies, medicine and equipment; and, assisting political subdivisions with the creation of urban search and rescue teams. In addition, the MEMA director is authorized to create mobile support units to reinforce disaster organizations in stricken areas. MEMA's director also serves as a liaison to the emergency management agencies of other states and the federal government.[159]

Louisiana

Governing statutes

The Louisiana Homeland Security and Emergency Assistance and Disaster Act outlines the specific responsibilities of key state entities and emergency responders and provides for the coordination of activities among state agencies and local and federal governments. The law establishes the Louisiana Office of Homeland Security and Emergency Preparedness (LOHSEP), confers emergency powers on the governor and parish and municipal governments, and requires the establishment of the Louisiana Emergency Management Plan (EOP).[160]

Roles and responsibilities

In Louisiana, parish and municipal governments' chief executives by law have overall responsibility for the direction and control of emergency and disaster operations and are assisted by a local homeland security and emergency preparedness director.[161] Their responsibilities include the development and implementation of emergency management programs to provide for rapid and effective action to "direct, mobilize, staff, train and coordinate use of local resources."[162]

Louisiana's governor has overall responsibility for emergency management in the state and is assisted in these duties by the LOHSEP director in meeting dangers to the state and people presented by emergencies or disasters. The governor is authorized, for example, to declare a disaster or emergency if he or she finds that one has occurred (or the threat is imminent) and coordinate delivery of all emergency services (public, volunteer, and private) during a natural disaster.[163] By making a disaster or emergency declaration, the governor activates the

state's emergency response and recovery program (which is under the command of the LOHSEP director). This authorizes the governor to, among other things: (1) utilize all available resources of the state government and of each political subdivision of the state as reasonably necessary to cope with the disaster or emergency; (2) direct and compel the evacuation of all or part of the population from any stricken or threatened areas within the state if deemed necessary for the preservation of life; and, (3) prescribe routes, modes of transportation, and destination in connection with evacuation.[164]

The LOHSEP, within the Military Department and under the authority of the governor and the adjutant general, is responsible for emergency preparedness and homeland security in the state.[165] The LOHSEP prepares and maintains a homeland security and state emergency operations plan (EOP), which establishes the policies and structure for the state's management of emergencies and disasters. The EOP prescribes the phases of emergencies and disasters—preparedness, response, recovery and prevention (mitigation)—and outlines the roles and responsibilities of the state's Emergency Support Functions (ESFs), which mirror those in the National Response Plan. The EOP is an all-hazards plan, assigning responsibilities for actions the state will take to provide for the safety and welfare of its citizens against the threat of natural and man-made emergencies and disasters. The EOP is designed to coordinate closely with the federal National Response Plan as well as parish Emergency Operations Plans.[166]

New Orleans

The City of New Orleans Comprehensive Emergency Management Plan ("New Orleans Plan") is consistent with the State of Louisiana Emergency Management Plan. The plan reflects the principle that "City government bears the initial responsibility for disaster response and relief."[167] It is therefore the Mayor of the City of New Orleans who must initiate, execute, and direct the operations during any emergency or disaster affecting the City of New Orleans.[168]

FEMA

According to the New Orleans Plan, "[i]f it becomes clearly evident that local resources are inadequate to fully manage the effects of an emergency or disaster, the Mayor may request state and/or federal assistance through [LOHSEP].[169] The New Orleans Office of Emergency Preparedness ("NOOEP") will coordinate with the LOHSEP to assure the most effective management of such assistance."[170]

The plan also says, "The authority to order the evacuation of residents threatened by an approaching hurricane is conferred to the Governor by Louisiana statute."[171] But this power "is also delegated to each political subdivision of the State by Executive Order."[172] "This authority empowers the chief elected official of New Orleans, the Mayor of New Orleans, to order the evacuation of the parish residents threatened by an approaching hurricane,"[173] according to the plan.

For example, New Orleans Mayor Ray Nagin, according to the plan, is responsible for giving the order for a mandatory evacuation and supervising the actual evacuation of the population. The city's Office of

Emergency Preparedness "must coordinate with the state on elements of evacuation" and "assist in directing the transportation of evacuees to staging areas."[174]

The New Orleans Plan states, "The safe evacuation of threatened populations . . . is one of the principle reason for developing a Comprehensive Emergency Management Plan."[175] The city's evacuation plan states, "The city of New Orleans will utilize all available resources to quickly and safely evacuate threatened areas."[176]

The plan also directs "[s]pecial arrangements will be made to evacuate persons unable to transport themselves or who require specific life saving assistance. Additional personnel will be recruited to assist in evacuation procedures as needed."[177] The evacuation plan further warns that "[i]f an evacuation order is issued without the mechanisms needed to disseminate the information to the affected persons, then we face the possibility of having large numbers of people either stranded and left to the mercy of the storm, or left in areas impacted by toxic materials."[178]

Threats and vulnerabilities related to hurricanes

General threats — frequency of hurricanes and vulnerable coastal areas in the U.S.

Hurricanes threaten the United States, particularly the coastal areas along the Gulf of Mexico and Atlantic Ocean, virtually every year. While Florida is the state most frequently hit, other states — particularly Texas, Louisiana, and North Carolina — have frequently been struck by hurricanes, according to the records of the National Hurricane Center (NHC).[179] The coastal areas of these and other states are among the most vulnerable to storm surge, which carries the greatest potential for loss of life in a hurricane. Storm surge is the water that swirling hurricane force winds push toward the shore as the storm advances. Combined with normal tides, this can increase the average water level by 15 feet or more.[180]

Flooding is also a serious threat to lives and property a hurricane. The NHC reports that, although storm surge has the greatest potential to take lives, in the last 30 years more people have died from hurricane-induced inland flooding.[181] Tornadoes can also add to the destructive power of a hurricane. While not all hurricanes produce them, according to the NHC, studies have shown that more than half of the hurricanes that reach landfall produce at least one tornado.

Specific vulnerabilities of New Orleans— inherent vulnerability to flooding

Metropolitan New Orleans is built on subsiding swampland on the delta of the Mississippi River, which makes the city inherently vulnerable to flooding.[182] The City of New Orleans is shaped like a bowl, with an average elevation of 6 feet below sea level.[183] Some elevations are as high as 12 feet above sea level, and some elevation are as low as 9 feet below sea level.[184] The Mississippi River, which flows through the middle of New Orleans, is on average 14 feet above sea level, and Lake Pontchartrain, which establishes the northern border of New Orleans, is on average one foot above sea level.[185]

New Orleans and its surrounding areas have experienced numerous floods from both the Mississippi River and hurricanes.[186] A major flood on the Mississippi River completely inundated New Orleans in 1927, and others following severe rainstorms damaged parts of the city in 1979 and 1995.[187] Several hurricanes have hit New Orleans, including Hurricane Betsy in 1965, Hurricane Camille in 1969, Hurricane Georges in 1998, and Hurricane Lilli in 2002.[188] The greatest threat from hurricanes is not wind, but storm-surge, which accounts for most of the damage and deaths caused by hurricanes.[189]

Levees designed, built to address vulnerabilities

After Hurricane Betsy in 1965, federal and state governments proposed a number of flood control projects to deal with the threat of hurricanes and the flooding they might cause in New Orleans.[190] These included a series of control structures, concrete floodwalls, and levees along Lake Pontchartrain and several other waterways.[191] One of the major projects is formally called the Lake Pontchartrain and Vicinity, Louisiana Hurricane Protection Project.[192] This project included levees along

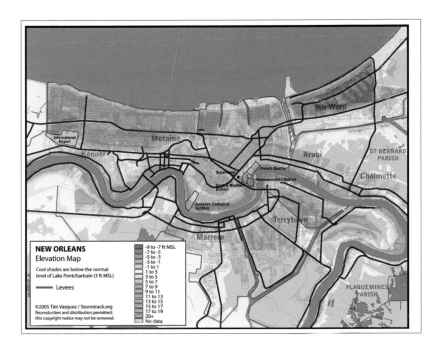

the Lake Pontchartrain lakefront, the 17th Street Canal, the London Avenue Canal, the Orleans Avenue Canal, the Intercoastal waterway, the Industrial Canal, the Mississippi River Gulf Outlet, and others.[193] Although the project was federally authorized, it was a joint federal, state, and local effort with shared costs.[194]

1 Exec. Order 12148, 44 Fed. Reg. 43239, 3 C.F.R. at 412, (1979 Comp.).

2 *See* Keith Bea, Cong. Res. Serv., Order No. RL 33064, *Organization and Mission of the Emergency Preparedness and Response Directorate: Issues and Options for the 109th Congress*, App. B: Evolution of Federal Emergency Authorities (Sept. 7, 2005) [hereinafter Bea, *Organizational Mission*].

3 *See Id.* at App. B; U.S. Gov't Accountability Off., Pub. No. GAO/T-RCED-93-46, *Disaster Management: Recent Disasters Demonstrate the Need to Improve the Nation's Response Strategy* (May 25, 1993) [hereinafter GAO, *Recent Disasters*].

4 *See* Keith Bea, Cong. Res. Serv., Order No. RL 31670, *Transfer of FEMA to the Department of Homeland Security: Issues for Congressional Oversight*, App. A: Summary of FEMA Authorities (Dec. 17, 2002) [hereinafter Bea, *Transfer of FEMA*].

5 *See* U.S. Gov't Accountability Off., Pub. No. GAO/RCED-93-186, *Disaster Management: Improving the Nation's Response to Catastrophic Disasters* (July 23, 1993) [hereinafter Bea, *Disaster Management*].

6 *See* Bea, *Transfer of FEMA*; GAO, *Disaster Management*.

7 Homeland Security Act of 2002, Pub. L. No. 107-296, Title V, 116 Stat. 2135 (2002).

8 *See* Bea, *Organization and Mission*; Federal Emergency Mgmt. Agency [hereinafter FEMA], News Release, *National Disaster Medical System* (Apr. 21, 2004) *available at* http://www.fema.gov/news/newsrelease.fema?id=11927 (last visited Jan. 21, 2006).

9 *See* Bea, *Transfer of FEMA*.

10 *See* FEMA, *A Guide to the Disaster Declaration Process* (undated) *available at* http://www.fema.gov/pdf/rrr/dec_proc.pdf (last visited Jan. 21, 2006).

11 Interviews by Select Comm. Staff with City of New Orleans officials in New Orleans, LA (Nov. 3-10, 2005) [hereinafter Select Comm. New Orleans Interviews].

12 *See* Elizabeth B. Bazan, Cong. Res. Serv., Order No. RL 33090, *Robert T. Stafford Disaster Relief and Emergency Assistance Act: Legal Requirements for Federal and State Roles in Declarations of an Emergency or a Major Disaster* (Sept. 16, 2005).

13 Select Comm. New Orleans Interviews.

14 Keith Bea, Cong. Res. Serv., Order No. RS 21227, *The Emergency Management Assistance Compact (EMAC): An Overview*, 2 (Feb. 4, 2005).

15 *See Id.* at 1-5.

16 *See Id.* at 1-2.; http://www.emacweb.org (last visited Jan. 21, 2006).

17 Robert T. Stafford Disaster Relief and Emergency Assistance Act [hereinafter Stafford Act] 42 U.S.C. § 5122(1) (2005).

18 *See* FEMA, *The Disaster Process and Disaster Aid Programs*, (Apr. 4, 2005) *available at* http://www.fema.gov/library/dproc.shtm (last visited Jan. 22, 2006) [hereinafter, FEMA, *Disaster Process*].

19 Keith Bea, Cong. Res. Serv., Order No. RL 33053, *Federal Stafford Act Disaster Assistance: Presidential Declarations, Eligible Activities, and Funding*, 3-4 (Sept. 27, 2005).

20 *See* FEMA, *Disaster Process* (FEMA allows that, when an obviously severe or catastrophic event occurs, Governors may request a major disaster declaration prior to conducting a damage assessment).

21 *See* FEMA, *Disaster Process* (Specifically, FEMA provides three categories of disaster assistance: (1) individual assistance; (2) public assistance; and (3) hazard mitigation assistance. Individual assistance is a combined FEMA-State program that provides money and services to people in the affected area whose property has been damaged or destroyed and whose losses are not covered by insurance. Individual assistance from FEMA can consist of funds to rent temporary housing, grants to repair damage that is not covered by insurance, and grants for "necessary and serious needs" such as medical or funeral expenses. Individual assistance can also include federally subsidized loans from the U.S. Small Business Administration (SBA) to repair or replace homes, personal property or businesses that sustained damages not covered by insurance); *See* FEMA, *Disaster Process* at 4 (Public assistance funds, through grants or SBA loans, the repair, restoration, reconstruction or replacement of public facilities or infrastructure damaged or destroyed by a disaster. Eligible recipients include state and local governments and certain private nonprofit organizations, such as educational, medical, rehabilitation or permanent custodial care facilities. Recipients may use their public assistance funds for projects such as debris removal and repair of road systems, bridges, and/or water control facilities); *See* FEMA, *Disaster Process* at 4-5 (Hazard mitigation assistance supports measures to reduce or eliminate long-term risk to people and property from natural hazards and their effects. For eligible projects, the federal government pays up to 75 percent of the costs with states providing a 25 percent match. Eligible mitigation measures under this program include buying or relocating property located in high hazard areas (such as flood plains); elevating flood-prone structures; and, seismic rehabilitation of existing structures).

22 *See* Directive on Management of Domestic Incidents, 39 WEEKLY COMP. PRES. DOC. 10 280 (Feb. 28, 2003) (Known as Homeland Security Presidential Directive/HSPD-5).

23 *See* U.S. Dep't of Homeland Security, *National Response Plan* (Dec. 2004) at i [hereinafter NRP].

24 *See* U.S. Gov't Accountability Off., Pub. No. GAO-05-652, *Homeland Security: DHS' Efforts to Enhance First Responders' All-Hazards Capabilities Continue to Evolve*, 11-12 (July 11, 2005) [hereinafter GAO: *DHS' Efforts to Enhance Capabilities*].

25 *See NRP* at 1.

26 *See Id.* at 11.

27 DHS, *National Incident Management System*, 2 (Mar. 1, 2004) *available at* http://www.dhs.gov/interweb/assetlibrary/NIMS-90-web.pdf (last visited Jan. 22, 2006).

28 *Id.* at ix, 1-4.

29 *See NRP* at xi-xiii.

30 *Id.* at 11.

31 *See Id.* at ESF-i-iv.

32 *Id.* at ESF#1-1-5.

33 *Id.* at ESF#2-1-12.

34 *Id.* at ESF#3-1-8.

35 *Id.* at ESF#4-1-5.

36 *Id.* at ESF#5-1-5.

37 National Response Coordination Center (NRCC); Regional Response Coordination Center (RRCC); Joint Field Office (JFO).

38 *NRP* at ESF#6-1-8.

[49] *Id.* at ESF#7-1-6.

[50] *Id.* at ESF#8-1-13.

[51] *Id.* at ESF#9-1-7.

[52] *Id.* at ESF#10-1-13.

[53] *See Id.* (Depending on whether an incident affects the inland or coastal zone, either EPA or DHS/USCG serves as the primary agency for ESF 10 actions. For incidents affecting both, EPA is the primary agency with DHS/USCG serving as the deputy).

[54] *Id.* at ESF#11-1-12.

[55] *Id.* at ESF#12-1-6.

[56] *Id.* at ESF#13-1-9.

[57] *Id.* at ESF#14-1-6.

[58] *Id.* at ESF#15-1-5.

[59] *See* GAO, *Recent Disasters* (The notion that FEMA distinguishes "catastrophic" disasters from other incidents and makes specific plans for a different, proactive response to them builds on its experiences, problems, and lessons learned in past disasters, particularly Hurricane Andrew in south Florida in 1992. In that disaster, FEMA was too reactive—waiting for state and local governments to identify what they needed and then ask for it—when the hurricane had clearly overwhelmed the ability of state, local, and voluntary agencies to adequately provide victims with essential services, such as food and water, within 12 to 24 hours. Summarizing its review of FEMA's response to Hurricane Andrew, GAO described the [then] federal strategy for responding to such disasters as deficient because it lacked provisions for the federal government to (1) immediately, comprehensively assess damages and the resulting needs of disaster victims and (2) provide food, shelter, and other essential services when victims' needs outstripped what state, local and voluntary agencies could themselves provide).

[60] *Id.* at 43.

[61] *NRP* at CAT-3.

[62] *See Id.* at CAT-1-3 (According to the catastrophic incident annex, DHS is developing a "more detailed and operationally specific NRP Catastrophic Incident Supplement" (CIS) to this annex. The supplement will be designated "For Official Use Only" and published independently of the NRP base plan and annexes. As of November 2005, DHS had not yet published the CIS); *See* Letter from Henry A. Waxman and Charlie Melancon, Members of Congress, to Michael Chertoff, Secretary of Homeland Security, Nov. 1, 2005 (on file with the Select Comm.) *available at* http://www.democrats.reform.house.gov/Documents/20051101103226-17173.pdf (last visited Jan. 22, 2006).

[63] *See NRP* at CAT-2-4.

[64] *See Id.* at CAT-3-5.

[65] *See Id.* at CAT-1.

[66] *Id.* at CAT-1.

[67] *Id.* at 3-4.

[68] *See* DHS, *Fact Sheet: Homeland Security Operations Center (HSOC)* (July 8, 2004) *available at* http://www.dhs.gov/dhspublic/display?theme=30&content=3813 (last visited Jan. 22, 2006) [hereinafter HSOC Fact Sheet]. (Specifically, participants in the HSOC include the FBI, U.S. Coast Guard, Postal Inspection Service, CIA, U.S. Secret Service, DC Metropolitan Police Department, Defense Intelligence Agency, Federal Protective Service, New York Police Department, National Security Agency, Customs and Border Protection (DHS), Los Angeles Police Department, Immigration Customs Enforcement (DHS), U.S. Department of Energy, U.S. Environmental Protection Agency, Drug Enforcement Agency, U.S. Department of Interior (U.S. Park Police), U.S. Federal Air Marshal Service, Alcohol, Tobacco, and Firearms, U.S. Department of Defense, U.S. Department of State, U.S. Department of Transportation, U.S. Department of Veterans Affairs, National Capitol Region, Transportation Security Administration, National Geospatial Intelligence Agency, U.S. Department of Health and Human Services, FEMA, National Oceanic Atmospheric Administration, Public Affairs (DHS), State and Local Coordination Office, Science and Technology Directorate, Geo-spatial Mapping Office, Information Analysis Office, and the Infrastructure Protection Office).

[69] *NRP* at 24; *HSOC Fact Sheet.*

[70] See *NRP* at 70 (A National Special Security Event (NSSE) is a designated event that, by virtue of its political, economic, social, or religious significance, may be the target of terrorism or other criminal activity).

[71] *See Id.* at 22-23; *HSOC Fact Sheet.*

[72] *NRP* at 27-28, 91.

[73] *Id.* at 27-28, 40; Interview by Select Comm. staff with Michael Lowder, Deputy Director, Response Division, FEMA, in Washington, DC (Jan. 5, 2006).

[74] *NRP* at 28, 68.

[75] Stafford Act at § 5143(a).

[76] *NRP* at 4, 7.

[77] *Id.* at 34.

[78] *Id.* at 33-34.

[79] Joint Chiefs of Staff, Department of Defense, Joint Publication 3-26, *Homeland Security* [hereinafter Joint Chiefs, *Homeland Security*], (Aug. 2. 2005) at IV-4, *available at* http://www.dtic.mil/doctrine/jel/new_pubs/jp3_26.pdf (last visited Jan. 22, 2006).

[80] *NRP* at 42.

[81] Joint Chiefs, *Homeland Security* at IV-1.

[82] Steven Bowman et al., Cong. Res. Serv., Order No. RL 33095, *Hurricane Katrina: DOD Disaster Response* at 2 (Sep. 19, 2005). [Hereinafter *Katrina: DOD Response*].

[83] Department of Defense, Directive 3025.1, *Military Support to Civil Authorities* (Jan. 15, 1993).

[84] 32 U.S.C. § 901 (2005).

[85] Joint Chiefs, *Homeland Security* at vii, IV-10-IV-15; *NRP* at 37.

[86] Bowman, *Katrina: DOD Response* at 3, 4.

[87] Civil support for incidents in Hawaii and the Pacific territories is provided by U.S. Pacific Command.

[88] Joint Chiefs, *Homeland Security* at IV-12; Bowman, *Katrina: DOD Response* at 3, 4.

79 Bowman, *Katrina: DOD Response* at 3, 4.

80 Joint Chiefs, *Homeland Security* at IV-10-12.

81 Lt. Gen. H Steven Blum, Chief, National Guard Bureau, *Types of Duty*, 1 (undated) (on file with the Select Comm., No. MMTF 00415-05).

82 *Id.*

83 *Id.*

84 Letter from Bob Riley, Governor of Alabama, to Donald Rumsfeld, Secretary of Defense (Sept. 2, 2005) (on file with the Select Comm.); Letter from Haley Barbour, Governor of Mississippi, to Donald Rumsfeld, Secretary of Defense (Sept. 4, 2005) (on file with the Select Comm.); Letter from Kathleen Babineaux Blanco, Governor of Louisiana, to Donald Rumsfeld, Secretary of Defense (Sept. 5, 2005) (on file with the Select Comm.); Memorandum from Gordon England, Deputy Secretary of Defense to Secretary of the Army and Acting Secretary of the Air Force (Sept. 7, 2005) (authorizing Title 32 status for Katrina Disaaster Relief activities, on file with the Select Comm.).

85 Departments of the Army and the Air Force, Headquarters, Army Regulation 130-5 AFMD 10, *Organization and Functions of the National Guard Bureau* (Dec. 30, 2001).

86 *Hearing on Hurricane Katrina: Preparedness and Response by the Department of Defense, the Coast Guard, and the National Guard of Louisiana, Mississippi, and Alabama Before Select Comm.,* [hereinafter *Oct. 27, 2005 Select Comm. Hearing*] 109th Cong. (Oct. 27, 2005) (written response to questions for the record of Lt. Gen. H Steven Blum).

87 Chris Doane & Joe DiRenzo III, *Protecting Our Ports: A Coast Guard Operational Commander's Perspective of the Maritime Transportation Security Act of 2002 in* 2004 U.S. COAST GUARD: THE SHIELD OF FREEDOM, 124 (2004).

88 District Eight, U.S. Coast Guard, *District Eight Facts, available at* http://www.uscg.mil/d8/d8facts.htm (last visited Jan. 26, 2006).

89 *See* Debra Spar and James Dail, *Essays: The Democratic Accountability of Non-Governmental Organizations: Of Measurement and Mission: Accounting for Performance in Non-Governmental Organizations,* 3 Chi. J. Int'l L. 171, 180 note 1 ("Strictly defined, NGO stands for "non-governmental organization" and would thus include any group that does not fall under the purview of the government. Taken to the extreme, this would include private companies, religious congregations, and trade unions. For the most part, however, the term NGO is used to refer to organizations that (1) are tax exempt, (2) have a decisionmaking body separate from the government, (3) consist, at least in part, of volunteer and donations, (4) have a charter or mandate within a specific development arena, and (5) consist of a formal organization (in other words, are registered as organizations.").

90 36 U.S.C. § 300101 (2005).

91 American Red Cross Museum, *History: The Federal Charter of the American Red Cross, available at* http://www.redcross.org/museum/history/charter.asp (last visited Jan. 22, 2006).

92 *Id.*

93 *Id.*

94 American Red Cross, *2004 Corporate Annual Report, Introduction,* 4, *available at* http://www.redcross.org/pubs/#report (last visited Jan. 23, 2006).

95 *NRP* at 3.

96 *Id.* at 12, ESF #6-5.

97 *Id.* at ESF #6-5.

98 *Id.* at 2

99 *Id.* at ESF #6-3.

100 *Id.*

101 American Red Cross, *Tropical Storm and Hurricane Action Plan,* 1 (undated) [hereinafter American Red Cross, *Storm Action Plan*].

102 *Id.*

103 American Red Cross, *American Red Cross Responsibilities Under the Federal Response Plan* (Aug. 2001) (Internal Red Cross planning document on file with the Select Comm.).

104 American Red Cross, *Interim Shelter Operations Management Toolkit,* iii (Sept. 2005) (It is not clear to what extent this document was utilized in the Red Cross's response to Hurricane Katrina).

105 American Red Cross *Storm Action Plan* at 2 ("The chapters serving the affected area provide the initial incident response in their respective communities, report their activities and assessments and are augmented by human and material resources and guidance, in a coordinated manner, from the service area or national headquarters.").

106 Interview by Select Comm. staff with Joseph C. Becker, Sr. Vice Pres., Preparedness and Response, American Red Cross in Wash., D.C. (Oct. 14, 2005) [hereinafter Oct. 14, 2000 Red Cross Interview].

107 *Id.*

108 American Red Cross, *Storm Action Plan* at 20 (chart entitled, "Hurricane Response Plan Routine Business Model Structure").

109 *Id.* at 3.

110 *Id.* at 3

111 *Id.* at 4.

112 *Id.* at 5.

113 *Id.*

114 Oct. 14, 2000 Red Cross Interview.

115 American Red Cross *Storm Action Plan* at 3

116 *Id.* at 7.

117 *Id.* at 9.

118 *Id.* at 9-18.

119 *Id.*

120 *Id.* at 9.

121 *Id.* at 9.

122 *Id.* at 12.

23 *Id.*

24 *Id.*

25 *Id.* at 15.

26 *Id.* at 16.

27 *Id.*

28 *See NRP* at 6 (incidents typically managed at the lowest possible level), 8 (roles of local chief executive officer and governor), 15 (concept of operations); FEMA *supra* note 10; DHS *supra* note 27 at ("most incidents are managed locally"); Bazan *supra* note 12 (summary—federal resources supplement state and local).

29 *See* GAO: *DHS' Efforts to Enhance Capabilities* at 7-8.

30 Keith Bea, et al., Cong. Res. Serv., Order No. RL 32287, *Emergency Management and Homeland Security Statutory Authorities in the States, District of Columbia, and Insular Areas: A Summary*, 6 (Mar. 17, 2004) [hereinafter Bea, *Statutory Authorities*].

31 *See* Emergency Management Assistance Compact, *Intrastate Mutual Aid Legislation, available at* http://www.emacweb.org/?150 (last visited Jan. 23, 2006) (for a list of states that have intrastate mutual assistance compacts).

32 *See* Keith Bea, Cong. Res. Serv., Order No. RS 22235, *Disaster Evacuation and Displacement Policy: Issues for Congress*, 1-2 (Sept. 2, 2005) [hereinafter Bea, *Disaster Evacuation Policy*].

33 *NRP* at 8.

34 *See* Bea, *Disaster Evacuation Policy* 132 at 1-2.

35 *See* Bea, *Statutory Authorities* at 4.

36 *See* Bowman *Katrina: DOD Response* at 7-8.

37 *See* Bea, *Statutory Authorities* at 10.

38 *Id.* at 5-6.

39 *See* Keith Bea, Cong. Res. Serv., Order No. RL 32678, *Louisiana Emergency Management and Homeland Security Authorities Summarized* (Sept. 2, 2005) [hereinafter Bea, *Louisiana Authorities*].

40 *See* Keith Bea, Cong. Res. Serv., Order No. RL 32316, *Mississippi Emergency Management and Homeland Security Authorities Summarized* (Sept. 2, 2005) [hereinafter Bea, *Mississippi Authorities*].

41 *See* Keith Bea, Cong. Res. Serv., Order No. RD 21777, *Alabama Emergency Management and Homeland Security Statutory Authorities Summarized*, 1-5 (Sept. 2, 2005) [hereinafter Bea, *Alabama Authorities*] (a third statute, the Emergency Interim Succession Act, applies when continuity of government operations come into question and provides for the succession of powers for legislators and officers of political subdivisions).

42 *State Chief Executives Emergency Response: Hurricanes & Other Disaster Emergencies: State Of Alabama Experience* (on file with the Select Comm., Nos. 000659AL-000666AL).

43 *Id.*

44 Preparedness Division Technological Hazards Branch, *State of Alabama, State of Alabama Emergency Operations Plan* [hereinafter *AL Emergency Operations Plan*] 4-5 (Oct. 1, 2000).

45 *Id.* at 2-3.

46 Interview by Select Comm. Staff with Bruce Baughman, Director, State of Alabama Emergency Management Agency, in AL (Oct. 11-12, 2005).

47 *See* Bea, *Alabama Authorities* at 2.

48 *See AL Emergency Operations Plan*.

49 *Id.* at 1.

50 *See* Bea, *Alabama Authorities* at 2.

51 Miss. Code Ann. §§ 33-15-11 to 33-15-53 (2004).

52 *Id.*

53 *Id.* at § 33-15-2.

54 *See* Bea, *Mississippi Authorities* at 2.

55 *Id.* at 5.

56 The Disaster Improvement Grant Program Plans Sec., Miss. Emergency Mgmt. Agency, Miss. Emergency Operations Plan, Volume II Miss. Comprehensive Emergency Mgmt. Plan, p. Basic-2 (May 14, 199) (change log updated through Feb. 2003).

57 Miss. Code Ann. § 33-15-11 (2004).

58 *See* Bea, *Mississippi Authorities* at 1; Bea, *Alabama Authorities* at 4.

59 *See* Bea, *Mississippi Authorities* at 2-3; Miss. Code Ann. § 33-15-7 (2004).

60 *See* Bea, *Louisiana Authorities* at 1-3.

61 Office of Homeland Security and Emergency Preparedness, State of Louisiana, *Emergency Operations Plan*, 7 (April 2005) [hereinafter *LA Emergency Operations Plan*].

62 *Id.* at 7.

63 *Id.* at 9.

64 Louisiana Homeland Security and Emergency Assistance and Disaster Act , LA. REV. STAT. ANN. § 724 D (2003).

65 *Id.* at §§ 724-725.

66 *LA Emergency Operations Plan* at 1.

67 Office of Emergency Preparedness, City of New Orleans, *Comprehensive Emergency Management Plan*, (2004) at 7 [hereinafter *N.O. Emergency Management Plan*].

68 *Id.* at 4.

69 *Id.*

70 *Id.*

71 *Id.* at 51.

72 *Id.*

73 *Id.*

[174] *Id.* at 54.

[175] *Id.* at 48.

[176] *Id.* at 50.

[177] *Id.*

[178] *N.O. Emergency Management Plan* at 45.

[179] *See* Eric S. Blake, et al., Tropical Prediction Center, U.S. Dep't of Commerce, NOAA Technical Memorandum NWS TPC-4, *The Deadliest Costliest, and Most Intense U.S. Tropical Cyclones from 1851 to 2004 (and Other Frequently Requested Hurricane Facts* Aug. 2005) *available at* http://www.nhc.noaa.gov/paststate.shtml (last visited Jan. 24, 2006).

[180] *See* National Hurricane Center, *Hurricane Preparedness: Storm Surge, available at* http://www.nhc.noaa.gov/HAW2/english/storm_surge.shtml (last visited Jan. 24, 2006).

[181] *See* National Hurricane Center, *Hurricane Preparedness: Inland Flooding, available at* http://www.nhc.noaa.gov/HAW2/english/inland_flood. shtml (last visited Jan. 24, 2006).

[182] Anu Mittal, U.S. Gov't Accountability Off., Pub. No. GAO-05-1050T, *Testimony Before the Subcommittee on Energy and Water Development, Committee on Appropriations, House of Representatives, Army Corps of Engineers: Lake Pontchartrain and Vicinity Hurricane Protection Project,* 2 (Sept. 28, 2005); R.B. Seed, et al., U. of Calif. At Berkely and Am. Soc'y of Civil Engineers, Rept. No. UCB/CITRIS – 05/01, *Preliminary Report on the Performance of the New Orleans Levee System in Hurricane Katrina on August 29, 2005,* 1-4 (Nov. 2, 2005) (support for subsidence); IEM, Inc., IEM/TEC04-070 r5, Southeast Louisiana Catastrophic Hurricane Functional Plan, 5 (Jan. 5, 2005) [hereinafter IEM, *Southeast Louisiana Hurricane Plan*] (support for "bowl" topography "Hurricane Pam").

[183] IEM, *Southeast Louisiana Hurricane Plan* at 5; *Hearing on Hurricane Katrina: Who's In Charge of the New Orleans Levees? Before Senate Comm. on Homeland Security and Governmental Affairs* [*Dec. 15, 2005 Senate Hearing*], 109th Cong. (Dec. 15, 2005) (written statement of Max. L. Hearn, Executive Director, Orleans Levee District) at 1.

[184] New Orleans District, U.S. Army Corps of Engineers, *Un-Watering Plan Greater Metropolitan Area, New Orleans, Louisiana,* 1 (Aug. 18, 2000) (While we use the term "sea level," the technical measurement used by the Corps is National Geodetic Vertical Datum (NGVD) which was developed by observing the mean sea level height at various locations around North America).

[185] New Orleans District, U.S. Army Corps of Engineers, *NGVD Datum Plane* (Apr. 15, 2005) *available at* http://www.mvn.usace.army.mil/pao/ response/NGVD.asp (last visited Jan. 25, 2006).

[186] Mittal, *Testimony* at 2.

[187] *See* FEMA, Disasters: Louisiana Severe Storm, Flooding Declared May 10, 1995, *available at* http://www.fema.gov/news/event.fema?id=2250 (last visited Jan. 25, 2006).

[188] Mittal, *Testimony* at 2.

[189] Richard D. Knabb, et al., National Hurricane Center, Dep't of Commerce, *Tropical Cyclone Report: Hurricane Katrina 23-20 August 2005,* 11, (Dec. 20, 2005); Mittal, *Testimony* at 2.

[190] *Dec. 15, 2005 Senate Hearing* (written statement of Max. L. Hearn, Executive Director, Orleans Levee District at 2); R.B. Seed, et al. at 1-3.

[191] Mittal, *Testimony* at 2.

[192] Flood Control Act of 1965. Pub. L. No. 89-298, § 204, 79 Stat. 103, 1077 (1965) (The Flood Control Act of 1965 authorized this project).

[193] *Dec. 15, 2005 Senate Hearing* (written statement of Col. Richard P. Wagenaar) at 1-2; Mittal, *Testimony* 182 at 3; The Industrial Canal is also known as the Inner Harbor Navigation Canal.

[194] Interview by Select Comm. Staff with David Pezza, U.S. Army Corps of Engineers, (Dec. 9, 2005); Mittal, *Testimony* at 3.

"Preparing for an event like Hurricane Katrina or any natural disaster, we should never feel like we are completely prepared. We can always do better."

Robert R. Latham, Jr.
Executive Director,
Mississippi Emergency Management Agency
Select Committee hearing, December 7, 2005

PRE-LANDFALL PREPARATION AND KATRINA'S IMPACT

As Hurricane Katrina entered
the Gulf of Mexico, Gulf coast
states and the federal government
prepared for landfall in the region.

Pre-landfall preparation by FEMA

The Federal Emergency Management Agency (FEMA)
positioned an unprecedented number of resources in
affected areas prior to Katrina's landfall. Indeed, FEMA's
efforts far exceeded any previous operation in the agency's
history. A staggering total of 11,322,000 liters of water,
18,960,000 pounds of ice, 5,997,312 meals ready to eat
(MREs), and 17 truckloads of tarps were staged at various
strategic locations in and near the Gulf region prior to
Katrina's landfall.[1] FEMA also pre-positioned 18 disaster
medical teams, medical supplies and equipment, and nine
urban search and rescue task forces (US&R) and incident
support teams.[2] Rapid Needs Assessment Teams also were
deployed to Louisiana on the Saturday before landfall.[3]
In Louisiana alone, on August 28, a total of 36 trucks of
water (18,000 liters per truck) and 15 trucks of MREs
(21,888 per truck) were pre-staged at Camp Beauregard.[4]

FEMA's Hurricane Liaison Team, which consists of
FEMA, the National Weather Service, and state and local
emergency management officials and is tasked with
coordinating closely with FEMA Headquarters staff by
phone and video conferencing systems, was activated and
deployed to the National Hurricane Center on August 24
in anticipation of Hurricane Katrina's making landfall.[5]
FEMA's Mobile Emergency Response Support detachments
were pre-positioned in Louisiana, Mississippi, and Alabama
to provide emergency satellite communications capability.[6]
According to former FEMA Director Michael Brown,
prior to landfall, FEMA reached out to other agencies for
assistance, such as the Department of Defense (DOD) for
potential movement of strategic airlift support.[7]

By 10 a.m. on Monday, August 29, the morning Katrina
made landfall, 31 teams from the National Disaster
Medical System (NDMS) had been deployed to staging
areas in Anniston, Alabama; Memphis, Tennessee;

Houston, Dallas; and New Orleans, including 23 Disaster
Medical Assistance Teams.[8] The teams, trained to handle
trauma, pediatrics, surgery, and mental health problems,
brought truckloads of medical equipment and supplies
with them. By September 1, 72 hours after landfall, FEMA
had deployed more than 57 NDMS teams and 28 US&R
teams with nearly 1,800 personnel to save lives and render
medical assistance. FEMA had also supplied generators
and thousands of cots and blankets.[9]

Pre-landfall preparation in Mississippi

Preparations for Hurricane Katrina in Mississippi
involved an array of actions, including county and
state preparedness and disaster response training in
the months leading up to the storm; the establishment
of local, state, and federal command structures by way
of emergency proclamations; activation of emergency
operations centers (EOCs); evacuations, many of them
mandatory, of the areas and types of homes most in
danger from a hurricane; and, the opening of emergency
shelters to which those evacuating could flee. Preparation
by the military in Mississippi largely took place through
activation of the state's National Guard and some initial
requests for Emergency Management Assistance Compact
(EMAC) assistance with security, engineering support, and
helicopters.

Following a request from Governor Haley Barbour, on
Sunday, August 28, President Bush issued an emergency
declaration for Mississippi.[10] Following a further request
from Barbour, on Monday, August 29, President Bush
declared a major disaster in Mississippi.[11]

Disaster preparedness training — Mississippi

For several years, Mississippi's Emergency Management
Agency (MEMA) has been using federal emergency
preparedness grant funds to improve its counties' abilities
to prepare for and respond to disasters. In 2000, 43 of
Mississippi's 82 counties had active county emergency
management programs; MEMA used DHS emergency

management performance grant funds, including a $1.3 million allocation in fiscal year 2005, to increase this to 79 active county programs in 2005.[12] In addition, the MEMA reported that, as of early 2005, over 1,200 first responders had received training in the National Incident Management System (NIMS).[13]

During the summer of 2005, the director of MEMA, Robert Latham, his key staff, and most of Mississippi's county emergency management directors underwent training in NIMS and the NIMS Incident Command System (ICS).[14] At approximately the same time, the FEMA officials who would later lead the federal response in Mississippi (Bill Carwile and Robert Fenton) also participated in extensive ICS training. Fenton was described by Carwile as having been involved for a long time in developing training for subjects such as the ICS and as an expert in how to adapt it for large scale operations, such as the response to Katrina. Carwile and Latham said they believe their training in the ICS and the ability it gave them to quickly establish a unified command were positive elements of the state's preparation for and response to Katrina.

Establishment of command structures in Mississippi

Mississippi issued its first Hurricane Katrina situation report on August 23 and, through Thursday, August 25, continued monitoring the storm.[15] According to this situation report, during these three days, MEMA conducted executive planning sessions to develop an EOC activation timeline as well as plans for protective actions and a proactive response.[16] It also established contact with a FEMA logistics cell and began encouraging the public to prepare for the storm.

On Friday, August 26, Mississippi activated its National Guard, and MEMA activated its EOC on Saturday, August 27.[17] At that time, it also deployed County Liaisons to six counties (Jackson, Harrison, Hancock, Pearl River, Stone, and George) and activated its State Emergency Response Team (SERT) for deployment to Camp Shelby the next day, August 28. The SERT established forward operations at Camp Shelby at 3 p.m. on August 28. According to the MEMA Director's brief, as of about 7 p.m. on August 28, 18 counties and 11 cities and towns had issued local emergency proclamations; by early morning of August 29, this had increased to 41 counties and 61 cities and towns.[18]

FEMA's liaison arrived at the state's EOC on Saturday, August 27. FEMA's Emergency Response Team-A (ERT-A) arrived the same day, August 27, when the state activated its EOC.[19] On August 28, MEMA reported that FEMA was deploying resources to a Regional Mobilization Center in Selma, Alabama, and that FEMA's ERT-A would be able to supply large quantities of water and ice to the hardest hit areas.[20]

Evacuations in Mississippi

Although the governor could order mandatory evacuations, longstanding practice in Mississippi rests that authority with local governments.[21] However, the state is generally included in any discussions about evacuation orders because, once a city or county chooses to make such an order, state responsibilities for managing traffic (including contra flow) and opening shelters can come into play.[22] In preparing for Hurricane Katrina, the state worked through the MEMA liaisons it dispatched to the counties along or near the Gulf coast as well as a representative it had stationed in Louisiana's EOC (because of contra flow agreements between Mississippi and Louisiana that provide for evacuations out of southeast Louisiana through Mississippi).

AP PHOTO/ROGELIO SOLIS

Emergency shelters—Mississippi

On August 27, MEMA urged Mississippi's coastal counties not to open local shelters in order to encourage people to evacuate north.[73] MEMA described coastal county shelters as an option of "last resort." On Sunday, August 28, MEMA reported that Red Cross shelters were open and on standby in the coastal counties.

Mississippi began opening shelters as early as August 28. MEMA reported 51 shelters open with 475 persons registered at that time and 36 additional shelters available on standby as needed.[24] In addition, MEMA indicated the Jackson Coliseum had been open as a shelter (and individuals were authorized to bring pets) and three special needs shelters had been established.[25] According to the Director's brief, also on August 28, MEMA reported the Red Cross had begun opening shelters that morning, bringing the total available shelters to 68 prior to the opening of the Jackson Coliseum.[26]

By August 29, just prior to landfall, MEMA reported 7 shelters were open with 7,610 persons registered in them. An additional 31 shelters were available on standby to open based on need.[27] The Jackson Coliseum opened as expected the day before and by early morning August 29 was reported by MEMA to be at capacity. Similarly, all Red Cross central Mississippi shelters were reported to be full as of 4:30 a.m. on August 29.[28] Two additional special needs shelters opened, bringing their total to five.[29]

Military preparation in Mississippi

Military preparation in Mississippi began as early as August 26 when, as noted earlier, the Governor activated the state's National Guard.[30] Mississippi's National Guard has over 12,000 troops, with Army and Air National Guard components, both under the direction of the Adjutant General (TAG), Major General Harold A. Cross.[31] Throughout the preparation and response to Katrina, Mississippi's Guard reported to and received taskings (or mission assignments) from MEMA.[32] The Mississippi National Guard has an Operations Plan, (OPLAN MSSTAD) on top of MEMA's Comprehensive Emergency Management Plan, that was used during Hurricane Katrina.[33] Refined and updated in an order issued to Mississippi Guard on June 1, 2005, this operations plan was validated during Hurricane Dennis, July 7 to 10, 2005.[34]

On August 27, Mississippi's Guard accelerated its preparations by alerting state emergency personnel to assemble for hurricane operations on the Mississippi Gulf coast under Joint Task Force Magnolia.[35] In doing so, Mississippi's National Guard assembled and pre-positioned at all three coastal county EOCs its special "hurricane strike" squads; each squad consisted of 10 military police (MPs), 15 engineers and five trucks.[36] In addition, the Guard placed on alert the following units from throughout the state:

223rd EN BN – Camp McCain, MS (Grenada, MS)
890th EN BN – Home Station Armories (located in the coastal region)
112th MP BN – Camp Shelby, MS (Hattiesburg, MS)
367th MAINT. CO – Home Station (Philadelphia, MS)
1687th TRANS CO – Home Station (Southaven, MS)
1387th QM WATER - Home Station (Leland, MS)
210th FINANCE – Home Station (Jackson, MS)
172nd AW – Home Station (Jackson, MS)
186th ARW – Home Station (Meridian, MS)[37]

Cross noted that these assets "were sufficient for a Category II storm, but as Katrina approached the Gulf coast on August 28, it became apparent that additional forces from outside the state would be required."[38] As a result, that afternoon, he initiated requests for assistance via the EMAC. The first such request, relayed to the on-site National Guard Bureau Liaison Officers (LNO) was for an additional MP Battalion, two more Engineering Battalions, and 3 CH-37 helicopters.[39] That same day, August 28, the National Guard Bureau Joint Operations Center in Washington, D.C., sent LNOs to Mississippi, with the first going to Mississippi's Joint Force Headquarters, followed by officers sent to the three coastal county EOCs and to MEMA's Operations Cell to facilitate out of state National Guard assets.[40]

In addition, Cross established at Gulfport a Forward Operations Center that eventually combined state and federal (including active duty) logistics support personnel.[41] In response to questions regarding the Guard's preparations, including the EMAC assistance it received, Cross said, "This greatly assisted in the command and control and situational awareness of all operations. As forces flowed into the state, more liaison teams were established in each county EOC that had Guard operations in that county. This was a very efficient system since the National Guard headquarters was linked directly with each county for coordination of relief efforts."[42]

The Guard's preparation in Mississippi was not, unfortunately, without incident. Prior to the storm's landfall, Sgt. Joshua Russell, Detachment 1, Company A, 89th Engineers, was killed when attempting to rescue an elderly couple in Harrison County.[43]

Pre-landfall preparation in Alabama

Final preparation for Katrina in Alabama began in earnest four days prior to landfall when it became evident the path of the storm pointed towards the Gulf coast. Three days prior to landfall, the Governor's staff participated in frequent videoconference calls with personnel from FEMA, the National Hurricane Center, including its director Max Mayfield, senior staff at the White House, and senior staff from the Governors' offices from Louisiana and Mississippi.[44] The Governor's staff indicated they were satisfied with the federal support they received and that Max Mayfield's briefings were particularly valuable.[45]

In Alabama's southernmost counties, Baldwin and Mobile, preparations began five days before the storm, when they started regular consultations with the National Hurricane Center, the State of Alabama Emergency Management Agency, and the National Weather Service in Mobile to discuss the storm's likely path and strength.[46] Information was then disseminated to all local officials and first responders and staff prepared to activate the EOCs.[47]

On August 28, 2005, Governor Riley wrote to President Bush, asking that he "declare an emergency disaster declaration for the State of Alabama as a result of Hurricane Katrina beginning on August 28, 2005 and continuing."[48] That same day President Bush "declared an emergency . . . for the State of Alabama."[49]

The next day, Monday, August 29, Riley wrote to President Bush again, this time asking him to "declare an expedited major disaster . . . as a result of Hurricane Katrina beginning on August 28, 2005 and continuing."[50] That same day, President Bush issued a major disaster declaration for Alabama."[51]

Establishment of command structures in Alabama

On Friday, August 26, Riley declared a state of emergency to handle what was then thought would be a surge of evacuees from the Florida panhandle. The state went into what they call Level II response and expected to receive 10 to 15 percent of Florida's evacuees.[52] A Level II response activates the Alabama EOC on a 24-hour basis, and all relevant agencies are activated and necessary personnel are assigned to staff the EOC.

One day later, on Saturday, August 27, a Level I response was activated.[53] The EOC was operating in full force, with desks staffed for each ESF. A FEMA Emergency Response Team - Advance (ERT-A) was on site late in the day. An ERT-A team is a small FEMA contingent with capabilities for planning, operations, communications, and logistics. A total of five to eight people from the Atlanta-based FEMA region IV were on site at the EOC. The Alabama Emergency Management Agency (AEMA) expressed some frustration with FEMA's late arrival. AEMA officials believed that had FEMA been on site sooner with a larger contingent, Alabama may have been able to acquire needed resources and commodities more quickly.

President Bush spoke to Riley on Saturday, August 27, two days prior to landfall, to ensure the Governor had everything he needed. The Governor's staff indicated they felt they were better prepared for Katrina than they were for Hurricanes Dennis and Ivan.[54] In addition to implementing many of the lessons learned from previous hurricanes, the Governor's staff believes one key element of the state's response to Katrina was the state's proactive communications strategy.

On Friday, August 26, as the storm gathered in the Gulf, the Governor personally visited all of the counties in the Gulf, holding numerous press conferences to urge local residents to evacuate pursuant to the mandatory evacuation orders.[55] In Alabama, the failure to obey a mandatory evacuation order is a misdemeanor enforced by county or municipal police.[56]

The Alabama EOC is divided into five clusters of desks and each desk is equipped with computers, telephony and other management tools.[57] The five clusters are:

- emergency services (ESF #s 1, 2, 3, 4, 9, 13)
- human services (ESF #s 6, 8, 11)
- infrastructure and support (ESF #s 10, 12)
- operations support (ESF #s 14, 15) and
- information and planning (ESF #s 5, 7).

There is a station for each ESF function and stations for all of the involved agencies, federal and state, including FEMA, EMAC, Army Corps of Engineers, National Guard, Alabama State Police, among others.[58]

One of the tools Alabama uses to respond to local disaster needs is the EM-2000 incident log, a Lotus Notes-based system which captures, in log book fashion, emergency events and requests from each of the 67 counties.[59] Each activity or request logged into the system gets assigned to one of the desks in the EOC for attention.

If a report comes in regarding individuals who are trapped and in need of rescue, the event will be assigned to the personnel in the emergency services cluster. Multi-ESF teams involving state police (ESF #13), transportation (ESF #1), and urban search and rescue (ESF #9) huddle to coordinate the optimal response. Events can be reported and tracked by ESF, by status, by county, and by a number of other custom data elements. Documents related to information requests, as opposed to action requests, are later scanned and attached. The EM-2000 data files appear to serve as the central universe of actions and documents related to the state's response to the storm.

Applying the lessons learned from Hurricane Ivan, the state upgraded the tracking system used to determine hospital bed vacancies, giving state officials real-time visibility of surge capacity and making it possible to better direct those with special medical needs to appropriate sites.[60] The state health office also has the capability to conduct daily conference calls with county health staff to assess status and needs. Health officials staff their own emergency operations center, linked by computer and phone to the main state EOC in Clanton.

Evacuations in Alabama

Even before any evacuations began, AEMA and state transportation officials participated in the FEMA regional Evacuation Liaison Team conference calls, during which emergency managers from Florida, Louisiana, and Mississippi shared information on the status of evacuation routes, road closures, traffic volumes, hotel availability, and other interstate implications of significant population migrations in the region.[61]

On the morning of August 29, Shelby County, Alabama, posted a message on the statewide EM2000 system saying the "Shelby County Humane Society will house animals during the emergency. Can house small animals as well as farm animals for a short duration."[62] More than 50 pets were evacuated from Mississippi and brought to Maxwell Air Force Base, where they were taken in by families on the base until the pet owners could be located.[63]

Pre-landfall preparation in Louisiana

On Saturday, August 27, Louisiana Governor Blanco wrote to President Bush, requesting that he "declare an emergency for the State of Louisiana due to Hurricane Katrina for the time period beginning August 26, 2005, and continuing."[64] Later that same day, President Bush declared an emergency for the state of Louisiana.[65] William Lokey was named Federal Coordinating Officer.[66]

On Sunday, August 28, in recognition of the potential catastrophic impact of Hurricane Katrina, Blanco asked President Bush, prior to landfall, to "declare an expedited major disaster for the State of Louisiana as Hurricane Katrina, a Category V Hurricane approaches our coast . . . beginning on August 28, 2005 and continuing."[67] The next day, President Bush declared a major disaster for Louisiana.[68]

Establishment of command and safeguarding of assets

The State of Louisiana took a number of steps to prepare for the arrival of Hurricane Katrina, including getting the EOC up and running with its full staff complement by the afternoon of Friday, August 26.[69] The EOC conducted communications checks with all the state agencies and parishes on Thursday, August 25 – four days before landfall.[70]

The state EOC then began holding regular conference calls with all state agencies, key parishes, federal agencies, other states, and the Red Cross to coordinate pre-landfall activities among all the different authorities.[71] These calls began at 5:00 p.m. on Friday, August 26, with five calls on Saturday, four calls on Sunday, and a final call Monday morning as the storm hit but before communications went out. In addition, several state agencies moved key assets northward, stockpiled critical supplies, positioned teams to do post-landfall damage assessments, or otherwise prepared for the hurricane.[72] The Louisiana Department of Fish and Wildlife coordinated with the Louisiana National Guard in advance to get boats placed on trailers and pre-positioned at Jackson Barracks in New Orleans in anticipation of flooding and the need for waterborne search and rescue.[73]

There were also preparations at the parish level. As noted, the parishes participated in conference calls with the state. Plaquemines Parish, one of the southern parishes most exposed to the storm, parked vehicles on high ground, gathered administrative records and moved them north, transferred prisoners to upstate facilities, and set up an emergency command post in a local high school.[74] Jefferson Parish, part of metropolitan New Orleans, also took a number of preparatory steps. According to Emergency Management Director Walter Maestri, they implemented their "Doomsday Plan" to hunker down in their EOC with a skeleton crew to minimize the number of people exposed to the hurricane's damage.

The Louisiana National Guard (LANG) and other state agencies went on alert and began staging personnel and equipment.[75] By Saturday, August 28, the day prior to landfall, the LANG had pre-positioned 9,792 MREs and 13,440 liters of water at the Superdome, the "shelter of last resort." The state also had positioned teams north, out

of harm's way, prior to landfall, and the first requests for EMAC teams were issued as well.

On Saturday, August 28, the New Orleans Regional Transit Authority (RTA) fueled up its fleet based at its Eastern New Orleans facility and moved buses not providing service to higher ground on a wharf near downtown New Orleans.[76] Buses that were providing regular service were also eventually moved to the wharf as well.

Evacuations in Louisiana

The state was actively involved in executing the Southeast Louisiana evacuation plan, with the Department of Transportation and Development and the Louisiana State Police working to manage traffic and implement "contraflow" — making all highway lanes outbound to maximize traffic flow and minimize traffic jams.[77] The Governor was personally involved in monitoring contraflow, which ran from Saturday at about 4:00 p.m. to Sunday at about 6:00 p.m.[78]

State officials coordinated the contraflow with the states of Mississippi and Texas, since Louisiana interstates fed into these states.[79] In a conference call at 6:30 a.m. Saturday morning, it was recommended that the evacuation plan for southeast Louisiana be implemented.[80] The state began staging assets necessary to execute an evacuation, including alerting and activating National Guard troops, pre-deploying traffic cones and barriers to key locations, and coordinating plans among all of the parishes.[81] Some parishes had already begun evacuation proceedings. By 6:00 p.m. on Sunday, August 28, traffic was light, so contraflow was halted, but residents could still evacuate on the outbound lanes once the highways were returned to their normal configuration.[82]

Up to 1.2 million Louisiana residents followed the evacuation orders and evacuated themselves in their private vehicles.[83] However, it later became apparent that thousands of residents, particularly in New Orleans, did not evacuate or seek shelter, but remained in their homes.

The parishes began declaring evacuations on Saturday, August 27 at 9:00 a.m. These declarations had been coordinated among the state and parishes in advance as part of Louisiana's emergency evacuation plan, which call for the most southern parishes to evacuate first so that, as

AP PHOTO/CHERYL GERBER

Emergency shelters in Louisiana

Louisiana also set up shelters as part of its evacuation plan. A "Sheltering Task Force" led by the Department of Social Services and the Department of Health and Hospitals, coordinated its activities with the state EOC and parishes through the aforementioned conference calls.[89] Specific shelters were designated along the main evacuation routes, including both general population shelters and special needs shelters.[90] These efforts were coordinated with both Mississippi and Texas, which set up shelters once Louisiana shelters began to fill.[91]

Several parishes also established "shelters of last resort" for residents that could not evacuate or had delayed leaving. Parish officials Ebbert and Maestri told Select Committee staff they purposefully designate these shelters at the last minute so people will not use them as an excuse to avoid evacuation.[92] New Orleans, which had already designated the Superdome as a shelter for the special needs population, also designated that facility as a "shelter of last resort" on Sunday, August 28.[93] The Louisiana National Guard pre-positioned 9,792 MREs and 13,440 liters of water at the Superdome.[94] Also in New Orleans, the RTA began running special service from 12 sites across the city to take riders to the Superdome.[95] The RTA also ran at least 10 paratransit vehicles to the Superdome and then on to the Baton Rouge area for "special needs" citizens; each of these vehicles made at least two trips.[96] All service ceased at approximately 7:00 p.m. Sunday night, approximately 11 hours before Katrina was due to make landfall and as conditions worsened.[97] Jefferson Parish also designated four facilities as "shelters of last resort."[98] According to Maestri, unlike the Superdome, these locations in Jefferson Parish did not have any prepositioned medical personnel or supplies but they did have pre-positioned food and water.

they drive north, they do not encounter traffic bottlenecks in New Orleans or Baton Rouge.[84] While some parishes (e.g., Plaquemines and St. Charles) began the process with "mandatory" evacuation orders, most parishes began with "recommended" evacuation orders and upgraded these to "mandatory" orders later on Saturday or Sunday.[85] Some of the parishes farther north (e.g., St. Tammany, Tangipahoa) declared mandatory evacuation orders only for residents living in low lying areas or manufactured homes.[86]

Some parishes also asked nongovernmental organizations to help evacuate those residents that did not have their own vehicles. Both New Orleans and Jefferson Parish have a program called "Brother's Keeper" run by the parishes in conjunction with local churches and the Red Cross. According to Maestri, the parish had a phone bank in the EOC manned by volunteers that help take the calls and match up riders with drivers once the evacuation was announced.[87] By Sunday evening, most of the parishes reported empty streets and had declared dusk-to-dawn curfews.[88]

Pre-landfall preparations by DOD, the National Guard, U.S. Army Corps of Engineers, and U.S. Coast Guard

DOD

In preparation for the last part of the 2005 hurricane season, the Secretary of Defense approved a standing order on August 19 that allowed the commander, U.S. Northern Command, to use military installations and deploy Defense Coordinating Officers (DCO) as needed to coordinate directly in support of FEMA in affected states. As the force provider to Northern Command, the U.S. Joint Forces Command issued general instructions on August 20 on how it would task units in support of any Northern Command requests to support FEMA.[99]

On August 23, Northern Command began tracking the tropical depression that became Hurricane Katrina. On August 24, the Office of the Secretary of Defense (OSD), Northern Command, and the National Guard Bureau participated in a teleconference with FEMA on what would be needed to respond to Katrina. Joint Forces Command issued a warning order to military services to be ready to support requests for assistance. Northern Command issued a similar warning order on August 25, the day Katrina struck Florida as a category 1 storm.[100]

On August 26, Northern Command issued an execute order, setting initial DOD relief actions into motion. The initial response was focused on Florida, but DCOs were also activated for Georgia, Alabama, and Mississippi.[101]

On August 27, Northern Command received its first mission assignment from FEMA, to provide Barksdale Air Force Base in Louisiana as a federal operational staging area. The same day, the Corps of Engineers positioned teams and supplies in Alabama, Louisiana, and Mississippi. In New Orleans, the commander of the Corps' New Orleans District evacuated most of his staff to alternate locations to be ready to respond when the storm passed. Other active military units ordered similar evacuations of personnel and equipment. In addition, the Louisiana National Guard aviation officer requested helicopter support from the National Guard Bureau, and support was coordinated through the EMAC.[102]

On August 28, DCOs were deployed to Mississippi and Louisiana. Northern Command took several additional steps to organize military assets that might be needed, including deployment of Joint Task Force-Forward (eventually Joint Task Force-Katrina) to Camp Shelby, Mississippi and a general alert to DOD assets potentially needed, particularly aviation assets.[103]

On the day Katrina made landfall, August 29, the Deputy Secretary of Defense led an 8:30 a.m. meeting to get damage assessment for DOD facilities and review resources that might be required from DOD to support hurricane relief. The Secretary of Defense was briefed on DOD's readiness and Northern Command issued several more alerts in anticipation of requests for assistance.[104]

National Guard

At the beginning of each hurricane season, National Guard Bureau (NGB) personnel participate in an interagency conference to assess potential response shortfalls and identify potential solutions that could be resolved through EMAC requests.[105] NGB planners conducted this EMAC conference in the spring of 2005 with participants from Alabama, Arkansas, Florida, Georgia, Louisiana, Maryland, Michigan, Mississippi, North Carolina, New York, and South Carolina. The Joint Staff J3 Joint Director of Military Support (JDOMS) also participated. The participants in these conferences believe that EMAC is capable of providing most military capabilities needed by states for hurricane disaster relief operations.

The role of the NGB grew in preparation for Guard response to Hurricane Katrina. On August 24, it issued an executive order calling on its Joint Staff to provide proactive planning and staffing support to states potentially affected by then-tropical storm Katrina. NGB Liaison Teams (LNOs) were sent to Alabama, Mississippi, and Louisiana.[106] On Wednesday, August 24, the first teleconference between NORTHCOM, the Joint Staff, Guard Headquarters, and FEMA was held to discuss DOD support to federal authorities.

The Joint Operations Center at the NGB geared up as the operations center for Katrina response.[107] The heads of the Army and Air National Guard also use this center for coordination of effort. During Hurricane Katrina preparation and response, the Joint Operations Center provided daily intelligence updates, logs of current operations, daily teleconferences, and coordination with states on logistical assistance; maintained communications with states and other agencies; and, coordinated Guard aviation assets.

On August 25, the NGB began hosting daily teleconferences with the operations officers of the Gulf states' Adjutant Generals. The Adjutant Generals reported their preparations to respond, and were asked if they needed out of state assistance.[108] Some of them had already contacted or were contacted by other nearby states to arrange for assistance via the EMAC in the form of personnel and equipment that might be needed.[109]

On Sunday, August 28, reports into NGB by state Adjutant Generals indicated that 4,444 Army National Guard and 932 Air National Guard in Florida, Alabama,

Mississippi, and Louisiana were ready to respond. Both General Bennett C. Landreneau of Louisiana and Cross of Mississippi requested additional aircraft from EMAC via NGB.[110] Consequently, these requests were considered state-to-state requests for assistance, not federal requests involving FEMA or OSD, even though NGB facilitated the assistance. On Monday, August 29, NGB noted that 65 Army National Guard aircraft were in position in Florida, Alabama, Texas, Louisiana, and Mississippi.

Louisiana National Guard

The Louisiana National Guard is an integral part of managing emergencies in the state. The Adjutant General, Landreneau, wears two hats, as he is head of both the National Guard and the Louisiana Office of Homeland Security and Emergency Preparedness (LOHSEP).[111] The National Guard plays a significant role in emergency command and control because of the dual role of the Adjutant General. Also, many of the personnel who staff the state's EOC are guardsmen.

On Friday, August 26, Blanco authorized the mobilization of 2,000 Louisiana guardsmen.[112] The next day, Landreneau called an additional 2,000 to active duty.[113] By the end of the day on Saturday, 3,085 Louisiana National Guard troops had been fully activated. Coordination also began with other states for additional aviation assets for search and rescue and EMAC support, if needed.

Before Katrina hit, Louisiana National Guard soldiers screen residents entering the Superdome.

The Louisiana National Guard participated in a number of preparation missions, including law enforcement, traffic control, shelter support and security, and securing operations at the Superdome.[114] Many guardsmen were also embedded with state and parish officials and later used their radios to help these officials reestablish some minimal level of communications.[115] Before Katrina hit, guardsmen provided support for general purpose shelters and special needs shelters by providing medical personnel.[116]

Alabama National Guard

The Alabama National Guard has 13,200 troops, with Army and Air National Guard components falling under its Adjutant General, Major General Mark Bowen.[117] The Adjutant General is also a member of the Governor's Cabinet, but is not dual-hatted as the emergency response coordinator. Although he participates in the state's EOC, Bowen's chain of command is a direct line to the governor. The Alabama Guard has developed and is organized around mission oriented joint force packages, (i.e., hurricanes, snow and ice storms). Task forces typically include security forces, engineers, medical, communications, special operations forces, logistics and a command and control cell. Alabama also has a voluntary state militia that is administered by the National Guard. They are used to augment the Guard force and have approximately 2,000 to 3,000 members.

During the Alabama National Guard's preparation phase, which began six days before Katrina hit, Guard assets monitored the storm track and began discussions with the NGB.[118] By August 26, Riley ordered 3,000 Alabama National Guard soldiers and airmen to state active duty and requested Secretary of Defense approval of 180 days of military duty.[119] Approval was granted by DOD on September 7 and was retroactive to August 29.[120]

Two days before the storm, a National Guard liaison officer was dispatched to the state EOC in Clanton.[121] On August 28, two National Guard Task Forces were formed, gathered pre-positioned supplies (food, water, ice, gas) from Maxwell Air Force Base, and equipment, including generators,

AP PHOTO/DAVE MARTIN

fuel trucks, and aviation assets.[122] Guard assets also began deployment to assist Mobile and Baldwin County Emergency Management activities.[123]

Mississippi National Guard

The Mississippi National Guard has 12,041 troops, with Army and Air National Guard components falling under Adjutant Major General Harold A. Cross.[124] The Adjutant General reports directly to the Governor, but is not dual-hatted as the state emergency management officer. Mississippi's emergency response is handled by the state's emergency management agency, MEMA.

On August 28, 2005, the Mississippi National Guard alerted state emergency personnel to assemble for hurricane operations on the Mississippi Gulf coast under Joint Task Force Magnolia.[125] National Guard special "hurricane strike" squads were pre-positioned at all three coastal county EOCs. Recommended but voluntary evacuation of civilians brought bumper-to-bumper traffic along Highway 49 northbound, from the beach in Gulfport to Jackson. By Sunday evening, numerous mandatory evacuation orders were in effect, and Mississippi National Guard Soldiers took shelter at Camp Shelby, 62 miles north of the predicted landfall area. These Guard personnel moved south after the storm had passed to begin assisting with response and recovery efforts.

U.S. Army Corps of Engineers

The Army Corps of Engineers (USACE), another active duty military unit, provided substantial resources to prepare for and respond to Hurricane Katrina. Under the National Response Plan, the USACE, as the lead federal agency for public works and engineering (ESF #3), provides relief and response support to FEMA.[126] To meet these responsibilities, USACE has pre-awarded competitively bid contracts for all of these functions to allow quick deployment of resources prior to and immediately after an event.[127] These pre-awarded contracts are part of USACE's Advanced Contracting Initiative (ACI), which has been in place for about six years.

USACE took a number of preparatory steps in anticipation of the hurricane season in general and for Hurricane Katrina specifically.[128] Over the summer, the USACE New Orleans District participated in an annual hurricane preparedness exercise conducted by the regional headquarters. In July 2005 the district sponsored a hurricane preparedness conference for federal, state, and local emergency managers.

In addition, USACE had equipment and supplies, including those needed to repair levees, pre-positioned in various locations along the Gulf of Mexico.[129] When Katrina approached, the New Orleans District monitored the situation and evacuated most staff, establishing a temporary district headquarters in Vicksburg, Mississippi. The district commander and eight staff remained in New Orleans, retreating to a bunker designed to withstand a category 5 hurricane. Their objective was to monitor the levee system, stay in contact with local officials, and provide post-storm assessments to the USACE chain of command.

U.S. Coast Guard

Well before arriving in the Gulf of Mexico, Hurricane Katrina was closely watched by Coast Guard officials as the storm approached and eventually passed through southern Florida. By Thursday, August 25, the Seventh Coast Guard District, based in Miami, had prepared for Katrina's arrival by partially evacuating Coast Guard boats, aircraft, and personnel, and closely monitoring Katrina's progress across the Florida peninsula.[130] As Katrina cleared the Seventh District, the Eighth District was busy executing hurricane plans in anticipation of Katrina's arrival.[131]

On August 27, the Eighth Coast Guard District's Incident Management Team (IMT), based in New Orleans, relocated to St. Louis in accordance with Coast Guard hurricane plans.[132] The Eighth District set heightened readiness for all units, ordered the evacuations of personnel and dependents from units along the Gulf coast in the anticipated impact zone, and closed the entrance to the lower Mississippi river to all commercial maritime traffic.

On August 28, the Coast Guard activated personnel to support air and swift boat operations under ESF-1, and positioned liaison officers at FEMA regions IV and VI, and to state EOCs in Florida, Louisiana and Mississippi.[133]

The Coast Guard's computer hub in New Orleans dropped off-line, resulting in no computer or internet connectivity to all coastal ports within the Eighth District Coast Guard units resorted to using phone and fax machines to communicate.

The Eighth District Commander requested additional Coast Guard air assets and personnel to support rescue and recovery operations.[134] Coast Guard aircraft and crews from Louisiana, Alabama, Florida, New Jersey, Massachusetts, North Carolina, Georgia, and Texas were pre-staged to provide rapid support.[135] Eighth District Commander Rear Admiral Robert Duncan contacted Blanco to discuss damage assessments and response efforts.[136]

Sector New Orleans operations and critical communications personnel evacuated to Alexandria, Louisiana. Non-essential Coast Guard personnel and dependents in the New Orleans area evacuated to the Naval Air Station in Meridian, Mississippi.[137] Coast Guard helicopters originally located in New Orleans relocated to Houston and Lake Charles, Louisiana to avoid Katrina's path, and prepared to begin rescue operations. All Coast Guard cutters and small boats relocated to safe locations, or traveled out to sea to avoid the storm.

In Mississippi, a Coast Guard Incident Management Team was established in Meridian.[138] Duncan contacted Barbour to discuss damage assessments and response efforts. Non-essential personnel and dependents from the Gulfport and Lockport areas relocated to Naval Air Station Meridian.[139] In Alabama, helicopters from Aviation Training Center Mobile deployed to Shreveport and Jacksonville for storm avoidance, and prepared to respond. Also, a Transportable Multi-mission Communications Center was pre-staged at Sector Mobile to provide temporary communication support. Non-essential Coast Guard personnel and dependents relocated to Maxwell Air Force Base.[140]

On August 29, the day Katrina made landfall, the Sector New Orleans Incident Management Team was established in Alexandria, LA.[141] Outside of the forecasted area of impact, Coast Guard Disaster Assistance Teams from Ohio, Kentucky, St. Louis, Pittsburgh, and Miami were pre-positioned to the region to respond as soon as conditions permitted.

During normal conditions, there are 15 helicopters assigned within the Eighth Coast Guard District, along with four fixed-wing aircraft and 16 cutters. Within 12 hours of Hurricane Katrina making landfall, the Coast Guard assigned 29 helicopters, eight fixed-wing aircraft, and 24 cutters to the area to support rescue operations.[142]

Pre-landfall preparations by the American Red Cross

The Red Cross' Gulf coast-area preparation was far along two days before Katrina made landfall in the Gulf coast. As of 2:00 p.m. on August 27, Carol Hall of the Red Cross reported to the White House and the Department of Homeland Security, among other governmental organizations that it "has every resource at its disposal on alert/moving in anticipation of this event to include personnel, equipment, and materials."[143] According to Hall, key aspects of this preparation included:

- Chapters across the region opened shelters in support of evacuations in all states.
- 275,000 HeaterMeals were staged in Baton Rouge, LA.
- 225,000 HeaterMeals were staged in Montgomery, AL.
- 15 sites were identified to bring in big kitchens with the support of Southern Baptists to provide 300,000-meals-per-day feeding capability.
- All 14 Disaster Field Supply Center warehouses loaded supplies, including 50,000 cots, 100,000 blankets, comfort and clean-up kits.
- All vehicles in the Red Cross fleet across the country were placed on alert for possible deployment and were dispatched to staging areas.
- All 8 Emergency Communications Response Vehicles (ECRVs) deployed to staging areas.
- Red Cross staff deployed to NRCC, Region VI RRCC, Region IV RRCC, ERT-As and other ESF #6 posts.

Red Cross volunteers unload supplies in preparation for Katrina.

By August 28, the Red Cross started to understand the magnitude of Katrina. One of its Disaster Operations Reports remarked, if Katrina makes landfall at its current pressure, "it will be the most intense storm to hit the US mainland."[144] On the same day it was reported, "For the first time ever, an ESF6 coordination center will be set up tomorrow at American Red Cross national headquarters to coordinate the deliver [sic] mass care services with our governmental and non-governmental organization partners."[145]

As Katrina made landfall on August 29, the Red Cross was fully staffing all of the relevant state and federal EOCs, including Alabama, Louisiana, Florida, Mississippi, Georgia, South Carolina, Tennessee, FEMA Regions IV and VI's RRCC, FEMA's NRCC, as well as ERT-A teams in Florida, Alabama, Mississippi, and Louisiana.[146] Sites for 25 kitchens to feed as many as 500,000 people were identified and pre-staged.[147]

Trajectory and impact of Hurricane Katrina

Finding: The accuracy and timeliness of National Weather Service and National Hurricane Center forecasts prevented further loss of life

Timeline of Hurricane Katrina and NWS Warnings to Federal, State and Local Officials

At 5:00 p.m. Eastern Daylight Time (EDT) (4:00 Central Daylight Time (CDT), the National Weather Service (NWS) reported that Katrina's projected path had shifted 150 miles to the west (toward Mississippi) and projected that Katrina would make landfall as a category 4 storm.[148] By 10:00 p.m. CDT that same night, the NWS projected that landfall was most likely at Buras, Louisiana, 65 miles south-southeast of New Orleans.[149] NWS proved extremely accurate; the final landfall location was only 20 miles off from Friday's forecast.[150] Since meteorological conditions that affect the track and intensity of the storm were relatively stable, NWS was especially certain of the accuracy of its prediction, even 56 hours from landfall.

At 10:00 a.m. CDT, on Saturday, August 27, the National Hurricane Center (NHC) issued a hurricane watch for southeast Louisiana, including New Orleans, which was extended to Mississippi and Alabama later that afternoon.[151] Later that evening, between 7:30 and 8:00 p.m. CDT, 35 hours before landfall, Max Mayfield, the director of the NHC called state officials in Louisiana, Mississippi, and Alabama to inform them of the storm's intensity and its potential to be devastating and catastrophic.[152] At Governor Blanco's urging, Mayfield also called Ray Nagin.[153]

Despite media reports indicating Mayfield encouraged Nagin to immediately order a mandatory evacuation, Mayfield "just told [officials] the nature of the storm [and that he] probably said to the Mayor that he was going to have some very difficult decisions ahead of him."[154] Similarly, Mayfield said that the "purpose of [his] calls there to the Governors of Louisiana and Mississippi was really just to make absolutely sure that they understood how serious the situation was . . . ."[155]

In public advisories issued at 10:00 p.m. CDT Saturday, 32 hours before prior to landfall, NHC warned of storm surge forecasts.[156] At 7:00 a.m. on Sunday, August 28, NWS advisories characterized Katrina as a "potentially catastrophic" storm.[157] Additionally, at 4:00 p.m. CDT on Sunday, the storm surge was predicted to be 18 to 22 feet, and locally as high as 28 feet with "large and battering" waves on top of the surge, meaning "some levees in the greater New Orleans area could be overtopped."[158]

Although it was reported that Mayfield cautioned the levees would be breached, no such warning was issued. "What I indicated in my briefings to emergency managers and to the media was the possibility that some levees in the greater New Orleans area could be overtopped, depending on the details of Katrina's track and intensity," Mayfield said.[159]

Also on Sunday, August 28, the NWS office in Slidell, Louisiana, which is responsible for the New Orleans area, issued warnings saying, "most of the area will be uninhabitable for weeks...perhaps longer" and predicting "human suffering incredible by modern standards."[160] Ultimately, NWS and NHC proved remarkably accurate in capturing Katrina's eventual wrath and destruction.

It is important to note, the hurricane risk to New Orleans and the surrounding areas was well-recognized and predicted by forecasters long before Hurricane Katrina. "The 33 years that I've been at the Hurricane Center we have

always been saying — the directors before me and I have always said — that the greatest potential for the nightmare scenarios, in the Gulf of Mexico anyway, is that New Orleans and southeast Louisiana area," Mayfield said.[161]

The NWS and NHC are not without critics though. AccuWeather Inc., a private weather service company, has said the public should have received earlier warnings that Gulf coast residents, and New Orleans residents in particular, were directly in Katrina's path.[162] AccuWeather issued a forecast predicting the target of Katrina's landfall nearly 12 hours before the NHC issued its first warning, and argued the extra time could have aided evacuation of the region.[163]

Responding to this criticism, Mayfield said premature evacuation can lead too large of an area to evacuate, causing unnecessary traffic and congestion on the roads.[164] As Mayfield testified, "the mission here of the National Hurricane Center and then the National Weather Service, is to provide the best forecast that we possibly can, and then the emergency managers at the local and state levels will use that, then they will call for evacuations."[165]

Ultimately, as Mayfield tried to convey, NHC and NWS can only forecast, issue warnings, and provide timely information to the state and local decision-makers who determine who and when to evacuate. The timeliness and accuracy of the forecasts saved lives. No government can blame inadequate response or lack of advanced warning.

Katrina makes landfall

Hurricane Katrina made landfall at Buras, Louisiana on the southeast corner of Louisiana, at 6:10 a.m. CDT, on Monday, August 29.[166] Katrina had maximum sustained winds of 121 mph and was unusually large, measuring approximately 400 miles across. Its eye was at least 30 miles wide. Though it had weakened from a category 5 to a strong category 3 storm by landfall, the damage and loss of life

from the storm was staggering, with effects extending from Louisiana through Mississippi, Alabama, Georgia, and the Florida panhandle.[167] The three states most directly affected — Alabama, Mississippi, and Louisiana — each suffered significant damage, with NHC noting that many of the most severely affected areas along the Gulf coast could take years to completely rebuild.[168]

Alabama — impact of Hurricane Katrina

Though Alabama was not where Hurricane Katrina made landfall, damages there were substantial. According to the NHC, "despite being more distant from the eye of Katrina, the storm surge over Dauphin Island, Alabama destroyed or damaged dozens of beachfront homes and cut a new canal through the island's western end."[169] Two deaths were reported during Hurricane Katrina in Alabama. However, these deaths were the result of an auto accident and unrelated to the Hurricane.[170]

Katrina caused significant damage along its coast with a wave surge of 13.5 feet, exceeding the 100-year flood level of 12 feet.[171] Bayou La Batre and (as noted above) Dauphin Island received the brunt of the storm in Alabama, losing 800 and 200 homes, respectively.[172] The storm caused wind damage as far north as Tuscaloosa County. Mobile Bay spilled into downtown and flooded large sections of the city, destroying hundreds of homes. The sheer power of the storm dislodged a nearby oil drilling platform, which became caught under the U.S. Highway 98 bridge.[173]

As of early January 2006, federal assistance to Alabama had exceeded $500 million.[174] Specifically, FEMA reported

FEMA

that, to date, it had provided $117 million in assistance to individuals and families (for housing and rental assistance) and $348 million for public assistance, crisis counseling, disaster unemployment assistance, and various mission assignments to other federal agencies during the disaster response. The public assistance funds were provided for, among other things, infrastructure costs, debris removal, and road and bridge repair. The costs for mission assignments to other federal agencies included the use of military aircraft for rapid needs assessments, shipments of ice (280 truckloads), water (186 truckloads), MREs (103 truckloads), generators (11 truckloads), cots (27 truckloads), and blankets (32 truckloads). The Small Business Administration (SBA) has approved over $68 million in loans to homeowners, renters, and businesses.

Mississippi — impact of Hurricane Katrina

In reporting casualty and damage statistics for Hurricane Katrina, NHC noted that "the storm surge of Katrina struck the Mississippi coastline with such ferocity that entire coastal communities were obliterated, some left with little more than the foundations upon which homes, businesses, government facilities, and other historical buildings once stood."[175] According to the NHC, the Hancock County EOC recorded a storm surge of as high as 27 feet; this surge likely penetrated at least six miles inland in many portions of the Mississippi coast and up to 12 miles inland along bays and rivers.[176] Even in areas that may have been spared the destruction of the storm surge, hurricane force winds wreaked havoc—according to Pearl River County EMA Director Bobby Strahan, for example, his EOC (one county inland) twice registered wind speeds of 135 miles per hour.[177]

All told, at least 231 Mississippians died during Hurricane Katrina.[178] In the three coastal counties alone,

66,000 may have been displaced from their homes due to flooding and/or structural damage to their homes.[179] At peak levels on August 31, Mississippi's power companies reported 958,000 customers were without power and that over 19,000 households were still powerless as of the end of September.[180]

Damages to Mississippi's economy were also substantial—the state's agricultural, forestry, gaming, maritime, and poultry industries all suffered extensive damages.[181] For example, the state reported that its two biggest crops—poultry and forestry—were very hard hit, with at least two years' worth of timber destroyed (worth $1.3 billion) and the value of the poultry industry dropping by six percent due to hurricane damage (including the estimated loss of 8 million birds and damage to 2,400 of the state's 9,000 poultry houses, 300 of which were totally devastated).[182] The state's dairy industry suffered losses estimated to exceed $6 million, and 20 percent of the expected rice and corn harvests may have been lost.[183]

The costs and volume of response and clean-up activity in Mississippi reflect the enormous damage Katrina left behind. For example, a month and a half after landfall, the state reported the total cost of assistance it received via EMAC was over $327 million ($176 million in civilian costs and $151 million in National Guard expenses).[184]

According to the National Emergency Management Association (NEMA, which administers the EMAC[185]), commonly requested resources included firefighters, search and rescue personnel, HAZMAT personnel, emergency medical technicians, state police, sheriffs, fish and wildlife personnel, corrections personnel, livestock inspectors, bridge inspectors, airport maintenance personnel,

FEMA

mbulances, medical doctors, registered nurses and Jational Guard Troops.[186] In total, at least 33 states aided ne law enforcement response effort in Mississippi through ne EMAC.[187]

Federal costs in Mississippi have also been ubstantial.[188] FEMA reports that, as of January 4, 2006 had disbursed in Mississippi just over $1 billion in ssistance via its Individuals and Households Program nd obligated to the state and local governments $666 nillion in public assistance to repair things like roads and ridges. SBA, FEMA reports, has approved home, business, nd economic injury loans totaling over $529 million. ISACE has installed nearly 50,000 temporary roofs nrough its Operation Blue Roof program (making that ffort 99 percent complete) and, in addition to the efforts f local governments and contractors, removed more than 3 million cubic yards of debris. While just over 30,000 EMA travel trailers and mobile homes are now occupied n Mississippi, four shelters housing 759 people remained pen at year's end.

Louisiana — impact of Hurricane Katrina

On August 28, at 10 a.m. CDT, the NWS field office in New Orleans issued a bulletin predicting catastrophic damage to New Orleans, including partial destruction of half of the well-constructed houses in the city, severe damage to most industrial buildings rendering them inoperable, the creation of a huge debris field of trees, telephone poles, cars, and collapsed buildings, and a lack of clean water.[189] As previously noted, NWS predicted the impact on Louisiana would be a human suffering incredible by modern standards." Unfortunately, much of what the NWS predicted came to pass.

With intense gale-force winds and massive storm surge, the effect of Hurricane Katrina on Southeast Louisiana was indeed catastrophic. After 11:00 a.m. CDT on August 29, several sections of the levee-system in New Orleans breached, and 80 percent of the city was under water at peak flooding, which in some places was 20 feet deep. The extensive flooding left many residents stranded long after

[38] *Id.*

[39] *Oct. 27, 2005 Select Comm. Hearing* (written response to questions for the record of Major General Harold A. Cross); *see also*, E-mail correspondence from LTC Rodney Neudecker, Mississippi Sr. Army Advisor Guard, to Lt. General Russel L. Honoré, Commander, Joint Task Force Katrina (Aug. 28, 2005; 11:26 a.m.); *see also*, E-mail correspondence from LTC Rodney Neudecker, Mississippi Sr. Army Advisor Guard, t Lt. General Russel L. Honoré; *see also*, Commander, Joint Task Force Katrina (Aug. 28, 2005; 4:42 a.m.).

[40] E-mail correspondence from LTC Rodney Neudecker, Mississippi Sr. Army Advisor Guard, to Lt. General Russel L. Honoré, Commander, Join Task Force Katrina (Aug. 28, 2005; 11:26 a.m.); E-mail correspondence from Lt. Col. Rodney Neudecker, Mississippi Sr. Army Advisor Guard, Lt. General Russel L. Honoré; *see also*, Commander, Joint Task Force Katrina (Aug. 28, 2005; 4:42 a.m.).

[41] E-mail correspondence from Lt. Col. Rodney Neudecker, Mississippi Sr. Army Advisor Guard, to Lt. General Russel L. Honoré, Commander, Joint Task Force Katrina (Aug. 28, 2005; 11:26 a.m.); E-mail correspondence from LTC Rodney Neudecker, Mississippi Sr. Army Advisor Guard to Lt. General Russel L. Honoré; *see also*, Commander, Joint Task Force Katrina (Aug. 28, 2005; 4:42 a.m.).

[42] *Oct. 27, 2005 Select Comm. Hearing* (written response to questions for the record of Major General Harold A. Cross).

[43] *Oct. 27, 2005 Select Comm. Hearing* at 26 (statement of Major General Harold A. Cross).

[44] *See generally*, Daily Video Teleconferences amongst officials dated Aug. 25 – Sept. 4, 2005 [hereinafter "Daily VTC"]. State and local officials from each of the impacted areas met daily with officials from, among other agencies, FEMA, and the National Hurricane Center.

[45] Interview by Select Comm. Staff with Toby Roth, Chief of Staff to Governor Barbour, and Dave Stewart, Policy Advisor to Governor Barbour, i Montgomery, AL (Oct. 12, 2005) [hereinafter *Roth / Stewart Interview*].

[46] FEMA, Chronology and Time Line, (DHS-FEMA-070-0001256).

[47] *Hearing on Hurricane Katrina: Preparedness and Response by the State of Alabama Before Select Comm.*, 109th Cong. (2005) at 86 (statement Leigh Ann Ryals) [hereinafter *Nov. 9, 2005 Select Comm. Hearing*]; *see also*, *Nov. 9, 2005 Hearing* at 93 (statement Walter Dickerson).

[48] Letter from Bob Riley, Governor of Alabama, to George W. Bush, President of the United States (Aug. 28, 2005).

[49] Letter from George W. Bush, President of the United States to Bob Riley, Governor of Alabama (Aug. 29, 2005).

[50] Letter from Bob Riley, Governor of Alabama, to George W. Bush, President of the United States (Aug. 28, 2005).

[51] *See*, Letter from George W. Bush, President of the United States to Bob Riley, Governor of Alabama (Aug. 29, 2005); *see*, Alabama; Major Disaster and Related Determinations, 70 Fed. Reg. 71,540-71,541 (Aug. 29, 2005, as amended Nov. 29, 2005).

[52] Level I being the highest (a declared disaster) and Level IV being the lowest (daily operating level). The AL EOP is in the process of being revised. The State of Alabama, with a view to being NRP and NIMS compliant, has reversed its ordering of the activation levels, i.e., Level I is now Level IV. *See*, E-mail correspondence from Bill Filter, Alabama Emergency Management Agency, Operations Department, to Select Comm Staff (Nov. 8, 2005).

[53] Interview by Select Comm. Staff with Charles Williams, Division Chief of Preparedness and Tim Payne, Branch Chief Emergency Managemen Program Coordinate, in Clanton, AL (Oct. 11, 2005) [hereinafter *Williams / Payne Interview*].

[54] *Williams / Payne Interview; see also, Roth / Stewart Interview*.

[55] *Roth / Stewart Interview*.

[56] *See*, ALA. CODE §§ 31-9-6 (4); 31-9-8 (4); 31-9-14 and 31-9-15 (2005).

[57] *William / Payne Interview*.

[58] *Id.*

[59] EM2000 messages from Aug. 23 through Sept. 15 were provided to the Select Comm. *See generally*, EM/2000 Tracker System Message Databas (Aug. 23 – Sept. 15, 2005).

[60] Interview by Select Comm. Staff with Dr. Donald E. Williamson, MD, Alabama State Health Director, in Montgomery, AL (Oct. 12, 2005) [hereinafter *Williamson Interview*].

[61] Meeting Summaries, FEMA Regional Emergency Liaison Team Conference Calls (Aug. 28, 2005 – Sept. 02, 2005).

[62] Alabama Emergency Management Agency, EM/2000 Tracker System Message 05-1839, (Aug. 29, 2005) (Doc. No. 002771AL). The AEMA Situation Report (SitRep) #8 also contained the following: "The Department has a list of 15 facilities across the state that will house animals evacuated because of the hurricane. The list, along with contact information and type of animal is posted on the Department website as well on the EM2000. Some of these facilities will house small animals such as dogs and cats; however, most only house horses. The total number animals that can be accommodated is over 2,000. Late this morning it was reported that just under 100 horses were being sheltered." Alabam Emergency Management Agency / Emergency Operation Center, Situation Report #8 (Doc. No. 000235AL) (Sept. 1, 2005).

[63] Alabama Emergency Management Agency / Emergency Operation Center, Situation Report #12 (Doc. No. 000312AL) (Sept. 5, 2005).

[64] Letter from Kathleen Babineaux Blanco, Governor of LA, to George W. Bush, President of the United States (Aug. 27, 2005).

[65] Louisiana: Emergency and Related Determinations, 70 Fed. Reg. 53,238 (Aug. 27, 2005, as amended Sept. 7, 2005).

[66] Louisiana: Emergency and Related Determinations, 70 Fed. Reg. 53,238 (Aug. 27, 2005, as amended Sept. 7, 2005).

[67] Letter from Kathleen Babineaux Blanco, Governor of LA, to George W. Bush, President of the United States (Aug. 28, 2005).

[68] Louisiana; Major Disaster and Related Determinations, 70 Fed. Reg. 72,458 (Aug. 29, 2005, as amended Dec. 5, 2005).

[69] Interview by Select Comm. Staff with LTC William Doran, Chief, Operations Division, LA Office of Homeland Security and Emergency Preparedness (LOHSEP), in Baton Rouge, LA (Nov. 7, 2005) [hereinafter *Doran Interview*]; *see* Interview by Select Comm. Staff with Jim Ballou Operations Division, LA Office of Homeland Security and Emergency Preparedness (LOHSEP), in Baton Rouge, LA (Nov. 7, 2005) [hereinafte *Ballou Interview*].

[70] Interview by Select Comm. Staff with Rex McDonald, Information Technology and Communications Director, Department of Public Safety and Corrections, in Baton Rouge, LA (Nov. 7, 2005) [hereinafter *McDonald Interview*].

[71] Audio recordings of Hurricane Katrina Conference Calls, LA State Emergency Operations Center (Aug 26-28, 2005).

[72] *See* Ballou Interview; *see also*, Doran Interview.

[73] Interview by Select Comm. Staff with General Joseph B. Veillon, Louisiana National Guard Commander for Task Force Minnow, in New Orleans, LA (Nov. 3, 2005) [hereinafter *Veillon Interview*].

[74] Interview by Select Comm. Staff with Dr. Walter Maestri, Emergency Manager for Jefferson Parish, in New Orleans, LA (Nov. 8, 2005) [hereinafter *Maestri Interview*].

[5] *Superdome Personnel, MREs, and Water from 28 Aug. – 3 Sept.*, Table: provided by staff from LA Governor Blanco's office (Dec. 2005).

[6] *Hearing on Rebuilding Highway and Transit Infrastructure on the Gulf Coast following Hurricane Katrina: State and Local Officials Before the House Subcommittee on Highways, Transit and Pipelines*, 109th Cong. (Oct. 27, 2005) at 1 (statement by William J. DeVille) [hereinafter *Oct. 27, 2005 T&I Hearing*].

[7] Audio recordings of Hurricane Katrina Conference Calls, LA State Emergency Operations Center (Aug. 26-28, 2005).

[8] *Id.*

[9] Audio recordings of Hurricane Katrina Conference Calls, LA State Emergency Operations Center (Aug. 26-29, 2005).

[10] *Id.*

[11] *Id.*

[12] *Id.*

[13] Interview by Select Comm. Staff with Andy Kopplin, Chief of Staff to Governor Blanco, in Baton Rouge, LA (Nov. 6, 2005) [hereinafter *Kopplin Interview*].

[14] Audio recordings of Hurricane Katrina Conference Calls, LA State Emergency Operations Center (Aug. 26-28, 2005).

[15] *Id.*

[16] *Id.*

[17] *Maestri Interview.*

[18] Audio recordings of Hurricane Katrina Conference Calls, LA State Emergency Operations Center (Aug. 26-29, 2005).

[19] *Id.*

[20] *Id.*

[21] *Id.*

[22] Interview by Select Comm. Staff with Terry Ebbert, Director of Homeland Security for the City of New Orleans, in New Orleans, LA (Nov. 9, 2005) [hereinafter *Ebbert Interview*]; *see also, Maestri Interview.*

[23] Audio recordings of Hurricane Katrina Conference Calls, Louisiana State Emergency Operations Center (Aug. 26-29, 2005).

[24] Table: Superdome Personnel, MREs, and Water from 28 Aug. – 3 Sept., provided by staff from Louisiana Governor Blanco's office (Dec. 2005).

[25] *Oct. 27, 2005 T&I Hearing* (statement of William DeVille).

[26] *Id.*

[27] *Id.*

[28] *Maestri Interview.*

[29] E-mail correspondence from Chairman, Joint Chiefs of Staff, to Department of Defense, et al (Aug. 19, 2005). This subject of this e-mail was a "Severe Weather Execute Order (EXORD) for DOD Support to Federal Emergency Management Agency (FEMA)."

[40] Department of Defense OASD HD, Hurricane Katrina/Rita/Ophelia Interim Timeline (Aug. – Sept. 2005) (Nov. 2, 2005) at 2 [hereinafter *DOD Timeline*]; *see also, Oct. 27, 2005 Select Comm. Hearing* at 3 (written statement by Timothy J. Keating).

[41] *DOD Timeline* at 2.

[42] *Id.* at 2-3.

[43] *DOD Timeline* at 3; *see* Col. Kranepuhl – Chief Operations, US Army, 1A Commander's Hurricane Assessment (Aug. 29, 2005), First US Army (Doc No. MMTF 00346-05) (Aug. 29, 2005); *see also,* Col. Kranepuhl – Chief Operations, US Army, 1A Commander's Hurricane Assessment (Aug. 30, 2005), First US Army (Doc No. MMTF 00349-05) (Aug. 30, 2005).

[44] *DOD Timeline* at 4.

[45] *Oct. 27, 2005 Select Comm. Hearing* (written response to questions for the record of LTG H Steven Blum).

[46] United States National Guard, Hurricane Katrina: National Guard After Action Review (Dec. 21, 2005) at 1.

[47] Interview by Select Comm. Staff with General H Steven Blum, Chief, National Guard, in Arlington, VA, (Oct. 19, 2005) [hereinafter *Blum Interview*]; *see also,* Interview by Select Comm. Staff with LT General Daniel James, III, Director of Air National Guard, in Arlington, VA, (Oct. 19, 2005) [hereinafter *James Interview*; *see also,* Interview by Select Comm. Staff with LT General Clyde A. Vaughn, Director of Army National Guard, in Arlington, VA, (Oct. 19, 2005) [hereinafter *Vaughn Interview*].

[48] United States National Guard, Hurricane Katrina: National Guard After Action Review (Dec. 21, 2005) at 1; *see also,* Blum Interview; *see also,* James Interview; *see also,* Vaughn Interview.

[49] *Oct. 27, 2005 Select Comm. Hearing* (written response to questions for the record of General Landreneau; *see also,* Interview by Select Comm. Staff with Major General Cross, State Adjutant General of MS, in Jackson, MS (Oct. 12, 2005) [hereinafter *Cross Interview*].

[50] United States National Guard, Hurricane Katrina: National Guard After Action Review (Dec. 21, 2005) at 10.

[51] *See,* Interview by Select Comm. Staff with Scott Wells, Field Officer, FEMA [hereinafter *Wells Interview*], in Baton Rouge, LA (Nov. 9, 2005); *see also,* Interview by Select Comm. Staff with Stephen Dabadie, Chief of Staff to LA Adjutant General Landrenau, LA National Guard, in Baton Rouge, LA (Nov. 4, 2005) [hereinafter *Dabadie Interview*].

[52] Louisiana Nat'l Guard, *Overview of Significant Events Hurricane Katrina* at 4 (Dec. 7, 2005) [hereinafter *LANG Overview*].

[53] *Id.* at 5.

[54] *See, Dabadie Interview; see also,* Interview by Select Comm. Staff with Gordon Nelson, LA Dep't of Transportation and Development, in Baton Rouge, LA, Nov. 4, 2005 [hereinafter *Nelson Interview*].

[55] Interview by Select Comm. Staff with Jiff Hingle, Plaquemines Parish Sherriff, in New Orleans, LA (Nov. 7, 2005).

[56] *Nelson Interview.*

[57] Interview by Select Comm. Staff with Mark Bowen, Adjutant General, AL National Guard, in Montgomery, AL, Oct. 12, 2005 [hereinafter *Bowen Interview*].

[58] Alabama National Guard, AL National Guard Katrina Response Notebook, 4-1.

[59] *Bowen Interview.*

[60] *Id.*

[61] Alabama National Guard, AL National Guard Katrina Response Notebook, 4-1.

[62] *Bowen Interview.*

[123] *Id.*

[124] *Oct. 27, 2005 Select Comm. Hearing* (written response to questions for the record of General Harold A. Cross).

[125] *Id.*

[126] Briefing to Select Comm. Staff with US Army Corps of Engineers, in Washington, D.C. (Oct. 28, 2005) at 7 [hereinafter *ACE Briefing*]; *see also, Hearing on Hurricane Katrina: The Role of Federal Agency Contracting in Disaster Preparedness Before Select Comm.*, 109th Cong. (Nov. 2, 2005) at 1-2 (written statement of Col. Norbert Doyle) [hereinafter *Nov. 2, 2005 Select Comm. Hearing*].

[127] Briefing to Select Comm. to Invest. the Preparation for and Response to Hurricane Katrina Staff with US Army Corps of Engineers, in Washington, DC (Oct. 28, 2005) at 7 [hereinafter *ACE Briefing*]; *see also, Hearing on Hurricane Katrina: The Role of Federal Agency Contracting in Disaster Preparedness Before Select Comm.*, 109th Cong. (Nov. 2, 2005) at 1-2 (written statement of Colonel Norbert Doyle) [hereinafter *Nov. 2, 2005 Select Comm. Hearing*].

[128] *Hurricane Katrina: Who's In Charge of the New Orleans Levees? Before Senate Committee on Homeland Security and Governmental Affairs*, 109th Cong. (Dec. 15, 2005) at 4 (statement of USACE/Col Wagenaar) [hereinafter *Dec. 15, 2005 Senate Hearing*].

[129] *Dec. 8, 2005 Senate Hearing* at 4 (statement of USACE/Col Wagenaar).

[130] United States Coast Guard, Coast Guard Atlantic Area situation report, 270024Z (Doc. No. DHS-USCG-0002-0000006) (Aug. 26, 2005; 8:24 p.m. EDT). Note: the Atlantic Area is the Portsmouth, Virginia Command. Note: this report was created at 0024 Zulu Time. Zulu Time is the same as Greenwich Mean Time (GMT). During the summer months, the time in Portsmouth is GMT-4 hours.

[131] United States Coast Guard, Coast Guard Atlantic Area situation report, 270024Z (Doc. No. DHS-USCG-0002-0000006) (Aug. 26, 2005; 8:24 p.m. EDT).

[132] United States Coast Guard, Coast Guard District Eight situation report, 271638Z (Doc. No. DHS-USCG-0002-0000003) (Aug. 27, 11:38 a.m. CDT). Note: District Eight is the New Orleans, Louisiana Command, which was relocated to St. Louis, Missouri during Hurricane Katrina. Note: This report was created at 1638 Zulu Time. Zulu Time is the same as Greenwich Mean Time (GMT). During the summer months, the time in St. Louis is GMT -5 hours.

[133] United States Coast Guard, Coast Guard District Eight situation report, 290413Z (Doc. No. DHS-USCG-0001-0004044) (Aug. 28, 11:13 p.m. CDT).

[134] United States Coast Guard, Coast Guard Atlantic Area situation report, 290413Z (Doc. No. DHS-USCG-0001-0004044) (Aug. 29, 2005; 12:13 a.m. EDT).

[135] United States Coast Guard, Coast Guard District Eight situation report, 290413Z (Doc. No. DHS-USCG-0001-0004044) (Aug. 28, 2005; 11:13 p.m. EDT).

[136] United States Coast Guard, Coast Guard District Eight situation report, 290413Z (Doc. No. DHS-USCG-0001-0004044) (Aug. 28, 2005; 11:13 p.m. EDT).

[137] United States Coast Guard, Coast Guard District Eight situation report, 281534Z (Doc. No. DHS-USCG-0002-0000008) (Aug. 28, 2005; 10:34 a.m. CDT).

[138] *See generally, Hurricane Katrina: Always Ready: The Coast Guard's Response to Hurricane Katrina Before Senate Committee on Homeland Security and Governmental Affairs*, 109th Cong. (Nov. 9, 2005) (statement of Rear Admiral Robert Duncan) [hereinafter *Nov. 9, 2005 Senate Hearing*].

[139] United States Coast Guard, Coast Guard Atlantic Area situation report, 290900Z (Doc. No. DHS-USCG-0001-0004053) (Aug. 29, 2005; 05:00 a.m. EDT).

[140] United States Coast Guard, Coast Guard District Eight situation report, 281534Z (Doc. No. DHS-USCG-0002-0000008) (Aug. 28, 2005; 10:34 a.m. CDT).

[141] United States Coast Guard, Coast Guard District Eight situation report, 291541Z (Doc. No. DHS-USCG-0001-0004058) (Aug. 29, 2005; 10:41 a.m. CDT).

[142] Briefing to Select Comm. Staff with Coast Guard regarding Response and Recovery Operations and Authorities, in Washington, D.C. (Oct. 27, 2005).

[143] E-mail correspondence from Carol Hall, American Red Cross, to Kirstjen M. Nielsen, et al, (Doc. No. WHK-16197) (Aug. 28, 2005; 2:48 p.m.).

[144] American Red Cross, Disaster Operations Summary Report #7, Aug. 28, 2005; update as of 5:00 p.m. at 2.

[145] *Id.* at 3.

[146] American Red Cross, Disaster Operations Summary Report #9, Aug. 28, 2005; update as of 3:00 p.m. at 3.

[147] American Red Cross, Disaster Operations Summary Report #9, Aug. 28, 2005; update as of 3:00 p.m. at 2.

[148] National Hurricane Center, Nat'l Weather Serv., *Hurricane Katrina Discussion No. 14*, (Aug. 26, 2005) (5:00 p.m. EDT).

[149] National Hurricane Center, Nat'l Weather Serv., *Hurricane Katrina Probabilities No. 15*, (Aug. 26, 2005) (11:00 p.m. EDT).

[150] *Hearing on Hurricane Katrina: Predicting Hurricanes: What We Knew About Katrina and When Before Select Comm.*, 109th Cong. (Sept. 22, 2005), [Hereinafter *Sept. 22, 2005 Select Comm. Hearing*] (statement of Max Mayfield).

[151] *Id.* at 3 (written statement of Max Mayfield).

[152] *Id.* at 5 (statement of Max Mayfield).

[153] *Id.* at 51-52 (statement of Max Mayfield).

[154] *Id.* at 52 (statement of Max Mayfield)

[155] *Id.* at 51 (statement of Max Mayfield).

[156] *Id.* at 3 (written statement of Max Mayfield).

[157] *Id.* at 59-60 (statement of Max Mayfield)

[158] *Id.* at 3 (written statement of Max Mayfield).

[159] *Id.*

[160] Public Advisory, National Weather Center (New Orleans, LA), Urgent Weather Message: Devastating damage expected (Aug. 28, 2005; 10:11 a.m. CDT).

[161] John Pain, *Federal Forecasters Got Hurricane Right*, ASSOC. PRESS, Sept. 16, 2005.

[162] *Id.*

[163] *Id.*

[64] *Id.*

[65] *Sept. 22, 2005 Select Comm. Hearing* at 47 (statement of Max Mayfield).

[66] *Id.* at 12 (written statement of Max Mayfield) (reporting that Katrina made landfall as a Category 4 storm with 140 mph winds. The NHC's final report on Katrina, released Dec. 20, revised this information. Regardless, "it was the costliest and one of the five deadliest hurricanes to ever strike the United States," the NHC report said); Richard D. Knabb, et al, National Hurricane Center, *Tropical Cyclone Report, Hurricane Katrina, 23-30 Aug. 2005* at 1 (Dec. 20, 2005) [hereinafter *NHC Katrina Report*].

[67] *NHC Katrina Report* at 3, 7-9.

[68] *Id.* at 11.

[69] *Id.*

[70] EM 2000 Message no. 05-1878, (Bates no. AL002716); *Nov. 7, 2005 Select Comm. Hearing* at 30 (statement of Governor Bob Riley).

[71] Garry Mitchell, *Katrina's painful blow to coast Alabama's top story in 2005*, ASSOC. PRESS, Dec. 24, 2005.

[72] *Id.*

[73] Alabama Emergency Management Agency / Emergency Operation Center, Situation Report #5 (Doc. No. 000205AL) (Aug. 30, 2005); *see also,* Kathleen Koch, *Katrina Drenches Mobile*, CNN, Aug. 30, 2005.

[74] Federal Emergency Management Agency, *Katrina Disaster Aid to Alabama Surpasses $516 Million,* (FEMA Release No. 1605-162) (Jan. 17, 2006) *available at* http://www.fema.gov/news/newsrelease.fema?id=22538 (last visited Jan. 26, 2006).

[75] *NHC Katrina Report* at 11.

[76] *Id.* at 3, 7-9. Wind speed estimates calculated using KTS to mph converter at http://www.disastercenter.com/convert.htm.

[77] Interview by Select Comm. Staff with Bobby Strahan, Director, River County EMA, in Washington, D.C. (Nov. 29, 2005) [hereinafter *Strahan Interview*].

[78] Interview with Robert Latham, Director, MS Emergency Management Agency, in Washington, D.C. (Jan, 2006) [hereinafter *Latham Interview*].

[79] Virginia W. Mason, Congressional Research Service, (CRS Publication RL33141) *Hurricane Katrina Social-Demographic Characteristics of Impacted Areas,* (Nov. 4, 2005) at 2.

[80] *See,* Mississippi Emergency Management Agency, Hurricane Situation Report #22 (Aug. 31, 2005; *see,* 12:00 p.m.); FEMA-MEMA, Joint Field Office Situation Report SITREP 30 / FEMA-1604-DR-MS (Sept. 25, 2005 07:00 a.m. – Sept., 26, 2005 06:59 a.m.

[81] *NHC Katrina Report* at 11.

[82] *See* Press Release, State's agriculture exceeds $6 billion, MS State Univ., Office of Agricultural Communications, Dec 15. 2005, *available at* http://msucares.com/news/print/agnews/an05/051215all.html (last visited Jan. 26, 2006); *see also,* Press Release, Timber industry salvages profits, MS State Univ., Office of Agricultural Communications, Dec 15. 2005, *available at* http://msucares.com/news/print/agnews/an05/051215forest.html (last visited Jan. 26, 2006); *see also,* Press release, Katrina leaves damaged crops, fuel frustrations, MS State Univ., Office of Agricultural Communications, Dec 15. 2005, *available at* http://msucares.com/news/print/cropreport/crop05/050902.html (last visited Jan. 26, 2006); *see also,* Press release. Katrina drops poultry's estimated farm value, MS State Univ., Office of Agricultural Communications, Dec 15. 2005, *available at* http://msucares.com/news/print/agnews/an05/051215poultry.html (last visited Jan. 26, 2006).

[83] *See* Press Release, State's agriculture exceeds $6 billion, MS State Univ., Office of Agricultural Communications, Dec 15. 2005, available at http://msucares.com/news/print/agnews/an05/051215all.html (last visited Jan. 26, 2006); *see also,* Press Release, Timber industry salvages profits, MS State Univ., Office of Agricultural Communications, Dec 15. 2005, *available at* http://msucares.com/news/print/agnews/an05/051215forest.html (last visited Jan. 26, 2006); *see also,* Press release, Katrina leaves damaged crops, fuel frustrations, MS State Univ., Office of Agricultural Communications, Dec 15. 2005, *available at* http://msucares.com/news/print/cropreport/crop05/050902.html (last visited Jan. 26, 2006); *see also,* Press release. Katrina drops poultry's estimated farm value, MS State Univ., Office of Agricultural Communications, Dec 15. 2005, *available at* http://msucares.com/news/print/agnews/an05/051215poultry.html (last visited Jan. 26, 2006).

[84] Mississippi EMAC, Cost Tracker as of Oct. 10, 2005 (Oct. 11, 2005).

[85] *See,* Keith Bea, *The Emergency Management Assistance Compact (EMAC): An Overview* (Jan. 5, 2006) (CRS Publication RS21227) at 1-2.

[86] *See, Emergency Management Assistance Compact (EMAC),* EMAC Request, MS: Katrina (unaudited draft), Nov. 3, 2005 [hereinafter *EMAC Requests*]

[87] *See, EMAC Requests.*

[88] *See* Federal Emergency Management Agency, Weekly Katrina Response Update for Mississippi, Jan. 6, 2006, (FEMA Release No. 1604-202) (Jan. 17, 2006), *available at* http://www.fema.gov/news/newsrelease.fema?id=22242 (last visited Jan. 26, 2006).

[89] Public Advisory, National Weather Center (New Orleans, LA), Urgent Weather Message: Devastating damage expected (Aug. 28, 2005; 10:11 a.m. CDT).

[90] *NHC Katrina Report* at 10-11.

[91] Fox News, *Five Deaths Linked to Polluted Flood Water*, Sept. 7, 2005, *available at* http://www.foxnews.com/story/0,2933,168630,00.html (last visited Jan. 26, 2006).

[92] *See,* Hearing After the Hurricanes: Impact on the Fiscal Year 2007 Budget, Before House Budget Comm. 109th Cong. (Oct. 6, 2005) (statement by Douglas Holtz-Eakin).

[93] *Dec. 14, 2005 Select. Comm. Hearing* at 44 (statement of Kathleen Babineaux Blanco).

[94] *See* FEMA, By the Numbers: Recovery update in Louisiana, (FEMA Release No. 1603-294) (Jan. 17, 2006) *available at* http://www.fema.gov/news/newsrelease.fema?id=22551 (last visited Jan. 26, 2006).

[95] *See* FEMA, By the Numbers: Recovery update in Louisiana, (FEMA Release No. 1603-294) (Jan. 17, 2006) *available at* http://www.fema.gov/news/newsrelease.fema?id=22551 (last visited Jan. 26, 2006).

"[Hurricane Exercise] Pam was so very prescient. And yet Katrina highlighted many, many weaknesses that either were not anticipated by Pam, or were lessons learned but not heeded.

"That's probably the most painful thing about Katrina, and the tragic loss of life: the foreseeability of it all."

Chairman Tom Davis
Select Committee Hearing, December 14, 2005

HURRICANE PAM

The Hurricane Pam exercise reflected recognition by all levels of government of the dangers of a catastrophic hurricane striking New Orleans

One of the key planning and preparedness steps many of the local, state, and federal officials involved in the response to Katrina in Louisiana took part in was the July 2004 exercise commonly known as "Hurricane Pam." FEMA funded and participated in this disaster simulation exercise in which a fictional, strong category three — with qualities of a category four — hurricane named Pam hit the New Orleans area. Emergency officials from 50 parish, state, federal, and volunteer organizations faced this scenario during the five-day exercise held at the Louisiana State Emergency Operations Center in Baton Rouge.[1]

The purpose of the exercise was to help officials develop joint response plans for a catastrophic hurricane in Louisiana. While many found the Pam exercise to be useful in executing a better response to Katrina, the exercise also highlighted lessons learned that were not implemented and did not anticipate certain weaknesses that Katrina exposed.

The Hurricane Pam scenario focused on 13 parishes in southeast Louisiana — Ascension, Assumption, Jefferson, Lafourche, Orleans, Plaquemines, St. Bernard, St. Charles, St. James, St. John, St. Tammany, Tangipahoa, and Terrebonne. Representatives from outside the primary parishes, including officials from Mississippi's Emergency Management Agency (EMA), participated because hurricane evacuation and sheltering involve communities throughout Louisiana and into Arkansas, Mississippi, and Texas.[2]

The Hurricane Pam exercise scenario was prescient. The virtual storm brought sustained winds of 120 mph, up to 20 inches of rain in parts of Southeast Louisiana, and storm surges that topped the levees and flooded the New Orleans area. The exercise assumed that:[3]

- 300,000 people would not evacuate in advance;
- 500,000 to 600,000 buildings would be destroyed;
- Phone and sewer services would be knocked out and chemical plants would be flooded;
- 97 percent of all communications would be down;
- About 175,000 people would be injured, 200,000 would become sick, and more than 60,000 would be killed;
- About 1,000 shelters would be needed for evacuees;
- Boats and helicopters would be needed for thousands of rescues because many residents would be stranded by floodwaters;
- A catastrophic flood would leave swaths of southeast Louisiana uninhabitable for more than a year.

The Pam simulation was designed and run by a private contractor, Baton Rouge-based Innovative Emergency Management Inc. (IEM). FEMA issued the Request for Proposal in 2004 asking for speedy execution of the catastrophic planning project. IEM was awarded the contract for more than a half million dollars in May 2004 and was told by FEMA it had 53 days to mount the exercise. As it can take up to eight months to write an emergency plan, 6 to 12 months to train on the plan, and about one year to issue the report, Pam was clearly a different type of plan in scope, execution, and timing. According to IEM President Madhu Beriwal, Hurricane Pam was a "planning exercise" designed to develop usable information in a much shorter timeframe.[4] FEMA and Louisiana officials accelerated the planning process because of the overwhelming consensus that a category five hurricane hitting New Orleans was one of the most likely and devastating disaster scenarios our nation faced, Beriwal explained.

This effort was part of FEMA's larger initiative for conducting catastrophic disaster planning, in which it chose 25 disaster scenarios based on priority of risk. A hurricane hitting New Orleans was picked as the first scenario to be studied. According to Beriwal, "We were still fairly early in the process" of developing a formal response plan for New Orleans when Katrina made landfall.[5]

In July of 2004, IEM held its first workshop. The initial eight day workshop had over 300 participants from federal, regional, and local agencies. The first three days were dedicated to establishing the specifics of the disaster scenario and pre-landfall planning, the remaining five days to post-landfall logistics.

Officials were presented with a hurricane scenario designed by Louisiana State University (LSU) researchers. Ivor Van Heerden, an LSU professor who used computer modeling to help create a realistic hurricane, said, "It was a slow moving category three storm, something that could quite easily happen, and designed so that it totally flooded the city, so that the participants could try to understand the full impacts of a flooded New Orleans."[6] Indeed, experts involved in the Hurricane Pam exercise were struck by the similarity of the simulation to the actual destructive conditions wrought by Katrina. According to Beriwal, Pam's slow-moving category three "made it virtually equal in force and devastation to Katrina's category four based on its surge and wind capacity."[7] And, of course, Katrina itself was later recategorized as a strong category 3.[8]

During the Pam simulation, participants broke into groups and devised responses as the disaster scenario unfolded. The workshop focused on issues ranging from search and rescue and temporary sheltering to unwatering, debris removal, and medical care. Not all issues, however, were covered in the workshop. Beriwal said while issues related to security and communications were on the agenda, the development of a plan to coordinate the displacement of school children took precedence.[9] Beriwal also said the issue of pre-landfall evacuation was not addressed, although Exercise Pam did make the basic presumption that the state and locals were responsible for pre-landfall evacuations. Apparently FEMA directed IEM to emphasize post-landfall and recovery issues in the Pam exercise as pre-landfall evacuation had always been a focal point in prior emergency disaster planning sessions.[10]

The Southeast Louisiana Catastrophic Hurricane Plan was the product of these series of workshops. The Plan was "designed to be the first step toward producing a comprehensive hurricane response plan, jointly approved and implemented by federal, state, and city officials."[11] By January 2005, IEM sent a draft planning document to the state and localities based on the planning derived from the July workshop. The delivery of the draft was expedited to give the Southeast Louisiana emergency management planners time to prepare for the 2005 hurricane season. Indeed, IEM scurried to make the plan available at this early date so officials could use it and *translate* it into individual detailed operational plans.[12] Beriwal noted

the plan was not meant to provide operational detail but rather was designed to provide general guidance, a sort of "to do list" for state and localities.[13] Beriwal further characterized the exercise as a "work in progress." She described IEM's role as "facilitator and assessors of consequences."[14]

The plan itself outlines 15 subjects that emergency managers should address during and after a catastrophic storm hitting New Orleans. The report is detailed in certain respects. It includes diagrams for makeshift loading docks to distribute water, ice, and food to storm victims — color-coded to show where pallets, traffic cones, and trash bins would be placed. Yet in other places the report is less specific; it does not identify, for example, what hospitals or airports would be used.

Numerous action plans ranging from debris removal, to sheltering, to search and rescue were developed. For example, state transportation officials took the lessons learned from the Pam exercise and previous hurricanes and revised the state's contraflow plan.[15] The revisions included making adjustments to traffic lights, cessation of construction, and greater coordination with the private sector. State officials reported that Hurricane Pam greatly improved the state's contraflow evacuation plan.[16] In fact, federal, state, and local officials across the board agreed the contra flow plan was a success story of Katrina emergency response. Over 1.2 million were evacuated in the 48 hours prior to landfall.[17]

As part of the Pam exercise, planners also identified lead and support agencies for search and rescue and established a command structure that would include four areas with up to 800 searchers. For example, "[t]he search and rescue group developed a transportation plan for getting stranded residents out of harm's way."[18] "The medical care group reviewed and enhanced existing plans."[19] "The medical action plan included patient movement details and identified probable locations, such as state university campuses, where individuals would receive care and then be transported to hospitals, special needs shelters or regular shelters as necessary."[20]

Workshops subsequent to the initial five-day Hurricane Pam exercise were held in November 2004 and August 2005. A second Hurricane Pam Exercise was planned for the summer of 2005, but did not take place, apparently due to lack of funding.[21] Agencies had anticipated expanding on aspects of response and recovery that were not explored in the 2004 exercise.[22]

Finding: Implementation of lessons learned from Hurricane Pam was incomplete

While state and local officials turned some lessons from the Hurricane Pam exercise into improvements of their emergency plans, other important changes were not made. State health officials said the exercise had helped them better prepare for evacuation of hospital patients and special needs people.[23] Since Pam was a catastrophic hurricane with flooding of New Orleans, it required them to consider the issue of evacuating New Orleans hospitals and the Superdome's special needs shelter.[24] Subsequent to the exercise, medical officials held planning sessions focused on post-landfall care and evacuation. The contingency plan for the medical component was almost complete when Katrina made landfall.[25] Officials said although the plan was not yet finalized, it proved invaluable to the response effort.[26]

Further, in the aftermath of Katrina, varying opinions have surfaced as to the roles and responsibilities established during the Hurricane Pam exercise. Some state and parish officials said they saw Pam as a "contract" of what the various parties were going to do, and the federal government did not do the things it had committed to doing.[27] According to Dr. Walter Maestri, the Jefferson Parish Director of Emergency Management, he understood that FEMA may not provide help until 48-72 hours later—but then he expected help.[28] That is, once the state cleared the roads, he anticipated that FEMA trucks would arrive with large quantities of water, food, and ice. Although these were the parish's planning assumptions, he said FEMA did not get substantial relief to the parish until 11 days after landfall.[29] Dr. Maestri also said the Hurricane Pam documentation makes it clear what FEMA was supposed to do, but FEMA did not do those things.[30]

Beriwal said, however, the plan derived from the Pam exercise was intended as a "bridging document" designed to serve as a guide and roadmap to be used by emergency operational officials at the state and local level. In other words, it was up to state and local officials to take the plan and turn it into more detailed individual operational plans.[31]

Yet, according to Scott Wells, Deputy Federal Coordinating Officer from FEMA, there were several Hurricane Pam Exercise "to do" items state or local governments did not complete.[32] For example, the state was supposed to develop more detailed concepts and plans in several areas: (1) search and rescue, (2) rapid assessment teams, (3) medical evacuation, (4) sheltering and temporary housing, (5) commodity distribution, and (6) debris removal.[33] The state's previous Louisiana Office of Homeland Security and Emergency Preparedness Deputy Director had laid these six areas out as priorities for the state to work on.[34] In Wells's view, the only one of these where the state made some progress was medical evacuation.[35]

Wells also said, however, that the need to shelter special needs people in the Superdome showed the state and city had not taken steps (which they had agreed to do after the Pam Exercise) to coordinate the movement and sheltering of these people further north, away from the Gulf.[36] As a result of the exercise and subsequent planning workshops, the state was supposed to develop "hasty plans" to address all these areas.[37] He said although he had tried to get state officials to focus on these hasty plans just before landfall, they would not do so.[38] According to Wells, the state had also agreed to learn and exercise a unified command through the incident command system.[39] Wells said the state did not do so, which led to major command and control problems during Katrina.[40]

Conclusion

Hurricane Katrina highlighted many weaknesses that either were not anticipated by the Pam exercise or perhaps were lessons learned but simply not implemented. For example, Hurricane Pam has been criticized for its emphasis on managing the aftermath of the catastrophe and not creating initiatives that would diminish the magnitude of the catastrophe. Indeed, much of the recrimination over the Hurricane Katrina response came because government authorities apparently failed to have a plan in place to assist in evacuating individuals without transportation. Nor did they appear to have an adequate sheltering plan in place. With Hurricane Pam's striking resemblance to Katrina in force and devastation, many have been left wondering at the failure to anticipate, and plan for, these essentials. Is a plan that leaves 300,000 in a flooded city and results in 60,000 deaths acceptable? ■

1. Press Release, Fed. Emer. Mgmt. Agency (FEMA), *Hurricane Pam Exercise Concludes* (July 23, 2004) *available at* http://www.fema.gov/news/newsrelease.fema?id=13051 (last visited Jan. 12, 2006) [hereinafter July 23, 2004 FEMA Press Release].

2. *Id.*

3. Ron Fournier and Ted Bridis, *Katrina What Planners Feared; Hurricane Simulation Predicted 61,290 Dead*, AP, Sept. 10, 2005 [hereinafter Sept. 10, 2005 Fournier Article]; David R. Baker, *Hard Times in Big Easy Efforts Intensify to Evaluate Living, Recover Dead*, SF CHRONICLE, Sept. 9, 2005.

4. Interview by Select Comm. staff with Madhu Beriwal, IEM, Inc., in Wash., DC (Jan. 6, 2006) [hereinafter Beriwal Interview].

5. John McQuaid, *'Hurricane Pam' Exercise Offered glimpse of Katrina Misery*, TIMES-PICAYUNE (New Orleans), Sept. 9, 2005.

6. *Id.*

7. Beriwal Interview.

8. Associated Press, *Hurricane Katrina Was Weaker Than First Thought At Landfall*, USA TODAY, Dec. 20, 2005 *available at* http://www.usatoday.com/weather/hurricane/2005-12-20-katrina-strength_x.htm.

9. Beriwal Interview.

10. *Id.*

11. Sept. 10, 2005 Fournier Article.

12. Beriwal Interview.

13. *Id.*

14. *Id.*

15. Interview by Select Comm. staff with Gordon Nelson, LA Dep't of Trans., in Baton Rouge, LA (Nov. 4, 2005).

16. *Id.*

17. *Hearing on Hurricane Katrina: Preparedness and Response by the State of Louisiana Before Select Comm.*, 109th Cong. (Dec. 14, 2005) at 77 (statement of Kathleen Babineaux Blanco, Governor of LA).

18. July 23, 2004 FEMA Press Release.

19. *Id.*

20. *Id.*

21. Beriwal Interview.

22. Interview by Select Comm. Staff with Jeff Smith, State Coordinating Officer, LA. Office of Homeland Sec. and Emerg. Preparedness, in Baton Rouge, LA (Nov 7, 2005).

23. Interview by Select Comm. Staff with Jimmy Guidry, Med. Dir., LA Dept. Health and Hospitals, in Baton Rouge, LA (Nov. 7, 2005).

24. *Id.*

25. *Id.*

26. *Id.*

27. Interview by Select Comm. Staff with Walter Maestri, Dir. of Emer. Mgmt., Jefferson Parish, in New Orleans, LA (Nov. 8, 2005).

28. *Id.*

29. *Id.*

30. *Id.*

31. Beriwal Interview.

32. Interview with Select Comm. Staff, Scott Wells, Dep. Fed. Coordinating Officer, in Baton Rouge, LA (Nov. 9, 2005).

33. *Id.*

34. *Id.*

35. *Id.*

36. *Id.*

37. *Id.*

38. *Id.*

39. *Id.*

40. *Id.*

AP PHOTO/BILL FEIG, POOL

"What happened to us this year, however, can only be described as a catastrophe of Biblical proportions. We in Louisiana know hurricanes and hurricanes know us. We would not be here today if the levees had not failed."

Kathleen Babineaux Blanco
Governor, State of Louisiana
Select Committee Hearing, December 14, 2005

Summary

The levees protecting New Orleans were not built to survive the most severe hurricanes. It was a well-known and repeatedly documented fact that a severe hurricane could lead to overtopping or breaching of the levees and flooding of the metropolitan area. In fact, for years the U.S. Army Corps of Engineers (USACE) has had a written plan for unwatering (i.e., draining) New Orleans in such a contingency. This well-known threat was the motivation for FEMA to sponsor the "Hurricane Pam" exercise. The potential for Katrina to be "the Big One" and breach the levees was also the key reason for the National Weather Service, Governor of Louisiana, and Mayor of New Orleans to issue such dire warnings.

Once construction of the levees was completed by USACE, the responsibilities for operating and maintaining the levees were split among many local organizations, which is the standard cooperation agreement for carrying out flood control projects nationwide. The costs of constructing these projects are shared, with operation and maintenance being a 100 percent local responsibility. These include levee boards in each parish, as well as separate water and sewer boards. The number of organizations involved, and disagreements among them, makes accountability diffuse and creates potential gaps and weaknesses in parts of the flood protection system. In one case, improvements to levee strength which may have mitigated or prevented some of the critical breaches that flooded downtown New Orleans were rejected by the competing local organizations. There also appear to have been lapses in both maintenance and inspections of selected levees, including those that breached. Also, prior to Hurricane Katrina, residents along those same levees reported they were leaking, another potential lapse in maintenance.

Despite the well-known importance of the levees, and the consequences of failure, the local levee boards responsible for maintaining and operating the levees did not have any warning system in place. While federal regulations require that they monitor levees during periods of potential flooding, the requirement is impractical to implement during a hurricane. In addition to no warning system, the loss of communications and

situational awareness, and only sporadic reports of flooding from a variety of sources, made it difficult to confirm that there were breaches in the levees and then to assess the damage. These factors, as well as physical difficulties of getting to the breach sites, combined to delay repair of the levee breaches.

The ultimate causes of the levee breaches, and subsequent flooding of New Orleans, are yet to be determined. At least four forensic investigations are under way to examine scientific evidence and determine the reasons for levee breaches. These include investigations by USACE's Engineer Research and Development Center, the National Science Foundation (NSF), the American Society of Civil Engineers (ASCE), and Louisiana State University (LSU). Possible causes include (1) the design was not appropriate for the purpose, (2) the storm exceeded levee design standards, (3) the levees were not actually built to the original design standards, (4) the levees were not properly maintained, or (5) a combination of these and other factors.

Finding: Levees protecting New Orleans were not built for the most severe hurricanes

New Orleans is protected from flooding by a system of levees

As noted in the BACKGROUND chapter, hurricanes threaten the Gulf coast every year, and New Orleans is particularly vulnerable because of its location and topography.[1] The majority of the metropolitan area is below sea level. Over the years, the city has continued to sink, due to drainage, subsidence, and compaction of the soils.[2] As an example of previous damage, Hurricane Betsy brought extensive destruction to New Orleans when it made landfall in Louisiana in September, 1965.[3] Unfortunately, many of the descriptions and

photos from Hurricane Betsy sound and look familiar to our nation as it considers the damage from Hurricane Katrina, forty years later. According to USACE's after action report on Hurricane Betsy…

- She left in her wake a path of devastation unparalleled by any other storm in the recorded history of Louisiana.[4]
- Betsy inundated over 5,000 square miles in Louisiana, including highly populated urban areas in Orleans and St. Bernard Parishes.[5]
- Extensive flooding was caused by overtopping and breaching of existing protection levees in Orleans, Plaquemines, and St. Bernard Parishes.[6]

- As Betsy's winds and tidal surge rolled inland, entire buildings were swept away from their foundations and floated as far as 10 miles away.[7]
- Betsy left 81 dead, over 17,600 injured, and caused the evacuation of 250,000 to storm shelters.[8]
- Betsy left thousands homeless in south Louisiana. Returning refugees often found only a pile of debris where their homes had stood just days before.[9]
- Betsy left numerous towns in south Louisiana with no means of communication.[10]

After Hurricane Betsy in 1965, federal and state governments proposed a number of flood control projects to deal with the threat of hurricanes and the flooding they

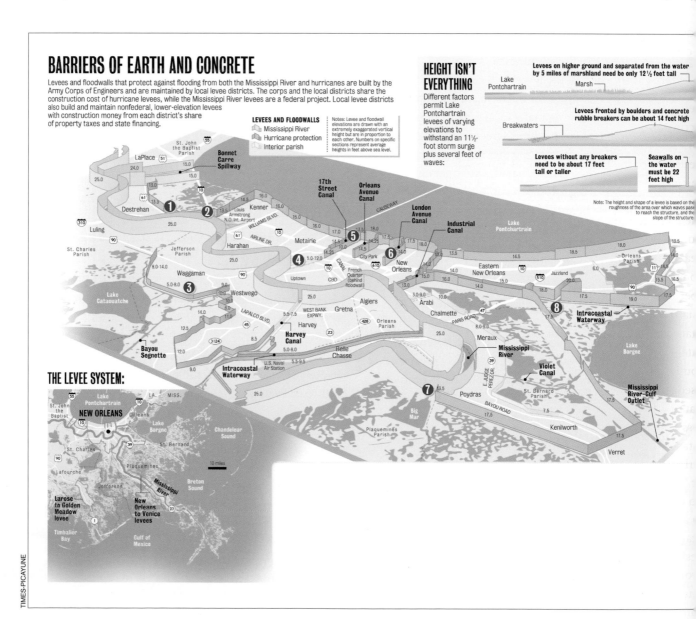

BARRIERS OF EARTH AND CONCRETE

Levees and floodwalls that protect against flooding from both the Mississippi River and hurricanes are built by the Army Corps of Engineers and are maintained by local levee districts. The corps and the local districts share the construction cost of hurricane levees, while the Mississippi River levees are a federal project. Local levee districts also build and maintain nonfederal, lower-elevation levees with construction money from each district's share of property taxes and state financing.

HEIGHT ISN'T EVERYTHING

Different factors permit Lake Pontchartrain levees of varying elevations to withstand an 11½-foot storm surge plus several feet of waves:

A FAILURE OF INITIATIV

might cause in New Orleans.[11] These included a series of control structures, concrete floodwalls, and levees along Lake Pontchartrain and several other waterways.[12] One of the major projects is formally called the Lake Pontchartrain and Vicinity, Louisiana Hurricane Protection Project.[13] This project included levees along the Lake Pontchartrain lakefront, the 17th Street Canal, the London Avenue Canal, the Orleans Avenue Canal, the Intercoastal waterway, the Industrial Canal,[14] the Mississippi River Gulf Outlet, and other areas.[15] Although the project was federally authorized, it was a joint federal, state, and local effort with shared costs.[16]

Levees were designed for a "standard" hurricane, not the most severe hurricanes

The levees protecting New Orleans were not designed to withstand the most severe hurricanes. According to USACE's plans for unwatering New Orleans, "the hurricane protection system is not designed for the largest storms and as a result, the metropolitan area is vulnerable to flooding from hurricane storm surges."[17] USACE originally designed the levees around New Orleans to protect against a hurricane intensity that might occur once every 200-300 years.[18] This protection level was used by USACE, in consultation with the U.S. Weather Bureau,[19] to develop specific criteria for a "standard project hurricane."[20] The "standard project hurricane" is a statistical compilation of many combined hurricane parameters or characteristics intended to simulate a natural hurricane occurrence in southeast Louisiana. The standard project hurricane was used not only for the Lake Pontchartrain project, but also nationwide for all hurricane protection projects where the loss of human life is possible.[21] According to USACE, the "standard project hurricane" was used to design the New Orleans levees and is roughly equivalent to a fast moving, "moderate," category 3 hurricane.[22] However, there is no direct comparison of the "standard project hurricane" to a specific category on the Saffir-Simpson Hurricane Scale—which did not exist when the levees were designed.[23] As shown in the table below, the "standard project hurricane" is equivalent to a hurricane with category 2 winds, category 3 storm surge, and category 4 barometric pressure.[24]

Table 1:
Comparison of "Standard Project Hurricane" with Saffir Simpson Scale

	"Standard project hurricane"	Saffir-Simpson category 2 hurricane	Saffir-Simpson category 3 hurricane	Saffir-Simpson category 4 hurricane
Central pressure (1)	27.6 Hg	28.50-28.91 Hg	27.91-28.47 Hg	27.17-27.88 Hg
Wind speed (2)	100 mph	96-110 mph	111-130 mph	131-155 mph
Radius of maximum winds (3)	30 miles	N/A	N/A	N/A
Average forward speed (3)	6 knots	N/A	N/A	N/A
Storm surge	11.2-13 feet (4)	6-8 feet	9-12 feet	13-18 feet

GAO ANALYSIS OF USACE AND NOAA DATA.[25]

Table Notes: The shaded areas indicate those parameters with the closest match between the standard project hurricane and the Saffir-Simpson Scale.

(1) Central pressure is measured in inches of mercury (Hg) or millibars.

(2) Wind speed for the standard project hurricane was measured as the maximum 5-minute average wind speed. The Saffir-Simpson Scale uses the maximum 1-minute average wind speed, a lower threshold.

(3) USACE estimated the radius of maximum winds and the average forward speed for a standard project hurricane, and the Saffir-Simpson Scale does not take either of these parameters into account.

(4) The standard project hurricane calculated maximum surge heights for different geographic areas within the Lake Pontchartrain area. The maximum surge height for the South Shore of Lake Pontchartrain—where the 17th Street, London Avenue, and Industrial Canals are located—was estimated at 11.2 feet.

In addition, there is no "standard" hurricane — the actual forces that levees need to withstand are a function of several factors. According to the preliminary NSF study, "the actual wind, wave and storm surge loadings imposed at any location within the overall flood protection system are a function of location relative to the storm, wind speed and direction, orientation of levees, local bodies of water, channel configurations, offshore contours, vegetative cover, etc. They also vary over time, as the storm moves through the region."[26] Similarly, USACE documents indicate that "[o]vertopping will depend upon the intensity of the storm, the track that the center or "eye" of the storm follows and the speed at which it travels along the track."[27]

Although the Lake Pontchartrain project is named a hurricane "protection" project, a number of factors other than saving lives and property are included in the design of such projects. For example, in addition to protecting urban and community lives and health, the design of such projects must include environmental and economic effects, and ensure that benefits of the completed project outweigh its cost of construction.[28] In discussing the design of the Lake Pontchartrain project in a 1978 hearing, USACE District Commander for New Orleans,

Colonel Early Rush, stated "Even though economists may, and in this case did, favor protection to a lower scale to produce a higher ratio of benefits to projected costs, the threat of loss of human life mandated using the standard project hurricane."[29]

Potential for Katrina to breach levees was well-known, leading to urgent warnings

Even with its hurricane protection system, it was common knowledge that New Orleans was susceptible to hurricane-caused flooding.[30] The risks of a major hurricane and flooding in New Orleans had been covered in the general media — by Scientific American (October 2001) and National Geographic (October 2004) — as well as in emergency management literature.[31] A recent article in the Natural Hazards Observer stated:

> When Hurricane Katrina came ashore on August 29, she ended decades of anticipation. There were few hazards in the United States more studied by scientists and engineers and there was ample warning that a strong storm could cause the City of New Orleans to flood.[32]

Emergency planners in the local area were particularly knowledgeable about this potentiality. A November 2004 article in Natural Hazards Observer — written by Shirley Laska, of the Center for Hazards Assessment, Response and Technology, at the University of New Orleans — laid out the hypothetical case that Hurricane Ivan had hit New Orleans. The article cites a fictional situation that is now all too real to the nation.[33]

> New Orleans was spared, this time, but had it not been, Hurricane Ivan would have… caused the levees between the lake and the city to overtop and fill the city "bowl" with water from lake levee to river levee, in some places as deep as 20 feet… Recent evacuation surveys show that two thirds of non-evacuees with the means to evacuate chose not to leave because they felt safe in their homes. Other non-evacuees with means relied on cultural traditions of not leaving or were discouraged by negative experiences with past evacuations. Should this disaster become a reality, it would undoubtedly be one of the greatest disasters, if not the greatest,

to hit the United States, with estimated costs exceeding 100 billion dollars. Survivors would have to endure conditions never before experienced in a North American disaster. Hurricane Ivan had the potential to make the unthinkable a reality. Next time New Orleans may not be so fortunate.[34]

Because of the well-known potential for flooding, USACE has had a plan for several years for draining New Orleans — Unwatering Plan, Greater Metropolitan Area, New Orleans, Louisiana, dated August 18, 2000. This plan provides details on the hurricane protection system and describes methods to get the water out after catastrophic flooding from a hurricane. The premise of the plan is that a category 4 or 5 hurricane may produce storm surge water levels of sufficient height to overtop the existing protection system.[35] The plan lays out a series of scenario that could occur, and suggests appropriate emergency responses to unwater the area.[36] For example, in one case…

> There is catastrophic flooding due to complete overtopping of the levees and floodwalls and inundation of the protected area. There will be extensive and severe erosion of levees and perhaps complete breaches. Due to the high water levels, all of the pumping stations will probably be flooded with major damages . . . . The levee districts and drainage departments may be dysfunctional to some degree.[37]

In more recent years, well before Hurricane Katrina, questions were raised about the ability of the Lake Pontchartrain project to withstand more powerful hurricanes than the "standard project hurricane," such as a category 4 or 5 hurricane. USACE had discussed undertaking a study of modifications needed to increase the strength of the existing levees, but no formal study wa undertaken.[38]

As discussed earlier in the HURRICANE PAM chapter, FEMA sponsored the "Hurricane Pam" exercise to look at the response to and recovery from a catastrophic hurricane hitting New Orleans and flooding the city. In that scenario "It was a slow moving Category three storm, something that could quite easily happen, and [the exercise scenario was] designed so that it totally flooded the city, so that the

A FAILURE OF INITIATI

rticipants could try to understand the full impacts of a
ooded New Orleans" according to Ivor Van Heerden, the
SU professor who used computer modeling to help create
realistic hurricane for the exercise.[39] Again, the key reason
r that exercise was the well-known potential for levee
ilure and catastrophic flooding in the metropolitan area.

As Katrina turned and began its track toward New
rleans, the potential for the levees overtopping or
reaching and flooding New Orleans resulted in a number
dire warnings from federal, state, and local officials. As
so discussed in the EVACUATION chapter, the National
eather Service issued a warning on Sunday, August 28,
ating that Katrina was "a most powerful hurricane with
nprecedented strength," that "devastating damage" was
pected, that "most of the area will be uninhabitable
r weeks," and that there will be "human suffering
credible by modern standards."[40] Governor Blanco
so made dire predictions, stating in several interviews
n Saturday and Sunday that flooding in New Orleans
as a major concern. On Saturday at approximately 8:00
m., she appeared on CNN and said that in New Orleans
t]he storm surge could bring in 15 to 20 feet of water.
eople in the city of New Orleans] will not survive that
indeed that happens."[41] Similarly, in a news conference
n Sunday morning, Mayor Nagin said, "The storm surge
ost likely will topple our levee system."[42]

inding: Responsibilities
r levee operations and
aintenance were diffuse

SACE oversees design and construction then
rns levees over to local sponsors

veral organizations are responsible for building,
erating, and maintaining the levees surrounding
etropolitan New Orleans. USACE generally contracts
design and build the levees.[43] After construction,
SACE turns the levees over to a local sponsor.[44] USACE
gulations state that once a local sponsor has accepted
project, USACE may no longer expend federal funds
construction or improvements. This prohibition does
ot include repair after a flood. Federally authorized
ood control projects, such as the Lake Pontchartrain
oject, are eligible for 100 percent federal rehabilitation

if damaged by a flood.[45] The Mississippi River levees are
the exception to the arrangement just described. USACE
operates and maintains these levees. These levees generally
withstood Hurricane Katrina, except for a breach south of
New Orleans in Plaquemines Parish—the parish that took
the full force of Hurricane Katrina at landfall.[46]

The local sponsor has a number of responsibilities. In
accepting responsibilities for operations, maintenance,
repair, and rehabilitation, the local sponsor signs a
contract (called a Cooperation Agreement) agreeing to
meet specific standards of performance.[47] This agreement
makes the local sponsor responsible for liability for
that levee.[48] For most of the levees surrounding New
Orleans, the Louisiana Department of Transportation
and Development was the state entity that originally
sponsored the construction. After construction, the state
turned over control to local sponsors.[49] These local
sponsors accepted completed units of the project from
1977 to 1987, depending on when the specific units
were completed.[50] The local sponsors are responsible for
operation, maintenance, repair, and rehabilitation of the
levees when the construction of the project, or a project
unit, is complete.[51]

Local sponsors do not have control over all factors
that could affect their parts of the levee system

The local sponsors include a variety of separate local
organizations. For example, different parts of the
Lake Pontchartrain and Vicinity, Louisiana Hurricane
Protection Project, were turned over to four different
local sponsors — to include the Orleans, East Jefferson,
Lake Borgne, and Pontchartrain levee districts.[52] In
addition, there are separate water and sewer districts that
are responsible for maintaining pumping stations.[53] The
USACE unwatering plan notes these arrangements by
stating that, among other factors, "the political boundaries
with internal local levees have resulted in this series of
loops or bowls of low lying ground encircled by levees
and floodwalls. Each of these areas is served by its own
drainage collection and pumping stations."[54]

The different local organizations involved had the
effect of diffusing responsibility and creating potential
weaknesses. For example, levee breaches and distress were
repeatedly noted at transition sections, where different
organizations were responsible for different pieces and

thus two different levee or wall systems joined together. According to USACE, "[a]t sections where infrastructure elements were designed and maintained by multiple authorities, and their multiple protection elements came together, the weakest (or lowest) segment or element controlled the overall performance."[55] Similarly, a scientist working on the NFS study, Raymond Seed, stated there needs to be better coordination of these transition sites.[56] Peter Nicholson, head of an ASCE team investigating the levees, said in response to a question of whether transition sections mattered:

> Well, certainly we find that each individual organization will do as they see fit, and when the two sections of the flood control system operated or owned, designed, maintained by each of those different organizations come together, they may be in two different manners. They may have two different heights. They may be two different materials.[57]

The different organizations also have different agendas, and sometimes these can thwart efforts to improve the safety of the overall system. Seed also provided an example where USACE had suggested improvements to the strength of the system that were rejected by the competing organizations. According to Seed:

> No one is in charge. You have got multiple agencies, multiple organizations, some of whom aren't on speaking terms with each other, sharing responsibilities for public safety. The Corps of Engineers had asked to put flood gates into the three canals, which nominally might have mitigated and prevented the three main breaches that did so much destruction downtown. But they weren't able to do that because, unique to New Orleans, the Reclamation Districts who are responsible for maintaining the levees are separate from the Water and Sewage District, which does the pumping. Ordinarily, the Reclamation District does the dewatering pumping, which is separate from the water system. These guys don't get along.[58]

While required inspections of levees were done, some deficiencies in maintenance were not fully addressed

Both USACE and the local sponsors have ongoing responsibility to inspect the levees. Annual inspections are done both independently by USACE and jointly with the local sponsor.[59] In addition, federal regulations require local sponsors to ensure that flood control structures are operating as intended and to continuously patrol the structure to ensure no conditions exist that might endanger it.[60]

Records reflect that both USACE and the local sponsor kept up with their responsibilities to inspect the levees. According to USACE, in June 2005, it conducted an inspection of the levee system jointly with the state and local sponsors.[61] In addition, GAO reviewed USACE's inspection reports from 2001 to 2004 for all completed project units of the Lake Pontchartrain project. These reports indicated the levees were inspected each year and had received "acceptable" ratings.[62]

However, both the NSF-funded investigators and USACE officials cited instances where brush and even trees were growing along the 17th Street and London Avenue canals levees, which is not allowed under the established standards for levee protection.[63] Thus, although the records reflect that inspections were conducted and the levees received acceptable ratings, the records appear to be incomplete or inaccurate. In other words, they failed to reflect the tree growth, and of course, neither USACE nor the local sponsor had taken corrective actions to remove the trees.

In addition, there was apparently seepage from one canal before Hurricane Katrina, indicating problems had developed in the levee after construction. Specifically, residents of New Orleans who live along the 17th Street Canal said water was leaking from the canal and seeping into their yards months before Hurricane Katrina caused the levee system to collapse. The leaks, they said, occurred within several hundred feet of the levee that later failed.[64] National Public Radio, which reported the story, said:

> State and federal investigators say that a leak may have been an early warning sign that the soil beneath the levee was unstable and help explain why it collapsed. They also say if authorities had investigated and found that a leak was

undermining the levee, they could have shored it up and prevented the catastrophic breach.[65]

National Public Radio also reported that work orders confirm that the Sewerage and Water Board had visited the location of the seepage a number of times. However, both USACE and the Orleans Levee District, with shared responsibilities for inspecting the levees, reported that they had not received any reports of seepage at the site.[66]

Finding: The lack of a warning system for breaches and other factors delayed repairs to levees

Actual levee breaches caused catastrophic flooding in New Orleans

Katrina made landfall as an "extraordinarily powerful" hurricane.[67] Katrina was expected to be a category 4 or 5 storm, although a recent updated analysis from the National Weather Service concluded it made landfall at the upper end of a category 3 hurricane (with estimated maximum sustained winds of 110 knots) near Buras, Louisiana.[68] While Katrina had weakened from its peak intensity of category 5, it remained a very large hurricane — the extent of tropical-force and hurricane-force winds were as large as predicted when Katrina was at maximum intensity.[69] Due to Katrina's large size, it is possible that sustained winds of category 4 strength briefly affected the extreme southeastern tip of Louisiana.[70] However, the sustained winds over all of metropolitan New Orleans and Lake Pontchartrain likely remained weaker than category 3

strength.[71]

The storm surge, not the winds, is the most destructive part of a hurricane,[72] and Katrina produced a massive storm surge. A precise measurement of Katrina's storm surge in the New Orleans area is difficult to measure, in part because of the widespread failures of tide gauges. However, various efforts are under way to make a definitive determination, particularly near the levees.[73] While the surge varied by location, some preliminary estimates are that the storm surge off Lake Borgne, which abuts New Orleans, was approximately 18-25 feet.[74]

One of the highest credible reports of storm surge came from the Hancock County, Mississippi, emergency operations center, where the storm surge was 27 feet.[75] One reason for the large size of the storm surge was that Katrina, although making landfall as a strong category 3, had already generated large northward propagating swells when it was a category 4 and 5 hurricane during the 24

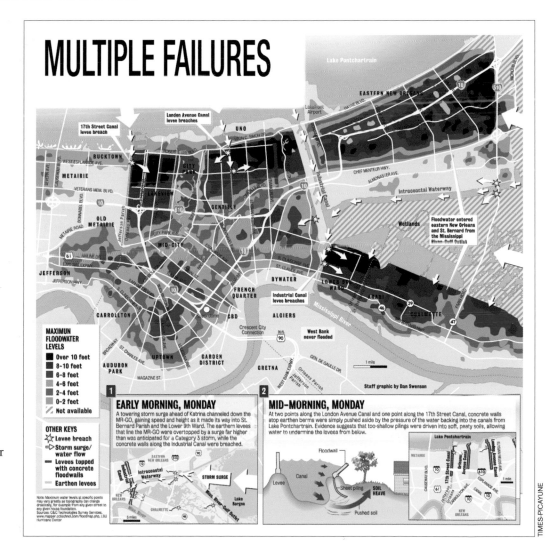

hours before landfall.[76] One of the instrument buoys located south of Dauphin Island, Alabama, measured a wave height of 55 feet — which matches the largest significant wave height ever measured by such a buoy.[77]

Because the eye of Katrina passed just slightly to the east of New Orleans, the hurricane threw unusually severe wind loads and storm surges on the flood protection systems.[78] The surge overtopped large sections of the levees during the morning of August 29 east of New Orleans, in Orleans and St. Bernard Parish, and it also pushed water up the Intercoastal waterway and into the Industrial Canal. The water rise in Lake Pontchartrain strained the floodwalls along the canals adjacent to its southern shore, including the 17th Street Canal and the London Avenue Canal.[79] Breaches along all of these canals led to flooding of 80 percent of New Orleans to depths up to 20 feet.[80] The flooding of central New Orleans led to the most widespread and costly damage of the hurricane. It also led to the difficulties encountered by emergency responders that are documented elsewhere in this report.

The lack of warning systems and degraded communications prevented situational awareness of the breaches in the levees, and delayed repairs

Despite the well-known importance of the levees, and the consequences of failure, the local levee boards responsible for maintaining and operating the levees do not have any warning system in place.[81] Federal regulations require local sponsors to ensure that flood control structures are operating as intended and to continuously patrol the structure *during flood periods* to ensure that no conditions exist that might endanger it.[82] However, it would be impractical to monitor the levees during a hurricane. The Executive Director of the Orleans Levee District, Max Hearn, stated:

> As the hurricane approached, and as water levels began to rise, District employees monitored the water levels and patrolled the flood control system. As weather conditions deteriorated and became unsafe, the District's employees were pulled into sheltered areas to ride out the storm.[83]

Again, with the large number of local organizations involved, it was not always clear who would be responsible for monitoring the levees and sounding the

alarm if there was a breach. According to one scientist, "If the lines of responsibility and who is in charge aren't clear, it is very hard to decide who needs to be issuing warnings and public notices...."[84]

Given that Hurricane Katrina led to the loss of power and severely degraded communications, as discussed in the COMMUNICATIONS and COMMAND AND CONTROL chapters, it is not clear that any warning system would have survived or have been effective. In the absence of communications that would have provided situational awareness, there were many rumors of flooding and its causes that had to be confirmed before assessment teams and repair teams could be dispatched. There were many sources of these reports of flooding.

■ Monday August 29, at 6:00 a.m., floodwaters began flowing into Jackson Barracks, according to Louisiana National Guard officers. Jackson Barracks is near the Orleans Parish – St. Bernard Parish line, and the floodwaters were determined later to be from the Industrial Canal breach. By late Monday morning, the floodwaters were 8-10 feet deep at Jackson Barracks, requiring the Louisiana National Guard to abandon their operations center and re-establish it at the Superdome.[85]

■ Monday, August 29, at 7:30 a.m., the state Emergency Operations center (EOC) received reports of flooding in the last conference call before communications were lost. Jefferson Parish relayed unconfirmed reports of significant flooding in the east bank. New Orleans reported extensive flooding in the east and on the lake front. St. Bernard Parish reported "overtopping" of the Industrial Canal and 3 feet of water in Arabi. When the State Coordinating Officer (SCO) Jeff Smith asked if those flooding rumors were confirmed, the parish deputy sheriff said they were confirmed and noted that his building was surrounded by white caps. Smith also stated he was aware of 3-4 feet of floodwaters at Jackson Barracks.[86]

■ Monday, August 29, morning (exact time unknown), USACE district commander first heard sporadic reports about levee overtopping and breaches.[87] The sources of these early reports included local radio stations and a USACE employee reporting overtopping at the Industrial Canal.[88] Later that day, the USACE district commander issued a situation report, noting flooding with 4-5 feet of water in Kenner (Jefferson Parish); flooding with 10 feet of water in Arabi (St. Bernard Parish); and water coming into Lakeview (New Orleans) from the 17th Street Canal. The report also said that there was a one-block section of the Industrial Canal that had breached.[89]

Monday, very late evening (exact time unknown), off duty police officers began calling their police stations from their residences to report flooding near the 17th Street and London Avenue Canals, according to the New Orleans Police Department. Deputy Chief Lonnie Swain said that these reports were the department's first knowledge that flooding was moving into central New Orleans — they had been aware of flooding in East New Orleans (from Lake Pontchartrain) and the Lower Ninth Ward (from the Industrial Canal).[90]

Beyond these reports known to the National Guard, the EOC, and the New Orleans Police Department, USACE was trying to determine the detailed status of the levee system. However, the USACE district commander in New Orleans also suffered from a lack of communications capabilities.[91] As noted earlier, there is no early warning system for levee breaches in New Orleans.[92] On Monday at about 3:00 p.m., the commander and a team ventured out to conduct early assessments of the situation. They were unable to conduct a thorough review because of the high winds, debris, and flooding. Although they had to return to the bunker, it was clear to them at that point that New Orleans had suffered catastrophic flooding and they began to review plans for unwatering New Orleans.[93]

On Tuesday, August 30, at about 9:00 a.m., the USACE district commander was able to get a helicopter and see the extent of the flooding from the air.[94] The USACE district office began to develop more detailed plans for repairing the levees after the airborne reconnaissance on August 30.[95] USACE has authority to provide a variety of emergency response actions when levees fail or are damaged.[96] Any repairs to federally constructed levees are funded 100 percent by the federal government.[97]

There were also physical barriers that made assessments and repair difficult. Specifically, emergency repair operations to close some of the breaches were seriously hampered by lack of access roads. USACE regulations generally require access roads on top of levees to allow

FEMA

for inspections, maintenance, and flood-fighting operations, and most USACE levees built in the United States meet this requirement.[98] However, in New Orleans, exceptions were made to these regulations because of its highly urban nature. Access roads were foregone when it was decided to use I-walls in the levee crowns to minimize right-of-ways into surrounding neighborhoods.[99] When Hurricane Katrina led to the breaches in the levees, the lack of access roads atop the levees resulted in very significant increases in time and cost to repair the damaged areas.

Poor communications, difficulties in doing assessments, and physical barriers all served to delay efforts to repair the levees. Levee repairs did not begin until Wednesday, when USACE began marshalling resources — such as contractors, materials, and equipment — at the 17th Street Canal site.[100] The Louisiana National Guard was also involved in these early efforts to conduct emergency repairs of the 17th Street Canal. That afternoon, USACE began dropping 3,000 pound sandbags into the breach.[101] The next day contractors started delivering sand, gravel, and rock to the breach site on a newly-built access road. At both the 17th Street Canal and the London Avenue Canal, Army Chinook and Blackhawk helicopters dropped 7,000 pound sandbags—an average of 600 per day—into the breaches. One breach took over 2,000 sandbags before engineers could see the bags under the water surface. According to one witness before the Select Committee, the need for sand was so great that USACE broke into a local business and "took" $580,000 worth of sand.[102] One week later, the 17th Street Canal breach was closed.[103]

Once the levee repairs were underway, USACE turned its attention to unwatering New Orleans and other flooded areas.[104] Since at least 2000, USACE has had a detailed plan for unwatering greater New Orleans in the event of flooding. These unwatering plans were also discussed in the "Hurricane Pam" exercise (discussed previously).[105] The exercise assumed the levees did not breach, however there was flooding due to overtopping which inundated New Orleans with at least 10 feet of water. The purpose of the USACE unwatering mission was to remove water from flooded areas (New Orleans), seal off canals from Lake Pontchartrain, repair breaches, create a series of deliberate breaches in the levee system (to help drain them), and pump out final excess with existing and temporary pumps.[106]

Through an emergency contracting process, USACE contacted four companies to complete the unwatering activities and, according to USACE, only one company—Shaw Environmental of Baton Rouge—could respond in a timely manner.[107] Projections made prior to Hurricane Katrina that it would take nine weeks to unwater New Orleans proved unfounded.[108] On October 11 (43 days after Katrina landfall) USACE reported that all floodwaters had been removed from the city of New Orleans.[109]

Finding: Ultimate cause of levee failures is under investigation, results to be determined

Several investigations are under way to assess causes of levee failure

There are at least four ongoing "forensic" investigations to determine the cause of the levee breaches around New Orleans. These are being done by USACE's Engineer Research and Development Center; the Center for the Study of Public Health Impacts of Hurricanes, LSU; the National Science Foundation, and ASCE. Each of these investigations has somewhat similar charters and overlapping membership.[110]

■ Interagency Performance Evacuation Task Force (IPET). The USACE Chief Engineer appointed the IPET, headed by the Engineer Research and Development Center, to examine and analyze data in a variety of areas (e.g., Geodetic Reference Datum, Storm and Surge Wave Modeling, Hydrodynamic Forces). At the request of the Secretary of Defense, the results will be analyzed independently by ASCE and the National Research Council.[111]

■ Louisiana State University (LSU). The Hurricane Center was appointed by the State of Louisiana to lead the state's forensic investigation of the Hurricane Katrina levee failures. The investigation team includes engineers and coastal scientists conducting analysis of the storm surge levels, levee construction, and levee failures.[112]

■ National Science Foundation (NSF). NSF assembled a Levee Investigation Team consisting of leading national and international experts in major disasters.[11] Participating teams of scientists are from the University of California, Berkeley; the Geo-Institute of ASCE; the Coasts, Oceans, Ports and Rivers Institute of ASCE; and the Hurricane Research Center of LSU.[114]

■ American Society of Civil Engineers (ASCE). ASCE assembled an independent team of experts, consisting of professional engineers with a wide range of geotechnical engineering expertise in the study, safety, and inspection of dams and levees. The purpose of the team is to collect data and make observations to determine why certain sections of the levee system failed and others did not.[115]

Preliminary results suggest some levees did not withstand forces they were designed to withstand

Some of the investigators testified or released reports on their preliminary findings. For example, at a November 2, 2005, Senate Hearing, witnesses included Paul Mlakar, of IPET; Ivor Van Heerden, of LSU; Raymond Seed of the University of California, Berkeley, representing the NSF; and Peter Nicholson of the University of Hawaii, representing the ASCE.[116] These witnesses (except Mlakar) testified on the preliminary findings from their investigations. In addition, the NSF and ASCE investigators released a joint interim report, with initial findings, at that hearing.[117] A month after the Senate Hearing, IPET released an interim report with a summary of its field observations, which generally concurred with the NSF/ASCE interim report.[118] In evaluating the causes of levee and floodwall failure, these preliminary reports indicated the impact of the hurricane, and thus the potential causes of the breaches varied by location.[119]

According to preliminary information from NSF, ASCE and LSU, most of the levees and floodwall breaches on the east side of New Orleans were caused by overtopping, s the storm surge rose over the tops of the levees and/or their floodwalls and produced erosion that subsequently ed to breaches.[120] A variety of factors led to overtopping f the Industrial Canal and the Mississippi River Gulf Outlet (MR-GO). An LSU Scientist, Hassan Madhriqui, aid that MR-GO worked as a funnel which increased the height of the storm surge and "caused floodwaters to tack up several feet higher than elsewhere in the metro rea and sharply increased the surge's speed as it rushed hrough the MR-GO and into the Industrial Canal."[121] The vertopping eroded the backside of the canals, scoured ut the foundations, and led to their collapse and thus ajor flooding of adjacent neighborhoods. According to eed, "A majority of them [levee breaches] were the result f overtopping, and that simply means that the hurricane as bigger than the levees were built to take…."[122]

In contrast, there was little or no overtopping along most of the levees in the vicinity of Lake Pontchartrain. The only breach along Lake Pontchartrain was in New Orleans East, which was probably due to overtopping. But n the drainage canals that feed into Lake Pontchartrain – the 17th Street and London Avenue Canal — there was o overtopping, and the failures were likely caused by eaknesses in the foundation soil underlying the levees, he weakness in the soils used to construct the earthen vee embankments themselves, or weaknesses caused y vegetation growing along the levees. These were the most costly breaches, leading to widespread flooding of entral New Orleans — to include the downtown area nd several large residential neighborhoods.[123] According o Van Heerden of LSU, "the surge in Lake Pontchartrain asn't that of a category 3 storm, and nor did it exceed he design criteria of the standard project hurricane."[124] icholson of ASCE concurred with this assessment, dding, "If the levees [on Lake Pontchartrain] had done hat they were designed to do, a lot of the flooding of ew Orleans would not have occurred, and a lot of the uffering that occurred as a result of the flooding would ot have occurred."[125]

However, these findings are preliminary.[126] Most of he investigations will not issue their final reports until he spring or summer of 2006. For example, the USACE PET report is scheduled to be completed in June 2006.[127] ossible causes of the levee breaches include a design not ppropriate for the actual application (indicating a shared eficiency), storm conditions simply too overwhelming

for the designed levees to withstand (indicating an act of nature), levee walls not secured deeply enough into the soil or otherwise improperly constructed (indicating a USACE deficiency); improper maintenance of the levees (indicating a local deficiency); or a combination of factors.

Conclusion

Hundreds of miles of levees were constructed to defend metropolitan New Orleans against storm events. These levees were not designed to protect New Orleans from a category 4 or 5 monster hurricane, and all the key players knew this. The original specifications of the

levees offered protection that was limited to withstanding the forces of a moderate hurricane. Once constructed, the levees were turned over to local control, leaving the USACE to make detailed plans to drain New Orleans should it be flooded.

The local sponsors — a patchwork quilt of levee and water and sewer boards —were responsible only for their own piece of levee. It seems no federal, state, or local entity watched over the integrity of the whole system, which might have mitigated to some degree the effects of the hurricane. When Hurricane Katrina came, some of the levees breached — as many had predicted they would — and most of New Orleans flooded to create untold misery.

The forces that destroyed the levees also destroyed the ability to quickly assess damage and make repairs. The reasons for the levee failures appear to be some combination of nature's wrath (the storm was just too large) and man's folly (an assumption that the design, construction, and maintenance of the levees would be flawless). While there was no failure to predict the inevitability and consequences of a monster hurricane — Katrina in this case — there was a *failure of initiative* to get beyond design and organizational compromises to improve the level of protection afforded. ■

1 *See* Eric S. Blake, et al., Tropical Prediction Center, U.S. Dep't of Commerce, NOAA Technical Memorandum NWS TPC-4, *The Deadliest Costliest, and Most Intense U.S. Tropical Cyclones from 1851 to 2004* (and Other Frequently Requested Hurricane Facts, (Aug. 2005) *available at* http://www.nhc.noaa.gov/paststate.shtml (last visited Jan. 24, 2006); Anu Mittal, U.S. Gov't Accountability Off., Pub. No. GAO-05-1050T, *Testimony Before the Subcommittee on Energy and Water Development, Committee on Appropriations, House of Representatives, Army Corps of Engineers Lake Pontchartrain and Vicinity Hurricane Protection Project* [hereinafter GAO *Hurricane Protection Project*] at 2 (Sept. 28, 2005); R.B. Seed, et al., U. of Calif. at Berkely and Am. Soc'y of Civil Engineers, Rept. No. UCB/CITRIS – 05/01, *Preliminary Report on the Performance of the New Orleans Levee System in Hurricane Katrina on August 29, 2005* [hereinafter *Report on Levee Performance*] at 1-4 (Nov. 2, 2005) (support for subsidence); IEM, Inc., IEM/TEC04-070 r5, *Southeast LA Catastrophic Hurricane Functional Plan [SE LA Functional Hurricane Plan]* at 5 (Jan. 5, 2005).

2 U.S Army Engineer District, New Orleans, *Un-watering Plan Greater Metropolitan Area, New Orleans, LA* [hereinafter *Un-Watering Plan*] at 1 (Aug. 18, 2000).

3 New Orleans District, U.S. Army Corps of Engineers, *Hurricane Betsy, September 8-11, 1965: After Action Report,* 1-5 (July 1966) (Included as App. E in *Un-Watering Plan*).

4 *Id.* at 2.

5 *Id.* at 4.

6 *Id.* at 32.

7 *Id.* at 24.

8 *Id.* at 5.

9 *Id.* at 29.

10 *Id.* at 26.

11 *Hearing on Hurricane Katrina: Who's In Charge of the New Orleans Levees? Before U.S. Senate Committee on Homeland Security and Governmental Affairs* [hereinafter *Senate Hearing: Who's in Charge of Levees*], 109th Cong. (Dec. 15, 2005) at 2 (written statement of Max. L. Hearn, Executive Director, Orleans Levee District); *Report on Levee Performance* at 1-3.

12 GAO *Hurricane Protection Project* at 2.

13 Flood Control Act of 1965. Pub. L. No. 89-298, § 204, 79 Stat. 103, 1077 (1965) (The Flood Control Act of 1965 authorized this project).

14 The Industrial Canal is also known as the Inner Harbor Navigation Canal.

15 *Senate Hearing: Who's in Charge of Levees* at 1-2 (written statement of Col. Richard P. Wagenaar, Commander and District Engineer, New Orleans District, U.S. Army Corps of Engineers); GAO Hurricane Protection Project at 3.

16 Interview by Select Comm. Staff with David Pezza [hereinafter Pezza Interview], U.S. Army Corps of Engineers (Dec. 9, 2005); GAO *Hurricane Protection Project* at 3.

17 *Un-Watering Plan* at 1.

18 GAO *Hurricane Protection Project* at 4; U.S. Army Corps of Engineers, Release No. PA-05-08, *News Release: U.S. Army Corps of Engineers Hurricane Relief Support and Levee Repair,* (Sept. 3, 2005) (hurricane protection projects were designed to withstand forces of a hurricane that has a 0.5 percent chance of occurrence in any given year).

19 The U.S. Weather Service is now the National Weather Service.

20 GAO *Hurricane Protection Project* at 4-5.

21 *Hearing on Hurricane Protection Plan for Lake Pontchartrain and Vicinity Before the House Comm. on Public Works and Transportation Subcommittee on Water Resources* [hereinafter *1978 Hearing on Protection Plan for Lake Pontchartrain*], 95th Congress, 45 at 16, (Jan. 5, 1978) (statement of Col. Early Rush, District Engineer, US Army Engineer District, New Orleans) (When USACE designs flood protection projects, it models forces that were expected from the most severe combination of meteorological conditions reasonably characteristic of the region approaching from different paths. This is one of the reasons why, there is a great deal of variability among the heights of the different parts of the flood protection system).

22 USACE *News Release: Levee Repair;* GAO *Hurricane Protection Project* at 1, 4; Anu K. Mittal, U.S. Gov't Accountability Office, Pub. No. GAO-06-322T, *Testimony Before the Committee on Homeland Security and Governmental Affairs, U.S. Senate: Hurricane Protection: Statutory and Regulatory Framework for Levee Maintenance and Emergency Response for the Lake Pontchartrain Project* [hereinafter GAO *Hurricane Protection: Statutory Framework*] at 2 (Dec. 15, 2005); *Un-Watering Plan* at 3.

23 GAO *Hurricane Protection: Statutory Framework* at 4-5.

24 *Id.*

25 *Id.* at 5.

26 *Report on Levee Performance* at 1-3, 1-4.

27 *Un-Watering Plan* at 6.

28 U.S. Water Resources Council, *Economic and Environmental Principals for Water and Related Land Resources Implementation Studies* at iv, vi, 12 (Mar. 10, 1983) (These guidelines apply to USACE, among other agencies, and require calculations of impact on (a) national economic development, (b) environmental quality, (c) regional economic impact, and (d) other social effects. The last category includes "urban and community impacts: life, health, safety" and others).

29 *1978 Hearing on Protection Plan for Lake Pontchartrain* at 16 (statement of Col. Early Rush).

30 *See* Eric Lipton, *White House Was Told Hurricane Posed Danger,* N.Y. TIMES, Jan. 24, 2006 at A6.

31 William L. Waugh, Jr., *The Disaster That Was Katrina,* NATURAL HAZARDS OBSERVER, Vol. XXX No. 2, Nov. 2005 at 7-8.

32 *Id.*

33 Shirley Laska, *What if Hurricane Ivan Had Not Missed New Orleans?,* NATURAL HAZARDS OBSERVER, Vol. XXIX No. 2, Nov. 2004 at 5-6.

34 *Id.*

35 *Un-Watering Plan* at 1.

36 *Id.* at 7.

37 *Id.*

38 GAO *Hurricane Protection Project* at 8.

Bob Marshall, *Hurricane Pam Exercise Offered Glimpse of Katrina Misery*, TIMES PICAYUNE (New Orleans) Sept. 9, 2005.

National Weather Service, New Orleans, LA, Urgent *Weather Message, ...Devastating Damage Expected...*, 10:11 a.m. CDT (Aug. 28, 2005).

Interview of Kathleen Babineaux Blanco, Governor of LA, CNN Saturday Night, (Aug. 28, 2005) (8:00 p.m. ET).

Press Conference by C. Ray Nagin, Mayor of New Orleans, and Kathleen Babineaux Blanco, Governor of LA, MSNBC, et al, Aug. 28, 2005.

Pezza Interview; *Senate Hearing: Who's in Charge of Levees* at 2 (written statement of Director Hearn); *Report on Levee Performance* at 6-1; GAO *Hurricane Protection Project* at 3.

Pezza Interview; *Senate Hearing: Who's in Charge of Levees* at 2 (written statement of Director Hearn); *Report on Levee Performance* at 6-1; GAO *Hurricane Protection Project* at 3.

33 U.S.C. §701t (2005) (They are eligible as long as they are active in USACE's Rehabilitation Inspection Program. To be eligible, they have to pass annual inspections by USACE, which was the case for the Lake Pontchartrain project).

Pezza Interview.

Pezza Interview; *Senate Hearing: Who's in Charge of Levees* at 3 (written statement of Director Hearn); GAO *Hurricane Protection: Statutory Framework* at 6.

Hearing on Hurricane Katrina: Why Did the Levees Fail? Before U.S. Senate Committee on Homeland Security and Governmental Affairs [hereinafter *Senate Hearing: Why Did Levees Fail*], 109th Cong. (Nov. 2, 2005) (statement of Raymond B. Seed, Professor of Civil and Environmental Engineering, University of California, Berkley).

Senate Hearing: Who's in Charge of Levees (written statement of Col. Wagenaar at 2); GAO *Hurricane Protection: Statutory Framework* at 6.

Pezza Interview; GAO *Hurricane Protection: Statutory Framework* at 8.

Pezza Interview; GAO *Hurricane Protection: Statutory Framework* at 9.

Senate Hearing: Who's in Charge of Levees (written statement of Col. Wagenaar at 2); GAO *Hurricane Protection: Statutory Framework* at 6.

Senate Hearing: Why Did Levees Fail (statement of R.B. Seed).

Un-Watering Plan at 4.

Interagency Performance Evaluation Task Force, *Interim Report to Task Force Guardian, Summary of Field Observations Relevant to Flood Protection in New Orleans* [hereinafter *Interim Report on Flood Protection in New Orleans*], LA at 7 (Dec. 5, 2005).

Senate Hearing: Why Did Levees Fail (statement of R.B. Seed).

Senate Hearing: Why Did Levees Fail (statement of Peter Nicholson, Associate Professor, Civil and Environmental Engineering, University of Hawaii).

Senate Hearing: Why Did Levees Fail (statement of R.B. Seed).

Pezza Interview; *Senate Hearing: Who's in Charge of Levees* at 3 (written statement of Director Hearn).

Pezza Interview; GAO *Hurricane Protection: Statutory Framework* at 9.

Senate Hearing: Who's in Charge of Levees at 2 (written statement of Col. Wagenaar).

GAO *Hurricane Protection: Statutory Framework* at 10.

Pezza Interview; *Report on Levee Performance* at 2-2.

Frank Langfitt, *Residents Say Levee Leaked Months Before Katrina National Public Radio*, NATIONAL PUBLIC RADIO, MORNING EDITION (Nov. 22, 2005) *available at* http://www.npr.org/templates/story/story.php?storyId=5022074 (last visited Feb. 1, 2005).

Id.

Id.

Richard D. Knabb, et al., National Hurricane Center, Dep't of Commerce, *Tropical Cyclone Report: Hurricane Katrina 23-30 August 2005* [hereinafter NHC: *Hurricane Katrina*] at 1, (Dec. 20, 2005).

Id. at 1.

Id.

Id. at 7.

Id. at 8.

Id. at 11; GAO *Hurricane Protection Project* at 2.

NHC: *Hurricane Katrina* at 8.

Report on Levee Performance at 1-4.

NHC: *Hurricane Katrina* at 8.

Id. at 9.

Id.

Report on Levee Performance at 1-2; NHC: *Hurricane Katrina* at 9 (Additional support that the surge severely strained the levee system).

NHC: *Hurricane Katrina* at 9.

Id.

Pezza Interview.

GAO *Hurricane Protection: Statutory Framework* at 9.

Senate Hearing: Who's in Charge of Levees at 4 (written statement of Director Hearn).

Senate Hearing: Why Did Levees Fail (statement of R.B. Seed).

Interview by Select Comm. Staff with General Joseph B. Veillon, Assistant Adjutant General for Air, LA Air Nat'l Guard in Baton Rouge, LA (Nov. 3, 2005).

Audio recordings of Hurricane Katrina Conference Calls, LA State Emergency Operations Center (Aug. 26-29, 2005).

Senate Hearing: Who's in Charge of Levees at 4 (written statement of Col. Wagenaar).

Id. at 5.

Richard P. Wagenaar, Col., New Orleans District, U.S. Army Corps of Engineers, *Situation report: Event Hurricane Katrina*, (Aug. 29, 2005).

Interview by Select Comm. Staff with Lonnie Swain, Deputy Police Superintendent, New Orleans Police Dep't, in New Orleans, LA, (Nov. 9, 2005).

Senate Hearing: Who's in Charge of Levees (written statement of Col. Wagenaar).

[92] Pezza Interview.

[93] *Senate Hearing: Who's in Charge of Levees* (written statement of Col. Wagenaar).

[94] *Id.* at 5.

[95] *Id.* at 6.

[96] Flood Control Act of 1941 § 5, 33 U.S.C. § 701n (2005) (Authorizes USACE to conduct emergency operations and rehabilitation activities when levees fail or are damaged and allows USACE to provide emergency operations to include technical assistance and direct assistance—providing sandbags and pumps, emergency contracting, and levee reinforcement. USACE administrative policies, guidance, and operating procedures for natural disaster preparedness, response, and recovery activities are set out in 33 C.F.R. Part 203 (2005).); *see Senate Hearing: Who's in Charge of Levees* at 3 (written statement of Col. Wagenaar); also GAO *Hurricane Protection: Statutory Framework* at 14-15.

[97] GAO *Hurricane Protection: Statutory Framework* at 10.

[98] U.S. Army Corps of Engineers, Manual No. 1110-2-1913, *Engineering and Design: Design and Construction of Levees* 8-9 (Apr. 30, 2000).

[99] *See Interim Report on Flood Protection in New Orleans* at 12-13.

[100] Lieutenant Colonel Pease, U.S. Army Corps of Engineers, US Army Corps of Engineers Support to Hurricane Katrina Response, (Aug. 31, 2005)

[101] *Id.*

[102] *Hearing on Hurricane Katrina: Voices from Inside the Storm Before Select Comm.*, 109th Cong., (Dec. 6, 2005) (statement of Harry Alford, President, National Black Chamber of Commerce).

[103] *Senate Hearing: Who's in Charge of Levees* (written statement of Col. Wagenaar).

[104] *Id.*

[105] *See Un-Watering Plan; SE LA Functional Hurricane Plan* at 6-7.

[106] *U.S. Army Corps of Engineers, USACE/ESF#3: Hurricane Season 2005* at 23 (Oct. 28, 2005) (on file with the Select Comm.).

[107] *Hearing on Hurricane Katrina: The Federal Government's Use of Contractors to Prepare and Respond Before the Select Comm.*, 109th Cong., (Nov. 2, 2005) (written statement of Norbert Doyle, Col., Principal Assistant Responsible For Contracting (Acting), U.S. Army Corps Of Engineers).

[108] Shirley Laska, *What if Hurricane Ivan Had Not Missed New Orleans?*, NATURAL HAZARDS OBSERVER, Vol. XXIX No. 2, Nov. 2004 at 6.

[109] NHC: *Hurricane Katrina* at 9; *see SE LA Functional Hurricane Plan* at 6.

[110] *Senate Hearing: Why Did Levees Fail* (statement of Sen. Susan M. Collins, Chairman).

[111] *Senate Hearing: Why Did Levees Fail* (written statement of Paul F. Mlakar, Ph.D., P.E., Senior Research Scientist, U.S. Army Research and Development Center).

[112] Louisiana State U. Hurricane Center, *Newsbriefs*, http://hurricane.lsu.edu/newsbriefs.htm (last visited Jan. 29, 2006).

[113] *Senate Hearing: Why Did Levees Fail* (statement of Peter Nicholson).

[114] *Senate Hearing: Why Did Levees Fail* (statement of R.B. Seed).

[115] *Report on Levee Performance* at 1-1.

[116] *See Senate Hearing: Why Did Levees Fail.*

[117] *Senate Hearing: Why Did Levees Fail* (statement of Sen. Collins).

[118] *See Interim Report on Flood Protection in New Orleans.*

[119] *Report on Levee Performance* at v; *Senate Hearing: Why Did Levees Fail* (written statement of Paul F. Mlakar).

[120] *Report on Levee Performance* at iv; *Senate Hearing: Why Did Levees Fail* (statement of Ivor L. van Heerden, Ph.D., Deputy Director, LA State U. Hurricane Center).

[121] *Report on Levee Performance* at 1-5; Matthew Brown, *Katrina may mean MR-GO has to go*, TIMES-PICAYUNE (New Orleans), Oct. 24, 2005 at 1; *Senate Hearing: Why Did Levees Fail* (statement of Ivor L. van Heerden).

[122] *Senate Hearing: Why Did Levees Fail* (statement of R.B. Seed).

[123] *Report on Levee Performance* at 1-5; *Senate Hearing: Why Did Levees Fail* (written statement of Paul F. Mlakar) and (statement of Ivor L. van Heerden).

[124] *Senate Hearing: Why Did Levees Fail* (statement of Ivor L. van Heerden).

[125] *Senate Hearing: Why Did Levees Fail* (statement of Peter Nicholson).

[126] *Report on Levee Performance* at cover, v.

[127] U.S. Army Corps of Engineers, Release No. PA-05-18, *News Release: Interagency Performance Evaluation Task Force – Testing Report on Sheet Pile Foundation Lengths in New Orleans Levees*, (Dec. 9, 2005).

AP PHOTO/RICK BOWMER

"At the local level, I think the biggest failure was leadership didn't take into account the fact that poor residents had no way of evacuating. I also think Governor Blanco should have called for a mandatory evacuation sooner and that Mayor Nagin should have coordinated better with Amtrak."

Terrol Williams
New Orleans Citizen and Evacuee
Select Committee Hearing, December 6, 2005

"We estimate that over 1 million people, or approximately 90 percent of the affected parishes' populations, evacuate[d] in about a 40-hour period. I don't know of any other evacuation that has occurred with that many people under these circumstances with that high of percentage of people being evacuated in that short of a time period."

Colonel (Ret.) Jeff Smith
Deputy Director, Louisiana Office of Homeland Security
and Emergency Preparedness
Select Committee Hearing, December 14, 2005

EVACUATION

Failure of complete evacuations led to preventable deaths, great suffering, and further delays in relief

Summary

Evacuation is a critical part of emergency preparation for a hurricane. Such preparation includes both detailed evacuation planning and implementation of the evacuation plan in potentially affected areas once a hurricane is projected to make landfall. The states of Alabama, Mississippi, and Louisiana, and many of their localities (e.g., New Orleans) have hurricane evacuation plans and years of experience implementing them.

In Alabama and Mississippi, the state or localities declared mandatory evacuations as Hurricane Katrina approached, and implementation of their evacuation plans went relatively well. In Louisiana, the state and local implementation of evacuation plans for the general population also went well, resulting in one of the largest emergency evacuations in history.

Two of Louisiana's most populous localities, New Orleans and Jefferson Parish, declared mandatory evacuations late or not at all. While the definition of "mandatory" evacuation and the associated obligations and liabilities that local governments assume are still being debated, early designation of the evacuation of New Orleans as mandatory could have increased the number of people that left, resulting in a more complete evacuation, saving lives, and reducing suffering. New Orleans city officials, who were responsible for executing an evacuation plan and who had the authority to commandeer resources to assist in the evacuation, failed to evacuate or assist in the evacuation of more than 70,000 individuals who did not leave either before the announcement of the mandatory evacuation or before the storm hit. Those who did not evacuate included many who did not have their own means of transportation. Despite the declaration of a mandatory evacuation on Sunday before landfall, New Orleans officials still did not completely evacuate the population. Instead, they opened the Superdome as a "shelter of last resort" for these individuals.

Problems sheltering this population, beyond emergency planners' general preference for evacuation, were exacerbated by inadequate preparations for a large population at the Superdome. For those with medical or special needs, New Orleans and other institutions also failed to evacuate them, but instead sheltered them — a decision that also had negative consequences and is discussed in detail in the MEDICAL CARE chapter. Those individuals in all states who had the means to evacuate, but did not do so, must also share the blame for the incomplete evacuation and the difficulties that followed.

The failure of a more complete evacuation led to catastrophic circumstances when Katrina made landfall, particularly in New Orleans where the force of the hurricane breached the levee system in multiple locations throughout the metropolitan area. As the resulting floodwaters spread through low lying urban areas,

thousands of people who were trapped in their homes climbed to their roofs or fled into flooded streets. Fortunately, thousands of these people were saved by a massive and heroic search and rescue effort. But many were not as fortunate, and hundreds of people died in their homes or other locations, presumably from drowning. Those who were in the Superdome, or those that found shelter and high ground at other locations, suffered horrible conditions. The floodwaters, which had been anticipated and even predicted from a large hurricane such as Katrina, furthered the misery and delayed the immediate relief of the remaining population.

The incomplete evacuation and floodwaters also required a post hurricane evacuation, for which federal, state, and city officials had not prepared. Because of a lack of preparations, planning had to be accomplished in emergency circumstances, where communications and situational awareness were in short supply. Requirements for buses kept growing as a lack of willing drivers and diversions of buses continued to delay the evacuation of the Superdome and other locations. Finally, the combination of more buses and supplemental airlifts resulted in a complete evacuation of New Orleans.

Finding: Evacuations of general populations went relatively well in all three states

Evacuation is a critical part of emergency preparation for a hurricane

Because of the destructive forces of hurricanes, evacuation planning is very important. Preparation for an approaching hurricane includes both detailed evacuation planning and implementation of that plan in potentially affected areas once a hurricane is projected to make landfall. Federal Emergency Management Agency (FEMA) officials told

Select Committee staff that emergency planners prefer evacuation to sheltering people within affected areas because the sheltered population is subject to the most intense dangers of the storm and because it may be a slow and difficult operation to get relief personnel and supplies back into hurricane ravaged areas.

The state of Louisiana has an evacuation plan, which was revised following Hurricane Ivan in 2004. The evacuation for that storm had caused massive traffic jams leading out of New Orleans. Those traffic jams were

the result of the southernmost parishes trying to evacuate at the same time as Orleans and Jefferson Parishes, the two most populous parishes. The new plan called for a staged evacuation with the southernmost parishes evacuating first, followed by Lower Orleans and Jefferson Parishes, and then Upper Orleans and Jefferson Parishes, facilitated by the implementation of contraflow (one-way outbound traffic) on the highways leading out of New Orleans.[1]

In addition to the Louisiana state plan, local governments have emergency evacuation plans. The City of New Orleans Comprehensive Emergency Management Plan ("New Orleans Plan") provides: "The authority to order the evacuation of residents threatened by an approaching hurricane is conferred to the Governor by Louisiana statute."[2] But this power "is also delegated to each political subdivision of the State by Executive Order."[3]

The New Orleans Plan further explains: "This authority empowers the chief elected official of New Orleans, the Mayor of New Orleans, to order the evacuation of the parish residents threatened by an approaching hurricane."[4] Under this authority, the Mayor of New Orleans is responsible for giving the order for a mandatory evacuation and supervising the actual evacuation of his population. The Mayor's Office of Emergency Preparedness must "[c]oordinate with the State . . . on elements of evacuation and "[a]ssist in directing the transportation of evacuees to staging areas."[5]

The importance of evacuations is expressed in the New Orleans Plan: "The safe evacuation of threatened populations . . . is one of the principle reasons for developing a Comprehensive Emergency Management Plan."[6] In furtherance of that goal, "[t]he city of New Orleans will utilize all available resources to quickly and safely evacuate threatened areas."[7]

Mississippi also has a state evacuation plan, one that takes account of local plans because of the key role that counties play in declaring evacuations. According to the testimony of the Director of the Mississippi Emergency Management Agency (MEMA), Robert Latham, the authority to make decisions about mandatory evacuations in Mississippi rests with local governments.[8] However, the state is generally included in any discussions about evacuation orders because, once a city or county chooses to make such an order, state responsibilities for managing traffic (including contraflow) and opening shelters can come into play.[9] In preparing for Hurricane Katrina, the Mississippi officials worked through the MEMA liaisons it dispatched to the counties along or near the Gulf Coast as well as a representative it had stationed in Louisiana's emergency operations center (because of contraflow agreements between Mississippi and Louisiana that provide for evacuations out of southeast Louisiana through Mississippi).[10]

Alabama also has an evacuation plan and recently revised it. Lessons learned during Alabama's response to Hurricanes Ivan and Dennis helped refine the state's actions as Katrina neared. Having been criticized for triggering evacuations that turned out to be unnecessary, Alabama officials practiced to reduce the time required to reverse traffic flows on the major routes and encouraged

AP PHOTO/JOHN DAVID MERCER, POOL

county and local officials to define smaller evacuation zones within their jurisdictions to better target evacuation actions. According to Governor Riley:

> On Katrina there was an evacuation plan that was a little more moderate than I had hoped for, and we convinced everyone in the room to expand it. The time before, as I said earlier, we got some criticism because we may have expanded it too much. We have gone back and built a zone type process. But we take all of the local team, because you have to have local buy-in because it won't work if you don't.[11]

Alabama state and county officials testified that one of their difficulties in planning evacuations is that Army Corps of Engineers data used as the basis for evacuation plans and models is outdated. According to Alabama Emergency Management Agency (AEMA) Director Bruce Baughman:

> The two coastal counties have had studies done by the [Army] Corps of Engineers. Those studies were about five years old. In the case of Mobile County, the data did not include the windfields. So it doesn't give you complete information when you are trying to make decisions on clearance times …. [I]t is based upon dated information. Baldwin County has grown by leaps and bounds so that you have got a higher population. And not only that, before Labor Day, you have got probably 100,000 people … as far as outside individuals that are tourists down in that area, and that is not computed into your clearance

AP PHOTO/CHERYL GERBER

times. What we have done is we have taken the data that is available that is between 22 and 24 hour clearance times for those two counties, and generally we allow 26 to 28 hour clearance times. But that is a best guess. What we need to do is based upon some real time data, so other studies need to be done in that particular area. That used to be funded out of the Hurricane Preparedness Program, and those studies are lagging way behind.[12]

Mississippi declared mandatory evacuations which generally went well

Mississippi evacuations were generally mandatory and went relatively well. Five Mississippi counties — Hancock, Jackson, Harrison, Stone, and Pearl River — issued mandatory evacuation orders on or before August 28 for specific areas or zones of their counties and/or those living in mobile homes.[13] For example, Harrison County first issued a mandatory evacuation order for its zones A and B, which include all of its Gulf-front and low-lying areas, at 10 a.m. on August 28; it strongly advised, but did not mandate, that residents in its highest elevations (zone C) evacuate the county.[14] According to Governor Haley Barbour, he has the authority to usurp county officials' decisions — that is, order a mandatory evacuation if they have not — but he chose not to do so because county

STATE OF MISSISSIPPI

officials are closer to the situation than he is.[15]

During the evacuation, Mississippi Department of Transportation personnel collected and reported traffic flow information along evacuation routes, including areas where contraflow was in place for those evacuating Louisiana. At 7 p.m. on August 28, traffic counts were "consistently high" and the contraflow areas showed a continuous increase in traffic.[16] According to traffic counts, by 11 p.m. that evening, traffic along the evacuation/contraflow routes had decreased substantially.[17]

Rep. Gene Taylor asserted, however, that evacuation planning ought to include providing people with gasoline especially at the end of the month:

> The other thing that I find interesting is that in all these scenarios that I'm sure you've thought out, did FEMA bother to realize that it is the 28th of the month, a lot of people live on fixed income, be it a Social Security check or a retirement check, they've already made their necessary purchase for the month. What they couldn't envision is having to fill up their gas tank one more time, at almost 3 bucks a gallon just to get the heck out of there. What I think no one is really focused on is a heck of a lot of people who stayed behind were people with limited means.[18]

Former Undersecretary Brown strongly opposed the suggestion that FEMA should have supplied gasoline:

> Congressman, FEMA is not there to supply gasoline, transportation; it is not the role of the federal government to supply five gallons of gas for every individual to put in a car to go somewhere. I personally believe that is a horrible path to go down. And while my heart goes out to people on fixed incomes, it is primarily a Sate and local responsibility.[19]

Whether providing gasoline should be a federal or state and local responsibility, there may very well have been victims of Hurricane Katrina who did not evacuate because at the end of the month they had run out of money for gasoline and found no other way to get gasoline or evacute.

Alabama mandatory evacuations also went relatively well

Alabama began implementing the evacuation early, and its evacuation also went well. Even before any Alabama evacuations began, AEMA and state transportation officials participated in the FEMA regional Evacuation Liaison Team conference calls during which emergency managers from Florida, Louisiana, and Mississippi shared information on the status of evacuation routes, road closures, traffic volumes, hotel availability, and other interstate implications of significant population migrations in the region.[20]

As it became clear Katrina would have a significant impact on the Alabama coast, Baldwin County emergency management officials called for a voluntary evacuation of all coastal, flood-prone, and low lying areas at 5 p.m. on Saturday, August 27.[21] State emergency management officials asked the Governor to declare a mandatory evacuation for threatened areas of Baldwin and Mobile Counties on Sunday, August 28.[22] According to the announcement released by the Governor's office, "In Baldwin County, the order calls for the evacuation of those on Plash Island, the Fort Morgan peninsula, and all areas south of Fort Morgan Road for Gulf Shores. The order also calls for the evacuation of those living in Perdido Key and south of Perdido Beach Boulevard. Those in all low lying and flood-prone areas south of I-10 in Baldwin County and those living along the Mobile Bay area and other water inlets also fall under the evacuation order."[23] Governor Riley testified:

... [W]e made it voluntary 36 hours out, and then shortly thereafter we made it mandatory. As it comes closer, as the cone begins to funnel in and we have a higher likelihood that it is going to happen, we make it mandatory. We ask people to leave. We do everything we can to encourage them to leave. But, again, the limiting factor is the amount of time. The difference between trying to evacuate our beaches before Labor Day and after Labor Day is like daylight and dark, because we have so many more vacationers there. And then when you layer on top of that the number of people that will be coming out of the Florida panhandle that will come through Alabama, if we don't start it three days early, you just physically do not have the capacity to take care of it.[24]

Alabama did not implement reverse lane strategies (i.e., contraflow) in response to Hurricane Katrina, as road closures were limited and traffic volume never warranted it. The state reported 118,900 applications for evacuation assistance by Alabama residents, of which 23,853 were by out of state residents.[25]

Louisiana evacuation of general population was very successful

The Louisiana evacuation for the general population, including contraflow, worked very well. Governor Kathleen Babineaux Blanco and other state officials labeled the implementation of this evacuation as "masterful" and as one of the most successful emergency evacuations in history.[26] Based on National Weather Service reports of Katrina's "dramatic shift" toward Louisiana on Friday, the state had less time than planned to prepare for contraflow and had to implement it in a compressed timeframe.[27]

Nevertheless, the contraflow planning and implementation went smoothly. The state effectively used conference calls to coordinate among the parishes. Some parishes declared some level of evacuation for the entire parish as early as Saturday morning, August 27, at 9:00 a.m. These were generally the lower parishes (LaFourche, Plaquemines, St. Bernard, and St. Charles), which was consistent with the Louisiana state plan for getting these populations to evacuate ahead of the metropolitan New Orleans population.

The parishes generally started with the declaration of a "recommended" evacuation and changed these to a "mandatory" evacuation as Katrina got closer. The state also coordinated closely with Mississippi and Texas on traffic and/or sheltering issues. For example, Friday afternoon Blanco called Barbour to coordinate that portion of the contraflow plan that involved highways leading out of Louisiana into Mississippi, and Governor Barbour agreed to the contraflow plan.[28]

Finding: Despite adequate warning 56 hours before landfall, Governor Blanco and Mayor Nagin delayed ordering a mandatory evacuation in New Orleans until 19 hours before landfall

Terms for voluntary and mandatory evacuations lack clear definitions

A wide variety of terms were used to describe the levels of evacuation orders, indicating a lack of clarity and a potential point of confusion for the resident population. For example, the different parishes used a wide variety of terms to describe the level of evacuation imposed before declaring a mandatory evacuation. These terms included a "precautionary" evacuation, a "voluntary" evacuation, a "recommended" evacuation, a "highly recommended" evacuation, and a "highly suggested" evacuation.[29] It appeared many of these officials were bending over backward to avoid using the term mandatory.

Throughout our discussions in all three states, Select Committee staff were unable to find a clear and consistent definition of mandatory evacuation. However, there was a consensus among almost all officials in all three states that even under a mandatory evacuation, authorities would not forcibly remove someone from their home. For example, in the case of Louisiana, both Blanco and LOHSEP Deputy Director Colonel Jeff Smith emphatically rejected the idea that people could be forcibly removed from their homes even under a mandatory evacuation order. Blanco said, "Well, in the United States of America you don't force people [out of their homes], you urge them."[30] Smith said: "It is America. You can't force people on to buses; you can't go into their houses at gunpoint and leave [sic]."[31]

Under Alabama state law, a mandatory evacuation declaration by the Governor is required before counties can take certain actions to ensure maximum compliance with local orders by those at risk.[32] But, regarding the practical meaning and effect of "mandatory" versus "voluntary" evacuations, Riley said:

We probably need to come up with a better definition of what mandatory is. We call it a mandatory evacuation because everyone else calls it a mandatory evacuation. But do we arrest anyone? No. Do we send people door to door? Absolutely. We have a phone system, that they can explain to you in just a moment, where we have an automated system that calls every resident, asks them to leave, advises them with a phone message of how important it is. We keep doing it until we get in touch with everyone. Do you ever get to the point that everyone is going to leave? I don't think so.[33]

Nevertheless, it is clear to the Select Committee that declaring a mandatory evacuation delivers a more powerful statement to the public than declaring a voluntary or similarly worded evacuation. A mandatory evacuation implies that individuals do not have a choice, that the government will not be able to protect them and provide relief if they remain, and it generally conveys a higher level of urgency.

Federal, state, and local officials recognized the potential for catastrophe and flooding and communicated that potential among themselves and to the public

Regardless of the various terms used for evacuations, federal officials fully informed Blanco and New Orleans Mayor C. Ray Nagin about the threat to New Orleans. On the evening of August 27, National Hurricane Center Director Max Mayfield called Blanco and later spoke to Nagin about the power of Hurricane Katrina.[34] Also on Sunday, President Bush called Blanco to express his concern for the people of New Orleans and the dangers they faced and urged a mandatory evacuation.[35] On Sunday, the Slidell Office of the National Weather Service, issued a very strongly worded warning at approximately 10:00 a.m.:

Devastating damage expected . . . Hurricane Katrina . . . a most powerful hurricane with unprecedented strength . . . rivaling the intensity of Hurricane Camille of 1969… Most of the area will be uninhabitable for weeks . . . perhaps longer. At least half of well constructed homes will have roof and wall failure. All gabled roofs will fail . . . leaving those homes severely damaged or destroyed… Water shortages will make human suffering incredible by modern standards.[36]

State and local officials also urged the public to evacuate by foretelling the potentially catastrophic consequences. For example, beginning on Saturday, August 27, Blanco publicly urged citizens to evacuate the city, expressing her concern for the strength of the levees against at least a Category 4 storm.[37] In several interviews on Saturday and Sunday, Blanco stated that flooding in New Orleans was a major concern. On Saturday at approximately 8:00 p.m., she appeared on CNN and said that in New Orleans "[t]he storm surge could bring in 15 to 20 feet of water. [People in the city of New Orleans] will not survive that if indeed that happens."[38] In the Sunday morning papers, it was reported that she had said the water levels could reach as high as 20 feet.[39] In a television interview on Sunday, Blanco was asked if the 15 foot levees could survive the storm, and she replied: "I don't think anything can tolerate a storm surge of 15-20 feet."[40]

In a Fox News interview on Sunday, Nagin was very specific about the threat. He said whether the levees would hold was the "big question."[41] He said he hoped people who stayed in the French Quarter would go up to their homes' second or third story and bring something to chop through their roofs.[42] He expressed his worry that "[the levees] have never truly been tested the way they're getting ready to be tested. If there's a breach and if they start to fail, it probably will create somewhat of a domino effect which would pour even more water into the city."[43]

Blanco's staff also called ministers on Saturday to urge them to tell their congregations to get out.[44] And apparently, the Mayor and his staff did similar things.[45] But these steps were clearly insufficient.

The declarations of a "mandatory" evacuation were delayed or never made in metropolitan New Orleans

Neither Blanco nor Nagin, however, ordered a mandatory evacuation until Sunday morning. According to the Saturday newspapers, Nagin said "he will make a decision about evacuations and other emergency procedures [Saturday] about noon."[46] At a news conference on Saturday, Nagin announced: "Ladies and Gentlemen, this is not a test. This is the real deal."[47] But as late as Saturday afternoon, according to news reports, Nagin was consulting city lawyers about legal liability to the city's businesses for lost revenue from evacuating customers.[48]

In addition, despite express authority to commandeer resources and enforce or facilitate the evacuation of the City of New Orleans and despite recognition of the probability that Hurricane Katrina would cause breaches of the levees and flooding of the city, Blanco and Nagin did not exercise those authorities by declaring a mandatory evacuation and enforcing it or using state and city resources to facilitate the evacuation of those who could not or would not, absent extraordinary measures and assistance, evacuate. This extraordinary storm required extraordinary measures, which the Governor and Mayor did not take.

Finally, on Sunday morning at around 11:00 a.m. central time — 19 hours before projected landfall, Nagin announced the issuance of a mandatory evacuation order.[49] According to the New Orleans Plan, that gave the Mayor the authority to "direct and compel, by any necessary and reasonable force, the evacuation of all or part of the population from any stricken or threatened area within the City if he deems this action necessary for the preservation of life, or for disaster mitigation, response, or recovery."[50] As previously noted, the New Orleans Plan also recognizes that "[t]he safe evacuation of threatened populations when endangered by a major catastrophic event is one of the principle reasons for developing a Comprehensive Emergency Management Plan" and that "[s]pecial arrangements will be made to evacuate persons unable to transport themselves or who require special life saving assistance."[51]

In a joint news conference on Sunday morning, Blanco and Nagin continued to express their concerns and explain the reason for the Mayor's issuing a mandatory evacuation order. Their comments raise the question as to why, given the severity of the predicted catastrophe, the mandatory evacuation was not ordered sooner.

Mayor Nagin: Ladies and gentlemen, I wish I had better news for you. **But we are facing a storm that most of us have feared.** I do not want to create panic. But I do want the citizens to understand that this is very serious, and it's of the highest nature. And that's why we are taking this unprecedented move.

The storm is now a Cat 5, a Category 5, as I appreciate it, with sustained winds of 150 miles an hour, with wind gusts of 190 miles per hour.

The storm surge most likely will topple our levee system. So we are preparing to deal with that also. So that's why we're ordering a mandatory evacuation . . . .

. . . .

This is a once in probably a lifetime event. The city of New Orleans has never seen a hurricane of this strength to hit it almost directly, which is what they're projecting right now.[52]

During the press conference Blanco stated:

I want to reiterate what the mayor has said. This is a very dangerous time. **Just before we walked into this room, President Bush called and told me to share with all of you that he is very concerned about the citizens. He is concerned about the impact that this hurricane would have on our people. And he asked me to please ensure that there would be a mandatory evacuation of New Orleans.**

The leaders at the highest ranks of our nation have recognized the destructive forces and the possible awesome danger that we are in. **And I just want to say, we need to get as many people out as possible.** The shelters will end up probably without electricity or with minimum electricity from generators in the end. **There may be intense flooding that will be not in our control, which would be ultimately the most dangerous situation that many of our people could face.**

Waters could be as high as 15 to 20 feet. That is what the Miami National Weather Service, the National Hurricane Center, has shared with us. That would probably be ultimately the worst situation. We're hoping that it does not happen that way. We need to pray, of course, very strongly, that the

hurricane force would diminish. But just remember, even if it diminishes to 1, there were six people lost in Florida when it was a Category 1 hurricane. So there's still imminent danger. There seems to be no real relief in sight, and it has been startling to see how accurate the path was predicted, and how it is following the predicted path.

So we have no reason to believe right now that it will alter its path.

Hopefully, you know, it could move just a little bit in one direction or another and not keep New Orleans in its sights. But we don't know that that would happen. That would be — we would be blessed if that happened.[53]

Jefferson Parish — the other major component of metropolitan New Orleans — never did declare a mandatory evacuation, except for the lower parts of the parish on the Gulf Coast. In a conference call among parish officials, Jefferson Parish President Aaron Broussard said he did not have the "resources to enforce" a mandatory evacuation.[54] Resource or enforcement issues, however, were not raised by any of the other parishes that declared mandatory evacuations. In addition, no one requested that the state or federal government provide resources to supplement those of the parish to implement a more complete evacuation.

STATE OF LOUISIANA

A FAILURE OF INITIATIV

Finding: The failure to order timely mandatory evacuations, Mayor Nagin's decision to shelter but not evacuate the remaining population, and decisions of individuals led to incomplete evacuation

Earlier mandatory evacuation could have helped get more people out

While the Mayor and the Governor recognized the dangers and expressed them to the public, they did not implement evacuation procedures for all of the citizens of New Orleans that reflected the seriousness of the threat. The results demonstrate the flaw of the evacuation — tens of thousands of citizens did not get out of harm's way.

Specifically, the failure to order a mandatory evacuation until Sunday, the decision to enforce that order by "asking" people who had not evacuated to go to checkpoints for bus service, and then using that bus service to take people only as far as the Superdome did not reflect the publicly stated recognition that Hurricane Katrina would "most likely topple [the] levee system" and result in "intense flooding" and "waters as high as 15 or 20 feet," rendering large portions of the city uninhabitable.[55] As a result, more than 70,000 people remained in the City to be rescued after the storm.[56]

While Blanco, Nagin, and Broussard, and leaders from other parishes carefully managed the phased contraflow evacuation, that only facilitated the evacuation of those who had the means to evacuate the city. Nagin testified that, on Saturday, August 27, he "called for a strong voluntary evacuation, urging all citizens that were able to evacuate the city."[57] Although Nagin was rightly proud of the achievement of the contraflow evacuation of the region, he also conceded that "it probably wasn't as good as we — all of our citizens needed."[58]

Some citizens of New Orleans believed that a mandatory evacuation should have been called earlier and that the government needed to assist people to evacuate. New Orleans citizen and evacuee Doreen Keeler testified, "[i]f a mandatory evacuation [order] would have been called sooner, it would have been easier to move seniors

AF PHOTO/MARI DARR-WELCH

out of the area and many lives would have been saved."[59] She further testified that "[g]oing to [senior citizens] with, yo, this is a mandatory evacuation, you do not have a choice, you have to leave, I feel would definitely help me to get my senior citizens out without waiting as long as I did in order to leave. And I think that if by some miracle there was any type of evacuation plan available, it could have been put into play earlier if a mandatory evacuation had been called."[60]

New Orleans citizen and community leader Dyan French asked: "Why would you get in the public media and ask a city, where 80 percent of its citizens ride public transit, to evacuate? What [were] they supposed to do? Fly?"[61] New Orleans citizen and evacuee Terrol Williams observed, "I think, unfortunately, a lot of the destruction that we saw, that persons were unable to safely evacuate, was because they were basically poor,"[62] which was echoed by Doreen Keeler: "They suffered through it because they had no way of getting out."[63]

New Orleans citizen and evacuee Leah Hodges complained that "[t]he stray animals from the animal shelter, most of whom would have been euthanized, were evacuated 2 days before the storm, and the people were left to die. Buses that could have gotten our people, who otherwise could not get out, were left to flood, and people were left to die."[64] And Barbara Arnwine, Executive Director for the Lawyers Committee for Civil Rights, testified: "We know that people were not able to evacuate because some people just didn't own cars."[65]

In contrast to New Orleans, officials in adjoining Plaquemines Parish cited their early declaration of a mandatory evacuation as the key to achieving a high evacuation rate. Plaquemines Parish President Benny Rousselle (according to Plaquemines Parish Sheriff Jiff Hingle) declared a mandatory evacuation on television at 9:00 a.m. on Saturday, August 27.[66] Sheriff's deputies started working the intersections to turn off traffic lights and expedite outbound traffic.[67] On Sunday, August 28, Placquemines Parish Sheriff's deputies went door-to-door to warn people to evacuate and to identify those who needed help doing so.[68] Hingle said these efforts resulted in Plaquemines Parish having an evacuation rate of 97 to 98 percent, which helped account for the small number of fatalities there — only three.[69]

The shelter of last resort for those who could not or would not evacuate was inadequate

A critical part of evacuation planning is accounting for those who cannot evacuate on their own, including those without access to private transportation. State and local emergency operations plans task transportation agencies with primary responsibility to assemble buses and other resources to operate this response function. For example, Alabama's Mobile County EOP states: "The principle mode of transportation during an emergency situation will be private vehicles. There will be citizens in Mobile County that do not have private vehicles nor are able to obtain transportation. These people will be looking to the City and County government to provide this emergency transportation. The Mobile County Emergency Management Agency has been given the responsibility of managing and coordinating this task."[70] An annex to the Baldwin and Mobile County plans is more explicit:

> Evacuation preparedness plans consider all persons who do not have access to a private vehicle and therefore would have to rely on public transportation for evacuation. Local governments

attempt to arrange for adequate resources to meet the demand for public transportation. Planning for adequate special needs emergency transportation for residents in private homes is usually the responsibility of local emergency management officials, while transportation for those in health-related facilities is the responsibility of the individual facilities. Although detailed information concerning residents of private homes may be difficult to obtain, each local government is developing procedures for maintaining an up-to-date roster of persons likely to need special assistance. Non-ambulatory patients will require transportation that can easily accommodate wheelchairs, stretchers, and, possibly, life-sustaining equipment. Lack of resources for these needs could result in critical evacuation delays and increased hazards for the evacuees. The Special Needs population for each county changes from year to year and requires public cooperation and assistance to maintain an up-to-date listing.[71]

Similarly, the New Orleans Plan specifically addresses the issue of those without access to transportation. The plan states that "[s]pecial arrangements will be made to evacuate persons unable to transport themselves…. Additional personnel will be recruited to assist in evacuation procedures as needed."[72] The New Orleans Plan further warns that "[i]f an evacuation order is issued without the mechanisms needed to disseminate the information to the affected persons, then we face the possibility of having large numbers of people either stranded and left to the mercy of the storm, or left in areas impacted by toxic materials."[73]

Specifically, the New Orleans Plan provides that "[t]ransportation will be provided to those persons requiring public transportation from the area," placing the Regional Transit Authority as the lead agency for transportation, supported by multiple federal, state, and local agencies, including the Orleans Parish School Board, New Orleans Equipment Maintenance Division, Louisiana Department of Transportation, Louisiana National Guard, Port of New Orleans, U.S. Coast Guard, New Orleans Public Belt Railroad, and Amtrak.[74] The tasks allotted to the RTA include: "plac[ing] special vehicles on alert to be utilized if needed[,] [p]osition[ing] supervisors and dispatch[ing] evacuation buses [and i]f warranted by scope of evacuation, implement[ing] additional service."[75] The New Orleans Plan expressly acknowledges that "[a]pproximately 100,000 Citizens of New Orleans do not have means of personal transportation."[76] Following the mandatory evacuation order, city officials sent the police and fire department through the city "asking" people to go to checkpoints where buses circulating through the city would pick them up — but only to take them to the Superdome which had been opened as a refuge of last resort that day.[77]

Despite the New Orleans Plan's acknowledgement that there are people who cannot evacuate by themselves, the city did not make arrangements for their evacuation. Instead, city officials decided to shelter them in New Orleans. As stated previously, emergency planners prefer evacuation to sheltering, because the sheltered population is subject to the most intense dangers of the storm. Evacuation is also favored because it may be slow and difficult to get relief personnel and supplies back into hurricane ravaged areas.

In addition, New Orleans preparations for sheltering these individuals were woefully inadequate. On Sunday

morning, New Orleans officials, instead of working to move individuals out of New Orleans and out of harm's way, were drafting a plan to seize private facilities to create additional "refuges of last resort."[78] Ultimately, city officials designated only the Superdome as such a refuge.

As will be discussed later in this chapter, the Superdome proved to be inadequate for the crowds that had to take refuge there. Only at the last minute did the City ask for food and water and medical personnel for the Superdome. As discussed in the MEDICAL CARE chapter, some of the federal medical assistance teams were called in so late they did not make it to the Superdome before landfall. On Sunday morning, the New Orleans Director of Homeland Security, Terry Ebbert, predicted "nightmare" conditions in the Superdome.[79]

Individuals share the blame for incomplete evacuation

The role of the individual was also an important factor in metropolitan New Orleans' incomplete evacuation. In Louisiana, state and parish officials said that it is generally the individual's responsibility to evacuate or identify themselves as having special needs if they need help. State and parish officials noted varying degrees of cooperation with evacuations among the individuals in the general population. They said many residents evacuate early on their own, even before an evacuation is declared. These individuals watch the weather reports when a hurricane is in the Gulf and make their own informed choices.

Some residents play "hurricane roulette."

Officials know from experience, however, that some percentage (from 10-25 percent) will not evacuate. The Governor and other state officials said some residents play "hurricane roulette."[80] That is, against the advice of the authorities, they stay and take the risk that the hurricane will hit somewhere else or that they will be lucky and relatively unaffected.

Select Committee staff heard similar comments in Mississippi. Testimony from county emergency management officials as well as Mississippi's governor indicated that "hurricane fatigue" as well as the expense of repeatedly evacuating when storms threaten may have caused some to not heed the mandatory evacuation orders. For example, Barbour testified that various areas in the state had undergone mandatory evacuations for Hurricane Ivan in 2004 and Hurricane Dennis earlier in 2005, but in both instances the storms ultimately made landfall farther east, sparing Mississippi.[81]

Both state and parish officials in Louisiana said the older population, some of whom might be classified as special needs, make up a substantial portion of those playing "hurricane roulette." They said there are a few reasons for this. First, many of the older residents had experience "sitting out" earlier hurricanes such as Betsy (1965) or Camille (1969) and reasoned they could "sit out" Katrina. Second, some of them were just "set in their ways" and would not listen to others' advice, even that of their own adult children, to evacuate. In addition, Katrina was originally headed for the Florida Panhandle, and its turn to the west caught many residents by surprise. Finally, it was the end of the month, when people did not have money for gas to evacuate.[82]

Regardless of their reasons for not evacuating, those that had the means to evacuate and did not do so must share some of the blame. Many of these people paid for their poor choices with their lives — as rising floodwaters drown them in their homes. Others who stayed, but could have left, suffered the less severe consequences of walking through floodwaters to crowded shelters or other high ground. These individuals suffered in horrible conditions — some with shelter and food and water and some without any of these — while they awaited evacuation, which they could have done for themselves earlier.

Finding: The incomplete pre-landfall evacuation led to deaths, thousands of dangerous rescues, and horrible conditions for those who remained

AP PHOTO/PAUL SANCYA

Failure of complete evacuation resulted in hundreds of deaths and severe suffering for thousands

Contrary to Blanco's claim that "[t]he word 'mandatory' doesn't mean any more than us getting up, saying, get out[,]"[83] the delay in calling a mandatory evacuation and not enforcing or facilitating that evacuation had real consequences for the city and for the protection of

"Hurricane Fatigue" — May have caused some people to not heed the mandatory evacuation orders.

A FAILURE OF INITIATIV

ordinary people. As noted above, many residents believed that an earlier declaration of a mandatory evacuation would have helped get more people out. The President of the Louisiana Nursing Home Association also told Select Committee staff that at least one nursing home had been unable to evacuate its patients prelandfall because it could not find bus drivers by the time the mandatory evacuation order was issued.[84]

While these warnings were sufficient to motivate more than a million citizens to evacuate using the state's revised, well-planned and executed, phased contraflow evacuation plan, more than 70,000 people did not evacuate.[85] Those who did not evacuate were exposed first to the dangers of drowning in the flood waters after the breach of the levees and then to deprivation of food, water, and shelter as they awaited rescue from other locations.

The anticipated flooding of New Orleans, unfortunately, occurred in an environment where a population of more than 70,000 had not evacuated, with thousands of these people remaining in their homes. Hundreds of these people died as floodwaters enveloped low lying neighborhoods in waters above the roof lines.[86] In tours of the affected areas, Select Committee staff noted the debris lines from the floodwaters were halfway up the roof of many single-story houses in St. Bernard Parish. The parish Director of Homeland Security and Emergency Preparedness Larry Ingargiola told Select Committee staff that during the storm, he had answered emergency cell phone calls from desperate people trapped in their attics, who had no way to escape the rising floodwaters.[87]

As stated before, many of these deaths were the result of hurricane roulette — individuals making decisions not to evacuate, or, for the poor population and those who procrastinated, not to seek shelter in the Superdome or other refuges of last resort in other parishes. As discussed in the MEDICAL CARE chapter,, there were also many deaths among those in medical and nursing home facilities.

An analysis of these deaths indicates that the flooding had a broad impact across all neighborhoods in New Orleans and the immediate surrounding parishes. The Knight Ridder news organization, using preliminary data from the Louisiana Department of Health and Hospitals, reviewed the location, ethnicity, sex and age of the victims. The results of their analysis were published in the Baton Rouge *Advocate* newspaper on December 30, 2005.[88] According to the analysis, "[t]he bodies of at least 588 people were recovered in neighborhoods that engineers say would have remained largely dry land had the [levees] not given way. . . ."[89] However, according to Orleans Parish coroner Dr. Frank Minyard, "[t]he cause of death for many will never be known because their bodies were too badly decomposed by the time they were recovered."[90] Dr. Minyard, however, did estimate that 20 percent of Katrina's New Orleans victims drowned,[91] and scores of others died of other causes awaiting rescue, trapped by floodwaters. Similarly, St. Bernard Parish Coroner, Dr. Bryan Bertucci, is cited as saying that most of the parish's 123 victims drowned in their homes.[92]

The analysis found that the victims of Hurricane Katrina were roughly proportionate to the pre-landfall population (based on census data) in terms of ethnicity, sex, and wealth. In terms of ethnicity, the dead in New Orleans were 62 percent black, compared to 66 percent for the total parish population.[93] The dead in St. Bernard Parish were 92 percent white, compared to 88 percent of the total parish population.[94] The percentage of the dead by sex was approximately the same as the overall population.[95] In terms of wealth, the analysis found that the percentage of dead bodies found in poorer New Orleans and St. Bernard Parish neighborhoods—as measured by poverty rates and median household incomes—was roughly equivalent to their percentage in the overall population.[96]

The finding about wealthier residents comports with statements by Louisiana First Assistant Attorney General Nicholas Gachassin, Jr. who said that many New Orleans area residents with the wealth and the means to evacuate and who decided not to do so paid for that decision with their lives.[97] Gachassin said that there were approximately 250,000 vehicles left in New Orleans, which he said demonstrated that there were many people with the means to leave the city who chose not to do so.[98] Similarly, the *Advocate* article stated that "at many of the addresses where the dead were found, their cars remained in their driveways, flood-ruined symbols of fatal miscalculation."[99]

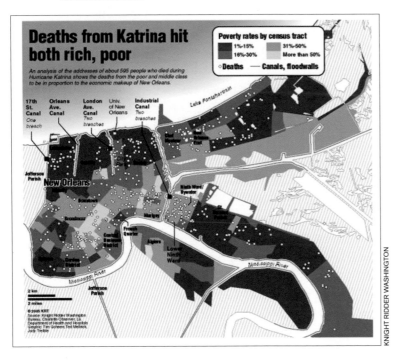

Failure of complete evacuations required heroic search and rescue efforts

The fortunate ones — among those who had stayed in their homes — were those that were able to climb to their roofs or flee into flooded streets. Many of these individuals had to use tools or other objects to chop through their roofs to escape the rising floodwaters. Thousands of these people were saved by a massive and heroic search and rescue effort. The U.S. Coast Guard alone reported that it rescued more than 33,000.[100] The Louisiana National Guard reported initial rescues of more than 25,000.[101] These people were pulled out of the floodwaters into boats or plucked from roofs into helicopters operated by a wide array of government agencies, non-governmental organizations, and citizen volunteers. State rescuers included personnel from the Department of Wildlife and Fisheries, local police, and the National Guard.[102] Federal rescue personnel included the Coast Guard, the Department of Defense, and several law enforcement agencies. All 28 of FEMA's Urban Search and Rescue teams (who come from a variety of states and local governments across the nation) were also involved in the rescues. The chapters on THE MILITARY and LAW ENFORCEMENT have more details on the search and rescue efforts by the military and law enforcement, respectively.

STATE OF LOUISIANA

The massive search and rescue effort, while necessary under the circumstances, distracted emergency managers and diverted key assets from other critical missions. According to National Guard officials involved in search and rescue, the entire focus of Monday and Tuesday was on saving lives; that was the Governor's top priority.[103] While the Select Committee does not question Blanco's urgency and priority on saving lives *after* the flooding took place, the same urgency and priority on a more complete evacuation of New Orleans *before* the flooding would have saved lives. If there had been a more complete evacuation, the number of flood victims requiring search and rescue would have been greatly reduced. This would have allowed federal, state, and local emergency response officials to focus earlier on re-establishing communications and situational awareness, and moving commodities into hard hit parishes beyond New Orleans. Many of the helicopters used for search and rescue could have been utilized for these tasks.

Those in shelters or on high ground suffered through horrible conditions

Those who escaped to shelters or high ground suffered horrible conditions at a number of locations including the Superdome, the Convention Center, and the Cloverleaf, where they arrived through a number of different means. Some had walked or driven before landfall, some had walked after the floodwaters reached their homes, and some had been dropped off by search and rescue boats or helicopters. Each of the locations had their own miserable conditions.

New Orleans opened the Superdome as a "refuge of last resort."[104] As such, it was set up to allow people to survive a storm passing over; it was not intended to house, feed, and water thousands of people for several days. A cadre of more than 200 New Orleans Police and the Louisiana National Guard searched all people entering the Superdome for weapons and contraband.[105] In addition, FEMA and the National Guard had prepositioned food and water in the Superdome, and some additional food and water was trucked in at the last minute.[106] Some of the people arriving had listened to the Mayor's suggestion and had brought a three day supply of food and water, sleeping bags, and clothes. Those who came to the Superdome after the flooding brought nothing but the clothes on their backs.

The conditions in the Superdome soon deteriorated. The initial calm situation Sunday night changed early Monday morning when the dome's roof opened up and the building lost power. While the Superdome was still structurally sound, the hole in the roof scared people; it made noise and water started coming in.[107] The National Guard had to suddenly move thousands of people from the field up into the seating sections.[108] Later, after the flooding, the power went out across the city.

Without power, the only lighting in the Superdome was emergency lighting that ran off the emergency generator. This was not the same as full lighting, and with no power, the air conditioning was also not working. Related to the power outage, the water system went out, causing the toilets to back up, creating an awful stench that grew progressively worse as the days wore on.

Many people could not stand the heat and smell and gathered outside on the surrounding walkway area, which thus became very crowded. Although the situation was bad and deteriorating, there was never a shortage of food and water; they were distributed twice a day at first and continuously later.[109] In general, people were hot, it smelled, and they were anxious to leave. This deteriorating situation led to the increasing urgency among officials and the population to evacuate the Superdome.[110]

Conditions were also unbearable in the Convention Center. The Select Committee was unable to determine exactly when the Convention Center became a shelter and when officials became aware of the deteriorating

AP PHOTO/RON HAVIV/VII

AP PHOTO/DAVID J. PHILLIP

People initially went to the Convention Center after the breaches of the levees late Monday night or early Tuesday morning. As the floodwaters rose, people left their homes and headed for higher ground. The Convention Center is near the Mississippi River levee, one of the higher elevation in New Orleans. The National Guard estimated that there were 19,000 people there.[114] Conditions in the Convention Center were notably worse than the Superdome in several ways. Like the Superdome, the Convention Center had no electrical power, no lighting, no air conditioning, and no functioning toilets. But unlike the Superdome, the Convention Center had no authorities or security on hand no weapon screening, no food and no water.[115]

AP PHOTO/ERIC GAY

AP PHOTO/ERIC GAY

conditions there. None of the officials who spoke with the Select Committee staff were willing to take responsibility for the operation of the Convention Center as a "shelter," and none claimed that they knew about the situation until Wednesday morning or afternoon, August 31.

While these officials stated that the Convention Center was never designated as a shelter like the Superdome, Mayor Nagin's testimony suggested that the city had sanctioned that location. In his prepared statement, the mayor stated that "[t]he swelling crowd at the Superdome and the number of people needing shelter required us to open the Convention Center as another refuge."[111] Brown was widely criticized for saying on Thursday night that he only found out that afternoon about the people at the Convention Center.[112] Late that same night, however, the city of New Orleans finally requested that the National Guard secure and evacuate the Convention Center in conjunction with the New Orleans Police Department the next day.[113]

Other high ground spots became spontaneous gathering points with miserable conditions. Many people went to these locations on their own, because their houses were flooded and they were looking for dry land. In addition, many people were dropped off at these sites by rescuers. Because of initial emphasis on saving lives, people were just dumped off there by helicopters or boats without any initial concerns for providing them with food or water.

Unlike the Superdome or the Convention Center, there was no shelter from the sweltering sun. Specific locations

A FAILURE OF INITIATIV

here evacuees found themselves included the Cloverleaf (where two highways met), the Industrial Canal levees, the Mississippi River levees, and Broad Street levees. These locations had generally not been manned with security personnel such as police, nor had there been any plans to supply them with food, water, or medical treatment.

MA

The "Cloverleaf" on the interstate was one of the worst locations. The site was being used for medical triage and evacuation, so there was initially some food and water there, at least for the medical patients. However, additional people arrived on their own or by the helicopters or boats that rescued them from the water. The supply of food and water was not sufficient for the crowd, which eventually grew to 6,000-7,000 people.[116]

Flooding further hampered relief efforts for those not initially evacuating

Efforts to provide relief to those stranded at the Superdome, Convention Center, the Cloverleaf, and other positions of high ground were stymied by the floodwaters. Simple tasks, such as trucking food and water to these locations, were complicated by flooded highways that necessitated the use of high clearance vehicles or long detours. Some of these sites were very difficult to supply or evacuate later because they were "islands" completely surrounded by water. As mentioned in the COMMUNICATIONS and the COMMAND AND CONTROL chapters, the lack of communications, situational awareness, command and control, and effective logistics systems further hampered efforts to identify many of these locations and coordinate relief. The floodwaters also complicated efforts to conduct a post landfall evacuation, as discussed in the next section.

Finding: Federal, state, and local officials' failure to anticipate the post-landfall conditions delayed post-landfall evacuation and support

Federal, state, and local officials had not prepared for post landfall evacuation despite predictions of extensive flooding

While these victims endured horrendous conditions, hundreds of city buses and school buses that could have been used for evacuation sat useless, flooded or without drivers. Nagin testified that the school buses belong to the New Orleans school district and, to his credit, he is now considering a cooperative agreement with the school district to move the school buses out of the area for the next storm.[117] Nagin also testified that the RTA buses were "always staged, or have been staged, in an area that has been high and dry throughout every storm that has ever hit the City of New Orleans; and we expected the same for this event. Unfortunately, those buses flooded also because 80 percent of the city went under water."[118] He testified that he had had trouble getting drivers even for the 20 buses that had taken residents to the Superdome prelandfall "because most [drivers] had evacuated" and that the National Guard was not available to drive buses.[119]

FEMA

By the time Hurricane Katrina made landfall at 6:10 a.m. central time on Monday, August 29, approximately 10-12,000 people were sheltered in the Superdome.[120] The massive flooding led to urgent search and rescue operations throughout the city and in other parishes as well. Those search and rescue operations moved tens of thousands of people off of their roofs and out of the flood waters to shelter or high ground. As the flood waters rose, people also self-evacuated from the city to the Superdome, the Convention Center, and other high ground around the city.

As previously noted, the Governor and the Mayor were well aware of the probability of levee breaches and flooding in New Orleans following a Category 4 or 5 hurricane. Federal officials were also aware of that probability. When Brown was asked by Select Committee Member Congressman Hal Rogers: "Was it known by you and others that the flood wall around New Orleans was only rated to take a category 3 hurricane,"[121] he replied, "Yes. That was a fact that came out in [the Hurricane Pam Exercise] that the levees may or may not hold, that the storm surge may or may not top them, they could top — the storm surge could top the levees without breaking and they could top and also break the levees. So we knew both of those were potential."[122] As Vice Mayor of Newport News, Virginia, and city planner Charles Allen testified before the Select Committee: "[I]t is clear from information in the news that the U.S. Government, in the form of the U.S. Weather Service [sic], the Federal Emergency Management Agency, and the U.S. Corps of Engineers [sic] understood the magnitude of this storm."[123]

Planning for the post landfall evacuation had to be done in emergency environment

Despite the advance knowledge of extensive flooding, the first task order for buses by the federal government to evacuate New Orleans post landfall was not issued until 1:30 a.m. on Wednesday, August 31.[124] Although Blanco claims that Brown told her that he had 500 buses standing by and that she was concerned when those buses did not materialize sooner,[125] the Select Committee found no other evidence that any such buses were, in fact, "standing by" or that Brown had made such a statement to Blanco.

Developing a plan to evacuate the Superdome and other locations after the flooding was a complicated endeavor. That planning included determining the number of buses needed, accessible routes to the

FEMA

Superdome and other locations, security needs, and the ultimate destination of those evacuated. This planning occurred in a highly degraded environment that included limited communications that prevented a full understanding of the scope of the needs and even the visibility of deployed resources. Repeatedly, during the daily video teleconferences, state and federal officials expressed their frustrations with the level of communications.[126]

In assessing the needs for the Superdome alone, Homeland Security Operations Center (HSOC) Spot Report Number 30, prepared at 2:00 a.m. on Wednesday, August 31, (even after the federal task order for buses) reflects that (1) there are 12-15,000 people at the Superdome, (2) the water is not rising as rapidly as previously feared, (3) the loss of electricity does not appear imminent, (3) the intention was to begin evacuations that day and continue them over the next few days, (4) alternate shelters have not been identified, and (5) two days of food and water is on hand.[127] According to that document, neither the means of egress to the buses for the Superdome population nor the alternative location to which they would be evacuated had been determined.[128] Options for egress from the Superdome included walking once the State Police can verify a route, constructing temporary bridging, "construct[ing] a sandbag dyke to allow for walk[ing] out," "us[ing] DOD landing craft to shuttle . . . to buses," and using helicopters for short flights to buses.[129] Alternative shelter included "stadiums in the State college system but other options are possible."[130] As we now know, many of the buses took people to the Astrodome in Houston. But as of Wednesday morning, FEMA officials were still concerned that Blanco had not spoken to Texas Governor Rick Perry to confirm that part of the plan.[131]

The planning process for the post-landfall evacuation did not really begin until Tuesday, August 30. Blanco testified that she did not realize the full consequences of the levee breaches until Tuesday morning, when she was able to travel to New Orleans and see the effects of the flooding for those sheltered in the Superdome.[132] At the noon video teleconference, Smith asks only that

[Y]ou realize what's going on and the sense of urgency here needs to be ratcheted up. Everybody is being fully cooperative, but in the deployment of some of these Federal assets, especially transportation for the evacuation effort that we're trying to coordinate, we don't need anything to slow that down. The push of the resources and so forth to date has not been an issue, but we don't need to let it become an issues [sic] because we're going to literally have tens of thousands of people that we've got to push these supplies too [sic].[133]

Later that day and into the evening, FEMA official Phil Parr and others sheltered in the Superdome, apparently unaware of the evacuation planning at the EOC, began their own planning to evacuate the Superdome as they observed the rising waters around the building and realized that people would not be able to walk out of the dome and return home.[134] According to Parr, the team inside the Superdome devised a plan involving the use of helicopters to airlift people away from the Superdome. They concluded that they needed at least nine helicopters, of which the Louisiana National Guard had three.[135]

They communicated this plan to the FEMA Regional Response Center (FEMA RRC) in Denton, Texas and got initial approval for it, with the RRC searching for the assets to implement it.[136] They believed their plan would have been able to move virtually all of the evacuees from the Superdome at that time in about 30 hours.[137] The next day, Parr learned that Commander of Joint Task Force Katrina Lt. General Russel L. Honoré had stopped that plan as he came to Louisiana to lead Joint Task Force Katrina.[138]

At the same time, there remained some doubt about the consequences of the levee breaches. General Don Riley of the Army Corps of Engineers reported at the noon video teleconference on Tuesday, August 30, that "[t]he lake [Pontchartrain] level may recede quickly enough before we can get anything in there [to fill the breach] and then we can turn that pump station on with the city and turn that water around and pump it back into the lake.[139] FEMA Federal Coordinating Officer (FCO) Bill Lokey discussed at the same video teleconference that they were "developing the distribution plan [for commodities] that we can get them out to the communities as the water does recede in some areas . . . ."[140] The FEMA Acting Director for Response during Hurricane Katrina, Ed Buikema, also said that on Tuesday and Wednesday, August 30 and 31, there was still some hope that the breaches in the levees could be repaired quickly.[141]

By the Wednesday, noon video teleconference, the numbers at the Superdome had swollen to approximately 23,000.[142] Reggie Johnson from the U.S. Department of Transportation reported that there were 455 buses under contract and "it looks like we've got about 200 that are currently in place, with the remainder that should be coming in on a staggered basis."[143] The next day, Johnson reported:

120 buses . . . departed for [the] Houston Astrodome last night. And there are 300 buses in the New Orleans area. You may not see those because actually they're staging at what's called the Poker Palace Texaco refueling site, and that's in a place in Louisiana, and I understand that they are drawing down from that site. They're bringing in about 40 buses at a time. There are 155 buses that were requested, and they are en route and should arrive at the truck stop by midnight tonight. We have not received any other requests . . . .[144]

1 State of LA and U.S. Dep't of Homeland Security, <u>Louisiana Citizen Awareness & Disaster Evacuation Guide</u> [hereinafter *LA Evacuation Flyer*]; *see also,* State of LA, <u>Emergency Operations Plan,</u> (Apr. 2005) [hereinafter *LA State Plan*]; <u>Supplement 1A: Emergency Operations Plan:</u> <u>Southeast Louisiana Hurricane Evacuation and Sheltering Plan</u> (Rev. Jan. 2000) [hereinafter *LA State Evacuation Plan*].

2 City of New Orleans, <u>Comprehensive Emergency Management Plan,</u> (2004) at 51 [hereinafter *New Orleans Plan*].

3 *Id.*

4 *Id.*

5 *Id.* at 54.

6 *Id.* at 48.

7 *Id.* at 50.

8 *Hearing on Hurricane Katrina: Preparedness and Response by the State of Mississippi Before Select Comm.,* 109th Cong. (2005) at 63-64 (statements by Haley Barbour, Governor of MS, and Robert R. Latham, Jr., Exec. Dir., MS EMA) [hereinafter *Dec. 7, 2005 Select Comm. Hearing*].

9 *Id.*

10 *Id.* at 34 (statement of Robert R. Latham, Jr., Exec. Dir., MS EMA).

11 *Hearing on Hurricane Katrina: Preparedness and Response by the State of Alabama Before Select Comm.,* 109th Cong. (2005) at 46 (statement of Bob Riley, Governor of AL) [hereinafter *Nov. 9, 2005 Select Comm. Hearing*].

12 *Id.* at 122-123 (statement of Bruce Baughman, Dir., AEMA).

13 Director's Brief, Director of MS Emergency Management Agency, Brief as of 1900 hours, Aug. 28, 2005 (MEMA -0010688) (Aug. 28, 2005) at

14 *Dec. 7, 2005 Select Comm. Hearing* at 2 (written statement of Brent Warr); *see also id.* at 157 (statement of Benjamin J. Spraggins, Dir., Harrison County EMA).

15 *Id.* at 64, 74 (statement of Haley Barbour).

16 Director's Brief, Director of Mississippi Emergency Management Agency, Brief as of 1900 hours, Aug. 28, 2005 (MEMA -0010688) (Aug. 28, 2005) at 3.

17 *See generally,* Director's Brief, Director of Mississippi Emergency Management Agency, Brief as of 0430 hours, Aug. 29, 2005 (MEMA -0010696 (Aug. 29, 2005).

18 September 27 hearing at 68-9.

19 *Id.* at 70.

20 Meeting Summaries, FEMA Regional Emergency Liaison Team Conference Calls (Aug. 28, 2005 – Sept. 02, 2005).

21 Baldwin County, AL, Hurricane Katrina Time Line of Events (Doc. No. 002553AL). The notation on the Time Line reads "volunteer evacuation" which Select Comm. Staff interpreted as a "voluntary evacuation."

22 Memo to Files, Alabama Emergency Management Agency EM/2000 Tracker System message 05-1675, (Aug. 28, 2005). Two days before the request for a mandatory evacuation in Alabama, AEMA officials had already requested transportation assistance for purposes of coordinating evacuation traffic flow out of Florida. Memo to Files, Alabama Emergency Management Agency EM/2000 Tracker System message 05-1611, (created Aug. 26, 2005; completed Aug. 28, 2005).

23 Press Release, Office of Gov. of AL, Governor Riley Orders Evacuation for Parts of Mobile and Baldwin Counties (Doc. No. 002580AL); Press Release, Office of Gov. of AL, Governor Riley Orders Evacuation for Parts of Mobile and Baldwin Counties (Aug. 28, 2005), *available at* http:// www.governorpress.alabama.gov/pr/pr-2005-08-28-02-katrina_evac_order.asp (last visited Jan 21, 2006).

24 *Nov. 9, 2005 Select Comm. Hearing* at 28 (statement of Bob Riley).

25 Memo to Files, Evacuee Population Presently in AL by County as of 9/28/05, AL Emergency Management Agency (Oct. 10, 2005) (Doc. No. 002576AL).

26 *Hearing on Hurricane Katrina: Preparedness and Response by the State of Louisiana Before Select Comm.,* 109th Cong. (2005) at 67 (statement of Kathleen Babineaux Blanco) (Blanco: "I am very happy to talk about our evacuation process, because it is the one thing that we did masterfully.") [hereinafter *Dec. 14, 2005 Select Comm. Hearing*]; *id.* at 94 (statement of Kathleen Babineaux Blanco, Governor of LA) (Chairman Davis: "This was the most successful evacuation you ever had, right?" Blanco: "Absolutely without a doubt.").

27 *Id.* at 68-69 (statement of Jeff Smith, State Coordinating Officer and Deputy Dir., LA Office of Homeland Security and Emergency Preparedness).

28 *Dec. 7, 2005 Select Comm. Hearing* at 61 (statement of Haley Barbour).

29 *See* Audio recordings of Hurricane Katrina Conference Calls, Louisiana State Emergency Operations Center (Aug. 26-28, 2005).

30 *Dec. 14, 2005 Select Comm. Hearing* at 138 (statement of Kathleen Babineaux Blanco).

31 *Id.* at 88 (statement of Jeff Smith). However, despite this insistence that forcing people out of their homes prelandfall was not an option, it was apparently still a very live option post landfall and may have been carried out, even if not ordered. *See* E-mail correspondence from John Jordan, Military Assistant to then FEMA Director Michael Brown, to Michael Brown, et al. (Sept. 4, 2005) (10:33 a.m.) ("Appears state is reluctant to execute a true mandatory evacuation – i.e., forced if necessary. Therefore, State is pushing for shelters (includes all life support) in [New Orleans] to house citizens that will not leave voluntarily."); *see* E-mail correspondence from John Jordan, Military Assistant to then FEMA Director Michael Brown, to Michael Brown, et al. (Sept. 5, 2005) (9:13 a.m.) ("Governor Blanco has decided not to force any evacuations in New Orleans. Resident are still encouraged to evacuate. Buses were sent through NO on previously in deified evac routes today and no additional residents would board buses for voluntary evacuation. It appears that the evacuation phase of operations is winding down or may be completed. Since FEMA did not anticipate reversal of decision for mandatory evacuation, crisis-action planning is now underway to provide this support."); *see* E-mail correspondence from John Jordan, Military Assistant to then FEMA Director Michael Brown, to Michael Brown, et al. (Sept. 5, 2005) (10:04 a.m.) ("Evacuations are slowing to a trickle."); *see* E-mail correspondence from John Jordan, Military Assistant to then FEMA Director Michael Brown, to Michael Brown, et al. (Sept. 6, 2005) (11:17 a.m.) ("Decision by Governor Blanco to not force any evacuations in New Orleans remains in place. Mayor of New Orleans is not forcing evacuations in NO and is not prohibiting residents from returning. Residents are still strongly encouraged to evacuate. . . . [S]ince NO is not being fully evacuated, requirements exist to provide all commodities to the remaining population."). *See also Hearing on Hurricane Katrina: Voices from inside the Storm Before Select*

Comm., 109th Cong. (2005) at 18 (statement of Terrol Williams) ("I was [in my mother's home] for about a week until September 8th or so, at which point a rescue crew comprised of State and local police as well as armed military officers forced me to evacuate. They arrived in a truck and two tanks and confiscated my weapons. I didn't resist them, and the officers weren't rough with me . . . . The rescue team took me to the Convention Center . . . . and from there I was immediately taken by helicopter to the airport. The next morning I was put on a Delta 757 airplane. . . . Passengers weren't told where they were going until after the plane had taken off.") [hereinafter *Dec. 6, 2005 Select Comm. Hearing*].

See ALA. CODE §§ 31-9-6 (4); 31-9-8 (4); 31-9-14 and 31-9-15 (2005).

Id. at 22 (statement of Bob Riley).

Dec. 14, 2005 Select Comm. Hearing at 65 (statement of Hal Rogers) ("Saturday evening at 7:30, Max Mayfield, the head of the National Hurricane Warning Center, personally, for the second time in his 36-year career, personally, called the mayor [of New Orleans] and the [Louisiana] Governor, all the Governors, by phone to reiterate the severity of this upcoming storm. 8 p.m., Mayfield telephones Mayor Nagin."); *see also id.* at 72 (statement of Kathleen Babineaux Blanco) ("On Saturday morning, indeed, Max Mayfield didn't call until – in fact he didn't call until Saturday night.").

Press Conference by C. Ray Nagin, Mayor of New Orleans, and Kathleen Babineaux Blanco, Governor of LA, MSNBC, et al. Aug. 28, 2005 (Blanco: "Just before we walked into this room, President Bush called . . . and asked me to please ensure that there would be a mandatory evacuation of New Orleans.") [hereinafter Nagin-Blanco Press Conference].

Public Advisory, National Weather Center (New Orleans, LA), Urgent Weather Message: Devastating damage expected (Aug. 28, 2005; 10:11 a.m. CDT).

Interview of Kathleen Babineaux Blanco, CNN Saturday Night, (Aug. 28, 2005) (8:00 p.m. ET) (Blanco: "We are very concerned about the people in the City of New Orleans and some of the people in the region as well, who have not actually gotten the message. They went to bed last night thinking the hurricane was going to Florida. And some have just gotten busy in their day and not gotten – you know, had any media contact, and don't even know this is happening. So, we're hoping that by tonight, that they're watching you and getting the message that it's a real threat. It's very serious. We want them to get out of town.").

Id.

Gordon Russell, *Ground Zero*, TIMES-PIC. (New Orleans), Aug. 29, 2005 at 1.

Interview of Kathleen Babineaux Blanco, ABC News Good Morning America, (Aug. 28, 2005).

Interview of C. Ray Nagin, At Large with Geraldo Rivera, Fox News Channel, (Aug. 28, 2005) (10:00 p.m. ET).

Id.

Id.

Dec. 14, 2005 Select Comm. Hearing at 74 (statement of Kathleen Babineaux Blanco).

Id.

Mark Schleifstein, *Katrina Puts End to Lull*, TIMES-PIC. (New Orleans) Aug. 27, 2005 at 1.

Bruce Nolan, *Katrina Takes Aim*, TIMES-PIC. (New Orleans) Aug. 28, 2005 at 1.

Id.

Nagin-Blanco Press Conference.

New Orleans Plan at 12.

Id. at 48, 50.

Nagin-Blanco Press Conference (emphasis supplied).

Id. (emphasis supplied).

Audio recordings of Hurricane Katrina Conference Calls, Louisiana State Emergency Operations Center (Aug. 28, 2005) (12:00 p.m.) (statement of Aaron Broussard).

Nagin-Blanco Press Conference.

Dec. 14, 2005 Select Comm. Hearing (written statement of Jeff Smith). This figure was arrived at based upon the reported number of individuals evacuated by officials from New Orleans.

Id. at 162 (statement of C. Ray Nagin).

Id.

Dec. 6, 2005 Select Comm. Hearing at 23 (statement of Doreen Keeler).

Id. 90 (statement of Doreen Keeler).

Id. at 49-50 (statement of Dyan French).

Id. at 61 (statement of Terrol Williams).

Id. (statement of Doreen Keeler).

Id. at 64 (statement of Leah Hodges).

Id. at 137-138 (statement of Barbara Arnwine).

Interview by Select Comm. Staff with Sherriff Hingle, Plaquemines Parish Sherriff, in New Orleans, LA (Nov. 7, 2005).

Id.

Id.

Id.

Mobile County, AL, *Comprehensive Emergency Operations Plan*, Mobile County Emergency Mgmt. Agency (July 1, 2004) at FSF1-11.

Baldwin County, *Emergency Operations Plan*, Annex O: "Alabama Hurricane Evacuation Study, Technical Data Report for Mobile and Baldwin Counties" (May 2001).

New Orleans Plan at 50.

Id. at 45.

Id. at 50, 24.

Id. at 54.

Id. at 55.

[77] *Dec. 14, 2005 Select Comm. Hearing* at 172 (statement of Terry Ebbert, Dir. of Homeland Security, City of New Orleans).

[78] *See* Audio recordings of Hurricane Katrina Conference Calls, LA State Emergency Operations Center (Aug. 26-28, 2005).

[79] *Id.* (statement of Terry Ebbert).

[80] *Dec. 14, 2005 Select Comm. Hearing* at 73 (statement of Kathleen Babineaux Blanco).

[81] *Dec. 7, 2005 Select Comm. Hearing* at 62 (statement of Haley Barbour).

[82] *Hearing on Hurricane Katrina: The Role of the Federal Emergency Management Agency Before Select Comm.*, 109th Cong. (Sept. 27, 2005) at 67-69 (statements of Michael Brown and Gene Taylor) [hereinafter *Sept. 27, 2005 Select Comm. Hearing*].

[83] *Dec. 14, 2005 Select Comm. Hearing* at 74 (statement of Kathleen Babineaux Blanco).

[84] Interview by Select Comm. Staff with Joseph Donchesse (Pres., LA Nursing Home Assoc.) in Baton Rouge, LA (Nov. 10, 2005).

[85] *See generally Dec. 14, 2005 Select Comm. Hearing* (written statement of Jeff Smith).

[86] John Simerman, *Breaches took toll: N.O. ruin greatly increased*, ADVOCATE (Baton Rouge) Dec. 31, 2005 at 1A, 8A [hereinafter *Breaches Article*].

[87] Interview by Select Comm. Staff with Larry Ingargiola, St. Bernard Parish Director of Homeland Security and Emergency Prepaedness, in St. Bernard Parish, LA (Nov. 3, 2005).

[88] *Breaches Article*, 1A; *see also*, Knight Ridder Tribune News, *Most Katrina Victims Older; many white*, ADVOCATE (Baton Rouge) Dec. 30, 2005 at 9A [hereinafter *Analysis Article*].

[89] *Breaches Article* at 1A.

[90] *Breaches Article* at 8A.

[91] *Id.*

[92] *Id.*

[93] *Analysis Article* at 9A.

[94] *Id.*

[95] *Id.*

[96] *Id.* ("The comparison showed that 42 percent of the bodies found in Orleans and St. Bernard parishes were recovered in neighborhoods with poverty rates higher than 30 percent. That's only slightly higher than the 39 percent of residents who lived in such neighborhoods, according to the census data. Similarly, 31 percent of the bodies turned up in areas with poverty rates below 15 percent, where 30 percent of the population lived. The median household income in neighborhoods where Katrina victims were recovered was about $27,000 a year, just under the $29,000 median for the overall area. One-fourth of Katrina deaths fell in census tracts with median incomes above $35,300. One-fourth of the area's pre-storm population lived in tracts with median incomes above $37,000.").

[97] Interview by Select Comm. Staff with Nicholas Gachassin, Jr., First Assistant Attorney General, LA Department of Justice, in Baton Rouge, LA (Nov. 6, 2005).

[98] *Id.*

[99] *Analysis Article* at A3.

[100] *Hearing on Hurricane Katrina: Preparedness and Response by the Department of Defense, the Coast Guard, and the National Guard of Louisiana, Mississippi, and Alabama Before Select Comm.*, 109th Cong. (2005) at 2 (written statement of R. Dennis Sirois), [hereinafter *Oct. 27, 2005 Select Comm. Hearing*]; *see also id.* at 37 (statement of R. Dennis Siros).

[101] LA Nat. Guard, *Overview of Significant Events Hurricane Katrina* at 23-24 (Dec. 7, 2005) [hereinafter *LANG Overview*].

[102] *Dec. 14, 2005 Select Comm. Hearing* (written statement of Jeff Smith).

[103] *See* Interview by Select Comm. Staff with General Brod Veillon, LA National Guard Commander for Task Force Minnow, in New Orleans, LA (Nov. 3, 2005); *see also* Interview by Select Comm. Staff with Colonel Barry Keeling, LA National Guard Commander of Task Force Eagle, in New Orleans, LA (Nov. 3, 2005).

[104] Nagin-Blanco Press Conference (Nagin: "At noon today, the Superdome will then be opened up as a refuge of last resort, where we will start to take citizens that cannot evacuate.").

[105] *LANG Overview* at 6.

[106] *See* Interview by Select Comm. Staff with Jacques Thibodeaux (LtC, LA Nat'l Guard) in New Orleans (Nov. 3, 2005) [hereinafter Thibodeaux Interview]; *see* Interview by Select Comm. Staff with Mark Mouton (Col, LA Nat'l Guard) in New Orleans, LA (Nov. 3, 2005) [hereinafter Mouton Interview]; Interview by Select Comm. Staff with Scott Wells (Field Officer, FEMA) in Baton Rouge, LA (Nov. 9, 2005) [hereinafter Wells Interview]; *see also* E-mail correspondence from David Passey (Dep't Homeland Security) to Cindy Taylor (Dep't Homeland Security), et al. (Aug. 28, 2005) (Doc. No. DHS 007265) ("Seven trucks (5 water and 2 MREs) are less than 2 hours away from the Superdome.").

[107] Thibodeaux Interview; Mouton Interview.

[108] *Id.*

[109] *Id.*

[110] *Id.*

[111] *Dec. 14, 2005 Select Comm. Hearing* at 3 (written statement of C. Ray Nagin).

[112] *See FEMA Chief Mike Brown* (NPR: All Things Considered broadcast, Sept. 5, 2005) (playing audio clip from CNN interview by Paula Zahn, CNN anchor, and Michael Brown, FEMA Director:

"Mr. MICHAEL BROWN (FEMA Director): We just learned about that today. And so I have directed that we have all available resources to get to that Convention Center to make certain that they have the food and water. And I'll tell you...

Ms. PAULA ZAHN (CNN): But, sir, you're not telling me that you just...

Mr. BROWN: ...also—and I will tell you...

Ms. ZAHN: ...learned that the folks at the Convention Center didn't have food and water until today are you?

Mr. BROWN: Paula, the federal government did not even know about the Convention Center people until today [Thursday, Sept. 2,

2005]."); *see NBC Today Show* (NBC television broadcast Sept. 10, 2005) (New Orleans co-host, Lester Holt: "That's right Campbell. If you'll recall, Michael Brown, the head of FEMA, acknowledged it was about 24 hours after those first TV reports of people holed up here [the New Orleans Convention Center] without food, in need of water, that he found out about it. That opened him up to a lot of criticism."); *see,* Editorial Opinion, *Bush: First the Head of FEMA; Would you trust your safety to Michael Brown?,* DAILY NEWS (Phila.), Sept. 7, 2005, at 17 ("Here was a clueless bureaucrat [Mr. Brown] who didn't seem to believe the horror stories coming out of the New Orleans convention center."); *see, Leadership: Some tragedy avoidable,* CHARLESTON GAZ. (W. Va.), Sept. 3, 2005, at 4A ("FEMA Director Michael Brown admitted that he did not know until Thursday that thousands of people had been stranded at the New Orleans Convention Center for days without water of foods, as well as in the Superdome. How could he not know? Anyone listening to local radio knew.").

[3] LA Nat. Guard, *Timeline of Significant Events Hurricane Katrina* at 7 (Dec. 7, 2005) [hereinafter *LANG Timeline*].

[4] Thibodeaux Interview; Mouton Interview; *LANG Overview* at 23-24.

[5] Thibodeaux Interview; Mouton Interview.

[6] Interview by Select Comm. Staff with Gordon Mitchell (LA State Police) in Baton Rouge, LA (Nov. 4, 2005).

[7] *Dec. 14, 2005 Select Comm. Hearing* at 200, 202 (statement of C. Ray Nagin). It is important to remember, however, that the school district is already a support agency for transportation under the New Orleans Plan.

[8] *Id.* at 201 (statement of C. Ray Nagin). There was evidence that a portion of the RTA bus fleet was saved by being moved to the wharf by the Mississippi River. Email from Leo Bosner to Linda Mammett-Morgan, et. al., transmitting Final Version DHS 0230 Situation Report input for Sept. 2, 2005, Doc. No. DHS-FEMA-0051-03122-03151 at 03128 (Sept. 02, 2005). According to RTA General Manager William DeVille, 197 of the RTA's 372 buses were destroyed. *Hearing on Rebuilding Highway and Transit Infrastructure on the Gulf Coast following Hurricane Katrina: State and Local Officials Before House Subcomm. on Highways, Transit and Pipelines of the Comm. on Transportation and Infrastructure,* 109th Cong. (2005) (statement of William J. DeVille). Whether the buses were available or not, no drivers were apparently available.

[9] *Dec. 14, 2005 Select Comm. Hearing* at 201 (statement of C. Ray Nagin).

[0] Thibodeaux Interview; Mouton Interview.

[1] *Sept. 27, 2005 Select Comm. Hearing* at 57 (statement of Rep. Hal Rogers).

[2] *Id.* at 58 (statement of Michael Brown).

[3] *Dec. 6, 2005 Select Comm. Hearing* at 107 (statement of Charles Allen).

[4] E-mail correspondence from Tony Robinson, Response and Recover Division Director, FEMA, to Jeff Smith, Col. Dep. Dir. LA Off. of Homeland Security and Emergency Preparedness, (Sept. 15, 2005).

[5] *Dec. 14, 2005 Select Comm. Hearing* at 131 (statement of Kathleen Babineaux Blanco).

[6] *See generally* Daily Video Teleconferences amongst officials dated Aug. 25 – Sept. 4, 2005 [hereinafter "Daily VTC"]. State and local officials from each of the impacted areas met daily with officials from, among other agencies, FEMA, and the National Hurricane Center.

[7] Memorandum of Spot Report regarding FEMA Co-ordination Calls, Doc. No. DHS-FEMA-00510001220–21 (Aug. 31, 2005).

[8] *Id.*

[9] *Id.*

[0] *Id.*

[1] E-mail correspondence from Gary Jones, FEMA, to Edward Buikema, FEMA Acting Director for Response during Hurricane Katrina, (Aug. 31, 2005) ("Jack Colley just advised me that Gov Perry has not received a call from Gov Blanco regarding this plan [to move LA evacuees to the Houston Astro Dome]. Jack said he heard that she was going to make the call early this morning, again this has not happened.").

[2] *Dec. 14, 2005 Select Comm. Hearing* at 155-156 (statement of Kathleen Babineaux Blanco) (Chairman Davis: "One last question, when did you realize that the tens of thousands of people in the Superdome would have to be evacuated out of New Orleans . . . .?" Blanco: "I recognized it on Tuesday [Aug. 30], when I was able to do – well, I knew about it before, but I had, you know, with my own eyes, made an evaluation.").

[3] Daily VTC (Aug. 30, 2005) at 10.

[4] Interview by Select Comm. Staff with Phil Parr, Dep. Fed. Coord Officer, FEMA in Washington, DC (Dec. 8, 2005) [hereinafter "Parr Interview"]; *see generally Dec. 14, 2005 Select Comm. Hearing* (statement of Phil Parr).

[5] Parr Interview.

[6] *Id.*

[7] *Id.*

[8] *Id.*

[9] Daily VTC (Aug. 30, 2005) at 11-12.

[0] *Id.* at 14 (emphasis supplied).

[1] Interview by Select Comm. Staff with Edward Buikema, FEMA acting Director for Response during Hurricane Katrina, in Washington, DC (Jan. 6, 2006) [hereinafter "Buikema Interview"].

[2] Daily VTC (Aug. 31, 2005) at 3.

[3] *Id.* at 26.

[4] Daily VTC (Sept. 1. 2005) at 9.

[5] Executive Order, Louisiana Governor Kathleen Babineaux Blanco, Emergency Evacuation by Buses, Exec. Order No. KBB 2005-31 (Aug. 31, 2005).

[6] E-mail correspondence from Miles Bruder, LA State Official, to "All Gov. Staff" regarding co-ordination of bus service (Aug. 31, 2005).

[7] Daily VTC (Sept. 1, 2005) at 8.

[8] *Id.*

[9] *Id.*; Executive Order, Louisiana Governor Kathleen Babineaux Blanco, Emergency Evacuation by Buses, Exec. Order No. KBB 2005-25 (Sept. 2, 2005). Note, this differs from the Executive Order issued on Aug. 31, 2005, in that it waves the commercial drivers license requirement for bus drivers.

[0] VTC (Sept. 1, 2005) at 9.

[1] *Id.* at 11.

[152] Parr Interview.

[153] Buikema Interview.

[154] VTC (Sept. 1, 2005) at 14.

[155] *See generally, Id.* Daily VTC (Sept. 2, 2005).

[156] *Id.* at 4-5.

[157] *Id.* at 5.

[158] *Id.* at 5-6.

[159] *Id.* at 3.

[160] *Id.* at 5.

[161] *Id.* at 3.

[162] Interview by Select Comm. Staff with Jim McVaney, Director of Government Relations for Air Transport Association, in Washington, DC (Oct. 24, 2005).

[163] *Id.*

[164] *Id.*

[165] *Id.*

[166] *Id.*

[167] *Hearing on Hurricane Katrina: The Role of the Department of Homeland Security Before Select Comm.*, 109th Cong. (Oct. 19, 2005) at 48 (statement of Michael Chertoff); *see also* H. R. Conf. Rep. No. 105-297, at 127 (1997) (appropriating $500,000 for a "comprehensive analysis and plan of all evacuation alternatives for the New Orleans metropolitan area"); *see also* H.R. Conf. Rep. No. 106-379, at 151 (1999) (directing FEMA to develop an evacuation plan for the New Orl eans area). Whatever plans resulted from these federal directives, they were clearly inadequate.

"*The one-two combination of a catastrophic hurricane and massive flood overwhelmed the normal disaster relief system. Some things worked well. But there were shortcomings that we must urgently address.*

"*This tragedy has emphasized how critical it is that we ensure our planning and response capabilities perform with seamless integrity and efficiency in any type of disaster situation – even one of cataclysmic nature.*"

Michael Chertoff
Secretary, U.S. Department of Homeland Security
Select Committee Hearing, October 19, 2005

Critical elements of the national response plan were executed late, ineffectively, or not at all

Summary

Similar to the troubled national responses to Hurricanes Hugo and Andrew in 1989 and 1992 respectively, the federal government failed to recognize the magnitude of the situation presented by Hurricane Katrina prior to landfall, adequately project future needs, fully engage the President, and respond in a proactive and timely manner. While the Federal Emergency Management System had evolved since Andrew to include a developed protocol for responding proactively to catastrophic disasters, important aspects of the National Response Plan were poorly executed, which contributed to the inadequate federal response to Hurricane Katrina.

With the creation of the Department of Homeland Security (DHS) and the development of the National Response Plan (NRP), an additional layer of management and response authority was placed between the President and FEMA, and additional response coordinating structures were established.[1] The Secretary of Homeland Security became the President's principal disaster advisor responsible for enabling the President to effectively utilize his authority under the Stafford Act to direct all federal agencies, particularly the Department of Defense (DOD), to respond in a coordinated and expeditious fashion. As part of these changes, critical response decision points were assigned to the Secretary of Homeland Security.[2] Secretary Chertoff executed these responsibilities late, ineffectively, or not at all. These secretarial authorities include:

- The designation of an incident of national significance (INS);
- The authority to convene the Interagency Incident Management Group (IIMG);
- The designation of the principal federal official (PFO); and

- The invocation of the national response plan's catastrophic incident annex (NRP-CIA).

There was plenty of advance warning by the National Weather Service, and the consequences of a category 4 hurricane striking New Orleans were well-documented. Fifty-six hours prior to landfall, Hurricane Katrina presented an extremely high probability threat that 75 percent of New Orleans would be flooded, tens of thousands of residents may be killed, hundreds of thousands trapped in flood waters up to 20 feet, hundreds of thousands of homes and other structures destroyed, a million people evacuated from their homes, and the greater New Orleans area would be rendered uninhabitable for several months or years.[3] An August 28 report by the department's National Infrastructure Simulation and Analysis Center concluded: "Any storm rated Category 4 or greater . . . will likely lead to severe flooding and/or levee breaching, leaving the New Orleans metro area submerged for weeks or months."[4]

Under these conditions it seems reasonable to expect the criteria for designating an INS would have been met, the appointment of a PFO would be necessary to coordinate an unprecedented federal response, the IIMG would be convened to provide strategic guidance and recommendations to the Secretary and the President, and the NRP-CIA would be invoked to shift the federal response posture from a reactive to proactive mode in order to save lives and accelerate assistance to overwhelmed state and local systems. According to a recent letter submitted by DHS (see Appendix 7) in response to the preliminary observations of the Comptroller General (see Appendix 6), DHS viewed the NRP-CIA as applicable only to no-notice or short-notice events. And the Select Committee acknowledges that the State of Louisiana expressed its satisfaction with the supplies and that former FEMA Director Michael Brown directed that commodities be "jammed up" the supply chain.

While the NRP-CIA may be particularly applicable to a no-notice event, the Annex itself reflects only that a catastophic incident may occur with little or no warning.

And the pre-positioning of supplies to the satisfaction of state and local authorities, while an appropriate measure for a disaster without catastophic consequences, was clearly not sufficient for the catastrophic consquences of Hurricane Katrina.

Instead, absent a catastrophic disaster designation from Chertoff, federal response officials in the field eventually made the difficult decisions to bypass established procedures and provide assistance without waiting for appropriate requests from the states or for clear direction from Washington. These decisions to switch from a "pull" to a "push" system were made individually, over several days, and in an uncoordinated fashion as circumstances required. The federal government stumbled into a proactive response during the first several days after Hurricane Katrina made landfall, as opposed to the Secretary making a clear and decisive choice to respond proactively at the beginning of the disaster. The White House Homeland Security Council (HSC), situated at the apex of the policy coordination framework for DHS issues, itself failed to proactively de-conflict varying damage assessments. One example included an eyewitness account of a levee breach supplied by a FEMA official at 7:00 p.m. on August 29. The White House did not consider this assessment confirmed for 11 more hours, when, after 6:00 a.m. the next morning, it received a Homeland Security Operations Center (HSOC) Situation Report confirming the breach.

The catastrophic nature of Katrina confirmed once again that the standard "reactive" nature of federal assistance, while appropriate for most disasters, does not work during disasters of this scale. When local and state governments are functionally overwhelmed or incapacitated, the federal government must be prepared to respond proactively. It will need to anticipate state and local requirements, move commodities and assets into the area on its own initiative, and shore up or even help reconstitute critical state and local emergency management and response structures.

The need for assistance is extreme during the initial period of a catastrophic hurricane, yet the ability of state and local responders to meet that need is limited. That is why it is so important for the federal government, particularly DOD resources, to respond proactively and fill that gap as quickly as possible. Because it takes several days to mobilize federal resources, critical decisions must be made as early as possible so that massive assistance can surge into the area during the first two days, not several days or weeks later. The CIA-NRP was drafted to meet this specific and well known requirement, yet Chertoff never invoked it for Katrina.

In contrast, the Emergency Management Assistance Compact (EMAC), a critical part of the national emergency management framework, successfully provided unprecedented levels of response and recovery personnel and assets to the Gulf coast in record time following Hurricane Katrina. EMAC is designed by statute to be adaptable and scaleable to meet the changing needs of each event. EMAC was widely praised for its quick and effective process for putting vital resources into every aspect of the response.

Finding: It does not appear the President received adequate advice and counsel from a senior disaster professional

Although the Select Committee's access to White House documents, communications, and staff was not as comprehensive as we had hoped, the information we did receive suggests the President could have received better disaster advice and counsel.

The Stafford Act places the federal government's disaster response authorities with the President. Similar to military matters, the President is the commander in chief of federal disaster response. Yet, unlike the military, which provides the Chairman of the Joint Chiefs of Staff as the President's primary professional military advisor, the President does not have regular access to a senior disaster professional to advise him during disasters or on disaster response issues. The President lacks this resource even though catastrophic disasters may strike with little or no warning and require early Presidential involvement to reduce the loss of life, human suffering, and extensive property damage.[5]

Under the Homeland Security Act, the Secretary of Homeland Security reports to the President and is the department's top disaster official; yet emergency management is just one of the Secretary's many responsibilities.[6] According to Chertoff's testimony before the Select Committee, he is not a hurricane expert, nor does he have much experience with disasters.[7]

However, according to White House and FEMA documents, it appears the White House took several steps to improve the flow of information and strategic advice into the President. For example, HSC staff solicited regular situation reports from almost every federal agency for the White House situation room. The HSC commenced 24-hour operations the morning Katrina hit New Orleans.[8] In addition, White House officials attempted to pressure the HSOC to convene the IIMG on the Saturday before Katrina made landfall.[9]

The IIMG consists of high level officials from all the major federal agencies, and it is intended to assess the magnitude of crisis situations, project future requirements for federal assistance, develop plans for meeting those requirements, recommend to the Secretary and the President appropriate courses of action, and provide strategic advice.[10] The Secretary did not convene the IIMG until three days later, roughly 36 hours after landfall.[11]

Within the emergency management community, there are a handful of potential catastrophes that keep disaster professionals awake at night. Perhaps the most troubling

of these has been a category 3 or larger storm striking New Orleans because of its high likelihood of occurrence, the extreme vulnerability of the city to long term flooding, and the difficulty of evacuating a large urban population over limited evacuation routes. As a result, this scenario has been studied, planned, and exercised perhaps more than any other potential catastrophic disaster in the country. A senior disaster professional would be well aware of the consequences of such a storm, recognize the challenges of responding to such a disaster, and appreciate the need for timely and proactive federal assistance.

Comments such as those the President made about not expecting the levees to breach do not appear to be consistent with the advice and counsel one would expect to have been provided by a senior disaster professional. Furthermore, it seems reasonable to expect delays in recognizing the need for and then requesting DOD mission assignments may have been avoided if the President had been advised of the need for early presidential involvement.

> *Comments such as those the President made about not expecting the levees to breach do not appear to be consistent with the advice and counsel one would expect to have been provided by a senior disaster professional.*

AP PHOTO/SUSAN WALSH

Finding: Given the well-known consequences of a major hurricane hitting New Orleans, the Secretary should have designated an incident of national significance no later than Saturday, two days prior to landfall, when the National Weather Service predicted New Orleans would be struck by a Category 4 or 5 hurricane and President Bush declared a Federal Emergency

The consequences of a major hurricane, defined as a category 4 or greater storm, striking New Orleans were well-known within Louisiana, the emergency management community, and DHS.[12] FEMA officials selected New Orleans as the first project for its catastrophic disaster preparedness program precisely because of its high probability of occurrence and horrific consequences.[13] The New Orleans levee system was designed to withstand, in essence, a category 3 storm. Anything larger would exceed the levees' design capacity and likely cause catastrophic flooding of the city. FEMA's Hurricane Pam exercise predicted the storm would inundate 75 percent of the city up to 20 feet and cause 60,000 deaths.[14]

Two days before landfall the National Weather Service predicted Katrina would strike New Orleans as a category 4 or 5 hurricane. The governors of Louisiana and Mississippi declared state emergencies and the President issued an emergency declaration for Louisiana. At this point in time, it was extremely likely FEMA's worst case hurricane scenario was about to unfold. Chertoff should have declared an INS in recognition of the severity of the situation and to allow for the immediate convening of the IIMG, designation of the PFO, and invocation of the NRP-CIA.

Finding: The Secretary should have convened the IIMG on Saturday, two days prior to landfall, or earlier to analyze Katrina's potential consequences and anticipate what the federal response would need to accomplish

The purpose of the IIMG is to anticipate evolving requirements and provide strategic recommendations or courses of action for the Secretary and President to consider as part of a national response to a major incident. The IIMG replaces the Catastrophic Disaster Response Group from the old Federal Response Plan and was created to fill an important operational planning gap. During a major incident, the NRP expects the response organization to be focused on the current and subsequent 24-hour operational period and unable to assess the overall disaster situation, project future needs, and develop effective plans to protect life and property. The NRP utilizes the IIMG, a group of experienced high level professionals with agency decision making authority, to look at the big picture, anticipate what will be needed several days in advance, and develop plans to fulfill those requirements. Those plans can then be provided to the operational commanders and implemented in a timely manner.[15]

The "single biggest failure" of the federal response was that it failed to recognize the likely consequences of the approaching storm and mobilize federal assets for a post-storm evacuation of the flooded city. If it had, then federal assistance would have arrived several days earlier.

The authority to convene the IIMG is the Secretary's,[16] yet Chertoff did not execute that authority early enough for the IIMG to perform this function during the critical pre-landfall period and initial days of the disaster. According to an e-mail between top FEMA officials on Sunday, the day before landfall, White House officials were pressuring the head of the HSOC, Matthew Broderick, to convene the IIMG.[17] Because the Secretary did not activate the IIMG until roughly 36 hours after landfall, despite the White House pressure, we will never know what the IIMG would have done, given the hurricane forecast and well-known consequences of a category 4 storm, in anticipation that the New Orleans levees would likely breach and force the rescue and evacuation of tens of thousands of victims from the flooded city.

If Chertoff had convened the IIMG, then perhaps on the Saturday or Sunday before landfall, when FEMA officials were deploying emergency response teams and moving tons of commodities into the surrounding region, the IIMG would have begun to accelerate DOD's involvement, develop plans to evacuate the Superdome, and pre-stage buses and boats outside the region for immediate deployment after the storm passed. Instead, the FEMA operational teams did not begin planning these critical actions until three days later, Tuesday evening, and the buses and boats did not arrive in large quantities until Thursday.[18]

According to Colonel Jeff Smith, Deputy Director for Emergency Preparedness with the Louisiana Office of Homeland Security and Emergency Preparedness

LOHSEP), the "single biggest failure" of the federal response was that it failed to recognize the likely consequences of the approaching storm and mobilize federal assets for a post-storm evacuation of the flooded city. If it had, then federal assistance would have arrived several days earlier.[19]

By not convening the IIMG prior to landfall, the Secretary robbed himself and the President of the opportunity to receive professional advice and strategic options for proactively addressing the unfolding catastrophic disaster. The threat stream presented by Katrina was clear days before landfall, the potential consequences were well-known, and important tools for dealing with the situation were available yet not utilized.

Finding: The Secretary should have designated the Principal Federal Official on Saturday, two days prior to landfall, from the roster of PFOs who had successfully completed the required PFO training, unlike FEMA Director Michael Brown. Considerable confusion was caused by the Secretary's PFO decisions

According to the NRP, "the PFO is personally designated by the Secretary of Homeland Security to facilitate federal support to the established Incident Command System (ICS) Unified Command structure and to coordinate overall federal incident management."[20] During large multi-state disasters such as Katrina, the PFO's role becomes particularly important for providing a coordinated federal response, as the FCOs appointed by the President for each state only control operations within their respective states. The Secretary should have begun this coordination earlier and appointed a PFO on Saturday.

The Secretary's eventual designation of Brown as PFO on Tuesday evening was highly unusual and elicited a concerned and confused reaction from Brown.[21] In order

to prepare PFO-designates to fulfill the responsibilities and functions of the PFO, the department conducts a formal training program, and maintains a roster of individuals approved and qualified to serve as a PFO. The NRP requires that "[u]nless extenuating circumstances dictate otherwise, all PFO-designates should satisfactorily complete this training program prior to performing PFO-related responsibilities."[22]

According to DHS officials, Brown had not taken the required PFO training program and was not on the approved PFO roster.[23] Coast Guard Admiral Thad Allen had successfully completed the training program, as had all of the other individuals designated by the Secretary to serve as PFO for past INS designations and National Special Security Events.[24] It is unclear why Chertoff deviated from the requirements of the NRP and designated an untrained individual to serve as PFO for such a catastrophic disaster.

There was confusion over the role and authority of the PFO

The Secretary was confused about the role and authority of the PFO. According to Chertoff's testimony, he designated Brown PFO because Brown was his "battlefield commander."[25] Yet, the NRP specifically states, "The PFO does not direct or replace the incident command structure established at the incident, nor does the PFO have directive authority over the SFLEO [Senior Federal Law Enforcement Officer], FCO [Federal Coordinating Officer], or other federal and state officials."[26] Furthermore, the Stafford Act places all emergency response authorities with

Brown had not taken the required PFO training program and was not on the approved PFO roster.

the President and requires that the President designate a FCO for each disaster or emergency declaration.[27] As a result, the legal authority to "command the battlefield," as the Secretary put it, resides with the FCO, not the PFO.

The apparent confusion over the authority and role of the PFO does not seem to have been recognized until almost two weeks after Chertoff selected Allen to replace Brown as PFO. It was at that time that the unprecedented decision was made to appoint Allen the FCO for Louisiana, Mississippi, and Alabama *in addition* to PFO. This step was necessary because DHS eventually recognized Allen, as the PFO only, did not have the legal authority to commit the expenditure of federal funds or direct federal agencies under delegated authority from the President.[28] As described above, only the FCO has that authority. This confused and unprecedented series of actions by the department prompted the resignation and departure of Bill Carwile, one of FEMA's most well respected FCOs, who was serving as FCO in Mississippi.[29]

Finding: A proactive federal response, or push system, is not a new concept, but it is rarely utilized

What is a push system?

In response to most disasters, the federal government provides assistance in response to state requests. This reactive approach is often referred to as a "pull" system in that it relies on states knowing what they need and being able to request it from the federal government.[30] States may make these requests either before disasters strike because of the near certainty that federal assistance will be necessary after such an event, *e.g.*, with hurricanes, or afterwards, once they have conducted preliminary damage assessments and determined their response capabilities are overwhelmed.

Unlike the bulk of the disasters requiring FEMA's response, catastrophic disasters require the federal response to be more proactive. This proactive response is referred to as a "push" system, in which federal assistance is provided and moved into the affected area prior to a disaster or without waiting for specific requests from the state or local governments.[31]

Implementing a push system—a proactive federal response—does not require federalization of the disaster or the usurping of state authority. Although a push system is a proactive response by the federal government, it still requires notification and full coordination with the state. The coordination process, however, should not delay or impede the rapid mobilization and deployment of these critical federal resources.[32]

A proactive response, or push system, is nothing new. In 1992, the nation's management of catastrophic disasters was intensely criticized after Hurricane Andrew leveled much of South Florida and Hurricane Iniki destroyed much of the Hawaiian island of Kauai.[33] In particular, a 1993 GAO report points to the slow delivery of services vital to disaster victims as a major flaw in the response to Hurricane Andrew in South Florida.[34] The report then contrasts this with the more effective response to Hurricane Iniki in Hawaii, where FEMA implemented a push system and sent supplies to the island of Kauai before local officials requested them.[35] This occurred despite being implemented in an ad hoc manner—rather than as part of an orderly, planned response to catastrophic disasters.[36] Furthermore, the long-standing authority for a proactive federal response resides in the Stafford Act. The current plan for how to utilize that authority is the NRP-CIA.

The pre-positioning of assets and commodities is a distinct action from the push or pull of those assets

The federal government will often pre-position life-saving and life-sustaining disaster equipment and supplies prior to landfall of a hurricane as close to a potential disaster site as possible. This pre-positioning of supplies can substantially shorten response time and delivery of initial critical disaster supplies to the field.

Although part of a proactive response, this pre-positioning of disaster supplies and assets is not in and of itself a push of commodities. Once assets are pre-positioned to go into the field, they still need to be mobilized and deployed into the field either proactively by pushing the commodities to the state or reactively by waiting for a request from the state.

Operational procedures for a push are not well exercised, practiced, or utilized

The majority of declared disasters are not catastrophic. Because of this, the pull system is most commonly used during disasters and training exercises and, therefore, is more familiar to disaster response personnel. In fact, the NRP-CIA has never been appropriately exercised.[37] As a result, federal personnel have little experience or comfort with instituting a proactive response.

Additionally, if the Homeland Security Secretary does not invoke the NRP-CIA, federal personnel have no clear instruction to switch from a reactive approach to a proactive approach. Without this clear direction, federal personnel can be uncomfortable pushing resources into the state because of the inherent risks, such as complicating the disaster response by diverting needed resources from other areas or wasting millions of dollars in a duplication of effort.

Finding: The Secretary should have invoked the Catastrophic Incident Annex (NRP-CIA) to direct the federal response posture to fully switch from a reactive to proactive mode of operations

Perhaps the single most important question the Select Committee has struggled to answer is why the federal response did not adequately anticipate the consequences of Katrina striking New Orleans and, prior to landfall, begin to develop plans and move boats and buses into the area to rescue and evacuate tens of thousand of victims from a flooded city. At least part of the answer lies in the Secretary's failure to invoke the NRP-CIA, to clearly and forcefully instruct everyone involved with the federal response to be proactive, anticipate future requirements, develop plans to fulfill them, and execute those plans without waiting for formal requests from overwhelmed state and local response officials.

The NRP-CIA was specifically written for a disaster such as Katrina. According to the NRP:[38]

■ A catastrophic incident results in large numbers of casualties and displaced persons.

■ The incident may cause significant disruption to the area's critical infrastructure.

■ A credible operating picture may not be achievable for 24 to 48 hours or longer. As a result, response activities must begin without the benefit of a complete needs assessment.

■ Federal support must be provided in a timely manner to save lives, prevent human suffering, and mitigate severe damage. This may require mobilizing and deploying assets before they are requested via normal NRP protocols.

■ Large-scale evacuations, organized or self-directed may occur.

■ Large numbers of people may be left homeless and may require prolonged temporary housing.

It is clear the consequences of Hurricane Katrina exceeded all of these criteria and required a proactive response. According to the NRP, "Upon recognition that a catastrophic incident condition (e.g. involving mass casualties and/or mass evacuation) exists, the Secretary of DHS immediately designates the event an INS and begins, potentially in advance of a formal Presidential disaster declaration, implementation of the NRP-CIA."[39] On Monday evening, when DHS received reports the levees had breached in multiple locations, it should have been clear to the department the nation's worst case hurricane scenario had occurred and a proactive federal response was required.[40] Chertoff never invoked the NRP-CIA.

Smith, LOHSEP Deputy Director for Emergency Preparedness, believed, "the biggest single failure of the federal response was the Department of Homeland Security's failure to recognize that Katrina was a catastrophic event and implement the catastrophic incident annex to the National Response Plan...Had DHS recognized Katrina for the event that it was, a truly catastrophic event, had DHS implemented the catastrophic incident annex to the NRP, Louisiana should have had a significant number of federal troops and federal assets, days prior to their actual arrival. . . . Instead federal troops did not arrive in number until Saturday, after the evacuations of the Superdome, Convention Center and cloverleaf were complete."[41]

Finding: Absent the Secretary's invocation of the NRP-CIA, the federal response evolved into a push system over several days

Even though Chertoff never invoked the catastrophic annex, federal officials in the field began, in an ad hoc fashion, to switch from a pull response to a push system because of the operational demands of the situation. The switch was uncoordinated but widespread by the end of the first week. This has occurred in previous disasters. As previously mentioned, the response to Hurricane Iniki in Hawaii implemented an ad hoc push system as FEMA sent supplies to the island of Kauai before local officials requested them.[42] Similarly, the response to Katrina evolved into an ad hoc push system, even though the NRP-CIA was not invoked.

The following Mississippi and Louisiana examples illustrate the switch to a push response and several other important principles of effective emergency management. First, they demonstrate the importance of having qualified and experienced professionals in charge of operations. Second, these officials need to have the authority to commit resources as they see fit without waiting to seek approval from above. And, third, federal officials need to have good working relationships with their state counterparts. In the first example, Carwile had been the FCO in Florida during the 2004 hurricane season and developed a close relationship with the Florida Director of Emergency Management Craig Fugate. It is clear from e-mails and numerous staff interviews that Carwile did not hesitate to authorize and Fugate provided any and all assistance to Mississippi without formal requests from Mississippi authorities.[43]

On August 30, FEMA worked with Florida officials to push response assets into Mississippi. In an e-mail to Brown and Carwile, Fugate informed them Florida was pushing search and rescue teams into Mississippi. He noted the EMAC paperwork was not keeping up with the need, so they were working off of verbal requests. Specifically, he wrote, "To both of you, you need it, you got it from [F]lorida. [T]he paper work (sic) can follow."[44]

On Thursday, September 1, Carwile and Fugate continued to push resources into Mississippi without clear mission requests:

[5:42 a.m. e-mail from Fugate to Carwile]

I'm out of water and ice from my stocks. I've directed Mike DeLorenzo [with the Florida Division of Emergency Management] to start purchasing and shipping product into the coastal Mississippi Counties. Not sure I have an EMAC mission, but our folks on the ground have concerns if they run out.
Not sure how much and when, but will try to keep you updated on progress. If this works, will continue until told to stop.

So far we have only been shipping water and ice. No food or baby products.

Craig

_____

Craig Fugate, Director
Florida Division of Emergency Management

[10:26 a.m. reply from Carwile to Fugate]

Craig:

You are doing the right thing. Thanks. Know Robert [Robert Latham, Director of the Mississippi Emergency Management Agency] would concur. Will police up paperwork later – you have my guarantee.

Food is also critical. Need MRE [meals ready to eat] and/or heater meals if you have any. Water, ice, food in eastern counties should be your priority. Recommend Allen coordinate with MGen Cross (TAG, MS) for integration into their distribution system.

Also, know FL is providing law enforcement. Need all you can send. Public safety major concern (looting, etc.). Have used Dixie Co. body bags (250) got more?

Thanks, old friend, Bill

In Louisiana, FEMA response personnel tried on a number of occasions to push commodities and assets into the field. In cases where it was clear there was a need for life-saving and life-sustaining commodities but no clear state distribution system set up, FEMA acted proactively to provide assistance. For example, Louisiana FCO Bill Lokey noted there were situations where stranded individuals were not in immediate danger, but needed food and water. When FEMA gained access to several helicopters, FEMA began ferrying food and water to people stranded on high ground even though there was no formal request by the state to perform this function. In addition, FEMA contracted with over 100 ambulances to transport hospital evacuees. This mission was not requested by the state, but FEMA responded proactively because the situation demanded immediate action.[45]

Although there are numerous examples of a push system being implemented at times, there were also a number of times when state or local officials expressed frustration that requests for assistance were not processed because they did not follow the formal request process. For example, according to Louisiana and FEMA officials, state and local officials verbally requested specific assets or commodities during conference calls that were never fulfilled.[46] In these cases no immediate action was taken because FEMA officials assumed the state would follow on the verbal requests with official written requests. If the catastrophic annex had been invoked, then perhaps FEMA would have expected requests outside the normal process and acted on them.

Finding: The Homeland Security Operations Center failed to provide valuable situational information to the White House and key operational officials during the disaster

During Hurricane Katrina, the roles and responsibilities of the HSOC were unclear. One of the primary roles performed by the HSOC is to maintain an accurate picture of events as an incident unfolds by gathering and integrating information from multiple sources, including the National Response Coordination Center (NRCC), the Coast Guard, and other DHS elements.[47] Specifically, the NRP has designated the HSOC as the national-level hub for information sharing management during domestic incidents. The HSOC provides primary situational awareness to the Secretary, the IIMG, and the White House.

Perhaps the single most important piece of information during Katrina was confirmation of the levee breaches in New Orleans. Beyond the importance of the information itself, the implications of the information determined whether or not Katrina would be just another bad storm in New Orleans or the nation's worst-case hurricane disaster. Because DHS failed to anticipate the likely consequences of the storm and procure the buses, boats, and aircraft that were ultimately necessary to evacuate the flooded city prior to Katrina's landfall, the next critical decision point of the federal response became

On Monday evening the HSOC failed to conclude levees breached in New Orleans despite a FEMA eyewitness report and the presence of numerous Coast Guard air assets over New Orleans, which had the ability to communicate to most anywhere in the country.

FEMA

confirmation of the levee breaches. If the levees breached and flooded a large portion of the city, then the flooded city would have to be completely evacuated.[48] Any delay in confirming the breaches would result in a delay in the post-landfall evacuation of the city.

On Monday evening the HSOC failed to conclude that levees had breached in New Orleans despite a FEMA eyewitness report and the presence of numerous Coast Guard air assets over New Orleans, which had the ability to communicate to almost anywhere in the country. According to the commander of the Coast Guard's Air Station New Orleans, Captain Bruce Jones, there were nine Coast Guard helicopters, including the helicopter he piloted, operating over New Orleans by Monday evening, and Rear Admiral Duncan was flown over the city in a Coast Guard Falcon aircraft to assess the situation.[49]

In addition, a Coast Guard C-130 from Clearwater, Florida arrived over the city Monday evening after it heard the radio chatter from the rescue helicopter operations and diverted from its mission to reconnoiter the status of off shore oil rigs. The C-130 was able to communicate with all of the helicopters, and it could patch some communications through to the Coast Guard's division eight headquarters temporarily established in St. Louis. The division headquarters could then patch those communications through to a landline and reach almost any destination from there. The one important exception was calling into Baton Rouge, which was not possible.[50]

According to Marty Bahamonde, a FEMA External Affairs official, and the Coast Guard, he was flown over New Orleans early Monday evening for the specific purpose of providing situational awareness to Brown and DHS headquarters.[51] Captain Frank M. Paskewich said his unit took Bahamonde up in the helicopter because they were under the impression he had a direct line of communication into the White House. They thought Bahamonde could get the information regarding the status of the levees and flooding in the city to Washington faster than they could through the Coast Guard chain of command.[52] Bahamonde's observations were received in the HSOC a few hours after his over flight and became a Monday 10:30 p.m. HSOC spot report that was sent to the White House situation room shortly after midnight.[53] This spot report can be found in **Appendix 2**. However, it is not clear if the other Coast Guard observations, including Duncan's reconnaissance flight, reached the HSOC on Monday evening or at all.

FEMA

Because the HSOC failed to confirm the levee breaches on Monday, the first federal decision to procure buses was made by Deputy FCO Phil Parr, who was at the Superdome on Tuesday when he saw the water reaching the Superdome and realized it would become an island and have to be evacuated. At that point he began to develop an evacuation plan and requested hundreds of buses.[54]

The HSOC's role is not only to provide situational awareness and policy advice to top officials within DHS, but also to provide situational information and address lower level coordination issues. Yet, interviews suggest that while information was flowing upwards to the HSOC and onto the Secretary, it was less clear what valuable information was flowing down to key officials on the ground during the disaster. Edward Buikema, FEMA's former Acting Director of Response, and Mike Lowder, Deputy Director of Response, both stated that while situational reports were continually flowing up the ladder from FEMA headquarters to the HSOC, no information was flowing back down from the HSOC to the NRCC.[55]

Finding: The White House failed to de-conflict varying damage assessments and discounted information that ultimately proved accurate

In response to document requests to White House Chief of Staff Andrew Card[56] and the Office of the Vice President,[57] the Select Committee received and reviewed 22,830 pages of Katrina-related documents.[58] Of this production, 16,482 pages were from staff of the President's Homeland Security Council Prevention, Preparedness and Response (PPR) directorate, headed by Kirstjen Nielsen. The remaining 6,348 pages were produced by the Office of the Vice President.

Homeland Security Council (HSC) staff received a continuous paper flow in the hours and days before Katrina made landfall and after. Of the 16,482 pages produced, almost all of the documents are repeated numerous times. The most commonly found documents include:

- HSOC Situation Reports
- HSOC Spot Reports
- Louisiana Office of Emergency Preparedness Situation Reports
- Mississippi Emergency Management Agency Situation Reports
- Alabama Emergency Management Agency Situation Reports
- E-mails from DHS Watch Officer to White House HSC Staff
- FEMA executive briefing slides
- FEMA Hurricane Liaison Team (HLT) Advisories
- FEMA National Situation Reports
- FEMA Regional Situation Reports
- DOE Energy Reports from Office of Electricity Delivery and Energy Reliability
- DOT Situation Reports
- Federal Highway Administration (FHWA) Status Reports
- Talking Points from both DHS and the White House
- National Disaster Medical System (NDMS) Reports
- Coast Guard briefing materials
- National Guard briefing materials
- Pipeline Situation Reports
- FAA Emergency Operations Division Reports
- HHS Operations Center Situation Reports
- HUD briefing materials
- White House Press Office materials, and
- Red Cross Disaster Operations Summary Reports

The HSC was situated at the apex of the policy coordination framework for responding to Hurricane Katrina.[59] A HSC chart has Chertoff, and the IIMG through the Secretary, seemingly reporting into the HSC. As the coordinator of policy, it would seem to follow that HSC was directly involved in the Katrina response:

Hurricane Katrina
Policy Coordination Framework for Response

WHITE HOUSE HOMELAND SECURITY COUNCIL

Not really, according to Deputy Homeland Security Advisor Ken Rapuano, who twice briefed Select Committee members and staff. "We don't do operations at the White House," Rapuano said on January 27. "We're a transit site for information. DHS is the operating agency for response, and we were working closely with them . . . . At the time we believed we were fully supporting the [federal, state, and local response] requirements. Now we know differently."[60]

As discussed previously in the Investigation Overview chapter, the Select Committee grew frustrated by the White House's slow response to requests for information and documents. On the one hand, it is true the Rapuano briefings the Select Committee ultimately received in lieu of more complete document production offered a wide array of acknowledged failures and lessons learned. On the other, the White House's decision to withhold documents and communications raising concerns about executive priviledge, leaves the Select Committee no choice but to find, based on the information we have received, that a *failure of initiative* plagued the White House as well.

Failure to resolve conflicts in information and the "fog of war," not a lack of information, caused confusion

The White House did not suffer from a lack of information. At 1:47 a.m. on August 29, before Katrina made landfall, DHS forwarded an infrastructure advisory to the White House Situation Room and HSC staff indicating the risks associated with a potential levee

Some agencies had well developed standard operating procedures while others had none at all. The U.S. Army Corps of Engineers and the Department of Transportation had previously developed significant operating procedures that covered agency responsibilities under the NRP.[85] Both agencies had used these operating procedures during training exercises to ensure an understanding of operating procedures prior to real time application.[86] These agencies executed their responsibilities under the NRP fairly well. Other agencies lack sufficient operating procedures for their responsibilities under the NRP. Many, when asked for operating procedures, referred to related sections of the NRP. Since the NRP is not an operational plan, this led to problems with execution of Emergency Support Function (ESF) responsibilities.[87]

While DOD, the Department of Health and Human Services (HHS), and the Coast Guard performed admirably in many respects, there were problems adequately coordinating their activities with other federal, state, and local agencies through the NRP structure.

AP PHOTO/ERIC GAY

For example, DOD by-passed the NRP mandated unified command, taking requests from the states directly, absent the necessary input and coordination by FEMA. This was apparent in the evacuation of the Superdome. Parr completed a plan to evacuate the Superdome Wednesday morning with the support of the Louisiana National Guard. Shortly before implementation of the plan, Parr was informed of the decision by General Honoré of Northern Command to proceed with a different evacuation plan. Unknown to Parr, Blanco had requested DOD's involvement in the evacuation the day before. The Governor's request was made outside the unified command and without the knowledge of FEMA officials, resulting in a duplication of efforts and a delay in the evacuation. Additionally, Parr stated that the actual evacuation under Honoré's plan resulted in an additional 24 hour delay to evacuees.[88]

In another case, HHS activated the National Disaster Medical System without prior notice or consultation with Alabama, thereby removing 200 beds from the inventory the state believed on hand, and to which state officials were still directing patients. Likewise, Coast Guard search and rescue operations were bringing survivors from Mississippi unannounced to already full hospitals until Alabama sent its own personnel forward to help triage cases and coordinate the direction of Coast Guard flights. This resulted in confusion over available hospital beds for victims through the Gulf coast and delay in the medical response.[89]

Additional failures to adhere to the NRP were apparent in the lack of communication between the NRCC and the HSOC, which disrupted the overall information flow and situational awareness.

Finding: Once activated, the Emergency Management Assistance Compact (EMAC) enabled an unprecedented level of mutual aid assistance to reach the disaster area in a timely and effective manner

EMAC provided invaluable interstate mutual aid in support of Hurricane Katrina by deploying more than 67,891 personnel (19,481 civilians and 48,477 National Guard) to Louisiana and Mississippi.[90] EMAC facilitated mutual assistance from 48 states, the District of Columbia, the Virgin Islands and Puerto Rico.

In support of Hurricane Katrina, more than 2,188 resource requests (missions) were filled.[91] Record number of National Guard troops, local responders, and health/medical personnel were deployed through the compact. EMAC also works in cooperation with the federal government by co-locating personnel, when requested, in the NRCC or Regional Response Coordination Center

Not only did senior DHS officials fail to acknowledge the scale of the impending disaster, they were ill prepared due to their lack of experience and knowledge of the required roles and responsibilities prescribed by the NRP.

(RRCC) in order to share information on EMAC activities in the affected states, monitor the availability of needed resources being offered by assisting states, and facilitate overall emergency response and recovery activities.

Through state statute, EMAC addresses the legal issues of liability, workers compensation, reimbursement, and professional licensure—prior to a disaster or emergency when resource needs and timing are critical.[92] State and territory members must pre-designate personnel with the authority to request and commit resources. Standard operating procedures exist for compact members and training and exercise of state personnel is required. While formalized protocols are in place, EMAC is designed to be adaptable and scaleable to meet the changing needs of each event.

Following each large scale activation of the compact, a review and evaluation of the response is conducted and standard operating procedures revised and updated to reflect lessons learned and best practices. For example, lessons learned from the 2004 Florida hurricanes led to an overhaul of some operational procedures related to mobilization and deployment of resources, an enhanced automation system to provide more accurate data and electronic tracking of resources, and a new standardized EMAC training curriculum and updated operations manual.[93] These enhancements were either in progress or completed prior to Hurricane Katrina.

In Mississippi, EMAC assistance was considered a success. The assistance in Mississippi included help from other states' security agencies (such as their state police) as well as various states' National Guards (troops and hard assets).[94] (See the MILITARY chapter for more detail.)

Louisiana state officials also viewed EMAC assistance as very successful. One state official said there were almost 500 EMAC agreements for assistance. Although the EMAC response from surrounding states varied, state officials applauded EMAC for successfully getting law enforcement manpower assistance. According to state police officers

Ralph Mitchell and Joseph Booth, Arkansas, Tennessee, New Jersey, and California all sent law enforcement officers through EMAC.[95]

FEMA officials also noted the general success of EMAC. Because of the magnitude of the disaster, however, Louisiana was unable to handle all of the EMAC requests, requiring FEMA to become more involved in the process than normal. In particular, FCO Scott Wells noted some state offers of assistance through FEMA were rejected by Louisiana. He said these offers were rejected by SCO Smith because of concerns about the costs to the state.[96]

Finding: Earlier presidential involvement might have resulted in a more effective response

Similar to other large scale disasters, the catastrophic nature of Katrina required early presidential involvement to direct federal agencies in a massive coordinated response. In practice, it takes presidential action to quickly deploy the logistical capability of the military to meet the tremendous food, shelter, and medical needs of large affected populations. According to the Government Accountability Office's (GAO) review of hurricanes Hugo (1989, SC and NC), Andrew (1992, FL and LA), and Iniki (1992, HI):

> Often, when a catastrophic disaster leaves a gap between what volunteers can provide and the needs of disaster victims, DOD is the only organization capable of providing, transporting, and distributing sufficient quantities of the items needed to fill that gap. . . . While we clearly see a major role for DOD in providing mass care, we do not advocate turning over the entire disaster response, relief, and recovery operations to the military.[97]

Similar to other large scale disasters, the catastrophic nature of Katrina required early presidential involvement to direct federal agencies in a massive coordinated response.

Instead, the GAO recommended increased presidential involvement in the disaster and an improved process for FEMA to request DOD assistance as the solution for enabling DOD to provide relief during the critical first few days of a catastrophic disaster.[98] The Stafford Act authorizes the President, not the director of FEMA or the Homeland Security Secretary, to direct federal agencies to save lives and protect property and support state and local response efforts.[99] While the Stafford Act requires the President to delegate *the coordination* of response efforts to a federal coordinating officer (FCO), the law does not give the FCO *command* authority over other federal agencies. As a result, the FCO is not in a position to direct the operations of large departments such as DOD. Only the President appears able to promptly engage active duty military forces and achieve a unity of effort among all the federal agencies responding to a catastrophic disaster.

During Hurricane Katrina this problem was apparent in FEMA's and DHS' inability to promptly task major mission assignments to DOD. For example, FEMA did not approach DOD about taking over the logistics mission until Thursday, September 1, according to staff interviews with senior FEMA officials.[100] In response, Colonel Chavez with the Assistant Secretary for Homeland Defense Paul McHale instructed FEMA that the request had to go to Secretary of Defense Donald Rumsfeld.[101] Although details and

planning still needed to take place, the Secretary of Defense supported approval of the request on Friday, and Principal Deputy Assistant Secretary of Defense Pete Verga approved execution orders on Saturday, September 3.[102] Out of this request, according to McHale, DOD found additional mission assignments that it could undertake and proposed them to FEMA. Seven other mission assignments were negotiated and approved over the next few days with senior DHS officials, including Deputy Secretary Michael Jackson and the Director of Operations Coordination Brigadier General Matthew Broderick (USMC-Ret).[103] But by the time all of these missions were assigned, it was one week since Katrina had made landfall.[104]

Conclusion

Hurricane Katrina exposed numerous deficiencies in the existing national framework for emergency management, including specific mistakes that delayed an appropriate federal response. Confusion accompanied the implementation of the NRP, resulting in key elements of the plan executed late, ineffectively, or not at all. Not only did senior DHS officials fail to acknowledge the scale of the impending disaster, they were ill prepared due to their lack of experience and knowledge of the required roles and responsibilities prescribed by the NRP. The Secretary of DHS failed to declare an INS, convene the IIMG, and properly designate the PFO in a timely manner. The White House failed to de-conflict varying damage assessments and discounted FEMA-supplied eyewitness information that ultimately proved accurate. Furthermore, the government was limited to a reactive response due to failure to activate the NRP-CIA. Despite failures of the system, portions of the national framework were successful, including EMAC, which proved invaluable in providing necessary levels of mutual aid assistance. ∎

Although the Select Committee's access to White House documents, communications, and staff was not as comprehensive as we had hoped, the information we did receive suggests the President could have received better disaster advice and counsel.

Homeland Security Act of 2002, Pub. L. No. 107-296, Title V, 116 Stat. 2135 (2002) [hereinafter Homeland Security Act].

Dep't of Homeland Security, *National Response Plan*, (Dec. 2004) [hereinafter *NRP*].

State of Louisiana, *Southeast Louisiana Hurricane Planning Project*, (Sept. 5, 2005) [hereinafter *Southeast LA Planning Project*].

E-mail correspondence from Stephen York, Department of Homeland Security, to Andrew Akers, Homeland Security Operations Center (HSOC), Senior Watch Officer, et al. (Aug. 28, 2005) (11:59 a.m.) [hereinafter Aug. 28, 2005 York E-mail]; http://www.cnn.com/2006/POLITICS/01/24/katrina.levees.ap/ (last visited Jan. 28, 2006).

1993 GAO Report.

Homeland Security Act.

Hearing on Hurricane Katrina: The Role of the Department of Homeland Security Before Select Comm., 109th Cong. (Oct. 19, 2005) (written statement of Michael Chertoff, Secretary of Homeland Security) [hereinafter *Oct. 19, 2005 Select Comm. Hearing*].

See E-mail correspondence from Kirstjen Nielson, White House Homeland Security Council, to Tom Ryder, Department of Energy (Aug. 29, 2005) (10:58 a.m.).

E-mail correspondence from Michael Lowder, Deputy Director of Response, FEMA, to Patrick Rhode, FEMA, et al. (Aug. 28, 2005) (7:48 p.m.) [hereinafter Aug. 28, 2005 Lowder E-mail].

[0] *NRP* at 22.

[1] Briefing for Select Comm. Staff by the White House in Washington, DC (Dec. 13, 2005).

[2] Aug. 28, 2005 York E-mail; E-mail correspondence from Andrew Akers, DHS, to Paul Perkins, HSOC, et al. (Aug. 29, 2005) (1:47 p.m.) [hereinafter Aug. 29, 2005 Akers E-mail].

[3] Interview by Select Comm. Staff with Madhu Beriwal, Pres., Innovative Emergency Management in Washington, DC (Jan. 6, 2005).

[4] *Southeast LA Planning Project*.

[5] *NRP* at 22-23.

[6] *Id.* at 22.

[7] Aug. 28, 2005 Lowder E-mail.

[8] *Hearing on Hurricane Katrina: Perspectives of FEMA's Operations Professionals Before the Senate Comm. on Homeland Security and Governmental Affairs,* 109th Cong. (Dec. 8, 2005) at 70-73 (testimony of Philip Parr, Deputy Federal Coordinating Officer, FEMA Joint Field Office, Austin, TX) [hereinafter *Dec. 8, 2005 Senate Comm. Hearing*].

[9] *Hearing on Hurricane Katrina: Preparedness and Response by the State of LA Before Select Comm.*, 109th Cong. (Dec. 14, 2005) at 18 (statement of Colonel Jeff Smith) [hereinafter *Dec. 14, 2005 Select Comm. Hearing*].

[0] *NRP* at 33.

[1] *See* E-mail correspondence from Ken Hill, Executive Secretary, DHS to Michael Jackson, Deputy Secretary, DHS, et al., (Aug. 30, 2005) (8:22 p.m.); E-mail correspondence from Michael Brown, Undersecretary for Emergency Preparedness and Response to Sharon Worthy, Special Assistant, DHS (Aug. 30, 2005) (11:00 p.m.).

[2] *NRP* at 34.

[3] *Jan. 6, 2006 Buikema Interview*.

[4] *Id.*

[5] *Oct. 19, 2005 Select Comm. Hearing,* (written statement of Michael Chertoff).

[6] *NRP* at 33.

[7] Stafford Act, §§ 5143, 5170(a)-(b), 5192.

[8] *NRP* at 33-34.

[9] *Jan. 6, 2006 Buikema Interview*.

[0] Interviews by Select Comm. Staff with New Orleans officials in New Orleans, LA (Nov. 3-10, 2005).

[1] *Id.*

[2] *NRP* at 342.

[3] *1993 GAO Report* at 3.

[4] *Id.*

[5] *Id.* at 7.

[6] *May 25, 1993 Senate Armed Forces Comm. Hearing* (Statement of J. Dexter Peach).

[7] Interview by Select Comm. Staff with Bill Lokey, Federal Contracting Officer for LA, FEMA , in Washington, DC (Jan. 23, 2006) [hereinafter *Jan. 23, 2006 Lokey Interview*].

[8] *NRP* at Catastrophic Incident Annex.

[9] *Id.* at CAT-4.

[0] *DHS HSOC Spot Report of Marty Bahamonte, Regional Director, External Affairs, Region One, FEMA (Aug. 29, 2005)* [hereinafter *Aug. 29, 2005 HSOC Spot Report*]; Interview by Select Comm. with Bruce Jones, Captain, Coast Guard New Orleans Air Commander in Washington, DC (Jan. 10, 2006).

[1] *Dec. 14, 2005 Select Comm. Hearing* at 18 (testimony of Colonel Jeff Smith).

[2] *1993 GAO Report* at 7.

[3] E-mail correspondence from William Carwile, DHS, to Craig Fugate, Director, Florida Division of Emergency Management (Aug. 30, 2005).

[4] *Id.*

[5] *Jan. 23, 2006 Lokey Interview*.

[6] Interviews by Select Comm. Staff with FEMA and Louisiana officials in New Orleans, LA (Nov. 3-10, 2005).

[7] *NRP.*

[8] *Southeast LA Planning Project*.

[9] Briefing for Select Comm. Staff by U.S. Coast Guard in Washington, DC (Jan. 10, 2006) [hereinafter *Jan. 10, 2006 Coast Guard Briefing*].

50 *Id.*

51 *Hearing on Hurricane Katrina in New Orleans: a Flooded City, a Chaotic Response Before the Senate Committee on Homeland Security and Governmental Affairs,* 109th Cong. (Oct. 20, 2005) at 9-13 (testimony of Marty Bahamonde, Regional Director, External Affairs, Region One, FEMA) [hereinafter *Oct. 20, 2005 Senate Comm. Hearing*]; *Jan. 10, 2006 Coast Guard Briefing.*

52 *Jan. 10, 2006 Coast Guard Briefing.*

53 E-mail correspondence from Michael Inzer, HSOC, to Bethany Nichols, et al. (Aug. 30, 2005) (12:02 p.m.) [hereinafter Aug. 30, 2005 Inzer E-mail]; *Aug. 29, 2005 HSOC Spot Report.*

54 Interviews by Select Comm. Staff with FEMA and Louisiana officials in New Orleans, LA (Nov. 3-10, 2005); *Dec. 8, 2005 Senate Comm. Hearing* at 70-73 (testimony of Philip Parr).

55 *Jan. 6, 2006 Buikema Interview.*

56 Letters from Select Comm. to Andrew H. Card, Jr., White House Chief of Staff, Sept. 30, Oct. 13, and Dec. 1, 2005.

57 Letters from Select Comm. to I. Lewis Libby, Jr., then Chief of Staff to the Vice President, Oct. 13, 2005, and to David S. Addington, Counsel to the Vice President, Oct. 4 and Dec. 7, 2005.

58 The Executive Office of the President produced 16,482 pages of documents and the Office of the Vice President produced 6,348 pages of documents.

59 *Hurricane Katrina – Policy Coordination Framework for Response,* Office of the Vice President document supplied to the Select Comm.

60 Briefing for Select Comm. Staff by the White House in Washington, D.C. (Jan. 27, 2006) [hereinafter *Jan. 26, 2006 White House Briefing*].

61 Aug. 28, 2005 York E-mail.

62 Aug. 29, 2005 Akers E-mail; DHS National Infrastructure Simulation & Analysis Center, *Fast Analysis Report (Update to Reflect Category 5 Status) to DHS IP on Hurricane Katrina, Gulf Coast* (Aug. 28, 2005).

63 *Id.* at 1.

64 E-mail correspondence from Stephen York, DHS, to Andrew Akers, HSOC SWO, et al. (Aug. 28, 2005) (12:14 p.m.); Homeland Security Operations Center, *Diagrams of New Orleans Levee Systems and Scenarios.*

65 E-mail correspondence from Insung Lee, HSOC, to Frank DiFalco, et al. (Aug. 29, 2005) (2:20 p.m.). HSOC report received at the White House Aug. 29, 2005 at 2:20 p.m.

66 E-mail correspondence from Tom Holz, to Bethany Nichols, et al. (Aug. 29, 2005) (6:13 p.m.); HSOC, *Hurricane Katrina SITREP #7.* HSOC report received at the White House, Aug. 29, 2005 at 6:13 p.m.

67 Aug. 30, 2005 Inzer E-mail; *Aug. 29, 2005 HSOC Spot Report.*

68 *Id.*

69 *Jan. 27, 2006 White House Briefing.*

70 *Oct. 20, 2005 Senate Comm. Hearing* (testimony of Marty Bahamonte, Regional Director, External Affairs, Region One, FEMA).

71 *Id.* at 27.

72 *Id.*

73 *Id* at 28.

74 *Id.*

75 *Jan. 27, 2006 White House Briefing.*

76 *Id.*

77 *Id.*

78 Daily Video Teleconference amongst officials dated Sept. 2, 2005 [hereinafter Sept. 2, 2005 Daily Video Teleconference].

79 *Hearing on Hurricane Katrina: The Role of the Federal Emergency Management Agency Before Select Comm.,* 109th Cong. (Sept. 27, 2005) at 213 (testimony of Michael Brown, then Director of FEMA) [hereinafter *Sept. 27, 2005 Select Comm. Hearing*].

80 David D. Kirkpatrick and Scott Shane, "Ex-FEMA Chief Tells of Frustration and Chaos," *The New York Times,* Sept. 15, 2005, A1.

81 *Id.*

82 *Sept. 27, 2005 Select Comm. Hearing* at 104.

83 Sept. 2, 2005 Daily Video Teleconference.

84 *Jan. 26, 2006 White House Briefing.*

85 U.S. Army Corps of Engineers, *ESF #3 Field Guide* (June 2001).

86 Briefing for Select Comm. Staff by Department of Transportation in Washington, DC on Oct. 31, 2005; Interview by Select Comm. Staff with U.S. Army Corps of Engineers in Washington, DC on Oct. 28, 2005.

87 *NRP* at 5.

88 *Dec. 8, 2005 Senate Comm. Hearing* at 70-72 (testimony of Philip Parr).

89 Interviews by Select Comm. Staff with Alabama Officials in Clanton and Montgomery, AL on October 11-12, 2005.

90 Beverly Bell, NEMA, "EMAC Strides in 2005 Set a Precedent for Future," (Jan. 30, 2006) http://www.mema.org/newsletterwork/temamain.html.

91 Interviews by Select Comm. Staff with Louisiana Officials in New Orleans, LA (Nov. 3-10, 2005).

92 *See* Emacweb.org.

93 Interviews by Select Comm. Staff with Louisiana Officials in New Orleans, LA (Nov. 3-10, 2005).

94 *Hearing on Hurricane Katrina: Preparedness and Response by the State of Mississippi Before Select Comm.,* 109th Cong. (Dec.7, 2005) at 2 (statement of Haley Barbour, Governor, State of Mississippi).

95 Interviews by Select Comm. Staff with FEMA Officials in New Orleans, LA (Nov. 3-10, 2005).

96 *Id.*

97 *Hearing on Disaster Management: Recent Disasters Demonstrate the Need to Improve the Nation's Response Strategy Before the Subcomm. On Nuclear Deterrence, Arms Control and Defense Intelligence of the Senate Comm. on Armed Forces,* 103rd Cong. (May 25, 1993) at 11-12 (statement of J. Dexter Peach, Assistant Comptroller General) [hereinafter *May 25, 1993 Senate Armed Forces Comm. Hearing*].

U.S. Gov't Accountability Off., Pub. No. GAO/RCED-93-186, *Disaster Management: Improving the Nation's Response to Catastrophic Disasters*, 2 (July 1993) [hereinafter *1993 GAO Report*].

Robert T. Stafford Disaster Relief and Emergency Assistance Act, 42 U.S.C. §§ 5170(a)-(b), 5192 (2005) [hereinafter Stafford Act].

⁰ *See* Interview by Select Comm. Staff with Edward Buikema, former Acting Director of Response, FEMA [hereinafter *Jan. 6, 2006 Buikema Interview*], in Washington, DC (Jan. 6, 2006).

¹ E-mail correspondence from Col. Richard Chavez, Senior Military Advisor for Civil Support, to Thomas Kuster, CIV, OSD-Policy (Sept. 2, 2005) (9:38 a.m.).

² DOD and FEMA, *MOD 8 to EXORD for DOD Support to FEMA for Hurricane Katrina*, on file with the Select Comm., No. MMTF 00028-05.

³ Correspondence from Paul McHale, Assistant Secretary of Defense for Homeland Defense, to Chairman Davis (Jan. 25, 2006).

⁴ *Jan. 6, 2006 Buikema Interview.*

FEMA

"*FEMA pushed forward with everything it had in order to help the states respond after landfall …Every single team, every single program of FEMA, was pushed to its limit to respond to Hurricane Katrina.*"

Michael D. Brown
Former FEMA Director, Select Committee Hearing,
September 27, 2005

DHS and the states were not prepared for this catastrophic event

Summary

It is clear the federal government in general and the Department of Homeland Security (DHS) in particular were not prepared to respond to the catastrophic effects of Hurricane Katrina. There is also evidence, however, that in some respects, FEMA's response was greater than it has ever been, suggesting the truly catastrophic nature of Hurricane Katrina overwhelmed a federal response capability that under less catastrophic circumstances would have succeeded.

Nevertheless, DHS' actual and perceived weaknesses in response to Katrina revived discussion of the value of incorporation of FEMA into DHS. Many experts and Members of Congress debated the policy and operational ramifications of bringing FEMA into DHS during consideration of the Homeland Security Act of 2002 (HSA).

The HSA transferred FEMA functions, personnel, resources, and authorities to the DHS Emergency Preparedness and Response (EP&R) Directorate. The emergency management community has complained since 2003 that FEMA was being systematically dismantled, stripped of authority and resources, and suffering from low morale, in part because of the Department's focus on terrorism. Others have said that FEMA's placement in DHS enabled the Secretary of Homeland Security to augment FEMA's resources with other DHS personnel and assets, all within an integrated command structure.

The cycle of emergency management begins with preparedness and mitigation, flows into response, and ends with recovery. The four cornerstones to comprehensive emergency management – preparedness, response, recovery, and mitigation – are interdependent and all vital to successful emergency management.

Preparedness encompasses those pre-disaster activities that develop and maintain an ability to respond rapidly and effectively to emergencies and disasters. All levels of government need to be prepared to respond to disasters. International Association of Emergency Managers President Dewayne West described preparedness as "what emergency managers do every day in order to be able to respond."[1] Emergency management officials at different levels of the government expressed concerns that distancing preparedness efforts from response, recovery, and mitigation operations could result in an ineffective and uncoordinated response.[2]

Following Hurricane Katrina, emergency management professionals in the Gulf coast region have questioned whether DHS and state preparedness for catastrophic events has declined over the past years due to organizational changes within DHS and a shift in programmatic priorities. In particular, the decline in preparedness has been seen as a result of the separation of the preparedness function from FEMA, the drain of long-term professional staff along with their institutional knowledge and expertise, and the diminished readiness of FEMA's national emergency response teams.

In the Gulf coast region, emergency managers expressed the view that FEMA's disaster response capabilities had declined since its inclusion in DHS, in part due to subsequent organizational changes within DHS and FEMA. The emergency management community has suggested that FEMA's readiness for a large disaster has declined despite extensive preparedness initiatives within the federal government, pointing to the separation of preparedness functions from response, recovery, and mitigation.

FEMA

Additionally, the tremendous damage and scale of Hurricane Katrina placed extraordinary demands on the federal response system and exceeded the capabilities and readiness of DHS and FEMA in a number of important areas, particularly in the area of staffing. The response to Hurricane Katrina required large numbers of qualified personnel at a time when FEMA's professional ranks had declined. FEMA response officials in both Mississippi and Louisiana testified that the department's inability to field sufficient numbers of qualified personnel had a major impact on federal response operations. In addition, FEMA had lost, since 2002, a number of its top disaster specialists, senior leaders, and experienced personnel, described as "FEMA brain drain." Many emergency management professionals had predicted this 'drain' would have a negative impact on the federal government's ability to manage disasters of all types.

In addition, emergency management professionals said the degraded readiness of FEMA's national emergency response teams reduced the effectiveness of the federal response to Hurricane Katrina. The diminished readiness of the national emergency response teams has been attributed to a lack of funding for training exercises and equipment. Emergency management professionals note the need for trained people, who have experience working together with their federal colleagues and state counterparts prior to a disaster, as a part of national emergency response teams. Emergency responders should not meet each other for the first time right before or after a major catastrophe. A decline in the readiness of these teams along with appropriate staffing added to an ineffective response.

Finding: While a majority of state and local preparedness grants are required to have a terrorism purpose, this does not preclude a dual use application

The "all hazard" versus "just terrorism" debate plays out in the interpretation of permissible uses for homeland security grant funding and efforts to make equipment purchases and exercise scenarios fit terrorism-related criteria while still being of some general use in day-to-day emergency response. For example, funding to exercise response capabilities for WMD-related scenarios might be used to

test evacuation planning and other "all hazard" response functions, with the WMD element little more than pretext.

This concern is evident at the local level. Alabama conducts or participates in approximately 50 training exercises each year ranging from "table top," classroom-like discussions to full scale exercises involving all members of the emergency management community, including federal, state, and local officials. According to Alabama officials, federal DHS funding restrictions dictate that almost all of these exercises involve a terrorism-based threat or scenario, despite the fact that all emergencies largely involve the same set of procedures — evacuations, loss of power, communications difficulties, need for shelter, food, and water, and inter-governmental coordination.[3]

State officials also voiced a concern that in the post-9/11 environment undue emphasis is placed on terrorism-based hazards.[4] Alabama's hazard risk profile includes terrorism, but state emergency management officials believe natural disasters pose a much more likely, perhaps inevitable, risk.[5] Although lately, hurricanes have hit the state with some regularity, Alabama is susceptible to a wide variety of other natural disasters, including earthquakes, tornadoes, floods, and droughts. With nuclear facilities located within the state, Alabama Emergency Management Agency (AEMA) officials are also on alert for nuclear-related emergencies. Special plans and precautions have also been funded to prepare for risks posed by an Army chemical weapons storage and incineration facility.[6]

According to Colonel Terry Ebbert, the Director of Homeland Security & Public Safety for the City of New Orleans, DHS' all hazards focus is unsubstantiated.

> [T]he Office of Domestic Preparedness restricted any use of grant funding for preparing, equipping, training, and exercising to enhance the preparedness of first responders operating in

a potential WMD environment. Most allowable expenditures under the UASI program remain closely linked to the WMD threat to the exclusion of many other forms of enhanced readiness.[7]

When Ebbert submitted a request to purchase a number of inexpensive, flat-bottomed, aluminum boats to equip his fire and police departments, with the intent of having them available to rescue people trapped by flooding, the request was denied. Ebbert concluded that the rules on what is permitted and reimbursable are unaltered while the newly stated focus on an "all hazards" approach to preparedness remains "elusive."[8] Ebbert recommended that "existing limitations imposed on the availability of Federal preparedness funding should be broadened."[9]

DHS officials are particularly sensitive to the charge that the agency has stopped state and local governments from purchasing equipment not exclusively suited to terrorism preparedness. Former Office of Domestic Preparedness (ODP) Director Suzanne Mencer stressed the dual use capability of many grants: "The grants don't prohibit a city from buying equipment for use in a natural disaster if it can also be used in a terrorist attack."[10] Mencer said some locals see the WMD wording and think it prohibits items, such as radios, that could also be used in a natural disaster: "They can still meet their needs in almost all instances if they look at the broader picture and not [just] the wording in the grant."[11] When asked about state and local complaints in Alabama and elsewhere, former director of ODP's Preparedness Programs Division, Tim Beres, noted that in fiscal 2004, grants paid for more than $1 billion worth of dual-use equipment, including $925 million for interoperable communications equipment and $140 million in chemical protection suits.[12]

DHS continues to develop and refine its guidelines to states and localities, in accordance with Presidential Directives, which require grants to be used in support of catastrophic events regardless of their cause.[13] Although a July 2005 Government Accountability Office (GAO) report found many state preparedness officials and local first responders believed DHS planners focused excessively on anti-terrorism criteria in their grant, training, and exercise programs, the auditors concluded that 30 of the 36 essential capabilities first responders need to

fulfill the critical tasks generated by the department's 15 catastrophic emergency planning scenarios would apply to both terrorist and non-terrorist incidents.[14] The GAO auditors concluded that DHS planning supported an all hazards approach.[15] Indeed, according to GAO auditors, in response to state and local complaints that DHS required too much emphasis on terrorism-related activities, DHS increasingly promoted flexibility to allow greater dual usage within the grant program requirements for fiscal year 2005.

DHS' growing dual use flexibility is reflected in its most recent grant guidelines. Specifically, the FY2006 guidance points out the numerous dual-use target capabilities (identified in the National Preparedness Goal) to be attained through DHS grant funding.[16] The guidance further states:

> [f]unding remains primarily focused on enhancing capabilities to prevent, protect against, respond to, or recover from CBRNE [Chemical, Biological, Radiological, Nuclear and Conventional Explosives], agriculture, and cyber terrorism incidents. However, in light of several major new national planning priorities, which address such issues as pandemic influenza and the aftermath of Hurricane Katrina, the allowable scope of SHSP [State Homeland Security Program] activities include catastrophic events, provided that these activities also build capabilities that relate to terrorism.[17]

Finding: Despite extensive preparedness initiatives, DHS was not prepared to respond to the catastrophic effects of Hurricane Katrina

As a result of various changes within DHS and FEMA, the emergency management community suggested FEMA's preparedness and readiness for a large disaster would decline despite extensive preparedness initiatives within the federal government. For example, during an April 2005 House Subcommittee hearing on DHS preparedness efforts, Dave Liebersbach, then President of the National Emergency Management Association (NEMA), expressed

FEMA's operational budget baseline (for non-Stafford Act disaster funding) had been permanently reduced by 14.8 percent since joining DHS in 2003. In addition to the permanent baseline reduction, he claimed FEMA lost $80 million and $90 million in fiscal years 2003 and 2004 respectively from its operating budget.[36] Brown argued these budget reductions were preventing FEMA officials from maintaining adequate levels of trained and ready staff.

Brown also said FEMA no longer managed numerous functions that were essential to meeting its statutory responsibilities, and therefore did not have the tools to successfully accomplish its mission. For example, the National Response Plan is a fundamental element of coordinating the federal government's response to disasters. Given FEMA's response mission, the Homeland Security Act of 2002 specifically assigned FEMA responsibility for "consolidating existing Federal Government emergency response plans into a single, coordinated national response plan."[37] However, instead of assigning this function to the organization responsible for executing the plan during a disaster (i.e. FEMA), the department initially assigned it to the Transportation Security Administration, which then relied on an outside contractor.

When some in the first responder community reacted negatively to the contractor's draft plan, the department transferred the NRP's development to another area of the department, the Integration Staff within the Secretary's office. The resulting plan made a number of departures from the existing Federal Response Plan, including the introduction of the Incident of National Significance (INS), the Principal Federal Official (PFO), the Interagency Incident Management Group (IIMG), the Homeland Security Operations Center (HSOC), and the Catastrophic Incident Annex (NRP-CIA).[38] The emergency management community expressed concerns about each of these newly created structures, which ultimately proved problematic or experienced difficulties achieving their intended purposes during the response to Hurricane Katrina.

Brown also identified what he believed were the most important goals for achieving FEMA's mission of leading the federal government's response to disasters. Several of the issues he identified for improvement proved to be critical problem areas in the Katrina response. The requirements he identified in March 2005 included the following:[39]

1. Improve logistics capability and asset visibility.
2. Implement a comprehensive and integrated multi-year catastrophic planning strategy.[40]
3. Establish a National Incident Management System Integration Center to improve command and control capabilities at the federal, state, and local levels.
4. Recruit, train, credential, deploy and retain a disaster workforce with the appropriate skill mix and management structure to support the operational requirements of all disaster related functions.
5. Ensure appropriate numbers, skills, and grades of employees to support current and long-term mission needs.

Senior DHS and Office of Management and Budget officials vigorously dispute the claim that FEMA's budget has been cut at all. They argue that any transfers from the FEMA budget reflect the transfer of functions carried out by DHS for FEMA, start up costs of the Department, and the use of unobligated funds. According to Andrew Maner, Chief Financial Officer for DHS, the core of the budget adjustments cannot be classified as permanent reductions to FEMA's base budget, as Brown claims.[41] For example, Maner said the transfer of $30.6 million was a transfer of unobligated balances from the 2002 Olympic Games to help fund the start-up of the new Department. The transfer of such unobligated balances was authorized by Congress in H.J. Res. 124, which became law on November 23, 2002 (P.L. 107-294), to pay for "the salaries and expenses associated with the initiation of the Department."[42] Also, Maner noted the $28 million transfer to ODP reflects efforts to complete the transfer of funds accompanying former FEMA functions that have been assumed by other DHS entities.[43]

Regardless of the impact, if any, of these budget adjustments on FEMA capabilities, the tremendous damage and scale of Hurricane Katrina placed extraordinary demands on the federal response system and exceeded the capabilities and readiness of DHS and FEMA in a number of important areas, including staffing. Hurricane Katrina consisted of three separate major disaster declarations, three separate statewide field operations, two directly-affected FEMA regional operations, and the full activation of national level resources such as the National Response Coordination Center (NRCC), the HSOC, and the IIMG. In addition, most FEMA regional offices were actively supporting atrina operations or assisting their regions receive Gulf Coast evacuees. These operations required large numbers of qualified personnel from what had become a relatively small agency of approximately 2,500 positions.

AP PHOTO/JOHN BAZEMORE

Ultimately, FEMA officials turned to federal agencies like the U.S. Forest Service and city firefighters from across the country to staff FEMA positions in the state.

FEMA response officials in both Mississippi and Louisiana testified that the department's inability to field sufficient numbers of qualified personnel had a major impact on federal response operations.[44] The Federal Coordinating Officer (FCO) in Mississippi, Bill Carwile, described how managing the personnel shortfall was perhaps his most difficult challenge. While he was able to deploy division supervisors to the coastal counties, he needed similar qualified employees for the devastated cities of Gulfport, Biloxi, and Pascagoula. Ultimately, FEMA officials turned to federal agencies like the U.S. Forest Service and city firefighters from across the country to staff FEMA positions in the state.

Despite those measures, Carwile stated, "We never had sufficient personnel to meet requirements."[45] According to Scott Wells, Deputy FCO for Louisiana, a 90-person FEMA regional office "is woefully inadequate" to perform its two primary disaster functions, operating a regional response coordination center and deploying people to staff emergency response teams in the field.[46] "You cannot do both. Pick one," he said.[47] Wells added, "We had enough staff for our advance team to do maybe half of what we needed to do for a day shift….We did not have the people. We did not have the expertise. We did not have the operational training folks that we needed to do our mission."[48]

In addition to having an inadequate number of qualified personnel, FEMA had lost a number of its top disaster specialists, senior leaders, and most experienced personnel. Both critics and supporters of FEMA's merger with DHS have acknowledged "FEMA brain drain" in recent years and its negative impact on the federal government's ability to manage disasters of all types.[49] Since 2003, for example, the three directors of FEMA's preparedness, response, and recovery divisions had left the agency, and departures and retirements thinned FEMA's ranks of experienced professionals. At the time Hurricane Katrina struck, FEMA had about 500 vacancies and eight out of its ten regional directors were working in an acting capacity.[50]

At least two factors account for FEMA's loss of seasoned veterans. First, like other government agencies, many of FEMA's long-term professionals are reaching retirement age.[51] And second, job satisfaction was second to last in 2005, according to the Partnership for Public Service, a nonprofit group that promotes careers in federal government.[52] Regardless of the reasons for the exodus, Brown and senior DHS officials were unable to maintain their ranks of disaster professionals, through employee retention, development, or recruitment, and this failure hindered the response to Hurricane Katrina.[53]

The disastrous effect of this manpower shortage was compounded in Hurricane Katrina by the difficulty of getting federal workers where they needed to be because of security concerns. In Louisiana, media reports and rumors of violence and general lawlessness delayed the deployment and placement of federal response workers. The Governor's Chief of Staff Andy Kopplin said there were approximately 1,000 FEMA employees deployed and on their way to New Orleans Wednesday, August 31, 2005, many of whom turned back due to security concerns.[54]

Finding: The readiness of FEMA's National Emergency response teams was inadequate and reduced the effectiveness of the federal response

One of the most critical links in the federal response system is the team of FEMA personnel that deploys to a disaster site to establish a unified command with state officials and directs federal operations. These national emergency response teams are the conduits through which federal disaster assistance is requested by and delivered to a state. They are intended to be on call and deploy at a moment's notice, since many disasters provide no advance warning. In prior years, according to Carwile, "We were then able to build a team to about 125 individuals, hand picked, from around the country, and we were able to routinely exercise that team because we had the funding in place to do so on the plan, against several scenarios."[55] The team had a robust operational plan, was sent to the Winter Olympics in Salt Lake City, and received dedicated satellite communications equipment. It appeared to be a well-equipped, well-trained team at a high state of readiness.[56]

Carwile testified that by 2004, the readiness of FEMA's emergency response teams had plummeted dramatically.[57] Funding for the teams dried up after 2002. They lost their dedicated communications equipment. Teams were split up into ever smaller units. Team training and exercises ceased.

In a June 30, 2004 memorandum, FEMA's top disaster response operators, the cadre of Federal Coordinating Officers, warned then FEMA Director Brown that the national emergency response teams were unprepared because no funding was available for training exercises or equipment.[58] In a few short years, FEMA's emergency response teams had been reduced to names on a roster. It appears no actions were taken to address the problems identified in the memorandum.

Asked whether or not implementing the recommendations would have made a difference in Katrina, Carwile responded, "I felt very fortunate because many of my colleagues with me in Mississippi had been with me on a national team in years past. It was kind of coincidental . . . but I can't help but believe that trained and ready teams, people who have worked together, would not have made some difference in a positive way."[59] Wells described the situation in Louisiana in this way: "We need to really train together as a team. We need to work as a team. What you have with this National Response Plan in the field is we have no unity of command."[60]

The requirement for trained people, who have experience working together with their federal colleagues and their state counterparts, is a constant theme of federal, state, and local emergency professionals. Numerous officials and operators, from state and FEMA directors to local emergency managers told the same story: if members of the state and federal emergency response teams are meeting one another for the first time at the operations center, then you should not expect a well-coordinated response.[61]

Conclusion

For years emergency management professionals have been warning that FEMA's preparedness has eroded. Many believe this erosion is a result of the separation of the preparedness function from FEMA, the drain of long-term professional staff along with their institutional knowledge and expertise, and the inadequate readiness of FEMA's national emergency response teams. The combination of these staffing, training, and organizational structures made FEMA's inadequate performance in the face of a disaster the size of Katrina all but inevitable. ■

International Ass'n of Emergency Managers, *Press Release: IAEM Announces Recommendations for Improved Emergency Response,* (Oct. 25, 2005) (on file with Select Comm.).

Hearing on The National Preparedness System: What are we preparing for? Before the House Comm. on Transportation and Infrastructure, Subcommittee on Economic Development, Public Buildings, and Emergency Management, 109th Cong. (Apr. 14, 2005) at 61-62 (statement of Dave Liebersbach, Pres., Nat'l Emergency Mgmt. Assoc.) [hereinafter *Apr. 14 Preparing Hearing*]; Memorandum from Michael Brown, Dir., FEMA to Michael Chertoff, Sec'y, Dept. of Homeland Sec. (March 2005) [hereinafter March 2005 Brown Memo]; Interview by Select Comm. Staff with Ed Buikema, Dir., Response Div., FEMA, in Wash., D.C. (Jan. 6, 2006).

Hearing on Hurricane Katrina: Preparedness and Response by the State of Alabama Before Select Comm., 109th Cong. (Nov. 9, 2005) at 75 (statement of Bruce Baughman, Dir., Ala. State Emergency Mgmt. Agency) [hereinafter *Nov. 9, 2005, Select Comm. Hearing*].

Interview by Select Comm. Staff with senior AL emergency management officials, in Clanton, AL (Oct. 11, 2005).

Id.

Nov. 9, 2005 Select Comm. Hearing at 75 (statement of Bruce Baughman, Dir., Ala. State Emergency Mgmt. Agency).

Hearing on Hurricane Katrina: Preparedness and Response by the State of Louisiana Before Select Comm., 109th Cong. (Dec. 14, 2005) at 174 (written statement of Col. (Ret.) Terry Ebbert, Dir., Homeland Sec. for New Orleans) [hereinafter statement of Terry Ebbert] [hereinafter *Dec. 14, 2005 Select Comm. Hearing*].

Dec. 14, 2005 Select Comm. Hearing at 174 (statement of Terry Ebbert).

Id. at 174-75 (statement of Terry Ebbert).

Shane Harris, *Federal Emphasis on Terrorist Threat Frustrates Local Disaster Response Officials,* NAT'L JOURNAL, Oct. 20, 2005 at 4 *available at* http://www.govexec.com/dailyfed/1005/102005nj1.htm (last visited Jan. 26, 2006).

Id.

Id.

Directive on Management of Domestic Incidents, 39 WEEKLY COMP. PRES. DOC. 10 280 (Feb. 28, 2003) (Known as Homeland Security Presidential Directive/HSPD-5); Directive on Management of National Preparedness, 39 WEEKLY COMP. PRES. DOC. 1822 (Dec. 17, 2003) (Known as Homeland Security Presidential Directive/HSPD-8).

Government Accountability Office [hereinafter GAO], Pub. No. GAO-05-652, *Homeland Security: DHS' Efforts to Enhance First Responders' All Hazards Capabilities Continue to Evolve* (July 2005) 26-30.

Id. at 39-41.

Dep't of Homeland Sec., *FY 2006 Homeland Security Grant Program: Program Guidance and Application Kit,* (Dec. 2005). Those capabilities include planning, community preparedness and participation, communications, critical infrastructure protection, on-site incident management, citizen protection: evacuation and in-place protection, emergency operations center management, critical resource logistics and distribution, urban search and rescue, volunteer management, emergency public information and warning, responder safety and health, triage and pre-hospital treatment, public safety and security response, medical surge; medical supplies management and distribution, environmental health, mass prophylaxis, mass care, firefighting operations and support, hazardous material response, structural damage assessment and mitigation, economic and community recovery, restoration of lifelines. *Id.*

Id.

Apr. 14 Preparing Hearing at 90 (statement of Dave Liebersbach, Pres., Nat'l Emergency Mgmt. Ass'n).

Id.

GAO, GAO-03-119, *High-Risk Series: An Update* (Jan. 2003); Congressional Research Service [hereinafter CRS], Rep. No. 31670, *Transfer of FEMA to the Department of Homeland Security: Issues for Congressional Oversight* [hereinafter CRS Rep. No. 31670] at 5 (Dec. 17, 2002).

Exec. Order No. 12127, 3 C.F.R. 1979 (1979); Exec. Order No 12,148, 44 Fed. Reg. 43239 (1979).

CRS Rep. No. 31670 at 5 (2002).

March 2005 Brown Memo; Letter from Michael Brown, Dir., FEMA to Tom Ridge, Sec'y, Dep't of Homeland Sec. (Sept. 15, 2003); National Emergency Mgmt Ass'n, *Priority Congressional Issues: 2004 Mid Year Conference,* (Feb. 10-13, 2004).

Spencer S. Hsu and Julie Tate, *Brown's Turf Wars Sapped FEMA's Strength,* WASH. POST., Dec. 22, 2005.

Letter from Michael Brown, Dir., FEMA to Tom Ridge, Sec'y, Dep't of Homeland Sec. (Sept. 15, 2003).

Letter from David Liebersbach, Pres., Nat'l Emergency Mgmt. Ass'n to Honorable Don Young and Honorable James Oberstar (July 27, 2005).

March 2005 Brown Memo.

March 2005 Brown Memo.

James J. Carafano and David Heyman, THE HERITAGE FOUND, *DHS 2.0: Rethinking the Dep't of Homeland Sec.,* Dec. 13, 2004 at 14.

Paul C. Light, *Katrina's Lesson in Readiness,* WASH. POST, Sept. 1, 2005 at A29.

James Carafano, Ph.D., and Richard Weitz, Ph.D., THE HERITAGE FOUND, *The Truth About FEMA: Analysis and Proposals,* Dec. 7, 2005.

Id.

Id.

Hearing on Hurricane Katrina: The Role of the Department of Homeland Security Before Select Comm., 109th Cong. (Oct. 19, 2005) at 4-5 (written statement of Michael Chertoff, Sec'y, Dep't of Homeland Sec.).

Press Release, Int'l Assoc. of Fire Chiefs, *Secretary Chertoff Announces Reorganization, Plans for DHS* (Aug. 1, 2005) (on file with Select Comm.).

March 2005 Brown Memo.

Homeland Sec. Act of 2002, Pub. L. No 107-296, 116 Stat. 2135 (2002).

U.S. Dep't of Homeland Sec., *Nat'l Response Plan* (Dec. 2004).

March 2005 Brown Memo.

Briefing for Select Comm. Staff with Madhu Beriwal, Pres., Innovative Emergency Mgmt., in Wash., D.C. (Jan. 6, 2006) (discussing how funding for FEMA staff to participate in subsequent Hurricane Pam implementation workshops had been cut).

Briefing for Select Comm. Staff with Andrew Maner, Chief Fin. Officer, Dep't of Homeland Sec., in Wash., D.C. (Jan. 18, 2006) [hereinafter Briefing with Andrew Maner].

[42] Briefing with Andrew Maner; FEMA, *Reductions to FEMA Base*, FY 2003-2005 (Jan. 18, 2006) (on file with Select Comm.).

[43] According to OMB data, a total of 448 employees (full-time equivalents, or FTEs) were transferred from FEMA to various DHS offices in 2003
  • 42 FTEs were transferred from FEMA's salaries and expenses budget account to DHS's Departmental Operations account;
  • 206 FTEs were transferred from FEMA's Working Capital Fund to DHS's Working Capital Fund; and
  • 200 FTEs were transferred from FEMA's Office of Inspector General to DHS's Office of Inspector General. (GAO, GAO-04-329R, *Transfer of Budgetary Resources to the Dep't of Homeland Sec. (DHS)* at 22 (Apr. 30, 2004) (on file with Select. Comm)).

And since the establishment of the Department, the following programs have been transferred from FEMA to other Departmental entities (OMB, Funding Chart (Oct. 4, 2005) (on file with Select Comm.):
• Emergency Management Performance Grants
• National Strategic Stockpile
• Citizen Corps
• Other grants for emergency management
• Inspector General
• FIRE Act Grants
• First Responder Grants
• Metropolitan Medical Response System grants

Moreover, according to information provided to the Select Comm. by DHS, the funding transfers that Brown referenced in his testimony Before the Select Comm. break down as follows (Briefing with Andrew Maner; FEMA, *Reductions to FEMA Base, FY 2003-2005* (Jan. 18, 2006) (on file with Select Comm.)):

FY 2003 –
• Unobligated balances from FY 2002 – $30.6 million (*Id.*) (DHS start-up costs)
• FY 2003 appropriations – $12 million (DHS start-up costs) (Of the $12 million in FY 2003 appropriations, $10 million had been allocated for Salaries and Expenses for preparedness functions and $2 million had been allocated for the programs of another management account – Emergency Management Planning and Assistance.)
• Transfer of Office for National Preparedness functions to Office of Domestic Preparedness/Bureau of Transportation Security - $10.6 million
• Transfer to the Transportation Security Administration to fund a shortfall from the Liberty Shield Supplemental – $5.5 million
• Transfer to the DHS Office of Inspector General for audits and investigations of the Disaster Relief Fund – $21.4 million

FY 2004 –
• FEMA share of DHS e-government initiatives (mostly to maintain DisasterHelp.gov website) – $2.6 million
• FEMA share of other DHS central services – $2.8 million
• Transfer to Inspector General for audits and investigations of the Disaster Relief Fund – $22 million
• National preparedness functions transferred to ODP – $28 million
• General reduction to base funding for Departmental management – $34 million

FY 2005 –
• Reduction for management cost savings realized from efficiencies attributable to the creation of DHS – $11.7 million
• $18,501 million for Working Capital Fund

[44] *Hearing on Hurricane Katrina Response and Initial Recovery Operations: Mississippi Before Select Comm.*, 109th Cong. (Dec. 7, 2005) at 7 (written statement of William Carwile, former FEMA Fed. Coordinating Officer, State of Miss.) [hereinafter *Dec. 7, 2005 Select Comm. Hearing*]; *Hearing on Hurricane Katrina: Perspectives of FEMA's Operational Professionals Before the Senate Committee on Homeland Security and Governmental Affairs*, 109th Cong. (Dec. 8, 2005) at 57-58 (statement of Scott Wells, Deputy, FEMA Fed. Coordinating Officer, State of LA) [hereinafter *Perspectives FEMA Hearing*].

[45] *Dec. 7, 2005 Select Comm. Hearing* at 7 (written statement of William Carwile, former FEMA Fed. Coordinating Officer, State of Miss.).

[46] *Perspectives of FEMA Hearing* at 57 (statement of Scott Wells, Deputy, FEMA Fed. Coordinating Officer, State of LA) [hereinafter statement of Scott Wells].

[47] *Id.*

[48] *Id.* at 57-58.

[49] Spencer Hsu, *Leaders Lacking Disaster Experience*, WASH. POST, Sept. 9, 2005 at A1.

[50] Interview by Select Comm. Staff with William Lokey, FEMA Fed. Coordinating Officer in Wash., D.C. (Jan. 26, 2006); FEMA Regions I, II, III, IV, V, VI, VIII, and IX with Acting Directors; *See, e.g.*, Region VIII Acting Director, *available at* http://www.fema.gov/about/bios/maurstad.shtm (last visited Jan. 30, 2006).

[51] Justin Rood, *FEMA's Decline: An Agency's Slow Slide From Grace*, GOVERNMENT EXECUTIVE (Oct.1, 2005).

[52] www.ourpublicservice.org/usr_doc/2003-rankings.pdf (last visited Jan. 28, 2006).

[53] *Id.*

[54] Interview by Select Comm. Staff with Andy Kopplin, Chief of Staff, Office of the Governor of LA, in New Orleans, LA (Nov. 6, 2005).

[55] *Perspectives of FEMA Hearing* at 60 (statement of William Carwile, former FEMA Fed. Coordinating Officer, State of Miss.) [hereinafter statement of William Carwile].

[56] *Id.* at 60.

[57] *Id.* at 65-68.

[58] *Id.* at 59 (statement of Senator Joseph Lieberman).

[59] *Id..* at 67 (statement of William Carwile).

[60] *Id.* at 58 (statement of Scott Wells)

[61] *See id.* at 67 (statement of William Carwile).

FEMA

"The sheer force of Hurricane Katrina disabled many of the communications systems that state and local authorities and first responders rely upon to communicate with each other and with FEMA. This was not an issue of interoperability, but of basic operability, resulting from wind, flooding, loss of power, and other damage to infrastructure."

Michael Chertoff
Secretary, U.S. Department of Homeland Security
Select Committee Hearing, October 19, 2005

COMMUNICATIONS

Massive communications damage and a failure to adequately plan for alternatives impaired response efforts, command and control, and situational awareness

Summary

Massive inoperability—failed, destroyed, or incompatible communications systems—was the biggest communications problem in the response to Katrina. It was predicted and planned for by some, while others experienced problems with their operations or were caught relatively unprepared. The loss of power and the failure of multiple levels of government to take the initiative to adequately prepare for its effect on communications hindered the response effort by compromising situational awareness and command and control operations, particularly in New Orleans and along the Mississippi Gulf coast. The Federal Emergency Management Agency (FEMA) could have pre-positioned mobile communications in New Orleans but did not because it believed that it should first be *asked* to do so by local authorities. In turn, poor situational awareness, and its resulting effect on command and control, contributed to the negative effects of inaccurate or unsubstantiated media reports because public officials lacked the facts to address what the media reported. To deal with the loss of power, some state and local governments had redundant communications and other means to communicate, such as satellite phones, which were invaluable. But they also experienced certain problems due to technical difficulties, high winds, and exceptionally high demand that at times overtaxed their capacity.

Where communications were operable or soon were restored, long debated and unresolved issues with interoperability among federal, state, and local communications systems complicated the efforts of first responders and government officials to work together in managing the response to Katrina. In recent years, local and state governments in each of the affected states have received several million dollars in federal funding to address communication interoperability issues. Despite

claims of an "austere fiscal environment,"[1] at each level of government, internal debate, parochial interests, and a general lack of prioritization and coordination between affected jurisdictions regarding the formation and implementation of interoperable communications policies and plans severely hindered the rescue, response, and recovery efforts at all levels of government.

Finding: Massive inoperability had the biggest effect on communications, limiting command and control, situational awareness, and federal, state, and local officials' ability to address unsubstantiated and inaccurate media reports

Massive inoperability was the biggest communications problem in the response to Katrina. By all accounts, destruction to regional communications companies' facilities and the power systems on which they depend was extraordinary. For example:

A downed communications tower, Plaquemines Parish, LA.

■ More than three million customer telephone lines were knocked down in Louisiana, Mississippi, and Alabama.[2] As of September 28, 2005, over 260,000 customer lines remained out of service, including 238,000 in Louisiana and 22,000 in Mississippi.

■ The entire communications infrastructure on the Mississippi Gulf coast was destroyed.

■ Significant damage was inflicted both on the wire line switching centers that route calls and on the lines used to connect buildings and customers to the network.

■ Thirty-eight 911 call centers went down. Thirty days after landfall, two call centers in Louisiana remained out of service.

■ Two telephone company switches in New Orleans responsible for routing 911 calls for the surrounding parishes were knocked out by flooding, resulting in one of the most significant losses of capacity in and around New Orleans.

■ Local wireless networks also sustained considerable damage, with up to 2,000 cell sites out of service.[3] A month after landfall, approximately 820 cell sites remained out of service, the majority within New Orleans and other areas of Louisiana.[4]

■ Over 20 million telephone calls did not go through the day after the hurricane.

■ 37 of 41 broadcast radio stations in New Orleans and surrounding areas were knocked off the air (2 AM and 2 FM stations continued to broadcast).

After surviving Hurricane Katrina's initial blow, the radio communications system for the New Orleans police and fire departments dissolved as its radio towers lost their backup power generators in the ensuing flood.[5] The New Orleans Police Department's communications system failed and was inoperative for three days following the hurricane. At one point, hundreds of New Orleans first responders were trying to communicate on only two radio channels on a backup system, forcing them to wait for an opening in the communications traffic to transmit or receive critical information. The New Orleans Police Department headquarters, and six of the eight police districts' buildings were out of commission due to flooding, limiting (or precluding) their ability to establish command and control by performing basic law enforcement functions because their communications were destroyed.

The Louisiana State Police reported the devastation caused by the storm "severely hampered the ability of emergency responders operating on the state system to communicate with other emergency services personnel." The State Police currently operate a statewide analog wireless communications system originally installed for

Six of the eight police districts' buildings were out of commission due to flooding, limiting (or precluding) their ability to establish command and control by performing basic law enforcement functions because their communications were destroyed.

voice communications and last upgraded in 1996. It is use by about 70 agencies with a total of over 10,000 subscriber Its infrastructure consists of 46 tower sites and 28 dispatch consoles. In a report issued December 7, 2005, the State Police reported, in addition to the effect it had on the state system, storm damage to communications systems the loca governments maintained was "severe and debilitating," further restricting communications between emergency responders. The equipment at its 46 towers depends on electricity and, when that was lost, keeping them running was nearly impossible once it became necessary to refuel the generators operating them because debris and flood waters hampered their refueling efforts.[6]

Mississippi experienced problems similar to the other affected Gulf states. Most of its state and first responder communications capabilities were inoperable during and in the immediate aftermath of the storm, forcing the various responders to rely on satellite phones and radios (which experienced their own problems due to wind damage and interference). According to Mississippi Emergency Management Agency (MEMA) Director Rober Latham, the entire communications infrastructure of the state's Gulf coast was destroyed by Hurricane Katrina, systems elsewhere across the state were inoperable, and those systems that were working were overloaded, resulting in delays processing local governments' requests for assistance. As a result, often the only communications capability present in Mississippi — for both MEMA as well as the affected counties — was through satellite phones and radios, which operate by connecting to satellites rather than routing calls through land-line or cellular towers.[7] FEMA, for its part, deployed a Mobile

Emergency Response Support detachment (MERS)[8] to the state Emergency Operations Center (EOC) in Jackson, Mississippi, to provide satellite communications systems for its operations in the Gulf coast counties. However, despite the presence of MERS and hand-held satellite phones in all of the affected counties' EOCs, the Federal Coordinating Officer for Mississippi, Bill Carwile, testified that communications capabilities were far short of what was needed to be effective.[9]

The majority of site problems were due to lack of power. Some sites had T-1 (high speed data) telephone land-line problems, but the design of the system generally allows access to more than one site in the area, so the radio/telephone calls were routed from the secondary power site. This created some delays in accessing the system, but was not a critical factor. Cellular telephone service was generally available throughout Alabama's affected areas, but several tower sites were overloaded or not fully operational after Katrina made landfall. This was not a major problem because the Alabama Emergency Management Agency (AEMA) does not consider cellular telephone service a primary source of communications during emergency response. Instead, AEMA has a cache of pre-programmed Southern LINC radios that are activated during disasters, programmed with specific groups for users (such as Mutual Aid, Logistics, Emergency Management Assistance Compact (EMAC), Staging, etc.) and have telephone capability. There were approximately 15 LINC portable units activated and delivered for use in the field for this disaster.

The importance of power, fuel, and communications to disaster response and situational awareness

The near total failure of regional communications degraded situational awareness and exacerbated problems with agency coordination, command and control, logistics, and search and rescue operations. Reliable communications are critical to the preparation for and response to a catastrophic event because of the effect they have on establishing command and control and maintaining situational awareness.[10] Without functioning communications systems, first responders and government officials cannot establish meaningful command and control, nor can they develop the situational awareness necessary to know how and where to direct their response

and recovery efforts. Similarly, without the ability to call for help, citizens cannot seek emergency assistance, alert responders or others to their whereabouts and needs, or receive updates or instructions from officials.

Katrina interoperability problems were masked to some degree by the larger and more serious breakdown of operability resulting from the destruction of facilities or power outages. Restoring phone service requires more than waiting for the flood waters to recede and restoring power. While many cables may be salvageable, the electronics that pass the signals across those lines will need to be replaced. As noted by Jim Gerace of Verizon Wireless: "It's essentially analogous to putting a PC in your bathtub. It's not going to work once it dries."[11]

In Louisiana, the winds and flooding degraded the quality of available communications, reducing most communications to the limited number of available satellite phones. Additionally, the communications infrastructure that remained intact was soon overwhelmed by the heavy communications traffic during the response.[12] FEMA officials reported "there were no status reports coming into the EOC Monday."[13] Deputy Federal Coordinating Officer Scott Wells stated that if the Coast Guard was doing flyovers of New Orleans, those reports did not get to the EOC on Monday.[14] Additionally, failed communications affected responders' ability to share information up and down the chain of command. According to Louisiana officials, "Two or three days after the storm, state police were running into division commanders in the New Orleans Police Department who reported that they had not talked to anyone above their rank since the storm."[15]

The Alabama communications infrastructure fared better than in Mississippi and Louisiana. The AEMA has various communications capabilities, with redundant backups, to ensure it maintains a high level of connectivity throughout the state. The EOC had equipment and trained personnel to communicate over all types of communications networks, including satellite, 800 MHz digital phone service, amateur radio, and others. AEMA staff viewed communications systems and capabilities during Katrina as strengths, although the goal of true interoperability within and among county emergency response and law enforcement agencies remains elusive to this day.[16] The state has little ability to mandate what types of communications technology each county procures. AEMA makes recommendations, but with so many different counties all with communications equipment in various stages of their life cycle, the EOC must be able to process all types of communications. The AEMA integrates these systems with various bridging technologies. Several attempts have been made in the past to build a state-wide/state-owned system, but lack of funding has prevented construction of this system. Nevertheless, state and county emergency management officials concluded their communications capacity functioned reasonably well during their response to Hurricane Katrina.[17]

Power is the most dominant factor for any

FEMA

telecommunications system[18] and hurricanes virtually always knock out the power, even if only for a short period of time. Very often these power outages can last for several days or more following powerful storms. For Hurricane Katrina, the Department of Homeland Security (DHS) was aware the power outages caused by the storm could go on for weeks after the storm, possibly longer. On August 28, the DHS National Infrastructure Simulation and Analysis Center issued and provided to the White House (among others) a "Fast Analysis Report" predicting the storm's likely impact on the Gulf coast area based on conditions as of August 27 when Katrina was still a Category 5 storm. In the report, DHS made a number of predictions about the storm's impact on power supplies, including:

■ Electric power loss is likely to affect over 2.6 million customers;

■ Restoring power could take more than 2 weeks for most of the affected areas **excluding New Orleans and the coastal areas** and may be hampered by flooding or other obstacles;

■ The New Orleans region could have power outages lasting 16 weeks if excessive flooding occurs, disabling existing pumping stations up to 10 weeks and entailing power repairs that may take up to 6 weeks to complete.[19]

As predicted, the affected states all suffered severe damage to their power and communications infrastructures. During Hurricane Katrina, the City of New Orleans lost two primary tower sites and had to evacuate the police and fire communications centers because of flooding. Associated with the loss of the communications centers was the loss of all 911 capabilities and the federally funded New Orleans Maritime Interoperable Committee's (NOMIC) interoperable bridging capability. Colonel Terry Ebbert, the Homeland Security Director for New Orleans, testified "Over 2,000 police, fire, and Emergency Medical Services (EMS) personnel were forced to communicate in a single channel mode, between radios, utilizing only three mutual aid frequencies."[20]

The government's ability to communicate depends upon the viability of the commercial network's infrastructure. Ninety percent of communications assets are privately owned and operated.[21] Verizon Wireless serves the Gulf coast with two major switching stations in Baton Rouge and Covington, Louisiana. These serve as the links between cell phone antennae scattered throughout the region and the rest of the global network. While the stations themselves remained operational during and after landfall, the Covington facility lost connectivity with the cell towers due to two breaks in the connecting fiber-optic ring run by BellSouth.[22] Normally, a fiber-optic link provides redundancy: if one link is cut, information can still travel along the other route. Katrina, however, knocked out both sources because of physical damage to the fiber-optic cable. In one case, the fiber-optic cable that transported calls and internet traffic to and from New Orleans and ran along the Lake Pontchartrain Causeway was severed. Additionally, at least 20 cell towers went down due to either power loss or flooding. Verizon Wireless installed backup generators at many of the towers, but not at all, reportedly, due to local zoning restrictions.[23] Refueling remote generators also proved lifficult if not impossible. Verizon Wireless reported a umber of its generators were stolen, one of Nextel's fuel rucks was stopped at gunpoint and its fuel taken for other urposes while en route to refuel cell tower generators, nd the Mississippi State Police redirected a fuel truck arrying fuel designated for a cell tower generator to fuel enerators at Gulfport Memorial Hospital.[24]

Other power and telecommunications companies

FEMA

eported similar problems due to exhausted fuel supplies, lisruption of natural gas supply lines, or refueling lifficulties due to flooding or security concerns. BellSouth eported that on September 1, 112 of its central offices vere running on emergency generators, an additional 7 were completely down, and an additional 32 had no onnectivity to the backbone network.[25] These central ffices served as 911 tandems, and when they went down, hey created outages of 911 service in as many as 13 ouisiana parishes.[26] In Gulfport, Mississippi, company fficers at Alabama Power and Southern Nuclear's Watson lectric Generating Plant watched as a 30-foot storm surge ose 20 feet within the plant and flooded the 50-kilowatt ackup generator that normally would have started vhen the power failed. The nerve center for the region's ower company had no backup power to supply to the ommunity.[27]

The loss of power — a common and altogether xpected result of a hurricane — need not mean n affected area has no communications capability ntil the utility companies are able to restore normal lectricity service. A well-planned and robust emergency ommunications system should be sustainable at easonable levels of operation even after electrical power

is lost.[28] Resources to sustain operations include backup generators and fuel, redundant systems, self-healing networks, access to multiple technologies, common radio frequencies for wireless communications, sufficient spectrum bandwidth to support communications needs, and the proper equipment and infrastructure to make it all work.[29] Regular land-line telephone connections can function after local power is lost if central switches maintain power and lines are not damaged; telephone switches can usually operate until their backup generators run out of fuel or are knocked out by flooding. Similarly, cell towers carrying commercial phone service and public safety radio communications can continue to function with back-up power, usually batteries.

Destruction to communications capability hindered command and control and severely limited situational awareness

"It sounds like it can happen again. How many local governments have a communications plan when everything fails?"

REPRESENTATIVE TAMMY BALDWIN (D-WI),
query during hearing, U.S. House of Representatives,
Sept. 7, 2005

In myriad ways, the vast destruction to the communications infrastructures, particularly those in Mississippi and Louisiana, negatively affected first responders and local and state governments' attempts to establish command and control. It also limited — and sometimes precluded — them from achieving and maintaining situational awareness. In New Orleans and along the Gulf coast, the National Guard and first responders were forced to rely on paper relays or face-to-face communications to convey critical information between emergency operation centers and the field.[30] This drastically slowed the pace at which those in the EOCs became aware of situations throughout their respective areas of

AP PHOTO/RIC FRANCIS

With communications knocked out, police relied on two-way radios.

responsibility. It delayed the delivery of direct assistance where it was most needed, and it hindered the ability to forward requests to state or federal agencies that might have been able to help. In the Louisiana state EOC, the communications problems were so severe that state officers could not reliably communicate with local officials, others in the state government, or federal officials, exacerbating the already severe problems with situational awareness.

On Tuesday, August 30, FEMA Deputy Federal Coordinating Officer Phillip E. Parr traveled by helicopter to the New Orleans Superdome.[31] His mission there was threefold: (1) form a unified command with the state as represented by the Louisiana National Guard, and the City of New Orleans; (2) maintain visibility of commodities ordered; and (3) build out a base from which FEMA teams could be formed to locate and assist in the hardest hit parishes. But according to Parr his ability to accomplish those goals were hindered by the lack of appropriate communications as mentioned in his statement: "To accomplish these goals we were to meet a Mobile Emergency Operations and Communications Vehicle and use that as a base of operations and communication. Due to extensive flooding in the city our communications vehicle was unable to enter the Dome and this severely hampered our operations."[32]

First responders' ability throughout the Gulf coast to communicate across a broad range (or distance) and gain control of an incident was compromised when power was lost and many had only their mobile (cellular) phones available. Because these phones run on batteries, they lose power the longer first responders have to use them in lieu of other means and, as a result, have shorter and shorter ranges over which they can operate as their batteries run down.

In Mississippi, Major General Harold A. Cross, the state's Adjutant General, told Select Committee staff the National Guard forward operating units on the coast were unable to establish and maintain meaningful communications with MEMA or Governor Barbour for the first 48 hours following landfall.[33] As a result, their initial activities were based on executing pre-landfall assignments and reacting to events on the ground as they found them. They acted with initiative. Exacerbating the situation, and unknown to Cross, the company providing the satellite service to his phones (Mobile Venture Satellites) had not informed the Guard it had changed the

contact numbers on two of the Guard's satellite phones. As a result, no one attempting to reach these phones — one with the Guard's Director of Military Assistance, Lieutenant Colonel Lee Smithson (the officer responsible for coordination of the Guard's materials and assets during the response and recovery effort), and another at the Stennis Space Center commodities distribution center — could get through. The Guard did not learn of the change until two days into the response when the state National Guard's Assistant Adjutant General, Gen. Playnt, finally spoke with Smithson to ask why he was not answering his satellite phone. Smithson contacted the satellite phone company, and was only then informed of the number change.[34] Because of this failure to notify the Guard of two number changes, those who needed to reach two of the most important people or places involved in the response did not have the correct numbers to do so. This contributed to the problems and delays experienced during commodity coordination and distribution efforts experienced in Mississippi.[35] These types of problems are further discussed in the COMMAND AND CONTROL chapter.

FEMA pre-positioned communications assets, but not in New Orleans, where the need became exceptionally critical

FEMA partially anticipated the communications infrastructure, particularly the parts dependent on electric power, would be needed in the Gulf coast and pre-positioned with each of the three states' EOCs a MERS detachment.[36] MERS detachments are designed to provide rapid multi-media communications, information processing, logistics, and operational support to federal,

A FAILURE OF INITIATIV

state, and local agencies during catastrophic emergencies and disasters. They do so, in part, by providing mobile telecommunications, operational support, life support, and power generation for on-site disaster management; this includes satellite, telephone, and video hook-ups.[37]

Former FEMA Director Michael Brown testified, in hindsight, FEMA should have pre-positioned a MERS detachment in New Orleans. Brown stated:

> In terms of communications, one of the things that I didn't mention in the litany of things that we prepositioned is something called our MERS unit, our Mobile Emergency Response System [sic]. Those are vehicles that are command and control units that have satellite hook-ups, telephone hook-ups, video hook-ups; enable us to do communications. I prepositioned those in all three states so that we would have communications wherever we needed it. I eventually sent one of those command units — in fact, it's one of the largest ones we have, called Red October — I eventually sent one of those into New Orleans for Mayor Nagin to use.
>
> In retrospect, I wish I'd done that four days earlier. Had I done it four days earlier, though, guess what? It probably wouldn't have gotten there. So I'm now second-guessing myself, and perhaps I should have prepositioned it there before Katrina made landfall. But again, that's not the role of the federal government; that's Mike Brown Monday morning quarterbacking, having seen everything that took place and trying to figure out, okay, now seeing everything that did not work in Louisiana, if I had known that beforehand, what could I have done?[38]

As a result, one of the federal assets that might have allowed FEMA and the local and state governments to work around the damage to the communications systems and sooner gain situational awareness about conditions in New Orleans was not present. Arguably, this instance of a failure of initiative — leaving a MERS detachment outside of the city — exacerbated the degree to which the massive damage to the local communications infrastructure delayed the ability of FEMA to learn of or confirm events on the ground in New Orleans and act accordingly.

"Communications and coordination was lacking, preplanning was lacking. We were not prepared for this."

WILLIAM M. LOKEY, FEMA Federal Coordinating Officer in Louisiana, testimony before U.S. Senate, Jan. 30, 2006

Poor situational awareness and its resulting effect on command and control contributed to the negative effects of inaccurate media reports because public officials lacked access to the facts to address media reports. Throughout the early days of the response, media reports from New Orleans featured rampant looting, gunfire, crime, and lawlessness, including murders and alleged sexual assaults at the Superdome and Convention Center. Few of these reports were substantiated, and those that were—such as the gunfire—were later understood to be actually coming from individuals trapped and trying to attract the attention of rescuers in helicopters.

Officials on the ground in New Orleans interviewed by Select Committee staff stated the media greatly exaggerated reports of crime and lawlessness and that the reports from the Convention Center and Superdome were generally unsubstantiated. Of the six deaths in the Superdome, none were crime-related (five were due to medical reasons and one was a suicide).[39] In some cases, the media's coverage of its own performance - well after the fact - showed many of these reports from the early days after Katrina were false. In December, *ReasonOnline* reported that:

> On September 1, 72 hours after Hurricane Katrina ripped through New Orleans, the Associated Press news wire flashed a nightmare of a story: "Katrina Evacuation Halted Amid Gunfire…Shots Are Fired at Military Helicopter."
>
> The article flew across the globe via at least 150 news outlets, from India to Turkey to Spain. Within 24 hours commentators on every major American television news network had helped turn the helicopter sniper image into the disaster's enduring symbol of dysfunctional urbanites too depraved to be saved.
>
> Like many early horror stories about ultra-violent New Orleans natives, whether in their home city or in far-flung temporary shelters, the A.P. article turned out to be false. Evacuation from the city of New Orleans was never "halted,"

state. AEMA officials considered their communications redundancy to be one area that worked well in their response to Katrina.[44] Southern LINC, the company whose network Alabama uses as its primary radio system, had a representative on site at the state EOC during this period that provided outage updates (as noted earlier, the AEMA has a cache of pre-programmed LINC radios that it activates during disasters and which also provide telephone capability).

In Mississippi, Gulf coast county governments had taken steps (including using DHS preparedness grant funds) to ensure some communications capability would likely survive a disaster. For example, despite the catastrophic damage suffered by the Gulf coast, Harrison County's Enhanced Digital Access Communication Systems (EDACS)[45] remained operational at nearly 100 percent capacity during and after Katrina's landfall. One interoperability success story from Mississippi was that although the Harrison County EDACS was not capable of linking to FEMA or to the MEMA EOC in Jackson, Mississippi, it was capable of linking with similar systems utilized by the Florida State Police and the Florida Fish & Wildlife Agency who arrived in Mississippi shortly after Katrina's landfall. These Florida state agencies were able to quickly reprogram their EDACS radios to communicate over the county's network. Within two weeks of landfall, the Harrison County EDACS system was able to expand to allow first responder communications within the adjoining Jackson and Hancock counties.[46]

MEMA Director Latham testified that Mississippi had satellite radios permanently mounted in the three coastal counties (Harrison, Hancock, and Jackson) and that 30 other counties also had these radios.[47] All MEMA personnel had access to a mobile satellite radio for communications throughout the state. This proved fortunate because often the only communications capability in Mississippi after the storm—for both MEMA and the affected counties—was through satellite phones and radios, which operate by connecting to satellites rather than routing calls through land-based lines or cellular towers.[48] The Harrison County EOC was only able to use its cellular communications system for approximately 12 hours until the battery on the cell tower died. They were unable to use the satellite system at the Harrison County EOC because it was damaged during the storm. Additionally, and currently, MEMA has a mobile operations unit, which it can deploy to disaster areas

and allows communication across all bands.[49] Despite problems the satellite systems experienced (discussed below), Latham noted they did allow the state to learn vital information it needed about conditions in the counties and their assistance needs.[50]

Unlike the three coastal counties, Pearl River County fared better at maintaining communications capability during and after the storm. Pearl River County had two satellite phones in its emergency operations center. According to its Emergency Management Director, Bobby Strahan, these worked throughout the response but did prove problematic early on because it took a long time for any calls to go through.[51] In addition, Strahan reported the county has four high band repeater systems strategically placed throughout the county which allow all of its first responders (including police, fire, and EMS) as well as its schools to communicate. All of these systems' locations had generator backup systems which functioned properly during Katrina. In addition, Pearl River County was able to sustain communications within the county and, to a limited extent, with portions of adjacent Hancock County because it had used DHS grant funds to buy a mobile communications center (trailer) that allowed it to communicate with agencies throughout the county as well as with MEMA's mobile operations unit.[52]

In Louisiana, most of the parishes did not have satellite phones because they chose to discontinue the service after the state stopped paying the monthly fees for the phones.

Others were caught relatively unprepared to deal with the communications problems that resulted from the hurricane's damage or found their existing capabilities were insufficient. In Louisiana, most of the parishes did not have satellite phones (as their counterparts in Mississippi did) because they chose to discontinue the service after the state stopped paying the monthly fees for the phones. In 1999, the state began using federal funding to provide each parish emergency management office with a satellite telephone and paid the $65.00 monthly fee, bu discontinued doing so for the parishes in August 2004. As a result, all but three parishes—Orleans, Plaquemines, and Jefferson—discontinued their satellite phone service.[53] Larry Ingargiola, Director, Office of Homeland Security and Emergency Management, St. Bernard Parish, told Select Committee staff the parish returned the satellite phones when the state stopped paying the monthly service fee. After Katrina hit, the state sent the phones back to St. Bernard because there was no other means of communication available to the parish.[54]

The failure of 911 call centers in New Orleans also illustrates how others were unprepared to deal with communications problems. Identifying where calls to a 911 call center will be routed if it is rendered inoperable is a basic preparation for Public Safety Answering Points (PSAPs) such as 911 call centers.[55] Although the technology to switch calls to 911 to an alternative location exists,[56] many 911 call centers in Louisiana did not have protocols in place to identify where their calls should go and had not arranged for any rerouting. As a result, numerous calls to 911 in the immediate aftermath – especially as the floodwaters in New Orleans were rising — simply dropped.[57]

In Mississippi, MEMA Director Latham testified the state found it did not have enough satellite radios when only its satellite systems were operable.[58] As a result, during its response to Katrina, MEMA purchased additional portable satellite phones for its State Emergency Response Team (in the future, Mississippi indicated these additional phones can be issued to local authorities as a redundant system in disasters).[59] Some Mississippi responders also found their satellite communications capabilities were not sufficiently capable of withstanding high winds. Specifically, though they generally remained operable and the state relied on them during its response to Katrina, Mississippi's satellite communications capabilities suffered because the hurricane force winds—at times sustained over 130 miles per hour—lifted the antennas in each of the coastal counties, causing satellite communications there to fail because the antennas were no longer properly targeted. As a result, for several days, these counties lost their ability to communicate with the state EOC in Jackson or FEMA about their needs for assistance or the status of any commodities requests they had made before the storm.[60] Because of the lessons it learned from the damage to its satellite systems in Katrina, Mississippi is investigating for future use in its counties' EOCs the omni-directional antennas it has in place on all

of its state EMA and Department of Wildlife, Fisheries, and Parks vehicles. According to Latham, these antennas would not be affected by strong winds and would allow constant communications.[61]

Responders in Louisiana similarly experienced certain problems that can plague satellite-based communications. Specifically, satellite phones are technically capable of transmitting calls virtually anywhere on earth, but they may have trouble doing so when the user is inside a building or when the weather is cloudy. According to the Louisiana State Police report, "heavy cloud coverage and system inundation" limited the effectiveness of the portable satellite phones delivered to several troop headquarters in the affected areas.[62] Even when weather conditions permit smooth transmissions of signals for satellite communications, this is meaningless if the caller does not know how to use the satellite phone, or the phone does not work at all. As Mayor Nagin noted during Congressional testimony, "I have a huge box of satellite phones that did not work."[63]

For the systems that were functioning after the storm as well as those that were eventually restored, problems with interoperability further exacerbated rescue efforts. As Colonel Ebbert testified, "[T]here was no voice radio contact with surrounding parishes or state and federal agencies. Lives were put at risk and it created a direct operational impact on their ability to maintain control of the rapidly deteriorating situation within the city, carry out rescue efforts and control the evacuation of those people who had failed to heed the call for evacuation."[64]

Despite hundreds of millions in federal funding for technology and communications, the absence of true communication interoperability within and between affected jurisdictions severely hindered rescue and response efforts at all levels of government

Many in the industry, media, and government have long focused on the problem of "interoperability." FEMA officials claimed they did not know for days about the thousands of people at the New Orleans Convention Center, first responders in helicopters could not talk to crews patrolling in boats, and National Guard Commanders in Louisiana and Mississippi had to use runners to relay orders.

Finding: The National Communications System met many of the challenges posed by Hurricane Katrina, enabling critical communication during the response, but gaps in the system did result in delayed response and inadequate delivery of relief supplies

The federal government's use of the National Communications System (NCS) prior to, during, and after Katrina's landfall to coordinate assets and personnel proved effective, but like the efforts of the Gulf states, it too was overwhelmed by the magnitude of the damage left in Katrina's wake.

Following the Cuban Missile Crisis, President Kennedy established the National Communications System by a Presidential Memorandum on August 21, 1963.[82] On April 3, 1984, President Ronald Reagan signed Executive Order 12472, which broadened the NCS' national security and emergency preparedness capabilities and superseded President Kennedy's original 1963 memorandum. The NCS expanded from its original six members to an interagency group of 23 federal departments and agencies, and began coordinating and planning NS/EP telecommunications for the federal government under all circumstances, including crisis or emergency, attack, recovery, and reconstruction. As mandated by

the Executive Order, the NCS also includes an industry component called the National Coordinating Center for Telecommunications (NCC), a joint industry-government body within the NCS. The operational mission of the NCC is coordination of restoring and reinstituting national security and emergency preparedness communications in an emergency situation. During Hurricane Katrina, the NCC operated a 24-hour watch center and conducted daily analysis and situational monitoring of ongoing events, and coordination of government and industry response capabilities.[83]

In addition to the Executive Order, the NCS has a specific communications role in the National Response Plan (NRP). Specifically, the NCS is the lead agency responsible for the communications component of Emergency Support Function 2 (ESF 2), which "ensures the provision of Federal communications to Federal, State, local, tribal and private-sector response efforts during an Incident of National Significance." In support of ESF 2, the NCC is tasked to function as a central point of coordination and information sharing among communications infrastructure operators.

To facilitate coordination of industry and government operations during an emergency, the NCS maintains and operates several priority service programs, which help ensure critical calls are completed in the event of congestion damage to the national commercial communications infrastructure. They include the Government Emergency Telecommunications Service (GETS), which provides authorized users a higher rate of call completion during periods of outages or congestion resulting from disasters. During and after Hurricane Katrina, the NCS issued 1,000 new GETS access code numbers to first responders and emergency recovery officials in the affected states. Between August 28 and September 9, the GETS system was utilized to make over 35,000 calls.[84] The NCS also operates a wireless counterpart to GETS, the Wireless Priority Service (WPS) program. It provides priority treatment for calls made during periods of wireless network congestion by emergency response personnel with national security and emergency preparedness responsibilities. During Katrina, the NCS enabled and distributed over 4,000 WPS cellular phones.[85]

In Gulfport, MS., video conferencing was used to coordinate disaster aid.

The NCS operates the Telecommunications Service Priority (TSP) program, which establishes a regulatory, administrative and operational framework for restoring and provisioning priority communications services. Through this program, service vendors are authorized to give priority to restoration and provision of service to those with TSP assignments. Following Hurricane Katrina, the NCS completed more than 1,500 TSP assignments helping to restore emergency response capabilities in the Gulf states.[86]

The NCS also maintains the Shared Resources High Frequency Radio Program (SHARES), which provides a single, interagency, voluntary message handling system using over 250 High Frequency (HF) radio frequencies when other communications are unavailable. A network of government, military, and Military Affiliate Radio Service (MARS) radio stations (an organized network of Amateur Radio stations affiliated with the different branches of the armed services to provide volunteer communications), and more than 90 federal, state, and private industry organizations participate in the SHARES program. Within days following Katrina's landfall, the NCS coordinated participation by 431 SHARES stations across the nation and assisted first responders conducting search and rescue missions by relaying information to appropriate government agencies; relayed logistical and operational information between FEMA's EOCs in Georgia, Mississippi, and Louisiana; relayed health and welfare messages between volunteer agencies in Georgia and the national headquarters of the American Red Cross in Washington, DC; established radio contact with deployed U.S. Navy ships detailed to New Orleans; and provided frequency coordination between federal agencies, Louisiana and Mississippi's EOCs, and the Civil Air Patrol.[87]

Additionally, the NCS coordinated the frequencies used by the nearly 1,000 Amateur Radio Emergency Services (ARES) volunteers across the nation who served in the Katrina stricken area providing communications for government agencies, the Red Cross and the Salvation Army. Emergency communications were conducted not only by voice, but also by high-speed data transmissions using state-of-the-art digital communications software known as WinLink. In Mississippi, FEMA dispatched Amateur Radio operators to hospitals, evacuation centers, and county EOCs to send emergency messaging 24 hours

FEMA dispatched Amateur Radio operators to hospitals, evacuation centers, and county Emergency Operations Centers to send emergency messaging 24 hours per day.

per day. According to Bay St. Louis Mayor Edward A. "Eddie" Favre, amateur radio operators were especially helpful in maintaining situational awareness and relaying Red Cross messages to and from the Hancock County EOC.[88] At airports in Texas and Louisiana, radio amateurs tracked evacuees and notified families of their whereabouts. The Red Cross deployed amateur radio volunteers at its 250 shelter and feeding stations, principally in Mississippi, Alabama, and Florida.[89] The Salvation Army operates its own Amateur Radio communications system using Amateur radio volunteers, known as SATERN. During the Hurricane Katrina response and recovery effort, SATERN joined forces with the SHARES program and received over 48,000 requests for emergency communications assistance utilizing federal frequencies made available via the SHARES program.[90]

Following landfall, the NCS activated the SHARES network on August 29, and worked with The U.S. Northern Command (NORTHCOM) to identify and deploy communications assets, and by September 2, all NCS ESF 2 systems were in place to receive communications requests from the affected region. The NCS dispatched satellite communications vans to various locations, including New Orleans City Hall, the Louisiana State Police headquarters in Baton Rouge, the New Orleans Airport, and the Louisiana National Guard in Jefferson Parish; dispatched AT&T and MCI cellular communication vans to the state EOCs in Mississippi and Louisiana; and identified and delivered satellite handsets to first responders in all three affected states. Additionally, the NCS designed and installed a new E-911 system in Plaquemines Parish, and provided an interim digital Land Mobile Radio system to the eight parishes surrounding New Orleans.[91]

Like all levels of government, the NCS was not able to address all aspects of the damage to the communications infrastructure of the Gulf states. Although the NCS performed several important functions prior to and during the response efforts, the "historical magnitude of Hurricane Katrina stressed the processes and procedures of the NCS and required ESF 2 to perform functions . . . which it [had] never done before."[92]

Conclusion

The extent of destruction and damage to the communications infrastructure and services caused by Katrina exceeded that of any other natural disaster experienced by the Gulf coast states. Simply put, Katrina's devastation overwhelmed government resources at all levels. The loss of power and the failure of various levels of government to adequately prepare for the ensuing and inevitable loss of communications hindered the response effort by compromising situational awareness and command and control operations.

Despite the devastation left by Katrina, this needn't have been the case. Catastrophic disasters may have some unpredictable consequences, but losing power and the dependent communications systems after a hurricane should not be one of them. The parish officials in Louisiana who declined to spend $65 per month for satellite phones showed a failure of initiative when they gave up those assets. Why such a "penny wise-pound foolish" decision was allowed to stand defies explanation. The same satellite phones that were given up by some of the parishes eventually were returned to them after Katrina's landfall because they had no other means of communicating with those bringing help to people in need. Similarly, those in the 911 call centers who could not reroute calls for help showed a failure of initiative by not taking the steps necessary to ensure calls to them were not in vain, simply because predictable things — power losses and flooding — happened after a hurricane.

Catastrophic disasters may have some unpredictable consequences, but losing power and the dependent communications systems after a hurricane should not be one of them.

Issues with interoperability have existed for years. Government officials and emergency service agencies are well aware of the need to establish and maintain robust emergency communications systems. Modern day National Guard units should not have to rely upon runners to relay messages. Governors should be able to communicate with their generals. Police commanders should be able to communicate with their officers in the street. Despite knowledge of interoperability problems and the seriousness of the consequences of failure to address them, and because of often parochial desires for duplicative, expensive, and diverse stand alone communications systems, officials responsible for providing for public safety spent millions on other priorities.

Disasters start and end at the local level. If first responders want interoperability with their counterparts in the future, their leaders need to communicate. Federal authorities need to establish standards. State and local officials need to take the initiative to make responsible use of federal, state and local funding to develop communications systems that can grow with their communities. These officials need to fulfill the public trust given to them. They need to lead. ∎

Hearing on Hurricane Katrina: Preparedness and Response by the State of Louisiana Before Select Comm., 109th Cong. (Dec. 14, 2005) at 3 (written statement of Col. Terry Ebbert, USMC (ret), Director of Homeland Security & Public Safety, City of New Orleans) [hereinafter *Dec. 14, 2005 Select Comm. Hearing*].

Hearing on Ensuring Operability During Catastrophic Events Before the Comm. on Homeland Security Subcomm. on Emergency Preparedness, Science, and Technology, 109th Cong. (Oct. 26, 2005) at 1 (written statement of Dr. Peter M. Fonash, Deputy Manager, National Communications System, DHS) [hereinafter *Oct. 26, 2005 Comm. on Homeland Security Hearing*].

Id. at 6.

Hearing on Public Safety Communications from 9/11 to Katrina: Critical Public Policy Lessons Before the Comm. on Energy and Commerce, Subcomm. on Telecommunications and the Internet, 109th Cong. (Sept. 29, 2005) at 3 (written statement of Kevin J. Martin, Chairman, Federal Communications Commission) [hereinafter *Sept. 29, 2005 Energy & Commerce Comm. Hearing*].

Matthew Fordahl, *Communication Breakdown: From 9/11 to Katrina*, ASSOC. PRESS, Sept. 13, 2005.

LA State Police, *Louisiana Totally Interoperable Environment* at 2-3 (Dec. 7, 2005).

Hearing on Hurricane Katrina: Preparedness and Response by the State of Mississippi Before Select Comm., 109th Cong. (Dec. 7, 2005) at 3-4 (statement of Robert R. Latham, Jr., Executive Director, Mississippi Emergency Management Agency) [hereinafter *Dec. 7, 2005 Select Comm. Hearing*].

See http://www.fema.gov/rrr/mers01.shtm (last visited Jan. 26, 2006).

Dec. 7, 2005 Select Comm. Hearing at 7 (statement of William L. Carwile, III, former Federal Coordinating Officer, Hurricane Katrina Response and Initial Recovery Operations: Mississippi).

[9] Command and control are two key aspects of emergency management involving unity of command and effort among local, state, and federal authorities as well as an accepted chain of command. (*See* DHS *National Response Plan*, (Dec. 2004) at 1 [hereinafter *NRP*].) Situational awareness simply refers to the extent to which the various responders—local, state, or federal officials, for example—have accurate, reasonably reliable information about conditions in the affected area and can use that information to guide their response efforts.

[1] Stephen Lawson, *Cell carriers tackle Katrina damage*, IDG NEWS, (San Fran.), Sept. 1, 2005.

[2] Interviews by Select Comm. Staff with FEMA, Louisiana state and local officials in New Orleans, LA (Nov. 3-10, 2005).

[3] Interviews by Select Comm. Staff with FEMA officials, New Orleans, LA (Nov. 9-10, 2005).

[4] Interviews by Select Comm. Staff with Scott Wells, FEMA, in New Orleans, LA (Nov. 9, 2005).

[5] Interview by Select Comm. Staff with Gordon Mitchell and Ralph "Joey" Booth, Louisiana State Police in Baton Rouge, LA (Nov. 9, 2005).

[6] Interviews by Select Comm. Staff with Jerry McRay, Branch Chief, Information Technology Systems, Alabama Emergency Management Agency EOC officials in Clanton, AL (Oct. 11, 2005).

[7] Interviews by Select Comm. Staff with Alabama Emergency management Agency EOC officials in Clanton, AL (Oct. 11, 2005).

[8] *Hearing on Communications in a Disaster Before the Senate Comm. on Commerce, Science & Transportation*, 109th Cong. (Sept. 22, 2005) (statement of Hossein Eslambolchi, President, AT&T Global Networking Technology Services and AT&T Labs) [hereinafter *Sept. 22, 2005 Senate Commerce Comm. Hearing*].

[9] DHS National Infrastructure Simulation and Analysis Center, *Fast Analysis Report (Update to Reflect Category 5 Status) to DHS IP on Hurricane Katrina, Gulf coast* at 1-2 (Aug. 28, 2005) (emphasis supplied).

[0] *Dec. 14, 2005 Select Comm. Hearing* at 3 (written statement of Col. Terry Ebbert).

[1] *Hearing on Hurricane Katrina Before the Comm. on Energy & Commerce*, 109th Cong. (Sept. 7, 2005) (statement of Kenneth P. Moran, Acting Director, Office of Homeland Security Enforcement Bureau, Federal Communications Commission).

[2] Joab Jackson, *Telecom infrastructure was no match for Katrina*, WASH. TECH., Nov. 7, 2005 [hereinafter *Telecom Infrastructure Article*].

[3] *Id.*

[4] Interview (telephone) by Select Comm. Staff with Anthony Melone, Vice President of Network Operations Support, Verizon Wireless (Jan. 27, 2006); *See also*, E-mail correspondence from Hans Leutenegger to Anthony Melone and Select Comm. Staff (Jan. 30, 2006) (9:45 a.m.).

[5] BellSouth *Press Release* (Sept. 2, 2005). Prior to Katrina, BellSouth Corporation served 1.9 million lines in Louisiana. Approximately 1.03 million lines (54.2%) were initially affected. In Mississippi, approximately 438,000 (39.8%) were affected, and in Alabama 93,000 (5.5%) of the state's 1.7 million lines were effected. By Sept. 2, approximately 144,000 remained out of services in New Orleans due to long term displacement. BellSouth News Release, Sept. 2, 2005.

[6] *Hearing on Communications Interoperability Before the Senate Comm. on Commerce, Science & Transportation*, 109th Cong. (Sept. 29, 2005) at 5-6 (written statement of Chief Willis Carter, First Vice President of the Assoc. of Public Safety Communications Officials-Int' and Chief of Communications, Shreveport Fire Department, Shreveport, LA) [hereinafter *Sept. 29, 2005 Senate Commerce Comm. Hearing*].

[7] Julia Harwell Segars, *Katrina's Wrath*, OPTIMIZE, Oct. 2005.

[8] Congressional Research Service Report RL32594, *Public Safety Communications Policy*, by Linda K. Moore (Updated Jan. 5, 2006).

[9] *Id.*

[40] Interview by Select Comm. Staff with Major General Harold A. Cross, Adjutant General, Mississippi National Guard in Jackson, MS (Oct. 13, 2005).

[41] *Hearing on Hurricane Katrina: Perspectives of FEMA's Operations Professionals Before the Senate Comm. on Homeland Security and Governmental Affairs*, 109th Cong. (Dec. 8, 2005) at 3 (statement of Phillip E. Parr, Deputy Federal Coordinating Officer, FEMA Joint Field Office, Austin, TX) [hereinafter *Dec. 8, 2005 Senate Homeland Security and Governmental Affairs Comm. Hearing*].

[42] *Id.*

[43] Interview by Select Comm. Staff with Maj. Gen. Harold A. Cross, Adjutant Gen., Mississippi National Guard at Jackson, MS (Oct. 13, 2005).

[44] Interview by Select Comm. Staff with Lt. Col. Lee Smithson, Mississippi National Guard, in Gulfport, MS (Jan. 19, 2006).

[45] *Id.*

[46] *See* http://www.fema.gov/rrr/mers01.shtm (last visited Jan. 26, 2006).

[47] *Id.*

[38] *Hearing on Hurricane Katrina: The Role of the Federal Emergency Management Agency Before Select Comm.*, 109th Cong. (Sept. 27, 2005) at 32-33 (statement of Michael D. Brown, former Dir., FEMA) [hereinafter *Sept. 27, 2005 Select Comm. Hearing*].

[39] Interview by Select Comm. Staff with Colonel Mark Mouton and Lieutenant General Jacques Thibideaux, Louisiana National Guard, in New Orleans, LA (Nov. 3, 2005).

[40] Matt Welch, *They Shoot Helicopters, Don't They? How journalists spread rumors during Katrina*, REASON ONLINE, Dec. 2005, *available at* http://www.reason.com/0512/co.mw.they.shtml, (last visited Jan. 25, 2006) [hereinafter *Media Rumors Article*].

[41] *Telecom Infrastructure Article.*

[42] *Media Rumors Article.*

[43] Briefing for Select Comm. Members and Staff by Mayor Favre, Bay St. Louis, MS, in Hancock County, MS (Jan. 20, 2006).

[44] Interview by Select Comm. Staff with Bruce Baughman, Dir., State of Alabama Emergency Management Agency, in Clanton, AL (Oct. 11, 2005).

[45] This simulcast trunked radio system consisting of three 20 channel sites and two 10 channel sites was installed in 2003 to serve law enforcement, fire, emergency medical, emergency management, and public utility services in Harrison County, which includes the cities Gulfport and Biloxi, MS.

[46] E-mail correspondence from Benjamin J. Spraggins, Dir., Harrison County Emergency Management Agency, to Select Comm. Staff (Feb. 1, 2006) (2:53 p.m.).

[47] *Dec. 7, 2005 Select Comm. Hearing* at 56 (statement of Robert R. Latham, Jr.).

[48] *Id.* at 3-4.

[49] *Id.* at 7 (statement of Bobby Strahan, MCEM, Director, Pearl River County Emergency Management Agency).

[50] *Id.* at 97 (statement of Robert R. Latham, Jr.).

[51] Interview (telephone) by Select Comm. Staff with Bobby Strahan, MCEM, Director, Pearl River County Emergency Management Agency (Nov. 29, 2005).

[52] *Id.; Dec. 7, 2005 Select Comm. Hearing* at 2, 7-8 (statement of Bobby Strahan).

[53] Interview by Select Comm. Staff with Matt Farlow, Information Technology Divisions Chief, LA Office of Homeland Security and Emergency Preparedness (Nov. 4, 2005).

[54] Briefing for Select Comm. Staff by Larry Ingargiola, Director, Office of Homeland Security and Emergency Management, St. Bernard Parish, in St. Bernard Parish, LA (Nov. 3, 2005).

[55] *Sept. 22, 2005 Senate Commerce Comm. Hearing* (written statement of Kevin J. Martin).

[56] *Id.*

[57] *Id.*

[58] *Dec. 7, 2005 Select Comm. Hearing* at 35 (written statement of Robert R. Latham, Jr.).

[59] *Id.*

[60] *Id.* at 1 (written statement of Benjamin J. Spraggins; *Id.* at 4 (written statement of Robert R. Latham, Jr.).

[61] *Id.* at 4 (written statement of Robert R. Latham, Jr.).

[62] LA State Police Report, *Louisiana Totally Interoperable Environment* at 3 (Dec. 7, 2005).

[63] *Hearing on Hurricane Katrina: Hurricane Katrina Evacuations Before the Senate Comm. on Homeland Security and Gov't Affairs,* 109th Cong. (Feb. 1, 2006) (testimony of C. Ray Nagin, Mayor of New Orleans, LA).

[64] *Dec. 14, 2005 Select Comm. Hearing* (written statement of Col. Terry Ebbert).

[65] *Sept. 29, 2005 Senate Commerce Comm. Hearing* at 1 (written statement of Dereck Orr, Program Manager of Public Safety Communications, Nat'l Institute of Standards and Technology).

[66] *Sept. 22, 2005 Senate Commerce Comm. Hearing* at 5 (statement of Sen. Rockefeller).

[67] *Oct. 26, 2005 Comm. on Homeland Security Hearing* (written testimony of Dr. Linton Wells II, Acting Ass't Sec'y of Defense, Networks and Information Integration, and DOD Chief Information Officer).

[68] *Sept. 29, 2005 Senate Commerce Comm. Hearing* at 2 (written statement of David Boyd, Deputy Director, Office Systems Engineering & Development, DHS).

[69] Correspondence from Colonel Henry L. Whitehorn, Superintendent, LA State Police, to Select Comm. (Dec. 29, 2005) [hereinafter Col. Whitehorn correspondence].

[70] *Dec. 14, 2005 Select Comm. Hearing* at 3 (written statement of Col. Terry Ebbert).

[71] Louisiana State officials claim for "Louisiana to achieve true interoperability, the initial acquisition cost infrastructure and equipment is $552,680, 423" thus rendering "the achievement of true interoperability at the state level virtually impossible." *See also* Col. Whitehorn correspondence.

[72] *Dec. 14, 2005 Select Comm. Hearing* at 3-4 (written statement of Col. Terry Ebbert); Col. Whitehorn correspondence.

[73] Matthew Fordahl, *U.S. Lacks Unified Emergency Radio System*, ASSOC. PRESS, Sept. 13, 2005 [hereinafter *Radio System Article*].

[74] Col. Whitehorn correspondence.

[75] The COPS Office was created by Title I of the Violent Crime Control and Law Enforcement Act of 1994 (P.L. 103-322). The mission of the COPS Office is to advance community policing in all jurisdictions across the United States. The COPS Office awards grants to state, local and tribal law enforcement agencies throughout the United States so they can hire and train law enforcement officers to participate in community policing, purchase and deploy new crime-fighting technologies, and develop and test new and innovative policing strategies.

[76] Congressional Research Service Memo, FEMA Hazard Mitigation, *COPS and ODP Grants Awarded in Alabama, Louisiana and Mississippi in Fiscal Years 2003-2005* (Dec. 21, 2005).

[77] *Id.*

[78] Interview (telephone) by Select Comm. Staff with Gilbert Moore, COPS Program External Affairs Office (Sept. 27, 2005).

[79] *Radio System Article.*

[80] Interview by Select Comm. Staff with Gregg Meffert, Chief Information Officer, City of New Orleans, in Wash., DC (Oct. 18, 2005).

Dec. 14, 2005 Select Comm. Hearing at 3 (written statement of Col. Terry Ebbert)

The NCS began in 1962 after the Cuban missile crisis when communications problems among the United States, the Union of Soviet Socialist Republics, the North Atlantic Treaty Organization, and foreign heads of state threatened to complicate the crisis further. After the crisis, President John F. Kennedy ordered an investigation of national security communications, and the National Security Council (NSC) formed an interdepartmental committee to examine the communications networks and institute changes. This interdepartmental committee recommended the formation of a single unified communications system to serve the President, Department of Defense, diplomatic and intelligence activities, and civilian leaders in order to provide better communications support to critical government functions during emergencies. The NCS mandate included linking, improving, and extending the communications facilities and components of various federal agencies, focusing on interconnectivity and survivability. *See* NCS website: http://www.ncs.gov/faq.html (last visited Jan. 31, 2006).

Oct. 26, 2005 Homeland Security Comm. Hearing at 3 (written statement of Dr. Peter M. Fonash).

Interview by Select Comm. Staff with Dr. Peter M. Fonash, in Wash., DC (Jan. 27, 2006).

Oct. 26, 2005 Homeland Security Comm. Hearing at 3 (written statement of Dr. Peter M. Fonash).

Id.

Id. at 4.

Briefing for Select Comm. Staff by Edward A. Favre, Mayor, Bay St. Louis, MS, in Bay St. Louis, MS (Oct. 13, 2005).

Hearing on Back to the Drawing Board: A First Look at Lessons Learned from Katrina Before the Government Reform Comm., 109th Cong. (Sept. 15, 2005), at 257-58 (written statement of Jim Haynie, President, National Association for Amateur Radio).

Sept. 29, 2005 Energy & Commerce Comm. Hearing (written statement of Harold Kramer, Chief Operating Officer, American Radio Relay League).

Oct. 26, 2005 Comm. on Homeland Security Hearing at 9 (written statement of Dr. Peter M. Fonash).

Id. at 7.

AP PHOTO/STEVEN SENNE

"Natural disasters will always be chaotic situations. But with proper planning and preparation, it is possible to respond quickly to restore order and begin recovery efforts."

Bob Riley
Governor, State of Alabama
Select Committee hearing, November 9, 2005

Command and Control was impaired at all levels, delaying relief

Summary

Command and control are key aspects of emergency management, and the federal government has taken several steps, most notably developing an Incident Command System (ICS), to promote unity of command among local, state, and federal authorities. However, during and immediately after Hurricane Katrina made landfall, there were lapses in command and control within each level of government, and between the three levels of government.

Local governments' command and control was often paralyzed by the complete destruction of their entire emergency management infrastructure. While state command and control facilities (such as the Emergency Operations Centers (EOCs)) were generally intact after the storm, the magnitude of the storm and a variety of operational factors impaired their unity of command. The federal government also struggled to maintain unity of command across different agencies and within individual agencies. These problems exacerbated the challenges of coordinating across all levels of government and prevented overall unity of command.

One of the factors that impaired command and control was the lack of communications and situational awareness. While the reasons for these deficiencies were detailed previously (see the COMMUNICATIONS chapter), their impact was to paralyze normal command and control mechanisms. Local governments in many locations in Louisiana and Mississippi lost all communications capabilities for some period. This prevented them from communicating their situation and needs to the state level.

The state EOC in Louisiana experienced its own communications problems. State officials in the EOC could not reliably communicate with local officials, other state officials, or federal officials. Similarly, the federal government lost some communications, and initial efforts to bring in supplemental capabilities to improve command and control were unsuccessful. Other key factors that impaired command and control can be traced to a lack of sufficient qualified personnel, inadequate training, and limited funding.

The lack of effective command and control, and its impact on unity of command, degraded the relief efforts. Delays and otherwise poor assistance efforts caused by a lack of command and control are documented in this and other chapters. They include:

- delayed and duplicative efforts to plan for and carry out post landfall evacuations at the Superdome;
- uncoordinated search and rescue efforts that resulted in residents being left for days without food and water;
- separate military commands for the National Guard and Department of Defense (DOD) active duty troops;
- confusion over deliveries of commodities because some officials diverted trucks and supplies without coordination with others;

- lack of clarity as to who was assisting hospitals to evacuate; and
- the collapse of the New Orleans Police Department and its ability to maintain law and order.

Finding: Command and Control was impaired at all levels of government

Command and control are key aspects of emergency management

Command and control are key aspects of emergency management, and the federal government has taken several steps to promote unity of command among local, state, and federal authorities. For example, the National Incident Management System (NIMS) was developed in 2004 to enable all responders, regardless of jurisdictions or discipline, to effectively and efficiently work together. The NIMS "provides a nationwide template enabling federal, state, local, and tribal governments and private-sector and nongovernmental organizations to work together effectively and efficiently to prevent, prepare for, respond to, and recover from domestic incidents regardless of cause, size, or complexity."[1]

In addition, NIMS incorporated the ICS, which has been in existence since the early 1970s. ICS is the standardizing scalable concept designed to provide for an integrated and organized structure while eliminating jurisdictional boundaries.[2] The National Response Plan (NRP) calls for the implementation of NIMS and the ICS upon activation of the NRP to ensure maximum flexibility of operation during the situation at hand.[3]

Optimal levels of coordination occur when there is unity of command, unity of effort, and an accepted chain of command. Unity of effort encompasses the concept that all parties to a mission should be focused upon the same agreed-to objectives and should work together to achieve them. Unity of command is the concept that an individual has only one superior to whom he or she is directly responsible, creating a clear line of supervision and command and control.

Chain of command furthers the concept of unity of command, creating a line of authority from the lowest ranking individual to those in command, establishing a highly effective and efficient system. It requires that order are given only to those directly below an individual in the chain of command and orders are received from only those directly superior in the chain of command. Those a the appropriate level in the chain of command can then, as authorized, coordinate their activities with peers in their partner organizations.

Many local governments lost command centers o otherwise could not establish unity of command

Achieving unity of command — with local, state, and federal authorities all acting together seamlessly to plan and conduct emergency operations — is often a challenge during a major disaster. It was particularly so when Hurricane Katrina made landfall. Local

governments' command and control was often paralyzed by the complete destruction of their entire emergency management infrastructure.

In Alabama, local counties had the least problems with command and control. Because Katrina turned to the west and hit Mississippi and Louisiana the hardest, Alabama counties were able to maintain their emergency management infrastructure. Both Baldwin and Mobile counties still had operating EOCs and generally were able to stay in contact with the state EOC.[4]

In Mississippi, there was a massive storm surge that destroyed government facilities, making it very difficult for the local communities to establish command and control. According to FEMA's Federal Coordinating Officer (FCO) for Mississippi, Bill Carwile, much of the emergency management and public safety infrastructure was destroyed in the coastal counties.[5] Mayor of Waveland Tommy Longo said the city staged at various points around the city some of the resources it expected to need to respond to the storm's damage, and it also staged some of these resources about 10 miles north of the city as a backup in the event of a catastrophic event.[6] Despite the city's preparations, the hurricane destroyed these resources. The storm decimated all of Waveland's public buildings, severely limiting its ability to provide command and control and to mount a response to the storm.[7]

Similarly, Hancock County lost its EOC—the location from which it expected to provide command and control for the county's response to the storm—because of severe flooding early on in the hurricane.[8] Pearl River County also lost its EOC in the early hours of the storm due to wind and water damage that knocked out its emergency backup generator and caused other damage, making the center inoperable.[9]

In Louisiana, there was a similar level of destruction to the basic emergency management infrastructure at the parish level. Many of the parish EOCs and public safety facilities were wiped out or flooded.[10] While Jefferson Parish was hard hit, it was in better shape to respond because it had protected its EOC. Jefferson Parish Emergency Manager Dr. Walter Maestri explained the EOC was in a hardened facility — an old incinerator with cement walls — with the command center, living quarters, and emergency generator all on upper floors.[11] While the EOC suffered immediate problems with communications being down, and it eventually had a shortage of fuel for its generator, it was able to keep operating at some level.[12]

Lack of command and control was particularly a problem in New Orleans. The authorities in the city lost their command and control facilities after the levee breaches and subsequent flooding. The city abandoned its EOC when City Hall was flooded and the emergency generator was flooded, cutting out power.[13] As discussed in more detail in the LAW ENFORCEMENT chapter, the New Orleans Police Department headquarters and district stations were flooded, crippling command and control for that department.[14] Similarly, the Louisiana National Guard, with headquarters at Jackson Barracks in New Orleans, lost its command and control due to flooding and had to abandon its operations center and re-establish it in an elevated parking structure at the Superdome.[15] According to Lieutenant General H Steven Blum, Chief of the National Guard Bureau, "…Jackson Barracks flooded at the most inopportune time, and he [Major General Landreneau—the Louisiana Adjutant General] had to relocate in the middle of trying to gain situational awareness and coordinate the response."[16] Thus, in New Orleans, for at least some period of time, emergency managers, the police, and the military lost command and control over their own personnel and lost unity of command with the other local, state, and federal agencies that needed to be involved in the relief efforts.

Even where there was still some infrastructure in place and communications were less of a problem, local command and control suffered from lack of clarity. The most notable example of this was at the Superdome in New Orleans. Although there were both National Guard and New Orleans Police Department officials on site to physically establish a unified command and personally talk to each other face to face, there was no consensus on who was in charge. Louisiana National Guard officers who ran security operations at the Superdome, Colonel Mark Mouton and LtC. Jacques Thibodeaux said the New Orleans Police Department had the lead for command and control.[17] They stated that the National Guard was there in support of the police.[18]

These statements directly conflict with New Orleans Police Department comments that the National Guard had the lead for command and control at the Superdome. Deputy Chief Lonnie Swain, the senior New Orleans Police Department officer at the Superdome, said the National Guard always had the lead for command and control at the Superdome and the police were there in support of the military.[19] In support of this position, New Orleans officials said the Superdome was a state facility, so a state agency (the National Guard) would naturally be in charge.[20]

One FEMA official, Deputy FCO Scott Wells, also said there was no clear unity of command at the Superdome.

He said he arrived there on Wednesday, August 31, and when he tried to contact the leadership at the location to coordinate FEMA activities, he found "nobody in charge, and no unified command."[21] For example, he said there was no organization or structure to collect requests, prioritize them, and pass them on to the next appropriate echelon. He described the conditions as "chaotic" and said there appeared to be no one planning the next steps.[22]

The Cloverleaf was another location in New Orleans where the command and control structure was unclear. Louisiana State Police officials Ralph Mitchell and Joseph Booth stated that one government agency (they did not know which one) set up a medical triage and treatment center at the Cloverleaf on Wednesday, August 31.[23] Crowds grew there as people came to the dry land on their own accord or were dropped off by the helicopters or boats that rescued them from the water.

On Thursday, September 1, medical patients were evacuated, but the rest of the crowd grew to about 6,000-7,000 people. By Thursday afternoon and evening, the crowd started getting restless. At one time, there were 60 state police officers there, in addition to National Guard troops. The two officials — who had been on site — said they did not know who was in charge of command and control or which agency had set up the medical triage center there in the first place.[24] Later on Thursday night and Friday morning, some relief came from FEMA and the National Guard, and the Cloverleaf was completely cleared by Saturday, September 3.[25]

The Convention Center, discussed in more detail in the EVACUATION chapter, suffered from no official presence at all. There was not even an attempt to establish command and control there until the rescue mission arrived on Friday, September 2 (four days after landfall).[26]

While there may have been some type of command structures set up at both the Superdome and the Cloverleaf, they do not appear to have been effective. The fact that the senior officials who were stationed at or visiting these locations disagreed on who was in charge, could not find out who was in charge, or did not know who was in charge, shows there was a significant lapse in command and control and demonstrates there was little unity of command at these locations in New Orleans.

State government unity of command was impaired by the magnitude of Katrina and other operational factors

While state command and control facilities (such as their EOCs) were generally intact after landfall, the magnitude of the storm and a variety of operational factors impaired their unity of command.

Again, Alabama encountered the fewest command and control problems because it was least affected by Katrina. According to Alabama Emergency Management Agency (EMA) Director Bruce Baughman, the state EOC was up and running, with effective command and control throughout the hurricane and its aftermath. Unlike Louisiana (discussed below) where the parishes and EOC lost use of their emergency management software, Alabama used its software effectively. The software, known as "EM 2000," was used by county EOCs to send requests for assistance and by the state EOC to task appropriate state or federal agencies and to track the status.[27] Select Committee staff were able to review the EM 2000 database and confirm the system was effectively used to track and close out many of the local requests.

Many examples demonstrate the effectiveness of Alabama's EOC and the EM 2000 system. On August 29 at 9:30 p.m. the Mobile Police Department requested vehicles for search and rescue operations. This task was marked complete in the EM 2000 database in a little over one hour at 10:41 p.m.[28] Earlier on August 29, Baughman ordered 40 truck loads of ice and 40 truck loads of water from Lipsey Water. This task was marked complete by 2:00 p.m. the next day.[29] At 6:41 p.m. on August 29, Baldwin County EMA requested, through EM 2000, five generators for use at water wells. This task was marked complete at 9:16 am the next morning.[30]

When some FEMA requests were made, however, they were not immediately addressed. On August 29, Mobile

of days after landfall, when situational awareness was weak and before more deliberate planning could take place.[37] FEMA went ahead and developed the hasty plans, but without the benefit of state EOC personnel participating. He said such state personnel should have participated because they had expertise in state and local conditions and capabilities.[38]

The only exception to this was the commodity distribution hasty plan. Wells said that was the only plan the state worked with FEMA to develop before landfall.[39] As another example, Wells cited the incident (covered in more detail in the MILITARY chapter) where the Louisiana Adjutant General requested DOD active duty forces directly without going through or even notifying FEMA.[40] Instead of practicing unity of command, Wells said the state bypassed FEMA for federal assistance, then later complained FEMA did not know what was going on, and that FEMA could not coordinate the federal effort.[41]

County EMA Director Walter Dickerson requested two EMA operations personnel and two FEMA logistics personnel to augment his staff. This need was not addressed until September 21.[31] Similarly, on August 30, when Monroe County requested shelter supplies from EMA, it had to wait for six days for the task to be closed. 50 cots were needed in addition to a self-contained shower and bath trailer.[32]

The Select Committee encountered severe disagreements about whether the State of Louisiana maintained effective unity of command. Some FEMA officials were very critical of Louisiana's command and control. Michael Brown, Director of FEMA during Katrina, called the state of Louisiana "dysfunctional" and said it did not have unity of command.[33] Brown cited this as one of the main reasons for delays in relief efforts in Louisiana and New Orleans.[34]

In addition, Wells said there was no unity of command in the EOC. Wells was particularly critical of the state for not practicing unity of command with the federal government's planning and coordination efforts.[35] Wells said state officials were "preoccupied with the evacuation" and would not participate in critical pre-landfall "hasty" planning in other areas such as (1) search and rescue, (2) rapid assessment teams, (3) medical evacuation, (4) sheltering and temporary housing, (5) commodity distribution, and (6) debris removal.[36]

According to Wells, these "hasty plans" would have helped guide the course of activities for the first couple

Other FEMA officials were not as harsh in their criticisms of Louisiana. Bill Lokey, the FEMA FCO in the state EOC, said there was at least a minimum level of command and control and unity of command, to the extent the various parties were working together to set common priorities for common objectives.[42] Lokey attributed any lack of unity of command and control to a variety of operational factors (detailed below) and the catastrophic nature of the event.[43]

Similarly, another FEMA official who was in the EOC and in New Orleans, Deputy FCO Phil Parr, said some level of chaos occurs in any disaster, so it was not particularly unusual that the EOC seemed chaotic under the circumstances.[44] As discussed in the next section, Lokey and Parr both stated that not only was the state government overwhelmed by the magnitude of the disaster, but the federal government was overwhelmed as well.[45]

Louisiana state officials, including State Coordinating Officer (SCO) Jeff Smith, countered FEMA criticisms by saying the EOC was fully functional.[46] Smith said it was always clear who was in charge at the EOC: the SCO.

Michael Brown, Director of FEMA during Katrina, called the state of Louisiana "dysfunctional" and said it did not have unity of command.

He also maintained the EOC and the state did maintain unity of command.[47] In response to then-FEMA Director Brown's comment that he arrived at the EOC and could not figure out who was in charge, Smith said that such comments were "just plain bull."[48] Smith stated — and Lokey concurred — that the SCO and FCO worked closely together throughout the crisis.[49] Smith also provided the Select Committee with a photo taken during the crisis of Lokey and Smith together in the EOC.[50] According to Smith, "if FEMA Director Michael Brown had wanted to find out who was in charge of the EOC, all he had to do was find his FEMA FCO, because I was standing right next to him."[51]

The Select Committee attempted to make an independent determination of the effectiveness of command and control in the EOC by listening to conference calls between the EOC and parishes.[52] Based on a review of pre-landfall conference calls, the EOC appeared to be organized and unified to the limited extent this could be determined through these calls.[53] For example, the SCO was clearly in charge of coordinating state and parish activities and managing all discussions and decisions in an orderly and logical fashion.[54] Participation in the calls was very broad, to include multiple state agencies, more than a dozen key parishes, federal agencies, other states, and the American Red Cross. In addition, every organization got its opportunity to talk, and there was time for each organization to ask questions. It appeared pre-landfall decisions and issues were fully vetted among the participants. However, these conference calls do not cover the period just after landfall — the most critical and challenging time for establishing and maintaining command and control.[55]

Despite the disagreements over the degree of effective command and control in the state EOC, federal and state officials both cited several operational factors that made unity of command difficult to maintain. Among the most significant factors were a lack of communications and situational awareness and a lack of sufficient qualified personnel, inadequate training, and limited funding. These are described later in this chapter as separate findings. The other operational factors impairing command and control in the state EOC, described by a number of federal and state officials, included the following:

- **Katrina's late turn toward Louisiana:** State officials indicated that Katrina had taken a "dramatic shift" toward Louisiana on Friday (August 26). They said they were not fully aware of the situation until Saturday and were therefore not as prepared as they otherwise would have been.[56]

- **Overwhelming number of requests:** The size of Katrina and the destruction she wrought was immense, including the flooding of New Orleans and subsequent problems with security and the post-landfall evacuation. All of these circumstances led to an overwhelming number of requests for assistance.[57]

- **Overcrowding in the EOC:** The EOC building and main room were very crowded by the large contingent of state and federal officials.[58] The EOC main room has a capacity of about 50 people, but there were about 200 people. The EOC building as a whole was also overcrowded with about 750-1,000 people in it. There were only 12 Emergency Support Function (ESF) rooms for 15 ESFs. State officials cited the size of the current Joint Field Office (JFO) (in an old department store with thousands of staff) as an indication of the amount of physical space and number of people needed to run an operation the size of Katrina.[59]

- **EOC Information Technology was overloaded:** The Information Technology system was overloaded by the number of additional computers logged in and the volume of information processed. This was slowing down and destabilizing the system, and officials had to add two servers in the middle of the response.[60]

- **Deviation from normal procedures:** Due to the overwhelming number of requests and degraded

FEMA should have been more sympathetic and provided more assistance when it was clear Louisiana was overwhelmed by the size of Katrina's devastation.

communications, officials had to deviate from normal procedures for requesting assistance.[61] The federal government contributed to this problem by also deviating from normal procedures. Specifically, other federal agencies tasked FEMA directly rather than putting requests to the parishes in the first place so they could go through the normal process (e.g., from the parish to the state and then to FEMA to be mission-assigned to other federal agencies.)[62]

■ **Freelancing by other federal, state, and local agencies:** State officials said, and a FEMA official confirmed, that federal agencies were "freelancing," or just showing up without coordinating with the appropriate authorities at FEMA or the state. They would bypass the command structure and just appear in the EOC.[63] In addition, several freelancers showed up from other state and local agencies, again, without coordinating with the appropriate authorities. They too would just appear in the EOC not knowing what to do.[64]

■ **Visits by politicians and celebrities:** Several elected officials from the state and national levels showed up in the EOC. While they just wanted to see what was going on and were trying to help, their presence distracted the EOC personnel.[65] There were similar visits by celebrities such as Oprah Winfrey and Sean Penn.[66] Most visits by elected officials and celebrities had large media crews covering them, further distracting the EOC personnel from their more urgent tasks.[67]

State officials who directed operations in the EOC — Col. William Doran and Mr. Jim Ballou — noted that with all of these operational factors, it would be easy for an outsider to conclude the EOC was a chaotic place.[68] In response to criticism from FEMA's Michael Brown, these two state officials (as well as the SCO Smith) said some level of confusion was to be expected in the EOC under the circumstances. They said FEMA should have been more sympathetic and provided more assistance when it was clear Louisiana was overwhelmed by the size of Katrina's devastation.[69]

Federal government also lacked unity of command across and within agencies

Like the states, the federal government also struggled to maintain unity of command across and within agencies. According to Louisiana SCO Smith, the federal government did not follow its own plan, the NRP, which calls for a unified command. In his prepared statement before the Select Committee, Smith stated "[a]nyone who was there, anyone who chose to look, would realize that there were literally three separate Federal commands."[70] Smith's statement goes on to describe these three separate command structures:

■ FCO and Joint Field Office (JFO): This was the unified joint command with the FCO (Lokey) and SCO (Smith) located initially at the state EOC, then moved to the Joint Field Office (in the old department store) once that was established.[71] The FCO, by doctrine, is the individual that is supposed to be in charge of all federal response operations, and only the FCO has the authority to obligate federal funds.[72]

■ Principal Federal Official (PFO): Smith said that "[t]he Primary [sic] Federal Officer (PFO) by doctrine is not supposed to be an operational person directly involved in response activities . . . . The PFO in Katrina went operational and began directing and guiding response operations and to a large degree left out the Federal Coordinating Officer (FCO)."[73] This was inconsistent with the NRP: "The PFO cell was operating on its own, communicating directly with the Governor, communicating directly with the Mayor of New Orleans and a myriad of other local elected officials," Smith said.[74]

■ Joint Task Force Katrina: This command was intended to serve DOD active duty forces. According to Smith, "[w]henever the task force commander of Hurricane Katrina, General Honoré, came onto the scene, he was also operating independently with little regard whatsoever for the Joint Field Office, which should have been the only unified command."[75]

The Select Committee found ample evidence supporting the view that the federal government did not have a unified command. For example, FEMA officials Lokey and Wells supported Smith's position, saying the PFO was not supposed to have an operational role and was not supposed to bypass the FCO.[76] They stated the initial PFO, Michael Brown, followed protocol. However, the second PFO, Coast Guard Admiral Thad Allen, immediately began directing operations and established a separate command in New Orleans, set apart from the SCO and FCO in the Joint Field Office. Both FEMA officials said Allen's direction of operations as a PFO exceeded his authorities as enumerated in the Stafford Act.[77]

Eventually Allen was appointed FCO in addition to PFO.[78] As Smith noted, "DHS in essence acknowledges that there was a problem …when DHS appointed the PFO as the FCO as well. DHS discovered the PFO did not have the authority to obligate money. Only the FCO has authority to obligate money."[79] This issue also arose in an April 2005 national level exercise sponsored by DHS called TOPOFF 3, where there was confusion over the different roles and responsibilities performed by the PFO and FCO.[80] The PFO issue is also discussed in detail in the NATIONAL FRAMEWORK chapter.

FEMA officials also acknowledged that DOD frequently acted on its own, outside the established unified command. Lokey said Honoré was directing activities from his JTF Katrina command ship (the USS Iwo Jima, docked pier-side in Orleans) without coordinating with the FCO at the state EOC and later the Joint Field Office.[81] He said Honoré, like the PFO was coordinating directly with local parishes and was accepting taskings from them, which violated established federal protocols.[82] Requests for assistance are supposed to go from the local level, to the state SCO, then to the FEMA FCO, and if appropriate, then to the Defense Coordinating Officer for DOD support.[83] Some may forgive Honoré for bypassing this process because it was broken and therefore unworkable after Katrina (as we discuss in the NATIONAL FRAMEWORK chapter). In fact, Lokey praised Honoré for "doing what had to be done to get things moving."[84] However, one of the results of Honoré's *modus operandi* of acting independently was further impairing FEMA's ability to maintain unity of command across the federal government. Assistant Secretary of Defense Paul McHale testified that "[m]ilitary command and control was workable, but not unified."[85] Additional difficulties between FEMA and DOD are discussed in the MILITARY chapter.

In addition to the problems with establishing and maintaining a unified command with DOD, FEMA struggled to establish a unified command with other organizations within DHS. According to Wells, the Coast Guard did not fuse their command in the search and rescue operation with the state and FEMA. Wells stated that for "the U.S. Coast Guard, who had junior officer representation but no authority to direct search and rescue air operations, all operations were directed by senior Coast Guard officers from another location. These officers refused to meet and conduct joint search and rescue operations with FEMA and state agencies."[86] Captain Bruce Jones, the Coast Guard officer in charge of air operations, commented that airborne search and rescue was sufficiently coordinated between the Louisiana National Guard's Task Force Eagle at the Superdome and the Coast Guard's air operations center at Belle Chasse Naval Air Station and that having two incident command was an effective way to divide the work load.[87] Regardless of the positive outcome of saving lives, there was not unit of command across the function of search and rescue.

In addition to its problems coordinating with other federal agencies, FEMA had problems coordinating its own activities. Because most communications systems were impaired, Lokey could not talk directly with his advance team leader in New Orleans, Parr.[88] Thus, they were unable to coordinate their activities. As another example, Lokey and his staff in the EOC did not know another FEMA official, Marty Bahamonde, was in New Orleans during and immediately after landfall until they were informed by FEMA headquarters on late Monday, August 29. Before that time, they did not even know Bahamonde was there or what his function was.[89] More generally, Lokey said the federal government and particularly FEMA, were overwhelmed.[90] Overwhelmed organizations cannot achieve unity of command.

Louisiana EOC conference calls provide additional evidence there was a lack of coordination within FEMA.[91]

Once emergency communications were restored and the Louisiana EOC restarted its conference calls with the parishes on September 9, it was clear FEMA activities were not well-coordinated. The September 9 call recorded a discussion in which Smith stated FEMA's "right hand is not always knowing what the left hand is doing."[92]

Parish officials agreed with this assessment and provided several examples. They noted the local FEMA representatives (situated in the parish EOCs) were working hard to resolve their problems, but that "other FEMA people just keep showing up."[93] The call indicates some FEMA officials were making commitments to various local elected officials, without coordinating with the FEMA FCO, the state EOC, or the parish EOC. One parish official said this situation was "creating downright chaos."[94]

Temporary housing was cited as a particular area where FEMA coordination was unacceptable to the state and parishes. According to Smith, a FEMA regional housing team was not coordinating with the JFO. Smith said he "blew his top" that morning because these FEMA regional officials were bypassing the state and parish EOC process in planning for temporary housing. FEMA needs to have appropriate state and parish representatives involved in any FEMA discussions of temporary housing, he said. Smith told the parishes the FEMA FCO needs to "ride herd" on the FEMA regional housing group so they follow established procedures.[95]

Finding: Lack of communications and situational awareness paralyzed command and control

Localities, without communications, could not participate in unified command

One of the key factors that impaired command and control was the lack of communications and situational awareness. While the reasons for these deficiencies were detailed previously (see the COMMUNICATIONS chapter), their impact was to paralyze normal command and control mechanisms. Many local governments in Mississippi and Louisiana lost all communications capabilities for some period. This prevented them from communicating their situation to the state level.

Alabama, as noted before in this chapter and the COMMUNICATIONS CHAPTER, experienced relatively few communications problems. Federal and state

officials alike concluded their communications capacity functioned well during their response to Katrina.[96] The Alabama EMA has various communications redundancy programs to ensure that it maintains a high level of connectedness throughout the state. The EOC has equipment and trained personnel to communicate over all types of communications networks, including satellite, 800 MHz digital phone service, amateur radio, and others. Communications systems and capabilities are viewed by AEMA staff as a strength, and during Katrina, this redundancy proved effective. That said, the goal of true interoperability within and among county emergency response and law enforcement agencies remains elusive since each county has its own authority and timetable to procure communications technology.[97]

In Mississippi, most land-based communications systems, including cellular phones, were inoperable. According to Mississippi's EMA Director, Robert Latham, voice and data systems statewide were also inoperable.[98] As a result, often the only communications capability present in Mississippi — for both the state EMA as well as the affected counties — was through satellite phones and

radios, which operate by connecting to satellites rather than routing calls through land-based lines or cellular towers. Despite FEMA efforts to bring in additional communications capabilities to the affected counties' EOCs, Carwile reported that communications capabilities were far short of what was needed to be effective.[99]

To illustrate the problem in Louisiana, the EOC uses conference calls as a way to provide command and control and ensure unity of effort among the state and effected parishes. However, after the conference call during landfall on Monday morning, August 29, the parishes lost their communications capabilities and were unable to convene another conference call until 11 days later, on Friday, September 9.[100] Even then, the participants in the conference call noted that it was still hard to make regular phone calls.[101]

State of Louisiana officials lost local input to unified command, and were unreachable for coordinating activities

The state EOC in Louisiana experienced its own communications problems, with officials in the EOC unable to communicate reliably with local officials, other state officials, or federal officials.[102] In one conference call, Smith noted that part of the problem was the state EOC had not been wired for the volume of communications required for a major catastrophe.[103] Many e-mails noted the difficulty of communicating with the state EOC. As one example, a U.S. Northern Command (NORTHCOM) e-mail that laid out the procedures for requesting DOD assistance through the Defense Coordinating Officer in the EOC also emphasized the EOC telephone appeared to be continuously busy.[104]

Federal government also lost communications and failed in initial efforts to improve command and control

Similarly, the federal government lost some communications, and initial efforts to bring in supplemental capabilities to improve command and control were unsuccessful. For example, FEMA has a mobile command and control suite, named Red October, which is housed in an oversized tractor trailer.[105] Lokey and his staff said during Hurricane Katrina, Red October was pre-deployed to Shreveport, in northern Louisiana, to keep it out of harm's way but also to allow rapid movement into Baton Rouge or New Orleans after the hurricane passed.[106] Red October, once deployed and opened up, had a command and control suite with about 30 work stations and robust communications.

As the situation unfolded in New Orleans, and the flooding destroyed much of the command and control capability of the city, FEMA officials decided to move Red October to New Orleans to provide on-site command and control to its advance team and to help connect with New Orleans and National Guard authorities at the Superdome.[107] However, while some tractor trailers were able to get into the flooded city, Red October was unable to do so because of its oversized dimensions. Other FEMA communications vehicles, such as the Mobile Emergency Response Support detachments, noted in the COMMUNICATIONS chapter, were not capable of driving through the floodwaters without damaging their sensitive electronic equipment. Therefore, FEMA was unable to use these to restore command and control with its forward team in New Orleans, led by Parr.[108]

Finding: A lack of personnel, training, and funding also weakened command and control

A lack of sufficient personnel hindered command and control

The lack of trained, professional personnel at both the state and federal level greatly hindered the response. According to FEMA, the Louisiana Office of Homeland Security and Emergency Preparedness (LOHSEP) had an inadequate staff, both in numbers and training. "There were too few professional staff" provided by the state, according to Wells.[109] The FCO Operations Chief, Tony Robinson, agreed, saying the EOC had only 40 full-time trained staff, leaving only 20 staff to operate in 12 hour shifts.[110] Twenty people were far too few to run the EOC during a large disaster and the state should have developed a surge capacity, Robinson said.[111]

Wells said LOHSEP's supplemental staff were inadequately trained, and LOHSEP relied too heavily on the Louisiana National Guard troops to work the EOC.[112]

He characterized the guardsmen as well meaning but not trained to be professional emergency managers.[113] Wells cited this as one of reasons the state EOC personnel did not understand the unified command under the ICS.[114] Robinson also said the ability to effectively operate decreased as the state's cadre of professional emergency managers was augmented by these inexperienced guardsmen.[115] FEMA was also significantly short on available trained staff to send into the field.[116] Finally, Wells stated that "[w]e did not have the people. We did not have the expertise. We did not have the operational training folks that we needed to do our mission."[117]

A lack of training also hindered command and control

In Louisiana the lack of adequately trained personnel was also a major impediment to utilizing ICS and achieving effective command and control over state and federal resources. Wells said the state personnel lacked overall discipline, lacked clear control lines of authority, lacked a clearly understood command structure, and lacked consistency in operational procedures.[118] "If people don't understand ICS, we can't do ICS. And if we can't do ICS, we cannot manage disasters," he stated in testimony before the Senate.[119]

Valuable time and resources were expended to provide on-the-job training in ICS to state personnel assigned to the emergency operations center in Baton Rouge.[120] Wells noted that state officials hired a consultant to teach their EOC staff about ICS <u>after landfall</u>.[121] Specifically, the state hired former FEMA Director James Lee Witt as a consultant, and one of Witt's staff (a former FCO) was training the state staff in the EOC on Tuesday and Wednesday, August 30 and 31.[122] Wells said it was ridiculous to try to teach unified command after the hurricane had hit when everyone in the EOC should have already known it by then; at that point, it was too late, and the training created additional confusion in the EOC, Wells said.[123]

In Mississippi, ICS issues were less of a problem. According to Carwile, "[t]here had been training previous to Hurricane Katrina by the Mississippi Emergency Management Agency on down to the county emergency managers. So, it worked well."[124]

Inadequate funding cited as reason for inadequate personnel and training

As addressed more fully in the FEMA PREPAREDNESS chapter, the lack of adequate staff and insufficient training are directly attributable to limited funding for FEMA operations. For example, the funding for training exercises is, and has been deficient. This is evident in the lack of coordination of FEMA staff. According to Carwile, training funding for national emergency response teams dried up in 2003.[125] Teams sent to the Gulf coast never had an opportunity to train together beforehand. Prior to activation, the teams were nothing more than names on rosters. This contributed greatly to the inefficient and timely delays in the initial federal response. Senator Joe Lieberman described the training and funding issues as "a FEMA disaster waiting to happen because we weren't giving [FEMA] the resources to get ready for this."[126]

Senator Joe Lieberman described the training and funding issues as "a FEMA disaster waiting to happen because we weren't giving [FEMA] the resources to get ready for this."

Finding: Ineffective command and control delayed many relief efforts

The lack of effective command and control, and its impact on unity of command, degraded the relief efforts. Moreover, the problems experienced individually by the local, state, and federal governments exacerbated the challenges of coordinating across all levels of government and prevented overall unity of command.

The evacuation of the Superdome provided one of the clearest examples of how ineffective command and control and the lack of unity of command hindered urgently needed relief. It was planned multiple times by different parties. On the day after Katrina's landfall, Parr worked with the Louisiana National Guard to devise a

plan for evacuating the Superdome through the use of Chinook and Blackhawk helicopters.[127] After working through most the night, the plan was ready for execution Wednesday morning. Parr and the Louisiana National Guard officer working with him estimated it would take 30 hours to completely evacuate the Superdome. However, earlier that day Blanco had instructed Landreneau of the Guard to contact Honoré of Northern Command to arrange for active duty military support of response operations in Louisiana.[128]

This request was made outside the unified command and without the knowledge of FEMA and Parr. During the early morning hours of Wednesday, Landreneau instructed Louisiana National Guard officials at the Superdome to cease planning for the evacuation as Honoré would be "taking charge" of the evacuation project, thus bypassing the unified command and requirements that state requests to federal agencies go through FEMA to further coordinate and limit duplication.[129] Parr said this resulted in the

evacuation of the Superdome population 24 hours later than would have occurred under the joint National Guard / FEMA plan put together at the Superdome.[130]

Other delays and poor assistance efforts caused by a lack of command and control, mainly in Louisiana, include:

■ Search and Rescue. Search and Rescue efforts were uncoordinated. During the critical first days after Katrina and the flooding, there was no unity of command between the various local, state, and federal agencies participating in search and rescue efforts. While heroic efforts by these agencies immediately saved lives, there was little coordination of where the victims should be or actually were taken. This resulted in victims being left in shelters or out in the open on high ground for days without food and water. For more details, see the EVACUATION chapter.

"All levels of government have "a fundamental lack of understanding for the principals and protocols set forth in the NRP and NIMS."

■ Military Support. Much of the military support was also uncoordinated. The Louisiana National Guard and DOD active duty forces, under Joint Task Force Katrina, were under separate commands. Federal attempts to bring them under the same command were rejected by the Governor. This resulted in delays in the arrival of DOD active duty troops—troops that provided a robust reservoir of manpower and a wide array of capabilities. For more details, see the MILITARY chapter.

■ Medical Evacuations. There was confusion over which agencies or personnel were supposed to assist with hospital evacuations. Hospitals reported that Army and FEMA officials came and surveyed the situation and never returned despite saying that they would. This resulted in delays in evacuating patients, with sometimes fatal consequences. For more details, see the MEDICAL CARE chapter.

■ Lawlessness in New Orleans. The New Orleans Police Department, in addition to losing hundreds of its personnel who did not report to duty, lost command and control over those that still reported to work. This resulted in delays in determining where problems were, dispatching officers to those locations, and otherwise planning and prioritizing operations to restore law and order. For more details, see the LAW ENFORCEMENT chapter.

Conclusion

In responding to Hurricane Katrina, elements of federal, state, and local governments lacked command, lacked control, and certainly lacked unity. Some of the reasons for this can be traced back to the magnitude of the storm, which destroyed the communications systems that are so vital to effective command and control. In addition, the magnitude of the storm created so much damage across such a wide area that it overwhelmed agencies and individuals who were struggling to mount an organized response.

But some of the lapses in command and control can be traced back to agencies and individuals demonstrating a *failure of initiative* to better protect their command and control facilities, better clarify command and control relationships on location, and better follow established protocols for ensuring unity of command. This problem of not following protocols is summed up well in a recent DHS-IG report on an exercise involving federal, state, and local governments: all levels of government have "a fundamental lack of understanding for the principals and protocols set forth in the NRP and NIMS."[131]

Finally, to some degree, lapses in command and control can be traced to a lack of sufficient qualified personnel, inadequate training, and limited funding. In total, these factors paralyzed command and control, leading to an agonizingly disjointed and slow response to the disaster. ■

[99] *Id.* at 7 (written statement of William L. Carwile).

[100] *See* Audio recordings of Hurricane Katrina Conference Calls, LA State Emergency Operations Center (Aug. 26 – Sept. 9, 2005).

[101] *See* Audio recordings of Hurricane Katrina Conference Calls, LA State Emergency Operations Center (Sept. 9, 2005).

[102] Macdonald Interview.

[103] *See* Audio recordings of Hurricane Katrina Conference Calls, LA State Emergency Operations Center (Sept. 9, 2005).

[104] E-mail correspondence from Clair Blong (DHS/FEMA NORAD USNORTCOM IC) to FEMA-NRCC and FEMA-HSOC Staff (Sept. 01, 2005 7:51 p.m.), citing e-mail correspondence from Nanette Nadeau (DAF NORAD USNORTHCOM), to Clair Blong, Sept. 01, 2005 (Doc No. DHS-FEMA-0028-0000685).

[105] Lokey Interview; *see also* Parr Interview.

[106] *Id.*

[107] *Id.* It is not clear which FEMA official ultimately approved this decision.

[108] Lokey Interview; *see also* Parr Interview.

[109] *Dec. 7, 2005 Select Comm. Hearing* at 5 (written statement of William L. Carwile).

[110] Interview by Select Comm. Staff with Tony Robinson, FEMA JFO Operation [hereinafter Robinson Interview], in Baton Rouge, LA (Nov. 10, 2005).

[111] Robinson Interview.

[112] Wells Interview.

[113] *Id.*

[114] *Id.*

[115] Robinson Interview.

[116] Wells Interview.

[117] *Dec. 8, 2005 Senate Hearing* at 58 (statement of Scott Wells).

[118] Wells Interview.

[119] *Dec. 8, 2005 Senate Hearing* at 46 (statement of Scott Wells).

[120] Wells Interview.

[121] *Dec. 8, 2005 Senate Hearing* at 46 (statement of Scott Wells).

[122] Wells Interview.

[123] *Id.*

[124] *Dec. 8, 2005 Senate Hearing* at 48 (statement of William L. Carwile).

[125] *Id.*

[126] *Dec. 8, 2005 Senate Hearing* at 61 (statement of Senator Joseph Lieberman).

[127] Parr Interview.

[128] *Id.*

[129] *Id.*

[130] *Dec. 8, 2005 Senate Hearing* at 70-72 (statement of Phil Parr).

[131] *DHS IG Report* at 1, 12.

NATIONAL GUARD

"In the early hours of Hurricane Katrina, and without regard to their own safety, and in many cases, knowing their own homes were probably destroyed, these great citizens of Louisiana began to go out, by helicopter and boat, to begin the massive search and rescue operations.

"Pulling residents from rooftops, out of attics, and directly from the water, the men and women of the Louisiana National Guard were there, saving thousands of lives …"

Major General Bennett C. Landreneau
The Adjutant General, State of Louisiana
Select Committee hearing, October 27, 2005

The military played an invaluable role, but coordination was lacking

Summary

The active and reserve components of the United States Armed forces have a long and proud history of providing essential aid to the civilian populace of this country in the aftermath of natural disasters. There are several reasons the nation continues to rely on the military to perform this role. One is that the military is able to provide essential, life saving services more quickly and more comprehensively than any other entity when local and state response capabilities are overwhelmed, including the ability to provide helicopter and boat rescue, shelter, food, water, and medical support. Importantly, much of this capability is vested with the National Guard, and is thus an asset under the control of the governor of each respective state or territory and the District of Columbia.

As robust as the military capability is, there are limitations, many of which are highlighted in the specific findings below. The most important limit to the military's ability to manage domestic disaster response is the nation's traditional reliance on local control to handle incident response. The federal government, with the Department of Defense (DOD) serving as part of the federal response team, takes its directions from state and local leaders. Since that is our nation's tradition, DOD does not plan to be the lead agency in any disaster situation and expects to assist as local authorities request and direct. Furthermore, DOD lacks the detailed knowledge of local conditions essential to effective relief operations.

Even so, the element of the U.S. military with the longest tradition of service — the militia, now called the National Guard — is a particularly valuable asset to each state, territory, and the District of Columbia. Units can be called to active duty by the order of the governor and serve as the state's chief executive directs. Thus, the National Guard is responsive and will possess knowledge of local conditions. In contrast, the processes by which active military forces are brought to a region are lengthy and burdensome. When they arrive, these forces will not have detailed local knowledge and will be prohibited by law

NATIONAL GUARD

from performing law enforcement functions. In addition, there will be two distinct military chains of command — one for federal troops and one for National Guard troops under state command.

This dual chain of command structure, lengthy federal troop activation system, and, in the case of Katrina, devastated local authorities, contributed to a poorly coordinated federal response to Katrina. It would not be possible to anticipate all problems and prevent all the difficulties that ensued from a storm of this magnitude, but better planning, more robust exercises, and better engagement between active forces and the National Guard both before and during disaster response would have helped prevent human suffering. Two new organizations created after September 11, 2001, the Department of Homeland Security (DHS) and DOD's Northern Command, are integral parts of this process, and the growing pains were evident to the Select Committee. Northern Command is charged with managing the federal military response to disasters and DHS is in charge of the overall federal effort. Northern Command has taken strides, but needs better integration with FEMA and with the National Guard effort at disasters and emergencies. Clearly, more needs to be done.

Even though there were problems, the military played an invaluable role in helping the citizens of Louisiana, Alabama, and Mississippi respond to the devastation of Katrina and saved countless lives. Indeed, as Assistant Secretary of Defense for Homeland Defense Paul McHale testified:

"The Department of Defense's response to the catastrophic effects of Hurricane Katrina was the largest military deployment within the United States since the Civil War."[1]

NATIONAL GUARD

There is no doubt DOD resources improved the national response to Katrina. Although trained and equipped for war fighting, there is enough commonality of expertise and equipment that made for a significant military contribution to the majority of Emergency Support Functions (ESFs) of the National Response Plan. DOD is the only federal department with supporting responsibilities in each of the fifteen ESFs.[2]

The Hurricane Katrina response also reinforced the National Response Plan's designation of the National Guard as the military's first responders to a domestic crisis.

"In contrast to Hurricane Andrew (1992) in which National Guard forces constituted 24% of the military response, National Guard forces represented more than 70% of the military force for Hurricane Katrina."[3]

Number of National Guard and active Duty Personnel in Joint Operational Area of Hurricane Katrina

Date	National Guard	Active Duty
August 26	2,505	n/a
August 27	2,633	n/a
August 28	4,091	n/a
August 29	7,522	n/a
August 30	8, 573	1,000
August 31	11,003	2,000
September 1	13,113	3,000
September 2	16,928	4,011
September 3	22,624	4,631
September 4	30,188	10,952
September 5	32,760	15,204
September 6	42,990	17,417
September 7	45,420	18,342
September 8	48,560	19,749
September 9	50,116	21,408
September 10	50,116	21,168
September 11	48,045	22,028
September 12	48,280	22,670
September 13	45,791	22,232
September 14	45,063	18,690

SOURCE: NORTHERN COMMAND TIMELINE

Despite the immediacy of required action, confusion created by multi-intergovernmental agency activities and dual military responses, the men and women of the armed services came when they were called. And whether on the ground, in the air, or on the water, they worked extremely hard to save and offer aid to the victims of Hurricane Katrina.

There are a number of specific areas where better coordination mechanisms could have greatly improved the execution of military support during Hurricane Katrina. The protocols associated with sharing essential information, the coordinated movement of personnel and equipment, and prior joint planning and training are vital to an effective and comprehensive response.

Finding: The National Response Plan's Catastrophic Incident Annex as written would have delayed the active duty military response, even if it had been implemented

The National Response Plan (NRP) creates confusion about federal active duty military involvement due to unresolved tension between the possible need for active duty military assistance when state and local officials are overwhelmed, and the presumption that a governor will use his or her understanding of the situation on the ground to decide whether and when to ask for active duty military support.

A foundational assumption of the NRP's Catastrophic Incident Annex (CIA) is that local and surrounding jurisdictions' response capabilities may be insufficient as they could be quickly overwhelmed by an event. Despite this guiding assumption, NRP-CIA policy assumes that state/local incident command authorities will be able to integrate federal resources into the response effort. The NRP-CIA fails to reflect whether in a catastrophic incident DHS should rely upon the same principle — the presence of local and state first responders for the first 48-72 hours of an emergency — as the non-catastrophic incident portion of the NRP. This failure would have delayed the federal military response and prevented full integration of the National Guard and active duty missions, even if the NRC - CIA had been involved.

Whether there exists an effective local and state response for the first 48-72 hours of a disaster is a critical element in determining the need for and extent of military involvement. Some point out that in cases of a major catastrophe, the President through the Stafford Act can designate and deploy federal resources without following NRP procedures. This view does not address if the NRP procedures in place in the event of a major catastrophe – whether or not the President chooses to federalize the response — are sound.

Recognizing that federal resources might be required to augment overwhelmed state and local response efforts, the NRP-CIA establishes protocols to pre-identify and rapidly deploy essential resources that are urgently needed to save lives and contain incidents. Under the NRP-CIA, normal procedures for a number of the Emergency Support Functions (ESF) may be expedited or streamlined to address urgent requirements. These include: medical teams, urban search and rescue teams, transportable shelter, medical and equipment caches, and communications gear. Standard procedures regarding requests for assistance may be, under extreme circumstances, temporarily suspended.

One of the planning assumptions of the NRP-CIA is that a detailed and credible common operating picture may not be achievable for 24 to 48 hours after the incident. As a result, the NRP-CIA calls for response activities to begin without the benefit of a complete situation and critical needs assessment. Moreover, under this Annex, notification and full coordination with states should not delay or impede the rapid mobilization and deployment of critical federal resources.

Finding: DOD/DHS coordination was not effective during Hurricane Katrina

The Department of Homeland Security and the Department of Defense share responsibility for ensuring the security and safety of America. Since the establishment of DHS after 9/11, both departments have sought to define their roles and responsibilities.

McHale testified at a recent congressional hearing that he was the Defense Department's principal liaison with DHS.[4] A memorandum of understanding between DHS and DOD assigns 64 DOD personnel to DHS to fill critical specialties, principally in the areas of communications and intelligence. There is also a Homeland Defense Coordination Office at DHS headquarters, as well as around-the-clock DOD presence in the DHS Homeland Security Operations Center.

Despite these efforts to integrate operations, gaps remained in DOD/DHS coordination. During a BRAC Commission hearing conducted August 11, 2005, a commissioner asked Peter F. Verga, Principal Deputy Assistant Secretary of Defense (Homeland Defense), of the existence of any document issued by DHS that would help DOD determine the requirements for military assistance to civilian authorities. Verga replied: "To my knowledge, no such document exists."[5]

On August 30, an e-mail generated in the Office of the Secretary of Defense (OSD) indicated concern about the flow of information between DOD and FEMA and a lack of understanding of what was an official request for assistance and what was not.[6] Another e-mail from DHS to DOD on this day indicated Secretary Chertoff was requesting updated information on the levees in New Orleans, shelter information, and search

Communications between DOD and DHS, and in particularly FEMA, during the immediate week after landfall, reflect a lack of information sharing, near panic, and problems with process.

and rescue missions DOD was performing. The OSD response expressed wonder at why DHS was asking for this information, as FEMA had not yet even generated requests for these missions for DOD.[7] Communications between DOD and DHS, and in particularly FEMA, during the immediate week after landfall, reflect a lack of information sharing, near panic, and problems with process.[8] As time went on, and FEMA and DOD worked out Requests for Assistance (RFAs), and communications and information sharing did improve.[9]

These problems are indicative of a dispute between DOD and DHS that still lingers. DOD maintains it honored all FEMA requests for assistance in the relief effort, refusing no missions.[10] FEMA officials insist that notwithstanding the official paper trail, DOD effectively refused some missions in the informal coordination process that preceded an official FEMA request.[11] Therefore, when DOD thought a mission was inappropriate, FEMA simply did not request the assistance from DOD.

The reliance of FEMA on DOD during the Hurricane Katrina response, although not anticipated in scope, became at its most basic, a takeover of FEMA's responsibilities as the logistics manager for the federal response. According to Secretary McHale:

> During Katrina, the federal military remained under FEMA's control. It meant that the Defense Department, which had the resources to appraise the situation and prioritize its missions more quickly than could FEMA, actually drafted its own requests for assistance and sent them to FEMA, which copied them and sent them back to the Department of Defense for action.[12]

Finding: DOD, FEMA and the state of Louisiana had diffculty coordinating with each other, which slowed the response

The process for requesting DOD active duty forces has several layers of review and is understandably not well understood or familiar to state officials who rarely would need to request DOD support. Even though state officials do not routinely work with DOD, requests for

DOD assistance are generated at the state level. These go from the state to FEMA's Federal Coordinating Officer (FCO), who in turn requests assistance from the Defense Coordinating Officer (DCO). The DCO passes these requests on to the joint task force, which routes them through Northern Command to the Office of the Secretary of Defense Executive Secretariat, to the Joint Directorate of Military Support on the Joint Staff. At each stage, the request is validated to ensure it can be met and that it is legal to provide the assistance. Once vetted, the request is tasked to the services and coordinated with Joint Forces Command, and forces or resources are then allocated to the joint task force, which in turn gets the support down to the user level by way of the DCO. This process is in place not only to satisfy DOD internal requirements, but to ensure maximum coordination with both FEMA and the state.

DOD's process for receiving, approving, and executing missions was called bureaucratic by Louisiana officials.[13] Despite the multiple layers of paperwork requirements described above, the Select Committee could not definitively determine the origin of the request for DOD to provide active duty forces. Louisiana officials said their Adjutant General made the request directly of General Russel L. Honoré — without coordinating the request through FEMA — the established process to request all federal assistance.[14] This request outside of normal channels may reflect frustration with the bureaucratic process.

Current FEMA FCO Scott Wells told Select Committee staff this direct state request to DOD was indicative of Louisiana not having a unified command during Katrina and created coordination problems during the response and recovery efforts.[15] Without a unified command, the system for requests for assistance was difficult. This difficulty was compounded by the scarcity of telephone

ommunication capability remaining in Louisiana, resulting in a communications chokepoint at the EOC in aton Rouge where the telephone was continuously busy.

Prior to the arrival of Honoré, senior FEMA fficials were unable to get visibility on their requests. or example, former Undersecretary for Emergency reparedness and Response and FEMA Director, Michael rown, testified that he did not know what happened to ome of his requests for assistance.[16]

While DOD officials testified in October that DOD as "leaning forward" and taking quick action prior to atrina's landfall, FEMA officials said the DOD process ppeared cumbersome.[17] Louisiana Governor Blanco's hief of Staff Andy Kopplin said DOD was, in his pinion, slow and overly bureaucratic.[18] It appears that lthough DOD may have been doing the best it could ith the system it had, Hurricane Katrina was of such nagnitude that more rapid response was necessary. lthough acknowledging that General Honoré operated utside normal FEMA-led channels, FEMA FCO William okey praised him for getting things done that Louisiana nd FEMA could not.[19]

Finding: National Guard and DOD response operations were comprehensive, but perceived as slow

National Guard response

"I am particularly proud of the timeliness and magnitude of the National Guard's efforts in advance of Hurricane Katrina and our response in its immediate aftermath. National Guard forces were in the water and on the streets of New Orleans rescuing people within four hours of Katrina's passing. More than 9,700 National Guard Soldiers and Airmen were in New Orleans by the thirtieth of August. The National Guard deployed over 30,000 additional troops within 96 hours of the passing of the storm."[20] *Lieutenant General H Steven Blum, Chief, National Guard Bureau*

When reports on the catastrophic damage in ouisiana and Mississippi began to flow in, the National Guard Bureau did not hesitate to act. The NGB took

responsibility for coordinating the flow of Guard resources and personnel from all 50 states to speed up the process and increase efficient use of resources as requirements from coastal states grew beyond their ability to coordinate individual state-to-state compacts.[21] The NGB Joint Operations Center (NGBJOC) worked closely with the Army National Guard Crisis Response Cell and the Air National Guard Crisis Action Team to source and move these forces into the Gulf Coast.

Initially, this operated via a "push" methodology with supporting states pushing available forces based on requirements identified by the Adjutants General in the supported states.[22] As situational awareness improved, this gradually transitioned to a "pull" process whereby supported states submitted requests for forces through the NGBJOC to be sourced by the supporting states.

NGB operated its Joint Operations Center around the clock to coordinate all National Guard actions associated with information sharing between Office of the Secretary of Defense, the Army and the Air Force, Northern Command, state emergency operations centers, and other DOD liaison officers. This coordination supported National Guard response activities in the affected states.[23] One of the challenges of Katrina for the Department of Defense was the lack of protocols set by Northern Command for information flow between the separate DOD entities.[24]

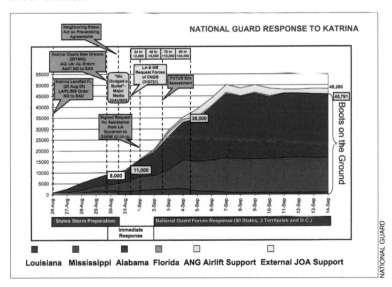

On Tuesday, August 30, state Adjutants General reported the following troop deployments to the NGB: 5,149 to Louisiana, 2,826 to Mississippi, 1,066 to Alabama, and 753 to Florida for a total of 9,794.[25] At this time, Louisiana and Mississippi were supplemented by Guardsmen from nine other states. In position and responding were 64 Army National Guard aircraft, that reported 186 search and rescue missions performed, 1,017 patients moved, 1,910 evacuees, 91 cargo movements, and 29 food and water movements.

On August 31, at 7:21 a.m., Lieutenant General Blum and Army National Guard Director Lieutenant General Clyde A. Vaughn placed a phone call to Louisiana State Adjutant General Landreneau.[26] The following is a record of their conversation:

General Blum: Benny, how are things going?
General Landreneau: Sir, we've had a difficult night.
General Blum: What do you need?
General Landreneau: We need 5K soldiers to help out. The armory is flooded. My command and control is at the Superdome. We have a lot of undesirables here trying to cause trouble.
General Vaughn: Hey Benny, can we drive to the Superdome?
General Landreneau: No sir, we are cut off by the rising water, along with the armory.
General Vaughn: Where do you want us to send the incoming soldiers?
General Landreneau: Sir, send them to the intersection of Interstate 310 and State 10.
General Blum: Benny, when's the last time you got any sleep?
General Landreneau: Well sir, I think two days ago.
General Blum: Listen, you need to get some rest, you sound exhausted.
General Landreneau: I'll try Sir, but every time I lay down someone gets me up for a little emergency.
General Blum: Try and get some rest, this is an ongoing effort and we need your energy.
General Vaughn: Benny, we're going to push help so be ready.[27]

On Wednesday, August 31, Blum set up a teleconference with all state Adjutants General at noon to coordinate "full capabilities of National Guard to be deployed as rapidly as possible to save life and limb."[28] Every state Adjutant General reported their Guard forces deploying or available for deployment.[29]

On Thursday, September 1 at 11:30 a.m., Secretary of Defense Rumsfeld and Blum met with President Bush to

NATIONAL GUARD

discuss the National Guard response.[30] At this briefing, the President agreed with Rumsfeld that the National Guard was responding effectively to the disaster and chose not to federalize Guard troops.[31] At 1:15 p.m., Blum was asked to be part of a DHS press conference with Chertoff and McHale, to discuss federal assistance to the Gulf. At 5:30 p.m., after coordinating with McHale and Rumsfeld, Blum departed for Belle Chasse, Louisiana, and immediately met with Louisiana State Adjutant General Landreneau at the Superdome. Later that evening, Blum met with Governor Kathleen Blanco to discuss troop and resource requirements in Louisiana.[32]

Also during this time, federal officials considered ways to structure a unified command. According to Deputy Homeland Security Advisor Ken Rapuano, federal officials discussed with Blanco federalizing the National Guard.[33] President Bush ultimately offered Blanco a "Memorandum of Agreement Concerning Authorization, Consent and Use of Dual Status Commander for JTF Katrina," making Honoré, as commander of Joint Task Force Katrina, a member of the Louisiana National Guard.[34] An excerpt from a DOD letter drafted for Governor Blanco to President Bush explained how the command would have been structured under the proposal:

In order to enhance Federal and State efforts, and if you grant permission, I would like to appoint the Regular Army officer commanding the Federal Joint Task Force Katrina to be an officer in the Louisiana National Guard. I would assign him to command the National Guard forces under my command.[35]

Thus, President Bush's proposal would not have put National Guard troops under federal control. Rather, the proposal would have put Honoré under Blanco's command in the chain-of-command over National Guard troops in Louisiana. In this proposal, Honoré would have served in two capacities — first, as the commander of federal troops ultimately answering to the President, and second, as the commander of the Louisiana National Guard, answering to Blanco. This proposal was intended to establish a single command for all military operations in Louisiana.

Blanco wrote to President Bush on September 3, declining this proposal. The Governor only agreed to the importance of creating a single military commander for federal forces that "could enhance the contribution of over 25 National Guard states currently being commanded by the Louisiana State Adjutant General."[36] As a result, federal troops remained under one command — Honoré and Northern Command, while the National Guard remained under the separate command of Landreneau and the Governor.

Administrative matters proved to be a challenge as well for National Guard troops deploying under Emergency Management Assistant Compacts (EMAC) with various states. Since these forces were activated in state-to-state agreements they were on state active duty and subject to the rules and entitlements authorized by their respective home states. This plethora of statuses made administration problematic for the National Guard, and led to a request that these forces be activated under Title 32 of the U.S. Code. This federal status permits uniform administration while allowing continued command and control by the Governor.[37] Numerous state Adjutants General suggested the National Guard Bureau request that guard troops be activated under Title 32.[38] In response, the National Guard Bureau strongly advocated for the use of Title 32:

> not only because it allowed Governors to retain control, but because it was the right thing to do for the soldiers and airmen. Each state has a different way of handling pay and benefits under State Active Duty. We had soldiers and airmen operating under 54 different payroll systems and receiving different benefits such as medical care and disability coverage. Our forces needed the protection provided by DOD entitlements.[39]

Between September 2 and September 5, the governors of Alabama, Mississippi, and Louisiana sent letters to the Secretary of Defense asking for all National Guard assets to be put under Title 32.[40] Blum then discussed putting the Guard on Title 32 status with McHale and together, they submitted a formal Title 32 request to Rumsfeld.[41] On September 7, Deputy Secretary of Defense Gordon England approved Title 32 status retroactive to August 29.[42]

On September 8, the NGB noted 50 States, two territories, and the District of Columbia had contributed forces in support of operations in Louisiana and Mississippi. National Guard forces reached peak deployment numbers for Katrina relief with over 50,000 personnel mobilized on this day.[43]

Army National Guard

> "Four hours after landfall, Army National Guard helicopters are performing rescue missions, with 65 helicopters positioned in Florida, Texas, Louisiana, Mississippi and Alabama." ***Northcom Timeline: Hurricane Katrina 1/3/06***[44]

The Army National Guard contributed heavily to the Katrina response, including the primary priority of search and rescue, evacuation, and commodity distribution. Distribution of water, ice, and food from military stockpiles in the days immediately following landfall was done at both designated and undesignated distribution sites. The Army Guard also provided much needed military transportation, helped clear debris from roads and residences, and provided assistance to law enforcement.[45] Unlike their active duty counterparts, the National Guard is not restricted from performing law enforcement duties under federal law, and thus rendered considerable assistance to civilian law enforcement efforts.[46] According to the daily log of Mississippi National Guard activities prepared for the Select Committee, the majority of the mission requests were for security, a mission that would only increase in the weeks following landfall.[47]

The following chart contains the number of Army National Guard present in the Gulf States.

Date	Number of Army Guard Personnel In Katrina Joint Operational Area
August 26	922
August 27	1,701
August 28	4,444
August 29	6,908
August 30	9,668
August 31	10,428
September 1	14,284
September 2	18,678
September 3	24,548
September 4	29,588
September 5	33,608
September 6	38,093
September 7	39,736
September 8	40,667
September 9	42,164
September 10	42,257
September 11	42,264
September 12	41,530
September 13	40,928
September 14	41,119
September 15	38,831

NATIONAL GUARD BUREAU AFTER ACTION REVIEW OBSERVATIONS TIMELINE, 12/21/05

Air National Guard

August 30: "The Air National Guard launches its first Air National Guard JTF-Katrina mission. A C-17 crew assigned to the 172nd Fighter Wing, Mississippi ANG flew its first sortie in support of Hurricane recovery. The mission lasted for 3 days. They airlifted 85 civilians from Gulfport."
Northcom Katrina Timeline 12/22/05

The Director of the Air National Guard Lieutenant General Daniel James III, told the Select Committee the efforts of the Air National Guard during Hurricane Katrina represented "the largest military airlift operation supporting disaster relief in the United States."[48]

But the Air National Guard brought more than evacuation, rescue, and airlift capabilities to the response. The Air National Guard also has an emergency medical

capability. ANG medics treated over 13,000 patients by September 19.[49] Expeditionary Medical Support (EMEDS) units provided medical personnel and equipment to support up to 10 major trauma surgeries without re-supply.[50] The Air National Guard also has a large civil engineering capability in its Rapid Engineer Deployable Operational Repair Squadron Engineer (RED HORSE) Squadrons.

Date	Number of Air Guard Personnel In Katrina Joint Operational Area (includes Air Guard in transit from outside wings transporting personnel, supplies and equipment)
August 26	8
August 27	932
August 28	932
August 29	933
August 30	956
August 31	960
September 1	972
September 2	2,464
September 3	3,998
September 4	4,596
September 5	6,613
September 6	5,770
September 7	5,952
September 8	5,735
September 9	4,347
September 10	4,581
September 11	4,125
September 12	4,109
September 13	4,112
September 14	3,477
September 15	3,512

NATIONAL GUARD BUREAU AFTER ACTION REVIEW OBSERVATIONS TIMELINE, 12/21/05

Some of the highlights of ANG activity in the first few days following landfall include:

August 29   Aero-medical Evacuation Squadron positioned to respond in Mississippi 50 ANG medical personnel at Naval Air Station New Orleans

August 30   The ANG launches its first Air National Guard JTF Katrina mission. A C-17 crew assigned to the 172nd FW, Mississippi ANG flew its first sortie in support of Hurricane recovery. The mission lasted for three days.

They airlifted 85 civilians from Gulfport. All ANG Airlift and Tanker units put on alert and places all air crew on Title 32 status

Texas ANG starts reconnaissance, activates search and rescue personnel and security forces to Louisiana

ANG establishes Tanker Airlift Control Center

August 31   ANG sources a NORTHCOM request for ANG Combat Weather Team to New Orleans

ANG reports 700 ANG Civil Engineer and 350 Red Horse personnel available

Tennessee and Oklahoma ANG help evacuate 143 patients from the New Orleans Veterans Hospital

The 259th ATCS Louisiana Air National Guard deploys their MSN-7 Mobile Control Tower to the Superdome[51]

September 1   First Air Force, composed of ANG wings across the country, is tasked to lead for planning, orchestrating and overseeing all Air Force support to Joint Task Force Katrina.[52] Gulfport, Mississippi is designated the main operating base for sustained ANG Hurricane relief efforts, including evacuation.

ANG Expeditionary Medical Support (EMEDS) units, civil engineering units arrive in Mississippi and New Orleans

On this day ANG Para-rescuemen are credited with 48 air saves and 250 boat saves in New Orleans. ANG Combat Controllers provide air movement for 750 helicopter sorties where 3,000 people are evacuated. From September 1 through 9, ANG from Alaska and Oregon pushed through 3,169 military and civilian helicopter sorties at multiple landing zones in New Orleans. ANG aircraft and crew would fly 2,542 sorties, airlifting 21,874 people and 11,110 pounds of cargo in support of hurricane relief.[53]

September 2   149th Air National Guard Surgical Team established field hospital in parking lot adjacent to New Orleans Convention Center.[54]

The National Guards of other states also played key roles in the Hurricane Katrina response. Through Emergency Management Assistance Compacts (EMAC), Louisiana and Mississippi were able to request and receive assistance from scores of states from across the country. While the EMAC process is a direct state-to-state relationship, both FEMA and the National Guard Bureau participated in negotiations to facilitate the identification and procurement of specific types of assistance from other states. There was a consensus among federal, state, and local officials that EMAC worked well. These troops served in Title 32 status, and were therefore commanded by the respective Governors of Louisiana and Mississippi and paid with federal funds.

Louisiana

The Louisiana National Guard conducted roving patrols, manned checkpoints, and supported the New Orleans Police Department in the parishes. The Army National Guard also secured key infrastructure sites, including levees,[55] and provided support for general purpose shelters and special needs shelters with medical personnel. One of the Guard's largest missions was to provide security and other support at the Superdome. Approximately 250 Guardsmen were at the Superdome,  searching entrants for weapons, providing them with food, water, and medical attention, and attempting to maintain law and order.

After Katrina hit, the National Guard was deeply involved in search and rescue operations to save people after the levees breached and many areas flooded.[56] Their role included both helicopter and boat sorties to rescue people from roofs and floodwaters and take them to high ground. They were also part of the more deliberate post-flood activities to go house to house and search for survivors and victims.

The National Guard also had a law enforcement mission beyond the shelters (e.g., the Superdome) to help restore law and order through street patrols and other activities in support of the overtaxed New Orleans Police Department.[57] One of the National Guard's law enforcement missions was to secure the Convention Center and generally maintain order there as occupants were evacuated. They provided food, water, and medical treatment, and searched evacuees as they boarded buses. Because the National Guard was never federalized, they could fully participate in all law enforcement missions.

Finally, the National Guard played a key role in logistics and transportation, using their high-clearance vehicles and helicopters to ferry personnel and supplies into and out of flooded areas.[58] For example, they transported and distributed food into the Superdome and supported the evacuation of its occupants.

The Louisiana National Guard received much assistance from many states across the country through EMAC.[59] Examples of the specific deployments included 2,426 infantry from Pennsylvania, 1,016 military police from Puerto Rico, 580 security troops from Michigan, 500 support troops from Arkansas, 535 security troops from Massachusetts, 350 security forces from Tennessee, 315 transportation and logistics troops from Alabama, 310 maintenance troops from Illinois, 250 air traffic controllers from Texas, and 221 truckers from South Carolina. In total, Louisiana made 451 EMAC requests, and 29,502 National Guard troops responded from other states to undertake these missions.

Alabama

The Alabama National Guard headquarters began monitoring Hurricane Katrina on August 23 and actively engaged in discussions with the National Guard Bureau on August 25. When Katrina became a Category 3

hurricane on August 27, the Alabama Guard increased staff at the state emergency operations center. EOCs along the Alabama Coast for the 20th Special Forces Group, 711th Signal Battalion, and 16th Theater Support Command were opened and manned. When FEMA designated Maxwell Air Force Base as a federal staging area for supplies, the Alabama National Guard sent troops there to help prepare for distribution.[60] Governor Riley declared a state of emergency on August 28, which formally activated the state National Guard.[61]

On August 29, the Alabama Emergency Management Agency (AEMA) received requests for commodities from Mobile, Baldwin, Butler, and Washington counties, and the Alabama Guard took control of all recovery and relief operations in coastal Alabama to include county distribution points. When AEMA requested special boat teams for search and rescue, and security, the Alabama National Guard responded. The Guard also performed damage assessment tasks. The Alabama National Guard had developed mission specific force packages for emergencies like hurricanes, snow and ice storms, and chemical and biological attacks. These force packages include security forces, engineers, medical, communications and logistical equipment, and trained personnel.[62]

The Alabama National Guard deployed approximately 750 soldiers and airmen within Alabama, but also provided 2,000 soldiers to locations in Mississippi and Louisiana in response to immediate EMAC requests for support on August 29 and 30.[63]

Mississippi

On August 29, in the rear area operations center in Jackson, it was recorded that the Mississippi National Guard had activated 2,736 Army National Guard soldiers, and 1,003 Air National Guard members to provide security, search and rescue, and debris removal operations.[64]

In his testimony before the Select Committee, Mississippi Adjutant General, Harold A. Cross, made the following observations:

> During and immediately after landfall, National Guard search and rescue operations began on the Gulf Coast. My personnel night

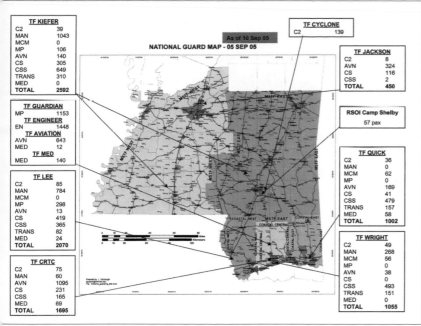

TF KIEFER
C2	39
MAN	1043
MCM	0
MP	106
AVN	140
CS	305
CSS	649
TRANS	310
MED	0
TOTAL	2592

TF GUARDIAN
MP	1153

TF ENGINEER
EN	1448

TF AVIATION
AVN	643
MED	12

TF MED
MED	140

TF LEE
C2	85
MAN	784
MCM	0
MP	298
AVN	13
CS	419
CSS	365
TRANS	82
MED	24
TOTAL	2070

TF CRTC
C2	75
MAN	60
AVN	1095
CS	231
CSS	165
MED	69
TOTAL	1695

NATIONAL GUARD MAP - 05 SEP 05 — As of 10 Sep 05

TF CYCLONE
C2	139

TF JACKSON
C2	8
AVN	324
CS	116
CSS	2
TOTAL	450

RSOI Camp Shelby — 57 pax

TF QUICK
C2	36
MAN	0
MCM	62
MP	0
AVN	169
CS	41
CSS	479
TRANS	157
MED	58
TOTAL	1002

TF WRIGHT
C2	49
MAN	268
MCM	56
MP	0
AVN	38
CS	0
CSS	493
TRANS	151
MED	0
TOTAL	1055

MISSISSIPPI NATIONAL GUARD

ground reconnaissance on the 29th and aerial reconnaissance early the next morning clearly revealed a disaster of unprecedented proportion all along the Gulf Coast of Mississippi and significant damage as far as one hundred and fifty miles inland. After reporting this initial surveillance to Governor Barbour, I immediately directed my rear operations center to activate all remaining available Mississippi National Guardsmen and to execute the movement of pre-planned assistance from other states. In addition, I requested assistance through the National Guard Bureau from other states, up to division sized strength. Accordingly, the 4,533 Mississippi National Guard soldiers and airmen were ultimately augmented by 11,839 National Guard personnel from 36 states under EMAC agreements.[65]

The Mississippi National Guard personnel on standby at Camp Shelby moved forward after the storm had passed to a scene of unbelievable destruction. Hurricane Katrina was by all accounts the worst storm in nearly a century, but Cross was prepared.[66] As soon as the storm abated somewhat, Mississippi National Guard personnel deployed from Camp Shelby into the devastated Mississippi coast to provide security, search and rescue and debris removal operations.[67] Even so, Cross recognized his own resources would be insufficient to assist along the whole coast of the state and he needed help from the National Guard of other states. In that regard, General Cross said:

EMAC agreements negotiated with 40 states creating a division-sized force within 96 hours eliminated need for Title 10 forces. The first out of state National Guard units to arrive in Mississippi were units from Alabama. 483 soldiers arrived on 30 August with an additional 359 soldiers arriving on 31 August. This Alabama National Guard Force consisted of combat engineers, military police, security forces, and communications assets. Their quick response was due to the fact that the Alabama National Guard was already postured to respond to Katrina in the event it impacted Alabama. The personal relationship between the adjutants general of the two states allowed for the rapid response of forces.[68]

MISSISSIPPI NATIONAL GUARD
DAILY RECAP

DATE	MSARNG	MSANG	TOTAL MSNG	OUT OF STATE	TOTAL DAILY SUPPORT
27-Aug-05	110	0	110	0	110
28-Aug-05	1006	0	1006	0	1006
29-Aug-05	2556	532	3088	0	3088
30-Aug-05	3089	633	3722	483	4205
31-Aug-05	3133	676	3909	842	4648
1-Sep-05	3289	633	3922	842	4764
2-Sep-05	3451	671	4122	1,040	5,165
3-Sep-05	3495	671	4166	2,563	6,729
4-Sep-05	3481	704	4185	10,568	14,753
5-Sep-05	3497	702	4199	10,568	14,767
6-Sep-05	3521	702	4223	10,568	14,791
7-Sep-05	3529	1022	4551	10,615	15,166
8-Sep-05	3549	1017	4566	10,723	15,289
9-Sep-05	3563	894	4457	10,723	15,180
10-Sep-05	3555	963	4518	10,721	15,239
11-Sep-05	3530	1003	4533	10,665	15,198
12-Sep-05	3474	1003	4477	11,895	16,372
13-Sep-05	3443	1003	4446	10,638	15,084
14-Sep-05	3354	1003	4357	10,579	14,936
15-Sep-05	3339	1003	4342	9,270	13,612
16-Sep-05	3325	1003	4328	9,270	13,598
17-Sep-05	3321	1003	4324	8,393	12,717
18-Sep-05	3254	1003	4257	8,397	12,654
19-Sep-05	3172	1003	4175	8,197	12,372
20-Sep-05	3159	1003	4162	5,664	9,826
21-Sep-05	3159	1003	4162	4,587	8,749
22-Sep-05	3158	1003	4161	4,364	8,525
23-Sep-05	3158	1003	4161	1,867	6,028
24-Sep-05	2332	686	3018	1,620	4,638
25-Sep-05	2332	686	3018	1,618	4,636
26-Sep-05	2060	876	2936	928	3,864
27-Sep-05	1990	876	2866	848	3,714
28-Sep-05	1983	1227	3210	824	4,034
29-Sep-05	1626	1227	2853	824	3,677
30-Sep-05	1626	1227	2853	817	3,670
1-Oct-05	1626	1227	2853	817	3,670
2-Oct-05	1626	1227	2853	817	3,670
3-Oct-05	1626	1227	2853	809	3,662
4-Oct-05	1626	1227	2853	581	3,434
5-Oct-05	1626	1227	2853	580	3,433
6-Oct-05	1626	1227	2853	588	3,441
7-Oct-05	1626	1227	2853	588	3,441
8-Oct-05	1626	1227	2853	232	3,085
9-Oct-05	1626	1227	2853	232	3,085
10-Oct-05	1626	866	2492	157	2,649
11-Oct-05					

SOURCE: MISSISSIPPI NATIONAL GUARD

As of: 10/11/2005 3:26

The initial requests for assistance from Cross were through personal relationships with other State Adjutant Generals.[69] General Blum, held a video teleconference on August 31 to solicit assistance from each of the 54 states and territories for both Louisiana and Mississippi. States responded rapidly to the urgent need and decided to worry about the authorizing paperwork later. In most cases, EMAC documentation followed after individual states provided the assets requested by Louisiana or Mississippi.[70] As noted earlier, all National Guard troops were retroactively placed in Title 32 status on September 7 by Deputy Secretary of Defense England.[71]

Out of state National Guard support in Mississippi through EMAC process

State	National Guard Assistance
Alabama	1,500 Security Forces, 7 Tactical planners and engineers, 2- CH47s with crew for S and R, 2-UH60s with crew for S and R, 300 Sleeping Bags and 80 cots, Engineering Brigade, MP Battalion, 1,450 personnel for TF, 37 personnel from Air Refueling Wing, CBCS Communications support, Ministry Team, Ground Safety Manager, EMEDS personnel
Arizona	Family Assistance Personnel, Medical support
Arkansas	100 soldiers, MP Company, 25 Heavy Trucks with 75 soldiers
California	Fire Team, Aircraft Maintenance personnel, medical support personnel
Colorado	MP Company, 50 Signal company personnel
Delaware	MP Security Company, 100 personnel to assist command and control, EMEDS personnel
Florida	4-UH60s, rescue teams, infantry battalion, 50 ambulances with crew, 15 cooks, OH-58 with crew, logistics aides, safety personnel, aircraft maintainers
Georgia	2- UH1s, 2 CH47s with crew, 1,500 Task Force personnel, Fire Vehicle, Cable/Copper Repair personnel
Idaho	Refuelers
Illinois	Security Forces, EMEDS personnel, public health personnel
Indiana	2,300 soldiers, 40 tankers
Iowa	Medical Support Battalion
Kansas	Air Refueling personnel, Emergency Medical teams, Guard Fire Fighters, Ministry Team, Internist, 25 EMEDs personnel and supplies
Kentucky	50 Heavy trucks with 150 soldiers, 24 person refueling team, food service personnel, Medical Preventative Medicine personnel, communications and LNO personnel
Kentucky	Water Purification Equipment with Operators, Ministry Team, medical personnel
Maine	Preventative Medicine Team, Cable repair personnel Security personnel
Maryland	MP Security Company, 104 Personnel for S and R and ice and water distribution
Massachusetts	Medical Officers
Michigan	MP Security Company, construction engineers, EMEDS personnel
Minnesota	Ministry Teams, Mental Stress Team, medical support
Missouri	2-C130 Aircraft with Crew, medical personnel
Montana	Public Affairs Team
Nebraska	Security Forces, Priest, Ground Safety Manager, ARW personnel
New Hampshire	EMEDS personnel, bioenvironmental personnel
New Jersey	Medical Support Personnel, bioenvironmental personnel
New York	8 UH6s, 2 CH7, 6 UH1 and 130 personnel, Rabbi, EMEDS personnel
North Dakota	Water Purification Equipment with Operators, 72 personnel from fighter wing
Ohio	119 soldiers for debris removal, etc., 1,300 Task Force soldiers, aviation assets, generators, 3 OH-58 with crew, aircraft maintenance personnel, food service personnel, EIS Management Team, tactical support personnel, EMEDS personnel, Air wing personnel
Oklahoma	25 personnel/Air Mobility, Fire Vehicle, Medical Support personnel
Oregon	Chief of Safety, Medics, EMEDS personnel
Pennsylvania	SatCom with personnel, AVC ATS Company, Food Services, Medical Support Personnel, EMEDS personnel
Puerto Rico	Air wing personnel
Rhode Island	Units to load and unload aircraft
South Carolina	Bioenvironmental Engineer
Tennessee	ATS Co. with Tower, TTCS, 3 MP Security Companies, fixed wing support teams, engineering battalion, logistics control cell, Mobile Emergency Operations Center, EIS Teams, 26 personnel from air refueling wing, aviation assets, Forklift loader, Fire Vehicle, EIS Management Team, EIS Repair Team, 26 Security personnel
Utah	Ministry Teams
Vermont	Bioenvironmental personnel
Virginia	447 Light Infantry for security and recovery, EMEDs personnel
West Virginia	Airlift Wing support

| Wisconsin | EMEDs personnel |
| Wyoming | Medical Support, Bioenvironmental Engineer |

MISSISSIPPI EMAC COST TRACKER DATED OCTOBER 10, 2005

Cross also coordinated closely with all other state entities involved, including the Mississippi Department of Public Safety, in order to maintain a coordinated law enforcement effort. Cross noted that coordination between Guard engineering companies with various utility companies to clear roads and restore electricity and phone services was instrumental in getting power restored to the majority of coastal counties well in advance of projections.[72]

The National Guard provided immediate and continued support to the people of Mississippi during Hurricane Katrina.[73] National Guard accomplishments included: 3,900 miles of roads cleared of fallen trees and debris; 1.2 million meals ready to eat (MRE) and 1 million gallons of water delivered via air (over 2,000 missions); 39 million pounds of ice, 6.4 million gallons of water, and 2.7 million MREs distributed to central distribution points in 37 counties; 200 presence patrols and more than 600 search and rescue missions conducted; law enforcement assistance provided, resulting in 72 arrests; aircraft logged over 1,995 hours and delivered 2.57 million pounds of cargo. Emergency medical assistance from the Air National Guard assisted hundreds of Mississippi citizens.

Department of Defense response

The day after Katrina made landfall, England led an early roundtable session to get damage assessments for DOD facilities and review resources that may be required of DOD to support hurricane relief.[74] The Secretary of Defense was briefed on DOD's response and Northern Command issued several more alerts in anticipation of requests for assistance.

While Honoré arrived on Wednesday, August 31, as the commander of the newly established Joint Task Force Katrina to supervise federal military operations, the first active duty Navy and Air Force personnel arrived in Louisiana late Thursday, September 1, and active duty Army personnel started to arrive early Friday, September 2.[75] These active duty personnel helped the Louisiana National Guard and the New Orleans Police Department (NOPD) control the crowds during the evacuation of the Superdome, maintain law and order in the streets, and eventually conduct secondary searches, going door to door looking for survivors or bodies and assisting those who had not yet escaped.

NATIONAL GUARD

The support provided by DOD was invaluable, according to a wide variety of officials.[76] DOD active duty forces were involved in search and rescue, but generally after the initial rescues from roofs by helicopters and boats. They were involved in the more deliberate search activities where mixed teams, to include National Guard, law enforcement, Coast Guard, and DOD worked together going house to house and searching for hold-outs and dead bodies.[77]

DOD also took over FEMA's logistics distribution functions. According to FEMA Acting Director for Response during Hurricane Katrina, Edward G. Buikema, FEMA initially approached DOD about this mission on Thursday, September 1.[78] On that date, Colonel Richard Chavez informed FEMA Acting Director of Operations Ken Burris the request "would require a Secretary DHS [sic] to Secretary DoD call to initiate and significant General Counsel input."[79] The formal Mission Assignment was prepared the next day at 6:15 p.m.[80] and by 7:41 p.m., McHale informed DHS Deputy Secretary Michael P. Jackson that "SecDef agreed to support your RFA for broad logistics support" and that DOD was "working on the specific language — and a planning staff to implement it."[81] Execution of the mission apparently began the next day, September 3, according to written orders signed by Principal Deputy Secretary of Defense for Homeland Defense Pete Verga.[82]

While the immediate life saving measures taken by the Coast Guard crews were laudable, the failure to systemically communicate the location of the rescued citizens to local authorities resulted in some rescued persons being effectively stranded, lacking food, water, and shelter for extended periods.

The first heavy lift aircraft to arrive at the New Orleans Airport was a Coast Guard C-130.[116] It brought water and food to the area on approximately August 31, which was subsequently forwarded to Zephyr Field, the Superdome, and Air Station New Orleans to be distributed by helicopters on their return flights to flooded areas. The Coast Guard initiated this effort because it recognized tha victims placed on higher ground "islands" had not yet been completely evacuated and required water and food, as temperatures during the day were nearing one hundre degrees. Once again, the effort was laudable but fell shor of the need, as some evacuees remained in distress.

On the afternoon of September 1, additional communications were re-established when Coast Guard Cutter SPENCER arrived on-scene in New Orleans.[117] SPENCER took tactical control of Coast Guard surface forces in New Orleans and, on September 2 established a Vessel Traffic System (VTS) to control marine vessel traffic in the area. The SPENCER's communications capabilities include satellite, medium frequency, high frequency, and very high frequency voice and data communications (surface – to - surface communications, and surface - to - air voice and data links).

On September 2 and 3, Joint Field Operations (JFOs) were established.[118] In Louisiana, however, there were Coast Guard and urban search and rescue personnel at

and the Louisiana Department of Wildlife and Fisheries.[113] A Coast Guard officer dispatched vessels. Crews returned to the site for food and rest.

On the second day of operations, August 30, drop off locations were chosen by helicopter pilots and established at the Superdome, Lakefront Airport, the "Cloverleaf" (an area along I-10), the University of New Orleans, Zephyr Field, and New Orleans Airport.[114] This information was communicated to the FEMA representative at Zephyr Field, who coordinated resources to assist survivors at each location. Notwithstanding this effort to coordinate, the hand-off was not effective, leaving many "rescued" persons without sustenance or shelter for extended periods. In addition, as larger numbers of survivors were placed at each location, requests were made for larger Department of Defense and National Guard helicopters, including MH-53s (from the USS Bataan) and CH-47s to shuttle them from dry land islands to locations accessible by bus for further evacuation; the helicopters began arriving on the same date.

On August 31, a Coast Guard liaison officer arrived at Task Force Eagle (the National Guard command center for air operations) at the Superdome.[115] The National Guard also received rescue requests at this site, and tasking orders would be passed to Coast Guard helicopters that arrived at that location.

e state EOC in Baton Rouge before the formalized JFO
as established. A cadre of Coast Guard personnel from
rt Arthur, and others, who had been evacuated from
ew Orleans, was already in the EOC handling search and
scue coordination.

By September 20, the Coast Guard had organized and
ordinated the rescue or evacuation of 33,544 people.[119]
the height of Katrina operations, over 33 percent
Coast Guard aircraft were deployed to the affected
gion.[120] Despite coordination difficulties, the Coast
uard's efforts were heroic and saved countless lives.

NATIONAL GUARD

inding: The Army Corps of ngineers provided critical esources to Katrina victims, but re-landfall contracts were not dequate

e Army Corps of Engineers ("USACE" or "Corps"),
other active duty military unit, provided critical
sources to respond to Hurricane Katrina. The Corps
ovided relief and response support to FEMA in
cordance with the National Response Plan as the
ad federal agency for public works and engineering
mergency Support Function #3). Some of the Corps'
ecific missions related to Hurricane Katrina included
oviding water and ice to regional warehouses, providing
nergency power, providing emergency roof repair, and
moving debris.

During Katrina and the aftermath, USACE provided
2 million liters of water, 232 million pounds of ice,
stallation of about 900 large generators, repairs to
0,000 roofs, and removal of a million cubic yards
debris.[121] USACE had pre-awarded competitively
d contracts for all of these functions to allow quick
ployment of resources prior to and immediately after an
ent.[122] These pre-awarded contracts are part of USACE's
lvanced Contracting Initiative (ACI) which has been in
ace for six years.

Due to the magnitude of the destruction, USACE
e-awarded contracts for roofing repair and debris
noval were not adequate, and additional contracts were
vertised and awarded using shortened but competitive
ocedures.[123] In addition, FEMA tasked USACE to

provide structural safety evaluations of low-rise and non-
public buildings in New Orleans and other locations.
To date, USACE has completed assessments of 47,800
of an estimated 80,000 to 100,000 units.[124] Given the
large number of uninhabitable or unusable buildings,
FEMA has recently tasked USACE with demolition of
buildings.[125] To date, USACE is still developing estimates
and conducting planning for the demolition mission.

Finding: The Department of Defense has not yet incorporated or implemented lessons learned from joint exercises in military assistance to civil authorities that would have allowed for a more effective response to Katrina

The Department of Defense participates in several
command and control exercises involving responses
to domestic emergencies, ranging from the combatant
command level to the national level.[126] In the past these
have included Northern Command exercises UNIFIED
DEFENSE (2003,2004), ARDENT SENTRY (2005),
DETERMINED PROMISE (2003, 2004), VIGILANT
SHIELD (2005), DILIGENT ENDEAVOR (2003),
DILIGENT WARRIOR (2004), NORTHERN EDGE (2003),
SCARLET SHIELD (2004), DARK PORTAL (2004) and
TOPOFF (2003, 2005). Many of these exercise scenarios
were designed to overwhelm local and state assets to
evoke a response under the National Response Plan,
including the employment of DOD assets.

Hurricane Katrina was a test of the recently established
(post - 9/11) United States Northern Command, and its
ability to oversee and coordinate the largest use of active
duty and Guard military in a domestic action in recent

history. Although Northern Command has conducted numerous exercises with the National Guard in state and local exercises, the lessons learned during these events were not consistently applied to the military response to Katrina.

NORAD/NORTHCOM ARDENT SENTRY 05 was a combined exercise with TOPOFF 3, conducted April 4-9, 2005.[127] The overall goal of this exercise was to conduct a joint service and interagency exercise that would provide realistic training opportunities for all agencies in incident management. Canadian forces also participated as part of the North American Aerospace Defense Command (NORAD). Another objective was to plan, deploy, and employ DOD forces in support of civilian authorities' operations in accordance with the National Response Plan and DOD policy. The lessons learned during this exercise offered a preview of problems that would surface again during the Katrina response. Some of Northern Command's recommendations for improvement were as follows:

> Conduct strategic effects-based planning between DOD and DHS for each Incident Annex in the National Response Plan.

> Investigate requirement for integrated "National Strategic Communications Plan" in coordination with interagency partners.

> Develop national capability to electronically produce, staff, validate, approve and track mission accomplishment of mission assignments.

> Determine requirements for a "National Common Operating Picture" in coordination with DHS, Department of Justice, and other Federal agencies.[128]

TOPOFF 2 also contained findings that, if corrected, would have enhanced the federal response to Katrina.[129] From uncertainty between federal and state roles to the lack of robust and efficient local emergency communications and the need to improve data collection from military agencies, TOPOFF 2 findings were telling predictors of some of the challenges the military faced.

Northern Command predicted in its ARDENT SENTRY/ TOPOFF 3 Master Executive Summary, that "this exercise success is due in part to scenario constraints that could provide a false sense of security and lack of incentive to initiate or aggressively participate in the integrated

regionally-based planning that is so essential."[130] Just over four months later, Katrina struck.

After Katrina, DOD officials reflected on the value of prior exercises. McHale commented that government training exercises "have not been sufficiently challenging."[131] Other Pentagon officials noted that in many cases, top officials, from Cabinet-level secretaries and generals to governors and mayors, do not participate and these simulations do not last long enough.[132] The Government Accountability Office, in a November 29 briefing also noted key players are not always involved in drills, the lessons from previous training and exercises are not retained, and the training and exercises are more targeted at terrorist events than natural disasters.[133]

The lack of implementation of lessons learned and the training necessary to learn them resulted in less than optimal response by all military components. Oxford Analytica took the following view:

> After Katrina made landfall, the NORTHCOM-led military support mission suffered many of the same planning failures, unclear lines of authority, communication breakdowns, and shortages of critical resources that were experienced by the civilian agencies, such as the Department of Homeland Security.[134]

Finding: The lack of integration of National Guard and active duty forces hampered the military response

"Title 10 versus 32 versus 14…again."[135]
Coast Guard Vice Admiral Jim Hull, NORTHCOM

"Advance planning between active-duty personnel and the Guard is vital – in contrast to the cooperation that . . . unfolded during Katrina 'on the fly' – albeit by 'superb leaders'."[136] **Washington Post, October 13, 2005, quoting Assistant Secretary of Defense Paul McHale**

In a speech on October 21, McHale indicated planning by the National Guard was not well integrated with the

overall military, and the Joint Staff did not have a grasp of the National Guard's plans.[137] Interestingly, a September 14 e-mail originating in the Joint Chiefs of Staff (JCS) offices commended the Bureau's efforts to provide operational information to JCS.[138] McHale stated that National Guard plans were not well integrated with overall DOD plans. The Joint Staff acknowledged that the NGB was providing timely and accurate reports, but Northern Command was apparently more focused on active operations and therefore did not have a well informed view of the significant National Guard effort in the region. The Joint Staff e-mail went on to say that Northern Command's briefings are too active duty focused and lack unity of effort.[139] In the same speech, McHale said DOD did not understand how to integrate with the plans of the National Guard.[140] The reverse was also true, despite past lessons learned.

In the TOPOFF 3 exercise in April 2005, it was clear the National Guard and the National Guard Bureau would be part of a large scale emergency response. The New Jersey National Guard noted that "although TOPOFF 3 began as an exercise with minimal National Guard involvement, it quickly evolved into one that heavily relied upon Guard participation, and identified a need early on for assistance from the National Guard Bureau."[141]

At the time of Katrina landfall, however, the National Guard did not have adequate knowledge of DOD planning guidance developed at Northern Command, including concept of operations plans and functional plans for military support to civilian authorities.[142] The National Guard After Action Report on TOPOFF 3 found that numerous members of the Guard operational leadership did not have adequate knowledge of these plans.[143]

At an after action meeting of state Adjutants General, the Adjutants General agreed coordination between active duty and National Guard in the response operation needed to be improved. According to the meeting report, "there was a lack of coordination of Joint Task Force Katrina operation with the National Guard Headquarters of the supported states."[144]

The National Guard Bureau also reported lines of command, control, and communications lacked clear definition and coordination between federal military forces and National Guard forces operating under state

control, resulting in duplicate efforts. For example, elements of the 82nd Airborne Division moved into a sector already being patrolled by the National Guard.[145] The meeting report also stated:

> Federal troops often arrived prior to being requested and without good prior coordination. This resulted in confusion and often placed a strain on an already overburdened disaster response system. A specific case in point was the Marine Corps amphibious units which landed in Mississippi without transportation, requiring National Guard transportation assets to move them to New Orleans increasing the burden on an already stretched support system.[146]

The National Guard 38th Infantry Division, composed of smaller Guard units from many states, reported they never formally coordinated with Northern Command.[147] Members of the 82nd Airborne Division, the first active duty personnel to arrival in New Orleans on September 3, had a similar experience. In a September 9 e-mail, a soldier in the 82nd indicated coordination of evacuation efforts in New Orleans was very poor.[148]

> We're conducting boat patrols using Coast Guard boats but coordination is very difficult . . . . National Guard seems to move in and out of sectors doing what they want then just leaving without telling anyone . . . . And this is in 4 days of operations.[149]

Despite the lack of integration in Washington, D.C. and in Louisiana, active and reserve forces worked well together in Mississippi. Notably, the Governor of Mississippi did not request active duty military assistance, relying instead on Mississippi and other National Guard personnel provided through EMAC.

However, in the DOD effort to lean forward, Honoré contacted Cross immediately to offer any help needed, and remained in contact with him daily in person or on the phone.[150] On September 3, Northern Command and JTF Katrina received confirmation from the Secretary of Defense that JTF Katrina was to assume responsibility for logistical operations in Mississippi and Louisiana in response to FEMA's request.[151] All DOD operations in the state of Mississippi were conducted with Cross' consent.[152]

One of the most important roles played by DOD in Mississippi was the delivery of military stocks of food and water that started to arrive in Gulfport on September 1. In his testimony before the Committee, Cross noted:

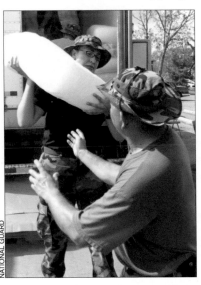

By the end of the second day after landfall, my intelligence reports indicated that the previously assumed flow of food and water was severely restricted. Many pre-planned distribution points were inaccessible and many hundreds of people were stranded by flood waters, blocked roadways or lack of fuel for transportation. These desperate civilians were primarily observed by aerial reconnaissance in Hancock County. Upon realization that food and water was not going to arrive by normal means in time, I offered an immediate airlift of food and water utilizing our helicopters and our rations and immediately requested through US NORTHCOM an emergency airlift of military stocks of MRE's. Within a day, massive amounts of MRE's began arriving at Gulfport just in time to be disseminated to prevent starvation. Almost 1.7 million MRE's were flown in to my position thanks to the quick reaction of Lieutenant General Joe Inge of Northern Command.[153]

Air Force personnel and aircraft from the 920th Rescue Wing and 347th Rescue Wing, as well as Special Operations Command aircraft arrived at the Jackson Air National Guard Base the day after landfall, and along with National Guard, performed search and rescue mission in the first days.[154]

The USS Bataan, the USS Truman, the USS Whidbey Island, and other vessels supported Navy and Marine Corps operations in Mississippi, delivering personnel, equipment, and commodities.[155] The USS Bataan had six helicopters, one land craft, extensive logistics supplies, and trauma medical capabilities that were used for search and rescue in both Mississippi and Louisiana.[156] According to a September 1 e-mail from Colonel Damon Penn, Mississippi's Defense Coordinator, a total of 19 active duty and National Guard teams were conducting search and rescue missions on the Mississippi coast.[157]

The Naval Construction Battalion Center at Gulfport was severely damaged during Katrina, and although most of the 800 "Seabees" were evacuated before the hurricane struck, remaining personnel and other Seabees deployed by the Navy helped with Hurricane Katrina recovery operations.[158] Gulfport-based Seabees, who linked up with the National Guard at their Joint Operations Center in Gulfport, coordinated with the National Guard to clear roads and assisted in removing debris.[159] The Seabees also set up logistics centers to distribute food and water and provide emergency medical services.[160] Two active-duty Seabee battalions from Port Hueneme, California, their subordinate detachments from both coasts, and Reserve Seabee volunteers joined those already in Gulfport, Mississippi, forming a total Seabee force of about 3,000 sailors by September 9.[161] The Seabees were also joined by 100 Mexican Marines and 215 Canadian Navy personnel who helped them work on FEMA temporary housing sites, nursing home repair, and repairs to public buildings schools and construction sites.[162]

On September 5, 1,000 Marines from the I Marine Expeditionary Force (MEF), Camp Pendleton, California, arrived at Biloxi, and 1,000 Marines from the II MEF Camp Lejeune, North Carolina, arrived Stennis Space Center.[163] These Marine units, commanded by Marine Corps Reserve Major General Douglas V. Odell, Jr., assisted in the transportation of large amounts of commodities, as well as providing personnel and quipment to assist in recovery operations in Hancock County as directed by Cross.[164] "Without concern for service lines and or 'Title of Authority,' [Major General] Odell accepted the mission and executed all requirements, until directed by his higher headquarters to move to New Orleans," Cross said.[165]

On September 8, the USNS Comfort arrived in Pascagoula to offer medical assistance and facilities.[166] Four days later, the Northern Command suggested to the Joint Chiefs of Staff that the Comfort be withdrawn because there was "very limited usage;" estimated at fewer than a dozen patients."[167]

According to Cross' response to questions by the Select Committee, the Mississippi National Guard maintained a very good relationship with DOD forces. "Active duty units that responded always took a subordinate, support role and these units coordinated directly with the Mississippi National Guard Forward Operations Center."[168]

In Louisiana, airborne search and rescue was another area where National Guard and DOD integration was lacking. As noted in the National Guard Bureau's After Action Report, National Guard and DOD active duty (as well as other) helicopters were conducting rescue missions over New Orleans with no preplanning for command and control. The different helicopters had different radios and used different frequencies, creating a dangerous situation for mid-air collisions in an area with little or no air traffic control.[169] Beyond the safety issue, National Guard and DOD active duty assets operated under their own tasking orders, which sometimes led to duplication.[170] Search and rescue coordination problems are discussed in more detail later in this chapter.

Another Louisiana example illustrating integration problems is the area of communication. The 35th Infantry Division, a National Guard unit, arrived at Belle Chasse Naval Air Station on September 6, and the 82nd Airborne Division, a DOD active duty unit, was to provide them with some communications support. Specifically, the 35th Infantry Division had forwarded its frequency and network requirements and the 82nd Airborne Division was to provide frequency management support providing specific frequencies to use. However, after the arrival of the 35th, there was still confusion over what frequencies to use because many systems were already using the assigned frequency. The 35th Infantry Division did not have the proper equipment to de-conflict the

frequency use, and could not obtain it until September 12, almost a week later.[171] For more information on communication difficulties during Hurricane Katrina, see chapter on COMMUNICATIONS.

Finding: Northern Command does not have adequate insight into state response capabilities or adequate interface with governors, which contributed to a lack of mutual understanding and trust during the Katrina response

"There must be a strong agreement between state and federal leadership as to the operational objectives. State concerns about maintaining sovereignty must be respected."[172] **General H Steven Blum, Chief, National Guard Bureau**

"Admiral Keating, who heads US NORTHCOM, a newly created military body overseeing homeland defense, has told lawmakers that active-duty forces should be given complete authority for responding to catastrophic disasters. . . . The head of the Washington State National Guard, General Timothy Lowenberg, suggested in emails to colleagues that Admiral Keating's suggestion amounted to a "policy of domestic regime change."[173] **Wall Street Journal, December 8, 2005**

On Friday, September 1, the President offered to place Honoré under the joint command of Northern Command and Governor Blanco. Under this proposal, Honoré would have commanded both active duty U.S. military forces and the Louisiana National Guard, subject to the command of the Governor with respect to the Guard and Northern Command with respect to the federal active duty troops. Governor Blanco declined this offer, leaving Honoré and Northern Command in charge of the federal active troops and Landrenau and Blanco in charge of the Louisiana National Guard.

The Governors of the Gulf states chose not to relinquish command of the National Guard units in their respective states. While better coordination of the military effort may have resulted if one commander were in charge of all aspects of military support, the Governor had confidence in Landreneau and saw no need for an added layer of command.

The Department of Defense was eager to assist the Gulf states. The establishment of JTF Katrina to coordinate the military response and the command's desire to help made state sovereignty an issue during the Katrina response.[174] Florida, Alabama, and Mississippi declined active duty military assistance, but active duty units pre-positioning at active duty bases in Mississippi operated smoothly with the Mississippi National Guard. Therefore, the issue of federalism played out in Louisiana. Resolving this issue may have slowed the active duty military response and contributed to tension in the state-federal relationship. In the end, there was a dual military response to Hurricane Katrina in Louisiana. Honoré commanded the active duty military response, and Landreneau commanded the Louisiana National Guard response.

The failure of DOD, governors, and other state officials to actively participate in joint planning for emergencies, both natural and man-made, that occurred within Northern Command's area of responsibility contributed to the tension. There were too few "civilian authorities" in DOD's military assistance to civilian authority planning. As Northern Command lamented it did not have adequate insight into the states, the Gulf governors also lacked insight into the operations of Northern Command.

In Northern Command's Master Exercise Summary Report on ARDENT SENTRY/TOPOFF 3, concern was expressed that Northern Command "does not have adequate insight into state response capabilities (responders, medical systems, National Guard, etc.) and other federal capabilities (contracts, FEMA, DHHS, etc). . . . This lack of understanding could contribute to off-target planning for potential active duty DoD roles and missions." [175]

DOD understands the different capabilities of Transportation Command, Forces Command, 1st Army, 5th Army, the Air Force, the Marine Corps, the Navy and role and capabilities of Joint Forces Command, Northern Command and Joint Task Force Katrina, but the Governor of Louisiana did not. In a September 19 interview with Gannett News Service, Blanco commented on the difficulties of communicating her request for troops. She said others asked, "Did you ask for this; did you ask for that[?] It got to be a very difficult little game," she said.[176]

> *DOD and DHS have not adequately defined what is required for military assistance to civilian authorities during large disasters.*

One cause of this misunderstanding is that DOD and DHS have not adequately defined what is required for military assistance to civilian authorities during large disasters. According to McHale, "It has never been the plan, nor has the Department of Defense been trained, resourced and equipped to provide a first responder capability."[177]

According to a September 2003 report to Congress on DOD's role in supporting homeland security missions:

> [The] Chairman [of the] Joint Chiefs of Staff, **maintains visibility** of National Guard assets performing homeland security missions. . . . Moreover, NORTHCOM and PACOM must have **insight** into state-controlled National Guard operations to facilitate coordination between Title 10 and Title 32 or State Active Duty military operations, which might be occurring in the same area, at the same time, towards a common goal. [emphasis added][178]

Honoré was not familiar with emergency operational procedures and personnel within the Katrina states. According to Blum, granting him a state commission without the knowledge and understanding of the state's operational environment would not necessarily have added anything to the response.[179] The Gulf coast governors, with their close relationships to state Adjutant General and common experiences with past emergencies, shared that view.[180]

Admiral Keating, the Commander of Northern Command has acknowledged that there are advantages to having a National Guard officer in command of homeland response:

> The advantages of using a N[ational] G[uard] officer during a disaster are: (1) the overwhelming majority of forces that respond to disasters are/will

be National Guard who will usually be on the scene in a state active duty status before DOD is requested to respond; (2) the NG is familiar with the local area and the local culture; (3) the NG usually has close ties with first responders such as local and state law enforcement, fire departments, etc.; and (4) the local community knows and relies upon the NG because they are part of the community. . . . NG personnel are more likely to have more experience working with local responders than the active component. A disadvantage of using a NG officer is: NG commanders might not be familiar with federal capabilities brought to the table, especially those from Navy and Marines.[181]

Some of the Adjutants General from the Gulf states and round the country believe the much needed integration, rust, and increased understanding by state officials of vhat constitutes joint military assistance would improve f Northern Command were a National Guard Command, ed by an experienced National Guard officer.[182]

Northern Command's mission is to "deter, prevent, nd defeat threats and aggression aimed at the United tates."[183] It also has a mission to "provide defense upport of civil authorities."[184] During a national mergency within the United States, NORTHCOM equires policies and procedures for interaction with tate officials. The absence of these policies hampered the atrina response.

The Select Committee does not believe there is a simple nswer to improving state and federal integration. Local ontrol and state sovereignty are important principles ooted in the nation's birth that cannot be discarded nerely to achieve more efficient joint military operations n American soil.

Finding: Even DOD lacked situational awareness of post-landfall conditions, which contributed to a slower response

The Department of Defense has significant assets for the collection of intelligence, as well as communications and satellite equipment needed in all military operations. These assets are at the very heart of conducting comprehensive and directed military operations around the world, and were not optimally used during the Katrina response. For example, the Select Committee found little evidence that DOD satellite imagery was used to great advantage to target relief to the hardest hit areas, nor was information resulting from DOD aerial damage assessment flights properly disseminated. Lack of a unified data collection system among DOD military and civilian personnel also forced the Department to rely on other sources.

Department of Defense documents indicated an unusual reliance on news reports to obtain information on what was happening on the ground in the days immediately following landfall. It appeared the Department also relied on the press for initial damage assessment in New Orleans. Reliance on often unsubstantiated press stories appeared to make DOD reactive instead of a leading participant in the response.

Department of Defense documents indicated an unusual reliance on news reports to obtain information on what was happening on the ground in the days immediately following landfall.

DOD e-mail and JTF Katrina Commander's Assessments cited press as the source of the information on looting, the situation at the Superdome, other shelters, and the New Orleans Hyatt.[185] E-mail from private sources to Honoré and McHale about people needing to be rescued at Xavier University and the Salvation Army Building in New Orleans were acted on. In the Xavier case, Honoré dispatched a reconnaissance team based on this information.[186] An e-mail dated August 30 from a colonel from the National Guard Bureau noted that Northern Command, First Army, and Fifth Army commanders could not make contact with the Louisiana State Adjutant General.[187]

Keating stated that the biggest challenge for Northern Command was "gaining and maintaining situational awareness as to the catastrophic disaster."[188] This also came as no surprise to McHale, who commented that "early situational awareness was poor, a problem that should have been corrected following identical damage assessment challenges during Hurricane Andrew."[189]

Finding: DOD lacked an information sharing protocol that would have enhanced joint situational awareness and communications between all military components

According to a National Guard assessment, JTF Katrina "had limited visibility on in-transit forces" being deployed. There was no system in place to track all active duty or Guard "forces and material from ports of embarkation" through distribution.[190] For example, an August 29 e-mail generated in the Office of the Secretary of Defense indicated concern over a Navy ship that announced its deployment without legal authority or Secretary of Defense approval.[191]

Information flowing up from the National Guard state headquarters or the National Guard Bureau also did not always make its way to the JTF Katrina commander. An August 31 e-mail confirmed that 1st Army and 5th Army headquarters could not communicate directly with the Louisiana Defense Coordinating Officer, which prevented the JTF Katrina commander from knowing what Guard assets were streaming into New Orleans at the time. On September 1, a general officer at NORTHCOM complained he had not been getting e-mail from the DCOs for two days.[192]

The Office of the Assistant Secretary of Defense for Homeland Defense also had problems keeping track of what DOD capabilities were being utilized and what tasks had been performed for the Homeland Defense Secretary. In a September 4 e-mail, some questions posed were:

How many MREs have been made available by DoD? . .
What is the # of hospital beds on USN ships?. . .
What is the status of aerial surveillance capability? . . .
What is [the] status of the New Orleans Police Department?
How linked up is the Guard with NOPD?[193]

There was also a request: "Need a daily DoD roll-up matrix: What we're doing, Who's doing it, [and w]hat's the progress?[194]

During the TOPOFF 3 and ARDENT SENTRY 05 exercises, NORTHCOM learned that

> . . . the ground rules for the channel of communications between USNORTHCOM, NGB J[oint] O[perations] C[enter] and State National Guard JOCs is largely undefined. There is not an agreement that delineates reporting responsibilities for force readiness and disaster response planning. Needed is a framework and an agreed on channel of communications to ensure the flow of information between USNORTHCOM, NGB and State National Guard JOCs is timely and complete.[195]

Yet, during Katrina, the National Guard Bureau learned NORTHCOM did not standardize reporting guidelines.[196] E-mails, logs, and daily briefings indicated a great flow of information between DOD component headquarters and the National Guard Bureau. There also appeared to be numerous mechanisms to assist in integrating federal and state operations. These included the establishment of a National Guard desk at the National Military Command Center, Guard representation in the Northern Command Joint Operations Center, web portals, daily conference calls, and e-mail situation updates to key leaders.[197] However the Select Committee could find no eporting requirements for sharing important information between DOD entities. Blum, however, noted that "these efforts, while effective, cannot be expected to overcome the inability of forces on the ground to effectively share information."[198]

Finding: Joint Task Force Katrina command staff lacked joint training, which contributed to the lack of coordination between active duty components

Hurricane Katrina required the Army, Air Force, Navy, and Marine Corps to work together in an emergency mission in the continental United States. Although skilled and trained in war-fighting missions abroad, conducting joint missions in this country, quickly, and under tremendous public pressure, posed integration challenges. One of the findings in an after action report from the Department of the Navy stated: "Service cultural issues seemed to dominate in a negative fashion."[199]

The core element of the JTF is formed by the 1st Army Staff. There is a perception that JTF is in essence, an Army T[ask] F[orce], with joint augmentation and that this disposition colors their decision making processes and view of the conduct of operations. . . . In a crisis, organizations play to their strengths and [tend] to disregard unfamiliar capabilities or concepts.[200]

Retired Coast Guard Vice Admiral Jim Hull was asked by Northern Command to assess the command's Katrina response. Hull's observations were critical of JTF Katrina, noting that the capabilities of 1st Army headquarters, which formed the nucleus of JTF Katrina, "was not organized or resourced to operate as a Joint Task Force."[201] Specific challenges ranged from inexperienced personnel to lack of communications and equipment. "The JTF is an ad-hoc organization doing the best it can without the resources necessary to make it an optimal enabler," he said. Hull noted that as Honoré made command decisions away from his headquarters, his staff was not always informed. "We track General Honoré's location by watching CNN," JTF Katrina staff said.

AP PHOTO/BILL HABER

The Department of the Navy Emergency Preparedness Liaison Officer Program in a September 12 After Action Report listed key problems within JTF Katrina:

Joint Doctrine was largely ignored. In the melee of the first few days where lives literally hung in the balance, perhaps this was a necessary course of action. However, as the Active Duty Force began to develop, the JTF Katrina headquarters never transitioned from the very tactical mindset of life saving to the operational mindset of sustaining and enabling a Joint Force. Since the Forward Command Element (General Honoré) was unable to communicate, they became embroiled and distracted with the tactical and were unable to focus on even the most basic of operational issues.... Other units who were responding from outside the area to integrate with what was called a "Joint" task force expected certain doctrinal norms which materialized very slowly or not at all.[202]

The report also remarked that since the JTF did not establish a commander for all land components, 1st Army, 5th Army, and the Marine Corps were unclear on JTF Katrina expectations, causing confusion and lack of coordination between land forces in New Orleans.[203] The effects of the difficulties with creating and sustaining a truly joint effort were visible on the ground in Louisiana, especially during later evacuation efforts, and the patrolling of New Orleans parishes.

Finding: Joint task force Katrina, the National Guard, Louisiana, and Mississippi lacked needed communications equipment and the interoperability required for seamless on the ground coordination

Reliable communications were the exception in the aftermath of Katrina. Even Honoré experienced communications problems. Honoré moved into Camp Shelby before he had the communications equipment necessary to support JTF Katrina.[204] Honoré's staff was frustrated at the lack of communications equipment. According to a Navy after action report, "At this stage it is believed that when the commander leaves Camp Shelby in the morning and returns in the evening, the staff's only access to communicate with him is through a borrowed Nextel cell phone and his Blackberry.[205] The Navy reported the USS IWO JIMA did have task force-capable communications equipment during the first ten days of the storm that would have been of great help to General Honoré.[206]

Blum also noted that "one critical area where we lack integration is in interoperable communications. National Guard units do not have the equipment necessary to effectively share information with Title 10 forces. This caused significant challenges on the ground that then bubbled up the chains."[207]

At the time of Katrina, Northern Command had yet to establish standardized communications architecture or to identify the system and information requirements to be used during homeland response operations.[208] Oxford Analytica reported:

Since September 11, emergency response planners have recognized that during a major disaster, local communications systems would be disrupted or disabled, and communication between federal, state, and local officials is a particularly weak link in coordinating emergency response. Katrina showed that little has been accomplished to fix this disconnect. Within the military, the National Guard was hindered by a shortage of communications equipment. These shortcomings suggest that the Pentagon does not assign homeland defense a sufficiently high priority.[209]

The loss of communications infrastructure in Mississippi and Louisiana due to hurricane forces caused a great deal of confusion for days following landfall. Communication outages that occurred in state emergency offices also caused problems in situational awareness. The state Adjutant General of Mississippi on the Gulf coast could not reach the Mississippi Emergency Management Agency in Jackson until two days after landfall.[210] When cell phones and towers were destroyed or lost power, states were not equipped with backup communications capabilities even with Guard forces. According to Cross:

One of the biggest lessons learned was the need to adequate, redundant communications systems with an emphasis on satellite backhaul capability in the event of cellular and landline failure. Obviously, this type of equipment requires resourcing. The Mississippi National Guard received $29,100 for fiscal year 2005 for Military Support to Civil Authorities. $8,000 of this amount was applied to pay the satellite phone service bill for the seven satellite phones currently on hand. In order for the Mississippi National Guard to be prepared to respond to catastrophic events, it must be funded accordingly.[211]

The Louisiana National Guard also experienced problems with lost or weak communications infrastructure.[212] Immediately after Hurricane Katrina passed, the Industrial Canal levee broke, flooding the National Guard headquarters at Jackson Barracks. The Guard had to abandon its headquarters operations center and establish a new one, including new communications connections, at the Superdome. Re-establishing these communications was greatly facilitated by the arrival of the state's Weapons of Mass Destruction (WMD) Civil Support Team (CST) and its emergency communications suite.

However, the National Guard in Louisiana was also plagued by problems with the state's 800 MegaHertz public safety radio system, which it shares with the state's law enforcement and other public safety agencies. State officials said this system was about 11 years old and limited to 48 channels.[213] They said it was not designed to handle thousands of calls, so the volume of calls after Hurricane Katrina overloaded the system. In addition, one of the state's three 800 MegaHerz relay towers, the Buras tower in Plaquemines Parish, was toppled by the hurricane, which further degraded the capacity of the system.[214] Louisiana National Guard officials cited the weaknesses in this system as one of the reasons they had problems communicating with the state's Emergency Operations Center in Baton Rouge.[215]

The National Guard Bureau confirmed that its liaison teams should also be deployed with significant mobile communications.[216] The Louisiana NGB Liaison Officer was equipped with a satellite phone, which was critical during the first days of response.[217]

Finding: EMAC processing, pre-arranged state compacts, and Guard equipment packages need improvement

Although there was a consensus among federal, state, and local officials that Emergency Mutual Assistant Compacts worked very well, the current EMAC approval process is cumbersome, and therefore not fast or suited to a large scale emergency. While initial Adjutant General to Adjutant General coordination allowed for rapid deployment of National Guard forces during Katrina, the sheer size of the emergency pointed out weaknesses in the current system.

As key communications infrastructure was taken out, the ability to negotiate state-to-state compacts became difficult, if not impossible. In the hours immediately following landfall, when it was needed most, offers of assistance from states all over the country were delayed in the EMAC process, as other states' invaluable assets were not immediately visible to the states affected.

The National Guard Bureau stepped in to help the Gulf state Adjutants General prior to landfall, and increased its management of requests for National Guard forces throughout the response, but some states still used the standard EMAC process through the National Coordinating Committee (NCC). As both the National

The current EMAC approval process is cumbersome, and therefore not fast or suited to a large scale emergency.

Guard Bureau and the NCC tried to anticipate requests, this dual track approach for requesting troops caused confusion and duplicated efforts. Better coordination between the NGB and the NCC was needed.[218]

In addition, not all National Guard personnel are trained in the EMAC process. Louisiana National Guard officers seemed to lack the knowledge and experience necessary to manage the tremendous surge of requests for assistance, as well as field offers from other states under EMAC. This inexperience was one of the reasons the National Guard Bureau played an unusually large role in the EMAC process.[219]

More familiarity with the EMAC procedures and assets by Northern Command and other federal forces would also have enhanced joint response efforts and given them a better appreciation of National Guard capabilities.[220]

Finding: Equipment, personnel, and training shortfalls affected the National Guard response

Needed equipment and manpower

The Army National Guard relied heavily on its aviation units and found that helicopter hoist-equipped aircraft resulted in immediate and successful search and rescue operations. Current Army doctrine, however, does not provide sufficient numbers of hoist-equipped aircraft to its Guard counterpart, nor stage them regionally to support responses to events of significant size.[221] For example, the Mississippi National Guard needed more airlift and helicopters immediately. Cross suggested pre-arranged state compacts for hurricane assets, especially search and rescue aviation assets, would make these assets more readily available and not run the risk they could not be obtained through EMAC requests.[222]

The Air National Guard also relied heavily on its airlift capabilities during Hurricane Katrina. The Air National Guard flew 351 missions with C-130s between August 30 and September 6.[223] Air National Guard personnel reported that:

> The C-130 is the ANG work horse, moving equipment for the National Guard such as CST's, EMEDS, and civil engineering equipment into areas with moderate to heavy infrastructure damage...the Guard can't have enough of them for responding to major homeland emergencies...they are essential.[224]

> New aircraft like the C-17 are better suited to carry over-size equipment such as the Rapid Engineer Deployable Operational Repair Squadron Engineer (RED HORSE) Squadrons, but the limited number of C-17s in inventory require its use to take care of war fighting requirements overseas. This 404-person mobile construction squadron does it all: rapid damage assessment, repair, contingency heavy construction operations such as roads and ramps.[225] Red Horse Squadrons were invaluable during Katrina.[226]

At the time of Katrina's landfall, Northern Command had not yet articulated specific requirements or capabilities that National Guard forces need during major homeland disasters.[227] Without established formal requirements, the equipment deemed necessary for the National Guard to assist civilian authorities in Katrina had not been purchased by the Department of the Army and the Department of the Air Force. The military departments only establish units and procure equipment for which formal mission requirements have been validated, like Title 10 warfighting missions abroad. Northern Command has yet to determine — with or without input from DHS — which specific military assets should be dedicated to provide military assistance to civilian authorities, in part because DHS has not articulated the requirement to DOD in any formal manner.[228] Therefore, at the present time, DOD does not require the purchase of equipment specifically for homeland defense or military assistance to civilian authorities for the National Guard.

Attempts to rent needed equipment were complicated by the great demand for heavy machinery created by the storm. Cross noted that contractors responding to other federal, state, and local requests for assistance leased the same type of equipment sought by the National Guard,

leaving little available for National Guard use.[229]

In a National Guard After Action Review dated September 2005, it was strongly recommended that the Department of Defense "identify the Continental United States mission as a valid requirement and equip it as a valid tasking."[230]

> "I was there. I saw what needed to be done. They were the fastest, best capable, most appropriate force to get there in the time allowed. And that's what it's all about." **General Blum**[231]

Hurricane Katrina required significant National Guard manpower, and quickly. With the current level of 457,000 personnel in the National Guard, the Katrina response demonstrated the Guard response was not hindered by the deployment of Guard troops to support the War on Terrorism. According to Blum, although National Guard from the affected states were deployed overseas, Guardsmen from surrounding, and then other states quickly supplemented the effort.[232] At landfall, over 40 percent of the Mississippi Guard, some 4,200 troops, were deployed overseas. Fortunately, critical engineering units and military police units were home.[233] In Louisiana, Blanco asked for the immediate return of Louisiana National Guard troops from Iraq, but the National Guard Bureau was satisfied it could provide sufficient troops from other states to meet the needs of Louisiana more quickly than trying to extract Louisiana troops from combat operations in Iraq.[234] The Joint Staff and Center for Army Lessons Learned were very impressed at the ability of the Guard to mobilize and move a Corps worth of personnel and equipment in four days.[235]

Nonetheless, organizational challenges surfaced in this rapid deployment. The National Guard forces flowing ld into the staging areas at Alexandria, Louisiana, and to the Naval Air Station New Orleans at Belle Chasse arrived so quickly that the number of Guardsmen assigned who process and task these units was too small.[236] The capabilities of each unit were not readily known by the U.S. logistics personnel tasking officers, causing further delays. A lack of well defined personnel and equipment packages by the Department of Defense to support civilian authorities in large disasters degraded instant tasking of units deployed to Louisiana.[237] General DOD development of regional strike forces composed of various National Guard units would have done a great deal to mitigate the effects of a large natural disaster or other catastrophic event: "Hurricane equipment packages for the Guard should be developed by the Department of Defense to help them provide more adequate assistance to civilian authorities in the future, Cross said."[238]

Current law hindered some congressionally mandated National Guard Civil Support Teams' response

Congress established WMD Civil Support Teams (CSTs) to deploy rapidly to assist local incident commanders in determining the nature and extent of an attack or incident; provide expert technical advice on WMD response operations; and help identify and support the arrival of follow-on state and federal military response assets.[239] The first 10 teams were funded as part of the National Defense Appropriations Act for FY 1999. Each team consists of 22 highly skilled, full-time National Guard members who are federally resourced, trained, and exercised in chemical, biological, and nuclear specialties, and skilled in reconnaissance, medical support, logistics, administration, communications, air liaison, and security.[240]

In these capacities, especially the use of their communications vehicles, the National Guard CSTs proved invaluable to the Katrina response. On September 2, a JTF Katrina official relayed a report from the National Guard Bureau that CSTs from Connecticut, North Carolina, Nebraska, Utah, Arkansas, West Virginia, Indiana, Kansas, Alabama, and the District of Columbia were on route to the Gulf Coast.[241]

During Katrina, there was confusion regarding the legal aspects of CST deployment, as some states interpreted the law to mean they were only authorized to be used for WMD incidents, and only in their states.[242] This interpretation delayed deployment of these vehicles to Mississippi. Lieutenant Colonel Smithson of the Mississippi National Guard said, "CSTs saved the day, I just wish they were here sooner."[243] Clarifying that they are available for use beyond WMD events would have greatly enhanced states abilities to react quickly to the Katrina disaster.[244]

Guard personnel categories caused confusion

Multiple types of duty status of National Guard personnel presented some legal challenges in the proper employment of forces.[245] State military lawyers interpreted laws, regulations, and policies pertaining to the various statuses and units of assignment very differently, which caused unnecessary delays. Delays in the Title 32 approval process, previously identified, added to the difficulty. The National Guard Bureau May 23, 2005 after action report on TOPOFF 3 found:

> As highlighted in Operation Winter Freeze, [the Democratic National Convention, the Republican National Convention] and [the] G-8 summit, and further during Ardent Sentry 05 events, the T[itle] 10/ T[itle] 32 approval process must be standardized. Current process is lengthy, largely undefined, and requires excessive time periods for approval.[246]

E-mails from various state Adjutants General began to arrive at the National Guard Bureau immediately after landfall inquiring about changing all Guard response to Title 32.[247] The National Guard Bureau agreed with these suggestions and began to actively discuss this status change with the Department of Defense.[248] On September 2, 4 and 5 respectively, Governor Riley of Alabama, Governor Barbour of Mississippi, and Governor Blanco of Louisiana wrote to the Secretary of Defense to formally ask that all National Guard personnel responding in their states be put on Title 32, Chapter 9, a new operational section of Title 32 that allows for the National Guard to perform homeland missions under governor control.[249]

The Select Committee believes the Guard response in Katrina would have been more effective had the decision to place National Guard troops in Title 32 status been made earlier by the governors, the National Guard Bureau, and the Secretary of Defense.

1   *Hearing on Hurricane Katrina: Preparedness and Response by the Department of Defense, the Coast Guard, and the National Guard of Louisiana, Mississippi, and Alabama Before Select Comm.*, 109th Cong. (Oct. 27, 2005) (written statement of Paul McHale, Assistant Secretary of Defense for Homeland Defense at 4) [hereinafter *Oct. 27, 2005 Select Comm. Hearing*].

2   *Id.* at 8.

3   *Id.* at 6.

4   *Joint Hearing on Role of the Military and National Guard in Disaster Responses Before the House Armed Services Subcommittee on Terrorism, Unconventional Threats and Capabilities and the House Homeland Security Subcommittee on Emergency Preparedness, Science, and Technology,* 109th Cong. (Nov. 9, 2005) at 7 (written statement of Paul McHale, Assistant Secretary of Defense for Homeland Defense) [hereinafter *Nov. 9, 2005 Joint Armed Services and Homeland Hearing*].

5   *Hearing Before Base Realignment and Closure Commission* (Aug. 11, 2005) at 34 (statements of Harold Gehman, 2005 BRAC Commissioner, and Peter Verga, Principal Deputy Assistant Secretary of Defense for Homeland Defense) [hereinafter *Aug. 11, 2005 BRAC Commission Hearing*].

6   E-mail correspondence from Col. Richard Chavez, Senior Military Advisor for Civil Support to Anthony Capra, Office of Assistant Secretary of Defense for Homeland Defense, et al., (Aug. 30, 2005) (12:18 p.m.).

7   E-mail correspondence from InSung Oaks Lee, Senior Watch Officer, Department of Homeland Security [hereinafter DHS] to Homeland Security Operations Center [hereinafter HSOC] Federal Emergency Management Agency [hereinafter FEMA] mailing list, et al. (Aug. 30, 2005) (10:43 a.m.).

8   *See generally* E-mail correspondence from Anthony Capra, OASD Homeland Defense, Department of Defense [hereinafter DOD] Desk to Michael Ritchie, Office of the Secretary of Defense, Policy, (Aug. 29, 2005) (12:15 p.m.); E-mail correspondence from Anthony Capra, OASD Homeland Defense Desk, DOD Desk to DOD HD Coordination Group, et al. (Aug. 30, 2005) (10:54 a.m.); E-mail correspondence from Col Richard Chavez, Senior Military Advisor for Civil Support, DOD to Anthony Capra, OASD Homeland Defense Desk, DOD Desk, et al. (Aug. 30, 2005) (12:18 p.m.); E-mail correspondence from Anthony Capra, OASD Homeland Defense Desk, DOD Desk to Col. Richard Chavez, Senior Military Advisor for Civil Support, DOD (Aug. 30, 2005) (11:36 a.m.); *see also* E-mail correspondence between DOD HSOC and FEMA HSOC (Sept. 3-4, 2005).

9   *See generally* E-mail correspondence between policy staff of Office of Secretary for Defense (Sept, 5, 2005).

10 *Oct. 27, 2005 Select Comm. Hearing* at 10 (written statement of Adm. Timothy Keating, Commander, North American Aerospace Defense Command [hereinafter NORAD] and U.S. Northern Command [hereinafter NORTHCOM]).

11 *See Hearing on Hurricane Katrina: The Role of the Federal Emergency Management Agency Before Select Comm.*, 109th Cong. at 34-35, 162 (Sept. 27, 2005) (statement of Michael Brown, Former Director, FEMA) [hereinafter *Sept. 27, 2005 Select Comm. Hearing*].

12 Mark Sappenfield, *Battle Brews Over a Bigger Military Role*, CHRISTIAN SCI. MONITOR, Dec. 13, 2005 at 3.

13 Interview by Select Comm. Staff with Andrew Kopplin, Chief of Staff to Gov. Kathleen Blanco, State of LA [hereinafter Kopplin Interview] in Baton Rouge, LA (Nov. 6, 2005); Interview by Select Comm. Staff with Jeff Smith, LA State Coordinating Officer, in Baton Rouge, LA (Nov. 7, 2005).

14 Kopplin Interview; Interview by Select Comm. Staff with Col. Stephen Dabadie, Chief of Staff to Maj. Gen. Bennett C. Landreneau, The Adjutant General, State of LA [hereinafter Dabadie Interview] in Baton Rouge, LA (Nov. 4, 2005).

15 Interview by Select Comm. Staff with Scott Wells, Deputy Federal Coordinating Officer, FEMA, in Baton Rouge, LA [hereinafter Wells Interview] (Nov. 9, 2005).

16 *Sept. 27, 2005 Select Comm. Hearing* at 34-35, 84, 109, 112, 113, 126, 161 (statement of Michael Brown, Former Director, FEMA).

17 *See Oct. 27, 2005 Select Comm. Hearing* at 127 (statement of Adm. Timothy Keating, Commander, NORAD-NORTHCOM and statement of Paul McHale, Assistant Secretary of Defense for Homeland Defense); Interview by Select Comm. Staff with Bill Lokey, Federal Coordinating Officer for LA, FEMA in Washington, DC [hereinafter Lokey Interview] (Dec. 2, 2005); Wells Interview.

18 Kopplin Interview.

19 Lokey Interview.

20 *Nov. 9, 2005 Joint Armed Services and Homeland Hearing* (written statement of Lt. Gen. H Steven Blum, Chief, National Guard Bureau [hereinafter NGB] at 2-3).

21 Interview by Select Comm. Staff with Lt. Gen. H Steven Blum, Chief, NGB, Lt. Gen. Daniel James, III, Director, Air National Guard, and Lt. Gen. Clyde A. Vaughn, United States Army, Director, Army National Guard [hereinafter Blum, James, and Vaughn Interview] in Arlington, VA (Dec. 19, 2005).

22 *Oct. 27, 2005 Select Comm. Hearing* (written response to questions for the record of Lt. Gen. H Steven Blum, Chief, NGB).

23 *See* NGB, *Hurricane Katrina, National Guard After Action Review Observations, National Guard Timeline* at 17 [hereinafter *National Guard Timeline as of Dec. 21, 2005*] (Dec. 21, 2005).

24 Interview by Select Comm. Staff with Brig. Gen. Pete Aylward, NGB, Liaison Officer assigned to Lt. Gen. Russell Honoré, First US Army, Commanding General, in Arlington, VA (Jan. 5, 2006); Memorandum from Acting Deputy Secretary of Defense Gordon England for Secretaries of the Military Departments, Chairman of the Joint Chiefs of Staff, Undersecretaries of Defense, Commander, United States Northern Command, Assistant Secretaries of Defense, and General Counsel, DOD (Sept. 9, 2005).

25 See National Guard Timeline as of Dec. 21, 2005 at 13.

26 Director of Army National Guard, *DARNG Katrina* [hereinafter Dec. 19, 2005 Army National Guard Binder] (Dec. 19, 2005).

27 *Id.*

28 *See* Dec. 19, 2005 Army National Guard Binder; National Guard Timeline as of Dec. 21, 2005 at 14; E-mail correspondence from Lt. Gen. H Steven Blum, Chief, NGB to National Guard Adjutants General, et al. (Aug. 31, 2005) (10:01 a.m.).

Blum, James, Vaughn Interview; E-mail correspondence from Maj. Gen. Francis Vavala, The Adjutant General, State of Delaware, to Lt. Gen. Steven Blum, Chief, NGB, (Aug. 31, 2005) (11:45 a.m.); E-mail correspondence from Lt. Gen. Clyde A. Vaughn, Director, Army National Guard (Sept. 1, 2005) (10:43 a.m.); E-mail correspondence from Maj. Gen. Douglas Burnett, The Adjutant General, State of Florida, to Lt. Gen. Steven Blum, Chief, NGB, (Sept. 4, 2005) (7:21 p.m.); E-mail correspondence from Lt. Col. Chuck Larcom, Senior Army Advisor, Rhode Island, to Lt. Gen. Russel Honoré, First US Army, Commanding General (Sept. 1, 2005) (11:19 a.m.); E-mail correspondence from Lt. Gen. Steven Blum, Chief, NGB to National Guard Adjutants General, et al. (Aug. 31, 2005) (10:01 a.m.). E-mail correspondence from NGB Chief to all Adjutant Generals regarding deployment coordination for Hurricane Katrina Relief (Aug. 31, 2005).

National Guard Timeline as of Dec. 21, 2005 at 17.

See Blum, James, Vaughn Interview; National Guard Timeline as of Dec. 21, 2005; Nicole Gaouette, et al., *Government's Response Plan Proves to be a Disaster*, STAMFORD ADVOCATE, Sept. 15, 2005 at A1.

National Guard Timeline as of Dec. 21, 2005 at 17.

10 U.S.C. § 333 (2005).

E-mail correspondence from Jon Sims, DOD Office of General Counsel to Paul McHale, Assistant Secretary for Defense for Homeland Defense (attached Memorandum of Agreement Concerning Authorization, Consent, and Use of Dual Status Commander for JTF Katrina) (Sept. 2, 2005) (11:45 p.m.).

Draft Letter from Governor Kathleen Blanco, State of LA, to President George W. Bush (Sept. 3, 2005).

Letter from Governor Kathleen Blanco, State of LA, to President George W. Bush (Sept. 3, 2005).

Letter from Governor Bob Riley, State of Alabama, to Donald Rumsfeld, Secretary of Defense (Sept. 2, 2005) [hereinafter Sept. 2, 2005 Letter from Gov. Riley to Sec. Rumsfeld]; Letter from Governor Haley Barbour, State of MS to Donald Rumsfeld, Secretary of Defense (Sept. 4, 2005) [hereinafter Sept. 4, 2005 Letter from Gov. Barbour to Sec. Rumsfeld]; Letter from Governor Kathleen Blanco, State of LA, to Donald Rumsfeld, Secretary of Defense (Sept. 5, 2005) [hereinafter Sept. 5, 2005 Letter from Gov. Blanco to Sec. Rumsfeld].

E-mail correspondence from Maj. Gen. Gus Hargett, The Adjutant General, State of Tennessee (Sept. 2, 2005) (6:07 p.m.); E-mail correspondence from Maj. Gen. David Poythress, The Adjutant General, State of Georgia (Sept. 2, 2005) (4:35 p.m.); E-mail correspondence from Maj. Gen. Mason Whitney, The Adjutant General, State of Colorado (Sept. 2, 2005) (17:28 p.m.).

Oct. 27, 2005 Select Comm. Hearing (written response to questions for the record of Lt. Gen. H Steven Blum, Chief, NGB).

Sept. 2, 2005 Letter from Gov. Riley to Sec. Rumsfeld; Sept. 4, 2005 Letter from Gov. Barbour to Sec. Rumsfeld; Sept. 5, 2005 Letter from Gov. Blanco to Sec. Rumsfeld.

Dec. 19, 2005 Blum, James, Vaughn Interview; National Guard Timeline as of Dec. 21, 2005 at 24.

Memorandum from Gordon England, Deputy Secretary of Defense, to Francis Harvey, Secretary of the Army, and Acting Secretary of the Air Force (Sept. 7, 2005).

National Guard Timeline as of Dec. 21, 2005 at 29.

Oct. 27, 2005 Select Comm. Hearing (written response to questions for the record of Adm. Timothy Keating, Commander, NORAD-NORTHCOM).

See NGB, *Chief's Battle Update Brief Covers 04 1400 September 2005*, (Sept. 4, 2005); NGB, *Chiefs Battle Update Brief Covers 01 September 2005*, (Sept. 1, 2005).

Oct. 27, 2005 Select Comm. Hearing (written response to questions for the record of Lt. Gen. Steven Blum, Chief, NGB); Steve Bowman, Lawrence Kapp, and Amy Belasco, Hurricane Katrina: DOD Disaster Response, CRS Report for Congress, RL33095 at 10 (Sept. 19, 2005).

See Mississippi National Guard, *Hurricane Katrina August 2005-November 2005* [hereinafter "Mississippi National Guard Daily Logs"].

Blum, James, and Vaughn Interview.

Air National Guard, *NGAUS ANG Breakout*, Lt. Gen. Daniel James, III, Director, Air National Guard [hereinafter Sept. 19, 2005 NGAUS ANG Breakout] (Sept. 19, 2005).

U.S. Air Force, *Expeditionary Medical Support*, Office of the Air Force Surgeon General, Air Force Medical Evaluation Support Activity at 5.

National Guard Timeline as of Dec. 21, 2005 at 14-15.

E-mail correspondence from Maj. Gen. Scott Mayes, 1st Air Force, Command and Control, to Adm. Timothy Keating, Commander, NORAD-NORTHCOM, et al. (Aug. 30, 2005) (2:40 p.m.).

National Guard Timeline as of Dec. 21, 2005; Army National Guard Aviation, *Hurricane Katrina – Aviation Support* (Aug. 29, 2005) (attached to E-mail correspondence from Maj Karl Konzelman, NGB to Lt. Gen. Russel Honoré, First US Army, Commanding General, et al. (Aug. 30, 2005) (10:32 a.m.)); Sept. 19, 2005 NGAUS ANG Breakout.

E-mail correspondence from Fletcher Thornton, Joint Operations Center, HQ, First U.S. Army (Sept. 2, 2005).

See NGB, *Chief's Battle Update Brief, Covers 04 1400 September 2005*; Louisiana National Guard, *Overview, Hurricane Recovery, Focus of Effort*.

Interview by Select Comm. Staff with Col. Barry Keeling, Commander of Task Force Eagle, LA National Guard, [hereinafter Keeling Interview] in New Orleans, LA (Nov. 3, 2005); Interview by Select Comm. Staff with General Brod Veillon, Commander of Task Force Minnow, LA National Guard, [hereinafter Veillon Interview] in New Orleans, LA (Nov. 3, 2005).

Interview by Select Comm. Staff with Lt. Col. Jacques Thibodeaux, LA National Guard [hereinafter Thibodeaux Interview], in New Orleans, LA (Nov. 3, 2005); Dabadie Interview.

Id.

Email correspondence from Angela Copple, EMAC Coordinator, National Emergency Management Association regarding numbers of personnel assisting by State (Nov. 3, 2005) (2:49 p.m.).

Alabama National Guard, *Hurricane Katrina Binder* at Tab 1, p. 3-4, and Tab 4.

Governor Bob Riley, State of AL, Press Release: *Governor Riley Declares State of Emergency Due to Approaching Hurricane, Requests Federal Assistance*, Aug. 28, 2005.

Alabama National Guard, *Hurricane Katrina Binder* at Tab 1 at p. 6, and Tab 4.

Id. at Tab 4.

Briefing Memorandum prepared for *Hearing on Hurricane Katrina: Preparedness and Response by the State of MS Before Select Comm.*, 109th Cong. (Dec. 7, 2005) [hereinafter *Dec. 7, 2005 Select Comm. Hearing Briefing Memorandum*].

Oct. 27, 2005 Select Comm. Hearing at 3-4 (written submission of Maj. Gen. Harold A. Cross, The Adjutant General, State of MS).

"The members of the public safety community aggressively moved into areas immediately after the storm passed and saved many lives and brought order. This was a very difficult mission as much of the public safety infrastructure, police and sheriff's stations, patrol cars, and communications had been destroyed in the coastal communities."

William L. Carwile, III
Hurricane Katrina Federal Coordination Officer for Mississippi
Select Committee hearing, December 7, 2005

The collapse of law enforcement and the lack of effective public communications led to civil unrest and further delayed relief

Summary

A wide variety of conditions led to lawlessness and violence in areas hit by Hurricane Katrina. Lack of food, water, and electricity. Uncertainty about evacuations. Even the loss of hope. Looting occurred in several locations. In some cases, people looted stores for their survival and to diminish suffering, taking items such as food, water, clothing, flashlights, batteries, and camping supplies. At least some police departments were involved in breaking into stores and commandeering supplies needed for their departments, as well as those needed for feeding people in shelters before state or federal assistance arrived. One New Orleans physician said police helped him break into a pharmacy to get needed medications and supplies. In other cases, people looted for purely criminal purposes, apparently taking items for personal use or resale that would not be needed or were useless without electricity (e.g., televisions).

General unrest and lawlessness arose in crowded areas where people were uncertain about their survival, or rescue, or prospects for evacuation. In some areas, the collapse or absence of law enforcement exacerbated the level of lawlessness and violence. Several police departments lost dispatch and communication

capabilities, police vehicles, administrative functions such as booking, and jails to confine arrested suspects. Tremendous additional burdens were imposed on the police, like search and rescue operations, that took priority over normal police functions. The extent of crime and lawlessness is difficult to determine, partly because of the loss of police record keeping during the disaster and partly because of unsubstantiated reporting by the media.

The breakdown of law enforcement was particularly notable in New Orleans. Despite the well-known threat from flooding, the New Orleans Police Department had not taken basic steps to protect its resources and ensure continuity of operations. For

example, communications nodes, evidence rooms, and even emergency generators were housed in lower floors susceptible to flooding. When the levees broke and the floodwaters overtook police headquarters and district offices, the department lost its command and control and communications functions. Police vehicles believed to be moved out of harm's way were lost to the floodwaters. Hundreds of New Orleans Police Department officers went missing — some for legitimate reasons and some not — at a time they were needed most. This left the city unable to provide enough manpower and other resources to maintain law and order at shelters and on the streets.

Looting broke out in the downtown section of the city, particularly along Canal Street. There were also reports, currently under investigation by the Louisiana Attorney General, that New Orleans police officers were involved in stealing vehicles from a car dealership. Even when police were present to restore law and order, they did not have the resources to arrest, book, and detain suspects. Other parts of the city, according to witnesses, were relatively calm despite the lack of law enforcement personnel.

Public communications is a key aspect of emergency management, and this function has its own emergency support function in the NRP. In Louisiana, and particularly

New Orleans, the federal, state, and local governments did not appear to have a public communications strategy to utilize the media. This problem was particularly severe in the area of law enforcement and crime. While the media played a positive role in many aspects — such as providing situational awareness to government authorities — it also played a negative role in the often unsubstantiated reporting of crime and lawlessness, undermining the accuracy and value of that awareness.

AP PHOTO/LM OTERO

New Orleans Mayor Ray Nagin and Police Chief Eddie Compass

Media reports of violence often gave credence to rumors that were either false or highly exaggerated. Public officials did not have a strategy to get ahead of the "information curve" to use the media to the public's advantage and help quell rumors. In fact, Mayor Ray Nagin and the Chief of Police repeated rumors of rampant criminality to the national media, contributing to the exaggerated image of utter lawlessness. Many of these reports, particularly of unchecked violence in the Superdome, appear to have been unsubstantiated. Nevertheless, the hyped media coverage of violence and lawlessness, legitimized by New Orleans authorities, served to delay relief efforts by scaring away truck and bus drivers, increasing the anxiety of those in shelters, and generally increasing the resources that needed to be dedicated to security.

Law and order were eventually restored as local law enforcement officers were removed from search and rescue, reassigned to law enforcement missions, and supplemented first by state National Guard troops, then by other state and local police through the Emergency Management Assistance Compact (EMAC) process. The National Guard played a substantial role in providing security and restoring law and order. The Louisiana National Guard was deployed before landfall, and provided security at the Superdome that helped maintain order there. Once looting broke out in New Orleans, guardsmen also patrolled the streets to restore law and order.

The Alabama National Guard was also deployed before landfall, providing a security task force for Mobile and Baldwin counties. National Guards from other states sent units through the EMAC process to perform security or law enforcement duties. For example, Arkansas provided 310 guardsmen from a military police company to provide security in Mississippi.

While not immediately deployed, Department of Defense (DOD) active duty forces also played a role in restoring and maintaining law and order. For example, the U.S. Army's 82nd Airborne arrived in New Orleans on September 3 (five days after landfall) and, according to the city's Director of Homeland Security, had a "calming effect" on the populace by their mere presence on the street. Precautions were taken to prevent DOD active duty forces from direct law enforcement missions, thereby avoiding Posse Comitatus issues.

Civilian law enforcement agencies from other states and localities also provided personnel through the EMAC process to supplement beleaguered state and local police. For example, South Carolina provided 118 law enforcement personnel with equipment to Mississippi.

Federal law enforcement agencies also played a major role in restoring law and order after Hurricane Katrina. Specific agencies included the U.S. Attorney's Office, the Federal Bureau of Investigation (FBI), the Drug Enforcement Agency (DEA), the Bureau of Alcohol, Tobacco, Firearms and Explosives (ATF), the U.S. Marshal Service (USMS), the U.S. Secret Service, U.S. Customs and Border Protection, the U.S. Border Patrol, U.S. Immigration and Customs Enforcement, and the Federal Air Marshal Service (FAMS). The first priority for most of these agencies was implementing continuity of operations plans — locating their people, securing their workplaces and sensitive information, getting supplemental manpower from other field offices, and otherwise fully restoring their mission capabilities. These federal agencies then turned to assisting state and local law enforcement agencies.

These agencies brought a wide array of capabilities and tactical teams to help restore and maintain law and order. Most of the federal personnel were deputized as state law enforcement officials, so they could fully partner with local police by participating in patrols, investigating crimes, and arresting suspects. The FBI deployed its Critical Incident Response Group and ATF deployed one of its Special Response Teams. ATF located and inspected federal firearms and explosives licensees to determine if their facilities were secure. USMS assisted with evacuating prisoners from flooded jails into federal facilities. FAMS provided security at the New Orleans Airport.

Federal agencies also helped establish interagency and intergovernmental mechanisms — such as common credentialing and a Law Enforcement Coordination Center — to coordinate the activities of the multitude of federal, state, and local law enforcement agencies. Finally, these federal agencies provided equipment, supplies, and other resources to local law enforcement agencies to help them start rebuilding their capabilities.

Finding: A variety of conditions led to lawlessness and violence in hurricane stricken areas

Several conditions led to lawlessness and looting

A wide variety of conditions led to lawlessness and violence in areas hit by Hurricane Katrina. Bobby Strahan, Pearl River County Emergency Management Agency Director, said the lack of critical commodities for those residents who did not evacuate (or returned quickly) and crowds seeking shelter at a limited number of facilities with generators may have been behind some of the post-landfall requests for security and law enforcement assistance.[1] According to Strahan, Pearl River experienced some looting and other crimes in the immediate aftermath of the storm. Once the county was able to secure and distribute limited amounts of food, ice, and water (what it could gather on its own plus assistance from the state of Florida), these security problems largely dissipated.

Similarly, those who did not evacuate (or returned quickly) may have contributed to significant security challenges at some of Mississippi's healthcare facilities in the affected areas. According Dr. Brian Amy, the State Health Officer of Mississippi, most of those facilities had generators and a limited power supply.[2] This caused them to quickly attract the attention of displaced residents, who were drawn to the lights and the possibility they might seek shelter there, and created what Amy termed an "overflow" situation resulting in security issues at the facilities.[3] In Louisiana, officials cited the lack of food, water, electricity, and uncertainty about evacuations as reasons for lawlessness and looting.[4] Even Governor Kathleen Blanco said she sympathized with people who looted stores to survive.[5]

Looting occurred in several locations. Mississippi experienced some looting, armed robbery, and crowd control problems immediately after the storm.[6] Security-related requests the state received from local officials included: (1) nighttime military police (MP) security at pharmacy and drug dispensing operations in several coastal cities; (2) help with security issues at an understaffed shelter that was about to receive evacuees from New Orleans; (3) law enforcement personnel to deal with reported theft and carjacking threats at a medical center in Biloxi; and (4) additional National Guard protection to deal with looters at the South Mississippi Regional Center in Long Beach.[7]

In Louisiana, state police officials said looting was most concentrated in the New Orleans area.[8] However, major looting was generally limited to the Canal Street area and ended by Tuesday, August 30. According to these officials, in some cases people looted stores for their survival, taking items such as food, water, clothing, flashlights, batteries, and camping supplies. In other cases, people looted for criminal purposes, apparently taking items for

their personal use or resale that would not be needed or were useless without electricity (e.g., televisions). Once most perpetrators realized they had no way to transport their loot and no place to store it, they often abandoned it. State police officials said several blocks away from the looting area, many large electronic items and appliances were found abandoned in their original boxes.

At least some police departments were involved in breaking into stores and taking supplies. Plaquemines Parish Sheriff Jiff Hingle said his officers broke into stores and commandeered food, water, and medicine.[9] Some of these items were needed to sustain the sheriff's office and other emergency personnel. Most of the items taken,

As an institution… the New Orleans Police Department disintegrated with the first drop of floodwater.

When the levees broke, the floodwaters overtook police headquarters and district offices. As a result, the department lost its command and control and communications functions. The dispatch and 911 call center ceased to function. Most police vehicles had not been moved out of harm's way and were lost to the floodwaters. The flooding created impassable roads which prevented the New Orleans Police Department from using their few remaining vehicles in most parts of the city. This left officers to patrol without any communications or transportation. With no command and control or guidance, there was no unified command or clear priorities within the department. One reporter who was on the scene wrote that "As an institution… the New Orleans Police Department disintegrated with the first drop of floodwater."[24]

Missing police officers led to a law enforcement manpower shortage

Further, hundreds of New Orleans Police Department officers went missing — some for understandable reasons and some not — at a time they were needed the most. This left the city unable to provide enough manpower and other resources to maintain law and order at shelters and on the streets.

All New Orleans Police Department officers are required to reside within the city limits, so a majority of the city's officers were personally affected by Katrina.[25] Whether it was damage to their homes or the health and safety of family members, many New Orleans Police Department officers, like members of the general public, were trapped in their homes and needed to be rescued during the critical days and hours after the levees failed and the flood waters rose.

Dereliction of duty by New Orleans Police Officers factored significantly into the department's inability to marshal an effective response. Original reports indicated that up to 320 officers (of its 1,750-officer force) resigned, were terminated, or are under investigation for abandoning their duties.[26] However, on December 14, Mayor Nagin testified that as of that date, 133 officers had been terminated or resigned after Hurricane Katrina, and said many of the original reports did not account for nearly 100 officers who were trapped or stranded on rooftops and unable to report to duty for that reason.[27] Regardless, the New Orleans Police force was severely depleted.

As a result, many residents were unable to obtain police assistance. Calls for help to the city's 911 system went unanswered.[28]

Some of the officers were also apparently involved in criminal activities. Officials from the Louisiana Attorney General's office said they are investigating thefts of luxury vehicles from a car dealership allegedly perpetrated by New Orleans Police Department officers.[29] The dealership, Sewell Cadillac Chevrolet, reported that several police officers had absconded with several brand new Cadillac Escalades.[30]

The Louisiana State Police provided relatively quick assistance. Although the New Orleans Police Department had lost its command and control capabilities, the Louisiana State Police operated under its own broad law enforcement statutory mandate. Thus, state police were able to move into the affected area quickly. As the significance of Katrina became evident, state police ceased other law enforcement activities to focus on New Orleans' needs.

Police had limited resources to stop looting in downtown New Orleans

Given the situation, police had limited resources with which to stop the looting.[31] And even when police were present to restore law and order, they did not have the resources to arrest, book, and detain suspects. One major problem was the loss of the booking and jail systems. Booking and jailing are done not by the New Orleans Police Department, but by the parish criminal sheriff. Sheriffs in each parish are constitutional positions independent from the parish president or mayor or police. The sheriff's booking offices and jails were flooded and therefore useless. While criminals, such as looters, could be apprehended by law enforcement officers, there was nowhere to book them or jail them. Many people originally apprehended for looting were just let go.

Finding: Lack of a government public communications strategy and media hype of violence exacerbated public concerns and further delayed relief

Governments appeared to lack any public communications strategy and media and public officials fed rumors

Public communications is a key aspect of emergency management, and this function has its own emergency support function in the NRP. In Louisiana, and particularly New Orleans, the federal, state, and local governments did not appear to have a public communications strategy to deal with the media. This problem was particularly severe in the area of law enforcement and crime.

The media played a positive role in Hurricane Katrina in many aspects — such as providing situational awareness to government authorities and the public. And many media reports of violence were substantiated and responsibly reported. For example, MSNBC provided live coverage of looters, including police officers, ransacking a local Wal-Mart in New Orleans.[32]

However, other media reports were based on rumors that were either false or highly exaggerated, undermining the value of the situational awareness being provided. CNN reported repeatedly on September 1, for example, that evacuations at the Superdome were suspended because "someone fired a shot at a helicopter."[33] State and local officials later said much of the "rampant shooting" reported was actually from trapped individuals who were firing weapons into the air to attract rescuers.[34]

According to state officials, rumors and reports of people shooting at helicopters were difficult to substantiate at the time.[35] But in the end, there were no bullet holes found in any helicopters. Again, people firing into the air may have been the origin of this rumor. Other reports of people shooting at helicopters taking patients to hospitals were never verified, nor were stories of two babies found with their throats slit in Convention Center bathrooms or of the man who heard a rape victim scream, ran outside for help, and was shot and killed by troops.[36]

State law enforcement officials expressed frustration over media reports of crime.[37] Many of these officials deployed to its emergency operations center. This EMAC team is called an "A-Team."

4. A-Team arrives at state emergency operations center and begins coordinating state-wide EMAC resource requests. These resource requests are broadcast to all members of the compact soliciting assistance.

5. States willing to assist respond to the broadcast and coordinate with the A-Team the specifics of the transaction, including costs. The A-Team helps the affected state choose from available resources.

6. Formal requisitions are finalized specifying, as precisely as possible, the resources that will be made available and their costs.

7. Resources are sent to the affected states.

8. Responding state submits reimbursement request.

9. Affected state reimburses responding state.

EMAC is executed by eight components:[61]

1. Requesting state – EMAC state, operating under a governor declared emergency, requests assistance.

2. Assisting state – EMAC state, responds to a request for assistance.

3. Authorized representative – state official empowered to request assistance or commit state resources in response to a request.

4. Designated Contact – EMAC subject matter expert within each member state.

5. National Coordination Group (NCG) – national EMAC group during non-emergencies. The NCG stands ready to activate EMAC as emergencies develop.

6. National Coordinating Team (NCT) – when the Department of Homeland Security and FEMA activate their National Response Coordination Center (NRCC) to coordinate the federal response and recovery operations during emergencies, EMAC deploys a NCT to serve at the NRCC in Washington, D.C. From the NRCC, the NCT coordinates EMAC's national response.

7. Regional Coordinating Team (RCT) – If FEMA activates a Regional Response Coordination Center (RRCC) a parallel EMAC RCT is

deployed. From the RRCC, the RCT coordinates deployed EMAC components responding throughout the affected region.

8. Other member states – during times of emergencies EMAC members are charged with monitoring the situation and to stand ready to assist as appropriate.

In supporting the response to Hurricane Katrina, a two-person EMAC A-Team was deployed to Baton Rouge, Louisiana on Sunday, August 28.[62] Jeff Smith was identified as the Louisiana state EMAC coordinator.[63] In Mississippi, Bill Brown, Operations Branch Chief, Mississippi Emergency Management Agency, coordinated EMAC.[64] On August 29, the A-Team was increased to four people, and shortly thereafter the team increased to eight members in Louisiana and nine members in Mississippi.[65] Through EMAC, a sizable contingent was deployed to assist Louisiana and Mississippi in the aftermath of Katrina.[66]

In Louisiana, 27,727 personnel were deployed through EMAC by September 13, and during the same time frame, in Mississippi, 18,247 people deployed.[67] There were 680 requests for assistance in Louisiana and 723 in Mississippi.[68] The total estimated cost for Louisiana is $201.8 million and for Mississippi, $314.1 million.[69] EMAC's total Katrina response involved processing 1,403 requests for assistance and 46,288 personnel deployment for a total estimated cost of $515.9 million.[70] The most commonly requested resources included: firefighters, search and rescue personnel, HAZMAT personnel, emergency medical technicians, state police, sheriffs, fish and wildlife personnel, corrections personnel, livestock inspectors, bridge inspectors, airport maintenance personnel, ambulances, medical doctors, registered nurses and National Guard troops.[71]

EMAC officials have acknowledged a significant population of "self-deployed" personnel, a large majority of which were local and state police officers who deployed to the scene, in what is believed to be a spontaneous response to media reports of lawlessness in southeastern Louisiana.[72] Due to the *ad hoc* nature of these "self-deployed" officers, specific figures are not known. As the ranks of EMAC deployed law enforcement officials and officially deployed federal law enforcement officials continued to grow in the region, the number of "self-deployed" personnel is believed to have declined rapidly.

Without an official deployment, the "self-deployed" personnel were acting without proper authority, without liability protection, and without eligibility for expense reimbursement.

National Guard played a key role in restoring and maintaining law and order

Law and order were eventually restored as local law enforcement officers were supplemented, first by state military troops. The National Guard played a substantial role in providing security and restoring law and order. The Louisiana National Guard was deployed before landfall, and provided security at the Superdome that helped maintain order there. Once looting broke out in New Orleans, they also patrolled the streets. The Mississippi National Guard was vital to restoring order and providing

security in the aftermath of the storm. According to Carwile, for example, a "massive National Guard presence" helped quell problems with isolated looting in the western affected counties (Pearl River and Hancock) within days after the storm.[73] The Alabama National Guard was also deployed before landfall, providing a security task force for Mobile and Baldwin Counties.

National Guards from other states also sent units through the EMAC process to perform security or law enforcement duties. In Mississippi, nearly 11,000 troops from 19 other states' National Guards joined more than 2,500 Mississippi National Guard troops in missions related to law enforcement (as well as other missions) by September 10, 12 days after landfall.[74] For example, Arkansas provided 310 guardsmen from a military police company to provide security in Mississippi.[75]

Similarly, the Louisiana National Guard's security forces were supplemented by thousands of guardsmen from other states. Through EMAC, Louisiana was able to request and receive assistance from scores of states from across the country. Examples of the larger deployments included 2,426 infantry from Pennsylvania, 2,016 military police from Puerto Rico, 580 security troops from Michigan, 500 support troops from Arkansas,

535 security troops from Massachusetts, and 350 security troops from Tennessee.

Assistant Secretary of Defense Paul McHale, in his testimony before the Select Committee, provided details on the extent of assistance provided by the National Guard. He stated that "when violence erupted in New Orleans, the National Guard Bureau coordinated the deployment of 4,200 National Guard MPs, 1,400 each day every day for 3 days in a row, a law enforcement presence nearly three times of the size of the New Orleans Police Department."[76]

There was a general consensus among federal, state, and local officials that EMAC worked very well for National Guard troops. Regarding military alone, by November 3, for Louisiana, there were a total of 451 EMAC requests and 29,502 Guardsmen who came from other states. Many of these out-of-state Guardsmen performed security and law enforcement functions and, like the Louisiana National Guard, operated under the Louisiana governor's Title 32 authority.

DOD active duty forces played an important, but less active, role in maintaining law and order

While they were not immediately deployed, DOD active duty forces also played a role in restoring and maintaining law and order. For example, the U.S. Army's 82nd Airborne arrived in New Orleans on September 3 (five days after landfall) and, according to the city's Director of Homeland Security, had a "calming effect" by their mere presence on the street. Precautions were taken to prevent DOD active duty forces from direct law enforcement missions, thereby avoiding Posse Comitatus issues. For more details on the use of the military, see the MILITARY chapter.

Law enforcement personnel from other states also played a key role in restoring and maintaining law and order.

Civilian law enforcement agencies from other states and localities also provided personnel through the EMAC process to supplement beleaguered state and local police. In Mississippi, local, state, and FEMA officials noted that assistance from Florida's law enforcement and emergency management agencies (as well as law enforcement from other states), plus the delivery of commodities Florida pre-positioned in the panhandle, were key to providing security and restoring order in southern Mississippi after landfall.[77]

Florida, in particular, was instrumental in the early days and received high praise from Mississippi officials for the manner in which that state's teams provided security, established an incident command structure in the coastal counties, and conducted some of the first search and rescue missions the night after the storm.[78] As noted earlier, Florida helped alleviate some of Mississippi's security problems by sending into the state some of the commodities it had pre-positioned in the panhandle region in anticipation of the hurricane striking farther east than it eventually did. Florida's supplies of food, water, and ice helped relieve the situation in Mississippi.[79]

While Florida and Alabama were among the first states to provide Mississippi with law enforcement assistance, they were not alone. Mississippi received assistance from Arkansas, South Carolina, and Georgia's state police or other state law enforcement agencies.[80] For example, South Carolina provided 118 law enforcement personnel with equipment to Mississippi.[81]

Louisiana also benefited from a very large influx of law enforcement personnel from other states. Like their counterparts in Mississippi, local, state, and federal officials involved in Louisiana's response to Katrina said EMAC was critical to restoring law and order.

The EMAC process was not always smooth. For example, a sheriff from Michigan and a sheriff from Alabama were at the Louisiana border but could not assist because no EMAC request had been made.[82] The Jefferson Parish Sheriff had apparently not made a request through the state EOC for the assistance — a requirement for providing law enforcement assistance through EMAC.[83]

Also, as late as September 2, EMAC requests simply had not been made. According to Josh Filler, the Director of DHS' Office of State and Local Government Coordination on the September 2 video teleconference:

> My office has received numerous phone calls from law enforcement organizations across the country — major city police chiefs, national sheriffs — who want to help, but we have encouraged them not to self-deploy to New Orleans or to Louisiana, but to work through the system, but they are saying that their States are not receiving requests for assistance.[84]

Finding: Federal law enforcement agencies were also critical to restoring law and order and coordinating activities

The first priority for federal law enforcement agencies was to implement their continuity of operations plans and locate their affected personnel

Prior to August 30, federal law enforcement worked to prepare their coastal offices for Katrina's landfall. Immediately after the hurricane, these law enforcement agencies implemented their continuity of operations plans and began the process of locating personnel living in the affected areas.

On August 26, the Federal Bureau of Investigation's (FBI) Jackson Field Office notified its Resident Agencies in Hattiesburg, Pascagoula, and Gulfport to implement their hurricane plans.[85] Hurricane shutters were installed, vehicles were secured, computers were bagged, and safes were locked. The traditional FBI operations of the Jackson Field Office were moved to its Oxford Resident Agency, in northern Mississippi.[86] FBI air assets and personnel who remained on the coast were utilized to determine the damage and security of the Mississippi offices.[87]

Within 12 hours after the hurricane subsided, the Jackson Field Office was in contact with all of its personnel.[88] The Jackson Field Office established a Command Post at Keesler Air Force Base in Biloxi. On August 29, the Special Agent-in-Charge (SAC) of New rleans surveyed the damage to the New Orleans Field Office.[89] Sixty percent of the top floor was uncovered. Due the sensitivity of documents housed in the Field Office, e SAC and the four agents remained at the building. The C ordered the move of the New Orleans Division to the uisiana State Police headquarters in Baton Rouge.[90] All I personnel living in Louisiana were accounted for by ptember 4.[91]

On August 23, the Bureau of Alcohol, Tobacco, rearms and Explosives (ATF) began Hurricane Katrina eparations.[92] ATF headquarters coordinated with Field ivisions in Houston, New Orleans (which includes e state of Mississippi), Nashville (which includes the te of Alabama), Tampa, and Miami.[93] Headquarters dered the evacuation of ATF personnel in New Orleans d Mississippi prior to the hurricane, and a list was mprised of personnel who chose to stay on the coast.[94] l ATF personnel leaving the affected area were instructed contact their supervisors after the storm. Due to the mage to the ATF facilities, a continuity of operations site as activated on August 30 in Mandeville, Louisiana.[95]

On the same day, ATF began contacting all ATF rsonnel living in the affected area.[96] The New Orleans ivision Office was relocated to Shreveport, where it sumed responsibility over Louisiana and Mississippi.[97] e Biloxi Field Office was relocated to a public safety mpound behind the Harrison County Sheriff's epartment.[98] The Mobile Field Office was moved to ookley Air Force Base, an inactive base in the Mobile ea.[99] ATF established a Critical Incident Management sponse Team in Baton Rouge to coordinate ATF perations.[100]

On August 26, in anticipation of Katrina's landfall, e New Orleans Field Division Special Agent-in-Charge dered the Drug Enforcement Administration's (DEA) eld Division closed and all DEA personnel were asked evacuate the area.[101] The New Orleans Field Division d the Gulfport Resident Office were severely damaged the hurricane.[102] DEA established teams responsible r locating all Field Division personnel following e storm.[103] On August 31, command centers were tablished at the Baton Rouge District Office and in obile. DEA headquarters chose the Office of Aviation Addison, Texas to serve as a logistical command nter for the field divisions throughout the country. On ptember 1, the New Orleans Field Division established operations center at a high school in Mandeville,

Louisiana, to house firearms and sensitive items from the New Orleans Field Office.[104]

On August 29, the United States Marshals Service (USMS) activated an Emergency Operations Center in Washington, D.C. in preparation for Hurricane Katrina.[105] USMS also placed four Operational Management Teams (OMT) on standby. Following Katrina, the OMTs began accounting for all USMS personnel in Louisiana, Mississippi, and Alabama.[106] Operational Medical Personnel were also deployed to the coast to assist USMS personnel.[107] OMT created a command post in Pineville, Louisiana and Jackson, Mississippi. On August 30, USMS deployed personnel and surveillance planes to survey the hurricane damage to USMS facilities.

Prior to landfall, U.S. Immigration and Customs Enforcement (ICE) pre-deployed Federal Protective Service (FPS) personnel located in Texas.[108] FPS was able to move into the affected area the day after the hurricane to assist FEMA. ICE's Gulfport office sustained no major damage and due to backup generators, was utilized as a staging site and provided assistance to ICE employees affected by the hurricane, as well as other state and local law enforcement.[109] From landfall until September 2, ICE's New Orleans field office worked to account for ICE personnel assigned to the New Orleans, Lake Charles, Lafayette, Baton Rouge, and Gulfport offices and obtain needed supplies.

On August 26 and 27, U.S. Customs and Border Patrol (CBP) ordered the ports of Mobile and New Orleans, and the Hammond Louisiana Air and Marine Branch to activate their hurricane preparedness plans.[110] CBP moved its air assets to Shreveport and Dallas. CBP's Mission Critical Team relocated from New Orleans to Shreveport and on August 29 began to locate CBP personnel living in the affected area.[111] CBP created a Forward Deployed Operations Command Center at the air hanger in Hammond to coordinate all CBP missions.[112] By September 4, all CBP employees were located.[113]

While the Federal Air Marshal Service (FAMS) did not need to implement a continuity of operations plan for a specific office, they are responsible for meeting their nationwide primary mission, while coordinating in preparation for severe weather and flight disruptions.[114] In anticipation of these disruptions due to Katrina, FAMS began monitoring the hurricane's track the week of August 21.[115]

From August 26 to August 29, Federal Bureau of Prisons (BOP) personnel from the Office of Emergency Preparedness, in Washington, D.C. and BOP's South Central Regional Office in Dallas monitored Hurricane Katrina's path.[116] The Office of Emergency Preparedness is responsible for coordinating the evacuation and for supporting corrections institutions in the areas affected by the hurricane. On August 30, BOP opened a command center to help the Louisiana Department of Public Safety and Corrections with transporting inmates out of the New Orleans area.[117]

AP PHOTO/RIC FRANCIS

While working to reconstitute themselves, federal law enforcement agencies supplemented state and local law enforcement with forces and supplies

While surveying office damage and locating personnel, federal law enforcement worked to assist state and local law enforcement with additional forces and supplies. While it is impossible to account for every federal law enforcement agent or officer who responded to requests for assistance by state and local law enforcement, or even by hurricane victims, there were specific assets brought to bear by federal law enforcement that should be highlighted to illustrate the degree of coordination with entities outside the federal government.

On August 30, FBI headquarter officials put their Field Offices on alert that additional personnel were needed in the affected area.[118] Ten Special Weapons and Tactics (SWAT) agents from the Houston Division were deployed to New Orleans to assist the New Orleans Police Department (NOPD) SWAT.[119] These agents brought a boat that enabled them to transport personnel

and supplies. On September 1, the Critical Incident Response Group deployed agents from the Dallas, Atlanta, Baltimore, and Houston SWAT teams and Hostage Rescue Teams (HRT) to continue to help NOPD control its affected area.[120] The Violent Gang Task Force from the New Orleans Division worked out of the Gretna Police Department.[121] Over 30 more agents coordinated with NOPD to back up NOPD SWAT, FBI SWAT, and HRT Special Agents.[122]

The FBI Command Post at Keesler Air Force Base in Biloxi, Mississippi communicated with the Mississippi Bureau of Criminal Investigations, the Mississippi Highway Patrol, the Homeland Security Director for the State of Mississippi, and local police and sheriffs to respond to requests for assistance.[123] The FBI was able to create a Virtual Command Center for the Law Enforcement On-Line Internet site.[124] All law enforcement nationwide were able to log onto the website and receive daily situation reports regarding FBI relief efforts.[125]

AP PHOTO/ANN HEISENFELT

The first group of ATF personnel detailed to the affected area arrived on September 2.[126] Thirty-four members of Special Response Teams (SRT), tactical teams specifically trained to handle high risk law enforcement and civil unrest, from the Dallas and Detroit Field Offices and seven SRT support staff were deployed to Algiers, Louisiana.[127] The SRT members were sent to New Orleans to assist the NOPD, whose SWAT teams were down to 25 percent capacity.[128] On September 6 and 7, 10 ATF agents were deployed to Biloxi, and 30 ATF agents were deployed to Gulfport.[129] These agents performed investigative roles, as well as assisting local police with firearms-related calls.[130]

From August 30 to September 12, 251 DEA Temporary
Duty agents reported from Miami, Atlanta, St. Louis,
Houston and Dallas to provide law enforcement
and search and rescue support in New Orleans.[131]
On September 4, DEA deployed personnel from the
Atlanta Field Division, as well as the Houston Mobile
Enforcement Team (MET), self-contained, specially
trained teams of eight to twelve agents that specialize
in law enforcement missions involving violence.[132]
These agents were then joined by the Charlotte MET on
September 5, and the Miami MET on September 7. The
METs helped state and local departments in conducting
routine law enforcement tasks, including patrols as well as
search and rescue missions.

On September 1, five USMS Marshals from the Training
Academy in Glynco, Georgia were deployed to provide
security at the Biloxi Airport.[133] USMS deployed an
additional four Marshals to the airport on September 3.
USMS supported NOPD by working with the 1st and 5th
districts in New Orleans and responded to backlogged 911
calls. In addition, USMS redirected NOPD National Crime
Information Center traffic to the USMS Communications
Center. USMS deployed more personnel to Mississippi
on September 5 to help local police and sheriff
departments.[134] They provided security for 11 search and
rescue teams, operated a missing persons task force and
a task force to locate sex offenders, and protected the
Mississippi gulf coast's fuel depot in Collins.

On September 2, ICE began its support of local law
enforcement in New Orleans' 4th District.[135] The 4th
District was still populated at that time, as it had not
taken on water. The New Orleans Special Response Team
(SRT), ICE's tactical team, was in the city on September 1.
SRT teams from Chicago and San Antonio, consisting of
12 to 18 members, arrived the afternoon and evening of
September 2. By midnight of September 2, there were over

100 ICE agents in New Orleans preparing to assist in the
response to the hurricane.

Throughout the week, ICE agents were tasked with
patrols and shifts with local law enforcement, worked to
curtail looting, assisted with evacuations, and followed
up on the approximately 6,000 911 calls made during and
after the hurricane.[136] ICE's Tampa Field Office provided
three inflatable Zodiac boats that helped ICE personnel
assist with transportation for fire departments and
medical personnel and respond to rescue calls. ICE agents
and logistical teams assisted the Mississippi Highway
Patrol, county sheriffs, and city police forces in Mississippi
with patrols, rescues, and searches.[137]

On the morning of August 30, the Border Patrol's
Tactical Unit pre-deployment site survey team left for
the affected area.[138] This deployment was pursuant to a
request for CBP to assist in evacuating the Superdome and
for riot control. However, the agents also worked other
law enforcement functions and relief operations, such as
distributing water, assisting with minor medical care, and

helping evacuees onto buses and helicopters. CBP had 100 agents, along with CBP vehicles, emergency equipment, and lifesaving supplies in Louisiana by September 1.[139] On September 2, Border Patrol agents were sent to provide security at the Louisiana State University Hospital, which served as the regional triage center. Border Patrol agents were also deployed to the New Orleans Airport to assist with crowd control and security.

A day after Katrina made landfall, FAMS responded to reports of deteriorating conditions at Louis Armstrong New Orleans International Airport.[140] The airport was starting to receive evacuees and was therefore becoming a shelter. As a response, FAMS sent personnel – drawing from its Houston Field Office – to the airport to assist as necessary.[141] Conditions at the airport continued to deteriorate as thousands of displaced persons sought refuge there.[142] There was no food, water, restroom facilities, or security. Consequently, when FAMS personnel began to arrive, they needed to help restore order.[143] On September 1, FAMS began initial deployment, including 54 from the Houston Field Office, arriving in-person by car. Also by late evening, evacuation flights out of the airport were fully operational. By September 2, FAMS personnel at the airport expanded their mission to include interim law enforcement activities as well as all necessary activities to operate the airport.[144]

On September 3, the Secret Service was asked by NOPD and the Louisiana State Police to take control of the credentialing process for state and local law enforcement in the New Orleans area.[145] The need for secure credentials for NOPD was a primary concern, as many police officers had lost their official identification badges during the hurricane.[146]

On September 5, the Louisiana Department of Public Safety and Corrections requested that BOP provide 1,000 beds and transportation for Louisiana state inmates.[147] BOP, along with USMS transferred 964 inmates to the United States Penitentiary Coleman-II, Florida.[148] From August 30 to September 7, BOP transported approximately 2,500 inmates or detainees in Louisiana to facilities outside of New Orleans.[149] In addition, BOP provided clothing, food, and water from Texas correctional institutions to the Louisiana State Police headquarters in Baton Rouge.[150]

Obtaining peace officer status presented problems for some federal law enforcement entities responding to the hurricane

The process for federal law enforcement being deputized or sworn in as a peace officer under state law in Louisiana and Mississippi proved cumbersome for some entities. The general concern was that in the process of assisting state or local law enforcement, or victims of the hurricane, federal law enforcement officers might find it necessary to make arrests outside of their federal jurisdiction. Due to the lack of an across-the-board policy on how to deal with federal law enforcement during a state of emergency, some federal law enforcement entities were required to seek advice from their individual Office of the General Counsel on how to proceed. The process was more difficult in Louisiana, where it became necessary to fly in representatives from the Louisiana Office of the Attorney General to the affected area to swear in the law enforcement officers or agents in person. Still other federal law enforcement agents were deputized by the Louisiana State Police.

Under Louisiana law, FBI agents have qualified immunity that protects them when responding to felonies committed in their presence or when assisting state officers.[151] However, FBI agents did not specifically have peace officer status when responding to Hurricane Katrina

AP PHOTO/ANN HEISENFELT

in Louisiana.[152] Governor Blanco granted the Louisiana Office of Attorney General authority to deputize FBI agents, and all FBI agents deployed to Louisiana were deputized by a representative of the office.

FBI agents deployed to Mississippi did not receive peace officer status until September 9, when Governor Barbour wrote a letter to all state and federal law enforcement officers.[153] The letter granted federal law enforcement officers working in cooperation with local law enforcement "the authority to bear arms, make arrests and to make searches and seizures, in addition to any other power, duty, right and privilege as afforded forces of the State of Mississippi."[154]

Prior to ATF agents being deployed to the affected area, DOJ examined the capabilities of ATF agents in assisting state and locals with law enforcement functions.[155] ATF agents are not afforded automatic peace officer status in the states of Louisiana and Mississippi. As ATF agents conducted their core statutorily required mission, DOJ determined ATF agents did not need to receive peace officer status.

Pursuant to federal statute, USMS "may exercise the same powers which a sheriff of the State my exercise . . . ."[156] USMS received further state law enforcement powers when the Director of USMS received an order from U.S. Attorney General Alberto Gonzales requesting the Director to "take all necessary and appropriate steps within available resources to provide the assistance" to Mississippi.[157]

The Louisiana Attorney General's Office coordinated the peace officer status for ICE agents deployed to Louisiana.[158] ICE agents were required to fill out paperwork and were sworn in by the Louisiana State Police every time a new rotation of ICE agents arrived in Kenner, Louisiana. ICE agents were sworn in as peace officers in Mississippi by the Hancock Sheriff's Department.

Border patrol agents were deputized by the state of Louisiana with law enforcement status on September 2.[159] Agents were not sworn in as peace officers in Mississippi.[160] On September 3, CBP's Office of Chief Counsel determined that CBP officers and Border Patrol agents could make arrests for state crimes in Louisiana, Mississippi, Alabama, Florida, and Texas, if the officer or agent was acting in his or her official capacity.[161]

On September 3, Louisiana began to deputize FAMS personnel as Louisiana State Police Officers, giving them full authority to enforce local and state laws.[162]

Emergency Support Function #13 (ESF-13) of the National Response Plan

DOJ, along with the Department of Homeland Security (DHS), is responsible for the Emergency Support Function #13 (ESF-13) of the National Response Plan.[163] ESF-13 covers Public Safety and Security and tasks DOJ and DHS with integrating federal non-investigative/non-criminal law enforcement public safety and security capabilities and resources to "support the full range of incident management activities with potential or actual Incidents of National Significance." The Office of the Deputy Attorney General and the Office of Legal Counsel assist in coordinating DOJ's ESF-13 responsibilities. The Bureau of Alcohol, Tobacco, Firearms and Explosives is responsible for DOJ's day-to-day actions with respect to ESF-13.

After the hurricane, ESF-13 requests were processed through the Law Enforcement Coordination Center (LECC) in Baton Rouge, because the LECC had working knowledge of the available regional resources.[164] The LECC determined whether the request could be met under ESF-13. The LECC (1) confirmed the requestor could not perform the mission, (2) determined whether the request was valid for ESF-13, (3) determined whether there were available federal law enforcement resources; and (4) approved or declined the request. The LECC then forwarded the approved request to Washington, D.C. Each requested agency coordinated with FEMA to establish funding.

Federal law enforcement coordination required communication between the U.S. Department of Justice, U.S. Department of Homeland Security, and the governors of the affected states

The Attorney General of the United States may "appoint officials . . . to detect and prosecute crimes against the United States."[165] The Attorney General may also approve the request of a state governor for federal law enforcement assistance if the Attorney General concludes that such "assistance is necessary to provide an adequate response to a law enforcement emergency."[166]

DOJ also has the authority under the Stafford Act to provide for non-operational assistance. In the case of a major disaster or an emergency, the President may direct the Department to "utilize its authorities and resources granted to it under Federal law (including personnel, equipment, supplies, facilities, and managerial, technical and advisory services) in support of State and local efforts."[167]

On Friday, September 2, Gonzales sent a memorandum to the heads of DOJ's law enforcement agencies, asking each agency to continue coordinating with state and local law enforcement.[168] The Attorney General specifically requested that: (1) the Federal Bureau of Investigation continue to deploy agents and tactical assets, (2) the Drug Enforcement Administration prepare to deploy its Mobile Enforcement Teams, (3) the Bureau of Alcohol, Tobacco, Firearms and Explosives establish a Violent Crime Impact Team in Baton Rouge, Louisiana, and (4) the United States Marshals Service conduct prisoner transport operations and provide court security.

On September 3, Gonzales received a letter from Mississippi Governor Barbour requesting the "deployment of Deputy U.S. Marshals to the State of Mississippi in support of law enforcement requirements created by the effects of Hurricane Katrina."[169] The same day, Gonzales responded in writing to Barbour that his request was approved, and an order authorizing the Director of the U.S. Marshals Service to "take all necessary and appropriate steps within available resources to provide the assistance so requested by [Governor Barbour]" was issued.[170]

The same day, Gonzales received a letter from Blanco requesting the deployment of the USMS and/or other Department of Justice personnel to the area affected by Hurricane Katrina.[171] On September 4, Gonzales responded in writing to Blanco that her request was approved, and an order authorizing the Deputy Attorney General to "take all necessary and appropriate steps within available resources to provide the assistance so requested by [Governor Blanco]" was issued.[172]

On September 6, Gonzales and DHS Secretary Michael Chertoff received a letter from Blanco requesting "the deployment of Immigration and Customs Enforcement officers, Customs and Border Protection personnel and/or other Department of Homeland Security personnel . . . in support of the law enforcement challenges created by the effects of Hurricane Katrina."[173] Gonzales responded in writing to Governor Blanco on September 7, saying that after consulting with DHS, he approved Blanco's request and deployed the appropriate law enforcement personnel.[174] Chertoff also responded to Blanco on September 7, stating that DHS law enforcement would "continue to provide assistance" with state and local authorities in Louisiana.[175]

The Law Enforcement Coordination Center in Baton Rouge, Louisiana coordinated the efforts of all federal law enforcement in the greater New Orleans area and assisted the New Orleans Police Department in reorganization

During the first week following the hurricane, local, state, and federal law enforcement working in New Orleans began daily 9:00 a.m. meetings at the Harrah's Casino in downtown New Orleans.[176] These meetings enabled the law enforcement entities to meet face to face and coordinate critical missions. The New Orleans Police Department (NOPD) District Captain for each city district attended the meetings, along with the Bureau of Alcohol, Tobacco, Firearms, and Explosive (ATF), the Drug Enforcement Agency (DEA), the Federal Bureau of Investigations (FBI), and U.S. Immigration and Customs Enforcement (ICE).

Michael J. Vanacore, Director of International Affairs ICE, and Michael Wolf, Special Agent-In-Charge for the FBI's Critical Incident Response Group, were detailed by their respective agencies to Baton Rouge to coordinate the federal law enforcement response to Hurricane Katrina in Louisiana.[177] The two men were designated as Co-Senior

During the first week following the hurricane, local, state, and federal law enforcement working in New Orleans began daily 9:00 a.m. meetings at the Harrah's Casino in downtown New Orleans.

deral Law Enforcement Officers (SFLEO) and stood up
e Law Enforcement Coordination Center (LECC) at LSP
eadquarters in Baton Rouge.[178]

Vanacore arrived at the Louisiana State Police (LSP)
eadquarters in Baton Rouge on Sunday, September 4.[179]
t the time, Vanacore understood his role was to work
ith the ICE New Orleans Agent-in-Charge, Michael Holt,
nd report to ICE headquarters in Washington, D.C. on
CE's mission in the area affected by the hurricane. Late
at evening, Vanacore was informed of the decision to
esignate him SFLEO. He was instructed he would share
FLEO responsibilities with Wolf. Wolf arrived in Baton
ouge on Monday, September 5. The same day, Vanacore
eviewed an unsigned letter designating him and Wolf as
FLEO.

Vanacore and Wolf had their first meeting late on
eptember 5.[180] On September 6, it was clear to Vanacore
nd Wolf they needed an operations center to coordinate
ederal law enforcement efforts in New Orleans.[181] The
enter was then designated the LECC. The LECC did
ot have command and control over the federal law
nforcement missions. Rather it served as the point of
ontact for all federal law enforcement in the greater
ew Orleans area. The missions of the LECC were to
oordinate efforts to reestablish the NOPD and efforts
f all law enforcement agencies' deployed resources to
e New Orleans area. According to Vanacore, the main
ission of the LECC was to ensure officer safety.[182]

On September 6, officials from the LECC, including
anacore, met with the Mayor of New Orleans, the City
f New Orleans Homeland Security Director and counsel
or the Mayor.[183] Officials also met with the NOPD
recinct captains.[184] Vanacore reported the Mayor's office
nd NOPD were "very helpful" and worked well with
e LECC.[185] The LECC had little communication with
e Louisiana Governor's Office, but Vanacore and Wolf
oth said interaction with the Governor's office was not
ecessary to achieve LECC's goals.[186]

Wolf brought additional FBI agents with him to Baton
ouge, as well as a Blue Whale Command, the FBI's
nobile command station, specially equipped with office
nd communication equipment.[187] Vanacore stated the
nobile command center was invaluable to standing up
e LECC.[188] By September 7, the LECC was gathering
nd centralizing information, to ensure there were not
uplicate law enforcement missions.[189]

The LECC divided the federal law enforcement entities
by New Orleans police districts.[190] Each federal law
enforcement agency was responsible for coordinating with
the precinct captain of the district.[191]

The LECC also began daily 8:00 a.m. meetings with
representatives from state and federal law enforcement.[192]
ICE, FBI, DEA, ATF, USMS, U.S. Customs and Border
Protection, including the Border Patrol, the National
Guard, the U.S. Attorney's Office from New Orleans and
Baton Rouge, the Office of the Louisiana Attorney General,
LSP, NOPD, and the New Orleans Fire Department were
all represented at the meetings. The City of New Orleans
Homeland Security Director also attended the daily
meetings. In addition, the U.S. Secret Service, the Sheriff's
Association, and the Federal Air Marshals participated
on a limited basis. CBP and FBI provided helicopters to
transport attendees to and from New Orleans and the
LECC for the meetings.[193]

The daily meetings commenced with Wolf reporting
the number of arrests and incidents from the prior day.[194]
There was then a roll call of all attendees to report their
force numbers. Vanacore summarized the daily events
on his blackberry and communicated to Jon Clark at ICE
headquarters in Washington, D.C. Wolf communicated
with FBI Headquarters.[195]

As the LECC worked from Baton Rouge, it became
apparent to Vanacore and Wolf that in order to achieve its
goals, the LECC needed to be located in New Orleans.[196]
On September 9, the LECC and NOPD moved into the
Royal Sonesta Hotel on Bourbon Street.[197] The LECC and
NOPD each had a conference room and an additional
room was used to receive incoming 911 telephone calls.[198]

The LECC worked with NOPD to assist in "standing
up" the police department. There were eight NOPD district
offices in New Orleans.[199] Four were rendered useless
due to insufficient power, and four were flooded. LECC
acquired air conditioning compressors and generators for
the district offices that needed power. Temporary office
spaces were procured to replace the flooded offices. The
evidence and property rooms for the NOPD were under
water and contained mold. The LECC assisted NOPD with
procuring contractors to recover and process the evidence
and property, and clean NOPD headquarters.

As a result of stolen uniforms, destroyed homes,
and displaced New Orleans police officers, NOPD was
patrolling the city without proper uniforms.[200] The LECC
was able to procure temporary battle dress uniforms off

the Federal Supply Schedule maintained by the General Services Administrations (GSA) for acquisitions by federal agencies. By using GSA for the uniforms, the NOPD did not have to utilize its local procurement process, which would have required three separate bids before purchasing new uniforms.

In addition, the LECC located photographers to create credentials for LECC and NOPD guards and officials at the Royal Sonesta.[201] LECC provided lights and generators to assist 15 police checks points. Supplies were provided for crime scene processing, including gloves and masks to protect police from mold.

Both Vanacore and Wolf reported the LECC had a positive working relationship with NOPD and that the department was receptive to LECC's assistance.[202]

Conclusion

First the levees were breached—and then law and order. As Katrina left people scrambling for food, for water, for supplies – for survival — lawlessness and violence, both real and imagined, spread, creating yet another problem for authorities who were burdened enough already.

How did this happen? For starters, the lack of basic necessities for residents who did not evacuate, or went back to their homes too quickly, contributed. As we saw in Pearl River County, once there were sufficient amounts of food, ice, and water, order was restored. Another problem was the uncertainty about evacuations. Confusion reigned, especially in places like the Superdome and the Convention Center, where conditions were terrible, nerve frayed, people desperate.

Compounding these difficulties was the collapse or absence of law enforcement. The police, in some cases, were unable to function or were diverting their attention to search and rescue operations. The New Orleans Police Department had known of the threat that could arise from flooding, yet failed to properly protect its resources or come close to continuity of operations. There was also a dereliction of duty by some New Orleans officers when, of course, their presence was needed most.

The federal, state, and local governments also lost another battle, this one with the media. Rumors spread, as fast as the fear. Some turned out to be true, but many did not, resulting in exaggerated reports that scared away truck and bus drivers who could have furnished people with much-needed supplies. Authorities needed to be on top of this situation, not a victim of it.

Fortunately, the National Guard in all three affected states were able to help out overburdened local authorities. About 20 other states added support, an effort that prevented a dire situation from being much worse. DOD active duty forces also came through, their mere presence serving to reduce tensions. Federal law enforcement agencies played an important role, as well, with additional forces and supplies.

For an exhaustive account of all federal law enforcement actions in response to Hurricane Katrina from August 23 to September 12, 2005, please see Appendix 5. ■

1. Interview by Select Comm. Staff with Bobby Strahan, Dir. Pearl River County Emergency Mgmt. Agency, State of Miss., in Wash., D.C. (Nov. 29, 2005) [hereinafter Interview with Bobby Strahan].

2. *Hearing on Hurricane Katrina: Preparedness and Response by the State of Mississippi Before Select Comm.*, 109th Cong. (Dec. 7, 2005) at 11 (statement of Dr. Brian Amy, State Health Officer, Miss. Dep't of Health) [hereinafter *Dec. 7, 2005 Select Comm. Hearing*].

3. *Id.*

4. Interview by Select Comm. Staff with Maj. Ralph D. Mitchell, Jr., Region 1 Commander, La. State Police and LtC. Joseph Booth, Deputy Superintendent, La. State Police, in Baton Rouge, LA (Nov. 9, 2005) [hereinafter Interview with Mitchell and Booth].

5. *Hearing on Hurricane Katrina: Preparedness and Response by the State of Louisiana Before Select Comm.*, 109th Cong. (Dec. 14, 2005) at 103 (statement of Governor Kathleen Blanco, State of LA) [hereinafter *Dec. 14, 2005 Select Comm. Hearing*].

6. EM2000 Messages, Nos. MEMA-0011924, MEMA-0012244, MEMA-001228, MEMA-0012312, MEMA-0013022 (on file with Select Comm.).

7. *Id.*

8. Interview with Mitchell and Booth.

9. Interview by Select Comm. Staff with Jiff Hingle, Sheriff, Plaquemines Parish, LA, in New Orleans, LA (Nov. 8, 2005) [hereinafter Interview with Jiff Hingle].

10. Interview by Select Comm. Staff with David Tranter, Deputy Attorney Gen. and Gen. Counsel, State of AL Emergency Mgmt. Agency, in Clanton, AL (Oct. 11, 2005).

11. EM2000 Messages, No. MEMA-0011924 (on file with Select Comm.).

12. Tiger Team Katrina Report, LA Nat'l Guard at 27 (Nov. 2, 2005) (on file with Select. Comm.).

13. Interview by Select Comm. Staff with LtC. Jacques Thibodeaux and Col. Mark Mouton, LA Nat'l Guard, in New Orleans, LA (Nov. 3, 2005) [hereinafter Interview with Thibodeaux and Mouton].

14. *Dec. 7, 2005 Select Comm. Hearing* at 5 (Statement of William L. Carwile, former FEMA Fed. Coordinating Officer).

15. *Id.* at 125-26 (Statement of Mayor Tommy Longo, Waveland, Miss.).

16. *Id.* at 125-27 (Statement of Mayor Tommy Longo, Waveland, Miss.).

17. Interview by Select Comm. Staff with Hancock County Emergency Operations Ctr. personnel, in Hancock County, Miss. (Oct. 11-14, 2005).

18. Interview with Bobby Strahan.

19. Interview with Jiff Hingle.

20. *Id.*

21. Dan Baum, *Deluged, When Katrina Hit, Where Were the Police?*, THE NEW YORKER, Jan. 9, 2006 at 54 [hereinafter Deluged Article].

22. *Id.*

23. *Id.*

24. *Id.* at 52.

25. Interview by Select Comm. Staff with Lonnie Swain, Deputy Chief, New Orleans Police Dep't, in New Orleans, LA (Nov. 9, 2005) [hereinafter Interview with Lonnie Swain].

26. Interview with Mitchell and Booth.

27. *Dec. 14, 2005 Select Comm. Hearing* at 226 (statement of C. Ray Nagin, Mayor, City of New Orleans, LA).

28. Interview with Mitchell and Booth.

29. Interview by Select Comm. Staff with Thomas Enright, Assistant Attorney Gen., Public Prot. Div., LA Dep't of Justice, in New Orleans, LA (Nov. 8, 2005) [hereinafter Interview with Thomas Enright].

30. Deluged Article at 54.

31. Interview with Lonnie Swain.

32. *Stealing for Salvation*, (MSNBC Television News Broadcast, Aug. 31, 2005).

33. Robert E. Pierre and Ann Gerhart, *News of Pandemonium May Have Slowed Aid*, WASH. POST, Oct. 5, 2005 [hereinafter Pandemonium Article].

34. Interview with Thibodeaux and Mouton; Interview by Select Comm. Staff with Terry Ebbert, Dir., Homeland Sec., City of New Orleans, in New Orleans, LA (Nov. 9, 2005) [hereinafter Interview with Terry Ebbert].

35. Interview with Thibodeaux and Mouton; Interview with Terry Ebbert; Interview by Select Comm. Staff with Nicholas Gachassin, First Assistant Attorney Gen., LA Dep't of Justice, in Baton Rouge, LA (Nov. 6, 2005) [hereinafter Interview with Nicholas Gachassin].

36. David Carr, *More Horrible Than Truth: News Reports*, N.Y. TIMES, Sept. 19, 2005 [hereinafter Carr Article].

37. Interview with Nicholas Gachassin; Interview with Thomas Enright.

38. Daily Video Teleconferences among officials dated Aug. 25 – Sep. 4, 2005 at 15 [hereinafter Daily VTC]. State and local officials from each of the impacted areas met daily with officials from, among other agencies, FEMA, and Nat'l Hurricane Center.

39. *Id.* at 6.

40. *Dec. 14, 2005 Select Comm. Hearing* at 214 (Statement of Terry Ebbert).

41. *Id.* at 226 (Statement of Mayor Ray Nagin, City of New Orleans, LA).

42. Carr Article; Susannah Rosenblatt and James Rainey, *Katrina Takes Toll on Truth, News Accuracy*, L.A. TIMES, Sept. 27, 2005; Beth Gillin, *Katrina Spawned Rumors; Media Ran with Them*, PHILA. INQUIRER, Sept. 28, 2005.

43. *Id.*

44. *Id.*

45. Interview with Thibodeaux and Mouton.

46. *Hearing on Hurricane Katrina: Preparedness and Response by the Department of Defense, the Coast Guard, and the National Guard of Louisiana, Mississippi, and Alabama Before Select Comm.*, 109th Cong. (Oct. 27, 2005) at 196 (statement of Lt. Gen. H Steven Blum, Chief of the Nat'l Guard Bureau) [hereinafter *Oct. 27, 2005 Select Comm. Hearing*].

47. Pandemonium Article.

48. Interview with Thibodeaux and Mouton.

49 Telephone Interview by Select Comm. Staff with Capt. Jeff Winn, New Orleans Police Dep't., New Orleans, LA, in Wash., D.C. (Jan. 26, 2006).

50 *Id.*

51 *Id.*

52 *Oct. 27, 2005 Select Comm. Hearing* at 196-97 (statement of Lt. Gen. H Steven Blum, Chief of the Nat'l Guard Bureau).

53 Interview with Thibodeaux and Mouton; Interview with Nicholas Gachassin; Interview with Terry Ebbert.

54 Interview with Nicholas Gachassin.

55 Interview by Select Comm. Staff with Andy Kopplin, Chief of Staff, Office of the Governor of LA, in New Orleans, LA (Nov. 6, 2005).

56 EMAC Operations Manual (Oct. 2005) [hereinafter EMAC Ops Manual]; Telephone Interview by Select Comm. Staff with EMAC personnel, in Wash., D.C. (Dec. 13, 2005) [hereinafter Telephone Interview with EMAC]; EMAC website: What Is EMAC. www.emacweb.org/?9 (last visited Jan. 26, 2006).

57 EMAC Ops Manual; Telephone Interview with EMAC; EMAC website: What Is EMAC. www.emacweb.org/?9 (last visited Jan. 26, 2006).

58 Emergency Management Assistance Compact, Pub. L. No. 104-321, 110 Stat. 3877 (1996). Hawaii has not ratified EMAC. (E-mail correspondence from EMAC personnel to Select Comm. Staff (Dec. 13, 2005) (5:14 p.m.)).

59 EMAC Ops Manual.

60 EMAC website: How Does EMAC Work. www.emacweb.org/?142 (last visited Jan. 26, 2006).

61 *Id.*

62 Telephonic Interview with EMAC.

63 *Id.*

64 *Id.*

65 *Id.*

66 *Id.*

67 E-mail correspondence from EMAC personnel to Select Comm. Staff (Dec. 19, 2005) (5:25 p.m.).

68 Presentation Materials prepared by EMAC personnel, EMAC Responses to Hurricanes Katrina and Rita (Oct. 4, 2005).

69 *Id.*

70 *Id.*

71 Master Log of EMAC Requisitions (unaudited draft).

72 Telephone Interview with EMAC.

73 *Dec. 7, 2005 Select Comm. Hearing* at 5 (Statement of William L. Carwile, former FEMA Fed. Coordinating Officer); Interview by Select Comm. Staff with William Carwile, former FEMA Fed. Coordinating Officer, in Wash., D.C. (Dec. 6, 2005).

74 Hurricane Situation Report 54, Miss. Emergency Management Agency (Sept. 10, 2005 at 1500 hours); updated Miss. Guard numbers from Miss. Nat'l Guard Daily Recap (Oct. 11, 2005).

75 EMAC Assistance to Miss., Nat'l Emergency Mgmt. Ass'n (Nov. 3, 2005).

76 *Oct. 27, 2005 Select Comm. Hearing* at 133 (statement of Paul McHale, Assistant Sec'y of Def. for Homeland Def.).

77 *Dec. 7, 2005 Select Comm. Hearing* at 111 (statement of William L. Carwile, former FEMA Fed. Coordinating Officer).

78 Interview by Select Comm. Staff with Col. Marvin E. Curtis, Jr., Assistant Comm'r, Dep't of Public Safety, State of Miss., in Jackson, Miss. (Oct. 2005).

79 *Dec. 7, 2005 Select Comm. Hearing* at 111 (statement of William L. Carwile, former FEMA Fed. Coordinating Officer) ("[I]n addition to the relief we got from the things that Mississippi brought to bear, the state of Florida which prepositionalized things up at the Panhandle, they bought us time too, because it would have been much worse had it not been for the things we got from Florida.").

80 Hurricane Situation Reports, Miss. Emergency Mgmt. Agency (Sept. 2, 2005 at 1200 hours; Sept. 6, 2005 at 0200 hours); *Dec. 7, 2005 Select Comm. Hearing* at 2 (Statement of Governor Haley Barbour, State of Miss.).

81 EMAC Assistance to Miss., Nat'l Emergency Mgmt. Ass'n (Nov. 3, 2005).

82 E-mail correspondence from Patrick Rhode to Casey Long and Brooks Altshuler (Sept. 2, 2005) (6:46 p.m.).

83 *Id.*

84 Daily VTC at 9 (Sept. 2, 2005).

85 Telephone Interview by Select Comm. Staff with Federal Bureau of Investigation [hereinafter FBI] personnel, in Wash., D.C. (Dec. 15, 2005) [hereinafter Dec. 15 Telephone Interview with FBI]; The Jackson Field Div. covers the entire state of Miss. and has 10 Resident Agencies located in: Southaven, Oxford, Tupelo, Columbus, Greenville, Meridian, Hattiesburg, Macomb, Gulfport, and Pascagoula (E-mail correspondence from FBI personnel to Select Comm. Staff (Dec. 5, 2005) (6:10 p.m.)) [hereinafter Dec. 5 E-mail from FBI].

86 Dec. 15 Telephone Interview with FBI.

87 Interview by Select Comm. Staff with FBI personnel, in Wash., D.C. (Nov. 28, 2005) [hereinafter Nov. 28 Interview with FBI]; Dec. 15 Telephone Interview with FBI.

88 Dec. 15 Telephone Interview with FBI.

89 Nov. 28 Interview with FBI.

90 Dec. 5 E-mail from FBI.

91 Telephone Interview by Select Comm. Staff with FBI personnel (Jan. 27, 2006).

92 Bureau of Alcohol, Tobacco, Firearms and Explosives [hereinafter ATF] Summary of Significant Activity (Nov. 18, 2005) [hereinafter ATF Summary of Significant Activity].

93 ATF Summary of Significant Activity; Interview by Select Comm. Staff with ATF personnel, in Wash., D.C. (Nov. 29, 2005) [hereinafter Interview with ATF].

94 Interview with ATF.

95 ATF Summary of Significant Activity.

96 *Id.*

7 Interview with ATF; E-mail correspondence from ATF personnel to Select Comm. Staff (Dec. 7, 2005) (11:47 a.m.) [hereinafter E-mail from ATF]. The office in Shreveport oversaw the administrative functions of the Shreveport, Little Rock, Jackson, and Oxford, Miss. Field Offices. (E-mail from ATF).

8 Interview with ATF.

9 E-mail from ATF.

00 Interview with ATF; Telephone Interview by Select Comm. Staff with ATF personnel, in Wash., D.C. (Dec. 1, 2005).

01 Response from the U.S. Dep't of Justice, to Chairman Tom Davis, Select Comm., and Charlie Melancon, U.S. Congressman (Nov. 23, 2005) [hereinafter Nov. 23 Dep't of Justice Response].

02 Hurricane Katrina Drug Enforcement Agency [hereinafter DEA] COOP Assessment (DAG000000223) (Jan. 26, 2006).

03 Nov. 23 Dep't of Justice Response.

04 Nov. 23 Dep't of Justice Response; Interview by Select Comm. Staff with DEA, in Wash., D.C. (Nov. 28, 2005).

05 Nov. 23 Dep't of Justice Response.

06 Response from the U.S. Dep't of Justice, to Chairman Tom Davis, Select Comm., and Charlie Melancon, U.S. Congressman (Dec. 8, 2005) [hereinafter Dec. 8 Dep't of Justice Response]; Interview by Select Comm. Staff with U.S. Marshal Service [hereinafter USMS] personnel, in Wash., D.C. (Dec. 8, 2005) [hereinafter Interview with USMS]. An Operational Mgmt. Team (OMT) oversees USMS' national response. There are OMTs located throughout the United States. A Chief Deputy, the highest ranking career Marshal in the district is in charge of the OMT. Each OMT has a core group of eight personnel. (Interview with USMS).

07 Dec. 8 Dep't of Justice Response.

08 Interview by Select Comm. Staff with U.S. Immigration and Customs Enforcement [hereinafter ICE] in Wash., D.C. (Nov. 16, 2005) [hereinafter Nov. 16 Interview with Interview with ICE].

09 Interview by Select Comm. Staff with ICE personnel, in Wash., D.C. (Dec. 2, 2005) [hereinafter Dec. 2 Interview with ICE].

10 U.S. Customs and Border Prot. [hereinafter CBP] Timeline Aug. 24-Aug. 30 (Dec. 8, 2005) [hereinafter CBP Timeline Aug. 24-Aug. 30]; CBP Hurricane Katrina Support and Operations PowerPoint (Sept. 20, 2005).

11 CBP Timeline Aug. 24-Aug. 30.

12 Interview by Select Comm. Staff with CBP personnel, in Wash., D.C. (Dec. 6, 2005) [hereinafter Interview with CBP]; CBP Timeline Aug. 30-Sept. 13 (Dec. 21, 2005) [hereinafter CBP Timeline Aug. 30-Sept. 13].

13 E-mail correspondence to Select Comm. Staff from CBP personnel (Jan. 26, 2006) (1:35 p.m.).

14 Fed. Air Marshal Serv. [hereinafter FAMS] Timeline prepared for Select Comm. Staff (Nov. 29, 2005) [hereinafter FAMS Timeline].

15 Interview by Select Comm. Staff with FAMS personnel, in Wash., D.C. (Nov. 29, 2005) [hereinafter Interview with FAMS]; FAMS Timeline.

16 Interview by Select Comm. Staff with Fed. Bureau of Prisons [hereinafter BOP] personnel, in Wash., D.C. (Dec. 5, 2005) [hereinafter Interview with BOP]; Dec. 8 Dep't of Justice Response.

17 Dec. 8 Dep't of Justice Response.

18 Nov. 28 Interview with FBI.

19 Nov. 23 Dep't of Justice Response.

20 Telephone Interview by Select Comm. Staff with FBI personnel (Jan. 27, 2006) [hereinafter Jan. 27 Telephone Interview with FBI]; Nov. 23 Dep't of Justice Response.

21 Nov. 23 Dep't of Justice Response. There are four Rapid Deployment teams located in: New York City, Wash., D.C., Los Angeles, and Miami. The teams are comprised of 160 people with different specialties. They are equipped to respond and be self sufficient for seven days on their own. (Telephone Interview by Select Comm. Staff with FBI personnel, in Wash., D.C. (Dec. 5, 2005) [hereinafter Dec. 5 Telephone Interview with FBI]).

22 Nov. 23 Dep't of Justice Response.

23 Dec. 15 Telephone Interview with FBI.

24 Nov. 23 Dep't of Justice Response. The Law Enforcement On-Line Internet site is not available to the general public. Law enforcement entities from around the country must have a password to access the FBI's information. (Dec. 5 E-mail from FBI).

25 Dec. 5 Telephone Interview with FBI.

26 ATF Summary of Significant Activity.

27 ATF Summary of Significant Activity; Interview with ATF.

28 Interview with ATF.

29 ATF Summary of Significant Activity.

30 ATF Summary of Significant Activity; Interview with ATF.

31 Response from U.S. Dep't of Justice, to Chairman Tom Davis, Select Comm., and Charlie Melancon, U.S. Congressman (Dec. 21, 2005). The day by day breakdown is as follows: Aug. 30 (24), Aug. 31 (17), Sept. 1 (32), Sept. 2 (16), Sept. 3 (33), Sept. 4 (38), Sept. 5 (11), Sept. 6 (13), Sept. 7 (39), Sept. 8 (10), Sept. 9 (6), Sept. 10 (5), Sept. 11 (4), Sept. 12 (4). (Id.).

32 Nov. 23 Dep't of Justice Response.

33 Dec. 8 Dep't of Justice Response.

34 Id. Police Dep'ts included: Pass Christian Police Dep't, Gulfport Police Dep't, Biloxi Police Dep't, Long Beach Police Dep't, and Harrison County Sheriff's Dep't.

35 Dec. 2 Interview with ICE.

36 Id.

37 Dec. 2 Interview with ICE; E-mail correspondence from Ronald R. Grimes, DHS to Gerald Garren, et al, (Sept. 6, 2005) (5:27 p.m.). Miss. entities assisted by ICE: Miss. Highway Patrol, Gulfport Police Dep't, Harrison County Sheriffs Office, Waveland Police Dep't, Bay St. Louis Police Dep't, Long Beach Police Dep't, Pass Christian Police Dep't, Hancock County Sheriffs Office, and Jackson County Sheriffs Office. (Id.; Dec. 2 Interview with ICE).

38 CBP Timeline Aug. 24-Aug. 30.

39 CBP Timeline Aug. 30-Sept. 13.

140 Interview with FAMS.

141 FAMS Timeline.

142 Interview with FAMS.

143 FAMS Timeline.

144 Interview with FAMS. This included, meeting arriving buses, helicopters, trucks, and ambulances; canvassing evacuees for information on those left behind in New Orleans; handwriting manifests for the New Orleans International Airport departing flights; pre-screening and loading passengers; crowd control; baggage handling; air traffic control; operating heavy equipment to facilitate blocking and dispatching aircraft; hand-carrying hundreds of sick, injured and elderly passengers on to departing aircraft; working with FEMA triage personnel to carry patients on stretchers for medical evaluation; delivering patients to the "Expected to Die" and morgue holding areas; and assisting in other medical emergencies. (*Id.*).

145 Additional Info. Relating To Secret Service [hereinafter USSS] Contributions Toward Response and Recovery Efforts Associated With Hurricane Katrina (Dec. 5, 2005) [hereinafter Dec. 5 Additional Info. Relating to USSS]; Additional Info. Relating To USSS Contributions Toward Response and Recovery Efforts Associated With Hurricane Katrina (Dec. 7, 2005).

146 Dec. 5 Additional Info. Relating to USSS.

147 Dec. 8 Dep't of Justice Response.

148 Interview with BOP; Dec. 8 Dep't of Justice Response.

149 Dec. 8 Dep't of Justice Response. A total of 54 BOP personnel were responsible for the transportation. These personnel were detailed from the Federal Correction Complex (FCC) in Beaumont, TX; FCC Forrest City, Arkansas; FCC Yazoo City, MS; FCC Oakdale, LA; the United States Penitentiary in Pollock, LA; the Federal Detention Center in Houston, TX. (*Id.*).

150 Dec. 8 Dep't of Justice Response; Interview with BOP.

151 Dec. 5 Telephone Interview with FBI; Dec. 5 E-mail from FBI (citing LA. REV. STAT. ANN. § 9:2793.1 (2005)).

152 Dec. 5 E-mail from FBI.

153 Dec. 5 E-mail from FBI; Dec. 5 Telephone Interview with FBI; Letter from Haley Barbour, Governor, State of Miss., to all state and local law enforcement officers (Sept. 9, 2005) [hereinafter Sept. 9 Governor Barbour letter]. The Governor's request was made under the Emergency Law Enforcement Assistance provisions of the Justice Assistant Act of 1984, 42 U.S.C. §§ 10501-10513, which authorizes the U.S. Dep't of Justice to provide law enforcement assistance to a state. (*Id.*).

154 Dec. 5 E-mail from FBI (citing order issued pursuant to MISS. CODE ANN. § 33-15-1 (2005)); Sept. 9 Governor Barbour letter. The Governor's request was made under the Miss. Emergency Mgmt. Law § 33-15-11(10). (*Id.*).

155 Interview with ATF.

156 28 U.S.C. § 564 (2005).

157 Order No. 2778-2005 from Alberto R. Gonzales, U.S. Attorney Gen. to USMS, Dir., Sept. 3, 2005 [hereinafter Gonzales Order to Dir. USMS].

158 Dec. 2 Interview with ICE.

159 CBP Timeline Aug. 30-Sept. 13.

160 Interview with CBP.

161 CBP Timeline Aug. 30-Sept. 13.

162 FAMS Timeline.

163 Nov. 23 Dep't of Justice Response.

164 E-mail correspondence from Bill Mercer to Bill Mercer (ODAG) (Sept. 8, 2005) (6:04 p.m.).

165 Nov. 23 Dep't of Justice Response (citing 28 U.S.C. § 533).

166 Nov. 23 Dep't of Justice Response (citing 42 U.S.C. § 10501).

167 *Id.*

168 Memorandum from Alberto R. Gonzales, U.S. Attorney Gen., to Heads of Fed. Law Enforcement Agencies (Sept. 2, 2005).

169 Letter from Haley Barbour, Governor, State of Miss., to Alberto R. Gonzales, U.S. Attorney Gen. (Sept. 3, 2005). The Governor's request was made under the Emergency Law Enforcement Assistance provisions of the Justice Assistant Act of 1984, 42 U.S.C. §§ 10501-10513, which authorizes the U.S. Dep't of Justice to provide law enforcement assistance to a state. (*Id.*).

170 Letter from Alberto R. Gonzales, U.S. Attorney Gen., to Haley Barbour, Governor, State of Miss. (Sept. 3, 2005); Gonzales Order to Dir. USMS.

171 Letter from Kathleen Blanco, Governor, State of LA, to Alberto R. Gonzales, U.S. Attorney Gen. (Sept. 3, 2005). The Governor's request was made under the Emergency Law Enforcement Assistance provisions of the Justice Assistant Act of 1984, 42 U.S.C. §§ 10501-10503, which authorizes the U.S. Dep't of Justice to provide law enforcement assistance to a state. (*Id.*).

172 Letter from Alberto R. Gonzales, U.S. Attorney Gen., to Kathleen Blanco, Governor, State of LA (Sept. 4, 2005); Order No. 2779-2005 from Alberto R. Gonzales, U.S. Attorney Gen. to Deputy Attorney Gen. (Sept. 4, 2005).

173 Letter from Kathleen Blanco, Governor, State of LA, to Alberto R. Gonzales, U.S. Attorney Gen. and Michael Chertoff, Sec'y, Dep't of Homeland Sec. (Sept. 6, 2005). The Governor's request was made under the Emergency Law Enforcement Assistance provisions of the Justice Assistant Act of 1984, 42 U.S.C. §§ 10501-10503, which authorizes the U.S. Dep't of Justice to provide law enforcement assistance to a state. (*Id.*).

174 Letter from Alberto R. Gonzales, U.S. Attorney Gen., to Kathleen Blanco, Governor, State of LA (Sept. 7, 2005).

175 Letter from Michael Chertoff, Sec'y, Dep't. of Homeland Sec., to Kathleen Blanco, Governor, State of LA (Sept. 7, 2005).

176 Dec. 2 Interview with ICE.

177 Nov. 16 Interview with ICE; Dec. 2 Interview with ICE; Interview by Select Comm. Staff with FBI personnel, in Washington, D.C. (Dec. 6, 2005) [hereinafter Dec. 6 Interview with FBI].

178 Dec. 2 Interview with ICE; Nov. 23 Dep't of Justice Response.

179 Dec. 2 Interview with ICE.

180 *Id.*

181 Dec. 2 Interview with ICE; Dec. 6 Interview with FBI.

182 Dec. 2 Interview with ICE.

183 *Id.*

184 Dec. 2 Interview with ICE; Dec. 6 Interview with FBI.

85 Dec. 2 Interview with ICE.
86 Dec. 2 Interview with ICE; Dec. 6 Interview with FBI.
87 Nov. 28 Interview with FBI; Dec. 2 Interview with ICE.
88 Dec. 2 Interview with ICE.
89 Dec. 2 Interview with ICE; Dec. 6 Interview with FBI.
90 *Id.*
91 Dec. 2 Interview with ICE; Dec. 6 Interview with FBI; Dec. 5 E-mail from FBI. The assignments were as follows: District 1: ATF/ DEA, District 2: FBI/Border Patrol's Tactical Units (BORTAC), District 3: Federal Protective Service, District 4: ICE, District 5: USMS/DEA/BORTAC, District 6: FBI/ATF, District 7: FBI/DEA/BORTACT, and District 8: ATF. (Dec. 5 E-mail from FBI).
92 Dec. 2 Interview with ICE; Dec. 6 Interview with FBI.
93 Dec. 2 Interview with ICE.
94 *Id.*
95 Dec. 6 Interview with FBI.
96 Dec. 2 Interview with ICE; Dec. 6 Interview with FBI.
97 Dec. 2 Interview with ICE; Dec. 6 Interview with FBI; Dec. 5 E-mail from FBI.
98 Dec. 6 Interview with FBI.
99 *Id.*
00 *Id.*
01 *Id.*
02 Dec. 2 Interview with ICE; Dec. 6 Interview with FBI.

"It's like being in a Third World country.

We're trying to work without power.

Everyone knows we're all in this together.

We're just trying to stay alive."

Mitch Handrich
Registered Nurse Manager at Charity Hospital[1]

Medical care and evacuations suffered from a lack of advance preparations, inadequate communications, and difficulties coordinating efforts

Summary

Public health preparedness and medical assistance are critical components to any disaster response plan

Hurricane Katrina tested the nation's planning and preparedness for a major public health threat and highlighted the importance of strong cooperation and partnerships among health agencies at all levels of government. The threat of any type of disaster emphasizes the need for planning and practice. Public health preparedness and medical assistance are critical components to any disaster response plan — the faster the health community responds, the more quickly control strategies can be developed and appropriate treatments can be identified. And the faster human suffering is diminished.

The annual hurricane season is a continuous challenge to public health infrastructures and a strain on resources. As seen in the preparation for and response to Katrina, medical personnel, supplies, and equipment were in constant need in the Gulf coast region. Despite deficiencies in coordination, communication, and capacity, public health and medical support services

effectively treated a massive and overwhelming evacuee population. Federalized teams of medical first responders were deployed to the affected region to provide assistance. Millions of dollars worth of medical supplies and assets were consumed. Some Department of Health and Human Services (HHS) assets, like the Federal Medical Shelters, had never been used or tested prior to Katrina but were deployed and were, for the most part, considered effective.

Despite difficulties, the medical assistance and response to Hurricane Katrina was a success. Thousands of lives were saved because of the hard work and enduring efforts of public health officials and medical volunteers. Poor planning and preparedness, however, were also too big a part of the story, resulting in delays and shortages of resources, and loss of life in the region.

This chapter outlines what medical personnel and supplies were pre-positioned, and deployed post-landfall, to the affected area and how those assets were utilized. It explains the plans in place prior to Hurricane Katrina for health care facilities and shelters. The findings in this chapter conclude several deficiencies in public health and medical response plans exist at all levels of government and within medical care facilities. Ultimately, better planning and initiative would have resulted in a more proactive, coordinated, efficient, and effective response.

Personnel

HHS and the Department of Homeland Security (DHS) have the capabilities to mobilize and deploy teams of medical personnel to disaster areas. HHS controls the Public Health Service Commissioned Corps, the Medical Reserves Corps, and personnel from its agencies such as the Centers for Disease Control and Prevention (CDC), National Institutes of Health, Substance Abuse and Mental Health Services Administration, and the Food and Drug Administration. DHS, specifically FEMA, has direct control over the National Disaster Medical System (NDMS), which supplies and organizes teams of medical personnel in each state who stand ready to deploy at any moment. Unfortunately, limited numbers of personnel were pre-positioned prior to landfall, and most deployments were delayed until after the storm hit and the magnitude of devastation was realized.

Supplies

In addition to medical personnel, HHS, FEMA, and the Department of Defense (DOD) have medical supplies at their disposal to respond to a public health emergency. HHS has control over the Strategic National Stockpile (SNS), a national repository of pharmaceuticals and medical supplies. NDMS personnel teams are always accompanied by large caches of supplies and drugs. DOD has a mobile medical unit capability as well. Limited amounts of supplies, however, were staged in the region prior to landfall. Several officials argued the magnitude of the storm's devastation could not have been predicted, and the amount of supplies needed was unknown until the fog cleared. Despite that argument, more supplies and personnel could have been pre-positioned prior to landfall.

AP PHOTO/BILL HABER

Evacuation plans, communication, and coordination must be executed well for effective response

During the days following Hurricane Katrina, around the clock media coverage of patients and staff trapped in New Orleans hospitals inundated television screens across the country. The nation watched in horror. How long would it take for evacuations to begin? And why had these hospitals not evacuated before the storm?

The Select Committee focused part of its medical investigation on these questions, as well as the overarching issues of impaired communications and lack of coordination. The Select Committee acknowledges this chapter does not tell the story of every hospital devastated by Hurricane Katrina. Nor does it include every detail of the communications and coordination difficulties which impeded the medical response.

Rather, this chapter provides findings based on an in-depth examination of specific plans in place before the storm, and a timeline of events that *actually* took place after the storm. Similarly, the Select Committee recognizes this section of the report focuses on the evacuations of New Orleans medical facilities in particular. Because New Orleans hospitals and facilities experienced the most complete failure of equipment and communications, and because the need to evacuate New Orleans hospital patients was so extreme, the Select Committee chose these institutions as its focal point.

Evacuations

As it stands, Louisiana hospitals and nursing homes are responsible for having and implementing their own emergency evacuation plans. The Louisiana Hospital Association (LHA) does not provide specific emergency response or evacuation guidance and said, with respect to protecting patients and staff, the primary priority for all hospitals is to "shelter in place" versus evacuate. Hospitals are, however, expected to comply with requirements set forth by the Joint Commission on Accreditation of Healthcare Organizations.[2]

The majority of hospital CEOs, as well as state and local medical personnel with whom the Select Committee met, cited time and money as two key factors influencing their decision about whether to evacuate patients from a shelter or medical facility prior to a hurricane. Time is critical given that the majority of hospital and Department of Veterans Affairs Medical Center (VAMC) plans call for evacuation decisions to be made anywhere from 36 to 72 hours in advance of a hurricane's projected landfall — hospitalized patients require a significant amount of time and staff to be moved safely. In the case of Hurricane Katrina, the then Methodist Hospital CEO, Larry Graham, said when he realized Hurricane Katrina was going to hit New Orleans, there simply was not enough time to evacuate patients.

The second much-discussed factor, cost, is perhaps even more critical to the decision. Expenses for evacuating a hospital are astronomical, and in the case of for-profit hospitals, these costs are not reimbursable by FEMA. In

Time is critical given that the majority of hospital and Department of Veterans Affairs Medical Center (VAMC) plans call for evacuation decisions to be made anywhere from 36 to 72 hours in advance of a hurricane's projected landfall

most cases hospitals say that given their cost/risk analyses, it makes the most economic sense to ride out a storm and protect patients within the hospital rather than evacuate them. For example, going to Code Grey alone (without factoring in evacuation expenses), costs Louisiana State University's hospitals $600,000 per day.[3] Many members of the New Orleans medical community likewise made the point, had Hurricane Katrina not resulted in such catastrophic flooding, their facilities would have been prepared, and their decision not to evacuate patients would have been the most prudent course of action. With the factors of time and money in mind, this chapter seeks to understand evacuation plans in place prior to Katrina, and preparedness levels of hospitals and the government to fully evacuate New Orleans medical facilities.

Communication and Coordination

Medical responders and coordinating officers from the government, hospitals, and private entities, cited non-existent or limited communication capabilities as a primary obstacle to their response. Emergency plans in place prior to Hurricane Katrina did not prevent oversights and confusion in procedures for ensuring functional and efficient communications equipment in the event of a disaster. A comparison of the VAMC plans for Louisiana, Mississippi, and Alabama, for example, demonstrates they are not standardized — some pieces of VAMCs' communications plans do clearly outline the who, what, where, and when of keeping communication systems operating, while other VAMC plans leave many questions unanswered. Most VAMC and hospital emergency plans, reviewed by Select Committee staff do not have one separate section devoted to communications preparation.

The LHA and its hospitals rely on multiple phone service providers, and all LHA hospitals rely on an emergency two-way radio such as Hospital Emergency Area Radio (HEAR) or 800 MHz radio.[4] This chapter describes how VAMC and hospital emergency plans address emergency communications and equipment, as well as exactly how such plans and equipment failed medical responders when they most needed it.

One of the most common and pervasive themes in the response to Hurricane Katrina has been a systematic failure of communications at the local, state, and federal levels — a failure that hindered initiative. The accounts of New Orleans medical facilities and special needs shelters are no exception, underscoring how failed communications with the outside threatened the safety of medical staff and the lives of their patients. It was difficult to ascertain a clear timeline of communication capabilities and failures for medical first responders and personnel. Institutions did not have time to collect information for hourly or even daily reports of how communication equipment and systems were working or not. Medical responders and personnel simply did not have adequate communications capabilities immediately following the hurricane. The majority of cell phones were rendered inoperable because they could not be recharged. Satellite communications were unreliable, and the distribution of satellite phones appeared insufficient.

Government agencies also encountered problems with coordination due to red tape and general confusion over mission assignments, deployments, and command structure. On a large scale, command structure presented problems when HHS, the coordinating agency for Emergency Support Function 8 (ESF-8), and NDMS, the system that houses most of the resources needed for a medical response, did not share an understanding of who controlled NDMS during the emergency. Confusion resulted when these two entities were operating separately, albeit with efforts to coordinate with each other. On a smaller scale, e-mails from first responders and medical personnel immediately following the storm reflect coordination problems. Misunderstandings about deployment orders and mission assignments resulted in streams of e-mails expressing uncertainties and frustrations.

ESF-8 Background

HHS is the "principal agency for protecting the health of all Americans and providing essential human services, especially for those who are least able to help themselves."[5] As such, HHS plays a role in the emergency management process. Under the National Response Plan (NRP), ESF-8 provides for the federal government to augment state and local resources and assist in response. Upon activation, ESF-8 "provides the mechanism for coordinated federal assistance to supplement state, local, and tribal resources in response to public health and medical care needs (to include veterinary and/or animal health issues when appropriate) for potential or actual Incidents of National Significance and/or during a developing potential health and medical situation."[6]

The Assistant Secretary for Public Health Emergency Preparedness serves on behalf of the Secretary to coordinate the HHS preparation for, response to, and efforts to prevent public health and medical emergencies or disasters. ESF-8 is tasked with the assessment of public health and medical needs, including behavioral health, conducting public health surveillance, and the provision and deployment of medical care personnel and medical equipment and supplies.[7]

As the designated primary agency for ESF-8, HHS is responsible for:

■ Orchestrating federal support within their functional area for an affected state;

■ Providing staff for the operations functions at fixed and field facilities;

■ Notifying and requesting assistance from support agencies;

■ Managing mission assignments and coordinating with support agencies, as well as appropriate state agencies;

■ Working with appropriate private-sector organizations to maximize use of all available resources;

■ Supporting and keeping other ESFs and organizational elements informed of ESF operational priorities and activities;

■ Executing contracts and procuring goods and services as needed;

■ Ensuring financial and property accountability for ESF activities;

■ Planning for short-term and long-term incident management and recovery operations; and

■ Maintaining trained personnel to support interagency emergency response and support teams.[8]

While HHS has a number of internal assets to supplement state, local, and tribal government entities, the NRP lists a number of additional external assets for HHS to use in coordinating the federal response. Support agencies under ESF-8 include DHS (FEMA and NDMS), DOD, VA, and the Department of Transportation (DOT).

Finding: Deployment of medical personnel was reactive, not proactive

Federalized teams were deployed and provided assistance in several locations after landfall

Thousands of people in the Gulf region were treated and hundreds of lives were saved due to the services provided by medical personnel in response to Hurricane Katrina. However, with few medical personnel teams pre-positioned prior to landfall, public health officials scrambled to mobilize and deploy personnel teams after the storm hit the Gulf coast. As a result, medical assistance in some areas was unnecessarily delayed by hours, even days. Personnel and supplies are readily available to decision-makers. With a few exceptions, the deployment of medical personnel was reactive, not proactive as most assets were not utilized until after the need was apparent. Ultimately, public health and medical support services were effectively but inefficiently delivered. Below is a comprehensive assessment of when and where medical personnel were deployed in the Gulf coast region to provide medical treatment and care.

FEMA

NDMS

FEMA is home to the NDMS. The mission of NDMS is to maintain a national capability to deliver quality medical care to the victims and responders of a domestic disaster.[9] NDMS has medical, mortuary, and veterinarian assistance teams located around the country. These specialized teams include:

- 45 Disaster Medical Assistance Teams (DMATs), groups of professional and paraprofessional medical personnel capable of providing medical care following disasters;
- 11 Disaster Mortuary Operational Response Teams (DMORTs), which consist of private citizens with specialized training and experience to help in the recovery, identification and processing of deceased victims;
- Four National Medical Response Teams, to deal with the medical consequences of incidents potentially involving chemical, biological or nuclear materials;
- National Pharmacy Response Teams and National Nurse Response Teams, which include pharmacists and nurses to assist in mass-dispensing of medications during disasters along with mass vaccination campaigns.
- Five Veterinary Medical Assistance Teams, clinical veterinarians, pathologists, animal health technicians, microbiologists and others who assist animal disaster victims and provide care to search dogs; and
- Three International Medical Surgical Response Teams, highly specialized teams, trained and equipped to establish free standing field surgical facilities anywhere in the world.[10]

Fully operational DMATs have the ability to triage and treat up to 250 patients per day for up to three days without resupply.[11] Within four hours of alert status, DMATs should be able to field a full 35-person roster. Within six hours after activation, DMATs should be deployment ready.[12]

Before Hurricane Katrina made landfall, NDMS only staged nine of its 45 DMATs in the Gulf coast region.[13] Three DMATs and a Management Support Team were pre-positioned in each of the following locations: Anniston, Alabama, Memphis, Tennessee, and Houston, Texas. According to FEMA officials, the Superdome in New Orleans was the first NDMS assignment because it was a designated special needs shelter.[14] DMAT Oklahoma 1 (OK-1 DMAT) was pre-staged in Houston, Texas on August 27 in anticipation of the storm. OK-1 DMAT efforts will be discussed more thoroughly in a later section of this chapter. In addition to OK-1 DMAT, other teams at the Superdome included NM-1, CA-6, and RI-1.

WA-1 DMAT from Washington was one of the few teams activated and deployed prior to landfall. It was staged in Houston and was poised to move to its mission assignment post-landfall, which ended up being Louis Armstrong International Airport in New Orleans (New Orleans Airport).[15]

FEMA activated OR-2 DMAT from Oregon on August 30 and immediately began treating patients when the team arrived at the New Orleans Airport on the afternoon of September 1.[16] As previously mentioned, every DMAT includes a large cache of medical supplies and equipment. It is much easier to move personnel than supplies. Although the OR-2 DMAT's cache left Portland on August 31, it took almost five days for the three trucks of supplies to reach the airport.

By August 31, three DMATs, WA-1, CA-4, and TX-4, had arrived at the New Orleans Airport, where evacuated patients were being received.[17] Eventually, eight DMATs would be stationed there to help provide medical care during the patient movement  operations in New Orleans.[18] The medical treatment provided and specific actions taken by the DMATs operating at the airport will be discussed in a later section of this chapter.

With Mississippi's hospital infrastructure decimated after Hurricane Katrina, nine DMATs and seven DMAT Strike Teams were sent to the state to provide medical care and augment the remaining functioning hospitals.[19] Mississippi's State Health Officer, Dr. Brian W. Amy, testified that, "through coordination with the National Disaster Medical System, we positioned DMAT teams at every affected hospital and Strike teams at overflow hospitals in the affected areas. Of the 17,649 reported injuries, DMAT teams treated 15,500 patients in the initial days after landfall."[20]

In general, at most locations DMATs were deployed, the teams were met with overwhelming demand for patient assessment and treatment. Many of the teams operated under extreme fatigue with limited medical supplies, inadequate amounts of food and water, intermittent electricity, and no air-conditioning.

DMORTs, teams of private citizens with specialized training and experience to help in the recovery, identification and processing of deceased victims, were sent to the Gulf coast to assist in the recovery process of dead bodies. A standard DMORT team is comprised of 31 medical and forensic volunteer personnel with specific training in victim identification, mortuary services, and forensic pathology and anthropology methods. DMORTs include a combination of medical examiners, coroners, pathologists, forensic anthropologists, medical records, fingerprint technicians, forensic odentologists, dental assistants, radiologists, funeral directors, mental health professionals, and support personnel.[21] Fully operational DMORTs should be able to deploy within 24 hours of notification.

With only two Portable Morgue Units (PMU) in

NDMS, one was sent to Louisiana and the other to Mississippi. PMUs are equipped to support DMORT services when no local morgue facilities are available. Each is manned by four DMORTs. FEMA did not have enough DMORTs and was forced to contract for additional personnel. HHS worked closely with DMORTs and FEMA by embedding Public Health Service (PHS) personnel in each team. A PHS senior officer and mental health officer were assigned to assist each DMORT.[22]

On Thursday, September 1, 27 Region II DMORTs prepared to leave for Anniston, Alabama, a site designated as the eastern staging point for the DMORT response.[23] On Monday, September 5, one week after landfall, HHS Assistant Secretary for Public Health Emergency Preparedness Stewart  Simonson requested "ample mobile mortuary services throughout the affected region."[24] An order for 200 mobile mortuary trucks was issued, with 130 designated to Louisiana and 70 to be delivered to Mississippi.[25] By the next day, mortuary services were being established in St. Gabriel, Louisiana with 96 personnel.[26] FEMA and Louisiana collaborated on drafting a body recovery plan which required the approval of then FEMA Director Michael Brown and Louisiana's newly appointed state medical examiner.[27] In Mississippi, mortuary services were established at the Naval Air Station in Gulfport. By September 6, one DMORT had set up facilities there.

U.S. Public Health Service Commissioned Corps

The U.S. Public Health Service Commissioned Corps, one of the seven uniformed services of the United States, is comprised of highly-trained and mobile health professionals who carry out programs to promote good health, understand and prevent disease and injury, assure safe and effective drugs and medical devices, deliver health services to federal beneficiaries, and supply health expertise in time of war or other national or international emergencies.

1,000 PHS Commissioned Corps Officers had been deployed to the region in support of the Hurricane Katrina medical response, making it the largest response in Corps history.

All Corps officers on deployment rosters were notified by the U.S. Surgeon General's office via e-mail on Saturday, August 27 that Hurricane Katrina could be a catastrophic event creating the need for medical assistance in the Gulf coast after landfall.[28] At the time of the e-mail, there was "no assessment of what will be needed at this point, but they will potentially ask the feds for medical, mental health, and pharmaceutical support, as well as EHOs, environmental and civil engineers to support the obvious needs for water, waste water and sewer, as well as infrastructure problems."[29] Commissioned Corps officers were asked to stand by and prepare for deployment as public health needs became apparent.

According to a briefing with U.S. Surgeon General, Vice Admiral Richard H. Carmona, PHS had pre-positioned 38 officers on Sunday, August 28 in Baton Rouge, Louisiana and Biloxi, Mississippi.[30] It was originally planned for the PHS officers to be stationed in New Orleans, but they were unable to get there before Hurricane Katrina made landfall. PHS officers were on the ground in New Orleans by late Monday, August 29.

Carmona suggested coordination with PHS, FEMA, and NDMS was difficult. HHS had trouble with tracking DMAT mission assignments and with staffing and communication. Despite the assignment of a Commissioned Corps officer liaison to FEMA to coordinate medical activities, coordination between the two agencies was lacking.[31]

PHS helped reestablish a public health infrastructure for some communities in the Gulf coast region. For example, when New Orleans Mayor Ray Nagin laid-off a majority of the city's public health employees, PHS helped to fill the gaps. "Public health services were never federalized—PHS just provided a federal presence. But the federal presence was absolutely stabilizing," Carmona said.[32]

By September 9, more than 1,000 PHS Commissioned Corps officers had been deployed to the region in support of the Hurricane Katrina medical response, making it the largest response in Corps history. More officers were deployed in response to Katrina than after 9/11 and the anthrax postal incident in 2001.[33] Commissioned Corps officers supplemented several medical response assignments. They worked side-by-side with the DMATs at the New Orleans Airport; staffed the Federal Medical Shelters at several locations in the Gulf coast; assisted with CDC activities; accompanied SNS assets; and helped provide mental health services to the affected region. In general, PHS is a valuable operational asset to HHS and was a critical component to the medical response to Hurricane Katrina. However, despite having the capability to mobilize Commissioned Corps officers at anytime, PHS failed to deploy a significant number of officers to the region prior to landfall.

Centers for Disease Control and Prevention

The CDC is a component of HHS that assists in carrying out its responsibilities for protecting the health and safety of all Americans and for providing essential human services, especially for those people who are least able to help themselves.[34] CDC controls the SNS, large quantities of medicine and medical supplies to protect the American public if there is a health emergency severe enough to cause local supplies to run out.

Before Hurricane Katrina made landfall, CDC activated the Emergency Operations Center (EOC) on August 25.[35] CDC personnel were on the ground in Louisiana with a Technical Advisory Response Unit (TARU) which accompanies SNS supplies.[36] In anticipation of the need to provide emergency medical services, 27 pallets[37] of medical supplies were pre-positioned on the ground prior to landfall.[38] On Sunday, August 28, these items were pulled from SNS with the mission assignment for some supplies to be delivered to the Superdome in New Orleans.[39] CDC also staffed and readied 12 teams of 20 people each to be deployed once the request from states for help was received.

CDC was responsible for deploying personnel and SNS assets, assisting state and local public health authorities with communicating food and water safety information, conducting disease surveillance, providing immunizations to displaced residents, and helping reestablish public health services in affected areas. Immediately following the hurricane, CDC's biggest concern was the risk of food-borne and water-borne illnesses.[40] CDC worked with the Louisiana Office of Public Health to assess reports on an outbreak of cholera and partnered with the Environmental Protection Agency and local health departments to assess environmental risks of toxins and chemicals in the water and air. CDC also worked with DOD to provide mosquito-control resources in most of the affected areas. Teams were deployed to both Louisiana and Mississippi on a mosquito spray mission.

CDC provided access to Influenza, Tetanus-Diptheria, Hepatitis A, and Hepatitis B vaccines to areas that were lacking them by coordinating the delivery, distribution, and administration of over three million doses of vaccine, with one million of the doses obtained from SNS.[41] When New Orleans lost its public health department due to layoffs, CDC sent over 100 medical personnel to help reestablish services, conduct surveillance, and improve communication.[42]

HHS Credentialed Volunteer Health Professionals

HHS designed a system that assists state and locals in verifying the credentials of volunteer healthcare workers. While stimulating the creation of over 900 medical teams, it also created confusion at the state level. Overall though, HHS was successful in mobilizing and credentialing medical professionals who volunteered in the Gulf coast following Hurricane Katrina. PHS set up a Katrina database to credential and verify medical professionals.

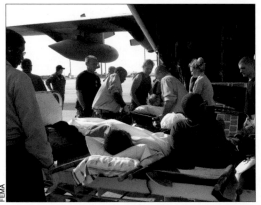

With the help of private companies, such as Kaiser Permanente, over 3,400 volunteers were processed and over 1,000 volunteers were deployed.[43] The database was linked to state databases and a national databank, allowing PHS to use existing information to help verify credentials. HHS also established a website (https://volunteer.hhs.gov) and toll-free number (1-866-KATMEDI) to help identify health care professionals and relief personnel to assist in Katrina relief efforts.[44]

The Medical Reserve Corps has a medical volunteer database where medical volunteers are pre-credentialed and can be activated within 24 hours. Carmona oversees this database as well as the response of the volunteers HHS calls upon. HHS was able to link its database to state databases in order to confirm volunteer credentials. Both HHS and Carmona stressed the importance of volunteers linking up with pre-existing rescue teams rather than acting independently. The Surgeon General's office likewise had generated a separate database for people who wanted to volunteer supplies or equipment.

Setting up a mechanism to allow individual medical personnel to volunteer was a useful tool initiated by HHS. The database was such a success that by September 3, an internal e-mail from HHS indicated "VOLUNTEERS SHOULD NO LONGER BE REFERRED TO KATRINARECOVERY@HHS.GOV, they should be directed to the https://volunteer.ccrf.hhs.gov/ and instructed to complete a volunteer application."[45] These credentialed volunteers heavily supplemented medical services in the Gulf coast region and were an important part of the medical response.

Substance Abuse and Mental Health Services Administration

As part of the public health and medical response, the Substance Abuse and Mental Health Services Administration (SAMHSA) mobilized personnel to support state mental health program directors in their efforts to conduct needs assessments, provide services, support ongoing administrative operations, access financial assistance and prepare for long-term assistance.[46] SAMHSA deployed Disaster Technical Assistance Center teams to provide information and supplement state and local disaster response planning, review disaster plans, conduct literature reviews, and offer mental health support services.[47] On Wednesday, September 7, SAMHSA created a "Crisis Hotline" to provide victims with 24 hour access to counseling and mental health resources.[48] Additionally, on Tuesday, September 13, HHS Secretary Micheal O. Leavitt announced $600,000 in emergency grants to Louisiana, Alabama, Texas, and Mississippi to ensure mental health assessment and crisis counseling are available in areas affected by Hurricane Katrina.[49] The states have used the money to support clinical assessment and provide psychiatric and nursing services, medications, brief interventions, crisis case management, and short-term residential support.

Finding: Poor planning and pre-positioning of medical supplies and equipment led to delays and shortages

Equipment and supplies were in heavy demand immediately following the hurricane and could not be quickly replenished by state, local, and federal resources. As detailed in other sections of this report, most shelters, hospitals, and flooded areas were without electricity and adequate supplies of potable water and food for days after Katrina made landfall. With only nominal amounts of medical supplies pre-positioned by FEMA and HHS, a great deal of medical provisions had to be supplied after Katrina made landfall. In areas like New Orleans, it took days to respond to the catastrophe and deliver medical supplies to the Superdome and Convention Center.

The delays were a result of poor planning. Obviously, supplies should be protected during the storm and staged in safe and secure locations for easy access post-landfall. Despite being unable to predict the magnitude of devastation from the storm, more supplies and equipment should have been pre-positioned and accessible to state and local officials immediately following landfall. Below is a detailed assessment of the different medical supplies and equipment that were provided to the Gulf coast in response to Hurricane Katrina.

States were heavily dependent on CDC/SNS for medical supplies

SNS 12-Hour Push Packages

As previously stated, the SNS is a national repository of antibiotics, chemical antidotes, antitoxins, life support medications, IV administration, airway maintenance supplies, and medical/surgical items.[50] The SNS has 12-hour Push Packages (Push Packs), caches of pharmaceuticals, antidotes, and medical supplies designed to provide response to a public health emergency within 12 hours. CDC estimates that each Push Pack costs $6 million, weighs almost 50 tons, and includes over 100 different kinds of supplies.[51] Push Packs are configured to be immediately loaded onto either trucks or commercial aircraft for the most rapid transportation. A Boeing 747 aircraft or seven tractor trailers are needed to move a

single Push Pack. A TARU accompanies the Push Pack to coordinate with state and local officials and ensure SNS assets are efficiently received and distributed upon arrival at the site.[52] TARU is simply a team of technical advisors to supervise the transfer of Push Pack contents to the receiving state.

Push Packs can be deployed at the request of a governor and independently of the NRP. Mississippi was the only state to request a Push Pack from CDC. The Push Pack arrived in Mississippi on Friday, September 2, four days after Katrina passed through the state.[53] As Amy testified, "within 12 hours of a call and my official request, eight tractor-trailers rolled into Mississippi loaded with medical supplies for affected Mississippi hospitals."[54] Push Packs were originally designed to respond to a bioterrorist attack, so they included items that were not relevant to treating the medical needs of Katrina evacuees. As a result, some of the Push Pack materials went unused. For this reason, CDC informed state and local officials they could request supplies and materials from SNS without requesting a full Push Pack.[55] Although Mississippi was the only state to request a Push Pack, other states still tapped resources and supplies from SNS. CDC figured out a way early on to prevent the waste of resources and ensure the most appropriate medical supplies were being allocated and delivered.

Also, CDC began to move towards more focused deliveries from existing inventories outside of SNS and acquired materials from private partners, as thousands of critical supplies were needed.[56] The Director for the Coordinating Office for Terrorism Preparedness and Emergency Response at CDC, Dr. Richard Besser, suggested creating Push Packs for major public health disruptions other than bioterrorism. This could ensure the most appropriate medical supplies and equipment arrive to the affected area first and would also prevent the waste of supplies that are not relevant to certain public health emergencies.[57]

Temporary medical operations staging areas were assembled and utilized

Federal Medical Shelters

Federal Medical Shelters (FMS) were a new component to the HHS hurricane response introduced following Katrina's landfall. These are rapidly deployed, minimal care medical kits capable of housing, triaging, and holding displaced patients. Each FMS is a 250-bed emergency shelter with a pharmaceutical suite, designed to provide care to patients for three days before the need to re-supply and re-stock materials.[58] An FMS is usually set up in a large space like an airport hanger or gymnasium with some provisions supplied by the SNS. FMS facilities are not designed for comprehensive community care needs; they are designed to offer last-resort care and support during situations in which normal, day-to-day operations are disrupted. FMS were developed to both augment hospitals and serve as quarantine stations.

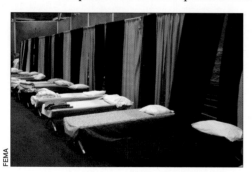

FEMA

Under the orders of Simonson, FMS began readying supplies and personnel on August 27, and one FMS was sent to Camp Beauregard, Louisiana on August 28.[59] From there, the FMS continued on to Louisiana State University (LSU) in Baton Rouge, and on the evening of Tuesday, August 30, the FMS at LSU began operations staffed by PHS commissioned Corps officers. FMS were also staged at Fort Polk Army Base in central Louisiana, Eglin Air Force Base near Pensacola, Florida, the Naval Air Station in Meridian, Mississippi, and the Mississippi Air National Guard Station in Jackson, Mississippi.[60] Additionally, the New Orleans Airport was the site of an FMS and helped provide acute medical care to evacuated patients from surrounding hospitals and the Superdome. The National Institutes of Health in Bethesda, Maryland set up a critical care facility for the sickest patients evacuated from the Gulf coast region.[61]

Essentially, these shelters were used to augment hospitals in the Gulf coast and help with the surge capacity of Katrina evacuees. Although Simonson thought the shelters were under-utilized in response to Katrina, he believed the exercise proved FMS are a valuable asset to be used in future public health emergencies. Despite this, only one was pre-positioned while most were readied and deployed in the days following landfall. Precious time was wasted because public health officials lacked initiative.

Prior to Katrina, FMS was only an idea on paper and had never been put into practice. The temporary medical shelters had never been tested in simulated drills or exercises, so it was initially unclear how FMS would perform and if their use would be effective.[62] Simonson said he believed HHS held two exercises to test FMS last year. He did not believe them to have been extensive or to have simulated disaster-like conditions.[63] The tests were held simply to time setup of facilities and processes. Despite the opportunity to truly test FMS at two federally mandated exercises, one in April 2005 and the other held in 2003, HHS did not seize the opportunity to assess and evaluate them.[64]

Expeditionary Medical Support Systems

The Air National Guard also supplied medical personnel and equipment to the Gulf coast region in response to Hurricane Katrina. Similar to FMS, Expeditionary Medical Support System's (EMEDS) mission is to provide front line, field hospital care in the event of a catastrophe or terrorist attack where local facilities are too overwhelmed to adequately treat patients.[65] EMEDS operate and function like brick and mortar hospitals and have operating rooms, dental, pharmacy and lab services, intensive care units, and other facilities and equipment. These mobile  hospitals have a 25-bed capacity and can be set up and ready to receive patients within 24 hours.[66] Traditionally, EMEDS are primarily for military personnel but, in response to Katrina, EMEDS were utilized to provide medical treatment to thousands of civilian victims.

STATE OF LOUISIANA

On Thursday, September 1, the Air Force deployed an EMEDS to provide medical assistance at the New Orleans Airport. Upon arrival, the EMEDS team set up and began

ssisting the DMATs who had already established a
make-shift facility.[67] At the New Orleans Airport EMEDS
teams helped other government agencies and civilian
medical teams provide treatment and health care to those
individuals transported to the airport. EMEDS teams
also assisted with aeromedical evacuations. According to
Colonel Richard Bachman, who directed the Air Force's
medical assistance in the Gulf region, "the EMEDS is to
set up rapidly, treat, stabilize, and then air evacuate people
out. It's a 25-bed hospital, but we took care of 2,500
people in two days, so the number of beds is essentially
irrelevant, because we weren't holding them and providing
long-term treatment….We never practiced hospital care in
an airport terminal without tents or [having] equipment
being overwhelmed by thousands of patients in the dark
without air conditioning."[68] Despite the unfavorable
conditions, EMEDS and other medical personnel stationed
at the airport completed an enormous patient movement
operation in a very brief window of time.

The Air Guard set up an additional mobile military
hospital at the Convention Center to take the place of
Charity Hospital and provide medical services to military
personnel while other facilities are out of commission.[69]
The Mississippi Air National Guard established an EMEDS
to augment services of the badly damaged Hancock
County Medical Center.[70] The EMEDS was set up in the
parking lot of that medical center and treated 47 patients
before it was demobilized in late September.

State Mobile Hospital Units

As one of the few self-contained mobile hospitals in the
U.S., the Carolina MED-1 mobile hospital was federalized
and deployed to Waveland, Mississippi. Carolina MED-
1 has complete emergency room and operating room
capabilities with 100 hospitals beds and functions exactly
like a brick and mortar hospital.[71] It was staffed by a team
of volunteers from the Carolina Medical Center, PHS
officers, and other medical volunteers. Waveland was
completely decimated by Katrina and was in desperate
need of medical facilities and personnel to treat residents.
In total, Carolina MED-1 treated almost 5,000 patients
and is considered one of the success stories of the medical
response to Hurricane Katrina. Amy described Carolina
MED-1 as an "invaluable asset to Mississippi's most hard
hit area in Hancock County."[72]

On Friday, September 2, Simonson wrote an e-mail
asking the state of Nevada to transport its mobile medical
facility (NV-1) to the New Orleans Airport.[73] He intended
NV-1 to serve as a federalized hospital facility to provide
medical care. Upon arrival at the airport, though, NV-1 was
told its assets were no longer needed and was eventually
directed to Gulfport, Mississippi where it was set up with
support staff from the Nevada Hospital Association, PHS
officers, and volunteer health professionals.[74] When asked
why he waited until September 2 to order NV-1 to New
Orleans, Simonson recalled there was some confusion as to
whether Mississippi had already requested use of NV-1.[75]
Simonson said ultimately NV-1 was used in Mississippi
and that it was difficult to initially assess where assets were
needed most.[76] In total, NV-1 saw almost 500 patients by
the end of September. Both of these mobile hospitals were
considered extremely valuable assets to the public health
response after Hurricane Katrina.

Finding: New Orleans was unprepared to provide evacuations and medical care for its special needs population and dialysis patients and Louisiana officials lacked a common definition of "special needs"

Defining "Special Needs"

New Orleans has the largest special needs population in
Louisiana. But the Louisiana Medical Director and State
Health Officer, Dr. Jimmy Guidry, and the Director of the
New Orleans Health Department, Dr. Kevin Stephens,
never offered a clear or consistent definition of "special
needs." According to Guidry, special needs people are

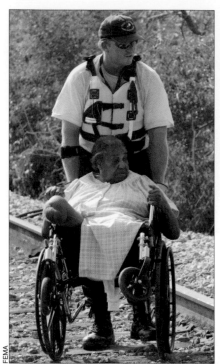

defined as not requiring hospital care, but not appropriate for a general population shelter either.[77] Stephens, on the other hand, indicated the state has a list outlining what criteria constitute a special needs patient. Among the most important, Stephens said, a patient with special needs is someone who requires intermittent electricity to sustain life.[78]

In fact, the list to which Stephens referred says the state of Louisiana has one set of criteria for classifying special needs persons, while Jefferson Parish has another.[79] The state defines Category I special needs persons as "patients who are acutely ill and need to be admitted to a hospital as a patient during an emergency evacuation of the area." Jefferson Parish classifies Category I special needs people as "patients who do not yet need to be admitted, but whose condition will probably deteriorate during an evacuation." These patients are to be taken to a trauma hospital. Aside from Jefferson Parish having a definition of Category I special needs that differs from the state's definition, confusion also arises in determining whether Jefferson Parish's criteria for Category II special needs people also applies to Louisiana. Category II is for "patients with limited needs and assistance who require special needs sheltering during an emergency evacuation of the area. These will be sent to non-trauma hospitals." Again, it is unclear whether this category is specific to Jefferson Parish or if it applies to the entire state.

Additionally, the Office of Emergency Preparedness (OEP) Director for Plaquemines Parish, Jesse St. Amant, was adamant that nursing home patients are considered "special needs patients."[80] Neither Guidry nor Stephens concurred, and nursing home patients are not listed within Louisiana or Jefferson Parish's special needs categories.[81]

Stephens stated New Orleans does not keep a list to identify special needs persons in advance of an emergency.[82] St. Amant, however, keeps a database of Plaquemines Parish's special needs patient population and interviews each patient about specific requirements for transportation, medications, and other special needs. He has pre-arranged contracts to address these needs and operates on an annual budget of approximately $300,000.[83] Stephens said New Orleans uses statistics from the health care community (such as the number of patients on dialysis) to reach its estimate that New Orleans has 1,000 special needs persons. Interestingly, a September 6 EOC Report indicated the state estimated *dialysis patients alone* were greater than this figure, saying the "State projects approximately 1,200 dialysis patients."[84] Additionally, the emergency coordinator in Jefferson Parish, which is an adjacent suburb of equivalent population to New Orleans, said they have a potential of 45,000 special needs patients—41,000 more patients than the estimate given by Stephens.[85]

Sheltering and Evacuating Special Needs Patients

State officials from the Governor's Office, the Department of Health and Hospitals (DHH), and the Department of Transportation and Development said all parishes, New Orleans included, were responsible for managing special needs evacuations.[86] New Orleans designated the Superdome as a special needs shelter, and Stephens said New Orleans' plan focuses on transporting special needs people from their homes to the Superdome. Special needs patients were to be collected throughout neighborhoods, using Rapid Transit Administration buses, and taken to the Superdome — despite the fact New Orleans does not keep a list of such patients.[87]

Guidry says the state bused 200 special needs people from the Superdome to LSU hospitals in Baton Rouge on Sunday before landfall.[88] According to state officials, the New Orleans plan never called for the use of school buses for evacuation, so in their opinion, criticisms about school buses lined up underwater and unused are unfair. Additionally, state officials say New Orleans never requested state assistance or buses to help with this effort (even though Guidry indicated the state did, in fact, assist in this manner).[89]

At the federal level, FEMA Deputy Federal Coordinating Officer Scott Wells said he interpreted special needs to be anyone needing assistance, whether they were impoverished or medically disabled.[90] To his knowledge, the state and the parishes made no significant attempts to evacuate special needs persons, although he indicated there may have been efforts to shelter them. The need to shelter special needs people in the Superdome showed the state and city had not taken steps (to which they had agreed during the Hurricane Pam exercise) to coordinate the movement and sheltering of these people farther north, away from the Gulf, Wells said.[91] The requirement for medical evacuations after the storm was an indication the pre-landfall evacuation was not successful.

Parish officials outside New Orleans also described their efforts to identify and evacuate special needs patients. According to the Plaquemines Parish sheriff, before the start of hurricane season, the parish solicits people to register if they have special needs for evacuation.[92] For Katrina, school buses were used to pick up and move these special needs registrants to a shelter in Belle Chasse, Louisiana. According to the Jefferson Parish emergency management director, their emergency operations plan also includes provisions for special needs people. The parish conducts a triage by telephone to determine which people with special needs require shelter within a parish hospital. Those who qualify are given a password for admittance. For Hurricane Katrina, there were 12,000 such people identified and sheltered.[93]

Dialysis Patients

Although dialysis patients were part of his definition of special needs persons, Stephens initially acknowledged the Superdome did not have the personnel, facilities, or supplies to provide dialysis.[94] Nor did it have food appropriate for diabetics. He said although dialysis patients were discouraged from going to the Superdome for this reason, several went anyway. Stephens further stated dialysis patients were among the first patients evacuated by helicopter.

In a subsequent meeting, however, Stephens gave completely different information. He said New Orleans has an evacuation plan specifically designed for dialysis patients so they know the medical facility to which they are assigned during an emergency.[95] He contradicted his early statement (dialysis patients *were* present in the Superdome) when he told the Select Committee the city's evacuation planning worked virtually perfectly, and no dialysis patients went to the Superdome. To his knowledge, Stephens said all dialysis patients were evacuated to their pre-assigned medical facilities. Of interest, the definition of Category II special needs persons, mentioned above for Jefferson Parish and possibly the entire state, includes "kidney dialysis" patients.[96]

The Superdome

Although Louisiana owns the Superdome, New Orleans runs it with assistance provided by the state, the Department of Health and Hospitals, and the Department of Social Services when needed.[97] The city is also responsible for drafting and implementing a plan for its use during an emergency.

AP PHOTO/BILL HABER

Since 1998, New Orleans has used the Superdome to shelter citizens with special needs during hurricanes.[98] For Hurricane Isadore in 2002, supplies were pre-staged, and the facility was staffed for 400 patients. Despite these preparations, though, only 27 special needs patients were identified and treated. During Hurricane Ivan, in September 2004, the Superdome was again opened as a special needs shelter and received just 32 patients.[99] The small number of special needs patients at the Superdome during these two hurricanes gave New Orleans officials a false indication of how many patients to expect for Hurricane Katrina. As a result, the city was ill-prepared.

The Superdome only contained enough personnel and supplies to care for approximately 1,000 people.

The city's plans call for the Superdome to house only special needs patients — not the general public.[100] For Hurricane Katrina, the special needs area was established in the southeast and southwest quadrant ballrooms, where some supplies were pre-positioned.[101] According to Superdome and Sports Arena General Manager Glen Menard, the Superdome's only "pre-positioned" supplies were goods leftover from a July event which the city requested remain in place.[102] Menard also said he placed two refrigerators and power generators in the southeast and southwest quadrants of the Superdome, which were designated as the medical care areas.

By the Sunday before landfall, over 400 special needs patients were evacuated to Baton Rouge using 10 para-transport vans and three city buses.[103] For the 8,000-10,000 people who remained in the Superdome, there were federal, state civilian, National Guard, and city medical personnel to provide care. But this contingent proved too small to provide care for the multitude of people who eventually sought refuge there. After the flooding, but before evacuation of the Superdome, it is estimated 23,000 people were sheltered there.[104]

As the crowd grew, it became increasingly difficult for the facility to care for special needs patients — the Superdome only contained enough personnel and supplies to care for approximately 1,000 people.[105] Section 132, next to the Superdome's First Aid Station, was used for evacuees in need of general medical attention.[106] With severe overcrowding of evacuees and flooding from roof leaks, the rest of the crowd was moved to elevated bleachers. Menard said eventually the special needs patients were further evacuated from the Superdome to the Sports Arena.

DMAT OK-1 departed from LSU to the Superdome on the evening of August 29.[107] Upon arrival, the National Guard told DMAT OK-1 it wasn't needed inside, redirecting the team to the Sports Arena, which is attached to the Superdome by two open-air walkways. DMAT OK-1 finally set up operations at the Sports Arena late that night and began receiving patients the morning

of August 30. The establishment of this DMAT came 36 hours after FEMA reported serious medical problems in the Superdome, including 400 people with special needs, 45 to 50 patients in need of hospitalization, and the rapid depletion of supplies.[108]

Evacuations finally began on August 31, and medical workers prepared records for their patients. In the end, though, those records were lost in the confusion. Evacuation of the Superdome concluded on September 3. Six people died in the Superdome—five for medical reasons and one from suicide.

Convention Center

Similar to the Superdome, the Ernest N. Morial Convention Center (Convention Center) is the property of the state of Louisiana. However, the Convention Center was never intended to serve as a shelter of any kind — special needs or otherwise — so there were no medical capabilities in place prior to the storm.[109] When asked by the media about conditions at the Convention Center, Brown said, "(W)e learned about that (Thursday) so I have directed that we have all available resources to get that convention center to make sure that they have food and water and medical care that they need."[110] The

AP PHOTO/ERIC GAY

Convention Center General Manager Warren Reuther, however, does not recall the provision of any medical assistance for the evacuees at his facility.[111]

Reuther is an appointee of Governor Kathleen Babineaux Blanco and says his responsibilities are to oversee the Convention Center and protect its assets.[112] Despite the fact the Convention Center was not intended as a shelter, evacuees seeking dry land arrived there, and upon finding the glass entry doors locked, broke in. Reuther estimates between 18,000 and 25,000, perhaps even 30,000 people, eventually gathered at the center.

A FAILURE OF INITIATIVE

During the storm, Reuther and approximately half a dozen of his public safety staff remained in place, attempting in vain to maintain order as evacuees filled almost every area of the building.[113] The Convention Center was quickly overwhelmed, running on reduced emergency power until all power was lost when fuel ran out on the night of August 30. Public bathrooms became overloaded, and problems were compounded by loss of water pressure. Hallways became the de-facto toilets. Walk-in refrigerators were emptied on the floor, and many evacuees began bringing their own food and alcohol into the building. Almost 32,000 chairs were broken or lost, 30,000 square yards of carpeting were destroyed, and the facility's infrastructure was damaged. Gunshots were reportedly heard, and Reuther and his staff were forced to hide from the crowds.

Evacuations at the Convention Center began Friday, September 2 and continued until Sunday, September 4. Despite Reuther's assertion medical assistance never

arrived, a DOD e-mail indicated medical teams were established and operating at the Convention Center on Saturday, September 3.[114] Medical needs were unclear because of poor communication and situational awareness. The number of evacuees continued to increase at the Convention Center as evacuations at the Superdome concluded. People left at the Superdome were directed to the Convention Center, where they would later be evacuated. Throughout the ordeal, Reuther saw no deliveries of food, water, or other supplies. At one point, he called Blanco but received no answer. He also never saw Nagin throughout the ordeal.[115]

Doctor's First-hand Account

Dr. Gregory Henderson is a Tulane University and Vanderbilt University School of Medicine graduate. He lives in New Orleans and is the Associate Chairman of the Ochsner Clinic Foundation Department of Pathology and Laboratory Medicine. He was set to begin his new job at Ochsner on September 1.[116]

Henderson happened to be attending a physician leader retreat for Ochsner staff on Friday, August 26 and Saturday, August 27, at the Ritz-Carlton hotel on Canal Street when the meeting was cut short because of the impending landfall of Hurricane Katrina.[117] He evacuated his family to Jackson, Mississippi and chose to stay at the hotel so he could remain close to their home.

By the morning of Tuesday, August 30, the Ritz-Carlton was surrounded by three to five feet of water and Canal Street was flooding.[118] There was a hotel announcement that anyone who needed medical care should report to the hotel's French Quarter Bar. Fortunately there was another medical conference involving medical specialists (seven physicians, a physician's assistant, and pharmacists) taking place at the hotel. The impromptu medical team had already started to organize a list of medicines and supplies they might need. Looking outside and talking to the police, he realized looting was occurring outside the hotel, and it appeared the looters were armed. Henderson, along with a family practice physician, pharmacist, and two officers from the New Orleans Police Department (NOPD), waded across Canal Street through waist-high water to the Walgreens pharmacy across the street. They were able to break into the pharmacy and began stuffing insulin, drugs, and medical supplies into plastic garbage bags. There was a confrontation with the looters, who were held back at gunpoint by the officers. Henderson was able to carry three bags of supplies back to the hotel.

He set up a make-shift clinic at the hotel for the next 24 hours. The majority of the patients were seeking prescription refills, a lot of which he did not have.[119] He subsequently opened another "clinic" when NOPD moved their operational headquarters and command and control center from the Ritz-Carlton to the Sheraton hotel across the street.

He was told by NOPD that Tulane, University, and Charity Hospitals were taking on water and basically inoperable and was asked by an NOPD captain if he could stay and take care of several hundred police officers who had set up camp at the Sheraton.[120] Henderson was dispatched with a team of armed officers and took additional supplies, including insulin, from a second Walgreens pharmacy. Many patients Henderson treated had "generalized anxiety disorders, not unexpected as most of the police had lost homes and some had lost family members and yet still were on the job." There

People were trapped inside hospitals, with a banner hanging from Charity Hospital that read, "Stop the lying and get us the hell out of here."

Methodist Hospital uses the Hurricane Preparedness Plan established by the New Orleans Office of Emergency Preparedness.[136] This plan suggests hospitals may begin evacuation preparations when there is a slow-moving Category 3, a Category 4, or a Category 5 hurricane within 72 hours of landfall (and is predicted to make landfall within 100 miles of New Orleans). The CEO or his designee has the authority to call for evacuation. Actual evacuations may begin up to 60 hours in advance. At 60 hours, the plan says, "Make arrangements for at least two flat-bottom type boats in the event of severe flooding conditions" and to fuel vehicles to capacity. The announcement of total or partial evacuation is called, if applicable, no later than 24 hours in advance. The Director of Facility Services, 12 hours prior to landfall, is to "ensure emergency vehicles and boats are in position and ready for immediate use."

There is also a section of the overall Hurricane Preparedness Plan devoted entirely to evacuations (The Hurricane Evacuation Plan) which states, "…evacuation from the Hospital will be a 'last resort' measure and will be carried out only when a mandatory evacuation is directed by the appropriate authority, or when a situation arises which places patients and staff unquestionably in harm's way. The threat of a direct strike by a major hurricane certainly creates such a situation, and evacuation may be necessary to protect the safety of patients and attending staff."[137]

If evacuation takes place prior to a hurricane, Methodist has written transfer agreements with two hospitals outside the major hurricane danger zone.[138] This section provides the contact information for Lifeguard Transportation Service, Inc. and Acadian Ambulance and Air Med Services — the two companies with whom the hospital has written transportation agreements. If these services are overwhelmed, the plan instructs the hospital to call the New Orleans Office of Emergency Preparedness.

As illustrated by these plans, hospitals and VAMCs lacked sufficient guidance for if and when they should evacuate their patients in anticipation of a hurricane. They also did not follow the limited guidance they did have.

Finding: New Orleans hospitals, VAMC, and medical first responders were not adequately prepared for a full evacuation of medical facilities

After New Orleans flooded, city medical centers needed to be evacuated. On September 2, *Good Morning America* showed the desperation of people trapped inside hospitals, reporting on a banner hanging from Charity Hospital that read, "Stop the lying and get us the hell out of here."[139] Flood waters prevented hospitals from receiving supplies o[r] personnel, and some private hospitals, such as Methodist, say medical supplies and fuel tanks being airlifted to them by their corporate headquarters were being intercepted by FEMA.[140] Many hospital emergency power generators were located at ground level or lower (often below sea level) and were subject to flooding. To make matters worse, fuel pumps were often placed at ground level, and fuel storage tanks (with limited fuel capacity) were frequently below ground level.[141] Three acute care hospitals in the New Orleans area remained operational, four maintained some limited function, and 21 were not operational, closed, or evacuated. In hospitals that lost power like Methodist, pulmonary ventilator systems and other medic[al] equipment requiring electricity became inoperable. Patien[ts] requiring ventilators were sustained by hand pumps.[142]

AP PHOTO/BILL HABER

State and FEMA urban search and rescue teams were se[nt] to help the hospitals evacuate, but they were intercepted by people trapped in th[e] floodwaters and on rooftops.[143] While Guidry said hospital evacuations were a huge logistical succes[s]

– they evacuated 12,000 patients by Saturday, September 3 — they did not seem like a huge success to the many patients awaiting rescue.

Hospital and VAMC Evacuation: Their Stories and Timelines of Events

Evacuations from VAMCs for Hurricane Katrina have received mostly favorable attention, particularly in comparison to the evacuation difficulties encountered by other New Orleans hospitals and shelters. "We had people on ventilators, we had liver patients, ambulatory patients, and every patient that we evacuated from every one of our facilities made it through this evacuation," VA Secretary R. James Nicholson said.[144]

On Monday, August 29, the VAMC Biloxi domiciliary patients and nine members of the medical staff were evacuated to VAMC Tuscaloosa, leaving 904 patients, staff, and family members sheltered in VAMC Biloxi.[145]

 VAMC Gulfport patients were transferred to other facilities before the storm made landfall. VAMC New Orleans did not mass evacuate prior to the storm, and during the two days that followed, August 30 and 31, its evacuation plans were activated. Five five-ton trucks were used in cooperation with DOD's air transport staff and HHS to evacuate 98 patients to the New Orleans airport on September 1. From there, the patients were flown to the Houston, Jackson, and Alexandria VAMCs. At this time, efforts were also underway to evacuate the remaining 94 patients and 367 staff and family members at VAMC New Orleans. By Friday, September 2, all patients, staff, and family members were evacuated from VAMC New Orleans.

Donald Smithburg, CEO of LSU Health Sciences Center/Health Care Services Division, and approximately 20 members of his staff provided a detailed account of the evacuation of their facilities, Charity Hospital (Charity) and University Hospital (University).[146] Smithburg went to Baton Rouge to staff the state EOC on the Saturday before the storm, and on Sunday at 7:00 a.m., he activated

Code Grey but decided against calling for evacuation.

At 5:30 a.m. on Monday morning, University lost electrical power. Charity followed, losing power at 8:00 a.m.[147] Both hospitals began using their emergency generators just two to three minutes after the power failures. Charity's generators and electrical equipment were located in the basement, and LSU officials said they knew Charity would probably lose emergency power if severe flooding occurred. The waters continued rising over the course of Monday, and late that night, Charity lost its emergency generators. Unlike Charity, University's emergency generator and electrical equipment were housed on the second floor, considered high enough to avoid flooding and low enough to avoid wind damage. University lost emergency power anyway, and both hospitals were left in darkness and without the means to care for their patients.

On Tuesday, August 30, Louisiana Wildlife and Fisheries evacuated nine of the 17 Intensive Care Unit (ICU) patients at University and four from the Charity campus.[148] Evacuation efforts were suspended, however, due to reports of gunfire and impending nightfall. On Wednesday, August 3, at 3:00 a.m., LSU received a request from the state OEP to prepare a patient roster. Officials were told patients should be triaged to red, yellow, and green status (red, critical; green, stable), and LSU staff gathered the necessary information manually. Later that morning, the state OEP notified them via the HEAR system to prepare for evacuation, but evacuation aid never arrived. At 11:00 a.m., Charity was notified its evacuation was to begin in 30 minutes, but by 4:00 p.m., they were still awaiting word from the National Guard regarding potential evacuation. That evening, the hospitals were notified the water level was too high for evacuation via the National Guard's five-ton trucks.

Further complications arose on Thursday, August 31 when LSU was told evacuation orders were on hold due to rumors of violence and potential harm to rescue workers.[149] An e-mail between HHS employees that morning confirms this: "Patient evacuation has been hampered by security issues on patient movement. It is unsafe for patient movement to continue without security provided."[150] LSU was told evacuations would resume after the arrival of federal troops. Smithburg said the Coast Guard and National Guard were evacuating people in the most immediate danger, so LSU was not a top priority.

FEMA

Evacuations for University and Charity patients and staff began on Friday, September 1 at 8:00 a.m. and noon, respectively. The U.S. Coast Guard arrived by helicopter. Patient evacuations were facilitated by the Coast Guard, Louisiana and Florida Wildlife and Fisheries, NOPD, and state police. HHS e-mails that morning also indicate, "today's priorities are Charity and University Hospitals."

A total of 167 patients were evacuated from University and approximately 200 from Charity.[151] LSU indicated that all of these patients were sent with paper records and three patients died due to the storm; two were ventilator patients who died on the roof of the hospital during evacuations.

Larry Graham, CEO for Pendleton Memorial Methodist Hospital (Methodist), monitored the storm on his own and stated he received no calls from the city or state government.[152] On Friday at 5:00 p.m., he believed the storm would miss New Orleans, but on Saturday, he realized there was going to be a problem. He began contacting all hospitals with which Methodist had transfer agreements, but none would admit patients due to concerns about how the storm might affect them. All of Methodist's agreements are with hospitals in Louisiana or Mississippi because all patient transport is handled via ground ambulance. He likewise indicated Methodist is a "for-profit" hospital, meaning it does not receive FEMA funding and is responsible for the costs of airlifting patients. Even with such funding, however, Graham is not sure evacuation measures are practical. In anticipation of Hurricane Ivan, Methodist evacuated over 30 ICU patients over a total of 45 hours. However by Saturday, August 27, Methodist did not have time for an evacuation of this scale.

Methodist housed a total of 750 people during Hurricane Katrina, including 130 patients.[153] Twenty-eight were ICU patients with 12 patients on ventilators, and 16 were dialysis patients. Chalmette Medical Center (Chalmette), Methodist's sister hospital located 12 miles away, evacuated its six ICU patients to Methodist. The remaining people at Methodist were staff, family, and people who had sought shelter in the hospital from the storm.

Like University and Charity, Methodist's emergency generators failed after the storm.[154] The generators were located on the roof, but the fuel pumps had flooded. Graham cut power in all areas that were deemed "not critical," and they hand-ventilated patients requiring oxygen. The next day, they began hand-carrying fuel to the generators. Chalmette's generators were located on ground level. At the time, however, Tim Coffey, the then CEO of Chalmette, believed the facility was sound.

On Sunday, August 28, ambulances were supposed to be en route to the hospital, but Graham said they were commandeered by government officials.[155] Methodist's parent company, Universal Health Services, Inc. (UHS), located in King of Prussia, Pennsylvania, was sending the hospital supplies, including fuel and water, via helicopter. The supplies never arrived because, as Methodist and UHS believe, FEMA intercepted the cargo. Army officers and FEMA officials arrived on Tuesday, and Graham informed them he needed assistance with evacuations. The officials assured him they would return but never did. Throughout the ordeal, Methodist had the assistance of 12 National Guardsmen as well as police forces that stayed for security reasons. Post-Katrina evacuations started taking place on Wednesday, August 31 because Methodist's corporate office contracted with private companies. The difficulties the hospital encountered were still enormous, though, as a September 2 e-mail from a Methodist doctor to HHS staff indicates:

"Contrary to what has been reported on the news, Methodist Hospital, including Albert and Maxine Barrocas have not been evacuated, and the details are grisly. FEMA has been intercepting supplies sent to the hospital, and patient and staff evacuations have essentially ceased.

If anyone can help bring attention to this problem, please help us. Below are some facts related to us by the staff at the hospital during one of the few occasions we have been able to talk to them.

- 600 People in hospital
- 13 patients on gurneys
- Staff is dehydrating
- FEMA is DIVERTING support being sent in by UHS (owners of hospital) away from the hospital

- Temperature is 110 degrees with humidity
- NO fuel left to operate th!!e hospital tower (sic)
- NO communication with National Guard to coordinate evacuation of patients
- Having to feed 500+ non-patient refugees — they are very close to rioting for the balance of food water and supplies
- NO power, NO communication
- Everything is manual — no xray — running out of supplies
- Patients are on the 2nd floor and 3rd floor — having to carry patients up the stairs and helicopters didn't come back
- Without power, the ventilator dependant patients are being manually bagged in 1 hour shifts by staff
- Refusing to take gurney patients
- FEMA is commandeering all supplies and all private efforts to get supplies including fuel, food, water
- Governor is misrepresenting what is going on
- Snakes in hospital
- Rashes on staff from water
- Losing nurses as result of dehydration
- Need FEMA to land on roof and prove what they are saying is correct
- No security—uprising for f!!ood, water and supplies (sic)
- Governor did not allow for the evacuation of hospitals and now won't help
- Uprising of refugees"[156]

Graham said the evacuations at Methodist were completed late on Friday, September 2.[157] He also stressed that mid-way through the evacuation, he learned patients who were triaged to the New Orleans Airport were not receiving adequate care. He began withholding patients who were supposed to be taken to the airport because Methodist was in a position to provide them with better care. He cited this as a primary "critical issue" — the evacuation of patients to locations unable to provide medical care. Coffey added that Chalmette doctors who went to the New Orleans Airport to offer their services were turned away by DMATs who said they were not credentialed in the NDMS physician database.

On September 20, an official from Tenet Healthcare (Tenet), Memorial Hospital's (Memorial) parent company, told CNN the National Guard evacuated some patients from Memorial before the flooding began on Tuesday, August 30.[158] The next morning, Wednesday, Tenet reported to CNN that it asked New Orleans local authorities for assistance in evacuating critically ill patients but was told it would have to hire private companies. Later that day, Tenet says local authorities and good samaritans provided limited assistance with evacuations by boat. On Thursday, helicopters hired by Tenet airlifted approximately 400 patients, employees, and evacuees from Memorial to another Tenet-owned hospital in Slidell, Louisiana. Tenet indicated flights were suspended overnight after reports of sniper fire, but evacuations resumed, and were completed, by the end of the day on Friday, September 2.

Louis Armstrong International Airport

The medical operation at the New Orleans Airport was chaotic due to lack of planning, preparedness, and resources

After patients were evacuated from medical facilities, most were taken to the New Orleans Airport, which served as a hospital for the sick, a refuge for thousands, and the hub of medical evacuations and airlifts.[159] There were two separate missions at the airport. The first was attending to the medial needs of evacuees and the second was processing evacuees not needing medical attention. According to OR-2 DMAT, evacuees who needed medical treatment were triaged, treated, and prepared for transports. People not requiring medical

AP PHOTO/RON HAVIV/VII

care were processed and prepared for transport to shelters in other states by commercial aircraft. In total, over 21,000 displaced persons not requiring medical care were evacuated.

"Overnight, we turned New Orleans' airport into the busiest helicopter base in the entire world. At any given time, there were at least eight to 10 helos off-loading on the tarmac, each filled with 10 to 40 survivors at a time, with 10 circling to land . . . It was a non-stop, never-ending, 24-hour-a-day operation," said Dr. Hemant Vankawala, a member of the Dallas DMAT deployed to the New Orleans Airport.[160]

Medical patients arrived by truck, bus, ambulance, and helicopter with little or no information or records about their conditions. The medical personnel at the New Orleans Airport were challenged by the sheer number of patients and the lack of information about patient medical histories. By August 31, three DMATs had arrived at the airport.[161] Eventually, eight DMATs would be stationed at the New Orleans Airport to help provide care during patient movement operations in New Orleans.[162] The Air Force also deployed an EMEDS team, on Thursday, September 1, to augment the medical assistance operation in place at the airport.[163] These EMEDS teams also assisted with aeromedical evacuations.

An OR-2 DMAT after-action report described medical facilities established in the upper and lower levels of the west terminal of the airport.[164] These facilities were supplied and staffed by DMATs and PHS officers. The flow of patients was constant, and it is estimated the entire medical operation at the New Orleans Airport treated approximately 3,000 patients who were eventually evacuated by military aircraft to other facilities. Some DMATs believe the number was much greater — as high as 6,000 to 8,000 patients.[165]

Despite the treatment and evacuation of thousands, the medical operation at the New Orleans Airport was chaotic due to lack of planning, preparedness, and resources.

FEMA officials did not conduct an adequate assessment of the situation before deploying DMATs. Upon arrival, many teams were confused about where to place assets and how to integrate into the existing operation. Many DMATs arrived before their cache of supplies, limiting their ability to do their work. According to Vankawala, medical personnel were operating with a limited amount of supplies and a generator with only partial power. "All we could do was provide the barest amount of comfort care. We watched many, many people die. We practiced medical triage at its most basic — black tagging the sickest people and culling them from the masses so that they could die in a separate area," Vankawala said.[166]

"We practiced medical triage at its most basic — black tagging the sickest people and culling them from the masses so that they could die in a separate area," Vankawala said.

TX-1 and TX-4 DMATs, which were among the first to arrive, had equipment that was not updated and could not link together other critical equipment, such as ventilators.[167] Similarly, one team member from OR-2 DMAT observed "five different models/brands of glucose monitors, all using their own proprietary test strips that weren't interchangeable. The CA-4 cache, which was current, arrived later and supplemented these caches."[168]

OR-2 DMAT reached the conclusion that, "there didn't appear to be a clear plan for dealing with the approximately 25,000 evacuees who arrived at the airport there was insufficient food, water, and sanitation."[169] One team member said evacuees were being taken from a dehumanizing experience (flooding and rescue) and placed into an equally dehumanizing environment at the New Orleans Airport.

Finding: The government did not effectively coordinate private air transport capabilities for the evacuation of medical patients

The Association of Air Medical Services (AAMS), comprised of 300 mostly private air transportation providers, represents 85 percent of all hospital transport capabilities.[170] In coordination with the Center for Transportation Injury Research, AAMS has a database called the Atlas and Database of Air Medical Services (ADAMS)— a web-based, interactive database listing these air medical services (rotary and fixed wing aircraft) and receiving hospitals. The database is updated annually, funded by the Federal Highway Administration, and receives technical support from the National Highway Traffic Safety Administration. In response to Hurricane Katrina, there was only one governmental request for access to ADAMS.[171]

Nevertheless, AAMS companies provided support for medical evacuations of both hospitals and nursing homes in Hurricane Katrina's aftermath. They were not used for pre-landfall evacuations and provided most of their resources without official contracts with hospitals.[172] Authorities were slow to establish a system for filtering evacuation requests. Confusion and indecision about evacuations led to delays.

AAMS said FEMA did not help their efforts.[173] On the morning of August 30, FEMA tasked Carla Brawley, a Department of Transportation contractor, to find and secure air medical resources.[174] Brawley contacted Acadian Air Ambulance (Acadian) flight coordinator, Mike Sonnier, to request resources. Acadian is the largest air ambulance provider in Louisiana. An AAMS after-action report stated,

> "According to Mr. Sonnier, sometime later that morning the National Guard Air Boss (name unknown) contacted Mr. Sonnier at Acadian and

AP PHOTO/UNIVERSITY OF ALABAMA AT BIRMINGHAM, STEVE WOOD

tasked him to serve as his civilian equivalent. Mr. Sonnier and Acadian air ambulance was then tasked with coordinating missions into and out of New Orleans airspace, coordinating requests for air evacuations from many of the New Orleans area hospitals, and also serving as the main contact between civilian providers and the lone FAA contracting officer that was tasked for this job by the Department of Transportation for FEMA."

By the end of the day, approximately 50 medical helicopters and 13 fixed-wing aircraft were in New Orleans.[175] While the first air evacuation took five hours, coordinators were in place to expedite the process on Wednesday. Over the next 96 hours, approximately 2,000 air medical evacuations were coordinated through AAMS members.[176] Acadian estimates it was responsible for 800 of these evacuations.[177] AAMS members accomplished these evacuations despite difficulties in communication and coordination. Poor use of assets and lack of coordination prevented additional evacuations. AAMS estimates it could have been able to move up to 7,000 patients if a better system had been in place.[178] "The first 72 hours was chaos," said one AAMS member.[179]

The majority of requests came directly from hospitals, such as Tulane University Hospital and Charity Hospital, because they were not receiving help through the Emergency Management Assistance Compact (EMAC).[180] On August 29, Hospital Corporation of America Division President Dave Smith requested AirHeart Air Ambulance of Sacred Heart Health System help with evacuations of Tulane. Smith said fuel for the generators was running low and floodwaters were approaching the facility.[181]

The following morning, Tuesday, Tulane University Hospital requested assistance with transporting "two specialty pediatric patients" from New Orleans to Little

Rock, Arkansas.[182] The Arkansas Children's Hospital and its affiliate, Angel One Transport, responded along with other children's hospitals.[183] Fixed wing aircraft were provided by two hospitals in Texas: Texas Children's Hospital in Houston and Cook Children's Hospital in Fort Worth, and Mercy Children's Hospital in Kansas City, Missouri. Additionally, Miami Children's Hospital provided a helicopter to assist with the evacuation of "13 critically ill PICU (Pediatric Intensive Care Unit) patients and family members." Tulane also directly contacted Florida-based Air Methods Lifenet Division that same day for evacuation assistance. In addition to these requests, personal networking also proved valuable in the absence of formal agreements. On August 31, a doctor who lived in Hawaii and had attended Tulane University, contacted a colleague at Tulane University Hospital. Together, these two doctors coordinated the assistance of Hawaii Air Ambulance. AAMS donated helipad coordinators to aid in efficiency and were able to evacuate 200 patients by noon on Friday, September 2.[184]

Compared to New Orleans, AAMS involvement in Mississippi was markedly different. Air Methods Lifenet Division summarized their experience in Mississippi by saying, "During the entire Katrina experience in Mississippi, there was no federal command and control or coordination of resources across the whole area. Attempts to coordinate with FEMA rescue operation center in Jackson, Mississippi were rebuffed by federal officials there who stated clearly that all air evacuations in Mississippi, medical and USAR, had been federalized. And that no civilian medical aircraft were needed."[185]

John Dickerson, the FEMA EOC representative in Mississippi, declined offers from one AAMS agency to provide 25 helicopters to Mississippi. The Mississippi EOC had requested support, through EMAC, from Florida air transport agencies.[186] Johnny Delgado, program manager of Baptist Health South Florida, Baptist Health Air Transport, and a Board Member of AAMS, had a crew and was ready to fulfill the request. They were en route to Gulfport, the meeting point for air medical evacuation support agencies, but were turned back. Dickerson told them because the response was now federal, private agencies are not allowed to assist. However, a different AAMS company dealt with the Mississippi EOC directly and was able to provide support to the state.[187]

Finding: Hospital and VAMC emergency plans did not adequately prepare for communication needs

The Biloxi, Mississippi VAMC Emergency Plan states when a hurricane is in the Gulf of Mexico and is 24 hours or less away from landfall, the Facilities Management Services (FMS) "will distribute emergency communications equipment. The facility's HF/VHF radios will be ready to be set up in the Director's Conference Room."[188] This part of the emergency plan does not, however, indicate which FMS team member is responsible for the distribution, including what specific equipment is to be distributed and to whom. Instead, the plan says FMS should develop its own Service Supplemental Hurricane Plan (SSHP) to address these issues.

The SSHP lists communication preparations and available equipment.[189] In addition to providing emergency communications equipment, the FMS is responsible for ensuring there are adequate linens, the Recreation Hall is set up as an employee shelter, and evacuation services are in place. VAMC Biloxi says its FMS team typically includes four to six people (two or three craftsman and two or three housekeepers) to handle this wide range of operations.[190]

The plan also lists the VAMC's communications capabilities but does not mention satellite phones discussed previously in the SSHP. It relies "primarily upon the use of telephones" and focuses on a telephone system designed exclusively for internal communications.[191] Two-way radios are designated for specific personnel, but the plan recognizes limits to radio capabilities, stating, "The limited number of radios and single voice transmission, however, combine to impose several restrictions." The radios are intended as back-up to the inter-office telephone system. The VAMC plan relies on landline telephones and the Hospital Emergency Area Radio (HEAR) Network System to communicate with the Emergency Medical Services (EMS) and outside world.

The VAMC New Orleans Emergency Management Plan also depends on the HEAR Network System for communication with area hospitals and ambulances.[192] The Chief of Police Services is to maintain a "pool" of Motorola radios, the exact number of which is not specified but will be used upon activation of the emergency plan. Radios should be distributed to 11 staff members, all of whom are designated in the plan. The plan also indicates radios will operate for about eight hours before needing to be charged and provides the frequency at which these radios operate. The failure response section does not mention potential power failures, and in turn, the inability to recharge the radios. Additionally, no section of the plan addresses when the two-way radios should be distributed in preparation for the storm. In fact, the Hurricane section of the plan fails to mention radios or refer the reader to the communications chapter.

The Veterans Health Information Systems and Technology Architecture (VISTA) Contingency Plan cites hurricanes as a "high probability" threat.[193] A telecommunications contingency plan included within the VISTA plan lists responsibilities and procedures for personnel in charge of communications during a telephone system failure. This plan indicates hand-held radios and/or cell phones will be used if landlines do not work and details who distributes the radios as well as who or what areas receives them. A total of 26 areas within VMAC New Orleans are to be provided with two-way radios (one radio per area), but there is no indication of how these radios should stay charged in the event power is lost. Additionally, "a cache of cellular phones are maintained by CIM Service Line Director . . . . " The exact number is not specified, but the plan states eight areas are designated as first priority to receive cellular telephones." As with the two-way radios, there is no planning for how to keep these cellular phones charged in the event that power is lost.

Charity and University use the Emergency Management Manual for the Medical Center of Louisiana at New Orleans.[194] The hospitals depend on two-way radios, cell phones, HEAR Radio, HRSO Radio, 800MZ Radio, and HAM Radio links for internal and external communications backup.

Methodist's Disaster and Emergency Preparedness Plan charges the Hurricane Preparedness Control Center with establishing and maintaining emergency communications.[195] The control center is assigned special telephone extensions as well as backup telephone numbers in case landlines fail. HEAR radio equipment, including the backup system, should be tested when a storm is more than 72 hours away. At 72 hours, the director of Facility Services is to designate the radio

operator's availability and "ensure operator adequately (sic) trained." At 60 hours before landfall, battery supplies are checked. When the storm is 24 hours from landfall, the director of Facility Services provides the maintenance supervisor with a two-way radio unit. When the storm is 12 hours away, the director of Facility Services should "position emergency equipment supplies and prepare for immediate operations" and conduct a "final check of the emergency power system." He or she is also supposed to ensure the radio operator is on duty and has contact on the HEAR system.

Methodist's plan takes into account the potential for flooding as a result of a Category 3, Category 4, or Category 5 hurricane stating, "Flooding conditions to some extent can almost certainly be expected to accompany a hurricane.[196] Several recent studies and surveys by hurricane forecasting experts indicate that the entire New Orleans area is extremely vulnerable to "catastrophic flooding" as a result of a major storm." If flooding is predicted or reported, the CEO is instructed to shut down telephone communications equipment and reassign communications attendants to the Control Center.[197] As such, all communications would obviously be lost.

These hospital and VAMC emergency plans lack a clear communications section, often leaving unanswered questions about what communications capabilities are in place, who is responsible for the equipment, and how to respond if power is lost. As a result, Gulf coast medical facilities were left without appropriate equipment or a proper understanding of how to implement an effective emergency communications plan.

Finding: Following Hurricane Katrina, the inability of VAMC New Orleans and hospitals to communicate impeded their ability to ask for help

Hospital executives said in Katrina's aftermath, hospital emergency area radio HEAR systems simply did not work.[198] Cell phones worked occasionally and allowed them to get in touch with the Louisiana Hospital Association, which in turn contacted the OEP on their behalf. The primary source of information was

> *Hospital executives said in Katrina's aftermath, hospital emergency area radio system (HEAR) simply did not work.*

television.[199] In an interview with CNN on September 30, Dr. Albert Barrocas, a physician at Methodist, said, "We were trapped, communications was a big issue. The fact that we could not bring family and patients together, a lot of them were separated. The majority were separated. We did not even know where these people were going to."[200]

The Director of VA Veterans Integrated Service Network 16 (VISN 16), Robert Lynch, tells a similar story. "There was no plan in Biloxi and New Orleans. Hard-working people did a lot of workarounds with a lot of creativity. We're going to learn from that," he said.[201] VISN 16 lost communications through its telephone landlines, operated by Sprint, during the storm. Lynch indicated that satellite phones worked sporadically and only when outside. In Biloxi, reports indicate only one cellular tower remained, and cell phone users could only make calls — not receive them. The VA worked around the communication failures by establishing a schedule for employees to be outside with satellite phones.[202]

Smithburg said that on Sunday at 7:00 a.m., the hospital set up an incident command center in its board room for communications.[203] The following day, the hospital went to Code Grey, and HAM operators arrived at the hospital. LSU had a point of contact at the OEP, but after the storm, LSU couldn't receive information from the OEP or FEMA. On Monday, August 29, Smithburg reported that Nextel and cell phone service were temporarily lost on the University campus, and text messaging was "intermittent."

Smithburg cited inadequate Health Resources and Services Administration grant funding as the primary reason for communication failure and said the LHA receives the federal grant money and allots it to Louisiana hospitals.[204] While the grants were helpful for supplying Motorola phones and a HAM network, he believes the funding for LSU was disproportionately small in comparison to its needs and patient load.

In the days following Hurricane Katrina, Gulf coast hospitals and VAMCs were responsible for hundreds of patients, some of whom were in critical condition. Without necessary communications capabilities, these facilities were almost completely isolated from first responders and the outside world. Incapacitated and without supplies, many struggled to provide care and keep patients alive until help arrived.

Finding: Medical responders did not have adequate communications equipment or operability

Inadequate communications and situational awareness among and within federal agencies contributed to a diminished understanding of the health needs of affected populations

On October 20, Stephens told the *Associated Press*, "Anything that could go wrong in communications went wrong."[205] Interviews with health officials and countless e mails from ESF-8 agency personnel support his statement. Immediately following Hurricane Katrina, cell phones and landlines were not working, blackberries were not dependable (and in some cases, unavailable), and satellite telephone capabilities were not sufficient.

In preparation for Hurricane Katrina, Stephens oversaw the placement of an incident command trailer inside the Superdome.[206] Immediately following the storm, he said landlines, the only mode of communication for his team, worked just five to 10 percent of the time. By Wednesday, cell phones began working intermittently but not enough to meet their communication needs, and despite his initial preparations, Stephens said these communication failures "weren't anticipated at all."

Colonel Kenneth K. Knight, Chief of the Air Force Medical Operations Center presented a timeline that showed similar difficulties — its communication systems were inoperable until September 1.[207] On this date, the Air Force medical response timeline says there were, "Few working landlines and cell phone success [was] spotty." It was not until four days after the storm, on September 2, the "cell phone network [was] improving."

Likewise, Colonel Falk, an Air National Guard Surgeon cited communications as the number one area needing nprovement.[208] Both the Air National Guard and Army National Guard experienced almost a total failure in communications. The Army satellite system was not working, and personal cell phones (service provided by Verizon) were the only means of contact. Likewise, the National Guard Bureau's "After Action Review" indicates communication failures adversely affected situational awareness. It states, "Lack of situational awareness was caused largely by the loss of communications. The lack of communications and difficulties with interoperability of equipment between forces as well as between the military and civilian leadership also hampered the rapid generation of EMAC requests. Poor communications also resulted in a lack of visibility of available assets in nearby states."[209]

National Guard Bureau Chief Lieutenant General Steven Blum indicated many guardsmen were equipped with outdated radios, and it was impossible for them to communicate with the Army's 82nd Airborne Division and 1st Calvary Division. "You don't want two units operating in the same area, doing the same function, that can't coordinate their efforts because they don't have the communications equipment," Blum said.[210]

The Deputy Assistant Secretary of HHS, Office of Public Health Emergency Preparedness, Dr. Robert Blitzer, said communications were initially a big problem.[211] The command center used land lines and cell phones, and Blitzer also ordered a mobile communications center, which was deployed from Washington, D.C. to Atlanta and then to Baton Rouge. Blitzer had not needed to deploy the mobile communications center for the previous four hurricanes that hit Florida. HHS Principal Deputy Assistant Secretary for Public Health and Emergency Preparedness, Dr. Gerald Parker, knew of just one satellite phone, located on the command bus, and said all SERT leaders "probably" had one.[212] Simonson said he thought there were two satellite phones per SERT, but for every satellite phone call that was successful, there were probably six failed attempts.[213]

Communication failures also affected NDMS. NDMS Chief Jack Beall said not only did his staff not have enough equipment, the operability of the equipment they had was "in and out."[214] Satellite phones worked only when trucks containing the satellite equipment were pointing in the right direction. But as Beall said, "When you have people dying, there's no time to mess with satellite phones." Overall, his Nextel cell phone was his best option for communicating, but when he or his staff worked in the Superdome, it was "total blackout." Efforts to remedy this problem began on September 3, with NDMS working to reach agreements with private cellular companies for the provision of "communications on wheels."[215]

OR-2 DMAT also cited communications as a key obstacle — particularly the operability of cell phones and interoperability of radios inside the New Orleans Airport.[216] "There is an over reliance on cellular phones for communications. The cellular infrastructure was severely damaged during Katrina and cell phone service was initially unavailable . . . . ," OR-2 DMAT reported. Radios also proved insufficient — the JT-1000 radios provided for the team could not contact radios in distant areas of the airport. Similarly, the team had no communication with security personnel via radio until the Forest Service provided Bendex King radios.

The breakdowns in communication experienced by government officials are illustrated in ESF-8 agency personnel e-mails. These e-mails show correspondence was almost non-existent until August 31, and difficulties sending and receiving messages persisted well into the first week of September. On August 31, a SERT member e-mailed the EOC and said, "My BB doesn't work at all, any communications with me will have to be through cell."[217] In Mississippi, a September 3 e-mail from the Gulfport Field Command Center indicates, "No phones or power as of now. Cells sometimes, Nextel service best. T-mobile not good for BBs at this area but do work other locations."[218] On September 5, a week after the storm, e-mails indicate that communications had not significantly improved. A CDC employee wrote the EOC saying, "Our folks in the field only have access to blackberry now. (The phone lines are going in and out and faxes are very difficult to send)."[219]

Much attention has been paid to lack of operability and the inability of first responders to connect with each other through the equipment they had. Some responders, however, were having difficulties just getting the equipment itself. A SERT team member on her way to Baton Rouge e-mailed HHS officials on September 5 saying she needed a cell phone and blackberry. A response from an HHS official states, "We do not issue Blackberry's to individuals for deployments (and we don't have any anyway), we have also exhausted our total cache of phones, so we have absolutely nothing to issue. If things change, I will advise you."[220] Likewise, the OR-2 DMAT report says there were an insufficient number of Motorola JF-1000 radios for their convoy, and other teams who did not have access to radios at all "encountered safety-related issues due to a lack of communications." The radios and satellite phones inside the FEMA trucks were also of no use to DMAT teams, as they had not been programmed.[221]

From lack of equipment, to inoperability, to failure to program satellite phones, communications proved to be one of the greatest obstacles to the Hurricane Katrina medical response. Critical time was wasted. And energy that should have been spent treating patients was instead spent on repeated, and often times unsuccessful, attempts to communicate.

Finding: Evacuation decisions for New Orleans nursing homes were subjective and, in one case, led to preventable deaths

"We see where there are gaping holes in our system. It has become clear that no one was evaluating these plans in any real sense. The system provides no check and balance."

—*Louisiana State Representative Nita Hutter*[222]

Like its hospitals, Louisiana's nursing homes (all privately owned, with the exception of two) are responsible for having their own evacuation plans.[223] These plans are required to be updated annually, and before the start of hurricane season each year, DHH sends a reminder letter. DHH also checks to ensure every Louisiana nursing home submits a plan; however, media reports indicate DHH cited only one nursing home in the past year for submitting an inadequate plan.[224]

Most plans encourage patients' families to help with evacuations, and several southeast Louisiana nursing homes have agreements with nursing homes in northern Louisiana for the transfer of residents after evacuations.[225] The statewide occupancy of Louisiana nursing homes is roughly 70 percent, which allows evacuated nursing homes to find bed space elsewhere. Before Hurricane Katrina's landfall, 19 nursing homes evacuated their residents. After the flooding in New Orleans, an additional

AP PHOTO/MARI DARR-WELCH

32 nursing homes evacuated. One nursing home, Saint Rita's, did not evacuate at all, and 35 residents died. Overall, it is estimated that 215 people died in New Orleans nursing homes and hospitals as a result of Katrina and failed evacuations.[226]

Three Louisiana Nursing Homes

Michael Ford is CEO and owner of three nursing homes in the New Orleans area — Riverbend Nursing and Rehabilitation Center (Riverbend), located in Plaquemines Parish, Metairie Health Care Center (Metairie), located in Jefferson Parish, and Waldon Health Care Center (Waldon) also located in Jefferson Parish.[227] Combined, these nursing homes house close to 360 patients. Ford is also the Vice President of the New Orleans region of the Louisiana Nursing Home Association (LNHA) and is a member of the Plaquemines OEP. According to Ford, all nursing homes' emergency plans must be approved by the state. Riverbend's emergency plan calls for the establishment of a pre-determined evacuation site, usually in a church gym in Kentwood, Louisiana, for both staff and patients. Ford has evacuated his nursing home patients once before, in anticipation of Hurricane Ivan, using an 18-wheel flat bed trailer equipped with air conditioning and a generator. The experience was trying, with the patients sitting "on a bus for eight hours to go one hundred miles," but he also says it gave him and his staff experience for Hurricane Katrina.

Ford received notice of the mandatory evacuation for Plaquemines Parish on the Saturday before Katrina made landfall. Jesse St. Amant, the OEP Director for Plaquemines Parish, declared the evacuation at 9:00 a.m. on August 27 and said, "If they don't leave, I tell 'em they're going to die in place."[228] Despite the difficulties moving patients for Hurricane Ivan, Ford listened to St. Amant and evacuated his nursing home in Plaquemines. Evacuation of Riverbend to the church in Kentwood was assisted by approximately 25 church volunteers, who

*'If they don't leave, I tell 'em
they're going to die in place."*

...oved patients by carrying them on mattresses. Ford
...ventually relocated all but 50 of his patients to a wing
...e rented at Kentwood Manor Nursing Home. The rest
...ere taken to one of Ford's other two nursing homes
...n Jefferson Parish. It took almost six weeks to find
...ccommodations and move everyone.[229]

Ford decided against evacuating Metairie, thinking
...would withstand the storm. Subsequent flooding,
...owever, forced him to evacuate 115 patients.[230] Using
...Wildlife and Fishery department boats and a Louisiana
...rmy National Guard two and a half ton truck, patients
...ere taken to higher ground on the interstate. Buses from
...he New Orleans' EOC collected some patients on the
...vening of August 29 and took them to a staging area
...n Baton Rouge, Louisiana. Ford had some pre-existing
...ontracts for housing his patients elsewhere, but he moved
...hem to the first available locations — all of which were in
...ouisiana. By mid November, patients from Metairie were
...oved to the Waldon facility (which was not evacuated
...or Katrina), where they remain today.

...t. Rita's Nursing Home

...he night before landfall, Ford had a phone conversation
...ith Mabel Mangano, who co-owns St. Rita's Nursing
...ome with her husband. "I'm staying," she told him.[231]
...Media reports indicate the Manganos were so confident
...bout the safety of St. Rita's, they invited staff, friends, and
...elatives to use it as a shelter.[232]

The Manganos and their 78 patients remained in the
...ursing home throughout the storm, and like many in

New Orleans, thought they were safe after the hurricane
passed.[233] But the floodwaters began to rise — eight to
nine feet in 30 minutes — and the Mangano's grandson
swam out and brought back a boat. They began putting
patients on mattresses floating like rafts.

On September 13, the Manganos were charged with 34
counts of negligent homicide.[234] Attorney General Charles
Foti's September 14 press release stated the "charges stem
from Mable Mangano and Salvador Mangano, Sr.'s alleged
failure to evacuate St. Rita's Nursing Home, contrary to
the facility's own evacuation plan and in violation of the
St. Bernard Parish's mandatory evacuation. Additionally,
subsequent to the mandatory evacuation order, authorities
offered to send two buses and drivers to evacuate residents
from the facility and the Manganos allegedly declined this
offer."[235]

The News-Star, a Monroe, Louisiana newspaper, says
despite these charges, "the Manganos did not abandon
St. Rita's during the flooding. Nor did they seal the fate
of their elderly residents by strapping them to their beds
before leaving, as was widely reported. They worked
alongside their staff and a few Good Samaritans during
the frantic rescue effort . . . ."[236] Parish residents may
soon be the judge.

Finding: Lack of electronic patient medical records contributed to difficulties and delays in medical treatment of evacuees

Although HHS partnered with the AMA to
establish a website allowing physicians and
pharmacists to electronically access the
prescription records of patients affected
by Katrina, few patients or health care providers
had access to medical records or a common
medical record system

As Hurricane Katrina tore through the Gulf coast region,
it destroyed millions of pages of paper files and patient
medical records in doctor offices, clinics and hospitals.
Thousands of patients displaced from the region by the
storm lacked medical records and were forced to depend
on memory and knowledge of their medical history,
allergies, and other important information.

Kindred Hospital in New Orleans was one of the few facilities in the Gulf coast with electronic patient medical records. When Kindred evacuated 54 patients following Katrina, the hospital was able to send patients' medical records electronically to other Kindred operated facilities in Baton Rouge and Houston where the patients had been transferred.[237] Additionally, Kindred was able to print and mail hard copies of a patient's electronic medical history for those who were evacuated to non-Kindred facilities.[238]

Eighty pediatric cancer patients from the Gulf coast were evacuated to St. Jude Children's Research Hospital (St. Jude) in Memphis, Tennessee.[239] The hospital was tasked with tracking down oncologists who fled flooded New Orleans with treatment records to ensure appropriate treatment for the pediatric patients. Additionally, doctors at St. Jude were forced to rely heavily on parents' recollection and notes of their children's treatments. "I honestly feel quite comfortable that the worst-case scenario is we delayed treatment" for some children, Dr. Joseph Mirro said. But there was "a lot of flying by the seat of your pants to get it right."[240]

According to Stephens, all medical files and documentation made regarding the treatment and medical attention provided to evacuees in the Superdome were lost.[241] This contrasts sharply with how patients' medical information was handled at the Astrodome in Houston. Thousands of the evacuees at the Superdome and Convention Center were transferred to the Astrodome without any paper or medical files. Volunteers in Houston were tasked with documenting patient information and registering evacuee to create new electronic medical records. The Harris County Hospital District created a large clinic in the Astrodome, which included 80 computer terminals to aid in registering patients and recording their medical history and information.[242] By September 9, records had been created for approximately 8,000 Katrina evacuees.[243]

Additionally, the American Medical Association (AMA National Community Pharmacists Association (NCPA), and several other organizations collaborated to launch the KatrinaHealth.org prescription medication network in September. The network is a secure online service to help physicians and authorized healthcare providers access medication and dosage information for Katrina evacuees.[244] The network allows and authorizes physician and pharmacies to provide prescription refills, or prescrib new medications.[245] It facilitates coordinated care and helps to avoid potential medical errors by providing acces to patient information. The AMA provides physician credentialing while NCPA provides authentification of pharmacists and pharmacies.[246]

Because the VA has developed an electronic patient record system for its facilities, electronic records for over 50,000 New Orleans VAMC patients were downloaded to tapes and transferred to the VAMC in Houston.[247] The Houston VAMC was able to reconfigure and restore them after the New Orleans VAMC evacuation. The records chi for the South-Central VA Healthcare Network said, "Every single thing on that computer was saved."[248]

Hurricane Katrina showed that physicians are often our "second" responders. They, too, need the support of sophisticated IT systems, enabling them to respond to a crisis quickly and retrieve and share critical records and

"I honestly feel quite comfortable that the worst-case scenario is we delayed treatment" for some children, Mirro said. But there was "a lot of flying by the seat of your pants to get it right."

information. The emerging public health threats of the 21st Century require the seamless flow of information at all levels of government. The need for better integration of IT into the healthcare industry was highlighted by thousands of Katrina evacuees with no medical patient records.

HHS has made recent efforts to support digital health recovery for the Gulf coast. In November, HHS announced partnerships with the Southern Governors' Association and DHH to accelerate electronic health records in Gulf states to create accessible, accurate medical records and medical information.[249] These partnerships will help physicians, medical practices, and hospitals rebuild medical records for their patients as they return to the region. However, National Coordinator for Health Information Technology, Dr. David Brailer, said, "Making patient data accessible to authorized physicians, whether it is following a hurricane or as part of routine care, remains a challenge that must be addressed."[250]

Finding: Top officials at HHS and NDMS do not share a common understanding of who controls NDMS under ESF-8

On a larger scale, the command structure between HHS and the NDMS was problematic. ESF-8 is implemented by the Assistant Secretary for Public Health Emergency Preparedness at HHS; however, NDMS is housed and operates under FEMA (DHS) authority. For Hurricane Katrina, NDMS was activated by FEMA on August 25.[251] According to the FEMA Office of General Counsel, activation of NDMS would certainly have "stood up" ESF-8.[252] However, there is no evidence of action under ESF-8 until August 27, when HHS first convened conference calls.[253] During a natural disaster or public health emergency, HHS and NDMS communication and coordination is essential for an effective response.

According to Simonson, coordinating the public health response under ESF-8 was "a strain without operational control and logistical support."[254] He says the relocation of NDMS left HHS with few operational assets. Despite HHS responsibility for coordinating the federal response to public health emergencies, HHS only

has PHS Commissioned Corps, SNS, and other smaller functions under its command. Unlike NDMS, none of HHS remaining assets are configured for a quick response. Instead, HHS assets are meant to sustain existing medical services and infrastructures. Simonson also indicated that without direct control over NDMS assets, the efficiency and effectiveness of ESF-8 is crippled. With modest operational assets, Simonson noted HHS lacked situational awareness, saying, "HHS lost its field network to FEMA when NDMS was moved to DHS."[255]

As executor of ESF-8, Simonson attempted to coordinate the pre-positioning of medical assets prior to Katrina's landfall.[256] He spoke directly to Stephens on Saturday, August 27 and Sunday, August 28 to ask what supplies the Superdome needed. As a result of those conversations, Simonson called then Acting Director of the Response Division Edward G. Buikema at FEMA to "aggressively advocate" DMATs, water, ice, and MREs be positioned in the Superdome prior to landfall. Simonson believed it would have been much easier to task NDMS if those assets had been under his direct control. When asked about attempts at coordination between the two agencies, Simonson said NDMS participated in ESF-8 conference calls, but despite its participation, acted as an asset of FEMA without coordinating mission assignments with him.

An e-mail from a U.S. Army Corps of Engineers Liaison at DOD, Mark Roupas, to Assistant Secretary for Defense for Homeland Defense Paul McHale on August 29, however, suggests Simonson did have a say in NDMS' activation. Roupas says: " . . . . DHHS is trying to decide which health care approach is better: 1) activate NDMS and move the patients out of the state or 2) move medical beds and personnel into the affected area and treat there. DHHS medical planners are meeting with Mr. Simonson at 6pm to discuss and decide which course of action to accept. If the decision is to move the patients via NDMS, then DHHS will activate the NDMS system. If the decision is to treat intrastate, then we should expect a formal RFA for -500 beds and personnel support."[257] This e-mail begs the question: how was the primary coordinator of medical response unaware that FEMA had activated NDMS on August 25?

Simonson believes ESF-8 should be more "clearly articulated."[258] He also believes the relocation of NDMS to DHS in 2003 undermined NDMS effectiveness.

Since its transfer, funding for NDMS has been stagnant, with millions of dollars being siphoned off to support "unidentified services."[259] NDMS has lost two-thirds of its staff since 2003. "There is room for substantial improvement in coordination between NDMS and the rest of ESF-8. Either ESF-8 should be directly responsible for NDMS or ESF-8 should be moved to where NDMS is located," Simonson said.[260]

Beall disagreed and told a much different story about the coordination between NDMS and HHS.[261] He said HHS has the authority to move NDMS and its assets under ESF-8 and that, to his knowledge, NDMS did not deploy any assets, with the exception of pre-positioning, without a direct order from HHS. He said HHS and NDMS were in close coordination throughout the operation, and that any coordination issues were more likely a result of internal difficulties within HHS — not between HHS and NDMS. He believes NDMS relocation to FEMA allows the system to "lean forward" more than it could under HHS.

How these two senior officials view the coordination and authorities for HHS and NDMS speaks for itself. Without a clear understanding of who has functional jurisdiction over NDMS, coordination of the system and all of its assets was certain to result in failures.

The OR-2 DMAT report illustrates command structure confusion, and general coordination problems, between NDMS and the DMAT teams it managed at the New Orleans Airport. OR-2 DMAT members reported a number of command-related issues, including:

■ ICS/NIMIS (or any form of an organized internal command and control structure) was not implemented by FEMA/NDMS at the airport. (Some attempts to use ICS were made by FEMA/NDMS following the arrival of a Forest Service overhead team, but were generally not that effective.)
■ There was no formalized unified command established between the many participating agencies until late in the response.
■ No safety officer was initially appointed at the command level (in a very unsafe environment).
■ Roles, responsibilities, and reporting structure of the two MSTs (Baton Rouge and Airport) were never clearly articulated. It was unclear what role the PHS representative at the airport had.

■ Liaisons with military and civilian entities participating in relief efforts at the airport were never established.
■ There did not appear to be any initial interfacing at a management level with knowledgeable local medical providers, public health officials, and local emergency providers.
■ There appeared to be a lack of communications between the Airport MST and Baton Rouge MST as well as NDMS headquarters.
■ Information was not being effectively communicated to the DMATs from either of the MSTs.
■ There was considerable friction between DMATs and the MSTs. An 'us and them' attitude was prevalent.
■ Only one fulltime FEMA/NDMS employee was present at the airport MST (arriving after operations had started). All other Airport MST staff were taken from onsite DMATs, reducing the number of team personnel for patient treatment and operations support.
■ Inexperienced leaders were placed in an overwhelming and chaotic environment that caused their effectiveness to rapidly deteriorate.
■ Management decisions that were being made were not based on the best interests of the patients.
■ There was inadequate equipment available to produce the copies and paperwork FEMA was requiring.[262]

The OR-2 DMAT report further states, "FEMA/NDMS operations at the airport were extremely disorganized compared to parallel military and Forest Service operations." Tensions between FEMA/NDMS and DMATs is an ongoing problem and "continues to compromise the efficiency of operations due to a lack of trust between both parties."[263]

Beall agreed there was tension and speculated DMAT members are accustomed to being in control of their environments and are not used to taking orders from federal officials.[264] He also said most of the FEMA NDMS officials deployed during Katrina and giving orders to DMATs were unseasoned and their inexperience contributed to the friction.

Historically, the mission of DMATs was to rapidly deploy and set up self-supporting field hospitals and provide medical care within the first 72 hours after a disaster before the arrival of other federal assets.[265] Alternatively, FEMA has historically operated under the assumption that state and local officials are the first line of defense during the initial 72 hours following a disaster until a federal response can coordinated. The NDMS response to Katrina suggests that FEMA was unable to support the historical rapid-deployment capability of NDMS.[266]

Finding: Lack of coordination led to delays in recovering dead bodies

The lack of coordination among agencies also contributed to delayed recovery of dead bodies in the Gulf coast region. According to ESF-8, HHS is responsible for victim identification and mortuary services. HHS has authority to ask DHS and DOD to assist in providing victim identification and mortuary services; establishing temporary morgue facilities; performing victim identification by fingerprint, forensic dental, and/or forensic pathology and anthropology methods; and processing, preparation, and disposition of remains.[267] The most experienced personnel in this area are a part of NDMS under the authority of FEMA and DHS. DOD also has significant expertise in mortuary affairs and mass fatality management.

Despite having this authority, HHS was slow to respond and coordinate efforts with DOD and DHS. On Sunday, September 4, DOD sent an e-mail to DHS recognizing the need to assist overwhelmed state and local authorities in victim identification. The e-mail provided a brief analysis of the situation in the Gulf coast region and said, "If this analysis is correct, it's not if, but when and how DOD will be asked to assist in the mortuary affairs response."[268] The e-mail further says DOD has developed "potential plans on what kind of requirements will be needed and how DOD can provide response support. Currently we have identified the potential missions of search and recovery, remains transport to establish human remains collection points, and assistance with DNA capture analysis."[269] The e-mail recommends a meeting between DHS, HHS, FEMA, and DMORT to discuss coordination among agencies and the commercial sector. It is unclear if and when this meeting took place. What is clear, however, is DOD essentially took the lead in coordinating an operational mortuary affairs plan, which was originally the responsibility of HHS.

Following the e-mail from DOD, HHS personnel recognized the need for an "integrated ESF-8 response" and devising a "coordinated way to collect and share information."[270] When asked why it took an e-mail from DOD six days after Katrina's landfall, Simonson responded, "HHS was not involved in discussions with actual body recovery. FEMA, DOD, and Kenyon International Emergency Services (Kenyon), a mortuary services contractor, were in discussions for recovery services and it was unclear who was in charge of the recovery effort."[271] ESF-8 is not responsible for recovering bodies but is responsible for mortuary services. As a result, HHS "had to wait for certain discussions to be made before going ahead with specific decisions. Everyone was frustrated with how slow the initial discussions were going."[272] Before HHS can coordinate victim identification and other mortuary services, FEMA, DOD, and state officials must have a recovery plan in place.

Body recovery was no less confused. For days, bodies went uncollected as state and federal officials remained indecisive on a body recovery plan. With state and local officials utterly overwhelmed by the disaster, they were initially more focused on rescuing Katrina's survivors than recovering dead bodies. By September 5, inaction was causing frustration. "Number 1 issue is body collection," Army Colonel John J. Jordan, military assistant to Brown at FEMA, wrote in an e-mail that day.[273] Jordan continued, "This issue must be addressed, and frankly, there is operations paralysis at this point. FEMA is pushing State to see what they want to do, and indications are that Governor is involved in some of the decisions, especially regarding interment." A week later, Blanco publicly blamed FEMA for the delay and its inability to sign a contract with Kenyon for body collection services.[274] Kenyon later signed a contract with the state.[275]

One week after landfall, on September 5, Simonson requested "ample mobile mortuary services throughout the affected region."[276] An order for 200 mobile mortuary trucks was issued with 130 designated to Louisiana and 70 to be delivered to Mississippi.[277] By the next day mortuary services were being established in St. Gabriel, Louisiana with 96 personnel.[278] FEMA and Louisiana collaborated on drafting a body recovery plan which required the approval of Brown, and the Louisiana "newly appointed" state medical examiner.[279] In Mississippi, mortuary services were established at the Naval Air Station in Gulfport. By September 6, one DMORT had set up facilities at the Naval Air Station. Body recovery was an enormous task that took several months to complete. Each home in the affected area was inspected twice for bodies. Mortuary services continue in the region as remains are identified and returned to families.

Finding: Deployment confusion, uncertainty about mission assigments, and government red tape delayed medical care

"Coordinating all of those agencies isn't a simple thing and [is] very difficult to practice. We sit down and do tabletop exercises where we go over who's going to do what, but a disaster of this magnitude is something that is very difficult to simulate or really practice. So, we rely on really well-trained, capable people that can adapt and adjust to whatever the situation is to get the job done."

— *Colonel Richard Bachmann, U.S. Air Force*[280]

In the wake of Katrina, first responders worked tirelessly — days and nights in miserable conditions — to provide medical care to thousands of hurricane victims. The coordination of these medical personnel, supplies, and equipment proved to be a daunting task. At one point, a frustrated member of the CDC Division of Emergency Operations wrote: "The approval process for a bottle of aspirin seems to be the same as for a 500 bed hospital."[281] From confusion about mission assignments and deployments, to broader misunderstandings about command structure, coordination was undoubtedly an obstacle to the Gulf coast medical response. Coordination efforts were impeded, and in turn, these impediments adversely affected the overall medical response.

Deployment Assignments

Hundreds of e-mails were sent from medical first responders to government officials expressing confusion and frustration over their deployment orders. On Friday, September 2, a PHS officer in Oregon sent an e-mail saying, "I've got supervisory approval and have had my bags packed and ready in the trunk of my car to leave at a moment's notice since Tuesday. Is there anything further you can tell me?"[282] On September 5, a Food and Drug Administration employee e-mailed the PHS coordinating officer saying,

> "I'm deploying tomorrow. I don't have any information about the mission and whether my role has changed from the original (FMCS MST 4

– there has been some issues with travel and just got my itinerary tonight so not sure if those issues were due to a change in assignment). I've gotten a phone call from a member of my team looking for direction and I don't know what to tell him. Please provide any information you can."[283]

Another PHS officer wrote, "Once again, sorry to bother you. However, what is the status of this mission? From the email I received earlier this week things were supposed to happen in 24-72hrs. At your earliest convenience, could I please get an update on this?"[284]

There was also confusion within government ranks regarding who had the authority to deploy officers and what officers had already been approved for deployment.[2] An internal PHS e-mail sent September 1 stated,

> "We are receiving reports from one Warden indicating that many of his staff are deployed. The problem is they are not on our Master list that we have been providing to OFRD. Can you provide me your latest deployed roster identifying the BOP officer/assets. I am thinking maybe these officers are on August or September rosters???"[286]

An August 30 e-mail from the chief of the Coast Guard medical division said,

> "I apologize for the confusion of the rosters with CG officers that were released earlier. It appears that all PHS officers were required to go to a website and register yesterday AM per the attached email. Many officers did this without knowing that registering automatically noted agency approval for a CCRF mission. I attempted to register without the agency approval box clicked in order to provide CG comments. The website only allowed submission with this box clicked positive . . . kind of a Catch-22."[287] A member of OFRD wrote FEMA saying, "This officer is stationed in AR and is not on our list of officers deployed. Who deployed him?"[288]

There was also limited visibility between agencies. An e-mail from a CDC employee to HHS/OS staff and CDC staff on September 9 stated, "Since OSHA is Labor Dept we have no visibility on their deployments at this time...could be they will link up with NIOSH team when ey all arrive, but we may well not know anything."[289] This correspondence reflects the absence of updated and accurate lists of who was available for deployment, who was not available, and who had already been deployed.

Mission Assignments

As late as September 22, evidence of confusion remained about who was in charge of what aspects of the response. An HHS incident manager wrote, ". . . . it appears that the OC for the 250 ambulances is no longer the State EMS Director Terry Bavousett, but has changed to the three names below. Please get your representative at the JFO to address this ASAP or the ambulances will end up at Reliant Park instead of the locations that Terry Bavousett has requested."[290] The FEMA liaison to CDC wrote, "I might be the only one — I doubt it — but I'm really confused with the structure within CDC/DEOC for this operation. Can you send out a team structure list of team leads as well as their DEOC schedule?"[291]

Clarity about missions was also lacking in the medical response to Hurricane Katrina—as evidenced by the lack of planning for the United States Navy Ship (USNS) Comfort. The USNS Comfort is a medical treatment facility with a primary mission of supporting medical needs for the military and serve as hospital facilities as part of a humanitarian effort.[292] It has a 1,000 bed capacity with 80 beds designated for an intensive care unit and 12 operating rooms. The Select Committee received varying cost estimates for operating costs for the USNS Comfort. According to the U.S. Northern Command, operating costs for the USNS Comfort are roughly $82,910 per day underway and $29,155 a day pier side.[293] However, a *Philadelphia Inquirer* article states, "When on full operational status, the daily costs exceeds $700,000 a day, according to the Navy."[294]

Originally destined for New Orleans to provide medical care to storm victims, the Comfort was redirected on September 9. "The Comfort is now headed for Pascagoula, Miss due to the lack of a medical mission in NO. Do not have anticipated arrival at that site, but OC will advise when they get the information. Decision has been made that two cruise ships will now be used to house state workers."[295] That same night, clarification about a mission assignment was never received. An e-mail exchange between HHS employees states, "USNS comfort

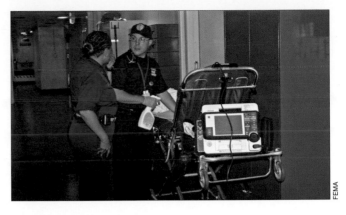

docked today in Pascagoula. I listened in to most of the conference call and nobody could seem to think of a mission for them. State Health Dpt was clear that they had nothing at this time."[296]

Additionally, the redirection of 250 ambulances required a significant number of approvals. An HHS incident manager wrote, "I have just been informed by FEMA HQ that Jack Colley or Dr. Sanchez the originators of the request will need to approve the change in the location of the delivery of the ambulances. Would you please contact your representatives at the JFO and ask that they confirm the location change with Reliant Stadium to the two staging areas noted in your e-mail with either the ESF# 7&8 representatives. GSA will then confirm back to you the delivery locations and times."[297]

Government Red Tape

Bureaucratic red tape also stood in the way of the medical response. The OR-2 DMAT report states, "The team was activated on the afternoon of Tuesday, August 30, and given instructions to be in Houston the next day, August 31. Because of the policy of making individual travel arrangements (see below), the last team member arrived in Houston shortly after midnight on September 1. The team departed for Baton Rouge in rental SUVs and vans at 5:00 a.m. on September 1. During the drive, team commanders had several phone conversations with other teams at the New Orleans Airport who stated the team was urgently needed due to the large number of patients. Instead of heading directly to the airport, the team was requested to first stage at LSU. After staging for nearly two hours, the team received an escort to the New Orleans Airport, arriving at approximately 3:30 p.m. Roughly 48 hours had elapsed since the activation order and the team arriving at the incident."[298] The report further says that because team members were deployed individually, their medical response was delayed.

On September 2, the Special Assistant to the Assistant Secretary of Defense for International Security Affairs, Jon G. Ferko, wrote McHale saying Blanco was withholding medical supplies until she received President Bush's word Louisiana would be reimbursed. The e-mail to McHale says:

Sir,

Some information that I thought you should know:

My brother is on the ground at the health and human services command center in Baton Rouge. He says the situation is 'grave' — he and his team are working desparately to save lives without medical supplies – he said he doesn't even have a bandaid.

His team spoke with the Governor of LA and she refuses to release ANY amount of funds for supplies until POTUS assures her of reimbursement. The team down there does not know who to work through to release funds – and this is the federal command team.

I felt that you should have this info – my brother actually called home in tears because they can't do anything to stop the loss of life....[299]

Conclusion

The numbers do not lie. Thousands of lives were saved, a tribute to the medical professionals and volunteers who worked around the clock under enormously grueling conditions. Yet, there is another, more sobering realization that can't be ignored either. Those numbers could — should — have been even greater. It wasn't a lack of effort that hindered their success. It was a lack of planning, lack of initiative, and lack of response.

There were not, for example, nearly enough medical personnel teams in position prior to landfall, which led to unnecessary delays in getting the right equipment and supplies to the right people. FEMA and HHS needed to plan for the worst. Instead, they scrambled for supplies in an effort that was often times uncoordinated. In too many cases, it was too late. Clearly New Orleans residents with "special needs" paid a disproportionate price. Neither the Louisiana Medical Director and State Health Officer, nor the Director of the New Orleans Health Department,

could clearly define the "special needs" population, much less adequately provide for it.

From the storm's impending landfall through the flooding of New Orleans, confusion grew over if, and when, hospital, VAMC, and nursing home evacuations should occur. Time was rushing by, lives were in jeopardy and even when evacuations were finally deemed necessary these institutions were not prepared to do it efficiently. One possible solution would have been better utilization of private firms to aid in evacuations. It was the answer in a few instances, but it could have been the answer in so many more. In all, an estimated 215 people died in New Orleans nursing homes and hospitals as a result of Katrina and failed evacuations.

Compounding problems for medical responders was poor communication and coordination. So poor, in fact, that at times, the only way to receive information was through television. And the lack of access to medical records, or a common, electronic medical record system, led to delays in treating evacuees. Suffering was also prolonged as attempts at coordination, within and between government agencies, proved frustrating and inadequate. Confusion arose over mission assignments and command structure. Medical officers and volunteers had little information about their deployment orders, many waiting for days with their bags packed and ready. And while some medical teams waited, without equipment or supplies to care for patients, state and federal officials squabbled over reimbursement.

Thousands of American men and women selflessly gave their time, money, and expertise to save lives. Unfortunately, lack of preparation, reticence to act, and confusion over coordination are all part of the story as well. Though there was the will, the medical response to Hurricane Katrina showed there wasn't always a way. The initiative of men like Mike Ford and Jesse St. Amant was the exception to the rule. ∎

Adam Nossiter, *It's Like Being in a Third World Country: Hospitals in flood zone struggle to save lives*, ASSOC. PRESS (New Orleans, LA) Aug. 31, 2005.

Interview by Select Comm. Staff with LA Hosp. Ass'n, in Baton Rouge, LA (Nov. 10, 2005) [hereinafter Nov. 10 Interview with LA Hosp. Ass'n].

Interview by Select Comm. Staff with LA State Univ. [hereinafter LSU] Health Care Services Div., in New Orleans, LA (Jan. 19, 2006). "Code Grey" refers to the section of the hospital's emergency management plan that prepares the hospital for extremely severe weather. (*Id.*). Nov. 10 Interview with LA Hosp. Ass'n.

HHS: What We Do *at* http://www.hhs.gov/about/whatwedo.html/ (last visited Jan. 27, 2006).

U.S. Dep't of Homeland Sec., *National Response Plan*, (Dec. 2004) at ESF #8 – Public Health and Med. Services Annex [hereinafter *NRP*].

Id.

Id. at ESF-iii.

Welcome to NDMS *at* http://ndms.dhhs.gov/ (last visited Jan. 27, 2006).

Press Release, Fed. Emergency Mgmt. Agency [hereinafter FEMA], NDMS Serves The Needs Of Hurricane Victims (Dec. 8, 2005) [hereinafter Dec. 8 FEMA Press Release].

Interview by Select Comm. Staff with FEMA and Nat'l Disaster Med. Sys. [hereinafter NDMS] (Nov. 30, 2005) [hereinafter Interview with FEMA and NDMS].

Disaster Medical Assistance Team (DMAT) Basic *at* http://www.fema.gov/preparedness/resources/health_med/dmat_basic.htm (last visited Jan. 5, 2006).

Interview with FEMA and NDMS.

Id.

Id.

After Action Report from OR-2 Disaster Med. Assistance Team [hereinafter DMAT] (Sept. 25, 2005) *available at*, http://www.democrats.reform.house.gov/story.asp?ID=984 (last visited Jan. 28, 2006) [hereinafter Sept. 25, OR-2 DMAT After Action Report].

Interview with FEMA and NDMS.

Press Release, FEMA, NDMS Demobilizes After Serving The Needs Of Hurricane Victims (Dec. 30, 2005).

U.S. Dep't of Health and Human Services [hereinafter HHS] and Miss. Dep't of Health [hereinafter MDH], *Hurricane Katrina Medical Support/Demobilization/Transition Plan for the State of Mississippi*, (Jan. 2006) at 3.

Hearing on Hurricane Katrina: Preparedness and Response by the State of Mississippi Before Select Comm., 109th Cong. (Dec. 7, 2005) at 2 (written statement of Dr. Brian W. Amy, Miss. State Health Officer) [hereinafter Dr. Brian Amy written statement].

"Disaster Mortuary Operational Response Team (DMORT)," *at* http://www.fema.gov/preparedness/resources/health_med/dmort.htm (last visited Jan. 5, 2006).

Interview by Select Comm. Staff with Vice Admiral Richard H. Carmona, U.S. Surgeon Gen., in Wash., DC (Nov. 22, 2005) [hereinafter Interview with Surgeon Gen. Carmona].

E-mail correspondence from Cliff Oldfield, Commander of DMORT Region II, to Barbara Butcher, Officer of Chief Medical Examiner, NYC et al. (Sept. 1, 2005) (2:27 p.m.).

E-mail correspondence from Keith Holtermann, Incident Manager ESF#8 7P-7A Watch, HHS, to EST-ESF08-A, et al. (Sept. 5, 2005) (9:46 p.m.).

Id.

E-mail correspondence from Keith Holtermann, Incident Manager ESF#8 7P-7A Watch, HHS, to Robert Blitzer, et al. (Sept. 6, 2005) (6:35 a.m.).

Id.

E-mail correspondence from John Mallos (OS) on behalf of CCRF-Response (OPHS), to CCRF-Response (OPHS) (Aug. 27, 2005) (6:02 p.m.).

Id.

Interview with Surgeon Gen. Carmona.

Id.

Id.

E-mail correspondence from Marc Wolfson (HHS/OS) to ASPA, et al., (Sept. 8, 2005) (12:06 p.m.).

About CDC: Home Page *at* http://www.cdc.gov/about/default.htm (last visited Jan. 27, 2006).

Interview by Select Comm. Staff with Dr. Richard E. Besser, Dir. of Coordinating Office for Terrorism Preparedness Emergency Response, Ctrs. for Disease Control and Prevention [hereinafter CDC], in Wash., DC (Nov. 17, 2005) [hereinafter Interview with CDC].

Id.

Press Release, HHS, HHS Supports Medical Response to Hurricane Katrina (Dec. 30, 2005). A pallet includes: "basic first aid material (such as bandages, pads, ice paks, etc.), blankets and patient clothing, suture kits, sterile gloves, stethoscopes, blood pressure measuring kits, and portable oxygen tanks." (*Id.*).

Interview with CDC.

E-mail correspondence from KC Decker, HHS/OS, to Andrew Stevermer, et al., (Aug. 28, 2005) (5:51 p.m.).

Interview with CDC.

Id.

Id.

Interview with Surgeon Gen. Carmona.

Press Release, HHS, HHS Releases Website and Toll Free Number for Deployment by Health Care Professionals (Sept. 3, 2005).

E-mail correspondence from Lakeisha Jones, HHS/OS, to Lakeisha Jones, et al., (Sept. 3, 2005) (6:02 p.m.).

Press Release, HHS, HHS Designates First Medical Shelters and Provides Vital Medical Supplies and Medical Assistance (Sept. 2, 2005) [hereinafter HHS Designates First Medical Shelters Release].

About SAMHSA DTAC *at* http://www.mentalhealth.samhsa.gov/dtac/about.asp (last visited Jan. 27, 2006).

48 Press Release, HHS, Crisis Hotline Available for Victims of Hurricane Katrina (Sept. 7, 2005).

49 Press Release, HHS, HHS Awards $600,000 in Emergency Mental Health Grants to Four States Devastated by Hurricane Katrina (Sept. 13, 2005).

50 Strategic National Stockpile at http://www.bt.cdc.gov/stockpile/ (last visited Jan. 7, 2006) [hereinafter Strategic Nat'l Stockpile website].

51 Interview with CDC.

52 Strategic Nat'l Stockpile website (last visited Jan. 7, 2006).

53 HHS Designates First Medical Shelters Release; E-mail correspondence from Stewart Simonson, Assistant Sec'y, Office of Public Health Emergency Preparedness, HHS, to MOL, HHS/OS, et al. (Sept. 2, 2005) (12:28 a.m.).

54 Dr. Brian Amy written statement at 5.

55 Interview with CDC.

56 *Id.*

57 *Id.*

58 *Id.*

59 Interview by Select Comm. Staff with Stewart Simonson, Assistant Sec'y, Office of Public Health Emergency Preparedness, HHS, in Wash., DC (Jan. 20, 2006) [hereinafter Interview with HHS].

60 Press Release, Am. Soc'y of Health-Sys. Pharmacists, Medical Shelters Provide Care to Hurricane Victims (Sept. 2, 2005) [hereinafter ASHP Press Release].

61 Delthia Ricks, *Outfitting Makeshift Hospitals: Medical Supplies are Being Sent from National Stockpile to Set Up Dozens of Temporary Centers,* Newsday.com, Sept. 6, 2005, *available at* www.newsday.com.

62 Interview with HHS.

63 *Id.*

64 ASHP Press Release.

65 News from The Adjutant General's Dep't *at* http://www.kansas.gov/ksadjutantgeneral/News%20Releases/2005/05-079.htm (last visited Jan. 7, 2006).

66 Master Sgt. Bob Haskell, *Air Guard Response to Katrina's Challenges,* THE OFFICER, Nov. 2005. [hereinafter Air Guard Response Article].

67 Sandra Basu, *DoD Provides Care to Spell Hurricane Relief,* U.S. Medicine, Inc, Oct. 2005, *available at* www.usmedicine.com [hereinafter DOD Provides Care Article].

68 *Id.*

69 Air Guard Response Article; Interview by Select Comm. Staff with Warren Reuther, Gen. Manager, Ernest N. Morial Convention Ctr. in New Orleans, LA (Dec. 20, 2005) [hereinafter Interview with Warren Reuther].

70 E-mail correspondence from Matthew Payne, HHS/OS to Robert Blitzer, HHS/OS, et al. (Sept. 28, 2005) (2:02 p.m.) [hereinafter Sept. 28 Matthew Payne E-mail].

71 *Id.*

72 Dr. Brian Amy written statement at 5.

73 E-mail correspondence from Stewart Simonson, Assistant Sec'y, Office of Public Health Emergency Preparedness, HHS, to Dep't of Public Safety personnel, State of Nevada, (Sept. 2, 2005) (6:08 p.m.).

74 Sept. 28 Matthew Payne E-mail.

75 Interview with HHS.

76 *Id.*

77 Interview by Select Comm. Staff with Dr. Jimmy Guidry, Med. Dir., Dep't of Health and Hosps., State of LA, in New Orleans, LA (Dec. 19, 2005) [hereinafter Dec. 19 Interview with Dr. Guidry].

78 Interview by Select Comm. Staff with Dr. Kevin Stephens, Dir., New Orleans Health Dep't., in New Orleans, LA (Dec. 19, 2005) [hereinafter Dec. 19 Interview with Dr. Stephens].

79 City of New Orleans Office of Emergency Preparedness, *Annex 1A La. Office of Homeland Sec. and Emergency Preparedness Shelter Operations Plan* (Revised July 2000) [hereinafter City of New Orleans Office of Emergency Preparedness].

80 Interview by Select Comm. Staff with Michael Ford, Vice President, New Orleans Region, LA Nursing Home Ass'n, Michella Ford, Facility Services Dir., Riverbend Nursing and Rehabilitation Ctr., and Jesse St. Amant, Dir., Emergency Preparedness, Office of Homeland Sec., Plaquemines Parish Gov't, in New Orleans, LA (Jan. 19, 2006) [hereinafter Jan. 19 Interview with Michael Ford, et al.].

81 City of New Orleans Office of Emergency Preparedness.

82 Nov. 9 Interview with Dr. Stephens.

83 Jan. 19 Interview with Michael Ford, et al.

84 E-mail correspondence from Lakeisha Jones, OS, to John Babb, OS, et al. (Sept. 6, 2005) (7:31 a.m.).

85 Interview by Select Comm. staff with Walter Maestri, Dir. of Emer. Mgmt., Jefferson Parish, in New Orleans, LA (Nov. 8, 2005).

86 Interview by Select Comm. Staff with Dr. Jimmy Guidry, Med. Dir., Dep't of Health and Hosps., State of LA, in Baton Rouge, LA (Nov. 7, 2005) [hereinafter Nov. 7 Interview with Dr. Guidry].

87 Nov. 9 Interview with Dr. Stephens.

88 Nov. 7 Interview with Dr. Guidry.

89 Interview by Select Comm. Staff with Gordon Nelson, Assistant Secretary for Operations, Dep't of Transp. and Dev. in Baton Rouge, LA (Nov. 4, 2005); Hurricane Katrina: Preparedness and Response by the State of Louisiana Before Select Comm., 109th Cong. (Dec. 14, 2005) at 242 (statement Ray Nagin, Mayor, City of New Orleans) [hereinafter *Dec. 14 Select Comm. Hearing*].

90 Interview by Select Comm. Staff with Scott Wells, Deputy Fed. Coordinating Officer, FEMA, in Baton Rouge, LA (Nov. 9, 2005).

91 *Id.*

92 Interview by Select Comm. Staff with Jiff Hingle, Sheriff, Plaquemines Parish, LA, in New Orleans, LA (Nov. 7, 2005) [hereinafter Interview with Sheriff of Plaquemines Parish, LA].

93 *Id.*

Nov. 9 Interview with Dr. Stephens.

Dec. 19 Interview with Dr. Stephens.

City of New Orleans Office of Emergency Preparedness.

Dec. 19 Interview with Dr. Guidry.

Interview by Select Comm. Staff with Glen Menard, Gen. Manager, New Orleans Superdome and Sports Arena, in New Orleans, LA, (Dec. 19, 2005) [hereinafter Dec. 19 Interview with Glen Menard].

Dec. 19 Interview with Dr. Stephens.

Dec. 19 Interview with Dr. Guidry.

Dec. 19 Interview with Glen Menard; Dec. 19 Interview with Dr. Stephens.

Dec. 19 Interview with Glen Menard.

Dec. 19 Interview with Dr. Stephens.

See generally, Daily Video Teleconferences among officials dated Aug. 25 - Sept. 4, 2005 [hereinafter *Daily VTC*]. State and local officials from each of the affected areas met daily with officials from, among other agencies, FEMA, and the Nat'l Hurricane Ctr.

Dec. 19 Interview with Glen Menard.

Telephonic Interview by Select Comm. Staff with Glen Menard, Gen. Manager of the New Orleans Superdome and the Sports Arena, in Wash., DC (Jan. 27, 2006).

Interview with FEMA and NDMS.

Larry Margasak, *Government Prepares for Next Big Disaster*, ASSOC. PRESS, Jan. 1, 2006.

Interview with Warren Reuther.

The Big Disconnect on New Orleans, CNN.com, Sept. 2, 2005, *available at* http://www.cnn.com/2005/US/09/02/katrina.response/ (last visited Jan. 30, 2006).

Interview with Warren Reuther.

Id.

Id.

E-mail correspondence from John J. Jordan, COL, U.S. Army to John Yingling, et al. (Sept. 3, 2005) (8:53 a.m.).

Interview with Warren Reuther.

Interview by Select Comm. Staff with Dr. Gregory S. Henderson, M.D., PhD., Ochsner Clinic Found., in New Orleans, LA (Jan. 19, 2006).

Id.

Id.

Id.

Id.

Id.

Id.

Id.

Id.

Dep't of Veterans Affairs, S. Cent. VA Health Care Network (VISN 16) Emergency Mgmt. Program Standard Operating Procedure, NO. 10N16-1 (Sept. 30, 2004) [hereinafter Sept. 30 Veterans Affairs Document].

Id.

Veterans Affairs Med. Ctr., Biloxi, State of Miss., *Miss. Emergency Plan (Section A)* (2005) at A-5 [Biloxi Veterans Affairs Med. Ctr. Plan].

Id. at A-7.

Veterans Affairs Med. Ctr., City of New Orleans, State of La., *Emergency Mgmt. Plan* at I-1 [New Orleans Veterans Affairs Med. Ctr. Plan].

Id. at I-7.

Id. at I-10.

Id. at III-6.

Med. Ctr. of LA at New Orleans (MCLNO), *the Emergency Management Manual* (2005) [hereinafter MCLNO Plan].

Id.

Id.

New Orleans Office of Emergency Preparedness, *Hurricane Preparedness Plan*, used by Pendleton Methodist Hosp. (2003) at 9 [New Orleans Hosp. Hurricane Plan].

Id. at 1.

Id. at 3.

Hospital Cries Out for Help New Orleans Charity Hospital (*Good Morning America* television broadcast, Sept. 2, 2005).

Interview by Select Comm. Staff with Larry Graham, former CEO, Pendleton Methodist Hosp. in New Orleans, LA (Dec.19, 2005) [hereinafter Interview with Larry Graham].

Nov. 10 Interview with LA Hosp. Ass'n.

Interview with Larry Graham.

Nov. 7 Interview with Dr. Guidry.

Elizabeth White, *Veterans Affairs' Hurricane Efforts Heralded*, ASSOC. PRESS, Sept. 9, 2005.

Briefing for Select Comm. Staff by Dep't of Veterans Affairs, in Wash., DC (Nov. 4, 2005); Press Release, Dep't of Veterans Affairs, VA Evacuates Patients from Hurricane Area (Sept. 2, 2005).

Interview by Select Comm. Staff with Donald Smithburg, CEO, LSU Health Sciences Ctr./Healthcare Services Div., in New Orleans, LA (Dec. 19, 2005) [hereinafter Dec. 19 LSU Interview].

Id.

Id.

Id.

[150] E-mail correspondence from KC Decker, HHS/OS to Erin Fowler, HHS/OS (Sept. 1, 2005) (9:06 a.m.).

[151] Dec. 19 LSU Interview.

[152] Interview with Larry Graham.

[153] *Id.*

[154] *Id.*

[155] *Id.*

[156] Email correspondence from Jennifer Young, HHS/OS to Alex Azar and Stewart Simonson, HHS/OS (Sept. 2, 2005) (10:50 a.m.).

[157] Interview with Larry Graham.

[158] *CNN NewsNight with Aaron Brown* (CNN Television Broadcast, Sept. 20, 2005).

[159] Sept. 25, OR-2 DMAT After Action Report.

[160] Hemant Vankawala, *A Doctor's Message from Katrina's Front Lines*, (National Public Radio, Sept. 2005), *available at* www.npr.org (last visited Jan 30, 2006) [hereinafter *A Doctor's Message*, Hemant Vankawala].

[161] Interview with FEMA and NDMS.

[162] Dec. 8 FEMA Press Release.

[163] DOD Provides Care Article.

[164] Sept. 25, OR-2 DMAT After Action Report.

[165] *Id.*

[166] *A Doctor's Message*, Hemant Vankawala.

[167] Sept. 25, OR-2 DMAT After Action Report.

[168] *Id.*

[169] *Id.*

[170] Briefing for Select Comm. Staff with the Assoc. of Air Med. Services personnel in Wash., DC (Oct. 18, 2005) [hereinafter Briefing with Air Med personnel]; Assoc. of Air Med. Services, Air Medical Community Response to Hurricane Katrina Disaster: Hospital Evacuation and Patient Relocation by Helicopter and Fixed Wing Aircraft Report (Jan. 9, 2006) [hereinafter Air Med. Report].

[171] *Id.*

[172] Briefing with Air Med. personnel.

[173] *Id.*

[174] Briefing with Air Med. personnel; Air Med. Report.

[175] *Id.*

[176] Briefing with Air Med. personnel.

[177] Air Med. Report.

[178] Briefing with Air Med. personnel.

[179] Briefing with Air Med. personnel.

[180] Briefing with Air Med. personnel; Air Med. Report.

[181] *Id.*

[182] Air Med. Report.

[183] *Id.*

[184] Briefing with Air Med. personnel; Air Med. Report.

[185] Air Med. Report.

[186] Briefing with Air Med. personnel; Air Med. Report.

[187] Briefing with Air Med. personnel.

[188] Biloxi Veterans Affairs Med. Ctr. Plan.

[189] Biloxi Veterans Affairs Med. Ctr. Plan (SSHP Appendix).

[190] *Id.*

[191] *Id.*

[192] New Orleans Veterans Affairs Med. Ctr. Plan.

[193] *Id.*

[194] MCLNO Plan.

[195] New Orleans Hosp. Hurricane Plan.

[196] *Id.*

[197] *Id.*

[198] Interview with Larry Graham.

[199] *Id.*

[200] *American Morning* (CNN Television Broadcast, Sept. 30, 2005).

[201] Stephen Losey, *Katrina Response Marred by Communication Failures*, FED. TIMES (Oct. 3, 2005) [hereinafter Communications Failures Article].

[202] Communications Failures Article.

[203] Dec. 19 LSU Interview.

[204] *Id.*

[205] Randolph Schmid, *Lack of Disease Outbreak Following Katrina 'Amazing,' to Health Director*, ASSOC. PRESS (Oct. 20, 2005).

[206] Dec. 19 Interview with Dr. Stephens.

[207] Interview by Select Comm. Staff with COL Kenneth Knight, Chief, Air Force Med. Operations Ctr., in Wash., DC (Oct. 13, 2005).

[208] Interview by Select Comm. Staff with COL Faulk, Air Nat'l Guard Surgeon, in Wash., DC (Oct. 7, 2005).

[209] National Guard Bureau, [*Hurricane Katrina: After Action Review Observations*] (undated).

[210] Communications Failures Article.

[1] Interview by Select Comm. Staff with Dr. Robert Blitzer, Deputy Assistant Sec'y, Office of Public Health Emergency Preparedness, in Wash., DC (Oct. 10, 2005).

[2] Interview by Select Comm. Staff with Dr. Gerald Parker, Principal Deputy Assistant Sec'y, Office of Public Health Emergency Preparedness, in Wash., DC (Oct. 10, 2005).

[3] Interview with HHS.

[4] Interview by Select Comm. Staff with Jack Beall, Chief, Nat'l Disaster Med. System, in Wash., DC (Jan. 23, 2006) [hereinafter Jan. 23 Interview with Jack Beall].

[5] *Id.*

[6] Sept. 25, OR-2 DMAT After Action Report.

[7] E-mail correspondence from Mark Hansey to EOC IST (Aug. 31, 2005) (3:12 a.m.).

[8] E-mail correspondence from Ron Burger to EOC Report (Sept. 5, 2005) (7:41 a.m.).

[9] E-mail correspondence from Edwin Shanley, CDC Liaison, to EOC Report (Sept. 5, 2005) (3:34 p.m.).

[10] E-mail correspondence from Robert Lavender, HHS/OS, to HHS personnel (Sept. 5, 2005) (3:24 p.m.).

[11] Sept. 25, OR-2 DMAT After Action Report.

[12] Roma Khanna, *Nursing Homes Left Residents With Weak Safety Net*, HOUSTON CHRONICLE (Dec. 11, 2005) [hereinafter Nursing Homes Article].

[13] Nov. 7 Interview with Dr. Guidry.

[14] Nursing Homes Article.

[15] *Id.*; Jan. 19 Interview with Michael Ford, et al.; Nov. 10 Interview with LA Hosp. Ass'n.

[16] *Katrina: New Orleans DA to Investigate Hospital Deaths*, NAT'L J. GROUP, AMERICAN HEALTH LINE (Jan. 18, 2006).

[17] Jan. 19 Interview with Michael Ford, et al.

[18] Jan. 19 Interview with Michael Ford, et al; Plaquemines Parish Gov't, *Phase 1 Mandatory Evacuation Notice* (Aug. 27, 2005) (9:00 a.m.).

[19] Jan. 19 Interview with Michael Ford, et al.

[20] *Id.*

[21] *Id.*

[22] *Reports Show Staff Tried to Save Lives at St. Rita's*, NEWS-STAR, Monroe, LA (Nov. 29, 2005) at 1A [hereinafter St. Rita's Article].

[23] Jan. 19 Interview with Michael Ford, et al.

[24] Press Release, Office of Attorney General, State of LA, Nursing Homes Owners Surrender to Medicaid Fraud Control Unit Investigators (Sept. 13, 2005).

[25] *Id.*

[26] St. Rita's Article.

[27] Marianne Kolbasuk McGee, *Storm Shows Benefit, Failures of Technology*, INFO. WEEK, (Sept. 12, 2005) [hereinafter Failures of Technology Article].

[28] *Id.*

[29] Lauran Neergaard, *Katrina Highlights Need for Computerized Medical Records*, ASSOC. PRESS (Sept. 13, 2005) [hereinafter Need for Computerized Medical Records Article].

[30] *Id.*

[31] Dec. 19 Interview with Dr. Stephens.

[32] Failures of Technology Article.

[33] *Id.*

[34] *"Katrina Health,"* available at www.katrinahealth.org (last visited Jan. 20, 2006).

[35] *Id.*

[36] *Id.*

[37] Need for Computerized Medical Records Article.

[38] *Id.*

[39] Press Release, HHS, HHS Enters Into Agreements to Support Digital Health Recovery for the Gulf Coast (Nov. 17, 2005).

[40] *Id.*

[41] Interview with FEMA and NDMS.

[42] E-mail correspondence from Pamela Williams, DHS, to Jay Lerner (Jan. 27, 2005) (6:41 p.m.).

[43] Interview with HHS.

[44] *Id.*

[45] *Id.*

[46] *Id.*

[47] E-mail correspondence from Mark Roupas, USACE Liaison to Paul McHale, HON, OSD (Aug. 29, 2005) (5:54 p.m.).

[48] Interview with HHS.

[49] Minority Staff Of House Comm. On Gov't Reform, Special Investigations Div., 109th Cong., *Report On The Decline Of The National Disaster Medical System* (2005).

[50] Interview with HHS.

[51] Jan. 23 Interview with Jack Beall.

[52] Sept. 25, OR-2 DMAT After Action Report.

[53] *Id.*

[54] Jan. 23 Interview with Jack Beall.

[55] Congressional Research Service [hereinafter CRS], Rep. No. 33096 at 5 (Oct. 4, 2002).

[56] *Id.* at 24.

[57] *NRP* at ESF#8.

[268] E-mail Correspondence from John Nesler, Dep't of Def. [hereinafter DOD] to Millard Bell, DHS (Sept. 4, 2005) (12:56 p.m.).

[269] *Id.*

[270] *Id.*

[271] Interview with HHS.

[272] *Id.*

[273] E-mail correspondence from John Jordan, U.S. Army to Army, DHS, and NORTHCOM personnel (Sept. 5, 2005) (10:03 a.m.).

[274] Lara Jakes Jordan, *Slow Removal of Katrina Bodies Caused by Louisiana Governor's Indecision*, Memos Say, ASSOC. PRESS (Oct. 27, 2005).

[275] *Id.*

[276] E-mail correspondence from Keith Holtermann, Incident Manager, HHS/SOC to FEMA and HHS personnel (Sept. 5, 2005) (9:46 p.m.).

[277] *Id.*

[278] E-mail correspondence from Keith Holtermann, Incident Manager, HHS/SOC to Robert Blitzer, HHS/OS and other personnel (Sept. 6, 2005) (6:35 a.m.).

[279] *Id.*

[280] DOD Provides Care Article.

[281] E-mail correspondence from Phil Navin, Div. of Emergency Operations, CDC to EOC Report and personnel (Aug. 30 2005) (8:00 p.m.).

[282] E-mail correspondence from Andy Hunt, Commander, USPHS to John Mallos, BSN, RN, LCDR, USPHS, OSG (Sept. 2, 2005) (1:06 p.m.).

[283] E-mail correspondence from David Elder, FDA to John Mallos, BSN, RN, LCDR, USPHS, OSG (Sept. 4, 2005) (11:17 p.m.).

[284] E-mail correspondence from John Mallos, BSN, RN, LCDR, USPHS, OSG to Kurt Kesteloot, Environmental Engineer, USPHS (Sept. 4, 2005) (6:18 p.m.).

[285] E-mail correspondence from John Mallos, BSN, RN, LCDR, USPHS, OSG to tsblumen@CHEQNET.NET (Sept 1, 2005) (7:58 p.m.).

[286] E-mail correspondence from Nick Makrides, BOP GOV to John Mallos, USPHS (Sept. 1, 2005) (8:32 a.m.).

[287] E-mail correspondence from Mark Tedaesco, USCG/USPHS to John Mallos, USPHS, OSG (Aug. 30, 2005) (5:12 p.m.).

[288] E-mail correspondence from John Mallos, BSN, RN, LCDR, USPHS, OSG to FEMA and HHS personnel (Sept. 5, 2005) (7:01 a.m.).

[289] E-mail correspondence from Robert Blitzer, OS to OS staff (Sept. 9, 2005) (10:35 a.m.).

[290] E-mail correspondence from Keith Holtermann, Incident Manager, HHS/SOC to HHS personnel (Sept 22, 2005) (2:48 a.m.).

[291] E-mail correspondence from Edwin Shanley, CDC Liaison to Debra Townes, CDC (Sept 7, 2005) (8:35 p.m.).

[292] http://www.comfort.navy.mil (last visited Jan. 26, 2006).

[293] Response from U.S.N. Command to Select Comm. Staff (Oct. 26, 2005).

[294] Henry J. Holcomb, *Rerouted: Sen. Lott of Miss. Steps into Divert Hospital Ship*, PHILA. INQUIRER, Sept. 10, 2005 at A01.

[295] E-mail correspondence from Bruce Burney, CDC to CDC personnel (Sept. 9, 2005) (7:41 a.m.).

[296] E-mail correspondence from Gregory Banner, HHS/OS to KC Decker, HHS/OS (Sept. 9, 2005) (10:39 p.m.).

[297] E-mail correspondence from Keith Holtermann, Incident Manager, HHS/SOC to HHS and TX personnel (Sept. 22, 2005) (12:44 a.m.).

[298] Sept. 25, OR-2 DMAT After Action Report.

[299] E-mail correspondence from Jon Ferko, Special Assistant to Paul McHale (Sept. 2, 2005) (1:27 p.m.).

"We were then lured to the so-called evacuation points. This was several days after the hurricane had struck. The city was flooded ... They loaded us onto military trucks after they told us they would take us to shelters where our basic needs would be met."

"We were in a wide open space along the interstate and under the Highway 10 causeway. The overpass provided little shade, however ... It was early September and still extremely hot. Our skin blistered. My mother's skin is still not fully healed."

Leah Hodges
New Orleans Citizen and Evacuee
Select Committee Hearing, December 6, 2005

SHELTER AND HOUSING

Long-standing weaknesses and the magnitude of the disaster overwhelmed FEMA's ability to provide emergency shelter and temporary housing

"Scooter: Please see below. The trailer idea is worse than I originally thought. Per the data below, the last batch of the trailers that we are now purchasing will be coming off the production line in approximately 3.5 years."

E-mail from Neil S. Patel, Staff Secretary to the Vice President, to Charles P. Durkin, Personal Aide to the Vice President, (apparently destined for Chief of Staff J. Lewis "Scooter" Libby, Jr.), September 9, 2005

AP PHOTO/BILL HABER

Summary

Like food and water, shelter is a basic human need. Hurricane Katrina transformed thousands of people's lives into a battle for survival — and, for some, finding adequate shelter proved at least as difficult as finding something to eat or drink.

Katrina, of course, was a powerful storm that hit vulnerable areas, requiring more than traditional solutions for immediate shelter and, later, temporary housing. Louisiana and Mississippi immediately were faced with thousands and thousands of the suddenly homeless, without the ability to provide emergency shelter or longer-term housing for all of them. Within a month, 44 states had played a role in sheltering the evacuees from Hurricanes Katrina and Rita.

But it is clear state and local governments in the areas most affected by the hurricanes were not adequately prepared. They failed to learn important lessons from the Hurricane Pam exercise, and lacked the necessary information about temporary housing. Shelters of last resort, designed for people to take refuge in the immediate hours before and after landfall (such as the Superdome), were not of sufficient capacity. Instead, the Superdome, itself located in a floodplain, had to bear a burden for which it was not prepared. The New Orleans Convention Centre, never planned as a shelter, became one out of sheer necessity and improvisation.

There was no comprehensive database of available shelters, which only complicated relief efforts. There were also delays in getting people out of shelters and into temporary housing. And FEMA's strategy of ordering 200,000 trailers and mobile homes shortly after the storm was blind to the nation's manufacturing capacity of 6,000 units per month.

Housing issues remain a tremendous concern for residents of the Gulf coast affected by Hurricane Katrina. Local elected officials in both Louisiana and Mississippi remain disappointed in FEMA's pace in setting up temporary housing. Debate over how long rental assistance will continue rages on. The question of where to build, or re-build, in the Gulf coast is the subject of great debate, both locally and nationally, as is who will pay for it. However, the long-term housing challenges in the Gulf coast are beyond the scope of the Select Committee's inquiry and are not covered in this report. Our charge was to examine the immediate response, not the recovery. We are certain the longer-term issues will continue to be discussed by others in Congress.

Finding: Relocation plans did not adequately provide for shelter. Housing plans were haphazard and inadequate

Shelter needs overwhelmed state and local governments

Initially, Hurricane Katrina displaced more than a million Gulf coast residents. As in most natural disasters, some evacuees only needed short-term shelter and were able to return home after the immediate crisis passed. However, because of the magnitude of the storm, hundreds of thousands remained displaced — for days, weeks, even months. Many are homeless today.

For example, Louisiana had 563 American Red Cross or state emergency shelters with a peak population of 146,292 in the early days following Hurricane Katrina's landfall.[1] Additionally, Louisiana had 10 special needs shelters that housed 2,480 persons.[2] In Mississippi, initial damage estimates projected 120,000 individuals needing emergency temporary housing.[3] A month after the storm, 44 states and the District of Columbia have been given emergency declarations to cover expenses related to sheltering evacuees forced from their homes by Hurricanes Katrina and Rita.[4]

In a catastrophic event like Katrina, many evacuees may be displaced for a longer than normal period of time or may permanently lose their housing. As FEMA and state officials learned from the Hurricane Pam exercise, temporary housing was an area of weakness.[5] Deputy FCO Scott Wells noted there were several follow-up items from the Hurricane Pam Exercise that state and local governments failed to execute, including developing more detailed concepts and plans on sheltering and temporary housing.[6] Similarly, Alabama state and local government plans lack information about temporary housing.[7]

FEMA

Finding: State and local governments made inappropriate selections of shelters of last resort. The lack of a regional database of shelters contributed to an inefficient and ineffective evacuation and sheltering process

The evacuation of millions of people prior to Hurricane Katrina's landfall created an urgent need to identify, and direct people to, suitable shelters. Officials had worried about the high number of people who would ignore hurricane evacuation orders in coastal areas.[8] Indeed, thousands of people in New Orleans did not obey the mandatory evacuation order. Shelters of last resort — places for persons to be protected from the high winds, storm surge, and heavy rains, but with little or no water or food — were needed for those who did not or could not evacuate the area.

A shelter of last resort is intended to provide the best available survival protection for the duration of the hurricane only.[9] In Louisiana, emergency operations plans required shelters of last resort to be located outside of the floodplain, or have the ability to locate on floors elevated above flood potential, and have a hurricane wind resistant structure.[10] The Superdome was used as a shelter of last resort even though it was located in a floodplain. In addition, the Superdome roof suffered extensive wind damage, demonstrating that it was not a hurricane wind resistant structure.

Many residents who took refuge in the Superdome found conditions there unbearable. Some tried to leave, only to find themselves trapped by the floodwaters that surrounded the hulking structure. Cleo Fisher, an 86-year-old resident of Bywater, told a local newspaper that he left the dome to try to get some heart medications.[11] He didn'

Evacuees tend to go to the most convenient and familiar shelter they can find, even though it may be inadequate.

et far — and, in fact, had to be rescued after he fell into he nearby water — but he did not want to return inside, ither.[12]

"It's worse than being in prison in there," he said. They don't have nothing for me."

Even some of the police officers and military personnel harged with keeping order inside the dome became ustrated with the lack of organization.

"This plan," said one police officer, "was no plan."[13]

Although some local emergency plans call for the lentification of local shelters, in a multi-state disaster, compilation of available shelters in the region may be hore appropriate. Government officials did not have a omprehensive database from which to identify suitable hd available shelters; therefore, identification of alternate helter locations was done on an ad hoc basis.[14] Because f the lack of a database of shelters, local, state, and federal officials have had a difficult time identifying the umbers and locations of displaced individuals.[15] This ck of information has complicated the relief effort, and d to the inefficient use of shelter resources.

The lack of a comprehensive means for tracking acuees has exacerbated difficulties in reuniting family embers and in determining accurate counts of people

FEMA

so as to more accurately provide for their needs[16] Out of human nature, evacuees tend to go to the most convenient and familiar shelter they can find, even though it may be inadequate. A database could be a helpful resource for planning and providing emergency public information. Similar initiatives have been proposed previously during the Cold War as part of civil defense, such as Crisis Relocation Planning.[17]

Finding: There was inappropriate delay in getting people out of shelters and into temporary housing — delays that officials should have foreseen due to manufacturing limitations

Dr. Gavin Smith told a congressional committee that "[w]ithout the rapid provision of temporary and permanent housing solutions, recovery will be slowed or fail to occur in a manner that meets the needs of disaster victims . . .."[18] Although temporary housing efforts in the wake of Katrina have far exceeded any previous effort, individuals remained in shelters for unacceptably long periods of time. Temporary housing efforts have fallen short of meeting demand. Federal, state, and local agencies failed to implement a successful program to shelter and place many evacuees in temporary housing.

FEMA established a Housing Area Command to oversee all temporary housing operations across Louisiana, Mississippi, and Alabama.[19] Although this group began identifying available land prior to landfall, temporary housing efforts suffered from delays. A Mississippi recovery official hailed FEMA for "the fastest deployment of temporary housing units to a disaster-stricken area since the program was established," but also noted the effort has not been good enough.[20] Specifically, he noted that operational and long-term planning and inter-organizational coordination remains unrealized, and the current approach is not sufficient to address the needs of communities and states following a catastrophic disaster like Hurricane Katrina.[21]

Due to the massive need for temporary housing, the federal government put together a plan that included a combination of old and new housing strategies, including housing people in trailers and on cruise ships.[22]

Housing still falls short of the overwhelming need. There are still delays in getting evacuees into trailers once they are delivered, due to among other things infrastructure, zoning and environmental issues.

Additionally, FEMA used hotels to serve as temporary emergency lodging, utilizing 85,000 rooms nationwide at the program's peak.[23] However, state and local officials complained of poor coordination by FEMA on these temporary housing solutions.[24] Immediately following the storm, FEMA contracted with cruise ships to provide transitional housing for hurricane victims close to the disaster area.[25] Many evacuees rejected this option, something that perhaps could have been avoided if there had been better coordination beforehand. Many individuals felt they needed to focus on finding jobs and obtaining permanent housing.[26]

Although FEMA began strategic housing planning before Katrina's landfall, and the private sector mobilized quickly to fill FEMA's manufactured housing demand, many issues also have plagued the relocation into this form of temporary housing. Mississippi Federal Coordinating Officer (FCO) William Carwile testified that over 24,000 travel trailers and mobile homes had been occupied in Mississippi.[27] FEMA logistics has reported that nine trains a week have been carrying approximately 90 trailers per train into the Gulf region. And, on January 11, 2006, FEMA announced that nearly 62,000 travel trailers and mobile homes were serving as temporary homes for Hurricane Katrina and Rita victims.[28] This number nearly tripled the number of units used following all of last year's Florida hurricanes and far outnumbered any housing mission in FEMA's history.[29]

Despite this commendable effort, housing still falls short of the overwhelming need. There are still delays in getting evacuees into trailers once they are delivered, due to among other things infrastructure, zoning, and environmental issues.[30] In Mississippi, the lack of working utilities for private sites and environmental and zoning issues with group sites have delayed the installation of travel trailers and mobile homes.[31]

FEMA's strategy of ordering 200,000 trailers and mobile homes shortly after the storm was blind to the nation's manufacturing capacity of 6,000 units per month. On Friday, September 9, staff to the Vice President and Office of Management and Budget (OMB) officials ratcheted up

concerns about FEMA's decision to rely on trailers and mobile homes to house displaced residents.[32] Special Assistant to the Vice President Marie Fishpaw wrote in an e-mail to Patel:

> FEMA have (sic) set up arrangements to order 200,000 units of trailers (and mobile homes) and committed up to $500 million to do so. They want to get 30,000 units (79% of the existing market) soon. FEMA plans to order another 100,000 units. OMB and OVP staff remain skeptical about this strategy. The nation can produce 6,000 units per month. There is probably some capacity for expansion (possibly by about 10%) to meet increased demand, but we don't know how much. That means most of these units won't be available for months. Further, some states, including Louisiana, are balking at the idea of large (25,000 units, as proposed by FEMA) trailer parks. We got all this info from OMB career staff.[33]

That message was then forwarded, apparently intended for then Chief of Staff to the Vice President, "I Lewis Libby, Jr.: "Please see below. The trailer idea is worse than I originally thought. Per the data below, the last batch of the trailers that we are now purchasing will be coming of the production line in approximately 3.5 years."[34]

Finding: FEMA failed to take advantage of HUD's expertise in large-scale housing challenges

FEMA has been working in partnership with the U.S. Department of Agriculture (USDA), the Department of Veterans Affairs (VA), and the Department of Housing and Urban Development (HUD) to meet the challenge of finding and securing sufficient rental assets to meet the huge demands created by mass evacuations. By early

FEMA has shown flexibility by allowing those individuals to be eligible for additional rental assistance, use of a voucher system similar to the one administered by HUD could have prevented this mistake.

In this case, FEMA failed to take full advantage of HUD's expertise and perspective on large-scale housing challenges, such as the agency's experience with voucher programs. HUD and public housing authorities have the expertise and infrastructure to help non-HUD clients during disasters.

ecember 2005, 5,000 displaced families had been placed n federal housing of some sort.[35] USDA has offered units om their own inventory, placing 974 families from ouisiana alone.[36]

Additionally, FEMA has concluded an inter-agency greement with the VA to rent unused VA housing units o evacuees, and FEMA is pursuing a similar arrangement ith Fannie Mae.[37] On September 12, 2005, FEMA signed n Interagency Agreement with HUD.[38] This agreement dentified and made available 5,600 HUD single-family omes.[39] Hundreds of disaster victims have made these omes their temporary residences, including 207 families Texas.[40]

FEMA and HUD have also partnered on the Katrina isaster Housing Assistance Program (KDHAP), a ansitional housing assistance program funded by FEMA nd administered by HUD and the network of public ousing authorities. Through KDHAP, HUD is providing ouchers to evacuees previously receiving public housing ssistance, as well as evacuees who were homeless prior to e hurricane.[41] By December 2005, nearly 15,000 families ceived rental assistance through KDHAP.[42]

In contrast, FEMA has used direct payments to acuees to provide rental assistance to more than 0,000 applicants, totaling more than $1.2 billion.[43] nfortunately, many displaced households received their itial rental assistance before receiving mailed guidance d did not use this assistance for housing, but instead ed it to meet other disaster-related needs.[44] Although

Conclusion

Despite this Herculean effort, state officials feel there has been a lack of coordination within the interagency community causing delay in relocating and housing people.[45] Although the federal government has shown some ingenuity in coming up with unique solutions such as lodging on cruise ships, and orchestrated the largest mobilization of temporary housing units in history, both of these solutions have proven inadequate.

Carwile, the Mississippi FCO, noted the need for taking a new look at housing solutions:

> In Mississippi, while temporary housing has been provided in numbers far exceeding any previous effort, this success is obscured by the overwhelming need and an exceptionally long period of time that people remain in shelters. New methodologies must be examined and implemented to take care of Americans in need of humane housing while in a catastrophic event.[46]

The devastation caused by Hurricane Katrina was heartbreaking enough for the people who lost their homes. Sadly, however, the days and weeks and months that followed provided little relief. The government plans for their shelter were far from adequate. ■

1 *Hearing on Housing Options in the Aftermath of Hurricanes Katrina and Rita Before the Comm. on Financial Services Subcomm. on Housing and Community Opportunity*, 109th Cong. (Jan. 13-14, 2006) at 3 (written testimony of Scott Wells, Federal Coordinating Officer for LA, FEMA) [hereinafter *Jan. 13-14, 2006 Financial Services Comm. Hearing*].

2 *Id.*

3 *Id.* (written testimony of James N. Russo, Federal Coordinating Officer for MS, FEMA) at 3.

4 FEMA, *2005 Federal Disaster Declarations*, http://www.fema.gov/news/disasters.fema?year=2005 (last visited Jan.12, 2006).

5 Interviews by Select Comm. Staff with FEMA and Louisiana State officials in New Orleans, LA (Nov. 3-10, 2005).

6 Interviews by Select Comm. Staff with FEMA officials in New Orleans, LA (Nov. 3-10, 2005).

7 Alabama Emergency Management Agency, *State of AL Emergency Operations Plan*, Oct. 1, 2000.

8 Timothy R. Brown, *Miss. Governor Declares State of Emergency as Katrina Nears*, LEDGER-ENQUIRER, Columbus, GA, Aug. 27, 2005.

9 State of LA Emergency Operations Plan Supplement 1B, *Southwest LA Hurricane Evacuation and Sheltering Plan*, (July 2000) at VI-1.

10 State of LA Emergency Operations Plan Supplement 1C: *Louisiana Shelter Operations Plan*, (July 2000).

11 Gordon Russell, *Refuges Find Dome An Intolerable Refuge*, NEW ORLEANS TIMES-PICAYUNE, Sept. 1, 2005, 5.

12 *Id.*

13 *Id.*

14 *DHS HSOC SPOT Report prepared by Matthew Thompson, NRCC* (Aug. 31, 2005).

15 Jan Moller, *La. seeks help compiling evacuee shelter database*, NEW ORLEANS TIMES-PICAYUNE, Sept. 10, 2005, A-7.

16 Shankar Vedantam and Dean Starkman, *Lack of Cohesion Bedevils Recovery*, WASHINGTON POST, Sept. 18, 2005, A01.

17 B. Wayne Blanchard, FEMA, *American Civil Defense 1945-1984: The Evolution of Programs and Policies*, (National Emergency Center Monograph Series Vol. 2, No. 2, 1985) at 19-20.

18 *Jan. 13-14, 2006 Financial Services Comm. Hearing* (written testimony of Dr. Gavin Smith, Director, Office of Recovery and Renewal, Office of Gov. Barbour) at 2.

19 FEMA News Release, *FEMA Contracts to Provide Housing Relief for Displaced Hurricane Victims*, Sept. 8, 2005.

20 *Jan. 13-14, 2006 Financial Services Comm. Hearing* (written testimony of Gavin Smith) at 1.

21 *Id.*

22 Rick Weiss, *Victims' Next Homes: Cruise Ships, Trailers*, WASHINGTON POST, Sept. 5, 2005, A15.

23 *Jan. 13-14, 2006 Financial Services Comm. Hearing* (written testimony of Scott Wells) at 4.

24 Audio recordings of Hurricane Katrina Conference Calls, LA State Emergency Operations Center (Aug. 26-28, 2005, Sept. 9, 2005).

25 FEMA, News Release, *Temporary Housing for Hurricane Katrina Evacuees Includes Cruise Ships, FEMA Reports*, Sept. 4, 2005.

26 Shankar Vedantam and Dean Starkman, *Lack of Cohesion Bedevils Recovery*, WASHINGTON POST, Sept. 18, 2005.

27 *Hearing on Hurricane Katrina: Preparedness and Response by the State of Mississippi Before Select Comm.*, 109th Cong. (Dec. 7, 2005) at 8 (written testimony of William L. Carwile, III, former Federal Coordinating Officer, Hurricane Katrina Response and Initial Recovery Operations: MS).

28 FEMA, *By the Numbers: FEMA Recovery Update for Hurricanes Katrina & Rita*, Jan. 11, 2006.

29 *Id.*

30 *Interview by Select Comm. Staff with Gary Moore, Director of Logistics, FEMA, in Washington, DC (Jan. 9, 2006).*

31 *Jan.13-14, 2006 Financial Services Comm. Hearing* (written testimony of James N. Russo) at 7.

32 *See* Aimee Curl, *Federal-Local Conflicts Keep Victims Out of FEMA Trailers*, FEDERAL TIMES, Jan. 16, 2006.

33 E-mail correspondence from Marie Fishpaw, Special Assistant to the Vice President, to Neil Patel, Staff Secretary to the Vice President, (Sept. 9, 2005) (1:41 p.m.).

34 E-mail correspondence from Neil Patel to Charles Durkin, (Sept. 9, 2005) (1:49 p.m.)

35 *Hearing on Housing Options in the Aftermath of Hurricanes Katrina and Rita Before the Comm. on Financial Services Subcomm. on Housing and Community Opportunity*, 109th Cong. (Dec. 8, 2005) at 12 (written testimony of David Garratt, Acting Director, Recovery Division, EMA) [hereinafter *Dec. 8, 2005 Financial Services Comm. Hearing*].

36 *Id.* at 12.

37 *Id.*

38 *Id.* (written testimony of Brian Montgomery, Assistant Secretary for Office of Housing/Federal Housing Commissioner, HUD) at 4.

39 *Id.*

40 *Id.* (written testimony of David Garratt) at 13.

41 *Id.* at 13-14.

42 *Id.* (written testimony of Brian Montgomery) at 6.

43 *Id.* (written testimony of David Garratt) at 6.

44 *Id.* at 6-7.

45 *Jan.13-14, 2006 Financial Services Comm. Hearing* (written testimony of Gavin Smith) at 1.

46 *Hearing on Hurricane Katrina: Perspectives of FEMA's Operational Professionals, Before the Senate Committee on Homeland Security and Governmental Affairs*, 109th Cong. (Dec. 8, 2005) at 37 (testimony of William L. Carwile, III, former Federal Coordinating Officer, Hurricane Katrina Response and Initial Recovery Operations: MS).

"[O]ne of the lessons that we need to learn from this catastrophic event is that we do need to get better about marshaling those assets and moving them around. I will tell you up front, FEMA has a logistics problem, we have a problem understanding all the time. I can point out where our stuff is and I can point out where it's supposed to go to; I can't always tell you that it actually got there."

Michael D. Brown
Former FEMA Director
Select Committee Hearing, September 27, 2005

LOGISTICS AND CONTRACTING

FEMA logistics and contracting systems did not support a targeted, massive, and sustained provision of commodities

Katrina overwhelmed the Federal Emergency Management Agency (FEMA) management and overloaded its logistics system. Response and relief personnel had little visibility into available federal assets and resources. The process for requesting assistance could not support the volume of requests, and the technology supporting that process proved inadequate. Federal, state, and local officials requested assistance outside existing channels with little coordination and communication. "[M]anagement by crisis would be the best way I could put it," said Kip Holden, Mayor of East Baton Rouge Parish.[1]

By September 9, Congress had passed legislation providing over $63 billion to the Department of Homeland Security (DHS) for disaster relief.[2] The circumstances and urgent needs created by Hurricane Katrina provided significant opportunity for fraud and mismanagement, and the DHS Office of Inspector General (OIG) estimates the cost to recover from the storm and rebuild the affected areas could exceed $200 billion.[3]

As of November 30, 2005, $19.3 billion has been obligated to needs resulting from Hurricane Katrina.[4] The funds have been used to relieve the immediate suffering of individuals and families, clear debris, reimburse federal agencies for the costs of technical and direct assistance, and support federal operations such as search and rescue, and delivery of consumables. The $19 billion has been obligated as follows:

- $8 billion for human service needs including unemployment compensation, personal needs that are not met by insurance, and temporary housing

(including vouchers for hotel/motel rooms and mobile homes);
- $2.2 billion for debris removal, public building repair and replacement, and damage inspections;
- $4.4 billion for technical and direct assistance provided by federal agencies;
- $14.7 million for inspections and hazard mitigation; and,
- $4.7 billion for administrative expenses, almost $3 billion of which has been obligated for mission assignment operations undertaken by other federal agencies at the direction of the federal officer responsible for coordinating response activities.[5]

Despite this outpouring of funds, procurement officials struggled to balance the competing and conflicting demands of local and elected officials. On October 21, New Orleans Mayor Ray Nagin complained about the time-consuming amount of federal oversight accompanying the federal dollars going to contracts and local governments. He said

> [t]he money is sitting in the doggone bank. . . . We can't use it, and as soon as they gave us the money, they sent a team of auditors and said, 'If you spend this money, we'll be watching you real close. . . .' So we're gun shy about how we use this money . . . .[6]

and

> [w]e just got these huge multinational companies that are using the shield of, 'We've got to work quick,' [rather than] trying to find local contractors.[7]

The Government Accountability Office (GAO) is undertaking a review of Katrina relief contracting

"[Hurricane Katrina] was beyond the capacity of the state and local governments, and it was beyond the capacity of FEMA. It was the largest natural disaster ever to strike the United States — 92,000 square miles. Logistics were falling apart."

activities. GAO's review includes acquisition planning, communication of responsibilities between various entities, contract management, and the use of emergency acquisition authorities. GAO briefed the Select Commitee on their review efforts, which will complement the findings of this report.

Finding: FEMA management lacked situational awareness of existing requirements and of resources in the supply chain. An overwhelmed logistics system made it challenging to get supplies, equipment, and personnel where and when needed

When President Bush authorized a federal emergency declaration for Mississippi and Alabama on Sunday, August 28, in response to these states' requests, then-FEMA Director Michael Brown said he began to "predeploy all the assets [including] the medical teams, the urban search and rescue teams, the emergency response, the management teams, the rapid needs assessment teams, prepositioning the water, the Meals Ready to Eat, the ice, the tarps."[8] However, given that landfall occurred on Monday, August 29, this was too late to begin the pre-deployment process.

FEMA leadership acknowledged this lack of planning. "[Hurricane Katrina] was beyond the capacity of the state and local governments, and it was beyond the capacity of FEMA," said Brown. "It was the largest natural disaster ever to strike the United States — 92,000 square miles. Logistics were falling apart."[9] When FEMA did arrive, representatives sometimes were empty-handed. "[W]hen FEMA finally did show up, everybody was angry because that is all they had was a Web site and a flier. They didn't have any real resources that they could give," reported Senator Pryor following visits and conversations with victims.[10]

Brown's testimony outlined some of the resources FEMA had in place. Prior to landfall FEMA had 14 trailer loads of Meals Ready to Eat ("MREs") at Camp Beauregard, Louisiana, four trailers in Moffit, 42 in Forth Worth, 15 trailer loads in Fullersville, 75 at two locations in Atlanta, three in Cumberland, Maryland, 15 in Charlotte, North Carolina, six in Eastover, South Carolina, 46 in Palmetto, Georgia, 15 in Homestead, Florida, at the airbase, 10 in Meridian, and two at the Superdome.[11]

Some suggested these resources should have been more readily available. Rep. Chip Pickering said "[most MREs] were [prepositioned] across the region, only a few in Meridian and a few in New Orleans, and that should have been closer, I think, to the storm."[12] Rep. Gene Taylor pointed out the provisions were too far away from the FEMA team, questioning

> [w]hat part of the FEMA plan envisioned that the first responders in Hancock County and in much of the Mississippi Gulf Coast would have to loot the local grocery store and loot the local Wal-Mart in order to feed themselves, would have to loot the local Wal-Mart in order to have a change of clothes? What part of your plan was that?[13]

Brown, however, strongly rejected the contention of having relief items in the immediate impacted areas, saying expectations must be realistic:

> [T]he last thing I'm going to do is to put equipment or manpower in place where they themselves become victims and then cannot assist the people they are there to assist. You cannot, you cannot physically — I don't think you can do it statutorily or any other way — say to any victim in this country that the minute you come out of your

abode, your home, your shelter, whatever it is, that the Federal Government is going to be there with a meal ready to eat for you. That is an unreasonable expectation. So what we do is we preposition those supplies so that we can move them in and help them. And that's why the FEMA plan, that's why the basic emergency management system says you should, as an individual, take personal responsibility and be prepared to be on your own for perhaps up to 2 or 3 days. If Congress expects the Federal Government to be able to supply every individual food and water immediately following a catastrophe or a disaster, then this committee in Congress needs to have a serious public policy debate about what the role of FEMA and the Federal Government is in disasters.[14]

According to the Director of the Mississippi Emergency Management Agency (MEMA), Robert Latham, the federal logistics system failed in the days immediately following Hurricane Katrina, leaving state officials without adequate supplies of food, water, and ice for emergency shelters.[15] FEMA representatives working with MEMA requested 450 trucks of water and ice, and 50 trucks of MREs. When less than 15 percent of the requested supplies arrived, state emergency responders were forced to purchase the commodities on the commercial market or obtain supplies from neighboring states.[16]

Mississippi officials had to deal with shortages of commodities for the first nine to ten days after landfall.[17] Fortunately, Mississippi officials had purchased supplies for Hurricane Dennis (July 2005) that were not used. Similarly,

FEMA

Florida officials had pre-positioned considerable resources to be used in the Florida Panhandle,[18] which, until Friday, August 26, was where Katrina was projected to make landfall. Commodities were provided by Governor Bush to Mississippi Governor Haley Barbour under the Emergency Management Assistance Compact (EMAC) and offered some relief to the victims in Mississippi's coastal counties.[19]

FEMA has a logistics problem, we have a problem understanding all the time. I can point out where our stuff is and I can point out where it's supposed to go to; I can't always tell you that it actually got there.

Federal Coordinating Officer (FCO) Bill Carwile speculated the shortages were the result of an overly centralized logistics system overwhelmed by the requirements of the three large disasters: Hurricanes Dennis, Katrina, and Rita. Mississippi officials asked permission to purchase (on their own) commodities from elsewhere to supplement those being provided by the centralized system. Carwile said he was authorized by FEMA Director Michael Brown to make these purchases.[20]

According to the Director of the Alabama Emergency Management Agency (AEMA), Bruce Baughman, a better contracting process for essentials and commodities is needed.[21] In the days before Katrina made landfall, when officials submitted commodity requirements for Alabama for items such as water, ice, MREs, these requests were unilaterally reduced by FEMA officials – often so reflexively that it appeared to be part of standard FEMA procedure. Baughman said their initial requests were carefully and precisely tailored to meet the actual needs of Alabama. Tim Payne, AEMA Branch Chief and Emergency Management Program Coordinator, said in advance of Katrina, their needs assessment concluded Alabama would require 100 trucks of water and 100 trucks of ice.[22] In response to this request, FEMA made available only 17 trucks of water and 16 trucks of ice.

Frequently during the Alabama response to Katrina, FEMA did not follow through with AEMA's requests for supplies and emergency support.[23] It appeared FEMA did not have the ability to track commodities within its own logistics system. To defend against commodity shortfalls in future emergencies, Alabama recently issued a Request for Proposals for key commodities and materials needed for an effective emergency response.[24] Baughman suggested having standing contracts in place and supplies

FEMA's logistics program is broken and needs to be fixed.

at the ready so the states would not again fall victim to an inadequate FEMA response or supply shortages due to other market competitors in times of crisis.[25]

Payne identified 12 categories of items that need to be on hand to effectively deal with an emergency.[26]

According to Brown, "one of the lessons that we need to learn from this catastrophic event is that we do need to get better about marshaling those assets and moving them around. I will tell you up front, FEMA has a logistics problem, we have a problem understanding all the time. I can point out where our stuff is and I can point out where it's supposed to go to; I can't always tell you that it actually got there."[27]

These problems are not new, however. FEMA's "bureaucratic slowness" in securing long-term housing and loans, removing debris, and getting basic assistance and reimbursement were "'huge problems that have been very frustrating," stated Florida Governor Jeb Bush before the House Homeland Security Committee.[28] Getting one truckload of ice from Atlanta to Florida in 2004 took a series of separate contracts that caused needless delays. "'FEMA's logistics program is broken and needs to be fixed. . . . I can say with certainty that federalizing emergency response to catastrophic events would be a disaster as bad as Hurricane Katrina," Governor Jeb Bush testified. "If you federalize, all the innovation, creativity and knowledge at the local level would subside.'"[29]

It should be noted FEMA used existing resources, procedures, and staff to organize and conduct a massive civil logistics operation beyond any this country has seen before. Over 11,000 trucks of water, ice, and meals were moved into the disaster region during the month after landfall. This is more than three times the number of trucks used during all hurricanes in 2004.[30] FEMA tried, but Katrina's magnitude exposed significant weakness and inefficiencies in the process.

Finding: Procedures for requesting federal assistance raised numerous concerns

Requests for federal assistance go through a standard process. Local government officials submit their requests to the state, and, if state officials cannot meet the request, they forward appropriate requests to federal officials.[31] In Louisiana, state and local emergency management officials manage requests for assistance during disasters using specially-designed commercial software called "E-Team."[32] E-Team is a web-based system and can be accessed from any computer with internet connectivity. According to Matt Farlow of Louisiana Office of Homeland Security and Emergency Preparedness (LOHSEP) Information Technology Division, Louisiana has used E-Team since 2000 and LOHSEP personnel are well-experienced in its use.[33] In addition to using E-Team to register and track parish requests, the Louisiana Emergency Operations Center (EOC) also uses it to send out e-mail alerts and notifications to parishes.

The parish-to-state process is much the same as the state-to-federal process. The parishes declare emergencies and request assistance from the state.[34] The parishes register their requests for assistance with the state directly via the internet with E-Team. However, according to state officials, not all parish officials know how to use E-Team well: "They don't know all the bells and whistles."[35] Parish officials can also register requests to the state by telephone or radio. If the parish communicates a request outside E-Team, by voice, e-mail, or fax communications, then the state EOC officials enter that request into E-Team.

The state receives the parish requests for assistance and determines whether the requests can be met from a nearby parish or with state resources.[36] If so, LOHSEP tasks that mission to another state agency. The state can also request assistance from nearby states through the EMAC.[37] When a state makes an EMAC request to another state, it is undertaking an obligation to pay that state for that assistance.[38] FEMA has a mechanism to later reimburse appropriate costs to the requesting state, which the state can use to repay the sending state. Finally, if the state cannot meet the request from its own or other state resources, the state can prioritize the various requests and pass them on to

EMA officials. The state is supposed to make such requests fter it has already reviewed its own capabilities.

FEMA officials determine whether to accept or reject he state request.[39] This determination is documented. A equest might be rejected for a number of reasons, such s not being appropriate, a state getting the resources rom elsewhere, or a state canceling a request while 'EMA officials are considering it. In some cases, a state equest might be made verbally to expedite assistance, but 'EMA officials expect the paperwork to soon follow. The aperwork from the state certifies that the state will pay its hare of the requested assistance.

Once FEMA accepts the request and agrees to meet it, fficials use a system called NEMIS (National Emergency Aanagement Information System).[40] FEMA does not use .-Team. NEMIS is used by FEMA officials to track the equest within the federal government and all requests 'EMA officials accept are entered into this system. 'EMA can meet the request from its own resources and apabilities, from other federal agencies, or from private ontractors. If FEMA officials task another federal agency vith the request, that is known as a "Mission Assignment" or MA), whereby the task is assigned to the other agency.

Mission Assignments to another federal agency ould also be passed on to a private contractor. This is lone because some agencies have more expertise and xperience in contracting for certain types of items. For xample, the U.S. Army Corps of Engineers (USACE) ontracts for debris removal.[41] Some federal agencies, ncluding FEMA, have pre-existing contracts that can be nodified quickly to add additional items. NEMIS is used o track the request and completion of the mission, as vell as to track spending and reimbursement later by 'EMA officials.[42]

AP PHOTO/MORRY GESH

In Louisiana there was widespread confusion about the process for obtaining federal assistance. In addition, the catastrophic nature of the disaster overwhelmed the existing procedures and systems

Louisiana state and parish officials said degraded communications and the effective loss of parish E-Team software forced them to deviate from normal procedures for requesting federal assistance.[43] These problems also made it difficult for the state EOC to check on the status of specific tasks assigned to state agencies. State officials complained about FEMA's non-automated process that made tracking status difficult. State officials also noted they had included FEMA on their E-Team license, but during Katrina the FEMA staff assigned to the EOC were not familiar with the E-Team system. This had not been the case in earlier hurricanes, when FEMA staff assigned to the EOC knew how to use E-Team.[44] State officials also complained about weaknesses in tracking the transportation and estimating arrival of FEMA-contracted commodities. FEMA officials have acknowledged these weaknesses.[45] Further, state officials said the federal government contributed to the problem when other federal agencies tasked FEMA directly rather than having requests go from parish to state to FEMA and then onto appropriate federal agencies.[46] According to Governor Blanco's chief of staff, Andy Kopplin, the governor had to go beyond the normal LOHSEP and FEMA process because these processes were too bureaucratic and impracticable.[47]

Parish officials were universally critical of FEMA for providing relief commodities late.[48] There were clearly misunderstandings of what constituted an official request for assistance. The Jefferson Parish Emergency Manager, Walter Maestri, said he directly communicated his needs before landfall in a conference call to the EOC, where FEMA personnel were present.[49] In his view, this constituted a request for assistance. However, both the State Coordinating Officer (SCO) and the FCO said while the purpose of these conference calls was to share information, they were not considered valid ways for a parish to make a request.[50]

New Orleans Director of Homeland Security, Col. Terry Ebbert, also said the existing systems for requesting assistance does not work during a catastrophic disaster.[51] The system assumes the parish knows what it wants,

New Orleans Director of Homeland Security, Terry Ebbert, was "shocked" to hear FEMA Director Michael Brown say the local parishes never got FEMA commodities because they never asked for them. In his opinion, FEMA officials should have known what was needed from their own experience.

the state knows what it wants, and both have the communications capabilities to make requests of FEMA. Ebbert said the current system is a "pull" system in which parishes must make requests to pull an item from the state and federal government. However, the parishes were too overwhelmed and their communications were too degraded to allow this to work. In a catastrophic disaster, FEMA needs a "push" system in which FEMA officials anticipate needs (e.g., for food, water, medical supplies, ice, tarps, generators) and push the commodities to the parishes without receiving the request. Under such disaster circumstances, it would be better to have too much of something than too little; the excess items can always be shipped elsewhere or stored for the next disaster.[52]

As such, Ebbert was "shocked" to hear FEMA Director Michael Brown say the local parishes never got FEMA commodities because they never asked for them.[53] In his opinion, FEMA officials should have known what was needed from their own experience. Similarly, Governor Blanco's chief of staff, Andy Kopplin, said the state had to go beyond both LOHSEP's and FEMA's bureaucratic processes for requesting and providing assistance.[54]

However, parish officials also acknowledged their emergency managers were overwhelmed. Plaquemines Parish Sheriff Jiff Hingle said his parish emergency manager was completely overwhelmed and unable to cope with the situation.[55] Hingle found he and the parish president had to make all requests for assistance through other channels because the normal system was not functional.

FEMA officials Scott Wells and Tony Robinson put much of the blame on the state, saying the standard request for assistance process was not working because the state was incapable of analyzing and prioritizing requests.[56] Wells and Robinson said many of the requests from parishes came up through channels to the EOC, but state officials appeared "overwhelmed" and they "lost control." The EOC did not attempt to prioritize such requests, did not try to

figure out if the requests could be met from state resources, and did not go through EMAC channels to see if other nearby states could provide the assistance. The EOC just passed the unfiltered requests on to FEMA officials. Wells said the FCO staff did a quick analysis of parish E-Team requests the EOC was passing on unfiltered to FEMA, and found many inappropriate items, such as writing tablets. According to Wells, these requests were inappropriate because the state should not be relying on FEMA for basic items that are otherwise easily obtainable.

Parishes were frustrated by the degraded communications and their desperate need for assistance. Robinson said while the parishes were still able to communicate requests to the EOC (via radio or other means), they were not able to use E-Team.[57] The EOC was not systematically entering the requests into E-Team, so the state could not track or check the status later, which led to many parishes becoming frustrated. The parishes probably blamed FEMA officials for any delays in getting assistance because they had communicated their requests and assumed the EOC had duly registered these requests and passed them on to FEMA officials. Many of the highly publicized parish requests for commodities such as for food and water assistance may have never even reached FEMA officials.

Some confusion arose because states and not the parishes are supposed to make requests to FEMA.[58] It was Louisiana's responsibility to take these parish requests, combine them with similar requests, determine whether the state could meet them, prioritize them, and, if appropriate, make requests to FEMA. That process, where the state enters the request into its E-Team system, allowing formal registry and tracking of status and completion, is the only way to provide an orderly processing of requests. Using verbal requests, without documenting them in a formal process, leads to chaos, particularly in a large disaster where there are hundreds

r thousands of local requests for assistance. If the parish
s unable to use E-Team because of communications or
ower difficulties, the state EOC (which, in fact, retained
ower during the hurricane and its aftermath) could have
till entered them into E-Team. Then the state should
erform its review, and, if appropriate, pass the request
n to FEMA. It was the state's job, not FEMA's, to take
own any parish requests from conference calls and enter
hem into the system. FEMA officials saw these conference
alls serving the function of information sharing and
ituational awareness, not substitutes for the parish-to-
tate and state-to-federal formal request process.

nteroperability between state and federal utomated systems

EMA FCO staff said there is no automatic or electronic
nterface between state systems (such as E-Team) and the
EMA system (NEMIS).[59] Both systems, if used correctly,
ave independent capabilities to track requests for
ssistance and determine their status. The two systems
neet in the EOC, where the E-Team requests are converted
nto NEMIS. However, there is no way for the state EOC
fficials to use E-Team to track the status of their request
n NEMIS, nor any way for the federal FCO officials to
se NEMIS to check information on the E-Team requests
riginating at the local level.

According to FEMA officials involved in the response to
Hurricane Katrina, the breakdown of a unified command
structure at the state EOC level hampered FEMA's ability
to meet state and local requests for commodities.[60]
Without a unified command, some state and local officials
began submitting commodity requests outside FEMA's
normal logistics channels. FEMA, in turn, started fulfilling
such requests on an "ad-hoc" basis before these requests
were properly authorized or logged into its logistics
system.[61] When supply requests and subsequent supply
distributions were not logged, FEMA could not accurately
keep track of the resources it staged at regional facilities.[62]
As a result, supplies and equipment were delivered not
according to specifications, delivered late, or not delivered
at all, and priority needs were not met.

In his testimony before the Select Committee, Brown
acknowledged these logistical problems and the need for a
better tracking system. He said if

[y]ou don't have a unified command, [you] kind
of go into an ad hoc mode. So we hear that, for
example, County X is requesting five truckloads
of Meals Ready to Eat, so we will then figure out
that, okay, we have got four available, so we are just
going to ship four into that county . . . .[63]

Then, "[another county] may send in a legitimate
request for five trailer loads [and] you think they are still
there because no one has yet entered in the [trailers] that
have gone out."[64]

When supply requests and subsequent supply distributions were not logged, FEMA could not accurately keep track of the resources it staged at regional facilities. As a result, supplies and equipment were delivered not according to specifications, delivered late, or not delivered at all, and priority needs were not met.

Management lapse

According to Holden, lack of "knowledge and understanding by many agencies paralyzed the efforts" to provide an orderly and efficient response, and required paperwork also "hindered immediate action and deployment of people and materials to assist in rescue and recovery efforts."[65] Pre-positioned federal assets critical to the operations of hospitals were never received. Resources from the Strategic National Stockpile, despite requests, were never locally deployed due to bureaucratic red tape.[66]

According to Carwile, "[i]n any operation, particularly in a chaotic environment, there needs to be a balance between 'going outside the system' and following a plan and a procedure."[67] Carwile suggested "there needs to be a well-disciplined, systematic approach based on a solid plan that is sufficiently flexible for a variety of situations. Experienced personnel know where the pitfalls are and can make decisions where flexibility is required. Doctrine, policies, training, and exercises should be developed that meet the needs of a trained and ready workforce."[68]

Even Brown experienced bureaucratic frustrations. Rather than have FEMA's food provision efforts oriented almost exclusively toward securing MREs, Brown sought to devise an arrangement in which distributors or retailers would deliver meals or groceries, like those that would ordinarily be conveyed to typical commercial outlets, directly to shelters. Brown testified he came to believe

> we were too focused on meals ready to eat. The issue was food, not the MREs. So we came up with what we thought was this brilliant idea that we would utilize Wal-Mart or some grocery

distribution system because they are accustomed to going to these 7-Elevens, [and other] convenience stores, to replenish them all the time . . . . [69]

Brown said FEMA started "trying to do a contract to do that very thing [but] ran into a bureaucratic wall [so much that] I finally had to scream at some people on the phone [']just make it happen, I don't care, just do the contract and make it happen.[']"[70]

According to Carwile, over the past four years, there has been no operational doctrine developed by FEMA. He said, as a consequence

> [t]here is no clear understanding of the responsibilities of each level (Washington, the Regions, and deployed Emergency Response Teams) and how they are to interact. This lack of operational doctrine results in unacceptable levels of overlap, double and triple ordering of resources, and long video teleconferences and conference calls [which can] disrupt field operations."[71]

Carwile believes "well-understood and defined operational methodologies based on doctrine would minimize the need for lengthy conferences and would achieve other efficiencies."[72]

Alabama officials said FEMA officials lacked management skills.[73] Nobody with FEMA seemed to know what assets existed and how to marshal them, they said. FEMA does not have a robust lessons learned/after action program to assist in the refining and reorganizing of processes. Instead, FEMA seemed to move from one emergency to the next without incorporating any formal reviews.

Alabama officials recommended FEMA adapt its training requirements to allow states to use monies targeted for state training exercises for after-action reviews of actual emergency-related operations.[74] One official echoed the thoughts of many AEMA personnel when he said the state was better prepared for Katrina by virtue of its experiences with previous hurricanes within the last year, notably Dennis (July 2005) and Ivan (September 2004).[75]

Carwile suggested the logistics supply system was overly centralized and recommended allowing the state to contract with private entities to provide logistical support and commodities distribution services, with the federal share of costs reimbursed by FEMA.[76]

Select Committee Members stated and Brown agreed [FE]MA should develop a formal planning and logistics [pr]ocess similar to that developed by the Department [of] Defense (DOD).[77] Some officials have suggested the [D]OD simply assume a larger role in logistics, or even [ta]ke control outright.[78] Although recognizing the value [of] DOD assistance, Brown indicated DOD involvement [wo]uld not be appropriate for smaller events. "I think that [th]e Army can help FEMA in that regard," Brown said. "I [wo]uld rather see it remain within FEMA because logistics [is] something that you need in every disaster, the smallest [on]e that FEMA might be involved in to the largest; and I [do]n't want to see us utilize the military in all of those."[79]

However, According to Carwile

[t]he factors contributing to the slow delivery of commodities should be examined and addressed for future disasters. Possible solutions [include] much better planning between State and Federal emergency management logisticians and operations personnel, the assistance and advice of DOD strategic logistics planners, and much more robust private sector partnerships, e.g., the US Army LOGCAP or USAF AFCAP programs. It is also possible for states to enter into their own contractual agreements with the private sector for procurement and delivery of response commodities. The federal share is reimbursable by FEMA and Florida routinely enters into such agreements.[80]

Rep. Bill Shuster pointed out the private sector provides [th]e best relief model and, while government agencies such [as] the DOD are excellent with logistics, "[s]ome of our [pr]ivate companies . . . are even better and our military [lea]rns from [these companies because they] know exactly [wh]at's in a truck. They know exactly where it's moving."[81]

For their part, private sector firms expressed the need [fo]r a get-it-done-and-ask-questions-later mentality. The [Di]rector of Business Continuity Global Security for Wal-[M]art said "[f]lexibility in our plans, flexibility in our [str]ucture, and flexibility of our Associates is paramount [to] success."[82] Southern Company's plans provide "for [fle]xible and decentralized authority to make decisions as [clo]se as possible to the disaster."[83] They demonstrated [cr]eativity in helping restore fuel service to Chevron [pu]mps, in helping expand their communications system

to assist other companies, and in the way they used their "family services plan" to provide emergency services to employees.[84]

Starwood hotels worked to engineer a way to pump water into the hotels, knowing the city's water system wouldn't be up and running for some time.[85] They also contracted at the last minute for security to protect their hotels from looting. IBM provided services to governmental and non-governmental organizations as needed on the ground.[86] These services ranged from temporary housing to websites and missing persons registries including the CNN Safe List, which it hosted.[87]

FEMA's Information Technology Systems are unable to support large-scale logistical challenges

The technology used to manage FEMA's logistics system may be partly to blame. FEMA's Logistics Information Management System III (LIMS III) is used to manage the agency's inventory of equipment and supplies.[88] A recent DHS OIG report found FEMA's computers were overwhelmed during the 2004 hurricane season, which hindered disaster-recovery efforts, delayed emergency supply shipments, and put emergency-response personnel at risk.[89] The report found during August and September 2004, when four hurricanes struck Florida, the IT system could not track essential commodities such as ice, water, and tents.[90]

According to the report, LIMS III is not integrated with other FEMA IT systems such as the database used to identify and deploy personnel to disaster sites.[91] Nor can it share information across federal, state, and local agencies. LIMS III was designed, however, to track "accountable property" such as bar-coded cellular phones and pagers, not "bulk commodities."[92] Although LIMS III contains information on the quantity and location of emergency supplies, it does not indicate when they will be shipped or when they should arrive.[93] In Florida, emergency personnel tracked items on spreadsheets and spent hours calling trucking companies to determine the status of goods in transit.[94]

Brown received this DHS report several weeks before Hurricane Katrina, but he and FEMA Chief Information Officer Barry West rejected the OIG's findings, calling the report's characterizations "inaccurate."[95] According to a FEMA spokesperson, "[FEMA's] [l]ogistics-support systems have presented us with some concerns over the past 18 months, and we are addressing this."[96]

During Katrina relief efforts, FEMA tested a system using global-positioning technology to track trucks transporting commodities.[97] FEMA also is installing an intranet-based electronic document system to replace paper documents and improve data sharing among agency officials via an intranet.

The DHS Emergency Preparedness and Response Directorate, which FEMA was part of, established an enterprise architecture office in 2003 and hired a chief enterprise architect in 2004 to develop a system to tie in the directorate's system with the rest of DHS.[98] Of the Katrina federal aid package, $4.6 billion is designated for FEMA logistics, search and rescue, and emergency supplies.[99]

Private sector fills void

Several tractor-trailers were strategically located throughout the region by various officials and organizations to collect local contributions, which were then sent to a warehouse for collection and distribution.[100] When the first of 14 packed trailer loads arrived, volunteers unloaded the first two and quickly realized much more assistance was needed to efficiently process the donations and prepare them for distribution.[101] A clear plan for the organized collection, sorting, storing and distributing of such a large volume of goods was not in place, however.

Local officials turned to the private sector. "Once we started seeing that we were going to have this enormous influx of material, we knew that there was no one better in the world for distribution and collection than Wal-

Mart Corporation. So we made some calls. And they immediately sent down some folks. And they showed us how to arrange a warehouse and they made it spin like a top," according to the Mayor of Fayetteville, Arkansas, Dan Coody.[102]

Several companies had existing disaster plans which eased the challenges they faced. Southern Company has a separate plan for each category of hurricane, and each year they conduct a major disaster simulation.[103] Before the storm hit, Southern Company had already pre-positioned trailers, caterers, laundry facilities, and 11,000 people for their response. Starwood developed a crisis management plan which "structures preparedness and response at the Corporate, Division, and Hotel level and defines responsibilities for each level of employee.[104] Wal-Mart keeps an Emergency Operating Center up and running 24 hours a day, every day of the year.[105] As one IBM executive noted "[a]dvanced planning of people, tools, and technology . . . is vital and important."[106] IBM had its Crisis Response Team on the ground four days in advance of Katrina, which worked with FEMA, the states, and private entities, providing a list of the services they could provide.

Ad Hoc response

In Fayetteville, Arkansas, individuals who had traveled there to stay with family or friends began to stop by the distribution center "in search of financial aid, food, clothes and other assistance," recalled Coody.[107] Officials had not anticipated receiving evacuees at the distribution center and were not sure how to respond. They had heard stories of survivors being bounced from place to place or from town to town, so they took it upon themselves to find answers, information, and assistance for everyone who needed it.

Officials and volunteers pulled boxes off pallets and made food and clothes available to these displaced individuals.[108] They moved all relief agencies into the distribution center offices to make a one-stop location where evacuees could get various types of assistance and support, and set up a "store" where people could shop for what they needed, free of charge.[109]

In addition, relief supplies were shipped from the Fayetteville distribution facility to the Salvation Army staging warehouse in Corsicana, Texas.[110] It was eventual

stined to aid the stricken areas of Louisiana and
ississippi. Many of these shipments were sponsored
local businesses and churches and were arranged by
aking direct contact with community members in the
ected areas. Fayetteville officials also learned many
ral areas were not receiving adequate support and were
ll in desperate need of various items that were in stock.
is spurred officials to focus their large-scale distribution
orts on rural Louisiana.

FEMA

Coody testified while Fayetteville had food, water,
eelchairs, baby supplies and many other items
pallets and ready to go, communicating and
ordinating the movement of supplies to these areas
s a challenge.[111] He said the distribution center had not
eived "any communications from the State or Federal
el about the needs in these areas."[112]
Although Fayetteville officials wanted to send goods
ere they were needed, arranging transportation also
oved to be a problem. Nonetheless, Coody recounted
me success in arranging deliveries including that they

asked J.B. Hunt and other trucking firms, ['c]an you
please donate your time and some drivers to load
up this trailer that we have . . . ready to go and take
it to a particular town in Louisiana?[']" And they
said, [']sure['], ...[113]

In another instance, Bogalusa, Mississippi had
quested water and baby food from Fayetteville.
incidentally, a truck arrived from Kansas City, and the
ver announced, "I have got a load of baby food and
ter and I am [being] told to get off the road because I
overloaded."[114] The mayor said

[as soon as] we saw what we had, we gave him a
map and we said, ['t]his is where you need to go,[']
and we sent [the items] on their way. As they pulled
into Bogalusa and off-loaded food [—] baby food,
adult food [—] and everything else, people started
opening packages and eating food directly off the
truck because they had not had any food in three
days.[115]

Coody reported the realization that Fayetteville had
the necessary supplies in stock previously but had "no
knowledge" or "no real infrastructure to get it there" was
disturbing, and "it broke our hearts."[116]

Finding: The failure at all levels to enter into advance contracts led to chaos and the potential for waste and fraud as acquisitions were made in haste

Concerns have been raised with respect to how FEMA
awarded its contracts in the immediate aftermath of
Hurricane Katrina and regarding the contract vehicles it
had in place before landfall.[117] In the weeks following
Katrina, more than 80 percent of FEMA's $1.5 billion
in contracts were awarded on a sole-source basis or
pursuant to limited competition.[118] Many of the contracts
awarded were incomplete and included open-ended or
vague terms. In addition, numerous news reports have
questioned the terms of disaster relief agreements made
in such haste. Questions have also been raised about
USACE's awarding of contracts with limited competition
for debris removal and clean up.[119]

In the face of the massive destruction caused by
Katrina, acquisition personnel acted to meet pressing
humanitarian needs, contacting firms in an effort to
provide immediate relief to survivors and to protect life
and property. Many of these firms were called into action
on a sole-source basis under acquisition provisions that
allow the government to acquire urgently needed goods
and services in emergency situations. These firms provided
emergency housing and shelter for victims and emergency
personnel, to start debris cleanup, and to secure property
from further damage.

The Shaw Group Inc., Bechtel National Inc., CH2M Hill, and Dewberry Technologies were engaged by FEMA to provide emergency housing and shelter for victims, to start the cleanup of hazardous waste, and begin restoration of the transportation infrastructure. Before Katrina struck, however, FEMA had only one contract in place relevant to the Katrina response for temporary housing. Immediately after the disaster, USACE competitively awarded contracts for debris removal to ACI/AshBritt, Inc., Environmental Chemical Corp., Central Environmental Services, and Phillips & Jordan, Inc. through an emergency competition, which resulted in the submission of 22 proposals.[120]

FEMA executed few, if any, written contracts during what officials called "the real nightmare emergency" (Aug. 29-Sept. 15).[121] The circumstances surrounding their contract awards made it difficult for FEMA to understand fully the contract specifics. FEMA simply instructed companies to begin work and submit vouchers for payment. FEMA used this method for the acquisition of food, ice, buses, and other supplies. This could raise issues of enforceability, which will need to be resolved when written contracts are issued.

FEMA's contracting practices were described by state and local officials as "problematic."[122] Louisiana officials cited lack of FEMA oversight and management in the awarding of contracts. Further, state officials suggested there were no performance-based standards under the contracts and suggested under "time and materials" contracts, the longer the contractor takes to perform the necessary service, the more money the firm stands to make.

Rep. Jefferson also conveyed complaints from Louisiana officials about FEMA's failure to contract out the mortuary and body recovery effort.[123] This was a particularly sensitive issue because New Orleans Mayor Ray Nagin was predicting thousands of casualties.[124] Sta[te] officials reported FEMA implemented a contract with Kenyon International in the immediate aftermath of the hurricane. According to officials, Kenyon was not given the support it needed from FEMA to meet its objectives and ended up pulling out of the contract. Ultimately, Louisiana contracted with Kenyon directly.[125]

When asked whether FEMA had contracts in place for disaster-related supplies, including tarps, ice, generators, and temporary shelters, Brown equivocated, stating they had some contracts in place for provision of MREs, wate[r], ice, temporary housing, and some of the trailers. In othe[r] cases, however, FEMA had to "start buying off the street [to] meet the demand."[126]

By the end of September, it was reported that 80 percent of the contracts — and half of the $3.2 billion spent — had been awarded without full and open competition.[127] The agency awarded 60 percent of its contracts without full competition in October 2005, 68 percent in November 2005, and 50 percent in the first h[alf] of December.[128]

The Select Committee heard testimony from representative companies that contracted with FEMA and USACE to provide immediate response and recovery requirements to the federal government. Carnival Cruise Lines provided temporary housing; The Shaw Group provided, among other services, "blue roof" emergency tarps to cover storm-damaged homes; Landstar System provided transportation support, including trucks for supplies and busses for evacuees; AshBritt provided debr[is] removal services; Innotech provided emergency package[d] meals.[129]

Typical contracting issues

The experiences of The Shaw Group are typical of the issues raised by contractors in the aftermath of Katrina. The company is a $3+ billion company with 20,000 employees worldwide. According to company officials, Shaw performed $800 million in federal work last year, and contracts for Hurricane Katrina and Rita relief have been the firm's biggest undertaking.[130] Shaw was originally awarded two separate $100 million contracts: the first by the USACE and the second by FEMA. Shaw

participating in competitive procurements for FEMA
requirements which, originally, were awarded on a
sole-source basis. USACE contracts (including blue roof
and rapid response contracts) were awarded on a non-
competitive basis.[131] Overall, most of Shaw's business
comes from USACE ($300 million), followed by DOD,
DOE, and the EPA.

The Friday before the storm, the Shaw Group was asked
by another firm to conduct damage assessments and
inspections.[132] They were also contacted by FEMA and
the USACE to begin work. They established a command
center in Baton Rouge run by a retired general who served
as the point of contact for all requests. FEMA placed a
contract specialist within Shaw's operations to help with
compliance and other issues. Officials were unsure if other
companies were offered FEMA assistance as well but said
they offered to provide Shaw personnel at FEMA.

FEMA

According to company officials, Shaw's existing blue
roof contract uses the highest number of workers from the
impacted areas of any firm project.[133] Last year, Shaw took
Louisiana contractors to Florida, which made preparations
and response for this event easier. Their rapid response
contract has expanded over the years and was activated by
the USACE. Shaw was not successful in a bid for a debris
removal contract.

Shaw officials raised several concerns, which were
typical of the issues raised by several contracting firms:[134]

Liability—Shaw officials expressed concern that
the federal government might hold them liable
for environmental issues arising from pumping
contaminated water out of the city.

■ *Changing Requirements*—FEMA tasked Shaw with
securing temporary housing, which the company began
doing, before FEMA officials changed their minds.
Although they did not lose money, the company did
lose time and goodwill.

■ *Contract Signing and Follow-through*—Shaw officials had
problems getting contracts signed by the appropriate
agency officials. Although all the contracts have since
been signed, payments from FEMA remain slow.
Because Shaw's subcontractors are generally small
businesses with tight cash flow, they cannot wait long
for payment. Shaw also had to turn down certain
projects because it had no indication from FEMA that
it would be paid. The Stafford Act requires that the
federal government give preference, if practicable, to
local businesses.[135] However, this was largely not done
and, according to Shaw officials, some local companies
have since gone out of business. For example, debris
removal contracts were given to Minnesota, California,
and Florida firms.

■ *Conflicts of Interest*—Shaw officials continue to struggle
with the propriety of working for FEMA and for the
parishes. Officials indicated complications could arise if
FEMA hires them to asses a situation, and then a parish
hires them for rebuilding using FEMA money.

■ *Bonding*—Shaw officials did not know what the
bonding requirements were for Katrina recovery work.
However, they noted few small subcontractors are
bonded to levels necessary to enable them to perform
major contracts.

Oversight and proposed reforms to address outstanding issues

Although some emergency awards were made on a sole-
source basis, they do not constitute the majority of those
awarded in support of the relief efforts. Nevertheless,
FEMA recognized the need to revisit non-competitive
contracts issued quickly immediately after the storm.[136]

Shortly after emergency needs arose, DHS's Chief
Procurement Officer (CPO) requested the OIG to begin
overseeing FEMA's acquisition process.[137] The DHS-
IG assigned 60 auditors, investigators, and inspectors

and hired additional oversight personnel. DHS-IG staff reviewed the award and administration of all major contracts, including those awarded in the initial efforts, and the implementation of the expanded use of government purchase cards.[138] The staff are continuing to monitor all contracting activities as the government develops its requirements and as the selection and award process unfolds. In addition, 13 different agency OIGs have committed hundreds of professionals to the combined oversight effort, with a significant part of the oversight provided by DOD, the various service audit agencies, and criminal investigative organizations.[139]

To ensure that any payments made to contractors are proper and reasonable, FEMA has engaged the Defense Contract Audit Agency (DCAA) to help it monitor and oversee payments made and has pledged not to pay on any vouchers until each one is first audited and cleared.[140] In addition, DHS's CPO met with each of the large Katrina contractors to impress upon them the need to ensure all charges are contractually allowable, fair, and reasonable. Finally, the GAO has sent a team to the Gulf coast area to provide an overall accounting of funds across the government and evaluate what worked well and what went wrong at the federal, state and local levels.

FEMA has indicated it will revisit non-competitive arrangements made immediately after the storm.[141] In addition, on September 16, FEMA instituted its Phase II plan. Under this arrangement, competitive procurements for relief efforts will be reconstituted and revitalized.[142] DHS officials indicated FEMA would formalize the original emergency agreements to establish clearly the terms and prices and then review all the requirements and decide whether any particular contract needs to be completed in the short term. If there is a continuing need for the requirement, the initial contract will be left in place only long enough for a competition to be held. The competitively awarded contracts will then replace the original arrangement. FEMA officials plan to ensure as much of the work as possible goes to local small firms.[143]

Procurement officials acknowledged the initial contracting response was poor, with little planning and inadequate resources.[144] However, these same officials stated the procurement system had sufficient flexibility to meet the challenge posed by Katrina.

Finding: Before Katrina, FEMA suffered from a lack of sufficiently trained procurement professionals. DHS procurement continues to be decentralized and lacking a uniform approach, and its procurement office was understaffed given the volume and dollar value of work

FEMA's grossly understaffed acquisition unit was not ready for the Katrina disaster.[145] FEMA had 55 acquisition slots, and procurement officials think it should have had minimum of 172.[146] Further, only 36 of the 55 slots were actually occupied. FEMA is one of the DHS agencies that are not under the control of the DHS chief procurement officer, thus the FEMA acquisition office reported to Michael Brown. As of the time of the interview, FEMA was relying upon staff from the central acquisition office, comprised of 60 acquisition personnel and led by a member of the Senior Executive Service. Regardless, the office was understaffed.[147]

Prior to Hurricane Katrina, the OIG had repeatedly cited as a major challenge the lack of consistent contract management for large, complex, high-cost procurement programs.[148] DHS procurement continues to be decentralized and lacking a uniform approach.[149] DHS has seven legacy procurement offices that continue to serve DHS components, including FEMA.[150] Notably, FEMA has not been reporting or tracking procurements undertaken by its disaster field offices, and its procurement office remains understaffed given the volume and dollar value of work. The CPO recently had established an eighth office called the Office of Procurement Operations to meet the procurement needs of the rest of DHS.[151]

FEMA had 55 acquisition slots, and procurement officials think i should have had a minimum of 172. Further, only 36 of the 55 slots were actually occupied.

Louisiana officials also noted a shift during the Katrina recovery of the personnel FEMA placed in charge of contracting and logistical decisions.[152] Instead of relying on FEMA's regional personnel, with whom the state is accustomed to working in the aftermath of a disaster, FEMA sent headquarters officials to the affected areas to make key contracting and logistical decisions, causing the process to become more bureaucratic. For example, adding individuals to FEMA's Individual Assistance Program has been problematic, according to local officials.[153]

In the past, the FCO from Region VI was able to add individuals in the field. With Katrina, however, state officials had to send the request to FEMA headquarters, which has become, some say, "gridlocked."[154] Further, as previously mentioned, Louisiana state and local officials also criticized FEMA contracting.[155] They said the focus seems to be shifting from the local FCO to FEMA headquarters and becoming more bureaucratic in the process.

Finding: Ambiguous statutory guidance regarding local contractor participation led to ongoing disputes over procuring debris removal and other services[156]

Under the Stafford Act,[157] federal contracts with private firms for debris clearance, distribution of supplies, reconstruction, and other activities must give preference, to the extent feasible and practicable, to organizations, firms, and individuals from the area affected by the disaster or emergency.[158] However, there is no statutory guarantee that, after a major disaster or emergency, recovery and reconstruction work will be awarded to businesses, organizations, and individuals, regardless of where they are from.

The award of federal contracts for disaster or emergency assistance activities are, in general, governed by the standard competitive bidding statutes that apply to all government contracting activities. The Stafford Act, however, contains a "local preference" provision, which can be implemented by the inclusion in a solicitation of

a clause creating a price preference for local firms or by a set-aside that only permits local firm to compete.[159] The implementation is at the discretion of the contracting officer. Significantly, the Stafford Act local preference is not a guarantee that local firms will be awarded recovery contracts.[160]

Similarly, prime contractors are often required to give preference to local subcontractors.[161] USACE Acting Principal Assistant Responsible for Contracting, Colonel Norbert Doyle, suggested there is some uncertainty as to the geographical preferences allowed and required by the Stafford Act.[162] Another official testified that different laws are necessary,[163] and stated "[the Stafford Act is] like bringing a donkey to the Kentucky Derby."[164]

Numerous public officials have complained about the small number of local firms given relief contracts, particularly with regard to debris removal. AshBritt, the Florida-based prime contractor for debris removal in Mississippi, was awarded a contract in early September by USACE.[165] According to AshBritt official Randy Perkins, the company was one of 22 firms that bid for USACE debris removal contracts. AshBritt won the Louisiana and Mississippi debris removal contracts, making the firm the only contractor for that job in those states. AshBritt was notified of the award 72 hours after the RFP was advertised.

The debris removal contracts have a $150 million ceiling at $30 million per year, and were intended by USACE to get work underway as soon as possible, with the agency reassessing the requests later.[166] USACE's delay in issuing RFPs was understandable given the disaster, according to Perkins.[167] He stated, it costs "hundreds of thousands of dollars to keep pre-existing contracts in

place, and firms receive no funding for this upkeep, which represents a free insurance policy for USACE," and few companies can secure the bond necessary to perform such a large-scale project.[168]

AshBritt official Perkins says he encountered political "fallout" from local officials because the company is not based in Mississippi or Louisiana.[169] The Select Committee was not able to substantiate his allegation, however. Perkins also discussed recieving mixed messages from local officials and "officials in D.C." While state officials told him "just get the debris out," he indicated officials in D.C. sent the message to "hire local workers." Although the company's contract with the government does not require it to hire local workers, Perkins says local contractors recieve 80 percent of AshBritt's payments to sub-contractors.[170] Although this percentage seems to differ from data provided in USACE progress reports, the Select Committee was not able to substantiate the actual level of debris removal work provided by the local sub-contracting community.

Brown suggested the scale of the disaster and the complexity of the response require a large firm's expertise:

Debris is a huge issue. Debris is one of those issues that is fraught with local politics. It's fraught with fraud, waste and abuse [and] in cleaning up debris in a situation like Katrina, you really have to have experts overseeing that global perspective because you have hazardous waste. You have the whole issue of private property versus public property . . . . So I would caution us about going down a path that says we're going to have all locals do it. I know, in my subdivision, the local garbage folks are very adept at picking up my trash twice a week, and they're pretty good about hauling out debris after a storm or something. But in the kind of debris removal we're talking about in Mississippi, Alabama and Florida from last year and this year, you really need to have a substantial company overseeing that, to not only protect the taxpayers, but to make sure it's done right.[171]

Later Brown said, "in a small town that's hit by a tornado and you have to clean up 45 blocks, city blocks, that's one thing. Here, where you're cleaning up entire cities, it's a different issue. So I would just caution that we approach that systematically."[172]

Even if this point is conceded, it appears that, despite the Stafford Act's preference provision, only a fraction of the money being spent in Mississippi is going to subcontractors based there, according to press reports citing documents from FEMA and USACE:[173]

- Of approximately $3.1 billion FEMA had awarded by Nov. 4, only $52.4 million, or about 1.7 percent, had gone to Mississippi firms.

- Of the $476 million that has been spent by the Corps of Engineers in Mississippi as of Nov. 2, about 28.5 percent has gone to Mississippi companies through direct contracts and subcontracts.

- Of the $164 million AshBritt has been paid so far by the Corps, only about $30 million, about 18 percent, has made it to Mississippi subcontractors.

However, Perkins said AshBritt has far exceeded its contractual requirements for hiring local, small, and minority-owned businesses.[174] "People don't understand that the general administrative costs are very high. It takes a lot to manage one of these projects," according to Perkins. "We have a tremendous amount of quality control people and logistical support and we need to pay for their housing."[175] He said the data released by USACE do not reflect the involvement of Mississippi businesses because there are several major contractors from the state that he called "team members," who are helping the company administer the overall contract. He said AshBritt also has provided "hundreds" of administrative jobs to Mississippians.

Use of local firms

Some have suggested FEMA's policies need to be changed to have local contractors in Gulf states ready to begin recovery work well before hurricane season.[176] For instance, instead of hiring the USACE to manage debris removal, states susceptible to hurricanes could prepare lists of businesses who meet federal standards to remove debris or haul trailers, thereby enabling local government to award their own contracts. Local governments are more likely to go with local contractors and local governments have been able to get the job done more quickly and cheaply.[177]

As of December 2005, of the nearly $8 billion expended by all direct contracts with the federal government, only five cents of every dollar reached Mississippi prime contractors.[178] Expenditure rates show DHS (including FEMA) has spent $4,150,359,361, with 3.5 cents for every dollar contracted directly to Mississippi businesses. A January 23, 2006 USACE report reported USACE awarded over $2.3 billion in Katrina contracts with 3.54 percent of total contract dollars going to Mississippi businesses.

Rep. Pickering noted

Congress wrote the Stafford Act to maximize the impact of federal dollars by giving preference to local contractors, strengthening the damaged economy and providing jobs to communities and victims of the disaster. . . . Mississippians have the ability, capacity and personal incentive to do this work. We want to rebuild and restore our home state, and these federal contracts will help our economy more through local contractors than sending the money to out-of-state corporations.[179]

Current federal policy discourages local governments from assuming responsibility for debris removal.[180] Local officials are responsible for a cost share of 10 to 25 percent (depending on the magnitude of the disaster) if they use their own contracts. However, if USACE contractors are used, the reimbursement for the life of the debris removal effort is 100 percent with no cost share. Communities removing their own debris have been notified they will incur a 10 percent cost share beginning March 16, 2006.[181]

Additionally, the specter of a federal audit can be very intimidating for local officials, especially for rural communities and those that have incurred major damage. Risk can be avoided by simply signing on with USACE, even if it is more costly and offers less control. For example, USACE is removing debris in Waveland, Mississippi and other locations at a reported cost of approximately $23 per cubic yard.[182] Nearby Gulfport hired its own contractor at $14.95 per cubic yard[183] and appears to be making faster progress.[184] Gulfport's action is particularly bold given their significant loss of ad valorem tax base. Finally, the $8.05 per cubic yard margin is particularly substantial given the 40 million cubic yard debris removal requirement in Mississippi alone.

Ambiguities regarding the implementation of local contractor preference under the Stafford Act should be resolved. In addition, clear, unambiguous remedies and penalties for failure to meet such statutorily mandated preferences may need to be considered.

FEMA response to local participation issue

In response to these concerns, FEMA plans a two-pronged approach.[185] First, FEMA will competitively award multiple five-year technical assistance contracts to small disadvantaged businesses for recovery work in the Gulf states, with evaluation preferences keyed to the location of both the prime contractor and subcontractors in the affected areas. Second, FEMA plans a full and open competition for multiple five-year contracts to provide technical assistance support on a national basis for disaster response and recovery. Under this competition, FEMA will require that these prime contractors meet significant small business subcontracting goals, including the preference for local businesses as provided under the Stafford Act.

Through this strategy, FEMA hopes to provide a diverse group of companies the opportunity to contract with FEMA for the Gulf coast hurricane recovery by adding prime contracting opportunities for small disadvantaged businesses with a geographic preference for those located in the Gulf states.[186] The national competition approach is intended to preserve subcontracting goals and opportunities for small and disadvantaged businesses as part of all prime contracts for future disasters. Both strategies will emphasize the importance of using local businesses, a critical piece of a successful economic recovery in a disaster-ravaged area. Select Committee staff did not receive detailed information on what efforts, if any, USACE is planning for its long-term Katrina-related acquisitions.

In addition, DHS representative Larry Orluskie said FEMA is changing some of its policies.[187] Recently, FEMA announced it will set aside $1.5 billion under 15 contracts worth up to $100 million apiece.[188] Acting FEMA Director David Paulison stated that priority would be given to local contractors on the five-year contracts for trailer maintenance.[189] Orluskie also cited the rebidding of several large, prime contracts as evidence that the agency is trying to be as transparent as possible in its contracting process.[190] Regarding the $100 million contracts held by Bechtel, Fluor, Shaw, and CH2M Hill, agency officials said the requests have been completed and will be awarded again in February 2006.[191]

Nevertheless, Carwile testified "[t]he Public Assistance program provided under Section 406 of the Stafford Act is far too cumbersome and time consuming in terms of getting funds through the states down to the impacted communities" and "could be totally revamped . . . ." He said "[t]he program is one of the most difficult and contentious aspects of disaster recovery," and "the entire issue of Federal reimbursement for debris removal should be addressed in a comprehensive manner."[192]

Finding: Attracting emergency contractors and corporate support could prove challenging given the scrutiny that companies have endured

When federal agency resources were overwhelmed and existing contractors unable to meet the huge demands created by the storm, federal officials turned to the private sector for assistance. In an effort to meet pressing needs by any means possible, federal officials looked to alternative sources for food, transportation, and housing. Many of the firms approached by agency officials had never contracted previously with the federal government. Housing was one resource in short supply. Officials considered a variety of options to shelter victims and first responders, and approached a number of cruise ship operators.

According to Carnival Cruise Lines representatives, on Wednesday, August 24, federal officials contacted the company regarding chartering ships.[193] Carnival found this

unusual given that the firm had never served as a federal contractor. "[W]e were watching just the total devastation, and we felt very strongly that it was a situation where we were in a position to help, and we very much wanted to help," stated Terry Thorton, a Carnival Vice President.[194]

The Military Sealift Command informed Carnival the RFP was being issued. Carnival indicated it wanted to "help" and responded to the RFP.[195] Thirteen ships were potentially available from Carnival and others. Four ships ultimately met the RFP requirements (which included a requirement for medical and pharmaceutical facilities), three belonging to Carnival. Carnival received the RFP at 9 a.m. Friday, and the initial response was due two hours later at 11 a.m. Carnival offered three ships, and negotiated all day with "best and final" offers provided at 9 p.m.

Carnival based its bid on projected cruise revenue for six months out, and agreed it would reduce the final bill and provide a refund if, after an internal audit by an independent accounting firm, it was found Carnival earned more than it would have in the cruise market.[196] To make the ships available, Carnival canceled approximately 100,000 existing reservations for which travel agent fees still had to be paid. Carnival makes its profit from ticket sales and "add-ons" (drinks, shore excursions, etc.) and not in the "time charter" business, which is a comprehensive package of food, beverages, and activities. In addition, it incorporated taxes into its offer,

which will be refunded if it is determined it does not owe taxes under U.S. law.[197]

Despite these provisions, numerous public officials and press reports have criticized the arrangement. Attention focused on the ships when FEMA revealed it intended to use them to house first responders. At the time, housing for first responders was in short supply, and FEMA sought out a variety of options. "I'm not sure that everyone on this panel would have made the same choice that FEMA made, but this was FEMA's choice as to how they wanted to house people . . . . And you've simply said, [']if you want us to do this, here's what the circumstances are,['] and FEMA said, [']that's okay with us,['] and we accept that," stated Rep. Jefferson.[198] When appreciation was expressed by Select Committee Members for Carnival's assistance, Carnival officials replied, "[t]hank you. Because honestly, that's one of the few times that we've really been thanked for the effort . . . ."[199]

The intense public scrutiny could limit the willingness of private sector companies to offer assistance during future disasters. Several firms expressed the view that the challenges associated with emergency contracting may not be worth the trouble. Finally, unfounded negative publicity harms company reputations. Public sector missions divert company assets from primary missions and could raise questions about whether a company was meeting its fiduciary duty to shareholders. Given the important role the private sector played in all aspects of the response and recovery, any loss of private sector involvement could be critical. ■

1   *Hearing on Recovering from Hurricane Katrina: Responding to the Immediate Needs of Its Victims Before Senate Comm. on Homeland Security and Gov't Affairs*, 109th Cong. (Sept. 28, 2005) at 58 (statement of Melvin Holden) [hereinafter *Sept. 28, 2005 Senate Comm. Hearing*].

2   Dep't of Homeland Sec., *Major Mgm't Challenges Facing the Dep't of Homeland Sec.*, Rpt. of the Inspector Gen., DHS FY 2005 Performance and Accountability Rpt. (Dec. 2005) at 110, *available at*, http://www.dhs.gov/interweb/assetlibrary/OIG_06-14_Dec05.pdf (last visited Jan. 28, 2006) [hereinafter *DHS IG Rpt.*].

3   *DHS IG Rpt.* at 111.

4   Amy Belasco, Cong. Research Service (CRS), *Reallocation of Hurricane Katrina Emer. Approps.: Defense and Other Issues* (Dec. 15, 2005) at CRS-3 [hereinafter *CRS Approps Rpt.*].

5   *Id.* at CRS-3–CRS-4.

6   Frank Donze, *Nagin decries slow pace of relief*, TIMES-PIC. (New Orleans, LA) Oct. 21, 2005 at 1.

7   James Varney, *Want answers? Don't ask FEMA*, TIMES-PIC. (New Orleans, LA) Oct. 22, 2005 at 1.

8   *Hearing on Hurricane Katrina: The Role of the Fed. Emer. Mgm't Agency Before Select Comm.*, 109th Cong. (Sept. 27, 2005) at 100 (statement of Michael Brown, former Undersecretary of Emergency Preparedness and Response) [hereinafter *Sept. 27, 2005 Select Comm. Hearing*].

9   Tom Gardner, *Former FEMA director shoulders greater share of blame for Katrina failures*, ASSOC. PRESS, Jan. 19, 2006.

10 *Sept. 28, 2005 Senate Comm. Hearing* at 82 (statement of Sen. Mark Pryor).

11 *Sept. 27, 2005 Select Comm. Hearing* at 65 (statement of Michael Brown). Note, each trailer contained 18,000 meals.

12 *Id.* at 150 (statement of Rep. Chip Pickering).

13 *Id.* at 65 (statement of Rep. Gene Taylor).

14 *Id.* at 66 (statement of Michael Brown).

15 Interview by Select Comm. Staff with Robert Latham, Director, Mississippi Emergency Management Agency, in Jackson, MS (Oct. 14, 2005) [hereinafter Latham Interview].

16 *Id.*

17 *Hearing on Hurricane Katrina: Perspectives of FEMA's Operations Professionals Before Senate Comm. on Homeland Security and Gov't Affairs*, 109th Cong. (Dec. 8, 2005) at 6 (written statement of William L. Carwile) [hereinafter *Dec. 8, 2005 Senate Hearing*].

18 *Id.*

19 *Id.*

20 *Id.*

21 Interview by Select Comm. Staff with Bruce Baughman, Director, Alabama Emergency Management Agency, in Clancy, AL (Oct. 11, 2005) [hereinafter Baughman Interview].

22 Interview by Select Comm. Staff with Tim Payne, Branch Chief and Emergency Management Program Coordinator, Alabama, in Clanton, AL (Oct. 11, 2005) [hereinafter Payne Interview].

23 Baughman Interview.

24 *Id.*

25 *Id.*

26 Payne Interview. These items included transportation, water, ice, materials handling equipment, cots plus bedding supplies, sandbags, meals, fuel, tarps, project management and logistics services, special needs beds, headquarters / office coordination capabilities.

27 *Sept. 27, 2005 Select Comm. Hearing* at 73 (statement of Michael Brown).

28 Frank Davies, *Gov. Bush: Keep Disaster Response Local*, HERALD (Miami), Oct. 20, 2005 at A-26 [hereinafter *Herald Article*].

29 *Id.*

30 Briefing for Select Comm. Staff by Gary Moore, Director of Logistics, FEMA (Jan. 9, 2006).

31 *See* Interview by Select Comm. Staff with Scott Wells, Deputy FEMA Federal Coordinating Officer, in Baton Rouge, LA (Nov. 9, 2005), [hereinafter Wells Interview]; *see also* Interview by Select Comm. Staff with Tony Robinson, FEMA Operations Officer, in Baton Rouge, LA (Nov. 10, 2005) [hereinafter Robinson Interview].

32 Interview by Select Comm. Staff with Matt Farlow, Chief Information Technology Division (LOHSEP), in Baton Rouge, LA (Nov. 4, 2005) [hereinafter Farlow Interview].

33 *Id.*

34 *Id.*

35 *Id.*

36 *See* Interview by Select Comm. Staff with LTC William Doran, Chief, Operations Division, Louisiana Office of Homeland Security and Emergency Preparedness (LOHSEP), in Baton Rouge, LA (Nov. 7, 2005) [hereinafter Doran Interview]; *see also* Interview by Select Comm. Staff with Jim Ballou, Operations Division, Louisiana Office of Homeland Security and Emergency Preparedness (LOHSEP), in Baton Rouge, LA (Nov. 7, 2005) [hereinafter Ballou Interview].

37 *See* Doran Interview; *see also* Ballou Interview.

38 *See* Wells Interview; *see also* Robinson Interview.

39 Robinson Interview.

40 *Id.*

41 *Id.*

42 *Id.*

43 *See* Doran Interview; *see also* Ballou Interview; *see also* Interview by Select Comm. Staff with Dr. Walter Maestri, Emergency Manager for Jefferson Parish, in New Orleans, LA (Nov. 8, 2005) [hereinafter Maestri Interview]; Interview by Select Comm. Staff with Jiff Hingle, Plaquemines Parish Sherriff, in New Orleans, LA (Nov. 8, 2005) [hereinafter Hingle Interview]; *see also* Interview by Select Comm. Staff with Terry Ebbert, Director of Homeland Security for the City of New Orleans, in New Orleans, LA (Nov. 9, 2005) [hereinafter Ebbert Interview].

44 Farlow Interview.

5 *Sept. 27, 2005 Select Comm. Hearing* at 110 (statement by Michael Brown); *see also* Interview by Select Comm. Staff with Bill Lokey, FEMA Federal Coordinating Officer, in Washington, DC (Dec. 2, 2005) [hereinafter Lokey Interview].

6 *See* Doran Interview; *see also* Ballow Interview; *see also* Lokey Interview; *see also* Interview by Select Comm. Staff with Phil Parr, Dep. Fed. Coordinating Officer, FEMA, in Washington, DC (Dec. 8, 2005) [hereinafter Parr Interview].

7 Interview by Select Comm. Staff with Andy Kopplin, Chief of Staff to Governor Blanco, in Baton Rouge, LA (Nov. 6, 2005) [hereinafter Kopplin Interview].

8 *See* Maestri Interview; *see also* Hingle Interview; *see also* Ebbert Interview.

9 Maestri Interview.

0 *See,* Interview by Select Comm. Staff with Jeff Smith, Deputy Director, Louisiana Office of Homeland Security and Emergency Preparedness, in Baton Rouge, LA (Nov. 7, 2005) [hereinafter Smith Interview]; *see also* Lokey Interview; *see also* Wells Interview.

1 Ebbert Interview.

2 *Id.*

3 *Id.*

4 Kopplin Interview.

5 Hingle Interview.

6 *See* Wells Interview; *see also* Robinson Interview.

7 *Id.*

8 *Id.*

9 Robinson Interview.

0 *Sept. 27, 2005 Select Comm. Hearing* at 106-107 (statement of Michael Brown).

1 *Id.* at 108 (statement of Michael Brown).

2 *Id.* at 110 (statement of Michael Brown).

3 *Id.* at 108 (statement of Michael Brown).

4 *Id.* at 110 (statement of Michael Brown).

5 *Sept. 28, 2005 Senate Comm. Hearing* at 5-6 (written statement of Melvin Holden).

6 *Id.* at 7 (written statement of Melvin Holden).

7 *Dec. 8, 2005 Senate Comm. Hearing* at 9 (written statement of William Carwile).

8 *Id.*

9 *Sept. 27, 2005 Select Comm. Hearing* at 164 (statement of Michael Brown).

0 *Id.* Note, Mr. Brown left FEMA shortly after this plan was devised. He testified that he was unaware of whether this proposal was ultimately implemented. *Sept. 27, 2005 Select Comm. Hearing* at 164 (statement of Michael Brown).

1 *Sept. 28, 2005 Senate Comm. Hearing* at 9 (written statement of William Carwile).

2 *Id.*

3 Baughman Interview.

4 Baughman Interview; *see also* Interview by Select Comm. Staff with David Tranter, General Counsel for Alabama Emergency Management Agency, in Clanton, AL (Oct. 11, 2005) [hereinafter Tranter Interview].

5 Interview by Select Comm. Staff with Toby Roth, Chief of Staff to Governor Barbour, in Montgomery, AL (Oct. 12, 2005) [hereinafter Roth Interview].

6 *Dec. 8, 2005 Senate Comm. Hearing* at 6 (written statement of William Carwile).

7 *Sept. 27, 2005 Select Comm. Hearing* at 149-150 (statement of Rep. Chip Pickering); *see also Sept. 27, 2005 Select Comm. Hearing* at 146 (statement of Michael Brown.).

8 *Sept. 27, 2005 Select Comm. Hearing* at 150 (statement of Rep. Chip Pickering).

9 *Id.* at 149-150 (statement of Michael Brown).

0 *Dec. 8, 2005 Senate Comm. Hearing* at 6 (written statement of William Carwile).

1 *Id.* at 163 (written statement of William Carwile).

2 *Hearing on Hurricane Katrina: What Can Government Learn from the Private Sector's Response Before the Senate Comm. on Homeland Security and Gov't Affairs,* 109th Cong. (Nov. 16, 2005) at 6 (written statement of Jason Jackson) [hereinafter *Nov. 16, 2005 Senate Comm. Hearing*].

3 *Id.* at 2 (written statement of David. M. Ratcliffe).

4 *Id.* at 5 (written statement of David. M. Ratcliffe).

5 *Id.* at 7-8 (written statement of Kevin T. Regan).

6 *Id.* at 3 (written statement of Stanley S. Litow).

7 *Id.*

8 Office of Inspector General, Dep't of Homeland Security, *Emergency Preparedness and Response Could Better Integrate Information Technology with Incident Response and Recovery* (Rpt. No. OIG-05-36), at 5 (Sept. 2005) [hereinafter *DHS IT Report*].

9 *See generally, DHS IT Report; see also* Laurie Sullivan, *FEMA's Foul-up; Report says agency's computer systems failed to track supplies during last year's hurricane season,* INFOR. WEEK, Oct. 3, 2005 [hereinafter *FEMA Foul Up Article*].

0 *FEMA Foul Up Article.*

1 *DHS IT Report* at 21.

2 *Id.* at 3.

3 *Id.* at 27.

4 *FEMA Foul Up Article.*

5 *DHS IG Report* at 46.

6 *FEMA Foul Up Article.*

7 *Id.*

8 *Id.*

[99] *Katrina Spending Highlights*, ASSOC. PRESS, Sept. 8, 2005.

[100] *Sept. 28, 2005 Senate Comm. Hearing* at 47 (statement of Dan Coody).

[101] *Id.*

[102] *Id.* at 79 (statement of Dan Coody). Mr. Coody further stated that Wal-Mart "immediately responded by sending two engineers to create a warehouse system for our facility, a distribution center supervisor and two additional employees to oversee the operation. During peak hours we had over 100 volunteers, city employees, Wal-Mart employees, and work release inmates working side by side to organize the donations. The trailers were unloaded by Saturday [September 10], and the donations were ready for shipment by September 15." *Sept. 28, 2005 Senate Comm. Hearing* at 2 (written statement of Dan Coody).

[103] *Nov. 16, 2005 Senate Comm. Hearing* at 2 (statement of David Ratcliffe).

[104] *Id.* at 2 (statement of Kevin T. Regan).

[105] *Id.* at 1-2 (statement of Jason Jackson).

[106] *Id.* at 22 (statement of Stanley S. Litow).

[107] *Sept. 28, 2005 Senate Comm. Hearing* at 48 (statement of Dan Coody).

[108] *Id.* at 2-3 (written statement of Dan Coody).

[109] *Id.* at 48 (statement of Dan Coody).

[110] *Id.*

[111] *Id.* at 49-50 (statement of Dan Coody).

[112] *Id.* at 80 (statement of Dan Coody).

[113] *Id.* at 80-81 (statement of Dan Coody).

[114] *Id.* at 81 (statement of Dan Coody).

[115] *Id.*

[116] *Id.*

[117] Renae Merle, *Lack of Contracts Hampered FEMA; Dealing With Disaster on the Fly Proved Costly*, WASH. POST, Oct. 10, 2005 at A01 [hereinafter *Contracts Article*].

[118] *Contracts Article.*

[119] *Nov. 2, 2005, Select Comm. Hearing* at 5 (statement of Chairman Tom Davis).

[120] Interview by Select Comm. Staff with Greg Rothwell, DHS Chief Procurement Officer, and Mui Erkum, Chief of Staff to Greg Rothwell, in Washington, D.C. (Sept. 19, 2005) [hereinafter Rothwell / Erkum Interview].

[121] *Id.*

[122] Smith Interview; *see also* Maestri Interview.

[123] Smith Interview.

[124] *Id.*

[125] *Id.*

[126] *Sept. 27, 2005 Select Comm. Hearing* at 100 (statement of Michael Brown).

[127] Chris Gosier, *Another Katrina casualty: Competition; No-bid Contracting Surges for Recovery Work*, FED. NEWS, Jan. 09, 2006 at 1 [hereinafter *No-bid Article*].

[128] *Id.*

[129] *See generally Nov. 2, 2005 Select Comm. Hearing.*

[130] Interview by Select Comm. Staff with Stephen Marlo, Vice President and Manager of Washington Operations and George Bevan, The Shaw Group, in Washington, D.C. (Oct. 25, 2005) [hereinafter Marlo / Bevan Interview].

[131] The blue roof program involves teams of contract personnel professionally installing high quality plastic sheeting over damaged roofs. This was first used extensively following Hurricane Andrew and again in Hurricane Georges in Puerto Rico, and, in 2004, in Florida. It enables families to reoccupy their houses until more permanent repairs can be made.

[132] Marlo / Bevan Interview.

[133] *Id.*

[134] *Id.*

[135] Robert T. Stafford Disaster Relief and Emergency Assistance Act, 42 U.S.C. §§ 5121-5206 (2005) [hereinafter Stafford Act].

[136] Rothwell / Erkum Interview.

[137] *Id.*

[138] *Id.* Procurement officials indicated that the $250,000 card threshold increase was unnecessary and did not plan to use it.

[139] Rothwell / Erkum Interview.

[140] *Id.*

[141] *Id.*

[142] *Id.*

[143] *Id.*

[144] *Id.*

[145] *Id.*

[146] *Id.*

[147] *Id.*

[148] *Id.*

[149] *See generally* Rothwell / Erkum Interview.

[150] Rothwell / Erkum Interview.

[151] Gov't Accountability Office, *Successes and Challenges in DHS' Efforts to Create an Effective Acquisition Organization* (GAO-05-179) (Mar. 2005) at 5.

[152] Smith Interview.

[153] *Id.*

[4] *Id.*

[5] *See* Smith Interview; *see also* Maestri Interview.

[6] During the Nov. 2, 2005 Select Comm. Hearing on contracting, Members posed questions that witnesses from DHS and FEMA were unable to answer. Although they committed to providing answers to these questions as well as additional information, agency personnel failed to do so despite repeated inquiries. *See generally, Nov. 2, 2005 Select Comm. Hearing.*

[7] Stafford Act. Note, the Stafford Act was first enacted in 1974.

[8] *See* Stafford Act at § 5150; *see also* Fed. Acq. Reg. (FAR) §§ 26.200 – 26.201.

[9] *See* Stafford Act at §§ 5121-5206, which directs that preference be given "to the extent feasible and practicable" to businesses and individuals from the affected areas.

[0] *See HAP Construction Inc.*, 98-2 CPD 76 (1998) (Gov't Accountability Office Decision No. B-280044.2) (Sept. 21, 1998).

[1] *See* Stafford Act at §§ 5121-5206.

[2] *Nov. 2, 2005 Select Comm. Hearing* at 88-89 (statement of Norbert Doyle).

[3] *Dec. 8, 2005 Senate Hearing* (statement of Scott Wells, Deputy Federal Coordination Officer, FEMA (citing press reports)

[4] Greta Wodele, *FEMA officials: Military delayed Superdome evacuation*, GOVEXEC.COM, Dec. 8, 2005.

[5] Interview by Select Comm. Staff of Randy Perkins, Managing Vice President of AshBritt Environmental, Inc., in Washington, D.C. (Nov. 14, 2005) [hereinafter Perkins Interview].

[6] *Id.*

[7] *Id.*

[8] *Id.*

[9] *Id.*

[0] *Id.*

[1] *Sept. 27, 2005 Select Comm. Hearing* at 150-151 (statement of Michael Brown).

[2] *Id.* at 153 (statement of Michael Brown).

[3] Joshua Cogswell, *Doling of storm funds rapped*, CLARION-LEDGER (Jackson, Mississippi) Nov. 13, 2005 at 1A [hereinafter *Storm Funds Article*].

[4] *Id.*

[5] *Id.*

[6] *See generally, Nov. 2, 2005, Select Comm. Hearing; see also Dec. 8, 2005 Senate Comm. Hearing.*

[7] *Id.; see also* Press Release, Rep. Chip Pickering, regarding Contracting (Nov. 3, 2005).

[8] Dep't of Homeland Security, *Report of U.S. Gov't Direct Contracts, including FEMA, as provided by the HCIC, as of December 12, 2005.*

[9] Press Release, Rep. Chip Pickering, regarding Contracting and the Stafford Act (Dec. 21, 2005).

[0] U.S. Army Corps of Engineers, *Small/Local Business Update* as of 1/23/06.

[1] *See, Mississippi; Major Disaster and Related Determinations* (FEMA-1604-DR, Amendment 12) (Aug. 29, 2005, as amended Dec. 21, 2005).

[2] Mike Brunker, *Dust flies over Katrina's Debris*, MSNBC, Jan. 29, 2006.

[3] Interview (Telephone) by Rep. Pickering Staff with Brent Warr, Mayor, Gulfport, MS from Washington, D.C. (Dec. 2005).

[4] Select Committee Members who toured the Gulf coast in January 2006 agreed with this assessment.

[5] *Storm Funds Article.*

[6] *Id.*

[7] *Id.*

[8] *Id.*

[9] *Id.*

[0] *Id.*

[1] *Id.*

[2] *Dec. 8, 2005 Senate Comm. Hearing* at 7-8 (written statement of William Carwile).

[3] Interview by Select Comm. Staff with Jon K. Waldron and T. Michael Dyer, outside counsel for Carnival Cruise Lines, in Washington, D.C. (Oct. 3, 2005) [hereinafter Carnival Counsel Interview].

[4] *Nov. 2, 2005 Select Comm. Hearing* at 170 (statement of Terry Thornton).

[5] Carnival Counsel Interview.

[6] *Id.*

[7] *Id.*

[8] *Nov. 2, 2005 Select Comm. Hearing* at 172 (statement of Rep. William Jefferson).

[9] *Id.* at 173-174 (statement of Terry Thornton).

FEMA

"While well intentioned, the volunteers never had a good grasp on security requirements for financial assistance distribution operations. On numerous instances, the ARC [American Red Cross] volunteers would simply find a vacant parking area and commence voucher distribution operations. Immediately, crowds would gather and would overwhelm the distribution site. The ARC would then call on the Guard for assistance.

"Repeated attempts were made to reinforce the need for prior coordination for site security. It was not until mid-September that the ARC started coordinating these operations."

Major General Harold A. Cross
The Adjutant General, State of Mississippi
In Response to Questions from Select Committee, November 22, 2005

CHARITABLE ORGANIZATIONS

Contributions by charitable organizations assisted many in need, but the American Red Cross and others faced challenges due to the size of the mission, inadequate logistics capacity, and a disorganized shelter process

Summary

Following Katrina's devastation, countless numbers of charities provided billions of dollars in relief to those in need. According to the Center on Philanthropy at Indiana University, as of January 9, 2006, private donations, including cash and in-kind gifts have reached $3.13 billion.[1] According to the Government Accountability Office (GAO), the efforts of charitable organizations in the Gulf coast represent the largest disaster response effort in United States history.[2]

Under the National Response Plan (NRP), the American Red Cross (Red Cross) is the primary agency responsible for Emergency Support Function (ESF) #6, Mass Care, Housing and Human Services. As the only nongovernmental organization with lead agency responsibilities under the NRP, the Red Cross plays the crucial role of helping to provide food and shelter to disaster victims.

Katrina, however, was too much for the Red Cross. The Red Cross was challenged to meet its responsibilities under the NRP, as its $2 billion relief operation was 20 times larger than any previous Red Cross mission. Like FEMA, the Red Cross did not have a logistics capacity sophisticated enough to deal with a catastrophe of Katrina's size. The Red Cross was dependent on FEMA and the Department of Defense (DOD) to provide critical commodities such as kitchen supplies, water, and food. The Red Cross was challenged by the sometimes disorganized manner in which shelters were established. Some shelters were unknown to the Red Cross until after they were already opened by local officials. The Red Cross was unable to staff some locally-operated shelters, including the Superdome, because charity officials were denied access.

Challenges aside, as of January 12, 2006, the Red Cross reported it had raised $2 billion for Katrina relief, by far the largest amount of money raised by a charity.[3] The Salvation Army had raised the second-highest amount, $295 million.[4] The Bush-Clinton Katrina Fund and Catholic Charities were the next-largest fund raisers, raising $137 and $100 million respectively.[5] Other major U.S. charitable organizations, including the United Way, have also contributed meaningfully to the response and recovery effort. One feature of the United Way's response has been its focus on restoring the network of local social service agencies in the region.[6]

Many of the charities responding to Katrina worked with each other to coordinate the delivery of a multitude of services, including providing food, shelter, and medical assistance.[7] Charities have shared information through daily conference calls and through electronic databases that allow multiple organizations to obtain information about services provided to hurricane victims.[8]

As much as any organization, public or private, the Red Cross played a substantial role in the immediate response to Hurricane Katrina. In what became a $2 billion, 220,000-person enterprise, the relief efforts undertaken by the Red Cross include the provision of financial assistance to 1.2 million families, encompassing more than 3.7 million hurricane survivors.[9] As of January 9, 2006, the Red Cross reported that since Katrina made landfall, it had provided hurricane survivors with nearly

3.42 million overnight stays in nearly 1,100 shelters across 27 states and the District of Columbia.[10] In coordination with the Southern Baptist Convention,[11] the Red Cross has served more than 52 million meals or snacks to hurricane survivors.[12] The Katrina response is larger — 20 times so — than any other Red Cross mission in its 125-year history.[13]

Pre-landfall actions

The Red Cross' Gulf coast-area preparation was far along two days before Katrina made landfall. As of 2:00 p.m. on August 27, the Red Cross reported to the White House and the Department of Homeland Security, among other governmental organizations that it "has every resource at its disposal on alert/moving in anticipation of this event to include personnel, equipment, and materials."[14] Key aspects of this preparation included:

- Chapters across the region are opening shelters in support of evacuations in all states.[15]
- 275,000 HeaterMeals staged in Baton Rouge, Louisiana.
- 225,000 HeaterMeals staged in Montgomery, Alabama.
- 15 sites being identified to bring in big kitchens with support of Southern Baptists to provide 300,000 meals per day feeding capability.
- All 14 Disaster Field Supply Center warehouses loading supplies including 50,000 cots, 100,000 blankets, comfort and clean-up kits.
- All vehicles in the Red Cross fleet across the country are on alert for possible deployment and are being dispatched to staging areas.
- All 8 Emergency Communications Response Vehicles (ECRVs) deployed to staging areas.
- Red Cross staff deployed to NRCC, Region VI RRCC, Region IV RRCC, ERT-As and other ESF #6 posts.[16]

By August 28, the Red Cross started to understand the potential magnitude of Katrina. One of its Disaster Operations Reports noted, if Katrina makes landfall at its current pressure, "it will be the most intense storm to hit the U.S. mainland."[17] Also on the same day it was reported, "For the first time ever, an ESF6 coordination center will be set up tomorrow at American Red Cross national headquarters to coordinate the deliver [sic] mass care services with our governmental and non-governmental organization partners."[18]

Post-landfall actions

As Katrina made landfall on August 29, the Red Cross was fully staffing all of the relevant state and federal Emergency Operations Centers (EOCs), including Alabama, Louisiana, Florida, Mississippi, Georgia, South Carolina, Tennessee, Federal Emergency Management Agency (FEMA) Regions IV and VI's Regional Response Coordination Center (RRCC), FEMA's National Response Coordination Center (NRCC), as well as Emergency Response Advance Element Teams (ERT-A) teams in Florida, Alabama, Mississippi and Louisiana.[19] Sites for 25 kitchens for a total daily capacity of 500,000 people were identified and pre-staged.[20] The Red Cross was also aware of the increasing population at the Superdome, a shelter of last resort it did not support.[21] Figure 1 shows Red Cross interactions with these various operations centers.

Figure 1:

Red Cross Involvement at Emergency Operations Centers

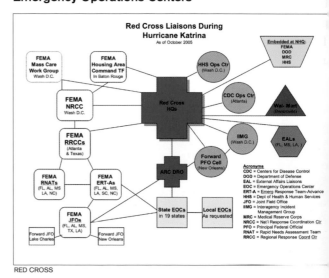

RED CROSS

Montgomery, Alabama Regional Headquarters

The day-to-day paid operations staff of the service area coordinates the fundraising and communications and provides the institutional knowledge of the affected area.[22] Armed with the right data, and knowledge of the area, the information and resources management cell can provide essential services to those in need.[23]

The Red Cross' temporary, regional disaster headquarters in Montgomery, Alabama serves Alabama, Mississippi, Louisiana, and the Florida panhandle.[24] The facility serves, "triple functions:" (1) a volunteer and staff shelter; (2) a warehouse for food and supplies; and (3) a temporary regional corporate headquarters – basically a hub for all relief operations in the Gulf coast region.[25]

The facility has been under lease for over a year, and was used during the 2004 hurricane season as a base of response operations for Hurricanes Dennis and Ivan.[26] Following Hurricane Katrina, the facility was re-opened Thursday, September 1, and was mostly operational within 24 hours and completely operational within 72 hours.[27] Skip Batchelor, a 20-year Red Cross veteran, said the facility would remain operational through October 2005.[28] The lifecycle of the emergency facility was, therefore, about two months.[29]

Located in an old K-Mart building, the facility houses all of the functions of a major corporation.[30] Having the appearance of large political campaign, there are hundreds of folding tables and chairs divided into work areas by function.[31] Some functional areas included:[32]

Warehousing. Approximately 30 percent of the facility served as storage location for food stuffs and supplies, including, cots, blankets, coolers, comfort kits, and meals ready to eat (MREs).

Staff Shelter. At its peak the facility housed 450 Red Cross personnel (staff and volunteers).

Transportation. The facility's parking lot was approximately 30 percent populated with large rental trucks, most supplied by Budget, which donated approximately 50 percent of the rental trucks free of charge. Numerous truck drivers reported each morning ready to drive goods to various points of service in the region. The Red

FEMA

Cross contracted with Shell to install an on site gasoline supply for its vehicles. The Red Cross was able to take advantage of wholesale pricing on this gasoline.

Information Technology (IT). Work stations had computer, internet and telephony capability. There was a central IT department that supported the entire facility.

Real Estate. The Red Cross leased other facilities to serve as points of contact for client interaction. Their real estate team located and secured these properties.

Chapter Outreach. Personnel attempted to coordinate the field needs with the resources available at headquarters.

Jobs and Training. Served as a clearinghouse for job opportunities and training for the displaced.

Financial Assistance. Analysis of client needs and eligibility for financial assistance.

FEMA interface. Provided assistance in connecting victims to FEMA.

Other NGO Coordination. Personnel worked to coordinate with the other key charities and non-government organizations (NGOs) to ensure that the clients are directed to and made aware of all of the potential relief resources. The key charities that clients are referred to include: Baptist Kitchens (food), Mennonites (home rebuilding), VOAD – Voluntary Organizations Active in Disaster (various local volunteers and other smaller relief entities, many of which are faith-based), Catholic Charities, and Habitat for Humanity (new homes).

Government Liaison. Government outreach to coordinate shelter operations, rescue and client outreach.

Volunteer Coordination. At its peak, the facility processed 45,000 volunteers.

Data Entry. There appeared to be 60 to 100 work stations for data entry, half of which are paid temporary workers and half are volunteers.

The ability of the Red Cross to rapidly open and operate such a sophisticated facility in a short amount time reflects the sophisticated planning regime the Red Cross has long had in place. The rapid standing up of the facility was described by Laura Howe a Birmingham-based Red Cross official as the equivalent of opening a Fortune 500 company in a couple days time.[33]

> **The Red Cross, much like FEMA, did not have a logistics capacity sophisticated enough to deal with a truly catastrophic disaster the size of Katrina**

The Red Cross was dependent on FEMA and DOD to provide certain supplies—particularly food in the form of MREs—so it suffered from all the weaknesses in the FEMA and DOD supply chain discussed earlier.

The flooding of New Orleans became a reality on August 30 and the Mayor declared that "80 percent of the city is under water and media sources report the water level is still rising, due in part to broken levees and failed water pumps in the city."[34] By 8:00 a.m. on August 30, the Red Cross was operating 254 shelters for 41,013 people and serving more than 63,000 meals a day.[35] According to the Red Cross' periodic reporting documentation, these numbers continued to grow. The largest number of meals served in a day occurred on September 4, when nearly 946,000 meals were provided.[36] Figure 2 shows the Red Cross daily statistics for the number of shelters in operation, their population, and the number of meals served per day.

Figure 2:
Red Cross Service Levels By Day

Date	Number of Shelters	Population	Number of Meals	Source
August 26	6	584	1,209	DOSR #2
August 27	3	252	3,884	DOSR #4
August 28	3	244	4,454	DOSR #6
August 29	239	37,091	N/A	DOSR #9
August 30	254	41,013	63,175	DOSR #1
August 31	259	52,719	114,413	DOSR #1
September 1	275	76,453	170,465	DOSR #1
September 2	308	94,308	N/A	DOSR #1
September 3	361	96,178	137,588	DOSR #1
September 4	397	106,970	945,886	DOSR #2
September 5	413	124,617	618,938	DOSR #2
September 6	490	125,941	485,983	DOSR #2
September 7	504	143,712	669,271	DOSR #2
September 8	527	138,294	683,826	DOSR #2
September 9	510	101,381	534,864	DOSR #3
September 10	468	97,892	501,318	DOSR #3
September 11	443	88,883	491,751	DOSR #3
September 12	445	74,890	444,793	DOSR #3
September 13	348	62,931	359,816	DOSR #3

Red Cross

Figure 3 shows the daily shelter population for Louisiana, Mississippi, Alabama, and a fourth category with the shelter population in all other states.

Figure 3:
Daily Shelter Population By State

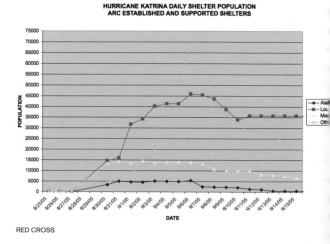

RED CROSS

The Red Cross was encouraged by its pre-landfall staging operation, deeming it largely a success.[37] That being said, the unprecedented devastation of Katrina, both in terms of property damage and number of individuals affected, was much larger than the Red Cross was equipped to handle. Its logistics system was not sophisticated enough – especially with regard to food service. Many problems were experienced in obtaining enough food to satisfy client needs. Many of the food orders processed through FEMA were either inexplicably canceled or never satisfied. On follow-up, it was discovered that many of the orders placed by the Red Cross with FEMA were not reflected in FEMA's systems.[38] FEMA's logistics system was not sophisticated enough to handle the volume Katrina triggered.

The Red Cross experienced substantial communication issues with FEMA.[39] The Red Cross relied on FEMA to provide food, fuel, mobile refrigeration equipment, portable toilets, and many other primary necessities to operate its shelters.[40] Ordinarily these needs are requested by the Red Cross through the respective states.[41] As Katrina gathered force the Red Cross compiled requests for Louisiana, Mississippi, and Alabama among other states.[42] These requests reflected predicted need levels for food, MREs, water, fuel, and other indispensable commodities.[43] In Mississippi, the Red Cross requests were cut substantially by FEMA middle management.[44] Joseph C. Becker, Senior Vice President of Preparedness and Response told Select Committee staff that the upper management of FEMA, including Dan Craig, the Director of the Recovery Division was responsive to Red Cross needs, but the middle level personnel, who were described as "FEMA's mushy middle" proved to be unnecessarily meddlesome.[45] FEMA's middle ranks, according to Becker, canceled orders, lost orders and were the root cause of many of the problems experienced in the field.[46] MREs were ordered and were to be used to feed people during the period before the feeding kitchens were up and running.[47] These MREs were canceled by FEMA under the logic that the Red Cross had also ordered food for the kitchens.[48]

The master log of official requests made by the Red Cross to FEMA under ESF #6 further reveals the ineffective logistics system.[49] The official requests, called Action Request Forms (ARFs), are processed through the FEMA logistics system.[50] A total of 99 ARFs were submitted to FEMA by the Red Cross. Red Cross resource requests are processed through the five emergency coordination centers – the NRCC at FEMA headquarters (18 ARFs), the Regional Response Coordination Center (RRCC) for FEMA Region IV in Atlanta, Georgia (22 ARFs), the RRCC

for FEMA Region VI in Denton, Texas (9 ARFs), the Joint Field Office (JFO) in Baton Rouge, Louisiana (30 ARFs), the JFO in Jackson, Mississippi (13 ARFs), and the JFO in Austin, Texas (7 ARFs).

Given the enormous nature of the Katrina relief effort, and the important role the Red Cross plays in the NRP, 99 requests is not an extraordinarily large number. FEMA, however, could not handle these requests. Only 22 of the 99 ARFs were deemed "Received" by the Red Cross, and 8 were canceled or withdrawn.

A careful review of the master log suggests that the logistics system did not work. Figure 4 is a table identifying logistics problems.

Figure 4:

Official Requests By The Red Cross to FEMA (selected).

Center	Date Requested	Resources Ordered	What Occurred
NRCC	August 30	700,000 MREs for AL and MS	Received only 400,000 and not until September 8 did 600,000 additional MREs arrive for MS.
NRCC	September 1	300,000 MREs for LA	Order canceled, then un-canceled, Product delivered on October 8.
NRCC	September 10	126 5-person security teams needed (630 total) for sites in MS	No security received.
Reg. IV	September 1-3	13 orders for "Kitchen Support," which includes refrigerator, propane, diesel, hand washing stations, porta potties, water buffalo, among other kitchen items.	Received, 10-14 days after request was approved. RC forced to purchase items independently to ensure continuous feeding.
Reg. VI	September 1	9 orders for "Kitchen Support" for Louisiana. Kitchens were for use in Alexandria, Baton Rouge, Bogor, Covington, Hammond, Kenner, and Prairieville.	Not received. Items purchased independently by Red Cross.

Chapter resources and self-reliance could be buttressed by extending chapter self-reliance to 72 hours. Each chapter is generally equipped to survive on its own for the first 48 hours. If expanded to 72 hours, FEMA should be able to assist the Red Cross at the national level in restocking the pipeline.[51]

The Red Cross was challenged by the sometimes disorganized manner in which shelters were established

While the Red Cross has an established role in operating shelters, many of the local governments set up ad hoc shelters without notifying the Red Cross. In other cases, the Red Cross was denied access to shelters.

The Red Cross has been criticized in both Mississippi and Louisiana for a variety of reasons, from excessive levels of bureaucracy to lack of sufficient shelters and food.[52] Becker said the root cause of many problems centered on substantial incongruities between the state and local political leadership on one hand and state emergency management personnel on the other.[53] Far too often state emergency management personnel and local political leadership were not aligned.[54] The Red Cross would receive one set of directions from the state and another from the locals.[55] Becker said, however, with independently elected sheriffs, mayors, and county and parish commissioners, this is not an easily avoidable problem.[56] Many complaints lodged at the Red Cross reflected their policy of not operating shelters in danger zones.[57] Local political leadership often feels compelled to open shelters in their locales even when the entire county or parish is subject to a mandatory evacuation order.[58] The Red Cross has trouble servicing these shelters, both from an access perspective (the roads are sometimes inaccessible) and from an identification perspective (sometimes nobody tells the Red Cross where the shelters are).[59]

The Mississippi National Guard had numerous issues with the Red Cross. The primary complaint was the Red Cross' failure to establish a formal operations section in accordance with the National Incident Management System combined with the fact that the Red Cross is staffed almost exclusively by volunteers. According to Major General Harold Cross, the Mississippi Adjutant General:

> While well intentioned, the volunteers never had a good grasp on security requirements for financial assistance distribution operations. On numerous instances, the ARC volunteers would

simply find a vacant parking area and commence voucher distribution operations. Immediately, crowds would gather and would overwhelm the distribution site. The ARC would then call on the Guard for assistance. Repeated attempts were made to reinforce the need for prior coordination for site security. It was not until mid-September that the ARC started coordinating these operations. Also, the ARC had volunteers who attempted to coordinate directly with subordinate Guard units for shelter and distribution site security. The Forward EOC operations officer met with ARC representatives on numerous occasions to define the requirements for security taskings. The ARC rarely adhered to these requirements. Consequently, the National Guard stayed in a reactive mode concerning security of distribution sites and shelters and hundreds of man hours were wasted. For future events, if the ARC would position a senior operations representative in the Forward Emergency Operations Center, many of the security issues would be resolved. This senior person should not rotate every few days.[60]

Cross also recommended the integration of NGO's like the Red Cross, into the Incident Command System.

GAO has testified the Red Cross did not provide relief in certain hard-to-reach areas because of safety policies.[61] Similarly, media reports indicate the Red Cross was slow to arrive in some small rural towns.[62] The Mississippi town of Pearlington, population 1,684, received no Red Cross support for weeks.[63] A Florida state disaster team set up a shelter, but the Red Cross said it was unsafe and declined to run it.[64] In Pearlington, the Red Cross declined to operate one shelter because it lacked a dehumidifier.[65]

Far too many shelters were unknown to the Red Cross, making it difficult for it to deploy resources.[66] Many of these shelters were within the danger or surge zones, including the Superdome. The Red Cross does not service these "shelters of last resort," as it would put its volunteer in harm's way.[67] After Katrina passed, the Red Cross did attempt to deliver provisions to the Superdome, but was denied access.[68] "The Homeland Security Department ha requested and continues to request that the American Re Cross not come back into New Orleans. Right now access

is controlled by the National Guard and local authorities.
. . . We cannot get into New Orleans against their orders,"
Renita Hosler, a Red Cross spokesperson, told *The
Pittsburgh Post-Gazette*.[69]

The Red Cross encountered many access problems
where local law enforcement would not permit entry
to establish a shelter.[70] The Select Committee asked the
Red Cross for an accounting of the shelters utilized as
compared to the pre-approved shelter list,[71] and for the
reasons behind any differences. The Red Cross provided
the Select Committee with a complete list of every
shelter in operation between the dates of August 25 and
September 30,[72] but will not provide a specific listing
explaining why certain pre-approved shelters were not
used. Lori Polacheck, of the Red Cross general counsel's
office said this was too difficult an undertaking.[73]

The Red Cross was challenged by the magnitude and
chaos of the evacuation of people before landfall and after
the flooding in New Orleans. People were moved, either
by government agencies or on their own initiatives, all
over the country in a haphazard way, making it difficult
for the Red Cross to track and care for the needs of
evacuees.

From the Red Cross' perspective, the transportation of
evacuees by FEMA was disorganized and uncoordinated.
As a primary provider in the feeding and sheltering of
the displaced, the Red Cross needed advance notice
of how many people it would be asked to serve. Many
problems were reported in this area. The information
communicated to the Red Cross by FEMA was unreliable.
There appeared to be no correlation between the
information communicated by FEMA and what actually
happened.[74] Howe noted that often airplanes of
evacuees would arrive without any warning. Conversely,
it seemed to Howe, whenever warnings of arrivals were
communicated, the arrivals often failed to materialize.[75]

This has been chronicled in the press. *The San Jose
Mercury News* reported on September 8 that a plan to
send 1,000 evacuees to California had been put on
hold.[76] The Red Cross, Catholic Charities, and the city
of San Francisco had spent days readying a shelter at
St. Mary's Cathedral.[77] On September 11 *The Columbus*

Dispatch reported a similar story; Columbus, Cleveland
and Cincinnati were set to take 1,000 evacuees on
September 8, but the in-bound flights were canceled
by FEMA.[78] Evacuees were scheduled by FEMA to be
transported to Ohio. Fred Strathman, a spokesman for
the Ohio Emergency Management Agency, indicated to
the newspaper that the plan to send evacuees to Ohio was
delayed twice by FEMA and then apparently canceled.[79]
A spokesman for the Red Cross of Greater Columbus,
Lynn Cook said, "Are we a little tired of pumping things
up and taking them back down? Yeah."[80] Similarly, *The
Courier-Journal* of Louisville, Kentucky reported that on
September 13, FEMA suspended evacuation flights due to
the unwillingness of evacuees to relocate so far from the
Gulf coast.[81] According to the newspaper, on September
5, federal officials told Louisville that 500 evacuees would
be arriving at any time.[82] The Red Cross had worked to
prepare a shelter and had stockpiled food and clothing.[83]
All for nothing.

More than any other hurricane, Katrina has produced a
large volume of seemingly permanent evacuees. The Red
Cross is now finding that a large number of evacuees are
not going home.[84]

The Red Cross has not escaped substantial public criticism

The Red Cross has not escaped substantial criticism.[85] The
most obvious casualty of this criticism came on December
13, when its president, Marsha Evans, announced her
resignation.[86] According to press accounts, even Evans
acknowledged the organization's response to Katrina and
Rita had been uneven, "eclips[ing] even our direst, worst-
case scenarios."[87]

At a December 13 hearing conducted by the House
Committee on Ways and Means Oversight Subcommittee
to review the response by charities to Hurricane Katrina,
Louisiana Representative Jim McCrery was extremely
critical of the Red Cross:[88]

Hurricane Katrina, and the subsequent flooding
of New Orleans, displaced roughly one million

shelters in facilities that do not meet our criteria for safety during landfall.

Consistent with State and local plans, and our practice in previous disasters, we were asked by state and federal officials not to enter New Orleans. While we were in constant communication with local and state authorities, it was not deemed safe for Red Cross personnel to re-enter the city of New Orleans. The Red Cross does not place our client evacuees, staff, volunteers, or resources in harm's way. It is our practice to heed evacuation orders and assist those in need of shelter outside of high-risk areas.

Additionally, it was the goal of local and state officials to fully evacuate the city of New Orleans after the storm passed. We were instructed by authorities that, in addition to issues of safety, if the Red Cross provided services to survivors within New Orleans, it would discourage people from heeding evacuation orders. At the direction of public officials, we entered New Orleans in a coordinated fashion to provide services at the earliest possible time.

This was a difficult scenario for the Red Cross. Eighty percent of our local Red Cross staff in the Southeast Louisiana Chapter lost their homes to Katrina, yet while they themselves were victims, they desperately wanted to provide support to their neighbors in need, and to this day they continue to do so. We are still engaged in active operations in the city.

Important assistance was provided by the Salvation Army, Catholic Charities, the United Way, and the National Voluntary Organizations Active in Disaster

As the only charitable organization with primary responsibility under the NRP, the Red Cross received a lot of Select Committee attention. Beyond the Red Cross, however, there was a vast network of charities that contributed meaningfully to the response efforts in the Gulf coast area. The important contributions of organizations such as the Salvation Army, Catholic Charities USA, the United Way, and the National Voluntary Organizations Active in Disaster (NVOAD) merit attention.

FEMA

Salvation Army

The Salvation Army has been at the site of most major natural disasters in America for more than a century.[100] It has developed areas of expertise in disaster response: mass feeding to survivors and emergency responders immediately after a disaster has occurred; sheltering those affected while tending to their spiritual and emotional needs; and then, the continuation of social service assistance to ensure the survivors have the means to move back into some semblance of the routine known before the disaster struck.[101]

In responding to those affected by Hurricane Katrina, the Salvation Army staged personnel and equipment in the states adjacent to the primary strike zone. Major Todd Hawks of the Salvation Army, summarized some of the key contributions the Salvation Army made to immediate response efforts:

- Loaded meals on 72 mobile canteens, each capable of providing 5,000 hot meals per day, and two 54-foot mobile kitchens, each capable of providing 20,000 hot meals per day. We intended to dispatch these mobile feeding units into those geographic areas determined by FEMA to be the hardest hit, and to dispatch additional units as needed.
- Mobilized 200 officers, employees, and volunteers to man these mobile kitchens.
- Prepared to dispatch portable shower units, trucks transformed into 1-stop shops called comfort stations, and emergency response command stations for officers to direct the response efforts.[102]

In the immediate aftermath of Katrina, the Salvation Army facilitated mass feeding, moving mobile feeding units into New Orleans, Biloxi, Gulfport, Mobile and numerous other affected communities within hours after the storm had passed.[103] In total the number of mobile canteens deployed numbered 178 and the number of field kitchens reached 11.[104] Since Katrina struck, the Salvation Army has served more than 5 million hot meals and more than 7 million sandwiches and snacks to survivors and first responders.[105] Although not a primary activity for the Salvation Army, at its highest point, it operated 225 shelters for more than 31,000 people.[106]

Catholic Charities

Catholic Charities USA is the membership association of one of the nation's largest social service networks. Catholic Charities agencies provide vital social services to people in need, regardless of their religious, social, or economic backgrounds.[107] As of January 6, 2006, Catholic Charities had allocated more than $56 million to over 60 local Catholic Charities and other Catholic organizations responding to the needs of families affected by the Gulf coast hurricanes.[108] In total, Catholic Charities USA has raised $137 million to assist the network's largest disaster response effort in its history.[109] Dozens of Catholic Charities agencies and Catholic organizations have each received disaster relief grants from Catholic Charities USA, ranging from $6,000 to $25 million.[110] Across the nation, more than 80 local Catholic Charities are working to meet the needs of hurricane victims.[111] Relief efforts have included: providing victims with food, financial aid, clothing, shelter, gas and retail store cards, and household

goods; helping with medical and prescription needs; offering clean up assistance; helping victims work with FEMA and other groups; and providing crisis counseling, case management, transportation, job placement, and temporary and long-term housing.[112]

United Way

United Way of America is the national organization that provides leadership to approximately 1,350 community-based United Way organizations. Each is independent, separately incorporated, and governed by local volunteers.[113] As of December 15, 2005, the United Way of America has raised $45 million to support hurricane response and recovery efforts.[114] Through its Hurricane Response and Recovery Fund, the United Way has focused its efforts on restoring the abilities of social service agencies in the Gulf coast region.[115] Many human services organizations in the Gulf coast states suffered tremendous damage to their facilities, which severely limited their ability to provide services to those in need.[116] United Ways throughout the affected areas have worked with partner agencies to ensure services such as emergency assistance, food, clothing, housing and transportation are available to those in need.[117]

National Voluntary Organizations Active in Disaster (NVOAD)

NVOAD is a national charity umbrella organization composed of approximately 40 charities that provide services following disasters.[118] As a designated support agency under ESF #6, NVOAD is responsible for sharing information with its member organizations regarding the severity of the disaster, needs identified, and actions taken to address these needs.[119] NVOAD coordinates planning efforts by many voluntary organizations responding to disaster.[120] Member organizations provide a more effective and efficient service to the community in need by agreeing to share information and combine resources.[121] This cooperation has proven to be an effective way for a multitude of organizations to work together in during an emergency.[122]

During the immediate response to Katrina, NVOAD organized daily conference calls with FEMA and other federal government representatives and its member

organizations operating in the Gulf coast region.[123] NVOAD also invited nonmember charitable organizations that were providing relief to hurricane victims to participate in these calls, which sometimes included more than 40 organizations at once. During these calls, both the federal government and charities were able to provide information and answer questions about services provided, needs identified, and the organizations' abilities to meet these needs.[124]

Conclusion

Since August 29, charitable donations to Katrina relief have exceeded $3 billion. Two-thirds of this amount has been raised by the Red Cross. With its $2 billion relief effort, the Red Cross has been able to fulfill many of its obligations under the National Response Plan. Katrina, however, overwhelmed the Red Cross. The Red Cross, like FEMA, did not have a logistics capacity sophisticated enough to fully support the massive number of Gulf coast victims. Among other challenges, the Red Cross was required to grapple with the sometimes disorganized manner in which shelters were established. While it has a well-defined role in operating shelters, many of the local governments set up ad hoc shelters without notifying Red Cross officials. In some cases, the Red Cross was denied access to shelters. Despite falling short of being universally present everywhere there was a need, the Red Cross and numerous other charitable organizations performed admirably and heroically in reaching the greatest number of people with impressive speed. ∎

[1] Center on Philanthropy at Indiana University, *Gulf Coast Hurricane Relief Donations*, http://www.philanthropy.iupui.edu/Hurricane_Katrina.html (Jan. 9, 2006) [hereinafter Center on Philanthropy – Donations]; Spreadsheet, Center on Philanthropy, *U.S. Organizations Providing Hurricane Relief Efforts* (Jan. 9 2005) [hereinafter Center on Philanthropy – Spreadsheet].

[2] *Hearing to Review the Response by Charities to Hurricane Katrina Before Subcommittee on Oversight of the House Committee on Ways and Means*, 109th Cong. (Dec. 13, 2005) (written statement of Cynthia M. Fagnoni, Managing Dir., Educ., Workforce and Income Sec., U.S. Gov. Accountability Office) [hereinafter *Dec. 13, 2005 Ways and Means Oversight Hearing* (written statement of Cynthia Fagnoni)].

[3] American Red Cross, *Facts at a Glance*, http://www.redcross.org/news/ds/hurricanes/2005/facts.html (Jan. 12, 2006) [hereinafter Jan. 12, 2006 Red Cross Facts at a Glance].

[4] Center on Philanthropy – Donations; Center on Philanthropy – Spreadsheet.

[5] Center on Philanthropy – Donations; Center on Philanthropy – Spreadsheet; *Dec. 13, 2005 Ways and Means Oversight Hearing* (written statement of Cynthia Fagnoni); Press Release, Catholic Charities USA, *Catholic Charities USA, 13 Other Major Nonprofits Reaffirm Commitment to Human Needs Aspect of Gulf Coast Recovery*, Jan. 6, 2005, http://www.catholiccharitiesusa.org/news/content_displays.cfm?fuseaction=display_document&id=743&location=3.

[5] Press Release, United Way, *United Way Receives $10 Million Grant From Lilly Endowment For Hurricane Recovery and Rebuilding*, Nov. 3, 2005 at http://national.unitedway.org/files/pdf/press_releases/Lilly_Endowment_Grant_FINAL_Nov_2005.PDF [hereinafter Nov. 3, 2005 United Way Press Release].

[7] *Dec. 13, 2005 Ways and Means Oversight Hearing* (written statement of Cynthia Fagnoni).

[8] *Id.*

[9] Jan. 12, 2006 Red Cross Facts at a Glance.

[10] American Red Cross, *Facts at a Glance*, http://www.redcross.org/news/ds/hurricanes/2005/facts.html (Jan. 9, 2006) [hereinafter Jan. 9, 2006 Red Cross Facts at a Glance].

[11] The Southern Baptist Convention provides the manpower and the kitchens, and the Red Cross provides supplies and logistics. Gabrielle DeFord and Maryann Sinkler, *Southern Baptists Help Feed Millions After Katrina*, Sept. 14, 2005, http:www.redcross.org.

[12] Jan. 9, 2006 Red Cross Facts at a Glance.

[13] *Hearing to Review the Response by Charities to Hurricane Katrina Before Subcommittee on Oversight of the House Committee on Ways and Means*, 109th Cong. (Dec. 13, 2005) (written statement of Joseph C. Becker, Senior Vice President Preparedness and Response, American Red Cross) [hereinafter *Dec. 13, 2005 Ways and Means Oversight Hearing* (statement of Joseph C. Becker)].

[14] E-mail correspondence from Carol Hall, American Red Cross, to Kirstjen M. Nielsen, et al. (Aug. 27, 2005) (2:48 p.m.) [hereinafter Aug. 27, 2005 Hall E mail].

[15] A complete list of all pre-approved shelters for Louisiana, Mississippi and Alabama was supplied to the Select Comm. The establishment of shelters is carefully planned for and part of the chapter disaster planning regime. See ARC 4496, Standards for Hurricane Evacuation Shelter Selection (Jan. 2002); ARC Shelter Operations Management Toolkit (Sept. 2005); Complete Shelter Listings for Alabama, Mississippi, and Louisiana.

[16] Aug. 27, 2005 Hall E-mail.

[17] American Red Cross, *Disaster Operations Summary Report (DOSR) #7* at 2 (Aug. 28, 2005).

[18] American Red Cross, DOSR#7 at 3 (Aug. 28, 2005).

[19] American Red Cross, DOSR#9 at 3 (Aug. 29, 2005).

[20] *Id.* at 2.

[21] *Id.* at 1.

[22] Interview by Select Comm. Staff with Laura Howe and Skip Batchelor, American Red Cross, in Montgomery, AL (Oct. 11, 2005) [hereinafter Oct. 11, 2005 Red Cross Interview].

[23] *Id.*

[24] *Id.*

[25] *Id.*

[26] *Id.*

[27] *Id.*

[28] *Id.*

[29] *Id.*

[30] *Id.*

[31] *Id.*

[32] *Id.*

[33] *Id.*

[34] American Red Cross, DOSR#11 at 2 (Aug. 30, 2005).

[35] *Id.* at 1.

[36] American Red Cross, DOSR#20 at 3 (Sept. 4, 2005).

[37] Oct. 11, 2005 Red Cross Interview; Interview by Select Comm. Staff with Joseph C. Becker, Sr. Vice Pres., Preparedness and Response, American Red Cross, in Wash., DC (Oct. 14, 2005) [hereinafter Oct. 14, 2005 Red Cross Interview]

[38] Oct. 11, 2005 Red Cross Interview; Oct. 14, 2005 Red Cross Interview.

[39] Oct. 14, 2005 Red Cross Interview.

[40] *Id.*

[41] *Id.*

[42] *Id.*

[43] *Id.*

[44] *Id.*

45 *Id.*

46 *Id.*

47 *Id.*

48 *Id.*

49 American Red Cross, ESF #6 Master Log at 2 (Dec. 22, 2005).

50 *Id.*

51 Oct. 11, 2005 Red Cross Interview; Oct. 14, 2005 Red Cross Interview.

52 Oct. 14, 2005 Red Cross Interview.

53 *Id.*

54 *Id.*

55 *Id.*

56 *Id.*

57 The Select Comm. reviewed planning documentation from individual Red Cross chapters. Disaster Response Plans were submitted from the following Red Cross chapters: Southeastern Louisiana (June 205), St. Bernard Parish Chapter (undated), Northwest Louisiana Chapter (June 2005), Northeast Louisiana Chapter (June 2005), Central Louisiana Chapter (Apr. 2002), South Central Mississippi Chapter (Sept. 2004), Mississippi Gulf Coast Chapter (Sept. 2005), Southeast Mississippi Chapter (Feb. 2003), and Alabama Gulf Coast Chapter (Jan. 1997). Statewide plans were received from the Red Cross in Alabama and Mississippi. The Red Cross is now organized into eight Service Areas, rather than by state. The state plans obtained by the Select Comm. from Alabama and Mississippi are now technically obsolete.

58 Oct. 14, 2005 Red Cross Interview.

59 *Id.*

60 *Hearing on Hurricane Katrina: Preparedness and Response by the Department of Defense, the Coast Guard, and the National Guard of Louisiana, Mississippi, and Alabama Before the Select Comm.*, 109th Cong. (Oct. 27, 2005) (written response to questions for the record of Maj. Gen. Harold A. Cross, the Adjutant General, State of Mississippi.); Mississippi National Guard, Hurricane Katrina Narrative, Daily Logs (Aug. 2005 – Nov. 2005).

61 *Dec. 13, 2005 Ways and Means Oversight Hearing* (written statement of Cynthia Fagnoni).

62 Martha T. Moore, *Red Cross in Critics' Cross Hairs*, USA TODAY, Oct. 17, 2005 [hereinafter Oct. 17 Moore Article].

63 *Id.*

64 *Id.*

65 *Id.*

66 Oct. 14, 2005 Red Cross Interview.

67 *Id.*

68 Oct. 14, 2005 Red Cross Interview; *Dec. 13, 2005 Ways and Means Oversight Hearing* (statement of Joseph C. Becker).

69 Ann Rodgers, *Homeland Security Won't Let Red Cross Deliver Food*, PITTSBURGH POST-GAZETTE, Sept. 3, 2005; *Dec. 13, 2005 Ways and Means Oversight Hearing* (Statement of Joseph C. Becker).

70 Oct. 11, 2005 Red Cross Interview; Oct. 14, 2005 Red Cross Interview.

71 Pre-approved Shelter Listings for Alabama, Mississippi, and Louisiana.

72 Hurricane Katrina Daily Shelter Populations, American Red Cross, Aug. 25, 2005 to Sept. 30, 2005.

73 Telephone Interview by Select Comm. Staff with Lori Polacheck, Senior Counsel, American Red Cross, Wash., DC (Jan. 23, 2005).

74 Oct. 14, 2005 Red Cross Interview.

75 *Id.*

76 Mary Anne Ostrom and Chuck Carroll, *Feds Hold Off On Sending 1,000 Evacuees to California; Families Want to Remain Closer to Home*, SAN JOSE MERCURY NEWS, Sept. 8, 2005 [hereinafter Sept. 8, 2005 Ostrom Article].

77 Sept. 8, 2005 Ostrom Article.

78 Robert Vitale, *With Few Evacuees Interested, Flights to Ohio Canceled*, THE COLUMBUS DISPATCH, Sept. 11, 2005 at A21 [Sept. 1, 2005 Vitale Article].

79 Sept. 1, 2005 Vitale Article.

80 *Id.*

81 Chris Kenning, *Evacuee Airlift Not Coming To City*, THE COURIER-JOURNAL (Louisville, KY), Sept. 14, 2005 at 1B [Sept. 14, 2005 Kenning Article].

82 Sept. 14, 2005 Kenning Article.

83 *Id.*

84 Oct. 11, 2005 Red Cross Interview; Oct. 14, 2005 Red Cross Interview.

85 *See generally*, Editorial, *Red Cross Operations Due For A Tune-Up*, MIAMI HERALD, Jan. 3, 2006 at A16; Jacqueline L. Salmon, *Red Cross Bolstering Minority Outreach; Recruitment a Priority After Storms Expose Sensitivity Gaps*, THE WASH. POST, Dec. 5, 2005 at A1; Jacqueline L. Salmon and Elizabeth Williamson, *Red Cross Borrowing Funds For Storm Aid – Loan of $340 Million Comes as Nonprofit Draws New Scrutiny*, THE WASH. POST Oct. 28, 2005 at A1; Oct. 17 Moore Article; Josh Getlin et al., *A Long Road To Recovery; Red Cross' Huge Effort Not Without Critics; Defenders Say The Scope Of The Storms Pushed The Short-Term Aid Expert Out Of Its League*, LA TIMES, Oct. 7, 2005, A1; Josh Getlin et al., *Fundraising Phenom – Red Cross – Is Under Fire*, LA TIMES, Oct. 6, 2005; Chad Terhune, *Along Battered Gulf, Katrina Aid Stirs Unintended Rivalry, Salvation Army Wins Hearts, Red Cross Faces Critics; Two Different Missions*, THE WALL STREET JOURNAL, Sept. 29, 2005 at A1; Associated Press, *Despite Katrina Efforts, Red Cross Draws Criticism*, USA TODAY, Sept. 28, 2005; Sean Gregory, *Trying To Get It Right This Time*, TIME, Sept. 26, 2005 at 24.

86 Press Release, American Red Cross, *Marsha J. Evans Steps Down As American Red Cross President and CEO* (Dec. 13, 2005).

87 David Cary, *American Red Cross President Resigns*, AP, Dec. 14, 2005.

88 *Hearing to Review the Response by Charities to Hurricane Katrina Before Subcommittee on Oversight of the House Committee on Ways and Means*, 109th Cong. (Dec. 13, 2005) (statement of The Honorable Jim McCrery) [hereinafter *Dec. 13, 2005 Ways and Means Oversight Hearing* (statement of Rep. McCrery)].

Dec. 13, 2005 Ways and Means Oversight Hearing (statement of Rep. McCrery).

Oct. 14, 2005 Red Cross Interview; Facts at a Glance, American Red Cross website (Jan. 9, 2006), http://www.redcross.org/news/ds/hurricanes/2005/facts.html.

Dec. 13, 2005 Ways and Means Oversight Hearing (statement of Joseph C. Becker).

American Red Cross, *2004 Annual Report* at 8. For a third party view of the Red Cross' finances, *see* Charity Navigator, http://www.charitynavigator.org.

Dec. 13, 2005 Ways and Means Oversight Hearing (statement of Joseph C. Becker).

Oct. 14, 2005 Red Cross Interview.

Id.

Id.

Dec. 13, 2005 Ways and Means Oversight Hearing (statement of Joseph C. Becker).

Id.

Id.

Hearing to Review the Response by Charities to Hurricane Katrina Before Subcommittee on Oversight of the House Committee on Ways and Means, 109th Cong. (Dec. 13, 2005) (statement of Major Todd Hawks, Public Affairs Secretary and Associate National Community Relations and Development Secretary, Salvation Army of America) [hereinafter *Dec. 13, 2005 Ways and Means Oversight Hearing* (statement of Todd Hawks)].

Dec. 13, 2005 Ways and Means Oversight Hearing (statement of Todd Hawks).

Id.

Id.

Id.

Id.

Nov. 3., 2005 United Way Press Release.

Catholic Charities, About, http://www.catholiccharitiesusa.org/about/index.cfm?cfid=6359238&cftoken=12248968.

Press Release, Catholic Charities USA, *Catholic Charities USA, 13 Other Major Nonprofits Reaffirm Commitment to Human Needs Aspect of Gulf Coast Recovery* (Jan. 6, 2005), http://www.catholiccharitiesusa.org/news/content_displays.cfm?fuseaction=display_document&id=743&location=3 [hereinafter Jan. 6, 2005 Catholic Charities Press Release].

Jan. 6, 2005 Catholic Charities Press Release.

Id.

Id.

Id.

Press Release, American Red Cross, *Salvation Army, and United Way, American Red Cross, Salvation Army, and United Way 'Put People First' When Addressing Needs Of Hurricane Katrina Victims – Three Organizations Prepare for Next Disaster* (Sept. 23, 2005) [hereinafter Sept. 23, 2005 Joint Press Release].

Center on Philanthropy – Donations; Center on Philanthropy – Spreadsheet.

Nov. 3, 2005 United Way Press Release.

Id.

Id.

Members of NVOAD are: Adventist Community Services, America's Second Harvest, American Baptist Men USA, American Disaster Reserve, American Radio Relay League, Inc. (ARRL), American Red Cross, Ananda Marga Universal Relief Team (AMURT), Catholic Charities USA, Center for International Disaster Information (formerly Volunteers in Technical Assistance), Christian Disaster Response, Christian Reformed World Relief Committee (CRWRC), Church of the Brethren-Emergency Response, Church World Service, Convoy of Hope, Disaster Psychiatry Outreach, Episcopal Relief and Development, Friends Disaster Service, Inc., Humane Society of the United States International Aid, International Critical Incident Stress Foundation, International Relief Friendship Foundation (IRFF), Lutheran Disaster Response, Mennonite Disaster Service, Mercy Medical Airlift (Angel Flight), National Emergency Response Team, National Organization for Victim Assistance, Nazarene Disaster Response, Northwest Medical Teams International, Presbyterian Church (USA), REACT International, Inc., Society of St. Vincent de Paul, Southern Baptist Convention, The Points of Light Foundation, The Salvation Army, United Church of Christ-Wider Church Ministries, United Jewish Communities, United Methodist Committee on Relief, United Way of America, Volunteers of America, and World Vision. *See* NVOAD, Members, http://www.nvoad.org/membersdb.php?members=National.

Dec. 13, 2005 Ways and Means Oversight Hearing (written statement of Cynthia Fagnoni); NVOAD, About, http://www.nvoad.org/about.php [hereinafter Website Materials, About NVOAD].

Id.

Id.

Id.

Id.

Id.

"Order is indeed the dream of man,
but chaos, which is only another word for dumb, blind, witless chance,
is still the law of nature."

WALLACE STEGNER
Crossing to Safety

"Nature, to be commanded, must be obeyed."

FRANCIS BACON

CONCLUSION

The preparation for and response to Hurricane Katrina should disturb all Americans. While the Select Committee believes all people involved, at all levels of government, were trying their best to save lives and ease suffering, their best just wasn't good enough.

In this report we have tried to tell the story of the inadequate preparation and response. We cover a lot of territory – from evacuations to medical care, communications to contracting. We hope our findings will prompt the changes needed to make all levels of government better prepared and better able to respond the next time.

The resolution that created the Select Committee charged us with compiling findings, not recommendations. But in reality that's a distinction without a difference. Moving from our findings to legislative, organizational, and policy changes need not be a long or difficult journey.

We are left scratching our heads at the range of inefficiency and ineffectivness that characterized government behavior right before and after this storm. But passivity did the most damage. The failure of initiative cost lives, prolonged suffering, and left all Americans justifiably concerned our government is no better prepared to protect its people than it was before 9/11, even if we are.

How can we set up a system to protect against passivity? Why do we repeatedly seem out of synch during disasters? Why do we continually seem to be one disaster behind?

We have not found every fact nor contemplated all successes and failures. What we have done over four months is intensely focus on a three-week period, uncovering a multitude of problems. We have learned more than enough to instruct those who will now have to draft and execute changes for the future.

We leave it to readers to determine whether we have done a fair and thorough job, and whether we identified and supported findings in a way that will foster change. Some predicted we would place disproportionate blame on one person or another, or that we would give some others a pass. We hope it is clear we have done neither.

We have not sought to assign individual blame, though it is clear in our report that some were not up to the challenge that was Katrina. Rather, we have tried to tell the story of government's preparation for and response to a massive storm, and identify lessons learned.

Our interaction with the White House illustrates this point. Some insist the White House's failure to provide, for example, e-mails to and from the White House Chief of Staff means we have insufficient information to determine why government failed. That view exalts political curiosity over the practical realities of a serious investigation.

While our dealings with the White House proved frustrating and difficult, we ended up with more than enough information to determine what went wrong there, to form a picture of a White House that, like many entities, was overcome by the fog of war. There is a big difference between having enough information to find institutional fault, which we do, and having information to assign individual blame, which, in the case of the White House, in large part we do not.

It's the former that's important if the goal is to be better prepared the next time. This was not about some individual's failure of initiative. It was about organizational and societal failures of initiative. There was more than enough failure to go around:

- Tardy and ineffective execution of the National Response Plan.
- An under-trained and under-staffed Federal Emergency Management Agency.
- A Catastrophic Incident Annex that was never invoked, and doubt that it would have done the job anyway.
- A perplexing inability to learn from Hurricane Pam and other exercises.
- Levees not built to withstand the most severe hurricanes.
- An incomplete evacuation that led to deaths and tremendous suffering.
- A complete breakdown in communications that paralyzed command and control and made situational awareness murky at best.
- The failure of state and local officials to maintain law and order.
- Haphazard and incomplete emergency shelter and housing plans.
- An overwhelmed FEMA logistics and contracting system that could not support the effective provision of urgently needed supplies.

The Select Committee encountered shortcomings and challenges even among those response elements that went relatively well and saved many lives. The military performed an invaluable role once forces were deployed, but encountered coordination problems with FEMA, the National Guard, and state officials. State-to-state emergency aid compacts were critical in restoring law and order and accelerating relief supplies, but too many people remain unfamiliar with the process. Contributions from charitable groups were enormously helpful, but they too were overwhelmed by the size of the storm.

Many of our findings are mixed in nature. Evacuations of general populations, for example, went relatively well in all three states. But declarations of mandatory evacuations in metropolitan New Orleans came late or not at all, and that, coupled with the decision to shelter but not evacuate the remaining population prolonged suffering. We saw heroic examples of medical care and patient needs being met under dire circumstances. But too often the deployment of medical personnel was reactive, not proactive.

The Select Committee acknowledges it was often torn between sympathy and incredulity, compassion and criticism. On the one hand, we understood Katrina was so big and so devastating that death and chaos were inevitable. We understood that top federal, state, and local officials overlooked some steps and some needs in the hours and days after landfall because they were focused on saving lives. But on the other hand, a dispassionate review made it clear that even an extraordinary lack of situational awareness could not excuse many of the shortcomings and organizational inaction evident in the documents and communications the Select Committee reviewed.

Leadership requires decisions to be made even when based on flawed and incomplete information. Too often during the immediate response to Katrina, sparse or conflicting information was used as an excuse for inaction rather than an imperative to step in and fill an obvious vacuum. Information passed through the maze of departmental operations centers and ironically-named "coordinating" committees, losing timeliness and relevance as it was massaged and interpreted for internal audiences.

As a result, leaders became detached from the changing minute-to-minute realities of Katrina. Information translated into pre-cast bureaucratic jargon put more than geographic distance between Washington and the Gulf coast. Summaries and situation reports describing the gross totals of relief supplies directed to affected areas did not say when or how or to whom those desperately needed supplies would be delivered. And apparently no one asked.

Communications aren't a problem when you're only talking to yourself.

The Select Committee believes too many leaders failed to lead. Top aides failed as well, primarily in mis-prioritizing their bosses' attention and action. Critical time was wasted on issues of no importance to disaster response, such as winning the blame game, waging a public relations battle, or debating the advantages of wardrobe choices.

We have spared our readers a rehashing of unflattering e-mails involving Michael Brown and Governor Blanco and others, as they have been given more than enough attention by the media. We will pause only briefly here to urge future responders to make people, not politics, their priority.

We further urge public officials confronting the next Katrina to remember disaster response must be based on knowledge, not rumors. Government at all levels lost credibility due to inaccurate or unsubstantiated public statements made by officials regarding law and order, levee breaches, and overall response efforts.

The media must share some of the blame here. The Select Committee agrees the media can and should help serve as the public's "first informer" after disasters. In the 21st century, Americans depend on timely and accurate reporting, especially during times of crisis. But it's clear accurate reporting was among Katrina's many victims. If anyone rioted, it was the media. Many stories of rape, murder, and general lawlessness were at best unsubstantiated, at worst simply false. And that's too bad because this storm needed no exaggeration.

As discussed in our report, widely-distributed uncorroborated rumors caused resources to be deployed, and important time and energy wasted, chasing down the imaginary. Already traumatized people in the Superdome and elsewhere, listening to their transistor radios, were further panicked.

"The sensational accounts delayed rescue and evacuation efforts already hampered by poor planning and a lack of coordination among local, state, and federal encies. People rushing to the Gulf coast to fly rescue helicopters or to distribute food, water and other aid eeled themselves for battle. In communities near and far, e seeds were planted that the victims of Katrina should e kept away, or at least handled with extreme caution," e *Washington Post* reported on October 5.[1]

Lt. Gen. H Steven Blum told the Select Committee 1 October 27, "We focused assets and resources based 1 situational awareness provided to us by the media, ankly. And the media failed in their responsibility to get right. …we sent forces and capabilities to places that dn't need to go there in numbers that were far in excess f what was required, because they kept running the same roll over and over….and the impression to us that were atching it was that the condition did not change. But the onditions were continually changing."[2]

E-mails obtained by the Select Committee reinforce the onclusion that top military officials were relying on news ports for information – information used to plan and ploy resources.[3]

The Select Committee does not mean to suggest e media is solely responsible for responders' ck of situational awareness, or the destruction of ommunications infrastructure that thrust television into e role of first informer for the military as well as the eneral public. Nor is the media solely responsible for porting comments from sources they believed to be edible – especially top officials.

The Select Committee does, however, believe such rcumstances make accurate reporting, especially in e period immediately after the storm, all the more nportant. Skepticism and fact-checking are easier when e sea is calm, but more vital when it is not.

As with so many other failures related to Katrina, hat's most vexing is that emergency managers should ave known such problems would arise among the chaos. r. Kathleen Tierney, head of the University of Colorado-oulder Natural Hazards Center, told Select Committee aff that misleading or completely false media reports ould have been among the most foreseeable elements Katrina. "It's a well-documented element of disaster sponse," she said. "What you do has to be based on nowledge, not rumor, and you're going to be faced with a t of rumors."[4]

Benigno Aguirre, sociology professor at the University Delaware Disaster Research Center, told the *Philadelphia Inquirer*, "It's discouraging for those who spend their lives studying disaster behavior that journalists so often get it wrong."[5]

Former FEMA Director Michael Brown told the Select Committee one of his biggest failures was failing to properly utilize the media as first informer.

"I failed initially to set up a series of regular briefings to the media about what FEMA was doing throughout the Gulf coast region," Brown said at the Select Committee's September 27 hearing. "Instead, I became tied to the news shows, going on the news shows early in the morning and late at night, and that was just a mistake. We should have been feeding that information to the press…in the manner and time that we wanted to, instead of letting the press drive us."[6]

Finally, a word about public communications. Both the message and the messengers were ineffective before and after Katrina. Messages to the public were uncoordinated and often confusing, leaving important questions unanswered. Federal, state, and local officials did not have a unified strategy for communicating with the public.

Risk communication is a well-researched field of study. There are accepted core principles for successfully communicating risks to the public. Information about threats should be consistent, accurate, clear, and provided repeatedly through multiple methods. It should be timely. It should be specific about the potential threat. It needs to get to people regardless of their level of access to information.

The Select Committee heard loud and clear from Gulf coast residents that the dangers of the coming hurricane could have been presented in a more effective manner, an issue which also carried racial and socioeconomic implications. If people don't hear a message from someone they trust, they will be skeptical.

Doreen Keeler, a New Orleans resident who evacuated before Mayor Nagin called for a mandatory evacuation, told the Select Committee local officials should have called for mandatory evacuations earlier, noting how difficult it was to convince the elderly residents of New Orleans to leave.[7] "If a mandatory evacuation would have been called earlier," she said, "it would have been easier to move seniors out of the area and many lives would have been saved. It took me almost 24 hours to get my in-laws to leave. Others tell the same story. The severity of the storm was not stressed by elected officials."[8]

The relevant "elected officials," we are sure, would contest that. In fact they did, in testimony before the Select Committee. But it's the public perception of what was stressed that's important here. The failure of initiative was also a failure of empathy, a myopia to the need to reach more people on their own terms.

Four and half years after 9/11, Americans deserve more than the state of nature after disaster strikes. With this report we have tried to identify where and why chaos ensued, so that even a storm the size of Katrina can be met with more order, more urgency, more coordination, and more initiative. ■

---

1   Robert E. Pierre and Ann Gerhart, *News of Pandemonium May Have Slowed Aid*, WASHINGTON POST, Oct. 5, 2005 at A8.

2   *Hearing on Hurricane Katrina: Preparedness And Response By The Department Of Defense, The Coast Guard, And The National Guard Of Louisiana, Mississippi And Alabama Before the Select Comm.*, 109th Congress (Oct. 27, 2005), (statement of Lt. Gen. H Steven Blum, Chief, Nat'l Guard Bureau).

3   *See* e.g., E-mail correspondence from 1A JOC Watch Battle Captain to Lt. General Russel Honoré (Aug. 29, 2005).

4   Interview by Select Comm. Staff with Kathleen J. Tierney, Director, Natural Hazards Research and Applications Information Center, Institute Behavioral Science, U. of Colorado at Boulder (Oct. 6, 2005).

5   Beth Gillin, *Katrina Spawned rumors; media ran with them*, THE PHILADELPHIA INQUIRER, Sept. 28, 2005 at A2.

6   *Hearing On Hurricane Katrina: The Role Of The Federal Emergency Management Agency Before the Select Comm.*, 109th Congress (Sept. 27, 2005), (statement of Michael D. Brown, former Undersecretary of Emergency Preparedness and Response, DHS).

7   *Hearing on Hurricane Katrina: Voices from Inside the Storm Before Select Comm.*, 109th Congress, (Dec. 6, 2005) (written statement of Doreen Keeler Tomlinson, resident of New Orleans, LA).

8   *Id.*

APPENDICES

GLOSSARY OF ACRONYMS AND ABBREVIATIONS

AAMC	Association of American Medical Colleges
AAMS	Association of Air Medical Services
ACI	Advanced Contracting Initiative
ADAMS	Atlas and Database of Air Medical Services
ADHS	Alabama Department of Health Services
AEMA	Alabama Emergency Management Agency
AEOC	Alabama Emergency Operations Center
AEW	Airborne Early Warning
AFB	Air Force Base
AGR	Active Guard and Reserve
AMA	American Medical Association
AMR	American Medical Response
ANG	Alabama National Guard
APCO	Association of Public-Safety Communications Officials
ARC	American Red Cross
ARES	Amateur Radio Emergency Services
ARF	Action Request Form
ARNG	Arkansas National Guard
ARW	Air Refueling Wing
ASAC	Assistant Special Agent-in-Charge
ASCE	American Society of Civil Engineers
ASDHD	Assistant Secretary of Defense for Homeland Defense
ASH	Assistant Secretary for Health
ASPHEP	Assistant Secretary for Public Health Emergency Preparedness (HHS)
ATCS	Air Traffic Control Squadron
AVCRAD	Aviation Classification and Repair Depot
ATF	Bureau of Alcohol, Tobacco, Firearms and Explosives (DOJ)
BAH	Board of Animal Health
BOP	Bureau of Prisons
BORSTAR	Border Patrol Search Trauma and Rescue
BORTAC	Border Patrol's Tactical Unit
BRAC	Base Realignment and Closure
BTS	Border and Transportation Security (DHS)
CAS	Client Assistance System
CBC	Construction Battalion Command
CBCS	Combat Communications Squadron
CBMU	Construction Battalion Maintenance Unit
CBP	United States Customs and Border Protection (DHS)
CBRNE	Chemical, Biological, Radiological, Nuclear, and High Yield Explosives
CCP	Citizen Corps Programs
CCRF	Commissioned Corps Readiness Force

CDC	Centers for Disease Control and Prevention (HHS)
CDT	Central Daylight Time
CEM	Comprehensive Emergency Management
CEMP	Comprehensive Emergency Management Plan
CERT	Community Emergency Response Teams
CEO	Chief Executive Officer
CG	Coast Guard
CIM	Clinical Information Management
CIMG	Crisis Incident Management Group
CIMRT	Critical Incident Management Response Team
CIMST	Critical Incident Management Support Team
CIP	Critical Infrastructure Protection
CIRG	Critical Incident Response Group
CIS	COPS in Schools
CJIS	Criminal Justice Information Services Division
CNU	Crisis Negotiation Unit
CO	Contracting Officer
COG	Continuity of Government
CONOP	Concept of Operations
COOP	Continuity of Operations
COLTS	Cells on Light Trucks
COPS	Community Oriented Policing Services
COW	Cells on Wheels
CP	Command Post
CPO	Chief Procurement Officer
CRAF	Civil Reserve Air Fleet
CRS	Congressional Research Service
CST	Civil Support Team
CS	Civil Support
CSEPP	Chemical Stockpile Emergency Preparedness Plan
DCAA	Defense Contract Audit Agency
DCO	Defense Coordinating Officer
DEA	Drug Enforcement Administration
DHH	Department of Health and Hospitals
DHS	United States Department of Homeland Security
DMAT	Disaster Medical Assistance Team
DMH	Department of Mental Health
DMORT	Disaster Mortuary Operational Response Team
DOC	United States Department of Commerce
DOD	United States Department of Defense
DOE	United States Department of Energy
DOJ	United States Department of Justice
DOSR	Daily Operations Summary Reports
DOT	United States Department of Transportation
DPS	Department of Public Safety
DRF	Disaster Relief Fund

RS	Department of Rehabilitation Services-Vocational Rehabilitation
TAC	Disaster Technical Assistance Center
USM	Deputy United States Marshall
VD	Digital Versatile Disc
WI	Disaster Welfare Information
CRV	Emergency Communications Response Vehicles
EO	Explosive Enforcement Officers
HO	Environmental Health Officer
LT	Evacuation Liaison Team
MA	Emergency Management Agency
MAC	Emergency Management Assistance Compact
MEDS	Expeditionary Medical Support System
MPG	Emergency Management Performance Grant
MWG	Emergency Management Working Group
MS	Emergency Medical Services
MT	Emergency Medical Technician
O	Executive Order
OC	Emergency Operations Center
OP	Emergency Operations Plan
	Executive Office of the President
PA	United States Environmental Protection Agency
PR	Emergency Preparedness and Response
RRS	Emergency and Rapid Response Services
RT	Emergency Response Team
RT-A	Emergency Response Team Advance Element
RT-N	National Emergency Response Team
RV	Emergency Response Vehicles
SAR-VHP	Emergency System for Advance Registration of Volunteer Health Professionals
SF	Emergency Support Function
SF-1	Emergency Support Function #1 – Transportation Annex
SF-2	Emergency Support Function #2 – Communications Annex
SF-3	Emergency Support Function #3 - Public Works and Engineering Annex
SF-4	Emergency Support Function #4 - Firefighting Annex
SF-5	Emergency Support Function #5 - Emergency Management Annex
SF-6	Emergency Support Function #6 - Mass Care, Housing, and Human Services Annex
SF-7	Emergency Support Function #7 - Resource Support Annex
SF-8	Emergency Support Function #8 - Public Health and Medical Services Annex
SF-9	Emergency Support Function #9 - Urban Search and Rescue Annex
SF-10	Emergency Support Function #10 - Oil and Hazardous Materials Response Annex
SF-11	Emergency Support Function #11- Agriculture and Natural Resources Annex
SF-12	Emergency Support Function #12 - Energy Annex
SF-13	Emergency Support Function #13 - Public Safety and Security Annex
SF-14	Emergency Support Function #14 - Long-Term Community Recovery and Mitigation Annex
SF-15	Emergency Support Function #15 - External Affairs Annex
AA	Federal Aviation Administration
AMS	Federal Air Marshal Service

FAR	Federal Acquisition Regulation
FBI	Federal Bureau of Investigation
FCI	Federal Correctional Institution
FCC	Federal Correction Complex
	Federal Communications Commission
	Federal Coordination Center
FCO	Federal Coordinating Officer
FDA	United States Food and Drug Administration (HHS)
FDOCC	Forward Deployed Operations Command Center
FEMA	Federal Emergency Management Agency (DHS)
FEOC	Federal Emergency Operation Center
FEL	Federal Explosive License
FFL	Federal Firearms License
FHWA	Federal Highway Administration (DOT)
FIRE	Assistance to Firefighters Program
FMA	Flood Mitigation Assistance
FMCS	Federal Medical Contingency Stations
FMS	Facilities Management Services
	Federal Medical Shelter
FORSCOM	United States Forces Command
FRP	Federal Response Plan
FPS	Federal Protective Services
FSS	Federal Supply Service
FTE	Full-time Employees
GAO	United States Government Accountability Office
GETS	Government Emergency Telecommunications Service
GIS	Geographic Information System
GSA	United States General Services Administration
HAZMAT	Hazardous Material
HCS	Health Care System
HD	Homeland Defense
HEAR	Hospitals Emergency Alert Radio
HF	High Frequency
HHS	United States Department of Health and Human Services
HIPAA	Health Insurance Portability and Accountability Act of 1996
HLT	Hurricane Liaison Team
HMGP	Hazard Mitigation Grant Program
HQ	Headquarter
HRT	Hostage Rescue Team
	Health Response Team
HSA	Homeland Security Act of 2002
	Alabama Homeland Security Act of 2003
HSC	Homeland Security Council
HSEEP	Homeland Security Exercise and Evaluation Program
HSGAC	Senate Homeland Security and Governmental Affairs Committee
HSOC	Homeland Security Operations Center

SOP	Homeland Security Overtime Program
SPD	Homeland Security Presidential Directive
UD	United States Department of Housing and Urban Development
AFIS	Integrated Automated Fingerprint Identification System
EM	International Association of Emergency Managers
TAC	Individual Assistance Technical Assistance Contracts
CE	United States Immigration and Customs Enforcement (DHS)
CS	Incident Command System
CU	Intensive Care Unit
DEN	Integrated Digital Enhanced Network
EM	Innovative Emergency Management, Inc.
HP	Individuals and Households Program
MG	Interagency Incident Management Group
O	Interoperability
MT	Incident Management Team
PET	Interagency Performance Evacuation Team
NS	Incident of National Significance
RS	Internal Revenue Service
SO	Information Security Officer
	Information Technology
AG	Judge Advocate General
CAHO	Joint Commission on Accreditation of Healthcare Organizations
DOMS	Joint Director of Military Support
FCOM	Joint Forces Command
FO	Joint Field Office
C	Joint Information Center
OC	Joint Information Operations Center
OC	Joint Operations Center
TF	Joint Task Force
PATS	Justice Prisoner and Alien Transportation System
DHAP	Katrina Disaster Housing Assistance Program
ANG	Louisiana National Guard
DPSC	Louisiana Department of Public Safety and Corrections
E	Law Enforcement
ECC	Law Enforcement Coordination Center
ES	Law Enforcement Services
ETPP	Law Enforcement Terrorism Prevention Program
FA	Lead Federal Agency
HA	Louisiana Hospital Association
IHEAP	Low-Income Home Energy Assistance Program
IMS	Logistics Information Management System
NHA	Louisiana Nursing Home Association
NO	Liaison Office
O	Liaison Officers
OHSEP	Louisiana Office of Homeland Security and Emergency Preparedness
RC	Logistics Readiness Center

LSP	Louisiana State Police
LSU	Louisiana State University
LSUHSC	Louisiana State University Health Sciences Center
LTG	Lieutenant General
MA	Mission Assignment
MARS	Military Affiliate Radio Service
MASH	Mobile Army Surgical Hospital
MBP	Mississippi Board of Pharmacy
MCI	Mass Casualty Incident
MCLNO	Medical Center of Louisiana at New Orleans
MCT	Mission Critical Team
MDAC	Mississippi Department of Agriculture and Commerce
MDEQ	Mississippi Department of Environmental Quality
MDT	Maintenance Down Time
MEF	Marine Expeditionary Force
MEMA	Mississippi Emergency Management Agency
MEOP	Mississippi Emergency Operations Plan
MERS	Mobile Emergency Response Support
MERV	Major Emergency Response Vehicle
MET	Mobile Enforcement Team
MG	Major General
MHz	Megahertz
MMD	Mississippi Military Department
MMRS	Metropolitan Medical Response System
MMWR	Morbidity and Mortality Weekly Report
MOU	Memorandum of Understanding
MP	Military Police
MRC	Medical Reserve Corps
MRE	Meals Ready to Eat
MR-GO	Mississippi River-Gulf Outlet Canal
MSCA	Military Support to Civil Authorities
MSDH	Mississippi State Department of Health
MSNG	Mississippi National Guard
MST	Management Support Team
MSY	Louis Armstrong New Orleans International Airport
MTSA	Maritime Transportation Security Act
MVMA	Mississippi Veterinary Medical Association
NAS	Naval Air Station
NASA	National Aeronautics and Space Administration
NBC	Nuclear, Biological and Chemical
NCC	National Coordinating Committee
	National Coordinating Center for Communications
NCG	National Coordination Group
NCH	Natural and Cultural Resources and Historic Properties
NCPA	National Community Pharmacists Association
NCS	National Communications System

NCT	National Coordinating Team
NDMS	National Disaster Medical System
NEMA	National Emergency Management Association
NEMIS	National Emergency Management Information System
NENA	National Emergency Number Association
NERPP	National Emergency and Regional Response Plan
NG	National Guard
NGB	National Guard Bureau
NGBJOC	Joint Operations Center at National Guard Bureau
NGO	Non-Governmental Organizations
NHS	National Hurricane Service
NIH	National Institutes of Health (HHS)
NIMS	National Incident Management System
NIOSH	National Institute for Occupational Safety Health
NIRT	Nuclear Incident Response Team
NOAA	National Oceanic and Atmospheric Administration (DOC)
NOMIC	New Orleans Maritime Interoperable Committee
NOOEP	New Orleans Office of Emergency Preparedness
NOPD	New Orleans Police Department
NORAD	North American Air Defense Command
NORTHCOM	United States Northern Command
NRCC	National Response Coordination Center
NRP	National Response Plan
NRP-CIA	National Response Plan - Catastrophic Incident Annex
NRP-CIS	National Response Plan - Catastrophic Incident Supplement
NRT	National Response Team
NSF	National Science Foundation
NSSE	National Special Security Event
NVOAD	National Voluntary Organizations Involved in Disaster
NWS	National Weather Service
OBP	Office of Border Patrol
ODP	Office of Domestic Preparedness
OEP	Office of Emergency Preparedness
OFO	Office of Field Operations
OFRD	Office of Force Readiness and Deployment
OIG	Office of Inspector General
OIO	Office of International Operations
OMB	Office of Management and Budget
OMT	Operational Management Teams
OPM	Office of Personnel Management
OPLAN MSSTAD	Mississippi National Guard Operations Plan
OSD	Operations Support Division
	Office of the Secretary of Defense
OSG	Office of the Surgeon General
OSHA	Occupational Safety and Health Administration
OTD	Operational Technology Division

OTU	Operational Training Unit
OVP	Office of the Vice President
PACOM	United States Pacific Command
PDM	Pre-Disaster Mitigation
PSAP	Public Safety Answering Point
PFO	Principal Federal Official
PHS	United States Public Health Service
PMU	Portable Morgue Units
POC	Point of Contact
POD	Plans of the Day
PPR	Prevention, Preparedness, and Response
PSAP	Public Safety Answering Points
RCPI	Regional Community Policing Institute
RCT	Regional Coordinating Team
RDD	Reportable Disease Database
RED HORSE	Rapid Engineer Deployable Operational Repair Squadron Engineer
RETCO	Regional Emergency Transportation Coordinator
RFA	Request for Assistance
RFP	Request for Proposal
RRCC	Regional Response Coordination Center
RTA	Regional Transit Authority
SAC	Special Agent-in-Charge
SAMHSA	Substance Abuse and Mental Health Services Administration
SAR	Search and Rescue
SATERN	Salvation Army Amateur Radio Communications System
SBA	United States Small Business Administration
SCO	State Coordinating Officer
SCHIP	State Children's Health Insurance Program
SEOC	State Emergency Operations Center
SERT	State Emergency Response Team
	Secretary's Emergency Response Team (HHS)
SFLEO	Senior Federal Law Enforcement Officers
SHARES	Shared Resources High Frequency Radio Program
SHSGP	State Homeland Security Grant Program
SLGCP	State and Local Government Coordination and Preparedness
SLOSH	Sea, Lakes and Overland Surges from Hurricanes
SMAC	Statewide Mutual Aid Compact
SMS	Short Message Service
SNS	Strategic National Stockpile
SOG	Special Operations Group
SOP	Standard Operating Procedure
SOU	SWAT (Special Weapons and Tactics) Operations Unit
	Statement of Understanding
SPEARR	Small Portable Expeditionary Aerospace Rapid Response
SRT	Special Response Team
SSA	Social Security Administration

SSHP	Service Supplemental Hurricane Plan
SHSS	State Homeland Security Strategy
SWAT	Special Weapons and Tactics
TAG	The Adjutant General
TANF	Temporary Assistance to Needy Families
TARU	Technical Advisory Response Unit
TDD	Training and Development Division
TDY	Temporary Duty
TERT	Telecommunications Emergency Response Taskforce
TMICC	Transportable Multi-mission Communications Center
TOC	Tactical Operations Center
TOPOFF	Top Officials
TRANSCOM	United States Transportation Command
TSA	Transportation Security Administration
TSP	Telecommunications Service Priority
TVA	Tennessee Valley Authority
UASI	Urban Areas Security Initiative
UHF	Ultra High Frequency
UHP	Universal Hiring Program
UHS	Universal Health Services, Inc.
UMC	University of Mississippi Medical Center
USACE	United States Army Corps of Engineers
USAID	United States Agency for International Development
USAR	United States Army Reserve
USCG	United States Coast Guard
USDA	United States Department of Agriculture
USMS	United States Marshals Service
USNS	United States Navy Ship
USP	United States Penitentiary
USPS	United States Postal Service
USS	United States Ship
VA	United States Department of Veterans Affairs
VAMC	Department of Veterans Affairs Medical Center
VFC	Vaccines for Children
VHF	Very High Frequency
VISN 16	Veterans Integrated Service Network 16
VISTA	Veterans Integrated Service Technical Architecture System
VOIP	Voice Over Internet Protocol
VOAD	Voluntary Organizations Active in Disaster
VTC	Video Teleconference
VTS	Vessel Traffic System
WCP	Working Capital Fund
WH	White House
WMD	Weapons of Mass Destruction
WPD	Witness Security and Prisoner Operations Division

HSOC SPOT REP

SPOT REP #:	#013
Date/Time (EDT):	08/29/05 @ 2230
Reference:	New Orleans Helicopter Overflight
Source of Information:	FEMA Teleconference – observations from Marty Bahamonte, FEMA Public Affairs. Participants included Patrick Rhode, Mike Lowder, Bill Locke, Mike Pawlowski and Mary Anne Lyle
Type of Incident:	Hurricane Katrina

Update	
Summary:	Marty Bahamonte of FEMA Public Affairs made two aerial over flights of the New Orleans area the afternoon of Monday, August 29, 2005. As additional information becomes available it will be reported.

He concluded the two immediate major problems would be:

1. Access to the city because roads are flooded to the north and east.
2. Housing

His observations include the following:

- The I-10 Twin Span bridges to the east of the City to Slidell are compromised in both directions for a stretch of five to seven miles. On the east side bridge sections are gone; on the west side bridge sections are buckled and askew.
- There is no way to enter New Orleans from the east. Highway 11 appears generally in tact but is under water where it enters the City and will require some repair but appears to be a quick fix.
- The western I10/I610 junction connecting Jefferson and Orleans Parrish is under water.
- Entrance from the north is not possible because as roads get into the city, they are under water.
- I10 to the west appears to have several underwater sections.
- The Airline Highway by the airport is above water.
- There is a quarter-mile breech in the levee near the 17th Street Canal about 200 yards from Lake Pontchartrain allowing water to flow into the City.
- The levee in Metarie is in tact.
- Only one of the main pumps is reported to still be working but cannot keep up with the demand and its longevity is doubtful.
- In the neighborhoods there are many small fires where natural gas lines have broken.
- Flooding is greatest in the north and east in New Orleans, Metairie |

	and north towards Slidell – an estimated 2/3 to 75% of the city is under water.
	• The flights did not go all the way north to Slidell so conditions there are not reported.
	• Some homes were seen with water to the first floor and others completely underwater.
	• Hundreds of people were observed on the balconies and roofs of a major apartment complex in the city. The location has been provided to City officials.
	• Downtown there is less flooding. Most buildings have windows blown out but otherwise appear structurally sound.
	• West and South of the City appear dry.
	• Lake Front Airport by Lake Pontchartrain is under water.
	• There is an oil tanker grounded in the Industrial Canal – two tugs were observed working with the ship.
	• The Coast Guard reported two other tankers aground but they were not observed.
	• The Coast Guard is flying rescue missions for people stuck on roofs. They reported seeing about 150 people but also said that as they lifted people out, they saw others breaking through the roofs of adjacent homes.
	• The Coast Guard will use night vision devices and continue rescue missions into the night.
	• Search and Rescue will need boats, in some locations high wheeled trucks may be usable. FEMA USR Teams are coordinating boat use with Louisiana Fish and Game officials.
	• The City reports about 300 people have been rescued by boat so far. These rescue operations will continue through the night.
	• Boat traffic is not restricted and movement of supplies by boat and barge is feasible.
	• The Inter Harbor Canal is not visible.
	• A few bodies were seen floating in the water and Coast Guard pilots also reported seeing bodies but there are no details on locations or numbers.
Significance:	
Actions/Follow-Up:	N/A
Miscellaneous:	
Prepared By:	Mathew Thompson NRCC Planning Section Analyst

SUMMARY OF WHITE HOUSE DOCUMENT REVIEW

These are examples of documents received by the White House (WH) Homeland Security Council (HSC) staff between August 27 and September 3. The items logged do not reflect the entire information flow to the White House, or all documents provided to the Select Committee. Rather, they are meant to illustrate the type and range of information known to the White House suggesting Katrina and the subsequent flooding of New Orleans (NO) was not a standard emergency event. Yet the enormity of Katrina seemed not to have been fully understood by the White House until at least Tuesday, August 30.

Facts Reported to White House Homeland Security Council Staff	Received	WHK Bates No. Begi
Red Cross notifies K. Nielsen at WH it expects Katrina to be a major hurricane. Red Cross stands ready to brief WH as requested.	8/27; 1:08 p.m.	5169
HSOC reports: New Orleans evacuation ordered. Superdome to open, Nagin to commandeer any property or vehicle necessary to provide shelter or transport.	8/28; 11:56 a.m.	12931
DHS infrastructure advisory sent to HSC. Advises likely flooding from Lake Pontchartrain due to surges from Cat 5 hurricane. If levee is breached, it is predicted to take 3 to 6 months to dewater New Orleans.	8/28; 11:59 a.m.	5217
DHS forwards to WH diagrams of NO levee system.	8/28; 12:14 p.m.	12922
DHS Advisory re transportation. Buses not in use should be moved to high ground. Surge is predicted to exceed 20 feet. Levees to be breeched.	8/28; 12:32 p.m.	5222
WH receives overview re capabilities of National Guard units from LA, AL, MS and FL.	8/28; 1:07 p.m.	9678
DHS forwards NO evacuation plan.	8/28; 5:00 p.m.	12934
HSOC reports: Katrina now Cat 5. Landfall expected at 8:00 a.m. 8/29. Coastal flooding as high as 28'.	8/28; 6:26 p.m.	5958
DHS sends WH comprehensive report [41 pages] on potential infrastructure impacts of a Cat 5 hurricane on the Gulf coast. Damage estimates predicted as high as $10 billion.	8/29; 1:47 a.m.	12072
HSOC reports: Katrina weakens to Cat 4. Coastal storm surge flooding of 18-22' above normal tide levels, locally as high as 28 feet. Some levees in New Orleans could be overtopped.	8/29; 6:10 a.m.	6509
DOD briefs WH re capabilities of DOD Civil Support.	8/29; 6:52 a.m.	9953
K. Nielsen advises federal agencies WH HSC will be available twenty-four hours a day through the duration of Hurricane Katrina. Bethany Nichols and Dan Kaniewski are identified as additional WH staff monitoring Katrina.	8/29; 10:58 a.m.	15770
DHS Watch Desk E-mails WH in re report from Maj Gen Landreneau. Extensive flooding along St. Claude and Claiborne avenues. Leak has developed in the Superdome. Five floors of windows at Charity Hospital have blown out and the first floor of the hospital is flooded. The 911 Centers in St. Bernard and Orleans parishes have been shut down.	8/29; 11:32 a.m.	14825
HSOC reports: Some LA Parishes have 8 to 10 feet of water. No levee failures reported. Approximately 15,000 evacuees in Superdome. It is estimated 300,000 LA residents will be without power. Unspecified numbers of LA and MS residents are stranded and awaiting evacuation in flooded areas.	8/29; 2:20 p.m.	16118
HSOC reports: Preliminary reports indicate the levees have not been breached. Assessment still pending. Army Corps estimates if NO experiences extensive flooding it could take months to dewater the city. Such flooding will preclude damage assessments and restoration.	8/29; 6:13 p.m.	6472

Facts Reported to White House Homeland Security Council Staff	Received	WHK Bates No. Begin
HSOC reports: Marty Bahamonde reports the following after a helicopter over flight: Access to the city is impeded due to flooding to the north and east. I-10 Twin Span bridges to the east of Slidell are compromised in both directions. Portions of this bridge are buckled, askew and in some cases gone. No ability to enter NO from the east. West I-10 and I-610 junction connecting Jefferson and Orleans Parish is under water. Entrance from the north is not possible because roads are under water. Quarter mile breach in the levee near the 17th St. Canal about 200 yards from Lake Pontchartrain allowing free water to flow into the city. Levee in Meterie is in tact. Only one of the main pumps is reported to be operable but its longevity is doubtful. Flooding is greatest in the north and east in New Orleans. Homes are completely underwater. Hundreds of people were observed on roofs and balconies. A few bodies were seen floating in the water.	8/30; 12:02 a.m.	7158
FEMA reports: No power; 911 system out; roof damage to Superdome; entire city flooded. St. Bernard & 9th Ward levee breached.	8/30; 6:00 a.m.	4057
HSOC reports: Levee breach, 17th St. at Canal Blvd – exceeds 100 meters in length. Much of downtown and east NO is underwater, the depth of which is unknown. Flooding to a depth of 8-10 feet in Meterie and 6 feet in 9th Ward.	8/30; 6:33 a.m.	11281
DHS Watch Officer E-mails WH and others that a 200 foot levee breach is being assessed.	8/30; 8:13 a.m.	6324
FEMA chart listing all task and ESF assignments.	8/30; 9:24 a.m.	6345
DHS Watch Officer E-mails WH with maps identifying locations of breached levees, highlighting two areas of concern, the levee at Tennessee St. and the levee at 17th St.	8/30; 10:23 a.m.	13330
K. Nielsen at WH e-mails Red Cross and acknowledges several federal partners have expressed a lack of situational awareness and are having problems getting logistics issues resolved.	8/30; 11:18 a.m.	16135
FEMA requests evacuation of 15-25K from Superdome.	8/30; 11:50 a.m.	12712
DHS Watch Officers advises WH – Martial Law reportedly declared in Jefferson and Orleans Parishes. National Guard to assume responsibility.	8/30; 11:51 a.m.	6325
DHS Watch Officers advises WH of distinction between the term "Martial Law" and "Law Enforcement Emergency" and further advises the latter term should be used.	8/30; 2:08 p.m.	14853
HSOC reports: Army Corps reports 300 foot levee breach 100 meters south of Hammond St. bridge; Water from Lake Pontchartrain is pouring into NO through this breach; additional multiple levee breaches in NO to include Tennessee St. breach.	8/30; 2:19 p.m.	4088
HSOC reports: Spot Report detailing levee breaches (maps included) south of Hammond St. bridge and near Tennessee St. bridge.	8/30; 3:07 p.m.	6850
New Orleans: No power in NO, no 911, entire city flooded except French Quarter and Business district; Superdome has roof damage; the following levee breaches are reported: St. Bernard & 9th, Haynes Blvd Pump Station, and 17th St. Canal. Jefferson Parish: People searching for food; gas and chemical leaks; toxic, deep flood waters.	8/30; 4:00 p.m.	4092

Facts Reported to White House Homeland Security Council Staff	Received	WHK Bates No. Begi
HSOC reports: Army Corps indicates 300 foot breach approximately 100 meters south of Hammond Street Bridge. Three hundred feet of the east flood wall is missing and water from Lake Pontchartrain is pouring into NO. Vehicles cannot access this breach location. The plan is for helicopters to dump sand into the breach site. Additional levee breaches in NO exist, including Tennessee Street.	8/30; 7:26 p.m.	6545
Memo from Sec. Chertoff distributed to Cabinet announcing Michael Brown as PFO.	8/30; 9:00 p.m.	6695
HSOC reports: Superdome needs to be evacuated; population is 12-15,000 people.	8/31; 2:00 a.m.	13833
HSOC reports: Waters continue to rise due to the breach of the 17th St. levee. 300 foot breach at present. Expectations are, without fixing the breach, flooding will not stop until it reaches lake level.	8/31; 5:47 a.m.	12484
FEMA reports: Total cumulative shelter population is 54,378.	8/31; 7:21 a.m.	12503
DHS Watch Desk advise re a recent report from Bob Patrick, FTA's NO Administrator: 200 to 250 Regional Transportation District employees were stranded at their Canal St. facility due to flooding. All were self evacuated via air mattresses whereby they were able to paddle to shallow water. From there they waded in shallow water to the Convention Center. Bob Patrick estimates the entire city of NO will be flooded by day's end.	8/31; 11:09 a.m.	14858
HSOC reports: Rising water at Superdome is threatening to flood the generator which will cause power failure. The State of LA has requested assistance in evacuating Superdome.	8/31; 12:54 p.m.	7080
HSOC reports: Astrodome site recommended as alternative shelter location for Superdome evacuees.	8/31; 6:25 p.m.	4177
HSOC reports: Significant flooding continues throughout NO. 17th St. levee breach in NO is ongoing and is currently two feet above flood stage. Southern region of MS is devastated and is currently out of fuel and water. Both Harrison and Hancock Counties experienced total destruction. 23,000 from the Superdome are being evacuated. 350,000 homes are estimated to have taken severe damage. Housing needs are estimated at 500,000 to 1 million. Widespread damage to utility systems and environmental impact will likely prevent habitation of the area for six month to one year. Pictures are included at bates nos. WHK7404 and 7405.	8/31; 6:31 p.m.	7388
HSOC reports: 11 hospitals in varying stages of damage. Most have no power.	9/1; 12:15 a.m.	7584
Commodity Status – listing locations and commodity supplies.	9/1; 1:00 a.m.	6692
HSOC reports: NOPD has suspended search and rescue efforts and are focusing on securing the city from lawlessness. Pipeline from Plaquemines Parish is leaking an estimated 240 barrels of oil a day. A fatality collection site is being established in Baton Rouge. Levee breaches have not been repaired or blocked. Army Corps projects it could take months to dewater NO once the flooding ceases.	9/1; 5:50 a.m.	6756
Aerial maps of flooded areas distributed by HSOC.	9/1; 5:52 a.m.	6775
K. Nielsen seeks update from DHS HSOC on news story re National Guardsman shot at the Superdome.	9/1; 10:06 a.m.	15834
FEMA chart listing all task and ESF assignments.	9/1; 11:05 a.m.	6580
K. Nielsen complains information arriving at WH HSC is stale, i.e., already updated by HSOC.	9/1; 11:24 a.m.	14760
K. Nielsen at WH requests DHS Watch Desk to follow up with a confirmation of the cause of the downed helicopter.	9/1; 12:41 p.m.	14903

acts Reported to White House Homeland Security Council Staff	Received	WHK Bates No. Begin
HS Watch Desk reports a downed helicopter.	9/1; 12:56 p.m.	14900
HS Watch Officer advises WH: NOPD reports Guardsman shot in Superdome bathroom following ı altercation with an evacuee.	9/1; 1:48 p.m.	12748
yover pictures sent to WH showing magnitude of damage.	9/1; 2:37 p.m.	10674
ostage situation at Tulane Hospital reported.	9/1; 2:47 p.m.	12750
A reports: Jefferson Parish has people on street searching for food. There are contaminated flood aters and the streets are impassable. Orleans Parish's 911 system is inoperable. Entire City of O is flooded except the French Quarter.	9/1; 4:00 p.m.	5654
vailability of generators and MREs are insufficient due to overwhelming demand.	9/1; 6:00 p.m.	11653
ational Guard deployed to assist with law and order. ignificant flooding continues in Jefferson, Orleans, and St. Bernard Parish. 7th Street Canal levee breach is being repaired. ɔod and water airdrops are taking place through affected area.	9/1; 6:14 p.m.	14138
-mail trail beginning with Richard Davis at WH-HSC asking for specific operational response plans r attending to hospitals in danger.	9/1; 7:24 p.m.	11831
ajeev Venkayya of WH HSC e-mails officials at DHS re standing water hazards and resources ᴠailable via CDC.	9/1; 8:43 p.m.	15373
SA personnel report trouble at MSY with maintaining order.	9/1; 10:19 p.m.	5588
an Ostergaard at DHS advises Richard Davis at WH that Katrina is a national disgrace.	9/1; 10:50 p.m.	15786
700 patients need to be evacuated from LA hospitals.	9/2; 4:21 a.m.	5183
HS Briefing Points report FPS officers have walked the perimeter of the Convention Center and there re approximately 1,000 people there. "New Orleans Officers on scene and tactically prepared."	9/2; 5:44 a.m.	10919
ed Cross is operating no feeding kitchens in NO due to security concerns. ed Cross will not ask its volunteers to risk their personal safety.	9/2; 6:00 a.m.	11756
/H advised of the willingness of states such as AK, AL and GA to receive evacuees.	9/2; 11:33 a.m.	15364
HS notifies WH, NO Convention Center population is 25,000 according to FEMA Region 6 RRCC. mited food and water is available.	9/2; 12:44 p.m.	5602
ed Cross estimates shelter population of 94,000.	9/2; 2:02 p.m.	16179
A reports: Jefferson: Downed power lines, downed telephone and light poles, downed trees and ınbs/debris and house debris. Lower water pressure or no water, gas/chemical leaks in air. Live wires, ɔ commercial power in drainage pumps stations, toxic water, still some deep water in some ɛighborhoods, animal/reptile issues. West Bank business/apartment building burning to the ground, reeping water from the 17th St. Canal. ɔrleans: No power, 911 system down, EOC on emergency power and cell phones, Bayou Bienvenue ɔporting 20 foot storm surge. Lost contact with 4 pump stations. Entire city flooded, except French ɔuarter/West. Bank/Business district. Superdome is structurally okay, some roof damage. t. Bernard: No power; 911 center down, structure damage, glass breakage at shelters, roof torn off ı high school gym shelter.	9/3; 12:00 p.m.	4522

EMERGENCY PREPAREDNESS AND RESPONSE GRANTS TO ALABAMA, LOUISIANA, AND MISSISSIPPI, FY 2003-2004

Emergency management assistance administered by FEMA includes providing funds for the reconstruction of damaged public facilities, cash grants to victims of disasters, and access to temporary housing, among other types of aid. FEMA also provides disaster planning and preparedness aid to state and local governments, and coordinates federal emergency management activities.

Prior to September 11, 2001, the federal government's role in supporting emergency preparedness and management was limited primarily to providing resources before large-scale disasters like floods, hurricanes, and earthquakes, and response and recovery assistance after such disasters. In response to the events of September 11, 2001, however, the federal government has provided billions of dollars to state and local governments for planning, equipment, and training to enhance the capabilities of first responders to respond to terrorist attacks and to a lesser extent natural disasters. Indeed, legislation and presidential directives call for DHS to place special emphasis on preparedness for terrorism, and DHS has directed that the majority of first responder grant funding be used to enhance first responder capabilities to prevent, protect against, respond to, and recover from terrorist attacks. Nonetheless, many grants can have all-hazards applications. The following is a summary of all FEMA Hazard Mitigation, COPS, and ODP grants awarded in Alabama, Louisiana, and Mississippi in Fiscal Years 2003-2004.

FEMA Hazard Mitigation Grant Programs

FEMA administers three programs that provide funds for activities that reduce losses from future disasters or prevent the occurrence of catastrophes. These hazard mitigation programs include the Flood Mitigation Assistance (FMA) program, the Hazard Mitigation Grant Program (HMGP), and the Pre-Disaster Mitigation (PDM) program.[1] These programs enable grant recipients to undertake activities such as the elevation of structures in floodplains, relocation of structures from floodplains, construction of structural enhancements to facilities and buildings in earthquake prone areas (also known as retrofitting), and modifications to land use plans to ensure that future construction ameliorates, and does not exacerbate, hazardous conditions.

Alabama, Louisiana, and Mississippi received a total of $67,313,169 through the three hazard mitigation programs in fiscal years 2003, 2004, and 2005. Following is a brief summary of the grants awarded in the three fiscal years:

- Alabama received a total of $27,516,469 over the three year period through the three FEMA-administered hazard mitigation programs, Louisiana received $31,221,099, and Mississippi $8,575,601;
- FMA grants: the state of Louisiana received $1,625,909, the state of Mississippi received $3,207,573 (Alabama received no FMA grants);
- HMGP grants: the state of Alabama received a total of $20,486,277, Louisiana received $29,595,190, and the state of Mississippi received a total of $5,368,030; and,
- PDM grants: the state of Alabama received a total of $6,530,977 in FY2004 — no PDM funds were received by Alabama in FY2003 or FY2005, and no PDM awards were made to Mississippi or Louisiana during the three year period.

EMA Hazard Mitigation Awards in FY2003

Flood Mitigation Assistance Program. A total of $1,100,109 was awarded to Alabama and Louisiana in FY2003 under authority of the Flood Mitigation Assistance (FMA) program. Mississippi received no funds through this program in FY2003. Baldwin County, Alabama received $143,770 under the FMA program and spent the funds on private structure elevation. No other county in Alabama received FMA funding. Louisiana received a total of $956,339 under the FMA program and all grant recipients, including Jackson, Terrebonne, and East Baton Rouge parishes, used the funding for private structure elevation.

Hazard Mitigation Grant Program. A total of $20,870,041 was awarded in FY2003 to two of the states under authority of Section 404 of the Stafford Act. No HMGP awards were provided in the state of Mississippi in FY2003. Alabama received $338,524 and Louisiana received $20,531,517. Of this amount, $13,565,975 was awarded to Terrebonne parish for elevation of private structures.

Pre-Disaster Mitigation Program. No PDM awards were made to Alabama, Louisiana, or Mississippi in FY2003.

EMA Hazard Mitigation Awards in FY2004

Flood Mitigation Assistance Program. A total of $646,947 was awarded to the three states in FY2004 under authority of the Flood Mitigation Assistance (FMA) program. Alabama received $282,136, Louisiana $76,500, and Mississippi $288,311. Again, the majority of the funding went to private structure elevation or private property acquisition.

Hazard Mitigation Grant Program. A total of $10,485,309 was awarded in FY2004 to the three states under authority of Section 404 of the Stafford Act. Alabama received $4,538,660 and mostly put it towards elevation of private structures or acquisition of private or public real property. Louisiana was awarded $5,921,463. Most notably, $1,810,500 was awarded statewide for the development of local multi-hazard plans. Assumption parish used its $15,000 to purchase generators. Louisiana State University used its $94,685 for public awareness and education. And Jefferson Parish put its $634,938 toward towards elevation of private structures.

Pre-Disaster Mitigation Program. Only one state, Alabama, received FMA funding in only one of the three years, FY2004. Most of the funds received by the state (83% of the $6,530,977) were awarded to the City of Birmingham for the acquisition of property in riverine flood plains.

EMA Hazard Mitigation Awards in FY2005

Flood Mitigation Assistance Program. A total of $4,685,750 was awarded in the three states in FY2005 under authority of the FMA program. Alabama received a total of $73,309. Louisiana received nearly $600,000, $400,000 of which went to the Louisiana Office of Homeland Security and Emergency Preparedness for salaries and expenses. And Mississippi's nearly $4,000,000 awarded funded private property acquisitions in the cities of Florence, Gulfport, Long Beach, Grenada, and Pearl River County.

Hazard Mitigation Grant Program. A total of $10,485,309 was awarded to the three states in FY2005 through the HMGP. Alabama received $15,609,093. The funding went to generators, warning systems, and acquisition of private or public real property and structures. Louisiana was awarded $3,142,210, which was used for public awareness and education in Terrebonne and Assumption parishes and elevation of private structures in Ouachita and Livingston parishes. And Mississippi was awarded $5,342,844, which it dispersed among several cities and counties, including Vicksburg, Lauderdale, Brandon, and Jackson. The funds were spent primarily on acquisition of private and public real property.

Pre-Disaster Mitigation Program. No PDM awards were made to Alabama, Louisiana, or Mississippi in FY2005.

Community Oriented Policing Services (COPS) Office

The COPS Office was created by Title I of the Violent Crime Control and Law Enforcement Act of 1994 (P.L. 103-322). The mission of the COPS Office is to advance community policing in all jurisdictions across the United States. The COPS Office awards grants to state, local and tribal law enforcement agencies throughout the United States so they can hire and train law enforcement officers to participate in community policing, purchase and deploy new crime-fighting technologies and develop and test new and innovative policing strategies.[2] The COPS Office has awarded more than $11.4 billion to over 13,000 law enforcement agencies across the United States since it started awarding grants in 1994.[3] As of the end of FY2004, the COPS Office has funded more than 118,000 community policing officers throughout the U.S.[4]

COPS Grant Programs

Below is a brief summary of the COPS grant programs under which funding was awarded to local law enforcement agencies in Alabama, Louisiana, and Mississippi. In summary:

- Alabama received $24,770,274 from FY2003 to FY2005 under the COPS Interoperability Communications, Law Enforcement Technology, Universal Hiring Program (UHP), COPS in Schools (CIS), and Homeland Security Overtime (HSOP) grant programs;
- Louisiana received $23,495,114 from FY2003 to FY2005 under the COPS Interoperability Communications, Law Enforcement Technology, UHP, CIS, Regional Community Policing Institute (RCPI) and Homeland Security Overtime (HSOP) grant programs; and
- Mississippi received $7,003,688 from FY2003 to FY2005 under the COPS Law Enforcement Technology, UHP, CIS, and HSOP grant programs.

COPS Interoperable Communications Grant Program. The Interoperable Communications Grant Program provides funding to local communities to help them develop effective interoperable communications systems for public safety and emergency service providers. The grant program funds projects that explore the use of equipment and technology to increase interoperability and data sharing among law enforcement, fire departments, and emergency medical services. Some examples of projects that have been funded include:

- Interoperability communications equipment for multidisciplinary and multijurisdictional public safety communication projects;
- Deployment of portable gateway networks;
- Technology to upgrade or enhance the ability of law enforcement to improve the timeliness, effectiveness and accuracy of criminal justice information exchanges; and
- Other technology that can be demonstrated to significantly increase interoperability within the public safety community.[5]

COPS Law Enforcement Technology Grant Program. The COPS Law Enforcement Technology Program provides funding for the development of automated systems that help state, local, and tribal law enforcement agencies prevent, respond to, and investigate crime. The funding can be used by law enforcement agencies to purchase technology that advances crime analysis, intelligence gathering, and crime prevention in their communities.[6] The technology grants allow law enforcement agencies to purchase technology that does not fall under the Interoperable Communications Grant Program.[7]

COPS Universal Hiring Program (UHP). UHP provides funding to state, local, and tribal governments for the salaries and benefits of newly hired officers who engage in community policing. Law enforcement agencies can use UHP funding to hire new law enforcement officers to work in community policing or to redeploy a comparable number of veteran officers into community policing. UHP funding can also be used to help law enforcement agencies partner with local communities to develop innovative ways to deal with long-standing problems. UHP was created in 1995 when COPS merged their Funding Accelerated for Smaller Towns (FAST) and Accelerated Hiring, Education and Deployment (AHEAD) programs.[8] Funds awarded under this program are used to pay 75 percent of a newly hired, entry-level officer's salary and benefits up to $75,000 per officer over the course of the three-year grant period. The agency is expected to pay the other 25 percent of the officer's salary and benefits, unless they are able to obtain a waiver because of extreme fiscal hardship.

COPS in Schools (CIS). The CIS grant program provides funding to local law enforcement agencies so they can hire new or additional school resource officers to engage in community policing activities in and around primary and secondary schools.[9] The CIS grant program provides an incentive for the local law enforcement agency to collaborate and develop partnerships with the school to use community policing efforts to combat school violence. Jurisdictions that apply for funding must show they have primary law enforcement authority over the schools identified in their application and do not have the ability to implement the program without federal assistance. Funds awarded under this program are used to pay the salary and benefits of a School Resource Officer up to $125,000 per officer over the course of the three-year grant period. Any costs over the $125,000 per officer are expected to be covered by the local jurisdiction.

Homeland Security Overtime Program (HSOP). HSOP provides funding to cover the overtime pay for officers engaging in homeland security and community policing activities.[10] The funds are meant to supplement the local law enforcement agency's current overtime budget. HSOP funds can be used to pay for officer overtime during homeland security training sessions or other law enforcement activities designed to prevent acts of terrorism or other drug-related violent crime. HSOP funds can be used to support overtime efforts for non-supervisory, sworn personnel. Funds cannot be used for civilian or community service officers. HSOP grantees are expected to contribute 25 percent in matching funds.

Regional Community Policing Institutes (RCPI). RCPI funds are used to establish Regional Community Policing Institutes. RCPIs are training centers funded by COPS that teach a range of courses from homeland security and domestic preparedness to police integrity. RCPIs also provide technical assistance for local law enforcement agencies.[11] There is a network of RCPIs across the United States that provide training to local law enforcement agents.[12] The Gulf Coast RCPI provides training and technical assistance in all aspects of community policing to local law enforcement in Louisiana, Alabama and Mississippi.

COPS Funding Awarded to Jurisdictions in Alabama

Fiscal Year 2003. In FY2003, jurisdictions in the state of Alabama received a total of $9,567,867 from the COPS Office. COPS funding awarded to jurisdictions in Alabama in FY2003 was done under three different grant programs, as shown in **Table 1.** A total of eight Law Enforcement Technology grants were awarded in Alabama, for a total of $1,855,820 in funding. A total of nine UHP grants were awarded in Alabama, for a total of $7,638,363 in funding. Only one HSOP grant was awarded in Alabama in the amount of $73,684.

Table 1: COPS Grants Awarded to Jurisdictions in Alabama in FY2003

Agency	Grant Program	Funding
Alabama Dept. Of Public Safety	Law Enforcement Technology	$174,000.00
Choctaw County Emergency Management Agency	Law Enforcement Technology	$198,700.00
City of Harselle	Law Enforcement Technology	$69,545.00
Huntsville Police Dept.	Law Enforcement Technology	$347,725.00
Jefferson County Sheriff's Dept.	Law Enforcement Technology	$469,750.00
Limestone County Board	Law Enforcement Technology	$49,675.00
Town of Rogersville	Law Enforcement Technology	$49,675.00
University of Alabama-Huntsville	Law Enforcement Technology	$496,750.00
Alabama Dept. Of Public Safety	UHP	$5,625,000.00
City of Troy	UHP	$70,021.00
Town of Coosada	UHP	$73,981.00
Jefferson County Sheriff's Dept.	UHP	$750,000.00
Lake View Police Dept.	UHP	$152,052.00
Madison Police Dept.	UHP	$450,000.00
Marengo County Sheriff's Dept.	UHP	$297,288.00
City of Troy	UHP	$70,021.00
Tuscaloosa County Sheriff's Dept.	UHP	$150,000.00
Mobile County Board of Commissioners	Homeland Security Overtime	$73,684.00
	Total Awarded	$9,567,867.00

Jurisdictions in Alabama received approximately 7.7 percent of the total amount of UHP funding awarded to all jurisdictions in the United States by the COPS Office in FY2003. However, jurisdictions in Alabama received slightly less than one percent of the total amount of Law Enforcement Technology funding awarded by the COPS Office for the fiscal year. Likewise, only 0.1 percent of the total amount of HSOP funding awarded in FY2003 by the COPS office went to Alabama.

Fiscal Year 2004. In FY2004, jurisdictions in Alabama received a total of $8,695,875 from the COPS Office. COPS funding awarded to jurisdictions in Alabama was done under four different grant programs, as shown in **Table 2**. Nine Law Enforcement Technology grants were awarded to jurisdictions in Alabama, for a total of $1,810,745 in funding. Three UHP grants were awarded in Alabama, for a total of $571,169 in funding. Four CIS grants were awarded in Alabama, for a total of $688,961 in funding. Only one Interoperable Communications Technology grant was awarded in FY2004 to Alabama, in the amount of $5.625 million.

Table 2: COPS Grants Awarded to Jurisdictions in Alabama in FY2004

Agency	Grant Program	Funding
St. Clair County Sheriff's Dept.	Law Enforcement Technology	$98,948.00
Jefferson County Sheriff's Dept.	Law Enforcement Technology	$98,948.00
Hanceville Police Dept.	Law Enforcement Technology	$19,790.00
Arab Police Dept.	Law Enforcement Technology	$14,842.00
Town of Douglas	Law Enforcement Technology	$9,895.00
Blount County Sheriff's Dept.	Law Enforcement Technology	$34,632.00
Lexington Police Dept.	Law Enforcement Technology	$49,474.00
Jefferson County Medical Examiner	Law Enforcement Technology	$494,739.00
Board of Trustees of the University of Alabama	Law Enforcement Technology	$989,477.00
City of Helena	UHP	$375,000.00
City of Midland	UHP	$121,169.00
Daphne Police Dept.	UHP	$75,000.00
Randolph County Sheriff's Dept.	COPS in Schools	$91,809.00
Scottsboro Police Dept.	COPS in Schools	$81,978.00
Wilcox County Sheriff's Dept.	COPS in Schools	$196,898.00
Marshall County Sheriff's Dept.	COPS in Schools	$318,276.00
Birmingham Police Dept.	Interoperable Communications Tech.	$5,625,000.00
	Total Awarded	$8,695,875.00

In FY2004, jurisdictions in Alabama received one percent of the total UHP funding awarded to jurisdictions nationwide by the COPS Office. Less than two percent of the total funding under the Law Enforcement Technology program and the CIS program went to jurisdictions in Alabama in FY2004. However, 6.8 percent of the total amount of funding awarded under the Interoperable Communications Technology program for FY2004 went to one jurisdiction in Alabama.

Fiscal Year 2005. In FY2005, a total of $6,506,532 in COPS funding was awarded to jurisdictions in the state of Alabama. Funding awarded to jurisdictions in Alabama were made under three different COPS grant programs, as shown in **Table 3**. Thirteen grants, for a total of $2,821,800 in funding, were awarded to jurisdictions in Alabama under the Law Enforcement Technology Program. One CIS grant was award in Alabama in the amount of $684,732. As in previous years, only one Interoperable Communications Technology grant was awarded in Alabama in the amount of $3,000,000.

Table 3: COPS Grants Awarded to Jurisdictions in Alabama in FY2005

Agency	Grant Program	Funding
Board of Trustees of the University of Alabama	Law Enforcement Technology	$147,996.00
Guin Police Dept.	Law Enforcement Technology	$39,466.00
Southside Police Dept.	Law Enforcement Technology	$19,733.00
Boaz Police Dept.	Law Enforcement Technology	$19,733.00
Morgan County Sheriff's Dept.	Law Enforcement Technology	$78,931.00
Shelby County Sheriff's Dept.	Law Enforcement Technology	$246,661.00
Mobile Police Dept.	Law Enforcement Technology	$246,661.00
Huntsville Police Dept.	Law Enforcement Technology	$295,993.00
Huntsville Police Dept.	Law Enforcement Technology	$493,322.00
Madison County Sheriff's Dept.	Law Enforcement Technology	$493,322.00
Morgan County Sheriff's Dept.	Law Enforcement Technology	$98,664.00
Jefferson County Criminal Courts	Law Enforcement Technology	$394,657.00
Tuscaloosa County Sheriff's Dept.	Law Enforcement Technology	$246,661.00
City of Tuscaloosa	COPS in Schools	$684,732.00
Mobile Police Dept.	Interoperable Communications Tech.	$3,000,000.00
	Total Awarded	$6,506,532.00

Three percent of the Law Enforcement Technology grant funds awarded nationwide by the COPS Office in FY2005 was awarded to jurisdictions in Alabama. Approximately 1.4 percent of all CIS funding awarded by the COPS Office for the fiscal year was awarded to a jurisdiction in Alabama. The Mobile Police Department received three percent of the Interoperable Communications Technology awarded by the COPS Office in FY2005.

Fiscal Year 2003. In FY2003, a total of $10,699,027 in COPS funding was awarded to jurisdictions in Louisiana. Funding awarded by COPS during the fiscal year was done under five different grant programs, as shown in **Table 4**. COPS awarded a total of eight Law Enforcement Technology grants in Louisiana, for a total of $2,493,685 in funding. COPS also awarded four UHP grants in Louisiana for a total of $2,039,523 in funding. Three grants under the HSOP were awarded in Louisiana for a total funding amount of $305,407. One grant was made to a jurisdiction in Louisiana under the Interoperable Communications Technology Program for $5,510,412, and under the RCPI Program for $350,000.

Table 4: COPS Grants Awarded to Jurisdictions in Louisiana in FY2003

Agency	Grant Program	Funding
Louisiana Commission on Law Enforcement and Admin.	Law Enforcement Technology	$1,490,250.00
Slidell Police Dept.	Law Enforcement Technology	$49,675.00
Vernon Parish Sheriff's Dept.	Law Enforcement Technology	$59,610.00
New Orleans Metropolitan Crime Commission	Law Enforcement Technology	$198,700.00
Jefferson Parish Sheriff's Dept.	Law Enforcement Technology	$49,675.00
St. Tammany Parish Sheriff's Dept.	Law Enforcement Technology	$99,350.00
Harahan Police Dept.	Law Enforcement Technology	$49,675.00
Lafourche Parish Sheriff's Dept.	Law Enforcement Technology	$496,750.00
Houma Police Dept.	UHP	$412,160.00
Lake Charles Police Dept.	UHP	$772,974.00
Port of New Orleans Harbor Police Dept.	UHP	$212,351.00
Ouachita Parish Sheriff's Dept.	UHP	$642,038.00
Slidell Police Dept.	Homeland Security Overtime	$40,033.00
Gretna Police Dept.	Homeland Security Overtime	$49,229.00
Ouachita Parish Sheriff's Dept.	Homeland Security Overtime	$207,345.00
New Orleans Police Dept.	Interoperable Communications Tech.	$5,510,412.00
Northwestern State University	RCPI	$350,000.00
	Total Awarded	$10,699,027.00

Jurisdictions in Louisiana received 1.3 percent of the total Law Enforcement Technology funding awarded by the COPS Office in FY2003. Also, jurisdictions in Louisiana received 2.1 percent of UHP funding awarded in the same fiscal year. Jurisdictions in Louisiana received less than one percent of HSOP funding awarded in FY2003. However, the New Orleans Police Department received 7.4 percent of the Interoperable Communications Technology funds awarded in FY2003. Northwestern State University received 1.7 percent of the RCPI funds awarded in FY2003 by the COPS Office.

Fiscal Year 2004. In FY2004, a total of $5,306,337 in COPS funding was awarded to jurisdictions in Louisiana. Like FY2003, grants awarded in the state of Louisiana were made under four different grant programs, as shown in **Table 5**. COPS awarded a total of six Law Enforcement Technology grants in Louisiana for the fiscal year, for a total of $1,335,795. COPS also awarded three grants under UHP in Louisiana for the fiscal year, for a total of $869,707. One grant was awarded to a local agency under the CIS program, for $101,394, and under the Interoperable Communication Technology Program, for $2,998,901.

Table 5: COPS Grants Awarded to Jurisdictions in Louisiana in FY2004

Agency	Grant Program	Funding
Rapides Parish Sheriff's Dept.	Law Enforcement Technology	$148,422.00
Lafayette Police Dept.	Law Enforcement Technology	$49,474.00
Sunset Police Dept.	Law Enforcement Technology	$19,790.00
Town of Grand Coteau	Law Enforcement Technology	$29,684.00
City of Bastrop	Law Enforcement Technology	$989,477.00
New Orleans Metropolitan Crime Commission	Law Enforcement Technology	$98,948.00
Terrebonne Parish Sheriff's Dept.	UHP	$360,686.00
Gretna Police Dept.	UHP	$75,000.00
Bossier Parish Sheriff's Dept.	UHP	$434,021.00
City of Westwego	COPS in Schools	$101,934.00
City of Shreveport	Interoperable Communications Tech.	$2,998,901.00
	Total Awarded	$5,306,337.00

Jurisdictions in Louisiana received less than one percent of the total amount of Law Enforcement Technology and CIS funds awarded by the COPS Office in FY2004. Less than two percent of all UHP funding in FY2004 went to jurisdictions in Louisiana. The City of Shreveport received 3.6 percent of the Interoperable Communications Technology funding awarded in FY2004.

Fiscal Year 2005. In FY2005, jurisdictions in Louisiana received a total of $7,453,750 in COPS funding. Like FY2003 and FY2004, awards made by the COPS Office to jurisdictions in Louisiana were done under three different programs, as shown in **Table 6**. Three awards were made under the Law Enforcement Technology grant program, for a total of $686,657. Only one award was made under the Interoperable Communications Technology Program, in the amount of $5,999,184. Two awards were made by the COPS Office under the RCPI program, for a total of $767,909.

Table 6: COPS Grants Awarded to Jurisdictions in Louisiana in FY2005

Agency	Grant Program	Funding
New Orleans Metropolitan Crime Commission	Law Enforcement Technology	$98,664.00
Bastrop Police Dept.	Law Enforcement Technology	$246,661.00
Northwestern State University	Law Enforcement Technology	$341,332.00
Baton Rouge Police Dept.	Interoperable Communications Tech.	$5,999,184.00
Northwestern State University	RCPI	$600,000.00
Northwestern State University	RCPI	$167,909.00
	Total Awarded	$7,453,750.00

Jurisdictions in Louisiana received 0.5 percent of the total amount of Law Enforcement Technology funding awarded by the COPS Office in FY2005. The Baton Rouge Police Department received six percent of the total amount of Interoperable Communications Technology funding awarded in FY2005. Also, Northwestern State University received five percent of RCPI funding awarded by the COPS Office for FY2005.

Fiscal Year 2003. In FY2003, a total of $3,251,953 was awarded by the COPS Office in Mississippi. As shown in **Table 7**, funds awarded to jurisdictions in Mississippi by the COPS Office were done under four different programs. Five Law Enforcement Technology grants were awarded in Mississippi during FY2003, for a total of $1,559,796. Seven UHP grants were awarded in Mississippi, for a total of $1,325,545. Only one CIS grant, for $94,513, was awarded in Mississippi in FY2003. Five HSOP grants were awarded in Mississippi for a total of $272,099.

Table 7: COPS Grants Awarded to Jurisdictions in Mississippi in FY2003

Agency	Grant Program	Funding
Columbia Police Dept.	Law Enforcement Technology	$248,375.00
Leake County Board of Supervisors	Law Enforcement Technology	$94,383.00
Simpson County Sheriff's Dept.	Law Enforcement Technology	$844,475.00
Warren County Sheriff's Dept.	Law Enforcement Technology	$248,375.00
Wilkinson County Sheriff's Dept.	Law Enforcement Technology	$124,188.00
Alcorn County Sheriff's Dept.	UHP	$75,000.00
DeSoto County Sheriff's Dept.	UHP	$299,067.00
City of Hattiesburg	UHP	$349,946.00
Pearl River Community College	UHP	$150,385.00
City of Sardis	UHP	$217,951.00
University of Southern Mississippi	UHP	$193,871.00
Vaiden Police Dept.	UHP	$39,325.00
Okolona Police Dept.	COPS in Schools	$94,513.00
Gulfport Police Dept.	Homeland Security Overtime	$139,759.00
Jackson County Sheriff's Dept.	Homeland Security Overtime	$68,948.00
City of Sardis	Homeland Security Overtime	$20,803.00
City of Starkville	Homeland Security Overtime	$22,896.00
Mississippi State University	Homeland Security Overtime	$19,693.00
	Total Awarded	$3,251,953.00

Less than one percent of the total amount of Law Enforcement Technology, CIS, and HSOP funds was awarded to jurisdictions in Mississippi in FY2003. Less than two percent of the UHP funds awarded by the COPS Office were awarded to jurisdictions in Mississippi.

Fiscal Year 2004. In FY2004, a total of $2,271,770 was awarded to jurisdictions in Mississippi by the COPS Office. As shown in **Table 8**, grants awarded to jurisdictions in Mississippi in FY2004 were done under three different programs. Three Law Enforcement Technology grants were made in Mississippi in FY2004, for a total of $444,557. Four UHP grants were awarded in Mississippi, for a total of $912,130. Four CIS grants were also awarded in Mississippi in FY2004, for a total of $915,083.

Table 8: COPS Grants Awarded to Jurisdictions in Mississippi in FY 2004

Agency	Grant Program	Funding
City of Jackson	Law Enforcement Technology	$98,948.00
Jackson County Sheriff's Dept.	Law Enforcement Technology	$98,948.00
Lee County Sheriff's Dept.	Law Enforcement Technology	$246,661.00
Booneville Police Dept.	UHP	$75,000.00
City of Mound Bayou	UHP	$204,501.00
Pearl River County Sheriff's Dept.	UHP	$412,500.00
City of D'Iberville	UHP	$220,129.00
Alcorn County Sheriff's Dept.	COPS in Schools	$103,192.00
Marion County Sheriff's Dept.	COPS in Schools	$251,769.00
Ripley Police Dept.	COPS in Schools	$195,082.00
Harrison County Sheriff's Dept.	COPS in Schools	$365,040.00
	Total Awarded	$2,271,770.00

Less than one percent of all of the FY2004 Law Enforcement Technology grant funding went to jurisdictions in Mississippi. Approximately 1.3 percent of UHP funding awarded by the COPS Office in FY2004 was awarded to jurisdictions in Mississippi. Less than two percent of all CIS funding for FY2004 went to jurisdictions in Mississippi.

Fiscal Year 2005. In FY2005, a total of $1,479,965 was awarded to jurisdictions in Mississippi by the COPS Office. As shown in **Table 9**, only two awards were made in Mississippi in FY2005, both under the Law Enforcement Technology program.

Table 9: COPS Grants Awarded to Jurisdiction in Mississippi in FY2005

Agency	Grant Program	Funding
Yazoo City Police Dept.	Law Enforcement Technology	$493,322.00
Southaven Police Dept.	Law Enforcement Technology	$986,643.00
	Total Awarded	$1,479,965.00

Approximately 1.1 percent of all Law Enforcement Technology funding went to the two jurisdictions in Mississippi that received funding in FY2005.

Office for Domestic Preparedness (ODP)

The Office for Domestic Preparedness (ODP) was transferred from the Department of Justice to the Department of Homeland Security (DHS) by Section 430, Title IV of the Homeland Security Act of 2002 (P.L. 107-296). ODP has primary responsibility for United States government terrorism preparedness.[13] ODP administers grants to state, local, and tribal first responder entities (such as law enforcement, emergency management, fire departments, and emergency medical services) that assist their preparedness activities. Since FY2003, ODP has awarded approximately $480 million to Alabama, Louisiana, and Mississippi first responders.

Since September 11, 2001 funding appropriated by Congress for DHS programs to enhance first responders' capabilities was largely emphasized enhancing capabilities to respond to terrorist attacks. The Homeland Security Act of 2002 and Homeland Security Presidential Directive-8, however, direct DHS to take an all-hazards approach to national emergency preparedness with a special emphasis on terrorism.[14] As a result, DHS grant guidance for the State Homeland Security Grant and the Urban Area Security Initiative grant programs, the two largest sources of DHS grants funds available to state and local first responders, is designed to support an all-hazards approach to planning, equipment, and training to enhance the capabilities of first responders to respond to terrorist attacks and to a lesser extent natural disasters.

ODP Grant Programs

A brief summary of ODP grant programs under which funding was awarded to first responder entities in Alabama, Louisiana, and Mississippi follows:

- Alabama received $216,130,186, from FY2003 to FY2005 under the ODP State Homeland Security Grant Program (SHSGP), the Critical Infrastructure Protection Program (CIP), the Citizen Corps Programs (CCP), the Law Enforcement Terrorism Prevention Program (LETPP), the Assistance to Firefighters Program (FIRE), and the Emergency Management Performance Grant Program (EMPG);
- Louisiana received $140,038,519, from FY2003 to FY2005 under the ODP State Homeland Security Grant Program (SHSGP), the Critical Infrastructure Protection Program (CIP), the Citizen Corps Programs (CCP), the Law Enforcement Terrorism Prevention Program (LETPP), the Assistance to Firefighters Program (FIRE), and the Emergency Management Performance Grant Program (EMPG); and
- Mississippi received $123,583,324, from FY2003 to FY2005 under the ODP State Homeland Security Grant Program (SHSGP), the Critical Infrastructure Protection Program (CIP), the Citizen Corps Programs (CCP), the Law Enforcement Terrorism Prevention Program (LETPP), the Assistance to Firefighters Program (FIRE), and the Emergency Management Performance Grant Program (EMPG).

State Homeland Security Grant Program (SHSGP). This assistance program provides financial assistance to states and U.S. insular areas to prepare for terrorist attacks involving weapons of mass destruction (WMD). The program authorizes purchase of specialized equipment to enhance state and local agencies' capability in preventing and responding to WMD incidents, and provides funds for protecting critical infrastructure of national importance. This program provides grant funds for designing, developing, conducting, and evaluating WMD exercises; developing and conducting WMD training programs; and updating and implementing each state's Homeland Security Strategy (SHSS).[15]

SHSGP funds may be used to plan for, design, develop, conduct, and evaluate exercises that train first responders, and to assess the readiness of state and local jurisdictions to prevent and respond to terrorist attacks. Exercises must be threat- and performance-based, in accordance with ODP Homeland Security Exercise and Evaluation Program (HSEEP) manuals. Exercises conducted with funds from this program must be managed and executed in accordance with HSEEP.[16]

Funds from this program may be used to enhance the capabilities of state and local first responders through the development of a state homeland security training program. Allowable training costs include establishment of WMD training capacities within existing training academies, universities, and junior colleges.[17]

States are the only authorized applicants, with the following state and local entities eligible to receive funding:

- Emergency management agencies or offices;
- Homeland security agencies or offices;
- Fire departments;
- Law enforcement agencies;
- Emergency medical services;
- Hazardous material-handling personnel;
- Public works agencies or offices;
- Public health agencies or offices;
- Governmental administrative agencies or offices; and
- Public safety communications agencies or offices.[18]

Citizen Corps Programs (CCP). On January 29, 2002, President Bush issued an executive order[19] which established the USA Freedom Corps. USA Freedom Corps' mission is to increase opportunities for citizens by expanding and enhancing public service. Within the USA Freedom Corps, the Citizen Corps program was established to coordinate volunteer organizations, with the mission to make local communities safe and prepared to respond to any emergency situation. Community Emergency Response Teams (CERT) is the only program of the four which Citizen Corps administers that provides grant funding to volunteer first responders.

CERT trains people to be prepared to respond to emergency situations in their own local communities. CERTs are groups of volunteers within communities that are trained by professional first responders to assist in the event of a disaster. CERT members give critical support to first responders, provide immediate assistance to victims, and organize spontaneous volunteers at a disaster site.

This program authorizes funding for training of CERT members only. The CERT program is a professionally instructed course taught by a team of first responders who have the requisite knowledge and skills. The course, taught to groups of citizens within their communities, consists of two and a half hour sessions held one evening a week, over a seven week period.[20] States apply for a grant under this program, while any community that has established a Citizen Corps Council is also eligible to receive funding from it.

Law Enforcement Terrorism Prevention Program (LETPP). In the FY2004 DHS appropriations, Congress directed ODP to establish a local law enforcement terrorism prevention grant program for states and localities.[21] This program provides funds to support activities to establish and enhance state and local efforts to prevent and deter terrorist attacks. Eligible program activities authorized include:

- Information sharing to preempt terrorist attacks;
- Target hardening to reduce vulnerability of selected high value targets;
- Threat recognition to identify potential or actual threats; and
- Intervention activities to interdict terrorists.

Approved costs for this program include, but are not limited to, personnel costs (including overtime as approved by the state administering agency), equipment, systems, and related expenses.[22] State and local law enforcement agencies are authorized to apply for grant funding under this program.

Assistance to Firefighters Program (FIRE). This program awards one-year grants directly to fire departments to enhance their abilities to respond to fires and fire-related hazards.[23] The program seeks to support fire departments that lack the tools and resources necessary to protect the health and safety of the public and firefighting personnel.[24] At least five percent of the funds go to prevention programs, and recipients agree to contribute a 30 percent nonfederal match if the cal population is greater than 50,000, or 10 percent if the local population is 50,000 or less. Grant recipients may not receive more than $750,000 for any fiscal year.[25] The program's grant application process is competitive, and applications are peer reviewed by state and local fire department officials.

FIRE program provides funds to support firefighter safety, fire prevention, emergency medical services, and firefighting vehicle acquisition. Individual fire departments are eligible to apply for grants under this program.

Emergency Management Performance Grant Program (EMPG). This program is designed to assist the development, maintenance, and improvement of state and local emergency management capabilities. It provides support to state and local governments to achieve measurable results in key functional areas of emergency management.[26]

EMPG funds are used for emergency management personnel costs, travel, training, supplies, and other routine expenditures for emergency management activities.[27] Funds from this grant program may also be used for consequence management preparedness projects and programs that develop and improve the capabilities of states and localities to prepare for, respond to, and recover from acts of terrorism involving WMD.[28]

States may use the funds provided through the EMPG to structure their individual emergency management programs based on identified needs and priorities for strengthening emergency management capabilities. States may also use EMPG funds to develop intrastate emergency management systems that encourage partnership building among government, business, and volunteer and community organizations.[29] State emergency management agencies or offices are eligible applicants and recipients of this grant program; additionally, state emergency management agencies may pass funds to emergency management offices at the local level.

ODP Funding Awarded to Alabama

Fiscal Year 2003. In FY2003, Alabama received a total of $61,348,493 from ODP. ODP funding awarded to Alabama in FY2003 was done under five different grant programs, as shown in **Table 10.**

Table 10: ODP Grants Awarded to Alabama in FY2003

Grant Program	Funding
State Homeland Security Grant Program	$31,200,000.00
Citizen Corps	$500,000.00
Critical Infrastructure Protection	$3,300,000.00
Assistance to Firefighters Program	$23,548,493.00
Emergency Management Performance Grant Program	$2,800,000.00
Total Awarded	$61,348,493.00

Fiscal Year 2004. In FY2004, Alabama received a total of $108,732,787 from ODP. ODP funding awarded to Alabama in FY2004 was done under five different grant programs, as shown in **Table 11.**

Table 11: ODP Grants Awarded to Alabama in FY2004

Grant Program	Funding
State Homeland Security Grant Program	$28,000,000.00
Citizen Corps	$600,000.00
Law Enforcement Terrorism Prevention Program	$8,300,000.00
Assistance to Firefighters Program	$68,932,787.00
Emergency Management Performance Grant Program	$2,900,000.00
Total Awarded	$108,732,787.00

Fiscal Year 2005. In FY2005, Alabama received a total of $46,048,906, in funding from ODP. ODP funding awarded to Alabama in FY2005 was done under five different grant programs, as shown in **Table 12.**

Table 12: ODP Grants Awarded to Alabama in FY2005

Grant Program	Funding
State Homeland Security Grant Program	$17,000,000.00
Citizen Corps	$200,000.00
Law Enforcement Terrorism Protection Program	$6,400,000.00
Assistance to Firefighters Program	$19,548,906.00
Emergency Management Performance Grant Program	$2,900,000.00
Total Awarded	$46,048,906.00

ODP funding Awarded to Louisiana

Fiscal Year 2003. In FY2003, Louisiana received a total of $51,048,654 from ODP. ODP funding awarded to Louisiana in FY2003 was done under five different grant programs, as shown in **Table 13.**

Table 13: ODP Grants Awarded to Louisiana in FY2003

Grant Program	Funding
State Homeland Security Grant Program	$32,200,000.00
Citizen Corps	$500,000.00
Critical Infrastructure Protection	$3,300,000.00
Assistance to Firefighters Program	$12,248,654.00
Emergency Management Performance Grant Program	$2,800,000.00
Total Awarded	$51,048,654.00

Fiscal Year 2004. In FY2004, Louisiana received a total of $51,159,534 from ODP. ODP funding awarded to Louisiana in FY2004 was done under five different grant programs, as shown in **Table 14.**

Table 14: ODP Grants Awarded to Louisiana in FY2004

Grant Program	Funding
State Homeland Security Grant Program	$28,000,000.00
Citizen Corps	$600,000.00
Law Enforcement Terrorism Prevention Program	$8,300,000.00
Assistance to Firefighters Program	$11,359,534.00
Emergency Management Performance Grant Program	$2,900,000.00
Total Awarded	$51,159,534.00

Fiscal Year 2005. In FY2005, Louisiana received a total of $37,830,331 from ODP. ODP funding awarded to Louisiana in FY2005 was done under five different grant programs, as shown in **Table 15.**

Table 15: ODP Grants Awarded to Louisiana in FY2004

Grant Program	Funding
State Homeland Security Grant Program	$17,700,000.00
Citizen Corps	$200,000.00
Law Enforcement Terrorism Prevention Program	$6,400,000.00
Assistance to Firefighters Program	$10,630,331.00
Emergency Management Performance Grant Program	$2,900,000.00
Total Awarded	$37,830,331.00

ODP Funding Awarded to Mississippi

Fiscal Year 2003. In FY2003, Mississippi received a total of $46,208,491 from ODP. ODP funding awarded to Mississippi in FY2003 was done under five different grant programs, as shown in **Table 16.**

Table 16: ODP Grants Awarded to Mississippi in FY2003

Grant Program	Funding
State Homeland Security Grant Program	$25,000,000.00
Citizen Corps	$400,000.00
Critical Infrastructure Protection	$2,700,000.00
Assistance to Firefighters Program	$15,908,491.00
Emergency Management Performance Grant Program	$2,200,000.00
Total Awarded	$46,208,491.00

Fiscal Year 2004. In FY2004, Mississippi received a total of $43,564,925 from ODP. ODP funding awarded to Mississippi in FY2004 was done under five different grant programs, as shown in **Table 17**.

Table 17: ODP Grants Awarded to Mississippi in FY2004

Grant Program	Funding
State Homeland Security Grant Program	$22,400,000.00
Citizen Corps	$500,000.00
Law Enforcement Terrorism Prevention Program	$6,700,000.00
Assistance to Firefighters Program	$11,564,925.00
Emergency Management Performance Grant Program	$2,400,000.00
Total Awarded	$43,564,925.00

Fiscal Year 2005. In FY2005, Mississippi received a total of $31,109,908 from ODP. ODP funding awarded to Mississippi in FY2005 was done under five different grant programs, as shown in **Table 18.**

Table 18: ODP Grants Awarded to Mississippi in FY2005

Grant Program	Funding
State Homeland Security Grant Program	$14,200,000.00
Citizen Corps	$200,000.00
Law Enforcement Terrorism Prevention Program	$5,200,000.00
Assistance to Firefighters Program	$9,209,908.00
Emergency Management Performance Grant Program	$2,300,000.00
Total Awarded	$31,109,908.00

[1] The programs are authorized in the following statutes: Flood Mitigation Assistance - 42 U.S.C. § 4104(c)-(d) (2005); Hazard Mitigation Grant Program - 42 U.S.C. § 5170(c) (2005); Pre-Disaster Mitigation - 42 U.S.C. § 5133 (2005).

[2] U.S. Dep't. of Justice, Cmty. Oriented Policing Servs. Office [hereinafter DOJ COPS Office], About Cmty. Oriented Policing Servs. Office, http:/ www.cops.usdoj.gov/Default.asp?Item=35, (last visited Oct. 25, 2005) [hereinafter About DOJ COPS Office website].

[3] DOJ COPS Office website, Message from the Dir., http://www.cops.usdoj.gov/Default.asp?Item=37, (last visited Oct. 25, 2005).

[4] About DOJ COPS Office website.

[5] DOJ COPS Office, COPS Fact Sheet: Interoperable Communications Tech., http://www.cops.usdoj.gov/mime/open.pdf?Item=947, (last visited Oct. 25, 2005).

[6] DOJ COPS Office, COPS Tech. Grants, http://www.cops.usdoj.gov/Default.asp?Item=58, (last visited Oct. 25, 2005).

[7] Telephone call by Select Comm. Staff with DOJ COPS Office personnel (Oct. 25, 2005).

[8] DOJ COPS Office, Universal Hiring Program, http://www.cops.usdoj.gov/Default.asp?Item=53, (last visited Oct. 25, 2005).

[9] DOJ COPS Office, COPS in Schools, http://www.cops.usdoj.gov/default.asp?Item=54, (last visited Oct. 25, 2005).

[10] DOJ COPS Office, Homeland Sec. Overtime Program, http://www.cops.usdoj.gov/default.asp?Item=1023, (last visited Oct. 25, 2005).

[11] Telephone call by Select Comm. Staff with DOJ COPS Office personnel (Nov. 21, 2005).

[12] DOJ COPS Office, Reg'l Cmty. Policing Insts., http://www.cops.usdoj.gov/default.asp?Item=229 (last visited Jan. 30, 2005) (The website provides a list of all Reg'l Cmty. Policing Insts. across the United States).

[13] Homeland Sec. Act (2002), Pub. L. No. 107-296, 116 Stat. 2135 (2002).

[14] Directive on Mgmt. of Nat'l Preparedness, 39 WEEKLY COMP. PRES. DOC. 1822 (Dec. 17, 2003) (Known as Homeland Sec. Presidential Directive/HSPD-8).

[15] Office for Domestic Preparedness, U.S. Dep't of Homeland Sec., *Fiscal Year 2004 State Homeland Security Grant Program: Program Guidelines and Application Kit,* 1 (2003).

[16] *Id.* at 3.

[17] *Id.* at 4.

[18] *Id.* at 2.

[19] Establishing the USA Freedom Corps, 67 Fed. Reg. 4869 (2002).

[20] Emergency Mgmt. Inst., Community Emergency Response Team Overview, http://training.fema.gov/emiweb/CERT/overview.asp (last visited Apr. 1, 2004).

[21] 2004 Dep't of Homeland Sec. Appropriations Act, Pub. L. No. 108-90, 117 Stat. 1137 (2003).

[22] S. REP. NO. 108-86 (2003).

[23] House REP. NO. 108-280 (2003) (In the conference report to accompany H.R. 2555, the Assistance to Firefighters grant program is to be administered by the Office of Domestic Preparedness. It also specifies that the grant administration process will not be changed from the present procedures, to include peer review and involvement by United States Fire Admin).

[24] Fed. Emergency Mgmt. Agency, U.S. Dep't of Homeland Sec., *FY2003 Assistance to Firefighters Grant Program Guidance,* 2 (2003).

[25] Floyd D. Spence Nat'l Def. Authorization Act for FY 2001, Pub. L. No. 106-398, § 1701, 114 Stat. 1654 (2000).

[26] 26 Fed. Emergency Mgmt. Agency, U.S. Dep't of Homeland Security, *FY2003 Emergency Management Performance Grant Program Guidance to States,* 2 (2003).

[27] *Id.* at 6.

[28] *Id.* at 8.

[29] *Id.* at 9.

KEY FEDERAL LAW ENFORCEMENT ACTIONS IN RESPONSE TO KATRINA

The Federal Bureau of Investigations established a Tactical Operations Center and utilized its Fly Teams to assist in fingerprinting victims and potential recovery contractors

The Federal Bureau of Investigations (FBI) accomplished core mission functions in response to the hurricane by establishing a Tactical Operations Center to support the FBI's tactical teams. In addition, FBI Fly Teams assisted FEMA's Disaster Mortuary Operational Response Team in identifying 112-115 hurricane victims by computerized fingerprint matching. FBI Fly Teams also assisted FEMA in identifying 458 criminal histories out of 2,900 potential hurricane recovery contractors through fingerprinting.

The FBI is the "principal investigative arm of the United States Department of Justice." The FBI's mission is to:

> [U]phold the law through the investigation of violations of federal criminal law; to protect the United States from foreign intelligence and terrorist activities; to provide leadership and law enforcement assistance to federal, state, local, and international agencies; and to perform these responsibilities in a manner that is responsive to the needs of the public and is faithful to the Constitution of the United States.[1]

The United States Attorney General can authorize the FBI to assist state and location authorities in a "law enforcement emergency."[2] The FBI may provide public safety support to state and local authorities in a presidentially declared "major disaster."[3]

The FBI's Law Enforcement Services Branch coordinates the Bureau's preparation for and response to a domestic emergency.[4] Staff from all offices within this branch were utilized after Hurricane Katrina. In addition, the FBI called upon its Administrative Services Division, Counterterrorism Division, Criminal Investigative Division, Cyber Division, Directorate of Intelligence, Finance Division, Information Technology Operations Division, and Security Division.

There are approximately 225 employees assigned to the FBI's New Orleans Field Office, which has jurisdiction over all FBI authority in the state of Louisiana.[5] The FBI has field offices in Jackson, Mississippi and Mobile, Alabama.[6] As part of the Jackson Field Office, the FBI has Resident Agencies in Pascagoula, Hattiesburg, and Gulfport, Mississippi.[7]

On August 26, the Jackson Field Office notified each supervisor at its Resident Agencies to implement their hurricane plans.[8] This required installing hurricane shutters, securing vehicles, bagging computers and equipment, and locking the safes. Authorized personnel on the Mississippi coast moved to the Jackson Field Office.

By 6:00 p.m. on August 29, the Jackson Field Office moved its traditional FBI operations to the Resident Agency in Oxford, Mississippi.[9] Also that evening, the FBI used an airplane to survey the damage to the Resident Agencies on the coast. The Jackson Field Office was able to electronically monitor the security alarms of its Resident Agencies in the affected area. FBI personnel who remained on the coast were dispatched to the Resident Agencies and confirmed that all offices were still secure.

On August 29, after Katrina's landfall, the Special Agent-in-Charge (SAC) of New Orleans and four other FBI agents surveyed the damage to the New Orleans Field Office.[10] The roof suffered significant damage, leaving sixty percent of the top floor uncovered. Due to the sensitivity of documents housed in the Field Office, the SAC and the four agents remained in the building to ensure its security.

Because of the damage to the building, the SAC decided to move the New Orleans Field Division to the Louisiana State Police (LSP) headquarters in Baton Rouge.[11] An Assistant Special Agent-In-Charge (ASAC) from the New Orleans Field Office went to Baton Rouge while the New Orleans SAC stayed in New Orleans. The Operational Technology Division

(OTD) left Quantico, Virginia, with 16 FBI personnel to deliver communication equipment to the affected area so the New Orleans Field Office could communicate with FBI headquarters.[12] FBI command vehicles — tractor trailers containing mobile offices — were deployed to Baton Rouge and the Jackson Field Office.[13]

Within 12 hours after Hurricane Katrina subsided, the Jackson Field Office was in contact with all of its personnel.[14] On August 30, OTD dispatched a mobile command post to Mississippi. The Jackson ASAC participated in another airplane survey of the area. The Jackson Field Office office manager left Jackson via car for the coast in order to assess damage to the Hattiesburg Resident Agency. While the Hattiesburg building remained secure, the Pascagoula Resident Agency sustained water damage to the ceiling, wall cavities, and carpet. The office was able to secure a temporary facility through the Navy free of charge. The Gulfport Resident Agency sustained similar water damage. The office was located on the top floor of a building and the attic of the building flooded. The FBI was able to work with government contractors to clean the office, and it was habitable by October 1.

The same day, Jackson Field Office personnel met with several military officials to determine where the temporary FBI command post should be located.[15] The FBI decided on Keesler Air Force Base, as there was a hotel on the property with showers and bathrooms. Some FBI personnel from the Jackson Field Office were also Air Force reservists and they had access to goods and services provided to Air Force employees.

On August 30, FBI headquarters officials put their Field Offices on alert that additional personnel were needed in the affected area.[16] Ten Special Weapons and Tactics (SWAT) agents from the Houston Division were deployed to New Orleans to assist the New Orleans Police Department (NOPD) SWAT.[17] The agents from Houston brought a boat that enabled them to transport personnel and supplies. The FBI SWAT agents relieved the New Orleans SAC and agents who had stayed to secure the New Orleans Field Office.

FBI personnel and equipment from Critical Incident Response Group (CIRG) and OTD arrived on August 31 in Baton Rouge and established a Command Post in Baton Rouge at the LSP headquarters.[18] Among the equipment were tents that FBI personnel used as shelter at the Command Post.[19]

By 2:00 a.m. on August 31, the FBI Command Post at Keesler Air Force Base was operational.[20] FBI agents from the Mobile and Miami Field Offices were deployed to work there. These agents assisted with health, safety, and welfare checks on other agents and citizens in the area. FBI sent employee assistance personnel, most of whom had crisis management backgrounds, to work with agents' family members. The first agents on the scene stayed the first week after the hurricane. After that, additional agents began rotating into the area. The second week, agents were deployed from FBI Headquarters to the Command Post. SWAT from the Little Rock Field Office were used to provide security at the Command Post and the Resident Agencies in Mississippi's affected area.

In a fortunate coincidence, the Command Post had an FBI employee who formerly worked for FEMA.[21] This employee checked in daily with FEMA in Jackson and on the coast and the Mississippi Emergency Management Agency. The Command Post also communicated with the Mississippi Bureau of Criminal Investigations, the Mississippi Highway Patrol, and the Homeland Security Director for Mississippi, who was also the former FBI Jackson Field Office SAC. The agents at the Command Post worked with local police and sheriffs to respond to requests for assistance.

On September 1, CIRG deployed agents from the Dallas, Atlanta, Baltimore, and Houston SWAT teams and Hostage Rescue Teams to continue to help NOPD control the affected area.[22] The FBI was able to create a Virtual Command Center for the Law Enforcement On-Line Internet site.[23] All law enforcement nationwide were able to log onto the website and receive daily situation reports regarding FBI relief efforts.[24]

The FBI established a Tactical Operations Center (TOC) in Sorrento, Louisiana on September 4.[25] Kenneth Kaiser, the Boston SAC, was deployed to Sorrento to oversee the TOC.

On September 3, the Laboratory Disaster Squad and the CJIS Fly Teams were deployed to St. Gabriel, Louisiana to assist with FEMA's National Disaster Medical System Center's Disaster Mortuary Operational Response Team (DMORT).[26] LSP, the National Guard, and local police were delivering deceased victims of the storm to St. Gabriel.[27] The DMORT was responsible for the handling of the bodies. The Fly Teams and the FBI's Evidence Recovery Teams worked together to submit the victims' fingerprints electronically to CJIS and the Integrated Automated Fingerprint Identification System (IAFIS) to search for identifying fingerprint matches.[28] In total, 750 unidentified bodies were brought to the DMORT and 112-115 bodies were identified using IAFIS.[29]

Also on September 3, a finance employee was sent from FBI headquarters to the FBI Command Post at Keesler Air Force Base.[30] This enabled the agents in Mississippi to purchase gas from the Air Force. By September 4, all FBI personnel living in the affected area of Louisiana were located.[31]

On September 5, CJIS Fly Teams helped FEMA fingerprint potential contractors for the Hurricane response.[32] This took place in Orlando and consisted of fingerprinting technology that identified if contracting applicants had criminal histories. The FBI and FEMA fingerprinted 2,900 potential contractors, detecting 458 criminal histories.

The FBI continued to deploy and assign personnel to assist state and local police.[33] The Violent Gang Task Force from the New Orleans Division worked out of the Gretna Police Department. Over 30 more agents coordinated with NOPD to back up NOPD SWAT, FBI SWAT, and HRT Special Agents. The FBI's Rapid Deployment Teams were sent to crisis sites to assist with administrative issues.

The FBI also utilized its air assets in responding to Hurricane Katrina.[34] They flew daily helicopter flights moving law enforcement personnel, equipment, supplies, and evacuees.[35] In addition, the FBI flew 12 missions utilizing its fixed wing assets for moving FBI personnel and equipment from Washington, D.C. to New Orleans and Jackson.[36] There were 1,200 FBI employees involved.[37] Seven hundred were deployed to the New Orleans area.

The Bureau of Alcohol, Tobacco, Firearms and Explosives secured buildings containing firearms, located and inspected all federal firearms and explosive licensees, recovered lost and stolen firearms, and dismantled explosives in the New Orleans area

---

Following the hurricane, the Bureau of Alcohol, Tobacco, Firearms and Explosives (ATF) established a Critical Incident Management Response Team (CIMRT). The CIMRT coordinates ATF's law enforcement operations and ensures that ATF continues its primary law enforcement missions. ATF located and secured buildings containing firearms, conducted inspections to ensure the safety of all individuals licensed to use firearms and explosives, worked to match stolen or lost firearms with their rightful owners, and dismantled explosives in New Orleans.

ATF's mission is to "conduct criminal investigations, regulate the firearms and explosives industries, and assist other law enforcement agencies."[38] This mission is in place so ATF's work can "prevent terrorism, reduce violent crime and to protect the public in a manner that is faithful to the Constitution and the laws of the United States." ATF's authority to respond to domestic emergencies is found in the Gun Control Act of 1968, the National Firearms Act, the Arms Export Control Act, and the Federal Explosives Laws.[39]

ATF's involvement in the preparation for Hurricane Katrina began on August 23.[40] Throughout that week, ATF headquarters in Washington, D.C. coordinated with its Houston, New Orleans (which includes the entire states of Louisiana and Mississippi), Nashville (which includes the state of Alabama), Tampa, and Miami Field Divisions to prepare for Katrina's landfall in Florida and the Gulf coast.[41] On August 25 and 26, ATF headquarters ordered the evacuation of ATF personnel in New Orleans and Mississippi, the New Orleans Special Agent in Charge (SAC) pre-identified those persons who were staying in the area, and those evacuating were instructed to call their immediate supervisor after the storm.[42]

On August 29, as Katrina made landfall, ATF headquarters began notifying the Field Divisions closest to New Orleans that assistance was needed.[43] These Field Divisions were asked to identify resources and personnel to be detailed to the affected area. Within eight hours, ATF identified the Nashville, Houston, and Dallas Field Divisions as those to detail personnel.[44]

The New Orleans Field Division and the Gulfport Resident Office were severely damaged by the hurricane.[94] Beginning immediately after the storm and continuing into Tuesday, the New Orleans Field Division began the process of reconstituting its field office by accounting for and identifying the whereabouts of all Field Division personnel — some of whom were in need of rescue.[95] DEA teams were established to facilitate the rescues. In all, 63 DEA employees and family members were rescued by DEA agents. The process of reconstituting its office allows DEA to be most helpful in undertaking other law enforcement roles and responsibilities related to the emergency at hand.[96] After the New Orleans Field Division personnel were located, DEA began assisting local law enforcement in the massive search and rescue effort.[97] Most of the Katrina-related DEA man hours were ultimately spent on search and rescue.[98]

On August 31, command centers were established at the Baton Rouge District Office and in Mobile.[99] At this time, DEA headquarters mobilized Field Divisions from around the country, including agents from the Miami, Atlanta, St. Louis, Dallas, and Houston divisions. These agents responded to Baton Rouge and Gulfport, Mississippi with supplies, including food, water, chain saws, generators, tarps, ice, gasoline, satellite phones, and vehicles.

Headquarters designated the Office of Aviation in Addison, Texas to serve as the Command Center for logistics purposes, instructing field divisions throughout the country to ship necessary supplies to Addison for eventual transportation to the field, principally the Baton Rouge and Gulfport areas.[100] The Addison facility continued to play a key logistics role throughout the DEA recovery effort, coordinating all transportation — including the use of seven DEA aircraft — and supplies for the field. The Command Center was staffed by 12 people from both the Office of Aviation and the Dallas Field Division, the Field Division with responsibility for the Addison Office.

Flight missions were conducted to transport personnel and supplies and to survey the damage.[101] Aerial photography surveys assisted the recovery assignments taking place in the field. Technical personnel were dispatched to re-establish communication links where necessary. The Office of Aviation flew over 280 missions with 14 pilots totaling 782 flight hours, providing transportation and commodity support to local, state, and federal law enforcement throughout the affected region.

On September 1, the New Orleans Field Division established an Operations Center in Mandeville, Louisiana at a local high school.[102] The Mandeville Operations Center coordinated the efforts of various federal, state, and local officials throughout the greater New Orleans area. The Mandeville center coordinated the removal of firearms and sensitive items from the New Orleans Field Office.[103] To assist SAC Renton, the DEA deployed Houston SAC James Craig.

Shortly after Craig's arrival, Renton and he met with New Orleans city officials, including Mayor Nagin and law enforcement officials to assess the law enforcement needs for the city.[104] It was determined that federal law enforcement agencies, such as DEA, FBI, and ATF, among others, would join the New Orleans Police Department (NOPD) and the Louisiana State Police in policing the city of New Orleans.[105] Each NOPD district was staffed by federal law enforcement representatives.

From August 30 to September 12, 251 DEA Temporary Duty agents reported from Miami, Atlanta, St. Louis, Houston, and Dallas to provide law enforcement and search and rescue support as needed.[106] On September 4, DEA deployed personnel from the Atlanta Field Division as well as the Houston Mobile Enforcement Team (MET).[107] METs are self-contained, specially trained teams of eight to twelve agents that specialize in law enforcement missions involving violence.[108] These agents were then joined by the Charlotte MET on September 5, and the Miami MET on September 7.[109] The METs helped state and local departments conduct routine law enforcement tasks, including patrols and search and rescue missions.

On September 1, it was determined the DEA would be in charge of acquiring necessary fuel for DOJ vehicles.[110] SAC Craig oversaw this effort, which involved the bulk purchase of gasoline to be utilized by all DOJ agencies during the recovery effort. DEA also coordinated the provision of motor vehicles for law enforcement purposes in the affected area. Working with the U.S. Marshals Service, DEA provided approximately 30 vehicles for state and local police departments. DEA also arranged for $200,000 from its asset forfeiture budget to be provided to its fleet management group to move seized vehicles into official use.

DEA supported the communications needs of the affected area by supplying Government Emergency Telephone System cards, satellite phones, and other communications equipment, including the installation of Wireless Priority Service.[111]

DEA's Office of Diversion Control played an important role throughout the response to Katrina.[112] The Acting Deputy Assistant Administrator for the Office of Diversion Control was identified to coordinate response activities. The goal was to maintain the availability of controlled substances for medical uses to the affected region.

On August 31, DEA Diversion Control staff convened to review previously negotiated agreements between DEA and FEMA, as well as agreements between DEA and the Centers for Disease Control (CDC).[113] These agreements facilitate delivery of needed supplies by allowing for the waiver of certain regulations in times of emergency. DEA established a point of contact within Diversion Control to coordinate, control and document allowances, waivers and regulatory controls. The Diversion Control website (deadiversion.gov) was re-tooled to handle those affected by Katrina.

On September 1, DEA established contact with the Boards of Pharmacy in Louisiana, Mississippi, and Alabama, as well as states receiving evacuees, including Florida, Texas, and Arkansas.[114] The Boards of Pharmacy were told DEA was making allowances for filling prescriptions upon presentation of a prescription bottle and based upon the professional judgment of the pharmacist.

On September 2, James Crawford, the Special Assistant to the Deputy Assistant Administrator for Diversion Control, began contacting major wholesalers to facilitate the processing of papers permitting these wholesalers to ship product under expedited procedures.[115] Throughout DEA's Katrina response, Crawford and the Diversion Control office worked to streamline processes to ensure Katrina victims received the products they needed.

On September 6, Crawford began working directly with the major chain pharmacies, such as Rite Aid, CVS, Walgreens, and Wal-Mart, to establish mobile replacement pharmacies and pharmacy trailers within shelter areas.[116] Diversion Control's efforts continued through October 27, at which time the New Orleans Divisional Office of Diversion Control was reestablished.

The United States Marshals Service was responsible for protecting the Strategic National stockpile, assisted in prisoner evacuations, accounted for and tracked federal judges in the affected area, and stood up a task force to locate violent parole and non-compliant sex offenders

---

The United States Marshal Service (USMS) focused on its core law enforcement missions following Katrina's landfall by locating and tracking federal judges in the affected area and creating a task force to locate violent parole and non-compliant sex offenders. USMS helped the Bureau of Prisons (BOP) relocate 920 Louisiana inmates and assisted FEMA in evacuating 3,510 individuals displaced by the hurricane. In addition, USMS helped the CDC protect the Strategic National Stockpile.

USMS is the oldest federal law enforcement agency in the United States, established by the Judiciary Act of 1789.[117] USMS is responsible for judicial and witness security, fugitive investigations, the transportation of prisoners and criminal aliens, asset forfeiture, federal service of process and prisoner services.[118]

On August 29, the Assistant Director for the USMS Operations Support Division ("Assistant Director") activated the USMS Emergency Operations Center (EOC) in Washington, D.C. in preparation for Hurricane Katrina.[119] The Assistant Director also placed four Operational Management Teams (OMT) and 33 USMS Inspectors, assigned to secure the Strategic National Stockpile, on standby.[120] CDC's Strategic National Stockpile contains large quantities of medicine and medical supplies to protect the United States in case a public emergency might result in the loss of local supplies.[121]

Following Katrina's landfall, USMS began accounting for USMS personnel. OMT worked with the Louisiana, Mississippi, and Alabama district offices to account for them.[122] Three Operational Medical Personnel were deployed to the coast of Mississippi and New Orleans to assist USMS personnel. Command posts were created by OMT at the Special Operations Group (SOG) Tactical Center at Camp Beauregard in Pineville, Louisiana, and at the District Office in Jackson, Mississippi.

Also on August 30, the Technical Operations Group Air Support Unit deployed six personnel, along with surveillance planes, which were used to assess the damage to the USMS facilities in New Orleans.[123] The federal court houses in New Orleans and Gulfport and Hattiesburg, Mississippi were damaged.[124] The Witness Security and Prisoner Operations Division (WPD) and Marshals from the Middle District of Louisiana Office helped the Orleans Parish evacuate prisoners

[46] Interview with ATF.

[47] ATF Summary of Significant Activity.

[48] Interview with ATF; E-mail correspondence from ATF personnel to Select Comm. Staff (Dec. 7, 2005) (11:47 a.m.) [hereinafter E-mail from ATF]; (E-mail from ATF) (The office in Shreveport oversaw the administrative functions of the Shreveport, Little Rock, Jackson, and Oxford, Miss. Field Offices).

[49] Interview with ATF.

[50] Id.

[51] Telephone call by Select Comm. Staff with ATF personnel, in Wash., D.C. (Dec. 1, 2005) [hereinafter Telephone call with ATF].

[52] ATF Summary of Significant Activity.

[53] Interview with ATF; Telephone call with ATF.

[54] Telephone call with ATF.

[55] Interview with ATF.

[56] Id.

[57] Telephone call with ATF.

[58] Id.; The Emergency Management Working Group was chaired by the Chief of Security and Emergency Programs Division (E-mail from ATF).

[59] Interview with ATF.

[60] ATF Summary of Significant Activity.

[61] Interview with ATF; Telephone call with ATF.

[62] ATF Summary of Significant Activity.

[63] Id.

[64] Interview with ATF.

[65] E-mail from ATF.

[66] ATF Summary of Significant Activity.

[67] Interview with ATF.

[68] ATF Summary of Significant Activity; Interview with ATF.

[69] Interview with ATF.

[70] Id.

[71] Telephone call by Select Comm. Staff with ATF personnel, in Wash., D.C. (Jan. 27, 2006).

[72] Interview with ATF; Interview by Select Comm. Staff with U.S. Immigration and Customs Enforcement [hereinafter ICE] personnel, in Wash., D.C. (Dec. 2, 2005) [hereinafter Dec. 2 Interview with ICE].

[73] Dec 2 Interview with ICE.

[74] Interview with ATF.

[75] ATF Summary of Significant Activity.

[76] Id.

[77] ATF Summary of Significant Activity; Interview with ATF.

[78] Interview with ATF.

[79] ATF Summary of Significant Activity.

[80] Interview with ATF.

[81] Id.

[82] ATF Summary of Significant Activity; Interview with ATF.

[83] ATF Summary of Significant Activity.

[84] E-mail from ATF.

[85] ATF Summary of Significant Activity.

[86] ATF Katrina Deployments Doc. (Nov. 29, 2005).

[87] Drug Enforcement Administration [hereinafter DEA] Mission Statement, http://www.usdoj.gov/dea/agency/mission.htm [hereinafter DEA website] (last visited Dec. 2, 2005).

[88] Response from the U.S. Dep't of Justice, to Chairman Tom Davis, Select Comm., and Charlie Melancon, U.S. Congressman (Dec. 8, 2005) [hereinafter Dec. 8 Dep't of Justice Response] (citing 21 U.S.C. §§ 801 et seq.).

[89] DEA website.

[90] Dec. 8 Dep't of Justice Response (citing 21 U.S.C. § 878 (a)(5)).

[91] Dec. 8 Dep't of Justice Response (citing 42 U.S.C. § 10501).

[92] Nov. 23 Dep't of Justice Response.

[93] Id.

[94] Hurricane Katrina Drug Enforcement Agency COOP Assessment (DAG000000223) (Jan. 26, 2006).

[95] Nov. 23 Dep't of Justice Response.

[96] Interview by Select Comm. Staff with DEA, in Wash., D.C. (Nov. 28, 2005) [hereinafter Interview with DEA].

[97] Interview with DEA.

[98] Id. From Aug. 30 through Sept. 28, DEA Special Agents assisted in over 3,400 search and rescues in LA and Miss. (Id.).

[99] Nov. 23 Dep't of Justice Response.

[100] Id.

[101] Id.

[102] Interview with DEA.

[103] Nov. 23 Dep't of Justice Response.

[104] Id.

[105] Interview with DEA.

06 Letter from U.S. Dep't of Justice, to Chairman Tom Davis, Select Comm., and Charlie Melancon, U.S. Congressman (Dec. 21, 2005) [hereinafter Dec. 21 Dep't of Justice Response]. (The day by day breakdown is as follows: Aug. 30 (24), Aug. 31 (17), Sept. 1 (32), Sept. 2 (16), Sept. 3 (33), Sept. 4 (38), Sept. 5 (11), Sept. 6 (13), Sept. 7 (39), Sept. 8 (10), Sept. 9 (6), Sept. 10 (5), Sept. 11 (4), Sept. 12 (4)).

07 Nov. 23 Dep't of Justice Response.

08 Interview with DEA.

09 Nov. 23 Dep't of Justice Response.

10 *Id.*

11 *Id.*

12 *Id.*

13 *Id.*

14 *Id.*

15 Dec. 8 Dep't of Justice Response (Wholesalers included: McKesson, Bergen/Amerisource and Cardinal Health).

16 *Id.*

17 United States Marshals Service [hereinafter USMS] Oldest Federal Law Enforcement Agency, http://www.usmarshals.gov/history/oldest.htm (last visited Jan. 21, 2006).

18 USMS Major Responsibilities of the USMS, http://www.usmarshals.gov/duties/index.html (last visited Jan. 21, 2006).

19 Nov. 23 Dep't of Justice Response.

20 Dec. 8 Dep't of Justice Response; Interview by Select Comm. Staff with USMS personnel, in Wash., D.C. (Dec. 8, 2005) [hereinafter Interview with USMS]; (Interview with USMS. (An Operational Mgmt. Team (OMT) oversees USMS' national response. There are OMTs located throughout the United States. A Chief Deputy, the highest ranking career Marshal in the district is in charge of the OMT. Each OMT has a core group of eight personnel).

21 Ctrs. for Disease Control and Prevention, Emergency Preparedness & Response, http://www.bt.cdc.gov/stockpile/ (last visited Jan 22, 2006).

22 Dec. 8 Dep't of Justice Response.

23 *Id.*

24 Interview with USMS. The courthouses are located as follows: C-600 U.S. Courthouse, New Orleans, LA 70130; 2012 15th Street, Suite 302, Gulfport, MS 39501; and 331 Federal Building, 701 Main Street, Hattiesburg, MS 39401. (E-mail correspondence from U.S. Dep't of Justice personnel to Select Comm. Staff (Dec. 8, 2005) (5:16 p.m.)).

25 Dec. 8 Dep't of Justice Response.

26 *Id.*

27 *Id.*

28 Interview with USMS.

29 Dec. 8 Dep't of Justice Response.

30 Dec. 8 Dep't of Justice Response; Interview with USMS.

31 Dec. 8 Dep't of Justice Response.

32 Dec. 8 Dep't of Justice Response; Interview with USMS.

33 Dec. 8 Dep't of Justice Response.

34 *Id.*

35 *Id.*; Dec. 21 Dep't of Justice Response. (The JPATS missions were conducted by 180 USMS personnel in 27 trips. The evacuees were moved to the following cities: Dallas, TX; San Antonio, TX; Corpus Christi, TX; Houston, TX; Smyrna, GA; Nashville, TN; Aurora, CO; Fort Smith, AR; and Phoenix, AZ. The evacuations cost a total of one million dollars. It took 3,216.7 work hours and 99.2 flight hours to complete the evacuations. 62 U.S. Air Force medics and 35 FAMS were transported to New Orleans on JPATS return trips).

36 Dec. 8 Dep't of Justice Response (JPATS flew the prisoners to Tampa, Florida for a total of 37.6 flight hours).

37 Dec. 8 Dep't of Justice Response; Interview with USMS.

38 Dec. 8 Dep't of Justice Response.

39 *Id.* (There were eight FEMA Strike Teams, each consisting of: FEMA Executive, Pub. Info. Officer, U.S. Army Corp of Engineers Representative, and a Community Relations Specialist).

40 *Id.*

41 Dec. 8 Dep't of Justice Response; Interview with USMS.

42 Dec. 8 Dep't of Justice Response.

43 Dec. 8 Dep't of Justice Response; Interview with USMS.

44 Dec. 8 Dep't of Justice Response.

25 *Id.* (Police Dep'ts included: Pass Christian Police Dep't, Gulfport Police Dep't, Biloxi Police Dep't, Long Beach Police Dep't, and Harrison County Sheriff's Dep't).

46 *Id.*

37 ICE website, http://www.ice.gov/graphics/about/index.htm (last visited Jan. 21, 2006).

38 Interview by Select Comm. Staff with ICE in Wash., D.C. (Nov. 16) [hereinafter Nov. 16 Interview with Interview with ICE]; E-mail from FAMS personnel to Select Comm. staff Dec. 5, 2005. (Oct. 16, 2005, FAMS was moved to the Transportation Security Administration (TSA) within DHS).

39 Nov. 16 Interview with ICE; E-mail correspondence from ICE personnel to Select Comm. Staff (Dec. 8, 2005) (8:51 a.m.).

30 Nov. 16 Interview with ICE.

51 ICE website, Federal Protective Service, http://www.ice.gov/graphics /fps/index.htm (last visited Jan. 27, 2006), E-mail correspondence from ICE to Select Comm. Staff (Jan. 4, 2006) (11:31 a.m.) [hereinafter Jan. 4 E-mail from ICE].

32 Jan. 4 E-mail from ICE.

33 *Id.*

44 *Id.*

Enclosure I: Statement by Comptroller
General David M. Walker on GAO's
Preliminary Observations Regarding
Preparedness and Response to Hurricanes
Katrina and Rita

transition so that victims are not just rescued, but can be taken to a place of shelter.

- Mass care—sheltering, feeding, and related services—following Hurricane Katrina required the integrated efforts of many organizations, including volunteer groups, charities and other nongovernmental groups, organizations providing mutual aid, and the military. Although many of these efforts were successful, it appeared that Hurricane Katrina seriously challenged the capacity of organizations such as the American Red Cross and FEMA to provide expected services to certain populations and in certain areas and at certain times. Housing beyond short-term shelters also became—and remains—a major problem, especially for victims who either cannot return to their community or require housing options in their community if they do return.

- Additional capability will be needed to effectively manage and deploy volunteers and unsolicited donations. Our early work indicates that because of the magnitude of the storms, volunteers and donations, including from the international community were not generally well integrated into the overall response and recovery activities. For example, there were challenges in integrating the efforts of the Salvation Army and smaller organizations, often local churches and other "faith-based" organizations. In addition, federal agencies involved in managing the international assistance were not prepared to coordinate, receive, distribute, or account for the assistance. Agency officials involved in the cash and in-kind international assistance told us the agencies had not planned for the acceptance of international assistance for use in the United States and, therefore, had not developed processes and procedures to address this scenario.

- Lastly, beginning and sustaining community and economic recovery, including restoring a viable tax base for essential services, calls for immediate steps so residents can restore their homes and businesses. Removing debris and restoring essential gas, electric, oil, communications, water, sewer, transportation and transportation infrastructure, other utilities, and services such as public health and medical support are vital to recovery and rebuilding. In less severe disasters, restoring these lifelines is easier. However, the magnitude and scope of Hurricane Katrina painfully makes visible the many challenges in effectively addressing these issues.

GAO will continue our work on a wide range of issues relating to the preparation, response, recovery, and reconstruction efforts related to the

Enclosure I: Statement by Comptroller
General David M. Walker on GAO's
Preliminary Observations Regarding
Preparedness and Response to Hurricanes
Katrina and Rita

hurricanes that I have discussed today. We have over 30 engagements underway and look forward to reporting on them throughout 2006. We will provide Congress and the American people with a comprehensive summary of what went well and why, what did not go well and why, and what, if any, specific changes are called for in the National Response Plan.

General Counsel

U.S. Department of Homeland Security
Washington, DC 20528

February 8, 2006

J. Keith Ausbrook, Esq.
Chief Counsel
House Select Bipartisan Committee on Katrina
2157 Rayburn House Office Building
Washington, DC 20515

Dear Keith:

We appreciated the opportunity to visit with you to discuss Mr. Walker's and the General Accountability Office's "preliminary observations" on the Department of Homeland Security's performance during Hurricane Katrina. As the Secretary has previously testified, the Department is not satisfied with many aspects of response for Hurricane Katrina and is working to remedy shortfalls in advance of the coming hurricane season. There are many appropriate criticisms regarding federal, state and local government entities involved in Katrina. Our meeting, however, addressed Mr. Walker's investigative methodology and the fact that several of his "preliminary observations" are not founded in any factual record. In the interest of brevity, we summarize certain of those issues below.

Premature Conclusions. First, Mr. Walker reached and announced conclusions regarding the Department without speaking with people in the Department actually involved in the decision-making process. Mr. Walker acknowledges this in his printed statement, which we understand to have been released to the press the day before his press conference: He states that he has "interviewed officials and analyzed information from the various involved federal agencies such as FEMA and the Department of Defense (DOD)"—but conspicuous by its omission is the interview of any officials from DHS headquarters. Indeed, Mr. Walker acknowledges that his report is only preliminary by qualifying his conclusions by describing them as "key themes . . . [that] *seem* to be emerging." (*See* Statement by Comptroller General, Feb. 1, 2006, at 3 (emphasis added)).

We do not believe it appropriate to reach conclusions regarding decisions purportedly made by top Department officials, *without* first speaking with the key personnel at DHS. For example, Mr. Walker opines on the Department's interpretation and use of the National Response Plan ("NRP") during Katrina. Robert Stephan, who is now our Assistant Secretary for Infrastructure Protection,

www.dhs.gov

was an author of the NRP and advised DHS leadership on the NRP during Katrina. Mr. Stephan was never consulted by Mr. Walker or his staff.[1]

Misunderstanding of Basic Roles and Responsibilities. Mr. Walker states that "no one was designated in advance to lead the overall federal response in anticipation of the event. . . ." The statement demonstrates a lack of understanding of the roles and responsibilities of the FEMA Director. Once the President declared an emergency, Mr. Brown had the authority necessary to direct the assets of the federal government under the Stafford Act. And he was doing so: the transcript of the FEMA video teleconference from the day before landfall, Sunday, August 28, reveals that the States, including Louisiana, along with our federal partners, were in fact coordinating through the FEMA Director and, indeed, expressed satisfaction at the level of pre-landfall federal support.[2] In fact, it is undisputed that unprecedented quantities of assets were indeed pre-positioned prior to landfall. *See* Attachment A (listing certain assets prepositioned before Hurricane Katrina).

Mr. Walker's conclusion also implies that there was some unmet need in the days prior to landfall—that DHS did not "lean forward." However, even a quick reading on the August 28, 2005 FEMA video teleconference transcript would have revealed that the States expressed satisfaction with the federal pre-positioning of assets, that Louisiana reported that the evacuation was going well, and that DOD was fully engaged, among other things. (In fact, Louisiana's Colonel Smith *directly refutes* Mr. Walker's conclusion that DHS was not leaning forward. *See* Attachment B for text of the Video Conference from August 28, 2005.)

Misunderstanding of the NRP. Mr. Walker also concludes that it was a mistake not to employ the NRP's Catastrophic Incident Annex (CIA), which he believes would have accelerated the response. First, as DHS NRP experts have advised, neither the CIA nor the Catastrophic Incident Supplement (CIS) was applicable—these documents were designed for no notice or short-notice incidents where anticipatory preparation and coordination with the State under the Stafford Act are not practicable. Second, the implementation mechanism for the CIA, the CIS, was not in force, and had not been disseminated or trained on at the time of Katrina. Third, the Department already had authority to "push" assets to the field under the Stafford Act without formally utilizing the CIA or CIS. *See* Attachment B (Instruction from Mike Brown: "I want to see that supply chain jammed up just as much as possible. . . . Just keep jamming those [supply] lines full as much as you can with commodities.") As noted, Katrina has demonstrated certain weaknesses and ambiguities in the NRP, particularly with regard to the Federal response to catastrophic events where State and local response capabilities are severely affected. The Administration will be addressing these issues as part of its lessons learned process.

---

[1] Just one example of a simple problem that could have been repaired: in his second paragraph, Mr. Walker states that he interviewed the "primary federal official." Of course, the NRP refers to a "*principal* federal official," or PFO, but not a "*primary* federal official." Additionally, as there were two PFOs named during Katrina response, it is unclear to whom he is referring.

[2] Mr. Walker did not request, and we have no indication that Mr. Walker has ever reviewed, this or any other FEMA VTC transcript.

Finally, Mr. Walker raises the issue of the declaration of an incident of national significance. The language of the NRP provides that ". . . all Presidentially declared disasters and emergencies under the Stafford Act are Incidents of National Significance. . . ." Secretary Chertoff's prior testimony before your committee already explained the purpose of the August 30 memorandum naming Mr. Brown as PFO. Of course, the Administration is continuing to review the language of the NRP to address any ambiguities or uncertainties in the use of particular terms.

Coast Guard. Mr. Walker gives well-deserved credit to the Coast Guard as a "federal responder . . . [that] 'lean[ed] forward' in proactive efforts anticipating a major disaster." In criticizing DHS, he fails to recognize that the Coast Guard is indeed part of this Department, and that the Secretary was in communication with the Coast Guard about their important life-saving efforts during Katrina. We refer you to the Secretary's testimony on this point.[3]

Preparedness and Planning. Mr. Walker points out that "training and exercises necessary to carry out these plans were not always developed or completed among the first responder community." Upon taking the helm of the Department, the Secretary recognized that preparedness required retooling and proposed, in the Department's Second Stage Review, that a new preparedness directorate be established. Because of the statutory 60-day waiting period, these changes were not in place at the time Katrina struck. Mr. Walker's report does not mention the pre-hurricane fixes proposed by the Secretary in 2SR, and his report is lacking for that reason as well.

We would be pleased to discuss any of these critiques with you in greater detail.

Sincerely,

Philip J. Perry
General Counsel

---

[3] "[O]ne of the things that I spoke to the Coast Guard at one point about was the need to make sure we were mapping areas where people might have just spontaneously collected to make sure we could get them food and water." *See* Secretary's Testimony to Committee (Oct. 19, 2005).

Exhibit A

Water (1 trucks = (approximately) 18,000 liters)

    5 trailers at Superdome = 90,000 liters of water

    211 trailers pre-staged around region = 3,789,000 liters of water

        39 trailers Beauregard, LA (702,000 liters)

        40 trailers Meridian, MS (720,000 liters)

        53 trailers Maxwell, AL (954,000 liters)

        20 trailers Saufley Field, FL (360,000 liters)

        29 trailers Homestead, FL (522,000 liters)

        30 trailers Mc Entire, SC (540,000 liters)

Ice (1 truck = (approximately) 40,000 pounds)

    114 trailers pre-staged around region = 4,560,000 pounds of ice

        22 trailers Beauregard, LA (880,000 pounds)

        16 trailers Maxwell AL (640,000 pounds)

        21 trailers Meridian, MS (840,000 pounds)

        54 trailers Craig Field/Selma AL (2,160,000 pounds)

        1 trailer Barksdale, LA (40,000 pounds)

    325 trailers in Cold Storage = 13,000,000 pounds ice in Cold Storage

        230 trailers Thomasville, GA (9,200,000 pounds)

        25 trailers Montgomery, AL (1,000,000 pounds)

        17 trailers Alexandria, LA (680,000 pounds)

        8 trailers Fort Worth, TX (320,000 pounds)

        45 trailers San Antonio, TX (1,800,000 pounds)

Meals Ready to Eat (MREs) (1 trucks = (approximately) 21,888 MREs)

    2 trailers Superdome (43,776)

    85 trailers pre-staged around region = 1,860,480 MREs pre-staged

        14 trailers Beauregard (306,432)

        30 trailers Maxwell, AL (656,640)

        10 trailers Meridian, MS (218,880)

        10 trailers Saufley, FL (218,880)

        15 trailers Homestead, FL (328,320)

        6 trailers Mc Entire, SC (131,328)

    97 trailers in Logistic Centers = 2,123,136 MREs pre-staged

        5 trailers Atlanta, GA (109,440)

        46 trailers Palmetto, GA (1,006,848)

        42 trailers Ft. Worth, TX (919,296)

        4 trailers Moffett, CA (87,552)

Logistics Center Rockville Shipments:

August 27th

    Three staging areas identified; Houston, TX; Memphis, TN; and Anniston, AL

        0800 hrs: Packaged and shipped 4 Patient Treatment Caches and 4 Pharmaceutical Caches to Houston, TX

        1750 hrs: Packaged and shipped 2 Patient Treatment Caches and 2 Pharmaceutical Caches to Memphis, TN

2000 hrs: Packaged and shipped 3 Patient Treatment Caches, 3 Pharmaceutical Caches and one Veterinary Medical Assistance Team (VMAT) Cache to Anniston, AL

August 28th

1300 hrs: Management Support Team (MST) Cache left LC-Frederick

1800 hrs: Packaged and shipped 3 Patient Treatment Caches and 3 Pharmaceutical Caches to Ft. McClellan, AL

2000 hrs: Packaged and shipped 3 additional Patient Treatment Caches and 3 additional Pharmaceutical Caches to Memphis, TN

August 29th

0130 hrs: Packaged and shipped 3 additional Patient Treatment Caches and 3 Pharmaceutical Caches to Memphis, TN

1000 hrs: Loaded on trailers and shipped 1 Disaster Portable Mortuary Unit (DPMU)

MOBILE EMERGENCY COMMUNICATIONS SUPPORT FOR HURRICANE KATRINA

As of August 29th, 2005:

All available MERS assets committed to Hurricane Katrina

MERS Denton, TX

Staged at Barksdale AFB; RNA and JFO build out team in LA EOC, Baton Rouge, LA

MERS Denver, CO

Convoys continue

MERS Maynard, MA

Equipment staged at McGee-Tyson

MERS Thomasville, GA

NDMS supported in Jackson, MS, all other sites operational

MERS Bothell, WA

Deploys additional equipment en route to LA

2000 hrs: Packaged and shipped 3 Patient Treatment Caches, 3 Pharmaceutical Caches and one Veterinary Medical Assistance Team (VMAT) Cache to Anniston, AL
August 28th
1300 hrs: Management Support Team (MST) Cache left LC-Frederick
1800 hrs: Packaged and shipped 3 Patient Treatment Caches and 3 Pharmaceutical Caches to Ft. McClellan, AL
2000 hrs: Packaged and shipped 3 additional Patient Treatment Caches and 3 additional Pharmaceutical Caches to Memphis, TN
August 29th
0130 hrs: Packaged and shipped 3 additional Patient Treatment Caches and 3 Pharmaceutical Caches to Memphis, TN
1000 hrs: Loaded on trailers and shipped 1 Disaster Portable Mortuary Unit (DPMU)

MOBILE EMERGENCY COMMUNICATIONS SUPPORT FOR HURRICANE KATRINA
As of August 29th, 2005:
All available MERS assets committed to Hurricane Katrina
MERS Denton, TX
Staged at Barksdale AFB; RNA and JFO build out team in LA EOC, Baton Rouge, LA
MERS Denver, CO
Convoys continue
MERS Maynard, MA
Equipment staged at McGee-Tyson
MERS Thomasville, GA
NDMS supported in Jackson, MS, all other sites operational
MERS Bothell, WA
Deploys additional equipment en route to LA

Exhibit B

Excerpts from August 28, 2005 videoteleconference:

MIKE BROWN: Okay. We'll move on now to the states. Louisiana?

COLONEL SMITH: Good morning, Mike. This is Colonel Jeff Smith here in Louisiana. We certainly appreciate those comments from the President, because I can tell you that our Governor is very concerned about the potential loss of life here with our citizens, and **she is very appreciative of the federal resources that have come into the state and the willingness to give us everything you've got**, because, again, we're very concerned with this.

I'm going to turn the briefing over for a moment to our Operations Officer, just to kind of give you a quick laydown of things. This is Colonel Bill Doriant.

COLONEL DORIANT: The Emergency Operations Center is at a Level 1, which is the highest state of readiness. We've got currently 11 parishes with evacuations, and climbing. Eight are mandatory, including a first-ever mandatory for New Orleans. We've got 38 parish declarations of emergency; also the state declaration and the Presidential declaration of emergency.

Evacuations are underway currently. We're planning for a catastrophic event, which we have been planning for, thanks to the help of FEMA, when we did the Hurricane Pam exercises. So we're way ahead of the game there.

Our priorities right now are sheltering, and then planning for search and rescue and commodities distribution after recovery.

That's all I have at this time.

COLONEL SMITH: I'll just tell you that the evacuation process is going much better than it did during Hurricane Ivan. Nobody anticipated that it would be easy. Nobody anticipated that there wouldn't be traffic jams. But by and large, it has gone much better than it did with Ivan. And, of course, we still have a contraflow in effect at this particular point in time, and we do still have heavy traffic coming out of New Orleans, but by and large that process is going very well.

We have established a unified command here with our federal coordinating officer. Our ERD-A team, ERD-N team is on the ground here. And, again, as our Operations Officer pointed out, we're spending a lot of time right now with the search and rescue, making sure that we marry the appropriate state assets and the federal assets, so we can have an effective search and rescue effort just as quickly as possible.

We're also taking a look at our sheltering needs, long-term sheltering needs, looking at sites to start bringing in the temporary housing. So we're not only fighting the current battle, managing expectations here with our local parishes, but we are also working with FEMA and our other federal partners to have the most effective response and recovery that we possibly can during this time.

So, again, I want to say thank you very much for all that you're doing. I think that at this point in time our coordination is as good as it can be, and we just very much appreciate the President and your commitments to resourcing our needs down here.

Any questions that you have, we'd be glad to take them now, unless you want to hold that until later. That's your call, Mike.

MIKE BROWN: Any questions? Colonel, **do you have any unmet needs, anything that we're not getting to you that you need or --**

COLONEL SMITH: **Mike, no.** (Inaudible) resources that are en route, and it looks like those resources that are en route are going to -- to be a good first shot. Naturally, once we get into this thing, you know, neck deep here, unfortunately, or deeper, I'm sure that things are going to come up that maybe some of even our best planners hadn't even thought about. So I think flexibility is going to be the key.

And just as quickly as we can cut through any potential red tape when those things do arise, you know, we just need to look at it. **We appreciate your comments. I think they were to lean as far, far as you possibly can, you know, without falling, and your people here are doing that.** And that's the type of attitude that we need in an event like this.

So, again, thank you very much.

MIKE BROWN: All right. I'll be in Baton Rouge probably about 4:00 this afternoon, so I'll see you sometime this evening.

*　　*　　*

MIKE BROWN: Any questions? (Missing) on the commodities that **I want to see that supply chain jammed up just as much as possible.** I mean, I want stuff (missing) than we need. Just keep jamming those lines full as much as you can with commodities.

My gut tells me we're -- that's going to be one of our biggest needs. So just (missing) up tight.

*　　*　　*

SECRETARY CHERTOFF: (Inaudible.) Yes. Hi, this is Secretary Chertoff. And, again, as it relates to the entire department, **if there's anything that you need from Coast Guard or any other components that you're not getting, please let us know.** We'll do that for you, OK.

MIKE BROWN: I appreciate it. (Missing.) Having been through many of these, the Coast Guard and ICE and all of the others have been incredibly good to us. And I hope we never have to call you and tell you that I can't get help from the Coast Guard or somebody. Thank you for those comments.

SECRETARY CHERTOFF: Secondly, **are there any DOD assets that might be available.** Have we reached out to them, and have we I guess made any kind of arrangement in case we need some additional help from them?

MIKE BROWN: We have DOD assets over here at the EOC. They are fully engaged, and we are having those discussions with them now.

Supplementary Report

to the Findings of the
Select Bipartisan Committee to Investigate
the Preparation for and Response to
Hurricane Katrina

Presented by the Select Committee on behalf of
Rep. Cynthia A. McKinney

Submitted this Monday, February 6, 2006

"Struggle is a never ending process.
Freedom is never really won.
You earn it and win it in every generation."

~ Coretta Scott King (1927-2006)

Contents

challenge faced by those dealing directly with the aftermath of the greatest natural disaster in our nation's history.

Government failed the people of the Gulf Coast. That appears to be the overriding theme of the Report. It is not something we did not know. We all saw it on our television screens. But the Report of the Select Committee is stunning for presenting us with a laundry list of failures. This must be qualified, of course, to acknowledge two major successes of government in this catastrophe. First, the largest pre-storm evacuation in our nation's history went of splendidly well for the millions who had the means to evacuate. Second is the heroic performance of first responders, the Coast Guard in particular, in rescuing tens of thousands of residents stranded in their homes. Their courage and dedication is truly to be commended.

Yet putting these two successes together, we immediately see that because the evacuation plan simply did not encompass those without their own means to evacuate, namely those living near or below the poverty line, without this major failing of an otherwise stunningly successful plan, there would not have been such an urgent need for rescue teams to conduct their daring feats of bravery.

The greater failure was the government's delayed and confused response. In general, poor coordination, poor planning and execution, and inadequate efforts at communication are cited in the Select Committee Report as causes of this failure. On its own terms, the Report also does a fair job of balancing, on the one hand, the fact that Hurricane Katrina simply overwhelmed existing capacity of the Federal Emergency Management Agency (FEMA), as well as relief organizations such as the Red Cross to cope with the scale of the catastrophe, with the overall inadequacy of preparation and planning.

Even more pointed is the Committee's conclusion that the lessons learned from the "Hurricane Pam" planning and preparedness exercise conducted in July 2004 were not applied to the response to Hurricane Katrina. The Hurricane Pam exercise was specifically designed to develop planning and response to a catastrophic hurricane hitting the Louisiana coast. It anticipated a scenario even worse than what actually happened before and after Hurricane Katrina. Given "Pam's striking resemblance to Katrina in force and devastation," the Report concludes, "many have been left wondering at the failure to anticipate, and plan for…essentials." Going back further, at a recent press conference, David Walker, Comptroller and head of the Government Accountability Office (GAO) stated that the GAO had made recommendations in the wake of hurricane Andrew in 1992, and that to date most of those recommendations had not been followed up on.[2]

After so many tens of billions of dollars have been spent in establishing and maintaining a new super-agency, the Department of Homeland Security, attentive Americans must ask not only how such a stunning failure of government response to a natural disaster is possible, but also how it is possible that in the process of expending vast sums on new bureaucratic infrastructure charged with enhancing our safety we now learn that lessons of the past were ignored in a way that led directly to the scenario of the present failure. The Committee's Report offers at least a large part of the answer when it points repeatedly to a failure to take initiative, which can easily be interpreted as a failure of leadership. As we read in the Report:

...a dispassionate review made it clear that even an extraordinary lack of situational awareness could not excuse the feckless, flailing, and organizational paralysis evident in the documents and communications the Committee reviewed.

Leadership requires decisions to be made even when based on flawed and incomplete information. Too often during the immediate response to Katrina, sparse or conflicting information was used as an excuse for inaction rather than an imperative to step in and fill an obvious vacuum.

This brings us to the content of the present report. Surprising as the quote above may be, coming from the Majority Party, it remains in keeping with the overall approach of many previous investigations into government failures, because it seeks to address the problem in predominantly bureaucratic terms. Over the years, there has been an almost cyclical pattern of crises or scandals followed by investigations that point out failures, followed by calls for bureaucratic reform.[3] Just as the 9/11 Commission called for a new czar to fight terrorism and got it, the call has already gone out in response to the failure of Hurricane Katrina for the selection of a right-hand man or woman to be the President's point person in coordinating natural disasters.[4] Yet it becomes clear as we proceed that the Secretary of Homeland Security had this authority and failed to exercise it in this disaster.

In this report we are less interested in engaging in a debate about what bureaucratic reforms are needed to fix the problem for the future than we are in addressing areas of omission in the Select Committee Report. In general, the Select Committee Report does not seem to acknowledge the full ramifications of Hurricane Katrina, and the way in which it represents a watershed moment for our nation. The testimony taken by the Select Committee was overwhelmingly from public officials, and this gave undue place to issues of personal and bureaucratic success or failure. The hearings took place during a period of intense confusion and agony for displaced survivors, who often spoke of bewilderment at the *ongoing* failure of the government to act. Moreover, while the Report cites agencies at all levels of government for failure, it generally omits the failure of *the White House or Congress* to respond to the long-term crisis which, collectively, Hurricane Katrina, the levee failures, and the inadequate response have spawned.

The death toll from Katrina stands at over 1,300. But the more astonishing figure is the number of missing, which varies between 3,000 and 6,600 souls, depending upon the source. According to the U.S. Department of Health and Human Services, about 500,000 people, including survivors and those who came to their rescue, may need mental health services.[5] The term "Katrina Stress" has become current, and the level of suicide among survivors is reportedly very high. Calls to the National Suicide Prevention hot line more than doubled in September of 2005,[6] and have stayed high.

Tens of thousands of evacuees living in hotels and motels with their accommodations provided by FEMA face eviction on March 1, 2006. Many have already been evicted. Attorneys for the Lawyers' Committee on Civil Rights have expressed concern that unless urgent action is taken, we may soon see a new class of "Katrina Homeless" in America.

1. HURRICANE KATRINA, POVERTY AND RACISM

Poverty and Race in New Orleans

Before Hurricane Katrina, there was another hurricane, a slow-moving economic hurricane bringing greater levels of poverty to the working-class cities like New Orleans. 2005 was the fourth consecutive year of increasing poverty in America, with one million additional Americans falling below the poverty line.[13] Seventy per cent of employees in the New Orleans Metropolitan Area are (or were) working class, defined as "those people with relatively little power at work" and whose incomes are typically below $40,000 per year. Poverty is something that happens to working class people, not middle class or corporate elite people. Specifically, those employed in the lowest-paid occupations such as health support, "food preparation, building maintenance, personal care, and sales" may have "occupations that pay from $12,000 to around $18,000 a year—at best not enough to bring a family of four out of poverty."[14] Being poor does not mean someone is not working. It means that a family is not earning enough income to really get by.

Below is a table of the 2004 demographics for employed adults from selected parishes within Metro New Orleans:

New Orleans Metropolitan Area: White and Minority Working Adults[15]				
Parish	White	%	Minority	%
Jefferson	155,422	74%	54,654	26%
Orleans	**64,066**	**34%**	**123,689**	**66%**
Placquemines	8,030	77%	2,050	23%
St. Bernard	25,959	90%	2,787	10%
St. Charles	16,776	77%	5,072	23%
St. James	5,072	56%	3,997	44%
St. John the Baptist	11,358	59%	7,890	41%
St. Tammany	80,178	89%	9,838	11%

In the 2000 census, over 67 % of the population of the City of New Orleans (Orleans Parish) was African-American, 28% were white, 3% Latino and 1.28% "of two races," perhaps representing the "Creole" population. [16] Creoles have historically been a privileged group within New Orleans Society, and the Mayor of New Orleans since 1978 has been a person of color, or rather a "creole of color." Ernest Nathan Morial (1978-1986), Sidney Barthelemy (1986-1994), Marc Morial (1994-2002) and C. Ray Nagin (2002-) have all been light-skinned Creoles. But outside of New Orleans they are widely perceived as black. The percentage of minorities (most of whom are black) living below the poverty line in the City of New Orleans is of course higher than the number of poor whites. But it may be surprising to some to learn that *for the Greater New Orleans Area in the wake of Katrina, a greater number of whites (85,000) live below the poverty line than do minorities (65,000).*

When the levees broke, the flooding in the City of New Orleans became the focus of media attention, and while other parishes experienced major flooding, Orleans Parish was hit the worst. With two thirds of the population of Orleans Parish being African-American, media cameras portrayed a situation where blacks were the primary victims. The drama unfolding in the City of New Orleans drew attention away from the complete destruction of Placquemines Parish which, stretching south along the Mississippi and surrounding wetlands, took the brunt of the storm surge, and the equally devastating flooding of St. Bernard's Parish.

Yet low income whites are not the only ones who experienced this invisibility. 124,000 Latinos made up three per cent of Louisiana's population. Throughout the Gulf Coast Region some 145,000 Mexicans live and work, and 40,000 Mexicans were displaced by Katrina out of New Orleans alone. Native Americans along the coast were hit terribly hard, including:

> the Parch Band Creek Indian Tribe in Alabama; the Coushatta Indian Tribe, Jena Band of Choctaw, and the Tunica-Biloxi Tribe in Mississippi. For one tribe near Chalmette, Louisiana, the local high school served as a tribal morgue, holding the bodies of Native American workers, including shrimpers and other fishermen, who were drowned in the flooding of New Orleans.[17]

Dr. Robin Rose of Oregon has been trying to get assistance for three small native groups in southern Mississippi had their communities literally washed away in the storm surge: the Pointe ou chien Tribe, the Iles des Jean-Charles Tribe and the Band of the Biloxi Chittamach are all tribes registered with the state, but because they have not been able to get Federal recognition, federal assistance has not been forthcoming.

Nearly 50,000 Vietnamese fisherman in Louisiana and the oldest community of Filipino shrimpers in the North America were displaced by the storm.[18] We heard very little about any of these peoples on *CNN* or *Fox* or *ABC*.

After the Select Committee Delegation stopped to visit the breach at the Industrial Canal along the western edge of the Lower Ninth Ward, where we witnessed the total destruction that was unleashed when the levee broke, releasing a twenty foot wall of water that leveled the immediate neighborhood (taking the highest death toll), our bus drove eastward to St. Bernard's Parish where the damage was basically just as severe. We were joined on the bus by St. Bernard Parish President, Junior Rodriguez, who told us that of over 6,000 homes in the parish, only four were not heavily damaged by the flood. Debris was everywhere and only a few homes were occupied. President Rodriguez did not mince words with our delegation, and he spelled out all the problems and runaround he was facing in dealing with FEMA, problems very similar to those facing the residents of Orleans Parish.[19]

The suffering of the residents of St. Bernard's parish, where 90% of the residents are white, draws to our attention to the fact that poverty is not racially specific, and nor is the vulnerability associated with it. When ex-FEMA Director Michael Brown testified before the Select Committee, Rep. Gene Taylor of Mississippi asked if he realized that Katrina hit at the end of the month, and that many of those living on fixed incomes, such as retirees, had already made their monthly purchases, and might not have foreseen the need to keep their gas tank full for the possibility of an evacuation. Taylor suggested that FEMA did not take into consideration that many of those who stayed behind, black and white, were persons of limited means. Poverty increases a person's likelihood of being a victim during the storm, and after.

Income or class divisions in America increasingly cut across ethnic and racial divisions. Consider that while minorities make up 37% of the workforce in the New Orleans Metropolitan Area, minorities hold fully 26% of higher-paying managerial and professional jobs. **_Across the United States, 75% of minorities do NOT live below the poverty line_**. Moreover, of the all those who do live below the poverty line in America, two-thirds are white. "Racism continues to operate and accounts for the fact that poverty is experienced _disproportionately_ among blacks and Hispanics (and among women because of sexism). But we should not allow this comparatively heavy burden among minorities to blind us to the full realities of poverty in America."[20]

Racial Stereotyping and Racism

Hurricane Rita didn't care if you were rich or poor, as the equal destruction of the homes of the very wealthy and working class residents of the Mississippi coast will testify. But the flooding of New Orleans—because it hit predominantly African-American neighborhoods the worst, and because poverty _is_ highest among blacks—seemed to reinforce widely held preconceptions that equate being "poor" with being "black." There was justifiable frustration expressed by many whites at the way the media shaped perceptions of the disaster by focusing on black poverty and black suffering while lower income whites in both rural and urban areas felt abandoned by emergency responders, as in many cases they were. Hurricane Rita, which struck the coasts of Texas and Louisiana on September 24, 2005, did little damage to cities or oil refineries, but it caused significant new flooding in rural areas and in other areas exacerbated rural flooding initially resulting from Hurricane Katrina, devastating many rural and mostly white communities and causing significant damage to hospitals. Undoubtedly part of the reason for a delay in meeting the needs of these communities was that responders were still overwhelmed by the magnitude of Katrina's impact.

At the same time, however, attributing black suffering primarily to poverty not only reinforces negative racial stereotypes of blacks, it also makes it very frustrating for blacks and other minority persons who have been the victims of treatment motivated by racial hatred if all of their suffering is simply attributed to their poverty, which is already assumed. The media coverage of the aftermath of the hurricane tended to reinforce such racial stereotypes of Blacks. For example, in one of his running commentaries, _CNN_ anchor Wolf Blitzer stated: "You simply get the chills every time you see these poor individuals …so many of these people, almost all of them we see, are so poor and they are so black."[21]

Racial stereotyping was starkly evident in the use of the term "refugees" that was typically used to describe black residents seeking to evacuate. The term "refugee" denotes a person crossing a national border in search of security. Thus the use of the term "refugee" to describe survivors may have served to create confusion in the minds of casual observers of television reports, by equating them with, for example, Haitian refugees seeking asylum in the United States, wave after wave of whom have been historically denied their requests for asylum. Workers and volunteers at evacuation shelters in Louisiana and Texas "heard loud and clear from those living there that the government, the media and everyone else should call them something other than refugees. 'We ain't refugees. I'm a citizen,' insists Annette Ellis." One day, after getting an earful from a crowd of 800 at the Bethany World Prayer Center in Baker, Louisiana, President Bush went live on television to urge the practice be stopped.[22] Usage of the term "refugee" fell precipitously. Here we must commend the President for at least taking some initiative.

Another area of apparent racial stereotyping involves reports of widespread looting. While blacks who commandeered supplies during the storm were called "looters", at least one television report showed white survivors "taking" supplies from a store. *USA Today* quoted one resident who compared the looters to cockroaches.[23] Most incidents of the goods taken during the storm were taken to address human needs in a crisis. Food and clothing were stolen for family and neighbors. Doctors who raided pharmacies for medicines to treat their patients are praised in the *Select Committee Report*. Dire circumstances make for dire methods. However, as one commentator writes, even violent crimes were undertaken for reasons that are understandable, given the circumstances. "Carjackers were looking for cars to get out. Pirates were looking for boats." Looting has occurred in many previous crises. Yet it was clear from their statements that neither none of the major players from Bush to Chertoff to Governor Blanco were prepared for Hurricane Katrina.

> I don't mean that they failed to anticipate the magnitude of the flooding; we knew that already. I mean that they have no idea how easily a natural disaster can turn human beings into a second-wave destructive force. They don't understand that disasters often bring out the worst in us, that the human dynamics are collective, and that 'responsibility' is quickly swamped. If you don't understand these dynamics, you can't plan for them. You end up pleading for 'personal responsibility' when what you needed was air drops and the National Guard.

> It's not like this hasn't happened before. The 1977 New York City blackout led to an epidemic of stealing. The mayor of Charleston, [South Carolina], during Hurricane Hugo says FEMA was clueless about law and order during that 1989 crisis. He thinks we need a military unit to take charge of these situations. That may be going a bit far, but we certainly need to think more systematically about the human dynamics of natural disasters. We run computer models of hurricanes, levee breaches, and flooding. What about isolation, desperation, looting, fighting, and shooting? It took the mayor of New Orleans three days to tell his cops to switch from rescue operations to controlling post-hurricane crime. Why? Because crime wasn't in the model.[24]

<u>Recommendation: When the *National Response Plan* and/or other disaster preparedness plans are revised, they need to be updated to anticipate looting as a highly probable and often rational</u>

response to scarcity by individuals in an emergency. Rights of property must not supersede the right to food, water and medicine, i.e. the right to survive, especially not during a declared emergency.

After Katrina, as the media hyped up reports of looting and presented black looting as mindless thuggery, an overall climate of fear was created, causing responders from both relief and law enforcement units, including the National Guard, to delay entry.

There still seem to be conflicting accounts of the level of street violence during the storm. The rumor of children being raped in the Superdome does indeed appear to have been just a wild rumor. But our office has received numerous calls claiming that some of the accounts that have now been dismissed as unsubstantiated by the media. One source says women at the Convention Center witnessed rapes, that women made sure to sit in groups, that inside the Convention Center, where it was pitch black, escaped prisoners roamed freely, and that at the height of it, only eight police officers were present before the rescue. During the Committee Delegation's meeting with first responders, the officer in charge of Special Forces at the Convention Center was asked how many people died. He could not say, he told us, but his men did remove any number of bodies, some with stab wounds. Survivors with direct experience who we have talked to are often loathe to get into the details, simply describing the conditions inside the Superdome or the Convention Center as "very bad."

Below we will also discuss below prisoners who had to escape from prisons in order to save their lives because they were left to die in the floodwaters. Regardless, the absence of any Federal forces on the ground in New Orleans for over a week, when National Guard forces were overstretched, left the situation in chaos.

Barbara Arnwine, President of the Lawyers Committee on Civil Rights, in testifying before the Select Committee, commented on the impact of rumors and stereotyping by saying that it is typical for rumors to spread in a crisis, but that in the case of Hurricane Katrina the rumors were racially charged. They amounted to allegations of massive criminal and subhuman activities by blacks. The rumors instilled fear and panic in aid workers, who then became reluctant to enter African-American communities to provide assistance. Ms. Arnwine believes that had their been a strong Federal presence sooner, providing security and communications, the rumors would have quickly died down.

Ms. Arnwine also noted that this did not apply only to New Orleans. Communities throughout the Gulf Coast Region saw no presence of staff from FEMA or its principal subcontractor, the Red Cross, for as long weeks after the storm in some cases. She pointed out that the majority African-American residents of Gulfport, Mississippi, a town whose majority of African-American residents have long been familiar with racial stereotyping and governmental indifference, were essentially overlooked by the Red Cross, which preferred to establish its operations either in white towns or in the white part of town. Thus African-American churches came to the rescue of those hardest hit by the storm, using their limited resources to provide food and medicine, as well as shelter and transportation.[25] Given the scale of need, some churches went bankrupt. Although a Federal policy was established to compensate the churches for their losses, Arnwine told the Committee that poor communication and racist assumptions concerning the likelihood of fraud have made it virtually impossible for these churches to get reimbursed.

Recommendation: FEMA or any agency that replaces it must be directed to produce impact and implementation policy studies aimed at producing emergency preparedness and response policies that address the particular needs of minority communities.

Recommendation: Congress should pass legislation to set procedures for protecting the civil liberties of minorities during an emergency situation. Armed forces and police should be on notice that individual acts of blatant discrimination or abuse of minorities will result in serious punishments, and systemic abuse will result in loss of financial support. Private relief organizations with discriminatory relief practices should be subject to review and possible loss of contracts.

FEMA's website directs viewers to support Operation Blessing, a $66 million dollar relief organization founded by religious businessman Pat Robertson. Shortly after Hurricane Katrina hit, Operation Blessing was featured prominently on FEMA's list of charitable organizations taking donations.[26] Only a week before Katrina hit, Robertson was brazenly calling for the assassination of a sitting head of state: Hugo Chavez of Venezuela. "We have the ability to take [Chavez] out, and I think the time has come that we exercise that ability," said Robertson.[27] When Ariel Sharon suffered a stroke in January, Robertson expressed similar ill, suggesting God had smote the Israeli Prime Minister when he told his television viewers: "He was dividing God's land, and I would say, 'Woe unto any prime minister of Israel who takes a similar course to appease the [European Union], the United Nations or the United States of America.'"[28] How can FEMA in good conscience direct traumatized disaster survivors into the hands of an organization run by a man who so plainly advocates murder by assassination and wishes death upon the suffering? We have no idea what Mr. Robertson did with the money, but we know this: Operation Blessing didn't show up to help out in mostly African-American neighborhoods.

In fact, African-Americans in New Orleans were on their own, much as the *Times-Picayune* predicted they would be. Writing in July 2005 the paper wrote:

> City, state and federal emergency officials are preparing to give the poorest of New Orleans' poor a historically blunt message: In the event of a major hurricane, you're on your own. In scripted appearances being recorded now, officials such as Mayor Ray Nagin, local Red Cross Executive Director Kay Wilkins and City Council President Oliver Thomas drive home the word that the city does not have the resources to move out of harm's way an estimated 134,000 people without transportation.[29]

Recommendation: Future emergency preparedness planning must include the provision of transportation for the elderly, the infirm and those without their own means of locomotion, as well as the placing of Disaster Recovery Centers (DRCs) as near as is feasible, to enable these evacuees to return to their homes as quickly and easily as possible.

When the storm hit, residents of Algiers, a mostly African-American community just north of Gretna, and of the Lower Ninth Ward, formed their own relief organization: the Common Ground Relief Collective (CGRC), in the absence of private of public relief assistance. On September 5th, a week after Katrina made landfall, local Algiers activist Malik Rahim and three of his colleagues started their efforts with just $50.

Mr. Rahim's name was among those on a list of speakers which our office suggested speakers for hearings, should any be held during the Select Committee's Delegation to the Gulf Coast on January 19-20, 2006. As the Select Committee elected not to hold hearings, we arranged a community event at a local church to take the testimony of the speakers.[30]

Sakure Kone, a member of CGRC spoke on behalf of Mr. Rahim at our meeting, and the section that follows is draw from his comments.

In flooded Algiers, the needs of the people were vast. The only thing working was the telephone. No stores, hospitals or clinics were open and there was no presence by officials. Malik Rahim put out a call by phone to his contacts across the country. Initially, paramedics arrived and met immediate needs by making door-to-door house calls. Mr. Rahim belonged to a local mosque: Mosque Bilal. At Mr. Rahim's suggestion, the officials at the mosque opened its doors to the public to serve as a free medical clinic. As more doctors, nurses and med students showed up to volunteer, the clinic became fully operational, seeing between 120 and 125 patients per day. The call had also gone out for food and water and these began arriving from all over the country. Mr. Rahim then set up a distribution center in his own home. To meet the intense demand, another distribution center and clinic was established across the river in the Lower Ninth Ward.

CGRC held discussions with government officials, but no governmental assistance to these efforts was forthcoming, perhaps due to CGRC's "no strings attached" policy with regard to assistance. "We were there for one purpose and one purpose only," said Kone, "and that is to meet the health, food and water needs of the community." Since September 5th, CGRC's volunteers have numbered 800, with 350 on hand as of January 19th, and a thousand more expected during spring break. CGRC currently serves over 300 meals at a time to local residents, and its volunteers have gutted, sanitized and refurbished dozens of homes, including homes in the Lower Ninth Ward that the City of New Orleans says it intends to bulldoze, though a court injunction has put a temporary halt on this.[31]

Stephen Bradbury also spoke at our New Orleans community meeting on January 19th, 2006. Bradbury works with the Association of Community Organizations for Reform Now (ACORN), which like CGRC helped to fill the needs of residents in the absence of public and private assistance in mostly African-American communities. Like CGRC, ACORN has undertaken the task of organizing volunteers to gut mold-infested houses gutting, seeking to refurbish a thousand houses by March 31st, 2006 as a first step toward allowing people to come back.

According to Mr. Bradbury, ACORN's focus since Hurricane Katrina has been to address three areas in which the rights of hurricane survivors have been or are still being violated:

1. <u>Right of access to information</u>: Federal, state and local governments have not stepped in to assist survivors to keep abreast of what is going on in their home. To meet this need, ACORN has set up the ACORN Katrina Survivors' Association, with centers in many of the cities where survivors were evacuated to.

2. <u>Right of return</u>: Government has a responsibility to try and ensure that those displaced by a natural disaster are located as close to their homes as possible. Yet not only were Katrina survivors evacuated to 44 states, some as far away as Washington State, but there has been a lack of interest in getting people back home, and survivors are being enticed to remain where they have been evacuated with everything from housing vouchers, clothing vouchers, Wal-Mart cards and so on. People relocated within Louisiana had a hard time even locating the Red Cross, unless they were in a shelter.

3. <u>Right to participate in decision-making</u>: ACORN is working on a daily basis to try to ensure people can come home and have a voice in decision-making. Government has an obligation to ensure that people have a role in the decision-making around the re-building of their homes "and that has not occurred in any way, shape or form." Neither the Governor's Commission, nor the Mayor's Committee had input from residents from low and moderate income families or from people who were not in New Orleans. The School Board has recently flaunted this by going ahead and saying that we will just be an all-charter school system, without input from the majority of people who will be impacted by their decision.

Mama D (Dyan French Cole) testified to the Select Committee about how she stayed at her residence throughout the disaster. Throughout the ordeal, she took in large numbers of evacuees and setting up a makeshift clinic with a local nurse on call to address illnesses. For this she was recognized by *CNN* as one of "Katrina's Heroes."

Many Americans may imagine that the functions performed by African-American churches and community self-help groups were actually provided by FEMA or the Red Cross. Where African-American survivors did get real outside help was after relocation, as Mr. Bradbury pointed out above. But the rumors and stereotypes that had been played up in the media followed them, and some were met with racism as renters refused to rent to "New Orleanians." Attacks against survivors have been reported in several cities.[32]

Many African-Americans and others are skeptical about the way in which families were split up and put on planes without being told where they were going, sending the African-American community from New Orleans into Diaspora. We must ask *qui bono*? Who benefits? In its eagerness to bulldoze the Lower Ninth Ward even as bodies are still being discovered in the debris, the Government of the City of New Orleans has been in a running legal battle with lawyers representing the displaced. It appears as if the City can scarcely wait to wipe the slate clean, deprive long-standing residents of their property rights, declare eminent domain and hand the survivors' property over to developers. It also seems clear that African-American communities are primarily the ones being targeted.

ASHÉ CULTURAL ARTS CENTER/BABA TUNJI

Patricia Thompson testified before the Select Committee that she was invited to evacuate before the storm but would not leave her daughters. During the flood, she gathered her children and grandchildren, fearing to lose them because some could not swim.

> We were told to go to the Superdome, the Convention Center, the interstate bridge for safety. We did this more than once. In fact, we tried them all for every day over a week. We saw buses, helicopters and FEMA trucks, but no one stopped to help us. We never felt so cut off in all our lives... We slept next to dead bodies, we slept on streets at least four times next to human feces and urine. There was garbage everywhere in the city. Panic and fear had taken over. The way we were treated by police was demoralizing and inhuman. We were cursed when we asked for help for our elderly, we had guns aimed at us by the police who are supposed to be there to protect and serve. They made everybody sit on the ground with their hands in the air, even babies... My 5-year-old granddaughter cried and asked her mama if she was doing right. I know the police were scared, but they had no right to treat everyone like hardened criminals.

Mama D asked the Committee why the responders showed up pulling guns on the survivors. "We had to hide. I didn't leave. We had to hide to save people," she said. "Police brutality? We are used to it."

Carla Nelson was a resident of Algiers, a mostly black community in Jefferson Parish. When lights and power were lost at her residence she and her family sought refuge. They learned on the radio that buses were being sent to evacuate people. Following these instructions, they went to the transport site only to be told that the buses there were there to transport residents of St. Bernard's Parish, which is 90% white. They were told to return at 6 p.m. Traveling in the dark, they sought out police who were flashing lights, but were told to return home, and threatened with jail if they did not have identification. They returned to the bus station as previously instructed but were stopped by a police car and surrounded by police with guns drawn and spotlights shining on their faces. One of the children was a 14 year old with attention deficit hyperactivity disorder (ADHD) and he was "freaking out," as he had never experienced this kind of intimidation. They were sent home, and each day, for several days, they made attempts to reach the bus station only to be turned back by Gretna police with lights and guns drawn. This incident was repeated at least four times. One time they ventured out in the morning hours and were accosted by a robber, and had to run and hide.

Finally, they reached an evacuation point where there were thousands of mostly African-American survivors in long lines. They got in line, realizing that the Gretna Police would not turn back thousands. One police officer apologized, and stated that the Police had been wrong to turn them away before. As they stood in line for two hours in the rain, the Police accosted a young African-American man and put him on the ground, guns to the head. People cried out, pleading with the officer not to not shoot him. One of the officers drew his gun and fired his gun in the air. This made it seem like someone in the line fired a gun; but no one in the line was armed. "Had it not been for a news helicopter overhead taking pictures, we would never have been able to get on the bus, as they were telling us that we could not board the bus because someone had shot the gun."

The buses transported them to the I-10 Causeway. The description of conditions at the Causeway as told by Ms. Nelson, who has never met Ms. Hodges, basically corroborate Ms. Hodges' story. There were thousands of people there, sick and elderly people. "It was like a camp, like some kind of camp, trash and debris up to your knees, feces, pampers, trash…" Ms. Nelson and family were detained there for nine hours. Others had been there for as long as 72 hours. The elderly were not given priority. When they died in their wheelchairs, all the authorities did was push them aside. Dead bodies were lined up on the opposite side of the street in a straight row covered up in yellow sheets. "Had it not been for the people of Calfax, TX and their 10 buses, we wouldn't have been here in Texas to this day. That's how much people were fighting to get on the bus. No consideration, no order, if you didn't make the bus, you'd be there for a few more days. I was determined to get on the bus and I did." Upon reaching Calfax, Texas they were given water and food. After several transfers, they reached Plano, Texas where they were issued housing with vouchers. As of January 2006, she and her family had not been back home to assess the damage.

Kevin Bush was removed from his home in the Lower Ninth Ward after the levee system collapsed and flood waters rose to the rooftops. He is a paraplegic who lives in a wheelchair. He was taken to the Superdome by military helicopter. Once there he was placed in a wheelchair by authorities and left to languish without food, water or medical care for five days. He survived, but due to this neglect, Mr. Bush has had to undergo multiple major surgeries to correct complications arising from the incident. Additional surgeries may become necessary.

Linda Bowie was a resident of the Upper Ninth Ward in New Orleans. In previous hurricanes her three daughters would usually remain behind to care for her mother. Thus before Hurricane Katrina she went with her three grandchildren to her 82 year old mother's house on Canal Street in the Sixth Ward. Her mother was seriously ill. They did not believe that they would need to evacuate. But when the flooding came on August 29th, they decided to try to evacuate, and went to the I-10 Bridge on Orleans Avenue at Durbanie.[34] There were thousands of people at this bridge, and at other bridges, dehydrating in the hot sun as helicopters flew overhead. When it got dark, they found a ride on a boat to a school that they had been told was an evacuation point. With helicopters everywhere, they expected to be evacuated, but they were not. They had paid the boat driver because they wanted to be sure he came back, which he did, taking them back to her mother's house. For the next several days, they repeated a similar pattern of travels. They disassembled her mother's hospital bed and traveled by boat to the bridge with the bed, her mother and a total of ten family members. But each time they reached the bridge, friends there would say that no one had come to evacuate them. Then she decided to try to reach the Superdome on her own, and found transport with the Fish and Wildlife Service staff.

At the Superdome there were military personnel everywhere, but they were mostly idle. "I am about to have a heart attack because my mother is dying on the bridge." She approached several of them and explained the situation. They gave her water because she was dehydrating. They explained that things would be okay because they had helicopters. So she returned to her mother's house and conveyed this message. The next day, she got into a confrontation with Homeland Security personnel who were blocking off the bridge at the North Claiburne overpass at I-10. Despite the presence of many responders, it did not seem as if anyone was getting any help. Her mother may have had a stroke that day. She tried calling a radio station for help. "After a hundred calls they assured us somebody was coming, helicopters will come. No helicopters came." The next day, they took the bed again the bridge, and once again she confronted the DHS personnel at the top of the bridge. After explaining the urgency of her mother's medical needs, one of them said "Well, let 'em die, that's one less nigger we gotta' worry about." "I got angry and they got angry and this nearly started a riot. We were told 'You niggers gotta' get outta' here or we're gonna' kill all y'all.'" She returned to her group lower down on the bridge and they pushed on to the Superdome.

> We were trying to gather people like Moses to get them to the Dome… On the way we saw all types of boats, trucks and official vehicles going everywhere, but no one stopped to check out our situation with the hospital bed. People were getting angry, starting to pitch things at the trucks. Seemed like everyone in the Guard had video cameras. It got ugly, with people screaming at the Guard.

At a stopping point, a helicopter landed nearby. She approached them and they called up a Humvee, loaded the mattress from the bed, and put her mother inside. One of Linda's sisters had to plead to be able to ride along. The Humvee drove off and she has not seen her mother since. Another of Linda's sisters is diabetic and had not had her medicine, so she was facing a diabetic coma without help. So once again she left her family behind and went to the Superdome. She had to fight her way up to the front to get inside. The first group they encountered very politely offered a police escort to go back and find her sister. Her sister was brought back to the infirmary, but since there was no medicine and there were no doctors:

> All we could do is pray for her. They did give her water, seven bottles, which was generous since there was no water inside or outside the Dome. There was no food. They said we had to go find a place inside. So we did. There was no

military presence inside of the Dome itself. There was military presence outside for the searches. Down on the ground there could have been police. It was horrible. We were way at the top.

While inside, her sister fell ill, and had to be taken back to the infirmary, where she had a seizure. Meanwhile Linda was able to find electrical power at a cellular phone station to power the device she needed to treat her son's asthma. The next day the buses came. "This was a worst nightmare, because that was where the military had barricades everywhere with thousands trying to get on the buses with no order." Managing to get on one of the buses, they were taken to the Astrodome in Houston. After her experience at the Superdome, Linda refused to go inside. She bought a ticket to Lawrenceville to visit her niece.

In mid-January, Linda and her sister met Governor Blanco. *CNN* covered the meeting where the Governor made a phone call to inquire about their mother's plight. Two days later they were contacted by David Lappin, a FEMA medic who had seen the story on *CNN*, and who said he didn't think she would live, and that all the doctors they visited said she was going to die. She was either taken to LSU Hospital in Baton Rouge, Terrbone General in Homa or, he said, they took her to Louis Armstrong Airport, where there was a place set up for critically ill patients whom the doctors deemed untreatable to let them die peacefully. But the medic doesn't know if she died or not, because when he left her she was still alive. Later both *CNN* and Governor Blanco's office called to tell her that they were doing DNA testing at the morgue. The results will be known soon, but Linda is seeking a forensic scientist for independent verification.

CBS's 60 Minutes interviewed eight people survivors who attempted to cross the Crescent-City Connection Bridge into Gretna and were turned back the Gretna Police. Many of them had been told that there were buses awaiting them for evacuation on the Gretna side of the bridge.

> With that assurance, they joined hundreds of other people who were walking toward the bridge to Gretna. Images taken that day by a *CBS News* crew driving across the bridge show groups of evacuees approaching a line of policemen holding shotguns. The police car was marked Gretna Police. Cathey Golden told *60 Minutes* that when her group reached the police line, they were told there were no buses, and stopped with a shotgun blast.

They sought an explanation. Larry Bradshaw, a white member of the mostly African-American group, says:

> The only two explanations we ever received was, one, 'We're not going to have any Superdomes over here,' and 'This is not New Orleans,' Bradshaw says. 'To me, that was code language or code words for, 'We're not having black people coming into our neighborhood.'[35]

There were about 200 people in the group, which was slow-moving because within the group were individuals in wheelchairs, on crutches or using strollers. After being turned back, the group camped out in the middle of the bridge. But at dusk that night the Gretna Police came back and confiscated their food and water. Survivor Lorrie Beth Slonsky said that a policeman:

Jumped out of his car with the gun aimed at us, screaming and cursing and yelling at us to get the blank-blank away. And just, just so rabidly angry. And we tried to reason, we tried to talk. And he was putting his gun in the face of young children and families. It said Gretna on the police car.[36]

These testimonials, and those relayed to the Select Committee by Attorney Ishmael Muhammed, reveal a consistent pattern of stranded African-American residents seeking evacuation points that they had been told about, only to be confronted with armed authorities who in many cases threatened them with weapons and used racial slurs. In two cases, we are told that white survivors were given priority status for getting onto transport vehicles being used for evacuation. There is a general pattern of military or police responders being idle and unresponsive to emergency requests, with the notable exceptions of several helpful and caring individuals.

We should also note that these survivors were not totally lacking means. Ms. Nelson had the money to hire a boat. Ms. Bowie had the money to buy a plane ticket.

In two of these cases, the Gretna Police are involved. Gretna Police Sheriff Harry Lee had set a policy back in the 1980s for his officers to observe special scrutiny for any blacks crossing the Crescent-City Connection bridge. The *New Orleans Gambit* quoted him as saying "It's obvious that two young blacks driving a rinky-dinky car in a predominantly white neighborhood, they'll be stopped." When blacks complained in April 2005 that Jefferson Parish police officers had a caricature of a young black man that they used for target practice, Sheriff Lee responded to questions by saying: "I've looked at it, I don't find it offensive, and I have no interest in correcting it."

Such blatant displays of racism are surely unworthy of officers in uniform. One means available to government to curb racial abuse is to establish procedures, because it is when procedures and regulations break down that individual authorities are left to act at their discretion, in which case the discriminatory judgment of those who harbor racial prejudices will come to the fore.

2.   FEMA and DHS

FEMA Before 9/11

When the Federal Emergency Management Agency (FEMA) was established in 1979 by President Jimmy Carter's Executive Order 12148, it brought together a range of organizations involved in disaster relief and preparedness, such as the National Weather Service Community Preparedness Program or the National Fire Prevention and Control Administration, and placed them under one umbrella. FEMA took over responsibility for relief and recovery during and after natural disasters from the Department of Housing and Urban Development (HUD). FEMA also took over civil defense operations from the Pentagon. Under President Bill Clinton, the FEMA Director became cabinet-level post tasked specifically with providing relief and recovery oversight, with Clinton naming James Lee Witt as FEMA Director in 1993.

As an independent agency, FEMA had handled such emergencies as the toxic dumping into Love Canal (Niagara Falls, NY) in the 1970s, the partial core breach at the Three Mile Island nuclear reactor in 1978, the Bay Area Earthquake of 1991 and Hurricane Andrew in 1992. In the aftermath of Hurricane Andrew, an interim report by the US Congress called FEMA a "political dumping ground, a turkey farm, if you will, where large numbers of positions exits that can be conveniently and quietly filled by political appointment."[37]

When James Lee Witt took charge of FEMA under Clinton in 1993, he ended political patronage in the organization, and removed unnecessary layers of bureaucracy, and "instilled in the agency a spirit of preparedness, of service to the customer, of willingness to listen to ideas of local and state officials to make the system work better."[38]

The success achieved by 1996 prompted the *Atlanta Journal-Constitution* to remark that "FEMA has developed a sterling reputation for delivering disaster-relief services, a far cry from its abysmal standing before … 1993."[39] During Witt's term of office (April 1993-January 2001), FEMA handled "approximately 348 Presidential declared disaster areas in more than 6,500 counties and in all 50 states and territories. Witt supervised the response to the most costly flood disaster in the nation's history…the most costly earthquake, and a dozen serious hurricanes."[40]

Recommendation: Congress should pass legislation to ban political patronage within Federal agencies; specifically within FEMA and DHS.

Upon entering office in January 2001, President Bush chose Joe Allbaugh as the new man to head FEMA. Allbaugh had run Bush's 2000 election campaign. The first person hired by Allbaugh was his long-time friend Michael DeWayne Brown, whom he appointed as General Counsel. Political patronage at FEMA was back. Unlike Witt, Allbaugh had no disaster management experience. While the same is widely said of Brown, in his testimony before the Select Committee he protested that he *did* have disaster management experience. As an undergraduate, Brown had served as assistant to the city manager of Edmond, Oklahoma, a 68,000 strong suburb of Oklahoma City where he worked with the emergency operations center to draft the emergency operation plan. Then from 1989 to 2001 Brown served as Judges and

Stewards Commissioner of the International Arabian Horse Association (IAHA). He resigned in the face of multiple lawsuits against the IAHA.[41]

Incorporation into DHS

In June of 2002, FEMA Director Joe Allbaugh resigned immediately upon being told that FEMA was about to be incorporated as one of 22 agencies within the new super-agency, the Department of Homeland Security (DHS), which was being created in response to the terrorist attacks of September 11, 2001. Brown was promoted to—or "slipped through"[42] to become—Undersecretary for Emergency Preparedness in charge of FEMA in January 2003. Although the Homeland Security Act of 2002 tasked FEMA with developing a National Response Plan, FEMA was to be stripped of its control preparedness grants totaling billions of dollars. Brown resisted, and in the ensuing years became a kind of antihero taking up the concerns and "huge angst" of the experienced members of his staff who worried that the new focus on terrorism inside DHS would leave their expertise underutilized. His resistance was not appreciated either within DHS or at the White House. The plan for FEMA under DHS Secretary Tom Ridge was to absorb what remained of FEMA into DHS's new Emergency and Response Directorate, eliminating the name FEMA entirely.[43] Brown managed to preserve FEMA's name at least. But over his objections that FEMA already had one, DHS built its own emergency operations command center. "Everybody wants a toy," Brown grumbled, "fancy screens and all that stuff."[44]

Morale at FEMA was plummeting, and experienced veterans began to depart from FEMA in droves. FEMA, with a staff of 2,500, was now tasked with preparing for disaster relief in the wake of terrorist attacks and/or the use of weapons of mass destruction, on top of natural disasters. As a series of tornadoes ripped through the Midwest in May of 2003, FEMA personnel who would otherwise have responded were instead preoccupied while being engaged in anti-terror, anti-WMD training exercises.[45]

Ridge had earlier seized control of the Justice Department's 150-man operation known as the Office of Domestic Preparedness (OPD). Despite plans to merge ODP into FEMA, Ridge decided instead to move it into his office. Then he gave ODP control over the preparedness grants that had formerly been controlled by FEMA.

> Ridge and his aides now believed that FEMA should be a response and recovery agency, not a preparedness agency. In an age of terrorism, they argued, preparedness needed a law enforcement component, to prevent and protect as well as get ready to respond.[46]

On September 15, 2003, Brown fired off an angry memo to Ridge, protesting that subsuming FEMA into DHS was ruining morale. He voiced the key concern of his staff, which was that Ridge's plan would separate preparedness from response, disrupting key relationships with first responders and leading to "an ineffective and uncoordinated response" to another major disaster.[47] In retrospect, these words make Brown look seem like a prophet that a hapless horse judge.

Brown's memo only did more damage. Ridge now reassigned the writing of the National Response Plan (NRP) to Admiral James M. Loy of the Coast Guard, who was also in charge of the Transportation Security Administration. Once completed, the NRP sparked an uproar within FEMA, and "among local, state and rival federal agencies." To FEMA officials it was awful; simplistic and top-down. According to FEMA's union chief: "'The gist was: We'll give orders and everybody will jump and say, Sir, yes, sir!'"[48] FEMA, which previously reported directly to the President, would now report to a "principal federal officer" under DHS. "'It was just another dad-gummed layer of bureaucracy,' Brown said."[49]

Indeed, the NRP actually involves *five* layers of bureaucracy. The following diagram, titled "EOCs [Emergency Operations Centers] / Coordination Centers,"[50] shows the levels of multi-agency centers for information sharing under the NPR. What is of concern is the number of offices information would theoretically have to travel through to get DHS in touch with a Local Center.

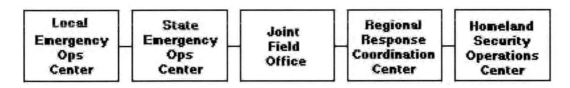

Hurricane Katrina was the first catastrophic event to be declared an "Incident of National Significance" under the *National Response Plan* (NRP). The NRP was designed using Incident Command System (ICS) management concepts.[51] ICS is a highly effective approach for localized emergencies that can spread rapidly, such as forest fires or epidemics, because it allows for rapid expansion or contraction of command structures. However, an incident with the capacity to wipe out infrastructure, including communications networks and local operations centers, as Hurricane Katrina did, can create a situation where over-reliance on local ops centers that may be compromised or may no longer exist can slow the process of gaining situational awareness at the highest levels of command. When ICS management concepts are clearly understood at all levels, ICS should be able to cope, but when they are not understood, the system becomes ineffective.

This appears to have played a role in the delayed response to Katrina, as the Secretary of DHS did not appear to grasp his role as the primary Incident Commander of the first ever Incident of National Significance, since he delegated that role to the head of the overstretched and under-resourced FEMA, rather than immediately deploying the far greater assets under his own control.

Similarly, because the NRP operates on principles based more in theory than upon past precedent, the challenge of integrating State and Federal forces is made unnecessarily problematic. This was evidenced in Governor Blanco's rejection of a White House proposal to place State and Federal forces under a single "dual status commander." This incident will be treated in detail below. Here, we point to that episode as an example of what happens when one side (the White House) is seeking to apply, incorrectly, abstract ICS concepts whilst the other side (the Governor) is falling back upon long-established precedents that are not sufficiently addressed within the abstract model of the NRP. The White House was applying ICS concepts incorrectly because it sought to create a two "mutually exclusive chains of command," which is precisely what ICS practices are meant to prevent.

Recommendation: The National Response Plan should either be overhauled or scrapped. A new plan should be developed that includes: 1) unambiguous command structures for military responders; 2) crystal clear clarification regarding the integration of the work of state and federal armed forces during an emergency to maximize the ability to deploy military assets in a pro-active manner; 3) pre-set standard operating procedures for non-military agencies operating in a crisis detailing what operations they can and should initiate without waiting for marching orders from a higher authority; 4) an integrated communications plan that puts all responders on the same page from the get-go, using Interoperable Communications technology.

Recommendation: The National Response Plan is color blind, and any future such national emergency response plans must include sensitivity training for *both* military and non-military responders so that responders are aware in advance of the specific needs and leadership patterns in communities of color.

Recommendation: Emergency response agencies like FEMA should offer diversity training to their employees, and establish direct working relationships with leadership figures in minority communities living in disaster prone areas such as flood planes so that those relationships are forged and ready to call upon *prior to* the emergency.

Brown's warnings that FEMA was falling apart were echoed in March of 2004 by James Lee Witt, who testified before Congress that "the ability of our nation to prepare and respond to disasters had been sharply eroded … I hear from emergency managers, local and state leaders and first-responders nearly every day that the FEMA they knew and worked well with has now disappeared." Aside from the issue of cronyism, and the lack of cabinet-level status for FEMA and disaster relief, two additional problems affected FEMA's ability to be an effective responder. The first of these was money. FEMA's budget was cut by nearly $80 million under the Bush Administration, and moreover "in 2005, nearly three of every four grant dollars from DHS to first responders went to programs exclusively focused on terrorism."[52] One expert calculates the ratio of DHS projects within focused on terrorism and WMD to those focused on hurricanes and natural disasters at over 28:1, commenting: "Surely as government bureaucrats write more documents and as commissions get underway in Washington, someone must recognize the corrosive effect of focusing on terrorism and WMD to the exclusion of more plausible, frequent, and frankly, more realistic scenarios."[53]

Upon the succession of Michael Chertoff, a man who is credited with authoring the Patriot Act, to replace Ridge as DHS Secretary on February 15, 2005, Brown bombarded Chertoff with memos seeking to undo what damage (in his view) Ridge had done to FEMA. "'I don't box in very easily,'" was Chertoff's cool response.[54] Chertoff proceeded with plans to strip FEMA of its preparedness mission. Chertoff:

> agreed with Brown's bureaucratic rivals that FEMA was too busy responding to daily disasters to focus on the long-term planning needed to prepare for a major catastrophe … Brown sent one last-ditch memo to Chertoff's deputy, warning that

under the new plan, 'FEMA is doomed to failure and loss of mission.' But his appeal was rejected ... On Sunday, Aug. 28, Brown was supposed to be finalizing his resignation letter. Instead he was on his way to Louisiana for Katrina and chuckling into his BlackBerry.[55]

At least Brown was taking the initiative, one day early.

<u>Recommendation: Congress should re-establish FEMA as an independent Federal agency, removing it from DHS; but give housing oversight back to HUD.</u>

Domestic Unpreparedness

"So far, all we've done is shovel money out the door to meet the humanitarian needs. But henceforth we've got to be very careful how we spend the money, and that means we're going to need a plan and somebody in charge."[56]
~ Sen. Charles E. Grassley, Chairman of the Senate Finance Committee

"With all due respect to the President, things are not going to bubble up from the bottom. There has to be some leadership here."[57]
~ Jack Kemp, former HUD Secretary under Bush Sr.

"The director...of the National Hurricane Center said this was the big one, but when this happened...Bush is in Texas, Card is in Maine, the vice president is fly-fishing. I mean, who's in charge here?"[58]
—Rep. Tom Davis, Chairman of the Select Committee

Indeed, Mr. Chairman, so nonchalant were top officials in the aftermath of Katrina that they did not even break from their vacations to attend to the disaster. While Bush, Brown and Chertoff had all been briefed on August 28th of the possibility of a levee failure,[59] Secretary Chertoff made a trip to Atlanta to visit the CDC to discuss avian flu on the 29th, the day of landfall, and did not become fully aware of the levee failures until mid-day on August 30th, some 30 hours after the initial breach. Chertoff did not declare Katrina an Incident of National Significance until August 30th, 36 hours after landfall, when he also designated Brown "principal federal officer." It must be asked why this was not called before the storm struck and whether it contributed to the delay in the response.[60]

Secretary of Defense Rumsfeld was busy taking in a baseball game in San Diego on the night of the 29th, in anticipation of Bush's visit to deliver a speech on the war in Iraq the next day. The President returned to Crawford Texas that night (August 30th). The same President who had flown from Crawford to Washington to intervene in Terri Shiavo's medical case did not visit the devastated areas until his fly-over on September 2nd, the fifth day after landfall, delivering the message "I am satisfied with the response. I am not satisfied with all the results" at a press conference. The next day, apparently forgetting what he had been told at the August 28th briefing, Bush stated: "I don't think anybody anticipated the breach of the levees."[61]

For her part, Secretary of State Rice was still taking in the sites on her New York City vacation two days after the storm when she took in a Broadway show, with some audience members booing her when the lights went up. She was reportedly accosted by angry citizens again the next day who found her buying thousands of dollars' worth of shoes. "A fellow shopper shouted, 'How dare you shop for shoes while thousands are dying and homeless!'"[62]

It certainly seems as if the folks over there at the White House have trouble reading:

1. "No one could have imagined them taking a plane, slamming it into the Pentagon… into the World Trade Center, using planes as a missile."
   –Condoleezza Rice, testifying before the 9/11 Commission, April 8, 2004.

   There were multiple and consistent warnings that Osama bin Laden was planning a major terrorist attack against the United States on or around September 11th, 2001 and that New York and Washington were likely targets. There had been warnings of threats to use planes as weapons since 1976. Rice actually joined President Bush in Genoa for the G-8 Summit in July of 2001 when Islamic terror groups had threatened to crash an airliner into the summit, prompting the closure of airspace over Genoa during the event.[63]

2. "Simply stated, there is no doubt that Saddam Hussein now has weapons of mass destruction."
   –Vice President Dick Cheney, August 26, 2002

   Former UN weapons inspectors accurately foretold that they had destroyed 95% and more of Iraq's WMD. US forces occupying Iraq for nearly three years now have not uncovered any conclusive evidence that Iraq continued to possess WMD in 2002.

3. "I don't think anybody anticipated the breach of the levees."
   –President Bush, September 2, 2005[64]

   There had been consistent warnings about the danger of a category 4 or 5 hurricane hitting New Orleans and flooding New Orleans since 1998,[65] and as noted above Bush, Brown and Chertoff were specifically briefed about this on August 28 2005.

The response to Hurricane Katrina by both DHS and the White House has been described as "staggeringly ineffectual" by one commentator writing days later, who pointed out that DHS Director Michael Chertoff seemed proud that only 2,800 National Guardsmen had reached New Orleans 72 hours after landfall, promising that the Army was "building capacity." DHS demonstrated that "it could organize an impressive press conference in Washington … But on the ground in Louisiana, where it counts … DHS is turning out to be the sum of its inefficient parts. The department looks like what its biggest critics predicted: a new level of bureaucracy grafted onto a collection of largely ineffectual under-agencies."[66]

DHS and FEMA unpreparedness and ineptness in the face of the hurricane-flood disaster was also apparent in the face of offers of international assistance. More than 90 countries and international organizations offered assistance in the first week following the disaster. But nearly all of these offers were "mired ... in bureaucratic entanglements." Although the State Department announced that no offers of aid were being turned away, a Swedish transport at the ready with water purification systems and a cellular network sat waiting for take-off orders for four days. A Canadian search-and-rescue team sat waiting for directions.[67] Actually, not all offers of aid were accepted. When Cuba volunteered a medical brigade with disaster relief experience in post-tsunami Sri Lanka, White House spokesman Scott McClellan answered with the message that Fidel Castro "needs to offer the people of Cuba their freedom." But the team members themselves continued to stand at the ready, and team member Dr. Delvis Marta Fernandez, a veteran hurricane responder at age 32, told reporters: "Let's get going. This is not political. This is a humanitarian emergency. People are dying and they need our help."[68]

Recommendation: Congress should take international politics out of disaster relief efforts by establishing a policy that no legitimate offers of foreign assistance will be refused.

Warnings of Levee Failure Since at Least 1998

The dramatic testimony of Mama D (Dyan French Cole) before the Select Committee concerning the failure of the levees attracted nationwide attention. She testified that the Seventeenth Street Canal was within a mile of her home and when the levee broke she heard two huge explosions. Reacting to this, major networks ran some rather patronizing stories on how a people who have suffered generations of oppression can develop a certain psychology of paranoia. But Mama D was not the only one who heard the explosions, many residents did.

> One such individual is Mr. Joe Edwards, Jr. who was interviewed by *ABC News* anchor and correspondent David Muir. He tells Mr. Muir, 'I heard something go boom! ...I know it happened. They blew it.' In addition to local New Orleans residents, like Mr. Edwards, Eugene Robinson of The Washington Post said on the September 18th edition of *Meet The Press*, 'I was stunned in New Orleans at how many black New Orleanians would tell me with real conviction that somehow the levee breaks had been engineered in order to save the French Quarter and the Garden District at the expense of the Lower Ninth Ward, which is almost all black...But these are not wild-eyed people. These are reasonable, sober people who really believe that.'

Commenting, author Cedric Muhammad's call for openness of mind on this issue:

> I think any reasonable and rational person with an open mind – not bound by ideology – would have to conclude that there is justification and various forms of evidence for considering the possibility that the levees were breached and the

Ninth Ward flooded for reasons other than that provided by the mainstream media and local, state and federal government including the Army Corps of Engineers.[69]

Moreover, as Mama D told MSNBC's Tucker Carlson, there were intentional levee breaches in 1927 and in the aftermath of Hurricane Betsy in 1965. In other words, New Orleans residents have historical precedents of intentional levee breaching to point to.

During the Great Mississippi Flood of 1927, which began on April 16th of that year, communities on both sides of the Mississippi River knew that their community would be spared if the other side broke. Levee patrols with shoot-to-kill orders were actually set up by both sides to catch any intruders who might be trying to dynamite their side of the levee. This was serious business. In Greenville, Washington County, Mississippi, the flood overtook the town, flooding an area 60 by 90 miles wide. Boaters rescued thousands of mostly poor African-American persons from rooftops and trees. They were deposited at the crown of the river levee. By April 25th:

> The situation in Greenville is dire. Thirteen thousand African Americans are stranded on the levee with nothing but blankets and makeshift tents for shelter. There is no food for them. The city's water supply is contaminated. The railway has been washed away, and sanitation is non-existent. An outbreak of cholera or typhoid is imminent.[70]

Local cotton magnate LeRoy Percy appointed his son Will to head the relief effort. But when Will arranged for the evacuation of the stranded survivors, the local whites feared that if the blacks were rescued, they wouldn't work the crops come harvest time. The steamboats that came to rescue the survivors removed only 33 whites. Will later tried to save face with the blacks who were stranded by employing them with the Red Cross in its relief effort.

> Red Cross relief provisions arrive in Greenville, but the best provisions go to the whites in town. Only African Americans wearing tags around their necks marked 'laborer' receive rations. National Guard is called in to patrol the refugee camps in Greenville. Word filters out of the camps that guardsmen are robbing, assaulting, raping and even murdering African Americans held on the levee.[71]

Later that summer African Americans began leaving, and over half left within the year. LeRoy Percy's cotton empire fell into ruin.

During the flood, as the waters moved south along the Mississippi, the decision was made to save the downtown businesses of New Orleans by blowing a 1,500-foot break in the Poydras levee, flooding St. Bernard and Placquemines Parishes. According to one expert, race did not play a factor in the decision to blow the Poydras levee, and in fact the decision was made following advice given five years earlier by the Army Corps of Engineers that if the city was ever seriously threatened, the levee should be blown.[72]

Historical memory has a tendency to turn events into legend. Since the flood of 1927 was a turning point for many black families in the south, the bitterness of those experiences are no doubt still associated with the flood, and the flood as we know is associated with the blowing of the levees. For the mostly white residents of St. Bernard and Placquemines Parishes who were intentionally flooded, the flood of 1927 was all about the blowing of the levees.

Hurricane Betsy in 1965 overtopped levees and led to the breaching of the Florida Avenue Levee, leading in turn to the flooding of the Lower Ninth Ward and neighboring Chalmette. While the Florida Avenue Levee was initially breached by the storm, it is our understanding that the Corps later intentionally breached some levee points in attempting to manage the drainage process.

Hurricane Katrina surely conjured up the haunting memories of these two events. As in the aftermath of Katrina, residents of the Lower Ninth died in their attics as waters rose above the eaves.

Mama D told the Select Committee said a former military official happened to be in the house at the same time and that he told her that what he had heard were two bombs. Our office has received numerous reports of others who claim to have heard explosions that sounded like bombs. We also were told that two young men reported being asked to step down from the levees so that they could be dynamited, but we were unable to get in contact with them. While one engineer we spoke with stated he could not explain how the levees failed, others we spoke to said that the intensity of the storm surge could certainly overtop the levees and possibly breach them. When asked if they could explain how all the four or more breaches occurred almost at the same time, we were told that uniformity of water pressure across the levee system could have reached critical levels at around the same time for all the levees that breached.

Dr. Iver Van Heerden[73] at the LSU Hurricane Center told us he was out at the levee breaches within 24 hours of landfall, taking samples and measurements. He found no evidence of any explosives. According to Van Heerden, researchers from the four separate investigations into the levee breaches that are mentioned in the Select Committee Report have met and have privately concluded that the reason the levees were breached was not due to poor maintenance but poor construction.[74] Specifically, the loose topsoil was not taken into consideration. Thus water was able at several of the sites to push out the loose topsoil under the levees, causing pressure bursts and breaching them starting from underneath. At one site the flood walls slid 45 feet. At each of the sites where there were levee breaches, the noise of the breach would have sounded like a huge explosion.

It is Minister Louis Farrakhan who may have initiated the controversy about intentional breaches. He noted that craters were seen at the breach sites where the walls had been.[75] The cratering he witnessed could have been caused by the water pushing out the earth underneath the levee wall before breaching the entire wall.

Probably the most suspicious fact about the Katrina levee breaches is that their water flow was aimed directly at African American communities (Orleans Parish at the 17th Street Canal; the Lower Ninth Ward at the Industrial Canal). As the Congressional Delegation Tour bus stopped on the bridge over the 17th Street Canal just up from the breach, we could see that the Jefferson Parish side of the canal, the side that didn't breach, had a built up earthen foundation with only a few feet of wall exposed. But on the Orleans Parish side (see photo, right), there was no earthen foundation surrounding the wall, which stood over 12 feet high from the ground. The thickness of the wall was only 11 inches. Each levee is maintained by the local parish government. The relative wealth of Jefferson Parish, a mostly white community, would have enabled it to invest in a much safer structure than what the Orleans Parish could afford. This would explain why the Orleans Parish side failed first.

One thing is certain about the levee breaches: there was amble discussion of the possibility of a levee failure prior to Katrina. Since 1998, the *Times Picayune* has run articles expressing concern about the possibility of a levee failure:

- October 4, 1998:[76] "[National Hurricane Center Director Jerry Jarrell] has two recurring nightmares of the worst-case hurricane that could hit the United States, and New Orleans is central to both. The first is a category 4 or 5 storm with winds as high as 150 mph that follows a path very similar to [Hurricane] Georges. After slamming into island after island in the Caribbean, creating havoc and killing hundreds of people, it moves northwest and cuts across the Miami metropolitan area, leaving damage similar to that caused by Hurricane Andrew in 1992. After clobbering Tampa Bay on a trek across Florida, it enters the Gulf, where it reintensifies before assailing New Orleans with a storm surge that overwhelms the city's levee system."

- June 1, 1999:[77] "New Orleans Office of Emergency Preparedness Director Frank Hijuelos said city residents should try to evacuate in advance of the first official evacuation requests, if they have the ability to leave and a place to go. He said that recommendation is based in part on computer modeling by Louisiana State University engineering professor Joe Suhayda and federal agencies that indicates a slow-moving Category 3, and Category 4 and 5 hurricanes cutting northwest over the metropolitan area will push a wall of water before it that will overtop the area's hurricane protection levees."

- June 2, 1999:[78] "The state's official hurricane emergency plan calls for the Superdome to be a staging area for National Guard and other emergency personnel in the hours after evacuation routes have been shut down and before a hurricane hits. Residents with special needs, such as medical patients with no transportation, are to be moved to the Dome and, if possible, evacuated by air or other means from the city. Once a hurricane is about to hit, the Superdome would be transformed into a 'refuge of last resort,' a bare-bones area where people caught on the street downtown could survive until the storm's fury subsided and they could be evacuated, Purpera said... New Orleans Office of Emergency Preparedness Director Frank Hijuelos said such an assumption by the public could be dangerous. If a major hurricane does hit, Hijuelos said, the accompanying storm surge could easily top hurricane protection levees, flooding streets with 17 feet of water or more. It could take weeks to remove the water, he said."

- June 23-27, 2002:[79] In a five part-series, the *Times-Picayune* offered its readers a comprehensive look at the dangers faced by the city. "It's only a matter of time before South Louisiana takes a direct hit from a major hurricane. Billions have been spent to protect us, but we grow more vulnerable every day."

- July 20, 2004: "Walt Zileski, warning coordination meteorologist for the National Weather Service's Southern Region headquarters in Forth Worth, Texas, said Hurricane Pam was fashioned after Hurricane Georges, which in 1998 turned east only hours before it would have followed for Pam... The water would be high enough in parts of New Orleans to top 17-foot levees, including some along Lake Pontchartrain and the Mississippi River-Gulf Outlet, Zileski said. Some of the water pushed into Lake Pontchartrain would flow through a gap in the hurricane levee in St. Charles Parish, flow across land to the Mississippi River levee and be funneled south into Jefferson and Orleans Parishes."

Additionally, in early 2001, FEMA had published its own report, ranking the possibility of a major hurricane hitting New Orleans as one of the three most likely catastrophes facing the country, alongside a terrorist attack in New York City and a major earthquake in San Francisco.[80] If President Bush did was not aware of the levee issue in New Orleans before he was briefed on the subject on August 28, 2005, somebody at the White House was not doing their job.

Not all Hurricanes are Treated Equal

We have seen above how FEMA's funding was cut, its staff demoralized and its mission called into question. Yet even in the midst of its being absorbed into DHS, FEMA did continue to have the ability to respond quickly and efficiently to a hurricane. Little more than a year prior to Katrina, Hurricane Charley crossed Florida from West to East on August 12, 2004. By Noon of August 16th, less than 4 days since landfall and 24 hours after the Hurricane dissipated off of Cape Cod, the White House website reported that the following resources had been mobilized:

- One hundred trucks of water, 280 trucks of ice, and 900,000 Meals-Ready-to-Eat for Jacksonville.

- 7,000 cases of food for Winter Haven.

- Urban Search and Rescue Teams and Disaster Medical Assistance Teams (DMATs) on the ground and setting up comfort stations, coordinating with FEMA community relations personnel.

- 4,100 National Guard troops in Florida, as well as thousands in nearby states.

- Tarps provided by the Army Corps of Engineers for "tens of thousands of owners of homes and buildings that have seen damage to their roofs."

- 300 medical personnel to be on standby.

- 1,000 additional community relations personnel deployed to Atlanta "for training and further assignment in Florida."

Additionally, survivors were notified that:

- "FEMA is coordinating with the Department of Energy and the state to ensure that necessary fuel supplies can be distributed throughout the state, with a special focus on hospitals and other emergency facilities that are running on generators.

- "FEMA is coordinating public information messages with Georgia, Tennessee, Alabama, and North Carolina so that evacuees from Florida can be informed when it is safe to return."

By August 15th, the White House web site boasted the following:

- "Registering approximately 136,000 assistance applicants;

- "Approving over 13,500 applications for more than $59 million in housing assistance;

- "Establishing 12 disaster recovery centers, which have assisted nearly 19,000 disaster victims;

- "Deploying medical teams that have seen nearly 3,000 patients;

- "Disbursing 1.2 million liters of water, 8.1 million pounds of ice, and 2 million meals and snacks;

- "Delivering over 20,000 rolls of plastic sheeting and nearly 170 generators; and

- "Treating more than 2,900 individuals through FEMA Disaster Medical Assistance Teams, supporting damaged hospitals"

FEMA appears to have responded in a timely and effective manner three months before an election in Florida, a state governed by Jeb Bush, the President's brother. ***Disaster relief checks were in the mail within a week.***[81] Additionally, after Hurricane Frances, FEMA was "very generous… especially in Miami-Dade [County] giving people money for…broken televisions, washers, driers, whole new wardrobes and rooms full of clothing… [and rooms] full of furniture."[82]

Let us contrast this with FEMA's dismal performance in the aftermath of Hurricane Katrina. Two days after landfall:

- White House pressure on FEMA to set up an interagency crisis management group in the days leading up to the storm were chided by FEMA staff. One staffer wrote to Brown: "Let them play their reindeer games as long as they are not turning around and tasking us with their stupid questions. None of them have a clue about emergency management."[83]

- FEMA regional director Marty Bahamonde wrote in an office e-mail: "The leadership from top down in our agency is unprepared and out of touch... I am horrified at some of the cluelessness and self concern that persists..."[84]

Three days after landfall:

- Secretary Chertoff told *NPR* that he had "'not heard a report of thousands of people in the Convention Center who don't have food and water,' even though every television viewer in the country had been hearing of those 25,000 stranded refugees for at least a day."[85]

Five days after landfall:

- FEMA Director Michael Brown notified an aide by e-mail that "no action from us" to use planes made available by airlines to evacuate victims had been made. But 30 minutes later he was informed that in fact FEMA had been "flying planes all afternoon and evening." Brown also mused that he wished Jeb Bush were Governor of Louisiana.[86]

- 9 stockpiles of fire-and-rescue equipment that had been "strategically placed around the country to be used in the event of a catastrophe" had still not been pressed into service.[87]

Additionally, FEMA's contracting was in disarray:

- FEMA had no plan for cleaning up the bodies, which after the storm were left decomposing in homes and on the streets. One week after the storm, FEMA asked Texas firm Kenyon International Emergency Services, Inc. to deliver mobile morgues (the morgue in New Orleans was flooded). But after several days of waiting, Kenyon decided to forget FEMA and signed a contract directly with the state of Louisiana.[88]

- FEMA ordered 1.6 million cases of meals-ready-to-eat (MREs) from the Pentagon, but demand rose to 2 million, but the Pentagon cut them off at 1.6: "We're happy that we're able to help the folks, [but]...we have to feed our troops too," said a Pentagon spokesperson.[89]

With FEMA officials themselves admitting that FEMA was nowhere near ready for Hurricane Katrina, and given Brown's unsuccessful attempts to protect FEMA's integrity as the authority on natural disaster response within DHS, FEMA was set up to fail when the big one hit. Nevertheless, we cannot ignore the disparities between the lavish treatment by FEMA of survivors of hurricanes Charley and Frances. FEMA, after all, speaks to a higher power, and that higher power was not only slow on the uptake, but slow on the delivery as well. If the nightmare were over for Katrina survivors, this would be a matter for policy debate. But the nightmare for the survivors continues.

"Duped" by FEMA: The Housing Fiasco

Many survivors who were aware of what was being offered and what assistance other survivors were receiving from FEMA, found themselves caught up in a second nightmare: the bureaucratic red tape that in many cases made it extremely difficult or even impossible to get assistance.

Jan Campbell[90] is a former FEMA employee who worked out of FEMA's operations center in Hyattsville, Maryland. She worked the phones on FEMA's regional intake and helpline. With hundreds of experienced employees having left FEMA over previous years, after Katrina hit FEMA was desperate to hire workers who could handle the phones for hundreds of thousands of survivors' calls. They were offered $15 per hour. "If you were alive they hired you," says Campbell. People were hired who later flunked criminal background checks. Well over a hundred in the Hyattsville office alone had already been on the job when they were fired over background checks. During their employment, these individuals had access to social security numbers. Training, which was supposed to take 10 days, was trimmed to 8 hours. Every day employees were threatened with firing. Most of the employees were African-American and many were single mothers.

For survivors who weren't in a hotel or in a shelter but not in their own home, the policy stated that they were entitled to an initial $2,000. But thousands of survivors could not access this entitlement because of *duplicate registrations*. Many of the survivors were low income minority persons from extended families, but those families had been split up in the mass evacuation into diaspora. The first thing entered into the computer was the person's telephone number. But what happened when a family of 2 or 3 or more adults were separated? The first to call in would typically receive the $2,000 of assistance, but the second or third to call in would give the same telephone number. They found themselves in "dupe status." Now they were stranded. The Red Cross might offer $300 and other services, but this would not last for long. Next, this survivor goes to apply for rental assistance. FEMA can't help them, because they're in dupe status.

There were other ways for survivors to find themselves in dupe status. The application process was available on the internet. But as often happens with online forms, many survivors were uncertain whether or not their form had been accepted after pressing the send button. So they reloaded the page and hit send a second time. Now they had unwittingly submitted a second application, and this landed them into dupe status.

Over 70,000 applicants landed in dupe status, and over half of these were New Orleans residents. FEMA management discouraged those on the phone from telling survivors why they were not eligible for checks. Five months after landfall, FEMA was still cleaning these applications up. But since the $2,000 assistance program was terminated in mid Fall of 2005, virtually anyone in dupe status did not receive the check unless their case was solved before the deadline.

Survivors were asked to provide proof of the residence they were living in at the time the hurricane hit. This required a lot of paperwork, especially for people who were far away from their residences. Sixty per cent of residents in the Lower Ninth Ward were illiterate, but no steps were taken to meet their special needs. FEMA employees had no social service background. Campbell's boss was a former warehouse worker. FEMA used satellite imaging to identify homes, but with so many homes destroyed they had to turn to other methods of verification such as checking phone books. If residences could not be verified, then the computer would display the words: "unable to verify," holding the application up. Survivors were not informed if there was a problem, and if they called in, staff could tell them about it, but there was no outreach so if they did not call in they did not know there was a problem. In November, a batch of faxes was lost in the mail system. But management instructed operators not to explain to survivors why their application had not yet been received or processed, but only to say: "Your case is still pending," and to ask them to send it back in.

A climate of suspicion pervaded the office. If someone called in and reported that they were unemployed, the computer showed: "refused to give income," which basically meant that FEMA thinks you are a crook. Office colleagues would hang up the phone proudly declaring "busted another crook." Applicants in the "refused to give income" category were sent to the Small Business Administration (SBA) for an SBA Loan, which requires filling out a 6 page form. Many elderly and disabled persons who did not have an employer found themselves in this situation, and were basically getting cheated out of any assistance. There were "so many ways to put people up a creek."

One man from East New Orleans had helped rescue 800 survivors, but then found himself forced to get on a plane to Tucson. He had no money. He could not get home. Since he could not prove that he lived in New Orleans, he then got hung up in asking for assistance when he was asked to provide proof of residency.

Phone operators were instructed not to spend more than 15 minutes on each call with the "customer." Staff were basically being told: "be quick, answer just what you're asked," and do not go over peoples' applications to be sure they get what they're entitled to. Because 15 minutes was often not enough to help someone solve a problem, unless you took time to go over the application with them, or to ask a Special Matters Expert (SME) for specific assistance, they were unlikely to receive everything to which they were legally entitled.

When rental assistance was obtained, survivors were told that it was good for 18 months. What they often weren't told was that they had to re-apply every 3 months. After the first three months, if they missed a rent payment, many landlords would turn them out in six weeks or less. Many checks were sent to the wrong address. Survivors had to apply for FEMA to reissue the check. *But FEMA can take up to nine months to reissue a check.*

Finally, people from New Orleans were the last to get trailers. 40,000 or more were needed, but only several thousands were made available. Every day, FEMA phone operators were instructed not to tell anybody about trailers. There was a systemic bias. There were 41,000 trailers along the Mississippi Coast and calls came in all the time from Mississippi residents asking for instructions on how to hook up their trailers. But Louisiana only got 1,700 trailers. [By the end of January, according to the *Washington Post*, Mississippi had 33,378 trailers, meeting 89% of the demand, where as Louisiana had only 37% of its trailer needs met.][91] And there were memos all the time giving phone numbers that survivors of Hurricane Rita in Texas, a hurricane that came a month after Katrina, could call to get a trailer, or get service for their trailer. The staff were grumbling among themselves: "How 'come these people in Texas are getting Cadillac treatment?"

"Most of the survivors were suffering from post-traumatic stress disorder (PTSD). I tried to help them when I could. We got yelled at routinely for 'having too much compassion… You're not here to do casework,' we were told." In November, Campbell raised a fuss at a meeting when survivors were about to be evicted from hotels. Staff phones had a button to transfer callers facing eviction to another program. But three quarters of the transfers did not go through, and staff were not provided a number to give directly to the callers who called back in. A day later, the number was provided to staff, but during that 24 hours most transferred calls got cut off.

One day, 20 employees passed out cold on two separate floors of the Hyattsville office. This event got coverage by *CNN*. The official explanation was that a gas can with a paper rag on it on the roof had caused the incident. Campbell didn't buy it. Campbell's co-workers told her she had gotten herself into trouble when she called the Hyattsville Fire Department to report that cartloads of paper were blocking exit doors in the building, which was against the fire code. She was terminated in early December because she "talked too long on the phone." She had shown too much compassion.

Ms. Campbell's story gives us a peek at the chaos inside of unhappy FEMA. This was not an organization that stood ready to deal with a hurricane of the magnitude of Katrina. This meant that as new policy was needed to cope, it had to be made on the run. That opened the door to all kinds of problems and irregularities, such as out of control spending with credit cards to purchase sleeping bags ($60,000 for 3,000); flip-flops ($223,000 worth in one purchase); and golf cart rentals at $1500 per month.[92] As well, FEMA trailers are said to be priced at up to $120,000 each in New Orleans, which is more than it would take to renovate an average house. One FEMA employee has been charged with looting from a client survivor.[93] Two others were indicted in scheme where they were taking kickbacks from food services contractors.[94]

But the clearest sign of chaos within FEMA has been its rolling deadline for evictions for tens of thousands of survivors who have been living in FEMA-subsidized hotels: from December 15th, to January 7th, to February 7th, and now to March 1st. The expensive hotel scheme itself was a stop-gap measure. But here again, we need to ask why the President or the Secretary of DHS did not step in to take charge. There have been options on the table, such as opening tens of thousands of existing dry housing units in New Orleans to survivors. After five months, FEMA finally announced at the end of January that it was in fact setting up a pilot program to relocate 20,000 survivors into government sponsored, rent-free apartments in New Orleans for 18 months (starting from August 29th, the day of landfall).[95] This was welcome news, but will FEMA's promise hold good? A FEMA official is said to have told the Subcommittee on Housing that the hotel deadline would be lifted altogether, but this did not turn out to be true. William Lokey, a field director for FEMA, told the Select Committee on December 14th that all survivors would be given return tickets to get back to their Gulf Coast homes, but FEMA has published no explicit policy and survivors we've talked to say they cannot access this program.

The other major option open to the government is to provide section 8 housing vouchers for survivors so that they can get established, find work, and start to rebuild their lives. Local and state government along the Gulf Coast needs to re-establish a tax base, but this will be very hard to do if residents don't return.

Tens of thousands of mostly African-American survivors face eviction on March 1st with no further promises of assistance.

3.   KATRINA AND THE CRIMINAL JUSTICE SYSTM

Law Enforcement

Governor Blanco's "shoot to kill" order was an extreme measure. Many survivors have expressed their bewilderment or dismay at being subject to curfews under armed patrols in the wake of the hurricane. Had there not been a failure of planning and coordination prior to the storm, would this extreme step have been taken? As suggested above, had disaster planning *anticipated* looting, it may have been possible for responding law enforcement officials, including National Guard, to be on the ground to ensure law and order sooner. But the problem in New Orleans goes deeper than that. Attorney Ishmael Muhammed made the following comment about Governor Blanco's decision during his testimony before the Committee:

> We know that there was a shoot-to-kill order given in an environment that already was problematic in terms of black people being killed by authorities. So, just using your common sense—the sense we all got a little bit of, at least—you give someone raring to go, before Katrina, in a disaster situation, a shoot-to-kill order and create an environment where everybody is a potential looter, you are going to have people getting shot down by police, by law enforcement authorities. And then you have account after account after account of people being killed. Then you have statements being made by law enforcement officials and government officials that the only—that all deaths are going to be identified as happening August 29th as the date and no identification is going to be made of what actually killed anyone, what actually made people—what actually was the reason that people died. Why is that? And then you have reports that 10,000 people may be dead, and all of a sudden we have a body count of a little over 1,000.

There were in fact numerous reports of actual and alleged police shootings and police brutality following Hurricane Katrina, including the following:

- "On the street right in front of the Convention Center, I see a circle of chairs around a black tarp. A body lies underneath it. It's been there since the night before. I pull the tarp back and see a black man lying in a pool of blood... Witnesses tell me what happened. Dwight Williams... says the night before, a New Orleans Police Department vehicle pulled up. 'For whatever reason, the gentleman made a move to the car,' he says. 'It took five seconds, the entire incident. The cop opened the door, shot him, and that was it."

- "Near the former St. Thomas housing development, a squadron of police, some in tactical gear, were clustered in an intersection... [A] man who appeared to be dead from a gunshot wound lay on the ground. It was unclear what had occurred. Police said there had been a shootout as they forced a reporter and a photographer out of a passing car at gunpoint... They took away a reporter's notebook and tossed the photographer's camera on the ground before returning and telling the pair to leave" (*Times-Picayune*, September 1, 2005).

- "New Orleans police shot and killed four men and wounded one on Sunday after looters fired on officers, a policeman said. The incident on Sunday morning, as the city began to clean up from the devastation of hurricane Katrina, resulted in four fatalities and one person in critical condition, said one policeman who asked not to be named. No police were wounded. 'Five men who were looting exchanged gunfire with police. The officers engaged the looters when they were fired upon,' said superintendent of New Orleans police, Steven Nichols. Asked for more details, he said only, 'The incident is under police investigation'" (Reuters, September 4, 2005).

- "Two New Orleans police officers repeatedly punched a 64-year-old man accused of public intoxication, and another city officer assaulted an Associated Press Television News producer as a cameraman taped the confrontations. After being questioned, officers Stuart Smith, Lance Schilling and Robert Evangelist were arrested late Sunday and charged with battery. They were also suspended without pay, released and ordered to appear in court at a later date, Capt. Marlon Defillo said." (Associated Press, October 10, 2005).

- "Police shot and killed a 38-year-old man who had been waving a knife Monday in New Orleans, witnesses said. The killing occurred about 4 p.m. on St. Charles Avenue in the south Garden District near downtown, after the man -- who has not been publicly identified -- left a Walgreens pharmacy carrying a knife, witnesses said. Some witnesses said they heard five or six shots, but 10 red cones were placed on the street. The cones are typically used to indicate where shell casings are found. The city's police force has been under increased scrutiny and strain in the wake of last summer's Hurricane Katrina, when some officers left their jobs and others continued to work long hours despite losing nearly everything in the storm. Since then, police have come under investigation for allegations of looting, stealing cars from a Cadillac dealership and the videotaped beating of a man that resulted in two officers being fired last week." (CNN, December 27, 2005)

The most controversial report involves conflicting stories of what happened on the Danziger Bridge on September 4, 2005. Here are some early accounts:

- "Police shot eight people carrying guns on a New Orleans bridge Sunday, killing five or six of them, a deputy chief said. A spokesman or the Army Corps of Engineers said the victims were contractors on their way to repair a canal." (Associated Press, September 4, 2005)

- "At least five people shot dead by police as they walked across a New Orleans bridge yesterday were contractors working for the US Defense department, according to a report by the Associated Press. A spokesman for the Army Corps of Engineer said the victims were contractors on their way to repair a canal, the news agency said, quoting a Defense Department spokesman. The contractors [were] crossing the bridge to launch barges into Lake Pontchartrain, in an operation to fix the 17th Street Canal, according to the spokesman" (The Australian, September 5, 2005).

New Orleans Police claim they caught eight snipers on a bridge who were shooting at relief contractors. There was a gun battle and five or six of the snipers were killed. Three months later, however, two families came forward with stories radically different from that of the police:

- "A teenager critically wounded that day, speaking about the incident for the first time, said in an interview that police shot him for no reason, delivering a final bullet at point-blank range with what he thought was an assault rifle. Members of another family said one of those killed was mentally disabled, a childlike innocent who made a rare foray from home in a desperate effort to find relief from the flood. The two families — one from New Orleans East and solidly middle class, the other poorer and rooted in the Lower 9th Ward — have offered only preliminary information about what they say happened that day. Large gaps remain in the police and civilian accounts of the incident." (*Los Angeles Times*, 11/24/05)

We anticipate additional stories and allegations about shootings to come forward. We have heard from many survivors with missing family members who fear that their loved ones were shot by police, National Guard, other military, or private contractors during the flood. Frank Minyard, Orleans Parish Coroner says: "If you murdered somebody in those days, you are probably going to get away with it."[96] In addition, there are countless reports of persons being arrested arbitrarily, or of children as young as twelve being taken off to prison for allegedly being in violation of curfew. This placed enormous strain on families seeking to reunite before evacuation when there was a child unaccounted for who later turned out to be in prison. One of the most egregious arrests was that of a 73-year old church deaconess with diabetes who had never in her long life been charged with a crime. She was charged with attempting to loot $63.50 worth of groceries at a deli. Eyewitnesses claim that she had paid for her groceries with a credit card and that the OPP officers were tied and frustrated because they were unable to apprehend young looters at a nearby store. "Not even the deli owner wants her charged," read the story. She was transferred form the parish jail to a state prison and a judge set her bail at $50,000, "100 times the maximum $500 fine under state law for minor thefts." She was released on September 16, 2005 after two weeks in jail, facing a court date in October.[97]

The New Orleans Police Department (NOPD) has a history marred by incidents of racist police brutality:

- In 1980, following the killing of a white police officer, police went on a rampage Algiers, a mostly African-American community, killing four citizens and injuring many more. "Some of the victims were tortured, including two who were dragged to swamps where the officers carried out mock executions."[98]

- In 1991, a Justice Department ranked citizen complaints of police brutality in New Orleans as the highest in the country.

- Between 1993 and 1998 over 50 NOPD officers were arrested for felonies including homicide, rape, and robberies.

- In 1995, an NOPD officer was convicted of robbery and an execution-style murdering three people at the restaurant: two employees and "an off-duty officer from her precinct working at the restaurant."

- In 1996 an NOPD officer was convicted of hiring a hit man to assassinate a woman who had filed a complaint of police brutality against him. He is currently serving a life sentence on death row. New Orleans is the only police department in the country with an officer on death row. In fact, two NOPD officers are currently on death row.

- In 1998 two NOPD officers were indicted "for allegedly beating two handcuffed men in custody."

- In the mid-1990s the pattern of violations by NOPD officers was so apparent that the Justice Department threatened a civil action. A reform process ensued, resulting in the arrest of 110 officers for a variety of criminal charges, the suspension of 600 officers for misconduct, the firing of 117 officers and 18 resignations—all this from a force with just 1,700 active duty officers.

- In 2004, despite attempts at reform, 8 officers were arrested on charges including aggravated assault, extortion and conspiracy to commit a robbery.

Experts report that the majority of those killed since Hurricane Katrina were killed by police. Given this pattern, Governor Blanco's "shoot-to-kill" directive during Hurricane Katrina must be called into question. It created conditions under which complaints against police brutality could be dismissed more arbitrarily than before.

To date, parts of the city are still patrolled by private mercenaries working for Blackwater. About 150 heavily armed mercenaries working for Blackwater made their appearance in New Orleans alongside other military responders after the hurricane. They are still there, and residents complain that their presence is a nuisance and intimidates residents. During her testimony before the Select Committee Governor Blanco denied having authorized the hire of mercenaries to join the relief effort. One Blackhawk employee stated that his company had been contracted by the Department of Homeland Security. He also claimed his comrade had been deputized by Governor Blanco's office. The report says: "The man then held up the gold Louisiana law enforcement badge he wore around his neck. Blackwater spokesperson Anne Duke also said the company has a letter from Louisiana officials authorizing its forces to carry loaded weapons."[99] Blackwater employees have demonstrated explicit examples of racial prejudices.

> Blackwater is not alone. As business leaders and government officials talk openly of changing the demographics of what was one of the most culturally vibrant of America's cities, mercenaries from companies like DynCorp, Intercon, American Security Group, Blackhawk, Wackenhut and an Israeli company called Instinctive Shooting International (ISI) are fanning out to guard private businesses and homes, as well as government projects and institutions.[100]

 All of this office's requests for more information about who hired Blackwater, and for what reason, have gone unanswered. However, one official of the City of New Orleans told Congresswoman McKinney that DHS sent them to the city.

It is nearly impossible to imagine "shoot-to-kill" orders and the hiring of private mercenaries to patrol the streets of wealthy or mostly white cities and neighborhoods. As we saw in some of the testimonials above, unarmed and non-violent African-American residents of New Orleans faced explicit acts of racial discrimination by the very forces sent to oversee their rescue.

Left to Die: The Plight of Prisoners

The now widely-publicized story of prisoners at the Orleans Parish Prison (OPP) who were abandoned in locked cells during the hurricane, with those on the lower floor facing floodwaters up to their necks, is actually just one more chapter to a long and sad story of prisoner abuse. Interviews with prisoners tell of open and pervasive drug use and beatings of prisoners by officers, or indifference by officers to prisoners beating other prisoners. The federal court has been monitoring Orleans Parish Prison ever since the 1969 filing of the lawsuit *Hamilton v. Morial*. Yet the conditions of the prison remain abysmal:

- In 1999, a pregnant female prisoner "reported being left in shackles during labor and another claimed she was denied an examination by a gynecologist despite bleeding immediately after childbirth."[101]

- In 2001, Shawn Duncan, being held on traffic charges, died of dehydration after he was held in restraints for 42 hours.[102]

- In 2003, two OPP guards were indicted after beating to death a prisoner who had been arrested on charges of public drunkenness.[103]

- "In 2004 OPP was one of the top five prisons with substantiated reports of sexual violence in the nation."[104]

- In each of the three months prior to Hurricane Katrina a prisoner died, two while under medical observation, one who committed suicide whilst under suicide watch.[105]

The Orleans Parish Prison is exceptional in a number of ways. Averaging around 7,000 prisoners on any given day (pre-Katrina), the OPP is the 8th largest local jail in the country. Only county jails in cities like New York, with populations many times that of New Orleans, house more prisoners. The OPP holds more prisoners than the largest state prison in Louisiana.[106] The cost of housing this many prisoners exceeds $100,000 *per day*, a bill that is currently being picked up by FEMA, according to experts. The irony of this is that while FEMA is preparing to evict needy survivors on March 1st, it is meanwhile paying top dollar to keep in jail many prisoners whose release dates have passed as well as many more who are only in on petty offenses.

Arrests in New Orleans are up from 48,000 per year in 1995 to 114,000 per year in 2004.[107] These numbers do not reflect an increase in violent crime in the city. In fact arrests for violent arrests are below half the rate for cities in the United States. The vast increase in arrests reflects a new policy of stopping at nothing to arrest citizens for petty crimes such as "public drunkenness, drug possession, disturbing the peace," obstructing a sidewalk, traffic violations or missed child support payments. Already the target of police harassment, most of these petty arrests target young African-American men, who often complain of being arrested on false charges. Under police sentencing rules, the arrested must spend at least 45 days in jail before sentencing. If prisoners are too poor to post bail, they languish in prison, saddled with court costs that can total $2,400 per year. Although the prison offers little by way of rehabilitation programs, prisoners are put to work for minimum wage at an aquaculture facility built by the prison.[108]

When Hurricane Katrina hit, the OPP had just completed a round of street sweeps, picking up people for petty crimes such as loitering. It had also taken in an influx of prisoners evacuated from other jails. When the city flooded, the prison was inundated with water and prisoners were trapped in cells with water up to their necks. Human Rights Watch researcher Corinne Carey commented that "Of all the nightmares during Hurricane Katrina, this must be one of the worst. Prisoners were abandoned in their cells without food or water for days as floodwaters rose toward the ceiling." Power went out early in the storm, and the toilets backed up, creating an unbearable stench. To let in air, inmates broke jail windows. Some set fire to blankets and shirts to hang outside as a cry for help. Inmates on the first floor had to get up onto the second bunk of their beds, but then the water rose to the ceiling and the female prisoners were then taken to the males' side of the dorm, but there the smoke from the fires that had been started meant that they remained in smoke-filled rooms for nearly two days.[109] Gas lines also broke and the women became nauseous.[110]

Some managed to escape, but many who did approached law enforcement officials at sites where people were congregating on bridges and turned themselves in. Some prisoners reported that dead bodies were seen floating in the floodwaters inside the prison. The prison was finally evacuated on September 2nd, five days after the storm. 450 of the inmates were taken to Jena Correctional Facility, and there have been many "extremely credible" complaints that once there they were tortured and abused, and were refused access to telephones.[111]

Corinne Carey researched the prison and at the end of September had reported that 517 prisoners remained unaccounted for.[112] It is hoped that further investigations by civil and human rights groups will clarify what became of the missing prisoners, though for some that may never be known.

It is shocking to learn that prisoners were evacuated from other jails prior to the storm into a jail that sat below the flood plain. The failure to evacuate the Orleans Parish Prison put prisoners and guards in serious jeopardy. At our community meeting in New Orleans, we heard from a man who had his jaw broken while being attacked by other prisoners during his ordeal of being caught in the flooded prison. He could barely endure the pain long enough to speak to us.[113] He had been arrested on a petty marijuana possession charge. Experts have reported that the OPP jail population has now swelled to 9,000, with 85 per cent of prisoners being held for petty offences. Many of these are being held *past their release date*, on the excuse that their paperwork was lost during the storm, or because their case has been backlogged. Anyone who endured the horrors of being trapped inside a flooded prison during a hurricane has already served a penalty far in excess of what any petty offense merits. More than that, their abandonment is an insult to their dignity as human beings.

It is beyond the pale that these prisoners are still incarcerated.[114] Six weeks after the storm, Human Rights Watch reported that many of those rounded up in the sweeps before the storm had not yet been brought before a judge.[115] OPP funding is based upon prison population, and if they were dismissed, the $100,000 daily allowance, currently supplied through FEMA, would immediately shrivel, resulting in lay-offs. It has been reported that the Louisiana State Legislature passed a law that sanctioned the detention of prisoners past their release date. Federal officials overseeing disaster relief need to take cognizance of this deplorable situation in which a city now desperate for funds and jobs has allowed its prison to even more pro-actively than before seek to incarcerate massive numbers of young African-American males as a means to the end of contributing to the local job market, and take action to remedy this travesty of justice.[116]

Let us end this gruesome tale on a positive note of recognition of the heroism of one of the guards. One of the women who suffered through this ordeal writes that "one woman … stayed with the inmates to the bitter end. Her name is: Colonel Joseph. She was a god sent Angel. So many deputies abandoned us."[117]

Recommendation: Future hurricane response plans should include evacuations for prisons susceptible to flooding.

4.   KATRINA, FEMA AND MARTIAL LAW

The Governor Rebuffs the President's Proposal

The term *posse comitatus* translates as "the formation of a posse." The experience of the founding fathers with the British model that combined the functions was enough to cause them to set that division sharply in administrative powers and civilian command of the military. This principle began to be eroded in the period following the end of the Civil War, and the effective occupation of areas of the south by federal troops who were holding military tribunals, carrying out executions of citizens and usurping local police and judicial control. Their excesses came to the attention of the post-war Congress and they passed the Posse Comitatus Act under the 45th Congress in 1878. The Act makes unlawful:

> …to employ any part of the Army of the United States, as a posse comitatus, or otherwise, for the purpose of executing laws, except in such cases and under such circumstances as such employment of said force may be expressly authorized by the Constitution or by act of Congress…[118]

Louisiana State Governor Kathleen Babineaux Blanco declared a State of Emergency for New Orleans on August 26, 2005, three days before Hurricane Katrina made landfall, extending until September 25. State Attorney General Charles Foti's office issued a clarification about Martial Law claims in the media, stating that no such term exists in state law. However the declaration of a state of emergency "gives authorities wide latitude to suspend civil liberties as they try to restore order and bring victims to safety"[119] Louisiana law does not have a martial law provision.

The declaration of a State of Emergency in Louisiana was equivalent to the suspension of *posse comitatus* and the establishment of martial law while the Guard was under state control. It allows the National Guard to perform police functions if there is a threat to life or property, or breakdown of law and order. Thus the early State of Emergency declared by Governor Blanco overcame *posse comitatus* considerations. The standard operating procedure has been that only when local Guard forces and police are unable to control the situation or when it is beyond their capabilities will federal armed forces be called in under 32 CFR 50i and 10 USC 331 seq.

There were numerous reports of National Guard troops being used in place of police and enforcing orders with the use of weapons. This was potentially legal under Louisiana law, which suspends the distinction between local police and state-commanded National Guard in restoring order and saving life and property once a formal emergency is declared.

On September 2, 2005, Governor Blanco was presented with a contract proposal from the White House that would have established "Mutually Exclusive Chains of Command." Governor Blanco refused to sign the Memorandum. Had the contract been signed, a "dual status commander" would have been designated to serve as commander of the Louisiana National Guard, subject to the orders of Governor Blanco, and *simultaneously* to provide "command and control over supporting Federal forces," including federalized National Guard units. "Such

A declaration of martial law generally comes from the President, but in an extreme situation, a local commander can impose martial law (32 CFR 501.2 and .4). The Army decides when it is no longer needed, though it should end as soon as necessity ceases (501.6).

Pre-empting both the Governor and the President, City of New Orleans Mayor Ray Nagin declared Martial Law to crack down on looters and told 1,500 police to do "whatever it takes" to regain control of the city. Nagin said that Martial Law means that officers don't have to worry about civil rights and Miranda rights in stopping the looters… "We will restore law and order," Blanco said, apparently confirming Nagin's decision.[127]

- "Martial law has been declared in New Orleans as conditions continued to deteriorate." (*CBS News*, August 30, 2005).

- "Martial law has been declared in Mississippi and Louisiana" (White House Spokesman Scott McClelland, August 31, 2005).

Despite these reports, the *Times-Picayune* noted that there is no such term as martial law in Louisiana State Law, adding however that when a state of emergency has been declared it provides powers similar to martial law.

Martial law replaces civilian control with military control. A Supreme Court case in 1946 lifted martial law declared in Hawaii during the attack on Pearl Harbor in 1941, forcing civil criminal cases into military courts. The decision ruled that the only legal basis for martial law rests on the complete breakdown of the functions of civil control. Additionally, an 1866 Supreme Court ruling on martial law held that it couldn't be instituted within the US when its civilian courts are in operation.[128]

On the surface of things, it would appear that *both* the President and the DHS were unclear about their roles and responsibilities, and the length and breadth of federal or executive powers. But this incident requires further study.

Recommendation: Congress should direct the Government Accountability office to investigate:

1) the degree to which confusion over roles, responsibilities and powers contributed to the tragic and unnecessary delay in dispatching Federal forces to the incident site; and

2) the Bush administration's claims that the Commander-in-Chief needs more power than the Constitution envisions or allows.

We now turn to the first of these issues.

Why the Delay?

Since governing legislation is clear, the question remains as to the source of the delay. The *Washington Post* ran the following story on September 3, 2005:

NEW ORLEANS, Sept. 3 -- Tens of thousands of people spent a fifth day awaiting evacuation from this ruined city, as Bush administration officials blamed state and local authorities for what leaders at all levels have called a failure of the country's emergency management. Louisiana did not reach out to a multi-state mutual aid compact for assistance until Wednesday, three state and federal officials said. As of Saturday, Blanco still had not declared a state of emergency, the senior Bush official said.

But this claim by the White House official was false. Governor Blanco had declared a State of Emergency ten days earlier on August 26th. On September 3rd—five days after landfall—the President finally authorized federal assets to move:

> President Bush authorized the dispatch of 7,200 active-duty ground troops to the area—the first major commitment of regular ground forces in the crisis—and the Pentagon announced that an additional 10,000 National Guard troops will be sent to Louisiana and Mississippi, raising the total Guard contingent to about 40,000. At a Pentagon news conference Saturday, Lt. Gen. Joseph Inge, the deputy commander of the Northern Command, said the active-duty ground forces would be used mainly to protect sites and perform other functions not considered law enforcement.[129]

From some of the statements made, however, it would appear that some intended to go *beyond* law enforcement:

> 'This place is going to look like a Little Somalia' stated Brigadier General Gary Jones, Commander of the Louisiana National Guard's Joint Task Force. 'We're going to go out and take this city back. This will be a combat operation to get this city under control.' (*Army Times*, Friday, September 2, 2005)

The mobilization was the largest military mobilization on US soil since the Civil War, with nearly 65,000 military personnel deployed to the region. In the absence of early federal support to stabilize the situation, State assets did not or could not restore law and order. The *Army Times* reported September 2nd that the National Guard began a massive operation to "fight insurgents in the city."

All indications suggest that it was only after receiving Blanco's letter on September 3rd that the President decided to act, and that the confusion over the unnecessary and unsigned Memorandum of Agreement lay at the heart of the situation.

Martial Law and FEMA

Aaron Broussard, President of Jefferson Parish, accused FEMA of deliberately sabotaging relief efforts. "New Orleans City Council President Oliver Thomas acknowledged that the city was surprised by the number of refugees left behind, but he said FEMA should have been prepared to assist. "Everybody shares the blame here," said Thomas. "But when you talk about the mightiest government in the world, that's a ludicrous and lame excuse. You're FEMA, and you're the big dog. And you weren't prepared either."[130]

The Memorandum of Understanding which the White House presented to Blanco did not seek to Federalize the Guard *directly*, but by placing Louisiana State Guard and Federal forces under one commander loyal to two sovereigns, it would have achieved virtually the same result, since ultimate authority rests with the Commander-in-Chief. The insistence on achieving a result tantamount to federalizing the Louisiana National Guard and other resources might be explained by examining martial law and readiness exercise planning involving FEMA.

The types of martial law planning that FEMA had been involved in from the 1980s forward will be found shocking to some. FEMA in those years was headed by Louis Guiffrida. Guiffrida had earlier helped to develop a plan at the National War College that included provisions for the "detention of at least 21 million American Negroes" in "assembly centers or relocation camps."[131]

In 1981, President Reagan had put Guiffrida in charge of the California Specialized Training Institute for Counterterrorism with funding from Federal Law Enforcement Assistance Administration (LEAA) of $425,000. Guiffrida designed plans for martial law with names like "Cable Splicer" and "Garden Plot," martial law plans that would have legitimized the arrest and detention of dissidents such as activists opposed to the war in Vietnam. In 1981, Guiffrida took charge of FEMA and created the Civil Security Division and a center for training civil defense personnel in military police methods. President Reagan also set up an Emergency Mobilization Planning Board (EMPB) to put National Security Council in charge of civil defense policy. This plan combined FEMA, the Pentagon and 10 federal agencies. Lt. Col. Oliver North served on the EMPB from 1982-1984 under Robert McFarlane, Assistant to the President for National Security Affairs.

When Attorney General William French Smith got wind of the plans to round up dissenters after being asked to review Executive Order 11490 (a sweeping order giving near dictatorial powers to the President during an emergency), he admonished McFarlane, writing: "I believe that the role assigned to [FEMA] on the revised Executive Order exceeds its proper function as a coordinating agency for emergency preparedness."[132]

North assisted FEMA in making martial law plans to counter civil unrest, according to his testimony during the 1987 Iran-Contra scandal.[133] Giuffrida's tenure FEMA did not last long. He resigned in 1985 under charges of mismanagement and embezzlement. The EMPB was dissolved soon thereafter. Yet one planning concept that was initiated in that period and which survives is Continuity of Government (COG). Continuity of Government essentially replaces Congress with appointed officials. During an emergency, COG replaces federal government with pre-selected executive agency teams that run affairs from secure locations, as Vice President Dick Cheney was reported to be doing well after 9/11. Command was said to rest with the National Security Council (NSC), FEMA and the Department of Defense.[134] We know of no clear indication that Continuity of Government has been lifted since September 11, 2001.

The obvious concern about the various plans just mentioned is that most of these plans appear to move in the direction of suspending the Posse Comitatus Act *indefinitely*. Moreover, both President Bush and Senator Mark Warner (VA) have recently renewed calls to undermine or reverse the *Posse Comitatus Act* of 1878.

Whatever his reasons, President Bush should be the one held responsible for the delay in deploying federal forces to the stricken region of the Gulf Coast. The President has no leg to stand on if he wishes to place blame for the delay on Governor Blanco, as we have seen above, for he did not need her consent in order to move forces. "Existing law is sufficient, and the Congress needs to investigate the New Orleans response by FEMA and government troops, as well as examine and reject the Bush administration's claims that they need more power than the Constitution envisions or allows."[135]

Recommendation: The Constitutional principle and practice of separating military and police functions has become a cornerstone of our democracy. Congress should re-affirm the Posse Comitatus Act in light of proposals to amend or overturn it being made by our President.

5. ENVIRONMENTAL CONCERNS

"Toxic Gumbo"

Hurricane Katrina left behind an environmental nightmare. In addition to scooping up and depositing toxic sediment sludge from the bottom of lakes, rivers and the Gulf of Mexico (as discussed below), Katrina struck 466 facilities handling large quantities of dangerous chemicals, and 31 hazardous waste sites along the Gulf Coast. Among the known contaminants and toxins that mixed with the floodwaters in New Orleans, are: oil, gasoline, hexavalent chromium, mercury, arsenic, chloroacetic acid, fecal bacteria from flooded sewage facilities (including E. coli),[136] household hazardous wastes,[137] pesticides and unattended corpses of the dead.

The United States Coast Guard reported more than 7 million gallons of oil and between 1 and 2 million gallons of gasoline from plants and depots in southeast Louisiana were spilled as a result of the hurricane. Spills of oil and other toxic chemicals pose a particularly serious public health threat when they dry and become airborne as invisible, breathable particulates. One of the first spill reports to come in was that of an oil tanker that had run aground and was leaking fuel.[138] Among the multiple oil spills from above-ground tanks was a tank breach at the Meraux Murphy Oil Refinery where over a million gallons of oil leaked into the floodwaters. Residents whose homes were flooded are being told not to return.[139]

Under the Resource Conservation and Recovery Act (RCRA) facilities that manage hazardous materials are required to have emergency plans to prevent waste or toxins from being released into the environment. The multiple spills suggest that adequate containment mechanisms were not constructed by the owners and companies of the leaking facilities.

The decision to pump the contaminated floodwaters out into Lake Pontchartrain will seriously compromise the fish and other organisms of the lake, and "will also undo the hard-won success of cleaning up Lake Pontchartrain to the point that portions were recently deemed safe for swimming."[140]

Superfund Sites Hit

Hurricane Katrina struck 16 superfund toxic waste sites, 3 of which were flooded, being in the environs of the City of New Orleans, one of them totally submerged. The flooded Superfund sites in Louisiana and Mississippi contained contaminants that include heavy metals associated with developmental problems and increased risk of cancer, and polycyclic aeromatic hydrocarbons, which are known carcinogens. These dangerous materials joined the rest of the dangerous contents of the "toxic gumbo" that mixed in the floodwaters and were then pumped into the Gulf of Mexico and Lake Pontchartrain. Here we have an example of a disaster compounding a disaster, as the toxic spills that created superfund sites (and there is nothing 'super' about them) should never have been allowed to happen in the first place and should have been cleaned up years ago.

In 1995, Congress allowed the taxation of crude oil and chemical feedstocks that provided revenue for the Superfund program to expire. Now comes an environmental catastrophe on the scale of Katrina and while the Superfund in its earlier incantation would have been the perfect vehicle for cleaning up the toxic mess in the Gulf, the work of cleaning up thousands of Superfund sites across the United States of America has come to a virtual standstill. The residents of the Gulf region thus face an uphill battle in getting federal assistance for clean-up, for if there is no money to restore local government, to get people housing so they can return and get jobs and rebuild the tax base, there is unlikely to be any money left for environmental cleanup. This is tragic, since the scale of the problem is simply too vast for local self-help groups or even for state and local government.

Testimonials from Independent Researchers

Independent researchers have reported environmental contaminants such as arsenic, benzo(a)pyrene and petroleum hydrocarbons exceeding Environmental Protection Agency and Louisiana Department of Environmental Quality Standards present in a one eighth inch layer of visibly distinct sediment covering most ground surfaces after the removal of floodwaters from New Orleans and environs.

Wilma Subra, President of Subra Company, an environmental research firm which she founded in 1981, is perhaps the foremost independent expert on this issue. A resident of Iberia, Louisiana, Subra has earned enormous respect in Louisiana and the Gulf Coast, even before Hurricane Katrina. Within 48 hours of Katrina's landfall, she was in the field, assessing the damage, taking test samples and assessing them, figuring out what community members would need to deal with resulting environmental hazards, working with other organizations to get necessary supplies to affected residents.

She has shared her data with the Environmental Protection Agency (EPA), and the EPA has shared its sampling data with her. Both sets of data matched perfectly. Where there is a disagreement is in the *interpretation* of the data. The EPA finds there is no long-term health risk, and has excused itself from the enormous task of removing the sediment sludge.

Wilma also spoke at the New Orleans community event.[141] The section that follows is drawn from Subra's presentation.

The key term to understand about why Hurricane Katrina has created an environmental emergency for the Gulf Coast is "sediment sludge." What is this? All of the historical discharges into the Gulf of Mexico and other water bodies throughout the 1900s wound up in the sediment layer at the bottom of these water bodies. These discharges included issue from untreated wastewater from treatment plants. The last time there was a storm surge even comparable to that of Hurricane Katrina was when Hurricane Betsy hit New Orleans in 1965.

Since that time, the degree of concentration of new chemical effluents in the sediment sludge is far greater than what it was at the time of Betsy.

The storm surge from Hurricane Katrina "scooped up" all this contaminated sediment in these water bodies, carrying it over land and spreading it all over everything. It was not deposited only in New Orleans. The line of contamination extends from Mobile Bay to the Louisiana-Texas line. On top of this, Hurricane Rita's storm surge deposited more contaminated sediment on areas already hit by Katrina and other areas. Wherever a storm surge came ashore *and* where there were breaches in the levees, the sediment sludge was spread all over. In some areas it is very sandy, like at the London Avenue Canal, and in other areas it is more silty, as at the Seventeenth Street and Industrial Canals.

What makes this sediment sludge dangerous is that it contains high levels of dangerous chemical such as:

- arsenic: a heavy metal and a suspected cancer-causing agent;

- polynuclear aeromatic hydrocarbons (PAHs): a big word, but the reader may be more familiar with the danger of waste from creosote facilities—PAHs comprise one of the chemical compounds in creosote that makes it toxic; and

- benzo(a)pyrene: a probable carcinogen, and the most toxic of these three.

Added to these chemicals are such organisms as:

- fecal choliforms: from untreated sewage;

- Staphylococcus aureus ("Staph"): an organism that gives you sore throat and skin infections; and

- salmonella: another bug that gives you food poisoning.

All of these organisms are alive and well in the sediment sludge. The sludge is very available, it is on the surface, and has been spread all over the yards and sidewalks. It is easy to kick up. When the organisms enter the lungs, and the affected person visits the doctor, the physician typically assumes that he is dealing with only one of these types of organisms, not more than one type. Hence the treatment typically fails because multiple types of organisms are causing the problem.

Exposure to these toxins can come through skin contact, resulting in skin rashes that do not respond to normal antibiotics; and inhalation, which can result in persistent respiratory problems and what local doctors are calling "Katrina cough."[142] While all the health agencies dispute this claim, all the medical doctors who have treated the responders, who have treated the people who return to their houses, say it is real, and it results mostly from recurrent, long-term exposure.

The local government has declared that in most areas it is safe for residents to return to their homes. But in reality, the presence of sediment sludge inside houses and on the yard means that returning residents are at risk of exposure to very toxic substances and contamination where the organisms are concerned.

In the aftermath of the Hurricane, Wilma Subra worked with the Louisiana Environmental Action Network (LEAN), a grassroots organization which at the time had very limited resources. Together with the Southern Mutual Health Association and Oxfam America, they assembled and began distributing kits for returning residents that included tybec suits, respirators, gloves, booties and essential cleaning supplies, advising residents to use the kits to avoid contact with the hazardous materials. They encouraged small children, pregnant women and the elderly not to go in until the hazardous material was cleaned up and addressed.

They approached FEMA and asked FEMA to take over and distribute the kits. FEMA declined. They asked the EPA. The EPA declined. So it was left up to LEAN, a local grassroots organization, to spearhead the enormous effort of providing these safety kits to returning residents. The kits were distributed through local community self-help groups like the Common Ground Relief Collective, and through local Churches, who in turn distributed them to their constituents.

The sediment sludge varies in depth. At the various sites of the levee breaches, the layer of sediment sludge deposited into residential areas could range from four to even as much as twelve feet. In most other affected areas away from these breaches the layer could be as thick as three to six feet, but once it dries it becomes a thin, dry layer of hazardous material that can easily become airborne upon contact. Over time, this material will travel. The delay in addressing this problem, with the refusal of the EPA to do the clean-up in spite of the fact that the EPA is the Incident Command agency responsible for clean-up, will mean that any clean-up effort will become more difficult over time, because the material will have gotten more spread around. Thus there is an urgent need for action at the federal level to get the clean-up effort started.

Monique Harden serves as International Policy Counsel for the National Black Environmental Justice Network. Ms. Harden also spoke at our community meeting, and below is a summary of her presentation.

What we are seeing in the Gulf Coast is a repeat of 9/11. In the aftermath of the attack on the World Trade Center the EPA was there saying the air quality was good when in fact it wasn't. And just recently we heard the news about a 9/11 rescue worker who died of black lung at the age of 34. Is this the future for New Orleans?

The Hurricane Relief Bill which was passed by Congress in the name of providing immediate aid to the affected region waived all public health and environmental laws. This was the opposite of what was needed to protect residents from harmful exposure. Since Katrina, the EPA has been going through this process of "assessing." This sounds good but means very little. Wilma Subra discovered the presence of arsenic and diesel fuel substances at levels above safety limits. Both of these materials can cause cancers in the long term. The presence of these toxic hazards on streets and sidewalks would, under existing regulations, qualify the entire region affected by the sediment sludge to be declared a Superfund site.

One would think that since we can easily demonstrate the presence of toxins at levels that would qualify our neighborhoods to get on the Superfund list, that we should be able to get the EPA interested in doing the clean-up. But so far, this has not been the case.

Recommendation: Congress should revive the Superfund program, which taxes polluters to pay for the environmental cleanup they are responsible for creating in the first place.

Looking at the data for arsenic, the EPA sets the screening level at 0.39 milligrams per kilogram. The screening level means further study is required. The Mississippi Department of Environmental Quality (DEQ) has a screening level of 0.4 milligrams, but the Louisiana DEQ sets the screening level at *12.0* milligrams per kilogram. There are states that will not allow children to play on soil with arsenic levels above 5.0 milligrams per kilogram. But in New Orleans and in places along the Gulf Coast, *average* levels of arsenic widely exceed 12 milligrams per kilogram. Now it is important for Members of Congress to understand how inadequate our system of environmental protection is. It's fine if you don't need it, but once you need it, you're in trouble. This is because the EPA sets no levels above which clean-up would be required. What's the *clean-up* level? No one can say. Even in terms of screening levels there is a problem, because in the case of Hurricane Katrina, the EPA has abandoned its own standards in favor of the more lax standards of States. So in Mississippi, arsenic samples above 0.4 milligrams per kilogram will merit further study. But in Louisiana the EPA only does further study if samples reach 12.0 milligrams per kilogram or higher.

The EPA and the Army Corps of Engineers have also declined so far to undertake the task of cleaning up the sediment sludge. Wilma Subra has been quoted as saying: "I get the impression that they don't want to remove anything, because if they do start removing, they set a precedent."[143]

The Failure of the EPA to Act

As soon as residents began returning to the region, returning residents and responders began reporting widespread cases of respiratory problems, asthmas and skin rashes. Law enforcement and emergency service personnel who waded for hours or days in the toxic floodwaters are now reporting medical problems that doctors are having a hard time diagnosing. These problems are being given names like "Katrina Rash" and "New Orleans Crud." Symptoms include terrible itching on the skin, abdominal cramps, high fevers. Says one responder: "They dumped us in New Orleans without the right equipment and they didn't give us shots or respirators." "I'm tired of my chest hurting," says a another.[144]

The Environmental Protection Agency failed to develop any broad strategic plan for dealing with the post-hurricane environmental clean-up and public safety, detailing goals and methods of achieving them. Tens of thousands of disaster responders and returning residents were allowed into damaged areas without receiving sufficient warnings or information about levels of contamination, health risks or necessary precautions. Given the comparatively enormous resources at their disposal, the refusal by the both the EPA and FEMA to assist in local efforts to protect residents and responders from exposure to toxins and contaminants that the EPA's own data shows are present in quantities exceeding safety limits is an outright scandal.

There is still time to act. With sufficient government testing, warning and support, the people of the Gulf Coast region could be protected from similar dangers arising from the above-mentioned post-hurricane environmental hazards.

Recommendation: Congress must pass legislation directing the Environmental Protection Agency to establish a comprehensive assessment and protection plan for the citizens of the Gulf Coast to protect the public from environmental contaminants and infectious materials that pose a threat to public health and safety in the aftermath of Hurricane Katrina.

The wetlands of the Gulf Coast are eroding. It took thousands of years for the sediments of the Mississippi River to build up the healthy marshes and barrier islands of the coastal wetlands. These wetlands serve as a natural shield, buffering the impact of storms. Yet over a million acres or 25% of the total number of acres of wetlands have disappeared since 1930 due to the diversion of the replenishing sediment and fresh water with the building of shipping canals and flood control works, among other causes. Every hour, a piece of land the size of two football fields is lost to the open water.[145] The "Coast 2050" plan envisions redesigning the flood control and shipping system to restore healthy sedimentation and replenish the wetlands. The price tag is usually estimated at between $14 and $25 billion for a 50 year project. One expert suggests that for every mile of wetlands passed by a storm surge, flooding would be reduced by a foot.[146] Congress needs to get involved and play a facilitating role in local efforts to restore one of America's greatest natural treasures.

Recommendation: Congress should establish a commission to work with scientists, engineers and state and local governments to explore the feasibility of the "Coast 2050"[147] plan to restore the coastal wetlands.

5. Conclusion: Bridges to Nowhere

A single weather event, Hurricane Katrina, has brought about the greatest population dislocation in the United States since the Great Depression of the 1930s. Katrina was not the strongest hurricane ever to hit the Gulf Coast, but it was perhaps the most destructive ever due to its extraordinary storm surge on the one hand, and due to human failures on the other. These failures are many and profound: the inadequacy of levees, the inadequacy of the evacuation plan, the inadequacy of the governmental response and a social environment characterized by widespread poverty, racial inequities and a history of racial discrimination. Without these failures, Hurricane Katrina, whose effect was compounded in mostly rural areas by Hurricane Rita, might have had an impact much more in keeping with most other hurricanes. Instead, Katrina's impact will be permanent and irreversible for many families and communities. The cleanup and reconstruction effort alone will likely take no less than a decade to accomplish, but the speed of that effort will also be determined by whether the American people step forward and exert sufficient pressure on their government to speed up the relief and reconstruction effort, or whether that effort is also shaped by human failure and a lack of compassion. President Bush has made a lot of easy promises, but has failed to live up to his words.[148]

As our tour bus for the Congressional Delegation made up of Select Committee Members, guest Members and their staff drove through the devastated Lower Ninth Ward of New Orleans, not far from downtown, one could still get a sense of the charm. Aside from the roads having been cleared, little had changed in four and a half months since a twenty foot wall of water was unleashed upon the is community of lower-income, mostly African-American residents. As we passed by heaps of debris, we were reminded that there were likely to be found more dead bodies (as indeed several have been even since our visit), it was possible to imagine the lifestyle of the residents of these cozy square wood houses.

Fourteen per cent of residents in the Lower Ninth were senior citizens. Another fourteen percent were handicapped. A full sixty percent owned their own homes, ranking the home ownership rate in this community among the highest in the country. At the same time, only forty per cent of residents were literate. These astonishing figures tell a tale of a community that was industrious, frugal and ill-served by the educational system. But most of all, you could tell just by looking that in spite of the fact that their homes were small, the people who lived here were proud of their community, and proud to contribute their part to the culture of New Orleans.

Another dramatic fact is that few of these residents left New Orleans very often. But now they are scattered to the four winds and 44 states, and of all the residents of New Orleans they face the longest odds of ever returning to their homes, most of which are beyond repair, let alone ever receiving compensation for the loss of their property. Numbers and dollar figures cannot begin to calculate the loss experienced by, say, a senior in her 80s who had rarely ever set foot outside New Orleans, but who now faces the challenge of starting a new life all over again in a strange community far away, separated from family and friends.

Hurricane Katrina, which struck the coasts of Louisiana, Mississippi and Alabama on August 29, 2005, was the first event to be declared an "Incident of National Significance" by the Secretary of Homeland Security, as empowered to do so under the NRP. The first priority listed in the event of an Incident of National Significance is "to save lives and protect the health and safety of the public, resources and recovery workers."

A mandatory evacuation was declared for the City of New Orleans in the aftermath of Hurricane Katrina. Yet more than 100,000 residents of New Orleans simply lacked the means to evacuate upon demand. There are many reasons why. The elderly, the disabled and the infirm required special assistance. Most self-supporting residents were low income earners and did not have their own means of transport to get out. Before the Hurricane Pam exercise in 2004, this issue seriously addressed, but funds for hurricane disaster planning were cut by the DHS.

For the low income, mostly black residents of Orleans Parish who had not heeded or could not heed evacuation calls, the order to evacuate was effectively meaningless. How would our 82 year-old grandmother with no care, living on a fixed income, and whose only family was based in the area about to be hit, get up and relocate out of the city. For starters, how would she pay for the hotel bills? For as many as five days after Hurricane Katrina, many of the bridges of New Orleans became bridges to nowhere, most with floodwaters on both ends. Thousands of survivors spent days stranded on a bridge, hopeful and expectant that one of the many helicopters flying overhead would stop and rescue them from the toxic floodwaters and the searing hot sun. Some black survivors report helicopters teasing them at the prospect of rescue and then leaving them and moving on to white neighborhoods. The conditions at the Convention Center, the Superdome, the I-10 / Causeway Cloverleaf resembled concentration camps—days of internment without adequate food, water or sanitation, and a growing sense of hopelessness. Yet all this wasn't all just about poor coordination. The Gretna Police *turned back* survivors seeking a way out by crossing the Crescent City Connection bridge, and subsequently confiscated their food and water—bridge to nowhere.

What we are left with is a spectacular failure of government. Prior to the flooding of New Orleans, Grover Norquist, President of Americans for Tax Reform and a close associated of indicted lobbyist Jack Abramoff, has publicly stated the following: "I don't want to abolish government. I simply want to reduce it to the size where I can drag it into the bathroom and drown it in the bathtub." It seems he got his wish, at least for the people of New Orleans. Hurricane Katrina should and undoubtedly will force us to reexamine prevalent notions of the market fundamentalists, who are ready and willing to fund any wars the government takes on, but who loathe paying for social programs or public infrastructure. It was under-funding that contributed to the flooding of New Orleans, and to the delinquent response. It may be under-funding that cripples the ability of tens of thousands of residents to return home and rebuild their lives.

Americans are generous when it comes to disaster. The $3 billion that has been raised by private entities for the relief effort eclipses the $2.2 raised for victims of 9/11. "But charity is episodic and driven by disaster. What is needed are structures of justice that perpetuate the goodwill intended in charity."[149]

The Gulf Coast provides America with a significant share of its energy supplies. This should be kept in mind as Congress and the White House decide how much relief and reconstruction monies are to be given, and in what form. Making a strong investment may pay greater dividends later. We can choose to leave New Orleans to the Donald Trumps and Prince Charles's of the world, who are already busy buying up property and planning their casinos and condominiums for the rich. In doing so we may be depriving tens of thousands of working people of their right of return, of their voting rights, of their property rights and yes, of their civil rights.

We can also choose to go half-way and assist only enough to restore things to the way they were before Katrina. But many working class survivors don't want to go back to how it was before. They see Katrina as an opportunity to fix what was broken. They dream of a New Orleans with its racial diversity restored, free of grinding poverty and crowded prisons, with strong levees[150] and comprehensive evacuation plans for future hurricanes. The Federal government should seek creative ways to assist in such a noble endeavor.

Summary of Recommendations:

- When the National Response Plan and/or other disaster preparedness plans are revised, they need to be updated to anticipate looting as a highly probable and often rational response to scarcity by individuals in an emergency. Rights of property must not supersede the right to food, water and medicine, i.e. the right to survive, especially not during a declared emergency.

- FEMA or any agency that replaces it must be directed to produce impact and implementation policy studies aimed at producing emergency preparedness and response policies that address the particular needs of minority communities.

- Congress should pass legislation to set procedures for protecting the civil liberties of minorities during an emergency situation. Armed forces and police should be on notice that individual acts of blatant discrimination or abuse of minorities will result in serious punishments, and systemic abuse will result in loss of financial support. Private relief organizations with discriminatory relief practices should be subject to review and possible loss of contracts.

- Recommendation: Future emergency preparedness planning must include the provision of transportation for the elderly, the infirm and those without their own means of locomotion, as well as the placing of Disaster Recovery Centers (DRCs) as near as is feasible, to enable these evacuees to return to their homes as quickly and easily as possible.

- Congress should pass legislation to ban political patronage within Federal agencies; specifically within FEMA and DHS.

- Recommendation: The National Response Plan should either be overhauled or scrapped. A new plan should be developed that includes: 1) unambiguous command structures for military responders; 2) crystal clear clarification regarding the integration of the work of state and federal armed forces during an emergency to maximize the ability to deploy military assets in a pro-active manner; 3) pre-set standard operating procedures for non-military agencies operating in a crisis detailing what operations they can and should initiate without waiting for marching orders from a higher authority; 4) an integrated communications plan that puts all responders on the same page from the get-go, using Interoperable Communications technology.

- Recommendation: The National Response Plan is color blind, and any future such national emergency response plans must include sensitivity training for both military and non-military responders so that responders are aware in advance of the specific needs and leadership patterns in communities of color.

- Recommendation: Emergency response agencies like FEMA should offer diversity training to their employees, and establish direct working relationships with leadership figures in minority communities living in disaster prone areas such as flood planes so that those relationships are forged and ready to call upon prior to the emergency.

- Congress should re-establish FEMA as an independent Federal agency, removing it from DHS; but give housing oversight back to HUD.

- Take international politics out of disaster relief efforts by establishing a policy that no legitimate offers of foreign assistance will be refused.

- Future hurricane response plans should include evacuations for prisons susceptible to flooding.

- Congress should direct the Government Accountability office to investigate:

  1) the degree to which confusion over roles, responsibilities and powers contributed to the tragic and unnecessary delay in dispatching Federal forces to the incident site; and

  2) the Bush administration's claims that the Commander-in-Chief needs more power than the Constitution envisions or allows.

- Recommendation: The Constitutional principle and practice of separating military and police functions has become a cornerstone of our democracy. Congress should re-affirm the Posse Comitatus Act in light of proposals to amend or overturn it being made by our President.

- Congress should revive the Superfund program, which taxes polluters to pay for the environmental cleanup they are responsible for creating in the first place.

- Congress must pass legislation directing the Environmental Protection Agency to establish a comprehensive assessment and protection plan for the citizens of the Gulf Coast to protect the public from environmental contaminants and infectious materials that pose a threat to public health and safety in the aftermath of Hurricane Katrina.

- The Federal government should establish a commission to work with scientists, engineers and state and local governments to explore the feasibility of the "Coast 2050" plan to restore the coastal wetlands.

SOURCE NOTES

Cover Art: by Ricardo Levins Morales, distributed by the Northland Poster Collective, who offered the Hurricane Katrina Poster and raise funds for the relief efforts. For More Information: Northland Poster: 1-800-627-3082; [http://www.northlandposter.com] (accessed February 6, 2006); Southern Partners Fund: [http://www.spfund.org] (accessed February 6, 2006).

[1] On July 22, 2005, on the anniversary of the release of the *9/11 Commission Report*, Rep. Cynthia McKinney hosted a Congressional Briefing entitled "The 9/11 Commission Report One Year Later: Did the Commission Get it Right?" at which over 30 independent experts discussed the omissions, errors and false premises of the Report.

[2] David Walker, Comptroller General of the United States made this observation at a press conference held jointly with Select Committee Chairman Tom Davis on Wednesday, February 1st, 2006.

[3] "…for those even slightly familiar with the current intelligence reform proposals, there is a more than vague sense, to use Yogi Berra's immortal phrase, '*Deja vu* all over again.' There has been a failure. Pearl Harbor. The unpredicted Soviet development of the Atomic Bomb, the Chinese Communist victory in 1949. Remember who lost China. The equally unpredicted North Korean invasion in 1950. The Bay of Pigs failure. Vietnam. The overthrow of the Shah in 1978. Samosa and Nicaragua a year later, not only unpredicted, but confidently declared by our intelligence estimates as impossible, or a scandal, and Iran-Contra comes to mind inevitably here, and some others in the 1970s. What happens next? A commission will be appointed, usually by the Executive, but post-Vietnam, often by the Congress. You will recall the Hoover Commission in the 1950s, the Church and Pike Commissions of the 1970s, and the Iran-Contra Joint Congressional Committee in the 1980s. Often forgotten are the Senate hearings of 1992, which tried to learn how we were so unprepared for Iraq's evasion of Kuwait, and led among other things to the late Senator Moynihan's very serious proposal for doing away with the CIA altogether, and Senator Arlen Spector's repeated and now accepted idea that the post of National Director of Intelligence and Director of the CIA be separated. The Committee, talking of this generic committee here, will labor long and hard and recommend inevitably that the agencies concerned coordinate their activities better and share their information" --David MacMichael, former CIA officer, speaking at the Congressional Briefing "The 9/11 Commission Report One Year Later: Did the Commission Get it Right?", July 22, 2005. While this quote concerns intelligence form, the conclusions of the Select Committee Report do tend to fit the pattern described.

[4] David Walker, Comptroller General of the United States, called for the appointment of one person to be the President's point person on disaster relief at a press conference held jointly with Select Committee Chairman Tom Davis on Wednesday, February 1st, 2006. Chairman Tom Davis joined this press conference and expressed overall consensus between the Select Committee and the GAO's report, although not necessarily on this specific point.

[5] Associated Press, "Holiday Depression Follows Katrina," December 7, 2005.

[6] Associated Press, "Katrina's aftermath tough on mental health," January 28, 2006.

[7] *Agence-France Presse*, January 12, 2006, "Bush Reaffirms Pledge To Rebuild Hurricane-Ravaged States."

[8] Cf. Freedberg, Sydney J Jr., "Disaster Inc.," *National Journal*, December 17, 2005.

[9] Fisher, William, "Report Finds 'Appalling Level of Fraud and Greed'," *Inter Press Service News Agency*, June 29, 2005. Halliburton has already been cited for overcharging the government hundreds of millions of dollars in contracts.

[10] Yen, Hope, "FEMA has yet to reopen no-bid Katrina contracts," Associated Press, November 11, 2005.

[11] *Democracy Now!*, "Workers in New Orleans Denied Pay, Proper Housing and Threatened with Deportation," December 16, 2006.

[12] Cf. also: Moran, Kate, "Building Owner Sues Jeff Parish over Seizure; Broussard had no right to take property for cleanup, he says," *Times-Picayune*, November 8, 2005. In the story, building owner George Ackel's property had been claimed by Jefferson Parish for cleanup operations and he was suing. As of the date of the piece, he had gotten no compensation.

[13] Raspberry, William, "Two Storms, Ample Warning", *Washington Post*, September 6, 2005.

[14] Zweig, Michael, "Talking Points on Class, Race and Gender in the U.S." (unpublished). Zweig is a professor of economics and Director of the Study of Working Class Life at the State University of New York at Stony Brook.

[15] Louisiana Works Department of Labor, "Louisiana Labor Diversity by Workforce", 2004, as cited by Zweig, ibid. Available online at: [http://www.laworks.net/forms/er/AffirmativeActionPublication.pdf] (accessed: February 2, 2006).

[16] As cited by *Wikipedia*, "New Orleans, Louisiana" at [http://www.wikipedia.org] (accessed: February 2, 2006).

[17] Dyson, Michael Eric, *Come Hell or High Water: Hurricane Katrina and the Color of Disaster*, New York, Basic Civitas, 2006: 143.

[18] Ibid. 143-144.

[19] Cf. *CNN*, "Katrina Victims 'Living in Barns': Parish President blasts FEMA over Temporary Homes," December 13, 2005.

[20] Zweig, op. cit.

[21] Shafer, Jack, "The Rebellion of the Talking Heads", *Slate.com*, September 2, 2005. Online at: [http://www.slate.com/toolbar.aspx?action=print&id=2125581] (accessed September 2, 2005).

[22] Pierre, Robert E. and Paul Farhi, "'Refugee': A Word of Trouble", *Washington Post*, September 7, 2005; C01.

[23] O'Driscoll, Patrick, "'The looters, They're like Cockroaches'", *USA Today*, September 2, 2005.

[24] Saletan, William, "The Thin Line Blew," *Slate.com*, September 4, 2005. Online at: [http://www.slate.com/id/2125575/nav/tap1/] (accessed September 4, 2005).

[25] Cf. Hudson, Audrey, "Storm Victims Praise Churches," *Washington Times*, December 2, 2005.

[26] Max, "Pat Robertson's Katrina Cash," *The Nation*, September 7, 2005; available only online at: [http://www.democracynow.org/article.pl?sid=05/09/07/1415225] (accessed February 5, 2006).

[27] *USA Today,* "Pat Robertson calls for assassination of Hugo Chavez," August 22, 2005.

[28] *CNN.com*, "Robertson suggests God smote Sharon Evangelist links Israeli leader's stroke to 'dividing God's land'," January 6, 2006. Online at: [http://www.cnn.com/2006/US/01/05/robertson.sharon/] (accessed February 5, 2006).

[29] Nolan, Bruce, "In Storm, N.O. Wants No One Left Behind," *Times-Picayune*, July 24, 2005.

[30] Community Forum, "Who is Cleaning up After Katrina?" held in New Orleans on January 19, 2006.

[31] CF. Nossiter, Adam, "Fight Grows in New Orleans on Demolition and Rebuilding," *New York Times*, January 6, 2005; and Nossiter, Adam, "New Orleans Delays Razing Houses 2 Weeks," *New York Times*, January 7, 2006.

[32] For example, see: Herrck, Thaddeus, "Teen Tension Trails Hurricane Evacuees into Houston School—With Influx of New Students Comes Insults, Brawls, Parents Protest the Cuffs," *Wall Street Journal*, December 2, 2005.

[33] Abdel Kouddous, Sharif and John Hamilton: "Three Displaced New Orleans Residents Discuss Race and Hurricane Katrina," *Democracy Now!* Wednesday, September 7th, 2005. Online at: [http://www.democracynow.org/article.pl?sid=05/09/07/1415225] (accessed February 5, 2006).

[34] The reader is advised that this is not the same bridge as the one where Ms. Hodges and Ms. Nelson stayed, which was at I-10 and North Causeway Boulevard.

[35] *60 Minutes on CBS*, "The Bridge to Gretna" (aired December 18, 2005). Transcript available online at: [http://www.cbsnews.com/stories/2005/12/15/60minutes/main1129440.shtml] (accessed February 2, 2006).

[36] *CNN*, "Racism, Resources Blamed for Bridge Incident," September 13, 2005.

[37] Gertz, Bill, 1992, "Mikulski Faults FEMA Officials, Calls for Probe", *Washington Times*, September 4, 1992 (as cited by [http://www.wikipedia.org] "James Lee Witt" (accessed February 1, 2006).

[38] *Atlanta Journal-Constitution*, February 12, 1996, "Short takes; Quick Witt Helps", (as cited by [http://www.wikipedia.org] "James Lee Witt" (accessed February 1, 2006).

[39] Ibid.

[40] *Wikipedia*, "James Lee Witt" online at: [http://www.wikipedia.org] (accessed February 1, 2006).

[41] Arends, Brett, "Brown pushed from last job: Horse group: FEMA chief had to be `asked to resign," *Boston Herald*, September 3, 2005.

[42] Cf. Pierce, Emily, "Brown 'Slipped' Through," *Roll Call*, September 12, 2005.

[43] Bennett, Jonathan, "Brown's Turf Wars Sapped FEMA's Strength: Director Who Came to Symbolize Incompetence in Katrina Predicted Agency Would Fail," *Washington Post*, December 23, 2005.

[44] Bennett, ibid.

[45] Center for Progressive Reform, "An Unnatural Disaster: The Aftermath of Hurricane Katrina Executive Summary", September 2005, p. 6.

[46] Bennett, op. cit.

[47] Bennett, ibid.

[48] Bennett, ibid.

[49] Bennett, ibid.

[50] *National Response Plan*, December 2004, Fig. 3, p. 17.

[51] Cf. United States Coast Guard, "Incident Command System," available online at: [http://www.uscg.mil/hq/g-m/mor/articles/ics.htm] (accessed February 6, 2006).

[52] Center for Progressive Reform, "An Unnatural Disaster: The Aftermath of Hurricane Katrina Executive Summary", September 2005, p. 6.

[53] Arkin, William, "Early Warning, William M. Arkin on National and Homeland Security, Michael Brown Was Set Up: It's All in the Numbers," *WashingtonPost.com* blog. Online at: [http://blogs.washingtonpost.com/earlywarning/2005/09/michael_brown_w.html] (accessed February 5, 2006). Arkin's specific numbers are: Hurricanes and Natural Disasters: 45; Terrorism and WMD: 1,287.

[54] Bennett, op. cit.

[55] Bennett, ibid.

[56] Gosselin, Peter G., "Bush is in No Hurry on Katrina Recovery," *Los Angeles Times*, October 17, 2005.

[57] Gosselin, ibid.

[58] Hsu, Spencer S. and Amy Goldstein, "Administration Faulted on Katrina: GAO Report Blames Bungled Response on Failures That Started at the Top," *Washington Post*, February 2, 2006; A05.

[59] Lush, Tamara, "For forecasting chief, no joy in being right Max Mayfield strives for accuracy, but worries about complacency," *St. Petersburg Times*, August 30, 2005.

[60] Landay, Jonathon S., et. al., "Chertoff Delayed Federal Response, Memo Shows," *Knight Ridder*, September 13, 2005.

[61] Froomkin, Dan, "A Dearth of Answers, *washingtonpost.com*, Thursday, September 1, 2005. Online at: [http://www.washingtonpost.com/wp-dyn/content/blog/2005/09/01/BL2005090100915.html] (accessed February 5, 2006).

[62] *Daily News*, "As South drowns, Rice soaks in N.Y.", September 2, 2005.

[63] *The Los Angeles Times*, "Italy Tells of Threat at Genoa Summit Plot: Officials there took seriously a report that terrorists would try to crash a plane to kill Bush and other leaders," September 27, 2001.

[64] Froomkin, Dan, "A Dearth of Answers, *washingtonpost.com*, Thursday, September 1, 2005. Online at: [http://www.washingtonpost.com/wp-dyn/content/blog/2005/09/01/BL2005090100915.html] (accessed February 5, 2006).

[65] Cf. Schleifstein, Mark, "Close Call Offers Lessons for Next Big Storm," *Times Picayune*, October 4, 1998.

[66] Naftali, Tim, "Department of Homeland Screw-Up", *Slate.com*, September 6, 2005 [http://www.slate.com/toolbar.aspx?action=print&id=2125494] (accessed September 6, 2006).

[67] Williamson, Elizabeth, "Offers of Aid Immediate, but U.S. Approval Delayed for Days", *Washington Post*, September 7, 2005; A1.

[68] Murray, Mary, "Katrina Aid from Cuba? No Thanks, says U.S. America Welcomes Foreign Help, Except from an Old Cold War Foe", *NBC News*, September 14, 2005. online at: [http://www.msnbc.msn.com/id/9311876/] (accessed February 1, 2006).

[69] Muhammad, Cedric, "Online Columnist Speculates that New Orleans Levee Breach May Have Been Intentional" *BlackElectorate.com*, September 29, 2005. Online at: [http://www.neworleansblack.com/indexarchive/9-29-05/9-29-05-index.php].

[70] From a summary of the PBS "American Experience" documentary *Fatal Flood*. Available online at: [http://www.pbs.org/wgbh/amex/flood/timeline/timeline2.html] (accessed February 5, 2006).

[71] Ibid.

[72] Cf. Barry, John M. *Rising Tide: The Great Mississippi Flood of 1927 and How Changed America*, New York: Simon & Schuster, 1998.

[73] Van Heerden testified before the Senate Committee on Homeland Security on Nov. 2nd, 2005.

[74] For a preview of one of these investigation's results, see: Nicholson, Peter, "Hurricane Katrina: Why Did the Levees Fail?" testimony on behalf of the American Society of Civil Engineers before the Committee on Homeland Security and Governmental Affairs, U.S. Senate, November 2, 2005.

[75] Muhammad, Cedric, "Online Columnist Speculates that New Orleans Levee Breach May Have Been Intentional" *BlackElectorate.com*, September 29, 2005. Online at: [http://www.neworleansblack.com/indexarchive/9-29-05/9-29-05-index.php].

[76] Cf. Schleifstein, Mark, "Close Call Offers Lessons for Next Big Storm," *Times Picayune*, October 4, 1998.

[77] Schleifstein, Mark, "Hurricane Plans Evaluated as Season Begins," *Times Picayune*, June 1, 1999.

[78] Schleifstein, Mark, "Hurricane, "Morial, State Dispute Dome as Shelter: Emergency Planners, Morial Disagree on Using Dome During Hurricane," *Times-Picayune*, June 2, 1999.

[79] *Times-Picayune*, "Special Report: Washing Away," June 23-27, 2002.

[80] Berger, Eric, "Keeping its Head Above Water, New Orleans Faces Doomsday Scenario," *Houston Chronicle*, December 1, 2001.

[81] Hartman, Thom, "You Can't Govern if you Don't Believe in Government," *Commondreams.org*, September 6, 2006; online at: [http://www.commondreams.org/views05/0906-21.htm] (accessed September 8, 2006). Emphasis not in the original.

[82] "Politicizing Disaster Relief; How FEMA Overcompensated Florida Citizens in the Run-Up to the Presidential Election," interview with *South Florida Sun Sentinel* reporter Megan O'Matz by Amy Goodman, *Democracy Now!* September 8, 2005.

[83] E-mail from Brown's deputy chief of staff, Brooks Altshuler to Brown, possibly dated August 30, 2005. Cf. Hsu, Spencer S., "Messages Depict Disarray in Federal Katrina Response," *Washington Post*, October 18, 2005.

[84] Associated Press, October 20, 2005, "FEMA Official: Agency Failed."

[85] Rich, Frank, "Fallujah Floods the Superdome," *New York Times*, September 4, 2005.

[86] Associated Press, October 17, 2005, "FEMA in Chaos from Start, Memos Show."

[87] Ahlers, Mike M., "Firefighting Gear Stockpile Unused", *Cnn.com*, September 6, 2005; online at: [http://edition.cnn.com/2005/WEATHER/09/03/katrina.unusedgear/index.html] (accessed September 6, 2005); citing the White House website: [http://www.whitehouse.gov/] (original page no longer available).

[88] Merle, Renae and Griff Witte, "Lack of Contracts Hampered FEMA," *Washington Post*, October 10, 2005; A01.

[89] Comment by James Lecollier, contracting officer at the Defense Logistics Agency, cf. Merle, ibid.

[90] The comments that follow are from notes taken during a personal visit from Ms. Campbell to our office on January 23, 2006.

[91] Hsu, Spencer S., "Post-Katrina Promises Largely Unfulfilled," *Washington Post*, January 28, 2006.

[92] Shane, Scott and Eric Lipton, "In Federal Buying Spree for Hurricane Relief, Agencies Often Paid Retail," *New York Times*, October 15, 2005; A14.

[93] Rioux, Paul, "FEMA Worker Charged with Looting: He was at Home to Install Trailer," *Times-Picayune*, January 10, 2006.

[94] Associated Press, "FEMA Employees Indicted in Kickback Scheme," January 27, 2006.

[95] Rochell Konigsmark, Anne, "FEMA to open apartments to displaced New Orleanians," *USA Today*, January 31, 2005.

[96] Possley, Maurice, "Keeper of Katrina's Dead," *Chicago Tribune*, November 8, 2005; cf. also Foster, Mary, "Katrina's Victims are Still Largely Nameless," *Associated Press*, October 6, 2005: "More than a month after Hurricane Katrina, the vast majority of the nearly 1,000 dead in Louisiana lie anonymously in a morgue—largely because authorities have released only a few dozen names, but also, perhaps, because many of the victims' families were scattered by the storm and are still picking up the pieces of their lives."

[97] McGill, Kevin and John Solomon, "A Sausage—Looted or Not—Lands Elderly Church Leader in Prison," Associated Press, September 15, 2005; and Simpson, Doug, "Grandmother Accused of Looting During Hurricane Katrina Released from Jail," Associated Press, September 16, 2005.

[98] This and the following points are taken from: Safer Streets, Strong Communities, "The New Orleans Criminal Justice System: An Opportunity to Rebuild" (2006 handout), citing *Times-Picayune* articles and a 1998 report by Human Rights Watch. Citations can be made available upon request.

[99] Scahill, Jeremy, "Blackwater Down," *The Nation*, October 10, 2005.

[100] Scahill, ibid.

[101] Perlstein, Michael, "Hearing Set on Mothers in Jail," *Times-Picayune*, May 4, 1999; as cited by Safe Streets, ibid.

[102] Young, Tara, "Murder suspect dies in prison: Ruptured Ulcer Killed Man, Doctor Says", *Times-Picayune*, March 5, 2002; as cited by Safe Streets, op. cit.

[103] WDSU Channel 6, "Orleans Criminal Sheriff's Deputies Indicted in Inmate's Death", June 2, 2005. Online at: [http://www.wdsu.com/news/4562307/detail.html] (accessed February 2, 2006).

[104] Department of Justice-Bureau of Justice Statistics, "Sexual Violence Reported by Correctional Authorities 2004", July 2005; as cited by Safe Streets, op. cit.

[105] Safe Streets, op. cit.

[106] Information taken by Safe Streets from the Louisiana State Prison website, online at: [http://www.corrections.state.la.us/LSP/general.htm] (access date unknown; page still active but subject to updates).

[107] Former OPP Chief Eddie Compass testifying before the New Orleans City Council, November 8, 2004. Transcript available in the New Orleans City Council Crime Summits 2004-2005, as cited by Safe Streets, op. cit.

[108] Safe Streets, op. cit.

[109] Kilborn, Julie H., Atty., "Evacuation of Women Inmates From Orleans Parish Prison," September 18, 2005. The author works in Baton Rouge, LA.

[110] Carey, Corinne, "Excerpts of Letters from Prisoners Abandoned to Katrina," Human Rights Watch, October 10, 2005.

[111] Human Rights Watch, "Louisiana: After Katrina, Inmates Face Prison Abuse", October 3, 2005.

[112] "Left to Die in a New Orleans Prison," Interview with Corinne Carcy, *Democracy Now!* September 28, 2005.

[113] Community Forum, "Who is Cleaning up After Katrina?" held in New Orleans on January 19, 2006.

[114] The American Civil Liberties Union (ACLU) is suing the OPP for records to determine why prisoners were abandoned to the storm, see: ACLU "Sheriff Illegally Withholding Records on Orleans Parish Prison, ACLU Lawsuit Charges," November 10, 2005.

[115] Human Rights Watch, "Louisiana: Justice Obstructed, Not Restored", October 14, 2005. See also: ACLU, "ACLUE Urges New Orleans City Council to Review Conditions at Prison," December 8, 2005. Testimony from prisoners who were never sentenced, prisoners who remain in prison past their release dates and prisoners who have been released has been available to our office.

[116] Also used for this section: Sothern, Billy, "Left to Die," *The Nation*, January 2, 2006; Human Rights Watch, "New Orleans: Prisoners Abandoned to Flood Waters", September 22, 2005.

[117] Carey, Corinne, "Excerpts of Letters from Prisoners Abandoned to Katrina," Human Rights Watch, October 10, 2005.

[118] Posse Comitatus Act 18 USC, Sec. 1385 and DoD Directive 5525,5; Limits to:10USC371 – drug enforcement support

Insurrection Act; 10USC331 – rebellions; 18USC831 – nuclear materials crimes; 10USC382 – chemical or biological WMD.

[119] Louisiana Homeland Security and Emergency Assistance and Disaster Act of 1993.

[120] Memorandum of Agreement Concerning Authorization, Consent, and Use of Dual Status Commander for JTF-Katrina.

[121] Department of Homeland Security, *National Response Plan*, December 2004, p. 9.

[122] Letter from Cathleen Babineaux Blanco, Governor of Louisiana to President George W. Bush, September 3, 2005.

[123] Roig-Franzia, Manuel and Spencer Hsu "Many Evacuated, but Thousands Still Waiting: White House Shifts Blame to State and Local Officials," *Washington Post*, September 4, 2005; A01. The report adds: "A senior administration official said that Bush has clear legal authority to federalize National Guard units to quell civil disturbances under the Insurrection Act and will continue to try to unify the chains of command that are split among the president, the Louisiana governor and the New Orleans mayor."

[124] Cf. Wayne, Leslie and Glen Justice, "FEMA Leader Under Clinton Makes it Pay," *New York Times*, October 10, 2005.

[125] Roig-Franza and Hse, op. cit.

[126] Department of Homeland Security, *National Response Plan*, December 2004, p. 7.

[127] WWLTV, Aug 31, 2005.

[128] Ex Parte Milligan 71 US 2 1866.

[129] Roig-Franza and Hse, op. cit.

[130] Roig-Franza and Hse, ibid.

[131] Ritt Goldstein, *Sydney Australia Morning Herald*, March, 2003; United States Civil Disturbance Plan 55-2, Secretary of the Army June 1, 1984. Operation Garden Plot, Civil Disturbance Control

[132] Ibid.

[133] *Washington Monthly*, "Which of these four is not like the other?" September 11, 2005; and Reynolds, Diana, "The Rise of the National Security State: FEMA and the NSC, Public Eye," *Covert Action Information Bulletin*, #33, Winter 1990.

[134] *New York Times*, November 18, 1991, "Continuity of Government planning"; *Washington Post*, October 2001, "Shadow Government Operating in Secret"; The Brookings Institute and the Heritage Foundation have published numerous studies on the post-attack use of COG.

[135] Remarks by Rep. Cynthia McKinney regarding her introduction of House Concurrent Resolution 274 in 2005 to reaffirm Congressional support for Posse Comitatus. Such a resolution passed the House in 2003.

[136] *ABC News*, "Sludge Contains High Content of Fecal Bacteria," September 16, 2005. "The analysis also found astonishing levels of bacteria. A measuring unit of normal soil has about 500 units of bacteria, while the sludge has 13.5 million. Samples of normal soil generally contain less than 200 units of fecal bacteria, but the sludge has 310,000." Cf. also: Palmer, Jioni J., "National Guard entrenched in muck on disaster's front lines," *Newsday*, September 19, 2005.

[137] Cf. *CNN.com*, "Storms turn everyday items to toxic trash," October 5, 2005.

[138] Testimony of Marty J. Bahamonde, office of Public Affairs, Federal Emergency Management Agency before the Senate Committee on Homeland Security and Governmental Affairs, Thursday, October 20, 2005.

[139] "Reinhabiting homes with visible oil contamination is not recommended because of the potential for skin exposure to oil substances. If people choose to reenter the affected area before remediation, they should take precautions to avoid contact with oil substances. Sensitive individuals, including children and people with recently healed or open wounds, should avoid all exposure to oil substances." —Centers for Disease Control and Prevention, "Health Consultation: Murphy Oil Spill," November 8, 2005; cf. also: Llanos, Miguel, "Residents at oil spill site told not to move back: Some in Katrina disaster area have, but EPA has 'serious concerns'," *MSNBC.com*, November 10, 2005; online at: [http://www.msnbc.com.msn.com/id/9994305] (accessed November 10, 2005).

[140] Center for Progressive Reform, "An Unnatural Disaster: The Aftermath of Hurricane Katrina Executive Summary", September 2005, p. 5.

[141] Community Forum, "Who is Cleaning up After Katrina?" held in New Orleans on January 19, 2006.

[142] Cf. Gold, Scott and Ann M. Simmons, "'Katrina Cough' Floats Around," *Los Angeles Times*, November 4, 2005; and Schaffer, Amanda, "Katrina Cough: the Health Problems of 9/11 are Back," *Slate.com*, online at: [http://www.slate.com/id/2130421/fr/rss/] (accessed November 15, 2005).

[143] Caputo, Anton, "How badly was the Big Easy polluted?" *Express-News* (San Antonia), February 5, 2006.

[144] Graham, George, "Mysterious Illness Could Have Katrina Ties," *Ruston Daily Leader*, (Ruston, LA), January 3, 2006.

[145] Environmental Defense Fund, "After Hurricane Katrina, Restoring Wetlands for Protection," September 8, 2005.

[146] Jackson, Patrick, "Lake faces aftermath of city catastrophe," *BBC News*, September 8, 2005.

[147] "Coast 2050," cf. the online report at: [http://www.coast2050.gov/] (accessed February 5, 2006).

[148] Hsu, Spencer S., "Post-Katrina Promises Largely Unfulfilled," *Washington Post*, January 28, 2006.

[149] Dyson, op. cit.: 203.

[150] Authors Kenneth R. Foster and Robert Giegengack have suggested that New Orleans should not be rebuilt where it sits below sea level, that the risk is too great for a repeat of Katrina or worse. Part of their skepticism, however, is based on their prediction that "the flood control system will be patched up in an ad hoc manner, [and] insufficient funds will be made available to bring the entire system up to the design goal of withstanding a Category 3 hurricane—much less the vastly greater funds needed to provide reliable protection against more intense storms." They also note that the goal of build levees to protect against a level 5 hurricane is not, "strictly speaking, a well-defined goal because a Category 5 hurricane has no defined upper limit to its wind speed and storm surge." –Foster and Giegengack, "Planning for a City on the Brink," Chapter 5 in *On Risk and Disaster: Lessons Learned from Hurricane Katrina*, Ronald J. Daniels, et. al., eds., Philadelphia: University of Pennsylvania Press, pp. 41-58.

UNITED STATES HOUSE OF REPRESENTATIVES
SELECT BIPARTISAN COMMITTEE TO INVESTIGATE THE
PREPARATION FOR AND RESPONSE TO HURRICANE KATRINA
FEBRUARY 15, 2006

ADDITIONAL VIEWS
PRESENTED BY THE SELECT COMMITTEE
ON BEHALF OF
REP. CHARLIE MELANCON
REP. WILLIAM J. JEFFERSON

TABLE OF CONTENTS

Hagin in the days before, during, and after the storm. The Committee received evidence that Mr. Brown warned the White House that he could not establish command and control; that he informed the White House that the levees failed on the day Katrina struck; and that he asked the White House for urgent help in managing the federal response. No "full and complete" assessment of the federal response to Hurricane Katrina is possible without reviewing these communications and the White House reaction. Yet when the White House refused to provide any of these communications, the Committee rejected our requests to subpoena them, effectively shielding the White House from scrutiny.

The federal agencies involved in the response to the hurricane provided more cooperation with the investigation than the White House. But there are also significant omissions in the documents they provided to the Committee. Defense Secretary Donald Rumsfeld, for example, refused to comply with the only subpoena the Committee issued. It is a telling mark of the Select Committee's deference to the executive branch that we lack even a basic log of the documents withheld by Secretary Rumsfeld and the Departments of Homeland Security and Health and Human Services.

The strongest part of the majority report is the assessment of the performance of Homeland Security Secretary Michael Chertoff. A major hurricane striking the Gulf Coast and New Orleans was one of the top three potential disasters facing the United States. Yet the evidence before the Select Committee shows that Secretary Chertoff was strangely detached in the key days before Katrina hit. He spent Saturday, August 27, at home and traveled on Tuesday, August 30 — the day after Katrina hit — to Atlanta for a bird flu conference. And he had the atrocious judgment to rely on Michael Brown as his "battlefield commander." The majority report correctly recognizes that Secretary Chertoff fulfilled his responsibilities "late, ineffectively, or not at all."

The majority report finds that Secretary Chertoff made a series of critical mistakes. According to the report, Secretary Chertoff "should have designated the Principal Federal Official on Saturday, two days prior to landfall"; he should have chosen someone "from the roster of PFOs who had successfully completed the required PFO training, unlike FEMA Director Michael Brown"; and he "should have convened the Interagency Incident Management Group on Saturday." The report calls his coordination with the Defense Department "not effective" and criticizes "the Secretary's failure to invoke the National Response Plan – Catastrophic Incident Annex, to clearly and forcefully instruct everyone involved with the federal response to be proactive, anticipate future requirements, develop plans to fulfill them, and execute those plans without waiting for formal requests from overwhelmed state and local response officials." Reviews by the Government Accountability Office and the White House itself reached similar conclusions.

What the majority report does not do, however, is draw the logical conclusion to its own findings and recommend Secretary Chertoff's removal from office. Our judgment, based on a careful review of the record, is that the Department of Homeland Security needs new and more experienced leadership.

The work that the Select Committee has started needs to be completed. Accordingly, we call for an independent commission, modeled after the 9/11 Commission, that will put politics aside and follow the facts wherever they lead. Only by finishing this job will the nation obtain the complete accounting that must precede true reform.

Finally, as representatives and residents of the Gulf Coast regions directly impacted by Hurricane Katrina, we feel compelled to emphasize that this catastrophe is far from over. There may be a tendency to view this Committee's report as the "closure" the nation needs to move on. But this report will not help a resident of New Orleans settle an insurance claim any faster, it will not move a family in Mississippi into a trailer, and it will not assist a worker from Alabama cover a mortgage with no job. There remain urgent and massive problems affecting the Gulf Coast region. Continuing and active engagement by Congress is essential.

I. COMMENTS ON MAJORITY VIEWS

The majority report includes over 90 findings. Taken together, these findings depict a deeply flawed response to one of the worst disasters in U.S. history.

The majority report finds massive failures in virtually every topic it addresses, including planning, execution, and leadership. As the majority report concludes, "[w]e are left scratching our heads at the range of inefficiency and ineffectiveness that characterized government behavior right before and after this storm." The majority report finds "shortcomings and organizational inaction evident in the documents and communications the Committee reviewed."

Some of these problems were obvious even before the investigation began. For example, Americans across the country saw for themselves during the televised coverage of the hurricane's aftermath that "FEMA management lacked situational awareness" and suffered from an "overwhelmed logistics system." And they saw how "massive" communications inoperability "impaired response efforts, command and control, and situational awareness."

Other problems were discovered during the Committee's investigation. The "Hurricane Pam" exercise had predicted how a massive hurricane could devastate New Orleans, and the majority report finds that officials failed to implement the lessons learned from this exercise. The majority report also finds that miscommunications between the Pentagon and Homeland Security Department created confusion and "near panic;" that "top officials" at the Departments of Health and Human Services and Homeland Security "delayed medical care" because they did not understand who controls the National Disaster Medical System; and that officials across the government "had varying degrees of unfamiliarity with their roles and responsibilities under the National Response Plan."

Overall, the majority report paints a picture of leaders who failed to lead and an executive branch that failed to execute, resulting in a passive, disorganized response.

An internal review by the White House came to similar conclusions. During a briefing to the Select Committee on December 15, 2005, Ken Rapuano, White House Deputy Homeland Security Advisor, summarized more than 60 specific findings from the White House review of the government's response to Hurricane Katrina.[1] These findings identified problems with almost every facet of the response, including planning, the military response, emergency communications, logistics, coordination with the private sector, training, public communications, environmental issues, shelter and housing, public health, and law enforcement.

---

[1] Letter from Rep. Charlie Melancon and Rep. Gene Taylor to Select Committee Chairman Tom Davis (Dec. 15, 2005) (summarizing the contents of Mr. Rapuano's briefing).

The Government Accountability Office also reached similar findings. On February 1, 2006, GAO reported that "responders at all levels of government — many victims themselves — encountered significant breakdowns in vital areas such as emergency communications as well as obtaining essential supplies and equipment."[2] According to GAO, the cause of these breakdowns was an absence of "clear and decisive leadership," "strong advance planning, training, and exercise programs," and "capabilities for a catastrophic event."[3]

What is most troubling about these findings is how closely they mirror problems identified after September 11, 2001. These same problems — a disjointed federal response, agencies that failed to share information, the absence of a clear chain of command, a lack of systems to communicate during the crisis — should have been resolved by the massive commitment of resources and government reorganization that took place after 9/11. The findings of the Select Committee, the White House, and the Government Accountability Office make clear that these problems have not been solved. What remains unclear is why the nation has made so little progress in preparedness, more than four years after 9/11.

In several areas, we have comments on specific findings made in the majority report. These are presented below.

A.   National Guard Performance

First and foremost, we wholeheartedly agree with the majority finding that the National Guard performed admirably under the most trying of circumstances. These citizen soldiers came to the aid of their communities even as many of them lost their homes and loved ones to the storm. This assessment is unanimous.

White House Deputy Homeland Security Advisor Ken Rapuano told the Select Committee on January 27, 2005: "The National Guard was the most functional and robust presence in the region, and they did an incredible job."[4] Phil Parr, the Deputy Federal Coordinating Officer for FEMA who was on the ground in New Orleans after Hurricane Katrina struck, testified before the Select Committee on December 14, 2005:

> I cannot say enough good things about the Louisiana National Guard. Every person I spoke to lost either something or everything. There was

---

[2] U.S. Government Accountability Office, *Statement by Comptroller General David M. Walker on GAO's Preliminary Observations Regarding Preparedness and Response to Hurricanes Katrina and Rita* (Feb. 1, 2006) (GAO-06-365R).

[3] *Id.*

[4] Briefing by Ken Rapuano, White House Deputy Homeland Security Advisor, to Select Committee (Jan. 27, 2005).

one gentleman who lost his wife, but he was still there working. They worked extremely hard. They were moving commodities. They kept control of the crowd. ... They were extremely professional. They were easy to work with. It was a pleasure. As a matter of fact, I'm even going to go so far as to say — because there's so many people I haven't mentioned and I'm not going to run down a list — but I worked with a National Guard unit in St. Bernard Parish from Colorado, also phenomenal people. So I just cannot say enough good things about working with the Louisiana National Guard.[5]

In an interview with the Select Committee staff on December 6, 2005, Mr. Parr explained further that, in addition to performing its own urgent mission, the National Guard was essentially making up for FEMA shortfalls.[6] For example, when FEMA failed to provide communications equipment to its officials in New Orleans, the National Guard made its own equipment available to FEMA. And when FEMA failed to provide vehicles so its officials could operate in flood conditions, Mr. Parr told the Select Committee that National Guard forces ferried FEMA officials back and forth across the street to attend meetings. The Guard was selfless and professional and did not allow adverse conditions to negatively affect its mission.

In particular, we acknowledge the sacrifice of Sergeant Joshua Russell of the Mississippi National Guard, who lost his life during the storm attempting to rescue an elderly couple. We agree with the testimony of Maj. Gen. Harold Cross, the Adjutant General of Mississippi, who stated:

> Sergeant Russell so highly represents the dedication and commitment of our National Guard. He swore to defend this country against all enemies, foreign and domestic. He'd already served in Iraq. He died facing forward to the enemy, in this case a natural disaster, and his last moments on this earth were spent helping others at the risk of his own life. He's a true American hero.[7]

---

[5] House Select Bipartisan Committee to Investigate the Preparation for and Response to Hurricane Katrina, *Hearings on Hurricane Katrina: Preparedness and Response by the State of Louisiana*, 109th Cong. (Dec. 14, 2005).

[6] Interview of Phil Parr, Deputy Federal Coordinating Officer, Federal Emergency Management Agency, by Select Committee Staff (Dec. 6, 2005).

[7] House Select Bipartisan Committee to Investigate the Preparation for and Response to Hurricane Katrina, *Hearings on Hurricane Katrina: Preparedness and Response by the Department of Defense, the Coast Guard, and the National Guard of Louisiana, Mississippi, and Alabama,* 109th Cong. (Oct. 27, 2005).

B.   FEMA's "Broken" Logistics System

We agree with the majority report that that FEMA's logistics system is inadequate. We concur that "FEMA management lacked situational awareness of existing requirements and of resources in the supply chain." This assessment came not only from the majority report, but the White House as well. In a briefing to the Select Committee on December 15, 2005, White House officials reported that their internal review had concluded that "priority needs were not met expeditiously," there was a "lack of real-time asset tracking," and FEMA's logistics system "failed to provide certain resources in an efficient and timely manner in order to meet the needs of victims and response personnel."[8]

FEMA officials agreed. For example, FEMA's top official in Mississippi, William Carwile, wrote in the days after the hurricane that the "system appears broken."[9] He described the same problems as officials in Louisiana, including a "dysfunctional" distribution system and inadequate supplies: "We were ordering 425 trucks of ice and 425 trucks of water a day and you're giving us 40."[10]

We add that the problems with FEMA's logistics system were well documented after the Florida hurricanes of 2004.[11] Solving these problems should have been a top priority for management at the Department of Homeland Security, and Congress should make this a key area for continuing oversight.

C.   Contracting Problems

We agree with the Select Committee's finding that "the failure at all levels to enter into advance contracts led to chaos and the potential for waste and fraud as acquisitions were made in haste." We also agree that "FEMA suffered from a lack of sufficiently trained procurement professionals," and that "procurement continues to be decentralized and lacking a uniform approach" at the Department of Homeland Security. We are disappointed, however, that the Committee did not go further in its examination of contracting issues. We recognize that this was

---

[8] Briefing by Ken Rapuano, White House Deputy Homeland Security Advisor, to Select Committee (Jan. 27, 2005).

[9] E-mail from William Carwile, Federal Coordinating Officer, Federal Emergency Management Agency, to Michael Lowder, Deputy Director of Response, Federal Emergency Management Agency, et al. (Sept. 2, 2005).

[10] House Select Bipartisan Committee to Investigate the Preparation for and Response to Hurricane Katrina, *Hearings on Hurricane Katrina: Preparedness and Response by the State of Mississippi*, 109th Cong. (Dec. 7, 2005). *See also Barbour Beseeches Congress,* Biloxi Sun Herald (Dec. 8, 2005).

[11] Department of Homeland Security, Office of the Inspector General, *Emergency Preparedness and Response Could Better Integrate Information Technology with Incident Response and Recovery* (Sept. 2005) (OIG-05-36).

caused in part by the Committee's short deadline, and we urge standing congressional committees to take up where the Select Committee left off.

On November 2, 2005, the Select Committee held a hearing on the government's use of contractors to prepare for and respond to Hurricane Katrina and other catastrophic events.[12] This hearing raised troubling questions about the government procurement system's ability to respond. The government and contractor representatives who testified were unable to answer many basic questions about the scope, price, and terms of contracts awarded in response to Hurricane Katrina.

For example, the witness from the Army Corps of Engineers was unable to provide an estimate of the government's average cost to install blue tarps on damaged roofs. When asked about reports that the government was being charged almost $2,500 for two hours of work installing blue tarps, Colonel Norbert Doyle, Acting Principal Assistant Responsible for Contracting, acknowledged the concern, stating: "That does seem like a lot of money."[13] He offered to have a "paper put together to explain what we think the average cost per roof really is," and to supply that to Committee members.[14] This document was never provided.

Similarly, the witness from FEMA, Senior Procurement Executive Patricia English, was unable to explain whether the installation of travel trailers for displaced residents could move at a more rapid pace, whether there were travel trailers at staging areas that had not been delivered to victims, or how long it would take for FEMA to renegotiate the sole source contract with Bechtel to provide temporary housing.[15] Although she offered to provide the Select Committee with responses to these and other questions, the Select Committee never received this information.

Ms. English also testified about the lack of adequate contingency contracts, agreeing that FEMA was not prepared to have "adequately responded to the disaster."[16] When she was asked to explain what percentage of contracts for response and recovery were taken up on an emergency basis rather than a contingency basis, she offered to get back to the Committee. The information was not provided.

---

[12] House Select Bipartisan Committee to Investigate the Preparation for and Response to Hurricane Katrina, *Hearings on Hurricane Katrina: The Federal Government's Use of Contractors to Prepare and Respond to Catastrophic Events*, 109th Cong. (Nov. 2, 2005).

[13] *Id.*

[14] *Id.*

[15] *Id.*

[16] *Id.*

In response to yet another unanswered question, this one regarding FEMA's policy for reimbursing localities for debris removal, Greg Rothwell, the Chief Procurement Officer for DHS, acknowledged that "many of our answers are going to frustrate the committee" and promised to provide requested information at a later date. The information was not provided.

The Select Committee also obtained evidence that FEMA failed to properly execute a contract to recover dead bodies after the storm. FEMA contacted a company called Kenyon International Emergency Services to perform body recovery, but then delayed the company from starting its work for several critical days. According to company officials, the federal handling of this contract was so poor that the company eventually chose to deal directly with Louisiana Governor Kathleen Blanco.[17] When asked why the federal government did not have a contingency contract in place for these services prior to the hurricane, FEMA Director Michael Brown testified:

> I don't know. And that was a mistake, one that we should look at and make sure we don't do in the future. I do know that, at some point, it was either 3,000 or 10,000 body bags were ordered. But that doesn't account for the fact that we should have had the contract with Kenyon in place before Katrina made landfall.[18]

As a result of this lack of information, Rep. Melancon wrote to Chairman Davis on November 9, 2005, requesting that the Committee submit 27 questions for the record to the witnesses who appeared at the hearing.[19] But the Select Committee received no responses to these questions.

Finally, although we agree with many of the majority findings on contracting, we strongly disagree that Congress should conduct less oversight. The majority report, referring specifically to the government's $236 million contract with Carnival Cruise Lines, finds that "intense public scrutiny could limit the willingness of private sector companies to offer assistance during future disasters." In fact, congressional oversight protected the interests of taxpayers by raising important questions about whether it was reasonable to pay Carnival over $214,500 to house a family of five for six months.[20]

---

[17] Briefing by Robert Jensen, President and CEO of Kenyon International, to Select Committee Staff (Sept. 28, 2005). *See also Company Accused Feds of Disaster Dithering; Body-Recovery Firm Instead Turns to State*, New Orleans Times-Picayune (Oct. 28, 2005).

[18] House Select Bipartisan Committee to Investigate the Preparation for and Response to Hurricane Katrina, *Hearings on Hurricane Katrina: The Role of the Federal Emergency Management Agency*, 109th Cong. (Sept. 27, 2005).

[19] Letter from Rep. Charlie Melancon to Select Committee Chairman Tom Davis (Nov. 9, 2005).

[20] *See, e.g.,* Letter from Rep. Henry A. Waxman, Ranking Minority Member, House Committee on Government Reform, to Michael Chertoff, Secretary of Homeland Security (Oct. 20, 2005).

In testimony at the Select Committee's hearing on November 2, 2005, Terry Thornton, Vice President of Carnival Cruise Lines, testified that "if the government has any concerns about the implementation of this profit neutrality provision, we would welcome any reviews by the Defense Contract Audit Agency requested by [Military Sealift Command]."[21] After watching the hearing that day, Captain Joe Manna, the primary contracting officer at Military Sealift Command, which oversees the contract, immediately telephoned the President of Carnival and arranged for audits to begin.[22] Without congressional oversight, this audit would not have happened.

D. Ineffective Law and Order

We agree with the majority finding that the "collapse of law enforcement and lack of effective public communications led to civil unrest and further delayed relief." We also agree that "the New Orleans Police Department was ill prepared for continuity of operations and lost almost all effectiveness."

In addition, we agree that "Federal law enforcement agencies were also critical to restoring law and order and coordinating activities." We note, however, that the situation could have been much improved had FEMA acted on an offer from the Interior Department in the immediate aftermath of the storm to provide an additional 400 law enforcement officials, including special agents and refuge officers from the Fish and Wildlife Service. Interior Department officials explained their frustration:

> Although DOI has 4,400 law enforcement officers — many of whom work in harsh environments and are trained in search and rescue, emergency medical services, and evacuation — DOI was not called upon to assist under the NRP until late September. Yet DOI had hundreds of officers readily deployable, many of whom were in the immediate area.[23]

For these reasons, we believe that law enforcement agencies both inside and outside the Department of Homeland Security should be better integrated into disaster response operations.

---

[21] House Select Bipartisan Committee to Investigate the Preparation for and Response to Hurricane Katrina, *Hearings on Hurricane Katrina: The Federal Government's Use of Contractors to Prepare and Respond*, 109th Cong. (Nov. 2, 2005).

[22] Briefing by Captain Joe Manna, Kenneth Allen, and Harry Eliot, Military Sealift Command; Louise Vitale, Department of the Navy; and Sina Lehmkuhler, Office of the Secretary of Defense, to Minority Staff, House Committee on Government Reform (Jan. 24, 2006).

[23] Letter from P. Lynn Scarlett, Assistant Secretary for Policy, Management and Budget, Department of the Interior, to Chairman Susan M. Collins and Ranking Member Joseph I. Lieberman, Senate Committee on Homeland Security and Governmental Affairs (Nov. 7, 2005).

E.   Success of Overall Evacuations

We agree with the majority finding that "evacuations of general populations went relatively well in all three states." We also agree that Louisiana's overall evacuation of the "general population was very successful" and "went smoothly." We disagree, however, with the suggestion that Louisiana state and local officials were responsible for "the failure of complete evacuations," and that this failure "led to deaths, thousands of dangerous rescues, and horrible conditions for those who remained." We do not believe 100% evacuation should be the standard operating assumption for disaster planning.

Louisiana state and local officials exceeded all expectations in executing their general evacuations. The majority report finds that more than a million people evacuated from southeastern Louisiana. Governor Blanco testified that of the 1.3 million people living in southeastern Louisiana, only 100,000 people, including first responders, remained in the area when Katrina made landfall.[24] In other words, more than 90% of the population evacuated. This was a significant accomplishment.

In testimony before the Select Committee, former FEMA Director Michael Brown criticized Louisiana officials for evacuation failures. But he offered his conclusion without first examining the facts. He said he was not sure how many people actually evacuated, and that he had not yet "had time to sit down and really look at those kinds of numbers." Yet, he said he "would have hoped for 80 percent."[25] In fact, Louisiana surpassed this goal.

We are not saying that evacuations cannot be improved. The majority report recognizes that even under mandatory evacuations, 10% to 25% of residents will refuse to leave, and authorities cannot forcibly remove these residents from their homes. We believe emergency planners should examine additional ways to encourage all residents to evacuate in such circumstances.

We also agree that evacuation of the special needs population was insufficient, and that evacuation of the city after it had flooded was chaotic and not well planned. We add that state and local officials should have better anticipated the basic needs of residents who evacuated to shelters of last resort. For example, they should have realized that flooding and power outages could have caused plumbing failures at the Superdome, and they should have pre-positioned portable toilets in advance. Nevertheless, we believe that these findings should be

---

[24] House Select Bipartisan Committee to Investigate the Preparation for and Response to Hurricane Katrina, *Hearings on Hurricane Katrina: Preparedness and Response by the State of Louisiana*, 109th Cong. (Dec. 14, 2005).

[25] House Select Bipartisan Committee to Investigate the Preparation for and Response to Hurricane Katrina, *Hearings on Hurricane Katrina: The Role of the Federal Emergency Management Agency*, 109th Cong. (Sept. 27, 2005).

accompanied by clear recognition that the evacuation of the general population exceeded all predictions.

F.   Inadequate Housing and Community Rebuilding

Nearly six months have passed since Hurricane Katrina made landfall, yet the housing situation in the affected areas of the Gulf Coast remains critical. In interviews with Select Committee staff in New Orleans in November, federal officials conceded that the housing mission is "failing."[26] Despite multiple requests, the Select Committee held no hearings on this critical issue, claiming that it was a long-term recovery problem outside the Committee's jurisdiction.

Securing temporary housing for displaced residents is an essential bridge in the transition from the relief phase to recovery. FEMA's confusion, indecision, and inefficiency in meeting the need for travel trailers, rental assistance, and hotel reimbursement have delayed that transition. These failures have prolonged the period in which displaced residents are dependent on federal assistance, and they have aggravated the adverse effects of other failures in the federal response.

Documents cited by the Select Committee show that top Administration officials identified temporary housing as a critical problem area shortly after the hurricane had passed. For example, an e-mail from the Vice President's office dated September 9, 2005, and stamped "VICE PRESIDENT HAS SEEN," stated:

> The trailer idea is worse then I originally thought. The last batch of trailers we are now purchasing will be coming off the production line in approximately 3.5 years. That means, most of these units won't be available for use for months.[27]

The Select Committee report quotes this message to show that the Administration recognized the shortcomings of FEMA's plan for trailer housing. It also finds that other federal agencies like Department of Housing and Urban Development were not fully utilized. But the report does not examine why the federal government has failed to develop a comprehensive rebuilding strategy for the Gulf Coast, or what happened to President Bush's promises of programs such as urban homesteading.[28]

---

[26] Interview of Capt. Tom Atkin, U.S. Coast Guard, Chief of Staff to Principal Federal Official Thad Allen, by Select Committee Staff (Nov. 9, 2005); Interview of Ted Monette, Deputy Principal Federal Official, Federal Emergency Management Agency, by Select Committee Staff (Nov. 9, 2005).

[27] E-mail from Neil Patel, Staff Secretary to the Vice President, to Charles Durkin, Personal Aide to the Vice President (Sept. 9, 2005) (addressed to I. Lewis "Scooter" Libby, Chief of Staff to the Vice President).

[28] *Post-Katrina Promises Unfulfilled*, Washington Post (Jan. 28, 2006).

As it turns out, the forecasts of shortcomings in FEMA's trailer program have been borne out. In Mississippi, hundreds of Gulf Coast residents are still living in tents. Although FEMA has been delivering trailers throughout the region, FEMA's efforts have been plagued by delay and inefficiency. In Mississippi, more than 33,000 trailers have been installed, but FEMA has a backlog of 34,000 repair requests and maintenance complaints.[29] In New Orleans, the trailers that have been installed meet just 37% of the demand for temporary housing.[30]

On October 28, 2005, Rep. Gene Taylor sent a letter requesting that the Select Committee hold a hearing on FEMA's administration of housing assistance programs.[31] At the Select Committee hearing on December 14, 2005, Reps. Taylor and Melancon renewed this request.[32] The Select Committee never held a hearing on housing, claiming that long-term recovery programs fell outside the limited jurisdiction of the Committee.

While years of recovery remain, the residents of the Gulf Coast cannot begin the hard work of rebuilding their communities until the need for temporary and permanent housing is addressed. We urge standing congressional committees to take up this critical issue immediately.

G. Cause of Levee Failures

The breach of the levees in New Orleans was the single most significant event affecting the course of the Hurricane's aftermath, but the Select Committee did not seek to determine why the levees failed, who was responsible, or how to ensure that new levee systems will protect the region in the future.

If the levees had not failed, New Orleans still would have suffered severe storm damage, but the flooding that devastated the city most likely would not have been so widespread. Moreover, even if there had been some flooding due to storm surge or overtopping, evacuees who had taken shelter at the Superdome or other shelters of last resort may have been able to return to their homes after waters receded, rather than having to leave the city entirely.

At the outset of the Select Committee's investigation, Chairman Davis and Rep. Melancon sent letters to multiple federal agencies requesting documents "relating to the construction, maintenance, or capacity to withstand a hurricane or flooding

---

[29] *Id.*

[30] *Id.*

[31] Letter from Rep. Gene Taylor to Select Committee Chairman Tom Davis (Oct. 28, 2005).

[32] House Select Bipartisan Committee to Investigate the Preparation for and Response to Hurricane Katrina, *Hearings on Hurricane Katrina: Preparedness and Response by the State of Louisiana*, 109th Cong. (Dec. 14, 2005).

of the 17th Street, London Canal, or Industrial Canal levees and storm walls."[33]
The Select Committee received some responsive documents from the Army Corps
of Engineers. Despite a request from the minority, however, staff did not conduct
interviews with the Army Corps of Engineers personnel most knowledgeable
about these issues.

The Select Committee's report does not resolve critical questions about levee
failures, noting instead that "the ultimate cause of the levee failures is under
investigation and results to be determined." It may be that the Select Committee
believed it could not resolve the complex engineering and liability questions in
the short timeframe established by the House for its review. It also may be that
the Select Committee felt it was more appropriate to leave these issues to the
various other entities currently examining them. But the Select Committee never
held a hearing on what these other organizations are learning or what they have
concluded to date.

Questions about why the levees failed are important not only to establish
accountability, but to help determine how to rebuild them. The reconstruction
process will not be effective unless residents and businesses are confident that
they will be protected from catastrophic flooding. Until Congress addresses this
critical failure in a comprehensive and detailed manner, the rebuilding effort will
be impeded.

H.   Environmental Issues

The Select Committee overlooked numerous environmental concerns that affected
the lead-up to the hurricane as well as the hurricane's immediate and long-term
effects. Although the Committee received a limited number of documents from
the Environmental Protection Agency, environmental issues were never addressed
in a hearing and are not a focus of the majority report.

Prior to Hurricane Katrina striking the Gulf Coast, there was massive
deterioration of Louisiana's coastal wetlands barrier islands that could have
protected the mainland against the full force of the incoming storm. This erosion
was caused by a huge reduction of sediment from the Mississippi River due to the
creation of levees and concrete liners, as well as a vast network of canals through
the marshlands built for shipping and oil development.[34]

In the immediate aftermath of the storm, independent test data showed
dangerously high mold counts and areas of toxic sediments, which pose a serious

---

[33] *See, e.g.,* Letter from Select Committee Chairman Tom Davis and Rep. Charlie Melancon to Lt.
Gen. Carl Strock, U.S. Army Corps of Engineers (Sept. 30, 2005).

[34] *See Gone with the Water*, National Geographic (Oct. 2004).

health risk to returning residents and workers.[35] For example, indoor sites had spore counts of up to 645,000 spores per cubic meter, rendering homes uninhabitable.[36] In addition, sediment testing "found pervasively high levels of arsenic, as well as high levels of other contaminants, including lead, banned pesticides, and cancer-causing polycyclic aromatic hydrocarbons at three specific sites."[37]

Contamination caused by the hurricane could also be exacerbated by recovery efforts. For example, much of the debris is being disposed of by burning, which has the potential to release toxic air pollutants such as mercury, or disposal into unlined landfills, which can allow groundwater contamination.[38]

The long-term challenges posed by global climate change are also key to understanding Katrina's implications for the future. Sea levels have already risen over the last century, and they are projected to rise further as the planet warms. Warmer ocean temperatures contribute to hurricane intensity. Recent studies have shown empirically that the increased frequency of more intense hurricanes over the past few decades is correlated with warmer ocean temperatures during that same period.[39] At a minimum, sea level rise from climate change will make coastal areas more vulnerable to storm damage, and if the frequency of more

---

[35] Natural Resources Defense Council, *New Private Testing Shows Dangerously High Mold Counts in New Orleans Air* (Nov. 16, 2005); Natural Resources Defense Council, *New Testing Shows Widespread Toxic Contamination in New Orleans Soil, Neighborhoods* (Dec. 1, 2005).

[36] Natural Resources Defense Council, *New Private Testing Shows Dangerously High Mold Counts in New Orleans Air* (Nov. 16, 2005).

[37] Natural Resources Defense Council, *New Testing Shows Widespread Toxic Contamination in New Orleans Soil, Neighborhoods* (Dec. 1, 2005).

[38] *See* Environmental Protection Agency, *Emergency Hurricane Debris Burning Guidance* (online at www.epa.gov/katrina/debris.html#emergency) (recognizing the difficulty of complying with federal regulations pertaining to burning debris and requiring segregation of hazardous wastes including batteries, which contain mercury, and PCBs "to the extent feasible"); Halcy Barbour, Governor of Mississippi, *Emergency Order* (Sep. 13, 2005) (waiving requirements for expansion of landfills and allowing structural debris to be disposed of through emergency burn sites); National Institute for Occupational Safety and Health, Centers for Disease Control, *NIOSH Interim Guidance on Health and Safety Issues Among Clean-Up Workers Involved with Handling and Burning Hurricane Debris* (Sept. 2005) (online at www.cdc.gov/niosh/topics/flood/ burningdebris.html) (explaining health and safety issues related to burning hurricane debris); *In Katrina's Wake*, Environmental Health Perspectives, v. 114, no. 1 (Jan. 2006) (noting that "the Louisiana Department of Environmental Quality has approved dozens of temporary debris disposal sites;" further noting that "monitoring in the area [of controlled burns] … has indicated some elevated levels of formaldehyde and acrolein in certain areas"); *Hurricane Bends Landfill Rules*, Washington Post (Oct. 30, 2005).

[39] *See* Emanuel, K., *Increasing Destructiveness of Tropical Cyclones Over the Past 30 Years*, Nature (2005); Webster, P.J., G. J. Holland, J. A. Curry, and H.R. Chang, *Changes in Tropical Cyclone Number, Duration, and Intensity in a Warming Environment*, Science (2005).

intense hurricanes also continues to increase, we will likely experience greater damage from hurricanes in the future.

Unfortunately, these important environmental issues were not examined by the Select Committee. The Select Committee also did not investigate the tremendous economic and environmental costs of the damage to oil and natural gas infrastructure in the Gulf, particularly to off-shore drilling platforms and seabed pipelines. For example, the Committee did not consider whether or how to ensure that new and rebuilt drilling infrastructure will be better able to withstand future storms.

The White House also raised some of these concerns. According to a briefing provided to the Select Committee on December 15, 2005, the White House concluded that there was a "lack of standards … to identify and communicate environmental risks to responders and general populations."[40] The White House also concluded that "environmental assessment teams were not prepositioned to respond."[41]

All of these issues are extremely serious and demand a coherent inquiry. But the Committee did not examine these critical questions.

I.   Investigation Overview

Chairman Davis and the Select Committee have worked diligently, and we appreciate the opportunities Democratic members from the affected region were given to participate in the investigation. We regret, however, that the majority report seriously mischaracterizes the structure of the Select Committee and the objections of the Democratic leadership, as well as the vigor of the Committee's pursuit of critical documents.

According to the majority report, the Select Committee was established with "minority subpoena authority." This is flatly wrong. The resolution establishing the Select Committee granted subpoena authority to the Republican chairman, but not to the Democratic minority. This was one of the primary reasons Minority Leader Nancy Pelosi and the Democratic leadership refused to appoint members. They were concerned that Republican-dominated control of the Select Committee would leave it vulnerable to partisan pressures. Democrats also objected to the five-month timeframe for the investigation, believing that an artificially short deadline would encourage agencies to stonewall and run out the clock.

Regrettably, the Democratic concerns proved prescient.

---

[40] Briefing by Ken Rapuano, Deputy White House Homeland Security Advisor, to Select Committee (Dec. 15, 2005).

[41] *Id.*

In large part, the success of an investigation hinges on access to documents and witnesses. The majority report recognizes that the Committee did not receive all the documents requested. But the report minimizes the significance of the missing documents, asserting that "we had more than enough to do our job." In fact, the Select Committee does not even know which documents the Administration is withholding. It is a telling indicator of the subservient position of the Select Committee that it was allowed to see only what the Administration wanted it to see and could not find out what had been withheld.

Based on obvious gaps in the documents provided to the Select Committee, we requested a series of meetings with officials at the Departments of Homeland Security, Defense, and Health and Human Services. We asked to have these agencies explain which documents they are withholding and why. We made this request on January 13, 2006.

Although the majority staff contacted these agencies, the agencies apparently ignored our request for briefings. As of February 11, 2006, we had received no briefing from any of the federal agencies regarding the documents they are withholding. The result is that the Select Committee does not have even the most basic log of the documents that have been withheld.

We have identified some of the holes in the record, although there are most likely many more. One major omission is that the documents provided to the Select Committee consistently lack communications to and from the agency head, which may be the most important agency records of all. As a result, the Select Committee has obtained little if any evidence documenting the basic flow of information to and from Homeland Security Secretary Michael Chertoff, Defense Secretary Donald Rumsfeld, or Health and Human Services Secretary Michael Leavitt regarding the Hurricane Katrina crisis. The Select Committee was informed that neither Secretary Chertoff nor Secretary Rumsfeld use e-mail, but we received no other records we requested, such as phone logs, e-mail records of assistants, or other internal communications that would show how Secretary Chertoff and Secretary Rumsfeld received information, communicated with other government officials, or gave orders. Nor did the Select Committee receive a set of Secretary Leavitt's e-mails, although e-mails to and from other officials at the Department make clear that Secretary Leavitt was sending and receiving e-mails relating to Katrina.

Another set of missing records involve FEMA's budget. When Michael Brown, the former FEMA Director, testified before the Committee, he asserted that FEMA had been "emaciated" by budget cuts that he had protested. On September 30, 2005, the Select Committee requested all "communications referring or relating to the budget request for fiscal year 2004, fiscal year 2005, and fiscal year 2006 for the Federal Emergency Management Agency to or from Undersecretary

Michael D. Brown."[42] Many of these documents were never provided by DHS. In fact, we would not even have known that the withheld documents existed, except that the *Washington Post* published an article on December 23, 2005, that described several of them.[43]

The most glaring gap in the record is the failure of the Select Committee to obtain documents from the White House. This omission — and its significance to the investigation — is discussed extensively in the next session. In this area too, the Select Committee was denied documents that were obtained by the press.[44]

We appreciate our ability to participate in the work of the Select Committee, and we recognize the efforts that Chairman Davis made to make the investigation bipartisan. But the fact remains that the investigation was far too deferential to the executive branch in resolving document disputes. These investigative failures would never have been tolerated if the recommendations of Leader Pelosi had been adopted.

II. FAILURE OF THE SELECT COMMITTEE TO EXAMINE WHITE HOUSE ACTIONS

As discussed in part I, the Select Committee has made many valuable findings about what went wrong with the response to Hurricane Katrina. Overall, the majority report is a comprehensive, detailed recitation of the problems that occurred. It is also a condemnation of the nation's progress in responding to catastrophic events since 9/11. We concur with the report's overarching conclusion that the response to Hurricane Katrina was "a national failure, an abdication of the most solemn obligation to provide for the common welfare." We also agree that Hurricane Katrina was "a failure of leadership."

Yet the findings of the majority report are nearly all phrased in the passive tense. The report catalogues what went wrong, but it rarely assesses <u>how</u> these failures occurred, <u>why</u> they were not corrected sooner, or <u>who</u> in particular was responsible. The majority report describes generic "institutional" failures, general "communications problems," and vague "bureaucratic inertia." With a few exceptions, however, the report fails to explain the causes of the failures or to hold anyone accountable.

---

[42] Letter from Select Committee Tom Davis to Michael Chertoff, Secretary of Homeland Security (Sept. 30, 2005).

[43] *See, e.g., Brown's Turf Wars Sapped FEMA's Strength,* Washington Post (Dec. 23, 2005) (describing several memos from FEMA Director Michael Brown to Homeland Security Secretary Michael Chertoff, including one that states: "A total of $77.9 million has been permanently lost from the base"). Michael Brown provided to the Committee some budget-related documents that he retained in his personal possession.

[44] *Id.* (describing e-mails between former FEMA Director Michael Brown and White House Deputy Chief of Staff Joe Hagin, including one from Mr. Hagin on Sunday, August 28, 2005, the day before Hurricane Katrina struck, stating: "You didn't get out in time").

The single biggest flaw in the Select Committee's investigation is its failure to obtain key information from the White House. The evidence received by the Select Committee revealed that the White House played a major role in orchestrating the response to Hurricane Katrina, but the Select Committee did not determine the extent to which White House officials were responsible for faults in the federal response. The White House, in effect, was shielded from meaningful scrutiny.

There are four basic questions about the role of the White House that the Committee's investigation identified but did not resolve: (1) How did White House officials, including Chief of Staff Andrew Card, respond to dozens of urgent warnings and requests for assistance from former FEMA Director Michael Brown? (2) Why were top White House officials missing in action or unaware of key facts in the crucial days before and after the hurricane hit? (3) Why did President Bush and other top Administration officials insist on asserting that the levees held until the day after the hurricane struck when in fact they failed almost immediately? and (4) Why did the top ranking homeland security official in the White House Situation Room leave his post on the evening Hurricane Katrina struck feeling "satisfied" that the federal response was well in hand?

These unresolved questions go to the heart of the federal response, but the Select Committee did not answer them. We discuss each in turn below.

A.   Communications with Michael Brown

During his testimony before the Select Committee on September 27, 2005, former FEMA Director Michael Brown explained that the White House played a central role in the response to Hurricane Katrina. He stated:

> I think this committee really needs to understand that the White House was fully engaged. The White House was working behind the scenes … to make things happen.[45]

Mr. Brown claimed to have based his conclusion on dozens of personal communications with top White House officials. He testified that he "exchanged e-mails and phone calls with Joe Hagin, Andy Card, and the president."[46] When asked how many communications he had with White House officials during this period, Mr. Brown replied: "I mean, 30 times, I mean, I don't know."[47]

---

[45] House Select Bipartisan Committee to Investigate the Preparation for and Response to Hurricane Katrina, *Hearings on Hurricane Katrina: The Role of the Federal Emergency Management Agency*, 109th Cong. (Sept. 27, 2005).

[46] *Id.*

[47] *Id.*

Mr. Brown testified that he had extensive access to the highest officials in the White House. As he testified at the hearing, "I mean, you know — look, I have no problem picking up the phone and getting a hold of Chertoff or Andy Card or Joe Hagin or the President. I don't have those problems."[48]

With respect to the substance of his communications, Mr. Brown testified that he told Mr. Card and others that "we needed help."[49] When asked exactly when the White House first learned that "a disaster was looming," Mr. Brown testified:

> Oh, they were aware of that by Thursday or Friday, because Andy Card and I were communicating at that point about — in fact, I remember saying to Andy at one point that this was going to be a bad one. They were focused about it. They knew it.[50]

In an interview with the *New York Times,* Mr. Brown claimed that he made a "blur of calls" after the hurricane struck, warning Mr. Card and others that "I can't get a unified command and control established" and that "things were going to hell in a handbasket."[51] He also stated that he "ask[ed] the White House explicitly to take over the response from FEMA and state officials."[52]

On February 10, 2006, Mr. Brown testified before the Senate Committee on Homeland Security and Governmental Affairs about his communications with the White House. He also appeared the next day, in closed session, before the House Select Committee to discuss these issues. In his statements before the Select Committee on February 11, Mr. Brown stated that he had "innumerable" conversations with White House officials in the days immediately preceding and following Hurricane Katrina, including the President; the Vice President; Mr. Card; Joe Hagin, Mr. Card's deputy; Francis Townsend, the Homeland Security Advisor; and Karl Rove, the deputy chief of staff and the President's political advisor. He stated that he kept the White House aware of the dire conditions in the Gulf Coast and sought White House help in tasking the Defense Department with essential response missions. He also stated that he made the White House aware of the frustrations he was encountering getting essential emergency support to the region in a timely manner.

Mr. Brown indicated that his communications with the White House were generally not successful in breaking through the red-tape and bureaucracy that

---

[48] *Id.*

[49] *Id.*

[50] *Id.*

[51] *Ex-FEMA Chief Tells of Frustration and Chaos,* New York Times (Sept. 15, 2005).

[52] *Id.*

was slowing down the federal response. He indicated that at one point Mr. Card responded to his requests by telling him to "go through the chain of command." He said he did not know why his calls to the White House failed to produce the results he wanted, but speculated that it could have been a result of the White House sending his requests back to the Department of Homeland Security to be processed through the chain of command.

Mr. Brown provided to the Committee several of the emails he sent to the White House. He indicated, however, that the emails that he had in his possession were an "incomplete" set of his email communications with the White House.

The questions raised by Mr. Brown's communications go to the core of the federal response. Mr. Brown had extensive communications with the top officials in the White House, in which he alerted them about conditions in the Gulf Coast and made urgent calls for help. Yet what the White House learned from Mr. Brown, what specific assistance he requested, and how the White House reacted remain shrouded in mystery.

B.   Laxity at the White House

Significant questions also remain unanswered regarding the conduct of senior White House officials. In the key days before and immediately after Hurricane Katrina, virtually the entire leadership of the White House was on vacation or out of Washington. President Bush was on a five week vacation in Crawford, Texas. Vice President Cheney was at his ranch in Wyoming. Chief of Staff Andrew Card was vacationing at his lakefront summer home in Maine. And Homeland Security Advisor Frances Townsend was also on vacation in Maine.[53]

Their absence is difficult to understand. A major hurricane hitting New Orleans had been identified as one of the top three catastrophic threats to homeland security.[54] As Chairman Davis stated: "The director ... of the National Hurricane Center said this was the big one. When this happened ... Bush is in Texas, Card is in Maine, the vice president is fly-fishing. I mean, who's in charge here?"[55]

The senior official left in charge at the White House was Deputy Homeland Security Advisor Ken Rapuano. Yet during a briefing he gave to the Select

---

[53] *Katrina's Aftermath: The Response; Put to Katrina's Test,* Los Angeles Times (Sept. 11, 2005).

[54] *See, e.g., Sharp Criticism of U.S. Response, Lack of Action to Prevent Disaster,* San Francisco Chronicle (Sept. 2, 2005); *Keeping Its Head Above Water,* Houston Chronicle (Dec. 1, 2001); *The Big One Is Coming,* Hartford Courant (Oct. 16, 2005); *Disaster Raises Question for California,* Dallas Morning News (Sept. 11, 2005); *Katrina's Aftermath: Government Response,* Houston Chronicle (Sept. 11, 2005); *Anarchy, Anger, Desperation: The Response,* San Francisco Chronicle (Sept. 2, 2005).

[55] *Administration Faulted on Katrina; GAO Report Blames Bungled Response on Failures That Started at the Top,* Washington Post (Feb. 2, 2006).

Committee on December 15, 2005, he conceded that he was not aware of key information. During the briefing he repeatedly emphasized that the major cause of the poor government response was that the National Response Plan relied on state and local officials to take the lead in organizing and coordinating the response.[56] In response to one question, Mr. Rapuano indicated that if federal officials did not hear from a local county in Mississippi, the federal agencies assumed that this meant that everything was under control, even if the county was so devastated that communications were impossible.

This assumption had catastrophic consequences and was completely unwarranted. The Select Committee obtained documents from the Department of Homeland Security demonstrating that federal officials had predicted before Hurricane Katrina that state and local authorities would be unable to conduct a response without federal help. The "Hurricane Pam" exercise was designed in 2004 to plan and prepare for "a catastrophic hurricane striking southeastern Louisiana."[57] The Scope of Work for this exercise predicted that such a "mega-disaster" would "quickly overwhelm the State's resources" and "creat[e] a catastrophe with which the State would not be able to cope without massive help from neighboring states and the Federal Government."[58] This document warned that "existing plans, policies, procedures and resources" were inadequate.[59]

Apart from the Hurricane Pam documents, the White House also received reports in the days directly before the storm struck warning that its effects would be catastrophic. For example, on the evening before the hurricane bore down on the Gulf Coast, the White House received a warning that "[a]ny storm rated Category 4 or greater on the Saffir-Simpson scale will likely lead to severe flooding and/or levee breaching, leaving the New Orleans metro area submerged for weeks or months."[60]

This evidence raises serious questions about how the White House could be so disengaged and so ill-informed. The threat of a major hurricane bearing down on New Orleans and the Gulf Coast called for the full attention of the President and his senior leaders. Yet for unexplained reasons, the response was left to a relatively junior official who was ignorant of basic information about the nature of the threat.

---

[56] Briefing by Ken Rapuano, Deputy White House Homeland Security Advisor, to Select Committee (Dec. 15, 2005).

[57] Federal Emergency Management Agency, *Combined Catastrophic Plan for Southeast Louisiana and the New Madrid Seismic Zone: Scope of Work* (2004).

[58] *Id.*

[59] *Id.*

[60] Department of Homeland Security, National Infrastructure Simulation & Analysis Center, *Fast Analysis Report* (Aug. 28, 2005).

C.   Misleading Statements about Levee Failures

FEMA and Coast Guard officials who were in New Orleans on Monday, August 29, the day the hurricane struck, personally observed levee failures and warned that two-thirds to three-fourths of the city had flooded. The White House was informed of these crucial facts, but for days and weeks after the hurricane, President Bush and other top Administration officials deflected criticism by insisting they were caught by surprise when the levees failed on Tuesday, August 30, the day after Hurricane Katrina. An important unanswered question is why these top officials persisted in making these misleading assertions.

The first official government report of the levee failure appears to have come at 8:14 a.m. on Monday, August 29, 2005, the morning Hurricane Katrina struck. At that time, the New Orleans office of the National Weather Services issued a bulletin warning against flash floods and stating: "A LEVEE BREACH OCCURRED ALONG THE INDUSTRIAL CANAL AT TENNESSEE STREET."[61] Within minutes, the report was picked up by radio and television news reports.[62] Later that day, additional press reports mentioned levee failures. For example, at 2:00 p.m., the New Orleans *Times Picayune* reported that "City Hall confirmed a breach of the levee along the 17th Street Canal."[63]

The same day, an urgent "Spot Report" was sent to the White House Situation Room. This Spot Report, issued by the Homeland Security Operations Center at 10:30 p.m., confirmed major breaches in the New Orleans levees: "There is a quarter-mile breech in the levee near the 17th Street Canal about 200 yards from Lake Pontchartrain allowing water to flow into the City."[64]

The Spot Report conveyed to the White House a worst-case scenario, including massive flooding that had already taken place and bodies scattered in the floodwaters. The report was based on the observations of Marty Bahamonde, the sole FEMA official in New Orleans, who had taken two Coast Guard helicopter flights that day to personally verify the damage. As the Spot Report continued:

- "[A]n estimated 2/3 to 75% of the city is under water."

---

[61] National Weather Service, *Bulletin: EAS Activation Requested; Flash Flood Warning* (Aug. 29, 2005).

[62] *See, e.g., Good Day Dallas,* KDFW-TV (Aug. 29, 2005; 8:21 a.m.) (reporting that "[t]he National Weather Service in New Orleans has reported a levee breach in New Orleans"); *Morning Drive Time,* ABC News (Aug. 29, 2005).

[63] *Rescuers Can't Get to Those Who Are Stranded,* New Orleans Times-Picayune (Aug. 29, 2005). *See also Hurricane Katrina Slamming Into Gulf Coast,* CNN (Aug. 29, 2005) (noting at 10:00 a.m. that a "levee breach occurred").

[64] Homeland Security Operations Center, *Spot Report #13* (Aug. 29, 2005) (WHK-4055) (DHS-FRNT-0001-0000002).

- "Some homes were seen with water to the first floor and others completely underwater."

- "Hundreds of people were observed on the balconies and roofs of a major apartment complex in the city."

- "Lake Front Airport by Lake Pontchartrain is under water."

- "The Coast Guard is flying rescue missions for people stuck on roofs. They reported seeing about 150 people but said that as they lifted people out, they saw others breaking through the roofs of adjacent homes."

- "A few bodies were seen floating in the water."[65]

The Spot Report was not the only evidence of levee failures reaching senior officials on Monday, August 29. At 9:27 p.m., Secretary Chertoff's chief of staff, John Wood, and others in the Secretary's office, received an e-mail from Brian Besanceney, the Assistant Secretary for Public Affairs, stating:

> [T]he first (unconfirmed) reports they are getting from aerial surveys in New Orleans are far more serious than media reports are currently reflecting. Finding extensive flooding and more stranded people than they had originally thought — also a number of fires. FYI in case tomorrow's sit reps seem more "severe."[66]

About an hour and a half later, FEMA Deputy Director Patrick Rhode sent an e-mail to DHS Deputy Secretary Michael Jackson. At 11:05 p.m., he wrote: "We just spoke with our first rep on the ground in New Orleans who did a helo tour and describes a 200 yard collapse of the levy on the south side of the lake which is accounting for much of the additional flooding."[67]

Despite all of these reports, President Bush has insisted repeatedly since the hurricane that the levees held until the following day, Tuesday, August 30. After touring Biloxi, Mississippi, on September 2, 2005, President Bush stated: "The

---

[65] *Id.*

[66] E-mail from Brian Besanceney, Assistant Secretary for Public Affairs, Department of Homeland Security, to John Wood, Chief of Staff, Department of Homeland Security, et al. (Aug. 29, 2005) (DHS-FRNT-0006-0000023).

[67] E-mail from Patrick Rhode, Deputy Director, Federal Emergency Management Agency, to Michael Jackson, Deputy Secretary of Homeland Security (Aug. 29, 2005).

levees broke on Tuesday in New Orleans."[68] According to the President, "New Orleans got hit by two storms, one the hurricane, and then the flood."[69]

During a press conference in New Orleans on September 12, 2005 — two weeks after the storm — President Bush explained the initial lax federal response by stating:

> When that storm came by, a lot of people said we dodged a bullet. When that storm came through at first, people said, whew. There was a sense of relaxation, and that's what I was referring to. And I, myself, thought we had dodged a bullet. You know why? Because I was listening to people, probably over the airways, say, the bullet has been dodged. And that was what I was referring to. Of course, there were plans in case the levee had been breached. There was a sense of relaxation in the moment, a critical moment.[70]

The President is not the only Administration official who has made this claim. Appearing on *Meet the Press,* Homeland Security Secretary Michael Chertoff stated: "what happened is the storm passed and passed without the levees breaking on Monday."[71] He claimed that when the levees broke on Tuesday, this "second catastrophe really caught everybody by surprise."[72] This statement appears to contradict not only the Spot Report, but other communications within the Secretary's own office that day.

Similarly, General Richard Myers, Chairman of the Joint Chief of Staff, stated at a September 6 briefing: "The headline, of course, in most of the country's papers on Tuesday were 'New Orleans dodged a bullet.'" He explained that on Tuesday, the day after the storm, "I called each of the chiefs of the services, one by one, and said we don't know what we're going to be asked for yet. The levees and the flood walls had just broken."[73] Since General Myers' briefing, the Defense

---

[68] White House, *President Tours Biloxi, Mississippi Hurricane Damaged Neighborhoods* (Sept. 2, 2005) (online at http://www.whitehouse.gov/news/releases/2005/09/20050902-6.html).

[69] *Id.*

[70] White House, *President, Lieutenant General Honore Discuss Hurricane Relief in Louisiana* (Sept. 12, 2005) (online at www.whitehouse.gov/news/releases/2005/ 09/20050912.html).

[71] *Meet the Press,* NBC News (Sept. 4, 2005).

[72] *Id. See also* Department of Homeland Security, *Press Conference with Officials from the Department of Homeland Security, Justice Department, Defense Department, the National Guard Bureau, U.S. Coast Guard and FEMA* (Sept. 1, 2005) ("[T]his has been a unique disaster in that we really had two disasters one after the other. We had the storm, but then before we could come in and begin the rescue effort and the evacuation effort and the effort to address people's needs, we had a second catastrophe. That was the levee breaking and the flood coming in").

[73] Department of Defense, *Defense Department Operational Update Briefing* (Sept. 6, 2005).

Department has adopted this false claim as fact in numerous subsequent press releases.[74]

Administration officials also made these claims directly to members of Congress. Chairman Davis led a congressional delegation to the Gulf Coast on September 18, 2005, during which Coast Guard Vice Admiral Thad Allen briefed the delegation, claiming that the levees were not breached until Tuesday, and repeating the line that New Orleans had "dodged the bullet."[75]

It is appalling to think that the President and his top advisors would mislead the public about the levee breaches to provide political cover for the slow federal response. But it is also hard to comprehend how the President and his top advisors could be misinformed for weeks about basic facts about what happened in New Orleans. Unfortunately, the Select Committee's investigation is unable to explain why these erroneous statements were made initially and repeated so frequently.

D.   Absence of Leadership in the Situation Room

President Bush allowed only a single White House official to talk to the Select Committee about the response to Hurricane Katrina. That official was Ken Rapuano, the deputy to Homeland Security Advisor Frances Townsend. Mr. Rapuano did not testify under oath or in public. None of his e-mails or other documents were provided to Congress. But he did brief the Select Committee in closed session in two parts, on December 15, 2005, and January 27, 2006.

Mr. Rapuano's briefings raised serious questions about the White House response. As described above, one question was how he could have been ignorant of the predictions that a hurricane hitting New Orleans and the Gulf Coast would incapacitate state and local officials. Other questions involve his conduct on Monday, August 29, the day the hurricane struck, and the seemingly passive White House response in the days following the hurricane.

With President Bush, Vice President Cheney, Chief of Staff Andrew Card, and Homeland Security Advisor Townsend on vacation, Mr. Rapuano was the senior official in the White House in charge of the federal response to Hurricane Katrina.

---

[74] *See, e.g.,* Department of Defense, *New Orleans "Unwatering" Task Force Speeds Progress* (Sept. 15, 2005) ("Since Hurricane Katrina flooded the city [on Tuesday] Aug. 30, engineers and workers have been feverishly damming up breached levees, strengthening canal walls and getting huge pumps on line"); Department of Defense, *82nd Airborne Division Becomes "Waterborne" in New Orleans* (Sept. 21, 2005) ("About 80 percent of the Crescent City was flooded after levees broke [on Tuesday] Aug. 30"); *New Orleans Is Dry, Says Corps of Engineers,* American Forces Press Service (Oct. 11, 2005) ("About 80 percent of New Orleans became flooded after the levees gave way [on Tuesday] Aug. 30, a day after Category 4 Hurricane Katrina hit the Gulf Coast").

[75] Briefing by Vice Admiral Thad Allen, U.S. Coast Guard, to Select Committee (Sept. 18, 2005).

Yet he told the Select Committee that he left the White House at 10:00 p.m. on the day the hurricane hit. During the briefings, he repeatedly emphasized the confused, conflicting, and incomplete information being received by the White House. But when asked to explain his decision to leave, he said he was "satisfied" with federal search and rescue efforts and with FEMA's response.

Mr. Rapuano also stated that he left the Situation Room on Monday evening under the assumption that "Michael Brown was satisfied with everything he got." When asked to explain the basis for his belief, Mr. Rapuano conceded that he had not actually communicated with Mr. Brown, but that his "impression" was based on communications with officials from the Department of Homeland Security. When asked to provide these communications, officials from the White House Counsel's Office interrupted and stated that Mr. Rapuano had no authority to negotiate with the Committee about documents.

Mr. Rapuano told the Select Committee that his top priority on Monday was search and rescue operations. And he asserted that he was confident when he left the White House that every available federal resource was being used to assist in this effort. But on January 30, 2006, just three days after Mr. Rapuano's briefing, a hearing in the Senate revealed that offers by the Interior Department for additional search and rescue resources — including 300 boats — were ignored immediately after Hurricane Katrina struck.[76] As the Interior Department explained:

> The areas of search and rescue and law enforcement illustrate the nature of the problem. … DOI's proactive offer to deploy shallow-water rescue assets utilizing flat-bottom boats operated by qualified Refuge Officers was not integrated into the NRP process, yet clearly these assets and skills were precisely relevant in the post-Katrina environment.[77]

Interior Department officials concluded: "Although we attempted to provide these assets, we were unable to efficiently integrate and deploy these resources."[78] Mr. Rapuano was never called back before the Select Committee to explain these inconsistencies.

Mr. Rapuano was specifically asked who was left in charge in the White House when he left at 10:00 p.m. He could not identify the individual, except to say that

---

[76] Senate Homeland Security and Governmental Affairs Committee, *Hearings on Hurricane Katrina: Urban Search and Rescue in a Catastrophe,* 109th Cong. (Jan. 30, 2006).

[77] Letter from P. Lynn Scarlett, Assistant Secretary for Policy, Management and Budget, Department of the Interior, to Chairman Susan M. Collins and Ranking Member Joseph I. Lieberman, Senate Committee on Homeland Security and Governmental Affairs (Nov. 7, 2005).

[78] *Id. See also FEMA Failed to Accept Katrina Help, Documents Say,* CNN (Jan. 30, 2006).

there would have been an unidentified "watch officer" manning the Situation Room.

These admissions by Mr. Rapuano call into question his actions and, by implication, the leadership emanating from the White House. It is astonishing that the White House would leave the response to one of the greatest disasters in U.S. history to a relatively junior staffer who would leave his post in the midst of confusion and conflicting reports without even identifying who would remain in charge.

Mr. Rapuano's briefing also raised unanswered questions about whether the White House provided essential leadership in the days after the hurricane. During the January 27 briefing, Mr. Rapuano was repeatedly asked to provide specific examples of orders or directives given by the White House to improve the disjointed federal response. He refused to provide a single example. Instead, he stated only that the White House had "engaged in discussions" about or "monitored" aspects of the federal response. Mr. Rapuano explained that "we don't do operations at the White House" and that his role was to "assess and monitor the situation" and to "coordinate and engage" when there were "operational gaps."

In a preliminary report to the Select Committee on February 1, 2006, Comptroller General David M. Walker concluded that someone should have been "directly responsible and accountable to the President" and should have been "designated to act as the central focus point to lead and coordinate the overall federal response."[79] Mr. Walker referred to an earlier GAO report emphasizing that "the nation needs presidential involvement and leadership both before and after a catastrophic disaster."[80]

Based on Mr. Rapuano's briefing, there is little evidence that such leadership was provided by the White House. There thus remain key unanswered questions about whether the White House fulfilled its responsibility to ensure that all branches of the federal government responded in an effective and coordinated manner.

E.   White House Refusal to Cooperate

During the course of the investigation, we made repeated attempts to get the documents and testimony needed to resolve these unanswered questions about the White House role. But we were consistently frustrated. With the exception of

---

[79] U.S. Government Accountability Office, *Statement by Comptroller General David M. Walker on GAO's Preliminary Observations Regarding Preparedness and Response to Hurricanes Katrina and Rita* (Feb. 1, 2006) (GAO-06-365R).

[80] U.S. General Accounting Office, *Disaster Management: Improving the Nation's Response to Catastrophic Disasters* (July 1993) (GAO-RCED-93-186).

Mr. Rapuano, President Bush refused to allow any White House officials to testify or be interviewed by the Select Committee. In addition, multiple efforts were made during the course of the Select Committee's investigation to obtain White House documents that would address these unanswered questions. In the end, these efforts were frustrated by the refusal of the White House to cooperate and the reluctance of the majority to exercise its authority under House Resolution 437.

On September 30, 2005, Chairman Davis and Rep. Melancon sent a document request letter to the White House. The request was broad, encompassing the full range of documents relevant to the Committee's inquiry. At the same time, the request identified a narrow subclass of documents that were of particular interest. These high priority documents included e-mails, internal memos, and other communications to and from top decision-makers in the White House. The letter asked the White House to give first priority to providing communications from "officials in the Office of the President, the Office of the Vice President, the Office of the White House Chief of Staff, and the Office of the Homeland Security Advisor."[81]

Although the letter requested an initial response within two weeks, the White House failed to respond. Rep. Melancon raised concern at the Select Committee's hearing on November 2, 2005, noting: "We also have no communications from the White House, even though Mr. Brown testified that he exchanged multiple e-mails with White House officials, including Chief of Staff Andrew Card."[82] In response, Chairman Davis cited not only the importance of these documents to the Committee's investigation, but his intent to issue a subpoena if necessary:

> I just want to commit to you and the other members of the committee, I'm going to seek a firm final deadline on all the prioritized requests. We need to get those documents to continue our work, and if they're not met — and I'll work on those deadlines with all of you. If we don't get them, I'm not hesitant to issue subpoenas; we have that power.[83]

When the White House again failed to produce the requested documents, Rep. Melancon reiterated his concern at the Select Committee's hearing on November 9, 2005.[84] In response, Chairman Davis promised to issue a subpoena by

---

[81] Letter from Select Committee Chairman Tom Davis and Rep. Charlie Melancon to Andrew H. Card, Jr., White House Chief of Staff (Sept. 30, 2005).

[82] House Select Bipartisan Committee to Investigate the Preparation for and Response to Hurricane Katrina, *Hearings on Hurricane Katrina: The Federal Government's Use of Contractors to Prepare and Respond*, 109th Cong. (Nov. 2, 2005).

[83] *Id.*

[84] House Select Bipartisan Committee to Investigate the Preparation for and Response to Hurricane Katrina, *Hearings on Hurricane Katrina: Preparedness and Response by the State of Alabama*, 109th Cong. (Nov. 9, 2005).

November 18: "I'm comfortable setting a firm deadline. ... I would think Friday, November 18th, the final day before we recess, is a reasonable date, and if the gentleman would agree, if the documents aren't produced by that date, I'm ready to proceed with subpoenas. The clock is ticking."[85]

When the White House again failed to produce the documents by the deadline, no subpoena was issued. Instead, representatives from the White House Counsel's office met with Select Committee staff on December 1, 2005.[86] At that meeting, the White House officials asserted that compliance would be impossible. They said responding to the document request would require the review of 71 million e-mail messages and take over one year. They could not explain, however, why other agencies had managed to comply or why they had not begun producing communications from at least the key individuals identified in the September 30 request letter.

During this meeting, the White House officials raised vague concerns about "separation of powers," claiming that it would be inappropriate and unprecedented for Congress to obtain the documents the Committee was seeking. When asked whether they were asserting a legal claim of executive privilege, they said they were not. When staff provided multiple examples of past precedents for this type of request — including testimony provided by White House chiefs of staff during the Clinton Administration — an official from the White House responded bluntly: "You're not getting Andrew Card's e-mails."[87]

Later that day, Chairman Davis and Rep. Melancon wrote to the White House objecting to these arguments.[88] To further limit the request, they identified an even smaller set of documents the White House should produce immediately. The letter requested communications from just a handful of individuals: Chief of Staff Andrew Card and his deputy Joe Hagin, Homeland Security Advisor Frances Townsend and her deputy Ken Rapuano, and two senior staff in each of their immediate offices. The request was further limited to communications from August 23 to September 15, 2005. The letter asked for these documents by December 6, 2005, and it made clear for the third time that our goal was "to avoid the issuance of subpoenas."[89]

---

[85] *Id.* (emphasis added).

[86] Meeting between Richard Klinger, Associate Counsel to the President; Robert F. Hoyt, Associate Counsel to the President; and Alex M. Mistri, Special Assistant to the President for Legislative Affairs, with Select Committee Staff (Dec. 1, 2005).

[87] *Id.*

[88] Letter from Select Committee Chairman Tom Davis and Rep. Charlie Melancon to Andrew H. Card, Jr., White House Chief of Staff (Dec. 1, 2005).

[89] *Id.*

On December 6, the White House wrote back refusing to provide the requested documents.[90] Instead, the White House offered a "background briefing" by a single White House official, Deputy Homeland Security Advisor Ken Rapuano. Although the White House said it would produce some e-mails from lower-level Homeland Security Council staffers, there was no commitment to produce any documents from the four specific officials identified in the December 1 request letter. There was also no explanation for the White House's decision to provide e-mails from some White House staffers but not others.

On December 13, Rep. Melancon issued a memorandum to all Select Committee members explaining his intent to move for a subpoena of the White House at the Select Committee hearing the next day. As the memo stated:

> It becomes impossible for the Committee to fulfill its mandate responsibly if the White House and other agencies are permitted to withhold key documents and run out the clock on the investigation. On multiple occasions, I have raised my concerns with the Committee that the White House and other agencies appear to be stonewalling the investigation. The Committee should not permit this to continue.[91]

When Rep. Melancon offered his subpoena motion on December 14, 2005, Chairman Davis opposed the motion, reversing the position he had declared publicly on three previous occasions. In explaining his reversal, Chairman Davis stated: "I don't think that Andy Card's e-mails are appropriate. We've researched this, in terms of executive privilege and the like. The President doesn't carry a blackberry with him. For all intents and purposes the Chief of Staff is the President. For these reasons I think that's too inclusive."[92] Chairman Davis also opposed obtaining e-mails from Joe Hagin, Frances Townsend, and Ken Rapuano, but he offered no explanation for his position on these officials.

After rejecting the subpoena motion, the Republicans on the Select Committee approved a separate motion accepting a closed briefing from the White House in lieu of any of the requested documents. The first briefing was provided by Mr. Rapuano on December 15 and the second on January 27.

Immediately after the first White House briefing on December 15, Reps. Melancon and Taylor wrote to Chairman Davis to renew their request for a

---

[90] Letter from William K. Kelly, Deputy Counsel to the President, to Select Committee Chairman Tom Davis and Rep. Charlie Melancon (Dec. 6, 2005).

[91] Memorandum from Rep. Charlie Melancon to Members of the House Select Bipartisan Committee to Investigate the Preparation for and Response to Hurricane Katrina (Dec. 13, 2005).

[92] House Select Bipartisan Committee to Investigate the Preparation for and Response to Hurricane Katrina, *Hearings on Hurricane Katrina: Preparedness and Response by the State of Alabama*, 109th Cong. (Dec. 9, 2005).

subpoena for the e-mails and communications of the four key White House officials. As they stated:

> The White House briefing made it clear that there were major flaws in the federal response. But the briefing did not explain why these failures occurred and who should be held accountable. Every time specific questions were asked about the role of key White House officials, Mr. Rapuano either declined to answer or gave only a general answer that provided no details.[93]

In the same letter, Reps. Melancon and Taylor asked Chairman Davis to schedule a hearing at which the four key White House officials would testify. That request was denied.

Late in the investigation, on February 10, 2006, Michael Brown testified before the Senate Committee on Homeland Security and Governmental Affairs, providing new details about his communications with the White House. After Mr. Brown completed his testimony, Chairman Davis subpoenaed him to appear the next day before the House Select Committee in closed session. During his appearance before the House Select Committee, Mr. Brown discussed his communications with White House officials. He also provided e-mails of some of these communications, although he described the e-mails as an "incomplete" set. The White House did not provide any of Mr. Brown's e-mails to the Select Committee. The White House also failed to provide any internal communications responding to Mr. Brown's e-mails and requests for assistance.

On September 15, the same day that House Resolution 437 passed the House, the President promised to cooperate fully in a congressional investigation. In a prime-time speech delivered in the French Quarter of New Orleans at the foot of historic St. Louis Cathedral, he stated:

> The United States Congress also has an important oversight function to perform. Congress is preparing an investigation, and I will work with members of both parties to make sure this effort is thorough.[94]

Ultimately, however, the President never kept this commitment. The White House withheld scores of critical documents, prevented all but a single White House official from even speaking to Congress, and made clear that a full and complete accounting would have to take a back seat to shielding White House actions through unprecedented and sweeping claims of executive privilege. When

---

[93] Letter from Rep. Charlie Melancon and Rep. Gene Taylor to Select Committee Chairman Tom Davis (Dec. 15, 2005).

[94] *Id.*

President Bush was asked on January 27, 2006, why the White House was not being more forthcoming, he stated: "that's just the way it works."[95]

F.   Congressional Precedents

The majority concludes that while it "was disappointed and frustrated by the slow pace and general resistance to producing the requested documents by the White House," the Select Committee "had more than enough to do our job." The majority has also asserted that its approach toward the White House was evenhanded and consistent with congressional precedents. We strongly disagree.

One of the most striking features of the Select Committee's approach toward the White House in this investigation is how dramatically it conflicts with congressional oversight during the Clinton Administration. During the Clinton Administration, the Government Reform Committee, the principal oversight committee in the House, issued over 1,000 unilateral subpoenas to investigate allegations against the Clinton Administration and the Democratic Party.[96]

Through these subpoenas and other requests, the Committee received exceptionally sensitive Administration documents, including descriptions of discussions between the President and his advisors, internal White House e-mails, and internal Administration deliberations.[97] At one point, the White House spent over $12 million to reconstruct internal White House e-mails for Committee review.[98] The Committee heard testimony from over 100 White House and agency officials, including three White House chiefs of staff.[99]

The treatment the Bush White House has received from the Select Committee is fundamentally different. The Select Committee has no idea what specific documents the White House is withholding from Congress. The Select Committee also has no idea whether the legal doctrine of executive privilege applies to any of these documents because we do not know what information they

---

[95] *Bush Reasserts Presidential Prerogatives; Eavesdropping, Katrina Probe Cited as Concerns,* Washington Post (Jan. 27, 2006).

[96] Minority Staff, Special Investigations Division, House Committee on Government Reform, *Congressional Oversight of the Clinton Administration* (Jan. 17, 2006).

[97] *Id.*

[98] Letter from Phillip D. Larsen, Special Assistant to the President and Director of the Office of Administration, to Rep. Ernest J. Istook, Jr. (Aug. 1, 2001).

[99] Deposition of Thomas F. McLarty, House Committee on Government Reform and Oversight (Sept. 5, 1997); Deposition of Erskine Bowles, House Committee on Government Reform and Oversight (May 5, 1998); Testimony of John Podesta, House Committee on Government Reform, *Hearing on the Controversial Pardon of International Fugitive Marc Rich* (Mar. 1, 2001) (H. Rept. 107-11).

contain. Although the minority requested briefings to answer these questions, those requests were denied.

III. OTHER FAILURES TO ASSIGN ACCOUNTABILITY

The White House may be the most extreme example in the majority report of a failure to determine responsibility for mistakes and assign accountability. But it is not the only example. Consistently throughout the report, problems in the response are identified without an assessment of cause and responsibility. We know from the majority report that "massive failures" in communications operability "impaired response efforts," we know that coordination with the Pentagon was not effective, and we know that poor planning and the failure to adequately preposition medical supplies led to delays and shortages. But we do not know who was responsible for these failures.

In the discussion below, we comment on several areas where further investigation is required to determine why specific mistakes were made and to hold those responsible to account.

A.   Delays in Deployment of Military Assets

The majority report contains multiple findings about problems in the Defense Department response to Hurricane Katrina. The report finds that "DOD/DHS coordination was not effective during Hurricane Katrina"; "DOD, FEMA and the state of Louisiana had difficulty coordinating with each other, which slowed the response"; and that various military organizations, including active duty troops, the National Guard, and the Coast Guard, each performed admirably, but that coordination among them was inadequate. But the Select Committee failed to insist on a full review of Defense Secretary Rumsfeld's responsibility for these problems.

At the Select Committee hearing on October 27, 2005, Defense Department officials claimed that they fulfilled every request for assistance they received in a timely manner. For example, Admiral Timothy Keating, the Commander of Northern Command, stated: "The United States Northern Command met every request for support received by FEMA."[100] Assistant Secretary of Defense for Homeland Defense Paul McHale testified: "The Department of Defense received 93 mission assignments from FEMA and approved all of them."[101] Mr. McHale further testified that the Defense Department moved quickly to accept a mission

---

[100] Select Bipartisan Committee to Investigate the Preparation for and Response to Hurricane Katrina, *Hearings on Hurricane Katrina: Preparedness and Response by the Department of Defense, the Coast Guard, and the National Guard of Louisiana, Mississippi, and Alabama* (Oct. 27, 2005).

[101] *Id.*

assignment from FEMA to take over logistics. When asked whether any time was lost waiting for approval of civilian mission assignments by Secretary Rumsfeld, Mr. McHale said, "I don't believe so. I think the time that elapsed was commensurate with the magnitude of taking on full logistical support throughout a three- or four-state area."[102]

This testimony was contradicted by FEMA officials. On January 5 and 6, 2006, Select Committee staff interviewed Ed Buikema, Acting Director of FEMA's Response Division, and Michael Lowder, FEMA Deputy Director of Response.[103] Mr. Buikema and Mr. Lowder were the senior FEMA officials responsible for coordinating logistics in response to Hurricane Katrina.

Both FEMA officials stated that on Thursday, September 1, 2005, three days after Hurricane Katrina made landfall, FEMA requested emergency assistance from the Defense Department pursuant to the National Response Plan.[104] In particular, they stated that FEMA issued a massive "billion-dollar mission assignment" to the Defense Department to deliver food, water, ice, and other essential commodities to all three states affected by the hurricane. The FEMA officials said that this urgent request included "logistical support," "airlift" assistance, and "commodity distribution." They characterized the request as a "blanket mission assignment" that was critical to a timely and effective emergency response.[105]

Both Mr. Buikema and Mr. Lowder stated that the Defense Department "rejected" this request.[106] The FEMA officials said they relayed their request to the Defense Department's Joint Director of Military Support, which told them that the Defense Department would not accept the mission assignment and that all requests for assistance by FEMA had to be personally approved by Secretary Rumsfeld. According to the FEMA officials, the Defense officials expressed concern that the involvement of active duty troops in providing emergency supplies raised legal issues that the Department had not resolved.

Both FEMA officials recounted that this unexpected rejection of their emergency request delayed critical assistance for days. They reported that they were forced to leave their command post at FEMA headquarters in order to negotiate with Pentagon attorneys about what assignments the Defense Department would and

---

[102] *Id.*

[103] Interview of Michael Lowder, Deputy Director of Response, Federal Emergency Management Agency, by Select Committee Staff (Jan. 5, 2006); Interview of Ed Buikema, Acting Director of Response, Federal Emergency Management Agency, by Select Committee Staff (Jan. 6, 2006).

[104] *Id.*

[105] *Id.*

[106] *Id.*

would not accept. These bureaucratic interagency negotiations continued throughout the weekend.

The FEMA officials did not personally communicate with Defense Secretary Rumsfeld during this period. But they told the Select Committee that they were informed during these protracted negotiations that Secretary Rumsfeld had to personally sign off on every mission assignment and that this added an extra layer of bureaucracy and review. According to one of the FEMA officials, "all FEMA mission assignments to DOD had to go to the Secretary of Defense."[107] This official also said that "had DOD fully engaged earlier, that would have helped."[108]

According to the FEMA officials, a final agreement on the Defense Department's mission assignment was not worked out until Monday, September 5 — one week after Hurricane Katrina struck. These accounts appear to be supported by documents. On Monday, September 5, Homeland Security Operations Center Director Matthew Broderick wrote to Assistant Secretary of Defense Paul McHale asking whether the renewed FEMA mission assignments to the Defense Department had been finally approved.[109]

The majority report describes the contradiction between the accounts of Pentagon officials, who claimed they approved every request for assistance, and the accounts of FEMA officials, who said their requests were denied. It recognizes that "communications between DOD and DHS, especially FEMA, … reflect a lack of information sharing, near panic, and problems with process. But the majority report fails to assign accountability for the delays in responding to FEMA's pleas for help.

On multiple occasions, the Select Committee tried to obtain documents that would allow the Committee to investigate these issues further. Chairman Davis and Rep. Melancon first requested documents from the Department of Defense on September 30, 2005.[110] In that letter, they made clear that the Defense Department should give first priority to producing documents from the Office of the Secretary of Defense.

When these documents were not produced, Chairman Davis and Rep. Melancon sent another letter requesting high priority documents from Secretary

---

[107] Interview of Michael Lowder, Deputy Director of Response, Federal Emergency Management Agency, by Select Committee Staff (Jan. 5, 2006)

[108] *Id.*

[109] E-mail from Matthew Broderick, Director, Homeland Security Operations Center, to Paul McHale, Assistant Secretary of Defense, et al. (Sept. 5, 2005).

[110] Letter from Select Committee Chairman Tom Davis and Rep. Charlie Melancon to Donald H. Rumsfeld, Secretary of Defense (Sept. 30, 2005).

Rumsfeld.[111] When the documents still had not been produced, Rep. Melancon offered a subpoena motion at the Select Committee's hearing on December 14, 2005. That motion was adopted, and the Select Committee directed Secretary Rumsfeld to turn over his communications on Katrina.[112]

Although the subpoena did prompt the production of some documents, including some of Secretary Rumsfeld's official correspondence, Secretary Rumsfeld continued to defy the subpoena with respect to his e-mails, notes, memoranda, and other documents. Secretary Rumsfeld withheld these documents "subject to a continuing review of the communication for legitimate issues of legal privilege and confidentiality," according to press accounts quoting Assistant Secretary of Defense Paul McHale.[113] The minority requested a meeting with Mr. McHale to determine precisely which documents were being withheld and why, but this request was denied. In response, Rep. Melancon wrote to Chairman Davis on January 23, 2006, to urge him to enforce the subpoena he had issued, but that request was also denied.[114] Our requests for an interview or direct testimony from Secretary Rumsfeld were denied as well.

Because Secretary Rumsfeld refused to comply with the Select Committee's subpoena, and because the Select Committee rejected our requests to enforce it, we were unable to determine why the Defense Department refused FEMA's requests for assistance or why protracted negotiations continued for more than a week after Hurricane Katrina struck.

B.   Failures in the Medical Response

Although evidence gathered by the Committee revealed that major failures were predicted in the nation's medical response system well before the storm hit, the Select Committee did not fully investigate why these breakdowns occurred or who was responsible for correcting these deficiencies before Katrina struck.

A report issued on December 9, 2005, by Rep. Henry A. Waxman, Rep. Bennie G. Thompson, and Rep. Charlie Melancon documented major failures in the medical response to Hurricane Katrina.[115] This report found that a key component of federal emergency response capacity — the National Disaster

---

[111] Letter from Chairman Tom Davis and Rep. Charlie Melancon to Donald H. Rumsfeld, Secretary of Defense (Dec. 7, 2005).

[112] House Select Bipartisan Committee to Investigate the Preparation for and Response to Hurricane Katrina, *Subpoena to Donald H. Rumsfeld, Secretary of Defense* (issued Dec. 14, 2005).

[113] *Pentagon May Resist Rumsfeld Subpoena with Legal Privilege*, Associated Press (Dec. 16, 2005).

[114] Letter from Rep. Charlie Melancon to Select Committee Chairman Tom Davis (Jan. 23, 2006).

[115] Minority Staff, Special Investigations Division, House Committee on Government Reform, *The Decline of the National Disaster Medical System* (Dec. 2005).

Medical System (NDMS) — experienced breakdowns in planning, supply management, communications, and leadership.

Evidence shows that the Administration was repeatedly warned about problems at NDMS. In 2002, an internal HHS report identified major gaps in the readiness of NDMS, including poor management practices, inadequate funding, and a lack of relevant doctrine and standards.[116] The review also pointed to deficiencies in communications, training, and transport that hindered the system's capability.[117]

In a 2005 report, a senior medical advisor to the Secretary of Homeland Security found that NDMS was rapidly degrading under mismanagement and neglect.[118] The report described federal medical capability as "fragmented and ill-prepared to deal with a mass-casualty event."[119] With respect to NDMS specifically, the report concluded that the system lacked the medical leadership and oversight "required to effectively develop, prepare for, employ, and sustain deployable medical assets."[120] The report called for a "radical transformation" of NDMS to enable it to fulfill its responsibilities under the National Response Plan.[121] Yet the Administration did not act on the report's recommendations.[122]

Given these multiple unheeded warnings, the minority requested hearings on the medical response to Hurricane Katrina, but no hearings were held. The minority also requested that the Select Committee interview ten key officials at the Department of Homeland Security and the Department of Health and Human Services who were responsible for the medical response. In response, the Committee interviewed two of these officials in late January, after most of the Committee's work was complete.[123] These two interviews were with Stewart Simonson, Assistant Secretary of Public Health and Emergency Preparedness at HHS, and Jack Beall, Chief of the NDMS Section of FEMA.

In speaking with Select Committee staff, Mr. Simonson and Mr. Beall gave sharply conflicting accounts of who was responsible for directing NDMS

---

[116] The CNA Corporation, *Assessing NDMS Response Team Readiness: Focusing on DMATs, NMRTs, and the MST* (Oct. 2002).

[117] *Id.*

[118] Department of Homeland Security, *Medical Readiness Responsibilities and Capabilities: A Strategy for Realigning and Strengthening the Federal Medical Response* (Jan. 3, 2005).

[119] *Id.*

[120] *Id.*

[121] *Id.*

[122] Minority Staff, Special Investigations Division, House Committee on Government Reform, *The Decline of the National Disaster Medical System* (Dec. 2005); *See also Review Warned of Medical Gaps Before Hurricanes*, Associated Press (Sept. 26, 2005).

[123] The Select Committee interviewed four other DHS and HHS officials about the medical response, but minority staff were not invited to participate.

operations during the response. Mr. Simonson stated that HHS had a limited role, since NDMS is housed within DHS. According to Mr. Simonson, HHS could not directly order the movement or operations of NDMS teams, but instead could only "advocate" for DHS to issue mission assignments that would place the teams where they were needed.[124] Mr. Beall denied this, stating that he and other NDMS officials "can't mission ourselves. We work for HHS. We just put the teams out there — then they belong to HHS."[125]

In its findings, the Select Committee identifies this critical confusion of roles, but it does not resolve the opposing accounts. Instead of determining who actually made critical decisions in the medical response, the majority report concludes that "the command structure between HHS and NDMS was problematic." While noting that more supplies and personnel could and should have been pre-positioned before the storm hit, the majority does not address why this was not done.

One way the Select Committee could have resolved this disconnect would have been to interview HHS Secretary Michael Leavitt — the person identified by the National Response Plan as responsible for overseeing the health and medical response to a disaster. Although the minority requested this interview, that request was denied. Without further investigation, it is impossible to know which officials controlled NDMS operations in the response and thus who should be held accountable.

Another way the Select Committee might have helped resolve this issue would have been to speak with the medical first responders on the ground who actually carried out orders. In his interview with staff on January 23, 2006, Mr. Beall informed the Select Committee that the Department of Homeland Security was planning to host a conference on January 26 and 27 in which all NDMS team leaders would gather in Washington D.C. to discuss the best way for NDMS to move forward in light of the problems experienced during Hurricane Katrina. Although not intended to be a backward-looking "lessons-learned" exercise, the conference promised to identify needed improvements, including resolving issues of command and control. We asked to have our staff attend this conference as observers and report back to the Select Committee. Although the majority initially responded positively to this request, the Administration refused to allow congressional investigators to attend.

Finally, the majority report does not fully address the inadequacy of medical supplies. Multiple accounts indicate that NDMS teams lacked critical medicines

---

[124] Interview of Stewart Simonson, Assistant Secretary of Health and Human Services for Public Health and Emergency Preparedness, by Select Committee Staff (Jan. 20, 2006).

[125] Interview of Jack Beall, Section Chief, National Disaster Medical System, Federal Emergency Management Agency, by Select Committee Staff (Jan. 23, 2006).

and equipment, such as ventilators, and that requests were delayed or ignored for days, diminishing the quality of medical care.[126] Team leaders report that NDMS officials regularly refuse requests for restocking and that, as a result, teams "almost always deploy with an insufficient cache."[127] The majority report finds that equipment and supplies "were in heavy demand and could not quickly be replenished." It also notes that many DMATs arrived without their caches. But it does not address why these problems occurred or who was responsible for addressing these preexisting deficiencies.

IV. FAILURE OF LEADERSHIP AT THE DEPARTMENT OF HOMELAND SECURITY

A major hurricane striking the Gulf Coast and New Orleans was one of the top three potential disasters facing the United States. Yet the evidence before the Select Committee shows that the Secretary of the Department of Homeland Security, Michael Chertoff, was detached and relatively disengaged in the key days before Katrina hit. He also had the atrocious judgment to rely on Michael Brown as his "battlefield commander," despite his lack of training. The majority report finds that Secretary Chertoff made a series of critical mistakes, especially with respect to a basic understanding and execution of the National Response Plan. Reviews by the Government Accountability Office and the White House come to similar conclusions. We agree with these findings and call for the replacement of Secretary Chertoff.

A.   Failure to Understand or Invoke National Response Plan

After the attacks of September 11, 2001, the Homeland Security Act transferred responsibility for responding to both natural and man-made disasters to a newly created Department of Homeland Security. As Secretary, Michael Chertoff was charged by the Act and by presidential directive with responsibility for managing the overall federal response to Hurricane Katrina. We agree with the majority report finding that Secretary Chertoff executed these responsibilities "late, ineffectively, or not at all."

In proposing a new Department of Homeland Security on June 6, 2002, President Bush observed that while "as many as a hundred different government agencies have some responsibilities for homeland security … no one has final accountability."[128] To provide this accountability, Congress passed the Homeland Security Act of 2002, which made the Secretary of Homeland Security

---

[126] Minority Staff, Special Investigations Division, House Committee on Government Reform, *The Decline of the National Disaster Medical System* (Dec. 2005).

[127] *Id.*

[128] White House, *Remarks by the President in Address to the Nation* (June 6, 2002) (online at www.whitehouse.gov/news/releases/2002/06/20020606-8.html).

responsible for "providing the Federal Government's response to terrorist attacks and major disasters," including "managing such response" and "coordinating other Federal response resources in the event of a terrorist attack or major disaster."[129]

Despite these statutory responsibilities, the chronology of Secretary Chertoff's actions shows a seeming disengagement from federal preparation and response efforts. In his testimony before the Select Committee, Secretary Chertoff reported that on Saturday, August 27, two days before landfall, he worked from home.[130] He also conceded that he missed a teleconference to discuss storm preparations on that day, although he claimed he received a subsequent briefing. Secretary Chertoff's testimony left the impression that he remained in close contact with his office during the day. But no communications were ever provided to the Select Committee to document this. Moreover, the Select Committee was informed that Secretary Chertoff does not use e-mail, which means that this vital means of communication was not available to him from home.

On the same day that Secretary Chertoff remained at home, Leo Bosner, a 26-year FEMA employee, stated that he was shocked by the lack of urgency at the Emergency Operations Center.[131] Mr. Bosner, who managed the night shift, said he sent a report to top officials before his shift ended on Saturday morning warning that Katrina was headed towards Louisiana with potentially catastrophic consequence. Yet when he returned for his shift on Saturday night, he said little had changed:

> We'd been expecting that, given our reports and so on, that there'd be some extraordinary measures taking place. So when we come in Saturday night and nothing much had happened — you know, we had a few medical teams, a few search teams were in place, but there was no massive effort that we could see. There was no massive effort to organize the city of New Orleans in an organized way that clearly had to be done. There was no massive mobilization of national resources other than the few that were out there. And I think most of us — I can't speak for everyone, but I know that I and a number of my colleagues just — we felt sort of shocked.[132]

---

[129] Homeland Security Act of 2002, Pub. L. No. 107-296, § 502.

[130] House Select Bipartisan Committee to Investigate the Preparation for and Response to Hurricane Katrina, *Hearings on Hurricane Katrina: The Role of the Department of Homeland Security,* 109th Cong. (Oct. 19, 2005).

[131] *Analysis: FEMA Official Says Agency Heads Ignored Warnings*, National Public Radio (Sept. 16, 2005).

[132] *Id.*

On Sunday, Secretary Chertoff participated in a video teleconference and in calls with governors. He testified that he was satisfied that Michael Brown had the resources and cooperation that he needed to handle the hurricane.[133]

Secretary Chertoff participated in a telephone call with the President on Monday, the day Katrina hit, but the call related primarily to immigration policy.[134] On Tuesday, Secretary Chertoff traveled to Atlanta for a briefing on avian flu.

The Select Committee report expresses particular concern that Secretary Chertoff failed to invoke the National Response Plan prior to Hurricane Katrina making landfall. The Homeland Security Act gives Secretary Chertoff responsibility for "consolidating existing Federal Government emergency response plans into a single, coordinated national response plan."[135] Homeland Security Presidential Directive 8, which was issued in December of 2003, stated:

> The Secretary is the principal Federal official for coordinating the implementation of all-hazards preparedness in the United States. In cooperation with other Federal departments and agencies, the Secretary coordinates the preparedness of Federal response assets, and the support for, and assessment of, the preparedness of State and local first responders.[136]

The majority report finds that Secretary Chertoff did not fulfill these responsibilities in preparation for Hurricane Katrina:

> Perhaps the single most important question the Select Committee has struggled to answer is why the federal response did not adequately anticipate the consequences of Katrina striking New Orleans and, prior to landfall, begin to develop plans to move boats and buses into the area to rescue and evacuate tens of thousands of victims from a flooded city. At least part of the answer lies in the Secretary's failure to invoke the National Response Plan – Catastrophic Incident Annex, to clearly and forcefully instruct everyone involved with the federal response to be proactive, anticipate future requirements, develop plans to fulfill them, and execute those plans without waiting for formal requests from overwhelmed state and local response officials.

---

[133] House Select Bipartisan Committee to Investigate the Preparation for and Response to Hurricane Katrina, *Hearings on Hurricane Katrina: The Role of the Department of Homeland Security,* 109th Cong. (Oct. 19, 2005).

[134] *Id.*

[135] Homeland Security Act of 2002, Pub. L. No. 107-296, § 502.

[136] White House, Homeland Security Presidential Directive/HSPD 8 (Dec. 17, 2003) (online at www.whitehouse.gov/news/releases/2003/12/20031217-6.html).

We agree with this finding. We also concur with the majority report's finding that Secretary Chertoff "should have invoked the Catastrophic Incident Annex to direct the federal response," as well as its finding that he "should have convened the Interagency Incident Management Group on Saturday, two days prior to landfall."

We also agree with the majority report's observation that this was a failure of leadership:

> We are left scratching our heads at the range of inefficiency and ineffectiveness that characterized government behavior right before and after this storm. But passivity did the most damage. The failure of initiative cost lives, prolonged suffering, and left all Americans justifiably concerned our government is no better prepared to protect its people than it was before 9/11.

B.   Misplaced Reliance on Michael Brown

We further agree with the majority report that Secretary Chertoff misplaced his trust in Michael Brown, the FEMA Director, to act as his "battlefield commander." The majority report finds that Secretary Chertoff "should have designated the Principal Federal Official on Saturday, two days prior to landfall." The majority report also concludes that Secretary Chertoff should have selected a Principal Federal Official "from the roster of PFOs who had successfully completed the required training, unlike FEMA Director Michael Brown." We agree with both findings. Failing to designate a qualified official prior to the hurricane left Michael Brown in charge by default.

During the Select Committee hearing on October 19, 2005, Secretary Chertoff testified that he relied on Mr. Brown to "manage this thing as the battlefield commander" who would "understand what the priorities were, which were first and foremost saving human lives, rescuing people, getting them food, water, medical assistance and shelter" and "execute those priorities in an urgent fashion."[137]

Prior to Hurricane Katrina, however, multiple reports had raised questions about Mr. Brown's leadership of FEMA. A report by the DHS Inspector General criticized FEMA's performance responding to four hurricanes in Florida in 2004, finding that the agency's systems for managing the personnel and equipment were

---

[137] House Select Bipartisan Committee to Investigate the Preparation for and Response to Hurricane Katrina, *Hearings on Hurricane Katrina: The Role of the Department of Homeland Security,* 109th Cong. (Oct. 19, 2005).

inadequate.[138] Instead of remedying these problems, Mr. Brown disputed the report's accuracy, claiming FEMA systems were "highly performing" and "well managed."[139] A report on the National Disaster Medical System found that under Mr. Brown's leadership, NDMS was "woefully underfunded, undermanned, and too remote from DHS leadership to gain the visibility it needs" due to "FEMA's inflexible and inappropriate management."[140] Mr. Brown's response to the report was to tell NDMS officials to "get over it."[141]

Despite these warnings, Secretary Chertoff left Mr. Brown in charge of mobilizing all preparations before Hurricane Katrina struck. And he did so despite Mr. Brown's evident lack of qualifications. As has been now widely reported, Mr. Brown did not have a background in emergency response prior to joining FEMA at the beginning of the Bush Administration. Instead, he had spent the previous decade as Judges & Stewards Commissioner of the International Arabian Horse Association.[142]

Mr. Brown's inability to manage a crisis is apparent from his e-mails that were provided to the Select Committee. Far from being an effective battlefield commander, Michael Brown's e-mails show that he was befuddled and disengaged. In the midst of the crisis, Mr. Brown found the time to exchange e-mails about his appearance, his reputation, and other nonessential matters. But few of his e-mails demonstrated leadership or a command of the challenges facing his agency.[143]

During the height of the crisis, it appears that Mr. Brown was reporting directly to the White House, effectively bypassing Secretary Chertoff and cutting him out of the chain of command. Secretary Chertoff testified that he repeatedly tried but failed to communicate with Mr. Brown. Secretary Chertoff testified that he grew increasingly frustrated on Tuesday:

> I would say that starting in the late morning — and the deputy and I both were trying to do this — rising in crescendo through the afternoon and late

---

[138] Department of Homeland Security, Office of the Inspector General, *Emergency Preparedness and Response Could Better Integrate Information Technology with Incident Response and Recovery* (Sept. 2005) (OIG-05-36).

[139] *Id.*

[140] Department of Homeland Security, *Medical Readiness Responsibilities and Capabilities: A Strategy for Realigning and Strengthening the Federal Medical Response* (Jan. 3, 2005)

[141] *Brown's Turf Wars Sapped FEMA's Strength*, Washington Post (Dec. 23, 2005).

[142] International Arabian Horse Association, *Former International Arabian Horse Association Judges & Stewards Commissioner, Michael Brown* (Sept. 7, 2005) (online at http://secure.arabianhorses.org/apps/index.cgi?page=pressrel&prid=41).

[143] Staff Report for Rep. Charlie Melancon, *Hurricane Katrina Document Analysis: The E-mails of Michael Brown* (Nov. 2, 2005).

afternoon I made it very clear to the people I was speaking to and communicating through that I expected Mr. Brown forthwith to get in touch with me because I insisted on speaking to him. I wound up speaking to his chief of staff. I rarely lose my temper, but I lost my temper to some degree with his chief of staff.[144]

Yet on Tuesday evening, Mr. Chertoff made another mystifying decision: he designated Michael Brown as Principal Federal Official in charge of the federal response.[145] The majority report asks why Secretary Chertoff "would have deviated from the requirements of the National Response Plan and designated an untrained individual to serve as PFO for such a catastrophic disaster." It answers this question by concluding that Secretary Chertoff "was confused about the role and responsibilities of the PFO." We agree.

It is also unclear why Secretary Chertoff retained Michael Brown for five days as the federal response continued to deteriorate. Secretary Chertoff testified before the Select Committee:

> On Thursday … the question that arose in my mind was whether I needed to supplement the battlefield management on the ground with some additional skills. And whether I ought to bring someone in with a different set of experiences to manage what I thought was the most troubled part of the operation. … And then ultimately on Friday I made the determination that I would put Admiral Allen in control of the entire operation."[146]

Ironically, on the same day Secretary Chertoff decided to relieve Mr. Brown of his duties, President Bush traveled to New Orleans and uttered his now-famous praise: "Brownie, you're doing a heck of a job."[147]

C.   Contrast with Hurricane Rita

There is a stark contrast between Secretary Chertoff's actions before Hurricane Katrina and his actions before Hurricane Rita, which struck Texas and the Gulf

---

[144] House Select Bipartisan Committee to Investigate the Preparation for and Response to Hurricane Katrina, *Hearings on Hurricane Katrina: The Role of the Department of Homeland Security,* 109th Cong. (Oct. 19, 2005).

[145] Memorandum from Michael Chertoff, Secretary of Homeland Security, *Designation of Principal Federal Official for Hurricane Katrina* (Aug. 30, 2005).

[146] House Select Bipartisan Committee to Investigate the Preparation for and Response to Hurricane Katrina, *Hearings on Hurricane Katrina: The Role of the Department of Homeland Security,* 109th Cong. (Oct. 19, 2005).

[147] *FEMA Director Faces a Wave of Destruction, Despair and Criticism,* Associated Press (Sept. 3, 2005).

inadequate.[138] Instead of remedying these problems, Mr. Brown disputed the report's accuracy, claiming FEMA systems were "highly performing" and "well managed."[139] A report on the National Disaster Medical System found that under Mr. Brown's leadership, NDMS was "woefully underfunded, undermanned, and too remote from DHS leadership to gain the visibility it needs" due to "FEMA's inflexible and inappropriate management."[140] Mr. Brown's response to the report was to tell NDMS officials to "get over it."[141]

Despite these warnings, Secretary Chertoff left Mr. Brown in charge of mobilizing all preparations before Hurricane Katrina struck. And he did so despite Mr. Brown's evident lack of qualifications. As has been now widely reported, Mr. Brown did not have a background in emergency response prior to joining FEMA at the beginning of the Bush Administration. Instead, he had spent the previous decade as Judges & Stewards Commissioner of the International Arabian Horse Association.[142]

Mr. Brown's inability to manage a crisis is apparent from his e-mails that were provided to the Select Committee. Far from being an effective battlefield commander, Michael Brown's e-mails show that he was befuddled and disengaged. In the midst of the crisis, Mr. Brown found the time to exchange e-mails about his appearance, his reputation, and other nonessential matters. But few of his e-mails demonstrated leadership or a command of the challenges facing his agency.[143]

During the height of the crisis, it appears that Mr. Brown was reporting directly to the White House, effectively bypassing Secretary Chertoff and cutting him out of the chain of command. Secretary Chertoff testified that he repeatedly tried but failed to communicate with Mr. Brown. Secretary Chertoff testified that he grew increasingly frustrated on Tuesday:

> I would say that starting in the late morning — and the deputy and I both were trying to do this — rising in crescendo through the afternoon and late

---

[138] Department of Homeland Security, Office of the Inspector General, *Emergency Preparedness and Response Could Better Integrate Information Technology with Incident Response and Recovery* (Sept. 2005) (OIG-05-36).

[139] *Id.*

[140] Department of Homeland Security, *Medical Readiness Responsibilities and Capabilities: A Strategy for Realigning and Strengthening the Federal Medical Response* (Jan. 3, 2005)

[141] *Brown's Turf Wars Sapped FEMA's Strength*, Washington Post (Dec. 23, 2005).

[142] International Arabian Horse Association, *Former International Arabian Horse Association Judges & Stewards Commissioner, Michael Brown* (Sept. 7, 2005) (online at http://secure.arabianhorses.org/apps/index.cgi?page=pressrel&prid=41).

[143] Staff Report for Rep. Charlie Melancon, *Hurricane Katrina Document Analysis: The E-mails of Michael Brown* (Nov. 2, 2005).

afternoon I made it very clear to the people I was speaking to and communicating through that I expected Mr. Brown forthwith to get in touch with me because I insisted on speaking to him. I wound up speaking to his chief of staff. I rarely lose my temper, but I lost my temper to some degree with his chief of staff.[144]

Yet on Tuesday evening, Mr. Chertoff made another mystifying decision: he designated Michael Brown as Principal Federal Official in charge of the federal response.[145] The majority report asks why Secretary Chertoff "would have deviated from the requirements of the National Response Plan and designated an untrained individual to serve as PFO for such a catastrophic disaster." It answers this question by concluding that Secretary Chertoff "was confused about the role and responsibilities of the PFO." We agree.

It is also unclear why Secretary Chertoff retained Michael Brown for five days as the federal response continued to deteriorate. Secretary Chertoff testified before the Select Committee:

> On Thursday ... the question that arose in my mind was whether I needed to supplement the battlefield management on the ground with some additional skills. And whether I ought to bring someone in with a different set of experiences to manage what I thought was the most troubled part of the operation. ... And then ultimately on Friday I made the determination that I would put Admiral Allen in control of the entire operation."[146]

Ironically, on the same day Secretary Chertoff decided to relieve Mr. Brown of his duties, President Bush traveled to New Orleans and uttered his now-famous praise: "Brownie, you're doing a heck of a job."[147]

C.   Contrast with Hurricane Rita

There is a stark contrast between Secretary Chertoff's actions before Hurricane Katrina and his actions before Hurricane Rita, which struck Texas and the Gulf

---

[144] House Select Bipartisan Committee to Investigate the Preparation for and Response to Hurricane Katrina, *Hearings on Hurricane Katrina: The Role of the Department of Homeland Security,* 109th Cong. (Oct. 19, 2005).

[145] Memorandum from Michael Chertoff, Secretary of Homeland Security, *Designation of Principal Federal Official for Hurricane Katrina* (Aug. 30, 2005).

[146] House Select Bipartisan Committee to Investigate the Preparation for and Response to Hurricane Katrina, *Hearings on Hurricane Katrina: The Role of the Department of Homeland Security,* 109th Cong. (Oct. 19, 2005).

[147] *FEMA Director Faces a Wave of Destruction, Despair and Criticism,* Associated Press (Sept. 3, 2005).

Coast just three weeks later. Before Hurricane Rita, Secretary Chertoff traveled with President Bush to NORTHCOM headquarters in Colorado to monitor preparations for the storm.[148] They spent the night there, and continued to manage the response from NORTHCOM headquarters as the storm made landfall.[149] Secretary Chertoff designated Hurricane Rita an Incident of National Significance the day before it struck landfall.[150] In addition, he named Coast Guard Admiral Larry Hereth to serve as Principal Federal Official for Hurricane Rita on September 22, 2005, two days before that hurricane struck.[151] Admiral Hereth had 32 years of experience managing federal operations.

During a briefing provided to the Select Committee by the White House on December 15, 2005, Deputy Homeland Security Advisor Ken Rapuano was asked about the differences in Secretary Chertoff's responses to the two hurricanes. He attributed them to the lessons learned from Hurricane Katrina, explaining that the Department had learned how devastating a hurricane could be.[152]

What Mr. Rapuano did not explain is why it took Hurricane Katrina to alert Secretary Chertoff to the consequences of a massive hurricane hitting New Orleans and the Gulf Coast. There were multiple reports prepared by the Department and other experts relating to the Hurricane Pam exercise warning that a "catastrophic hurricane" striking southeastern Louisiana would cause a "mega-disaster."[153] These documents warned that such a hurricane "could result in significant numbers of deaths and injuries, trap hundreds of thousands of people in flooded areas, and leave up to one million people homeless."[154] They also warned expressly that "the gravity of the situation calls for an extraordinary level of advance planning to improve government readiness."[155] In the face of these dire warnings, Secretary Chertoff's disengagement remains a mystery.

For these reasons, we fully agree with the majority report's concern that "given the advanced warning provided by the National Hurricane Center and the well-documented catastrophic consequences of a category 4 hurricane striking New Orleans, it is unclear why Secretary Chertoff did not exercise these responsibilities sooner or at all."

---

[148] *Hurricanes Katrina and Rita Were Like Night and Day*, Washington Post (Sept. 25, 2005).

[149] *Id.*

[150] *Id.*

[151] *Id.*

[152] Briefing by Ken Rapuano, Deputy White House Homeland Security Advisor, to House Select Committee (Dec. 15, 2005).

[153] Federal Emergency Management Agency, *Combined Catastrophic Plan for Southeast Louisiana and the New Madrid Seismic Zone: Scope of Work* (2004).

[154] *Id.*

[155] *Id.*

D.   Failure to Plan for Catastrophic Incidents

Beyond the mistakes Secretary Chertoff made in the days directly before and after Hurricane Katrina struck, the majority report also identifies longer-term planning deficiencies at the Department of Homeland Security. We agree with the majority's conclusions that these failures presaged and compounded the disaster.

We agree with the majority report's finding that "implementation of lessons learned from Hurricane Pam was incomplete." The possibility of a massive hurricane striking the Gulf Coast was considered one of the top three disasters the nation might face.[156] Yet FEMA Director Michael Brown testified before the Select Committee that his requests for additional funding to implement the lessons learned from the Hurricane Pam exercise were denied:

> QUESTION: You are under oath as saying you didn't get the money to implement what you learned from Hurricane Pam. And you're telling us that your numbers were depleted, your dollars were depleted, and you saw your department eviscerated. That's what you told this committee now.
>
> MR. BROWN: That's correct.[157]

The Select Committee did not receive an adequate rationale for this decision to deny the Hurricane Pam funding.

We also agree with the majority report's finding that "massive" communications inoperability "impaired response efforts, command and control, and situational awareness." As the majority report concludes, there was "a failure to adequately plan for alternatives." This problem was highlighted by the 9/11 Commission when communications problems arose at all three crash sites:

> The inability to communicate was a critical element at the World Trade Center, Pentagon, and Somerset County, Pennsylvania, crash sites, where multiple agencies and multiple jurisdictions responded. The occurrence of this problem at three very different sites is strong evidence that compatible

---

[156] *See, e.g., Sharp Criticism of U.S. Response, Lack of Action to Prevent Disaster*, San Francisco Chronicle (Sept. 2, 2005); *Keeping Its Head Above Water,* Houston Chronicle (Dec. 1, 2001); *The Big One Is Coming,* Hartford Courant (Oct. 16, 2005); *Disaster Raises Question for California,* Dallas Morning News (Sept. 11, 2005); *Katrina's Aftermath: Government Response,* Houston Chronicle (Sept. 11, 2005); *Anarchy, Anger, Desperation: The Response,* San Francisco Chronicle (Sept. 2, 2005).

[157] House Select Bipartisan Committee to Investigate the Preparation for and Response to Hurricane Katrina, *Hearings on Hurricane Katrina: The Role of the Federal Emergency Management Agency*, 109th Cong. (Sept. 27, 2005).

and adequate communications among public safety organizations at the local, state, and federal levels remains an important problem.[158]

To remedy this problem, the Homeland Security Act of 2002 gave the Secretary of Homeland Security responsibility for "developing comprehensive programs for developing interoperative communications technology, and helping to ensure that emergency response providers acquire such technology."[159]

Hurricane Katrina made clear that this responsibility was not met. The majority report concludes that "Joint Task Force Katrina, the National Guard, Louisiana, and Mississippi lacked needed communications equipment." It also finds that "medical responders did not have adequate communications equipment or operability." We agree with these findings.

To this list we would add FEMA. Several FEMA officials told the Select Committee that they had approximately 100 satellite telephones. Yet the Select Committee could not determine where even one of these satellite phones was deployed. To the contrary, we were informed that FEMA Director Michael Brown did not have one, FEMA public affairs official Marty Bahamonde did not have one, and FEMA Deputy Federal Coordinating Officer Phil Parr did not have one.[160] In fact, Mr. Parr told the Select Committee that FEMA was prevented from mobilizing its roving communications vehicle, a Multiple Emergency Operations Vehicle called the "Red October," to the Superdome because it was not designed to operate in flooded areas. He also said FEMA had no contingency plans for air dropping communications equipment into affected areas.[161]

We also agree with the majority report that Secretary Chertoff's coordination with the Defense Department "was not effective." In testimony before the Select Committee, Secretary Chertoff conceded there were major breakdowns with the Department of Defense, stating that the absence of adequate planning "goes to how well we work with the military when the military has large numbers of assets they can bring to bear on a problem, how fluid we are with them."[162] According to Secretary Chertoff, better planning with the military would have allowed the

---

[158] National Commission on Terrorist Attacks Upon the United States, *The 9/11 Commission Report*, p. 397 (2004).

[159] Homeland Security Act of 2002, Pub. L. No. 107-296, § 502.

[160] Interview of Phil Parr, Deputy Federal Coordinating Officer, Federal Emergency Management Agency, by Select Committee Staff (Dec. 6, 2005); Interview of Michael Lowder, Deputy Director of Response, Federal Emergency Management Agency, by Select Committee Staff (Jan. 5, 2006).

[161] Interview of Phil Parr, Deputy Federal Coordinating Officer, Federal Emergency Management Agency, by Select Committee Staff (Dec. 6, 2005).

[162] House Select Bipartisan Committee to Investigate the Preparation for and Response to Hurricane Katrina, *Hearings on Hurricane Katrina: The Role of the Department of Homeland Security,* 109th Cong. (Oct. 19, 2005).

federal government to "to respond hours and maybe even days earlier to some of the issues that were addressed on a Thursday and a Friday that might have been addressed on a Tuesday or a Wednesday."[163]

In addition to the planning failures noted in the majority report, we note that Secretary Chertoff failed to complete a required operational supplement to the National Response Plan for more than seven months. The National Response Plan issued in January 2004 established broad lines of authority for agencies responding to catastrophic events. It stated that a "more detailed and operationally specific" supplement would set forth in detail the precise role of each agency involved in federal response efforts.[164] But this Catastrophic Incident Supplement languished and was not completed until September 6, 2005 — seven days after Hurricane Katrina struck.

To investigate this delay, Chairman Davis and Rep. Melancon sent a letter to Secretary Chertoff on September 30, 2005, which requested a wide range of documents, including all previous drafts of the Catastrophic Incident Supplement.[165] When the Department did not provide them, Rep. Melancon reiterated the importance of these documents in a letter to Chairman Davis on January 10, 2006.[166] Although the Department provided the final draft, it did not provide any previous versions. As a result, the Select Committee was not able to analyze the negotiations between agencies to determine the cause of the delay.

In his testimony before the Select Committee, Secretary Chertoff conceded that one of the biggest failures was the failure to plan. He testified that the federal government "did not have the kind of integrated planning capabilities that you need to deal with the kind of catastrophe we faced in Katrina."[167] Over and over again, Secretary Chertoff pointed to a lack of planning as the key to the federal government's response failures. As he stated to Rep. Thornberry: "I think 80% or more of the problem lies with the planning. ... [I]t doesn't come naturally to civilian agencies for the most part to do the kind of disciplined planning for a complicated operation."[168] What Secretary Chertoff did not explain was why he failed in this critical planning function, which is his under the Homeland Security Act.

---

[163] *Id.*

[164] Department of Homeland Security, *National Response Plan* (Dec. 2004).

[165] Letter from Select Committee Chairman Tom Davis and Rep. Charlie Melancon to Michael Chertoff, Secretary of Homeland Security (Sept. 30, 2005).

[166] Letter from Rep. Charlie Melancon to Select Committee Chairman Tom Davis (Jan. 10, 2006).

[167] House Select Bipartisan Committee to Investigate the Preparation for and Response to Hurricane Katrina, *Hearings on Hurricane Katrina: The Role of the Department of Homeland Security,* 109th Cong. (Oct. 19, 2005).

[168] *Id.*

E.   "The Emaciation of FEMA"

Evidence before the Select Committee showed that FEMA's ability to respond to natural disasters significantly degraded following the enactment of the Homeland Security Act, which moved FEMA into the Department of Homeland Security. We agree with the majority report that both "DHS and FEMA lacked adequate trained and experienced staff for the Katrina response." As the head of the Department, Secretary Chertoff bears at least partial responsibility for this deterioration of FEMA.

Under the Clinton Administration and the leadership of James Lee Witt, FEMA was regarded as a premier, Cabinet-level, all-hazards planning and response agency. But after its transfer to the Department of Homeland Security in 2003, its capacity to respond deteriorated.

During his testimony before the Select Committee, Michael Brown testified that "one of my frustrations over the past three years has been the emaciation of FEMA."[169] He cited not only "brain drain" caused by the loss of senior career FEMA officials, but also what he euphemistically called a DHS "tax," which he described as "assessments imposed by DHS which is money that's drawn out of different programs used for DHS-wide programs."

Additional evidence obtained by the Select Committee supported Mr. Brown's assertions. For example, on January 5, 2006, the Select Committee conducted an interview with FEMA Deputy Director of Response Michael Lowder. He reported that the number of personnel on national emergency response teams had been cut from a high of 300 in the mid-1990s to a low of 50 today.[170]

Mr. Brown testified that he protested organizational and budgetary decisions that diminished the role of FEMA, and the importance of disaster response, within the Department of Homeland Security. He testified that "it has been a personal struggle over the past two or three years to keep that place together because of this resource problem."[171]

When asked whether he documented these concerns to his superiors, Mr. Brown replied: "I'm certain I did lay it out in writing. … I know I wrote to Secretary Ridge when he was secretary. I've done memos to Secretary Chertoff and Deputy

---

[169] House Select Bipartisan Committee to Investigate the Preparation for and Response to Hurricane Katrina, *Hearings on Hurricane Katrina: The Role of the Federal Emergency Management Agency*, 109th Cong. (Sept. 27, 2005).

[170] Interview of Michael Lowder, Deputy Director of Response, Federal Emergency Management Agency, by Select Committee Staff (Jan. 5, 2006).

[171] House Select Bipartisan Committee to Investigate the Preparation for and Response to Hurricane Katrina, *Hearings on Hurricane Katrina: The Role of the Federal Emergency Management Agency*, 109th Cong. (Sept. 27, 2005).

Secretary Jackson."[172] Mr. Brown also testified that he requested additional resources for disaster response in the Department of Homeland Security budget, but that those requests were denied.

The Select Committee was provided with a copy of a September 15, 2003, memo from Mr. Brown to then-Secretary Ridge, warning that removing some of FEMA's preparedness functions would "fundamentally sever FEMA from its core functions," "shatter agency morale," and "break longstanding, effective and tested relationships with states and first responder stakeholders."[173]

Despite multiple requests for similar documents directed to Secretary Chertoff, however, the Department of Homeland Security has failed to provide them. In a story that ran on December 23, 2005, the *Washington Post* quoted from memos sent from Mr. Brown to Secretary Chertoff warning that "this reorganization has failed to produce tangible results," and "a total of $77.9 million has been permanently lost from the base."[174] The report also cited an e-mail to Secretary Chertoff's deputy, warning: "FEMA is doomed to failure and loss of mission."[175] The Department did not provide these documents to the Select Committee.[176]

F.   GAO and White House Findings

Reports by the nonpartisan Government Accountability Office and the White House itself have largely come to the same conclusions as the Select Committee regarding Secretary Chertoff's actions. On February 1, 2006, GAO issued preliminary findings concluding as follows:

> No one was designated in advance to lead the overall federal response in anticipation of the event despite clear warnings from the National Hurricane Center. … [T]he DHS Secretary designated Hurricane Katrina as an incident of national significance on August 30th — the day after final landfall. However, he did not designate the storm as a catastrophic event, which would have triggered additional provisions of the National Response Plan (NRP), calling for a more proactive response. As a result,

---

[172] *Id.*

[173] Memorandum from Michael D. Brown, Under Secretary of Homeland Security for Emergency Preparedness and Response, to Tom Ridge, Secretary of Homeland Security (Sept. 15, 2003) (DHS-FEMA-0116-000001).

[174] *Brown's Turf Wars Sapped FEMA's Strength,* Washington Post (Dec. 23, 2005).

[175] *Id.*

[176] Michael Brown provided to the Committee some budget-related documents that he retained in his personal possession.

the federal posture generally was to wait for the affected states to request assistance.[177]

GAO went on to explain the importance of the Secretary's role in conducting the planning necessary to prepare for catastrophic disasters like Hurricane Katrina:

> Although the NRP framework envisions a proactive national response in the event of a catastrophe, the nation does not yet have the types of detailed plans needed to better delineate capabilities that might be required and how such assistance will be provided and coordinated. ... The leadership to ensure these plans and exercises are in place must come from DHS.[178]

GAO concluded that without such leadership from Secretary Chertoff, major breaches appeared in the chain of command:

> In the absence of timely and decisive action and clear leadership responsibility and accountability, there were multiple chains of command, a myriad of approaches and processes for requesting and providing assistance, and confusion about who should be advised of requests and what resources would be provided within specific timeframes.[179]

Ultimately, GAO concluded that "[n]either the DHS Secretary nor any of his designees, such as the Principal Federal Official (PFO), filled this leadership role during Hurricane Katrina."[180]

The White House came to similar conclusions, although it couched its findings in general terms rather than mentioning specific officials responsible. During a briefing to the Select Committee on December 15, 2005, the White House provided more than 60 specific findings from its own review of the government's response to Hurricane Katrina.[181] Some of the findings related to Secretary Chertoff's duties under the Homeland Security Act, including:

–   The National Response Plan did not function as planned.

–   National Response Plan command and coordination were incomplete.

---

[177] U.S. Government Accountability Office, *Statement by Comptroller General David M. Walker on GAO's Preliminary Observations Regarding Preparedness and Response to Hurricanes Katrina and Rita* (Feb. 1, 2006) (GAO-06-365R).

[178] *Id.*

[179] *Id.*

[180] *Id.*

[181] Briefing by Ken Rapuano, White House Deputy Homeland Security Advisor, to Select Committee (Dec. 15, 2005).

- Lack of comprehensive national strategy and plans to unite communications plans, architectures, and standards.

- No guidance for worst case effects to the communications infrastructure.

- Federal response did not inform nongovernmental organizations what resources were required and how to connect local, State, and Federal emergency managers.

- There was no Federal coordinating entity with a complete understanding of the interdependency of critical infrastructure sectors.

- Focus on terrorism rather than all hazards.[182]

G. New Leadership for the Department of Homeland Security

The discussion of Secretary Chertoff's response is in many ways the strongest part of the majority views. Unlike other areas, where the report eschews accountability, the majority makes affirmative findings that identify major shortcomings in Secretary Chertoff's actions. These findings are confirmed by the conclusions of GAO and the internal White House review.

Ultimately, though, the majority report does not draw the logical conclusion to its own findings. Former FEMA Director Michael Brown is the only federal official who has lost his job and been held accountable for the dismal federal response. He should not be alone. As the majority findings make clear, Secretary Chertoff provided ineffective leadership at a time of great crisis. We therefore recommend his replacement. We believe the President should appoint an official familiar with emergency management to the nation's top homeland security post.

V. THE NEED FOR AN INDEPENDENT COMMISSION

Given the key gaps that remain in the Select Committee's work, we recommend the creation of an independent commission based on the model of the 9/11 Commission. The Select Committee has significantly advanced public understanding of the response to Hurricane Katrina. But it failed to surmount White House intransigence and rarely assigned accountability for mistakes. These shortcomings can only be addressed by the appointment of a truly independent commission.

---

[182] *Id.*

The 9/11 Commission provides an excellent model. It examined fundamental questions, including whether advance warnings of the September 11 attacks were taken seriously, whether adequate preparation had been made for responding to such contingencies, and whether plans were executed to minimize the loss of American lives. The 9/11 Commission called the highest Administration officials to account, including Presidents Bush and Clinton, as well as Vice Presidents Cheney and Gore. The 9/11 Commission also obtained sworn testimony from various other White House officials, including National Security Advisor Condoleezza Rice and National Security Council Counterterrorism Advisor Richard Clarke, among others.

This is exactly the type of forceful and independent investigation that the American people — and especially the residents of the devastated Gulf Coast region — deserve with respect to Hurricane Katrina.

During the course of its investigation, the 9/11 Commission received and reviewed more than 2.5 million pages of documents and over 1,000 hours of audiotape. The 9/11 Commission interviewed over 1,200 individuals in ten countries, and it issued a best-selling report recommending fundamental changes to the makeup of the federal government.

We commend Chairman Davis for his leadership of the Select Committee. He made numerous efforts to work with us, and he tried to approach the investigation in a bipartisan manner. But in the end, the model of congressional Republicans investigating a Republican White House has serious deficiencies. The Select Committee could not — or would not — insist on compliance when the White House resisted its requests for information. It failed to enforce its single subpoena to Defense Secretary Rumsfeld. Indeed, the Select Committee could not get a full accounting of withheld documents from even a single federal agency.

For these reasons, we conclude that only an independent commission with sufficient authority to obtain critical documents and other information from the Administration will be able to tell the full story of Hurricane Katrina. This endeavor is critical not only for historical and accountability purposes, but also to ensure that the nation will not falter again in the event of a future disaster.

Charlie Melancon
Member of Congress
Louisiana's 3rd District

William J. Jefferson
Member of Congress
Louisiana's 2nd District

LIST OF ATTACHMENTS TO BE PUBLISHED LATER

Correspondence and Reports

Letter from Chairman Tom Davis and Ranking Minority Member Henry A. Waxman, House Committee on Government Reform, to Michael Chertoff, Secretary of Homeland Security (Sept. 9, 2005) (regarding the Hurricane Pam exercise).

Letter from Select Committee Chairman Tom Davis and Rep. Charlie Melancon to Michael Chertoff, Secretary of Homeland Security (Sept. 30, 2005) (initial request for DHS documents).

Letter from Select Committee Chairman Tom Davis and Rep. Charlie Melancon to Donald H. Rumsfeld, Secretary of Defense (Sept. 30, 2005) (initial request for Pentagon documents).

Letter from Select Committee Chairman Tom Davis and Rep. Charlie Melancon to Lt. General Carl A. Strock, U.S. Army Corps of Engineers (Sept. 30, 2005) (initial request for Army Corps documents).

Letter from Select Committee Chairman Tom Davis and Rep. Charlie Melancon to Michael O. Leavitt, Secretary of Health and Human Services (Sept. 30, 2005) (initial request for HHS documents).

Letter from Select Committee Chairman Tom Davis and Rep. Charlie Melancon to Andrew H. Card, Jr., White House Chief of Staff (Sept. 30, 2005) (initial request for White House documents).

Letter from Select Committee Chairman Tom Davis and Rep. Charlie Melancon to Kathleen Babineaux Blanco, Governor of Louisiana (Sept. 30, 2005) (initial request for Louisiana documents).

Letter from Select Committee Chairman Tom Davis and Rep. Charlie Melancon to Haley Barbour, Governor of Mississippi (Sept. 30, 2005) (initial request for Mississippi documents).

Letter from Select Committee Chairman Tom Davis and Rep. Charlie Melancon to Robert Riley, Governor of Alabama (Sept. 30, 2005) (initial request for Alabama documents).

Letter from Rep. Henry A. Waxman, Ranking Minority Member, House Committee on Government Reform, to Michael Chertoff, Secretary of Homeland Security (Oct. 20, 2005) (regarding Carnival Cruise Line contract).

Letter from Rep. Gene Taylor to Select Committee Chairman Tom Davis (Oct. 28, 2005) (regarding the need for a Select Committee hearing on housing).

Letter from Rep. Henry A. Waxman and Rep. Charlie Melancon to Michael Chertoff, Secretary of Homeland Security (Nov. 1, 2005) (regarding incomplete Catastrophic Incident Supplement to the National Response Plan).

Staff Report for Rep. Charlie Melancon, *Hurricane Katrina Document Analysis: The E-mails of Michael Brown* (Nov. 2, 2005).

Letter from Rep. Charlie Melancon to Select Committee Chairman Tom Davis (Nov. 9, 2005) (regarding unanswered contracting questions).

Minority Staff, Special Investigations Division, House Committee on Government Reform, *The Decline of the National Disaster Medical System* (Dec. 2005).

Letter from Select Committee Chairman Tom Davis and Rep. Charlie Melancon to Andrew H. Card, Jr., White House Chief of Staff (Dec. 1, 2005) (second request for White House documents).

Letter from William K. Kelly, Deputy Counsel to the President, to Select Committee Chairman Tom Davis and Rep. Charlie Melancon (Dec. 6, 2005) (White House refusal to provide requested documents).

Letter from Select Committee Chairman Tom Davis and Rep. Charlie Melancon to Donald H. Rumsfeld, Secretary of Defense (Dec. 7, 2005) (second request for Pentagon documents).

Letter from Select Committee Chairman Tom Davis and Rep. Charlie Melancon to David Addington, Chief of Staff, Office of the Vice President (Dec. 7, 2005) (second request for Vice President documents)

Memorandum from Rep. Charlie Melancon to Members of the House Select Bipartisan Committee to Investigate the Preparation for and Response to Hurricane Katrina (Dec. 13, 2005) (memo explaining need for subpoenas).

Letter from Rep. Charlie Melancon and Rep. Gene Taylor to Select Committee Chairman Tom Davis (Dec. 15, 2005) (requesting a hearing on White House compliance with Committee requests).

Letter from Rep. Charlie Melancon to Select Committee Chairman Tom Davis (January 10, 2006) (requesting that the Select Committee obtain drafts of the Catastrophic Incident Supplement to the National Response Plan).

Letter from Rep. Charlie Melancon to Select Committee Chairman Tom Davis (January 23, 2006) (regarding need to enforce the Defense Department subpoena).

Motions and Subpoenas

Select Bipartisan Committee to Investigate the Preparation for and Response to Hurricane Katrina, *Motion to Subpoena Harriet Miers, Counsel to the President* (Dec. 14, 2005) (motion by Rep. Melancon to subpoena White House documents, rejected by majority).

Select Bipartisan Committee to Investigate the Preparation for and Response to Hurricane Katrina, *Substitute Motion to Accept a Briefing from the White House* (Dec. 14, 2005) (handwritten motion adopted by majority in lieu of requested documents).

House Select Bipartisan Committee to Investigate the Preparation for and Response to Hurricane Katrina, *Subpoena to Donald H. Rumsfeld, Secretary of Defense* (issued Dec. 14, 2005).

Documents Provided to the Select Committee

Homeland Security Operations Center, *Spot Report #13* (Aug. 29, 2005) (WHK-4055) (DHS-FRNT-0001-0000002) (describing Bahamonde eyewitness account of flooding and levee failure).

E-mail from Brian Besanceney, Assistant Secretary of Homeland Security for Public Affairs, to John Wood, Chief of Staff, Department of Homeland Security, et al. (Aug. 29, 2005) (DHS-FRNT-0006-0000023) (regarding the severity of the storm)

E-mail from Patrick Rhode, Deputy Director, Federal Emergency Management Agency, to Michael Jackson, Deputy Secretary of Homeland Security (Aug. 29, 2005) (regarding the severity of the storm).

National Weather Service, *Bulletin: EAS Activation Requested; Flash Flood Warning* (Aug. 29, 2005) (online at www.srh.noaa.gov/data/warn_archive/LIX/FFW/0829_131705.txt) (first official government confirmation of levee failure).

American Government

UNIVERSITY PRESS OF FLORIDA

Florida A&M University, Tallahassee
Florida Atlantic University, Boca Raton
Florida Gulf Coast University, Ft. Myers
Florida International University, Miami
Florida State University, Tallahassee
New College of Florida, Sarasota
University of Central Florida, Orlando
University of Florida, Gainesville
University of North Florida, Jacksonville
University of South Florida, Tampa
University of West Florida, Pensacola

ORANGE GROVE TEXT *PLUS*

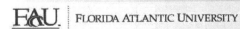

FAU. | FLORIDA ATLANTIC UNIVERSITY

American Government

TIMOTHY O. LENZ AND MIRYA HOLMAN

FLORIDA ATLANTIC UNIVERSITY DEPARTMENT OF POLITICAL SCIENCE

University Press of Florida

Gainesville · Tallahassee · Tampa · Boca Raton

Pensacola · Orlando · Miami · Jacksonville · Ft. Myers · Sarasota

ISBN 978-1-61610-163-3

Orange Grove Texts *Plus* is an imprint of the University Press of Florida, which is the scholarly publishing agency for the State University System of Florida, comprising Florida A&M University, Florida Atlantic University, Florida Gulf Coast University, Florida International University, Florida State University, New College of Florida, University of Central Florida, University of Florida, University of North Florida, University of South Florida, and University of West Florida.

University Press of Florida
15 Northwest 15th Street
Gainesville, FL 32611-2079
http://orangegrovetexts.org

Contents

CHAPTER 1: WHY GOVERNMENT? WHY POLITICS?

1.0 | What is Government?

Government can be defined as the institutions and processes that make and implement authoritative decisions for a society. The government unit can be a city, county, state, regional, national, or international government. The decisions, which include laws, regulations, and other public policies, are authoritative in the sense that individuals and organizations are legally obligated to obey the decisions or face some kind of sanction. In the U.S., government includes the **national** government institutions (Congress, the Presidency, the federal courts, and a broad range of federal bureaucracies), the 50 **state** governments (state legislatures, governors, state courts, and state bureaucracies), and the **local** governments (counties, cities, and other special government units such as school boards).

1.10 | *Why Government*

Is government necessary? Is it possible to live without government? Why do governments exist all over the world when people all over the world are so critical of government? These are old political questions that were first asked when people began thinking about life in organized societies. Questions about the need for government and the legitimate purposes of government are continually being asked because the answers reflect contemporary thinking about basic human values, including freedom, order, individualism, equality, economic prosperity, national security, morality and ethics, and justice. These values are central to government and politics in all countries although the values attached to them and their relative importance varies a great deal. Given the almost universal criticism of government, and a strong tradition of anti-government rhetoric in the United States, it is worth wondering "why government?"

One recurring theme in American government and politics is the conflict between two basic values: freedom and order. Freedom (or liberty) is highly valued in the American political tradition. Individual freedom is an essential element of democracy. Self-government requires individual liberty. In the U.S., freedom of religion, speech, press, and association are individual liberties that are guaranteed by the First Amendment to the U.S. Constitution. The language of the First Amendment, which begins with "Congress shall make no law….," reflects the most common understanding of individual liberty in the U.S. where freedom is usually defined as the absence of government limits.

Order is also a basic political value. One of the primary responsibilities of government is to create and maintain good public order. Good public order is commonly defined to include public safety (individuals are protected from crime, foreign invasions, and domestic disturbances) as well as behavior that a society considers appropriate conduct. Governments use law to create and maintain these aspects of good public order. These laws sometimes limit individual liberty in order to achieve order. Politics is often about where to strike the right balance between allowing individuals the freedom to do what they want, to live their lives without government restrictions, and giving government power to control behavior in order to maintain good public order. In American politics, debates are often framed as freedom *versus* order because the relationship between individual freedom and government power is considered a zero-sum relationship: an increase in one means a corresponding decrease in the other. The power problem illustrates this relationship.

1.12 | *The Power Problem*

The **power problem** refers to the need to grant government enough power to effectively address the problems that people expect government to address, while also limiting power enough so that government can be held accountable. The challenge is to give government enough power so that it can address or solve the problems that people want government to solve, such as providing public safety and national security and economic prosperity, while also limiting government power so that it can be held accountable by the people. Too little power can be a problem because weak governments or "failed states" can provide havens for criminals or terrorists. Too much power can be a problem because strong governments can threaten individual rights. Creating good government requires striking the right balance between granting *and* limiting power. Doing so is difficult because people have different views about the balance point. Politics is about reconciling individual, ideological, and partisan differences of opinion about the power problem.

1.13 | *Politics*

People have different opinions about whether their political system, or the political system of another country, allows too much individual freedom or provides too little public order. People also have different beliefs about what government should be doing. The U.S. Constitution does not say very much about the specifics of where to strike the balance between rights and powers. It mostly provides general guidelines about powers and rights. The Fourth Amendment provides the people a right "against unreasonable searches and seizures," but it does not say when a police officer's search or seizure is unreasonable. The Eighth Amendment prohibits "cruel and unusual punishment" but does not define it. Article I, Section 8 of the Constitution grants Congress power to provide for the "general Welfare of the United States," but it does not define general welfare.

The fact that the Constitution includes such general language means that some disputes about where the balance between government power and individual rights should be struck are more *political* than *legal*. In democratic political systems, politics is about different beliefs about how much power government should have and what government should be doing. Conservatives and liberals typically take different positions in political debates about government power, both the amount of government and its uses. Political opinions about the right balance between individual rights and government power are influenced by conditions. Is it a time of war or peace? Is the economy good or bad? Is there good public order or is it a time of crisis or disorder? These are the political conditions that determine public opinion. The Constitution does not say very much about government power during times of crisis or emergency. Article I Section 9 of the Constitution *does* provide that Congress may suspend the writ of habeas corpus "when in Cases of Rebellion or Invasion the public Safety may require it." But most questions about striking the right balance between granting and limiting power, or the balance between individual freedom and government power, or the right size and role of government, are left for each generation to decide depending on the particular circumstances they face.

American politics is often framed as debates about the *size* of government. These debates are familiar arguments about big government versus small government. But politics is actually more likely to be about the *role* of government—the purposes and uses of government power. The "big v. small" arguments tend to distract from the disagreements about what government should be doing. Politics is about whether government is too strong or too weak, too big or too small, doing too much or too little. Politics is also about whether government is doing the right things or the wrong things, whether specific public policies should change, and whether the government has the right priorities. Many of these political questions about the right size and proper role of government are actually questions about whether a political system is a just system.

1.14 | *Justice*

Justice is a basic concept that is hard to precisely define. It can be generally understood to mean that an individual is treated fairly. Politically, justice usually means that an individual is treated fairly by the government. The definition of *justice as fairness* includes the belief that individuals should get what they deserve: good or appropriate behavior is recognized and rewarded; bad or inappropriate behavior is recognized and punished. There are many definitions of justice, but most include a moral or ethical component—that is, definitions of justice commonly identify a particular set of values as important.

Justice is important politically because it describes a proper ordering of things, values, and individuals within a society. The nature of a just society or political system has been the subject of human inquiry since people first thought about living a good life in an organized society. Justice is a familiar subject in works of politics, philosophy, theology, and law. The Ancient Greek philosophers Plato and Aristotle described what they believed to be the attributes of a just society and the best form of government to achieve justice. The Founders of the American political system also thought a great deal about a just society and the best form of government. The Declaration of Independence explains why the American colonists were justified in fighting the Revolutionary War against Great Britain. It includes a long list of charges that the "king of Great Britain" acted so unjustly that the colonists were justified in taking up arms and breaking their political bonds with Great Britain. The Preamble to the U.S. Constitution also declares an interest in creating a form of government that promotes justice. It explains that the Constitution was established "in Order to form a more perfect Union, establish Justice, insure domestic Tranquility, provide for the common defence, promote the general Welfare, and secure the Blessings of Liberty to ourselves and our Posterity…"

The interest in justice was not limited to the founding era. Both sides in the Civil War claimed to be fighting for justice: the North fought against slavery, among other reasons, and the South fought for states' rights, among other reasons. The various civil rights movements of the 20th Century were also organized efforts to achieve a more just society for Blacks, women, and other minorities. Political theorists continue to explore the meaning and importance of justice. In *A Theory of Justice*, John Rawls argued that "justice is the first virtue of social institutions, as truth is of systems of thought."[1] The argument that justice is the most important virtue for our social, political, and governmental institutions to pursue reflects the continued value placed on justice in modern thinking about government and politics—but recognizing the importance of justice is much easier than actually defining it.

Political science studies individuals (and individual behavior) and systems (and the workings of institutions). At the individual level of analysis, justice is as simple as a person's expectation that she or he will be treated fairly. In this sense, justice is an expectation that a person will get what they deserve—whether it is recognition and reward for doing well and behaving appropriately, or sanctions for not doing well or behaving inappropriately. At the system level of analysis, a just political system is one that maintains a political order where individuals are treated fairly, where the system treats people fairly as is therefore a legitimate system of governance. One factor that complicates considerations of whether an individual is treated fairly or a political system is just is that fair treatment may be a universally accepted concept but views on what fair or just treatment is in a particular situation is a subjective value judgment.

What justice means is further complicated by the fact that there are different types of justice. *Retributive justice* is concerned with the proper response to wrongdoing. Retributive justice is most relevant to the criminal justice system and the theory and practice of punishment as reflected in sentencing policy. The *law* of retribution—*lex talionis*—reflects the concept of retributive *justice*—the belief that punishment should fit the crime. The biblical verse "life for life, eye for eye, tooth for tooth, hand for hand, foot for foot, wound for wound, stripe for stripe," embodies the principle of retributive justice. However, there is no consensus that the "an eye for an eye" principle of retributive justice should be interpreted literally to mean that justice requires taking an eye for an eye, a hand for a hand, a tooth for a tooth, or a life for a life. The alternative to this literal reading of retributive justice is the metaphorical interpretation. The metaphorical interpretation requires proportionality—a punishment that fits the crime. A just punishment must be proportionate to the crime, but justice does not require that punishment be identical to the crime.

A second type of justice is *restorative justice*. Restorative justice is also relevant to the criminal justice system. However, unlike retributive justice, which is primarily concerned with punishing an offender, restorative justice emphasizes the importance of restoring the victim (making the victim whole again) and rehabilitating the offender.

A third type of justice is *distributive justice*. Distributive justice is concerned with the proper distribution of values or valuables among the individuals or groups in a society. The valuables can be things of material value (such as income, wealth, food, health care, tax breaks, or property) or non-material values (such as power, respect, or recognition of status). Distributive justice is based on the assumption that values or valuables can be distributed equitably based upon merit. Political debates about economic inequality, a fair tax system, access to education, and generational justice (whether government policies benefit the elderly more than the young) are often conducted in terms of distributive justice: who gets what and who should be getting what.

1.2 | The State of Nature: Life Before or without Government

One of the most important concepts in western political thought is "the state of nature." The state of nature is used to explain the origin of government. The 17th Century English political philosopher Thomas Hobbes (1588-1679) believed that life in a state of nature (that is, without government), would be "solitary, poor, nasty, brutish, and short" because human beings are self-interested actors who will take advantage of others. Hobbes believed that it is simply human nature for the strong to take advantage of the weak. The competition for economic and political advantage results in a constant "war of all against all" that makes an individual's existence precarious. Hobbes and other social contract theorists believed that individuals who are living a precarious existence in the state of nature decide to enter into a social contract that

creates a government with enough power to maintain order by controlling behavior. The terms of the social contract include trading some of the individual freedom in the state of nature for order, security, justice, or other political values. His classic work *Leviathan* (1651) describes a strong government with power to create and maintain order. The word Leviathan comes from the biblical reference to a great sea monster—an image that critics of modern big government consider appropriate.

All ideologies include a view of human nature. Some ideologies are based on a negative view of human nature—one that describes humans as basically self-interested or even quite capable of evil. Some ideologies are based on a more positive view of human nature—one that describes humans as basically public-spirited or even benevolent. Ideologies with a more positive view of human nature assume that individuals are capable of getting along well without government, with minimal government, or with government that is much weaker than a Leviathan. For a view of human nature as capable of good or evil, that stresses the importance of education and socialization to develop the better instincts and moral conscience, read President Abraham Lincoln's First Inaugural Address, which appeals to Americans to be guided by "the better angels of our nature."

1.21 | *John Locke (1632-1704)*

In *An Essay Concerning the True Original, Extent and End of Civil Government*, the English political philosopher John Locke described life in the pre-government "state of nature" as a condition where "all men" are in "a state of perfect freedom to order their actions and dispose of their possessions and persons, as they think fit, within the bounds of the law of nature, without asking leave, or depending upon the will of any other man."²

Locke did not mean that "perfect freedom" gave individuals license to do whatever they wanted. The law of nature mandated that "no one ought to harm another in his life, health, liberty, or possessions." According to Locke, the natural state of man is to live free from oppression and the will of man—"living together according to reason without a common superior on earth" and "to have only the law of Nature for his rule." However, history teaches that some individuals inevitably gain power over others, and use their power to harm them. The use of power or might without right—the fear that might makes right—is one reason why individuals decide to leave the state of nature and live under government.

1.22 | *Jean-Jacques Rousseau*

In *The Social Contract*, Jean-Jacques Rousseau (1712-1778) wondered why people were born free but everywhere lived with government: "Man is born free, and everywhere he is in chains." The American political tradition of criticizing government raises the question whether government is necessary. *To govern* means to control. Government control is intended to create and maintain order. Why is government necessary to create order? In the history of western political thought, the alternative to government is life in what political philosophers call a *state of nature*. Life without government in a "state of nature" created problems or conditions that caused individuals to believe that living with government would be an improvement.

1.23 | *Influences on the American Founders*

John Locke believed that individuals decided to leave the state of nature and live under government because government offered greater protection of their rights including the right to life, liberty, and property. This natural rights-based understanding of the purposes of government greatly influenced the writers of the Declaration of Independence. The Declaration of Independence explained and justified the American Revolution as a necessary act—the right and duty of a free people to assert their natural or "unalienable Rights" to "Life, Liberty, and the Pursuit of Happiness" when confronted with tyrannical government. Some of the most important words and ideas in the Declaration of Independence can be traced to the writings of Locke. Natural rights are those that individuals have because they are human beings or because they are God-given rights. Natural rights are not created by human beings or government. Natural rights contrast with positive rights, which are created by an act of government.

1.24 | *The Social Contract Theory of Government*

Hobbes, Locke, Rousseau, are classical political philosophers who are social contractarians. They advocate a social contract theory that provides a justification for creating government and operating it as acts of self-government. According to social contract theory, people create governments by entering into written or unwritten agreements to live together under a particular form of government. The agreement is a *contract* because it binds the parties to specific rights (or benefits) an obligations, duties, and responsibilities. The agreement is *social* because it involves the members of a community or society deciding to create a binding agreement to live together under a form of government. In the U.S., the social contract is a written document: the Constitution. The terms of this social contract include individual rights and responsibilities as well as government powers and responsibilities. The people have a duty to obey the law. The government has a responsibility to provide safe streets, national security, and other public goods.

Social contract theory is identified with self-government because it is based on popular sovereignty. Popular sovereignty is the belief that the people are sovereign, that the people are the ultimate source of governing authority. Popular sovereignty describes political authority—the legitimate use of government power—as based on the consent of the governed. Government is based on the consent of the people; government is not imposed on the people. Social contract theory explains why it is rational for an individual to voluntarily give up the freedom of living in the state of nature and agree to live under a government that can tell them what they can and cannot do. The social contract explains why it is rational for an individual to accept a government with the power to take a person's life, liberty, and property.

John Stuart Mill elaborated on social contract theory in works that described liberal democracy as the major political development or advance of the 19th Century. His classic book *On Liberty* elevated the importance of individual liberty as a political value and advocated for stronger protection of individual liberty from restrictions by government and the rule of the majority. Mill is remembered today for his articulation of the *Harm Principle* as a way to determine the proper use of government power to limit individual freedom. The Harm Principle held that the only legitimate reason for using law to limit an individual's freedom was to prevent one person from harming another. The Harm Principle is considered a libertarian principle because it was developed in order to limit government power to restrict individual liberty. The Harm Principle is libertarian in the sense that it considers laws that are passed to prevent a person from harming themselves inappropriate—which means that paternalistic legislation such as laws requiring the wearing of seatbelts or motorcycle helmets or prohibiting the use of drugs would be considered inappropriate. The Harm Principle is also libertarian insofar as it considers moral regulatory policies (e.g., legislating morality) inappropriate use of government power.

The contract theory of government remains a strong influence on thinking about government. In *A Theory of Justice* (1971), the political philosopher John Rawls explains why it makes sense for individuals to give up their individual preferences (or personal freedom to do as they please) and agree to live under a government where they submit to the judgment, authority, or power of other members of the political community. Like Locke and Mill, Rawls believes that people create governments because they believe that life under government will more just, fairer, than life without government.

The idea of government based on a social contract has an especially strong appeal in the U.S. The enduring appeal is rooted in politics and economics. Its appeal can be traced to the fact that social contracts were part of both the **colonial** experience (e.g., the Mayflower Compact of 1620 and the Massachusetts Bay Charter of 1629) and the **founding** experience (e.g., the Constitution). Social contract theory remains politically appealing because it is based on the democratic idea of popular sovereignty, the belief that government power comes from the people and must be based the consent of the governed. The social contract theory of government is also influential because the U.S. is a capitalist country with an economic system that is based on individuals entering into private contracts with one another to provide a broad range of goods and service. A people familiar with using contractual agreements to order private affairs are likely to consider social contracts a legitimate way to order public affairs.

1.3 | Modern Government

Despite today's widespread and strong criticism of government, few people argue that government is unnecessary. Few people are anarchists. Anarchism is the political philosophy that believes government is unnecessary *and* that government power is illegitimate because it is based on force or compulsion. The term anarchism derives from a Greek word meaning without bosses. Anarchism is often considered chaos or extreme disorder. Anarchists do not advocate chaos, they simply believe that individuals can freely and voluntarily organize their lives to create social order and justice without being compelled or controlled by government. Anarchists have a positive or optimistic view of human nature. They believe that the human capacity for reason makes it possible for individuals to realize the benefits of voluntarily working together, and to voluntarily accept some controls on their behavior. Anarchists believe  that the private sector can provide the goods and services, as well as the good public order that most people have come to expect from the government.

The widespread acceptance of government as necessary—or at least a necessary evil—does not mean there is consensus on the size and role of government. American politics includes lively debates about the right size of government and the appropriate role for government—what government should be doing. From the founding era, to the development of the American political system, and continuing today there have been debates about the size, scope, and purposes of government. Criticism of government is one of the familiar themes of American politics. We love to hate government because we think the government is doing things it should not be doing, or not doing things that we think it should be doing. Which raises the question, what should government do? What are the criteria for determining whether government provides a good or service rather than having it provided by the private sector?

1.31 | Market Failures

Governments everywhere are expected to maintain good public order, provide national security, maintain public safety, and provide material prosperity and economic stability. In the U.S., how do we decide what the government (federal, state, or local) should do and the private sector should? In a political system based on limited government, and an economic system based on a market economy, there is a preference for goods and services to be provided by the private sector. The Subsidiary Principle is that wherever possible decisions should be made by the private sector rather than the government, and wherever possible decisions should be made by the lower level of government (local) rather than the higher level of government. The Subsidiary Principle does not mean that all government action is inappropriate, but it indicates that government action should be limited to situations where the private marketplace is unable to efficiently and equitably provide a good or service. One reason for government intervention in the market is when there is a market failure. The following aspects of market failures are discussed below: public goods, monopolies, externalities, information asymmetries, and equity.

A <u>public good</u> is one that, once provided, cannot be limited to those who have paid for it. Clean air, clean water, safe streets, and national security are often cited as examples of public goods. The government provides national security because it is hard to limit the benefits of being safe from foreign attacks or terrorism to those who have been willing to pay the costs of providing the benefits of national security. The government also acts to provide clean air (i.e., regulating air pollution) because it is hard to limit the breathing of clean air to those individuals who have voluntarily paid for the clean air. The fact that it is hard or even impossible to limit a good or a service to those who have paid for it raises the **<u>free rider</u>** problem: individuals have an economic incentive to enjoy the benefit without paying the cost. Clean air and national security are considered public goods because they are provided by the public (the government) through taxes or regulation.

A second market failure is **externalities**. In a perfect market, an economic transaction (the buying/selling of a good or service) will include the total cost of the good or service so there is no need for government intervention or regulation of a market transaction that does not affect parties other than the buyer and seller. Government intervention in the marketplace can be justified where market transactions have externalities. An externality occurs when a market transaction affects individuals who are not a party to the transaction. There are **positive externalities** and **negative externalities**. An example of a negative externality is the pollution that is caused by making or using a product but which is not reflected in its price. The price of a gallon of gasoline, for example, does not include the environmental degradation caused by using a gallon of gas to run a lawnmower or drive a car. The purchase price of a plastic toy or a steel car does not include the cost of the air pollution or water pollution that is caused by the manufacture or use of the toy or car because the factory may have been able to allow some of the cost of production to go downstream (if the plant is located along a river) or into the Jetstream (the high smokestacks at a steel plant can disperse air pollution into the atmosphere). The manufacturer and the consumer are not paying for all of the costs of production and consumption when water and air pollution are not included in the price of a good. Individuals who live downstream or downwind pay the price of dirtier air or dirtier water. These are negative externalities because the producer and consumer agree on a purchase price that negatively affects third parties to the market transaction.

Examples of positive externalities include education, vaccination, and crime control. Education can benefit an individual, and it could be limited to those who actually pay for it. But the benefits of education are not necessarily limited to the student (who pays the tuition and receives the education) and the school (which receives tuition). The third party benefits (the positive externalities) include employers who have a qualified workforce and society because democracy is presumed to require an educated citizenry. These have historically been arguments for public education.

Another example of a market failure is a **monopoly**. Free-market economic theory is based on competition. If a single business has a monopoly in a particular sector of the market, the lack of competition will result in market inefficiency or failure. In the absence of competition, there is no incentive to set a fair price or otherwise provide consumers with good service. In a small town or an urban neighborhood with two independent grocery stores, competition will keep prices in check because neither store can greatly increase the price of flour without losing customers to the other store. However, if one of the stores closes, the remaining store can charge higher prices and provide lower services because customers have no choice but to pay the higher price and put up with the level of service. Congress passed the Sherman Antitrust Act in 1890, which prohibited monopolies (or restraints of trade), because the industrial revolution resulted in sugar, steel, and monopolies that limited competition. The Standard Oil Company, for example, controlled about 90% of the oil refining in the U.S. "Big" government was used to keep "big" business in check where monopolies emerged in various sectors of the industrial economy. More recently in the information-based economy, the federal government (and, in fact, the European Union) has challenged Microsoft's domination of the software market.

A final market failure issue is **equity**. Markets are about economics. Politics can be about equity—the assurance that everyone in a society has fair access to certain goods and services that are available in the private market and public goods. Collective goods (or social goods) are those that *could* be delivered in the private sector based solely on a person's ability to pay for the good or service, but which are often provided by the government or subsidized by taxes as a matter of public policy. Public utilities such as water and sewage and electricity and telephone service, for example, could be provided by the private sector solely on the basis of an individual's ability to pay for them, but the political system considers these goods and services, including basic education and perhaps health care, social goods.

1.4 | Why Politics

Government obviously involves politics, and it is hard to talk about government without talking about politics, but government is not the same thing as politics. Politics exist wherever people interact with one another. Politics occurs in families, religious organizations, educational institutions, organized sports and entertainment, and the workplace. Political scientists focus on certain kinds of politics, the kinds that involve government and public policy, for example.

1.41 | *What is Politics?*

There are many different definitions of politics. The political scientist Harold Lasswell defined politics as the determination of "who gets what, when, how."[3] This definition focuses on politics as the authoritative allocation of scarce resources such as money, land, property, or wealth. David Easton defined politics as "the authoritative allocation of values for a society."[4] This definition of politics as the allocation of scarce resources is sometimes

thought to refer only to **material values** such as taxes or government benefits provided by education, health care, job training, veterans, or social welfare programs. However, politics is not limited to the authoritative allocation of scarce material valuables. Politics is also about values. Politics includes authoritative statements about non-material or **spiritual values**, which is why politics is often about religion, morality, values, ethics, patriotism, civics, honor, and education.

Politics includes government actions or policies that subsidize certain behaviors or values that are considered desirable and worthy of support in order to promote them: for example, marriage, child rearing, education, work. Politics also includes government actions or policies that regulate certain values or behaviors that are considered undesirable in order to control them or to discourage them: idleness; smoking or other tobacco use; consumption of alcohol; and gambling (although the discouragement of gambling is diminishing as governments rely on taxes from gambling). Politics also includes government actions or policies that prohibit certain behaviors or values by making them illegal: for example, drug usage; prostitution; or hate crimes.

In addition to material and spiritual values, politics includes the processes by which decisions are made. Process politics includes campaigns and elections, interest groups lobbying, voting behavior of individual citizens, the decision making of government officials in the legislative and executive branches of government, and even the decision making of judges. The following provides basic definitions and explanations of some of the terms that are essential to understanding American government and politics.

1.42 | *What is Political Science?*

<u>Political Science</u> is the branch of the social sciences (e.g., economics, sociology) that systematically studies the theory and practice of government. It includes the description, analysis, and prediction of the political behavior of individuals and organizations (such as political parties and interest groups) as well the workings of political systems. The discipline of political science has historical roots in moral philosophy, political philosophy, political economy, history, and other fields of study that traditionally examined normative (or value-based) beliefs about how individuals *should* live a good life in a good society. Modern political science is less normative and more "scientific" in the sense that it emphasizes the systematic study of government and politics. It examines empirical evidence or data on government and politics.

1.5 | **Political Values**

Politics and government are not limited to material values or valuables such as money, property, or other forms of wealth and possessions. Government and politics are also concerned with values. Some of the most important political values include individual rights such as freedom and equality, social order, public safety, ethics, and justice.

1.51 | *Personal Liberty (Individual Freedom)*

Freedom has become an especially important value in modern government and politics. Contemporary politics in the U.S. and elsewhere emphasizes individual liberty more than in the past when other values, such as maintaining good moral order, were relatively more important. Individual liberty is generally considered an individual's right to make decisions about his or her own life without government restrictions, limits, or interference. In this respect, individual liberty is an aspect of self-determination or personal autonomy where individuals are free to decide how to live their lives. There are, however, two broad concepts of liberty: a negative concept of liberty and a positive concept of liberty.

In *On Liberty*, John S. Mill differentiated between liberty as the freedom to act and liberty as the absence of coercion. Mill was describing the difference between negative liberty—the absence of constraints—and positive liberty, an individual's freedom to live life as he or she wants. In this sense, *negative* means the absence of legal limits and *positive* means the opportunity (to do something). In *Two Concepts of Liberty*, Isaiah Berlin elaborated on this distinction between positive liberty and negative liberty. Negative liberty refers to the condition where an individual is protected from (usually) governmental restrictions. Positive liberty refers to having the means, the resources, or the opportunity to do what one wants or to become what one wants to become, rather than merely not facing governmental restraints. The negative concept of liberty is the dominant concept in the American political and legal tradition in the sense that individual liberty is generally considered the absence of government restraints. The negative concept of liberty is reflected in the language of the Bill of Rights. For example, the First Amendment provides that "Congress shall make no law" restricting freedom of religion, speech, or press. The civil liberties guaranteed in the Constitution do not, as a rule, give individuals a right, they place limits on the government's power to limit individual freedom.

This distinction between negative and positive liberty is important. One reason why the U.S. Constitution has fallen out of favor as a model for other countries is because of the modern expectation that Constitutions guarantee positive rights and liberties.[5] Section 2 of The Canadian Charter of Rights and Freedoms provides that everyone has fundamental freedoms of "thought, belief, opinion and expression, including freedom of the press and other media of communication." South Africa's Constitution provides that everyone has the right to "freedom of artistic expression," human dignity, the right to life, and freedom from all forms of violence and torture. Germany's Constitution guarantees everyone the right "to the free development of his personality" and "the right to life." (Art.1(1)

> Think About It!
> Should Constitutions guarantee positive liberty?

1.52 | *Social Order*

Order is an important political value because one of the major responsibilities of government is to create and maintain good social order. The public expects government to fight crime, manage public demonstrations and protests, and prevent social unrest including civic disturbances, riots, or even domestic rebellions, and national security from foreign threats. The government's role in providing these aspects of physical order or conditions is less controversial than its role in providing good social order as it relates to standards of moral, ethical, or religious behavior. Moral regulatory policy can be very controversial because it involves values about which people may strongly disagree. The term culture wars refers to ideological battles over values related to public policies concerning issues such as abortion, gay rights, the definition of marriage, welfare, religion in public life, and patriotism.

1.53 | *Justice*

Justice is a basic concept that is central to most assessments of the legitimacy of a society. While it is hard to precisely define justice or a just society or political order, the concept of justice as fair treatment is a universal value shared by people everywhere. Justice means being treated fairly or getting one's just deserts whether they are rewards for doing well or sanctions for inappropriate behavior or punishment for illegal behavior.

1.54 | *Equality*

Equality is an important value in democratic political systems. Equality is an essential element of democracy. However, equality is actually a complicated and controversial concept whose meaning and significance has been debated from the founding era until today. Equality does not mean that everyone must be treated the same, or that it would be a good thing if everyone were treated the same. The words of the *Declaration of Independence* assert that we are all created equal and endowed by our creator with certain unalienable rights. But this has never been understood to mean that everyone is the same (in terms of abilities, for example) and should be treated the same as everyone else (regardless of merit). The natural inequality of age and ability, for instance, are contrasted with the political equality that is expressed by references to egalitarian principles such as "one person one vote" or equality under the law. This concept of political and legal equality is expressed in the Fourteenth Amendment, which prohibits the state governments from denying to any person within their jurisdiction the "equal protection of the laws." The Fourteenth Amendment was initially intended to prohibit racial discrimination, but its scope has been broadened to include prohibition against legal discrimination on the basis of gender or age. Government can treat people differently, but it cannot discriminate against individuals, which means inappropriately treating individuals differently.

1.55 | *Political Power, Authority, and Legitimacy*

Power, authority, and legitimacy are important concepts that are central to the study of politics and government.

Power can be defined as the ability to *make* another person to do what you want, to force others to do what you want. Power is using coercion or force to make someone comply with an order. Power is independent of whether it is proper or legitimate to demand that another person obey an order. A gunman has power to make a person comply with an order or demand to give up a wallet, for example, but this power is not considered legitimate.

Authority can be defined as the right to make other people do what you want. A person is authorized to make another comply with their demands. The authorization could be based upon a person's position as a duly elected or appointed government official. The word *authority* derives from the Latin word "auctoritas." In modern usage, authority is a particular type of power, po*wer which is recognized as legitimate, justified, and proper.* The sociologist Max Weber identified three types of authority: traditional, charismatic, and rational-legal. Traditional authority is based on long-established customs, practices, and social structures and relationships. Tradition means the way things have always been done. Power that is passed from one generation to another is traditional authority. Traditional authority historically included the hereditary right to rule, the claim of hereditary monarchs that they had a right to rule by either blood-lines (a ruling family) or divine right. The concept of a ruling family is based on traditional authority. The rise of social contract theory, where government is based on the consent of the governed, has undermined traditional authority and challenged its legitimacy. Democracies generally require something more than a ruler's claim that their family has, by tradition, ruled the people.

The second type of authority is charismatic authority. Charisma refers to special qualities, great personal magnetism, or the distinct ability to inspire loyalty or confidence in the ability to lead. Charismatic authority is therefore personal. In politics, charismatic authority is often based on a popular perception that an individual is a strong leader. The Spanish word caudillo refers to a dynamic political-military leader, a strong man. Charismatic leadership is sometimes associated with the cult of personality, where neither tradition nor laws determine power.

The third type of authority is rational (or legal) authority. Rational-legal authority depends on formal laws for its legitimacy. A constitution or other kind of law gives an individual or an institution power. A government official has power by virtue of being duly elected or appointed to office. Most modern societies rely upon this kind of legal-rational authority to determine whether power is legitimate. In the U.S., for example, the power of the presidency is vested in the office, not the individual who happens to be president.

Legitimacy refers to the appropriate ability to make others do what you want, the legal right to make others comply with demands. It is a normative or value-based word that indicates something is approved of. Political legitimacy is the foundation of governmental authority as based consent of the governed. The basis of government power is often subject to challenges to its legitimacy, the sense that the action is authorized and appropriate. Authority remains a contested concept because, while the conceptual difference between authority and power is clear, the practical differences may be hard to identify because of disagreements about whether a law is legitimate. In the U.S., the tradition of civil disobedience recognizes that individuals have some leeway to refuse to comply with a law that they consider illegitimate.

1.6 | Citizenship

A citizen is a member of the political community. Certain rights, duties, and obligations are attached to an individual's status as a citizen. Citizenship can be bestowed in a variety of ways. In some societies, one becomes a citizen by being born on the territory of the country or via parents who are citizens. Such citizenship is automatic in the United States (also known as jus soli or the 'right of soil'). There are also other forms of citizenship. You can choose to be a citizen, called naturalization, by learning about a political system, meeting some form of residency requirement, and taking an oath. In Germany – until the 1990s – citizenship was by blood (or 'right of blood'). Your parents had to be ethnically German for you to receive citizenship. There was no method by which a non-German could become a citizen until the late 1990s, when the law on citizenship was changed to allow naturalization. Other countries require citizens to pass certain economic requirements to become citizens.

Citizens have responsibilities as active members of a polity. Citizens are expected to obey the laws, vote, pay taxes, and if required submit to military service. Citizens also have rights and freedoms. Subjects, those subjected to the rule of the few or the one, have neither rights nor freedoms and their sole responsibility is to do what they are told. The actions of governments are binding on all citizens. One reason why individuals worry about government power is because the government can use its criminal justice powers to take a person's life or liberty (e.g., a sentence of death or imprisonment), and the government can use its civil justice powers to take a person's property (e.g., fines and eminent domain). Citizen vigilance is necessary to guard against government abuse of its substantial powers.

1.7 | The Forms of Government

One subject of interest to political science is the different forms of government. A simple description of the different forms of government is that there is government of the one, the few, and the many. Each of these three forms of government has a good variation and a bad variation.

Table 1.7 The Forms of Government

Form of Government	Good Variation	Bad Variation
The One	Monarchy	Tyranny/Autocracy
The Few	Aristocracy	Oligarchy (rich or powerful)
The Many	Polity/Democracy	Democracy (tyranny of majority)

The three forms of government refer to the basic system of government, the government institutions that are established by a political community. The U.S. system of government was intended by its founders to be a mixed form of government because it includes elements of all three forms: monarchy (the presidency); aristocracy (the Senate, the Electoral College, and the Supreme Court); and democracy (the House of Representatives; elections). The founders created a mixed form of government as part of the institutional system of checks and balances.

The system of checks and balances was designed to create a political system where institutions and political organizations provided a measure of protection against corruption and abuse of power. The Founders thought that the mixed form of government was the best way to avoid what historical experience seemed to indicate was inevitable: the tendency of a political system to become corrupt. The Founders were acutely aware of the historical problem of corruption, and the tendency of governments to become corrupt over time. History provided many examples of power corrupting individuals and governments. The awareness of corruption caused the Founders to worry about centralized power. Their worries were succinctly expressed by the 19th Century Italian-British figure, Lord Acton (1834-1902), whose famous aphorism warned: "Power tends to corrupt; absolute power corrupts absolutely."

The Founders believed the power problem of corruption could be avoided by dividing power so that no one person or institution had complete power. The Founders also realized that each form of government tended to become corrupt or decay over time. A monarchy (which might be a good form of government of one) was apt to turn into tyranny. An aristocracy (which might be a good form of government of the few best and brightest) was apt to turn into oligarchy (government of the rich or powerful). And a democracy (government of the many) was apt to decay into mobocracy, tyranny of the majority, or rule by **King Numbers**. So they created a mixed form of government.

The roots of American thinking about democracy can be traced to Classical (or ancient) Greece and the Roman Republic, the Age of Enlightenment, the Protestant Reformation, and colonial experiences under the British Empire. The ancient Greeks in the city-state Athens created the idea of the democratic government, practiced as a kind of democracy. The Romans developed the concept of the representative democracy, one where citizens elect representatives to act on their behalf.

The United States is a republic. A republic is a **representative democracy**. The diagram below describes the difference between direct and representative democracy.

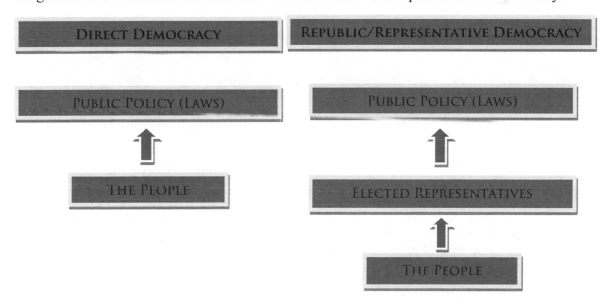

In a republic, individuals do not directly govern themselves. Voters elect representatives who, as government officials, make laws for the people. This contrasts with a **direct democracy,** where voters choose public policies themselves. Today, however, the term democracy is used generically to include direct and indirect democracy (or republican systems of government). The Constitution's original design provided for only limited democracy in the way the national government worked. The members of the House of Representatives were directly elected by the people, but the members of the Senate were selected by state legislators, the president was chosen by the Electoral College (not by popular vote of the people), and federal judges were nominated by the president and confirmed by the Senate to serve life terms. And only a small percentage of citizens (white male property owners) were originally allowed to vote in elections. The Constitution provided only limited popular control over government because the Founders were skeptical of direct democracy. Over time, the Constitution, the government, and politics become more democratic with the development of political parties, the direct election of senators, and an expansion of the right to vote.

1.8 | Summary: Why government and politics?

Government and politics occur almost everywhere because they are one of the ways that individuals organize themselves to achieve individual goals such as wealth, public safety, and education. Government and politics also help achieve shared social goals such as a sense of belonging to a community, national security, and the establishment of a just society. These material and non-material goals can be provided by, or protected by government. But they can also be threatened by government or even taken by it. Government can, for instance, take a person's life, liberty, or property. The fact that government can protect or threaten important values is one of the reasons why government and politics are almost continually debated and argued and sometimes even fought over. Individuals and groups have different ideas about government should be doing, and are willing to fight for control of government so that their ideas and beliefs can be acted upon or implemented in public policy.

1.9 | Other Resources

1.91| *Internet*

The Library of Congress: http://memory.loc.gov/ammem/index.html

For more information on the political theory of Thomas Hobbes and John Locke: http://www.iep.utm.edu/hobmoral/ and http://www.iep.utm.edu/locke/

The Declaration of Independence: http://avalon.law.yale.edu/18th_century/declare.asp

The U.S. Constitution: http://avalon.law.yale.edu/18th_century/usconst.asp

U.S. Government: http://www.usa.gov/

The Center for Voting and Democracy has links to articles related to elections and democracy, and links to organizations and ideas related to reforming the electoral system, and analysis of electoral returns. www.fairvote.org/

1.92 | In the Library

Berlin, Isaiah. 1958. *Two Concepts of Liberty*. Oxford: Clarendon Press.

Hobbes, Thomas. 1996. *Leviathan.* Richard Tuck, ed. New York: Cambridge University Press.

Locke, John. 1773. *An essay concerning the true original extent and end of civil government.* Boston: Edes and Gill.

Locke, John. 1988. *Two Treatises of Government.* Peter Laslett, ed. New York, Cambridge University Press.

Mill, John Stuart. 1869. *On Liberty.* London: Longman, Roberts & Green.

Plato. 1995. *The Last Days of Socrates.* Hugh Tredennick, ed. New York: Penguin.

Rawls, John. 1971. *A Theory of Justice.* Cambridge, MA: Belknap Press.

Rousseau, Jean-Jacques. 1762. *The Social Contract.*

Weber, Max. 1958. "The three types of legitimate rule." *Berkeley Publications in Society and Institutions*, 4 (1): 1-11. Translated by Hans Gerth.

Xenophon. 1990. *Conversations of Socrates.* Hugh Tredennick, ed. New York: Penguin.

KEY TERMS

Public Good

Power

Authority

Legitimacy

Government

Politics

Citizen

Justice

Social Contract

Direct Democracy

Representative

Democracy

Oligarchy

Monarchy

Polity

Tyranny

Aristocracy

Personal Liberty

1.0 | STUDY QUESTIONS

1.) What are the basic questions to be asked about American (or any other) government?
2.) Why do governments exist everywhere if governments everywhere are widely criticized?
3.) What is politics?
4.) What is meant by *power?*
5.) *What is political power?*
6.) Explain the concepts authority, legitimacy, justice, and democracy.
7.) Distinguish among the three concepts of democracy mentioned in the chapter, explaining in which of these senses the textbook refers to American government as *democratic.*

---

[1] John Rawls. 1971. *A Theory of Justice*. Cambridge, MA: Belknap Press of Harvard University Press.

[2] Locke, John. 1689. *Second Treatise of Civil Government*. "Chapter 2: Of the State of Nature."

[3] Harold Dwight Lasswell. 1935. *Politics Who Gets What, When and How*. Gloucester, MA.: Peter Smith Publisher Inc.

[4] *The Political System*. 1953. New York: Knopf, p.65.

[5] Law, David S., and Versteeg, Mila. 2012. "The Declining Influence of the United States Constitution." 87 New York University Law Review 3(June):762-858. Available at http://papers.ssrn.com/sol3/papers.cfm?abstract_id=1923556

CHAPTER 2: THE U.S. SYSTEM OF CONSTITUTIONAL GOVERNMENT

2.0 | The Constitution and Constitutional Government

This chapter examines the U.S. Constitution and the system of constitutional government. The primary goals are to describe the origin and development of the Constitution, explain the functions of a constitution, and describe and explain the contemporary workings of the U.S. system of constitutional government. In order to accomplish these goals, the chapter explores the political theory of the Constitution and the practical politics of governance with special emphasis on comparing how the constitutional system was intended to work with how it actually works today. The chapter's main theme is the tension between the American commitment to the Constitution and the enduring ideals embodied in it, and the pressures to adapt to political, economic, social, technological, and scientific change. The tensions between *continuity* (remaining true to basic principles) and *change* (meeting contemporary needs) exist in all political systems, but the tensions between the desire to stay the same and the forces of change are especially strong in the U.S. because Americans have an especially strong commitment to the Constitution as a foundational or fundamental document. This commitment to basic constitutional values is especially strong during times of great change and challenges, when it expressed as political appeals to return to the nation's founding values and the original understanding of the Constitution. This is a recurring theme in the American politics of the Constitution.

"We are under a Constitution but the Constitution is what the Court says it is."

-Charles Evans Hughes

"For as in absolute governments the king is law, so in free countries the law ought to be king; and there ought to be no other."

Thomas Paine, *Common Sense* **(1776)**

2.1 |The Constitution and Constitutional Government

A constitution is a governing document that sets forth a country's basic rules of government and politics. Constitutions are today almost universally recognized as an appropriate foundation for a political system, therefore most countries have a constitution. The expectation that a modern political system will have a constitution originates from the political belief that constitutional government is a good form of government—that constitutional government is a legitimate, rightful, or appropriate form of government. Constitutions are closely associated with government legitimacy because constitutions are considered one of the best ways to achieve the rule of law. The rule of law supports government *legitimacy* by requiring that government action be authorized by law, thereby making it possible to hold government officials legally accountable for their actions. The rule of law is one of the ways to achieve and maintain political legitimacy, the acceptance of a government as the appropriate authority. Political legitimacy increases compliance with the law because people are more willing to obey the law if they consider it legitimate.

Constitutional government is *government according to the rule of a basic or fundamental law.* Constitutional government is not merely government based on the rule of law. It is government based on a particular kind of the rule of law: the rule of a basic or fundamental law. The constitution provides the foundation for the system of government. Political systems based on constitutional government have a legal hierarchy of laws. In the U.S. system of constitutional government, the hierarchy of laws includes constitutional law, legislative or statutory law, and administrative or regulatory law. The legal hierarchy means that not all laws are created equal. Constitutional law trumps the other kinds of laws. Legislation (statutes passed by congress or a state legislature) cannot conflict with the Constitution. Administrative regulations, rules which are created by administrative or bureaucratic agencies, must be consistent with the legislation that created and authorized the administrative agency *and* regulations must not conflict with the

Constitution. The Constitution establishes the basic framework of government, allocates government powers, and guarantees individual rights. These basic aspects of government and politics are considered so important that they are provided for in the Constitution. One of the most important features of constitutional government is the fact that the Constitution cannot be changed by majority rule. The Constitution cannot be changed by *ordinary* laws—legislation passed by majority vote. Constitutional amendments require super majority votes. Diagram 2.1 below illustrates the hierarchy of laws in the U.S.

Diagram 2.1
The Hierarchy of Laws in the United States

2.2 | The Rule of Law

The rule of law is defined as the principle that governmental authority is exercised only in accordance with public laws that are adopted and enforced according to established procedures. The principle is intended to be a safeguard against arbitrary governance by requiring that those who make and enforce the law are also bound by the law. Government based on the rule of law is contrasted with government according to the rule of man. The rule of man describes a political system where government officials determine their own powers without reference to pre-existing laws.

The idea of government according to the rule of law has ancient roots. One source is classical Greek and Roman political thought. The writings of the ancient Greek political philosophers Plato and Aristotle described and analyzed different forms of good and bad government. Plato believed that the best form of government was the rule of man, specifically rule by a philosopher-king. He described a philosopher-king as a wise and good ruler—think of someone like Solomon, a wise person who not only *knew* what to do but was a *good* person who could be trusted to do what is right. Plato believed that rule by such a philosopher-king was the best form of government because the wise and good leader would be free to do what was right without being limited by laws or other government institutions with which power was shared.

Aristotle described a good form of government as one with institutions and laws. His description of a good form of government is more closely identified with the modern concept of government according to the rule of law. For example, Aristotle's good government was less dependent on a leader's character. He described a system of government that did not depend on getting a leader as good and wise as Solomon. Aristotle made government power less personal and more institutional: a leader's power was based on the authority of the office held rather than personal attributes such as physical strength, charismatic leadership, heredity or blood-lines, or some other personal attribute.

Western thinking about the rule of law also includes English and French political philosophers. The English political philosopher Samuel Rutherford's *Lex, Rex* (1644) advocated using law (*Lex*) to control the power of a monarch or other ruler (*Rex*). The English political struggles to bring the king under the law influenced American thinking about good government. The French political philosopher Montesquieu's *The Spirit of the Laws* (1748) provided the American Founders with specific ideas about how to create a system of government that guarded against the abuse of power. Montesquieu's main contribution to the U.S. system of constitutional government is the principle of the separation of powers—dividing government into three branches (the legislative, the executive, and the judicial branches).

During the colonial and revolutionary eras, Thomas Paine's *Common Sense* (1776) drew upon these sources for inspiration about how law could be used to control the power of the king, and indeed all government power. In this sense, Paine's political theory reflected the development of the rule of law to displace the rule of man. According to Paine,

> . . . the world may know, that so far as we approve of monarchy, that in America THE LAW IS KING. For as in absolute governments the King is law, so in free countries the law OUGHT to be King; and there ought to be no other.

The bold assertion that the king was not the sovereign ruler—a claim that the king was not above the law but rather subject to it—earned Thomas Paine a deserved reputation as a political radical. Remember that such statements could not only be considered treason, for which the penalty could be death, but they challenged the English monarchy's claims to the divine right to rule. One of the best statements of what the rule of law meant to the Founders is John Adams' statement in *The Constitution of the Commonwealth of Massachusetts*:

> "In the government of this commonwealth, the legislative department shall never exercise the executive and judicial powers or either of them: the executive shall never exercise the legislative and judicial powers, or either of them: the judicial shall never exercise the legislative and executive powers, or either of them: to the end it may be a government of laws and not of men."
>
> (The Constitution of the Commonwealth of Massachusetts, Part The First; Art. XXX)

Support for the rule of law continued to develop during the 19th century. The legal scholar Albert Venn Dicey's *Law of the Constitution* (1895) how it meant that everyone was under the law and no one was above it:

"... every official, from the Prime Minister down to a constable or a collector of taxes, is under the same responsibility for every act done without legal justification as any other citizen. The Reports abound with cases in which officials have been brought before the courts, and made, in their personal capacity, liable to punishment, or to the payment of damages, for acts done in their official character but in excess of their lawful authority. [Appointed government officials and politicians, alike] ... and all subordinates, though carrying out the commands of their official superiors, are as responsible for any act which the law does not authorise as is any private and unofficial person." (at 194)

2.3 | Is the Rule of Law Part of the American Creed?

The rule of law has become so important in American thinking about government that it is considered part of an "**American Creed**." A creed is a statement of beliefs. It is usually meant to refer to a statement of religious beliefs or faith but the American *political* creed refers to the widely-shared set of political beliefs or values about the best way to form and administer good government. The American Creed consists of the country's basic governing principles: the rule of law, popular sovereignty, checks and balances (principally the separation of powers and federalism), individual rights, and judicial review.

In fact, most governments today are at least officially committed to the rule of law—even if they do not live up to the ideal. The importance of the rule of law is reflected in the fact that non-governmental organizations (NGOs) such as the World Bank consider the rule of law an essential condition for political, social, and economic development. The World Bank's Law & Development/Law and Justice Institutions Programs link the rule of law with these important aspects of a nation's development. The almost worldwide acceptance of the rule of law as a basic principle of governing has made law one of the factors determining whether government power is legitimate. The distinction between power and authority is based on the difference between the illegitimate use of power or coercion and the legitimate use of power or coercion. When political power is exercised appropriately, based on the rule of law, it is considered authority. In Western political development, law has displaced older or traditional sources of authority such as heredity, divine right, or personal charisma.

2.31 | *Constitutional Democracy*

The U.S. is commonly called a democracy or a republic but it is actually a constitutional democracy or constitutional republic. The *constitutional* limits the *democracy*! The Constitution limits democracy as defined as majority rule. Congress may pass popular laws that ban flag burning or punish radical political speech or prohibit certain religious practices but even laws that have widespread public support can be declared unconstitutional. In the U.S. legal hierarchy, the Constitution trumps statues (even if they are popular). Democratic politics may be about popularity contests and majority rule but constitutional law. The Bill of Rights protects individual rights from majority rule. In fact, the Constitution is a counter-majoritarian document in the sense that it cannot be changed by a simple majority vote. Changing the Constitution requires extra-ordinary majorities. A constitutional amendment requires a two-thirds vote to propose an amendment and a three-quarters vote to ratify it.

2.32 | *Three Eras of Development*

American government can be divided into three eras or stages of political development: the founding era; the development of the system of government; and the emergence of the modern system of government.

- The *founding* era includes the colonial experience culminating with the Declaration of Independence and the Revolutionary War; the Articles of Confederation, which was the first form of government; and the creation of the republican system of government in1787.

- The *development* stage is not as clearly defined as the founding era. It extends from the early years of the republic to the Progressive Era (from 1890 to the end of World War I). It includes the early 1800s when the Marshall Court (1801-1835) issued landmark rulings that broadly interpreted the powers of the national government; the post-Civil War constitutional amendments abolishing slavery, prohibiting denial of the right to vote on account of race, and prohibiting states from denying equal protection and due process of law; and the Progressive Era policies regulating monopolies and working conditions (e.g. enacting child labor laws, workplace safety laws, and minimum wage and maximum hours laws. These developments changed the system of government and politics that was established by the Constitution. Political parties were organized. The powers of the president and the national government expanded. The public expected broader participation in politics and greater popular control over government.

- The *modern* era of American government is usually traced to the 1930s. The Great Depression was a national—indeed, an international—economic problem that the American public expected the national government to address. The development of a national economy further strengthened public expectations that the national government, more than the state governments, were responsible for the state of the economy. The public began to look to the federal government for solutions to problems. Organized crime was perceived as a national problem that required federal action. World War II and the subsequent Cold War also increased the power of the national government, which has primary responsibility for foreign affairs and national defense. The creation of a social welfare state and a national security state changed politics and governance. It altered the distribution of power between the national and state governments. It also expanded the power of the presidency and the rise of the administrative state—the expansion of the federal bureaucracy that Americans love to hate.

The following sections examine the founding era. The development and modern eras are examined in greater detail in the chapters on congress, the president, the judiciary, and federalism.

2.4 | The Founding Era

2.41 | *The Colonial Era*

People came to the new world primarily from England and Europe for a variety of reasons. Some came looking for greater political freedom. Some came for economic opportunity with the promise of free land. Some were entrepreneurs who saw the New World as a place to make money. Some were seeking a new start in life. Some fled religious persecution in their home land and were searching for freedom to practice their religion. In the 16th and 17th centuries, English joint-stock companies were formed under charters from the crown to promote commercial and territorial expansion in North America. The Virginia Company of London founded the Jamestown settlement in 1607. In New England, the Massachusetts Bay Company charter described explicitly religious political purposes. The First Charter of Virginia (1606), The Mayflower Compact (1620) and The Charter of Massachusetts Bay (1629) are documentary evidence of the colonial era belief that politics and government had explicitly religious purposes.[1] The colonial experience with charters creating communities also provided colonists with personal experiences creating or "constituting" governments. These experiences are one reason why the social contract theory of government has been so influential in shaping American thinking about government.

2.42 | *The Spirit of Independence*

Several factors fostered a spirit of independence in the colonies. The first factor is the **character** of the people who came to "the New World." In the seventeenth century, crossing the Atlantic Ocean was a long, difficult, and dangerous undertaking. The people who made the trip tended to be the hardier, more adventurous, or more desperate individuals, so the colonies were populated with people who had an independent streak. A second factor is **geography**. The large ocean between the rulers and the ruled created conditions that allowed a sense of colonial identity to develop. King James I (1600-1625) increased the independent spirit by allowing the colonists to establish assemblies such as the Virginia House of Burgesses. Each of the 13 colonies had a constitution. These conditions fostered expectations of individual liberty in self-government, religious practices, and economic activity. By the mid-1700s, local traditions and distance weakened colonial ties to the Crown. A third factor is **ideas**. The political philosophy of the Age of Enlightenment included an emphasis on reason, self-government, liberty, and equality. These ideas appealed to the colonists' and were used to challenge British imperial power in the New World.

A fourth factor is **economics**. The colonial economies differed from the British economy. Changes in the economic ties between England and the colonies increased support for political independence. During the colonial era the British economic policy was mercantilist. **Mercantilism** is the theory that the government controls and directs economic activity, particularly foreign trade, in order to maximize the state's wealth. The British controlled colonial industries and trade to increase imperial wealth. The British prohibited their colonies from trading with other imperial powers like the Dutch to ensure that British colonial gold and silver stayed within the empire. The American colonies initially benefited economically from this mercantilist arrangement. They had a buyer for the raw materials and other goods produced by the colonies. The American colonies produced wood for ships for the British fleet as well as tobacco, cotton, rice, and sugar for export. In return, the colonists could buy finished products like ships and rum. Mercantilism was responsible for the **triangle** trade: slaves were brought to America from Africa; sugar, cotton, and tobacco were exported to England; and manufactured goods, textiles, and rum were sent to Africa to pay for slaves.

This mercantilist arrangement changed as the colonial economy developed. The colonies started chafing against mercantilist policies as they believed they were no longer receiving competitive prices for their goods. Furthermore, as the New England economy developed into a manufacturing and trade economy, New England started taking England's place in the trade triangle, thereby reducing the need for the British Empire.

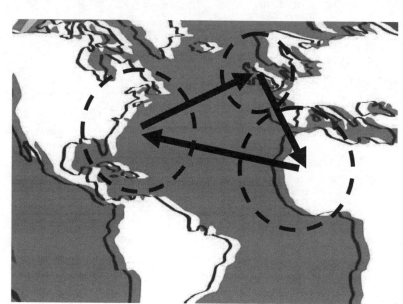

2.43 | *Trade and Taxation*

Despite the complaints about trade policies, the colonists were generally content with British governance until the **Seven Years War** (1756—1763). The long and expensive war with the French and Indians ended with the British in control of most of North America. The colonists thought this would open up even more cheap frontier land for them to settle but the British had other ideas. The Crown decreed in 1763 that there would be no further westward movement of British subjects because the Crown did not want to pay to defend settlers against Indians. The British Parliament taxed the colonists to pay for the very expensive war. **The Sugar Act** of 1764 taxed sugar, wine, coffee, and other products commonly exported to the colonies. The colonists resented these taxes and began to cry "no taxation without representation!"

Parliament further angered the colonists by passing **the Stamp Act** in 1765, which required all printed documents to bear a stamp. The printer had to pay for the stamp. In the same year, the Parliament passed the **Mutiny (Quartering) Act** that forced colonists to either provide barracks for British soldiers or house them in their homes. The colonists, who were already mad about paying taxes, started protesting that they have to pay for soldiers to live in their homes. The Sons of Liberty, which were organized by Samuel Adams and Patrick Henry to act against the Crown, looted the Boston tax collectors home. Violence spread throughout the colonies and the stamp act became virtually unenforceable.

In 1767, Parliament enacted **the Townshend Acts** that imposed duties on many products including tea. The Sons of Liberty started a boycott which prompted the British to send troops to Boston. When British soldiers fired on a crowd of protesters, killing five people, the event was depicted as the Boston Massacre. Paul Revere portrayal of the British captain ordering the troops to fire on the crowd inflamed colonial passions.

Paul Revere's engraving of the Boston Massacre

In 1772, still upset by the tea tax, Samuel Adams suggested the creation of Committees of Correspondence to improve communication among colonists. By 1774, twelve colonies had formed such committees which organized protests prior to the revolution and coordinated actions during the revolution. Despite colonial opposition, Parliament passed another tax on tea in 1773 and, consistent with mercantilist economic policy, granted a monopoly to the East India Company. The colonists responded by dumping tea into Boston Harbor. The "Boston Tea Party" enraged King George, who declared that it was time to force the colonies to fall into line. The King persuaded Parliament to pass **the Coercive Acts** or the Intolerable Acts, which allowed Britain to blockade Boston harbor and placed 4,000 more soldiers in Boston. These actions increased resentment on both sides of the Atlantic. All but one colony (Georgia) agreed to send delegates to a new continental congress to present a united message to the King.

2.44 | *The First and Second Continental Congresses*

The First Continental Congress that met in Philadelphia in September and October 1774 consisted of 56 delegates from every colony except Georgia. They <u>adopted a statement of rights and principles</u>, including colonial rights of petition and assembly, trial by peers, freedom from a standing army, and the selection of representative councils to levy taxes. The statement provided that the Congress would meet again in May 1775 if the King did not agree with their requests. King George refused the request of the Continental Congress. A second Continental Congress called a meeting in May of 1775, but before the delegates could meet fighting broke out at Lexington and Concord, Massachusetts. When the delegates at the Second Continental Congress convened on May 10, 1775 the atmosphere was more hostile toward Britain. King George sent 20,000 more troops. The Revolutionary War had begun in earnest.

> Think About It!
> Anti-war movements in the Revolutionary Era? Not everyone in the colonies supported the Revolutionary War. And not everyone in Britain thought it was a good idea to send troops to put down colonial rebellions. See the British political cartoon from 1775 describing King George's decision as being lead by obstinacy and pride:
> http://www.loc.gov/pictures/item/97514880/

2.45 | *The Declaration of Independence (1776)*

The Declaration of Independence was written to justify the colonists' taking up arms to overthrow an existing political system. It is a philosophical defense of the right of revolution. Thomas Jefferson, a Virginia farmer and lawyer, was the main author of the Declaration of Independence. The language that Jefferson used in the Declaration reflected John Locke's words and ideas about natural or God-given rights, popular sovereignty, the social contract theory of government based on the consent of the governed, and even a people's right to revolt against an unjust government. The following language from the Declaration of Independence explains these ideas:

> *"When in the course of human events, it becomes necessary for one people to dissolve the political bands which have connected them with another, and to assume among the powers of the earth, the separate and equal station to which the laws of nature and of nature's God entitle them, a decent respect to the opinions of mankind requires that they should declare the causes which impel them to the separation.*
>
> *We hold these truths to be self-evident: That all men are created equal; that they are endowed by their Creator with certain unalienable rights; that among these are life, liberty, and the pursuit of happiness; that, to secure these rights, governments are instituted among men, deriving their just powers from the consent of the governed; that whenever any form of government becomes destructive of these ends, it is the right of the people to alter or to abolish it...."*

The Declaration acknowledges that people should not be quick to revolt against a government. It is only after *"a long train of abuses"* intended to reduce the people to despotism that *"it is their right, it is their duty, to throw off such government, and to provide new guards for their future security..."* The Declaration listed the King's actions that aimed to establish "absolute tyranny" over the states. It then declared *"**That these United Colonies are, and of right ought to be, FREE AND INDEPENDENT STATES;** that they are absolved from all allegiance to the British crown and that all political connection between them and the state of Great Britain is, and ought to be, totally dissolved..."*

2.5 | The Articles of Confederation

The first American form of government was the <u>Articles of Confederation</u>. The Continental Congress approved the Articles of Confederation and they took effect in 1781 upon ratification by all thirteen states. A confederation is a loose association of sovereign states that agree to cooperate in a kind of voluntary "league of friendship." The Second Article of Confederation provided that "Each state retains its sovereignty, freedom, and independence, and every power, jurisdiction, and right, which is not by this Confederation expressly delegated to the United States, in Congress assembled." The Third Article provided that "The said States hereby severally enter into a firm league

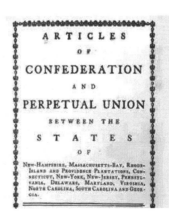

of friendship with each other, for their common defense, the security of their liberties, and their mutual and general welfare, binding themselves to assist each other, against all force offered to, or attacks made upon them, or any of them, on account of religion, sovereignty, trade, or any other pretense whatever."

In a **confederation,** political power is decentralized because the central (or national) government is weak and the state or regional governments are strong. The Articles of Confederation had major defects which were exposed during the Revolutionary War. The defects became more apparent after the Revolutionary War when the states no longer felt the need to work together to face the threat of the common enemy. The Articles had five major defects related to taxing power, an executive official, commerce, amendment, and the power to maintain domestic order.

- **Taxing**. The national government did not have the power to tax, which meant that congress (the main institution of the national government) had to beg the states to pay for the war and other government functions. It is hard today to imagine a government without the power to tax.

- **Executive**. The Articles did not provide a chief executive. The Revolutionary War was fought against a monarchy (an executive figure), and the natural reaction of the Founders was to create a new political system which did not have a single leader or executive figure who could become a monarch. The Declaration of Independence lists the colonists' grievances against King George. The Revolutionary War was fought against a monarch who was accused of tyrannical abuse of power. It was logical for the Founders to create a form of government where a representative body, a legislative institution more closely identified with democratic government, had the most power.

- **Commerce**. The Articles did not give the national government power much economic power. The states had power to regulate interstate and foreign commerce. Some states enacted laws which benefited economic interests in their state and discriminated against out of state or foreign business interests. These kinds of economic protectionist legislation limited trade. States could also coin money. Critics eventually saw state power over commerce and economics as a barrier to the development of a national economy and advocated giving the national government power over interstate and foreign commerce.

- **Amendment**. One of the most important challenges facing any political system is how to provide for change in response to different economic, social, or political circumstances. The Articles could be amended only by unanimous consent of congress and the state legislatures. This made it very difficult if not impossible for the government to adapt to circumstances that it faced.

- **Domestic Order**. Because power was decentralized, the national government did not have power to act to ensure domestic tranquility and order. Maintaining good public order is one of basic responsibilities of any government. The national government's ineffectual response to domestic disturbances such as Shays'

Rebellion and secessionist movements in some parts of the country exposed the weakness of the national government under the Articles.

The most famous of these domestic threats to public order were armed marches in Massachusetts. In the fall of 1786 and winter of 1787, Daniel Shays, a Revolutionary War veteran, lead around 1500 supporters on an armed march to stop mortgage foreclosures. Economic conditions were bad. High state taxes and high interest rates caused farmers to face bankruptcy and mortgage foreclosures. Shays and his supporters marched on the government to demand that it provide them with some relief from the bad economic conditions. The State of Massachusetts appealed to the national government for help in putting down **Shays' Rebellion**, but the national government could not act without the consent of the other states, which rejected the request for money to establish a national army. Order was finally restored when the governor of Massachusetts called out the state militia.

A scene at Springfield, during Shay's Rebellion, when the mob
attempted to prevent the holding of the Courts of Justice
—E. Benjamin Andrews, 1895

Shays' Rebellion alarmed government officials and political leaders who believed the national government needed to be given more power to respond to such threats to good public order. A constitutional convention was held in the summer of 1787 to "revise" the Articles of Confederation to correct its defects. However, the delegates to the convention decided to abolish the Articles of Confederation and create a new form of government. After lively debate, the delegates drafted a new constitution which created a new system of government, a federal republic with a stronger national government. Modern Americans tend to forget the central role that Shays' and other "unruly" individuals played in the creation of the republic. (Holton 2007) Radical popular action has been a part of the American political experience and tradition from the founding of the republic, through the civil war fought to preserve the union, to modern efforts to create a government that is responsive to the people.

2.5 | The U.S. Constitution

Although the delegates to the Constitutional Convention met in secret, the records of the convention debates reveal lively debates about what form of government to create. The convention debates and the subsequent debates over ratification of the new constitution were generally organized as a debate between the Federalists and the Anti-federalists. The Federalists supported ratification because they believed that the country needed a stronger national government. Their arguments for ratification were made in a series of famous essays written by James Madison, Alexander Hamilton, and John Jay called The Federalist Papers. The Anti-federalists opposed ratification of the Constitution because they believed that it gave the national government too much power. They preferred a political union where the states had more power. The Anti-federalists tend to be overlooked because they lost the argument. The Constitution was ratified. But the Anti-federalist Papers are worth reading in an era when American politics includes criticism of the size of the federal government.

The Declaration of Independence and the Constitution were written for two very different purposes. The Declaration is a philosophical defense of a people's right to overthrow an unjust government. The Constitution is a practical, working document that was written to create a more effective form of government. The Preamble of the Constitution states that "We, the people…" establish the Constitution "in order to form a more perfect Union, establish justice, insure domestic tranquility, provide for the common defense, promote the general welfare, and secure the blessings of liberty to ourselves and our posterity…" The Constitution created a new form of government, a "more perfect Union" that was more capable of accomplishing the things that the people expect government to do. Alexander Hamilton explained this purpose in Federalist *Number One*:

> AFTER an unequivocal experience of the inefficiency of the subsisting federal government, you are called upon to deliberate on a new Constitution for the United States of America. The subject speaks its own importance; comprehending in its consequences nothing less than the existence of the UNION, the safety and welfare of the parts of which it is composed, the fate of an empire in many respects the most interesting in the world.

Considering the passionate motives of those who supported or opposed the new Constitution, Hamilton worried that a spirit of self-righteous passion would make compromise and cooperation difficult, and that the intolerant spirit would tempt one side to attempt to dominate the other side by physical force rather than the force of argument.

In *To Secure These Rights: The Declaration of Independence and Constitutional Interpretation* (1995), Douglas Gerber argues that the purpose of the Constitution was to effectuate or make possible the Lockean liberal principles that were asserted in the *Declaration of Independence*. The *Declaration* asserted the existence of certain unalienable or natural rights; the Constitution created a system of constitutional government that provided the means to achieve the rights and protect them.

The main body of the Constitution establishes the basic framework of government. It provides for a republican system of government; elections and representation; and it grants and limits the powers of government. Article I provides the powers of the legislative branch. Article II provides the powers of the executive branch. Article III provides the powers of the judicial branch. The first ten amendments to the Constitution, commonly referred to as the Bill of Rights, provide for individual rights. The Bill of Rights includes important limits on the powers of government.

2.51 | *The Three Functions of the Constitution*

The U.S. Constitution does three things. It establishes the basic framework of the government; it allocates government powers; and it declares or guarantees individual rights.

Establish the basic framework of government. The Constitution creates a **republican** form of government, a **federal** system of government, and a system of government with the **separation of powers**. A republic is a type of democracy. It is an indirect democracy. Elected representatives make public policy for the people. The people control government by electing government officials.

A federal system is a two-tiered system of government where power is divided between a central government (the national or federal government) and the regional or state governments. Federalism is a *geographic* division of power between the national government and the state governments. The actual division of powers is specific in some areas of public policy (e.g., the national government has exclusive power over interstate commerce, coining money, and foreign affairs) but general in others (e.g., both national and state governments make crime, education, environmental, and tax policy). Furthermore, the division has changed over time. The federal government is involved with more areas of public policy than originally intended because the Founders intended to create a state-centered political system. Federalism is an important part of the Madisonian system of institutional checks and balances whereby the national and state governments check one another's powers.

The separation of powers is a functional division of power among the legislative, executive, and judicial branches of government. The separation of powers serves two purposes. First, it is part of the Madisonian system of checks and balances designed to prevent the concentration of power in the hands of one individual or one institution. Second, it contributes to good governance.

The checks and balances purpose is directly related to the intention to limit government power. In fact, it is sometimes considered evidence that the Founders intended to create an inefficient system of government. The separation of power's role in the system of checks and balances is to distribute power among three separate but interdependent branches to prevent any one individual or institution from getting too much power. The separation of powers is one of the Constitution's basic governing doctrines even though it is not specifically mentioned in the Constitution.

The three branches were not intended to be completely independent of one another. The French political philosopher Montesquieu, who was the main inspiration for the tripartite separation of powers, believed that each branch had to be sufficiently independent of the others so that one branch could not create, or abolish, any other branch. Separation of powers does not mean that each branch's powers are completely separate from the others. In fact, the system of institutional jealousy depends on some overlap so that each branch will guard against another branch poaching on its turf. Congress' power to enact laws can be checked by the president's veto. The president's veto can be overridden by a two-thirds majority vote in both houses of congress. The president is delegated power as commander-in-chief, but only congress has the power to declare war and to raise and support an army. The president has the power to nominate federal judges, ambassadors, and other high government officials, but the nominations must be confirmed by the Senate. And the Supreme Court has final authority to strike down both legislative and presidential acts as unconstitutional. The president nominates federal judges but they must be confirmed by the Senate. Congress determines the federal judiciary's budget and the organization of the federal court system. Over time, the president has become a very important participant in the legislative process. It is commonplace today to refer to *the administration's budget*, for instance, or *the administration's bill* in congress. Presidential legislation and judicial policy making are part of the modern vocabulary of government and politics.

The second reason for the separation of powers is that it contributes to good governance. The argument that the separation of powers contributes to good governance is based on the belief that each branch of government has a special institutional competence, and that good governance requires all three special competencies. The legislative branch's competence is representation (of districts, states, and interests), deliberation, and ultimately compromise to make laws for the nation. The executive branch's competence is action (the ability to act swiftly when needed) and administration (to justly administer the laws passed by congress). The executive is to ensure that the laws passed by Congress are uniformly applied, not enforced selectively against the minority party, racial or ethnic minorities, or the political opponents of the people who made the laws. The judiciary's competence in a political system with a tradition of individualized justice is dispute resolution: to conduct trials where laws are applied to individuals, and to interpret the laws when there are legal disputes about what the laws mean. The Founders thought that the separation of powers was a modern, political scientific contribution to good government. In *Federalist 47*, Madison praised the "celebrated" Montesquieu for popularizing the "invaluable precept in the science of politics." In contrast to the checks and balances purpose of the separation of powers, the good governance purpose emphasizes government efficiency/effectiveness more than inefficiency/limited government.

The Founders intended the legislative branch to make laws, the executive to carry them out, and the judicial branch to interpret the laws. But this is not exactly the way the system works. The modern national government does have three separate institutions but they actually share *law making* power. For instance, the terms *presidential legislation* and *legislating from the bench* are commonly used to describe what the modern presidency and judiciary actually do. Descriptions of how the modern government works typically include legislative policymaking, executive policymaking, and judicial policymaking.

The separation of powers is not essential for democracy. Modern democracies include presidential government and parliamentary government. The separation of powers is more common to presidential systems than parliamentary systems, which typically fuse legislative and executive powers. The prime minister, the executive figure, may be an elected member of the legislative body, the parliament. In parliamentary systems, one institution, the elected legislature or parliament, is the supreme governing body; the other institutions (the prime minister or the courts) are inferior to it. In separation of powers, each branch is largely independent of the other branches in the sense that the other branches are not created by, or dependent on, another branch for its existence. Congress cannot abolish the judiciary; the president cannot abolish congress. Accordingly, in a fusion of powers system such as that of the United Kingdom, the people elect the legislature, which in turn selects the executive (who is usually called the prime minister. The fact that a prime minister is selected by the legislative body, and is an elected member of that body, means that parliamentary systems fuse rather than separate institutional powers.

In the U.S., the separation of legislative and executive power is evident in the fact that Congress does not select the president, and the president is not a member of congress. The president is selected independent of Congress. In a parliamentary system, the tenure of a prime minister selected by a legislature is likely to end when the term of the legislature ends and a new parliament selects a new executive. In a presidential system the executive's term may or may not coincide with the legislature's term. However, legislative and executive powers can be informally fused when the president's party controls Congress. Party loyalty (to a president of the same party) can weaken a member of congress' institutional loyalty. The fusion can create problems. Party loyalty can undermine the institutional checks and balances if the majority party in congress supports the president.

Allocate Power. The second function of a Constitution is to allocate power. The Constitution *both* grants *and* limits government powers. The main grants of power to the national government are provided in Article I (legislative), Article II (executive), and Article III (judicial). Article one I, Section 8 provides a list of powers delegated to Congress. The main limits on the power of the national government are provided in the Bill of Rights. The challenge when writing a constitution is to strike the right balance between granting and limiting government power: a government that is too weak can be ineffectual or result in a failed state; a government that is too strong can threaten individual liberty.

Guarantee Individual Rights (or Freedoms). The third function of a constitution is to provide for individual rights. The U.S. Constitution, the 50 state constitutions, and the constitutions of other countries include provisions declaring or guaranteeing rights. In the U.S. Constitution, the Bill of Rights provides for freedom of speech, religion, and press, as well as providing protection against unreasonable search and seizure, due process of law, the right to a trial by jury, and protection against cruel and unusual punishment. These constitutionally protected rights are sometimes called civil liberties. Civil liberties are distinct from civil rights, which is a term that usually refers to individual rights that are provided in legislation rather than the Constitution.

Civil Liberties are the constitutional rights that limit the government's power to restrict individual freedom. Civil liberties are often called individual rights or individual liberties because they limit government power over individuals. Civil liberties include the First Amendment guarantees of freedom of religion, speech, and press; the Second Amendment right to keep and bear arms; the Fourth Amendment right against unreasonable search and seizure; the Fifth Amendment guarantee of due process of law; the Eighth Amendment prohibition against cruel and unusual punishment; and the Fourteenth Amendment guarantee of equal protection of the laws. Some of the most important civil liberties provisions are described in very general language: the protection against unreasonable search and seizure; the guarantee of due process of law; and the prohibition against cruel and unusual punishment. The meanings of these vague words are not precise. People disagree about their meaning. As a result, conflicts between individuals who claim a civil liberties freedom from government restriction and government claims that they have the power to restrict the freedom are often decided by the Supreme Court.

The term *civil rights* is often used generically to refer to individual rights and individual liberties. But there are two significant differences between civil liberties and civil rights. First, civil rights are statutory rights. They are provided in legislation, not the Constitution. Second, civil rights protect individuals against discrimination. Civil rights laws promote equality by prohibiting discrimination on the basis of race, gender, religion, ethnicity, or some other status or characteristic. Two examples of landmark civil rights laws are the 1964 Civil Rights and the 1965 Voting Rights Act.

2.52 | *The Bill of Rights*

When the Constitution was submitted to the states for ratification, it did not include a provision declaring or guaranteeing individual rights. The Federalists, who supported the Constitution, argued that a bill of rights was unnecessary because the powers of the newly formed national government were so carefully limited that individual rights did not have to be specifically mentioned in the Constitution. In fact, some Federalists argued that adding a bill of rights could actually be dangerous because listing specific individual rights that the government could *not* limit would inevitably be interpreted to mean that the government *could limit* any rights that were not actually mentioned in the bill of rights. Nevertheless, legislators in some states threatened to withhold ratification of the Constitution unless a bill of rights was added to the document.

The Anti-federalist George Mason, a constitutional convention delegate from Virginia, opposed the new constitution because it did not include a bill of rights. The Anti-federalist worries that the new constitution created a stronger national government but did not include a bill of rights threatened the ratification of the Constitution. In order to ease Anti-federalist worries, a bill of rights was proposed to limit the power of the national government. The first ten amendments were based on Mason's *Virginia Declaration of Rights*. In 1789, the First Congress of the United States adopted the first ten amendments to the Constitution. These amendments were ratified by the required number of states in 1791. The following is an edited version of the first ten amendments to the Constitution (the Bill of Rights):

First Amendment: *"Congress shall make no law respecting an establishment of religion, or prohibiting the free exercise thereof; or abridging the freedom of the speech, or of the press....."*

Second Amendment: *"A well-regulated Militia, being necessary to the security of a free State, the right of the people to keep and bear Arms, shall not be infringed."*

Fourth Amendment: *"The right of the people to be secure in their persons, houses, papers, and effects, against unreasonable searches and seizures, shall not be violated...."*

Fifth Amendment: *"No person shall...be subject for the same offence to be twice put in jeopardy of life or limb, nor shall be compelled in any criminal case to be a witness against himself, nor be deprived of life, liberty, or property, without due process of law; nor shall private property be taken for public use, without just compensation."*

Sixth Amendment: *"In all criminal prosecutions, the accused shall enjoy the right to a speedy and public trial, by an impartial jury of the State and district wherein the crime shall have been committed.....and to have the assistance of counsel for his defence."*

Seventh Amendment: *"In suits at common law, where the value in controversy shall exceed twenty dollars, the right of trial by jury shall be preserved..."*

Eighth Amendment: *"Excessive bail shall not be required, nor excessive fines imposed, nor cruel and unusual punishment inflicted."*

Ninth Amendment: *"The enumeration in the Constitution, of certain rights, shall not be construed to deny or disparage others retained by the people."*

Tenth Amendment: *"The powers not delegated to the United States by the Constitution, nor prohibited by it to the States, are reserved to the States respectively, or to the people"*

Until 2008, the Supreme Court had interpreted the Second Amendment as guaranteeing the states the power to maintain a well-regulated militia. As such, the Second Amendment was read as a *federalism* amendment: it protected the states from the federal government—particularly its military power. In _District of Columbia v. Heller_, the Supreme Court ruled that the Second Amendment guaranteed an individual right to keep and bear arms. As a result, the right to keep and bear arms has now been added to the list of civil liberties that individuals and organizations, such as the National Rifle Association, can use to challenge gun control and other regulatory policies enacted by the federal, state, or local governments.

Most of the provisions in the Bill of Rights apply to criminal justice. They list specific rights. The Ninth Amendment is different. It was added to the bill of rights to ease Anti-federalist worries that *not* listing a right mean that the right did not exist. What if the men who made up the list forgot to include a basic right? What if a future generation considered a right a fundamental right? The Ninth Amendment was intended as a statement that the Bill of Rights should not be read as an exhaustive list.

2.53 | *Civil Rights and Civil Liberties*

The relationship between religion and politics is one of the most controversial issues in American politics. During the colonial era, government and politics had explicitly religious purposes. The *First Charter of Virginia* (1606), the *Mayflower Compact* (1620), and *The Book of the General Lawes and Libertyes Concerning the Inhabitants of the Massachusetts* (1648), for example, describe government and politics as organized efforts to make people moral—as defined by organized religious beliefs. Some colonies had an established church—an officially recognized and government supported church. Massachusetts established the Congregational Church as the official church and some southern colonies established the Anglican Church as the official religion. Over time, the colonies moved away from establishing an official denomination and toward establishing Christianity or Protestantism.

The Constitution changed the relationship between church and state—or at least the relationship between religion and the federal government. Article VI of the Constitution provides that "no religious Test shall ever be required as a Qualification to any Office or public Trust under the United States." More important, the First Amendment prohibits Congress from making any law "respecting an establishment of religion or prohibiting the free exercise" of religion. The First Amendment guarantees freedom of religion, which includes the right of individuals and organizations to actively participate in politics, but it limits government support for religion. Political and constitutional debates involve providing public aid to religious schools, policies allowing or requiring organized prayer in public schools, religious displays of the Ten Commandments or crèches in public places, laws related to the teaching of evolution or creation science, and legislating morality. Civil liberties claims have been made to challenge the constitutionality of using law to promote morality by regulating obscenity, to prohibit certain sexual behavior, and to define marriage as a relationship between one man and one woman.

2.6 | Constitutionalism

This chapter began with an acknowledgement that having a constitution is today almost universally accepted as the best form of government. But having a document called a constitution does not mean that a political system is committed to constitutional government. Constitutionalism refers to the public and government officials' commitment to the values that are expressed in the Constitution. Without the commitment, a constitution is merely paper or words without much to back them up. With the commitment, a constitution acquires real political and legal force. Americans have an especially strong commitment to the Constitution. Support for the Constitution remains strong even in tough times of economic hardships, domestic disorder, or national security threats. In contrast, public support for the government varies a great deal, and in fact support for government institutions has declined over time. The enduring appeal of the Constitution and the belief in the founding values that are embodied in it (e.g., freedom; limited government; equality) remain a political constant even in times of great political change, conflict, and even turmoil. What explains the enduring appeal of the Constitution?

One explanation is that the enduring public support reflects a general commitment to the Constitution or to constitutional government rather than support for specific provisions of the Constitution or particular interpretations of them. This explanation is supported by studies of public opinion that reveal consistently low levels of knowledge about what is actually in the Constitution. A public opinion survey conducted by the Constitution Center revealed startlingly low levels of public knowledge about the Constitution: less than five percent of the American public could correctly answer even basic questions about the constitution.

The consistently high levels of public support for the Constitution do not mean there is general consensus about *what* specific provisions of the Constitution actually mean. In fact, the general consensus supporting the Constitution masks political conflict about what specific provisions of the Constitution mean and how to interpret them. For instance, both conservatives and liberals profess support for the Constitution and the values embodied in it. But they consistently disagree about the government's criminal justice powers, its economic regulatory powers, its moral regulatory powers, and its war powers. For instance, both sides in the debates about the role of religion in American government and politics appeal to the Constitution as supporting their side of the debate about school prayer.

Liberals and conservatives also disagree about *how* the Constitution should be interpreted. A Pew Research survey of public opinion about the Constitution revealed major differences between conservatives and liberals, an ideological divide that was so wide that it was described as a chasm. Conservatives believe the Constitution should be interpreted according to the original meaning of the words or the original intentions of those who wrote them. Liberals believe that the Constitution should be interpreted according to contemporary societal expectations. These differences reflect the tension between continuity and change, between adhering to certain beliefs and changing with the times. Particularly during hard times or times of crisis, conservatives are apt to blame political problems on departing the republic's political and constitutional founding values, and to call for a return to them as the solution to the problems.

2.61 | *The Relationship between the Constitution and the Government*

The relationship between the political system that was established by the Constitution and modern governance is both interesting and complicated. Public opinion reflects such strong support for the Constitution *and* such strong criticism of the government that it could be said that Americans love the Constitution but hate the government (that it created). Although it may seem surprising, venerating the Constitution can create governance problems. Reverence for the Constitution can create problems. Take, for example, constitutionalists. Constitutionalists believe the Constitution should be strictly or literally interpreted. Some religious constitutionalists believe that the Constitution was a divinely-inspired document. The belief that a document is divinely-inspired makes reasoned political analysis, including assessment of the problems of modern governance, difficult. Secular constitutionalists merely believe that the Constitution should be strictly interpreted. Some of the individuals who call themselves constitutionalists are advocates of the Tenth Amendment. The motto of these "Tenthers" is "*The Constitution. Every Issue. Every Time. No Exceptions, no Excuses*." These constitutionalists believe the solution to the nation's problems is to return to the *original* Constitution, not the

Constitution as it has come to be understood. This is one of the main points of the Tea Party movement.

Political and legal scholars disagree about whether the nation's problems can be solved by returning to the original understanding of the Constitution and how the government was intended to work. Appeals to return to "the" Founders views are misleading insofar as it presumes that there was one, single, unified voice. At a minimum there were basic differences between the Federalists and the Anti-federalists.

The bicentennial of the Constitution in 1987 produced a number of scholarly works that identified governance problems that could be traced to the Constitution, and recommended constitutional reforms to create "a more workable government."[2] Constitutionalists and some conservatives reject the argument that the constitutional design of government is flawed or that modern challenges require modernizing the Constitution. Those who advocate change write in the Jeffersonian tradition.

2.62 | Should Laws, Like Food Products, Have Expiration Dates?

Thomas Jefferson argued that laws, including the Constitution, should have sunset provisions. He thought that laws should last only twenty years—the lifespan of a generation—because one generation should not bind a succeeding generation. No society "can make a perpetual constitution, or even a perpetual law," because just as the earth "belongs always to the living generation," people are masters "of their own persons, and consequently may govern them as they please." The constitution and laws "naturally expire at the end of 19 years." the life span of a generation. Laws that are enforced longer are enforced as "an act of force, and not of right." Jefferson did not think that the problem of one generation binding another could be solved by claiming that each succeeding generation's decision not to repeal a law was tacit consent to it. This tacit consent might apply if the form of government "were so perfectly contrived that the will of the majority could always be obtained fairly and without impediment." But no form of government is perfect. Representation is likely to be "unequal and vicious," various checks limit proposed legislation, factions control government bodies and bribery corrupts them, and personal interests cause government officials lose sight of "the general interests of their constituents." So practically speaking, "a law of limited duration is much more manageable" than one that needs to be repealed.[3]

One contemporary critic of the constitutional design of American government, Sanford Levinson, thinks that venerating the founding era and the system of government created by the Constitution is, ironically, not in keeping with the founding values of the republic. In "Our Imbecilic Constitution," Levinson reminds us that the authors of the *Federalist Papers* advocated ratification of the new Constitution by "mock[ing] the 'imbecility' of the weak central government created by the Articles of Confederation." Levinson scolds those who call the modern American political system "dysfunctional, even pathological" for failing to even mention the Constitution's role "in generating the pathology." According to Levinson, slavery, the Senate system of providing equal representation to North Dakota and California, the Electoral College, and the separation of powers, all created problems but "the worst single part of the Constitution...is surely Article V, which has made our Constitution among the most difficult to amend of any in the world." Amendment is so difficult that the mere discussion of possible reforms is considered a waste of time. He considers it unfortunate that "most contemporary

Americans" have lost the ability to "think seriously" about whether the Constitution's provisions for governance still serve us very well" and instead "envelope" the Constitution "in near religious veneration."

Levinson blames the modern dysfunctional government on the decision to make the Constitution so hard to amend. Most of the 50 state constitutions are much easier to amend. He notes that fourteen states give the voters the opportunity call a constitutional convention at regular intervals. There have been more than 230 state constitutional conventions, and "each state has had an average of almost three constitutions." Levinson describes the framers' "willingness to critique, indeed junk, the Articles of Confederation" truly admirable, and he thinks that "we are long overdue for a serious discussion about [the Constitution's] own role in creating the depressed (and depressing) state of American politics."

2.63 | *Continuity and Change*

The U.S. Constitution is distinctive in at least two respects. First, it is the world's *oldest* continuing governing document. Second, the Constitution is a very *brief* document. The Constitution's brevity and longevity are related. The Constitution has lasted as long as it has partly because it is such a short document. It is a short document that is filled with general phrases describing government and politics. The Preamble declares its purpose as "to form a more perfect Union" and "establish Justice." creating "a more perfect Union." Article I gives Congress power to use whatever means "necessary and proper" to accomplish the things that Congress has power to do. The Bill of Rights has especially memorable but flowery phrases. The 5th Amendment prohibits government from denying any person **due process of law**. The 4th Amendment prohibits **unreasonable searches and seizures**. The 8th Amendment prohibits **cruel and unusual punishment**. These general provisions of the Constitution allow for, or perhaps require, interpretation to give them concrete meaning, interpretation to determine how they are to be applied in specific instances. Interpretation is a way to informally change the meaning of the Constitution— to accommodate change without requiring formal amendment or an entirely new constitution. The short and general Constitution has endured for more than 200 years with only 27 amendments—and the first ten amendments were adopted as the bill of rights in 1791. This means that the Constitution has undergone only minimal formal changes despite more than two centuries of major political, economic, social, technological, and scientific changes.

Which raises a question: Is the Constitution, an Eighteenth Century document, still relevant to Twenty-first Century government and politics? It is. But the informal accommodation to reflect change means that it is no longer possible to read the Constitution to understand how modern American government and politics actually work. The following are just some of the major political developments that are not even mentioned in the Constitution.

- **Political Parties**. The Constitution does not say anything about political parties even though parties play a central role in politics and government. Parties have also changed the way the Electoral College works.

- **Corporations**. The Constitution does not say anything about corporations even though they are important economic organizations that the Supreme Court has said are "persons" for the purposes of the Fourteenth Amendment.
- **The Fed**. The Constitution does not say anything about the Federal Reserve Board even though "the Fed" is a very important government body with control over monetary policy.
- **The Fourth Branch**. The Constitution creates three branches of government but the development of the federal bureaucracy has created a fourth branch of government.
- **Presidential Government**. The Founders created a system based on legislative government but presidential power has expanded greatly over time and the system developed in presidential government.
- **Presidential Legislation**. This term applies to, among other things, executive orders and executive agreements.
- **Judicial Review**. The Constitution does not explicitly give courts the power of judicial review, but this implied power to review the acts of other government officials to determine whether they are constitutional has greatly expanded the power of courts.
- **The Congressional Committee System**. It is impossible to understand how Congress works without describing the committee system and the party leadership system.
- **The Sole Organ Doctrine**. This doctrine is one of the key concepts for understanding the modern president's role in foreign affairs and national security policy.
- **A National-centered System**. The Founders created a state-centered political system, but the government has developed into a national-centered system.

> **Think About It!**
> Can a person read the Constitution to get a good understanding of how American government and politics work today?

> **Act on It!**
> Contact a local, state, or national government official (e.g., your member of Congress), and ask them whether they support any constitutional amendments.

2.7 | Continuity

One way to better understand the U.S. Constitution is to compare it to other constitutions. The constitutions of the 50 states are very different than the U.S. Constitution. Among other things, the state constitutions are much younger, longer and more detailed than the U.S. Constitution. The constitutions of other countries are even more varied. The ready electronic access to the constitutions of other countries makes it easy to compare the constitutions of the countries of the world. Reading a country's constitution to determine what form of government the country has, and to determine what civil rights and liberties it includes, provides insights into the political history of a nation. It is especially interesting to compare the civil rights and liberties provisions in the newer constitutions with those of older constitutions such as the U.S. Constitution because the U.S. played an important role in writing the constitutions of Germany and Japan after World War I and, more recently, the constitutions of Iraq and Afghanistan.

2.8 | Summary

This chapter examined the origins and development of the U.S. system of constitutional government. It includes the various factors that fostered colonial independence and the subsequent development of American government and politics. The primary theme is the distinctive tension in American political culture between continuity (preserving the original understanding of the Constitution and the founding era values) and change (adapting to the political, social, economic, and technological conditions of the times). One aspect of self-government is thinking about the system of government and politics so that, as informed citizens, we can answer two basic questions. How is it working for us? How can we help to form "a more perfect Union?"

2.9 | Additional Resources

2.91 | *INTERNET SOURCES:*

Primary documents are available at
http://www.loc.gov/rr/program/bib/ourdocs/Constitution.html

Montesquieu. *The Spirit of the Laws.* http://www.constitution.org/cm/sol.htm

Paine, Thomas. 1776. *Common Sense*
http://www.ushistory.org/paine/commonsense/singlehtml.htm

Rutherford, Samuel. 1644. *Lex Rex: Law Is King, or The Law & The Prince.*
http://www.lonang.com/exlibris/rutherford/

The Constitution of the Commonwealth of Massachusetts
http://www.netstate.com/states/government/ma_government.htm

The First Charter of Virginia (1606)
http://www.lonang.com/exlibris/organic/1606-fcv.htm

KEY TERMS:

Constitutions
Rule of Law
Mercantilism
The triangle trade
Seven Years War
The Sugar Act
The Stamp Act
Mutiny Act
The Townshend Acts
The Coercive Acts
Confederation
Shays' Rebellion
A republican system
of government
Federalism
Separation of powers
Checks and balances
The Bill of Rights

The Mayflower Compact (1620)
http://avalon.law.yale.edu/17th_century/mayflower.asp

The Charter of Massachusetts Bay (1629)
http://avalon.law.yale.edu/17th_century/mass03.asp

The Lawes and Libertyes of Massachusetts (1648)
http://www.commonlaw.com/Mass.html

The National Constitution Center:
http://www.constitutioncenter.org/

The constitutions of countries of the world:
www.constitution.org/cons/natlcons.htm

2.92 | *IN THE LIBRARY*

Amar, Akhil Reed. 2005. *America's Constitution: A Biography*. New York: Random House.

Beard, Charles. 1913. *An Economic Interpretation of the Constitution of the United States*. New York: Macmillan.

Berkin. Carol. 2003. *A Brilliant Solution: Inventing the American Constitution*. Harcourt.

Bowler, Shaun and Todd Donovan. 2001. *Demanding Choices and Direct Democracy*. University of Michigan Press.

Breyer, Stephen. 2006. *Active Liberty: Interpreting our Democratic Constitution*.

Dicey, Robert A. and Albert Venn. 1895. *Law of the Constitution*. 9th Edition, 1950. London: MacMillan.

Gerber, Douglas. 1995. *To Secure These Rights: The Declaration of Independence and Constitutional Interpretation*. New York: New York University Press.

Holton, Woody Holton. 2007. *Unruly Americans and the Origins of the Constitution*. New York: Hill and Wang.

Ketcham, Ralph. 2003. *The Anti-Federalist Papers and the Constitutional Convention Debates*. Signet Classics.

Kyvig, David E. 1998. *Explicit and Authentic Acts: Amending the U.S. Constitution, 1776- 1995*. University Press of Kansas.

Maier, Pauline. 1997. *American Scripture: Making the Declaration of Independence.* New York: Knopf.

---

[1] A repository of these historical documents is available at http://avalon.law.yale.edu/

[2] See, for example, *A Workable Government? The Constitution after 200 Years*. 1987. Ed. by Burke Marshall. New York: W.W. Norton & Company; *Reforming American Government: The Bicentennial Papers of the Committee on the Constitutional System.*1985. Ed. by Donald L. Robinson. Boulder, CO: Westview Press.

[3] Letter to James Madison," (September 6, 1789) In *The Papers of Thomas Jefferson*, Edited by Julian P. Boyd, et al. Princeton: Princeton University Press. 1950.
http://press-pubs.uchicago.edu/founders/documents/v1ch2s23.html

CHAPTER 3: CONGRESS

3.0 | Congress

Is Congress the Broken Branch of Government? Congress *is* the government institution that everyone loves to hate. Congress has been called the broken branch of government because nothing seems to make the Congress less capable of action than the need for action. Why? In the 19th Century, the Senate was considered the greatest deliberative body in the world. Today, Congress still debates issues but the quality of the debates rarely rises to the level of greatness. And congressional speeches are often delivered to an empty chamber—but one with a camera focused on the speaker. The way the modern Congress works, or does not work, exposes Congress to the charge that it is a perfectly good 19th Century institution!

The main purpose of this chapter is to explain the role Congress plays in the modern system of government. The chapter focuses on the following issues:

- The **Power** Problem with Congress: more accountability than effectiveness?
- The **Functions** of Congress. How Congress's role has changed over time.
- The **Organization** of Congress. How bicameralism, the committee system, and the party structure, affect the congressional decision making processes.

Information about the functions of Congress, the organization of Congress, and the members of the House of Representatives and the Senate is available at the following website: http://www.usa.gov/Agencies/Federal/Legislative.shtml

3.1 | The Power Problem

The power problem is the need to **grant** government enough power to effectively address the problems that people expect government to solve, while also **limiting** power so that it can be held accountable. A successful government is one that strikes the right balance between granting and limiting power. The main power problem with Congress is effectiveness: Congress is often unable to get anything done. Congress has been called "the broken branch" of government because the public (and many political scientists) consider it an inefficient or ineffective institution. Congress has plenty of critics. Public opinion polls generally reflect that the public does not hold Congress in very high regard because Congress does not seem to be making much headway toward solving the nation's problems. Public confidence in Congress as an effective institution is not high. The reasons for this criticism of Congress can be traced to its organization and operation. Congress is not designed to be an especially effective institution. It is designed as a representative institution where different interests and perspectives are represented, and decision-making requires negotiating, bargaining, and compromise. These democratic values (representation, bargaining, and compromise) are sometimes at odds with effective or decisive action.

CONFIDENCE IN CONGRESS
(% OF THOSE INDICATING A GREAT DEAL AND QUITE A LOT)

GALLUP 2010 Confidence Poll; "Now I am going to read you a list of institutions in American society. Please tell me how much confidence you, yourself, have in each one -- a great deal, quite a lot, some, or a little.

Are members of Congress smarter than tenth graders? A study of congressional speeches on the floor of the House and Senate concluded that the level of speech was at the tenth grade level— *and declining*! Descriptions of "sophomoric" talk do not instill public confidence in Congress.

Think about it! Are members of Congress sophomoric? Are they smarter than a 5th grader? Analysis shows they *talk* like 10th graders.
http://www.npr.org/blogs/itsallpolitics/2012/05/21/153024432/sophomoric-members-of-congress-talk-like-10th-graders-analysis-shows

3.2 | Change over Time

Congress' role in the U.S. system of government has changed a great deal over time. Congress does not play the same role that it did during the founding era. The Founders made Congress **the** law-making branch of the federal government. Article I Section I of the Constitution provides that "all legislative Powers herein granted shall be vested in a Congress of the United States, which shall consist of a Senate and House of Representatives." Congress was intended to be the *first branch* of government in the sense that it was intended to be the primary branch of the federal government. Congress was the most powerful (and therefore also the most dangerous) branch of government.

The political experiences of the Founders made it logical for them to create a political system where the legislative branch was most powerful. The Revolutionary War was fought against a monarchy. Many of the Founders remained wary of executive power. And the Founders believed that the legislative branch was more democratic, that it was a republican or representative institution during a time when republican or representative government seemed to be the wave of the future. Representative government was considered modern, one of the then-recent advances in the "science" of good government.

The Founders did not create three branches of government with equal power. The legislative, executive, and judicial branches were created equal in the sense that they have the same constitutional status. The Founders created a system of legislative government, not executive government or judicial government. But as the U.S. political system developed, the presidency accumulated a great deal of power in absolute terms and relative to Congress. Congress is still the **first** branch but it is not necessarily the **primary** branch of government. The modern system has developed into a political system based on executive governance rather than legislative governance.

This change has occurred over time. The 19th Century was the golden age of representative assemblies as governing bodies. The 20th Century was not kind to representative assemblies which lost favor to executive government—particularly parliamentary systems headed by prime ministers—in most countries of the world. The decline of congressional power relative to the president is certainly one of the most importance changes in the way the U.S. system of government works. Congress is no longer "the central institution" of the national government.[1] Congress is still a powerful institution. Compared to the representative assemblies in many other countries, Congress is a powerful institution because it plays both a lawmaking and a representative role. In most modern parliamentary systems, the representative body (the parliament) is largely limited to representation, with a prime minister who actually governs the country and makes policy for the nation.

Congress still performs many important functions, but its primary role, to be the lawmaker for the nation, has diminished. The modern Congress focuses less on making laws for the nation and more on **representation** and **oversight** of the administration. Representation of constituents (i.e., individuals in the district or state) and organized interests is a very important function of individual members of Congress and Congress as an institution. The importance of legislative oversight of the administration (and the bureaucracy) has increased as Congress has delegated more and more power to the president and the size of the federal bureaucracy has increased. But the president has taken the lead in many areas of public policy making—particularly global affairs such as national defense and foreign policy but also areas of domestic policy such as fiscal policy (the setting of budget priorities).

Congress lost power relative to the executive for a broad range of reasons. One of the general reasons is related to the nature of power in the U.S. system of government. Power is dynamic, not static. It is not a solid or fixed quantity. It is more like a liquid that flows to wherever it seems to be most effective. Power will flow to whichever *level* or government (national or state) seems more effective at addressing the problems facing the nation. And power will flow to whichever *branch* of government (legislative, executive, or judicial) which seems most effective. Or power will flow to the private sector if the public considers the private sector more effective at solving a problem than the public sector. Today, the general public sees the president as the nation's leader because the presidency seems to be a more effective institution.

3.3 | The Separation of Powers

In order to describe the way Congress works today, and to understand its current role, it is necessary to understand how the separation of powers works today. The separation of powers doctrine does not provide for a watertight separation of legislative, executive, and judicial powers. Although the Constitution delegates to Congress *all* legislative powers, Congress is not the only government body that makes laws. According to the Congress website, "The legislative branch is the law making branch of the government made up of the Senate, the House of Representatives, and agencies that support Congress." Congress is the only source of federal statutes or legislation, but there are other kinds of law, including executive orders, executive agreements, administrative regulations, and even case law. Presidents *make law* when they sign executive orders. The Supreme Court *makes law* when it interprets what the Fourth Amendment prohibition against "unreasonable searches and seizures" actually means when police officers are investigating individuals who are suspected of crimes. And administrative agencies such as the Federal Communications Commission and the Internal Revenue Service *make laws* through rulemaking actions that define indecency or determine whether a religious organization should be granted tax exempt status.

Just as the executive and judicial branches have some lawmaking powers, Congress also has powers over the other branches. The House of Representatives controls **appropriations** or the budget. Without funding, the other branches – particularly the executive branch – are hamstringed in their ability to act. The House also has the power of **impeachment**, or the formal charging of a government official with treason, bribery, other high crimes and misdemeanors. The Senate then acts as a court for the impeachment, with the Chief Justice of the Supreme Court presiding. The Senate also has the power to approve (or fail to approve) the most important of the presidential appointments, including federal judgeships, ambassadorships, and cabinet level posts. The Senate also approves all treaties. Congress also has the power to declare war.

3.4 | Constitutional Powers

Congress has two types of constitutional powers: enumerated powers and implied powers. **Enumerated powers** are those that are specifically mentioned. Enumerated powers are sometimes called delegated powers because they are powers that the Constitution actually delegates to government. **Implied powers** are those that are not specifically mentioned but which can be logically implied to flow from those that are enumerated.

3.41 | *Enumerated Powers*

The following are some of the enumerated powers granted in Article I, Section 8:

"The Congress shall have power
to lay and collect taxes, duties, imposts and excises, to pay the debts and provide for the common defense and general welfare of the United States; but all duties, imposts and excises shall be uniform throughout the United States;

To borrow money on the credit of the United States;

To regulate commerce with foreign nations, and among the several states, and with the Indian tribes;

To establish a uniform rule of naturalization, and uniform laws on the subject of bankruptcies throughout the United States;

To coin money, regulate the value thereof, and of foreign coin, and fix the standard of weights and measures;

To establish post offices and post roads;

To promote the progress of science and useful arts, by securing for limited times to authors and inventors the exclusive right to their respective writings and discoveries;

To constitute tribunals inferior to the Supreme Court;

To define and punish piracies and felonies committed on the high seas, and offenses against the law of nations;

To declare war, grant letters of marque and reprisal, and make rules concerning captures on land and water;

To raise and support armies, but no appropriation of money to that use shall be for a longer term than two years;

To provide and maintain a navy;

To make rules for the government and regulation of the land and naval forces;

To provide for calling forth the militia to execute the laws of the union, suppress insurrections and repel invasions; ... And

To make all laws which shall be necessary and proper for carrying into execution the foregoing powers, and all other powers vested by this Constitution in the government of the United States, or in any department or officer thereof."

> **Think about it!**
> Presidential nominees must be confirmed by the Senate. When was the last time the Senate rejected a presidential nominee to head an executive department? Or a Supreme Court nominee?
>
> http://www.senate.gov/artandhistory/history/common/briefing/Nominations.htm

3.42 | *Implied Powers*

Article I Section 8 is a list of Congress's enumerated powers. The list of specifically mentioned powers ends with the **necessary and proper** clause. (See above). The necessary and proper clause has been interpreted to mean that Congress can make "all laws which shall be necessary and proper" to achieve its enumerated powers. In effect, the necessary and proper clause gives Congress power to choose the means it considers necessary to achieve its legislative ends. For example, Congress has the enumerated power to raise an army, and the implied power to use a military draft to raise the army. Congress has enumerated power to regulate commerce and coin money, and the implied power to create the Federal Reserve System and the Department of the Treasury to perform these functions. The necessary and proper clause is sometimes called ***the elastic clause*** because it has been interpreted very broadly to allow Congress to choose the best means to accomplish its specifically mentioned powers.

The Supreme Court established the precedent for broadly interpreting the necessary and proper clause to give Congress implied powers in _McCulloch v. Maryland_ (1819). This landmark case involved a legal challenge to Congress' power to charter a national bank. Congress created a national bank. Maryland taxed the Baltimore branch of the national bank. The Supreme Court was asked to decide whether Congress had the power to create a national bank and whether a state could tax a branch of the bank. Chief Justice John Marshall ruled that the power to create a national bank was an implied power that flowed from Congress' delegated powers, including the power to regulate commerce. Congress could decide whether a national bank was a "necessary and proper" way to regulate commerce. Marshall, incidentally, was a prominent member of the Federalist Party, which supported a strong national government to promote economic development. The _McCulloch_ ruling established a precedent that the Court would broadly interpret the powers of Congress. As a result, Congress today legislates on many areas of public policy that are not actually mentioned in the Constitution as grants of power.

3.5 | What Does Congress Do?

Congress has four main roles or functions:

- **Lawmaking** for the nation (Legislating)

- **Representation** (of Constituents and Interests)

- **Legislative Oversight** (Investigating)

- **Constituency service** (Solving Constituent Problems)

3.51 | _Law-making for the nation_

The Constitution delegates all legislative power to Congress. It therefore is the only branch of government that can "make laws." Both the House and the Senate must pass a bill for it to become a law but they have different roles in the law making process. For instance, tax bills must originate in the House of Representatives. This provision of the Constitution reflects the Founders' belief that decisions to tax the people should originate with the government institution that was closest to the people. The members of the House are closer to the people than members of the Senate. Members of the House are directly elected by the people to serve two-year terms. The members of the Senate were originally chosen by state legislatures and served six-year terms.

3.52 | Representation

Congress is a representative institution. The members of the House and Senate are elected representatives of the people. Congress is institutionally designed to represent geographic districts. In the House of Representatives, the legislative districts are 435 geographic areas with about 650,000 people in each district. In the Senate, the districts are the 50 states. Representation is not limited to geography. Members of Congress also represent individuals and organized interests. In a large, populous nation such as the United States, representative institutions increase *political efficacy*. Political efficacy is the belief that it is possible for a person to participate effectively in government and politics. Representative institutions are one of the ways that government is designed to be responsive to public demands and interests. Efficacy is related to the belief that individuals and organizations can have an impact on government. In the U.S. system of republican government, congress is the institution that is designed to represent the people, deliberate on public policy options, and enact make laws for the nation.

There are three theories of representation: the **delegate** theory; the **trustee** theory; and the **politico** theory. The delegate theory is that members of Congress *should* act as instructed delegates of their constituents. According to this theory, elected representatives are not free agents: representatives have a political obligation to do what their constituents want. A legislator who votes on bills based strictly on public opinion polls from the district, for example, is acting as a delegate. The trustee theory is that members of Congress *should* do what they think is in the best interest of their constituents. According to this theory, elected representatives are free agents: they can vote according to what they think is right or best regardless of public opinion in the district. A trustee uses his or her judgment when deciding how to vote on a bill, for example. A trustee does not feel obligated to vote based on public opinion polls from the district.

Studies of Congress indicate that legislators are not typically either delegates or trustees. The **politico** theory of representation suggests that representatives *are* rational actors whose voting behavior reflects the delegate or trustee theory of representation depending on the situation.

Members of Congress are expected to represent their districts. The representation of districts includes representing individuals and organized constituents such as business interests that are located in the district. Members from agricultural districts are expected to represent agricultural interests. Members from urban districts are expected to represent urban interests. Members from manufacturing districts are expected to represent manufacturing interests, and members from districts where mining, forestry, or other natural resource interests are located are expected to represent those interests. Where one industry is especially important to a district, particularly in the House of When one interest is the dominant interest in a districts, a representative may be strongly identified with that single interest. For example, Congressman Norm Dicks represents Washington State's 6th Congressional District. The 6th District includes Tacoma's port district, the Puget Sound Naval Yard and other military installations, and a number of defense contractors. One of the companies, Boeing, which is the world's largest aerospace manufacturer, was headquartered in Washington State until it relocated to Chicago.

Representative Dicks serves on three key House Appropriations Subcommittees dealing with defense, Interior and the Environment, and Military Construction/Veterans. Representative Dicks' came to be called "The Representative from Boeing" because of his strong advocacy for Boeing. His representation of American Defense Contractors included strong opposition to the U.S. military's decision to award a major defense contract to build the new generation of airplane refueling tankers to a European and American consortium of airplane builders.

3.53 | *Constituency Service*

The third congressional role is related to representation. Constituency service is helping constituents solve problems that they may have with the government. All the Web sites of the members of the House of Representatives prominently list constituency service as one of the things that the member of congress does for the individuals or organizations in the district. Members of Congress maintain offices in their districts to help solve constituent problems: getting government benefits such as Social Security checks; getting Veteran's services; problems with government regulations of business; or who have kinds of problems or issues that constituents have with the government. This constituency *casework* often involves helping individuals or organizations cut through government red tape or bureaucratic procedures.

> **Act on It!**
> **Contact a member of congress, your representative, or one of your senators and ask them about a political issue of concern to you. How can you find a member of congress?**
> Go to the www.usa.gov
> Click on Legislative Branch
> Select House of Representatives or Senate
> Go to the Home Page and enter your zip code.

3.54 | *Legislative Oversight*

The fourth congressional role is oversight. Congress's oversight role consists of two primary functions:

- Oversight of the Laws

- Investigation of Scandals

The first oversight function is oversight of the laws being administered or executed by the President and the bureaucracy. The oversight of the laws is important because although Congress passes laws, the executive branch or the bureaucracy administers or carries out or implements the laws. This means that the body that makes the laws does not actually implement them. Congress oversees the administration of the laws by conducting hearings to determine how public policy is being implemented, to determine whether the president is implementing the laws the way Congress intended, or to determine whether the law needs to be changed based on information about how it is working, especially whether it is working well or not. The main method of legislative oversight is through congressional hearings at which members of the executive branch or independent regulatory agencies may be called to testify about how they are carrying out the laws passed by Congress.

Congressional hearings are the principal formal method by which committees collect and analyze information in the early stages of legislative policymaking. But there are other kinds of hearings as well: confirmation hearings (for the Senate, not the House), legislative hearings, oversight hearings, investigative hearings, or a combination of them. Hearings usually include oral testimony from witnesses, and questioning of the witnesses by members of Congress.

There are several types of congressional hearings. Congressional Standing (or Policy) committees regularly hold legislative hearings on measures or policy issues that may become public law. Agriculture committees hold hearings on proposed legislation related to agriculture policy. Banking and financial services committees hold hearings on bills related to the financial services sector of the economy. The armed services committees hold hearings on legislative proposals related to national defense and the military. The health, education, and labor committees hold hearings on bills related to these aspects of domestic policy. Sometimes a committee holds hearings on several bills before deciding on one bill for further committee and chamber action. Hearings provide a forum where witnesses from a broad range of backgrounds can appear to provide facts and opinions to the committee members. The witnesses include members of Congress, other government officials, representatives of interest groups, academics or other experts, as well as individuals directly or indirectly affected by a proposed bill. Most congressional hearings are held in Washington, but field hearings are held outside Washington.

Oversight hearings are intended to review or study a law, a public policy issue, or an activity. Such hearings often focus on the quality of federal programs and the performance of government officials. Hearings are also one way for Congress to ensure that executive branch is implementing laws consistent with legislative intent. A significant part of a congressional committee's hearings workload is dedicated to oversight. Committee oversight hearings might include examination of gasoline price increases, lead paint on toys imported from China, the safety of the food supply in the wake of e. coli contamination, indecent programming broadcast over the television or radio airwaves, the government's response to natural disasters, terrorism preparedness, Medicare or Medicaid spending or access to health care, or matters related to crime policy.

The second oversight function is investigation of scandals. Investigative hearings are similar to legislative hearings and oversight hearings, but they are specifically convened to investigate when there is suspicion of wrongdoing on the part of public officials acting in their official capacity, or suspicion of private citizens whose activities or behavior may warrant a legislative remedy. Congress might conduct investigate hearings to get additional information about use of steroids in

professional sports such as baseball, or to determine whether tobacco companies are "spiking" the nicotine content in cigarettes or whether tobacco company executives think nicotine is addictive. Congress has broad power to investigate and it has used it since the earliest days of the republic. Some of its most famous investigative hearings are benchmarks in American political history:

- The Teapot Dome Scandal in the 1920s
- The Army-McCarthy Hearings during the Red Scare in the 1950s
- The Watergate scandal in the 1970s
- The Church Committee Hearings on the CIA and illegal intelligence gathering in the 1970s
- The Iran-Contra Affair Hearings in 1987
- The National Commission investigating the 9/11 terrorist attacks
- The National Commission investigating the financial crisis

Investigative hearings gather information and issue reports that are often used to pass legislation to address the problems that the hearings examined. The National Commission on Terrorist Attacks Upon the United States was created to "investigate the facts and circumstances" relating to the terrorist attacks. The National Commission's Report was used to increase coordination of intelligence about terrorism. The Financial Crisis Inquiry Report submitted by the National Commission on the Causes of the Financial and Economic Crisis in the United States in January 2011 included among its recommendations regulation of certain financial transactions.

Confirmation hearings on presidential nominations are held in fulfillment of the Senate's constitutional role to "advise and consent." Senate committees hold confirmation hearings on presidential nominations to executive and judicial positions within their jurisdiction. When the President nominates the head of an executive agency—such as the Secretary of State, Interior, Department of Homeland Security, or Defense—the Senate must confirm the nomination. The Senate also must confirm the president's nominees for federal judgeships.

Confirmation hearings offer an opportunity for oversight into the activities of the nominee's department or agency. The vast majority of confirmation hearings are routine, but some are controversial. The Senate may use the confirmation hearing of a nominee for Attorney General to examine how the Administration has been running the Department of Justice and provide some guidance on how the Senate would like the Department to function. The Constitution also requires that the Senate consent to the ratification of treaties negotiated by the executive branch with foreign governments. Arms control treaties have historically been controversial. Recently, the Senate used the ratification of the Strategic Arms Reduction Treaty between the U.S. and Russia to exert power over the executive branch and to influence the foreign policy choices of the President.[2] Therefore, hearings provide an opportunity for different points of view to be expressed as a matter of public record. So confirmation hearings are one of the ways that the Senate performs its constitutional responsibilities in an important area of public policy.

One of Congress' implied powers is the power to issue subpoenas and to hold individuals in contempt of Congress for not complying with demands to testify or provide requested information. Most of the time individuals welcome an invitation to testify before Congress because it can be a valuable opportunity to communicate, publicize, and advocate their positions on important public policy issues. However, if a person declines an invitation, a committee or subcommittee may require an appearance by issuing a subpoena.

Committees also may subpoena correspondence, books, papers, and other documents. Subpoenas are issued infrequently, and most often in the course of investigative hearings. The subpoena power is an implied power of Congress. Congress has the enumerated power to legislate, and hearings and subpoenas are implied powers that are logically related to Congress' need for information related to legislation it is considering. But when Congress requests records from the executive branch, the president cite executive privilege as a constitutional power to refuse to give Congress the information it requests during an oversight investigation. In 2012, the <u>House Oversight and Government Reform Committee</u> demanded records related to Operation "Fast and Furious," a Bureau of Alcohol, Tobacco, Firearms and Explosives sting operation that was intended to track illegal gun running on the Mexican border. The operation lost track of guns that it had provided, and the guns ended up in the possession of a Mexican drug cartel. Congress demanded information about the program and how it went wrong.

House Oversight of Operation "Fast and Furious"

http://www.pbs.org/newshour/bb/law/jan-june12/holder_06-20.html

3.6 | Lawmaking, Representation, or Oversight?

Today, Congress devotes more time to representation and oversight and less time making laws for the nation. This shift has occurred more in some areas of public policy than in others. In foreign affairs and national security, for example, Congress generally follows the president's lead in formulating public policy. In domestic affairs, Congress typically exerts more influence over public policy. As individual members of Congress pay more attention to representation, oversight, and constituency service, they pay less attention to law making for the nation. As a result, Congress as an institution also focuses less on its traditional lawmaking role. This change is reflected in the congressional work schedule. Today's Congress spends much less time in session. For an interesting perspective by a member of the House of Representatives who left Congress and then returned after 33 years, listen to Congressman Rick Nolan's (Democrat-Minnesota) thoughts about why Congress no longer works (well).

Think About It! How does Congress work?

http://www.npr.org/2013/02/12/171837291/congressman-returning-after-33-years-says-congress-works-and-cooperates-less-now

3.7 | The Internal Organization of Congress

How an institution is organized affects *what* it does. The three most important aspects of the way Congress is organized are bicameralism, the committee system, and the party system.

3.71 | *Bicameralism*

Congress is a bicameral or two-house body. Bicameralism is part of the system of checks and balances and part of the functional differences in legislative governance. The House of Representatives and the Senate have different sizes, roles, and rules of operation. The House is larger and therefore has more formal rules of operation to govern debate. The Senate is smaller and relies more on informal rules, a tradition of open debate (including the infamous filibuster), and personal relationships. In order for a bill to become a law it must pass both houses of Congress—a fact that makes lawmaking in bicameral bodies much more complicated than in unicameral bodies.

3.72 | *The Committee System*

The key to understanding how Congress works is the committee system. Congress does most of its work in committees. The committee system is a form of division of labor. Most modern organizations operate with a system of division of labor where individuals are assigned different tasks in order to take advantage of specialization or expertise. The standing committees in Congress are an example of specialization. The jurisdiction of congressional committees such as the House of Representatives committee on agriculture, the committee on education and labor, the committee on financial services, and the committee on foreign affairs reflects their area of legislative expertise and authority. There are four basic kinds of committees: **standing committees, joint committees, conference committee,** and **select or special committees.** The House of Representatives committee system and the Senate committee system are similar but each body creates its own committee system.

- **Standing** committees are the most prominent of the committees. These are the permanent committees that focus on specific area of legislation, such as the House Committee on Homeland Security or the Senate Committee on Armed Forces. The majority of the day-to-day work in Congress occurs in these standing committees. Generally, sixteen to twenty members serve on each committee in Senate and thirty-one members serve on committees in the House. The majority party determines the number of committee members from each party on each committee, which ensures that the majority party will have the majority of committee members. Standing committees also have a variety of **subcommittees** that cover more precise subsections of the legislative issues addressed by the committee. Generally, subcommittee members have considerable leeway in shaping the content of legislation.
- **Joint** committees have members from the House and the Senate and are concerned with specific policy areas. These committees are set up as a way to expedite business between the houses, particularly when pressing issues require quick action by Congress.
- **Conference** committees are created to reconcile differences between the House and Senate versions of a bill. The conference committee is made up of members from both the House and the Senate who work to reach compromises between similar pieces of legislation passed by the House and the Senate.
- **Select** or special committees are temporary committees that serve only for a very specific purpose. These committees conduct special investigations or studies and report back to whichever chamber established the committee.

Senate Committee Hearing on the Banking Industry Subprime Mortgage
Crisis

3.73 | *The Political Party System*

The third organization characteristic that is essential for understanding how Congress
operates is the party system. The House and the Senate are organized differently but both
houses have party leadership structures. The **majority party** is the party with the most
seats; the **minority party** is the party with second number of seats. The majority party in
each house organizes the sessions of Congress and selects its leadership. The majority
party in the House of Representatives selects the Speaker of the House and the majority
party in the Senate choses the Majority Leader. The House of Representatives leaders are
chosen by the members of the House. The Senate leaders are chosen by the members of
the Senate.

Leadership in the House of Representatives

MAJORITY LEADER

COMMITTEE ON
RULES

MINORITY LEADER

MAJORITY WHIP

REPUBLICAN
STEERING
COMMITTEE

DEMOCRATIC
POLICY COMMITTEE

MINORITY WHIP

REPUBLICAN
CONGRESSIONAL
CAMPAIGN
COMMITTEE

DEMOCRATIC
CONGRESSIONAL
CAMPAIGN
COMMITTEE

REPUBLICAN
CONFERENCE

DEMOCRATIC
CAUCUS

The House is a much larger body than the Senate therefore the House relies more heavily on formal rules to function. Loyalty to the party organization, party leadership, and voting along party lines are also all more common in the House than in the Senate. The most powerful position in the House of Representatives is the **Speaker of the House,** which is the only leadership position in the House that is created by the Constitution. The Speaker is a member of the majority party and is elected by their party to oversee House business, interact with the Senate and the President, and is the second in line of presidential succession. In addition to the Speaker, the House leadership includes majority and minority leaders; majority and minority whips; party policy committees that the Republicans call a Steering Committee and Democrats call a Democratic Policy Committee; Republican and Democratic congressional campaign committees; and the Republican Conference and Democratic Caucus.

The Senate's presiding officer is determined by the Constitution, which sets forth that the vice-president of the United States is the ranking officer of the Senate. The vice-president is not a member of the Senate, so he votes only in the case of a tie. The **president pro tempore**, or the official chair of the Senate, is a largely honorary position awarded to the most senior senator of the majority party. The leader with power in the Senate is the majority leader, who is elected to their position by their party. The Senate, with far fewer members than the House, is a more causal organization that relies much less on formal structures of power for organization. As such, the majority party leader in the Senate has less power than the Speaker of the House. The Senate also lacks a rule committee, but has a largely similar structure to the House, in terms of the positions of power within each party.

LEADERSHIP IN THE SENATE

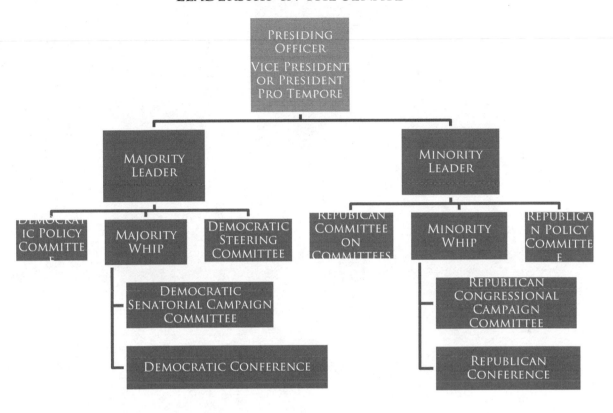

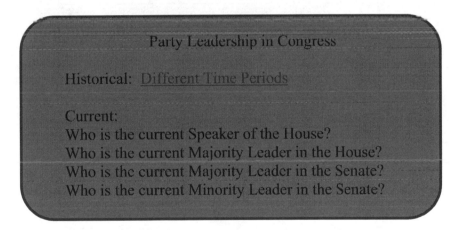

Party Leadership in Congress

Historical: Different Time Periods

Current:
Who is the current Speaker of the House?
Who is the current Majority Leader in the House?
Who is the current Majority Leader in the Senate?
Who is the current Minority Leader in the Senate?

3.8 | How a Bill Becomes a Law

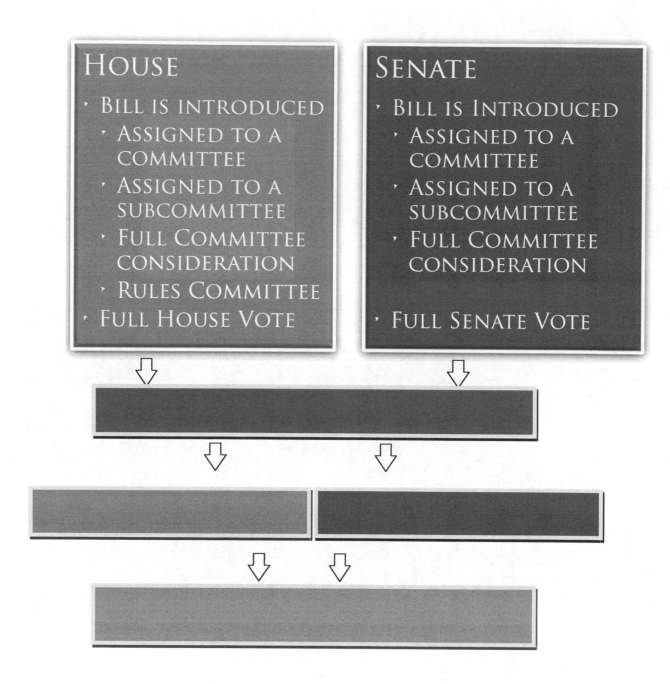

HOUSE
- BILL IS INTRODUCED
- ASSIGNED TO A COMMITTEE
- ASSIGNED TO A SUBCOMMITTEE
- FULL COMMITTEE CONSIDERATION
- RULES COMMITTEE
- FULL HOUSE VOTE

SENATE
- BILL IS INTRODUCED
- ASSIGNED TO A COMMITTEE
- ASSIGNED TO A SUBCOMMITTEE
- FULL COMMITTEE CONSIDERATION
- FULL SENATE VOTE

The process by which Congress makes legislation is complex and drawn out, involving a series of procedural steps that have been institutionalized overtime. The first formal step in either the House of Representatives or the Senate is to introduce the bill for consideration in the legislative body. The bill is introduced and assigned to a committee for consideration; once in the committee, the bill is assigned to an appropriate subcommittee. The subcommittee will study the bill, hold hearings for those individuals and interest groups concerned with the bill, and debate and edit provisions of the bill. The subcommittee sends the bill back to the full committee, who votes on whether to send the bill to the full House or Senate for consideration. In the House (and *only* in the House), the bill is then sent to the House Rules committee, where the rules governing debate and amendments on the bill are decided. Both the House and the Senate debate and vote on the bill. If the bills considered by the House and Senate differ, the bills are sent to a Conference committee, which crafts a single bill that both houses of Congress will find acceptable. The bill from the Conference committee is then sent back to both the House and the Senate for a final vote. If the bill passes both houses, the legislation is sent to the president for either approval (through signing) or a veto. If the president vetoes a bill, a two-third vote by both the House and the Senate can override the veto.

3.81 | *Sessions of Congress*

A term of Congress is divided into two sessions, one for each year. Congress has occasionally also been called into an extra or special session. A new session commences on January 3 (or another date, if Congress so chooses) each year.

> Think the Senate doesn't have a sense of humor? Senate history, art, and political cartoons are available at the Senate website:
> http://www.senate.gov/pagelayout/art/g_three_sections_with_teasers/exhibits.htm

3.82 | *Finding Legislation*

How can I find a federal law? Congress legislates on an extremely broad range of subjects ranging from domestic policy (clean air, clean water, obscenity or indecency on radio or television or the Internet, crime, health care) to foreign affairs (international trade, defense policy). One way to find a federal law is through http://thomas.loc.gov/. Select Multiple Previous Congresses; select Bill Summary Status; select Congress (of your choice); select Advance Search; type in search phrase (e.g. Venezuela, for legislation related to that country); select date, or date range; and hit search.

3.9 | **Additional Resources**

3.91 | *INTERNET RESOURCES*

A user friendly website for information about Congress is http://www.opencongress.org/

In order to get a sense of how important constituency service is to members of Congress, visit the website of your congressional representative or the site of another member of the House of Representative: http://www.house.gov/house/MemberWWW.shtml

Information about the organization, functions, and workings of Congress is available at http://www.usa.gov/Agencies/Federal/Legislative.shtml, http://www.house.gov/house/MemberWWW.shtml, and http://www.senate.gov/

The first C-SPAN coverage of the Senate occurred on June 2, 1986. The video, "Twenty-five Years of C-SPAN2 Coverage," is available at http://www.c-spanvideo.org/videoLibrary/blog/?p=834

The *Washington Post*'s "Today in Congress" section including committee hearings and votes. www.washingtonpost.com

3.92 | *IN THE LIBRARY*

Arnold, R. Douglas. 2006. *Congress, the Press, and Public Accountability*. Princeton University Press.

Dodd, Lawrence and Bruce Oppenheimer (eds). 2001. *Congress Reconsidered*, 7th ed. Congressional Quarterly.

Mayhew, David. 2000. *America's Congress*. Yale University Press.

O'Connor, Karen (ed). 2002. *Women and Congress: Running, Winning, Ruling*. Haworth.

Tate, Katherine. 2003. *Black Faces in the Mirror: African Americans and their Representatives in the U.S. Congress*. Princeton University Press.

TERMS:

Appropriations
Impeachment
Enumerated powers
Implied powers
Necessary and proper
Clause
Delegate
Trustee
Politico
Majority party
Minority party
Speaker of the House
President pro tempore
Standing committees
Joint committees
Conference committee
Select or special committees
Legislative oversight
Constituency service

STUDY QUESTIONS

1) Discuss the powers of Congress and the differences between the House and Senate.
2) What are the constitutional powers of Congress?
3) What roles do political parties play in the organization of Congress?
4) To what extent do the various leadership positions in the House and Senate make some leaders more powerful than others?
5) Describe a typical day of a member of Congress.
6) How representative is Congress? Discuss both the theories of representation and the demographic make-up of Congress. How has this changed over time?
7) What is the traditional process by which a bill becomes a law?
8) How can Congress exercise oversight of the executive branch? Have recent congresses taken this responsibility seriously enough?

---

[1] Theodore J. Lowi and Ginsberg, Benjamin (1996). *American Government.* Fourth Edition. New York: W.W. Norton & Company. p. 153.

[2] http://dosfan.lib.uic.edu/acda/treaties/salt2-1.htm

CHAPTER 4: THE PRESIDENCY

4.0 | Introduction

When the American public thinks of the presidency, they think of the President—the person whose name, face, character, and personality are prominently featured during the presidential campaign, and the person who upon taking office dominates media coverage of the federal government. The President *personifies* the government. The personal nature of the Presidency is reflected in the fact that Article II of the Constitution provides that "The executive Power shall be vested in a President of the United states of America." The modern President personifies the federal government. But the modern presidency is actually a vast institution that consists of a large number of offices, executive departments, and agencies. The presidency consists of an *individual* and an *office*. Understanding the role of the presidency in modern American government and politics requires learning about both the *President*, the individual who happens to occupy the Office of the President of the United States, and the *presidency*, the institution.

This chapter examines three main issues that are central to the presidency:

- The power problem: Accountability.
- The increase in presidential power: Presidential government?
- Management of the executive branch: Controlling the bureaucracy.

4.1 | The Power Problem

The power problem is the difficulty of striking that delicate balance between granting government enough power to be effective while also limiting power so that the people can hold government accountable. The power problem for Congress is on the effectiveness side of the scale. Congress is institutionally designed for representation of interests and deliberation; it is not designed for decisive, effective action. The power problem for the presidency is on the accountability side of the scale. The concentration of executive power in the hands of one individual or office may increase effectiveness, but the nature of modern presidential power makes it hard to hold presidents legally accountable for their use of power. The nature of the presidency, the discretionary nature of presidential power, and the fact that much of a President's political power is *personal* make it hard to hold a President legally accountable for the use of government power.

George Washington
1st President of the United States
(1789-1797)

4.12 | Is the Presidency Imperial or Imperiled?

The rule of law is a principle that is so widely accepted as the appropriate standard for evaluating government that it is considered part of the American "creed." Virtually all civics courses and introductions to American government contrast political systems based on the rule of law with those based on the rule of man. The rule of law is defined as the principle that governmental authority is legitimately exercised only in accordance with written, publicly disclosed laws adopted and enforced in accordance with established procedure. The rule of law principle is intended to be a safeguard against arbitrary governance by requiring that those who make and enforce the law are also bound by it. As the following description of presidential power indicates, the modern exercise of presidential power is difficult to reconcile with this principle.

4.13 | *INCREASED POWER*

Best Presidents	*Worst Presidents*
1. Lincoln	1. Buchanan
2. F. Roosevelt	2. A. Johnson
3. Washington	3. Pierce
4. T. Roosevelt	4. Harding
5. Truman	5. W. Harrison

Source: C-SPAN Survey of Historians on Presidential Leadership

The power of the president has greatly increased over time, and that the increased power of the president has presented some challenges. The modern presidency is much more powerful than the Founders intended it to be. For example, Abraham Lincoln did not aspire to be president. His ambition was to serve in the Senate. The great leaders of the day, men like Henry Clay, Daniel Webster, and John C. Calhoun, served in the Senate which was then the "greatest deliberative body in the world." The antebellum presidency was by contrast "a mundane administrative job that offered little to a man of Lincoln's oratorical abilities."[1] The modern president is not only more powerful than the president was in the early years of the republic but the modern president is more powerful relative to Congress. The Founders created a system of government that was based on legislative governance in the sense that Congress was intended to be the primary branch of government. The modern system of government has actually developed into a political system that works more like presidential or executive government. The presidency has become the primary branch of government, the most powerful branch of government with more authority over more areas of public policy than was the case when the country was founded. Presidential power increased for a variety of reasons. One reason is crises, both domestic and foreign, wars, and other threats to national security, concentrated power in the presidency because it was designed to act with greater speed than the other branches of government.

The increased power of the president has caused political scientists to regularly take the pulse of the presidency to determine whether it is too strong, too weak, or just about right. The term **Imperial Presidency** is used to refer to presidents who are too strong, too powerful for our own good. The term **Imperiled Presidency** is used to refer to presidents who are too weak, not powerful enough to govern effectively. In the 1960s, the increased power of the presidency caused some concern. The term Imperial Presidency was coined to describe a presidency that had grown too powerful, and resembled a monarchy insofar as it was becoming hard to control.[2] The Imperial label was initially applied to the presidencies of Lyndon Johnson (1963-1968) and Richard Nixon (1969-1974).

The Imperiled Presidency label was initially applied to the presidencies of Gerald Ford (1973-1976) and Jimmy Carter (1977-1980). President Ford seemed incapable of responding effectively to the economic crises caused by the OPEC oil embargo. The Organization of the Petroleum Exporting Countries oil embargo caused energy price increases and inflation.[3] The Ford administration's response to the threat included distributing "WIN" buttons, but the Whip Inflation Now buttons seemed a pathetically weak response to the economic threat of gas shortages. President Carter seemed incapable of responding effectively to national security threats. The Soviet invasion of Afghanistan in 1978 and the anti-American Iranian Revolution of

1979, which included taking of American hostages in Iran created the impression that the presidency had become too weak to respond strongly to these international threats.

40TH

<u>Ronald Reagan</u> campaigned for the presidency pledging to return to a stronger presidency, and his election as president (1981-1988) marked a return to a strong presidency with confidence in American leadership in foreign affairs and national security. However, Reagan's successor, George H. W. Bush (Bush the Elder or "41"), who served from 1989 to 1992, renewed concerns about an imperiled presidency. Ironically, Bill Clinton's tenure in office (1993-2000) raised questions about both an imperial and an imperiled presidency. Since the 9/11 terrorist attacks, President George W. Bush's (the Younger, "43," 2001-2008) tenure has renewed questions about an imperial presidency. The fact that presidential power seems so dynamic, subject to so much fluctuation, and evaluated so differently in terms of whether a strong president is good or bad, illustrates the difficulty assessing the role the modern president plays in the U.S. system of government.

4.2 | Presidential Power

One of the main questions debated during the constitutional convention of 1787 was whether the new government should have a single executive official. The recent memory of the Revolutionary War fought against monarchy made delegates to the constitutional convention wary of executive power. But the constitutional convention was called to remedy defects in the Articles of Confederation, one of which was the lack of an executive figure. The extended debate over executive power concluded with the creation of an executive office with considerable power and considerable checks and balances.

The president has both *legal* (or formal) powers and *political* (or informal) powers. The following is a diagram of presidential powers.

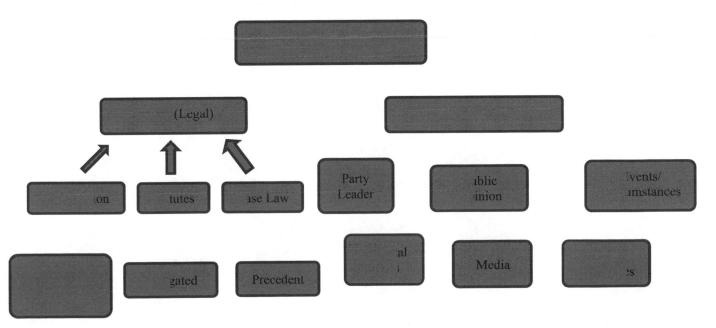

The legal powers are provided in the Constitution, statutes, and case law. The president's *constitutional* powers are set forth in Article II. Compared to Article I, which sets forth congress' powers, Article II is a short and general article. The statement that "the executive Power shall be vested in a President" is followed by brief descriptions of how the president is selected, who is eligibility to serve as president, a statement that the president is commander-in-chief, and a description of the president's appointment and treaty making powers. The president's *statutory* powers are extensive. As described below, congress has delegated broad powers to the president which greatly supplement the president's constitutional powers. The president's *case law* powers are based on court rulings, primarily Supreme Court precedents. One of the most intriguing aspects of presidential power is the fact that the president's formal constitutional powers have changed very little since the founding of the republic but presidential power has changed a great deal. The major changes have occurred in the president's statutory powers, case law powers, and in the political powers.

4.21| *The Legal Sources*

In order to understand the presidency, it is very important to recognize the difference between legal and political powers. In fact, the difference is one of the keys to explaining the modern presidency. The President's constitutional powers have remained surprisingly constant (or steady) for more than 200 years. In fact, the major amendment affecting presidential power is the 22nd Amendment and it actually reduced presidential power by limiting a president to serving two full terms in office—thereby making a President a lame duck as soon as the second term begins.

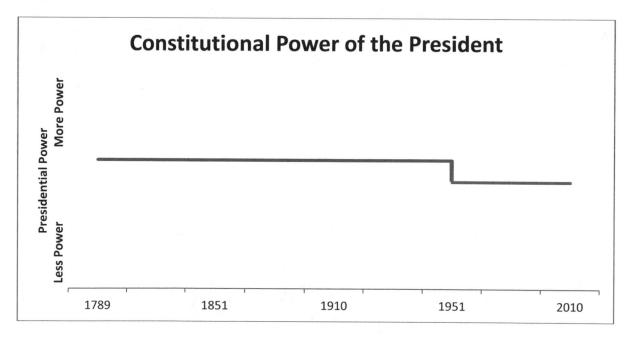

But presidential power has increased a great deal since the founding of the republic, *and* presidential power fluctuates considerably from one president to another. What does the static nature of the president's constitutional powers and the dynamic nature of presidential power say about presidential power? It suggests that the key to understanding changes in presidential power are developments in statutory and case law as well as politics.

4.22 | *The Article II Constitutional Power*

Presidents claim three kinds of constitutional powers: enumerated, implied, and inherent powers. The delegated powers are the least controversial. **Enumerated** powers are those that are actually mentioned or enumerated in the Constitution in Article II. The enumerated powers make the president the chief executive and Commander in Chief; give the president power to veto legislation, grant pardons, and make treaties and appoint ambassadors and other government officials including Supreme Court justices; and provide that the president shall from time to time report to Congress on the state of the union as well as to *"take Care that the Laws be faithfully executed, and shall Commission all the Officers of the United States."*

Some of these enumerated powers are shared with Congress. Treaties must be ratified by the Senate. Supreme Court appointments (and some other high level executive appoints such as the secretaries of the executive departments) must be confirmed by the Senate. The power of appointment provides a president with an extremely important role in the administration of the federal government. The President nominates the heads of the 15 Executive Departments, federal judges, and other government officials such as the head of the Federal Reserve Board. The Senate, however, must confirm a nominee in order for the person to be appointed as Secretary of Defense, Secretary of State, Attorney General, or Supreme Court Justice.

Implied powers are those that are not actually mentioned in the Constitution, but which are logically related to them. Implied powers are more controversial that enumerated powers because they are not actually mentioned, but merely implied. The following are examples of implied powers of the president.

- Firing. If the president has the enumerated power to appoint an official, then it is implied that the president also has the power to fire that official. The power to fire is considered a power that is logically related to the chief executive responsibility to manage the executive branch.
- Executive Privilege. Executive privilege is a president's power to refuse to disclose communications with his subordinates. The Supreme Court has recognized that this power exists in order to ensure that a president receives candid advice about public policy matters. Executive privilege limits the power of Congress or the courts to compel the president or his subordinates or advisors to disclose communications.
- Executive Agreements. Executive Agreements are international agreements between the leaders of countries. Executive agreements function like treaties but they do not require senate ratification, therefore the president' control over executive agreements is greater than control over treaties. The Supreme Court has ruled that the president's constitutional power over foreign affairs implies the power to enter into executive agreements.
- Executive Orders. An executive order is a presidential directive, usually issued to an executive branch official, which provides specific guidelines on how a policy is to be implemented. Executive orders are a way for the president to manage the executive

branch. In effect, executive orders are a form of law or policy making by the executive branch.

The most controversial kind of presidential power is **inherent** power. Inherent powers are not actually mentioned in the Constitution or even implied from enumerated powers. Inherent powers are powers that Presidents claim as inherent in the office, powers that the President has simply because the President is the President. Presidents have historically claimed that they have the power to do something (e.g., use military force) simply because they are President. The argument for inherent powers is that certain powers are inherent in the office and therefore do not require any specific legal authorization.[4] The inherent powers doctrine is controversial because it is practically impossible to hold Presidents legally accountable if they can claim that their actions do not need legal authorization.

4.23 | *Statutory Powers*

The president's powers are not limited to those that can be traced to the Constitution. The president also has statutory powers. Congress has delegated a broad range of powers to the president to act in domestic policy and foreign and national security affairs. Congress began delegating policy making powers to the president in the early years of the republic. During the 20th Century, Congress delegated so much policy making power to the president that political scientists refer to the modern president as the "chief legislator" because of the important role the president plays in the legislative process. The following list of statutory delegations to the president is merely a short list of congressional delegations of power to the president that shows how Congress has delegated to the president broad policymaking power in a broad range of areas.

4.24 | *Statutory Delegations*

Hostage Act of 1868.This 19th Century Act authorized the president to take "all actions necessary and proper, not amounting to war, to secure the release of hostages." It provided that the president may act quickly to secure the release of "any citizen of the United States has been unjustly deprived of his liberty by or under the authority of any foreign government." Furthermore, the president has the duty to attempt to secure the release of any hostage and can "use such means, not amounting to acts of war, as he may think necessary and proper to obtain or effectuate the release; and all the facts and proceedings relative thereto shall as soon as practicable be communicated by the president to Congress."[5]

Employment Act of 1946. This Act declared that it was the federal government's responsibility to manage the economy. It also delegated to the president the power "to foster and promote free competitive enterprise, to avoid economic fluctuations or to diminish the effects thereof, and to maintain employment, productivity, and purchasing power."[6] The Act was passed because of the significant increase in unemployment in the early 1930s and the perceived "planlessness" of economic policy.

Gulf of Tonkin Resolution (1964). This Act authorized the president "to take all necessary measures to repel any armed attack against the forces of the United States and to prevent further aggression." Congress gave the president a "blank check" to fight the war in Vietnam.[7]

Economic Stabilization Act of 1970. This Act authorized the president "to stabilize prices, rents, wages, and salaries by issuing orders and regulations he deems appropriate."[8]

Emergency Economic Stabilization Act of 2008. This Act authorized the president, acting through the secretary of the treasury, to spend up to $700 billion dollars to "rescue" or "bailout" distressed financial institutions.[9]

Authorizations for the Use of Military Force in Afghanistan and Iraq (2002) In response to the terrorist attacks on September 11, 2001, Congress authorized the president "to use all means that he deems appropriate, including the use of military force, in order to enforce the UN resolutions, defend the national security interests of the United States against the threat posed by Iraq, and restore international peace and security in the region."[10]

The cumulative effect of congressional delegations has been a great increase in the statutory powers of the president. Modern presidents have much more statutory power than early presidents. The chart below, "Statutory Powers of the President Over Time," describes the statutory powers of the president over time. The stepped increases indicate the statutory delegations of power.

Think about it!

Is it a good idea to give a president power to do "whatever he deems necessary" to solve a problem?

STATUTORY POWER OF THE PRESIDENT

4.24 | *Case Law Sources of Presidential Power*

A third legal source of presidential power is case law. Court rulings in cases involving presidential power are an important source of presidential power. The Supreme Court's rulings in cases involving national security and emergency powers are an especially important source of presidential power because the Court has generally supported an expansive reading of presidential power in these two circumstances. As a result, there is a large body of case law that supports presidential power. One of the most important case law precedents is *U.S. v. Curtiss-Wright Export Corporation* (1936). The case involved a major U.S. company in the business of selling weapons that challenged the President's power to issue an executive order banning companies from selling arms to two warring South American countries. The Court upheld the president's powers, and used the case to write into constitutional law the **Sole Organ** doctrine. The sole organ doctrine holds that the President is the sole organ of the nation in foreign affairs. The doctrine originates from a statement that Representative John Marshall made in the House of Representatives in 1799: "The President is the sole organ of the nation in its external relations, and its sole representative with foreign nations."[11]

Presidents have relied on the Court's expansive reading of presidential power in national security and foreign affairs. World War II, the Cold War, and the War on Terror provided presidents with many opportunities to use the sole organ doctrine to assert control over foreign affairs—particularly when challenged by Congress. The Court has generally upheld presidential claims, citing the sole organ doctrine. The enemy combatant cases that the Supreme Court decided in 2002, 2004, and 2008 were unusual, and controversial, precisely because they placed some limits on the President's power as commander-in-chief to decide how best to wage the war on terror.

4.3 | Political Sources of Presidential Power

4.31| *The Party Leader*

The emergence of political parties has fundamentally changed politics and government. Political parties changed government by making presidents the de facto political leader of the party to which they belong. The Republican and Democratic Parties have official leaders, but the President is the most politically visible member of a party and the party's highest elected official. Presidents use the political party as an asset to build public support for issues, to build political support for administration policies, and to organize support for electoral campaigns.

President Andrew Jackson was the first President to use a mass membership party as a base of support. He served during the time when political parties changed from caucuses (meetings of like-minded government officials) to mass membership organizations (parties with whom members of the public identified). The development of political parties created a new source of power for the president among the public and other government officials. For example, party loyalty is one reason why members of Congress will support legislation for a president who shares their political party. Not all presidents have been willing or able to use the party as a base of support. President Rutherford B. Hayes was a Republican but he did not consider himself beholden to either public opinion or the Republican Party. The Republican Party apparently felt the same way about President Hayes: "Almost without exception, party leaders were contemptuous of the Puritan President and they boycotted his wineless White House functions."[12]

In one important respect, party loyalty undermines the Madisonian system of institutional checks and balances. James Madison is the Founder who is most strongly identified with the argument that political power could be held accountable by a system of institutional checks and balances. The separation of powers into the legislative, executive, and judicial branches was supposed to make it harder for power to be abused because each branch would jealously guard its turf from poaching by another branch. Congress would protect its power from the executive or judicial branch; the President would protect executive power from encroachment by the congress or the courts; and the courts would protect their power from Congress or the President. Party loyalty can undermine the system of institutional checks: party loyalty can trump institutional loyalty. Members of Congress may support a president of their party more than Congress, and members of the courts might support a President who shares their ideology or policy beliefs. For instance, Republican members of Congress supported the expansion of presidential power during the tenure of Republican President George W. Bush. Diminished institutional loyalty to Congress has enabled the expansion of presidential power.

4.32 | *Personal Skills*

The fact that the Constitution vests the executive power in one person means that a President's power will depend, to some extent, on his or her personal skills, intelligence, experience, character, leadership, and management styles. The executive branch is a huge institution, and a president cannot assume that everyone will automatically do what he wants. A president can also be effective getting government officials, and members of Congress, to do what he wants by persuading them, by influencing them. Personal skills vary from one incumbent to another, which is one reason why presidential power fluctuates even though constitutional power remains constant.

4.33 | *Inaugural Addresses and Annual Messages*

There are several formal opportunities for the President to communicate with Congress and the American people, including inaugural addresses and the State of the Union. The President's inaugural address is an opportunity for a President to tell Congress, the American public, and the rest of the world what he intends to do as President. The State of the Union address originates from the constitutional requirement that the President

ANNUAL STATE OF THE UNION ADDRESS

"shall from time to time give to the Congress Information of the State of the Union, and recommend to their Consideration such Measures as he shall judge necessary and expedient." The State of the Union has changed over time, moving back and forth from a spoken to a written and back to a spoken address. The address focuses on what the president feels have been the highlights of the preceding year, as well as his goals for the year to come.

4.34 | *Events, Circumstances, Conditions*

Presidential power is also affected by the political events, circumstances, and conditions facing the nation. A President whose political party also controls Congress is usually in a better position than one who has to deal with a Congress controlled by the other party. Divided control of the federal government sometimes produces "gridlock," an inability of the House of Representative, the Senate, and the President to agree on public policies.

Crises have historically resulted in an increase in presidential power. In times of crisis, the public and other government officials look to the President for leadership and give him leeway to select the appropriate policy responses to the crisis. Wars and other threats to national security, economic crises, and other emergency conditions have also tended to increase presidential power. The Great Depression of the 1930s created an expectation that the national government respond to a national economic emergency. The President became the person held responsible for maintaining economic prosperity. The modern president who does not appear to be acting decisively to address problems is likely to suffer a loss of political support or public approval.

Public opinion polling records the effects of events or circumstances on public approval of the president. George W. Bush is a good example of the impact of events on presidential popularity. He began his tenure in office with approval ratings of around 50%. Immediately after the 9/11 terrorist attacks, his approval rating soared to nearly 90%. Since then, his approval rating has sunk to historic lows. When he left office, his approval rating was around 34%.

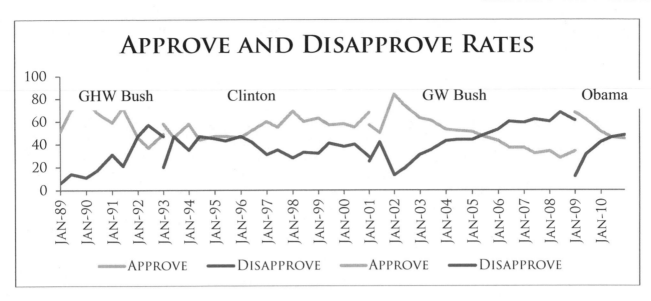

4.35 | Public Opinion

In a democracy, public opinion can serve as an important source of presidential power or an important limit on it. Strong public support adds to a President's formal powers, while weak public support subtracts from it. One of the most widely reported measures of public opinion about the president is the regular survey of job approval ratings. The President's popularity as measured by job approval is regularly measured and widely reported as a kind of presidential report card.[13] Unlike the constitutional and statutory powers, which are fairly constant, public opinion is dynamic.

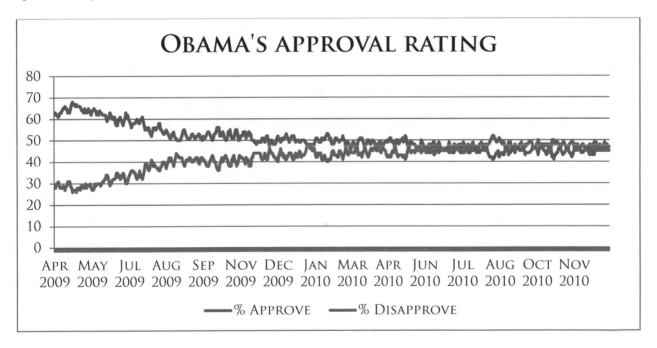

For example, Obama's approval ratings have followed the traditional pattern of high initial approval, with eventual declines in approval ratings and increases in disapproval ratings. The changes in approval ratings have resulted in Obama having less power when he pursues his policy agenda.

4.36 | *The MediA*

Presidents typically have a love-hate relationship with the media. Presidents love to use the media to get their message out, and Presidents love favorable coverage of themselves and their administration. But Presidents also hate *bad press*, any critical media coverage of them or their administration. The *love* side of the relationship is evident in the eagerness of any administration to provide favorable photo opportunities that reinforce the image of presidential leadership. The *hate* side of the relationship is apparent in statements by presidents from Thomas Jefferson to Richard Nixon. <u>*President Jefferson's Second Inaugural Address*</u> (March 4, 1805) includes strong condemnation of press coverage of his administration:

> "During this course of administration, and in order to disturb it, the artillery of the press has been levelled against us, charged with whatsoever its licentiousness could devise or dare. These abuses of an institution so important to freedom and science, are deeply to be regretted, inasmuch as they tend to lessen its usefulness…[T]hey might, indeed, have been corrected by the wholesome punishments reserved and provided by the laws of the several States against falsehood and defamation; but public duties more urgent press on the time of public servants, and the offenders have therefore been left to find their punishment in the public indignation.…..No inference is here intended, that the laws, provided by the State against false and defamatory publications, should not be enforced; he who has time, renders a service to public morals and public tranquillity, in reforming these abuses by the salutary coercions of the law; but the experiment is noted, to prove that, since truth and reason have maintained their ground against false opinions in league with false facts, the press, confined to truth, needs no other legal restraint; the public judgment will correct false reasonings and opinions, on a full hearing of all parties; and no other definite line can be drawn between the inestimable liberty of the press and its demoralizing licentiousness. If there be still improprieties which this rule would not restrain, its supplement must be sought in the censorship of public opinion."

(Courtesy of *The Presidency Project*, John Woolley and Gerhard Peters)

Richard Nixon had a difficult relationship with the media during his entire political career. President Nixon's relationship with the press became especially difficult when the press began investigating criminal activity related to Watergate and then reported on the widening scandal. The following excerpt from President Nixon's News Conference on Oct. 26th 1973 reveals his disdain for the press corps:

> Q. Mr. President, you have lambasted the television networks pretty well. Could I ask you, at the risk of reopening an obvious wound, you say after you have put on a lot of heat that you don't blame anyone. I find that a little puzzling. What is it about the television coverage of you in these past weeks and months that has so aroused your anger?
> THE PRESIDENT [to Robert C. Pierpoint, CBS News]. Don't get the impression that you arouse my anger. [Laughter]
> Q. I'm afraid, sir, that I have that impression. [Laughter]
> THE PRESIDENT. You see, one can only be angry with those he respects.

(Courtesy of The American Presidency Project: www.presidency.ucsb.edu
http://www.presidency.ucsb.edu/ws/index.php?pid=4022#ixzz1sa7xTDeJ)

4.4 | The Office: The Organization of the Executive Branch

The executive branch is organized around the various functions of the office of the presidency. The President is the head of the executive branch, with the vice-president and the white house staff under his direct supervision. The Executive Office of the President consists of the individuals who serve as the president's policy advisors. These individuals also manage the various policy offices that are located in the executive branch. The final component of the president's circle of advisors is the cabinet. The cabinet is an informal name for the heads of the fifteen executives departments—e.g., the Secretaries of State, Defense, Treasury and so on.

The growth of the executive branch has included what is commonly called the bureaucracy or the administrative state. As the chief executive officer, the president has a great deal of control over the administrative apparatus that produces regulations.

Department Head	Year	Responsibilities
Secretary of State	1789	Foreign policy
Secretary of the Treasury	1789	Government funds and regulation of alcohol, firearms, and tobacco
Secretary of Defense	1789	National defense, overseeing military
Attorney General	1870	Represents the U.S. government in federal court; investigates and prosecutes violations of federal law
Secretary of the Interior	1849	Natural resources
Secretary of Agriculture	1889	Farmers, food quality, food stamps and food security
Secretary of Commerce	1903	Business assistance and conducts the Census
Secretary of Labor	1913	Labor programs, labor statistics, enforcement of labor laws
Secretary of Health and Human Services	1953	Health and income security
Secretary of Housing and Urban Development	1965	Urban and housing programs
Secretary of Transportation	1966	Transportation and highway programs
Secretary of Energy	1977	Energy policy and research
Secretary of Education	1979	Federal education programs
Secretary of Veterans Affairs	1989	Programs for veteran's assistance
Secretary of Homeland Security	2002	Issues relating homeland security

4.41 | *The Origins of the Office of the Presidency*

The Treaty of Paris (1783) that ended the Revolutionary war left the United States independent and at peace but with an unsettled governmental structure. In 1777, during the war, the Second Continental Congress had drawn up the Articles of Confederation, a voluntary league of friendship among the states. The Articles government had inherent problems, which became increasingly apparent with the end of the war and the defeat of the common enemy (Great Britain).

During the economic depression that followed the revolutionary war, the viability of the American government was threatened by political unrest in several states, most notably Shays' Rebellion in Massachusetts. The Articles had created a weak federal government, one that consisted of a Congress but no president. The lack of an executive office was one of the perceived weaknesses of the Articles of Confederation. Individuals who presided over the Continental Congress during the Revolutionary period and under the Articles of Confederation had the title "President of the United States of America in Congress Assembled." This title was often shortened to "President of the United States." But these individuals had no important executive power. The Congress appeared institutionally incapable of functioning as a lawmaker for the nation, which was a barrier to the nation-wide development of commerce and economic development.

The constitutional convention was convened in 1787 to reform the Articles of Confederation, but the members decided to create an entirely new system of government. While most of the delegates agreed upon the need for an executive there was a long and lively debate about the nature and power of the office. The debates about executive power revealed the power problem: how to give government enough power to be effective while also limiting power so that it could be held accountable. The creation of the executive was shaped both the colonial experiences under the British monarchy, which made delegates wary of executive power, and the weakness of the Articles of Confederation, which made delegates think executive power was necessary. They ultimately created a government with an executive with considerable power but sufficient limits with a legislative-centered system of government so that the executive was made safe for republican government.

4.42 | Washington Thwarts a Threat

At the close of the Revolutionary War, a perilous moment in the life of the fledgling American republic occurred as officers of the Continental Army met in Newburgh, New York, to discuss grievances and consider a possible insurrection against Congress. They were angry over the failure of Congress to honor its promises to the army regarding salary, bounties and life pensions. The

officers had heard from Philadelphia that the American government was going broke and that they might not be compensated at all.

On March 10, 1783, an anonymous letter was circulated among the officers of General Washington's main camp at Newburgh. It addressed those complaints and called for an unauthorized meeting of officers to be held the next day to consider possible military solutions to the problems of the civilian government and its financial woes. General Washington stopped that meeting from happening by forbidding the officers to meet at the unauthorized meeting. Instead, he suggested they meet a few days later, on March 15th, at the regular meeting of his officers. Meanwhile, another anonymous letter was circulated, this time suggesting Washington himself was sympathetic to the claims of the disgruntled officers. On March 15, 1783, Washington's officers gathered in a church building in Newburgh. The fate of the American experiment with republican government may have been in their hands. General Washington unexpectedly showed up. Although he was not entirely welcomed by his men, he personally addressed them and appealed to their sense of responsibility to protect the young republic. See the Appendix, "George Washington Prevents the Revolt of the Officers." The fate of a nation plagued by a political military and a political commander in chief as president was avoided.

4.5 | Qualifications for Office

The constitutional qualifications to become president include being a natural-born citizen of the United States, at least thirty-five years old, and a resident in the United States for at least fourteen years. The Twenty-second Amendment also limits a president to serving two terms in office. The "natural-born" qualification means that some prominent individuals and successful politicians such as California Governor Arnold Schwarzenegger are not eligible to be president. And members of the "birther" movement question President Barack Obama's eligibility to serve as president. There is some discussion today of whether the requirement that a president be a natural-born citizen should be changed so that naturalized citizens who have lived in the country for a long time would be eligible to become president.

The informal, political requirements include having some government experience. The majority of presidents had prior experience as vice presidents, members of Congress, governors, or generals. Thirty-one of forty-two presidents served in the military. President Ulysses Grant's Civil War service as General-in-Chief and President Eisenhower's distinguished military career as Allied Commander during WWII are examples of how military service is seen as a political qualification for the presidency. During presidential campaigns government experience, or in an anti-government political climate, the lack of government experience is presented as a political qualification for office. Membership in one of the two major political parties is also an informal political qualification. Candidates usually must receive the backing of either the Republican Party or the Democratic Party because the U.S. has a two-party system which makes it hard for third or minor party candidates to be successful. In 1992, third-party candidate Ross Perot received nearly 19% of the popular vote.

4.6 | Selection of the President

Although people commonly refer to the **election** of the president, the president is actually

selected by the Electoral College. The way the president is chosen is very complicated and involves both election (popular votes cast in the fifty states) and selection (Electoral College votes). The United States is a republic (or indirect democracy), but the voters do not directly elect the President. Presidents are chosen indirectly by the **Electoral College**. This process is complicated and has been criticized for years.

4.61| ELECTIONS

Elections take place every four years on the Tuesday after the first Monday in November. Many states do provide early and absentee voting several weeks before election day. The U.S. does not have a single, national election for President. Presidential elections are actually 50 separate elections because each state conducts an election for President.

4.62 | The Campaign

The modern presidential campaign begins before the primary elections. A **primary election** is an election to determine who will be the political party's candidate for office. The two major political parties use primary elections to clear the field of candidates in advance of their national nominating conventions. In the 2012 presidential campaign, the incumbent President Obama did not face any Democratic Party challengers therefore he did not have to run in primary elections,

but the Republican Party held primary elections and caucuses as part of the process to determine who would receive the Republican Party nomination. Each party's nominating convention actually selects the party's nominee for president. The party's presidential candidate chooses a vice presidential nominee and this choice is rubber-stamped by the convention. The party also establishes a platform on which to base its campaign. Although nominating conventions

From L to R: Ronald Reagan (40st), Gerald Ford (38th), Jimmy Carter (39th), and Richard Nixon (37th)

have a long history in the United States, their importance in the political process has greatly diminished. The fact that primaries determine which candidate has the most delegates to the party convention means that modern conventions usually merely ratify the results of the primary elections, rather than actually choosing the party's nominee. However, the national party conventions remain important as a way of energizing the parties for the general election and focusing public attention on the nominees.

Nominees participate in nationally televised debates that are sponsored by the Commission on Presidential Debates. The Commission negotiates the terms of presidential debates, including setting the rules for determining which candidate are allowed to participate in the debates. The rules typically exclude candidates other than the nominees of the two major parties. But Ross Perot was a third party candidate who was allowed to participate in the 1992 debates. Modern presidential campaigns rely heavily on the media. Radio and television campaign ads show how candidates and parties "package" and "sell" themselves to the general public. The Museum of the Moving Image shows campaign ads from the 1952 presidential campaign between Republican Dwight Eisenhower and Democrat Adlai Stevenson until today. Examining campaign ads shows how parties and candidates present themselves, and they show how campaigns have changed over time.

4.63 | *The Electoral College*

The Electoral College may be the least-known and most misunderstood government institution in the American political system—except perhaps for the Federal Reserve Board which is another famously obscure government institution. The Founders agreed on the need for a president, but disagreed on the way to select one. While some favored national popular vote; others wanted Congress to choose the president. The Electoral College was created by the Founders because they did not trust people enough to allow them to directly elect the president. In a time of limited public education, limited communication, and a fear of sectionalism in American politics, the Founders believed that the average voter lacked the information to be an informed, unbiased judge

of candidates for the presidency. Consequently, they thought that the Electoral College would serve as a kind of council of wise elders who would choose the best person from among those who received the most popular votes in the presidential election. The College would review the people's choices and then decide for itself which of their preferences would be best. However, the Electoral College no longer performs this role because of the development of political parties.

Think about it!

This satirical news report on the Electoral College is accurate. Is this any way to select a President?

http://www.youtube.com/watch?v=BkqEdlRDKfo

Although the Constitution would allow state legislators to select the members of the Electoral College, the states have provided for the members of the Electoral College to be chosen by popular vote. At state party conventions, the state political parties choose party loyalists to serve as members of the Electoral College. Whichever party's candidate wins the most popular votes in the state gets to have its members cast the state's Electoral College votes. Because the members of the Electoral College are chosen by the parties, they usually cast their votes for their party's candidate.

Voters in each of the states cast their votes for president, but the Electoral College actually selects the President. Each state has the same number of Electoral College votes as it has members in the Congress. There are 535 members of Congress, so the Electoral College consists of 535 members plus three for the District of Columbia for a total of 538. When citizens cast their votes, the names of the presidential and vice presidential candidates are shown on the ballot. The vote, however, is actually cast for a slate of electors chosen by the candidate's political party. In most states, the ticket that wins the most votes in a state wins all of that state's electoral votes, and thus has their slate of electors chosen to vote in the Electoral College. Maine and Nebraska do not use this method. They give two electoral votes to the statewide winner and one electoral vote to the winner of each congressional district. Neither state has split electoral votes between candidates as a result of this system in modern elections.

The winning set of electors meets at their state's capital on the first Monday after the second Wednesday in December, a few weeks after the election, to vote, and sends a vote count to Congress. The vote count is opened by the sitting vice president, acting in his capacity as President of the Senate, and read aloud to a joint session of the incoming Congress, which was elected at the same time as the president. Members of Congress can object to any state's vote count, provided that the objection is supported by at least one member of each house of Congress. A successful objection will be followed by debate; however, objections to the electoral vote count are rarely raised.

In the event that no candidate receives a majority of the electoral vote, the House of Representatives chooses the president from among the top three contenders. However, each state delegation is given only one vote, which reduces the power of the more populous states.

4.64 | *Is It Time for a Change?*

The Constitution originally provided that the U.S. Electoral College would elect both the President and the Vice President in a single election. The person with a majority would become President and the runner-up would become Vice President. The elections of 1796 and 1800 exposed the problems with this system. In 1800 the Democratic-Republican plan to have one elector vote for Jefferson and not Aaron Burr did not work; the result was a tie in the electoral votes between Jefferson and Burr. The election was then sent to the House of Representatives, which was controlled by the Federalist Party. Most Federalists voted for Burr in order to block Jefferson from the

From L to R: George H.W. Bush (41st), Barack Obama (44th), George W. Bush (43rd), William (Bill) Clinton (42nd), and Jimmy Carter (39th)

presidency. The result was a week of deadlock. Jefferson, largely as a result of Hamilton's support, ultimately won. The Twelfth Amendment (ratified in 1804) required electors to cast two distinct votes: one for President and another for Vice President. It explicitly precluded from being Vice President those ineligible to be President: people under thirty-five years of age, those who have not inhabited the United States for at least fourteen years, and those who are not natural-born citizens.

The Electoral College remains controversial today because it is inconsistent with the general principles of democracy. The Electoral College system does not provide citizens with a constitutional right to vote for president. Furthermore, the candidate who gets the most popular votes can lose the Electoral College vote. This is what happened in 2000, when Al Gore received the most popular votes but George Bush received the most Electoral College votes.

Think About It!

What is the best way to choose a leader? Are there differences between "insiders" who are promoted up through the organizational ranks and "outsiders?" Is it a good idea to "roll the dice" with an outsider?

http://www.npr.org/2012/10/25/163626172/decision-time-why-do-some-leaders-leave-a-mark

And the Electoral College is biased in favor of less populous states and against more populous states. For example, the largest state by population, California, only has about one electoral vote for every 660,000 residents, while the smallest, Wyoming, has an electoral vote for about every 170,000. This means that a vote cast in one state is worth much more than a vote cast in another state. So how much is a vote for president worth? It varies a great deal depending on the state. *The New York Times* article, "How Much is Your Vote Worth?" describes why a vote for President cast in a state with a small population (i.e., Wyoming or North Dakota) is worth much more than a vote cast in a state with a large population (i.e., California, New York, or Florida).

One of the more innovative ways to think about using technology to change the way we elect the President is the creation of an electronic national primary election. The Americans Elect organization thinks that the current party politics does not serve people, and that the solution is to create an electronic, national primary election that gives voters more control over the selection of candidates and the political parties less control. What do you think of the idea?

4.7 | The Bureaucracy

One component of the federal government that requires some explanation is the federal bureaucracy. Much of the federal bureaucracy is located within the executive branch. The following provides a brief definition of bureaucracy, a description of the federal bureaucracy, and explanation of who controls the federal bureaucracy.

4.71 | *What is a Bureaucracy?*

A bureaucracy is a large organization whose mission is to perform a specific function or functions. Bureaucracies are organizations with three distinctive characteristics:

- Hierarchy. A bureaucracy structured hierarchically. It has a chain of command. At the top of the hierarchy are the policy makers. At the bottom of the hierarchy are the policy followers. Individuals in organizations have supervisors with higher ranks within the chain of command.
- Division of Labor. A bureaucracy is based on the division of labor. Individuals perform specific tasks rather than having everyone do everything the organization does. The division of labor allows organizations to develop expertise.
- Rules. A bureaucracy works according to written rules and regulations that determine what tasks individuals are assigned. An organization that is overly bureaucratic, which has too many strict rules and regulations, is sometimes said to have too much "red tape." Too many rules and regulations can limit an organization's performance of its mission.

It is important to note that this definition of a bureaucracy is not limited to government. Bureaucracy is the most common way of organizing individuals to perform functions in the private sector and the public sector. Corporations in the for-profit sector and the non-profit sector are bureaucracies. Political parties and interest groups are private sector bureaucracies.

In the public sector (i.e., government), the bureaucracy is the term for some of the officials who are responsible for administering the laws. The elected officials (the president and members of Congress) are not considered members of the federal bureaucracy. The political appointees that run the 15 executive departments (e.g., the departments of state, treasury, commerce, defense, and justice) are not the bureaucracy. The federal bureaucracy is the professionals or career officials who work in the mid and lower tiers of an organization. These individuals are not elected or appointed: they typically receive their jobs based on civil service tests. The federal bureaucracy consists of the people who carry out the organization's policies that are made by the upper management levels are the political appointees. Click on the organizational chart of any of the 15 executive departments to see the bureaucratic structure of the department.

The following figure represents a typical executive department bureaucratic organization.

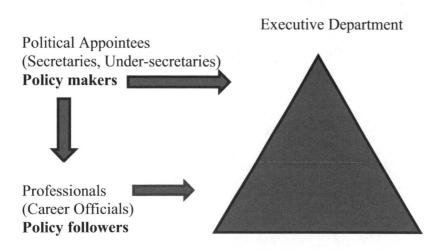

4.72 | Controlling the Bureaucracy

Controlling the bureaucracy is an important political issue for two reasons. First, the increase in the size of the federal government (the problem of big government) is measured largely in terms of the bureaucracy. We still have only one president and the size of Congress has been fixed at 535 for around a century. Big government is measured primarily in terms of the increased number of administrative departments and agencies and bureaus and independent regulatory commissions, the increased number of federal government employees, and the increased number of federal regulations. Second, the bureaucracy is an unelected "fourth branch" of government with policy making (or rule making) power. The bureaucracy does not fit easily into the tripartite separation of powers into the legislative, executive, and judicial branches. The following diagram illustrates how the bureaucracy makes "laws." Government agencies such as the Federal Communications Commission to not make legislation, but the agency (like all the executive departments and other regulatory commissions) has a rule making process and the rules that they make are legally binding and therefore have the same legal effect as laws passed by Congress.

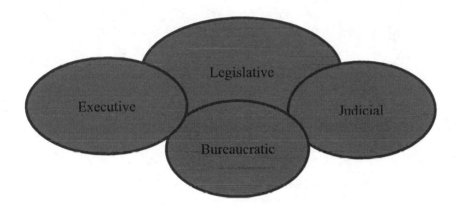

So who controls the bureaucracy? Congress creates the bureaucracy (the departments and agencies and commissions) and it can abolish bureaucracies. Congress also determines the budgets of the agencies, and the appointments of the heads of the 15 executive departments and the independent commissions must be confirmed by the Senate. The president plays an important role in controlling the federal bureaucracy. Article II of the Constitution vests the executive power in the president, and provides that the president has, with the advice and consent of the Senate, the power to appoint the heads of departments. These constitutional provisions make the president the chief executive with responsibility for managing the federal bureaucracy. Presidents use their power of appointment to control the federal bureaucracy.

4.8 | Conclusions

The development of the U.S. system of government from a congress-centered system to a president-centered system is one of the most important changes that have occurred over the more than 200 years of the existence of the republic. The increased power of the president, and the personal nature of modern presidential power, makes the power problem with the presidency even more important. The challenge is to find ways to hold executive power accountable. The personal and political nature of presidential power, and its roots in events, character, personal skills, and public opinion, presents a challenge for a system of government committed to the rule of law.

4.8 | Additional Resources

4.81 | *Internet Resources*

For a brief biography of your favorite or least favorite President, go to http://www.whitehouse.gov/about/presidents/georgewashington

The inaugural addresses of the presidents are available at the Avalon Project http://www.yale.edu/lawweb/avalon/presiden/inaug/inaug.htm and at The Presidency Project http://www.presidency.ucsb.edu/

The Annual Messages to Congress and the American Public are available at http://avalon.law.yale.edu/subject_menus/sou.asp.

The official Website of the White House is http://www.whitehouse.gov/government/cabinet.html

An electronic source of information about the presidency and presidential campaigns is available as an online class: http://www.ithaca.edu/looksharp/mcpcweb/unit5.php

The University of North Carolina site offers biographies of the presidents and first ladies including links to presidential libraries. www.metalab.unc.edu/lia/president/
The National Portrait Gallery's Hall of Presidents has information about and portraits of Presidents: www.npg.si.edu/exh/hall2/index.htm

4.82 | *In the Library*

ABBOTT, PHILIP. 2008. *ACCIDENTAL PRESIDENTS: DEATH, ASSASSINATION, RESIGNATION, AND DEMOCRATIC SUCCESSION (THE EVOLVING AMERICAN PRESIDENCY)*. PALGRAVE MACMILLIAN.

BRADLEY, RICHARD. 2000. *AMERICAN POLITICAL MYTHOLOGY FROM KENNEDY TO NIXON*. PETER LANG PUBLISHING.

DIONNE, E.J. AND WILLIAM KRISTOL (EDS). 2001. *BUSH V. GORE: THE COURT CASES AND THE COMMENTARY*. BROOKINGS INSTITUTION.

SAUER, PATRICK. 2000. *THE COMPLETE IDIOT'S GUIDE TO THE AMERICAN PRESIDENTS*. ALPHA BOOKS.

SCHLESINGER, ARTHUR M. 2004. WAR AND THE AMERICAN PRESIDENCY. NORTON, W. W. COMPANY, INC.

TARANTO, JAMES AND LEONARDO LEO (EDS). 2004. PRESIDENTIAL LEADERSHIP: RATING THE BEST AND THE WORST IN THE WHITE HOUSE. THE FREE PRESS.

WOODWARD, BOB. 2002. BUSH AT WAR. SIMON AND SCHUSTER.

TERMS

The rule of law
Imperial
Presidency
Delegated powers
Implied powers
Electoral College
Primary elections

STUDY QUESTIONS

1. Discuss how the relative powers of Congress and the presidency have changed over time.
2. What is the role of the president in the legislative process?
3. What situations have resulted in expansion of presidential powers?
4. How has the president's role as commander in chief of the military changed over time?
5. How do the president's cabinet and staff assist the president in exercising his duties and achieving his goals?
6. How does public opinion affect the presidency? How does the president use public opinion to achieve his policy goals?
7. If you were redesigning the Constitution from scratch, what existing presidential powers would you retain, which would you get rid of, and which would you modify? Why?

---

[1] Stephen B. Oates, 1994. *Abraham Lincoln: The Man Behind the Myths*. New York: HarperPerennial, p.76.

[2] Arthur M. Schlesinger, Jr. 1973. *The Imperial Presidency*. Boston and New York: Houghton Mifflin.

[3] http://www.opec.org/aboutus/history/history.htm

[4] Louis Fisher provides an excellent description of presidential claims of inherent powers. See http://loc.gov/law/help/usconlaw/pdf/Inherent-March07.pdf

[5] Quoted in *Dames & Moore v. Regan*, 453 U.S. 654 (1981). The Hostage Act was codified at 22 U.S.C. Sect. 1732 (1976).

[6] http://research.stlouisfed.org/publications/review/86/11/Employment_Nov1986.pdf

[7] http://avalon.law.yale.edu/20th_century/tonkin-g.asp

[8] http://www.presidency.ucsb.edu/ws/index.php?pid=3273

[9] http://www.house.gov/apps/list/press/financialsvcs_dem/press092808.shtml

[10] http://www.gpo.gov/fdsys/pkg/PLAW-107publ243/content-detail.html

[11] See *U.S. v. Curtiss-Wright Export Corp.*, 299 U.S. 304, 319 (1936). http://supreme.justia.com/us/299/304/case.html

[12] Wilfred E. Binkley. 1951. *American Political Parties*. Second Edition (New York: Alfred A. Knopf), p. 321.

[13] See http://www.presidency.ucsb.edu/data/popularity.php

CHAPTER 5: THE JUDICIARY

5.0 | The Judiciary

All countries have courts. Courts are considered an essential element of good government because of their role in the administration of justice and their role in upholding the rule of law. But courts do not play the same role in all countries. In some countries courts have a very limited role relative to the political institutions. In other countries courts have a broad role. Courts play a broad role in American government and politics—a role that has been controversial from the earliest days of the republic to current events. Today courts today rule on everything from "A" (abortion and agriculture and airlines) to "Z" (zoning and zoos). The Supreme Court's most controversial decisions on matters such as abortion, the death penalty, school prayer, obscenity and indecency, and sexual behavior have made the Court one of the primary targets in the **culture wars**. The term culture war refers to the political conflicts over values rather than economics. Courts and trials certainly have captured the public's imagination. The nation's history is marked by famous "trials of the century." And judges are prominent in popular culture as indicated by the number of TV Judges (e.g., *The People's Court*; *Judge Judy*; Judge Joe Brown; Judge Mathis; Judge Alex; and even Judge Wapner's *Animal Court*).

This chapter describes the role that courts play in the U.S. system of government and politics. It focuses on three main issues:

- The power problem for the federal courts is legitimacy: the legitimacy of judicial power in a democratic system of government.
- The increased power of the judiciary: the judiciary was originally called the "least dangerous" branch of government but court critics now refer to an "imperial judiciary."
- The courts as government institutions: the relationship between law and politics.

"Presidents come and go, but the Supreme Court goes on forever." President William Howard Taft

"It is emphatically the province and duty of the judicial department to say what the law is." Chief Justice John Marshall in *Marbury v. Madison*

The primary focus is on the U.S. Supreme Court but some attention is paid to organization and operation of the federal court system. The state court systems are only briefly mentioned. Information about the Supreme Court is available at http://www.supremecourt.gov/. Information about the federal court system is available at http://www.uscourts.gov/Home.aspx and the Federal Judicial Center.

5.1 | The Power Problem for the Federal Courts

The power problem for Congress is effectiveness: the modern Congress is not a particularly effective institution. The power problem for the presidency is accountability: it is difficult to hold presidents legally accountable for their actions. The power problem for the federal courts is **legitimacy**. Legitimacy has been an issue throughout the nation's history. The problem is that in democratic political systems there is a preference for policy making by elected government officials but federal judges are appointed to life terms. This makes the federal judiciary an undemocratic government institution. This is not necessarily a problem. But it is a problem if the courts have policy making powers.

The federal courts are not the only non-elected government institution with policy making power. The Federal Reserve Board is a non-elected government body with substantial power to make economic policy related to inflation and employment. When assessing the legitimacy of judicial power it is important to remember that the U.S. is not a pure democracy. It is a constitutional democracy. The Constitution actually places a number of very important limits on majority rule. In fact, the Constitution (particularly the Bill of Rights) is a counter-majoritarian document. The fact that courts interpret the Constitution means that courts sometime perform a counter-majoritarian role in the constitutional democracy. Much of the controversy surrounding the role of the courts in the U.S. system of government and politics is about the legitimacy of courts making policy. Judicial policymaking or legislating from the bench is considered inappropriate in a political system where the elected branches of government are expected to have the primary policymaking power. The power problem for the courts is about the boundaries between the political system and the legal system, the separation of politics and law. Keeping law and politics separate is complicated by the fact that the judiciary is expected to have some degree of independence from the political system so that courts can perform one of their most important roles: enforcing basic rule of law values in a constitutional democracy.

The C-SPAN presentation "Legal Scholars Examine the Role of Courts in Democracy" discusses the relationship between the courts and democracy: http://www.c-span.org/Events/Legal-Scholars-Examine-the-Role-of-Courts-in-Democracy/10737430324-1/

5.2 | The Political History of the Supreme Court

Judicial power is also controversial because courts have historically taken sides in many of the most important and controversial issues facing the nation. The Supreme Court has had four distinct eras based on the kinds of issues the Court decided during the era: the Founding Era (1790-1865); the Development Era (1865-1937); the Liberal Nationalism Era (1937—1970); and the Conservative Counter-revolution (since 1970). Although the specific issues that the Court decided during these four eras changed, what has remained the same is that the Court has addressed many of the major political controversies and issues of the day. The Supreme Court Timeline marks some of these eras and issues. The Supreme Court is usually referred to by the name of the Chief Justice who presided over it.

5.21 | *The Founding Era (1790-1865)*

During the Founding Era the Court was concerned with issues related to the way the new system of government actually worked, particularly issues related to the separation of powers and federalism. In fact, the Supreme Court took a side in the debates between the Federalists, who supported the national government, and the Anti-federalists, who supported state governments, by broadly reading the powers of the national government. The Marshall Court (1801-1835) established the power of the national government in a series of rulings that broadly interpreted the powers of the national government. It established the power of judicial review in *Marbury v. Madison* (1803). Judicial review is the power of a court to review the actions of government officials to determine whether they are constitutional. In *Marbury,* the Court declared a part of the Judiciary Act of 1789 unconstitutional. The Marshall Court also ruled that Congress had complete power over interstate commerce in *Gibbons v. Ogden*. This ruling meant that a state government could not regulate commerce among the states. The Marshall Court also established the precedent for broadly interpreting Congress' power under the Necessary and Proper Clause in *McCulloch v. Maryland* (1819).

Chief Justice Marshall was succeeded by Chief Justice Roger B. Taney. The Taney Court (1836–1864) is remembered mainly for rulings that upheld the powers of the states rather than the national government. Taney wrote opinions that supported the idea of **dual federalism**, the idea that the national and state governments had power over different areas of public policy, and that each level of government was supreme in its field. According to dual federalism, the national government is supreme in matters of foreign affairs and interstate commerce, for example, and the state governments are supreme in matters of public policy including interstate commerce, education, the regulation of morality, and criminal justice. So the Marshall Court emphasized national supremacy, and the Taney Court emphasized dual federalism. The Taney Court's ruling in *Dred Scott v. Sandford* (1857) contributed to the sense that the Civil War was inevitable because the Court limited Congress' power to limit the spread of slavery. In the years leading up to the Civil War, slavery was an issue that threatened the union. In *Dred Scott* the Court struck down the Missouri Compromise of 1820, a law passed by Congress to limit the spread of slavery in the territories.

5.22 | *Development and Economic Regulation (1865-1937)*

This Supreme Court era is noted for cases challenging the government's power to regulate the economy. In response to problems caused by the Industrial Revolution, the government increased regulation of business during the Progressive Era (roughly 1890 to WWI) and the New Deal Era (1930s). The regulations included anti-trust legislation, child labor laws, minimum wage and maximum hour laws, and workplace safety regulations. During this era the Court saw its role as protecting business from government regulation, and it used the power of judicial review to strike down laws that regulated business. The Court did not strike down all of these laws but in 1934 and 1935 it did declare unconstitutional many of the major provisions of the Roosevelt Administration's New Deal. The conflict between the national political system that supported increased government regulation of business and social welfare policies that were intended to end the Great Depression and provide a greater measure of income security, and a Court that ruled many of these policies unconstitutional, came to a head in the latter 1930s. The

Supreme Court's rulings limiting the government's power to regulate economic activity placed the Court in the middle of the most controversial issues of that era.

One reason for the New Deal era conflict between the political branches and the Court was an accident of history. President Franklin D. Roosevelt was unlucky in that he did not have the opportunity to appoint a member of the Supreme Court during his entire first term in office. Political change occurs regularly with the election calendar: every two years. But because the Justices are appointed to life terms, vacancies occur with retirements or death, so legal change occurs irregularly. President Roosevelt and congressional Democrats saw the election of 1932 as a critical election that gave them a mandate to govern. They became increasingly frustrated with Supreme Court rulings where a conservative majority (often by 6-3 or 5-4 margins) struck down major New Deal programs in 1935 and 1936. Roosevelt eventually proposed legislation to add another member to the Court for every sitting justice over the age of seventy, up to a maximum of six more members—which would have increased the size of the Court from nine to 15 members. This proposal was very controversial, because it was obviously an attempt to get the Court to change its rulings by "packing" the court with new Justices who would support New Deal policies of economic regulation. Although the Court's rulings striking down New Deal policies were unpopular, President Roosevelt's court packing plan was considered an inappropriate attempt to exert political control over the Court. The proposal died in Congress.

However, in 1937 the Court abruptly changed its rulings on economic regulation and began to uphold New Deal legislation. The Court announced that it would no longer be interested in hearing cases challenging the government's power to regulate the economy. The Court indicated that it would henceforth consider questions about the government's power to pass economic regulations matters for the political branches of government to decide. The Court also announced that in the future it was going to take a special interest in cases involving laws that affected the political liberties of individuals. In effect, the Court announced that it would use judicial restraint when laws affected economic liberties but judicial activism when laws affected political liberties. The Court further explained that it was especially interested in protecting the rights of "discrete and insular" minorities. This 1937 change is called **the constitutional revolution of 1937** because it was such an abrupt, major change in the Court's reading of the Constitutional and its understanding of its role in the system of government and politics.

5.23 | *The Era of Liberal Nationalism (1937-1970)*

In the middle years of the 20th Century, the Court participated in debates about civil liberties and civil rights by assuming the role of protector of individual liberties and promoter of equality. The Court's interest in civil liberties cases marks the beginning of the Court's third era. It began protecting civil liberties in cases involving freedom of expression (including freedom of religion, speech, and press); the rights of suspects and criminals in the criminal justice system; racial and ethnic minorities to equal protection of the laws; and the right to privacy. The Warren Court (1953-1969) is remembered for its judicial activism on behalf of civil liberties. Chief Justice Earl Warren presided over the Court's important civil liberties cases supporting individual freedom and equality in both **civil** law and **criminal** law. In the 1950s and 1960s, the Court's civil liberties rulings ordering school desegregation put the Court in the middle of debates about racial equality.

The Warren Court's civil law rulings included the landmark school desegregation case *Brown v. Board of Education* (1954), and landmark right to privacy cases such as *Griswold v. Connecticut* (1965). In *Griswold v. Connecticut* the Court held that the U.S. Constitution included an implied right to privacy that prohibited states from passing laws that made it a criminal offense to disseminate information about birth control devices— and by implication, the implied right to privacy limited government power to regulate other aspects of sexual behavior. The Warren Court also issued rulings that affected the freedom of religion. In *Engel v. Vitale* (1962), the Court ruled that it was unconstitutional for government officials to compose a prayer and require that it be recited in public schools. The prayer was "Almighty God, we acknowledge our dependence upon Thee, and beg Thy blessings upon us, our teachers, and our country." In *Abington School District v. Schempp* (1963) the Court held that mandatory Bible reading in public schools was unconstitutional.

The Warren Court's criminal law rulings were no less controversial than its civil law rulings. The Court broadened the rights of suspects and convicted offenders in the state criminal justice systems. *Gideon v. Wainwright* (1963) broadened the right to the assistance of counsel by holding that anyone charged with a felony had a right to be provided an attorney if he or she could not afford to pay for one. *Mapp v. Ohio* (1961) held that the Exclusionary Rule applied to state courts. The Exclusionary Rule prohibited the use of evidence seized in violation of the Constitution in order to obtain a conviction. *Miranda v. Arizona* (1966) may be the most famous of the Warren Court rulings on criminal justice. It required police officers to notify suspect of their constitutional rights before questioning them. These rights include the right to remain silent, the right to have the assistance of counsel, and notified that anything said can be used in a court of law against them.

These Warren Court rulings, and the Burger Court's ruling in *Roe v. Wade* (1973) that the right to privacy included the right to an abortion, put the Court in the middle of "the culture wars"—the political conflicts over value as opposed to economics. Judicial decisions about state laws defining marriage continue the tradition of judicial participation in the leading controversies of the day.

5.24 | *The Conservative Counter-Revolution*

One indication that the era of liberal nationalism has ended is the fact that today's Court has a different agenda than the Warren Court. Today's Court is conservative and the Justices are interested in different issues than the Warren Court. President Nixon's election in 1968 marked the beginning of the rightward change in the country's *political* direction. His appointment of four Justices marked the beginning of the rightward change in the Court's *legal* direction. The 1968 presidential campaigns made crime a national issue. Candidate Nixon portrayed judges as being soft on crime and he pledged that as president he would appoint judges who would get-tough-on-crime. President Nixon appointed four members of the Court, including Chief Justice Warren Burger. The Burger Court (1969–1986) changed the Court's ideological direction, most immediately in the area of criminal justice where President Nixon's appointment of four get-tough-on-crime Justices had an immediate impact on the Court's rulings. Crime policy is a good place to see the relationship between politics and the law because crime is one of the basic responsibilities of governments everywhere. People expect government to protect individuals from threats to their lives and property. Americans expect the government to provide safe streets, subways, and parks, and to ensure that people are secure in their homes. Preventing crime, investigating crimes, and arresting, prosecuting, and punishing those convicted of criminal acts is part of the national, state, and local government functions.

The election of conservative Republican presidents (Nixon, Ford, Reagan, Bush 41 and Bush 43), and even conservative Democratic presidents (Carter and Clinton) solidified the Court's rightward movement. Because the Justices are appointed by political figures through a political process (the President nominates a Justice and the Senate must confirm the nominee), it is not surprising that political changes are reflected on the Court. The selection of federal judges is an obvious contact point between law and politic, between the legal system and the political system.

The Rehnquist Court (1986–2005) was also a conservative court. The conservative bloc of Justices had a working majority on the Court. In civil law, some of the Rehnquist Court's rulings on federalism reflected the conservative backlash against the liberal expansion of the powers of the federal government. Politically, conservatives advocated New Federalism during the Nixon Administration. Legally, the conservatives on the Court revived the concept of federalism as a constitutional framework for allocating the powers of the national and state governments. Its rulings in *U.S. v. Lopez* (1995) and *U.S. v. Morrison* (2004), for example, limited Congress's use of the Commerce Clause power to regulate the possession of guns near schools and violence against women. In *Lopez*, the Court struck down the Gun Free School Zones Act of 1990. In *Morrison*, the Court struck down provisions of the Violence Against Women Act of 2000.

The Roberts Court (2005–present) has also established a record as a conservative Court. Chief Justice Roberts and Justice Samuel Alito were nominated in part because they had judicial records of supporting business interests. Since the late 1930s, business interests were overshadowed by all the attention paid to higher profile, hot-button issues such as abortion, school prayer, affirmative action, and the death penalty. Business cases are now an important part of the Supreme Court's docket and the Court has issued a number of rulings that are favorable to business interests. For example, the Roberts Court's 2010 ruling striking down major parts of the federal laws regulating independent campaign contributions (Citizens United v. Federal Election Commission) eased restrictions on corporate campaign contributions. The Roberts Court is also more supportive of the *Accommodationist* reading of the Establishment Clause of the First Amendment, which allows much more government support of religion than the *Wall of Separation* reading favored by the liberal Justices. And on matters of national security, including the war on terror, Justices Roberts and Alito reflect the conservative Justices support for broadly interpreting presidential power as Commander-in-Chief.

5.3 | The Increased Power of the Courts: Going from Third to First?

In the U.S., the judiciary is called the third branch of government for two reasons. First, the judiciary is provided for in Article III of the Constitution. Second and more important, the legislative and executive branches were intended to be more powerful than the judiciary. The judiciary was intended to be the weakest of the three branches of government.

Courts have always played an important role in American society. In *Democracy In America*, Alexis de Tocqueville (1835) famously said that "There is hardly a political question in the United States which does not sooner or later turn into a judicial one." But the power of the judiciary has increased over time, and modern courts play a much more important role in government and politics than the Founders intended. The increase in judicial power is reflected in the fact that the courts were originally described as the "least dangerous" branch of government (by Alexander Hamilton in *Federalist No. 78*) but now critics of the court attach the label "imperial judiciary" to the courts. As with Congress and the Presidency, the Supreme Court has changed over time as institutional norms and practices and customs became established. Hamilton thought the judiciary was the least dangerous third branch because the courts had neither the power of the purse (Congress controlled the budget) nor the power of the sword (the executive branch enforced the laws). However, over time, the Court has gained power in our political system. The following describes how that change occurred.

5.31 | The Early Years

In the early years of the republic the Court initially lacked power or prestige. Early presidents had a hard time finding Justices who were willing to serve on the Court because no one really knew what the Court would do, it was not considered an important or prestigious institution, and one of the Justices' duties (riding circuit to travel through the circuit courts) was very difficult during a period of this country's history when frontier travel was difficult and uncomfortable.

The Supreme Court first met in February 1790 at the Merchants Exchange Building in New York City, which then was the national capital. When Philadelphia became the capital city later in 1790 the Court followed Congress and the President there. After Washington, D.C., became the capital in 1800 the Court occupied various spaces in the U.S. Capitol building until 1935, when it moved into its own building.

The Court became a more prestigious institution during the Marshall Court Era. In *Marbury*, Chief Justice John Marshall argued that it was logical to read the Constitution to give the courts the power to interpret the laws. The Constitution is a law. In fact, the Constitution is the supreme law of the land. Therefore, the courts have the power to interpret the Constitution. This power of judicial review is a major source of the judiciary's power. It gives the courts the power to declare unconstitutional laws passed by Congress, executive orders or other actions of the President, administrative regulations enacted by bureaucracies, lower court judges, laws passed by state legislatures, or the actions of state governors, county commissioners, city officials, and school board policies. Courts have used judicial

Old Supreme Court Chambers

review to declare unconstitutional a federal income tax law, presidential regulations of the economy, state laws requiring that black children be educated separate from white children in public schools; public school policies supporting organized prayer; and laws defining marriage as a relationship between one man and one woman.

The Marshall Court ended the practice of each judge issuing his or her own opinion in a case and began the tradition of having the Court announce a single decision for the Court. This change created the impression that there was one Court with one view of what the Constitution meant, rather than a Court that merely consisted of individuals with differing points of view. Thus the Marshall Court enhanced the Court's prestige as an authoritative body with special competence to interpret the Constitution when disputes arose over its meaning. But the main reason for the expansion of the power of the courts is the power of judicial review.

5.32 | Judicial Review

Judicial review is the power of courts to review the actions of government officials to determine whether they are constitutional. It is a power that all courts have, not just the Supreme Court, and it is a power to review the actions of *any* government official: laws passed by Congress; presidential actions or executive orders; regulations promulgated by administrative agencies; laws passed by state legislatures; actions of governors; county commission decisions; school board policies; city regulations; and the rulings of lower courts. The Constitution does not explicitly grant the courts the power of judicial review. Judicial review was established as an implied power of the courts in the landmark case *Marbury v. Madison* (1803), where the Court for the first time ruled that a law passed by Congress was unconstitutional. The case was a minor dispute. President John Adams signed a judicial appointment for William Marbury. His commission was signed but not delivered when a new President (Thomas Jefferson) took office. When the new administration did not give Marbury his appointment, Marbury used the Judiciary Act of 1789 to go to the Supreme Court asking for an order to deliver his commission as judge. Chief Justice John Marshall's ruling in *Marbury v. Madison* used syllogistic

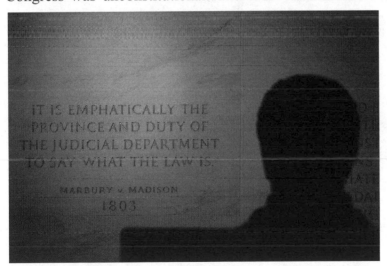

Statute of John Marshall in the foreground, shadowed, quotation from Marbury v. Madison (written by Marshall) engraved into the wall. United States Supreme Court Building.

reasoning to explain why it was logical to read the Constitution as implying that courts have the power to review laws and declare them unconstitutional if they conflicted with the Constitution. Syllogistic logic is a form of reasoning that allows inferring true conclusions (the "then" statements) from given premises (the givens or "if" statements). Marshall structured the logical argument for judicial review as follows:

[If] the Constitution is a law,
[and if] the courts interpret the laws,
[then] the courts interpret the Constitution.

Marshall further reasoned that courts have the power to declare a law unconstitutional:

[If the] Constitution is the supreme law of the land,
[and if] a law, in this case the Judiciary Act of 1789, conflicts with the Constitution,
[then] that law is unconstitutional.

Judicial review gives courts the power to review and declare unconstitutional laws passed by Congress, executive orders or other actions of the President, administrative regulations enacted by bureaucracies, lower court judges, laws passed by state legislatures, or the actions of state governors, county commissioners, city officials, and school board policies. Judges have used judicial review to declare unconstitutional a federal income tax law, presidential regulations of the economy, state laws requiring that black children be educated separate from white children in public schools, school board policies requiring the recitation of organized prayer in public schools, and laws making flag burning a crime.

Some of the Founding Fathers, particularly Federalists such as Alexander Hamilton, accepted the notion of judicial review. In *Federalist No. 78* Hamilton wrote: "A constitution is, in fact, and must be regarded by the judges, as a fundamental law. It therefore belongs to them to ascertain its meaning, as well as the meaning of any particular act proceeding from the legislative body. If there should happen to be an irreconcilable variance between the two, that which has the superior obligation and validity ought, of course, to be preferred; or, in other words, the Constitution ought to be preferred to the statute." The Antifederalists (e.g., Brutus in *Antifederalist #XV*) feared the judicial power would be exalted above all other, subject to "no controul," and superior even to Congress. Nevertheless, judicial review has become a well-established power of the courts.

5.33 | *Limits on Judicial Power*

Does judicial review make the courts more powerful than the legislative and executive branches of government because the courts can rule presidential and congressional actions unconstitutional? The courts do have the power to strike down presidential and congressional actions, which critics say makes the judiciary the most powerful, not the least powerful, branch of government. But there are limits on judicial power. The courts cannot directly enforce their rulings. Judges rely on individuals or other government officials to enforce their rulings. Judges cannot expect automatic compliance with their rulings. Opposition to desegregation of public schools after the 1954 *Brown v. Board of Education* was widespread. For example, in 1957 the Florida Legislature passed an Interposition Resolution that asserted that the U.S. Supreme Court did not have the authority to order states to desegregate public schools therefore Florida government officials did not have to comply with the Brown ruling.

Interposition is a doctrine that asserts the power of a state to refuse to comply with a federal law or judicial decision that the state considers unconstitutional. Compliance with the Court's rulings outlawing organized prayer in public schools has also been mixed. And police officer compliance with Court rulings on search and seizure is not automatic. The courts depend on compliance by executive branch officials, such as school board members, teaching, and police officers.

5.34 | *Two Concepts of Judicial Role: Restraint and Activism*

The legitimacy of judicial power is usually described in terms of two concepts of the appropriate rule for the judiciary: judicial restraint and judicial activism. **Judicial restraint** is defined as a belief that it is appropriate for courts to play a limited role in the government, that judges should be very hesitant to overturn decisions of the political branches of government, and that judges should wherever possible defer to legislative and executive actions. **Judicial activism** is defined as a belief that it is appropriate for courts to play a broad role in the government—that judges should be willing to enforce their view of what the law means regardless of political opposition in the legislative or executive branches. There are three main elements of judicial restraint.

- **Deference** to the Political Branches of Government. Judicial deference to legislative and executive actions is a hallmark of judicial restraint. When judges are reluctant to overturn the decisions of the political branches of government they are exercising judicial restraint. Judges who bend over backwards to uphold government actions are exercising judicial restraint. Judicial activists are less deferential to the political branches of government. Activist judges are more willing to rule that the actions of government officials—whether the president, the Congress, lower court judges, the bureaucracy, or state government officials—are unconstitutional.

- Uphold **Precedent**. Precedent is a legal system where judges are expected to use past decisions as guides when deciding issues that are before the court. Precedent means that judges should decide a case the same way that they have decided similar cases that have previously come before the court. When judges decide cases based on established precedent, they are exercising judicial restraint. Judges who rely on "settled law" are using judicial restraint. Activists are not as committed to uphold precedent. They are more willing to overturn precedents or create new ones that reflect changes in contemporary societal attitudes or values. Activist judges are less bound by what has been called the "dead hand of the past."

- Only **Legal** Issues. Courts are institutions that are designed to settle legal disputes. Advocates of judicial restraint believe that courts should only decide legal questions, that courts should not become involved with political, economic, social, or moral issues. One indicator of judicial restraint is when a court limits its cases and rulings to legal disputes. It is not always clear, however, whether an issue is a legal or a political issue. Cases that address campaigns, voting, and elections, for instance, involve both law and politics because voting is considered a right, rather than merely a political privilege. Judicial activists are less concerned about getting the courts involved with cases or issues that affect politics, economics, or social issues. They are willing to issue rulings that affect politics because they don't necessarily see a bright dividing line between politics and law.

5.35 | *Ideology and Roles*

It is important to note that the above definitions of restraint and activism do not mention ideology. Judicial restraint and activism are not intrinsically conservative or liberal even though restraint is often considered conservative and activism is often considered liberal. Sometimes the Supreme Court's activism is conservative. The Marshall Court was a conservative activist court. During the 1930s the Court was a conservative activist court. In fact, during most of the Supreme Court's history it activism has been primarily politically conservative. During the period 1937-1970 the Court's activism was generally liberal—which is why activism is today most often associated with liberalism. However, the Court has once again become a primarily conservative activist Court. The Rehnquist Court has been a conservative activist Court using federalism and the separation of powers to strike down federal legislation such as the Violence Against Women Act and the Gun Free School Zones Act and provisions of the Brady Handgun Control Act. And with its ruling in *Bush v. Gore* (2000), the Rehnquist Court intervened in the 2000 presidential election dispute in Florida to ensure that George W. Bush became President despite receiving fewer votes than Al Gore. The Roberts Court has continued the trend toward conservative activism. Its rulings have most notably ignored established precedent to overturn existing campaign finance laws and to create a new individual right to keep and bear arms.

5.4 | **Courts as Government Institutions**

A court can be defined as a government body designed for settling legal disputes according to law. In the U.S. courts have two primary functions: **dispute resolution** and **law interpretation**.

Dispute Resolution. The dispute resolution function of courts is to settle disputes according to law. This is a universal function associated with courts. Courts provide a place and a method for peaceably settling the kinds of disputes or conflicts that inevitably arise in a society. These disputes or conflicts could be settled in other ways. They could be settled by violence, vendettas, feuds, duels, fights, war, vigilantism, or political power. One justice problem with these methods of dispute resolution is that the physically strong, or the more numerous, or the more politically powerful will generally prevail over the physically weaker, the less numerous, or the less politically powerful. These alternative methods of dispute resolution tend to work according to the old maxim: Might makes right. The modern preference for settling disputes peaceably according to law rather than violence or political power has made the dispute resolution function of courts a non-controversial function because they are associated with justice.

Dispute resolution is the primary function of trial courts. A trial is a fact-finding process for determining who did what to whom. In a civil trial, the court might determine whether one individual (the respondent) did violate the terms of a contract to provide another individual (the plaintiff) with specified goods or services, or whether a doctor's treatment of a patient constituted medical malpractice, or whether a manufacturer violated product liability laws. In a criminal trial, the court might determine whether an individual (the defendant) did what the government (the prosecution) has accused him of doing. These are all examples of the dispute resolution function of courts.

The dispute resolution function of courts is familiar to most people as a courtroom trial where the lawyers who represent the two sides in a case try to convince a neutral third party (usually a jury) that they are right. In one sense, a trial is nothing more than a decision making process, a set of rules for making a decision. But a trial is a distinctive decision making process because it relies so heavily on very elaborate procedural rules. The rules of evidence (what physical or testimonial evidence can and cannot be introduced) are very complicated. The rules of evidence are important because the decision (the trial verdict) is supposed to be based solely on the evidence introduced at trial. Trials have captured the political and cultural imagination so much so that famous trials are an important part of the political culture of many countries including the U.S.

Law Interpretation. The second function of courts is law interpretation. Law interpretation is deciding what the law means when there is a disagreement about what a law means, conflicting provisions of a law, or even conflicts between two laws. An example of law interpretation is when courts decide whether a police officer's search of a person's car constitutes a violation of the Fourth Amendment's prohibition against "unreasonable search and seizure." Courts are asked to determine the meaning of "unreasonable." Another example of law interpretation is when courts decide whether the death penalty (or imposing the death penalty on minors or mentally handicapped persons with an I.Q. below 70) is unconstitutional because it violates the Eighth Amendment prohibition against "cruel and unusual punishment."

Law interpretation is primarily the function of *appellate courts*. Appeals courts do not conduct trials to determine facts; they decide the correct interpretation of the law when a party appeals the decision of a trial court. Law interpretation is a much more controversial function than dispute resolution because it involves judges making decisions about what the law means. The Supreme Court "makes" legal policy when it decides whether police practices related to search and seizure or questioning suspects are consistent with the Fourth Amendment warrant requirements or the Fifth Amendment due process of law. It makes legal policy when it decides whether the death penalty constitutes cruel or unusual punishment. It makes policy when it decides whether laws restricting abortion violate the right to privacy. It makes policy when it reads the Fourteenth Amendment Equal Protection Clause to require "one person, one vote." It also makes policy when it decides whether the traditional definition of marriage as the union of one man and one woman deprives gays and lesbians of the Equal Protection of the laws. The law interpretation function is often political and often controversial because it gets the courts involved with making policy.

The dispute resolution function is not very controversial. There is broad public support for the idea of government creating courts to peaceably settle conflicts according to law. Law interpretation is the controversial function of courts because it gets courts involved with policy making.

5.5 | The U.S. Court System

5.51 | *The Organization of the Federal Court System*

The U.S. has a federal system of government that consists of one national government and fifty state governments. It is sometimes said that the U.S. has two court systems: the federal court system and the state court systems. But it can also be said that the U.S. has 51 courts systems and 51 systems of law because each state has substantial autonomy, as an aspect of state sovereignty, to create its own court system and its own system of criminal and civil laws.

The Federal Court System consists of one Supreme Court, 13 Courts of Appeals, 94 District Courts, and some special or legislative courts (including a court of claims, a court of veterans appeals, and Foreign Intelligence Surveillance Courts).

5.52 | *The Supreme Court of the United States*

The Supreme Court (SCOTUS) is the highest court in the United States. It is also the head of the judicial branch of the federal government and as such has administrative and legal responsibilities for managing the entire federal court system. The Supreme Court consists of nine Justices: the Chief Justice and eight Associate Justices. The Justices are nominated by the President and confirmed with the "advice and consent" of the Senate to serve terms that last a lifetime or during "good behavior." Federal judges can be removed only by resignation, or by impeachment and subsequent conviction.

The Supreme Court is the only court established by the Constitution. All other federal courts are created by Congress. Article III of the Constitution provides that:

> The judicial Power of the United States, shall be vested in one supreme Court, and in such inferior Courts as the Congress may from time to time ordain and establish. The Judges, both of the supreme and inferior Courts, shall hold their Offices during good Behavior, and shall, at stated Times, receive for their Services a Compensation which shall not be diminished during their Continuance in Office.

5.53 | *The Supreme Court Jurisdiction*

The term *jurisdiction* refers to a court's authority to hear a case. The Supreme Court's jurisdiction is provided in the Constitution, statutes, and case law precedents.

Constitutional. Article III provides that judicial power "shall extend to all Cases…arising under this Constitution, the Laws of the United States, and Treaties…." The Court has both original and appellate jurisdiction, but the Court is primarily an appellate court. The Court's original jurisdiction (that is its authority to sit as a body hearing a case for the first time, as a kind of trial court) is limited to cases "affecting Ambassadors, other public Ministers and Consuls, and those in which a State shall be Party…" The Founders gave the Supreme Court original jurisdiction over cases where states are parties in order to remove the case from the geographic jurisdiction of a state. They believed it served the interests of justice to have a legal dispute between two states be decided by a federal court that was not physically located in a state. In all other cases, the Court has appellate jurisdiction; that is, it reviews the decisions of lower courts.

Statutory. Congress also has statutory authority to determine the jurisdiction of federal courts. The Federal Judicial Center lists "Landmark Judicial Legislation" related to the organization and jurisdiction of the federal courts from the Judiciary Act of 1789 to the creation of the federal circuit in 1982. Congress has attempted to prohibit the courts from hearing controversial issues by passing *court stripping* laws that prohibit federal courts from hearing cases involving flag burning or school prayer for instance. The Detainee Treatment Act limited the jurisdiction of courts to hear cases involving habeas corpus application of a Guantanamo Bay detainee.[1] The Constitution specifies that the Supreme Court may exercise original jurisdiction in cases affecting ambassadors and other diplomats, and in cases in which a state is a party. In all other cases, however, the Supreme Court has only appellate jurisdiction. The Supreme Court considers cases based on its original jurisdiction very rarely; almost all cases are brought to the Supreme Court on appeal. In practice, the only original jurisdiction cases heard by the Court are disputes between two or more states.

The power of the Supreme Court to consider appeals from state courts, rather than just federal courts, was created by the Judiciary Act of 1789. Under Article III, federal courts may only entertain "cases" or "controversies" which means federal courts are not supposed to hear hypothetical disputes.

Case Law Precedents. The Supreme Court also has authority to determine the jurisdiction of the federal courts. Its case law rulings and its administrative rules describe the kinds of cases or issues that federal courts hear. The Court's Rule 10 provides that a petition for certiorari should be granted only for "compelling reasons." One such reason is to resolve lower court conflicts. A lower court conflict occurs when different courts interpret the same law differently. An example of lower court conflict is the rulings upholding and striking down the Affordable Care Act. Other compelling reasons to accept an appeal are to correct a clear departure from judicial procedures or to address an important question of law. A writ of certiorari is a request to a higher court to review the decision of a lower court. The Court receives around 7,000 petitions each year, but issues only 75 or so decisions each year, so the Court has an elaborate screening process for determining which writs will be accepted. After the Court grants the writ of certiorari, the parties file written briefs and the case is scheduled for oral argument. If the parties consent and the Court approves, interested individuals or organizations may file amicus curiae or friend of the court briefs which provide the Court with additional information about the issues presented in a case.

5.54 | *The Supreme Court Term*

The Supreme Court meets in the United States Supreme Court building in Washington D.C. Its annual term starts on the first Monday in October and finishes sometime during the following June or July. Each term consists of alternating two week intervals. During the first interval, the court is in session, or "sitting," and hears cases. During the second interval, the court is recessed to consider and write opinions on cases it has heard. The Court holds two-week oral argument sessions each month from October through April. Each side has half an hour to present its argument—but the Justices often interrupt them as you can tell when listening to the Oyez audio recordings.

 After oral argument, the Justices schedule conferences to deliberate and then take a preliminary vote. Cases are decided by majority vote of the Justices. The most senior Justice in the majority assigns the initial draft of the Court's opinion to a Justice voting with the majority. Drafts of the Court's opinion, as well as any concurring or dissenting opinions, circulate among the Justices until the Court is prepared to announce the ruling.[2]

5.6 | The Selection of Federal Judges

Article II grants the President power to nominate federal judges, whose appointments must be confirmed by the Senate. The individual Justices and the Court as an institution are not political like Congress and the President. Partisanship, for example, is less apparent. But individual Justices and the Court are described in political terms primarily as conservative, moderate, or liberal rather than as members of a political party. Media accounts of the Court refer to the right wing, the left wing, and the swing or moderate Justices. Presidents nominate individuals who share their ideological views, and Senators also consider ideology when considering whether to ratify a nominee. Presidents generally get Justices who vote the way they were expected to vote but there are some prominent examples of Justices voting contrary to the expectations of the President who nominated them: Oliver Wendell Holmes disappointed President Theodore Roosevelt; Chief Justice Earl Warren disappointed President Eisenhower who expected Warren to be a traditional conservative but he presided over the most liberal Court in the Court's history; Justice Harry Blackmun became more liberal that President Nixon expected him to be; and Justice David Souter's voting record was more liberal than President George H. W. Bush expected.

 The Constitution does not provide any qualifications for federal judges. A member of the Court does not even have to be a lawyer. The President may *nominate* anyone to serve and the Senate can reject a nominee for any reason. But most members of the Court have been graduates of prestigious law schools and in recent years, individuals who have had prior judicial experience.

5.61 | *Demographics*

In addition to political factors such as party and ideology, and legal factors such as legal training, the Court's membership is examined in terms of demographic factors such as race, ethnicity, age, gender, and religion. The Court is not a representative institution. For the first 180 years, the Court's membership almost exclusively white male Protestant. In 1967 Thurgood Marshall became the first Black member of the Court. In 1981, Sandra Day O'Connor became the first female member of the Court. But it is interesting to note that the liberal Marshall was replaced by a conservative, Clarence Thomas, and the two female members of the Court did not share an ideological perspective. Justice Brandeis became the first Jewish Justice in 1916. In 2006 Samuel Alito became the fifth sitting Catholic Justice, which gave the Court a Catholic majority.

The Supreme Court of the United States, 2010

5.62 | *Senate Hearings*

As the courts have played a broader role in our system of government and politics, the confirmation process has attracted more attention from interest groups, the media, political parties, and the general public. One form of participation in the confirmation process is lobbying senators to vote to confirm or to reject a nominee. The Senate Judiciary Committee conducts hearings, questioning nominees to determine their suitability. At the close of confirmation hearings, the Committee votes on whether the nomination should go to the full Senate with a positive, negative or neutral report.

The practice of a judicial nominee being questioned by the Senate Judiciary Committee began in the 1920s as efforts by the nominees to respond to critics or to answer specific concerns. The modern Senate practice of questioning nominees on their judicial views began in the 1950s, after the Supreme Court had become a controversial institution after the *Brown v. Board of Education* decision and other controversial rulings. After the Senate Judiciary Committee hearings and vote, the whole Senate considers the nominee. A simple majority vote is required to confirm or to reject a nominee. Although the Senate can reject a nominee for any reason, even reasons not related to professional qualifications, it is by tradition that a vote against a nominee is for cause. It is assumed that the President's nominee will be confirmed unless there are good reasons for voting against the nominee. And so rejections are relatively rare. The most recent rejection of a nominee by vote of the full Senate came in 1987, when the Senate refused to confirm Robert Bork. A President who thinks that his nominee has little chance of being confirmed is likely to withdraw the nomination.

5.63 | *Vacancies*

The Constitution provides that Justices "shall hold their Offices during good Behavior." A Justice may be removed by impeachment and conviction by congressional vote. Only one Justice (Samuel Chase in 1805) has been impeached by the House and he was acquitted by the Senate. His impeachment was part of the era's intense partisan political struggles between the Federalists and Jeffersonian-Republicans. As a result, impeachment gained a bad reputation as a partisan measure to inappropriately control the Court rather than as a legitimate way to hold judges accountable as public officials. Court vacancies do not occur regularly. There are times when retirement, death, or resignations produce vacancies in fairly quick succession. In the early 1970s, for example, Hugo Black and John Marshall Harlan II retired within a week of each other because of health problems. There are other times when a great length of time passes between nominations. Eleven years passed between Stephen Breyer's nomination in 1994 Justice O'Connor's retirement in 2005. Only four Presidents have been unable to appoint a Justice: William H. Harrison, Zachary Taylor, Andrew Johnson, and Jimmy Carter.

The Chief Justice can give retired Supreme Court Justices temporary assignments to sit with U.S. Courts of Appeals. These assignments are similar to the senior status, the semi-retired status of other federal court judges. Justices typically strategically plan their decisions to leave the bench so that their successor will be appointed by a President who is most likely to nominate a person who will share their partisan or ideological views of the role of the Court. This is possible because the Justices have lifetime appointments. They decide when to retire, usually because of age and infirmity.

5.64 | *The Size of the Supreme Court*

The Constitution does not specify the size of the Supreme Court. Congress determines the number of Justices. The Judiciary Act of 1789 set the number of Justices at six. President Washington appointed six Justices—but the first session of the Supreme Court in January 1790 was adjourned because of a lack of a quorum. The size of the Court was expanded to seven members in 1807, nine in 1837, and ten in 1863. In Judicial Circuits Act of 1866 provided that the next three Court vacancies would not be filled. The Act was passed to deny President Johnson the opportunity to appoint Justices. The Circuit

Judges Act of 1869 set the number at nine again where it has remained ever since. In February of 1937 President Franklin D. Roosevelt proposed the Judiciary Reorganization Bill to expand the Court by allowing an additional Justice for every sitting Justice who reached the age of seventy but did not retire (up to a maximum Court size of fifteen). The Bill failed because members of Congress saw it as a court packing plan. Roosevelt was in office so long that was able to appoint eight Justices and promote one Associate Justice to Chief Justice.

5.7 | Deciding Cases: Is it Law or Politics?

One of the most frequently asked questions about the courts is whether judges decide cases based on law or politics. This question goes to the heart of the legitimacy problem. To answer the question let's look first at the Supreme Court as an institution. The Supreme Court has almost complete control over the cases that it hears. The Supreme Court controls its docket. It decides only 80-90 of the approximately 10,000 cases it is asked to decide each year. This means that the Court decides which issues to decide and which issues not to decide. This is, in a sense, political power.

The role of law and politics in an individual Justice's decision making is of more direct interest. Legal scholars identify a variety of influences or factors that explain judicial decisions. But there are two general models of judicial decision making: a legal model and a political (or extra-legal) model. The legal model of deciding cases explains judicial decisions as based on legal factors (the law and the facts of the case). The political model explains decisions as based on behavioral factors (demographics such as race, gender, religion, ethnicity, age), attitudinal factors (political, ideological, or partisan), or public opinion. The legal methods include the plain meaning of the words, the intentions of the framers, and precedent. The most political method is interpretation, where judges decide cases based on their own beliefs about what the law is or should be, or contemporary societal expectations of justice.

5.71 | *Understanding the Methods of Deciding Cases*

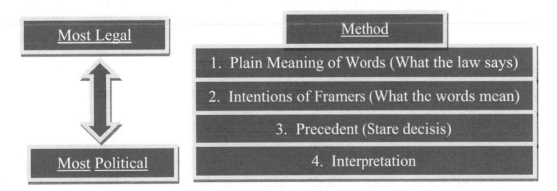

In a system of government based on the rule of law, it makes sense to expect that judges would decide cases based on the written law, whether it is the Constitution, a statue, or an administrative regulation. The following is a logical order in which judges decide cases.

5.72 | *Plain Meaning of the Words*

This method of deciding a case entails a judge reading the law to determine whether case can be decided by the plain meaning of the words. Sometimes the meaning of the law is plain. The Constitution requires that a President be 35 years old and a native born citizen. But some provisions of the Constitution are ambiguous. The Fifth Amendment provides that "No person shall be... deprived of life, liberty, or property, without due process of law…" The Eighth Amendment prohibits "cruel and unusual punishments." It is impossible to read the phrases "due process" or "cruel and unusual punishment" and arrive at a plain meaning of the words. Judges must use other methods to determine the meaning of these general provisions of the Constitution.

      Statutes can present a similar problem. The Communication Decency Act of 1996, for instance, made it a felony to "knowingly" transmit "obscene or indecent" messages to a person under age 18. It is easy to determine whether a person who was sent a message was under age 18; it is virtually impossible to define with any precision the meaning of "indecent," therefore the meaning of the word requires interpretation.

5.73 | *Intentions of the Framers*

If the plain meaning of the words (what the words say) is not clear, then a judge can rely on another method of deciding a case: the intentions of those who wrote the law. This method relies on determining the intentions of the frames, what the individuals who wrote the law intended the words to mean. In order to determine what the words of the Constitution mean, a judge could examine the Records of the Constitutional Convention, the writings or letters of the delegates to the Constitutional Convention of 1787, the Federalist Papers (a series of essays by James Madison, Alexander Hamilton, and John Jay supporting the adoption of the new Constitution), or the writings of the Anti-federalists (authors who opposed the ratification of the new constitution). In order to determine the meaning of the words in a constitutional amendment, a judge might examine the Congressional Record for evidence of the intentions of the framers. The congressional debates surrounding the adoption of the 13th, 14th, and 15th Amendments, for example, can provide a better understanding of the purposes of these three post-Civil War Amendments.

5.74 | *Precedent*

The U.S. legal system is based on **precedent** or *stare decisis*. *Stare decisis* is Latin for "let the previous decision stand." The system of precedent means a judge is expected to decide a current issue the way a previous issue was decided. Although precedent may seem like a legalistic way to decide cases, it is actually based on a common sense expectation of justice: an expectation that an individual will be treated the way other similarly situated individuals were treated. In this sense, precedent is a basic element of fairness.

      Precedent is a system where the past guides the present. But courts cannot always decide a case by looking backward at how other courts decided a question or legal issue. Sometimes a judge may think it is inappropriate to decide a current question the same way it was decided in the past. Attitudes toward equality and the treatment of women for example may have changed. Or attitudes toward corporal punishment may have changed. Rigidly adhering to precedent does not readily allow for legal change. And sometimes courts are presented with new issues for which there is no clearly established precedent. Advances in science and technology, for instance, presented the courts with new issues such as patenting new life forms created in the laboratory or the property rights to discoveries from the Human Genome Project. When the plain meaning of the words, the intentions of the framers, and precedent do not determine the outcome of a case, then judges sometimes turn to another method: interpretation.

Think about it!

Should judges make policy?

What does Justice Antonin Scalia say about reading the law?

http://www.pbs.org/newshour/bb/law/july-dec12/scalia_08-09.html

5.75 | *Interpretation*

Interpretation is defined as a judge deciding a case based on her or his own understanding of what the law should mean, or modern society's expectations of what the law should mean. Take, for example, the problem of deciding what the Eighth Amendment's prohibition against "cruel and unusual punishment" means. Should it refer to what people thought was cruel in the 18th Century, or should the standards of modern or civilized society be used to interpret what punishment is prohibited? Interpretation is controversial because it gives judges a great deal of freedom to decide what the law means. Interpretation is also called political decision-making, legislating from the bench, or activism because judges determine what the law means rather than those who wrote the law. This is sometimes called legislating from the bench, or judicial activism. Judicial restraint usually means judicial deference to the other branches of government, upholding precedent, and deciding only legal (not economic, social, or political) issues.

5.7 | **The 50 State Court System**

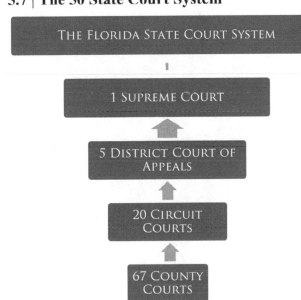

THE FLORIDA STATE COURT SYSTEM

1 SUPREME COURT

5 DISTRICT COURT OF APPEALS

20 CIRCUIT COURTS

67 COUNTY COURTS

The U.S. system of federalism gives each state substantive power to establish its own court systems and its own system of civil and criminal laws. Therefore the U.S. does not have two court systems (one federal and one state). It has fifty-one systems: one federal and 50 separate state court systems.

The Florida Supreme Court has responsibility for the administration or management of the entire state court system. These responsibilities include budgeting and allocation of judicial resources. The Supreme Court also has to hear appeals from death penalty sentences, cases in which a defendant receives capital punishment.

5.8 | Additional Resources

5.81 | *Internet Resources*

Landmark Supreme Court cases are available at www.landmarkcases.org

A gallery of famous trials (e.g., Socrates, Galileo, the Salem Witch Trials, John Peter Zenger, and the Oklahoma City Bomber) are available at htt://www.law.umkc.edu/faculty/projects/ftrials/ftrials.htm

Information about the organization and functions of the federal court system, including a court locator to find the federal courts in your area or information about serving as a juror, is available at http://www.uscourts.gov/

The full text and summaries of Supreme Court opinions, as well as audio recordings of the oral arguments before the U.S. Supreme Court are available at the Oyez Project: http://www.oyez.org/

Videos of the Justices explaining their views on how they see their individual job as Justices and the Court's role as an institution in their own words are available at the C-SPAN Web site: http://supremecourt.c-span.org/Video/TVPrograms.aspx

Information about the 50 state court systems is available at The National Center for State Courts: http://www.ncsconline.org/

For Information about Florida's death row, a virtual tour of a prison cell, or other information about convicted offenders on the death row roster is available at the My Florida Web site (click Government, Executive Branch, Department of Corrections): www.myflorida.gov The link to death row fact sheets is http://www.dc.state.fl.us/oth/deathrow/

Additional information about the Supreme Court is available at http://www.pbs.org/wnet/supremecourt/educators/lp4b.html and http://www.pbs.org/wnet/supremecourt/educators/lp4c.html

Demographic information about the Supreme Court Justices is available at http://www.fas.org/sgp/crs/misc/R40802.pdf

5.82 | *In the Library*

Ball, Howard. Supreme Court and the Intimate Lives of Americans: Birth, Sex, Marriage, Childrearing, and Death. New York University Press, 2004.

Bugliosi, Vincent et. al. The Betrayal of America: How the Supreme Court Undermined Our Constitution and Chose Our President. Thunder's Mouth Press, 2001.

Cooper, Philip. Battles on the Bench: Conflict Inside the Supreme Court. University Press of Kansas, 1999.

Dworkin, Ronald (ed). Badly Flawed Election: Debating Bush v. Gore, the Supreme Court, American Democracy. The New Press, 2002.

Garbus, Martin. Courting Disaster. Times Books, 2002.

Gregory, Leland H. Presumed Ignorant! Over 400 Cases of Legal Looniness, Daffy Defendants, and Bloopers from the Bench. Bantam Books, 1998.

Hall, Kermit (ed). Conscience and Belief: The Supreme Court and Religion. Garland Publishers, 2000.

Hammond, Thomas H., Chris W. Bonneau, and Reginald S. Sheehan. Strategic Behavior and Policy Choice On The U.S. Supreme Court. Stanford University Press, 2005.

Hansford, Thomas G. and James F., II Spriggs. The Politics of Precedent on the U.S. Supreme Court. Princeton University Press, 2006.

Hitchcock, James and Robert P. George (ed). The Supreme Court and Religion in American Life: From Higher Law to Sectarian Scruples (New Forum Books Series), Vol. 2. Princeton University Press, 2004.

Lazarus, Edward. Closed Chambers: The First Eyewitness Account of the Epic Struggles Inside the Supreme Court. Times Books, 1998.

Lipkin,, Robert. Constitutional Revolutions: Pragmatism and the Role of Judicial Review in American Constitutionalism. Duke University Press, 2000.

Lopeman, Charles S. The Activist Advocate: Policy Making in State Supreme Courts. Praeger, 1999.

McCloskey, Robert and Sanford Levinson. The American Supreme Court, 3/e. University of Chicago Press, 2000.

Mourtada-Sabbah, Nada. The Political Question Doctrine and the Supreme Court of the United States. Lexington Books, 2007.

Noonan, John T. Narrowing the Nation's Power: The Supreme Court Sides with the States. University of California Press, 2002.

Peppers, Todd C. Courtiers of the Marble Palace: The Rise and Influence of the Supreme Court Law Clerk. Stanford University Press, 2006.

Raskin, Jamin B. Overruling Democracy: The Supreme Court Versus the American People. Taylor and Francis, Inc., 2004.

Rehnquist, William H. The Supreme Court. Knopf, 2001.

Schwartz, Herman. The Rehnquist Court. Hill and Wang, 2002.

Starr, Kenneth. First Among Equals: The Supreme Court in American Life. Warner, 2002.

Toobin, Jeffery. The Nine: Inside the Secret World of the Supreme Court. Anchor, 2008.

Yarbrough, Tinsley. The Rehnquist Court and the Constitution. Oxford University Press, 2001.

5.83 | TERMS

Legitimacy
Judicial restraint
Judicial activism
Judicial review
dispute resolution
law interpretation
precedent

5.84 | DISCUSSION QUESTIONS

1. Discuss the importance of the Marshall Court.
2. Explain *stare decisis* and the role it plays in the American judicial system. What did William Rehnquist mean when he called *stare decisis* "a cornerstone of our legal system" but said that "it has less power in constitutional cases?" Do you agree with him?
3. Describe the racial, ethnic, and gender makeup of the federal courts. Does it matter that some groups are underrepresented and other groups are overrepresented? Why?
4. Discuss the criteria for nominating Supreme Court justices and the process by which the nominees are confirmed. How has the process changed in recent years?
5. Discuss the advantages and disadvantages of judicial activism and judicial restraint.
6. Compare and contrast the attitudinal, behavioral, and strategic models of judicial decision making. Explain which of these models most accurately captures how judges make their decisions.
7. What factors affect the implementation of court rulings? Should courts be given additional power to implement decisions?

[1] http://jurist.law.pitt.edu/gazette/2005/12/detainee-treatment-act-of-2005-white.php
[2] The Court's annual case schedule and docket are available at http://www.supremecourtus.gov/

CHAPTER 6: FEDERALISM

OUT OF MANY, ONE.

CHAPTER 6: FEDERALISM | 121

6.0 | Why Federalism?

What is federalism? Why have a federal system of government? How does the U.S. system of federalism work today? These are some of the questions that will be answered in this chapter. The chapter
- Defines federalism.
- Explains the logic of the U.S. system of federalism.
- Describes how the U.S. system of federalism works today, and
- Examines the power problem with federalism.

The general public does not think about federalism very much and therefore does not have much to say one way or another about federalism itself.[1] The average voter has stronger opinions about criminal justice policy, education, abortion, immigration, or national security policy than opinions about federalism. Federalism tends to be considered a technical matter of interest to government officials or political insiders more than the general public. Americans do, however, have strong opinions about "big government"—and opinions about big government are often directly related to federalism because "big government" is a euphemism for the federal government of "Washington." In fact, political opinion about public polices related to crime, education, abortion, the environment, health care, and immigration is usually related to opinions about federalism because they include opinions about whether the policies should be state or national government policies.

Federalism is a two-tiered system of government in which power is divided between a national (or central) government and subnational units (states, provinces, or regional governments). Therefore federalism is a geographic division of power. In the U.S., power is distributed between the national government and state governments. The number of states has grown from the original 13 to 50 today with the addition of Hawaii in 1959. In other countries with federal systems (e.g., Argentina, Australia, Canada, Germany, and India) the regional governments are called provinces. Constitutional federalism means that neither the national nor the state governments can abolish one another because both levels of government are the creatures of the constitution. A state such Alabama or Vermont or Wyoming is not a creature of the national government or a mere local administrative unit of the national government. In the U.S. system of federalism, both the national and state governments are sovereign political entities. Federalism is based on the concept of dual sovereignty: both the national and state governments have sovereignty. Sovereignty is defined as having the ultimate or highest authority. Is it possible to have two sovereigns with authority over the same geographic area and people? The idea of dual sovereigns does seem to conflict with the concept of sovereignty as ultimate government authority. In fact, this is the source of the power problem with federalism. The image below depicts political fighting over federalism in Australia, which is analogous to the 50 states fighting with one other in the U.S.

The **power problem with federal systems** of government is the need to strike the right balance of power between the state governments and the federal government. The Constitution provides for a federal system but with a few notable exceptions, such as the power to coin money and the power to regulate interstate commerce, which are exclusively federal powers, the Constitution does not specify what powers each has. As a result, American politics has historically included debates about which level of government should do what, and whether the federal government is getting too big. Finding the right balance of powers is both a legal (or constitutional) matter **and** a political matter. It is about law and politics. In fact, federalism is a good example of the challenge of adapting a Constitution that is more than 200 years old to modern times, the challenge of maintaining continuity with the federal system established by the Constitution while accommodating major economic, political, technological, scientific, and social changes.

Federalism is not the most common type of political system in the world. Most of the world's approximately 190 countries have unitary systems of government (that is one unit), not federal systems. So why does the U.S. have a federal system? The answer to this question is provided in the very origins of the word *federalism*. The word federalism comes from the Latin *foedus*, or covenant, where individuals or groups agree to join a political union with a government body to coordinate their interests and represent them. In the American political experience, the colonists had strong attachments to their colonial governments, just as people now have attachments to their state governments. The colonists were wary of giving too much power to a central government. Federalism was a way for government power to be divided between the states and a national government as part of the system of checks and balances.

Federalism serves three main purposes. First, it is part of the system of institutional checks and balances that was designed to control government power by dividing it between two levels of government. Second, creates a political system where interests can be represented in the national government. Members of Congress represent states and districts within states. Third, federalism creates a governance system where the states can serve as "laboratories of experimentation." If one or more states try a policy (e.g., education reform or health care reform) that works, the successful policy experiment can be adopted by other states. If one state's policy experiment fails then the costs are limited to one state—unlike what happens when the national government adopts a policy that fails.

"The question of the relation of the States to the Federal Government is the cardinal question of our constitutional system. At every turn of our national development, we have been brought face to face with it, and no definition either of statesmen or of judges has ever quieted or decided it." **Woodrow Wilson, 28th President of the United States**

6.1 | Comparing Systems of Government

One way to better understand federalism is to compare it with other types of government. There are three basic types of systems of government: unitary systems, confederal systems, and federal systems.

6.11 | Unitary Systems

A **unitary system** is, as the term suggests, a political system with one level of government. Power concentrated in one central government. The central government has sovereignty or the highest governing authority. The central government may create local or regional units to help govern but these units are "creatures" of the national or unitary government. They are created by the national government and they can be abolished by the national government—and the national government also can determine how much power the local units have because the local units do not have sovereignty.

In France, for example, the national government can abolish local governments or change their boundaries. This kind of national control over state governments does not exist in the United States, because the Constitution created a federal system where both the federal (national) government and the state governments have independent constitutional status. The Constitution provides for both a national government and state governments. The American states, however, are unitary systems. The states can create, alter, or abolish local governments such as cities, counties, school districts, port authorities, as well as the other kinds of special governments that states create.

Canada has a federal system that divides power between the federal parliament and provincial governments. Under the Constitution Act, Section 91 of the Canadian Constitution provides for federal legislative authority and Section 92 provides for provincial powers. One difference between Canadian and U.S. federalism is that the Canadian system provides that the provincial governments have specifically delegated powers and all the national government retains all residual powers. In the U.S. the national government has specifically delegated powers and the states retain all residual powers. All federal systems have political conflicts over which level of government has power over which areas of policy. Areas of Canadian conflict include legislation with respect to regulation of the economy, taxation, and natural resources. The actual distribution of powers evolves over time. The Australian system of federalism resembles the U.S. system in terms of the division of power between the national and state governments but Australia has a parliamentary system rather than the separation of powers.

6.12 | Confederal Systems

A **confederal system** (or a confederation) is a political system where the constituent units (the states, provinces, or regional governments) are more powerful than the central (or national) government. Power is decentralized. The central government is comparatively weak, with fewer powers and governing responsibilities than the units.

The Founders decided to create a federal system rather than a unitary or confederal system because of their political experience. The Revolutionary War was fought against the British monarchy, a unitary system with power concentrated in the national government. And the first U.S. form of government, the Articles of Confederation, was a confederal system that was widely viewed as flawed because it left the national government with too little power to address the problems facing the new nation. They considered federalism a form of government that was between the extreme centralization of a unitary system and the extreme decentralization of a confederation.

6.2 | The Articles of Confederation

The first U.S. government after the colonial era was a confederation: The Articles of Confederation. Congress adopted The Articles of Confederation in 1777 and they became effective upon ratification by the states in 1781. The following are some of the most important provisions of the Articles of Confederation.

Articles of Confederation

"To all to whom these Presents shall come, we the undersigned Delegates of the States affixed to our Names send greeting.

Articles of Confederation and perpetual Union between the states of New Hampshire, Massachusetts-bay Rhode Island and Providence Plantations, Connecticut, New York, New Jersey, Pennsylvania, Delaware, Maryland, Virginia, North Carolina, South Carolina and Georgia.

I.The Stile of this Confederacy shall be "The United States of America."

II.Each state retains its sovereignty, freedom, and independence, and every power, jurisdiction, and right, which is not by this Confederation expressly delegated to the United States, in Congress assembled.

III.The said States hereby severally enter into a firm league of friendship with each other, for their common defense, the security of their liberties, and their mutual and general welfare, binding themselves to assist each other, against all force offered to, or attacks made upon them, or any of them, on account of religion, sovereignty, trade, or any other pretense whatever."

X. [Authorizes a committee of the states to carry out the powers of Congress when Congress is in recess.]

The above language from the Articles of Confederation describes a union where most power resides with the constituent units, the states. It specifically refers to the political system as a union of states that join together in "a league of friendship." It stipulates that each state retains its "sovereignty, freedom, and independence." Article X authorizes a committee of the states to act for Congress when Congress is in recess. The language of the Articles suggests that the each state that joined the Confederation remained free to decide whether to leave the Confederation. Slavery and the nature of the union, specifically whether states could leave it, were the two main causes of the Civil War.

6.21 | *The Second Confederation*

Eleven southern states believed that secession was one of the powers retained by the states as sovereign and independent entities in the federal system created by the Constitution. The Constitution created a federal system, but it did not define whether states could leave the union. Political divorce was not mentioned. The North argued that the union was permanent—that once a state decided to join *the* United States the marriage was permanent. The South argued that the states retained the power to decide to leave the union. Their view of federalism left more power in the hands of the states which were united as *these* United States," a term that reflects their belief that federalism left considerable power with the states.

The Confederate States of America (1861-1865), or the Confederacy, was the government formed by eleven southern states. The United States of America ("The Union") believed that secession was illegal and refused to recognize the Confederacy as a legal political entity. The North considered the South a region in rebellion. The end of the Civil War in the spring of 1865 began a decade-long process known as Reconstruction. This "second civil war" involved extensive efforts to exert federal control over the states of the confederacy. Political resistance against federal authority was quite strong, and the struggle for the civil rights of newly freed slaves and Black citizens continued into the 20th Century as part of the civil rights movement. Determining the appropriate balance of power between the national and state governments remains a controversial political and legal issue.

6.3 | Federalism and the Constitution

The Constitution created a federal government with more power than the national government had under the Articles of Confederation. Specific powers were **delegated** to the national government. Article I, Section 8 of the Constitution lists powers granted to Congress. The list of powers delegated to Congress includes the power to coin money, tax, regulate interstate commerce, and raise and support armies.

The Constitution also took some powers that had belonged to the states under the Articles of Confederation and gave them to the federal government. The states were specifically prohibited from coining money and regulating interstate commerce because the Founders—principally the Federalists—believed that the national government had to direct the nation's economic development. Then there is the infamous Supremacy Clause, which provides that federal laws "shall be the supreme Law of the Land." The Supremacy Clause does not prohibit states from having laws that differ from the federal laws, but it does prohibit states from passing laws that conflict with federal laws.

All other powers—those not delegated to the national government, or prohibited to the states—were to be reserved (or left with) the states or the people. These are the **reserved** powers. The reserved powers are dictated by the 10th Amendment: "The powers not delegated to the United States by the Constitution, nor prohibited by it to the States, are reserved to the states respectively, or to the people." The language of the 10th

Amendment reflects the fact that there was some uncertainty about exactly which powers the Constitution delegated to a stronger national government. The Anti-Federalists worried that the new Constitution betrayed the Revolutionary War cause of fighting against a monarchy or strong central government. The Constitution did significantly increase the power of the national government. The 10th Amendment reassured the Anti-federalists that the states retained their traditional powers.

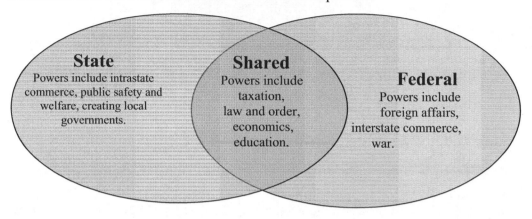

The first U.S. government after the colonial era was a confederation: The Articles of Confederation. Congress adopted The Articles of Confederation in 1777 and they became effective upon ratification by the states in 1781. The following are some of the most issues related to federalism.

The Constitution does not define or explain federalism because the states were pre-existing units of government. The Constitution also did not define the nature of the union, whether the union was permanent or states could decide to secede. The Constitution also did not provide specifics on the actual division of power between the national and state governments. The balance of power between the national and state governments was left to be determined by politics and by subsequent generations. In fact, the balance of power between the national and state governments has historically been determined more by politics than by the actual language of the Constitution. This is apparent in the way that federalism has been an important aspect of political events throughout the history of the United States. Federalism was a central element of the Civil War; the Civil Rights movements; the expansion of the rights of suspects and prisoners in the criminal justice system; the controversy over the right to privacy as it applies to abortion policy; and most recently, federalism has been an underlying issue involving the controversy over the definition of marriage.

6.4 | Why Federalism?

Federalism is part of the Madisonian system of institutional checks and balances. In *Federalist No 51*, Hamilton explained how dividing power between two levels of government in a "compound republic" checked government power:

> In a single republic, all the power surrendered by the people is submitted to the administration of a single government; and the usurpations are guarded against by a division of the government into distinct and separate departments. In the compound republic of America, the power surrendered by the people is first divided between two distinct governments, and then the portion allotted to each subdivided among distinct and separate departments. Hence a double security arises to the rights of the people. The different governments will control each other at the same time that each will be controlled by itself.

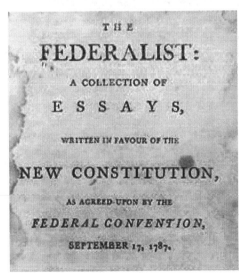

Hamilton was an ardent Federalist. He believed that one of the lessons of history was that threats to good public order came from a government that was too strong to hold government officials accountable and from government that was too weak to create or maintain good public order. Hamilton believed that federalism solved some of the problems of a weak national government under the Articles of Confederation, weaknesses that were exposed by Shays' Rebellion and other domestic disturbances by creating a stronger national government. Federalists also supported a strong national government to direct economic development. In *Federalist Number Nine*, Hamilton wrote:

> A FIRM UNION WILL BE OF THE UTMOST MOMENT TO THE PEACE AND LIBERTY OF THE STATES, AS A BARRIER AGAINST DOMESTIC FACTION AND INSURRECTION. IT IS IMPOSSIBLE TO READ THE HISTORY OF THE PETTY REPUBLICS OF GREECE AND ITALY WITHOUT FEELING SENSATIONS OF HORROR AND DISGUST AT THE DISTRACTIONS WITH WHICH THEY WERE CONTINUALLY AGITATED, AND AT THE RAPID SUCCESSION OF REVOLUTIONS BY WHICH THEY WERE KEPT IN A STATE

OF PERPETUAL VIBRATION BETWEEN THE EXTREMES OF TYRANNY AND ANARCHY....[THE CRITICS OF REPUBLICAN GOVERNMENT] HAVE DECRIED ALL FREE GOVERNMENT AS INCONSISTENT WITH THE ORDER OF SOCIETY....THE SCIENCE OF POLITICS, HOWEVER, LIKE MOST OTHER SCIENCES, HAS RECEIVED GREAT IMPROVEMENT. THE EFFICACY OF VARIOUS PRINCIPLES IS NOW WELL UNDERSTOOD, WHICH WERE EITHER NOT KNOWN AT ALL, OR IMPERFECTLY KNOWN TO THE ANCIENTS. THE REGULAR DISTRIBUTION OF POWER INTO DISTINCT DEPARTMENTS; THE INTRODUCTION OF LEGISLATIVE BALANCES AND CHECKS; THE INSTITUTION OF COURTS COMPOSED OF JUDGES HOLDING THEIR OFFICES DURING GOOD BEHAVIOR; THE REPRESENTATION OF THE PEOPLE IN THE LEGISLATURE BY DEPUTIES OF THEIR OWN ELECTION: THESE ARE WHOLLY NEW DISCOVERIES, OR HAVE MADE THEIR PRINCIPAL PROGRESS TOWARDS PERFECTION IN MODERN TIMES.

> Think About It!
> Do you agree with Hamilton's analysis of the threats to freedom in Federalist No.8, "The Consequences of Hostilities Between the States"?
> http://thomas.loc.gov/home/histdox/fed_08.html

Hamilton's call for a national government with enough power to create and maintain good public order as well as to promote economic development stands in sharp contrast with the Anti-federalists. The Anti-federalists were a loosely-organized group of individuals who advocated for what would today be called states' rights. They believed that the powers of the national government should be limited and that the states should be the primary political unit within the American system of federalism.

6.5 | The Political Effects of Federalism

Federalism has two principal effects on government and politics. First, it creates a large number of governments. Second, complicates government and politics.

6.51 | The Surprisingly Large Number of Governments

Although federalism is a two-tiered system of government, the U.S. actually has a large number of governments: one national government; 50 state governments; and thousands of local governments.

The Number of Governments in the United States	
Type	Number
Federal Government	1
States	50
Counties	3,043
Municipalities	19,372
Townships or Towns	16,629
School districts	13,726
Special Districts* <ul><li>Mosquito Control</li><li>Child Protective Services</li><li>Port Authority</li><li>Airport</li><li>Beach Taxing</li><li>Health Care</li><li>F.I.N.D (Florida Inland Navigation District)</li></ul>	34,683
TOTAL NUMBER OF GOVERNMENT UNITS:	87,504

*Examples of Special Districts in Palm Beach County, Florida

Think About It! What's in a name? Does it matter whether a municipality is a city or a town? Yes, it does.

Niagara Falls in Danger of Losing Status as City, Aid"
http://www.npr.org/2012/10/25/16
3653935/niagara-falls-in-danger-
of-losing-city-status-aid

Act on it!

One good thing about having a large number of governments is the increased access to government. Contact a local government official and ask a question about a public policy issue of interest to you.

Source: U.S. Department of Commerce, Statistical Abstract of the United States, 2003 (Washington, D.C.: U.S. Government Printing Office, 2003), 261

Federalism also complicates American government and politics. In unitary political systems, political debates focus on the substance of public policy. The debates focus on *what* public policy should be concerning foreign affairs, economics, crime, education, the environment, moral regulatory policy, or religion. All countries debate public policy on these controversial issues. In the U.S., federalism means that political debates are about *what* public policy should be and about *who* should be making public policy. We debate whether abortion should be legal, whether there a right to die, whether global warming exists and what public policy should be, whether the death penalty should be used for sentencing, whether organized prayer be allowed in public schools. We also debate who should be making the policy, whether the national or state governments should be making public policy. The U.S. system of federalism makes American politics doubly complicated: we debate what policy should be and who should make it.

Federalism has means that politics includes running debates about the proper distribution of power over public policy. Federalism and the distribution of power between the national and state governments have been part of many of the nation's most important political events: the Civil War; Progressive Era debates about social policy; the Great Depression of the 1930s; and the 20th Century Civil Rights movements. Federalism is also one of the issues that inspired the modern conservative movement in the latter 1960s as a reaction against the New Deal and Great Society expansions of national government power over domestic policies.

Debates about federalism are actually debates about one aspect of the **power problem**: how much power to centralize in the national government and how much power to leave decentralized with the states. The Constitution does not solve the power problem in the sense that it does not specify, except for certain areas such as coining money and regulating interstate commerce, whether the national government or the state governments have power to act in an area of public policy. The federalism dimension of the power problem has been dynamic. The actual distribution of power between the national and state governments changes depending on conditions and circumstances.

Crises usually result in centralization of power in the national government. Shays' Rebellion, the Great Depression; World War II and the Cold War, and terrorist threats to national security were all crises that resulted in increased power for the national government.

6.6 | Federalism is Dynamic

The balance of power between the national and state governments is dynamic. It is always changing, with the balance sometimes

> The PEW Center on the States provides data on economic mobility in the states. http://www.pewstates.org/research/data-visualizations/economic-mobility-of-the-states-interactive-85899381539

tilting toward the national government and sometimes tilting toward the states. But modern federalism does not work the way the Founders intended. The Founders created a political system where most government power was left in the hands of the states and the national government's powers were limited. It was a state-centered system. Over time, however, the powers of the national government expanded, and expanded relative to the states. The following describes the major historical changes in federalism.

6.61 | Dual Federalism

The first era of federalism is described as dual federalism. **Dual federalism** is a theory of federalism that describes both the federal government and the state governments as co-equal sovereigns. Each is sovereign in its respective areas of policymaking. The Supreme Court endorsed this understanding of federalism in an early case _Cooley v. Board of Port Wardens_ (1851). The question in this case was whether a state government could require that ships entering or leaving the Philadelphia harbor hire a local pilot. The Constitution gives the national government exclusive power to regulate commerce among the states. The Philadelphia Port traffic involved more than one state, so it was interstate commerce. The Court developed the **Cooley Doctrine** to decide whether a matter was for local or national regulation. According to the Cooley Doctrine, subjects that are "in their nature national, or admit only of one uniform system, or plan of regulation, may justly be said to...require exclusive legislation by Congress." Subjects that are not national and require local diversity of regulation are left to the states. The Cooley Doctrine assumes that the national and state governments have separate areas of responsibility. For example, the national government would have exclusive power over interstate commerce, national security, and foreign affairs, while the state governments would have exclusive power over schools, law enforcement, and road building.

The Cooley Doctrine still serves as a guide for determining whether the national or state governments have power to regulate, but it does not provide specific answers to questions about whether something required a single, uniform system of regulation. In fact, as both the national and state governments shared responsibility over more areas of public policy, debates about highway speed limits, legal drinking ages, educational policy, the regulation of airports, and immigration issues have challenged the idea that each level of government is supreme in it respective field.

6.62 | *Cooperative Federalism*

Cooperative federalism describes the national and state governments as sharing power over areas of public policy. Dual federalism is an outdated concept in the sense that there are so few areas of public policy that are exclusively either state or national, and so many areas of public policy where the federal government now acts. For example, all levels of government are involved in education, economics, transportation, crime, and environmental policy. The term **intergovernmental relations** is useful for understanding how modern federalism works because it captures how the national, state, and local governments interact with one another to make and administer policy.

One way to better understand the forces of change in the American political system is to examine economics. Economic changes have prompted the expansion of the federal government. The Industrial Revolution in the mid-19th Century fundamentally changed the American economy. The emergence of large national corporations created support for national government action to regulate these new centers of private power. During the Progressive Era (1890s until the World War I) the national government began to regulate industries such as the railroads, steel, banking, and mining. The federal government also passed social welfare legislation including child labor laws and minimum wage and maximum hour laws. In fact, today the federal government redistributes resources from wealthier states to poorer states. In today's economy, population mobility, the ability to relocate to states where the jobs are is an important economic indicator.

6.63 | *Expansion of Federal Power*

One measure of big government is the increased size and influence of the national government relative to the state governments. As the country changed from a local economy to a national economy, where businesses made and sold products and services across the country, public opinion shifted toward seeing the national government as the appropriate level of government to regulate business. During the 20th Century the power of the national government continued to expand relative to the states. The modern era of the U.S. political system began in the 1930s partly in response to an economic crisis. The

Great Depression created popular support for national government activism to remedy the problem of the economic depression. The trend toward centralizing power and responsibility for maintaining material prosperity has accelerated with the further development of a global economy, where businesses buy and sell in a world economy.

A second source of expansion of federal power is civil rights. The Civil War Amendments—the 13th, 14th, and 15th Amendments—expanded the federal government's role in promoting racial equality. The Fourteenth Amendment, which was ratified in 1868, prohibits a state from denying to any person within its jurisdiction the equal protection of the laws. This Amendment was intended to protect the rights of newly freed slaves from state laws that discriminated against them on account of race. The Fourteenth Amendment gave Congress power to pass "appropriate legislation" to enforce

the provisions of the Amendment. Congress used this power to pass civil rights legislation such as the Civil Rights Act of 1875 which outlawed racial discrimination in public accommodations. However, in the _Civil Rights Cases_ (1883), the Supreme Court declared the law unconstitutional because it regulated private behavior—the decisions of owners of hotels and restaurants not to serve Black customers. According to the Court, the Fourteenth Amendment, which was the basis for the Act, prohibited state action. The Court's landmark ruling in _Plessy v. Ferguson_ (1896) also limited the scope of federal civil rights laws by upholding state laws that required racial segregation.

The Civil Rights Movement of the 1950s and 1960s also relied on federal efforts to secure the civil rights of individuals who were the victims of discrimination. Some of these efforts relied on Congress, which passed laws such as the 1964 Civil Rights Act and the 1965 Voting Rights Act. Some of the efforts relied on the United States Supreme Court. Decisions in landmark cases such as Brown v. Board of Education (1954) made state actions supporting racial discrimination in public schools unconstitutional. In many parts of the country the use of federal power to enforce equal protection of the laws prompted strong resistance. The constitutional argument against this use of federal power to promote equality, particularly racial equality, was the states' rights argument.

Federalism was part of the background of the civil rights movement. The U.S. Supreme Court rulings in cases such as *Brown v. Board of Education*, in which they outlawed racial segregation in public schools, prompted a political backlash in the states, particularly in the South. The principal reason for the backlash was opposition to

Courtesy Kansas State Historical Society

Oliver L. Brown, et al. vs Board of Education of Topeka, Kansas, United States Supreme Court, May 17, 1954.

integration. However, there was also a strong **states' rights** opposition to integration. States' rights can be defined as a belief that a policy is the responsibility of a state government not the national or federal government. Florida was one of the southern states that cited states' rights reasons for opposing court-ordered desegregation. In 1957, the Florida Legislature passed an <u>Interposition Resolution</u> in response to *Brown v. Board of Education*. **Interposition** is a political doctrine that a state can interpose itself between the people of the state and the federal government when the federal government exceeds its authority. The Interposition Resolution declared that the U.S. Supreme Court exceeded its power when it declared racially segregated public schools unconstitutional.

Advocates of states' rights opposed the use of federal power to achieve greater racial equality in state politics, government, and society. George Wallace is an important political figure in the states' rights movement. He was a precursor of the modern conservative movement's criticism of big government, by which he meant a federal government with the power to order states to change their laws regarding race relations. He is a good example of how thinking about federalism is interwoven with thinking about civil rights in the U.S. Wallace was a forceful and articulate spokesperson for the conservative belief that the federal government's powers were limited to those specifically enumerated. He gave impassioned campaign speeches defending states' rights against a civil rights movement that relied heavily on "outside agitators" to bring about change. The outsiders were the federal government in general and the courts in particular.

> Think About It!
> Listen to one of Governor George Wallace's states' rights speech against the civil rights movement:
> http://www.youtube.com/watch?v=QW6ikSCDaRQ&feature=endscreen&NR=1

A third reason for the expansion of federal power is criminal justice policy. The development of a national economy made state borders less relevant for legitimate business and economic activity because goods were no longer made, marketed, and sold entirely within one state. Illegitimate businesses were also organized nationally. Organized crime, in particular, did not operate exclusively within a single state. The rise of organized crime presented a challenge to law enforcement which was historically state and local law enforcement. The rise of nationally organized criminal enterprises provided one of the justifications for the creation of the Federal Bureau of Investigation (FBI). The FBI has jurisdiction across the country, unlike local law enforcement whose jurisdiction (or legal authority) is geographically limited. Historically, criminal justice has been one of the areas of public policy reserved to the states under the U.S. system of federalism. The rise of organized crime, the war on crime, and the war on drugs made crime and policing a national political issue to be addressed by the federal government. Congress responded by passing more and more anti-crime legislation—a trend toward federalizing crime that continued throughout the 20th Century and into the 21st Century.

Think about it! Why does the U.S. have a federal law enforcement agency? The FBI tells the story of its creation and expansion in "A Brief History of the FBI."http://www.fbi.gov/about-us/history/brief-history

---

A fourth reason for the expansion of federal power is national security, national defense, and foreign policy. World War II and the Cold War increased the power of the national government. Threats to national security have historically been considered the primary responsibility of the federal government. The war on terror has continued to shift power to the national government relative to the states. For instance, the federal government increasingly uses the resources and information on local governments to find and track terrorist suspects. Terrorism is often an international threat—its support networks, funding, and training involve other countries, and terrorists seek to move easily across national borders—therefore the threat of terrorism typically increases the power to the federal government.

The economy, civil rights, national security, and crime are not the only reasons for the expansion of federal power. In environmental policy, Congress has passed major legislation such as the Clean Air Act and the Clean Water Act and established bureaucratic agencies the Environmental Protection Agency to implement the new federal environmental policies. In educational policy, Congress passed the No Child Left Behind Act. The Act increased the federal government's role in an area of public policy that was traditionally left to the states. In health care, President Obama signed the Patient Protection and Affordable Health Care Act on March 23, 2010. Twenty-eight states filed lawsuits claiming that parts of the Act, which critics called Obamacare, were unconstitutional because they exceeded the federal government's power. The Supreme Court upheld most provisions of the Act, including the mandate that individuals buy health insurance or pay a penalty/tax, in National Federation of Independent Business v. Sebelius (2012), but ruled that state sovereignty protected the states from certain provisions of the law that required states to adopt certain health care policies or lose federal Medicaid funding.

6.7 | The Conservative Backlash: New Federalism

Beginning in the latter 1960s, conservatives began criticizing the expansion of the federal government and the idea of cooperative federalism. Their criticism of "big government" included calls for returning some power to the states. Their advocacy of states' rights was intended primarily as a check on the expansion of the national government's power in domestic affairs. The Nixon administration's policies to support returning some powers to the states were called <u>New Federalism</u>.

The political support for New Federalism was also reflected in changes in the Supreme Court's rulings. The Court began to limit the powers of the federal government. From 1938 until 1995, the Court did not invalidate any federal statute on the grounds that the law exceeded Congress' power under the Interstate Commerce Clause. But in <u>United States v. Lopez</u> (1995), the Court ruled that some provisions of the Gun-Free School Zones Act, a federal law enacted in 1990 to curb gun violence, exceeded Congress's commerce powers and infringed on the states' reserved powers to provide safe schools. A conservative majority on the Rehnquist Court issued a number of important rulings that enforce constitutional provisions that limit congressional power in fields of public policy where the states have power to act. These rulings are based on the political conservative belief that federalism is a legal arrangement that protects the states and is part of the system of checks and balances that protects individual freedom.

The challenge is to adapt a more than 200 year old system of federalism to a modern environment that has experienced a great deal of political, economic, technological, and social change. Take, for example, economic change. The U.S. economy has changed from local to state to national and now, with globalism, international trade. How does a global economy affect the distribution of power between the national and state governments? How has the U.S. assumption of the role as the world's policeman, the Cold War, and the war on terror affected the distribution of power between the national and state governments? These economic and national security developments have increased federal power—an increase that sometimes, but not always, means a decrease in state powers.

Think about it!

Do we still need states? In a global economy, are political boundaries such as states merely an additional business expense?

Federalism is one aspect of the conservative backlash against the liberal centralization of power that occurred during the New Deal and Great Society eras. The backlash has not been inspired by opposition to big government in general. Conservatives supported big government for national security purposes, getting tough on crime, and moral regulatory purposes (e.g., sexual behavior, marriage, obscenity and indecency, and the definition of marriage). Even in economic policy, business groups with ties to conservative and Republican politics such as the U.S. Chamber of Commerce and the National Association of Manufacturers lobbied for the passage of federal laws that explicitly preempt state tort laws. Tort laws govern wrongful injury lawsuits such as product liability and medical malpractice litigation. The states traditionally had primary responsibility for tort laws as part of their reserved powers. The tort reform movement, of which the Chamber of Commerce and the National Association of Manufacturers are prominent supporters, advocates taking cases out of the state courts and into the federal courts. This is evidence that liberal and conservative attitudes toward federalism tend to be strategic rather than principled. A principled position is one that is taken regardless of whether it produces a preferred outcome. A strategic position is one that is taken because it produces a preferred outcome. Liberals tend to think that policies should be decided in the states when they think the state political systems will produce liberal policy outcomes. Conservatives tend to think that policies should be decided in the states when they think the state political systems will produce conservative policy outcomes. If a liberal (or a conservative) thinks the federal government will produce a preferred policy outcome, they are likely to think that the policy should be decided by the federal government rather than the states.

6.71 | *Immigration Policy*

Immigration is one of the issues that illustrate the potential conflict between national and state policy. Controlling undocumented immigrants is a pressing issue in some states, particularly states bordering Mexico and states with large numbers of undocumented immigrants. The key constitutional doctrine for understanding whether states have the power to act in an area or policy field is **preemption**. Federal law can preempt or trump state law. The preemption doctrine is based on the <u>Supremacy Clause</u>, Article VI of the Constitution, which provides that the Constitution, federal laws, and treaties shall be the "supreme Law of the Land." The Supremacy Clause guarantees national union. When deciding whether a state law conflicts with a federal law the Court does a "preemption analysis" consisting of three questions. Did Congress expressly state that federal law preempted state law? Does the state law conflict with federal law? Has Congress so extensively regulated the area of policy to have "occupied the field?" If Congress has enacted a comprehensive and unified federal policy in a field, then Congress has assumed responsibility for that field and left little or no room for state action. States can experiment with health care reform, education reform, and many other reforms in other areas of public policy.

Immigration policy is a special case because it has national security implications. Illegal immigration became a political issue when some states thought the federal government was unwilling or unable to enforce immigration laws. States adopted a variety of laws that were intended to discourage illegal entry and to discourage employment of illegal immigrants or undocumented aliens. Arizona, which shares a border with Mexico, is one such state. In 2010 it passed SB1070 an immigration control law that, among things, required Arizona police officers to determine the citizenship or immigration status of a person who was lawfully detained. SB1070 served as a model for other states including Alabama, Georgia, Indiana, South Carolina, and Utah. The Arizona law was challenged on the grounds that it was preempted by federal law. In <u>*Arizona v. U.S.*</u> (2012), the Supreme Court upheld one provision of the law and struck down three provisions.

The stated purpose of SB1070 was to use state resources to help the federal government enforce its immigration laws. The law 1) required law enforcement officers to check the immigration status of persons who they have a "reasonable suspicion" are in the country illegally; 2) required the warrantless arrest of individuals that law enforcement official have probable cause to believe have committed a crime for which the person could be deported; 3) made it a crime to not carry immigration papers in the state; and 4) made it a crime for illegal immigrants to seek a job or to work in the state.

The Court upheld provision number one but struck down the other three. The Court explained that the federal government's broad power over immigration and alien status is based on 1) its enumerated power in Art I, Sect. 8 cl. 4 to "establish an uniform Rule of Naturalization;" 2) its inherent sovereign power to control and conduct foreign relations; and 3) the Supremacy clause. The fact that Congress has created a single sovereign responsible for maintaining a comprehensive and unified system to keep track of aliens within the nation limits state sovereignty to legislate in a policy field that Congress has occupied. The dissenting Justices argued that the states have their own inherent sovereignty and can legislate on immigration matters of great concern to them.

Think About It!

What should public policy regarding undocumented aliens be? Who should make the policy?

6.8 | Summary

This chapter described federalism, explained the origins of the U.S. system of federalism, and described its development over time. The division of powers between the national and state governments has been controversial throughout the nation's history. Federalism has proven to be a dynamic form of government in the sense that the actual distribution of power between the national and state governments has varied a great deal over time. The Constitution provides for a federal system but, with the notable exception of foreign affairs and interstate commerce, it does not specify exactly what each level of government has power to do. As a result, the actual balance of power between the national and state governments changes. In this sense, federalism is dynamic. The federal government's power has increased, and it has increased relative to the state governments for a variety of reasons, including the development of a global economy. Because of the central role federalism plays in the system of checks and balances, changes in federalism raise important questions about where to strike the right balance between state and federal power.

6.9 | Additional Resources

6.91 | Internet Resources

One valuable resource for information about the states is the PEW Center On the States which describes and analyzes state policy trends, for example. See http://www.pewcenteronthestates.org/

The Tenth Amendment Center provides a contemporary view on states' rights: http://www.tenthamendmentcenter.com/

The Urban Institute's publication "Assessing the New Federalism" is an informative look at the place for cities in the U.S. system of federalism: www.urban.org/center/anf/index.cfm

Publius: The Journal of Federalism is an academic journal dedicated to the investigation of issues related to federalism: http://publius.oxfordjournals.org/

The National Council of State Legislators provides a variety of information about state legislatures, including ideas about the relationship between the state and federal governments: www.ncsl.org/statefed/afipolcy.htm

6.92 | *In The Library*

Berman, David. 2003. Local Governments and the States: Autonomy, Politics, and Policy. ME Sharpe.

Burgess, Michael. 2006. Comparative Federalism: Theory and Practice. Routledge, 2006.

Butler, Henry N. 1996. Using Federalism to Improve Environmental Policy (AEI Studies in Regulation and Federalism). American Enterprise Institute Press, 1996.

Cornell, Saul. The Other Founders: Anti-Federalism and the Dissenting Tradition in America, 1788-1828. University of North Carolina Press, 1999.

Doernberg, Donald. 2005. Sovereign Immunity And/Or the Rule of Law: The New Federalism. Carolina Academic Press.

Donahue, John.1997. Disunited States. Basic Books.

Elkins, Stanley and Eric McKitrick. 1995. The Age of Federalism: The Early American Republic, 1788-1800. Oxford University Press.

Gerston, Larry N. 2007. American Federalism: A Concise Introduction. M.E. Sharpe.

Karmis, Dimitrios. 2005. Theories of Federalism: A Reader London: Palgrave Macmillan.

Nagel, Robert F. 2002. The Implosion of American Federalism. Oxford University Press, 2002.

Noonan, Jr. John T. 2002. Narrowing the Nation's Power: The Supreme Court Sides with the States. University of California Press, 2002.

Remington, Micheal C. 2002. Federalism and the Constitution: Limits on Congressional Power and Significant Events, 1776 – 2000.

Schrag, Peter. 1999. Paradise Lost: California's Experience, America's Future. University of California Press.

Tarr, G. Alan, Robert F. Williams, Josef Marko (eds.). 2004. Federalism, Subnational Constitutions, and Minority Rights. Praeger.

Twight, Charlotte. 2002. Dependent on D.C.: The Rise of Federal Control Over Ordinary Lives. Palgrave.

Zimmerman, Joseph. 2002. Interstate Cooperation: Compacts and Administrative Agreements. Praeger.

TERMS:

Federalism
Unitary system
Confederation
Delegated powers
Reserved powers
The power problem
Dual federalism
Cooley Doctrine
Cooperative federalism
States' rights
Interposition

6.93 | STUDY QUESTIONS

Why have a federal system of government?

Discuss the allocation of federal and state powers.

Explain how the allocation of federal and state powers has changed over time.

Describe four areas where federal powers have grown into areas traditionally reserved for the states.

Discuss the current state of federalism in the United States.

What role did the civil rights movement play in the expansion of federal powers?

How is federalism dynamic?

Why did the Federalists believe that a strong federal government was necessary?

---

[1] Larry N. Gerston. 2007. American Federalism: A Concise Introduction. New York: M.E. Sharpe, Inc., p.87.

7.0 | The Media and Democracy

The media play an important role in all modern democracies. A free press is a strong indicator of whether a political system is democratic. In fact, freedom of the press is considered an essential condition for modern democratic government. Freedom of the press is vital for democracy because self-government requires an informed and educated citizenry. The **educative role** is one of the reasons why the press is the only business that is given constitutional protection (the First Amendment guarantees freedom of the press). But education is not the media's only function. In the U.S. system of government, the media are also expected to play a **watchdog role**. The institutional media are expected to play an important role in checking government power by investigating and reporting on government and public affairs. The modern mass media have also played a **socialization role** by presenting the same information and portraying cultural values to national audiences.

The importance of these roles in a democracy explains why the power of the press (or media) has been such a controversial issue throughout the nation's history. The power problem with the media is that a free press is not necessarily a fair press. How the press uses its substantial, and growing, power is controversial. Media bias—whether ideological or partisan—is a familiar theme in American politics because of the central role the media play in government and politics. This chapter examines the media's role in American democracy.

The media are unusual in that they are mostly private companies whose primary purpose is to make money, but they also are expected to serve a public function. Media companies exist to make money—which they do by providing entertainment, information (news), and advertising. The educative and watchdog functions of the media are not the primary roles of media companies. The history of the media reveals major changes in media technology and function. During the founding era, the press was not just political; it was an overtly partisan press. Handbills and flyers and papers were distributed to convince readers to support a person or a party. The emergence of powerful corporations in the railroad, banking, manufacturing, and oil sectors of the economy prompted calls for big government to act as a countervailing force to big business. The media played an investigative, watchdog role by alerting the public to business influence or abuses of power. In the modern era of government and politics, both campaigns and government rely heavily on public communications. The media provide the public with almost constant information about government and politics. But the relationship between the media and democracy has changed. During the founding era, the press was very partisan or closely aligned with political movements and parties. Today the mainstream media are often less obviously committed to one side in public debates, but questions remain about how the large corporate media conglomerates are using their power in an information age. The concerns about the power of the press, about media biases, remain.

"Were it left to me to decide whether we should have a government without newspapers or newspapers without a government, I should not hesitate a moment to prefer the latter."
Thomas Jefferson

"The man who reads nothing at all is better educated than the man who reads nothing but newspapers. The press is the toxin of the nation." **Thomas Jefferson**

"Why should a government which believes it is doing right allow itself to be criticized. It would not allow opposition by lethal weapons. Ideas are much more fatal things than guns."
Nikolai Lenin (1920)

"I'm as mad as hell, and I am not going to take this anymore."
UBS Evening News Anchor Howard Beale in the film Network (USA 1976)

7.1 | The Love-Hate Relationship

Despite the common assumption that the media are essential for democratic government, Americans have always been ambivalent about the press. Thomas Jefferson's comments on the newspapers of his day reflect the attitudes of the politicians of his day and today. Which of Jefferson's statements about the press quoted above do you think were made before he became president and was made after he became president? Attitudes toward the role of the press may depend on whether you are in office or not. The love-hate relationship is nothing new. In Jefferson's day, the press was intensely partisan and played an open, active role in politics.

7.2 | The Founding Era

The print press certainly played an important role in the founding of the American republic. The Trial of John Peter Zenger is an example of one of the famous American trials illustrating the importance of freedom of the press as a way to hold government officials accountable. In 1735, the editor and publisher of a newspaper called *The New York Weekly Journal* was tried on charges of sedition and libel for publishing articles that criticized William Cosby, the governor of the New York colony. The trial was an important event because it presented a challenge to the government's power to limit freedom of expression in order to maintain what the government considered good public order. The outcome of the case strengthened the colonists' commitment to two ideas: the idea that freedom of the press and trial by jury were important checks on the power of government.

7.21 | *The First Amendment*

The language of the First Amendment acknowledges the importance of freedom of the press: "Congress shall make no law....abridging the freedom....of the press...." The First Amendment establishes the unique role of the press as only business that is specifically protected by the Constitution. This special status is one reason why the press is sometimes called "the fourth estate"—a reference to the fact that the press is, along with congress, the president, and the judiciary, one of our political institutions. But just as Americans love to hate government, they love to hate the press.

7.22 | *The Hate Relationship – The Partisan Press*

Freedom of the press played an important role in the founding of the republic, but criticism of the press is almost as old as the republic. The early press focused on scandals and salacious stories in order to sell papers. Then, as now, scandals sold papers. The early press was sometimes called "the penny press" because the papers were very cheap. The penny press was political rather than professional. In the early days of the republic, the press was both political and partisan. A paper was identified with a particular point of view: it openly and explicitly and strongly either supported or opposed a political party; it took strong stands on political issues, candidates, or government officials. There was less news reporting and more of what we today would call editorial or analysis. Neither the reading public nor public officials expected a newspaper to strive for objectivity or neutrality—or to use the phrase popularized by Fox News, "Fair and Balanced" reporting.

7.23 | Libel Laws

In the early days of the republic, the *free press* was not expected to be a *fair press*. Newspapers became early targets of political criticism because the free press was not a fair press. Influential or prominent individuals and powerful government officials were often upset by what their critics in the press printed about them. Their response to what they considered bad press included support for the passage of laws against libel and slander. Libel and slander are false spoken or written statements that injure a person. The injury can be economic or reputational.

The Alien and Sedition Acts of 1798 are examples of early federal laws that limited freedom of the press despite the absolutist language of the First Amendment prohibiting congress from passing any law restricting freedom of speech or press. The Act made it a crime (seditious libel) to publish false or scandalous statements that tend to bring government into disrepute. The laws were passed by a Congress controlled by Federalists who did not appreciate what their political opponents—including Thomas Jefferson and other Anti-federalists—were saying about them. When Jefferson became president and the Democratic-Republican Party became the dominant political party, the Sedition Act of 1798 was repealed.

These early controversies involving the role of the press in American politics illustrate that early American attitudes toward the media were complicated. There was strong support for a free press able to criticize public officials, but strong criticism of the press for not being fair.

7.24 | *The Commercial Media*

In the 1830s, the partisan press changed to a commercial press with the emergence of came to be called the penny press. Advances in printing technology allowed newspapers to be produced at a far cheaper rate (one cent rather than 6 cents). The reduced cost of producing newspapers made news profitable. Papers made money by printing sensationalized accounts of crimes and disasters and scandals. This was **yellow journalism**, a pejorative reference to journalism that features scandal-mongering, sensationalism, jingoism, or other unethical or unprofessional practices and coverage.

7.25 | *Pulitzer, Hearst and the Spanish-American War*

The circulation battles over the New York newspaper audience between Joseph Pulitzer's *New York World* and William Randolph Hearst's *New York Journal* lead to increases in the sensationalism of the press. As a part of the battle for dominance for the New York media market, both newspapers sensationalized increasing tensions with Spanish-controlled Cuba. When the U.S. Naval ship *The Maine* exploded in a Cuban harbor, Hearst and Pulitzer both sensationalized the Spanish involvement in the explosion. The U.S. soon went to war with Spain and the Spanish-American war is considered the first press-driven war.

Pulitzer's coverage of the explosion   Hearst's coverage of the explosion

7.25 | *Muckraking*

Muckraker journalism emerged in the latter part of the 19th Century as an early form of investigative reporting. A muckraker is a journalist who digs around in the muck to expose corruption. The Industrial Revolution and the government's **laissez faire** policies toward corporations prompted journalists to expose public and private crime, fraud, waste, threats to public health and safety, graft, and illegal financial dealings.

7.26 | *The Professional Press*

Starting around 1900, the press began to be more professional. Joseph Pulitzer started a school of journalism at Columbia University. Journalism schools trained journalists to be objective, to separate facts from of opinion, to avoid biased coverage of public affairs. The byline, or putting the name of newspaper reporters on stories, allowed the public to hold reporters accountable for their work. During the 20th Century, the institutional print media, including the major national newspapers, and then the institutional broadcast media, added prestige to professional journalism and news reporting on public affairs.

The idea of an objective press was based on a belief that facts were distinct from values: objective journalists should have "faith in *facts*" and skepticism toward *values*; objective journalists should segregate facts and opinions/values."[1] This professional ethic encouraged journalists to consider the reporter separate from the news they reported and take pride in presenting the news (the facts) as objectively or neutrally as possible. The ideal of an objective *professional* press encouraged the view that the institutional press should function as a virtual "fourth branch" of government describing the world of government and politics. It also created the idea that news reporters would assume a critical role as **watchdog** journalists who investigate and publicize wrongdoing. Two of the most significant instances of the press performing the watchdog role are *The New York Times* reporting on the Pentagon Papers in 1971 and the *Washington Post* reporting on the Watergate Scandal in 1972. These stories contributed to President Nixon's famous hostility toward the press. Listen to the following audio recording of a December 14, 1972 conversation where President Nixon gave his Secretary of State, Henry Kissinger, advice about press relations after discussing how to handle press coverage of the Vietnam War. What does it reveal about a president's attitudes toward the press?

> Think About It!
> In the Nixon Tape "Nixon, Kissinger on 'Christmas Bombing'" President Nixon says to Kissinger:
> "Also, never forget. The press is the enemy. The press is the enemy. The press is the enemy. The establishment is the enemy. The professors are the enemy. The professors are the enemy. Write that on the blackboard 100 times. And never forget it."
> http://www.youtube.com/watch?v=h0vi2l0WxO8

7.3 | The Mass Media

The modern mass media are widely criticized by government officials, politicians, and the general public. The fictional character Howard Beale, the UBS network evening news anchor in the 1976 film *Network*, captured the criticism of the media's power in a famous, award winning rant during a television broadcast. Beale tells viewers to go to a window, open it, and shout out as loud as you can: "I'm mad as hell and I'm not going to take it anymore!" The Beale character's outburst resonated with public frustration with an increasingly powerful media in an era when three broadcast networks—ABC, CBS, and NBC—dominated the airwaves. The media today seem to be everywhere, a pervasive force in modern society. With the proliferation of media outlets, as the internet joined newspapers and television and radio, worries about media power have changed. There is less worry that three corporate media companies control access to information. There is more worry about too much information, too much entertainment, too much consumer-focused programming, and a segmenting of the information marketplace.

7.31 | *The New Media and the Fragmentation of the Media*

The media have become both consolidated, in terms of ownership, and fragmented, in terms of the types of media that are available. While in 1940, 83% of newspapers were independently owned, less than 20% of newspapers now are not a part of a chain or

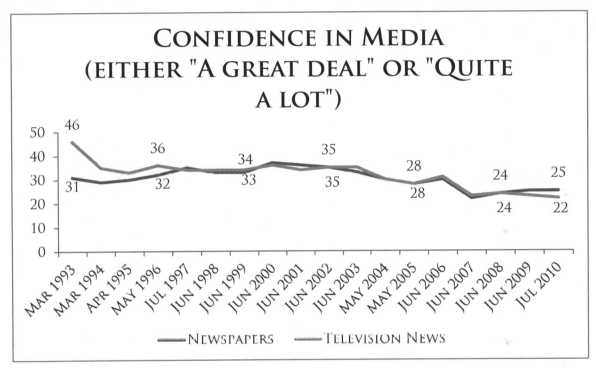

CONFIDENCE IN MEDIA (EITHER "A GREAT DEAL" OR "QUITE A LOT")

media conglomerate. At the same time, a wider menu of options has emerged for those seeking information. Twenty-four hour a day news reporting, internet news sources, and the increasing availability of news sources to match political ideologies has several consequences. First, scholars have found that as competition between news sources increases, the quality and in-depth coverage of news declines. Second, fragmentation may also lead to a decline in the ability of political leaders to hold the attention of the public. Third, the increased number of news outlets results in people seeking out news that reinforces their views. This makes people less open to alternative viewpoints, and more set in beliefs that may or may not be true. Generally, the increased fragmentation and competition have resulted in less confidence in the media in the U.S. As the figure above shows, less than a quarter of the American public has a great deal or quite a lot of confidence in either newspapers or television news.

7.32 | *The Mass Media*

The term mass media refers to media that are specifically designed to reach a large (that is, mass) audience such as the entire population of a nation or state. The term was coined in the 1920s with the development of nationwide radio networks and mass-circulation newspapers and magazines. The classic examples of mass media are the three television

networks—ABC, CBS, and NBC—before the emergence of cable television networks (CNN and ESPN began in the late 1970s) and the Internet. The programming of the three broadcast television networks was clearly intended to appeal to a national audience. The broadcast networks and the major newspapers (e.g., *The New York Times*, *Washington Post*, *Chicago Tribune*, and *Los Angeles Times*) are sometimes referred to as the "MSM " or mainstream media. Cable TV is a relatively recent addition to the mass media.

7.4 | i-Media

Communications technology is changing the media. The mass media are being replaced by individualized (i-media), which are smaller scale, niche audience, or specialized target media. These are sometimes called the "new media." Some internet media now reach audiences and markets on a scale that was previously limited to the very large mass media. These internet media include personal web pages, podcasts and blogs. The institutional media, whether it is print journalism or electronic journalism, is facing competition from various new media. The new media are not just competing for a market share previously controlled by the mass media; it is a competition that is revolutionizing the production of news and other programming content. The new media provide more user-generated content. These new media blur the distinction between professional and amateur journalism and change the traditional function of the mass media as "mediating" institutions—in a mass society of 300 million people, for example, the institutional press mediated between big government and the individual citizen.

7.41 | *The End of Institutional Press?*

For some time now declining newspaper subscriptions have raised serious questions about the future of newspapers. In "The Report on the State of the News Media in 2007," Arthur Ochs Sulzberger Jr, the publisher and chairman of The New York Times Company, responded to questions about the impact of technological changes on print journalism. He said, "I really don't know whether we'll be printing *The Times* in five years, and you know what? I don't care?"[2] This is a surprising statement for a newspaper man to make about the future of the print press.

The *Report* noted that technology was transforming the media in ways that may be as important the development of the television and radio, and perhaps even as important as the development of the printing press itself. Information technology is not just changing the way people get information. It may be fundamentally changing the relationship of the consumer or citizen to traditional institutions including government, education, and the media: "Technology is redefining the role of the citizen—endowing the individual with more responsibility and command over how he or she consumes information—and that new role is only beginning to be understood." Information technology has empowered individuals by making them less dependent on the institutional media to *mediate*. Political scientists use the term mediating to refer to those institutions in large, mass societies that stand between the state (i.e., big government) and the individual. For example, as the national government grows larger, the gap between a lone individual and big government increases. Mediating institutions provide individuals with information about government and check on government. The owners of newspaper, television, and internet companies, and the editors who work for them, filter, edit, or otherwise decide what is newsworthy and merits reporting. Information technology is making this traditional "mediating" role less important. But eliminating the mediating institutions leaves the individual citizen or consumer with more responsibility for determining the accuracy of the electronic information that is now so widely available and either free or cheap. These new or non-institutional media are part of trend toward "de-intermediation" that includes Wikipedia, We Media, YouTube, and the blogosphere.

7.42 | *I-Media and Politics*

The advent of new forms of media has had a strong effect on political action and political campaigning, particularly in the 2008 presidential election. A survey by the Pew Center for Internet & American Life[3] found that nearly three quarters of (74%) of internet users (55% of the general population) went online in 2008 to get involved in the political process or to get news and information about the election. 45% of internet users used the internet to watch a video related to the campaign and a third forwarded political content to others. These findings – and the increased prominence (and success) of political campaigns internet outreach suggests that traditional forms of media may not be connected people to political information as they have done in the past.

AS GAG-RULERS WOULD HAVE IT.
—Satterfield in the Jersey City *Journal*.

7.5 | Journalism as a Profession

The development of an independent, professional journalism began after the Civil War when newspapers were no longer as likely to be closely allied with a political party. The fact the newspapers became less partisan did not mean that the press became less political, however. Newspapers in the latter part of the 19th Century became very political during the Progressive Era (roughly the 1890s until World War I), but they tended to be political in the sense that they criticized political machines and political party bosses, or advocated on behalf of causes such as public corruption. As journalism became a profession, reporters were less partisan but still political. Investigative reporting of scandals or working conditions redefined the role of the press from a partisan press to an institutional press with the power to set the political agenda by calling public attention to an issue than needed political attention.

7.6 | The Media and the Political System

The media, including individuals working as reporters, editors, and producers, as well as media organizations, has a large amount of control over what the American public sees as the news. The approval of government action by the public is essential in a democracy, and the people must be aware of what the government is doing in order to approve. As such, the media's choice of what is newsworthy has very real implications for the health of the American democracy.

7.61 | *Reporting Political News*

Reporting political news and public affairs information is one of the core functions of media outlets, particularly those with a national focus. Washington, D.C. has the largest concentration of news professionals in the United States. There are more than 8000 reporters with Congressional press passes in Washington, covering political news for the American public.[4]

The president receives the most news coverage of any political figure. Presidents hold press conferences to shape public opinion and explain their actions. Today, a press secretary often briefs the media on a regular basis, instead of having regular press conferences with the president personally, a traditional started in the Eisenhower administration. Prior to that, many reporters maintained personal relationships with the president and received updates directly from him. Now, the majority of news about the president is received through a daily (or near daily) press release, accompanied by a press briefing where the president's press secretary answers questions about the press release. Many scholars feel that the president does get a lot of attention, but most of it is negative. Negative coverage encourages cynicism in the population at large and alienates people from politics.

Presidential press conferences, where the president answers questions directly from the press, are much rarer. Press conferences appear to be an opportunity for the media to directly ask the president a question get an answer from the president (rather than from advisers or spokespeople), but press conferences are actually carefully staged events. Government officials provide answers that they have scripted and rehearsed before the conference. The number of news conferences given by a president varies dramatically, depending on the administration. As the figure below shows, presidents in the early 1900s gave many more press conferences than modern presidents.[5] Richard Nixon and Ronald Reagan gave very few press conferences; Nixon's low numbers were partially due to the fact that he had bad previous experiences with the press and partially due to the scandal of Watergate. Reagan's low numbers were largely due to the fact that he preferred alternate venues for communicating with the press, including one-on-one interviews, answering questions on his way to or from the Presidential helicopter or during a photo session, or, as Sam Donaldson, White House reporter for ABC News said, "The reason we yell at Reagan in the Rose Garden is that's the only place we see him."[6]

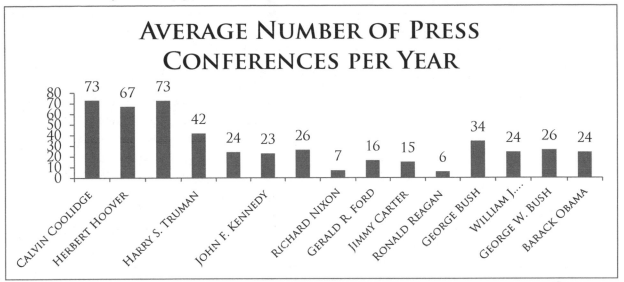

The media encountered challenges in covering George W. Bush's administration. President Bush prided himself on the "tightlipped, no leaks nature" of his White House. No one from the administration appeared in the media without prior approval, and no one talked about what went on behind closed doors. The administration was happy and the media were unhappy. Obama seems to prefer a more informal, off-the-cuff style of interaction with the press, and he has limited the number of formal press conferences

Media coverage of Congress is different than the coverage of the President. Congress has 535 members and is a decentralized institution. Public awareness of what Congress is doing and how it operates is rather low. Media coverage focuses on the leadership—the Speaker and majority and minority leaders. The chairs of committees engaged in reviewing important policies *may* get some attention from local stations and papers that report on local representatives.

One of the ways that the media **does** cover Congress is by investigations and scandals. When members of Congress do something scandalous (or illegal) the media give such affairs (and sometimes they are actually affairs) air time or print coverage. This kind of coverage is negative: it focuses on failures or misdeeds or scandals or partisan fights. The negative coverage is partly responsible for the public's negative perceptions of Congress as an ineffective branch of government. But media coverage of congressional committees doing their work, or the federal bureaucracy doing its work, is not usually considered newsworthy: it is considered as exciting as watching paint dry and not worthy of much attention.

The Media World At Your Fingertips
C-SPAN provides contact information for media organizations in the U.S. and other countries. Engage the media community in another country. Write a letter to the editor about the media organization's coverage of an issue of interest to you.
http://www.c-span.org/Resources/Media-Organizations/

7.7 | Media and Communications Law

There is an extensive body of law that governs freedom of the press. It includes statutory law (federal and state legislation), regulatory law (or administrative rulings and orders), and the case law (court rulings) on the First Amendment.

7.71 | *You can't say whatever you want*

Perhaps the most important thing to know about freedom of the press is that you are not free to publish whatever you want to. The Supreme Court has never said that the First Amendment gives an individual the right to say anything that he or she wants to say. For instance, libel and slander are not protected by the First Amendment. Libel is writing something that is false and injures another person. A person can be held responsible (financial or otherwise) for publishing something libelous and the government can punish individuals who publish factual information that is deemed harmful to national security. During the World War I era the Court upheld laws that punished individuals for criticizing U.S. participation in the war. One of the legal doctrines that the Court uses to determine when freedom of the press can be restricted is the <u>Clear and Present Danger Test</u>. The government can punish individuals for saying or publishing things that raise a "clear and present danger" of causing actions that the government has the power to prevent.

7.72 | *The Modern Media*

The growing role of the media, particularly the various forms of electronic communication, in modern American society has made communications a political issue. The government's role in communications has been controversial for decades. The federal government's media or telecommunications policy has three legal foundations:

7.73 | *Constitutional Law*

The First Amendment is the primary source of Constitutional protections for the media in the United States. It states that the "Congress shall make no law… abridging the freedom

of speech, or of the press." The Court has generally interpreted this right broadly and struck down attempted by the government to regulate the media. Freedom of the press has largely taken the form of protection from **prior restraint,** or the government banning expression of ideas prior to their publication. The most famous case upholding the press right to publish what it thinks is newsworthy is _New York Times v. United States_ (1971). This is the _Pentagon Papers_ case. The _New York Times_ and the _Washington Post_ had published excerpts of classified Department of Defense documents (the Pentagon Papers) examining the conduct of the War in Vietnam, and the papers planned additional publications. The Nixon administration sought an injunction against the publication of the documents, contending that the documents would prolong the war and embarrass the government. The Supreme Court explained that the First Amendment freedom of the press placed a heavy burden of proof on the government to explain why "prior restraint" (that is, an injunction that prohibiting publication) was necessary. And the Court ruled that the government had not met the burden of proof because it did not explain why publication of the documents would lead to immediate, inevitable, and irreparable harm to national security or other interests. As a result of the Court's rulings, the U.S. has one of the freest presses in the world.

Freedom of the press is not absolute. The government can limit freedom of the press if publication threatens national security interests. The government can legally prevent publication of certain strategic information such as the movement of troops during wartime. It can also legally censor publication of instructions on how build nuclear bombs. However, information technology has made such efforts to prevent publication practically difficult or even impossible. Information is now freely available on the Internet—even real time images of military actions. The War in Iraq illustrates how media technology has changed coverage of wars. The Pentagon adopted a policy of embedding journalists in military units. And soldiers with smart phones have repeatedly taken photos that exposed inappropriate or illegal behavior.

7.74 | _Statutory Laws_

The statutory basis for the federal government's media and telecommunications policy has its roots in two congressional acts, the Communications Act of 1934 and the Telecommunications Act of 1996. The Communications Act of 1934 established the **Federal Communications**

Commission (FCC) to oversee "interstate and foreign commerce in wire and radio communication." The FCC is considered one of the independent commissions because its members serve terms of office, can be removed only through impeachment, and no more than three of its five members can be from one political party.

The Communications Act went through a major overhaul when Congress passed the Telecommunications Act of 1996. The primary purpose of the Telecommunications Act was to deregulate the telecommunications industry. Prior to the 1996 Act, much of the telecommunications industry resembled a monopoly. People did not have a choice as to where they purchased their telephone service. The 1996 Act also relaxed laws on media ownership. Prior to the 1996 Act, a single company could not own more than twelve television stations or forty radio stations. The 1996 Act greatly relaxed this regulation, instead putting the cap of ownership at 35% of the national market for television and removing the cap entirely for radio ownership. As a result, major media companies like CBS, Fox, and Clear Channel greatly increased their shares of the media markets.

7.75 | *Administrative Regulations*

There are also administrative regulations that determine U.S. telecommunications and media policy. The **Federal Communications Commission** (FCC) is the primary source of these regulations, orders and policies. These regulations include the day-to-day actions of the FCC and the 1,899 employees that work for the FCC. This might include the approval of a merger of two telecommunications companies, fining companies for indecency, licensing amateur radio operators, and regulating some aspects of the internet.

7.76 | *The Fairness Doctrine*

One of the rules or regulations that the Federal Communications Commission promulgated was the fairness doctrine. The **fairness doctrine** required radio and television broadcast license holders to present controversial issues of public importance in a fair and balanced manner. The fairness doctrine is an example of an administrative regulation or "law" created by an administrative agency. It is a law in the generic sense that it is an official, binding policy that individuals or organizations are not free to decide whether to comply with it. The FCC's authority to issue regulations was upheld by the Supreme Court in *Red Lion Broadcasting Co. v. FCC* (1969).[7] Red Lion Broadcasting aired on a Pennsylvania radio station a 15 minute broadcast by Reverend Billy James Hargis as part of a Christian Crusade series. The broadcast accused an author, Fred Cook, of being a Communist and of writing a book to "smear and destroy Barry Goldwater." Cook demanded free time to reply under the Fairness Doctrine. Red Lion refused. The FCC ruled that the broadcast was a personal attack that violated the Fairness Doctrine. Red Lion challenged the Fairness Doctrine in court.

The Supreme Court upheld the constitutionality of the Fairness Doctrine on the grounds that Congress had the authority to regulate broadcast media because of the scarcity doctrine. According to the scarcity doctrine, the airwaves are public and the government can regulate them by licensing to prevent signal overlap. The scarcity doctrine is what differentiates the print media, which are not licensed by the government, from the broadcast media, which are. Cable TV is not subject to the same kinds of government licensing and regulation.

7.77 | Media Deregulation: Economic

The FCC repealed the fairness doctrine in 1987. The FCC is managed by five appointed commissioners. No more than three of the five commissioners can be of one political party. The three Republican commissioners, who reflected the broader Republican emphasis on deregulation of business, concluded that the doctrine had grown to inhibit rather than enhance debate. They maintained that the technology revolution had increased the media voices in the information marketplace and made the fairness doctrine unnecessary (and perhaps was even an unconstitutional limit on freedom of expression). One consequence of this economic deregulation of the media in the 1980s was the rise of conservative radio and television hosts/programs, such as Rush Limbaugh and Bill O'Reilly. The repeal of the fairness doctrine occurred at a time when conservatives were taking to the airwaves using a style of public discourse that would not have been possible under the regulatory schemes of the fairness doctrine, which would have required broadcasters to provide right to reply to programs that discussed controversial issues from one perspective or side.

The current FCC continues this economic deregulatory policy by allowing media mergers in the communications industry. The FCC's position is that emerging technology and marketplace competition is preferable to government regulation of this rapidly changing sector of the American economy. Congress has also supported this perspective in the Telecommunications Act of 1996.

7.78 | Media Re-regulation: Moral Regulatory policy and 'air' pollution

Media policy has traditionally divided the ideological left and right in American politics. It is not a matter of one side supporting government regulation and the other side opposing government regulation. The left and right are often divided over the purposes of government regulation. Liberals are generally more concerned about violence while conservatives are more concerned about sex. During the 1960s and 1970s, for example, the liberals on the Supreme Court generally supported civil libertarian claims that the First Amendment freedom of expression limited the government's power to restrict access to sexually explicit materials. The Justices increasingly required the government to provide evidence that its restrictions were necessary to prevent harm, and that the traditional argument that the government could restrict access to what it considered immoral materials was no longer valid. The result was a significant "deregulation" of morals or values based policies concerning access to sexually explicit materials.

This deregulation was one of the reasons for the conservative backlash against liberalism. Efforts to reregulate communications include federal laws aimed at increasing the government's power to regulate the media, particularly to protect minors, including the following.

- Communications Decency Act of 1996[8]

This law criminalized the "knowing" transmission of "obscene or indecent messages" to any person who was under 18 years of age. It defined obscene or indecent as any message "that, in context, depicts or describes, in terms patently offensive as measured by contemporary community standards, sexual or excretory activities or organs." The Supreme Court declared these provisions of the Act unconstitutional in *Reno v. American Civil Liberties Union* (1997) as the act violated the First Amendment.[9] In the ruling, Justice Stevens found that the act so restricted the ability of adults to engage in communication that is appropriate for them that cost outweighs the benefits of the law.

- Child Online Protection Act of 1998 (The "Son of CDA")[10]

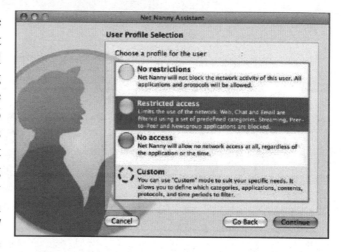

This Act required commercial Web site operators to take actions to prevent persons under 18 from seeing material harmful to children by demanding proof of age from computer users. The Act provided a fine of $50,000 and 6 month prison term for allowing minors to view harmful content, which it defined as harmful using "contemporary community standards."[11] The law was challenged in court. In *Ashcroft v. American Civil Liberties Union* (2004) the Supreme Court ruled that the law was unconstitutional because it limited the freedom of expression rights of adults. In 2007, U.S. District Judge Lowell A. Reed explained why he thought it was not a good idea to try to protect minors by limiting their rights as adults: "perhaps we do the minors of this country harm if First Amendment protections, which they will with age inherit fully, are chipped away in the name of their protection."[12]

- Children's Internet Protection Act of 2000.[13]

This Act required public libraries to and public schools to take measures to limit computer access to certain Web sites in order to protect children. The law was challenged by the American Library Association on the account that it required libraries to block access to constitutionally protected information. In *United States et al. v. American Library Association* (2003), the Supreme Court ruled that the law did not violate the First Amendment because the law did not require libraries to block access to information but simply made the government provision of financial assistance for obtaining internet service dependent on compliance with the law.

The FCC is entrusted with the responsibility of enforcing federal laws concerning obscenity, indecency, and profanity, as well as illegal actions by telecommunications companies, such as "mystery fees"[14] or "pay-to-play" programs.[15] The Enforcement Bureau of the FCC reviews public complaints and investigates to determine whether the facts warrant government action.[16] These investigations can result in   The difficulty determining what constitutes programming that warrants fines or other legal actions is illustrated by Michael Powell, the former Chair of the FCC, who stated the FCC's position on a television network broadcast of the popular film, *Saving Private Ryan* without censoring the soldiers' cursing. In response to public complaints about the primetime broadcast, and in an attempt to ease broadcasting company concerns about whether they would be subject to FCC disciplinary actions (fines or broadcast licensure revocation), Powell provided the following explanation of FCC policy.

STATEMENT OF MICHAEL K. POWELL, CHAIR
FEDERAL COMMUNICATION COMMISSION

Re: Complaints Against Various Licensees Regarding Their Broadcast on November 11, 2004, of ABC Television Network's Presentation of the Film "Saving Private Ryan,"

Today, we reaffirm that content cannot be evaluated without careful consideration of context. Saving Private Ryan is filled with expletives and material arguably unsuitable for some audiences, but it is not indecent in the unanimous view of the Commission.

This film is a critically acclaimed artwork that tells a gritty story—one of bloody battles and supreme heroism. The horror of war and the enormous personal sacrifice it draws on cannot be painted in airy pastels. The true colors are muddy brown and fire red and any accurate depiction of this significant historical tale could not be told properly without bringing that sense to the screen. It is for these reasons that the FCC has previously declined to rule this film indecent.

This, of course, is not to suggest that legal content is not otherwise objectionable to many Americans. Recognizing that fact, it is the responsible broadcaster that will provide full and wide disclosure of what viewers are likely to see and hear, to allow individuals and families to make their own well-informed decisions whether to watch or not. I believe ABC and its affiliated stations made a responsible effort to do just that in this case.

Fair warning is appropriately an important consideration in indecency cases. In complaints you often find that Americans are not excessively prudish, only that they are fed up with being ambushed with content at times and places they least expect it. It is insufficient to tell consumers not to watch objectionable content, if the "shock" value is dependent on the element of surprise. This is particularly true in broadcast television, where viewers are accustomed and encouraged to order their viewing by parts of the day—morning shows, daytime TV and late night have long been the zones in which expectations are set. When those lines are blurred, the consumer loses a degree of control, a degree of choice.

Context remains vital to any consideration of whether profanity or sexual content constitutes legally actionable indecency. The Commission must stay faithful to considering complaints within their setting and temper any movement toward stricter liability if it hopes to give full effect to the confines of the First Amendment."

7.8 | Which Way Are We Going?

The study of communication law and policy leads to the conclusion that for the past several decades (from the 1970s until today) policy has been moving in two different directions at the same time. One direction is toward deregulation (less government): policy has generally supported economic or business deregulation of telecommunications. In an era of deregulation of various industries (airlines; oil and natural gas), conservatives have argued that marketplace competition and technological innovation are solutions to problems with communications sector, not government regulation. The second direction is toward more regulation (more government): policy has supported more government regulation of telecommunications on behalf of social or values purposes. Conservatives worry about sex programming; liberals worry about depictions of violence.

Think about it!

Has communications technology made it possible for almost anyone to claim to be a journalist?

The conflict between economic deregulation and social re-regulation/regulation is apparent in a proposal made by the Chair of the FCC to extend the FCC's regulatory authority to cable television. Interest groups such as the Parents Television Council support the proposal to give the FCC authority to regulate explicit sex and violence and indecency. Tim Winter, the President of the PTC tried to put telecommunications in proper perspective when he stated that, except for the Pentagon, the FCC has "the most important role in our nation." His argument echoed some of the earliest founding statements about the relationship between the media and democracy, particularly his claim that the way we communicate (the public airwaves, electronic communication, cable, satellite, telephone) is "the essence of our democracy."

The advocates of expanding the FCC's authority over the communications sector by authorizing it to regulate cable as well as broadcast companies, have encountered strong opposition. Opponents of expanding the FCC's regulatory authority include the national Cable and Telecommunications Association. The Association believes that the best way to regulate the industry is to rely on the intensely competitive marketplace, not government intervention. In fact, despite the politics supporting increased government regulation of programming, the law is likely to present a significant hurdle. Blair Levin, the chief of staff to FCC Chairman Reed Hundt, thinks that the effort to extend the FCC's reach to include cable companies would ultimately lose in the courts. He also wryly commented that FCC Chair Martin's push for a la carte service subscriptions, which is related to family values selection, was likely doomed: "Every chairman of the FCC comes to realize there is a conflict between family values and market values."[17]

7.9 | Media Bias

The press has been charged with bias from the earliest days of the republic. The charge was certainly accurate during the founding era of the partisan penny press. Contemporary criticism of the media for being biased is partly the result of higher expectations of a professional press. The growing role of the media has increased scrutiny of the media and the ways in which they influence values, behavior, and public understanding of government and politics.[18]

Individuals in positions of power in either the private sector (heads of companies or unions or other organizations) or the public sector (national, state, or local government officials) are likely to be sympathetic to the charge of media bias because the institutional press has historically claimed a watchdog role, one that includes investigative reporting. The government watchdog role has made the media an "oppositional" force in the sense that the press investigates and serves as a watchdog for whatever administration is in control of government.

7.9 | Additional Resources

7.91 | Internet Resources

The Center for Media and Public Affairs at http://www.cmpa.com/ provides information about the public role of the media.

The Pew Research Center's Project on Excellence in Journalism at http://journalism.org/ One of the Pew Research Center's newer projects is the Pew Internet & American Life Project. It provides interesting perspectives on the cultural effects of the reliance on the Internet. See http://www.pewinternet.org/.

One useful source of information about the modern media is http://journalism.org/

One example of the new media is the fake news shows have blurred some of the distinctions between news and entertainment (Infotainment). http://www.colbertnation.com/the-colbert-report-videos/252013/october-08-2009/bend-it-like-beck

The University of California at Los Angeles website has both statutory law and case law relating to electronic law and policy http://www.gseis.ucla.edu/iclp/hp.html

The Annenberg Public Policy Center of the University of Pennsylvania conducts content analysis on TV coverage of politics. www.appcpenn.org

Newseum is the museum dedicated to the history of news and media, with a Web site that has interesting cyber exhibits, including coverage of the terrorist attacks of September 11, 2001, war correspondents, editorial cartoonists, women photographers, and front-page stories from around the country. www.newseum.org

7.92 | In the Library

Baker, C. Edwin. 2006. Media Concentration and Democracy: Why Ownership Matters. Cambridge University Press.

Bennett, W. Lance. 2004. News: The Politics of Illusion. Longman.

Bennett, W. Lance, Regina G. Lawrence, and Steven Livingston. 2007. When the Press Fails: Political Power and the News Media from Iraq to Katrina. University of Chicago Press.

Cook, Timothy. 1998. Governing with the News. University of Chicago Press.

Eshbaugh-Soha, Matthew. 2003. "Presidential Press Conferences over Time." American Journal of Political Science 47 (2):348–353

Fritz, Ben et al. 2004. All the President's Spin: George W. Bush, the Media, and the Truth. Simon and Schuster Trade.

Goldberg, Bernard. 2001. Bias: A CBS Insider Exposes How the Media Distort the News. Regnery Press.

Graber, Doris A. (ed). 1998. The Politics of News: The News of Politics. Congressional Quarterly Books.

Jamieson, Kathleen Hall. 2000. Everything You Think You Know About Politics…And Why You're Wrong. Basic Books.

Kovach, Bill and Tom Rosenstiel. 2007. Elements of Journalism: What Newspeople Should Know and the Public Should Expect. Crown Publishing.

Lieberman, Trudy. 2000. Slanting the Story: The Forces that Shape the News. New Press.

Prior, Markus. 2007. Post-Broadcast Democracy: How Media Choice Increases Inequality in Political Involvement and Polarizes Elections. Cambridge University Press.

Schechter, Danny. 2003. Media Wars: News at a Time of Terror. Rowman and Littlefield Publishers, Inc.

Shogun, Robert. 2001. Bad News: Where the Press Go Wrong in the Making of the President. Ivan Dee Press.
Summerville, John. 1999. How the News Makes Us Dumb. Intervarsity Press.

STUDY QUESTIONS

1. When covering Congress, who tends to be the focus of media coverage? Why?
2. Leonard Downie, Jr., the former executive editor of the Washington Post, does not vote because he thinks voting might lead to questions about his neutrality. Explain whether you think journalists can be neutral and also vote in elections?
3. Compare and contrast the print press and electronic media.
4. How much confidence does the public have in the media? Is this level of confidence sufficient to ensure a vibrant democracy?
5. What are the major periods of the media?
6. What is the media's relationship with the president?

Key Terms
Educative Role
Watchdog Role
Commercial Media

[1] Schudson, Michael. 1981. *Discovering the News: A social history of American newspapers*. New York: Basic Books.

[2] Quoted in The State of the News Media 2007, An Annual Report on American Journalism, http://stateofthemedia.org/2007/narrative_overview_intro.asp

[3] http://www.pewinternet.org

[4] A congressional press pass allows reporters to sit in the House and Senate press galleries, as well as providing some access to presidential press briefings. The process to get a congressional press pass is available here: http://www.senate.gov/galleries/daily/rules2.htm

[5] Gerhard Peters. "Presidential News Conferences." *The American Presidency Project*. Ed. John T. Woolley and Gerhard Peters. Santa Barbara, CA: University of California. 1999-2010. Available at: http://www.presidency.ucsb.edu/data/newsconferences.php.

[6] Steven V. Roberts, "Washington Talk: The Presidency; Shouting Questions At Reagan," *New York Times*, October 21, 1987.

[7] http://www.oyez.org/cases/1960-1969/1968/1968_2_2

[8] http://www.fcc.gov/Reports/tcom1996.txt

[9] http://www.oyez.org/cases/1990-1999/1996/1996_96_511

[10] http://www.ftc.gov/ogc/coppa1.htm

[11] http://www.gseis.ucla.edu/iclp/coppa.htm

[12] http://www.salon.com/21st/feature/1999/02/02feature.html

[13] http://www.fcc.gov/cgb/consumerfacts/cipa.html

[14] http://www.fcc.gov/eb/News_Releases/DOC-301874A1.html

[15] http://www.fcc.gov/eb/News_Releases/DOC-300325A1.html

[16] http://www.fcc.gov/eb/

[17] http://www.npr.org/templates/story/story.php?storyId=16783080

[18] http://www.stateofthenewsmedia.org/chartland.asp?id=200&ct=col&dir=&sort=&col4_box=1

8.0 | Public Opinion

James Madison believed that popular government—what is today called democratic government—requires an informed public. One of the most widely shared *modern* beliefs is that democracy requires an informed, educated, and active citizenry in order to work as a good form of government. The belief that knowledge can overcome ignorance and solve problems is at the foundation of many collective human endeavors whether in the world of science or the world of politics: the scientific community and the political community. It is an article of political faith that knowledge is power and popular information makes self-government possible. The importance of information explains why political scientists, government officials, members of political parties, business groups, organized labor, and so many other interest groups pay so much attention to public opinion. This chapter examines public opinion: what it is; how it is formed; how it is measured; and its role in politics, government, and public policy.

The power problem with public opinion is determining whether, to what degree, and how public opinion influences public policy. **Democratic theory** assumes that public opinion drives the political machine. But political practice (how politics and government actually work) and political science research raise important questions about the theory. The relationship between public opinion and public policy is not a simple "cause" and "effect" relationship as described in Figure 8.1 below. The relationship is complicated by several factors. One complicating factor is the fact that the U.S. is not a pure or direct democracy; it is a constitutional democracy that places limits on majority rule. A second complicating factor concerns the nature of public opinion. Is public opinion a *cause* (that is, does it determine government action) or an *effect* (is it the result of something else). Figure 8.1 describes the democratic assumption about public opinion as the cause of government action. But what if public opinion is itself the effect of something? Questions about who or what controls public opinion are central to the power problem with public opinion because they are central to the assumptions of the democratic theory of politics and government. Governments and other political actors try to control public opinion.

Figure 8.1 The Classic Systems Theory

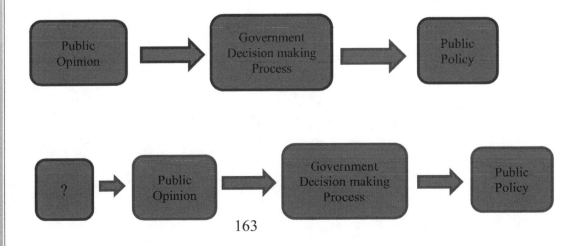

8.1 | Definition

Public opinion is defined as the aggregate of public attitudes or beliefs about government or politics. The following description and analysis of public opinion in the U.S. focuses on three main issues. The first issue is the political importance of public opinion in representative systems of government. The second issue is the role of public opinion in two models of democracy—the delegate and trustee models of democracy. The third issue is the nature of public opinion, particularly the formation, measurement, and control of public opinion.

8.2 | IMPORTANCE

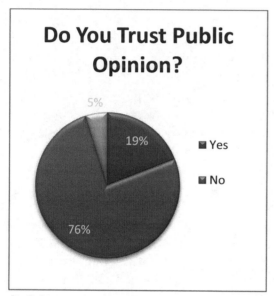

Public opinion is important in democratic political systems because democratic self-government is based on the consent of the governed. Democratic theory requires public policies to more or less reflect public opinion. Democracy assumes that the people are the ultimate source of governing authority. This is what is meant by popular sovereignty: the people are sovereign. Popular sovereignty is one of the basic principles of the U.S. system of representative government. The belief that government authority derives from the people means that public policies are supposed to be based on public opinion. Public opinion is supposed to directly or indirectly cause public policies to be enacted. Responsiveness to public opinion is one measure of a political system's legitimacy—the belief that a system of government is lawful, right, or just.

8.3 | TWO MODELS OF REPRESENTATION

The following describes two models of representation: the delegate model and the trustee model democracy. The two models describe how public opinion influences public policy in modern democracies and how public opinion should influence public policy.

8.31 | *THE DELEGATE MODEL*

According to the **delegate model**, public opinion is the principal source of government legitimacy because government power is only properly exercised when it is based on public opinion. It describes a strong linkage between public opinion and public policy. Public opinion is considered the cause of public policy; public opinion is considered the determinant of public policy. The delegate model of democracy is based on the delegate theory of representation. The delegate theory of representation describes elected government officials as obligated to do the will of the people—to represent the constituents who elect them to office. Government officials are instructed delegates in the sense that they are expected to do what the people want. The strong role of public opinion in the delegate model of democracy makes it a populist form of representative democracy. Populist means "of the people." A populist is a person, party, or philosophy that advocates for "the people" or "the common person" or "the middle class" as opposed to the elites.

8.32 | *THE TRUSTEE MODEL*

The **trustee model** allows government officials more freedom of choice to decide what is in the public interest. Government officials are not expected to act solely upon public opinion. The trustee model of democracy is based on the trustee model of representation, where a government official is not obligated to do what the people want, but can decide what is best. A representative is considered a trustee whose better access to information or good judgment may justify the representative's beliefs, actions, or votes differ from public opinion at any moment in time. The trustee is not required to do what public opinion polls indicate that the people want. The government officials are held accountable for their decisions in regular elections, but they have considerable freedom to choose courses of action that may in fact differ from the preferences of the public as measured by polls, for example. The trustee model is more elitist in the sense that elected representatives are expected to be the "better sorts" of the community, the leaders who are chosen to make good decisions about public policy without merely following public opinion.

8.4 | THE FOUNDERS' INTENTIONS

The Framers did not establish a direct democracy. They created an indirect democracy or **republic**, whereby the public selects individuals to represent their interests in government decisions. They believe that a republic was a better form of government than a direct democracy because they worried about majority rule. Absolute majority rule would be replacing monarchy—rule by King George—with democracy—rule by King Numbers. They were committed to popular government, but not one where majority rule applied to all aspects of government and politics. These views are described in Madison's *Federalist Papers Number 10* and *Number 51*.

Federalist Number 51 elaborates on the ways to limit the abuse of government power that is made necessary by human nature. Popular sovereignty is the primary way to limit the abuse of power, and the system of checks and balances (federalism and the separation of powers) is the

Ambition must be made to counteract ambition. The interest of the man must be connected with the constitutional rights of the place. It may be a reflection on human nature, that such devices should be necessary to control the abuses of government. But what is government itself, but the greatest of all reflections on human nature? If men were angels, no government would be necessary. If angels were to govern men, neither external nor internal controls on government would be necessary. In framing a government which is to be administered by men over men, the great difficulty lies in this: you must first enable the government to control the governed; and in the next place oblige it to control itself. A dependence on the people is, no doubt, the primary control on the government; but experience has taught mankind the necessity of auxiliary precautions.

secondary (or "auxiliary") limit on the abuse of power. Madison famously wrote that human nature makes government necessary, and makes it necessary to control government:

In *Federalist Number 10*, Madison explained that the Founders created a representative democracy that was not purely majority rule. They believed that the best form of government was one that was based on limited majority rule. The Constitution placed limits on the power of the people to do whatever they wanted. The constitution protected minorities, landowners, wealthier individuals, white males, from majority rule. This is the concept of a constitutional democracy. It is one which combines two conflicting goals: democracy suggests that the people can do as they will. Democracy suggests pure majority rule. Constitutional suggests limits on the power of a majority to do as it wills. It cannot do whatever it wants. This is one of the tensions in the U.S. system of government. Each generation must strive to achieve "that delicate balance" between granting the majority power to do what it wants and limiting majority rule to protect minorities. The Bill of Rights, for example, places limits on the power of the people as expressed in laws passed by Congress.

8.5 | THE NATURE OF PUBLIC OPINION

8.51 | *FORMATION OF PUBLIC OPINION*

One of the most interesting questions about public opinion is how people acquire their beliefs, attitudes, and orientations. Understanding public opinion begins with examining some of the main sources of public opinion, including political socialization, education, life experience, political parties, the media, and the government.

8.52 | *SOCIALIZATION*

Socialization is all the ways that people acquire attitudes, values, and beliefs. Socialization begins early. The agents of socialization include families, schools, friends, religious institutions, workplace colleagues, and the media. Children begin to form political attitudes very early in life. The family is a strong influence on thinking about government and politics. Children do not always or automatically identify with their parents' ideology or political party but a person's party affiliation is causally related to their parents. Socialization also occurs in settings other than the family. Some of the other agents of socialization can limit the influence of the family. For example, the fact that many children are now raised in families where both parents work means that the family's influence has decreased relative to other sources of socialization such as schools, friends, colleagues, and the media.

8.53 | *LIFE EXPERIENCES*

Not all political attitudes are fixed early in life. A person's adult experiences, desires, or needs can form new attitudes or change old ones. A change in a person's health can change attitudes about social welfare programs, for example. A change in a person's economic status, for better or worse, may affect attitudes. Times of general economic prosperity or an individual's need may shape a person's thinking about the appropriate role for government in the economy. Unemployment due to an economic down turn, or riches from entrepreneurial success, can change a person's thinking about the fairness of the marketplace as a mechanism for allocating resources.

In American politics, economics is one of the factors that have historically divided conservatives and liberals, Republicans and Democrats. A person's work experience as a business owner or manager, or an employee, can affect attitudes toward government and politics. Public opinion about economic issues, such as tax policies and spending policies and government regulation of business, is one of the ways we identify individuals as conservatives, liberals, or populists.

8.54 | *EDUCATION*

Education is also recognized as one of the major sources of socialization. Students acquire information and attitudes in schools. One of the reasons why issues such as school desegregation, school busing, school prayer, mandatory flag salutes or pledges of allegiance, and curriculum issues such as civics, values, tolerance, and evolution have been so controversial is because public schools have an educational mission and a socialization function. The impact of public schools is not just limited to academics. Educational institutions also play an important role in socialization, which is why school curriculum and policies have been considered worth fighting over.

8.55 | *GEOGRAPHY*

Regional differences have played an important role in some of the country's most important political experiences. Early in the nation's history, the geographic divisions were the result of distinctive economic systems in the northeast (manufacturing and shipping), the south (agrarian and plantation), and the interior frontier. By the middle of the 19th Century, the divisions between the industrial, non-slave North and the agricultural, slave-holding South resulted in the Civil War. The urbanization of the 20th Century produced major

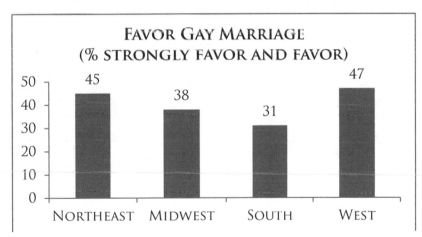

Pew Forum on Religion & Public Life. "Do you strongly favor, favor, oppose, or strongly oppose allowing gay and lesbian couples to marry legally?" October 9, 2009

difference of public opinion in urban and rural areas. Political geography still has an effect on attitudes and policy preferences. Generally, people in the Northeast and the West are more likely to support abortion rights, while those in the Midwest and South are more likely to favor restricting access to abortions. As the figure here shows, these regional trends are echoed in the support for gay marriage.

8.56 | *RACE AND ETHNICITY*

Ethnic and racial groups have differed in their political values throughout our nation's history. African Americans, mobilized by the Republican Party (the party of Lincoln) in post-Civil War period, were excluded from the political system in the South until the Civil Rights movements in the 19050s and 1960s and were eventually won over by the Democratic Party's support for the movement. Currently, African Americans support liberal policies and Democratic candidates.

In the late 1800s and early 1900s, Europeans from countries like Italy, Ireland, Germany, and Poland immigrated in large numbers to the United States. These groups became a part of Franklin Delano Roosevelt's New Deal coalition in the 1930 and they continued to be part of the Democratic Great Society coalition in the 1960s. Since then, however, conservatives such as Ronald Reagan have successfully appealed to these European ethnic groups which were identified as "Reagan Democrats." In recent decades, the political behavior of Hispanics has attracted a great deal of attention because they are the fastest growing ethnic group in the United States. Both the Democratic and Republican parties are interested in securing their political support. But this has been challenging because the term "Hispanic" includes a broad range of people with different backgrounds, experiences, and attitudes. Mexican-Americans, Cuban-Americans, and Puerto Ricans, for example are all considered Hispanic.

8.57 | GENDER

A person's gender can have a major effect on their political attitudes. During the last thirty years, women have been more likely to support liberal issues and the Democratic Party. The gender difference in party identification is the **gender gap**. Women are more likely to support the Democratic Party and men are more likely to support the Republican Party. Women are also more likely to support affirmative action policies, welfare policies, income assistance, reproductive rights (pro-choice views on abortion), and equal rights for gays and lesbians. Women have voted for the Democratic presidential candidate at a higher rate than men in every presidential election since Jimmy Carter's 1980 bid against Ronald Reagan. Women also register more frequently as members of the Democratic Party. As the figure below shows, the gender gap in party registration fluctuates with the year, but women remain consistently more likely to register as Democrats.

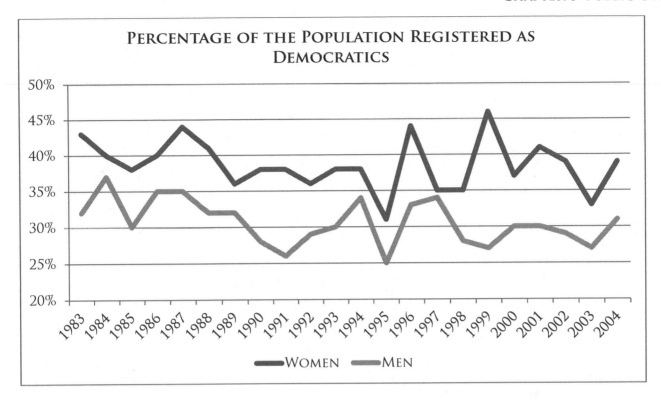

PERCENTAGE OF THE POPULATION REGISTERED AS DEMOCRATICS

8.55 | *THE MEDIA*

The media play a large and growing role in modern American society. In 1997, adult Americans spent around thirty hours a week watching television, and children spent even more time watching television.[1] The general consensus that the media have an impact on public opinion masks debates about the nature of that impact. Take, for example, socialization—the process by which individuals acquire information and form attitudes and values. The media are one important source of socialization in the sense that people acquire information and attitudes from the media. The traditional mass media have played an important in "mediating" between individuals and the government. The figure below described the mediating role.

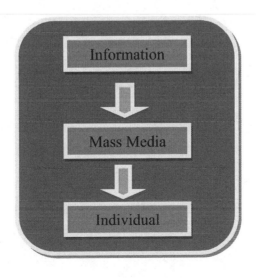

The traditional mass (especially newspapers) (especially the television The Mediating Role of the Mass Media media include the print press and the broadcast media and radio networks). The role the media play in American politics includes *setting the agenda*. The term setting the agenda describes how the media decide what issues the public should be thinking about. The media decide what constitutes "news" that is worth reporting. Media coverage of poverty, the rate of inflation, religion, crime, or national security has an impact on what the public thinks is important as well as how the public thinks about the government's performance. Media influence on the values and attitudes of minors has been especially controversial. The content of programming, particularly concerning sex and indecent language and violence, has been a political issue for some time. The federal government has undertaken a number of efforts to regulate the content on broadcast networks. Congress has passed legislation regulating programming. The Federal Communications Commission has implemented administrative regulations, including fines, which attempt to control indecent programming on the broadcast networks. And the Supreme Court has ruled on the constitutionality of these legislative and administrative restrictions on programs broadcast over the airwaves. More recently, efforts have focused on the Internet.

Not all of the debate is about the media's role in making sexually explicit or violent material more widely available. Another issue is the ideology. The ideological bias of the mainstream media is one of the recurring themes of commentary about the political role of the media in modern American society. This issue will be examined in greater detail in the section on the media.

8.56 | *THE GOVERNMENT*

The government is an important source of public opinion and it has a variety of ways to influence public opinion. Public schools, for example, teach civics—which included attitudes toward government politics. The government is also able to instill patriotic attitudes, and the use of controlled information about national security matters, for example, to influence public opinion. Presidents, for instance, benefit from the "rally around the flag" effect when the country faces a threat. The government's role in socializing is controversial, however, because it seems to reverse the causal order of democratic theory wherein public opinion determines public policy. And government influence on public opinions is often considered propaganda. Propaganda is one of the normative or value-laden terms like democracy, conservative/liberal, bureaucracy, or terrorism. It is often associated with illegitimate or improper government efforts to influence thinking about politics, such as brain-washing or overly emotional appeals that convinces individuals or groups to support a particular strong leader, a party, or an ideology. But the descriptive, dictionary definition of propaganda is that it is using words or speech intended to convince someone of a political position or point of view. In this sense, propaganda is persuasion or advocacy—which seems central to politics.

Some of the earliest discussions of public opinion were by economists who were interested in the workings of the market place. Adam Smith, the classical economist referred to public opinion in his work, *The Theory of Moral Sentiments* (1759). It is not surprising that economists who think about the role of supply and demand in the marketplace would think about public opinion. The English philosopher Jeremy Bentham also applied the concept of public opinion to thinking about the relationship between the government and the people. Bentham is associated with the utilitarian philosophy that the political and economic calculation of the public good or public interest is the greatest good for the greatest number. This variation of rule by "king numbers" was rejected by the Founders who did not trust the public enough to give the people direct democracy.

8.6 | IS PUBLIC OPINION A CAUSE OR AN EFFECT?

Are attitudes toward government and politics the cause of public policies, or are attitudes (public opinion) the result of other factors? In politics, power is the ability to make another person do what you want. Can political power be used to make a person think what you want? This is an especially important question when the subject is the government.

8.61 | RHETORIC

One important means of public communication is rhetoric. Rhetoric is the art of using language, both public speaking and writing, to communicate, to persuade, or to convince. In the 19th Century rhetoric was taught using collections of memorable political speeches and even "pulpit eloquence" such as *The American Orator*. The *Orator* was an influential book that trained individuals in proper public speaking techniques the way that other books trained people in proper etiquette.

8.63 | DYNAMIC OR STATIC

One of the most important things to remember about public opinion is that it is dynamic, not static. It changes—and perhaps more important, *it can be changed*. Public opinion about the president, for example, is very dynamic and responds to a broad range of factors. Public opinion about congress is more stable, but reflects general public assessments of how congress is performing as a political institution. Public opinion polls such as the <u>Gallup Poll</u> regularly ask people for their opinion about government.

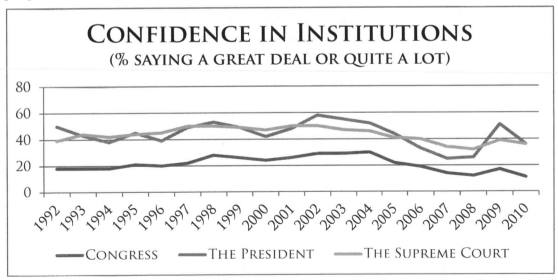

GALLUP 2010 Confidence Poll; "Now I am going to read you a list of institutions in American society. Please tell me how much confidence you, yourself, have in each one -- a great deal, quite a lot, some, or a little"

Sixty-nine percent of Americans say they have a great deal or fair amount of confidence in the Supreme Court, compared with 50% for Congress and 43% for the president. Public confidence in

Congress and the president has been trending steadily downward for decades. In contrast, public confidence in the Court has remained very stable.[2]

Political actors, such as candidates for office, government officials, party leaders, interest group leaders, and community activists are not limited to responding to public opinion. Political actors try to influence, change, and even to control public opinion. In government and politics information is power. Information about how people acquire their attitudes can increase the understanding of socialization.

8.64 | THE MARKETPLACE OF IDEAS

Understanding *how* people acquire their attitudes can make it possible to use that information to control *what* people think. This is the essence of the power problem with public opinion. Can public opinion (ideas and attitudes) be manufactured the way material products are made? Can ideas about candidates, parties, and issues be sold the way other products are sold to consumers? The marketplace is a familiar and powerful concept in the United States because the U.S. is a capitalist country where people are very familiar with the idea of a marketplace of goods and services. It is not surprising that the logic of the *economic marketplace* has been applied to politics. The *political marketplace of ideas* refers to the ability to pick and choose from among the competing ideologies and parties the way that consumers are able to pick and choose from among the competing sellers of goods and services.

The application of economic marketplace logic to the political marketplace raises some important questions about the nature of public opinion. One question is about the role of advertising. The conventional economic wisdom is that marketers and advertisers respond to consumer demands for products and services. But modern advertising also creates demand. The ability to create consumer demand, rather than just respond to consumer demands, is one reason why the government regulates the advertising of certain goods and services. Lawyer advertising is regulated by the government. Medical advertising, particularly of drugs, is regulated by the government. Advertising of tobacco products is heavily regulated by the government, particularly advertising campaigns that appeal to minors by using cartoon characters. The Federal Trade Commission's mission includes regulating business practices that are "deceptive or unfair" to consumers. It has a Bureau of Consumer Protection which prevents "fraud, deceptive, and unfair business practices in the marketplace." It investigates complaints about advertising.

8.65 | *THE GOVERNMENT IN THE MARKETPLACE OF IDEAS*

Of course, the government is also in the business of trying to control public opinion rather than merely responding to it. Governments frequently try to control what people think— about the issues, about candidates, about parties, about government officials, and about the government itself. The pejorative term for these efforts is propaganda; the modern term is public relations. In the 1930s and 1940s the government used newly emerging experts (in public relations, advertising, and film) to influence public opinion. An example of these propaganda programs to produce public opinion is the Roosevelt administration's New Deal WPA program, "By the People, For the People: Posters from the WPA, 1936-1943." One archive that includes short films that were produced by the government to build popular support for certain public policies, such as the Cold War or military service, is http://www.archive.org/details/americanoratoror00cook The "moving images" preserved here show government programs to shape the following thinking and behavior:

- For appropriate behavior for young people in the 1950s, watch "How to be a teenage in 1950";
- For messages encouraging patriotism and support for military service, watch the cartoon "Private Snuffy Smith"; http://archive.org/details/private_snuffy_smith
- For promoting health fears of sexual promiscuity, watch "Sex Madness:" http://archive.org/details/sex_madness
- The WWII removal and detention Japanese living in designated areas of the west coast of the U.S.: http://www.youtube.com/watch?v=_OiPldKsM5w

http://www.youtube.com/watch?v=PMrzGauQJdk

8.66 | *Nature or Nurture?*

Are political ideas something that an individual is born with or something that is acquired? Much of public opinion about government and politics is the result of nurture not nature; it is acquired through experience or learned from family, friends, school, and work. This is one reason why it is considered important for a democracy to provide equal access to information, public discourse about current events, and rational debates about political alternatives. Access to information ensures that individuals have an equal right to participate in politics—regardless of whether than right is actually exercises.

Public opinion is subject to manipulation by a variety of elites, governmental and non-governmental. The Declaration of Independence asserted that all men were create equal and endowed by their Creator with certain unalienable rights. This declaration of equality is generally understood to mean that each individual has legal and political equality, or the same rights rather than having rights based on status or power.

8.7 | **DEMOCRATIC THEORY AND POLITICAL REALITY**

The relationship between public opinion and public policy is more complicated than simply "public opinion causes or determines public policy." In most modern, western-style democracies, there are ongoing debates about the degree to which public opinion matters, the degree to which public opinion determines public policy. Critics of modern democracy argue that a group of elites, either officials in government or those individuals or organizations that are outside government with more money, power, or access to resources, essentially control public opinion and make public policy for their special interests, not the general public. Supporters of modern democracy acknowledge that not everyone has equal resources, and that wealth and power are unequally distributed. But they argue that power is sufficiently spread around so that no single set of elites—the wealthy, powerful, informed, or even government—can control public opinion and dominate the political process. These supporters of modern democracy are generally pluralists. Pluralists maintain that there are many elites and many groups that compete for influence, but which are unable to control public opinion or dominate the political process.

8.71 | *The Premise of Democratic Theory*

The premise (or basic assumption) of democratic theory is that an informed public makes choices about government officials and public policies. In other words, democratic theory assumes that elections determine who governs and what policies will be enacted into law. This is the argument that democratic government is legitimate because its authority is based on the consent of the governed. Is this assumption valid? There is empirical evidence that the assumption of an informed public is mistaken. Public opinion polls indicate that the American public is not well-informed about public affairs, candidates, or issues. Civics knowledge is rather low. The average voter has little information about public affairs, including the names of their representatives in city government, county government, state legislature, or congress. People do not pay much attention to politics. More attention is paid to social and cultural activities such as entertainment and sports than politics. The low levels of information about politics are the result of apathy (disinterest), the belief that participation in politics does not really matter very much (low levels of efficacy), time constraints (being busy with families and work). People have other priorities for allocating their scarce resources (time, effort, and money). It is much easier for professionals—people who have white collar jobs or information-related jobs such as journalism or academia—to keep up with public affairs than people who have blue collar jobs or jobs that do not involve working with information. There are information costs associated with becoming well-informed about public affairs and keeping up with the issues.

Think About It!

"Are You Smarter Than A 5th Grader?" Is Kelly Pickler?

http://www.youtube.com/watch?v=Cey35bBWXls

8.8 | **MEASURING PUBLIC OPINION**

8.81 | *POLLING*

Public opinion polling is one of the facts of modern life. Gallup polls are a familiar feature of modern politics. The widespread use of public opinion measurement around the world is evidence of the belief that public opinion is important for political and other purposes. Governments find surveys to be useful tools for gathering information about what the public thinks, for guiding public information and propaganda campaigns, and for formulating public policies. The US Department of Agriculture was one of the first government agencies to sponsor systematic and large scale surveys. It was followed by many other federal bodies, including the US information agency which has conducted opinion research throughout the world. It is frequently measured using survey sampling.

An opinion poll is a survey of opinion from a particular sample. Opinion polls are usually designed to represent the opinions of a population by asking a small number of people a series of questions and then extrapolating the answers to the larger group within certain confidence intervals.

8.82 | HISTORY

The first known example of an opinion poll was a local straw vote conducted by *The Harrisburg Pennsylvanian* in 1824. It showed Andrew Jackson leading John Quincy Adams by 335 votes to 169 in the contest for the presidency. This straw vote was not scientific. But straw votes became popular in local elections. In 1916, the *Literary Digest* conducted a national survey as part of an effort to increase circulation. The straw vote correctly predicted Woodrow Wilson's election as president. The *Digest* correctly called the following four presidential elections by simply mailing out millions of postcards and counting the returns. In 1936, the *Digest's* 2.3 million "voters" constituted a very large sample, but the sample included more affluent Americans who tended to support the Republican Party. This biased the results. The week before the election the *Digest* reported that Republican Alf Landon was far more popular than Democrat Franklin D. Roosevelt. At the same time, George Gallup conducted a much smaller, but more scientifically-based survey. He polled a demographically representative sample, and correctly predicted Roosevelt's landslide victory in the 1936 presidential election. The *Literary Digest* soon went out of business. The polling industry gained credibility and public opinion polling began to play a more important role in politics, particularly campaigning.

But public opinion polling has changed. In a 1968 book, *The Pulse of Democracy*, George Gallup and Saul Rae described public opinion polling as **taking** the pulse of democracy. By this, they meant that polling used social scientific methods to try to accurately measure what the public was thinking about public affairs. Today, polling is more likely to be conducted for the purpose of **making** the pulse of democracy, using social scientific methods to make public opinion. This is the argument made by David W. Moore in *The Opinion Makers* (2008). This change in the way information about how and what people think is used is directly related to the power problem with public opinion.

8.83 | METHODS

In the early days of public opinion polling, polls were conducted mainly by face-to-face interviews (on the street or in a person's home). Face-to-face polling is still done, but telephone polls have become more popular because they can be conducted quickly and cheaply. However, response rates for phone surveys have been declining. Some polling organizations, such as YouGov and Zogby use Internet surveys, where a sample is drawn from a large panel of volunteers and the results are weighed to reflect the demographics of the population of interest. This is in contrast to popular web polls that draw on whoever wishes to participate rather than a scientific sample of the population, and are therefore not generally considered accurate.

The wording of a poll question can bias the results. The bias can be unintentional (accidental) or intentional. For instance, the public is more likely to indicate support for a person who is described by the caller as one of the "leading candidates." Neglecting to mention all the candidates is an even more subtle bias, as is lumping some candidates in an "other" category. Being last on a list affects responses. In fact, this is one reason why election rules provide for listing candidates in alphabetic order or alternating Republican and Democratic candidates. When polling on issues, answers to a question about abortion vary depending on whether a person is asked about a "fetus" or and "unborn baby."

All polls based on samples are subject to sampling error which reflects the effects of chance in the sampling process. The uncertainty is often expressed as a margin of error. The margin of error does not reflect other sources of error, such as measurement error. A poll with a random sample of 1,000 people has margin of sampling error of 3% for the estimated percentage of the whole population. A 3% margin of error means that 95% of the time the procedure used would give an estimate within 3% of the percentage to be estimated. The margin of error can be reduced by using a larger sample, however if a pollster wishes to reduce the margin of error to 1% they would need a sample of around 10,000 people. In practice pollsters need to balance the cost of a large sample against the reduction in sampling error and a sample size of around 500-1,000 is a typical compromise for political polls.[3]

- **Nonresponse** bias. Some people do not answer calls from strangers, or refuse to respond to polls or poll questions. As a result, a poll sample may not be a representative sample from a population. Because of this selection bias, the characteristics of those who agree to be interviewed may be markedly different from those who decline. That is, the actual sample is a biased version of the universe the pollster wants to analyze. In these cases, bias introduces new errors that are in addition to errors caused by sample size. Error due to bias does not become smaller with larger sample sizes. If the people who refuse to answer, or are never reached, have the same characteristics as the people who do answer, the final results will be unbiased. If the people who do not answer have different opinions then there is bias in the results. In terms of election polls, studies suggest that bias effects are small, but each polling firm has its own formulas on how to adjust weights to minimize selection bias.
- **Response** bias. Survey results may be affected by response bias. Response bias is when a respondent gives answers that not reflect his or her actual beliefs. This occurs for a variety of reasons. One reason is that a respondent may feel pressure not to give an unpopular answer. For example, respondents might be unwilling to admit to socially unpopular attitudes such as racism, sexism, or they may feel pressure to identify with socially or politically popular attitudes such as patriotism, civic activism, or religious

commitment. For these reasons, a poll might not reflect the true incidence of certain attitudes or behaviors in the population. Response bias can be deliberately engineered by pollsters in order to generate a certain result or please their clients. This is one of the reasons why the term pollster suggests huckster, or a con artist. Even respondents may deliberately try to manipulate the outcome of a poll by advocating a more extreme position than they actually hold in order to support a position that they identify with. Response bias may also be caused by the wording or ordering of questions.

- **Question wording**. The wording of the questions, the order in which questions are asked, and the number and form of alternative answers offered influence results of polls. Thus comparisons between polls often boil down to the wording of the question. For some issues the question wording can produce pronounced differences between surveys. These differences could be caused by respondents with conflicted feelings or the fact that attitudes are evolving. One way in which pollsters attempt to minimize this effect is to ask the same set of questions over time, in order to track changes in opinion. Another common technique is to rotate the order in which questions are asked. One technique is the split-sample, where there are two versions of a question and each version presented to half the respondents.

- **Coverage** bias. Coverage bias is another source of error is the use of samples that are not representative of the population as a consequence of the methodology used, as was the experience of the *Literary Digest* in 1936. For example, telephone sampling has a built-in error because people with telephones have generally been richer than those without phones. Today an increased percentage of the public has only a mobile telephone. In the United States it is illegal to make unsolicited calls to phones where the phone's owner may be charged simply for taking a call. Because pollsters are not supposed to call mobile phones, individuals who own only a mobile phone will often not be included in the polling sample. If the subset of the population without cell phones differs markedly from the rest of the population, these differences can skew the results of the poll. The relative importance of these factors remains uncertain today because polling organizations have adjusted their methodologies to achieve more accurate election predictions.

8.9 | COMPARATIVE PUBLIC OPINION

Many of the issues that political scientists have identified as most important to understanding American government and politics are not unique to the United States. The comparative study of public opinion reveals the similarities and differences in how the peoples of the world think about politics and government.

8.91 | THE WORLD VALUES SURVEY

One source of comparative information about public opinion is the World Values Survey. The World Values Survey developed from the European Values Study (EVS) in 1981 which covered only 22 countries worldwide. Ronald Inglehart (The University of Michigan) is a leading figure in the extension of the surveys around the world. The survey was repeated after an interval of about 10 years in then again in a series of "waves" at approximately five year intervals. The

WVS was designed to provide a longitudinal and cross-cultural measurement of variation of values. The European origin of the project made the early waves of the WVS Eurocentric and notable for their especially weak representation in Africa and South-East Asia. In order to overcome this bias by becoming more representative, the WVS opened participation to academic representatives from new countries that met certain minimal survey standards. They could then exchange their data with the WVS in return for the data from the rest of the project. As a result, the WVS expanded to 42 countries in the 2nd wave, 54 in the 3rd wave and 62 in the 4th wave. Today the WVS is an open source database of the WVS available on the Internet. The Secretariat of the WVS is based in Sweden. The official archive of the World Values Survey is located in [ASEP/JDS] (Madrid), Spain.

The global World Values Survey consists of about 250 questions resulting in some 400 to 800 measurable variables. One of the variables measured is Happiness. The comparative "Perceptions of Happiness" are widely quoted in the popular media. Does the U.S. get a smiley face? The popular statistics website Nationmaster also publishes a simplified world happiness scale derived from the WVS data. The WVS website allows a user to get a more sophisticated level of analysis such as comparison of happiness over time or across socio-economic groups. One of the most striking shifts in happiness measured by the WVS was the substantial drop in happiness of Russians and some other Eastern European countries during the 1990s.

8.93 | *THE INGLEHART MAP*

Another result of the WVS is the Inglehart Map. A number of variables were condensed into two dimensions of cultural variation (known as "traditional v. secular-rational" and "survival v. self-expression"). On this basis, the world's countries could be mapped into specific cultural regions because these two dimensions purportedly explain more than 70 percent of the cross-national variance. The WVS also found that trust and democracy were values that crossed most cultural boundaries.

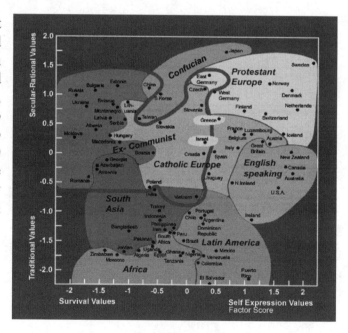

The Inglehart Map of the World

8.94 | *RELIGION AND ECONOMIC DEVELOPMENT*

The Pew Research Center's Global Attitudes Project has examined the relationship between a country's wealth and its religiosity. The results show that countries with a high per capita income tend to score low on religiosity.[4]

8.95 | *WEB SOURCES*

One valuable source of information about American public opinion, voting, and political participation is the "American National Election Studies" information available at http://www.electionstudies.org/

Public speaking continues to be an important influence on public opinion. An electronic source of important public speeches, including the "top 100" American speeches, as well as memorable film speeches, is the Web site http://www.americanrhetoric.com/. This Web site includes audio and video recordings of some of the most important American political speeches. Another resource which has archived some of the most memorable political speeches in the nation's history is the American Rhetoric: Top 100 Speeches Web site. See, for example, the famous Goldwater Speech delivered at the Republican Party Convention in 1964. http://www.americanrhetoric.com/speeches/barrygoldwater1964rnc.htm

8.96 | *IN THE LIBRARY*

Asher, Herbert. *Polling and the Public: What Every American Should Know*. Washington, DC: CQ Books. 2001.

Clem Brooks and Jeff Manza. Why Welfare States Persist: The Importance of Public Opinion in Democracies. University of Chicago Press, 2007.

Katherine Cramer Walsh. Talking About Race: Community Dialogues and the Politics of Difference. University of Chicago Press, 2007.

Robert Eisinger. The Evolution of Presidential Polling. Cambridge University Press, 2003.

Robert Erikson, et al. Statehouse Democracy: Public Opinion and Policy in the American States. Cambridge University Press, 1994.

Robert Erikson, Michael Mackuen, and James Stimson. The Macro Polity. Cambridge University Press, 2002.

Robert S. Erikson and Kent L. Tedin. American Public Opinion: Its Origins, Content, and Impact, 8/e. Longman, 2006.

George Gallup. The Gallup Poll Public Opinion. Scholarly Resources, published annually.

Gallup, George, and Saul Rae. 1968. The Pulse of Democracy. New York: Greenwood Press.

John Hibbing and Elizabeth Theiss-Morse. Stealth Democracy: American's Beliefs about How Government Should Work. Cambridge University Press, 2002.

Ole R. Holsti. Public Opinion and American Foreign Policy. University of Michigan Press, 2004.

Darrell Huff. How to Lie With Statistics. WW Norton, 1993.

Vincent Hutchings. Public Opinion and DemocraticHelen Ingram, et al (eds). Mediating Effect of Public Opinion on Public Policy: Exploring the Realm of Health Care. State University of New York Press, 2004.

Paul Lavrakas and Michael J. Traugott. Election Polls, the News Media and Democracy. Chatham House, 2000.

Walter Lippman. Public Opinion. Hard Press, 2006.

Moore, David W. 1992. The Superpollsters: How They Measure and Manipulate Public Opinion in America. Four Walls Eight Windows.

Moore, David W. 2008. The Opinion Makers. Boston: Beacon Press.

8.98 | STUDY QUESTIONS

1. How does race and ethnicity influence public opinion?
2. Looking at your own upbringing, in what ways were you socialized? Be sure to discuss specific people and events and how they shaped your political beliefs.
3. Define public opinion and discuss early efforts to measure it.
4. How do we measure public opinion? Be sure to discuss the different methods and their strengths and weaknesses.
5. The authors of the *Federalist Papers* noted that "all government rests on public opinion." What did they mean by this claim? Do you agree with them?

Willem E. Saris and Paul M. Sniderman (eds). Studies in Public Opinion: Attitudes, Nonattitudes, Measurement Error, and Change. Princeton University Press, 2004.

James A. Stimson. Tides of Consent: How Public Opinion Shapes American Politics. Cambridge University Press, 2004.

Jeffrey Stonecash. Political Polling: Strategic Information in Campaigns. Rowman and Littlefield, 2003.

Keith Warren. In Defense of Public Opinion Polling. Westview Press, 2001.

Robert Weissberg. Polling, Policy, and Public Opinion. Palgrave, 2002.

---

[1] Statistical Abstract of the United States, 1997 (Washington, DC: Government Printing Office, 1997), 1011.

[2] Survey Methods: Results are based on telephone interviews with 1,010 national adults, aged 18 and older, conducted Sept. 14-16, 2007. For results based on the total sample of national adults, one can say with 95% confidence that the margin of sampling error is ±3 percentage points. In addition to sampling error, question wording and practical difficulties in conducting surveys can introduce error or bias into the findings of public opinion polls.

[3] Note that to get 500 complete responses it may be necessary to make thousands of phone calls.

[4] http://people-press.org/reports/display.php3?ReportID=167

CHAPTER 9: POLITICAL IDEOLOGY

conservative is a man
[wi]th two perfectly good
[leg]s who, however, has
[ne]ver learned how to
[wa]lk forward."

Franklin Delano
[Ro]osevelt,
[32]nd President of the
[Un]ited States

[T]he trouble with our
[lib]eral friends is not that
[th]ey are ignorant, but
[tha]t they know so much
[tha]t isn't so."

[Ro]nald Reagan,
[40]th President of the
[Un]ited States

9.0 | What's in a Name?

Have you ever been in a discussion, debate, or perhaps even a heated argument about government or politics where one person objected to another person's claim by saying, *"That's* not what I mean by conservative (or liberal)? If so, then join the club. People often have to stop in the middle of a good political discussion when it becomes clear that the participants do not agree on the meanings of the terms that are central to the discussion. This can be the case with ideology because people often use familiar terms such as conservative, liberal, or socialist without agreeing on their meanings. This chapter has three main goals. The first goal is to explain the role ideology plays in modern political systems. The second goal is to define the major American ideologies: conservatism, liberalism, and libertarianism. The primary focus is on *modern* conservatism and liberalism. The third goal is to explain their role in government and politics. Some attention is also paid to other "isms"—belief systems that have some of the attributes of an ideology—that are relevant to modern American politics such as environmentalism, feminism, terrorism, and fundamentalism. The chapter begins with an examination of ideologies in general. It then examines American conservatism, liberalism, and other belief systems relevant to modern American politics and government.

9.1 | What is an ideology?

An <u>ideology</u> is a belief system that consists of a relatively coherent set of ideas, attitudes, or values about government and politics, AND the public policies that are designed to

implement the values or achieve the goals. Let's examine the parts of this definition. First, an ideology is a belief system: it consists of a *set* of ideas or values on a broad range of issues as opposed to a single belief about a single issue. These beliefs help people make sense of the world around them. People go through life with "mental images" of "how the world is or should be organized." These images constitute an ideology—a way to simplify, organize, evaluate and "give meaning to what otherwise would be a very confusing world."[1] Individuals who are daily bombarded with information can use ideology to help make sense of it. When people read about a terrible crime or crime statistics, ideology can provide a ready-made explanation for the cause of the criminal behavior as well as a predisposition to support a liberal or conservative public policy response to crime. A person who sees video of police officers beating someone on the streets on Los Angeles or elsewhere is apt to use ideology to provide a handy mental image of whether the use of force is justified or a case of police brutality. A person who reads about the latest data on unemployment can use ideology to provide a framework for thinking that the unemployment rate is too high or too low. A person who thinks about taxes is apt to use ideology to conclude that taxes are too high or too low without having to spend a great deal of time learning about economic policy. And finally, individuals who view actual images of bombing or read about the use of military force can use an ideological "mental image" to react to the action based on an ideological bias for or against the use of military force.

Second, an ideology has an action component. An ideology is about ideas and positions on public policies. A public policy is a plan of action to implement ideas or values or achieve specific goals. The commitment to acting on ideas differentiates an ideology from a philosophy. A philosophy is primarily concerned with ideas or values. For example, political philosophy is the study of fundamental questions about the government, politics, liberty, justice, equality, property, rights, law, and what constitutes a good or moral public order. Political philosophers examine questions about the legitimacy of government; the difference between power and authority; the nature of freedom and equality; civic duties and obligations; and the nature and scope of government power to limit individual liberty. The adherents of an ideology are committed to specific sets of values and to acting to achieve them in the realm of politics and government.

9.12 | *A Coherent Set of Ideas: Human Nature and the Role of Government*

An ideology is not just a set of ideas it is a *coherent* set of ideas. This means that the components of an ideology should be consistent with one another. One idea should not conflict with others. For example, ideologies typically include beliefs about human nature and beliefs about the appropriate role for government. In terms of human nature,

Think about It! Watch the trailer for the 1938 film *Angels with Dirty Faces*. What do you think the film says about human nature?
http://www.youtube.com/watch?v=Nld4DcRHME0

an ideology can describe human nature as basically 1) good or bad; and 2) fixed or flexible. The belief that human nature is basically good means that people are expected to do the right thing because they have a natural sense of right and wrong and will generally do what is right. The belief that human nature is basically bad means that people are by nature self-interested, that evil is part of human nature, and therefore people will often do wrong. The belief that human nature is fixed assumes that an individual's capacities and abilities are determined at birth: intelligence, aptitudes, and character are a matter of nature. The belief that human nature is flexible means that an individual's capacities and abilities can be developed by family, religion, culture, tradition, and education: intelligence, aptitudes, and character are a matter of nurture. Beliefs about the determinants of human behavior are of great political importance because they shape beliefs about the best form of government (e.g., whether democracy will work), the

Read about it!
What does Jefferson think about "egoistic," self-loving behavior?
http://etext.virginia.edu/etcbin/toccer-new2?id=JefLett.sgm&images=images/modeng&data=/texts/english/modeng/parsed&tag=public&part=228&division=div1

appropriate role of government (e.g., limited or broad), and they shape public policies. For instance, they determine criminal justice policies, particularly whether sentencing policies should emphasize punishment or rehabilitation.

James Madison is remembered as the architect of American government because he designed a form of government with elaborate institutional checks and balances. He believed that people were by nature self-interested and needed to have their ambitions checked. Thomas Jefferson wrote extensively about human nature, specifically about the question whether humans were self-interested egoists (individuals whose actions are based solely on "self-love") or whether they had a moral sense. He believed people had a natural moral sense. The question was whether it was based on religion, which would justify government support for religion, or a natural sense of moral obligation or conscience. These are some of the most profound political questions. In a June 13, 1814 Letter to Thomas Law, "The Moral Sense," Jefferson discusses his thoughts on the question.

In his First Inaugural Address (delivered March 4, 1861), President Lincoln spoke about human nature when he closed his Address with the hope that the divisiveness of the Civil War could be ended by appeals to "the better angels of our nature." Lincoln believed that without such appeals to our good nature, appeals to the worse angels of our nature would result in division, discord, and violence.

An ideology would be inconsistent if it included positive *and* negative views of human nature, or if it included both fixed and flexible views of human nature. Assessing the consistency of views on the role of government is more complicated. They typically include ideas about the appropriate *size* and the appropriate *use* of government power.

The size usually refers to small government or big government. The use refers to the purposes of government. With the notable exception of libertarianism, ideologies typically support small government for some purposes and big government for others. For example, modern conservatives believe in big government for national security, morals regulation, and crime. Liberals believe in big government to regulate business and to expand social and economic equality. American politics tends to focus on the *size* of government—which individual, ideology, or political party supports big government and which supports small government. However, the *role* of government—what government power is actually being used for—is probably more important than the size of government.

> Think About It!
> Are humans Hobbesian creatures who are violent by nature?
> What does Steven Pinker's 2007 TED Lecture, *The Myth of Violence*, say about human nature?
> http://www.ted.com/talks/lang/en/steven_pinker_on_the_myth_of_violence.html

9.13 |

The te   and politics. One of these two labels is usually attached to individuals, parties, interest groups, media articles and outlets, public policies, and government officials—including judges. But the fact that the terms conservative and liberal are commonly used does not mean that their meanings are clear. In fact, arguments are often about the meaning of words such as freedom, order, and justice—as well as conservative and liberal. The fact that our ordinary political vocabulary includes words whose meanings are not agreed upon explains why so many political arguments pause with the declaration, "That's not what I mean by liberalism/conservatism/order/justice!" Democracy requires a shared political vocabulary, and it works best when citizens know the meanings of the words they use to describe government and politics. Defining conservatism and liberalism is complicated by the fact that they have changed a great deal over time. Ideologies are dynamic, not static. They change over time. What it means to be a conservative or liberal changes over time, which is one reason why it is sometimes hard to know just what is in a name.

9.14 | *The Functions of Ideology*

In politics as in economics and sports, *organization* increases effectiveness. Ideologies organize interests. Ideologies can increase the effectiveness of individuals and ideas by organizing them in order to maximize their impact on public policy. In this respect, ideologies serve a purpose that is similar to political parties and interest groups. But ideologies both unite people and divide them. Ideologies do bring people together to work for shared ideas but they also move people apart by dividing them into opposing camps: believers and non-believers. The fact that ideologies both unite and divide, increase political cooperation and political conflict, is one reason why Americans are so ambivalent about ideology, why they have conflicting feelings about ideology. The ambivalent feelings about ideology can be traced to the earliest days of the republic when the Founders warned against "the mischiefs of faction." In *Federalist Number 9* Hamilton argued that a firm union was a safeguard against "domestic faction." In Federalist

Number 10 Madison described how to design a political system that "cured" the "mischiefs of faction." Worries about the harmful effects of factions have not gone away. Today's worries are about ideologies or parties or special interests divided Americans into competing camps that fight hard for their views rather than working toward the common good. The later chapters describe how organization can increase an individual's feelings of efficacy, the belief that individual participation in politics matters because it can make a difference. Ideology *can* play a similar role because it unites and organizes like-minded people to work on behalf of shared ideas.

9.2 | The Major Isms

The range of ideological debates in the U.S. is very limited compared to other democracies. American politics is practically limited to liberalism and conservatism. There are occasional references to other ideologies such as libertarianism, radicalism, socialism, and fascism, but these ideologies are for the most part outside the mainstream of political debate or they are considered the more extreme elements within liberalism or conservatism. The more extremist ideologies of the left and right ends of the political spectrum are not usually part of political discourse. In this sense, the two-ideology system mirrors the two-party system: both present voters with a limited range of political choices.

Liberalism and conservatism have changed a great deal over time. In the early 1800s, the conservative party was the Federalist Party, which advocated a strong federal government, and the liberal party was the Jeffersonian Republicans, which advocated states' rights. In the 1930s, conservatives supported states' rights while liberals supported expansion of the federal government. Since the mid-1960s four major issues have consistently divided conservatives and liberals:

- *National Security Policy.* Conservatives have generally been stronger supporters of national defense (anti-communism and anti-terrorism) policies than liberals.
- *Crime Policy.* Conservatives have supported getting tough on crime by strengthening police and advocating punishment. Liberals have generally been considered soft on crime by strengthening due process rights of suspects and advocating rehabilitation.
- *Moral Regulatory Policy.* Conservatives support moral regulatory policy related to abortion, pornography, sexual behavior, and public displays of religion. Liberals support deregulation of morals.
- *Economic Policy.* Conservatives have been more consistently pro-business and anti-tax. Liberals have generally been more pro-labor and more supportive of government regulation of business.

9.30 | Conservatism: Traditional and Modern

This is a conservative era in American politics. Conservatism has been the dominant, but not exclusive, force in national politics since the late 1960s[2] with the notable exception being the reaction to the Watergate scandal in the mid-1970s. However, conservatism is not a monolithic ideology. In fact, wherever two or more conservatives are gathered together the discussion invariably turns to who is the real, true conservative. The following describes the two main strains of conservatism: traditional conservatism (during the period from the 1930s until the mid-1960s) and modern conservatism (from the mid-1960s until today). There are three main differences between traditional and modern conservatism—their views on change, ideology, and the role of government.

9.31 | *Views on Change*

Traditional conservatism is closest to the original meaning of the word conservative, which is derived from the Latin *conservāre*—meaning to conserve by preserving, keeping, or protecting traditional beliefs, values, customs, or ways of doing things. Traditional conservatives defend the status quo against radical or revolutionary change or

Edmund Burke, 1771

the assumption that all change is reform (good change). Edmund Burke (1729-1797), the Irish-British political philosopher, is considered the father of traditional conservatism. He did not oppose change. In fact, he argued that a government without a means of changing lacked the necessary means for its own survival. However, Burke preferred slow or incremental change and opposed radical or revolutionary change.

Modern conservatism is a much stronger advocate for *change*. In fact, some conservatives call themselves radical conservatives. A radical is someone who advocates basic, even revolutionary change. Radicals can be leftwing or rightwing. When President Reagan called his administration a bunch of radicals he reminded voters that he was a movement conservative, a person who was committed to the cause of overturning liberal social, economic, and defense policies. In contrast to traditional conservatism, which rejected radical or revolutionary change of the right or left, modern conservatism advocates major, even radical or revolutionary change. However, the change is usually described as radical change from the liberal status quo, change that will bring the country back to the basics. This usually means that the solution for many of the contemporary social, economic, and political problems is to return to the Founder's original understanding of politics, government, and the Constitution. This recurring conservative theme is one of the main points of the Tea Party movement.

Traditional conservatism's skepticism about change is related to the belief in the importance of order. Traditional conservatives consider order the necessary condition for achieving or maintaining other important values such as individual freedom, private property, and justice—and without good order, these other values and valuables are unlikely to be attained. Traditional conservatives believe that order can be created and maintained by social institutions (family, schools, churches, and civic organization) as well as by government. In this sense, traditional conservatives are not anti-government.

They believe that government has a responsibility to maintain domestic order, to control crime, to preserve traditional values through moral regulatory policies, and to provide national security from foreign threats. But traditional conservatives believe that the primary responsibility for these activities lies with the private sector, the civil society, rather than the public sector (the government). The Burkean emphasis on order, social institutions, and civic responsibility made traditional conservatism less committed to other values such as individualism, individual liberty, and equality. A leading American traditional conservative is Russell Kirk (1918-1994). The Russell Kirk Center provides a good description of traditional conservative principles. They include belief in natural law, hierarchy, the connection between property rights and freedom, faith in custom and tradition, and skepticism of change.

9.32 | *Views on Ideology*

The second different between traditional and modern conservatism is that modern conservatism is much more *ideological*. Today's conservatives portray conservatism as an ideology that will solve the problems created by liberalism. The term *movement conservative* refers to those conservatives who consider themselves part of an organized cause to work for conservative ideas. These conservatives are part of a cause. Traditional conservatives were to a certain extent anti-ideological. They considered ideology problematic because it was extremism rather than moderation—and traditional conservatives were in the Aristotelian and Burkean traditions that emphasized conservatism as moderation rather than extremism. The word ideology was originally coined to refer to the scientific study of ideas. It was originally used to describe how the systematic study of ideas could lead to a better understanding of the political world the way that science increased understanding of the natural world. But by the middle of the 20th Century the word ideology was used to describe the ideas that were used to get and use political power. In fact, beginning in the latter 1950s, sociologists including Nan Aron, Seymour M. Lipset, Edward Shils, and Daniel Bell described ideology as assuming the role that religion played in traditional societies. In modern, Western-style secular democracies of the world ideology played the role of religion. They did not mean this as a compliment. They considered ideology at least partly an irrational, unthinking, and therefore unreasonable force in a political world where states had become very powerful, even totalitarian. The criticism of ideology was a reaction against the ideologies of the left and the right during the period from the 1930s to the 1960s. These critics of ideology came to be called neoconservatives, or new conservatives. Prominent neoconservatives were a group of former leftists who rejected ideologies of the left, which produced communism (e.g. The Soviet Union and China), and ideologies of the right, which produced fascism (Hitler's Germany and Mussolini's Italy). They associated ideology with totalitarianism.

9.33 | *Views on Role of Government*

The third difference between traditional and modern conservatives concerns the role of government. Modern conservative support for change and ideology has changed conservative thinking about the role of government. Conservatives are not antigovernment or even advocates of small government as much as they oppose what government has been doing. Specifically, conservatives oppose public policies that promote egalitarianism, social welfare, the due process model of justice, and the de-regulation of morals. The claim that conservatives are not antigovernment can be supported by examining conservative views on the four major policy areas that have consistently divided conservatives and liberals: national security; crime; economics; and moral regulatory policy. The conservative position is not antigovernment in these four areas. Conservatives are pro-government on national security, crime, regulation of morals, and even, to a lesser extent, economics. There *is* a libertarian strain within conservatism that is consistently antigovernment but mainstream conservatism does not take the libertarian position on the major policies.

The conservative movement's support for government is apparent in the principles and positions taken by leading conservative organizations such as The Heritage Foundation, the The American Conservative Party, and The American Conservative Union. The Heritage Foundation, for example, describes itself as a leading voice for conservative ideas such as individual freedom, limited government, traditional values, and strong national defense. It promotes the latter two values by support for "big" government. The American Conservative Party's principles are more anti-government in the sense that they more consistently advocate limited government. The principles include natural rights and individual liberty, the belief that law should be used to support liberty and mediate disputes where one person has harmed another, and the reminder that "[t]he armed forces and law enforcement exist to bolster private defense, not supplant it."

Ideologies include a commitment to acting on values. Conservatives use both the government and the private sector to achieve their goals, but they are especially committed to the private sector. The free market plays a central role as a means to achieve conservative goals. In fact, the market model is often presented as an alternative to a statist or government model for organizing society. The English political philosopher Adam Smith developed the marketplace model in *Wealth of Nations*. This book, which was published in 1776, the same year as the Declaration of Independence, is one of the most influential books ever written. Smith advocated an alternative to mercantilism, the conventional economic model of the day that the government should direct economic activity for the wealth of the empire. Smith described an economic system where the prices of goods were determined by the interactions of buyers and sellers in a competitive marketplace rather than the government. Over time, however, the logic of the marketplace model has been extended beyond economics to other, non-economic areas of society. For example, the economic free marketplace of goods has been expanded to politics where the free market place of ideas is based on the same logic as the economic free market. This is controversial because the marketplace model assumes that goods and services should be available on the basis of the ability to pay— but some things are valuable even though they are not highly valued in the economic marketplace. The philosopher Michael Sandel worries that the logic of the marketplace is now being applied to more and more non-economic settings. Listen to his argument about what money cannot buy and should not buy. Do you agree with him?

Michael Sandel, "'*What Money Can't Buy' and What it Shouldn't Buy*,"
PBS Newshour (June 11, 2012)
http://www.pbs.org/newshour/bb/business/jan-june12/makingsense_06-11.html

9.40 | Liberalism

A standard dictionary definition of a liberal is a person who believes in individual liberty. Therefore liberalism can be defined as an ideology that values individual liberty. This definition is not very helpful because it does not explain very much and because conservatives also believe in individual liberty. And liberals, like conservatives, believe in order. However, liberals and conservatives place different values on individual liberty and order. Liberals tend to value liberty more than order while conservatives tend to value order more than liberty.

Defining liberalism is complicated for some of the same reasons that defining conservatism is complicated: it is a set of ideas—not just one idea; the ideas have changed over time; and like conservatism, liberalism is not monolithic. Two main strains of liberalism are examined here: classical liberalism and modern liberalism.

9.41 | Classical Liberalism

Classical liberalism is rooted in the ideas of the English political philosopher John Locke (1632-1704). Locke's ideas greatly influenced the thinking of the American founders. His words about the importance of life, liberty, and property found their way into the Declaration of Independence. Locke emphasized the following five ideas:

- Reason. Humans should use their reasoning capacity to understand the natural and political world rather than *merely* relying on faith, custom, or tradition in order to organize society.
- Individualism. The importance of the individual as a political actor relative to groups, classes, or institutions included an emphasis on legal equality.
- Liberty. Freedom is valued more than order, or relative to obedience to authority.
- Social Contract Theory of Government. Individuals decide to leave the state of nature and create government based on the consent of the governed and created by a social contract.
- Property Rights. Economic rights (to property and contract) are related to political rights. The shift is toward a private sector economy rather than one run by the government is an aspect of the commitment to limited government.

Classical liberalism originated as a political theory that limited government. During much of the 20th Century classical liberalism was actually considered conservative because it was associated with the defense of property rights and the free market, and opposition to government regulation of the economy and the expansion of the social welfare state.

9.42 | *Modern Liberalism*

The main difference between classical liberals and modern liberals is that modern liberals abandoned the emphasis on limited government as the best way to protect individual rights. Modern liberals used government to achieve greater equality, liberty, and income security.

- Equality. The various civil rights movements of the 19th, 20th, and 21st centuries expanded equality for racial and ethnic minorities and women. Most recently, the gay rights movement has advocated for greater legal equality under the law. Egalitarianism became a more important goal for modern liberals. Laws were used to limit discrimination.

- Liberty. Modern liberals also used law to protect civil liberties. Radical political speech. Limits on government censorship. The right to privacy and deregulation of morals.

- Income Security. Modern liberals used government policies to pass social welfare programs (e.g., social security; Medicare; unemployment insurance; workers compensation). These policies were designed to increase income security for the young, the old, and the sick. Support for the creation of the social welfare state explains why modern liberals are called social welfare liberals to differentiate them from classical liberals.

One of the founders of modern liberalism is the 19th Century English political philosopher John Stuart Mill. In *On Liberty and Representative Government*, Mill explained a principle or rule for determining what government should be allowed to do,

> "The only purpose for which power can be rightly exercised over a member of a civilized community, against his will, is to prevent harm to others. His own good, either physical or moral, is not a sufficient warrant."

and what it should not be allowed to do, in a political system based on limited government. The rule has come to be called The Harm Principle. In fact, Mill was merely

> "The legitimate powers of government extend to such acts only as are injurious to others. But it does me no injury for my neighbor to say there are twenty Gods or no God. It neither picks my pocket nor breaks my leg."

restating the liberal idea developed by Thomas Jefferson (and John Locke before him):

The Harm Principle is libertarian in the sense that it limits government power over individuals. Mill accepted the basic principles of classical liberalism, particularly individual freedom, but he was more supportive of using government power to protect liberty and to promote equality. The origins of social welfare liberalism can be traced to this shift toward greater reliance on government to provide economic and social security. In modern American politics, liberals generally support government regulation to promote equality and economic security—the social welfare state—while conservatives generally support government regulation to promote law and order, national security, and morality—the national security and moral regulatory state.

One indication that this is a conservative era in American politics is the fact that liberalism has become a pejorative term, a negative term. Liberalism has been stigmatized as the "L-word" after been blamed for being soft on crime, for being weak on national defense, for undermining traditional values, and for being unduly critical of capitalism. In fact, the word liberal is so out of political favor today that liberals call themselves progressives. Progressive is a euphemism for liberal and Progressivism is a strain of liberalism.

Think About It!
Why are conservatives happier than liberals?
http://www.pbs.org/newshour/bb/business/july-dec11/makingsense_12-09.html

---

9.50 | Libertarian

Libertarianism is a simpler ideology than either conservatism or liberalism. Simply stated, libertarians value freedom and believe that individuals and groups can organize life with only minimal government. Libertarians have a positive view of human nature. The belief that government threatens freedom—that more government means less

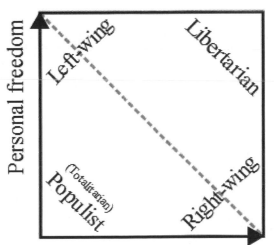

Nolan chart, 2d political spectrum. Diagonal line indicates classical 1d left-right political spectrum.

freedom—is reflected in The Libertarian Party motto: "Maximum freedom. Minimal Government." The familiar slogan, "That government is best which governs least!" is libertarian. Libertarians believe in minimal government: government should be limited to doing what is necessary to protect individuals from being harmed by others. Libertarians value freedom more than order, but they believe that order actually emerges from the competition of the marketplace. This is the basis of libertarian support for laissez faire policies in economic, political, and social affairs. Laissez faire is a French term for "let it be." In economics, laissez faire means allowing the competition of the marketplace, and the interaction of buyers and sellers, to operate without government intervention, regulation, or control. Libertarians rely on the private sector to produce order and prosperity. In politics, libertarians oppose using government power to promote values such as equality, patriotism, or morality. They also oppose immigration policies that limit the free movement of people across national borders. This is why libertarians can be conservative on some issues (opposed to using law to promote equality or create social welfare or to regulate business) and liberal on others (opposed to moral regulatory policy and opposed to laws promoting patriotism).

Libertarians take seriously the **harm principle** as a guide for limited government. The harm principle is libertarian insofar as it considers the only legitimate use of government power is preventing individuals from being harmed by others. Harm means physical harm to person or property or interests. The harm principle does not allow paternalistic legislation, using laws to prevention people from harming themselves by smoking, drinking alcohol or using drugs, eating unhealthy food, riding motorcycles without a helmet, or riding in a car without a seatbelt.

9.60 | Other Isms

9.61 | *Socialism and Communism*

<u>Socialism</u> is the belief that economic power is the basis of political power and that economic equality is essential for political equality. The belief that economic inequality causes political inequality provides the socialist justification for using government to actively promote equality through extensive government regulation or even government control of the economy. In order to achieve political equality, the government as redistributes resources through progressive taxation and social welfare program, at a minimum, and government control of the economy (both the means of production and the distribution of goods and services) at a maximum. <u>Karl Marx</u> is the most famous figure associated with socialism because he developed a comprehensive, systematic analysis of the relationship between economics and politics, thereby giving earlier socialist thinking an ideology or world view. For an American economist's critique of the rise and fall of socialism as an economic model read <u>Robert Heilbroner's analysis</u>.

Like conservatism and liberalism, there are many variations of socialism. In fact, in American politics the term socialist is often used in a generic sense to refer to any "big government" taxing and spending policies. In this sense, government spending as a share of the nation's Gross Domestic Product is a measure of how *socialistic* the country is. Socialists do support expansive government. But so do non-socialists. For example, the federal government's response to the Great Recession included the infamous Troubled Asset Relief Program (or TARP) of 2008 and the Emergency Economic Stabilization Act of 2008 which provided government bailouts for financial services companies and car manufacturers (GM and Chrysler). These policies were *socialistic* only in the sense that they increased government intervention in the private sector economy. But the bailouts were not socialistic in the sense that they were not aimed at promoting greater economic equality: critics called them Wall Street bailouts that Main Street would have to pay for. The key to identifying socialist policies that result in big government, as opposed to non-socialist policies that result in big government, is the social policies promote egalitarianism: economic equality.

Communism can be understood as an extreme version of socialism. It takes the socialist ideal of equality, and the government's responsibility to achieve it in the economic, political, and social sectors to the point where there is no distinction between a private sector and the public sector. Communism is *totalitarian* in the sense that it advocates **total** government power over society. Indeed, the word *totalitarian* means total control with no distinction between the public sector and the private sector. In a totalitarian system, the government is authorized to use its powers and laws to regulate individual behavior, family policy, business and labor, as well as all aspects of social life.

9.62 | Anarchism

In terms of the size of government, anarchism is at the opposite end of the ideological spectrum from communism. The key to understanding anarchism is the fact that the Greek origin of the term means "without rulers." Anarchists oppose all forms of government because governments by definition have the power to coerce individuals to join a community or require obedience to laws. Government use force—even the force of law—to ensure compliance rather than merely allowing individuals to freely, voluntarily join a political community. Anarchists believe that government is not necessary because people can use their capacity for reasoning to decide whether to freely and voluntarily agree to live in orderly and just societies without government requiring them to do so. Anarchists have a basically positive view of human nature which contrasts with Thomas Hobbes who believed that humans were by nature selfish, and the strong would take advantage of the weak. Anarchists believe that people will learn from experience that some rules are necessary for peaceful and prosperous coexistence and therefore will voluntarily accept rules that provide good order and justice without the force of law. Anarchists consider government power to compel individuals to obey the law illegitimate because it violates an individual's inherent right to be free from coercion by others. In today's political debate, anarchists are most often depicted as violent radicals who oppose government policies promoting international trade and globalism.

9.63 | Populism

The term populism refers to "of the people." Populists advocate on behalf of the common person who they depict as being unfairly treated by the rich and powerful or some other privileged elites. In this sense, populist movements tend to be protest movements representing farmers, the average American, or workers. Populism has been a recurring theme throughout American history. President Andrew Jackson was a populist who worked to bring the average person into a political process that was controlled by "the better sorts" of society. In the latter 19th and early 20th Century, agrarian populists defended rural/agrarian interests from the urbanization and industrialization that occurred with the Industrial Revolution. Populism often emerges as a reaction against major social, economic, or cultural changes (e.g., immigration) or economic crises (e.g., panics, depressions, or recessions). The cultural revolution of the 1960s spawned right wing populists such as George Wallace, Governor of Alabama and presidential candidate.

Listen to <u>Wallace's populist campaign message</u> making fun of northern urban elites (including the Washington press).

Today's left wing populism includes criticism of Wall Street (e.g., the Occupy Movement) and the growing economic inequality in the country. Today's right wing populism includes opposition to immigration, or at least the demand that the federal government defend the country's borders and enforce immigration laws, and opposition to efforts to change the traditional definition of marriage as a union between one man and one woman—for example, the Tea Party Movement's rallying cry is to "take back the Constitution" from the elites.

Tea Party Protest, Washington D.C. September 12, 2009

9.64 | *FEMINISM*

Feminism is a social or political movement that strives for equal rights for women. It is multi-faceted movement that has political, economic, social, legal, and cultural components. The *Stanford Encyclopedia of Philosophy* defines <u>feminism</u> and describes it by paying special attention to its various dimensions. Feminist theory describes and analyzes gender differences (and similarities) in order to better understand gender differences and gender inequality. From the perspective of political science, feminist theory is an attempt to explain relevant facts, include gender behavior, sexuality, and inequality. One relevant fact is the different gender political power relations. Feminism describes and critiques these political power relations. As such, feminist theory often promotes women's rights. The subjects of study include discrimination, stereotypes, objectification, and patriarchy. <u>Women's Studies</u> is a multidisciplinary academic field that includes anthropology, communications, economics, history, philosophy, political science, and sociology.

9.65 | ENVIRONMENTALISM

Environmentalism is a movement whose members advocate protecting the natural environment. Environmentalism is an example of modern issue politics advanced by individuals—policy entrepreneurs who take up a cause—and organizations (interest groups). The environmental movement began to have an impact on national politics in the 1960s and 1970s when they put the environment on the government's agenda. Senator Gaylord Nelson founded <u>Earth Day</u> on April 22, 1970. The <u>Environmental Protection Agency</u> also was created in 1970. The EPA is the primary federal government agency responsible for providing clean air and clean water. Why is the environmental movement political? Why is it controversial to provide clean air and clean water? Because doing so involves the allocation of scarce resources. Protecting the environment costs money and entails government regulation of business and consumer behavior. This explains the debate over global warming. Global warming is an example of an environmental issue that has become controversial because addressing it will require governmental regulation.

9.66 | FUNDAMENTALISM

Fundamentalism is not usually considered an ideology the way conservatism, liberalism, and libertarianism are ideologies. However, fundamentalism is an idea which has an important impact on modern American politics and the politics of other countries. <u>Fundamentalism</u> is usually defined as a movement within a religious denomination—a movement that reacts against modernity by advocating a return to the basics or the fundamentals of a particular faith. Religious fundamentalism is evident in most of the major religions of the world today. Christian, Islamic, and Judaic fundamentalists advocate a return to basic articles of faith, particularly those tenets of faith that are expressed or revealed in sacred texts such as the Bible or Koran.

Fundamentalism is not limited to religious movements. It can be secular as well. From a social science perspective, fundamentalism is a reaction against modernity, particularly science, secularism, and value relativism. **Secularism** is the belief that government and politics should be separate from religion, that religion is appropriate for the private (social) sphere, not the public (governmental) sphere. In the U.S., secularism is reflected in the idea that there should be a "wall of separation" between church and state. **Relativism** is the belief that values are subjective and conditional rather than universal and objectively true. Fundamentalists advocate restoring the traditional or fundamental belief that morals and values are universal truths that are not subject to evolving standards of modernity.

In the U.S., political fundamentalists advocate returning to the nation's founding values, political principles, and founding documents. Legal or constitutional fundamentalists advocate Originalism, the belief that judges should decide cases based on the original intentions of those who wrote the words of the Constitution rather than their interpretation of the words or the modern meanings of the words. Religious fundamentalists and secular fundamentalists tend to be conservative insofar as they work to return to or restore the values of the founding era.

9.67 | Terrorism

Terrorism is hard to define in a way that is universally accepted or which differentiates between acceptable and unacceptable uses of political violence. The old saying that one person's freedom fighter is another person's terrorist still applies to contemporary analyses of political violence. A basic definition of terrorism is the use of violence or the threat of violence to intimidate or coerce a people, principally for political purposes. Terrorism creates a climate of fear in a population in order to achieve a particular political objective.

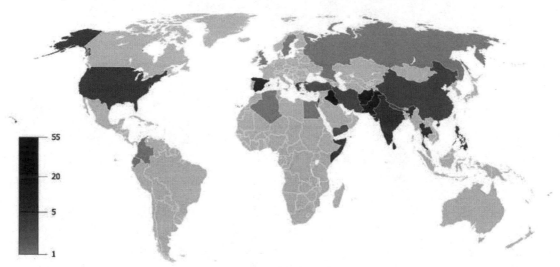

Number of terrorist incidents, by country, in 2009

U.S. law does define terrorism. Title 118 of the U.S. Code defines international terrorism as violent acts that "appear to be intended to" "intimidate or coerce a civilian population;" "to influence the policy of a government by intimidation or coercion," or to "affect the conduct of a government by mass destruction, assassination, or kidnapping."[3] It defines domestic terrorism as activities that "involve acts dangerous to human life that are a violation of the criminal laws of the United States or of any State;" "appear to be intended" to "intimidate or coerce a civilian population; to influence the policy of a government by intimidation or coercion; or to affect the conduct of a government by mass destruction, assassination, or kidnapping…"; and "occur primarily within the territorial jurisdiction of the United States."

An extremely broad range of individuals, political organizations, and movements have used terrorism: leftist and rightist; conservative and liberal; nationalistic and internationalist movements; religious and secular; defenders of the status quo and revolutionaries; populists and elitists; and even governments (though state institutions such as armies, intelligence services, and the police). Since the terrorist attacks of 9/11, the government has devoted a great deal of attention to terrorism. In fact, the Federal Bureau of Investigation describes protecting against terrorism its top priority.

Terrorism involves the use of political violence but not all political violence is terrorism. It is important to differentiate between legitimate and illegitimate uses of political violence. During the colonial era, mob actions were part of the American political experience with direct, participatory democracy. The Boston Tea Party in December 1773 was direct action intended to protest against British policies and to intimidate the British. Shays' Rebellion in the winter of 1786 and 1787 was an armed uprising by citizenry who demanded that the government be more responsive to the economic problems of average Americans who facing mortgage foreclosures.

The Tea Party movement played an important role in the 2010 mid-term elections. Conservatives and Republican candidates for national and state offices did very well. One controversy surrounding the Tea Party movement is the fact that individual members of the movement and Tea Party groups either implied or explicitly stated that the American political tradition includes demanding change through means other than the ballot box and regular elections. These alternative methods include violence and the threat of violence. The references to "Second Amendment" remedies for political problems are a reminder that the American political tradition includes famous examples of when political violence was accepted as a legitimate way to achieve political change or to oppose advocates of political change. Members of the Tea Party movement and advocates of gun rights, such as the National Rifle Association, remind the American public and government officials that the Declaration of Independence explained why individuals or organizations can take up arms when the government is tyrannical, exceeds its authority, or is not responsive to demands.[4]

9.60 | Why are there only two ideologies in the U.S.?

Individual freedom of choice is a powerful concept in the U.S. In economics, freedom of choice means a preference for free markets. The free marketplace of goods and services where consumers choose based on their preferences is a very familiar part of American culture. In the economic marketplace competition is believed to improve products and services. It is also considered a good thing for economic consumers to have a broad range of options from which to choose when purchasing a car, a house, health care, an insurance plan, or any other good or service. Americans consider economic choice a good thing—and economic consumers certainly have a great variety of goods and services from which to choose. At one time, television viewers had only three networks to watch. Now there is a seemingly endless menu from which to select. At one time, economic consumers had to choose from the big three American automobile manufacturers: Chevrolet, Ford, and Chrysler. Today's consumers have many more choices. Why then is political choice so limited? Why are American economic consumers presented with such a variety of goods and services but they are practically limited to choosing either a conservative or a liberal, either a Republican or Democrat? Must a person be either a conservative or a liberal? In a nation of 300 million people, is it possible to fit everyone into only two boxes? Are policies either liberal or conservative?

9.61 | WHAT ARE YOU?

The two-dimensional framework for thinking about ideologies and political parties has serious limitations. Must all people be fit into either the conservative or the liberal box? Must all issues be reduced to only two-dimensions? The limitations of the conservative and liberal framework have prompted searches for ways of thinking about ideology that provide for more than two options. One alternative framework that provides more than two categories is the World's Smallest Political Quiz. It makes a distinction between views on economic issues and views on personal issues. Take the quiz to see which of four ideological labels best describes you.   Do you think the results accurately label you? What do you think of the quiz? Do you think the organization that developed the questions is biased toward a particular ideology?

In recent years American politics has been described in terms of "Red States" and "Blue States." Red states are conservative Republican and blue states are liberal Democratic. The Pew Research Center developed a "Political Typology" quiz that provides more political colors than red and blue.

9.70 | Is Ideology A Good Influence or A Bad Influence?

It is not easy to provide simple definitions of complex terms such as conservatism and liberalism and describe their role in American government and politics. It is even harder to assess whether their role is positive or negative, whether ideologies are good or bad influences on government and politics. It is hard to objectively—that is, neutrally or without bias—assess an ideology's role because ideologies are prescriptive rather than descriptive terms. A **prescriptive** term is a normative or value-laden term. A prescriptive term is one that has a value judgment about its worth, whether it is desirable or undesirable, whether it is good or bad. A **descriptive** term is not a normative or value-laden term. The following illustrates descriptive and prescriptive statements that are (mostly) familiar to politics.

Descriptive Statements

Democracy is government of the people, by the people, and for the people.
Freedom is the right to do what you want.
Equality means treating everyone the same.
Conservatism is an ideology that values social order more than individual liberty.
Liberalism is an ideology that values individual liberty more than social order.
Socialism is an ideology that values equality.
Terrorism is the political use of violence.

Prescriptive Statements

Democracy is a good form of government.
Freedom is preferable to slavery.
Chocolate is better than vanilla.
Conservatism is preferable to liberalism.
Liberalism is preferable to conservatism.
Capitalism is a good economic system.
Socialism threatens freedom.
Violence is not a legitimate means to a political end.
Terrorism is unacceptable.

There are too many lawyers and laws in modern American society.

It is hard to conservatism and ideologies are considered than descriptive term is a normative A descriptive term without assessing

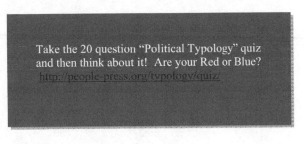
Take the 20 question "Political Typology" quiz and then think about it! Are your Red or Blue?
http://people-press.org/typology/quiz/

objectively assess liberalism because commonly prescriptive rather terms. A prescriptive or value-laden term. defines or explains value. In American

politics and government, people think of conservative or liberal or socialist as good or bad rather than merely as labels that describe *different* sets of beliefs and programs for acting on them. As a result, candidates for public office, government officials, public policies, and political events are viewed through prescriptive, ideological lenses. Capitalism and democracy are considered good; other economic and political systems are considered bad. Similarly, the Republican and Democratic parties are not merely described, they are assessed as good or bad based on ideological or policy preferences.

Prescriptive terms reflect biases for or against something—which makes it harder to study it objectively. Studying terrorism is complicated because it is a prescriptive term, and its prescription is pejorative (or negative): to call a person a terrorist, or to describe an action as terrorism, is to condemn the person or the action. A descriptive definition of democracy is that it is a political system where people control their government through elections or other means. But democracy is commonly used in a prescriptive sense: "Democracy is a good (or bad) form of government." To say that democracy is a good form of government is a positive normative statement. To say that democracy is a bad form of government is a negative normative statement. Attaching prescriptive labels to political terms sometimes makes it harder, not easier, to understand what is being described. The fact that the terms liberal and conservative, which are so important for understanding American politics and government, are so often used as prescriptive labels that are attached to individuals, parties, or policies can make it harder to understand American government and politics. When thinking about ideology, it is important to try to separate the descriptive thinking about the terms from the prescriptive or normative assessment of whether the ideology is good or bad. Doing so will increase the likelihood that ideology—the systems of beliefs and policies for acting on them—can increase understanding of government and politics and the public policies that emerge from the process.

Chapter 9:Key Terms

Ideology
Traditional
conservatism
Modern conservatism
Liberal
Classical liberalism
Terrorism
Libertarianism
Socialism
Communism
Anarchism
Feminism
Environmentalism
Fundamentalism

Chapter 9: Study Questions
1. What is the role of religion in ideology?
2. What is ideology?
3. How do liberalism, conservatism, and libertarianism likely influence thinking about stem cell research?
4. Briefly discuss the problems with the conservative and liberal labels.
5. Is ideology good or bad?
6. Describe some of the differences between conservatism and libertarianism.

9.8 | Additional Resources

The Center for Voting and Democracy has links to articles related to elections and democracy including voter turnout, links to organizations and ideas related to reforming the electoral system, and analysis of electoral returns. www.fairvote.org/

The World's smallest political quiz uses ten questions to place a person on the economic and social ideological spectrums. http://www.theadvocates.org/quiz

The Gallup Organization provides historical and current information about American public opinion. www.gallup.com

9.9 | In the Library

George W. Carey, et al. Freedom & Virtue: *The Conservative Libertarian Debate*. Intercollegiate Studies Institute, 1998.

Robert Erikson. *American Public Opinion: Its Origins, Content, and Impact*. Longman Pub Group, 2006.

William Flanigan. *Political Behavior of The American Electorate*. CQ Press, 2006.

Taegan D. Goddard. *You Won - Now What? How Americans Can Make Democracy Work from City Hall to the White House*. Scribner, 1998.

Gerald M. Mara. *The Civic Conversations of Thucydides and Plato: Classical Political Philosophy and the Limits of Democracy*. State University of New York Press, 2008.

Edwin Meese. *The Heritage Guide to the Constitution*. Regnery Publishing, 2005.

Deborah Stone. *The Samaritan's Dilemma: Should Government Help Your Neighbor?* Nation Books, 2008.

Howard Zinn. *A People's History of the United States: 1492 to Present*. Harper, 2001.

---

[1] Kenneth M. Dolbeare and Linda J. Medcalf. 1988. *American Ideologies Today*. New York: Random House, Inc. p.3.

[2] In *The Emerging Republican Majority* (New Rochelle, NY: Arlington House, 1969), Kevin P. Phillips predicted the rightward movement in American national politics based on his experience working with President Nixon's 1968 campaign.

[3] http://www.law.cornell.edu/uscode/uscode18/usc_sup_01_18_10_I_20_118.html

[4] See http://blogs.abcnews.com/thenote/2010/06/what-are-sharron-angles-2nd-amendment-remedies-to-reids-oppression.html

CHAPTER 10: POLITICAL PARTICIPATION

1960 Democratic National Convention

10.0 | Political Participation

One of the most important, and difficult, political questions is why governments have authority over individuals. Why can the government (or the *community* or the *majority*) tell people what to do and what not to do? This is the power problem stated in its simplest terms. In theory, democracy addresses this aspect of the power problem through *self-government*. Self-government requires the participation of an active and engaged citizenry. This chapter examines how voting, elections, and campaigns organize participation in politics and government in order to solve the problems that people expect government to solve. Political participation is not limited to voting. Good citizenship, full citizenship, is active and engaged citizenship. Efforts to increase political participation have resulted in a movement to increase civic engagement. The term **civic engagement** refers to a broad range of individual or collective actions that are intended to address issues of public concern. Civic engagement includes volunteerism, working with organizations, and participation in the electoral process. The latter part of this chapter provides examples of how to "do" civic engagement. The chapter begins with voting.

10.1 | Voting

Voting is one of the ways that citizens participate in a democracy. Voting is just one form of political participation. There are many other ways to participate in politics: writing a letter to a newspaper; posting to a Web site; making a campaign contribution; contacting a legislator; running for office; campaigning for a candidate; or lobbying government. But voting is the form of political participation that is most closely associated with meeting the responsibilities of citizenship because voting is an act of self-government. Voters select government officials to represent them and cast votes for or against issues that are on the ballot. There are many other forms of political participation: running for office, making campaign contributions, working for a party or candidate or issue, lobbying, or contacting government officials about an issue or problem which interests you. Even non-voting—the intentional refusal to participate in an election as a protest against the political system or the candidate or party choices that are available—can be a form of political participation. All these forms of participation are components of political science measures of how democratic a political system is.

10.11 | *Expanding the right to vote*

One of the most important developments in the American system of government has been the expansion of the right to vote. Over time, politics has become much more democratic. The Founders provided for a rather limited right to vote because they were skeptical of direct democracy and the ability of the masses to make good decisions about public policy or government leaders. In fact, the Founders were divided on how much political participation, including voting, was desirable. The Federalists generally advocated limited participation where only white male property owners could vote. A leading Federalist, Alexander Hamilton, advocated a system of representative government that resembled "a natural aristocracy" that was run by "gentlemen of fortune and ability."[1]

The Anti-federalists advocated broader participation. The Anti-federalist author writing under the name *The Federal Farmer* defined democratic participation as full and equal representation: "full and equal

---

[sidebar quotes, partially cut off:]

e vote is the most
erful instrument
devised by man for
king down injustice
destroying the
ble walls which
ison men because
are different from
r men."

don B. Johnson

ways vote for
ciple, though you
vote alone, and you
cherish the
etest reflection that
r vote is never lost."

n Quincy Adams

representation is that in which the interests, feelings, opinions, and views of the people are collected, in such a manner as they would be were all the people assembled." The Anti-federalist *Republicus* advocated an American democracy that provided for "fair and equal representation," which he defined as a condition where "every member of the union have a freedom of suffrage and that every equal number of people have an equal number of representatives."

Over time the right to vote was greatly expanded and the political system became much more democratic. Abraham Lincoln's *Gettysburg Address* is a memorable political speech because of what it said about democracy and equality. Lincoln famously defined democracy as government *of* the people, government *by* the people, and government *for* the people. He also brought equality back into American political rhetoric by emphasizing the political importance of equality that was first stated so memorably in the Declaration of Independence. The Declaration of Independence asserted that all men were created equal and endowed with unalienable rights. The Constitution did not include equality as a political value. It provided for slavery and allowed the states to limit the right to vote. The right to vote was expanded by constitutional amendments and by legislation. The constitutional changes included the following amendments:

- The 14th Amendment (1868) prohibited states from denying to any person with their jurisdiction the equal protection of the laws.
- The 15th Amendment (1870) prohibited states from denying the right to vote on the basis of race.
- The 17th Amendment (1913) provided for direct election of Senators.
- The 19th Amendment (1920) gave women the right to vote.
- The 24th Amendment (1964) eliminated the Poll Tax.
- The 26th Amendment (1971) lowered voting age to 18.

One of the most important *statutory* expansions of the right to vote is the Voting Rights Act of 1965. It made racial discrimination in voting a violation of federal law; specifically, outlawing the use of literacy tests to qualify to register to vote, and providing for federal registration of voters in areas that had less than 50% of eligible minority voters registered. The Act also provided for Department of Justice oversight of registration, and required the Department to approve any change in voting law in districts that had used a "device" to limit voting and in which less than 50% of the population was registered to vote in 1964. The Civil Rights Act of 1964 is a landmark civil rights statute that also expanded the right to vote by limiting racial discrimination in voting.

In addition to these government actions, the political system also developed in ways that expanded the right to vote and made the system more democratic. The emergence of political parties fundamentally changed the American political system. Political parties changed the way the president is chosen by effectively making the popular vote, not the Electoral College, determine who wins the presidency. There have been notable exceptions to the rule that the candidate who receives the most popular votes wins the election (the presidential elections of 1824, 1876, 1888) and 2000), but modern political culture includes the expectation that the people select the president.

10.12 | *How democratic is the United States political system?*

Democracy is a widely accepted value in the U.S. and elsewhere in the world. As more nations adopt democratic political systems, political scientists are paying attention to *whether* a country's political system is democratic as well as *how democratic* the political system is. Democracy is not an either/or value. There are degrees of democracy: a political system can be more or less democratic. Non-governmental organizations such as Freedom House and publications such as *The Economist* have developed comparative measures of how democratic a country's political system is. *The Economist* ranks the U.S. as 17th in the world.[2] This is a surprisingly low ranking for a nation that extols the value of democracy and promotes it worldwide. The low ranking on democracy is due to several factors:

- Voter Turnout. The U.S. has comparatively low rates of voter turn-out. European countries, for example, have much higher rates of voting.
- A Presidential System. The U.S. has developed into a system of presidential governance system where executive power is dominant rather than the more democratic legislative or parliamentary systems.
- National Security. The U.S. has developed extensive provisions for secrecy and national security and emergency powers which are hard to reconcile with democratic values.

10.13 | *Voter Turnout*

Voter turnout is the proportion of the voting-age public that participates in an election. Voter turnout is a function of a number of *individual* factors and *institutional* factors. Voter turnout is low in the United States. What does low mean? In many elections, less than half of the eligible voters participate in the election. The graph below shows the turnout rate for presidential elections from 1960 to 2008.

Think About It!

Should the U.S. try to increase voter turnout by either paying people to vote or by fining (or otherwise sanctioning) eligible voters who do not vote?

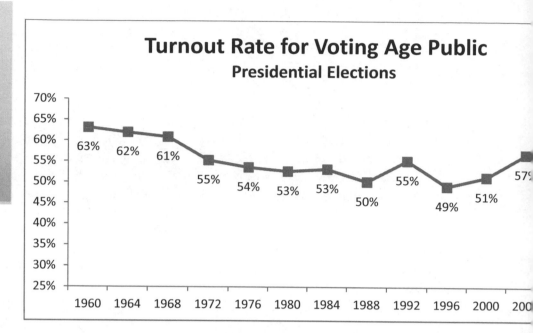

Turnout Rate for Voting Age Public
Presidential Elections

Voter turnout is also low compared to other western industrial democracies. Why is U.S. voter turnout low in absolute numbers (less than half) and comparatively? Some of the explanations focus on the individual while others focus on the electoral system.

10.14 | *Individual Explanations*

The individual explanations focus on an individual's motivations. The two main models of individual explanations for voting behavior are the rational choice model and the civic duty model.

The **rational choice** model of voting was developed by Anthony Downs, who argued that individuals are self-interested actors who use a cost-benefit analysis to determine whether it is in their self-interest to vote.[3] According to the rational choice model, a person's decision whether to vote is based on an individual's assessment of whether the vote will affect the outcome of the election, the expected benefit of voting and not voting, and the sense of civic duty (the personal gratification or satisfaction from voting. The rational choice model is based on the assumptions in economic models of human behavior.

The **civic duty** model describes non-material, non-rational incentives for voting. According to the civic duty model, a person votes out of a sense of responsibility to the political unit, or a commitment to democratic government and the obligations and duties as well as the rights of citizens to maintain self-government. Patriotic values and the commitment to the community or society are familiar expressions of civic duty.

In order to vote, the probability of voting, times the benefit of vote, plus the sense of duty to vote must outweigh the cost (in time, effort, and money) of voting. As the probability of a vote mattering in a federal election almost always approaches zero (because more than 100,000,000 votes are cast), duty becomes the most important element in motivating people to vote. According to the rational choice model, a person will vote if they think it is worth it; a person will not vote if they think it is not worth it.

According to this cost-benefit ratio, it may be rational not to vote. An individual with a greater commitment to civic duty or responsibility will weigh the relative costs differently and may conclude that voting is worth it.

The concept of political efficacy is central to understanding voting behavior. **Political efficacy** is the belief that one's participation matters, that one's decision to vote really makes a difference.   What is the likelihood that one vote will matter in a presidential election where more than 100, 000,000 votes are cast? The rational choice model suggests that voter turnout in the United States is low because individuals have thought about whether or not to vote and simply concluded that it is not worth their time and effort and money to vote.

Demographic factors affect whether or not someone turns out to vote. Demographic factors that are related to voter turn-out include income, education, race and ethnicity, gender, and age. Wealthy citizens have higher rates of voter turnout than poor citizens. *Income* has an effect on voter turnout. Wealthy citizens have higher levels of political efficacy and believe that the political works and their votes will count. On the other hand, people that make less money and have less wealth are less likely to believe that the political system will respond to their demands as expressed in elections. *Race* is also related to voter turnout. Whites vote at higher rates than minorities. *Gender* is also related to voter turnout. Women voted at lower levels than men for many years after gaining suffrage with the passage of the 19th Amendment in 1920, but today women vote at much higher levels than men do. *Age* is also important. There is a strong relationship between age and voter turnout. Older people vote at higher levels than younger people do, which helps explain why candidates for office and government officials are so sensitive to issues that affect seniors (such as reducing spending on Social Security or Medicare).

10 15 | *System Explanations*

The system explanations focus on aspects of the political system that affect voter turnout. These system factors include voter registration laws, the fact that elections are usually held on one day during the week, the large number of elections in our federal system, and the two-party system.

Eligibility. A person's eligibility for voting is provided for in the U.S. Constitution, state constitutions, and state and federal statutes. The Constitution states that suffrage cannot be denied on grounds of race or color (Fifteenth Amendment), sex (Nineteenth Amendment) or age for citizens eighteen years or older (Twenty-sixth Amendment). Beyond these basic qualifications, the states have a great deal of authority to determine eligibility and to run elections. Some states bar convicted criminals, especially felons, from voting for a fixed period of time or indefinitely. The National Conference of State Legislatures reports on felon voting rights in the states. The Sentencing Project reports that 5.8 million Americans are disenfranchised, denied the right to vote, because of a felony conviction. State felon voting laws have a disproportionate impact on African-Americans: one out of 13 African-Americans are ineligible to vote because of a felony conviction.

Voter Registration. Voter registration is the requirement that a person check in with some central registry in order to be allowed to vote in an election. In the U.S., the individual is responsible for registering to vote—sometimes well before the actual election. Furthermore, each state has different voter registration laws and moving from one state to another state requires reregistering to vote.[4] These registration laws reduce voter turnout. In some countries, the government registers eligible voters and actually fines eligible voters who do not perform their civic duty to vote in an election.

Think About It!

What should you expect when you show up at the polls to vote?

"What to Expect Before Heading to the Polls"

http://www.npr.org/templates/story/story.php?storyId=96538073

Voter Fatigue. Voter fatigue is the term for the apathy that the electorate can experience when they are required to vote too often in too many elections. The U.S. has a large number of government units (around 90,000) and Americans elect a large number of government officials—around one for every 442 citizens. Having a large number of elections—in the U.S. there is always an election somewhere—can reduce voter turnout.

The Two-party System. Finally, the two-party system can contribute to low voter turnout by increasing the sense that an individual's vote does not matter very much. In two-party systems, the parties tend to be primarily interested in winning elections. In order to win elections, the parties tend to compete for moderate voters with middle-of-the-road appeals because most of the voters are by definition centrists rather than extremists. This can be a winning electoral strategy, but it sometimes leaves voters thinking there isn't much real difference between the two major parties which compete by "muddling in the middle." Why vote if there is no real choice between the two candidates or parties? The two major American political parties tend to be interested primarily in winning elections, and only secondarily in advocating ideologies or issues. In contrast, countries with multiple party systems are more likely to have *rational* political parties. As used here, a rational party is one whose primary goal is advancing ideas, issues, or ideology; winning an election is secondary.

Listen to Southern Democrat Huey Long's critique of the Democratic and Republican Parties in the 1940 presidential election. George C. Wallace, the former Governor of Alabama and 1968 presidential candidate of the American Independent Party, famously said of the Democratic and Republican candidates for president: there is "not a dime's worth of difference between them."[5] Does it matter whether one votes for a Republican or Democrat when there really isn't much choice in a two-party system where the major parties don't differ much on the issues?

Election Tuesday? Why does the U.S. have elections on a Tuesday? The reason for Tuesday elections goes back to the days of horses and buggies when Monday elections would require traveling on the Sabbath and Wednesday was market day. So in 1845 Congress provided for Tuesday elections. Would changing from one-weekday elections to two-day weekend elections increase voter turnout by making it easier for people to fit voting into busy family and work schedules? It has in some countries. The U.S. has comparatively low rates of voter turnout but bills to change to weekend voting die in committee in Congress. Some states now allow early voting and a significant percentage of votes are now cast before prior to the day of the election. Should technology such as electronic voting be used to increase voter turnout?

10.2 | Elections

Elections are one way for people to participate in the selection of government officials. Elections also provide a means of holding government officials accountable for the way they use their power. Participation and accountability are two of the main reasons why elections are a measure of *whether* a political system is democratic and *how democratic* it is. In most cases, it is not as useful to describe a political system as democratic or non-democratic as it is to determine how democratic it is. Many countries of the world have political systems that are more or less democratic. Some countries are more democratic than others. The existence of free, open, and competitive elections is one measure of whether a country's political system is democratic.

10.21 | *Three Main Purposes*

Elections serve three main purposes in representative democracies (or republics, like the U.S.):

- **Selecting government officials**. The most basic purpose of an election in a democratic system is to select government officials. Elections provide an opportunity for the people to choose their government officials. The fact that voters choose their representatives is one of the ways that democratic or republican systems of government solve the power problem. Voting is part of self-government.
- **Informing government officials**. Elections also provide government officials with information about what the people what, what they expect, and what they think about government. Elections provide an opportunity for the voice of the people to be expressed and heard. Elections thus serve as one of the ways to regularly measure public opinion about issues, political parties, candidates, and the way that government officials are doing their jobs.
- **Holding government accountable**. Elections provide regular or periodic mechanisms for holding elected representatives, other government officials, and even political parties accountable for their actions while in power. The Founders of the U.S. system of republican government provided for elections as part of the system of checks and balances.

The political scientists who study voting and elections describe two theories of elections. One theory is the elections are **forward looking** in the sense that an election provides government officials with information about which direction the public wants the government to go on major issues. The second theory is that elections are **backward looking** in the sense that an election provides government officials with feedback about what has been done   in effect, an election is a referendum on government officials or the political party in power.

10.22 | *Too Much of a Good Thing?*

In the U.S., voters go to the polls to elect national government officials at all levels of government: national, state, and local. Voters indirectly elect the President (through selection by the Electoral College). Voters directly elect the members of the House of Representatives and the Senate. Voters directly elect state government officials such as governors, legislators, the heads of various executive departments, and in many states judges. And voters elect local government officials such as county commissioners, school board members, mayors and city council members, and members of special governing districts such as airport authorities. In addition, most states provide for referendums, elections where voters decide ballot issues. With more than 90,000 total government units in the U.S., elections are being held somewhere for some office or for some ballot measure almost all the time. Across the whole country, more than one million elected offices are filled in every electoral cycle.

10.23 | *Initiative and Referendum*

Elections are not limited to those that involve the selection of government officials. In the U.S., many state and local governments provide for ballot initiatives and referendum. A ballot initiative is an election where the voters decide whether to support or reject a proposed law. A referendum is an election where the voters go to the polls to approve or reject a law that has been passed by the state legislature or a local government body. The people vote for or against issues such as state constitutional amendments, county charters, or city charter provisions and amendments.[6]

The increased use of initiatives and referenda in states such as California has raised questions about whether direct democracy is preferable to indirect or representative democracy. In a representative democracy, the elected representatives of the people make the laws; in a direct democracy, the people make the laws. The recent trend toward initiatives and referendum has attracted the attention of people who study American politics. One organization that monitors and reports on what is happening in the states is the Ballot Initiative Strategy Center. This Center acts as a "nerve center" for "progressive" or liberal ballot initiatives in the states. The Initiative and Referendum Institute (IRI) at the University of Southern California studies ballot initiatives and referendums in the U.S. and elsewhere in the world. Technology has made it possible to use this form of direct democracy to make the political system more democratic by allowing the public more opportunities to participate in the adoption of the laws that government them.

10.24 | *Regulating Elections*

Elections are regulated by both federal and state law. The U.S. Constitution provides some basic provisions for the conduct of elections in Articles I and II. Article I, Section Four provides that "[t]he Times, Places and Manner of holding Elections for Senators and Representatives, shall be prescribed in each State by the Legislature thereof; but the Congress may at any time by Law make or alter such Regulations, except as to the Place of Chusing Senators." The 13th, 14th, and 15th Amendments also regulate elections by prohibiting states from discriminating on the basis of race or gender. The 15th Amendment states that the "right of citizens of the United States to vote shall not be denied or abridged by the United States or by any State on account of race, color, or previous condition of servitude."

However, most aspects of electoral law are regulated by the states. State laws provide for the conduct of primary elections (which are party elections to determine who the party's nominee will be in the general election); the eligibility of voters (beyond the basic requirements established in the U.S. Constitution); the running of each state's Electoral College; and the running of state and local elections.

10.25 | *Primary and General Elections*

Election campaigns are organized efforts to persuade voters to choose one candidate over the other candidates who are competing for the same office. Effective campaigns harness resources such as volunteers; money (campaign contributions); the support of other candidates; and endorsements of other government officials, interest groups and party organizations. Effective campaigns use these resources to communicate messages to voters.

Political parties have played a central role in election campaigns for most of the nation's history. However, during the last 30 years there has been an increase in candidate-centered campaigns and, more recently, independent organizations (such as super-PACS). Candidates who used to rely on political parties for information about voter preferences and attitudes now conduct their own public opinion polls and communicate directly with the public.

Before candidates can seek election to a partisan political office, they must get the nomination of their party in the **primary election.** A campaign for a non-partisan office (one where the candidates run without a party designation on the ballot), does not require getting the party nomination. A primary election is an election to determine who will be the party's nominee for office. A general election is the election to actually determine who wins the office. A primary election is typically an intra-party election: the members of a party vote to determine who gets to run with the party label in the general election. A general election is typically an inter-party election: candidates from different parties compete to determine who wins the office. Most state and local political parties in the United States use primary elections (abet with widely varying rules and regulations) to determine the slate of candidates a party will offer in the general election. More than forty states use only primary elections to determine the nomination of candidates, and primaries play a prominent role in all the other states.

There are four basic types of primary elections: **closed primaries, open primaries**, **modified closed primaries,** and **modified open primaries.** Closed primaries are primary elections where voters are required to register with a specific party before the election and are only able to vote in the party's election for which they are registered. Open primary elections allow anyone who is eligible to vote in the primary election to vote for a party's selection. In modified closed primaries, the state party decides who is allowed to vote in its primary. In modified open primaries, independent voters and registered party members are allowed to vote in the nomination contest.

10.3 | **National Elections**

The United States has a presidential system of government. In presidential systems, the executive and the legislature are elected separately. Article I of the U.S. Constitution requires that the presidential election occur on the same day throughout the country every four years. Elections for the House of Representatives and the Senate can be held at different times. Congressional elections take place every two years. The years when there are congressional and presidential elections are called presidential election years. The congressional election years when a president is not elected are called midterm elections.

The Constitution states that members of the United States House of Representatives must be at least 25 years old, a citizen of the United States for at least seven years, and be a (legal) inhabitant of the state they represent. Senators must be at least 30 years old, a citizen of the United States for at least nine years, and be a (legal) inhabitant of the state they represent. The president must be at least 35 years old, a natural born citizen of the United States and a resident in the United States for at least fourteen years. It is the responsibility of state legislatures to regulate the qualifications for a candidate appearing on a ballot paper. "Getting on the ballot" is based on candidate's performances in previous elections.

PRESIDENT AND VICE PRESIDENT
PRESIDENTE Y VICE PRESIDENTE

PRESIDENT AND VICE PRESIDENT +
PRESIDENTE Y VICE PRESIDENTE +
(Vote for One)
(Vote por Uno)

John McCain Sarah Palin	REP	← ◄
Barack Obama Joe Biden	DEM	← ◄
Gloria La Riva Eugene Puryear	PSL	← ◄
Chuck Baldwin Darrell Castle	CPF	← ◄
Gene Amondson Leroy Pletten	PRO	← ◄
Bob Barr Wayne A. Root	LBT	← ◄
Thomas Robert Stevens Alden Link	OBJ	← ◄
James Harris Alyson Kennedy	SWP	← ◄
Cynthia McKinney Rosa Clemente	GRE	← ◄
Alan Keyes Brian Rohrbough	AIP	← ◄
Ralph Nader Matt Gonzalez	ECO	← ◄

2008 Presidential Ballot in Palm Beach County, Florida

10.31 | *Presidential Elections*

The president and vice-president run as a team or ticket. The team typically tries for balance. A balanced ticket is one where the president and the vice-president are chosen to achieve a politically desirable balance. The political balance can be:

- Geographical. Geographical balance is when the President and Vice-president are selected from different regions of the country—balancing north and south, or east and west—in order to appeal to voters in those regions of the country.
- Ideological. Ideological balance is when the President and Vice-president come from different ideological wings of the party. The two major parties have liberal and conservative wings, and the ideological balance broadens the appeal of the ticket.

- Experience. A ticket with balanced political experience is one that includes one candidate with extensive experience in federal government and the other a political newcomer. Sometimes political experience (being a Washington insider, for instance) is considered an advantage; sometimes it is considered a handicap. Incumbency can be a plus or a minus. Balance can try to have it both ways.
- Demographics. Demographic balance refers to having a ticket with candidates who have different age, race, gender, or religion. Once again, demographic balance is intended to broaden the ticket's appeal.

The presidential candidate for each party is selected through a **presidential primary**. Incumbent presidents can be challenged in their party's primary elections, but this is rare. The last incumbent President to not seek a second term was Lyndon B. Johnson. President Johnson was mired in the Vietnam War at a time when that war was very unpopular. The presidential primary is actually a series of staggered electoral contests in which members of a party choose delegates to attend the party's national convention which officially nominates the party's presidential candidate. Primary elections were first used to choose delegates in 1912. Prior to this, the delegates were chosen by a variety of methods, including selection by party elites. The use of primaries increased in the early decades of the 20th Century then they fell out of favor until anti-war protests at the 1968 Democratic National Convention.

Police attacking protestors at the 1968 Democratic National Convention in Chicago, IL

Currently, more than eighty percent of states use a primary election to determine delegates to the national convention. These elections do not occur on one day: the primary election process takes many months. The primary election process is long, drawn-out, complex, and has no parallel in any other nation in the world. The presidential candidates begin fundraising efforts, start campaigning, and announce their candidacy months in advance of the first primary election.

It is purely historical accident that New Hampshire and Iowa have the first primary elections and are thus the focus on candidate attention for months prior to their January elections. New Hampshire had an early primary election in 1972 and has held the place of the first primary since that time. Iowa's primary is before New Hampshire, although the state uses a **caucus** to select delegates. Generally, the Iowa caucus narrows the field of candidates by demonstrating a candidate's appeal among party supporters, while New Hampshire tests the appeal of the front-runners from each party with the general public.

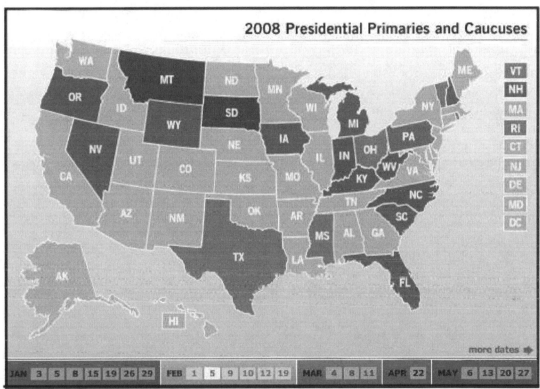

Dates of primary elections in 2008.

10.32 | *The Electoral College*

The president is not directly elected by the people. The popular vote does not actually determine who wins the presidency. When the voters in a state go to the polls to cast their votes for president (and vice president), they are actually voting for members of the Electoral College. The winner of a presidential election is the candidate who receives a majority vote of the members of the Electoral College.

With the possible exception of the Federal Reserve Board, the Electoral College may be the least-understood government body in the U.S. system of government. Each member of the Electoral College cast her or his vote for a presidential and vice-presidential candidate. Each state's members of the Electoral College are chosen by the state political party at that states party convention. The state parties choose party loyalists to be the party's members of the Electoral College if that party wins the popular vote in the state. This is why the members of the Electoral College almost always vote for the presidential candidate who wins the popular vote in that state. On rare occasion, a "faithless" Elector will not vote for the candidate who won the popular vote in their state. When voters in a state go to the polls to vote for a president, they actually each cast their votes for a slate of electors that is chosen by a party or a candidate. The presidential and vice-presidential candidate names usually appear on the ballot rather than the names of the Electors. Until the passage of the Twelfth Amendment in 1804, the runner-up in a presidential election (the person receiving the second most number of Electoral College votes) became the vice-president.

The winner of the presidential election is the candidate who receives at least 270 Electoral College votes. The fact that it is possible for a candidate to receive the most popular votes but lose the election by receiving fewer Electoral College votes than another candidate is hard to reconcile with democratic principles. It also does not seem fair in modern American political culture which includes an expectation that voters chose government officials. Abolishing the Electoral College and replacing it with a national direct system would also prevent a candidate from receiving fewer votes nationwide than their opponent, but still winning more electoral votes, which last occurred in the 2000 Presidential election.

State law regulates how the state's Electoral College votes are cast. In all states except Maine and Nebraska, the candidate that wins the most votes in the state receives all its Electoral College votes (a "winner takes all" system). From 1969 in Maine, and from 1991 in Nebraska, two electoral votes are awarded based on the winner of the statewide election, and the rest (two in Maine, three in Nebraska) go to the highest vote-winner in each of the state's congressional districts.

The Electoral College is criticized for a variety of reasons:

- It is undemocratic. The people do not actually elect a president; the president is selected by the Electoral College.
- It is unequal. The number of a state's Electors is equal to the state's congressional delegation. This system gives less populous states a disproportionate vote in the Electoral College because each state has two senators regardless of population (and therefore two members of the Electoral College). The minimum number of state Electors is three. Wyoming and California have the same number of senators. Wyoming has a population of 493,782 and 3 EC votes, 164,594 people per EC vote. California has a population of 33,871,648 and 55 EC votes, 615,848 people per EC vote.

Map of Electoral College Votes

- It spotlights swing states. The Electoral College system distorts campaigning because the voters in swing states determine the outcome of the election. As a result, voters who live in states that are not competitive are ignored by the political campaigns. Abolishing the Electoral College and treating the entire country as one district for presidential elections eliminate the campaign focus on swing states.

- It is biased against national candidates. The Electoral College also works against candidates whose base of support is spread around the country rather than in a state or region of the country which would enable them to win the popular vote in one or more states. This is what happened to Ross Perot. In 1992, Perot won 18.9% of the national vote, but received no Electoral College votes because his broad appeal across the country did not include strength in one or a few state.

Despite these long-standing criticisms of the Electoral College, abolishing it is unlikely because doing so would require a constitutional amendment—and ratification of a constitutional amendment requires three-quarters of the state legislature to support it. The less populous states are not likely to support an amendment to abolish the Electoral College in favor of direct popular election of the president because doing so would decrease the voting power of the less populous states. Small states such as Wyoming and North Dakota would lose power and more populous states such as California and New York would gain power.

10.33 | *Congressional Elections*

Congressional elections take place every two years. Each member of the House of Representatives is

2010 Florida Senate Campaign Debate: (From L to R: Marco Rubio, Charlie Crist, Kendrick Meek)

elected for a two-year term. Each Senator is elected for a six-year term. About one-third of the Senate is elected in each congressional election. Until the Seventeenth Amendment to the United States Constitution in 1913, Senators were elected by state legislatures, not the electorate of states.

10.34 | *House Elections*

Elections to the United States House of Representatives occur every two years on the first Tuesday after November 1 in even years. If a member dies in office or resigns before the term has been completed, a special House election is held to fill the seat. House elections are first-past-the-post elections—meaning the candidate who gets the most votes wins the election regardless of whether that person receives a majority of the votes cast in the election. The winner is the one who receives a plurality of the votes. Plurality means the most votes. It is not necessary for the winner to receive a majority (50% plus one) of the votes.

Every two years congressional elections coincide with presidential elections. Congressional elections that do not coincide with presidential elections are called mid-term elections—because they occur in the middle of a President's four-year term of office. When congressional elections occur in the same year as a presidential election, the party whose presidential candidate wins the election usually increases the number of congressional seats it holds. This is one of the unofficial linkages between presidential and congressional elections. The president and members of Congress are officially elected separately, but some voters go to the polls to vote for or against Republicans and Democrats so the president's popularity has an impact on congressional elections.

In 2010, Allen West (R) challenged incumbent and Ron Klein (D) in Florida District 22. West emphasized his military experience. A neighborhood campaign supporter produced a sign which framed the choice as "The Wimp or the Warrior."

There is a historical pattern that the incumbent president's party loses seats in mid-term elections. In mid-term elections, the president is not on the ballot. The president's party usually loses seats in mid-term elections. One reason for mid-term losses is the president's popularity has slipped during the two years in office. Another cause of mid-term election losses is the fact that voter turnout is lower in mid-term elections, and members of the president's party are less likely to vote in an election when *their* president is not on the ballot. These patterns of voting behavior illustrate the partisan linkages between congressional and presidential elections.

10.35 | *Gerrymandering*

Over time, congressional districts have become far less competitive. Congressional districts are drawn to protect individual incumbents and political parties. Another way to describe this is that congressional districts are drawn to create safe districts. A safe district is one that is not competitive; it is a safe district for the Republican Party or a safe district for the Democratic Party because the district boundaries are drawn to ensure that it contains a majority of Republicans or Democrats. One consequence of drawing safe districts is a reduction in voter choice. The Constitution requires that congressional districts be reapportioned after every census. This means that reapportionment or redistricting is done every ten years. The reapportionment is done by each state. In most cases, the political party with a majority in the state legislature controls redistricting. The fact that either one or the other major party controls the reapportionment encourages partisan gerrymandering.

Gerrymandering is drawing electoral district lines in ways that advantage one set of interests and disadvantage others. Historically, gerrymandering advantaged rural interests and disadvantaged urban interests. Voters in rural districts were over-represented and voters in urban districts were under-represented. Racial gerrymandering is done to advantage one race and to disadvantage others. Historically, racial gerrymandering over-represented white voters and under-represented Black voters. Racial gerrymandering is illegal because the Fourteenth Amendment prohibits states from denying people the equal protection of the laws. Partisan gerrymandering is drawing electoral lines to benefit the majority party and hurt the minority party. It is still practiced as a way for the majority party to use its political power.

One of the ways that the two major parties cooperate is in the creation of safe electoral districts. The Democratic and Republican parties have a vested interest in reducing the number of competitive districts and increasing the number of safe seats. The fact that more than nine out of ten Americans live in congressional districts that are not really competitive, but are safe seats for one party or the other, means that elections are not really very democratic. Redistricting to create safe seats for incumbents (those in office) gives an incumbent a great advantage over any challenger in House elections. In the typical congressional election, only a small number of incumbents lose their seat. Only a small number of seats change party control in each election. Gerrymandering to create safe districts results in fewer than 10% of all House seats actually being competitive in each election cycle—competitive meaning that a candidate of either party has a good chance of winning the seat. The lack of electorally competitive districts means that over 90% of House members are almost guaranteed reelection every two years.

"The Gerry-Mander." Boston *Gazette*, March 26, 1812.

This is a significant development because competitive elections are one measure of how democratic a political system is. The large number of safe districts makes a political system less democratic because there are fewer competitive elections. Creating safe seats for 1) Republicans and Democrats; and 2) incumbents in either party, results in conditions that resemble one-party politics in a large number of districts. If one party almost always wins a district, and the other party almost always loses, the value of political competitions is greatly diminished.

10.36 | *A Duopoly (or Shared Monopoly)*

The two major parties collude to create these political monopolies (technically they are duopolies because the two major parties control the political marketplace). The creation of a large number of safe seats makes districts more ideologically homogeneous, thereby making negotiating, bargaining, and ultimately the need to compromise less likely. A candidate who does not have to run for office in a politically diverse district is less likely to have to develop campaign strategies with broad public appeal, and once in office such a legislator is less likely to have to govern with much concern about accommodating different interests or representing different constituents.

10.4 | Campaigns

A political campaign is an organized effort to influence the decisions of an individual, group, organization, or government institution. Campaigns are one way that individuals, parties, and other political actors compete for popular support. Campaigning is a type of advertising: it is political advertising rather than commercial advertising. A candidate, political party, or interest group campaigns by providing the public with favorable information about their issues (this is positive campaigning) or unfavorable information about the opposition (this is negative campaigning). Political (or electoral) campaigns are organized efforts with three elements: message, money, and machine.

10.41 | *The Message*

The campaign message is usually a clear and concise statement that explains why voters should vote for a candidate or an issue. Some examples of campaign messages include the following:

- John Doe is a business man, not a politician. His background in finance means he can bring fiscal discipline to state government.
- Crime is increasing and education is decreasing. We need leaders like Jane Doe who will keep our streets safe and our schools educating our children.
- Jane Doe has missed over 50 congressional votes. How can you lead if you don't show up to vote?
- Jane Doe is not a Washington politician. She remembers where she came from and won't become part of the problem in Washington.
- Jane Doe knows how to keep Americans safe from terrorism.
- John Doe is an experienced leader.
- Vote Yes on Number Four to Protect Marriage.

The message is one of the most important aspects of any political campaign, whether it is an individual's campaign for office or a referendum on an issue. The media (radio, television, and now the new media) emphasize short, pithy, memorable phrases from campaign speeches or debates. These "sound bites" are the short campaign slogans or catchy messages that resemble bumper-stickers. Sound-bite campaigns and campaign coverage reduce political messages to slogans such as "Peace through Strength" (Ronald Reagan), "Its Morning in America" (President Reagan), and "Change We Can Believe In" (Barack Obama). The Museum of the Moving Image has archived presidential campaign ads. A memorable campaign slogan from the 1984 Democratic primary campaign was Walter Mondale's ad dismissing his main Democratic challenger, Gary Hart, with the catch phrase from a popular Wendy's commercial: "Where's the beef?" The implied charge was that the photogenic Hart lacked substance, particularly when compared to the dull but experienced Mondale. The mantra of Bill Clinton's presidential campaign in 1992 was "It's the economy stupid." This slogan stressed the importance of keeping the campaign focused on the state of the economy rather than other issues that sometimes distract Democrats. Candidate George W. Bush's campaign used the slogan "compassionate conservatism" to appeal to both conservatives and those who worried that conservatives did not care about the poor or disadvantaged.

Today's national and state campaigns are typically professional, sophisticated, carefully crafted campaigns to develop and control the image of a candidate. The marketing of political campaigns has been described as the "packaging" of a candidate and the "selling" of a candidate—even "The Selling of a President." The reference to selling a president is from Joe McGinniss' *The Selling of the President* (1968). McGinniss described how candidate Richard Nixon used Madison Avenue marketing professionals and strategies to win the White House. At the time, the idea that a political campaign could, or should, market and sell a candidate the way that beer, deodorant, and bars of soap were marketed and sold other products like beer or deodorant or a bar of soap was controversial. The idea of corporate advertising expertise being applied to democratic politics in order to influence what citizens thought of the president seemed inappropriate and threatening. Bringing marketing values to politics seemed to demean or diminish politics by treating people as consumers rather than as citizens. Political advertising also seemed threatening in the sense that it used psychology to manipulate or control what people think.

In the years since 1968, the marketing and advertising of candidates is widely accepted as the way to conduct a successful national campaign. Presidential campaigns develop a message or candidate "brand." After the Watergate Scandal exposed President Nixon's dishonesty, the Jimmy Carter campaign brand was honesty: "I will not lie to you." During the Carter Administration the Soviet Union invaded Afghanistan, Americans were taken hostages during a revolution in Iran that overthrew the Shah of Iran who was an ally of the United States, and a hostage rescue mission failed. These events, coupled with the loss of the Vietnam War, allowed presidential candidate Ronald Reagan to portray President Carter, the Democrats, and liberals as weak on national defense. The Reagan campaign theme "Peace through Strength" successfully branded Carter, Democrats, and liberals as weak on national defense and Reagan, Republicans, and conservatives as strong on national defense.

The comparison of campaigning and advertising is appropriate because many of the techniques and strategies that are used by Madison Avenue advertisers are mainstream politics. The similarities between the selling of a product or service and the selling of candidate are now acknowledged. In order to be successful, national campaigns spend a great deal of money on gathering information about political consumers so that candidates and parties can craft and present a message that is appealing.

10.42 | *Money*

Campaign finance has become more important as campaigns have changed from traditional *retail politics* to *wholesale politics*. The term retail politics refers to campaigns where candidates actually meet voters one-on-one, in small groups or communities, at town hall meetings, or other face-to-face settings such as walking a neighborhood. The term wholesale politics refers to campaigns where candidates address large audiences often using the print and electronic mass media.

The change to wholesale politics has increased the cost of campaigning by shifting from labor-intensive campaigning—where friends and neighbors and campaign workers and volunteers canvas a district or city or make personal telephone calls to individual voters—to capital-intensive campaigns where money is used to purchase television air time or advertising. The change from campaigns as ground wars to air wars has increased the cost of campaigning.

Fundraising techniques include having the candidate call or meet with large donors, sending direct mail pleas to small donors, and courting interest groups who could end up spending millions on the race if it is significant to their interests. The financing of elections has always been controversial because money is often considered a corrupting influence on democratic politics. The perception is that the wealthy can purchase access to government officials or pay for campaigns that influence public opinion. The fact that private sources of finance make up substantial amounts of campaign contributions, especially in federal elections, contributes to the perception that money creates influence. As a result, **voluntary public funding** for candidates willing to accept spending limits was introduced in 1974 for presidential primaries and elections. The Federal Elections Commission was created in the 1970s to monitor campaign finance. The FEC is responsible for monitoring the disclosure of campaign finance information, enforcing the provisions of the law such as the limits and prohibitions on contributions, and overseeing the public funding of U.S. presidential elections.

A good source of information about money matters in American campaigns and elections is The Center for Responsive Politics. The Center tracks money in politics as part of an "open secrets project." The recommendation to "Follow the money" has become all-purpose slogan that is applicable to criminal investigations and investigations of political influence and campaign ads. The saying comes from the Hollywood film *All the President's Men* which tells the story of how Washington Post reporters investigated the Watergate scandal. A secret source named Deep Throat advised the reporters to "Follow the Money."

The National Institute on Money in State Politics is still following the money trail to determine political influence in state politics. The U.S. Supreme Court's rulings in campaign finance cases has made "Follow the money" even more relevant in today's politics. In a series of rulings, the Court has said that campaign contributions are speech that is protected by the First Amendment and that government restrictions on campaign contributions are subject to strict scrutiny—which means that the government has to show that campaign finance laws serve a compelling interest in order to be upheld. As a result, corporations can make unlimited independent campaign expenditures. Even the existing requirements that contributions be publicly disclosed are now being challenged. The Campaign Finance Information Center's mission is to help journalist follow the campaign money trail in local, state, and national politics. The landmark Supreme Court ruling that has changed the campaign finance rules is *Citizens United v. Federal Election Commission* (2010).

http://www.oyez.org/cases/2000-2009/2008/2008_08_205

http://www.law.cornell.edu/supct/html/08-205.ZS.html

10.43 | *The Machine*

The third part of a campaign is *the machine*. The campaign machine is the organization, the human capital, the foot soldiers loyal to the cause, the true believers who will carry the run by

The War Room is a documentary that chronicles Bill Clinton's 1992 Presidential Campaign from an inside-look at his campaign staff.

volunteer activists, the professional campaign advisers, pollsters, voter lists, political party resources, and get-out-the vote resources. Individuals need organizations to campaign successfully in national campaigns. Successful campaigns usually require a campaign manager and some staff members who make strategic and tactical decisions while volunteers and interns canvass door-to-door and make phone calls. Large modern campaigns use all three of the above components to create a successful strategy for victory.

10.5 | The Media

Modern campaigns for national offices—the presidency, the Senate, and the House of Representatives—are largely media campaigns. They are conducted using the print media, electronic media, and the "new" media (the Internet and the social media). Communication technology has fundamentally altered campaigns. The development of the broadcast media (radio and television) changed political campaigns from "ground wars" to "air" wars. The term ground war refers to a campaign that relies heavily on candidates and their campaign workers meeting voters and distributing campaign literature. The term air war refers to campaigns that rely heavily on the mass media.

The following two quotes from the Museum of the Moving Image archive of presidential campaign ads illustrate the change in thinking about television campaign advertising:

- "The idea that you can merchandise candidates for high office like breakfast cereal is the ultimate indignity to the democratic process."
  Democratic presidential candidate Adlai Stevenson (1956)
- "Television is no gimmick, and nobody will ever be elected to major office again without presenting themselves well on it." Television producer and Nixon campaign consultant (and later President of Fox News Channel) Roger Ailes (1968)

10.51 | Who Uses Whom?

Campaign organizations have a complicated relationship with the media. They need and use each other but they have different, sometimes conflicting needs. The media like **good visuals** and compelling personal interest stories which capture the attention of the public and turn the general public into an audience. Campaigns like to provide such visuals. But the media (and campaigns) also like to play "gotcha." The media consider it a good story to catch a candidate's ignorance, mistake, or gaffe—or even to ask a question that might cause a candidate to make a mistake. The mistake might be

- Misspelling a word. Vice-presidential candidate Dan Quale spelled "potato" "potatoe."
- Ignorance. Not knowing the name of a foreign leader. Presidential candidate George W. Bush did not know the name of the leader of Pakistan.
- Misrepresentation. During the presidential primary campaign, Hillary Clinton misrepresented a trip to Kosovo as one where she landed at an airport under fire to convince voters that she had the experience to be commander in chief.

- Math problems. Announcing budget numbers that do not add up.
- Ignorance. Vice-presidential candidate Sarah Palin did not know the name of any Supreme Court decision that she disagreed with.

10.52 | *The Social Media*

Communication technology has changed national campaigns from primarily ground wars (walking the neighborhoods; kissing babies; shaking hands) to air wars (broadcast radio and television ads). Campaigns are now using social media to post material on Tumblr (videos and photos) or Spotify or Pinterest. According to Adam Fletcher, deputy press secretary for the Obama re-election campaign, "It's about authentic, two-way communication."[7] This may be true, but it may also be about a campaign strategy to try to reach people where they are: Online using social media. A presidential campaign that shares songs with the public may be less interested in actually creating two-way communication with the public than it is in establishing social connections with people by appearing to share tastes. Familiarity (with songs, photos and videos that are posted on Spotify, Flickr, Instagram, Twitter, Facebook, etc.) creates trust. Socialbakers, a social media analytics group, says the campaigns have to try to reach people wherever they are, and young people in particular are on-line more than reading newspapers or watching broadcast television networks.

10.53 | *The Age of Digital Campaigns*

The digital age is fundamentally changing campaign advertising. In the age of mass media, campaign ads that aired on the major television and radio networks were intended for the general audiences that were watching or listening to national programs. The digital age allows targeted advertising. Political intelligence companies such as Aristotle gather large files of detailed information about a person's behavior from commercial companies that keep track of consumption patterns or Internet searches, and then sell that data to campaigns. The campaigns, which then know where a person lives; what their demographics are; what they purchase; what they read; what their hobbies are; and other factors that might be related to how they think about politics, can tailor ads to very specific audiences. This digital information is very good for campaigns, but is it good for us? See the following PBS story about "How Campaigns Amass Your Personal Information to Deliver Tailored Political Ads." The digital campaigns are also developing ways to target "off the grid" voters, the voters who do not get their public affairs information from the traditional media sources (papers, television, and radio). Identifying such voters is one thing. Getting them to vote is another. Having a good ground game—people in neighborhoods, cities, districts, and states who can actually contact voters and get them out to vote—is still an important element of a successful presidential campaign strategy.

Think About It!
How much does a campaign know about me? See "How Campaigns Amass Your Personal Information to Deliver Tailored Political Ads."
http://www.pbs.org/newshour/bb/politics/july-dec12/frontline_10-29.html

President Obama's reelection campaign was successful because it combined air wars with a solid ground game in the states that it identified as the key swing states in the 2012 presidential election.

10.54 | *Campaign Fact Checking*

Candidates, parties, and organizations supporting or opposing a candidate, or an issue, say things which may not meet the standard of "the truth, the whole truth, and nothing but the truth." In an age of electronic communications, it is even more likely that Mark Twain, the American humorist, was right when he said, "A lie can travel halfway around the world while the truth is still putting on its shoes." As a result, a number of organizations have developed campaign fact-checking operations to hold campaigners accountable for what they claim as facts. One of these organizations is Factcheck.org. Its Web site provides running description and analysis of inaccurate campaign statements. Some of the more interesting false statements that they fact-checked were claims that Democratic presidential candidate Barack Hussein Obama was a radical Muslim who refused to recite the Pledge of Allegiance and took the oath of office as a U.S. Senate swearing on the Koran, not the bible.

10.55 | *Political Futures Market*

One of the more innovative and interesting perspectives on the measurement of public opinion as a predictor of the outcome of an election involves the application of economic perspectives. The "political futures" markets are designed to provide an economic measure of support for a candidate as a predictor of whether the candidate will win an election. One example of this approach is The Iowa Electronic Markets. These are real-money futures markets in which contract payoffs depend on economic and political events such as elections. These markets are operated by faculty at the University of Iowa Tippie College of Business as part of their research and teaching mission.

10.6 | How to "Do" Civic Engagement

The importance of fostering civic engagement in higher education is described in *Civic Responsibility and Higher Education* (2000), a book edited by Thomas Ehrlich. Ehrlich worked to promote including civic engagement along with the traditional academic learning in the mission of universities. The American Association of Colleges and Universities stresses the role that higher education plays in developing civic learning to ensure that students become an informed, engaged, and socially responsible citizenry. These efforts emphasize the importance of connecting classroom learning with the community. The connection has two points: usable knowledge and workable skills. The emphasis on usable knowledge includes promoting social science research as problem solving. The term ***usable knowledge*** refers to knowledge that people and policy makers can apply to solve contemporary social problems. (Lindblom and Cohen) The emphasis on workable skills is even more directly related to civic engagement. Today there are many organizations that advance the cause of linking academic study and social problem solving. One of these organizations is the W. K. Kellogg Foundation. This Foundation was created by the cereal company magnate. The Foundation emphasizes the importance of developing the practical skills that will enable individuals to realize the "inherent human capacity to solve their own problems." These skills include dialogue, leadership development, and the organization of effort. In effect, civic engagement develops the practical skills that can help people help themselves. How can you "do" civic engagement?

- Contact a government official. Contact a local, state, and national government official. Ask them what they think are the major issues or problems that are on their agenda. Contacting your member of Congress is easy. (See the Chapter on Congress.)
- Attend a government meeting. Attend the public meeting of a local government: a neighborhood association; a city council meeting; a county commission meeting; a school board meeting; a school board meeting; or a state government meeting (of the legislature or an executive agency).
- Contact an organization. Contact a non-government organization to discuss an issue of your concern, community interest, or the organization's mission. These organizations, political parties, and interest groups represent business, labor, professional associations, or issues such as civil rights, property rights, the environment, immigration, religion, and education.

10.7 | Summary

One aspect of the power problem is the government authority over individuals. The government's ability to tell an individual what to do is legitimate—that is, it is authority rather than merely power—if the government's ability is based on the consent of the government. Democracy, or self-government, requires an active and engaged citizenry in order to make government control over individuals legitimate. Political participation is one of the measures of how democratic a political system is. Therefore, political participation is also a measure of government legitimacy. Voting, elections, and campaigns provide opportunities for individuals to be active and engaged citizens.

10.8 | Additional Resources

10.81 | *In the Library*

Campbell, Angus, Philip Converse, Warren Miller, and Donald Stokes. 1960. The American Voter. New York: Wiley.

Civic Responsibility and Higher Education. 2000. Thomas Ehrlich. Editor.

Downs, Anthony. 1957. *An Economic Theory of Democracy.* New York: Harper Collins.

Green, Donald P., and Alan S. Gerber. 2008. *Get Out the Vote : how to increase voter turnout.* 2nd ed. Washington, D.C.: Brookings Institution Press.

Lewis-Beck, Michael S. 2008. The American Voter Revisited. Ann Arbor: University of Michigan Press.

Lindblom, Charles E., and David K. Cohen. 1979. *Usable Knowledge*. New Haven: Yale University Press.

McGinniss, Joe. 1968. *The Selling of the President*.

Schier, Steven. 2003. *You Call This An Election? America's Peculiar Democracy*. Washington, DC: Georgetown University Press.

10.82 | *Online Resources*

Each state has primary responsibility for conducting and supervising elections. For information about Florida elections go to the My Florida Web site http://www.myflorida.com/ and click on government, then executive branch, then state agencies, then department of state, then http://election.dos.state.fl.us/. Or you can learn about Florida election laws by going directly to the Florida Department of State Web site which provides information about voter registration, candidates, political parties, and constitutional amendment proposals.

Votesmart provides basic information about American politics and government. It is, in effect, American Government 101.

C-SPAN election resources are available at http://www.c-span.org/classroom/govt/campaigns.asp.

Dave Leip's Atlas of U.S. Presidential Elections provides interesting information about presidential elections. http://uselectionatlas.org/RESULTS/index.html
Rock-the-Vote is an organization dedicated to getting young people involved in politics. www.rockthevote.org/

Project Vote-Smart is a nonpartisan information service funded by members and non-partisan foundations. It offers "a wealth of facts on your political leaders, including biographies and addresses, issue positions, voting records, campaign finances, evaluations by special interests." www.vote-smart.org/

The U.S. Census Bureau has information on voter registration and turnout statistics. www.census.gov/population/www/socdemo/voting.html

C-Span produces programs that provide information about the workings of Congress and elections. www.c-span.org

Key Terms:
voter fatigue
open primaries
closed primaries
presidential primary
caucus
voter turnout
rational choice model
civic duty model
political efficacy
Individual explanations
System explanations
Voter registration
"Air" campaigns

10.9| STUDY QUESTIONS

1. What is the rational choice theory of voting?
2. What are the primary factors at the individual level that influence whether someone turns out to vote?
3. What are the institutional factors that depress voter turnout in the United States?

---

[1] Alexander Hamilton, in *The Records of the Federal Convention of 1787*, Vol. 2, ed. Max Farrand (New Haven, CT: Yale University Press, 1937), 298-299.

[2] For the methodology and results, see
http://www.economist.com/markets/rankings/displaystory.cfm?story_id=8908438

[3] See Anthony Downs. 1957. *An Economic Theory of Democracy*. New York: Harper Press.

[4] Declare Yourself has information on each state and the requirements for voter registration at http://www.declareyourself.com/voting_faq/state_by_state_info_2.html

[5] George C. Wallace. Stand Up For America. New York: Doubleday, 1976:212.

[6] The National Conference of State Legislatures provides detailed information about ballot initiatives in each state: http://www.ncsl.org/default.aspx?TabID=746&tabs=1116,114,802#802

[7] Quoted in "Campaigns Use Social Media to Lure Younger Voters," Jenna Wortham, The New York Times (October 7, 2012). www.nytimes.com Accessed October 12, 2012.

CHAPTER 11: POLITICAL PARTIES

11.0 | Why Political Organizations?

Why do people everywhere live, work, and play in groups? Why are large organizations—corporations, political parties, interest groups—the predominant actors in our political, economic, and social systems? Is there something *natural* about *social* organizations? And what is the role of individuals in political systems where groups are the dominant actors? Political scientists are not the only scholars who ask such questions. These are some of the oldest and most interesting questions that are asked by other social scientists (economists, sociologists, and anthropologists), philosophers, and natural scientists. Scientific research studies the phenomenon of grouping in the animal kingdom to learn why animals such as fish, birds, and elephants live in groups.[1] Social scientific research studies ideological, partisan, and other political groupings of people.

This chapter examines one form of political organization: political parties. Parties exist in all modern democracies but there is an underlying tension between democratic theory, which values individualism, and the political reality that organizations are the dominant actors in modern politics and government. The tension between individualism and organization is one reason why Americans are more skeptical of political parties than people in other western democracies where political parties tend to be stronger. Americans have such a strong commitment to individualism that there is a healthy skepticism about organizations, particularly large, powerful organizations whether in government, politics, or economics. In American politics and government, parties are considered a necessary evil. Their influence over voters and government officials is frequently questioned, but parties are also considered essential for organizing public participation in politics and control over government. The following sections explore these aspects of party politics in the U.S.

11.1 | What is a Political Party?

A **political party** is an organization of people with shared ideas about government and politics who try to gain control of government in order to implement their ideas. Political parties usually try to gain control of government by nominating candidates for office who then compete in elections by running with the party label. Some political parties are very ideological and work to get their set of beliefs implemented in public policy. Other political parties are not as ideological. A party may not be ideologically united because it represents a coalition of different interests. Or it may be more interested in gaining and holding power by having its members win elections than strongly advocating a particular set of beliefs.

Political organizations play an important role in government and politics around the world. It is impossible to understand American government and politics without understanding the role of political parties and interest groups. This is ironic because American culture values individualism, but political organizations such as parties and interest groups have come to play an extremely important role in our political and economic life. Parties and interest groups are linkage institutions. Linkage institutions are sometimes called aggregating or mediating institutions. The media are also a linkage (or mediating) institution. A linkage organization is one that links individuals to one another or the government. A linkage organization aggregates and collects individual interests. This is an important function in large scale (or mass) political systems because it is a way for individuals with shared interests to speak with a single or louder voice. Linkage organizations are also important because they mediate between individuals and government, they "mediate" between the lone (or small) individual and (increasingly) big government. The mediating role becomes more important as a country's population increases and as government get larger and larger. Intermediary organizations make it possible for individuals to think that they can have an impact on government. In this sense, political parties like other "mediating structures" actually empower people. Parties are part of **civil society**. The term civil society refers to the *non-governmental sector of public life*. Civil society includes political, economic, social, religious, cultural activities that are part of the crucial, non-governmental foundations of a political community: the family, neighborhoods, churches, and voluntary associations (including parties and interest groups). The Heritage Foundation is a conservative think tank. One of its goals is to promote these mediating structures as a way to empower people and limit government as envisioned by Peter Berger and John Neuhaus in *To Empower People: The Role of Mediating Structures in Public Policy* (1977). Civic engagement maintains these traditional mediating structures and supports their development.

The following sections examine political parties and their role in American politics pays some. Some attention is paid to the historical development of the U.S. party system, particularly the features of the two-party system.

11.2 | Roles in Modern Democracies

It is hard to imagine modern democracies without political parties. They exist in all democratic political systems. The freedom to form parties and compete in the electoral process is considered one of the essential measures of democracy because parties are considered vital elements of self-government. Political parties perform the following functions:

- Recruit and nominate candidates for office.
- Help run campaigns and elections.
- Organize and mobilize voters to participate in politics.
- Organize and operate the government.

The recruitment and nomination of candidates is one of the most important functions of political parties. In the past, party leaders in the U.S. exerted a great deal of control over the party's candidate for office. Party leaders and activists chose their party's nominee. Today, however, party control over nominations has been weakened by the increased use of primary elections to choose party candidates. In primary elections, the public votes for a party's nominee, which has opened the process and limited the influence of party officials and activists. The party's weakened control over the nomination process has weakened American political parties.

Political parties also organize and mobilize voters. This function is important in large countries because it can help organize the public in ways that increase an individual's sense of political efficacy. Political efficacy is the belief that a person's participation matters, that a person's vote can make a difference. In large scale democracies such as the United States, political parties organize individuals, synthesize their interests, and link or collect their views on government and politics into two or more perspectives. This collection or organization can magnify an individual's political voice. So political parties are not just divisive forces in politics; they can unite individuals with other like-minded people who share their thinking on government and politics.

The role of political parties does not end with an election. After an election, the parties work to organize and operate the government. The majority party in Congress and the party that wins the presidency work to organize the actions of the candidates who campaigned successfully and became government officials. The *Ins* generally support one set of public policies, and the *Outs* support an alternative set of public policies.

The above roles explain why political scientists see parties as vital elements of modern liberal democracies. Liberal democracies are a form of representative government that is based on individual rights and limited government with political participation organized by parties. But the American political tradition includes skepticism of parties. The fact that about one-third of voters consider themselves Independents rather than members of either of the two major parties (the Republican and Democratic parties) is evidence that Americans do not have a particularly strong attachment to parties. The Independents apparently think parties are not an essential element of modern democracy, or they associate political parties with the kinds of partisan bickering and fighting that prevent well-meaning people from working together to solve problems.

11.3 | Founding Era Opposition to Political Parties

Political parties have a familiar place in American politics today and they are accepted as established features of politics and government. However, this was not always so. The Constitution does not mention political parties. Indeed, political parties did not even exist when it was written. During the founding era, the groups that pursued a particular political interest were referred to as factions—and they were generally considered harmful influences whose power needed to be checked.

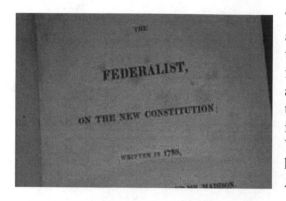

The Founders opposed political parties, and warned against their development in American politics. But they were not banned. The Founders felt that federalism and the separation of powers and checks and balances would keep factions from advancing their special interests and harming the public interest in the new republic. The anti-party views of George Washington and James Madison illustrate the early hostility to the emergence of political parties in the American political system.

11.31 | *George Washington*

George Washington's <u>*Farewell Address*</u> on September 19, 1796 is a famous statement warning against the spirit and actions of political parties. He warned against the development of state parties that created geographic divisions among Americans as well as "the baneful effects of the spirit of party generally," a spirit that was "inseparable from our nature," and existing in all forms of government, but "it is seen in its greatest rankness, and is truly their worst enemy," in popular forms of government:

> The alternate domination of one faction over another, sharpened by the spirit of revenge, natural to party dissension, which in different ages and countries has perpetrated the most horrid enormities, is itself a frightful despotism. But this leads at length to a more formal and permanent despotism. The disorders and miseries which result gradually incline the minds of men to seek security and repose in the absolute power of an individual; and sooner or later the chief of some prevailing faction, more able or more fortunate than his competitors, turns this disposition to the purposes of his own elevation, on the ruins of public liberty.
>
> ...[T]he common and continual mischiefs of the spirit of party are sufficient to make it the interest and duty of a wise people to discourage and restrain it. It serves always to distract the public councils and enfeeble the public administration. It agitates the community with ill-founded jealousies and false alarms, kindles the animosity of one part against another, foments occasionally riot and insurrection. It opens the door to foreign influence and corruption, which finds a facilitated access to the government itself through the channels of party passions. Thus the policy and the will of one country are subjected to the policy and will of another."

James Madison also considered factions and other social, economic, and political divisions) a vice. But he thought that banning factions would be a cure that was worse than the disease because factions were rooted in human nature. In *Federalist Number 51* he describes his ingenious solution to the problem of factions. He made factions, which were a problem, part of the solution. The system of checks and balances required so many different interests, parties, and factions that ***no one*** could dominate the political process and use government power against the others. So the political solution to the problem of factions was more of them. The way to guard against a united majority threatening the rights of the minority is to create a society with "so many separate descriptions of citizens as will render an unjust combination of a majority of the whole very improbable, if not impracticable." Madison specifically compared the problem of protecting political rights with the problem of protecting religious rights:

> "In a free government the security for civil rights must be the same as that for religious rights. It consists in the one case in the multiplicity of interests, and in the other in the multiplicity of sects. The degree of security in both cases will depend on the number of interests and sects; and this may be presumed to depend on the extent of country and number of people comprehended under the same government."

11.32 | *Parties and the Constitution*

As previously mentioned, the Constitution does not does not say anything about political parties. Parties developed after the Constitution was written. Shortly after the Constitution was written the Federalist and Anti-federalist Parties had emerged to compete for control of the federal government. The Federalist Party supported a strong national government, a strong executive in the national government, and commercial interest. The Federalist Party's geographic base was in New England. The Anti-federalist Party supported strong state governments, legislative government, and agrarian interests. Its geographic base was strongest in the South and West. Alexander Hamilton and Chief Justice John Marshall were strong Federalists. Thomas Jefferson and James Madison were Anti-federalists (a party which came to be called the Democratic-Republicans). The election of 1800 was a presidential contest won by Jefferson, and the landmark case of *Marbury v. Madison* (1803) began as a political contest over Federalist and Anti-federalist control of government. The Jeffersonians (or Democratic-Republicans) then became the dominant party, winning seven consecutive presidential elections from 1800 to 1824.

The fact that the Constitution does not say anything about one of the most important features of modern American government and politics is surprising. It also explains why it is not possible to read the Constitution to get a good understanding of how government and politics actually work. It is hard to understand American government and politics without understanding the role that political parties play.

11.4 | Party Systems

Modern governments typically have one-party systems, two-party systems, or multi-party systems. The U.S. has a two-party system.

11.41 | *One –Party Systems*

In **one-party systems**, only one political party is legally allowed to hold power. Although minor parties may sometimes be allowed in a one-party system, the minor party is legally required to accept the leadership of the dominant party. In a one-party system, the dominant party is usually closely identified with the government. The party organization and the government may not be identical, but sometimes party officials are also government officials so the separation between party and government may not be very great. In fact, in some one-party systems the party leadership position may be more important and powerful than positions within the government itself. Communist countries such as China and Cuba, and formerly the Soviet Union, are examples of one-party political systems. One-party systems are usually in countries without a strong democratic tradition.

Although there are few one-party systems, there is a variant called the **dominant party system** that is fairly common. A dominant party system is one where one party is so strong, so dominant, that even though other parties are legally allowed no other party has a real chance of competing in elections to win power. Dominant party systems can exist in countries with a strong democratic tradition in the country. The inability of any party other than the dominant party to compete in elections may be due to political, social and economic circumstances, public opinion, or the fact that the dominant party is entrenched in government and uses the government powers to preserve its privileged position. In countries with weak democratic traditions, the dominant party may remain in power by using political patronage (distribution of government jobs, contracts, or other government benefits to influence votes), voting fraud, or other manipulations of the electoral process. Where voting fraud is used to stay in power, the definition between a dominant and a one-party system is blurred. Examples of dominant party systems include the People's Action Party in Singapore and the African National Congress in South Africa. Mexico was a one-party dominant system with the Institutional Revolutionary Party until the 1990s. In the United States, the south was a one-party dominant region from the 1880s until the 1970s. It was controlled by the Democratic Party as a result of the Civil War: the Republican Party was the party of Lincoln.

11.42 | *Two –Party Systems*

A **two-party system** is one where there are two major political parties that are so strong that it is extremely difficult for a candidate from any party other than the two major parties to have a real chance to win elections. In a two-party system, a third-party is not likely to have much electoral success. The U.S. has a two-party system. The two major parties, the Republican and Democratic Parties, are the dominant parties. It is difficult for any third or minor party to win elections.

In the U.S., parties are mostly regulated by the laws of the individual states, which organize elections to both local and federal offices. No laws limit the *number* of political parties that may operate, so it is theoretically possible for the U.S. to develop a multi-party system. However, the country has had a two-party system since the early years of the republic. Third or minor parties do appear periodically. The fact that states have restrictive ballot access laws limits the development of third parties, but most are generally of only limited and temporary political significance.

In a two-party system, the typical ideological division is to have one party consisting of a right wing coalition and one party consisting of a left wing coalition. A coalition is a (usually temporary) combination or alliance of different interests that agree to unite to achieve shared goals. In the U.S., the Republican and Democratic parties are coalitions of interests. The Republican Party coalition consists of libertarians, economic conservatives, social conservatives, and national security and public order advocates. The Democratic Party coalition consists of racial and ethnic minorities, civil libertarians, organized labor, and the elderly. The components of the two major party coalitions can change over time. They are not necessarily permanent members of one party or the other. The two major parties are ideologically broad and inclusive because they need to position themselves to appeal to a broad range of the electorate.

One reason for a two-party system is the rules of the electoral game, specifically whether a country uses proportional representation (PR) **or single-member district plurality vote system** (SMDP). Proportional representation is a system where each party receives a share of seats in parliament that is proportional to the popular vote that the party receives. In a single-member district plurality vote system the person who gets the most votes in an election wins the seat. It is a winner-take-all election: The person who gets the most votes (i.e., the plurality) wins the election even if he or she did not win a majority of the votes. The United States uses this single-member district plurality system. For example, in a congressional election, the candidate who gets the most votes wins the senate seat or a house seat. The Electoral College also uses this winner-take-all system. The presidential candidate that receives the most popular votes in a state gets all of that state's Electoral College votes (with the exception of Nebraska and Maine which use a system of proportional representation). The winner-take-all system is not very democratic and it <u>disadvantages minor parties</u>.

Politics, like sport, is activity that is organized by rules. Election rules have a major impact on **how** the political game is played and **who** is likely to win. The winner-take-all system has the following effects on the way the political game is played:

- It tends to create and maintain a two-party system.
- It tends to make political parties more ideologically moderate because they must compete to win the most votes cast in an election or it will lose the election. Extremist or single-issue parties are unlikely to win elections.
- It increases political stability because tends the differences between the two major parties will not be as great as it would be in a political system where parties competed at the left or right extremes of the ideological spectrum. Maurice Duverger, the French sociologist described how the electoral rules had these effects on party politics.

Duverger's Law is a principle that a plurality election system tends to produce a stable, two party system.

An electoral system based on proportional representation creates conditions that allow new parties to develop and smaller parties to exist. The winner-take-all plurality system marginalizes new and smaller political parties by relegating to the status of loser n elections. A small third party cannot gain legislative power if it has to compete and win in a district with a large population in order to gain a seat. Similarly, a minor party with a broad base of support that is geographically spread throughout a state or spread across the nation is unlikely to attract enough votes to actually win an election even though it has substantial public support. For example, the Libertarian Party has supporters throughout the country, and may attract a substantial number of votes, but the votes are not enough to be the majority in a single district or a single state.

Duverger also believed the SMDP vote rule produces moderation and stability. Take, for example, the following scenario. Two moderate candidates (from two moderate parties) and one radical candidate are competing for a single office in an election where there are 100,000 moderate voters and 80,000 radical voters. If each moderate voter casts a vote for a moderate candidate and each radical voter casts a vote for the radical candidate, the radical candidate would win unless one of the moderate candidates gathered less than 20,000 votes. Consequently, moderate voters seeking to defeat the radical candidate/party would be more likely to vote for the candidate that is most likely to get more votes. The political impact of the SMDP vote rule is that the two moderate parties must either merge or one moderate party must fail as the voters gravitate to the two strong parties.

A third party usually can become successful only if it can exploit the mistakes of one of the existing major parties. For example, the political chaos immediately preceding the Civil War allowed the Republican Party to replace the Whig Party as the more progressive party. Loosely united on a platform of country-wide economic reform and federally funded industrialization, the decentralized Whig leadership failed to take a decisive stance on the slavery issue, effectively splitting the party along the Mason-Dixon Line. Southern rural planters, initially lured by the prospect of federal infrastructure and schools, quickly aligned themselves with the pro-slavery Democrats, while urban laborers and professionals in the northern states,

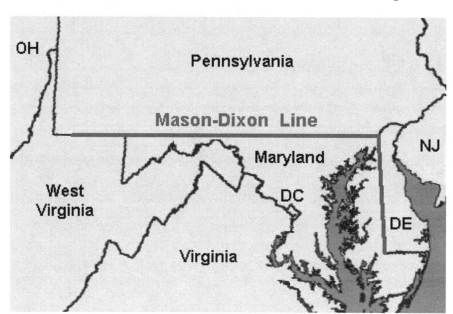

threatened by the sudden shift in political and economic power and losing faith in the failing Whig candidates, flocked to the increasingly vocal anti-slave Republican Party.

In countries that use proportional representation (PR), the electoral rules make it hard to maintain a two-party system. The number of votes that a party receives determines the number of seats it wins, so new parties can develop an immediate electoral niche. Duverger believed that the use of PR would make a two-party system less likely, but other electoral systems do not guarantee new parties access to the system.

11.43 | MULTI—PARTY SYSTEMS

Multi-party systems are systems with more than two parties. The Central Intelligence Agency's</u>World Factbook</u> provides a list of the political parties in the countries of the world. Canada and the United Kingdom have two strong parties and a third party that is electorally successful, may place second in elections, and presents a serious challenge to the other two parties, but has still never formally won enough votes to gain control of government. However, strong third parties can play a pivotal "king making" role if one of the two major parties needs its support in order get the most votes and gain control of government.

Finland is unusual in that it has an active three-party system in which all three parties routinely win elections and hold the top government office. It is very rare for a country to have more than three parties that are equally successful and have the same chance of gaining control of government (that is, "forming" the government or appointing the top government officials such as the prime minister). In political systems where there are numerous parties it is more common that no one party will be able to attract a majority of votes and therefore form a government, so a party will have to work with other parties to try to form a coalition government. Coalition governments, which include members of more than one party, are actually commonplace in countries such as the Republic of Ireland, Germany, and Israel.

In countries with proportional representation, the seats in a country's parliament or representative assembly would be allocated according to the popular votes the party received. The electoral districts are usually assigned several representatives. For example, assume the following distribution of the popular vote:

Party	Percent of the Popular Vote
Republican Party	36
Democratic Party	35
Libertarian Party	15
Green Party	14

The seats in the country's 100-member representative assembly would be allocated as follows:

Party	Seats in the Representative Assembly
Republican Party	36
Democratic Party	35
Libertarian Party	15
Green Party	14

Proportional representation makes it easier for smaller or minor parties to survive because they can win some seats in an election even though they never win enough votes to form a majority and control the government. Consequently, proportional representation tends to promote multi-party systems because elections do not result one winner (the candidate or party that get the most votes) and all the rest of the candidates are losers.

242|

11.5 | U.S. Political Parties

The U.S. has a two-party system. The two major parties are the Republican Party and the Democratic Party. There are, however, minor parties. Two well-established minor parties are the Libertarian Party and the Green Party. The following table includes the largest current largest parties. Each party was on the ballot in enough states to have had a mathematical chance to win a majority of Electoral College votes in the 2008 presidential election. Project Vote Smart provides a useful list of political parties in each of the 50 states.

12.51 | *Current Largest Parties*

Party Name	Date Founded	Founder(s)	Associated Ideologies	Current Party Chair
Democratic Party	1792/ 1820s	Thomas Jefferson/ Andrew Jackson	Liberalism, Progressivism, Social Liberalism	Tim Kaine
Republican Party	1854	Alvan E. Bovay	Conservatism, Neoconservatism, Economic Conservatism, Social Conservatism	Reince Priebus
Libertarian Party	1971	David Nolan	Libertarianism	Mark Hinkle
Green Party	1984	Howie Hawkins John Rensenbrink	Environmental Protection, Liberalism	Theresa El-Amin, Mike Feinstein, Farheen Hakeem, Julie Jacobson, Jason

| | | | | Nabewaniec, David Strand, and Craig Thorsen |

Act on It!#

Contact a political party in your state, or another state, and ask a party official a question about the party's position on an issue or about an issue that interests you.

11.6 | POLITICAL PARTY ERAS

Political scientists have identified distinctive party eras in the U.S. party system. A party era is a time period when the two major parties took different sides on the most important issues that were facing the nation during that time period. The following describes six party eras.

11.61 | *The First Era: the 1790s until around 1824*

The election of 1796 was the first election where candidates ran as members of a political party. The Federalist Party and the Anti-Federalist Party (or Democratic Republicans) differed on the question of the power of the national government. The Federalists generally supported a strong national government and the Jeffersonian Democratic Republicans supported state government. The election of 1800 produced a number of firsts. It produced "America's first presidential campaign."[2] It marked the beginning of the end for the Federalist Party. John Adams and the Federalist Party supported England, a strong national government, industrial development, and aristocracy. Thomas Jefferson and the Republican Party supported France, decentralized state governments, and agrarian society, and egalitarian democracy. Jefferson won the election of 1800 which was the first transition of power from one party to the opposition party and the beginning of a party system. By 1820, the Federalist Party had gone out of existence and James Madison (of the Democratic Republicans) was elected president in what came to be called the "Era of Good Feelings" because it was a period of one party-dominance (therefore there was little party competition).

11.62 | *The Second Era: from 1824 until the Civil War*

During the second era, Andrew Jackson and the Democrats were the dominant party. The Democrats advocated a populist political system that is often called **Jacksonian Democracy**. One feature of Jacksonian Democracy is governing based on political patronage. The familiar political slogan, "**To the victor go the spoils (of office),**" describes how the candidate that won an election was entitled to give government jobs (and other benefits) to the people (including the members of his or her political party) that supported the campaign. This was the era that produced political parties as mass membership organizations rather than political parties as legislative caucuses. The most important national political issues during this era were economic matters, such as tariffs to protect manufacturing and the creation of a national bank to direct economic development, slavery, and the territorial expansion of the republic. In the years 1854 to 1856, the Republican Party emerged to replace the Whig party as the second of the major political parties of the era.

11.63 | *The Third Era: from the Civil War to 1896*

During this party era, the Republican Party and the Democratic Party were divided on two major issues: Reconstruction of the South and the Industrial Revolution. The Republican Party was a northern party that supported manufacturing, railroads, oil, and banking as part of the broader support for the Industrial Revolution. The Republican Party supported the national government's <u>Reconstruction</u> of the South after the Civil War. The Democratic Party was based in the South. It opposed the use of federal power, including civil rights laws, to regulate the way that Southern states treated newly freed slaves. In terms of economic policy, the Democratic Party also supported rural or agrarian interests rather than urban and industrial interests.

11.64 | *Fourth Era: from 1896 to 1932*

The Republican Party was the dominant party during the fourth party era. It was strongly identified with big business, the northeast, and the west. The Democratic Party was largely limited to its base in the southern states of the old Confederacy. The early years of this era, the period from the 1890s until World War I, were the Progressive Era. The Progressive Era was a major reform era in American politics and government. It produced the civil service system, primary elections, nonpartisan elections, and direct democracy mechanisms such as referendum, initiative, and recall. The civil service system was an effort to replace the spoils system of political patronage with a merit selection system of government officials. Primary and nonpartisan elections weakened political parties by giving voters more control over the selection of candidates for office any by having candidates run without party labels. These reforms were intended to get politics out of the "smoke-filled back rooms" where party bosses chose candidates for office. Referendum and initiative were two electoral reforms that expanded direct democracy by allowing the public to vote on laws proposed by state legislatures or to initiate their own laws without having to rely on state legislatures. Finally, rRecall was a way for voters to vote government officials out of office.

11.65 | *The Fifth Era: from the 1930s until the latter 1960s*

During this era the Democratic Party was the dominant party. The era includes the major expansions of the federal social welfare state during the New Deal programs advocated by President Franklin D. Roosevelt and the Great Society programs advocated by President Lyndon Johnson. During this era, the Democratic Party became identified with the common person, minorities, and labor, while the Republican Party became identified with business and the wealthy. The New Deal issues included the national government's response to the Depression and foreign policy matters related to World War II and the Cold War. The Great Society issues focused on the expansion of the social welfare state and civil rights and liberties. Egalitarianism is one of the values associated with New Deal/Great Society liberalism.

11.66 | *The Sixth Era: from the latter 1960s—*

This era began as a conservative backlash or reaction against the liberalism of the New Deal and Great Society. Republicans opposed liberal Democratic policies that conservatives blamed for an increase in crime, social disorder (race riots, prison riots, and antiwar demonstrations), the loss of the War in Vietnam, loosening of sexual mores, school busing, affirmative action, the separation of church and state, inflation, and going soft on communism. Both of the major parties are coalitions of interests or viewpoints. During this era, the Republican Party was like a four-legged stool supported by following four legs:

- Anti-crime: Advocates of getting tough on crime.
- Anti-communism: Cold Warriors.
- Economic conservatives: advocates of the free market.
- Values voters: the conservatives who support traditional and religious values.

The values voters in the Republican Party focus on social issues. The values and lifestyles conflict between liberals and conservatives was called the culture wars. An important movement in the culture war was Patrick Buchanan's Address at the 1992 Republican Party Convention. Buchanan, a traditional conservative who lost the Republican Party nomination for president, gave a rousing speech that inspired the social conservative base of the Republic Party with the following declaration and call to action: "There is a religious war going on in this country. It is a cultural war as critical to the kind of nation we shall be as the cold war itself—for this war is for the soul of America."

On economic issues, Republicans during this sixth era took two main positions: de-regulation of business and opposition to taxes. On national security matters Republicans were staunch anti-communists who supported getting tough on the Soviet Union. These issues became the basis for the Republican Party's rise in national politics beginning with President Nixon's election in 1968. The Republican Party won the presidency five of the six presidential elections between 1968 and 1988. And until the mid-term elections in 2006, Republican President George W. Bush's party controlled both houses of Congress. Democratic President Obama's victory in the 2008 presidential election increased speculation that the country was entering a post-party era where party politics was less important than issue politics, but the intense partisan divisions that characterized governance since then have ended such speculation about post-party politics.

Nevertheless, the U.S. party system is dynamic, not static. It is constantly changing. The advanced age of the current party era has raised two related questions. Is the Sixth Party Era about to end? Does the increase in the percentage of the public that consider themselves independents indicate the emergence of a post-party era? The political forces that shape the two major political parties are still at work:

"The modern Democratic Party was shaped by the populism of the 1890s, the antibusiness reformism of the 1930s and the civil rights crusade of the 1960s. The Republican Party was formed by abolitionism in the 1850s, anti-tax revolts in the 1970s and 1980s and the evangelical conservatism of the 1990s and 2000s."[3] The constituent elements of the two major party coalitions change over time, but the parties typically consist of components or interests that are associated with the different sides of public policy debates or issues. As these coalitions change, they pressure the parties to change to accommodate their interests. This could result in a new dominant party era. However, the increase in the number of Americans who consider themselves Independents, and the ability of candidates to run for office using their own resources rather than the resources traditionally provided by a political party, has renewed speculation about the decline of political parties or even an end to the era of political parties. Is the political party over?

Are political parties anachronistic?

"Are Independents Just Partisans in Disguise"
http://www.npr.org/blogs/itsallpolitics/2012/08/22/159588275/are-independents-just-partisans-in-disguise

11.67 | PARTIES, CAUSES, AND MOVEMENTS

One of the keys to understanding the continued life of the U.S. two-party system is the relationship between political parties and movements (or causes). A political movement or cause is an organized campaign on behalf of an issue or policy. The American political experience includes many movements: anti-slavery; prohibition; women's rights; civil rights; anti-war; pro-life; the environment, etc. The Republican and Democratic Parties have causes or movements as part of their political bases. The Tea Party movement is an example of a recent movement within the Republican Party that advocated, among other things, a return to the original understanding of the Constitution.

The Democratic Party has incorporated the business reform movement of the 1930s and the civil rights movement of the 1950s and 1960s into its base. Government regulation of business and government advocacy of civil rights, particularly of minorities, are causes or movements that are associated with the Democratic Party. The Republican Party has incorporated the anti-communist movement of the 1950s and the religious revivalism of the 1980s and 1990s into its base. Political movements to strengthen national defense and promote Christian activism are causes that are generally at home in the Republican Party. Political movements often change the political parties as their ideas are incorporated into the party.

In fact, the movement-party dynamic explains **the continuity and change** in the American political system. The continuity is the fact that the two-party system of Republicans and Democrats has remained the same for almost 200 years. The change is the fact that what it means to be a Republican or Democrat changes over time as movements arise to bring new issues to the political system. The dynamic of the relationship between a political party and the causes and political movements that periodically arise from within elements of a political party help explain how political change occurs within a party system that has not changed very much in 200 years in the sense that we have had the same two major parties since the early decades of the 19th Century.

11.7 | Party Affiliation and Political AttituDES

Political party is related to political attitudes. Therefore, the origins of political partisanship (the identification with a political party) have been studied extensively. There is broad agreement that a person's identification with a political party is caused by upbringing, ethnicity, race, geographic location, and socioeconomic status. A person also identifies with a party because of ideology or positions on important issues. In order to better understand all of these factors, a Gallup Panel survey asked Americans who identified themselves as Republicans or Democrats (or said they leaned to either party if they initially said they were independents) to explain in their own words just what it is about their chosen party that appeals to them most. The following Gallup Polling data describe the appeal of the two major parties.[4]

Republicans justify their allegiance to the GOP most often with reference to the party's conservatism and conservative positions on moral issues. Beyond that, Republicans mention the party's conservative economic positions, usually defined as support for smaller government. Finally, a much smaller number of Republicans mentioned a variety of other things that appealed to them.

Republicans		Democrats	
	Percent		Percent
Conservative/More conservative	26	Social/Moral issue positions	18
Conservative family/moral values	15	Overall platform/ philosophy/ policies	14
Overall platform/ philosophy/ policies	12	Liberal/More liberal	11

Conservative on fiscal/economic issues	10	Help the poor	7
Favors smaller government	8	Disagree with the Republicans	5
Favors individual responsibility/self-reliance	5	Always been a Democrat	5
Always been a Republican	4	Antiwar	3
For the people/working people	3	Healthcare reform	2
Low taxes	3	Pro-environment/conservation	1
Favor strong military	3		
Pro-life on abortion	2		
More honest than the Democrats	2		
Disagree with the Democrats	2		
Other	3	Other	7
Nothing in particular (vol.)	5	Nothing in particular (vol.)	6
No opinion	6	No opinion	5

Asked of Republicans and independents who lean to the Republican Party. What is it about the Democratic Party that appeals to you most? Percentages add to more than 100% due to multiple responses.

Asked of Democrats and independents who lean to the Democratic Party) What is it about the Democratic Party that appeals to you most? Percentages add to more than 100% due to multiple responses.

The Democrats' justifications are somewhat different. Compared to the percentage of Republicans who mention conservatism as their rationale for identifying with the Republican Party, the percentage of Democrats who mention liberalism is relatively small. Democrats are most likely to mention that the Democratic Party appeals to them because it is for the working class, the middle class, or the *common man*. Democrats also tend to mention issues or party stances in general, and to a lesser extent mention specific issues such as the party's antiwar, pro-healthcare, and pro-environment stances.

11.8 | Summary

One example of how the U.S. political system did not develop the way the Founders intended is the development of political parties. The Founders worried about political parties as divisive forces. They saw parties literally dividing Americans into "parts" or parties. The two-party system has not changed for almost 200 years, but the two major parties have changed a great deal over time as political movements and third or minor parties arise to address new issues facing the nation. American political culture values individualism. Individualism produces skepticism about political parties, but parties are also considered important linkage institutions that organize public participation in politics. So despite a political culture that values individualism, despite skepticism about political organizations and partisanship, despite the rise of interest groups as alternative sources for campaign support, and despite the fact that around one-third of voters now consider themselves Independents, parties continue to play a central role in the modern system of government and politics. So despite the periodic claims that parties are dying, that American politics is entering a post-partisan era, and books entitled *The Party is Over*,[5] the party is not over. The reports that parties are dead bring to mind Mark Twain's famous quip about a newspaper report that he had died: "The reports of my death are greatly exaggerated."

KEY TERMS
political party
nomination process
one-party systems
two-party system
Duverger's Law
Multi-party systems

Study Questions

What are the roles and functions of political parties in America? Do parties play a worthwhile role in the American political system?

1) How are political parties organized in America? What effect does this have on the political system?
2) Trace the evolution of the political parties from the founding through the New Deal. How and why did the parties change during this period?
3) What role do political parties play in elections?
4) What are the major eras in the history of American political parties?
5) Compare and contrast the platforms, strengths, weaknesses, and strategies of the Republican and Democratic Parties.

11.9 | ADDITIONAL RESOURCES

Gov-Spot offers a list of many Political Parties and platforms for review. http://www.govspot.com/categories/politicalparties.htm

The University of Michigan Library Web site provides links to congressional party leadership and platforms. www.lib.umich.edu/govdocs/polisci.html

In the Library:

Bibby, John F. and L. Sandy Maisel. 2002. *Two Parties—Or More?* Westview Press.

Green, Donald, et al. 2002. *Partisan Hearts and Minds: Political Parties and the Social Identities of Voters*. Yale University Press.

Greenberg, Stanley B. 2004. *The Two Americas: Our Current Political Deadlock and How to Break It*. St. Martin's Press.

Sanbonmatsu, Kira. 2004. *Democrats, Republicans, and the Politics of Women's Place*.

University of Michigan Press.

[1] Jens Krause and Graeme D. Ruxton. 2002. *Living in Groups*. London: Oxford University Press.

[2] Edward J. Larson. 2007. *A Magnificent Catastrophe: The Tumultuous Election*

[3] Sam Tanenhaus, "Harnessing a Cause Without Yielding to It." *The New York Times* (November 9, 2008), p.3WK.

[4] http://www.gallup.com/poll/102691/Whats-Behind-Republican-Democratic-Party-ID.aspx

[5] Mike Lofgren. 2012. The Party Is Over. New York: Viking.

CHAPTER 12: INTEREST GROUPS

Lobbyist Bob Livingston (L) and former Speaker of the House Newt Gingrich (R)

12.0 | Interest Groups

MADNESS IS RARE IN INDIVIDUALS - BUT IN GROUPS, POLITICAL PARTIES, NATIONS, AND ERAS IT'S THE RULE.

- FRIEDRICH NIETZSCHE

"TEN PEOPLE WHO SPEAK MAKE MORE NOISE THAN TEN THOUSAND WHO ARE SILENT."

NAPOLEON BONAPARTE

Interest groups play an extremely important role in American politics and government. In fact, it is impossible to understand American government or politics without a basic understanding of interest groups. This chapter describes interest groups and their political activities. It also explains their role in politics, government, and the public policy process. The explanation of the increased role that interest groups play in modern politics and government includes assessments of whether their role is basically good or bad, beneficial or harmful, as well as whether interest groups are too powerful. The main question about interest groups is whether they advance their special interests to the detriment of the general, public, or national interest. This question is similar to questions about the role of political parties, and it produces similar skepticism about powerful special interests. In politics as in other areas of life, organization increases effectiveness. Like parties, interest groups are mediating institutions that organize public participation in politics, function as part of the system of checks and balances, and help civil society control government power. This chapter will help you decide whether group behavior is madness or whether groups give voice to individuals.

12.1 | What is an Interest Group?

An **interest group** is a collection of individuals or organizations that share a common interest and advocate or work for public policies on behalf of the members' shared interests. For these reasons, interest groups are also called advocacy groups, lobbying groups, pressure groups, or even special interest groups. What is the difference between an interest group and a political party? It is not size—although in the U.S. interest groups are smaller than the Republican and Democratic Parties. An interest group can have more or fewer members than a political party. A large organization such as The Association for the advancement of Retired People (AARP) has more members than some minor political parties.

The major difference between an interest group and a political party is that parties try to achieve their policy goals by running candidates for office in order to control government but interest groups usually do not. Both political parties and interest groups take positions on important public policy issues and work on behalf of their members' goals. But interest groups advocate for policies without actually running candidates in elections in order to try to take control of government. Interest groups typically lobby the government to adopt their positions. Lobbyists are the individuals who represent and advocate on behalf of an interest group. Political scientists agree that interest groups play an important role in American politics, but they do not agree on what exactly defines an interest group. One definition of an interest group focuses on membership: a group must have a significant number of members in order to be officially recognized as an interest group. Another definition focuses on efforts to influence public policy, not membership itself, so that an interest group is defined as any non-government group that tries to affect policy. The term interest group is sometimes used generically to refer to any segment of a society that shares similar political opinions on an issue or group of issues (e.g. seniors, the poor, consumers, etc.) even if they are not necessarily part of an organized group.

12.12 | *Types of Interest Groups*

There are many types of interest groups. Interest groups represent or advocate on behalf of almost every imaginable organized interest from A (abortion; airlines; agriculture) to Z (zoning and zoos). One major distinction between types of interest groups is the difference between public and private interest groups. A **public interest group** is one that advocates for an issue that benefits society as a whole. A **private interest group** is one that advocates for an issue that primarily benefits the members of the group. There are some overlaps between these two types because it is not always possible to separate public and private interests.

Common Cause, founded by Ralph Nader, was one of the first public interest groups. It promotes responsible government generally but it has a primarily liberal orientation. Three prominent public interest groups in the field of public health are the American Heart Association, the American Cancer Society, and the American Lung Association. A related type of public interest group is The Public Interest Research Group (PIRG), but it is a primarily liberal advocate on issues such as the environment, public transportation, and education. Groups whose primary purpose is advancing the economic interests of their members are private interest groups. The Indoor Tanning Association, for example, is a trade group that advocates for a specific industry. It lobbies to protect an industry from increased government regulation during a time when there is increased concern about skin cancer. During the protracted health care reform debates of 2009 that eventually resulted in the passage of the Patient Protection and Affordable Care Act (Obamacare), Congress considered proposals to pay for the expanded health with a "Botax," a tax on elective, cosmetic surgery. Doctors successfully lobbied against the Botax in the Senate health care reform bill, so a "tantax" was substituted—a tax on indoor sun tanning services. The Indoor Tanning Association opposed the proposed Tantax. In fact, the tanning industry has a broader lobbying and public information campaign to ease public concerns about the adverse health effects of tanning and thereby avoid further taxation and regulation. This campaign is a good example of a defensive strategy, one that is intended to prevent public policy actions that are adverse to a group's interests. The U.S. political system has many veto points where legislation can be stopped.

The number of organized interest groups began increasing in the post-World War II era, with group formation surging since the 1960s. The increased size of the federal government also meant that many of the interest groups went national in the sense that they focused their activities on Washington, DC.[1]

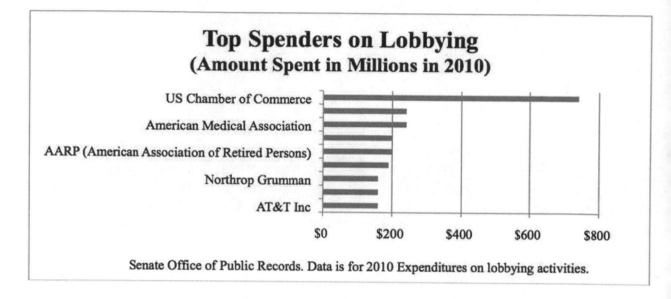

The following illustrate the types of interest groups and interest group activities:

- Business Groups. A corporation such as an aerospace manufacturer or a health care company that lobbies to win a government contract to buy airplanes or provide health care services. Corporations often hire a lobbying firm to advocate for their interests.

- Trade or Professional Associations. An employers' organization or trade or professional association that represents the interests of an entire industry (e.g., manufacturers or health care or insurance or legal services). An interest group that represents an entire sector of the economy might lobby for favorable tax policies or favorable regulatory policies.

- Labor Groups. Labor unions that represent organized labor and other employee rights groups advocate for public policies that benefit workers, such as minimum wage laws or workplace safety laws or health care. These groups can represent private sector workers or public sector workers.

- Demographic Groups. These are organizations that represent specific demographic segments of society such as senior citizens; racial, ethnic, or religious minorities; veterans; persons with disabilities; and immigrants. These groups typically lobby for retirement benefits, laws protecting against discrimination, pension benefits, handicap accessibility, religious freedoms and public support, and favorable immigration policies.

- Single Issue Groups. These are groups that were created specifically to advocate for a single-issue. Single-issue groups include those that advocate for women's rights, the environment, or advocate for or against abortion or gay rights.

- Ideological Groups. Ideological groups include organizations that advocate for conservatism, liberalism, or libertarianism, for example. Ideological groups also include think tanks, the research and policy organizations that often have a particular ideological perspective or a particular economic theory that informs their policy analysis and advocacy.

- Religious Organizations. Church Groups or organizations active on religious issues lobbying government for exemptions from zoning laws, tax laws, or employment rules and regulations.

12.13 | *Economic Interest Groups*

The greatest number of interest groups is economic interest groups including business, trade and other associations, labor, and professional associations.

- **Business**. Businesses such as General Motors, Microsoft, and Boeing lobby to influence public policy regarding employment, workplace safety, the environment, taxes, and trade policy, among others. In this era of cooperative federalism, where both the national and state governments regulate business and economic activity, corporations typically have a Public Affairs or Public Relations or Government Affairs division to conduct public relations campaigns, to make campaign contributions on behalf of candidates they support, and to lobby on behalf of the business' interests.

- **Trade Associations**. Businesses with a similar interest sometimes join trade associations to advocate on behalf of the entire industry or sector of the economy. The U.S. Chamber of Commerce, the National Federation of Independent Businesses, and the National Association of Manufacturers are trade associations. They are interest groups that represent business generally, or small business specifically, or the manufacturing sector specifically. The number of such business groups and their local, state, and national influence make them one of the more important political forces in U.S. politics. Business groups are generally members of the Republican Party coalition.

- **Labor**. Interest groups representing workers include labor unions that represent individuals who work on farms or the agricultural sector, manufacturing such as steel and auto manufacturing), and individuals who work in the service sector. Union membership in the U.S. is low, particularly compared with membership in other industrial democracies. Two of the oldest and most powerful labor unions are the AFL-CIO (The American Federation of Labor and Congress of Industrial Organizations) and the Teamsters. The influence of organized labor has greatly diminished over the past decades. One reason for their decline is the American economy has moved away from industry and manufacturing, which were the sectors of the economy where unions were strongest, toward an information and service sector economy, where unions were not organized. Industrial and manufacturing unions represented blue-collar workers. White-collar workers have not been heavily unionized. As the economy shifted toward the service sector, a labor union was created specifically to represent these "pink collar" workers. The Service Employees International Union (SEICU), which calls itself the largest and fastest growing union, organizes on behalf of health care and hospitality industry workers. Labor Unions are traditionally members of the Democratic Party coalition.

- **Professional Associations**. Professionals have organized themselves into some of the most influential interest groups in the U.S. These include such well known professional associations as the American Medical Association; the American Bar Association; the National Education Association; the National Association of Realtors; and engineering associations—the National Society of Professional Engineers and the American Engineering Association. The AEA's mission is to make the AEA "an AMA for engineers." The above "Top Spenders on Lobbying" graph shows that professional associations are the top spenders on lobbying. Each state controls occupational licensure. That is, a state licenses professionals to operate in the state. Therefore there are 50 state medical associations and state bar associations. Medicine, law, and engineering are among the most prestigious professions. Their professional associations can exert considerable influence over government regulation of their professions, including the licensing standards that determine access to the profession. One power question about these professional associations is whether they use their influence to protect the public/consumers (from untrained or unscrupulous doctors, engineers, lawyers, or financial advisors) or whether they use their political power to protect their members.

Act on It!
Civic engagement includes interacting with organizations that are such an important part of civil society. Contact an interest group to ask about an issue that you are interested in or an issue that the group supports

12.14 | *Ideological Groups*

Ideological groups are organized to advocate for a particular set of political beliefs. Ideological groups are harder to identify than economic groups. The American

Conservative Union calls itself the oldest membership-based conservative organization in the U.S. One of its most widely known actions is the rating of elected government officials. The American Civil Liberties Union might be considered an ideological organization but its advocacy of civil liberties is sometimes liberal and sometimes conservative. The Americans for Democratic Action calls itself the oldest independent liberal organization in the U.S. There is a large number of radical or fringe organizations that are active in American politics, if sometimes only on the Internet. One such radical right organization is the Guardians of the Free Republic.

12.15 | *Think Tanks*

Think tanks are organizations that are primarily interested in researching and promoting ideas. It is appropriate to think of think tanks as "think-and-do" tanks because they are interested in thought that produces action. Think tanks research and advocate public policies that are based on the ideas they support. The American Action Network is a conservative think tank. A former director of the Congressional Budget Office described its purpose, and the purpose of other think tanks: "Having good ideas is not enough. You actually have to sell them to the Congress, the president, the citizens." [2] Two prominent think tanks are the Brookings Institution, a think tank with a generally liberal orientation, and the American Enterprise Institute, a think tank with a generally conservative orientation.

12.2 | Incentives to join

Why do political groups exist? Why do people join groups? The Political Scientist James Q. Wilson identified three types of incentives to join a group: solidarity, material, and purposive.[3] Some interest groups provide more than one of these incentives for membership, but the different categories are useful for understanding the different kinds of interest groups.

12.21 | *Solidarity*

Solidarity incentives for a person to join a group are essentially social reasons. Individuals decide to join a group because they want to associate with others with similar interests, backgrounds, or points of view. The old saying, Birds of a Feather Flock Together, describes solidarity incentives. Church groups, civic groups such as the Elks Club, and groups whose members have shared ethnic backgrounds, are examples of groups whose members are motivated primarily by associational or shared interests.

12.22 | *Material*

Material incentives are essentially economic motives for membership. Membership is motivated by a tangible benefit. An individual who joins the Association for the Advancement of Retired People (AARP) to get motel, restaurant, or car rental discounts is motivated by a material incentive to join. A company that becomes a member of a trade association such as the Chamber of Commerce or the National Association of

Manufacturers in order to benefit from the trade association's lobbying is motivated by a material incentive. A study of interest groups in the United States and other countries found that a great majority (almost three-quarters) represents professional or occupational interests. The main motivation of such professional or occupational groups is economic or material interests.[4]

12.23 | *Purposive*

Purpose incentives are those that appeal to an individual's commitment to advancing the groups' social or political aims. Purposive groups attract members who join for reasons other than merely associating with others who share their interests, or solely because they want to obtain material benefits. Some of these purposive or issue advocacy groups are ideological. Ideological purposive groups advocate on behalf of ideas (e.g., conservative; liberal; libertarian) or causes (right-to-life; civil liberties; property rights; the environment; religious freedom). Purposive groups include the American Conservative Union, the American Civil Liberties Union, the Sierra

Club, and the two major interest groups who take different sides in the debate over abortion policy: The National Right to Life and the National Abortion Rights Action League (NARAL).

12.3 | What Do Interest Groups Do?

Much of what interest groups do falls under the large umbrella of lobbying. Lobbying is a broad term for an interest group's activities that seek to persuade political leaders and government officials to support a particular position. Lobbying occurs at all levels of government (local, state, national, and international), in all three branches of government (although technically groups do not lobby the courts), and in non-governmental settings. Interest group lobbying includes testifying at government hearings, contacting legislators, providing information to politicians, filing lawsuits or funding lawsuits or submit amicus curiae briefs with a court, and public campaigns to change public opinion or to rally members of the group to contact public officials.

12.31 | *Lobby Congress*

Congress, committee members, and individual members of congress are frequent targets of lobbying campaigns. Interest groups might lobby in the congressional setting by providing testimony at a committee or subcommittee meeting, contributing to an individual congressional representative's

campaign fund, or organizing a letter or phone-call campaign by members of the interest to convince a particular representative of the public support for a policy.

12.32 | *Lobby the Executive Branch*

Although the executive branch does not actually make the laws, interest groups target the executive branch in order to influence the formation of public policy or its implementation. Lobbying the executive branch may include contacting the president, members of the president's staff (including the chief of staff or policy advisors), cabinet level officials, or other high-ranking members of the executive departments (the political appointees that make policies). Interest groups also lobby the independent regulatory commissions. These agencies have rule making authority. The rule making process includes taking public comments about proposed regulations. Interest groups participate in this process in order to influence regulatory policy that affects them. Officials in the executive departments also play an important role in the development of the federal budget, so interest groups lobby them to support programs that the groups supports and oppose programs that the group is opposed to. Agricultural interests, food processors, and consumer groups lobby members of the Department of Agriculture, which plays an important role in congressional and administration food policy. Health care providers, insurance companies, and patient rights groups lobby officials in the Department of Health and Human Services, which play an important role in formulating and implementing health care policy (including Medicare and Medicaid). The telecommunications industry, consumer rights groups, and citizen groups interested in the content of broadcast programming lobby the Federal Communications Commission. The FCC is an independent regulatory agency that licenses broadcast companies and has some authority to regulate the content of broadcast programming and other aspect of the telecommunication industry.

Interest Groups are an important part of the policymaking process. They are one of the three major members of what political scientists call Issue Networks. The term Issue Network describes the patterns of interactions among three sets of participants in the policy making process: a congressional committee; an Executive Department; and interest groups. Each area of public policy has an Issue Network. Interest groups link the government—that is congressional committees and the executive departments or independent regulatory commissions—and the civil society (the interest groups). The following figure describes the Issue Network for defense policy. The arrows describe the mutual benefits the participants provide. Interest groups provide information to the legislative committees and executive departments that make public policy in their area of interest. Congressional committees provide budgets for programs that an interest groups supports. And executive departments support programs that interest groups support.

Figure 12.3   Issue Networks: Defense Policy

Congressional Committees
Senate Armed Services Committee
House Armed Services Committee

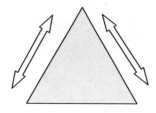

Executive Departments
The Department of Defense

Interest Groups
(Aerospace and Defense Industries)

12.33 | *"Lobbying" the Courts*

In an effort to maintain some separation of law and politics, it is considered inappropriate for interest groups to lobby the courts the way they lobby congress and the executive branch. Interest group efforts to influence the courts take two forms. The first is political litigation. Political litigation is using a lawsuit primarily to change public policy. An interest group may file a lawsuit on behalf of its members. The Sierra Club may file a lawsuit challenging a policy allowing development of a natural environment. The National Federation of Independent Businesses challenged the constitutionality of the Patient Protection and Affordable Care Act (Obamacare). A second way that an interest group can lobby the courts is by filing an *amicus curiae* brief (that is, a friend of the court brief) that advocates for one of the two sides in a case that is before the court. The major cases that the Supreme Court agrees to decide typically have a large number of amicus curiae briefs submitted for both sides. A third way that interest groups attempt to influence the courts is by sponsoring a lawsuit, providing legal resources for the actual parties. Taking a case all the way to the Supreme Court requires a great deal of time and money.

School Segregation Banned, the *Topeka State Journal*. *Courtesy Kansas State Historical Society*

STATE THE TOPEKA **JOURNAL** Home Edition
By Stauffer Publications, Inc.
Topeka, Kansas, Monday, May 17, 1954—Twenty-four Pages FIVE CENTS

SCHOOL SEGREGATION BANNED

Supreme Court Refutes Doctrine of Separate but Equal Education

High Tribunal Fails to Specify When Practice of Dual Schools Must Be Dropped by States

"Today, education is perhaps the most important function of state and local government. Compulsory school attendance laws and the great expenditures for education both demonstrate our recognition of the importance of education to our democratic society... WE CONCLUDE THAT IN THE FIELD OF PUBLIC EDUCATION THE DOCTRINE OF 'SEPARATE BUT EQUAL' HAS NO PLACE. SEPARATE EDUCATIONAL FACILITIES ARE INHERENTLY UNEQUAL."
Oliver L. Brown, et al. vs Board of Education of Topeka, Kansas, United States Supreme Court, May 17, 1954.

A good example of political litigation is the efforts of The National Association for the Advancement of Colored People (NAACP) to support lawsuits challenging the constitutionality of segregated public schools. The landmark Supreme Court ruling in Brown v. Board of Education was the result of an organized campaign to use the courts to change public policy. In fact, the various civil rights revolutions of the period 1940s-1960s relied heavily on political litigation. In the 1950s and 1960s, liberal public interest groups relied heavily on political litigation to change public policies related to prisoner rights, racial equality, freedom of expression, the right to privacy, and environmentalism. In the 1970s conservative public interest groups used political litigation to change public policies on abortion, property rights, freedom of religion, affirmative action, business and employer rights, and gun rights.

Today there are many conservative organizations that have adopted a legal strategy to achieve conservative policy goals:

- The Pacific Legal Foundation was created to challenge environmental regulations.
- The U.S. Chamber of Commerce established a National Chamber Litigation Center and the Institute for Legal Reform to advocate pro-business legal policies.
- The Christian Legal Society advocates against the separation of church and state.
- The Cato Institute advocates libertarian positions.
- The National Rifle Association advocates for gun rights.

The tort reform movement is an example of business groups going to court to change legal policies relating to torts—wrongful injuries such as medical malpractice and product liability.

"Judicial Hellholes," "Jackpot Justice," "Looney Lawsuits," and "Wacky Warning Labels Contest" are terms that have entered everyday vocabulary about civil law in modern American society. The American Tort Reform Association has even trademarked the epithet "Judicial Hellholes." The National Federation of Independent Businesses has created a Small Business Legal Center specifically to advocate in the courts: "The Legal Center is the advocate for small business in the courts. We do what

JUDICIAL HELLHOLES 2009 2010
ATR FOUNDATION

federal and state NFIB lobbyists do, but instead of lobbying legislatures we lobby judges through briefs and oral arguments in court. We tell judges how the decision they make in a given case will impact small businesses nationwide."[5]

The American Tort Reform Association's membership and funding come from the American Medical Association and the Council of Engineering Companies. The National Association of Manufacturers uses political litigation to change policies that it considers anti-business, such as product liability laws and campaign finance laws that limit campaign contributions. The U.S. Chamber of Commerce has established an Institute for Legal Reform which specializes in political litigation to advance pro-business legal policies. Whose side are the lawyers on? In criminal justice, the defense bar represents suspects who have been accused of a crime. In civil justice issues such as product liability and medical malpractice, the plaintiff bar generally represents consumers, employees, or patients. Lawyers for Civil Justice is a national organization of corporate counsel and defense lawyers advocating for tort reform. The Florida Chamber of Commerce created the Florida Justice Reform Institute to reform what it calls a wasteful civil justice system. Other business organizations advocating tort reform include America's Health Insurance Plans, American Hospital Association, Pharmaceutical Research and Manufacturing Association, and the National Federation of Independent Businesses.

12.34 | *Grassroots Lobbying and Protests*

Interest groups also engage in **grassroots lobbying**. Grassroots lobbying is a term for efforts to mobilize local support for an issue position the group has taken. Grassroots lobbying is usually contrasted with Washington lobbying. Washington lobbying is sometimes criticized as "inside-the-beltway" activity that focuses on the Washington political establishment to the neglect of the average American or Mainstreet America. Grass roots lobbying has an "outside-the-beltway" focus and therefore a reputation for being a more genuine reflection of public opinion that Washington lobbying campaigns. Grassroots lobbying consists of interest groups contacting citizens and urging them to contact government officials rather than having the interest group directly contact government officials.

The political appeal of appearing to be a grass-roots organization whose members come from the community has created the phenomenon called "astroturf" lobbying. Astroturf lobbying is where an interest group without a large membership portrays itself as having roots in the community. The membership is artificial, however, which is why the grassroots are called astroturf. In today's media age and celebrity culture, grassroots campaigns can use influential media personalities (such as Rachel Maddow or Glen Beck) to encourage their listeners or viewers to take action, thereby linking the national and electronic communities to the local or grassroots. The more extreme version of grassroots lobbying is organizing or supporting protests and demonstrations. Many national organizations have a day where they bring members to Washington, D.C. to call attention to their issues, whether advocating to put an issue on the policy agenda or to protest a change in public policy.

12.35 | *Lobbyists*

Interest groups frequently pay professional lobbyists to represent the organization to the public and the government. Professional lobbyists can either work directly for the interest group or they can be employees of public relations or law firms who are hired by the group for a specific campaign. One of the most seriously funny depictions of interest group efforts to influence public opinion and public policy, and the image of lobbyists is the Hollywood film *Thank You For Smoking*. The fictional film describes the efforts of

the tobacco lobby, the alcohol lobby, and gun lobby, which IN THE FILM are called the "MOD Squad: Merchants of Death." The *Youtube* video clip is available at: http://www.youtube.com/watch?v=iBELC_vxqhI

12.36 | *Campaigns and Elections*

Interest groups also participate in campaigns and elections. In elections of government officials, interest group activity includes the following:

- Candidate recruitment. Groups recruit candidates with specific views on political issues to support for office.
- Campaign contributions. Interest groups provide funding to support campaigns.
- Campaign resources. Interest groups with large memberships provide campaign workers.
- Public information. Interest groups rate candidates (e.g., on conservatism or liberalism) to provide information to voters about where a candidate stands on the issues).
- Get out the vote efforts. Groups can rally their members to go to the polls to vote for a particular candidate.

Of course, money is the mother's milk of politics. Money has become more important as politics has moved away from the grass roots **retail politics** (one-to-one or personal relationships) toward **wholesale politics** (mass appeal campaigns). Wholesale politics is more likely to be "air war" campaigns that are conducted on television, radio, and the Internet. One of the main ways that groups participate in elections is by providing money—raising and spending money on behalf of a campaign or political cause. There are a number of organizations that are created specifically to provide money for campaigns. A **Political Action Committee (PAC)** is a political arm of a business, labor, trade, professional, or other group. PACS are legally authorized to raise voluntary funds from employees or members of the group to contribute to a party or candidate. Many interest groups have PACs. Realtors have RPAC; doctors have AMPAC; supporters of abortion rights have NARAL-PAC and pro-life advocates have Right to Life PAC.

Political action committees (PAC) allow interest groups pool resources from group members and contribute to political campaigns and politicians. Under federal law, an organization automatically becomes a PAC by either receiving contributions or making expenditures more than $1000 for the purpose of influencing a federal election. Individual contributions to federal PACs are limited to $5,000 per year. However, the whole system of campaign finance law is currently in an unsettled state because the Supreme Court has ruled that campaign spending is a form of free speech that is protected by the First Amendment. As a result, the federal laws limiting the amount of money that an individual could spend on his or her own campaign were struck down. And in *Citizens United v Federal Election Commission* (2010) the Court ruled that corporate campaign contributions that were independent of a candidate's campaign could not be limited by the government. This ruling resulted in the creation of Superpacs. In addition, organizations that are listed under section 527 of the tax code as social welfare organizations can also engage in more campaign activity without regulation.

Not all campaigns are conducted to elect government officials. Some campaigns are referendums. A referendum is a political campaign where the public votes for or against an issue that is presented on the ballot. An example of a referendum election is one where the public votes whether to approve a tax increase. Interest groups are especially important players in referendum politics because groups organize public support for their side of the issue and public opposition for the side they oppose.

12.37 | *Providing Information*

Interest groups and lobbyists typically describe their function as providing useful information to the public and government officials. The general public and even members of Congress are usually not experts on an issue that they will be voting on. Lobbyists provide technical information about their fields of interest or expertise. Lobbyists for the American Medical Association provide information about health care and lobbyists for health insurance companies provide information about insurance. In this sense, lobbyists describe their role in the political process as an educative role: explaining technical or specialized matters to generalists. Lobbyists who represent large membership groups also "educate" members of Congress or the administration about how the general public or the group's members feel about a particular issue, bill, or law. This is also a representational role.

An interest group's strategy may also include conducting a public opinion campaign. Public opinion campaigns are efforts to change public opinion about an issue. Issue advocacy campaigns are political advertising campaigns to shape public opinion, to persuade the public to think about an issue the way that the group thinks about an issue. Oil companies that are worried about their public image can hire advertising companies to design campaigns that portray oil companies as "energy companies" that are deeply concerned about the environment, global warming, conservation, jobs, and the socially responsible production of energy. Oil spills such as the Exxon Valdez spill in Alaska and the British Petroleum oil well spill in the Gulf of Mexico in 2010 prompted extensive public relations campaigns to portray the two companies as good stewards of the environment. These kinds of well-financed public relations campaigns conducted by major corporations raise questions about the nature of public opinion in a democracy. Is public opinion the cause of public policy, or is public opinion made by these campaigns. Most interest groups today rely to some extent on direct mail, the use of computerized mailing lists to contact individuals who might share their interests.

12.38 | *Agenda Building*

Agenda building is the process by which new issues are brought to the attention of political decision-makers. There is a seemingly unlimited supply of problems or issues that someone or some group thinks the government should do something about. But public officials have limited resources (time, political capital, information, and money). Politics is the allocation of these scarce resources. Public officials must concentrate on a few important issues. Interest groups can convince politicians to put a new issue on the government's agenda.

12.39 | *Program Monitoring*

Program monitoring is when individuals or groups keep track of the government's actions to determine whether and how a bureaucracy or other administrative agency is implementing legislation. A group that monitors a program may find that a program or policy they supported is not being implemented as intended or is not being implemented well. Interest groups play a role in the policy process by monitoring policies.

12.4 | **Playing Offense or Defense?**

Sometime interest groups lobby *for* changes in public policy. They want to pass health care reform, make abortion illegal, increase regulation of Wall Street companies, enact policies to address global warming, or increase government support

for religious activity. Sometimes interest groups lobby *against* change in public policy. They want to stop health care reform, maintain legal abortions, stop government regulation, or prevent the passage of laws that provide more government support for religious activities.

Health care policy illustrates how some interest groups play offense (they support change) and others play defense (they oppose change). There are interest groups that are working hard to change the current employment-based health care system in favor of a public or national health care policy. The groups playing offense include organized labor unions, the American Association of Retired Persons (AARP), and even the American Medical Association, which has historically opposed the creation of public health care as a form of socialized medicine. The groups playing defense include health care providers, insurance companies, and organizations representing business such as the U.S. Chamber of Commerce. The high economic stakes—health care accounts for around 17 percent of the country's gross domestic product—make it hard to make any major changes in health care. For decades the interest group battles over health care reform have been a clash of titans—a conflict among big, powerful interest groups with a great deal at stake in the outcome: groups representing doctors, hospitals and other health care providers, insurance companies, and other business groups. Interest groups devote a great deal of money, time, and other resources to such conflicts. The debate over the health care reform proposed by the Obama administration attracted an unprecedented amount of money. For a description of the large sums of money spent on health care reform see "Exploring the Big Money Behind Health Care Reform."

Is it easier to play offense or defense? The political system makes it easier to play defense than offense. It is easier to prevent the government from acting than to prompt it to act.

- The separation of powers. Passing a federal law requires working with both the legislative and executive branches.
- Bicameralism. In order for a bill to become a law it must pass both houses of Congress.
- The committee system in Congress. The committee system is a functional division of labor that creates natural contact points for interest groups to participate in the policymaking process. Interest groups can lobby a committee to "kill the bill."
- Party politics. The "OUT" party often has a vested interest in opposing a bill proposed by the "IN" party.
- Federalism. The geographic division of power between the national and state governments is part of the system of checks and balances.

All of these attributes of the political system create many veto points at which an individual or organization can try to stop action. The multiple veto points make it easier to stop action than to successfully propose it and interest groups are important players in the defensive contests to stop change that they oppose.

12.5 | The Free Rider Problem

A large, active, and committed membership is a valuable resource. Candidates for office and elected government officials tend to listen to lobbyists that represent groups with large and active membership—particularly when the membership includes voters in the individual's district or state. The American Association of Retired Persons (AARP) is an influential demographic group because it has over 40 million members—and because older people have higher rates of voter turnout than younger people. But attracting and maintaining membership can be challenging.

One of the most important challenges to forming a membership-based group is the **free-rider problem**. The free-rider problem occurs when a person can benefit from an interest group's actions without having to pay for the costs of those actions. This creates an incentive to be a free rider, to receive benefits without paying costs. Free riders get what is for them a free lunch. The free-rider problem creates membership problems for groups that rely on material or purposive incentives for members to join their group. In fact, the free-rider problem is one reason why the government requires everyone to pay taxes that are used to provide certain goods and services.

A **private good** is something of value whose benefits can be limited to those who have paid for it. A private good is divisible in the sense that it can be provided to those who have paid for it but not to those who have not paid for it. Cars, computers, and phones are divisible goods. Health care, legal advice, and education are divisible services. A **public good** is something of value whose benefits cannot be limited to those individuals who have actually paid for it. In this sense, a **public good** is an indivisible good because once it is available its benefits cannot be limited to those who have actually paid for it. For these reasons, private goods are available for purchase in the marketplace based on the ability to pay while the government provides public goods. Safe streets, public order, peace, national security, and clean air or clear water are commonly considered public goods because they are indivisible: once provided, it is hard to limit national security or clean air to those who have paid for them.

Political debates about the role and size of government can often be reduced to arguments about whether some goods or services should be considered private goods, and available in the marketplace based on the ability to pay, or public goods that are provided by the government. Is education a public or private good? Does it depend on whether the education is primary or secondary education, or a college or professional education? Is health care a private or public good? The answers to these questions are political because they answer the age-old questions about what government should be doing.

12.6 | Are Interest Groups Harmful or Helpful?

Concern about the influence of interest groups is as old as the republic and as new as the coverage of health care reform. The Founders worried about factions. In *Federalist No. 10*, Madison worried about the apparently natural tendency of individuals to organize themselves into groups that advocate for their special or self-interest rather than the general or public interest. Madison believed that the most common source of factions was "the unequal distribution of property." He did not think that the "mischiefs of faction" could be eliminated; he thought they could be controlled if there were so many different factions that no one or two could dominate politics and use government and politics for their narrow self-interest and against the minority interests.

It is not easy to determine whether interest groups play a harmful or helpful role in modern American government and politics. It is easy to criticize special interests for working against the public interest. But there is often disagreement about what the public interest is. And it is not easy to measure the influence of groups. The Center for Responsive Politics[6] studies the activities and the influence of groups, with a special emphasis on political contributions and their influence on public policy. It is easier to measure activity (e.g., campaign contributions) than influence.

It is not simply that large groups are more influential than small groups, or that

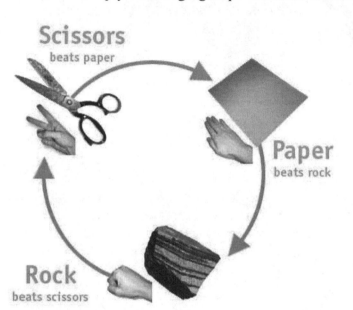

money is the sole determinant of influence. Money and numbers are important. But familiar game of **rock, scissors, paper** can help explain the relationships among the major kinds of resources that groups can mobilize. Interest group resources include numbers (the size of the membership), money (financial resources), and intensity (the members' commitment to the cause). If size alone—the number of members—were the sole determinant of influence, then consumers and workers would be much more influential than business interests because there are more of consumers and workers. And the poor would be much more influential than the rich. But size can be trumped by money. The U.S. Chamber of Commerce has less than 10% of the membership of the AARP but the financial resources of the Chamber's members make it an influential interest group. Money is a resource that is used to influence decision makers by making campaign contributions or by public relations campaigns that shape the way people think about an individual, issue, or party. So money can trump numbers. And finally, intensity of interest can trump numbers and money. An organization with a small number of members who are intensely interested or committed to their cause can trump numbers or money. Intensity is one of the keys to explaining the political influence of the National Rifle Association. NRA members are famously committed to the cause of advocating gun rights.

12.7 | Summary

It might be said of interest groups (and bureaucrats) that love them or hate them, we can't seem to live without them. The Founders worried about the "mischiefs" of faction, but groups have been integrated into the American political system at all levels (national, state, and local) and arenas (legislative, executive, and legal). Concerns about the power or influence of special interests remain valid, but it is not easy to determine whether groups are healthy or harmful. Members of Congress rely on interest groups to provide them with information about subjects being considered for legislation. Legislative committees take testimony from interest groups during committee hearings. Groups do provide a great deal of information to the public and to policymakers in both the legislative and executive branches of government. And like political parties, interest groups are linkage organizations that can increase political efficacy, the individual sense that participation matters, that participation can make a difference, that membership in a group increases citizen control over public policy in a democracy.

12.8 | Additional Resources

In order to get an idea of the number and type of interest groups see the list of some of the more important interest groups in the U.S., a list that is organized by the issues they represent or the public policy areas in which they lobby: "Political Advocacy Groups: A Directory of United States Lobbyists." http://www.vancouver.wsu.edu/fac/kfountain/

American Civil Liberties Union (ACLU) offers information on the entire Bill of Rights including racial profiling, women's rights, privacy issues, prisons, drugs, etc. Includes links to other sites dealing with the same issues. www.aclu.org

AFL-CIO is the largest trade union organization in America. Its Web site offers policy statements, news, workplace issues, and labor strategies. www.aflcio.org

Richard Kimber's Worldwide Index of Political Parties, Interest Groups, and Other Social Movements www.psr.keele.ac.uk/parties.htm

Mexican American Legal Defense and Education Fund (MALDEF) Web site offers information on Census 2000, scholarships, job opportunities, legal programs, regional offices information, and more. www.maldef.org

Native American Rights Fund (NARF) Web site offers profiles of issues, an archive, resources, a tribal directory, and treaty information, as well as a lot of other information. www.narf.org

The National Association for the Advancement of Colored People (NAACP) Web site offers information about the organization, membership, and issues of interest to proponents of civil rights. It also has sections on the Supreme Court, Census 2000, and the Education Summit and includes links to other Web sites. www.naacp.org

The National Rifle Association (NRA) offers information on gun ownership, gun laws, and coverage of legislation on associated issues. www.nra.org

National Organization of Women (NOW) Web site offers information on the organization and its issues/activities including women in the military, economic equity, and reproductive rights. It offers an e-mail action list and the ability to join NOW online. There is also a page with links to related sites. www.now.org

In the Library

Berry, Jeffrey and Clyde Wilcox. The Interest Group Society. Longman, 2008.

Biersack, Robert. After the Revolution: PAC's, Lobbies, and the Republican Congress. Addison Wesley, 2000.

Birnbaum, Jeffrey. The Money Men. Times Books, 2000.

Broder, David S. Democracy Derailed. Harcourt Brace, 2000.

Cigler, Allan J. and Burdett A. Loomis (eds). Interest Group Politics. CQ Press, 2006.

Dekieffer, Donald E. The Citizen's Guide to Lobbying Congress. Chicago Review Press, 2007.

Gray, Virginia and David Lowery. The Population Ecology of Interest Representation: Lobbying Communities in the American States. University of Michigan Press, 2001.

Hernnson, Paul S. Interest Group Connection: Electioneering, Lobbying, and Policymaking in Washington. Congressional Quarterly, Inc., 2004.

Keck, Margaret and Kathryn Sikkink. Activists Beyond Borders. Cornell University Press, 1998.

Rosenthal, Alan. Third House: Lobbyists and Lobbying in the States. Congressional Quarterly, Inc., 2001.

Strolovitch, Dara Z. Affirmative Advocacy: Race, Class, and Gender in Interest Group Politics. University of Chicago Press, 2007.

Key Terms:

interest group
lobbyists
Public interest groups
economic interest groups
grassroots lobbying
Political Action Committee (PAC)
agenda building
Program monitoring

STUDY QUESTIONS

1. What factors make an interest group successful? Provide examples.
2. Discuss and provide examples of how interest groups attempt to influence election outcomes.
3. Should there be additional limits on interest group participation in American politics?
4. What do interest groups do?
5. What are the different types of interest groups?
6. Should interest groups be protected under the First Amendment? Why or why not?

[1] See Allan J. Cigler and Burdett A. Loomis. 2007. *Interest Group Politics*. Seventh Edition. Washington, D.C.: CQ Press.

[2] Quoted in Jackie Calmes. "G.O.P. Group to Promote Conservative Ideas." *The New York Times*. (February 3, 2010). Available at http://www.nytimes.com/2010/02/04/us/politics/04conservative.html

[3] Chapter three of James Q. Wilson. 1973. *Political Organizations*. New York: Basic Books.

[4] See http://www.worldadvocacy.com/

[5] http://www.nfib.com/small-business-legal-center/about-the-legal-center/

[6] http://www.opensecrets.org/

CHAPTER 13: PUBLIC POLICY

13.0 | Public Policy

The previous chapters looked at American politics and government from a systems perspective. The classic democratic systems theory describes public opinion as the primary determinant of public policy. The chapter on public opinion studied the *demand* stage of the political process: how individuals and organizations and elections call the government's attention to issues or conditions or problems. The chapters on congress, the presidency, and the courts examined how these government institutions make decisions. This chapter examines the *response* stages of the process, the types of public policies, and some of the issues related to social science evaluation of public policy.

Figure 13: The Classic Systems Theory

13.1 | What is Public Policy

A **policy** is an official position on an issue or a plan of action that is intended to achieve certain results. It includes official positions taken by a government body, a private sector organization, a corporation, or even an individual. The following are policies:

- A congressional statute that makes it a crime for individuals to provide material support for organizations that the government labels terrorist organizations.
- An executive order such as "Don't Ask, Don't Tell" that directs the Department of Defense not to ask members of the military whether they are gays.
- Workplace safety rules and regulations.
- Corporate marketing practices for advertising tobacco or alcohol products to children.
- A company's personnel employment practices for hiring, firing, and promotion.
- An interest group's position on the environment or crime or some other issue.
- The personnel practices of non-profit organizations.
- A church's budget priorities or community outreach.
- A university's academic integrity code.
- A professor's grading of student class work.

The term **public policy** refers to governmental programs, rules, and courses of action. Public policies are stated in statutes, regulations, judicial rulings, executive orders and executive agreements, and even budgets. The study of public policy includes the process of decision making (*who* makes decisions and *how* they are made), the substance of a policy (*what* the official position is), and the analysis of its impact (whether a policy is effective). Public policy is also an academic and professional discipline that is studied and practiced in academic institutions and think tanks. The professional association of public policy practitioners, researchers, scholars, and students is the Association for Public Policy Analysis and Management. The academic discipline of public policy includes a broad range of social science fields including political science, economics, sociology, and public administration.

A government action is a public policy, but so is government inaction. A government decision **not** to take action on a matter such as global warming or health care or poverty is a public policy. The policy making process includes efforts to get the government to act (offensive strategies) and efforts to stop government action (defensive strategies). Gun control organizations lobby for gun control laws while the National Rifle Association lobbies against them or even for public policies that expand the right to keep, bear, and buy and sell arms.

Public policy is divided into two spheres: domestic and foreign policy. **Domestic policy** includes programs that affect individuals and organizations within a country. It includes a broad range of official positions on issues such as the economy, criminal justice, education, health care, transportation, energy production and consumption, and the environment. **Foreign policy** concerns a country's relations with other countries. U.S. foreign policy includes the economic, technological, informational, military, health, trade, and environmental relations with other countries. Some public policies affect both domestic and foreign affairs. Immigration policy, international trade policy, and national security policy for instance affect both domestic and foreign affairs. In fact, globalism has blurred the distinctions between domestic and foreign policy in a broad range of public policies.

"...POLICY IS MORE LIKE AN ENDLESS GAME OF MONOPOLY THAN A BICYCLE REPAIR"
- DEBORAH STONE. 2001. *POLICY PARADOX: THE ART OF POLITICAL DECISION MAKING,* PAGE 261.

13.2 | Policy Stages

The policy process has six stages: identifying a problem, agenda setting, policy formulation, policy adoption, policy implementation, and policy evaluation. Political efforts to influence public policy through education, lobbying, campaigning, campaign contributions, or other methods occur at all stages of the policy process.

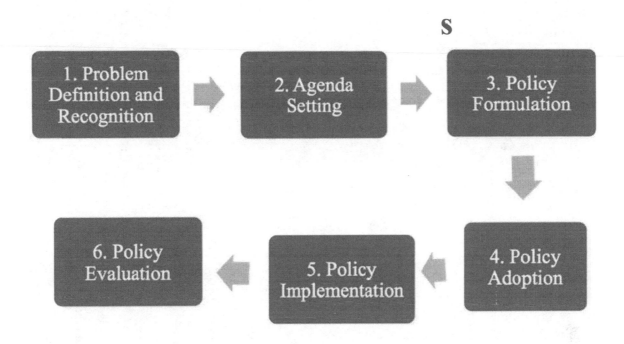

13.21 | *Problem Recognition*

Problem definition and recognition is the first stage of public policymaking. It is when individuals, interest groups, business interests, or even government officials consider something a problem that the government should solve. The problem might be air pollution, taxes, inflation, food and drug safety, crime, or bad roads or bad schools. Defining a problem and recognizing that it is appropriate for government to address it is the first stage in the policy process.

13.22 | *Agenda Setting*

Agenda setting is the second stage. **Agenda setting** is putting an issue, a condition, or a problem on the government's agenda for action. It is easy to get some issues on the government's "to-do" list. Maintaining safe streets, providing economic stability and prosperity, providing national security, and maintaining good public order are considered basic government responsibilities so it is usually not hard to get them on the government's agenda. Getting agreement on what policy to adopt is another matter, however. The increased number of mass shootings, particularly at schools, has put gun violence on the government agenda but specific policy proposals remain controversial.

Some issues are hard to get on the government's agenda because there is no agreement that they are issues that government should be involved with. Individuals and organizations may have to mount campaigns and lobbying efforts to get the government to pay attention to public transportation, health care, an unsafe street that needs some kind of traffic control device, or the need for a park or civic recreation center.

Agenda setting is the process of transforming a private matter into a public matter, making a private issue a public issue. It requires convincing people that an issue is political and that the government should enact a public policy to address it. Is workplace safety a public issue? The answer often depends on whether a job is, or is perceived to be, dangerous.

Think about it!
What are the deadliest jobs in America:

http://www.npr.org/blogs/money/2013/01/08/1688971
40/the-deadliest-jobs-in-america-in-one-graphic

13.23 | *Sex and Violence in the Media and Music*

Public campaigns to get the government to regulate indecent or violent programming on broadcast television and radio illustrate how issues get on the government's agenda and how they are kept off it. Individuals and organizations concerned about broadcast media depictions of sex and violence, and profane music lyrics, mounted sustained lobbying efforts to convince the government to put the issues on the government's agenda. The Federal Communications Commission licenses and regulates the broadcast media. The public, and therefore the government, is especially concerned about the impact of such materials on children.

Think About It! Should the government require labeling music and video games and television and radio programs the way the government requires labeling of food?
http://www.npr.org/templates/story/story.php?storyId=4279560

In the 1980s, organizations including the Parents Music Resource Center lobbied Congress to put offensive music lyrics on the federal government's agenda. Tipper Gore, at that time the wife of Senator Al Gore, bought an album, Prince's *Purple Rain*, for her daughter. Tipper Gore mistakenly thought the album was a children's album. She was offended by the explicit lyrics. In 1985, she testified before Congress that music should be labeled, primarily to protect children from an increasingly coarse culture where sex and violence were more explicit. The concerns about explicit lyrics were prompted by earlier concerns that watching violent television programming caused violent behavior in children. Congress listened to her testimony, complaints about the lack of family values in the music industry, and the testimony of musicians such as Frank Zappa who opposed government regulation of the music industry, and decided not to pass a law regulating music lyrics. Instead, Congress relied on the recording industry to voluntarily label music that contained offensive lyrics. This is an example of an unsuccessful effort to put an issue on the government's agenda but it did put the issue on the public agenda.

The question whether watching violent television programming, playing violent video games, listening to vulgar music lyrics, or visiting offensive Internet sites has a negative impact on attitudes or behavior remains an important public policy question.

13.24 | *Indecency and the Internet*

Unlike the efforts to label music, efforts to put Internet indecency on the government's agenda have been successful. As was the case with broadcast indecency, the debate focused on children. Stories about children being exposed to, or having access to indecent materials simply by doing a Google word search has prompted Congress to pass laws to protect minors from harmful material on the Internet. The Communications Decency Act of 1996 protected minors from harmful material on the Internet. The Act made it a criminal offense to knowingly transmit "obscene or indecent" messages to any person under 18 years old. The American Civil Liberties Union challenged the law in court arguing that the First Amendment protected freedom of expression from such federal laws. In *Reno v. American Civil Liberties Union*, 521 U.S. 844 (1997), the Court ruled that the law was unconstitutional. The Court had two main problems with the law. First, the law made it a criminal offense to send an indecent message, which was a severe penalty for such actions. Second, and more important, the Court considered the penalty especially severe for sending an indecent message because there is no agreement on what is indecent. Did the law make it a federal criminal offense to email or twitter an off-color joke to a minor?

The Court's ruling did not put an end to efforts to put Internet indecency on the government's agenda, and Congress passed the Child On-line Protection Act of 1998 to protect children from Internet material that was "harmful to minors." This Act was also struck down. Congress responded by passing the Children's Internet Protection Act of 2001. The Act was challenged by the American Library Association, which argued that it violated the First Amendment freedom of expression. In *United States v. American Library Association* (2003), the Supreme Court upheld the Act. Widespread public and parental concerns about the content of Internet materials that are available to minors keep the issue on the government's agenda.

13.25 | **Global Warming**

Global warming is an especially interesting case study of agenda setting. Using data showing increases in temperature, scientists and environmental organizations have been lobbying the government to take actions to reduce emissions that contribute to global warming. Business groups and conservative organizations have been lobbying against such government action. The initial defensive strategy was to deny the existence of global warning. Opponents of government action argued that temperature increases were part of natural, long-term cycles of temperature fluctuations that sometimes resulted in ice ages and sometimes resulting in warm periods. As a result, global warming is an example of political science—or more accurately politicized science. In fact, researchers worry that the politicization of "global warming" means that scientists cannot even use the term, that they will have to use the term "climate change" instead. This substitution of terms is similar to the way that the scientific theory of evolution became so political that science textbooks refer rather meekly to "life forms change." The Yale Project on Climate Change is an organization that is committed to "bridging science and society" on the matter of global warming. It includes an examination of how public opinion about global warming changed in response to the organized efforts to challenge the science.

13.26 | *Imported Goods*

The U.S. imports many consumer products. The safety of products imported from China became an issue when media reports of goods with the "Made in China" label included stories about imported pet food and toothpaste with chemical contaminants or other harmful ingredients, dangerous toys, drugs that were not tested the way that drugs with the "Made in the U.S.A." were tested. These stories attracted the attention of individuals and interest groups who lobbied government officials to 1) be more vigilant about the goods that were allowed into the country; and 2) increase government regulation and inspection of such goods. Parents who worry about imported toys with lead paint or heavy metals such as cadmium and imported dairy products contaminated with the chemical melamine can be effective advocates for putting the safety of imported products on the government's agenda. There is now a Web site for parents concerned about the safety of toys imported from China. It is one thing to get the safety of imported food or toys or drugs on the government's agenda and get a policy enacted, it is another to provide funding for agencies such as the Department of Agriculture, the Food and Drug Administration, or the Consumer Products Safety Commission, that are responsible for inspecting such items.

13.27 | *Food Policy*

The story of how food security and nutrition were put on the government's agenda is another example of how issues become political. In one sense, the consumption of food is a classic example of private good whose benefits can be limited to those who are willing and able to pay for it. But food is also considered an appropriate issue for government action. The case of policy is examined in greater detail in a separate chapter.

13.3 | Policy Formulation

The third stage of the policy process is policy formulation. Policy formulation is the government process of developing a policy to address the problem that has been put on its agenda. A broad range of political actors typically participate in forming policy. The issue network for a particular area of public policy includes the congressional committee, the executive department(s), and the interest groups. A key factor in policy formation is defining the problem because how a problem is defined can have a significant impact on the substance of the policy. The following are examples of how political problems can be, and often are, defined in very different terms.

- The price of gasoline. Is the price of a gallon of gasoline too high or too low? Are gas price increases caused by high rates of consumption (Americans tend to drive big cars and SUVs that do not get good gas mileage!) or by decisions to not exploit all sources of energy ("Drill, baby, drill!)?

- Health Care. Is the high cost of health care caused by too much or too little access to health care? Do consumers overuse health care because their employers are paying for some of the cost of health insurance? Or are health care providers the problem? Supporters of The Patient Protection and Affordable Care Act (Obamacare) defined the problem in terms of access and coverage; opponents defined the health care act's mandate to buy insurance as an infringement on individual freedom.
- Unemployment. Some people define unemployment as a problem caused by a lack of individual initiative. Others define unemployment as a problem caused by the structure of the modern economy.
- Crime. Crime can be defined as a problem caused by personal values or by poverty.
- Outsourcing. Do American businesses send jobs overseas because American worker wages are too high or because of tax incentives to do so?

In all of the above examples a problem can be defined in very different ways that determine what policy solution is appropriate. Defining the energy problem as a problem of over-consumption leads to energy policies that are intended to solve the problem by emphasizing conservation. Defining the energy problem as inadequate supply leads to policies that emphasize production. The individuals and organizations who participate in the formation of public policy work hard to maintain control over how the policy problem is defined in order to control the substance of the policy that is ultimately adopted.

13.31 | *Policy Adoption*

Policy adoption is the making of a law or laws that give the policy legal force. The government's process of deciding upon a course of action includes deliberation over evidence of the need for government action. In Congress and the executive branch, this could include hearings to take testimony about the nature of the subject being considered, calls for feedback from the public, lobbying by interest groups, citizens, or corporations. Individuals and organizations may provide evidence of the need for regulation, or evidence that regulation is not needed. If the public policy is to promote an activity by subsidizing it, then the focus is on getting the government to support policies that promote the activity. The policy adaptation stage can be very lengthy because the U.S.

system of government creates so many points at which supporters and opponents (in particular) can participate in the process. In Congress alone, the decision-making stages include subcommittees, committees, and the full body of each house. The executive branch decision making process can include executive departments with policy authority over the proposed policy.

The policy adaptation stage culminates with the passage of a law or administrative regulation that identifies the official purposes of the policy. Elected officials often publicly appear at the signing of a popular law, for example, and bureaucratic officials may support a public policy that increases the agency's budget or rule making authority over their area of expertise.

13.32 | *Implementation*

The fifth stage is implementation. Implementation is what happens after a policy is put into effect. Implementation is neither automatic nor simple. There are three common problems with implementation: ambiguity, communication, and resistance. The first common problem is *ambiguity*. Some policies are not very clear or precise: the statutory language may be vague or general. When a statute or regulation is vague, the individuals responsible for implementing the policy may not know what the policy requires. This problem is fairly common when Congress passes a general law that described its goals only in very general terms, and then requires the experts or specialists in the bureaucracy to actually define what the law requires or to determine the way to implement the goals of the law.

An example of this problem is a law passed by Congress declaring that federal policy supported clean air and clean water. These goals—clean air and clean water—require specific definitions that are provided by those authorized to implement the policy of clean air and clean water. Another example of the importance of implementation is the debates surrounding the  use of "enhanced interrogation" as part of the war on terror. The government's official position is that torture is illegal, but the individuals who are conducting field interrogations are sometimes left to define what treatment is torture and what is not torture knowing that there is some support for tough questioning that may cross an unclear line. In fact, police officers, military police, or the FBI and CIA interrogators may not even know what the policy is concerning legal methods of interrogation.

Having an official or general policy against torture does not eliminate the need to define what is, and what is not, torture. In fact any large organization needs clear *communication* of instructions throughout all of its levels if policies are to be implemented as intended. A common problem in government and private sector bureaucracies is need to clearly communicate policies throughout the organization's chain of command, from the top of the organization (the policy makers) to the bottom of the organization (the policy followers).

In addition to the problems of ambiguity and communication, *resistance* is a third problem with implementation. The implementation problem here is that the individuals who are entrusted with the responsibility to implement or carry out the intentions of the policy may not support it. Resistance or opposition to a policy can make implementation difficult. The police officer may oppose a Supreme Court ruling that the Constitution requires that individuals who are suspected of committing a crime must be notified of their rights before being questioned by the police. A public school teacher may oppose a Supreme Court ruling that that prohibits organized, spoken prayer in public schools or at school events. The political appointee on the Consumer Products Safety Commission may be opposed to further government regulation of business. The head of the Food and Drug Administration may claim that the FDA has the authority to regulate nicotine despite the tobacco lobby successfully stopped efforts to get Congress to pass a law that specifically authorized the FDA to regulate nicotine as a drug.[1]

The U.S. system of government creates special implementation problems that many other countries do not have. A country with a unitary form of government does not have to worry about independent local, state, or regional governments that may or may not implement a national policy. A country like the U.S. with a federal system of government has to take into consideration the fact that a state may not support a national policy and therefore not implement it. Furthermore, separation of powers means that the branch of government that makes a law (Congress) is not the branch of government that implements or carries it out (the executive), and the branch that makes a law is not the branch that interprets a law when there is a legal dispute about what it means (the courts). For example, a Democratic Congress may pass a law that a Republican President does not support, or simply interprets in a way that differs from the way the Congress understands the law. In contrast, a country with a parliamentary system does not have to worry about separate branches of government because the legislative and executive branches are formally connected. A good example of problems with implication is the 2007 political debate about the role of the Consumer Products Safety Commission in inspecting goods (ranging from pet foods to pharmaceutical ingredients to toys) imported from China. Republican President George Bush reflected the generally pro-business position of the Republican Party when he appointed an acting head of the CPSC who was did not support increased government regulation of the import business. Democrats in Congress supported increased regulation of import businesses, particularly those that imported dangerous toys from China where industry inspections and regulation are not a strict as in the United States.[2]

13.33 | *Budgeting*

In order for a policy to be successful it has to be built into the budget. Take the case of global warming. One way to address global warming is to increase spending on research to develop energy that less harmful to the environment. But if the problem definition stage has identified business, consumer, and ideological opposition to such efforts, then any energy policy that is adopted should include provisions to ensure compliance with the policy. For instance, an energy policy that included increased research might have a legal provision authorizing the Environmental Protection Agency to fine energy companies that do not spend a certain percentage of their research budgets on environmentally friendly policies. Such a legal provision has budgetary impacts, and in order to be successful Congress would have to allocate money to the EPA for enforcement of the law.

13.34 | *Policy Evaluation*

The above description of the stages of the policy process explains why politics does not start with government decision making and it does not stop with the adoption of a policy. Politics includes what happens after a bill has become a law. **Policy evaluation** is determining whether a policy is working as intended. This can be difficult because the subject can be complex (e.g., determining the cause of crime) and because of politics. Some evaluation is based on *anecdotal evidence*. Anecdotal evidence is stories from a few people that make their way to the ears of an evaluator. Politicians often cite compelling personal stories as evidence that a policy they support is working, or as evidence that a policy they support is not working. Sometimes horror stories and success stories are cherry-picked from the data. Evaluation also sometimes relies on *public opinion*. The political assumption is that a popular policy must be a good policy and an unpopular policy must be a bad policy. But public opinion—conventional wisdom—can be mistaken. Social scientists value evaluation that is based on *empirical evidence*: the systematic analysis of data. However, policies are assessed by a variety of individuals from a variety of perspectives and with a variety of goals in mind so it is not surprising that different methods of evaluation are used.

13.35 | *Unintended Consequences*

Public policies frequently have side effects or unintended consequences. Because policies are typically intended to apply to complex adaptive systems (e.g. governments, societies, large companies), making a policy change can have unintended or counterintuitive results. For example, a government may make a policy decision to raise taxes, in hopes of increasing overall tax revenue. Depending on the size of the tax increase, this may have the overall effect of reducing tax revenue by causing capital flight or by creating a rate that is so high that citizens have incentives to NOT earn the money that is taxed. The policy formulation process typically includes an attempt to assess as many areas of potential policy impact as possible, to lessen the chances that a given policy will have unexpected or unintended consequences. Because of the nature of some complex adaptive systems such as societies and governments, it may not be possible to assess all possible impacts of a given policy.

Policies are intended to affect human behavior. When thinking about how to get people to do what you want, it makes sense to think about their motivations. One of the most frequently used motivators is money: individuals are paid money to do things we want them to do (e.g., work) and fined for doing things we don't want them to do. But money is an imperfect motivator.[3]

A good example of unintended consequences is the public policy supporting wearing a helmet while riding a bicycle. The National Highway Traffic Safety Administration recommends that bicyclists wear helmets as a safety measure to protect against head injuries. Parents often require children to wear bicycle helmets. Should local governments require bicyclists to wear helmets while riding on bike paths? The intended consequence is reducing head injuries. The unintended consequences include increased rates of obesity, increased heart disease, and increased rates of diabetes because requiring helmets reduces bicycle riding (exercise). Some American cities are adopting bike sharing programs to increase the use of bicycles for urban transportation. Helmets present a problem for such programs. When a major considers a law requiring wearing helmets, the benefits (reduced head injuries) should be considered against the costs (decreased bicycling).

13.4 | TYPES OF POLICY

Public policies are intended to affect 1) the conditions under which people live and work; and 2), the human behavior of individuals and organization. Policies affect conditions by creating safe streets, national security, domestic public order, and economic stability. Policies affect behavior by creating incentives or disincentives to behave in certain ways. Public policy is intended to influence the decisions that people make. Two broad classifications of public policy are distributive policy and regulatory policy.

13.41 | DISTRIBUTIVE POLICIES

Distributive policies provide goods and services. Government programs that provide welfare, public education, highways, public safety, or other benefits such as tax deductions and credits are distributive policies. One subcategory of distributive policies that is politically controversial is *redistributive* policy. A redistributive policy takes resources from one group of individuals or states (e.g., wealthier, younger, employed, or urban) and transfers them to another group of individuals or states (poorer, older, unemployed, or rural). Social welfare programs are redistributive policies in which money or in-kind services such as food stamps or health care (under Medicaid) are provided to individuals who cannot provide them for themselves or to promote income equality and income security. Tax policies that provide for home mortgage interest deductions or reduced tax rates for interest income are also redistributive. One of the most important social welfare policies is Social Security. The Social Security Administration (SSA) Web site provides historical information about the creation of the program and its funding, as well as current information about social security rules, regulations, and policies. The fiscal stability of Social Security has become part of contemporary political debates about entitlements in an era where demographic changes are increasing the average age of the American public.

13.42 | REGULATORY POLICIES

Think about it!

Should the government take from one group of people (or states) and give to others?

Regulatory policies are those that are intended to change the behavior of individuals or organizations. These policies are generally thought to be best applied in situations where good behavior can be easily defined and bad behavior can be easily regulated and punished through fines or sanctions. Examples of regulatory policy include speed limits laws, "sin" taxes on alcohol, tobacco, or gambling, or tax credits for consumers who buy hybrid vehicles. Many countries have "population" policies, which are intended to either encourage people to have more children or discourage people from having more children. Population policies are important components of a country's economic policy because demographics is such an important factor linked to, among other things, a country's economic development. Demographics include the age distribution of a country's population. Having a larger or smaller percentage of younger or older people has great implications for public policies. China's one-child policy is an example of a national population policy whose primary objective was to control population increase. However, policies intended to solve one problem often have other, unintended consequences. China's one-child policy has controlled population growth, but it has created other problems that are just now emerging. Limiting births has serious long-term implications for a country's demographics because it affects the ratio of working age individuals to the young, elderly, and retired.

One policy response to the Great Recession was proposals to increase the regulation of the financial services sector of the economy in order to prevent another crisis in financial services that is so severe that it threatens to bring down the entire economy, and therefore requires a government bailout. The Obama administration proposed the creation of a Consumer Financial Protection Bureau. Democratic President Obama appointed Elizabeth Warren as a special assistant to create a Consumer Financial Protection Bureau. Her testimony (May 24, 2011) before the House of Representatives Subcommittee on TARP and Financial Services of the Committee on Oversight and Government Reform revealed sharp partisan differences on government regulation of financial services. In 2012, Warren was elected as a U.S. Senator from Massachusetts.

President Obama with Elizabeth Warren, a Harvard Law Professor who
participated in crafting legislation to regulate the financial industry.

13.5 | PUBLIC POLICY ISSUES

13.51 | SOCIAL POLICY

Social policy includes a broad range of public policies: social welfare policy (income or
service support), health care, and education. Social policy is often distributive policy
insofar as it entails taking resources from one group and providing them to another
groups, or from a general population to a particular population. Because of the
relationship between economic resources (income or wealth) and opportunity, social
scientists study the impact of economic inequality. The relationship between
income/wealth and education is particularly important because so much emphasis is
placed on education as the key to economic opportunity and political equality. Studies of
performance on standardized tests that are used to determine admission to colleges, for
example, reveal consistent correlations between family income and performance on
standardized tests.[4]

The importance of education is also reflected in the fact that states have
compulsory schooling laws and impose taxes to support public education. In terms of
public policy, there are important differences among primary, secondary, and college
education. Primary and secondary education are considered public goods in the sense that
society and the students benefit from the education. College is more complicated.
Receiving a college degree is a private good in the sense that it provides an individual
with certain benefits, but college is also a public good in the sense that higher education
is often part of a state's economic development strategy. In fact, reductions in state tax
support for college reflect a nationwide trend toward education policy that treats college
as more of a private good than a public good. This policy shift is occurring against the
background of another major change in thinking about education policy. More analysts
are questioning the economic wisdom of assuming that everyone should go to college. Is
there an education bubble similar to the real estate bubble that played an important role in
the Great Recession? Both sectors of the economy benefited from and relied on the
perception that values—properties and degrees—would continue to increase? Are sub-
prime mortgages, which played an important role in bringing about the Great Recession,
analogous to sub-prime college degrees?

Think About It!
What is the value of a college degree?
See the Public Broadcasting story "Assessing the
Value of College Education" at
http://video.pbs.org/video/1954954225

One important component of a country's social welfare policy is health care. The governments of all the major industrial democracies play a role in providing health care. The U.S. government plays a smaller and different role than the governments in other countries with similar economic and political systems. The high cost of health care in the U.S., measured as a percentage of a family's budget and as a percentage of the country's gross domestic product, has put health care reform on the political agenda. Republicans and Democrats have disagreed on the best solutions to the problems with the health care system.

From a national policy perspective, a basic question is whether the U.S. health care system rates good, fair, or poor. The answer depends in part on which of several measures are used to assess health care:

- Cost—the share of a country's Gross Domestic Product.
- Access—the percentage of people who have access to health care by, for example, insurance coverage.
- Performance—health measures such as infant mortality and life expectancy.

Organizations such as The Commonwealth Fund promote the creation of a more effective health care system. One politically relevant fact when thinking about health care (or virtually any other area of public policy) in the U.S. is federalism. The 50 states have their own role in the design and delivery of health care. Want more information about your state's health care system? The Commonwealth Fund State Scorecard 2009 provides an interactive map that enables a reader to quickly see where the state in which they reside ranks in terms of health care on various measures and by overall rank.

The question whether the U.S. has a good health care system prompts another question: Compared to what? Comparison is valuable because it provides benchmarks for evaluating policy. Health care systems can be studied from a number of different comparative perspectives. One comparison is *historical*: comparing the current system with the past system. A second approach is *comparative*: comparing the U.S. system with those in other countries. This comparative approach involves comparing and contrasting the health care systems in different countries. A third way is to compare the health care sector of the American economy with other sectors of the economy.

Comparative Health Care Systems

T. R. Reid compares the health care systems in countries with political and economic systems that are similar to the U.S. and countries with different systems. The results provide valuable benchmarks for determining the performance of different health care systems. http://www.npr.org/templates/rundowns/rundown.php?prgId=13&prgDate=8-24-2009

The comparative costs of health care are examined in this Public Broadcasting System story http://www.pbs.org/newshour/rundown/2012/10/health-costs-how-the-us-compares-with-other-countries.html

---

One comparison involves the use of medical technology. The American practice of medicine is noted for its advanced technology. The reliance on medical technology is a mixed blessing. It can produce amazing outcomes but it is very expensive. The love affair with medical technology has made the old-fashioned physical exam, a low-cost diagnosis, a "dying art." Dr. Abraham Verghese, a physician at the Stanford Medical School, described the problem in a semi-serious way: "I sometimes joke that if you come to our hospital missing a finger, no one will believe you until we get a CAT scan, an MRI, and an orthopedic consult. We don't trust our senses." Dr. Verghese's comment criticizes the modern medical profession for becoming so dependent on machines to tell them about the patient (the "I-patient") that doctors do not pay very much attention to the actual patient in the hospital bed.

A final comparison involves comparing health care with other sectors of the U.S. economy. The U.S. economy has a manufacturing sector, an agricultural sector, an educational sector, a criminal justice sector, a hospitality sector, a telecommunications sector, and even a **fast food sector**. Comparing the health care and fast food sectors may seem inappropriate because they are so different. But the fast food industry has developed and applied cost and quality control measures, as well as other organizational practices that might be applicable to the health care industry. The two sectors might seem so completely different that the one has little to say about the other, but from an organizational perspective, the attention that restaurant chains have paid to delivering a **good** (fast food) produce may be relevant to the delivery of a **service** (health care). Americans brought organizational skills to manufacturing, agriculture, and to the service sector (notably, through chain restaurants and lodging). But medicine—doctors and hospitals—have resisted the trend until recently. Doctors **were** self-employed; now three-quarters are employees. Hospitals are also becoming parts of chains. In "Big Med," Gawande describes how "[restaurant] chains have managed to combing quality control, cost control, and innovation" and asks whether their organizational principles can do the same for health care.[5]

Although health care is often described as a "system" it did not develop as a system but rather as a series of decisions made about individual aspects of health care (e.g., hospital regulations; insurance policies; drug regulations; physician licensing) over a long period of time. For example, the "system" is surprisingly dependent on tax policy. Taxes are used to raise money to fund government programs, to discourage certain activities (e.g., smoking), encourage certain behaviors (e.g., marriage; child rearing), or to redistribute wealth (progressive income taxes). The federal government's health care tax exclusion has grown over time to be an important foundation of large employers' provision of health care for employees.

> Think About It!
> Is a tax break the best policy for subsidizing health insurance coverage?
> http://www.npr.org/blogs/health/2012/12/04/166434247/the-huge-and-rarely-discussed-health-insurance-tax-break

13.53 | THE TOBACCO WARS

One of the early fights over health care policy was a political and legal campaign to regulate or even ban smoking and the use of other tobacco products. The term tobacco wars refers to the long-running battle between the tobacco industry (primarily growers, manufacturers, and sellers) and the anti-tobacco lobby (the American Medical Association, the American Heart Association, the American Lung Association, and other consumer and public health advocates). The fight over control of tobacco policy has been waged in all political arenas: city government, state government, and the federal government; congress, the executive branch, and the courts. In the past, the consumption of tobacco was considered a largely private choice to use nicotine. As the adverse health consequences of tobacco use were discovered, however, there was pressure to make tobacco a political issue, to put tobacco on the political agenda. The efforts included the use of political litigation, or the use of lawsuits that are intended to change public policy.

The result was a rather complicated system of regulation, which includes limits on the sale of tobacco products (not to minors), and limits on the advertising of tobacco products.

In order to understand how much public attitudes toward smoking have changed over the years it is useful to look at tobacco advertisements. What is especially striking about many of the early tobacco ads is that they explicitly claimed or strongly implied that smoking was healthful. Advertising campaigns used doctors and nurses to sell cigarettes. They even used images of infants who seemed to notice that mommy was especially enjoying a particular brand of cigarettes. These advertising campaigns seem shocking today.

13.54 | ENVIRONMENTAL POLICY

American politics today is increasingly organized around issues, areas of policy such as civil rights, health care, abortion, crime, education, national security, and the environment. Environmental policy is an example of issue politics. Environmentalism is a broad term that covers many areas of public policy such as air pollution, water pollution, and the conservation of land and other natural resources. Water policy has become a very important area of environmental politics. As the supply of clean water has become an increasingly scarce resource, water has become a contentious political issue for local, regional, state, and national government. Historically, water was fairly abundant in the Eastern part of the U.S. East of the Mississippi River where water was plentiful *wasting water* meant consuming it needlessly or using too much water. But in the arid regions west of the Mississippi River, where water was always a scarce resource, to waste water meant to not use it—to allow river water to flow unimpeded and unused downstream and eventually into the ocean was considered wasteful. Much of western urban development—big cities such as Los Angeles, Phoenix, Las Vegas, and San Diego—and agricultural development was made possible by massive dams and irrigation projects that transported water over long distances and even over or around high mountains to where it was needed for thirsty people or thirsty crops. As a result, it was said that in the American West water flows uphill—toward money.

Water flows over mountains to fields and cities in southern California.[6] On the great plains, the Ogallala (or High Plains) Aquifer that lies beneath much of the country ranging from South Dakota to Texas supports large scale industrial agriculture, but this use of ground water can be considered **mining** as much as **farming**.[7] Underground aquifers are mined for their water the way other minerals such as gold, copper, silver, and coal are mined. The way we think about water complicates efforts to reuse it. For example, the cognitive versus psychological content of water presents a serious challenge for policymakers and private sector organizations who want to change public opinion about recycling cleaned wastewater—particularly recycling sewage water for human consumption. The following National Public Radio story, *Water, water everywhere but not a drop to drink?*, explains why people think that cleaned wastewater is still dirty.

> Think About It!
> "Water, water everywhere but not a drop to drink?"
> http://www.npr.org/2011/08/16/139642271/why-cleaned-wastewater-stays-dirty-in-our-minds

As water became a political issue organizations have arisen to advocate on behalf of various water policies and practices. For example, the WateReuse Research Foundation is a non-profit corporation whose mission is to conduct and promote applied research on the science of water reuse, recycling, reclamation, and desalination. Water politics is not just about conservation or being green. It is a vital resource that has national security implications.

13.55 | ENERGY POLICY

The U.S. is a high-consuming nation. It is not just that the U.S. uses a lot of energy—it is, after all a country with a large population. The U.S. is a high-consuming country because Americans have a high per capita use of energy. The following World Bank data compares the per capita consumption of energy in various countries.[8]

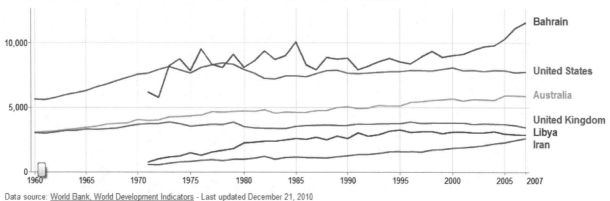

Energy use per capita
Primary energy use (before transformation to other end-use fuels) in kilograms of oil equivalent, per capita. More info »

Data source: World Bank, World Development Indicators - Last updated December 21, 2010

The U.S. per person consumption of energy is high compared to other countries. U.S. dependence of foreign oil has been an issue since the 1970s Arab Oil Embargoes. The U.S. has been talking about the need for energy independence ever since then.

> For a satirical view on political rhetoric about the importance of U.S. energy independence see The Daily Show's "An Energy-Independent Future." http://www.thedailyshow.com/watch/wed-june-16-2010/an-energy-independent-future

Energy policy is about producing enough energy, conservation of resources, environmentalism, national security, and economics. The discussion of renewable energy is part of a broader concern about sustainability—whether it is energy sources, fisheries, forestry, mineral deposits, or water supplies. In fact, the discussion has included some provocative comments about whether modern civilization as we know it is even sustainable.

Think About It!
Is modern civilization sustainable?
Is civilization a bad idea?
http://www.npr.org/blogs/13.7/2011/11/15/142339570/is-civilization-a-bad-idea

13.56 | SUSTAINABILITY

Sustainability is an important concept in environmental policy. Sustainable forestry practices harvest trees while keeping enough and healthy forests. Sustainable agriculture refers to farming practices that incorporate productivity with concern for maintaining water and soil quality. Marine sustainability refers to fishing practices that maintain sustainable stocks of fish and healthy natural fisheries. The Marine Stewardship Council is a global organization that works with fisheries, companies, scientists, conservation groups, and the general public to promote sustainable fisheries by labeling seafood as certified sustainable seafood. Do you care whether the fish you in the market or eat in a restaurant is obtained using sustainable fishing practices? Is the "certified sustainable" label about science or economics?

Think About It!
What Does "Sustainable" Fishing Mean?
http://www.npr.org/2013/02/12/171376617/conditions-allow-for-more-sustainable-labeled-seafood

13.6 | ADDITIONAL RESOURCES

13.61 | INTERNET RESOURCES

Congress funds the Congressional Research Service, which provides detailed descriptions and analyses of public policy issues. The Web site http://opencrs.com/
The Congressional Budget Office (CBO) Web site offers Congress's opinions on budget matters including statistics, reports, budget reviews, testimony, and more.
www.cbo.gov/

The American Enterprise Institute is a conservative think tank that addresses a variety of issues. Its Web site offers information on their calendar of events, a variety of articles, and links: www.aei.org

The Brookings Institution is the oldest think tank in America and has the reputation of being fairly moderate. Its Web site offers policy briefings, articles, books, The Brookings Review, discussion groups, and links. www.brookings.edu

The Cato Institute is a libertarian think tank promoting free market ideas. Its Web site offers a variety of articles and links. www.cato.org

U.S. Department of Health and Human Services offers information about public policies related to health and other issues under their purview. www.hhs.gov

Almanac of Policy Issues has a wide array of information about policy related issues and has numerous links to more information.
www.policyalmanac.org/social_welfare/index.shtml

13.62 | IN THE LIBRARY

Arthur Benabie. Social Security Under the Gun. Palgrave, 2003.
Rebecca Blank et. al. (eds). The New World of Welfare. The Brookings Institution, 2001.
Robert Bryce. Gusher of Lies: The Dangerous Delusions of "Energy Independence".
Public Affairs, 2009.
Paul K. Conkin. The State of the Earth: Environmental Challenges on the Road to 2100.
University Press of Kentucky, 2008.
Peter A. Diamond and Peter R. Orszag. Saving Social Security: A Balanced Approach.
Brookings Institution Press, 2004.
Diana M. Dinitto and Linda Cummins. Social Welfare: Politics and Public Policy. Allyn
& Bacon, Inc., 2004.
Barbara Ehrenreich. Being Nickeled and Dimed: On (Not) Getting By in America.
Metropolitan Books, 2001.
Peter J. Ferrara and Michael Tanner. A New Deal for Social Security. The Cato Institute,
1998.
Neil Gilbert and Amitai Etzioni. Transformation of the Welfare State: The Silent
Surrender of Public Responsibility. Oxford University Press, 2002.
Michael Katz. The Price of Citizenship: Redefining the American Welfare State.
Metropolitan Books, 2001.
David Kelly. A Life of One's Own: Individual Rights and the Welfare State. The Cato
Institute. 1998.
Sally Kneidel. Going Green: A Wise Consumer's Guide to a Shrinking Planet. Fulcrum
Publishing, 2009.
Jennie Jacobs Kronenfeld. The Changing Federal Role in U.S. Health Care Policy.
Praeger Publishing, 1997.
Kelly Lee et. al. (eds). Health Policy in a Globalising World. Cambridge University
Press, 2002.
Sanford Schram. After Welfare: The Culture of Postindustrial Social Policy. New York
University Press, 2000.
Robert Stevens and Rosemary Stevens. Welfare Medicine in America: A Case Study of
Medicaid. Transaction Publishers, 2003.

Joseph White. False Alarm (Century Foundation Book Series): Why the Greatest Threat to Social Security and Medicare is the Campaign to Save Them. Johns Hopkins University Press, 2003. David Zucchino. Myth of the Welfare Queen: A Pulitzer Prize-Winning Journalist's Portrait of Women on the Line. Touchstone Books, 1999.

KEY TERMS

Policy
Public policy
Domestic policies
Foreign policy
Agenda setting
Policy adoption
Policy evaluation
Distributive policies
Regulatory policies

STUDY QUESTIONS

1. How do issues get on the political and government agendas?
2. What issues are most likely to make it onto these agendas?
3. What are the stages of the policy process?
4. What are the challenges in implementing policy?
5. Describe the problem of unintended consequences.
6. How has policymaking changed over time?

---

[1] http://www.fda.gov/safety/recalls/default.htm

[2] For an idea of the many kinds of consumer products that the CPSC reviews see http://www.cpsc.gov/

[3] See http://www.pbs.org/newshour/bb/business/jan-june10/makingsense_04-15.html

[4] See http://economix.blogs.nytimes.com/2009/08/27/sat-scores-and-family-income/

[5] Atul Gawande, "Big Med," The New Yorker (August 13, 2012): 53-63.

[6] Quoted in Richard Knox, "The Dying Art of the Physical Exam," *All Things Considered, Morning Edition,* National Public Radio (September 20, 2010). http://www.npr.org/player/v2/mediaPlayer.html?action=1&t=1&islist=false&id=129931999&m=12998429 6

[7] http://www.kgs.ku.edu/HighPlains/OHP/index.shtml

[8] See http://www.google.com/publicdata?ds=wb-wdi&met=eg_use_pcap_kg_oe&idim=country:USA&dl=en&hl=en&q=energy+consumption#met=eg_use_pcap_kg_oe&idim=country:USA:ALB:AUS:ARG:BHR:IRN to examine the energy use of additional countries. The original data is available from http://data.worldbank.org/data-catalog/world-development-indicators?cid=GPD_WDI

14.0 | Economic Policy

What does economics have to do with politics? What is the relationship between capitalism and democracy? And how does the government make economic policy? These are important questions about government and the economy in all forms of government but the answers vary a great deal depending on the country's economic and political systems. This chapter examines three related issues about government and the economy.

- The relationship between economics and politics. It can be useful to think of the economic system as independent of the political system (in the same way that it can be useful to think of the legal system as separate from the political system) but economics like law) is not completely separate from politics. Government includes politics, economics, and law. This chapter explains how these systems work together.

- Economic Policy. The chapter examines fiscal policy and monetary policy, the two main components of economic policy that the government uses to achieve its goals.

- The relationship between economic power and political power. Does economic power create political power? Does economic inequality create political inequality? Does the distribution of income and wealth affect justice? These are all aspects of the power problem with economics.

14.1 | The Market Model and the Government Model

One aspect of the power problem is finding the right balance between the private sector and the public sector. The private sector is basically the market model for maintaining good social order, providing goods and services, and allocating scarce resources. The public sector is basically the government model for providing these functions. The tensions between the private sector/market model and the public sector/government model have been one of the recurring themes in American politics from the earliest days of the republic. The current debates about the size of the federal government, and the belief that government has gotten too big, can be traced to what happened to the size of the government during the 20th Century. It got bigger relative to the private sector. In *Government versus Markets: The Changing Economic Role of the State* (2011), Vito Tanzi compares government spending as a share of a country's national income in 1870 and 2007.[1] The numbers explain why the size of the national government and the size of the national debt have become such important political issues in American politics.

Table 14.1

Country	Share of National Income By Year	
	1870	2007
U.S.	7.3%	36.6%
Great Britain	9.4%	44.6%
Germany	10.0%	43.9%
France	12.6%	52.6%

The numbers reveal a clear trend toward bigger government, measured as a share of gross domestic product, in western democracies. There are two main concerns about the expansion of government. The first concern is that the expansion of government—that is, the public sector—results in the contraction of the private sector (that is, business and civil society). A second concern is that this expansion of government occurred during a period of population increases and high rates of economic growth and population increases in western countries. But times have changed. These same countries now face three new conditions that, taken together, present serious challenges for the economic and political systems. The first problem is low rates of population growth. Low rates of population growth also contribute to the second problem: comparatively low rates of economic growth. Third, demographic changes, specifically aging populations, mean that the countries will have an increase in the proportion of older workers and older citizens who require more social services such as Social Security and health care (Medicare). An aging population means a decrease in the ratio of working age people (the producers) to non-working age people (the consumers).

The population increases, increases in productivity, and high rates of economic growth produced prosperity. Prosperity and the belief that the pie was continually getting bigger and bigger meant that politics did not seem to be about scarcity and the need to allocate scarce resources. Economic conflicts between liberals and conservatives, Democrats and Republicans, were muted. The prospect of austerity has sharpened the debates and the conflicts because politics now seems to be a zero sum game where one person's (or side's) increase means another person's (or side's) decrease.

14.12 | Politics and *The Market*

One indication of the importance of economics is the large number of interest groups, think tanks, policy organizations, professional associations, and trade groups whose organizational missions include economic issues. Economic interest groups of all kinds lobby on behalf of their members: business, labor, professional associations, agriculture, manufacturing, service industries, and intellectual property. In fact, economics is so important that **The Market** is used as a metaphor for the economy, **Wall Street** is used as a metaphor for the financial services sector of the economy, and **Main Street** is used as a metaphor for the small business sector of the economy.

What is the Dow Jones Industrial Average?

The Dow Jones Industrial Average is one indicator of how the economy is doing. But the DJIA is no longer comprised of stock prices of industrial companies, as the name implies? The components of the Dow are changed every few years to reflect the breadth of the U.S. economy and to drop companies that are not doing well. In 2011, the 30 DJIA companies included four financial firms, two giant retailers, one restaurant chain, five consumer-products makers, two telecommunications firms, three drug companies, five high-tech firms and an entertainment conglomerate. It had only five traditional manufacturers— Caterpillar, Alcoa, United Technologies, 3M and General Electric — plus a couple of energy companies. The Dow is not merely a collection of the largest U.S. firms. It does not include Apple — which trades places with Exxon Mobil as the biggest company in America — or Google, which has a larger market capitalization (the number of shares outstanding multiplied by price) than Wal-Mart, which is listed on the Dow. And these companies are multinational companies that do business globally

---

14.13 | *The Relationship between Politics and Economics*

The 19th Century term political economy described the close relationship of politics and economics. Today the term economic policy is more commonly used to describe government positions on economic activities related to the production of good and the provision of services. The close relationship between politics and economics is reflected in public opinion polls that regularly ask people what they think are the most important issues facing the nation. The surveys consistently identify three issues:

- **Crime** (policies to provide public safety)
- **Economics** (policies to provide stability and prosperity)
- **National security** (foreign and defense policy)

The ranked order of the importance of these three issues varies depending upon circumstances. During good economic times, voters consider national security or crime policy more important than economics. During bad economic times (recessions, depressions, high inflation, or high unemployment), economics is likely to be ranked number one. During times of war, the threat of war, or terrorism, the public is most concerned about national security. And when crime rates are high or increasing, worries about public safety make crime a high priority issue. People everywhere expect protection them from foreign threats, crime, and economic insecurity. They can provide the protection themselves (e.g., self-defense or private security guards), they can rely on civil society organizations to provide it (e.g., neighborhood watch groups or militia), they can rely on businesses to provide it, or they can rely on the government to provide it. National security, crime, and economics are political because they are basic responsibilities that governments everywhere are created to address. The American political experience demonstrates the strong connections between economics and politics from the founding era until today.

14.2 | Economic History

14.21 | *The Founding Era*

Economic conditions played an important role in the founding of the Republic when economic instability, including steep increases in the cost of living, contributed to political instability. When Benjamin Franklin returned to America in 1762 after spending almost five years abroad he wrote: "The expence of living is greatly advanc'd in my absence. Rent of old houses, and the value of lands…are trebled in the past six years." Franklin was describing an early American real estate *bubble*. An economic bubble occurs when the value of an asset increases so fast that its price gets so high compared to other economic measures such as income that the price cannot be sustained and ultimately collapses. When the real estate bubble that Franklin described finally popped, credit was tightened, and a recession ensued. These were some of the bad economic times that caused political discontent that eventually contributed to the American Revolution.[2]

Scholars still debate the relative importance of political ideas and economic conditions on the American Revolution. Some scholars stress the importance of the colonists' commitment to political ideas including freedom, democracy, equality, and justice. Others stress the importance of economic conditions and the economic interests of the wealthy or property owning classes. Regardless of whether political ideas or economics were more important, economics contributed to the founding of the republic.

Shays' Rebellion is an often told story. In the fall of 1786 and winter of 1787, Daniel Shays and other Revolutionary War veterans conducted an armed march on the capital of Massachusetts. They were protesting mortgage foreclosures of their farms and businesses due to bad economic times, and demanded debt relief from the government. Political leaders were worried that bad economic conditions were creating political unrest that included mob violence. The fear of such unrest was one of the reasons for calling the Constitutional Convention in the summer of 1787. The national government's role in the economy was debated during the Convention. The Constitution they wrote gave the national government important economic powers, including the power to tax and spend, the exclusive power to coin money, the power to regulate interstate and foreign commerce, and the power to quell the domestic disturbances that resulted from bad economic times.

Economic issues remained important during the early years of the republic when political debates centered on the national government's role in the economy. In fact, differences of opinion about economic policy played an important role in the emergence of the first political parties. The Federalist Party supported a national government with a strong and active role in economic development. Alexander Hamilton was a Federalist who, as Secretary of the Treasury, advocated using the national government's power to develop a national economy. The other major political party, the Jeffersonians or Democratic-Republicans, believed that economic matters were the primary responsibility of the state governments. The two major parties still debate the government's role in the economy.

14.22 | *The Industrial Revolution*

In the U.S., the Industrial Revolution occurred in the middle years of the 19th Century. It changed the economy from a primarily agrarian and small-business economy, dominated by landowners and small entrepreneurial craftsmen, to an industrial economy where large corporations dominated various sectors of the economy. Big corporations developed in transportation (railroads), manufacturing (steel), energy (oil), and finance. The Industrial Revolution also changed the social and political systems.

> The struggles between small business (local and "mom and pop" hardware stores, electronic stores, clothing stores, and grocery stores) and big business occurred long before Wal-Mart and other big box stores put local businesses out of business. Listen to the story of "The Great A&P and the Struggle for Small Business in America."
> http://www.npr.org/player/v2/mediaPlayer.html?action=1&t=1&is list=false&id=139848775&m=139870174

14.23 | *The Progressive Era*

The Progressive Era extended from around 1890 until 1920. Progressives were social reformers who tried to address some of the problems caused by the Industrial Revolution. They believed that big government was necessary to regulate big business (corporations). Progressives advocated social welfare legislation to protect individuals from the economic insecurities of the marketplace. Progressive Era legislation included child labor laws, minimum wage and maximum hour laws, and workplace safety laws. The Progressive Era laid the groundwork for the expansion of the social welfare state in the 20th Century.

14.24 | *The Great Depression*

Dorothea Lange. 1936. "Migrant Mother"

In the 19th Century economic downturns were aptly called "panics" because they caused people rush to withdraw their money from banks, and when banks could not meet the demands of such runs on banks, panic ensued. The 1920s were called the Roaring Twenties because of the good economic times. The good times ended with a stock market crash in late October of 1929. A worldwide economic downturn in the 1930s was called the Great Depression. The Great Depression changed the relationship between government and the economy in the U.S. and elsewhere. The severe economic downturn depression caused high unemployment, bank and factory closings, bankruptcies, and a collapse of farm prices. The American people did not merely accept these hardships as part of the normal boom-and-bust business cycle. They expected government to do something about the shortage of jobs, food, and shelter and the government responded to public opinion with a major change in economic policy.

Nineteenth Century economic policy promoted economic development: the settling of the frontier; the expansion of the railroads; the development of manufacturing and oil industries; and the promotion of exports. Economic policy encouraged and rewarded entrepreneurial risk-taking more than protecting individuals from the economic insecurity of the business cycle, youth, old age, or infirmity. The New Deal policies of the Roosevelt administration (1933-1945) emphasized income security by providing disability benefits, unemployment insurance, and retirement benefits. Today these programs are collectively referred to as the **social welfare state**.

14.25 | *Ideology and the Role of Government in the Economy*

The Great Depression also challenged the prevailing laissez faire economic theory, which held that the government should not intervene in the marketplace because market competition will naturally provide order, stability, and prosperity. An ideology is a set of beliefs. One of those beliefs is about the government's role in the economy. The following describes four economic theories about the size and role of government in economic affairs.

Government and the Economy

Size	Small	Medium	Large
Theorist	Adam Smith	John Maynard Keynes	Karl Marx
Type of economic system	Free Market Model (Laissez faire)	Mixed Economy Regulated and Subsidized	Managed Controlled Government Model

Adam Smith's *The Wealth of Nations* (1776) is considered the most important early modern work describing a market alternative to the prevailing economic theory of mercantilism. Mercantilism is an economic theory that the government should direct, manage, and license economic activity for the good of the nation. The British Empire was built by mercantilist policies. The British government licensed economic activity in the American colonies for the good of the empire. Mercantilism is a statist theory because it relies heavily on government management of economic activity. Adam Smith was a revolutionary thinker because he challenged the prevailing wisdom of the day that government management of economic activity was essential to maintaining good social order, political stability, and economic prosperity. Mercantilism assumed that the government created order. In *The Wealth of Nations* Smith argued that the free market, while appearing chaotic and unrestrained, is actually guided by an invisible hand to produce the right amount and variety of goods. A "natural price" for a product is set by the following marketplace dynamics: A product shortage will increase the price, thereby stimulating more production; overproduction will decrease price, thereby causing less production until equilibrium is reached.

Smith assumed that humans were by nature self-interested. But he did not think that government power was the best way to control people. He believed that individual selfishness and greed were checked and balanced by other self-interested individuals. Competition, not government control, kept individuals in check and coincidentally benefited society as a whole. In this respect, Smith made selfishness an economic virtue the way that James Madison made selfishness a political virtue. According to Smith,

> It is not from the benevolence of the butcher, the brewer, or the baker that we expect our dinner, but from their regard to their own interest. We address ourselves, not to their humanity but to their self-love, and never talk to them of our own necessities but of their advantages. [As every individual strives to use his capital and his labor to greatest advantage] he "neither intends to promote the public interest, nor knows how much he is promoting it….[H]e intends only his own gain, and he is in this, as in many other cases, led by an invisible hand to promote an end which was no part of his intention…. By pursuing his own interest he frequently promotes that of society more effectually than when he really intends to promote it. I have never known much good done by those who affected to trade for the public good. It is an affectation, indeed, not very common among merchants, and very few words need by employed in dissuading them from it.[1]

Adam Smith (1723-1790) laissez faire theory challenged mercantilism which was the prevailing economic theory of the 18th Century. John Maynard Keynes was a British political economist who challenged laissez faire theory in the first half of the 20th

Century. In *The General Theory of Employment, Interest and Money* (1936), Keynes argued that governments should use fiscal policy (the taxing and spending powers embodied in the budget) to achieve economic stability and prosperity. His theories influenced President Franklin Delano Roosevelt's New Deal programs that used fiscal policy to end the Great Depression of the 1930s and Lyndon Johnson's Great Society programs in the 1960s. John Maynard Keynes lent his name to Keynesian economic theory which assumes that the government can and should intervene in the economy to 1) regulate the extremes of the boom-and-bust business cycle; and 2) provide economic stability.

The belief that Keynesian economic theory implemented during the New Deal helped the country out of the 1930s Depression made <u>Keynesian economics</u> the new prevailing theory of government and the economy.

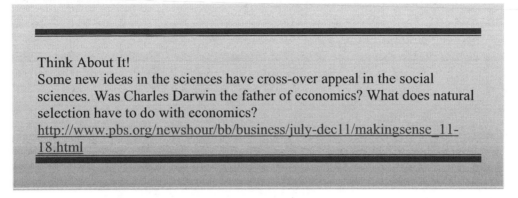

Think About It!
Some new ideas in the sciences have cross-over appeal in the social sciences. Was Charles Darwin the father of economics? What does natural selection have to do with economics?
<u>http://www.pbs.org/newshour/bb/business/july-dec11/makingsense_11-18.html</u>

14.3 | The Great Recession

The severe economic downturn that began in late 2007 was initially considered just another stage in the regular business cycle of expansion and contraction. The boom and bust business cycle is a familiar economic experience. Figure 14 below illustrates the business cycle with specific economic downturns noted, most notably the Great Depression, a severe and long-lasting economic downturn, and the Great Recession. The Great Recession officially ended with a return to economic growth. But the rate of growth has remained comparatively low, job creation has lagged behind other recoveries, and wages have remained stagnant. The lingering bad economic times suggest that the Great Recession was not part of the normal business cycle of expansion and contraction but rather an indication of a broader, structural change in the economy.

Figure 14.3
The Business Cycle (of Expansion, or Booms, and Contraction, or Busts)

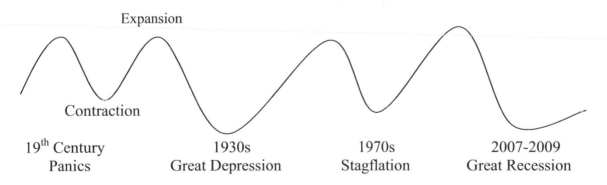

14.31 | *What's In a Name?*
What is a recession, and how is it different than a depression? And what is so great about the Great Depression and the Great Recession? In the 19th Century, financial crises were called "panics" because they often included a run on bank deposits. After the Great

Depression, economic downturns were called recessions partly because the word recession did not recall the bad memories of the 1930s. Government officials are not encouraged to use the word recession either because it reminds voters of bad economic times. In 1978 President Carter's economic advisor Alfred Kahn was chided by the administration for warning that efforts to fight inflation were likely to produce a recession. President Carter did not want one of his leading economic advisors talking about a looming recession during a reelection campaign. So when Kahn spoke publicly about the likelihood that fighting inflation would cause a recession, he simply substituted the word *banana* for the word *recession*. He warned, "We're in danger of having the worst banana in 45 years."[3]

The organization that officially designates economic conditions a recession is the National Bureau of Economic Research. The National Bureau of Economic Research (NBER) defines a recession as a "significant decline in economic activity spread across the economy, normally visible in real GDP, real income, employment, industrial production, and wholesale-retail sales." The NBER's Business Cycle Dating Committee maintains a chronology of the U.S. business cycle that identifies the dates of peaks and troughs that frame economic recession or expansion. The period from a peak to a trough is a recession and the period from a trough to a peak is an expansion. According to the chronology, the most recent peak occurred in March 2001, ending a record-long expansion that began in 1991. The most recent trough occurred in November 2001, inaugurating an expansion. A recession begins just after the economy reaches a peak of activity and ends as the economy reaches its trough. Between trough and peak, the economy is in an expansion. Expansion is the normal state of the economy. Most recessions are brief and they have been rare in recent decades. The NBER reported that the Great Recession officially started in December 2007 and ended in June 2009.

14.32 | *A Structural Change in the Economy?*

The depth and length of the economic downturn made economists and political officials wonder whether the downturn was not merely the normal business cycle but rather a structural change in the U.S. economy. A structural change is a major economic transformation similar to the Industrial Revolution, which brought about the change from an agrarian to an industrial economy, and then the post-industrial transformation from a manufacturing economy to an information- and service-economy. Figure 15 (above) leaves the direction of economic expansion and the shape of the next business cycle open because of uncertainty about whether the end of Great Recession will bring a return to the regular business cycle or whether the Great Recession marked a structural change in the economy.

To date, the economic recovery has produced disappointing job creation numbers and unemployment remains high by historical standards. One reason why the economic recovery has not produced more jobs is technology and the increased economic productivity it brings. In "The Great Stagnation: Why Hasn't Recent Technology Created More Jobs?" economists explain why technology can cause unemployment. The managing director of a U.S. manufacturing company, Vista Technologies, bluntly explained why his company and other companies prefer to buy equipment rather than hire employees.[4] He dreaded the hiring process: sifting through poorly written resumes;

interviewing applicants; paying for drug testing and mandated safety programs; and training new employees. Furthermore, during the period after the Great Recession the cost of capital became *relatively* much cheaper than the cost of labor because the federal government adopted monetary policy that kept interests rate (the cost of money) at historically low levels. The increase in labor costs was not due to wage increases as much as increased costs of employee benefits, mainly health care costs. One common business strategy to control costs is to purchase equipment and automate production rather than to hire new employees. This is why the comparatively lower cost of capital has had a negative effect on job creation. The negative impact is compounded by the fact that much of the equipment has been purchased from foreign manufacturers. Capital costs are also lower than labor costs because public policies such as accelerated capital depreciation provide tax breaks for capital investments.

There are two reasons why manufacturing no longer produces the jobs that it once did for: globalization and technology. Globalization has meant that U.S. manufacturing jobs have been sent abroad to low wage countries—first to Japan and more recently to China and India and other regions of the world. Technology has meant the increased use of computer-aided industrial production. Modern factories use robotics rather than more workers to increase production. The elimination of jobs and the resulting downward pressure on wages has had a significant impact on "the American dream" of upward mobility. In "Making It in America," Adam Davidson describes the "remnant workforce, the smaller workforce remaining in manufacturing in the U.S. He argues that this remnant workforce must be highly trained. During much of the 20th century, "simultaneous technological improvements in both agriculture and industry happened to create conditions that were favorable for people with less skill." The development of mass production "allowed low-skilled farmers to move to the city" and get jobs in highly productive factories. The change from an agricultural to an industrial economy adversely affected "the highly skilled craftsperson." By contrast, the loss of manufacturing jobs is ending one of the ways that low-skilled workers could join the middle class.[5]

14.33 | *Why the U.S. Business Cycle is So Closely Related to the Electoral Cycles*

The Great Recession had an immediate impact on politics and government. The initial reaction was a massive government bailout of businesses. The bailouts were followed by fiscal and monetary policies that were intended to stimulate the economy. One result of these economic policies was massive government deficits. The initial political reaction to the economic crisis and the massive increases in deficit spending was voter dissatisfaction. Barack Obama (Democrat) won the 2008 presidential election promising economic change. Voter anxiety about the economy resulted in big Republican gains in the 2010 mid-term and state elections—Republicans gained 69 seats in Congress. The political lesson of the Great Recession is that voters hold the government accountable for economic conditions. The public expects the national government to take decisive action in times of economic crisis to stabilize the economy.

Think about it!

"I want to have as few people touching our products as possible. Everything should be as automated as it can be. We just can't afford to compete with countries like China on labor costs..."

Dan Mishak, Managing Director, Vista Technologies

The political impact of economic downturns is greater in the U.S. than in other western democracies because the U.S. has a smaller social welfare safety net. In the U.S., the loss of a job means the loss of income. The problem of job and income loss is compounded by the fact that the U.S. has a system of health care insurance that is based on employment. The loss of a job often means the loss of health care insurance. As a result, unemployment greatly decreases income security in the U.S. This economic insecurity has made the U.S. political system very sensitive to the unemployment rate.

Furthermore, two major parts of the social welfare system, Social Security and Medicare, are not even designed to support unemployed young people. They provide income security primarily for the elderly. These aspects of the U.S. social welfare safety net explain why high rates of long-term unemployment for young people present such a serious economic and political challenge.

One additional factor strengthening the link between the business and political cycles is the fact that the U.S. economy is a consumer economy. Around two-thirds of the gross domestic product is consumer spending. The decades prior to the Great Recession were marked by high rates of individual consumption, high rates of debt, and low rates of savings. Economic downturns have a direct impact on personal income, thereby reinforcing downturns rather than working as a countervailing force. The belief that the Great Recession is part of a long-term structural change in the U.S. economy, and not merely yet another business cycle, has stimulated interest in changing economic policy to encourage production and saving rather than consumption. In order to be successful, a pro-production economic policy will have to change economic behavior. One strategy for increasing savings rates is increasing financial literacy. Even **Sesame Street** is being used to teach children (and adults) about financial literacy and the importance of delaying gratification in order to increase savings rates.

> "Are U.S. Wages Enough to Live On?"
> http://www.pbs.org/newshour/rundown/2012/05/are-us-wages-enough-to-live-on.html

14.4 | A Regular Cycle of Economic Crises?

The Great Recession began in the financial services sector of the economy. It had an immediate impact on government and politics. The passage of the Troubled Asset Recovery Program and the Emergency Economic Stabilization Act of 2008 are evidence of the close relationship between economics and politics. Economic problems tend to become political problems, and severe economic problems become major political problems. In the latter part of the 19th Century, economic downturns created populist and nativist reactions that included hostility toward immigrants, Catholics, Jews, and Blacks. The worldwide economic downturn in the early 1930s resulted in totalitarian governments in Germany, Japan, and Italy. In the 1970s the U.S. suffered from two economic problems that do not usually occur together: inflation and low growth. Inflation usually results from high growth, not low growth. The unusual combination of a stagnant economy and high inflation was caused by among other things an oil embargo that greatly increased energy costs and decreased economic growth. A new term, stagflation, was coined to describe the unusual economic conditions.

The economic problems of the 1970s decreased public confidence in American government and private sector institutions. The Great Recession produced a similar decrease in public confidence in institutions. But it has also had a significant impact on generational wellbeing, class, and social status. It has created a unique group: the formerly middle class. These are people who achieved middle-class status at the tail end of the long economic boom, and then lost it when they became the first ones to drop out of the middle class because they were the last ones whose upward mobility allowed them to join the middle class. This is politically significant because downward mobility conflicts with the American belief in **upward mobility**. Upward mobility is almost considered an American birthright, part of the American dream: if you have ability and work hard then you will prosper. **Downward mobility** includes career setbacks, lifestyle setbacks, housing setbacks, and social capital reversals. David Brooks, a conservative commentator, concluded that the "loss of a social identity, the loss of the status symbols that suggest an elevated place in the social order will likely produce alienation and a political response. If you want to know where the next big social movements will come from, I'd say the formerly middle class."[6]

The Great Recession has renewed questions about why the U.S. experiences repeated cycles of crises in the financial sector of the economy that require government bailouts. In the 1980s, the Savings and Loan industry required a government bailout. A dot-com bubble in the high-tech sector burst in 2000. The Great Recession was caused by, among other factors, banking and investment practices that included risky behavior, corruption, scandals, and fraud. It produced emergency legislation such as the Troubled Asset Relief Program whose government bailout provisions were intended to avoid a financial meltdown. This pattern of business crises followed by government bailouts is not the normal working of the marketplace where the rise and fall of businesses is considered natural.

Why do corporate executives engage in risky or bad business practices that jeopardize their company and the economy? The first answer that comes to mind is that even smart people make some mistakes. But this individual-level explanation overlooks organization-level explanations. The first organizational explanation is that some decision makers are insulated from the adverse consequences of their bad decisions. The Federal Deposit Insurance Corporation (the FDIC) is a federal program that guarantees bank deposits in savings accounts. A second organizational explanation is even more important in explaining risky corporate behavior particularly in the financial services sector of the economy: the separation of ownership and management in modern corporations. In the good old days of small business, the people who owned a business were the people who actually ran it. They were risking their money. The typical corporation is run by managers rather than owners. The managers of financial services companies are not using their own money. They are playing with (or risking) other people's money (investors). People in the financial services sector of the economy are more likely to engage in riskier behavior. This is not a new problem. It is an organizational problem that was recognized as early as 1932 in Adolf Berle's *The Modern Corporation and Private Property*. It is one of the reasons why the government provides insurance for bank deposits through the Federal Deposit Insurance Corporation (FDIC).

A second explanation is "the moral hazard." The moral hazard refers to a situation where a decision maker does not assume the costs or responsibilities of a decision and is therefore likely to make riskier decisions or more decisions than they would make if they knew that they would be responsible for their bad decisions. The fact that the FDIC insures bank deposits, and the fact that some companies are considered too big to be allowed to fail, means that the government is protecting bankers or other business leaders from the negative consequences of their risky or bad decisions. This is the moral hazard. The moral hazard is one explanation for the modern era pattern of financial crises and bailouts.

Think About It!

Does the Moral Hazard explain why bankers become "banksters?" "Banksters" is the title of an Economist article (July 7, 2012) about British bankers illegally manipulating an important interest rate called the LIBOR (London Interbank offer rate).
http://www.economist.com/node/21558260

Are the recurring financial crises evidence of recidivism?

Massachusetts Institute of Technology Finance Professor Andrew Lo discusses the recurring cycles of financial crises and government bailouts in the Public Broadcasting System story, "Evaluating and Preventing a Massive Financial Crisis."

14.41 | *Follow the Money*

When the *Washington Post* reporters Bob Woodward and Carl Bernstein were investigating the Watergate scandal in the early 1970s, they were advised by a secret source to "follow the money." Money often leaves an interesting trail. In 2008, New York State Governor Eliot Spitzer, an ambitious Democrat with a promising national career, unexpectedly resigned his office.

The media focused on the scandal angle of a high-profile political figure paying a great deal of money to high-priced prostitutes. The rest of the story was also interesting because it exposed to the general public how extensively the government monitors financial transactions. The government used sophisticated computer software that tracks

almost all financial transactions to discover that Spitzer paid large sums of money to high-priced prostitutes. Large cash transactions are easy to spot because banks are required to report transactions over $10,000. Computer software also tracks small financial transactions in order to detect pattern of suspicious activity.[7] The ability of the private sector and the government to track almost all financial transactions for good or ill raises serious questions about the use of such information in an age where information is power.

14.5 | Government's Economic Tool Box: Fiscal Policy

Fiscal policy is the government's use of taxing and spending powers to achieve policy goals. Fiscal policy is reflected in the budget. A budget is a political document because politics can be defined as "the authoritative allocation of scarce resources." The budget is where you see policy priorities. Senator and later Vice-president Joe Biden often people of his father's saying: "Don't *tell* me what you value. *Show* me what your budget is and I'll tell you what your values are." The federal government's fiscal policy is reflected in the federal government's annual budget for the fiscal year, which begins October 1st. A state's fiscal policy is reflected in the state's budget.

14.51 | *Who Makes Fiscal Policy?*

Congress and the president make fiscal policy. Until the early years of the 20th Century, Congress exerted almost complete control over fiscal policy because it has the power to tax and to spend. Congress passed the annual federal budget. Today the president plays an extremely important role in making fiscal policy. For instance, the president begins the annual budget process by introducing *the administration's* budget in Congress. Congress then holds committee hearings on the various budget proposals, debates the various provisions of the administration's budget priorities, assesses the administration's taxing and spending policies, and then adjusts the administration's priorities to reflect congressional priorities. Congress then enacts the federal budget for the fiscal year.

The politics of the budget includes debates about literally thousands of programs for law enforcement, social security, education, health care, national security and trade policy. But the most politically salient debates about the budget and fiscal policy center on the budget deficit. Deficit spending occurs when government spending exceeds revenue in a fiscal year and the year ends with red ink. If the government spends more than it taxes, the fiscal year ends with a budget deficit. The national debt is the cumulative budget deficits.

14.52 | *Budget Deficits*

Budget deficits are not usually accidents, mistakes, bad mathematics, or the result of incompetent accountants or emergencies. The red ink of budget deficit (spending more than tax revenue in a fiscal year) is usually intentional. Fiscal policy is the use of the taxing and spending policies to achieve public policy goals. Keynes believed that government should use fiscal policy to manage the business cycle, to moderate the extremes of expansion and contraction, to avoid the boom (the rapid economic expansion that leads to inflation) and bust (recession or depression). The term Keynesian economics refers to the government using taxing and spending policies to manage the economy. The logic of using fiscal policy to moderate the business cycle and achieve economic stability is fairly simple. During a time of rapid economic growth (a boom period), the government's fiscal policy could increase taxes and/or cut government spending. Increasing taxes and decreasing spending remove money from the economy, thereby slowing economic growth. It has a "deflationary" effect on the economy. During a downturn in the business cycle fiscal policy could decrease taxes and/or increase government spending. Cutting taxes and increasing spending puts more money into the economy, thereby stimulating economic growth. Deficit spending has an inflationary effect on the economy; austerity budgets have a recessionary effect on the economy. Fiscal policy is intended to have a counter-cyclical effect on the business cycle.

> The Budget Deficit and the National Debt
> http://www.pbs.org/newshour/bb/business/july-dec12/makingsense_10-25.html

14.53 | *Taxes*

Taxes are used for a variety of purposes: to raise money; to subsidize behavior or goals; to regulate behavior; to redistribute resources.

- **Raise Money**. The main purpose of taxing is to raise money to pay for the things that the government does: gas taxes provide money to build roads and bridges; real estate taxes provide money for schools; and income taxes provide money for fighting crime, fighting fires, and for national security.
- **Subsidize.** The government's power to tax is also used to *subsidize* behavior that the government wants to encourage or goals that it promotes. Tax policy can subsidize marriage, having and raising children, religious and charitable contributions, or conservation of national resources by promoting green energy sources. Taxes for these purposes are primarily to subsidize behaviors rather than to raise money.
- **Regulate**. The government also uses taxes to discourage or regulate behavior that it wants to discourage. The term "sin" tax refers to using tax policy to decrease smoking or gambling or drinking alcohol. Carbon emission taxes are intended to reduce air pollution.
- **Redistribution**. Tax policy is also used to redistribute wealth from some individuals or groups to others. Taxes can be used to redistribute income or wealth from richer persons to poorer persons, from younger individuals to older individuals, from wealthier states or regions of the country to poorer states or regions. Tax money used for social welfare purposes is redistributive.

Good tax policy, like beauty, is in the eye of the beholder. Economists generally prefer taxes that raise money to fund government programs with minimum disruption of market forces. The Tax Foundation is an organization that advocates for what it considers the principles of good tax policy: fairness; efficiency; and clarity. Efficiency and clarity are easier to measure than fairness because fairness, like beauty, is in the eye of the beholder. For example, in the U.S. system of federalism, federal tax revenues are taken from some (wealthier) states and redistributed to other (poorer) states based on a concept of fairness. Some states are net contributors and others are net benefactors of federal tax policies. One of the ironies of the pattern of distribution of federal tax policies is that the Red states tend to be benefactors, and Blue states tend to be contributors. Red states benefit, while Blue states pay. At an individual level, taxing and spending policies are also intended to affect behavior, to encourage certain behaviors by subsidizing them and discouraging others by taxing them. What do behavioral economists say about such efforts?

> What is behavioral economics and what do behavioral economists
> know about politics?
> http://www.npr.org/templates/story/story.php?storyId=12779692
> http://www.npr.org/templates/story/story.php?storyId=124361795
> http://www.econlib.org/library/Enc/BehavioralEconomics.html

14.54 | The Federal Budget Process

Congress and the president make fiscal policy. The federal budget process is a long and complicated process whose participants include Congress (including committees), the president (including various executive agencies, but most notably The Office of Management and Budget). The Center on Budget Priorities provides a good description of the three main stages of the federal budget process: 1) the Office of Management and Budget submits the administration's proposed budget to Congress; 2) Congress adopts a budget resolution; and 3) reconciliation of the budget resolution. The process is described in greater detail in the two boxes below:

> The Federal Budget Process
> As Described By
>
> The Office of Management and Budget:
> http://www.whitehouse.gov/omb/budget
>
> The Center on Budget Priorities:
> http://www.cbpp.org/cms/?fa=view&id=155

The Federal Budget: Timelines and Participants

Early fall

The executive departments and agencies send initial budget requests to the Office of Management and Budget (OMB).

November/December/January

The OMB reviews the initial requests, modifies them, and sends them back to the agencies. The OMB hears agency appeals. The OMB resolves appeals and assembles the final budget request.

February/March

The president submits the budget request to Congress. Administration and agency officials testify in support of the budget request before the House and Senate appropriations subcommittees (House and Senate). Public witnesses also participate in the hearings.

May

The House and Senate adopt budget resolutions prepared by the Budget Committees. The House and Senate Appropriations Committees make 302(b) allocations. "302(b) is the section of federal law that describes how each appropriations committees divides the overall level of discretionary spending provided in the Budget Resolution among its thirteen subcommittees.

June

The House Appropriations Subcommittees prepare appropriations bills and the Senate Appropriations Subcommittees revise them.

July-August

The House passes spending bills and the Senate passes revised spending bills.

September

Conference committees resolve differences between the House and Senate bills and agree on final versions of spending bills. The president signs or vetoes final bills.

October 1

The start of the fiscal year. If Congress has not passed all the appropriations bills, it passes continuing resolutions to maintain funding for any agencies whose funding has not been passed by the beginning of the fiscal year.

14.6 | The Government's Tool Box: Monetary Policy

Monetary policy is defined as using the money supply to achieve economic goals such as controlling inflation and maintaining employment. The money supply is the amount of money in private hands. Increasing or decreasing the money supply affects the rate of inflation and the amount economic activity. Monetarists argue that monetary policy, not fiscal policy is the key to controlling economic activity. Monetary policy is based on the assumption that the price of money, which is another way of saying the interest rate, is the key to economic activity. The price of money is another term for interest rates. Monetarists think that increasing the cost of money is likely to decrease economic activity, and decreasing the cost of money is likely to increase economic activity. Consequently, monetarists advise increasing interest rates during boom times in order to prevent or control inflation, and decreasing interest rates in bust times to prevent a recession or to get out of one.

The <u>Federal Reserve Board</u> has primary control over monetary policy. The Fed is an independent agency in the sense that Congress and the president have limited control over it because the members of The Fed are appointed for lengthy terms of office that do not coincide with presidential or congressional election cycles. This insulates The Fed from political, or more accurately, partisan control. The Federal Reserve Board (of Governors) consists of seven members who are appointed for 14-year terms. It includes an Open Market Committee, which consists of 12 Members (seven Governors and the heads of five regional banks.

The Fed is authorized to regulate banks and to set monetary policy. It is responsible for using monetary policy to achieve two economic objectives: Price Stability (controlling inflation) and Maximum Employment. Beginning in the fall of 2007, uncertainty in the financial markets created concern that the problems caused by sub-prime mortgage practices would turn into a full-blown nationwide or even global panic. Critics called the Troubled Asset Recovery Program (TARP) the Toxic Asset Recovery Program because the government was authorized to buy "troubled" financial assets. The Federal Reserve Board aggressively intervened in the capital markets in order bring about a measure of stability. The conservative Ben Stein reacted to the Fed's decisive action by saying, "God Bless the Fed." The sense of relief that the Chair of the Federal Reserve Board acted decisively to avert a collapse of the financial system, and perhaps a broader economic collapse, is an indication of the importance of The Fed's role in the U.S. economic system. Stein also used an interesting metaphor to explain why he supported the government's financial rescue package. Faced with the "terrifying prospect" of an industrial economy that was not working well, "we must turn to the federal government for relief. The private sector is the patient, not the doctor."[8]

Who is EDGAR, and what is he accusing me of?

"God Bless the Fed" Ben Stein

Information about how the government measures the rate of inflation/cost of living is provided in "Why Your Salary May be Affected by the Price of Lettuce," http://www.npr.org/blogs/money/2010/11/11/131251848/why-your-salary-may-be-affected-by-the-price-of-lettuce

14.61 | *The Undemocratic Fed*

One of the basic democratic principles is that policymakers should be elected representatives of the people. In democracies, elections choose to policymakers and hold them accountable. But The Fed is a policymaking body whose members are appointed for long terms. In this respect, The Fed is an undemocratic institution. In fact, supporters of The Fed defend it *because it is not political*. The Fed is designed to insulate economics from partisan politics. Although the Fed is an independent agency with some insulation from direct political control, it is a mistake to think of The Fed as an apolitical institution. Its views of what to do about inflation and unemployment are very political. The Fed makes choices about how much inflation is too much and how much unemployment is acceptable. This is how The Fed makes policy. The members of The Fed are bankers who bring a banking perspective to monetary policy. The Fed has been controversial since its creation. Libertarian Representative Ron Paul (Republican-Texas) is a vocal critic of The Fed. Does he make good points about its role in a democracy?

Think about it!
Is The Fed guilty of the charges made against it by critics such as Ron Paul: http://www.ronpaul.com/legislation/audit-the-federal-reserve-hr-1207/

14.7 | Poor Economic Vision?

The Great Recession caught most people by surprise even though the boom and bust of the business cycle was very familiar. This raises an interesting question. Why were some of the best and brightest minds working in the financial sector of the economy so shortsighted that they failed to foresee the problem that their actions were causing? There are at least three reasons for poor economic vision (or myopia): self-interest; ideology; and over-confidence.

14.71 | *Self-interest*

The first reason is **self-interest**. The financial services industry has an incentives structure that rewards risk-taking behavior. If an industry rewards making risky loans and selling high-risk financial products because they bring higher profits than safer loans and investments, then it is rational for people who work in the financial services to engage in such riskier rather than safer economic behavior.

14.72 | *Ideology*

A second reason is **ideology**. An ideology is a set of beliefs about how the world works. The economic beliefs are about how the economic world works. But what if the beliefs are mistaken? During the economic boom times of the late 1980s and 1990s Alan Greenspan, who was the Chair of the Federal Reserve Board from 1987 until 2006, was lionized as a great man with a deep understanding of how the financial (and broader economic) system worked. Then the Great Recession hit! Greenspan was forced to acknowledge that there were fundamental flaws in his ideological model of how the economic world worked.

Alan Greenspan's Confession

http://www.pbs.org/newshour/bb/business/july-dec08/crisishearing_10-23.html

One flaw is the *way* the financial services sector was de-regulated: bankers were allowed to make riskier investments but the government kept in place government protections against depositors losing money. Business deregulation is considered an element of conservative and Republican economic policy, but Democratic President Carter began the federal trend toward deregulation by deregulating the airlines and natural gas industries. Then in 1980 Monetary Control Act eliminated regulations of interest rates and usury laws, and the 1982 Garn-St. Germain Depository Institutions Act allowed Savings and Loan Institutions, which had historically been in the safe business of home loans, to get into riskier and therefore sometimes more profitable financial dealings. And in 1999, President Clinton further deregulated banking by signing the Financial Services Modernization Act, which repealed Depression Era limits on banking.

The problem is that the government deregulated risk-taking while continuing to subsidize financial security. For example, bank deposits are insured against loss in order to maintain public confidence in the banking system. In 1982, the Garn-St. Germain Depository Institutions Act deregulated savings and loan banks. Prior to 1982, these "thrift" banks were allowed to make residential (home) loans but not riskier commercial loans. They were also prohibited from using customer deposits to invest in the stock market. The savings and loans banks lobbied congress to change the law to allow them to use deposits for riskier and generally more profitable, investments. The ensuing savings and loan crisis of the 1980s required a massive government bailout to protect depositors from losing their money.

Business deregulation expanded because conservatives and liberals came to support business deregulation but for very different reasons. Conservatives supported deregulation because they thought government regulation was ineffective and counterproductive and limited growth. Liberals supported deregulation because they thought government regulators were actually serving powerful corporate interests rather than protecting consumers or the environment.

The **Capture Theory** explains why regulators do not do what they were created to do. According to the capture theory, government regulators are created to regulate an industry but they eventually are captured by the interest that they were created to regulate. This happens because regulators work with the regulated and eventually come to identify with them and the industry. It is a variation on the Stockholm Syndrome where hostages come to identify with their captors. The capture theory often creates a revolving door: government regulators quit their jobs to go to work in the industry they regulated. In effect, they change teams. Former airlines regulators go to work for the airlines industry. Former Internal Revenue Service officials go to work for tax and accounting firms. Goldman Sachs was called "Government Sachs" because so many former and future government officials worked for it. The capture theory and the revolving door explain why the Securities and Exchange Commission, the Commodities Futures Trading Commission, and even the Fed grew so close to the financial services sector that they were supposed to be regulating that they seemed to be representing Wall Street interests rather than protecting the public interest by regulating the industry. And then the government bailed out the industry when things went bad.

Since the 1980s Savings and Loan crisis the financial services industry developed innovative products such as securitized loans. Financial engineering and marketing offered high rates of return on financial products that were sold as low risk investments but which were actually very risky. Government bailouts once again prevented financial losses. But once the immediate crisis passed, and the collapse of the financial system was averted, Wall Street once again went back to business as usual. Paul Volcker, the former chair of The Fed, believes that financial regulation is necessary because of "Wall Street's recidivist tendencies." According to Volcker, the lesson of the history of financial crises is that bankers will use their positions to line their pockets.[9]

14.73 | Over-confidence

A third reason for the cycles of economic crises is over-confidence. Modern economists and government officials assumed that the development of knowledge of how markets and economies worked had become so advanced that technical expertise could be applied to manage the business cycle and stabilize economies. This created the belief that severe economic downturns like the Great Depression were a thing of the past. In hindsight, over-confidence in the theories of individual rationality and market rationality blinded observers to the risks of assuming markets were self-correcting.[10]

Ben Bernanke

The three main economic policy architects of the Bush administration's response to the Great Recession were the Secretary of the Treasury (Hank Paulson), the Chair of the Federal Reserve Board (Ben Bernanke), and Timothy Geithner (President of the New York Federal Reserve Bank). This three functioned as an economic SWAT team or first responders who formulated and coordinated the fiscal policy (i.e., bank bailout and troubled asset relief program) and the monetary policy (e.g., lowering interest rates) response to the financial crisis. The fact that President Obama, a Democrat, basically continued the economic policies of President Bush, a Republican, was not surprising because the Obama administration's response to the Great Recession was formulated by Ben Bernanke, the Chair of the Federal Reserve Board, and Timothy Geithner, the Secretary of the Treasury. Bernanke's and Geithner's backgrounds provide insights into their ideas about what the government should do when facing a financial crisis.

Bernanke is an economist whose research expertise is the Great Depression of the 1930s. His study led him to conclude that the Depression was prolonged and worsened by the government's weak and inconsistent response to the economic crisis. The lesson he learned from the history of the Depression is that government must act swiftly, decisively, and with greater rather than lesser force when facing a major economic crisis. He brought this background to the Bush administration's policy discussions of how to respond to the financial crisis.

Timothy Geithner

Geithner's public service began in 1988 as a civil servant in the Treasury Department. These were economic boom times in the United States. A long Bull Market made Wall Street and the Department of the Treasury very influential power centers for federal economic policy. Their ideas seemed to work. But Geithner's "formative experience was in figuring out how to contain the series of upheavals that swept the international financial community in the 1990s, from Japan to Mexico to Thailand to Indonesia to Russia, and threatened the boom."[11] These international financial crises revealed a new and unexpected vulnerability in the global financial system: one country's financial problems could quickly affect (or infect) countries halfway around the world. Globalism increased economic interactions, which could increase economic efficiency and prosperity, but it also made a country vulnerable to "infections" from abroad. Geithner's policy experience included defending "the long boom," the extended period of economic growth in the U.S., against foreign financial threats. His experience made him an institutionalist—an economist who thinks that government and private sector institutions (non-government organizations or NGOs) play important roles in preventing financial meltdowns.

Geithner believed that a massive government response to the financial crisis was necessary. It was supposed to operate like an economic SWAT team that used monetary policy, fiscal policy, and private money to recapitalize the financial markets in order to promote bank lending. Geithner came to believe in the need for a massive response to the economic crisis because of the lesson he learned when Japan's real estate bubble burst in the early 1990s. He believed that the government's wrong response to the economic crisis produced a "lost decade" of economic growth. He did not want that to happen in the U.S. As a professional student of international economic crises, particularly financial crises, Geithner made an interesting observation about what lessons are to be learned from crises: "You learn much more about a country when things fall apart. When the tide recedes, you get to see all the stuff it leaves behind." One of the conclusions to be drawn from the experience of the various international financial crises that have occurred during the era of globalization is that *none* of the governments—whether in Japan or Mexico or Indonesia or the U.S.—treated the problem as an economic problem that had nothing to do with government and politics.

14.8 | Economic Issues

14.81 | *Globalization*

During the latter years of the 20th Century and the early years of the 21st Century, a central element of the federal government's economic policy was the promotion of international trade. With the end of the Cold War, international trade became an increasingly important part of U.S. foreign policy. The General Agreement on Tariffs and Trade (known as GATT) was created to promote international trade by reducing tariffs. It was in effect from 1949 until 1993. GATT was replaced by the World Trade Organization in 1995. The WTO was created to supervise and liberalize international trade. It includes a framework for negotiating and formalizing trade agreements and a framework for resolving trade disputes. More than 150 countries are currently members of the WTO. The U.S. political and economic systems are still adjusting to the opportunities and challenges of globalization in part because the interrelated economies diminish domestic American control over economic conditions.

Globalization and the development of international trade systems have increased economic uniformity in international trade, but countries still have unique economic, political, and social systems that affect economic interactions. The development of a world economy is still facing "fault lines" or domestic pressures that resist uniformity. These include income and wealth inequality, trade imbalances, and financial systems with very different rules. For example, the financial systems in some countries emphasize formal rules and regulations while others operate with informal relationships. These differences can make it difficult to understand the rules of the international trade game. In *Fault Lines: How Hidden Fractures Still Threaten the World Economy*, Raghuram G. Rajan describes how different sets of national and international rules and incentive structures are now rubbing against one another in ways that made the Great Recession, which he describes as an "economic earthquake," a likely economic disaster. Even within the U.S., the "incentive structure" in the financial services sector effectively reduced the price of taking risks by providing very large financial rewards for profits.[12]

14.82 | *Global Economic Competitiveness*

The increase in international business and trade has increased the attention paid to comparative economic data. One of the sources of information about how the U.S. compares to other countries is the Organization for Economic Cooperation and Development (OECD). The OECD provides basic information on how countries provide social and economic policies.

There have historically been tensions between U.S. domestic economic policy and its international trade policy. The U.S. political system, like the political systems in other countries, responds to domestic political pressures by passing laws that benefit domestic business interests and disadvantage foreign interests. The term economic protectionism describes policies that favor domestic business over foreign business, or favor in-state business over out-of-state business. One common type of economic protectionism is tariffs. A tariff is a tax on imports, goods that are brought into a country. Import taxes can start trade wars, where countries retaliate against one another by passing tariffs. One amusing trade war involved a tax that France levied on chickens that were grown in the U.S. and imported to France. The U.S. then retaliated against France by taxing certain motor vehicles that were imported to the U.S. Since then, however, the auto industry has become global, and car parts are imported and vehicles are assembled in so many countries that it is sometimes hard to tell whether a car in a domestic or import. An American car company, such as Ford, has extensive foreign manufacturing plants, and it can actually be hurt by laws that place tariffs on imported vehicles or parts.

Globalization has increased attention paid to what makes a country competitive in the global economy. Where does the U.S. rank in an index of competitiveness? And what criteria are used to measure competitiveness? The World Economic Forum creates an annual Global Competitiveness Report. The Report for 2010-2011 ranked the U.S. fourth among the nations of the world. The bailout of the American automobile manufacturers as part of the Troubled Asset Recovery Plan focused attention on the comparative costs of manufacture in the U.S. David Leonhardt's article "73 Dollars and Hour: Adding it Up," compares the cost of auto manufacturing in the U.S. with other countries. The differences in wage rates, benefits, and retirement are significant.[13]

Globalization has meant that each nation's economy is more closely tied to others. Western democracies share common problems with budget deficits and national debt. Big budget numbers prompt the question, "How big is big?" A comparative perspective on national debt and deficit helps put economic data in perspectives.

Think about it!
Would it be more efficient to have one world currency?
President Nixon and Bretton Woods:
http://www.pbs.org/newshour/rundown/2012/05/why-isnt-there-a-single-world-currency.html

---

14.83 | *Markets and Values*

Markets allocate scarce resources. The market model is a way to efficiently determine the price of valuables, but what about values?

14.83 | *Equality*

The U.S. is a democracy. Equality is a democratic value. But Americans have always accepted a great deal of economic inequality. Why? Americans accept inequality if it based on merit: a meritocracy (or natural aristocracy based on ability) is considered compatible with democracy; inequality based on privilege is not. And an economic system that produces inequality is not considered unjust or unfair if it provides for economic mobility so that people can work their way up the ladder. Economic equality and economic mobility have become very important terms in current political debates about economic policy. Have liberals and Democrats declared war on the rich? Have conservatives and Republicans declared war on the poor? The debates are prompted by absolute measures of poverty and relative measures of mobility. PEW Charitable Trust's Center on the States describes family mobility and its political significance for the American dream in the wake of the Great Recession. The data from the PEW research project on mobility are discussed in the National Public Radio story, "Moving on Up More Difficult in America."

Growing inequality is not just an issue that affects individuals. It is an issue that has an aggregate impact on the economy. At some point, inequality has a negative impact on an economy, society, and political system. The increasing inequality in the U.S. over the last four decades is now a matter of debate about economic policy. The high costs of inequality are examined in a Public Broadcasting System *Newshour* story "Inequality Hurts" (aired September 28, 2011). How much inequality is too much? One way to answer this question is to compare the U.S. with other countries. The Central Intelligence Agency produces a great deal of information about the countries of the world. One interesting index is a measure of equality. See the "Distribution of Family Income—the GINI Index." Where does the U.S. rank in terms of income equality? Is there a relationship between a country's distribution of income (that is, its equal or unequal distribution of income) and justice or the sense of fairness?

14.84 | *Morality*

Conservatives advocate both the market model and traditional values. Is the free market consistent with the preservation of traditional values? Markets are based on freedom of choice in selecting goods and services. Moral regulatory policy has traditionally limited freedom of choice in order to preserve and maintain moral values. The Heritage Foundation is a leading conservative think and do tank. It advocates both markets and morality by advocating the morality of markets.

14.85 | *Summary*

This chapter examined the relationship between economics and politics. It described the historical impacts that economics have had on politics, the two major components of economic policy (fiscal and monetary policy), and it examined whether economic power and political power, with specific reference to questions about inequality and perceptions of justice.

14.9 | Additional Resources

14.91 | *Internet Resources*

"Fear the Boom and Bust: A Hayek vs. Keynes Rap Anthem"
http://www.youtube.com/watch?v=d0nERTFo-Sk

The von Mises Institute presents the theoretical argument for minimal government involvement in the economy: http://mises.org/etexts/ecopol.asp

President Franklin Delano Roosevelt's March 12, 1933 "Fireside Chat on Banking." http://www.presidency.ucsb.edu/ws/index.php?pid=14540#axzz1NlGuPlqw

15.92 | *In the Library*

Adam Smith's *The Wealth of Nations* (1776)

KEY TERMS

The Industrial Revolution
Social welfare policies
Fiscal policy
Monetary Policy
The Business Cycle

Study Topics
1. Why are economics and politics related?
2. Define fiscal policy and monetary policy.
3. Is The Fed an undemocratic institution?
4. What is the business cycle?

---

[1] *Government versus Markets: The Changing Economic Role of the State* (2011). Cambridge: Cambridge University Press.
[2] Quoted in Tim Arango, "The Housing-Bubble Revolution," *The New York Times* (November 30, 2008): 5WK. http://www.nytimes.com/2008/11/30/weekinreview/30arango.html?scp=1&sq=Housing-bubble%20revolution&st=cse
[3] Quoted in "Diagnosing Depression," *The Economist* (December 30, 2008). http://www.economist.com/finance/displaystory.cfm?story_id=12852043
[4] Quoted in Catherine Rampell, "Companies Spend on Equipment, Not Workers," *The New York Times* (June 9, 2011). Accessed at http://www.nytimes.com/2011/06/10/business/10capital.html?_r=1&hp
[5] Adam Davidson, *The Atlantic*. January/February 2012. pp58-70.
[6] David Brooks. "The Formerly Middle Class." *The New York Times*. November 17, 2008. Accessed at http://www.nytimes.com/2008/11/18/opinion/18brooks.html?_r=1&hp

[7] For a good description of how monitoring occurs, listen to the following report on National Public Radio: http://www.npr.org/templates/story/story.php?storyId=88116176

[8] Ben Stein, "What if a Slowdown Is a Never-Ending Story? *The New York Times* (November 23, 2008), BU8.

[9] John Cassidy, The Volcker Rule, *The New Yorker* 25-30, at 28 July 26, 2010.

[10] http://www.nytimes.com/2009/09/06/magazine/06Economic-t.html?_r=1&scp=2&sq=Krugman%20economists&st=cse

[11] This analysis is based on Joshua Green, "Inside Man," *The Atlantic* (April 2010): 36-51, 38.

[12] Rajan G. Raghuram (2010). *Fault Lines: How Hidden Fractures Still Threaten the World Economy* (Princeton University Press).

[13] http://www.nytimes.com/2008/12/10/business/economy/10leonhardt.html?_r=1&hp

"Do the food nazis want your Twinkies?"

"Should the government be the nutrition police?"

15.0 | Food Policy

Is Ketchup a vegetable? Are too many people getting food stamps? Is the government planning to take away my Big Gulps and make me eat broccoli? These are just some of the unusual ways that we talk about the politics of food. In 1981 the Department of Agriculture considered a proposal to reduce federal spending by defining ketchup as a vegetable for the federally subsidized school lunch program. The proposal was widely ridiculed by food activists who were promoting children's nutrition. Stories about welfare queens using food stamps to buy sodas and candy have been told for decades by critics of the welfare state who think that a program to help the truly needy has expanded beyond its original purpose. More recently, government policies to promote nutrition and good diet in order to reduce increasing rates of obesity have prompted worries about government plans to take our Twinkies, Big Gulps, and French fries. During a 1990 press conference, President George Herbert Walker Bush confessed that he had disliked broccoli ever since he was a child and now that he was president he was not going to eat it anymore. (The statement did not make broccoli growers very happy!) Then broccoli played a surprisingly central role in the political and legal debates over the constitutionality of The Patient Protection and Affordable Care Act (better known as Obamacare). Critics argued that argued if government could require a person to buy health insurance it could also require people to eat broccoli. In her concurring opinion in the Supreme Court ruling that upheld the constitutionality of Obamacare, Justice Ginsburg described the argument against the individual mandate as a parade of "broccoli horribles."[1]

This chapter examines the politics of food policy. Food policy is an area of federal policy that is often overlooked because the public, the political parties and interest groups, and the media pay more attention to higher profile issues such as national security, the economy, crime, and other issues such as education and health care. The government's role in ensuring food security (that is, an adequate supply of food) and food safety is not controversial. People expect the government to ensure that they have *enough* food and *safe* food. But food policy has become controversial as the government has begun to promote healthy diets by regulations that require labeling menus and limit portion sizes and proposals to tax certain items such as sweetened drinks. The chapter focuses on three aspects of food policy. First, it describes food policy. Second, it describes how diet and nutrition were put on the government agenda (i.e., the politics of food). Third, it describes the main government and non-government actors who make food policy as participants in the food issue network.

15.1 | Is Food a Private Good or a Public Good?

Why is food even a political issue? In one sense food is a classic example of a private good. Food is a divisible good (one whose benefits can be limited to those who pay for it). Private goods are available in the private sector based on the ability to pay. Food is a matter of private choice: an individual decides what to eat, how much to eat, and how much to pay for it. These decisions are based on a person's ability to pay and personal tastes. In this sense, food is provided according to the *market model* rather than the *government model*. But food is not considered a completely private good that is available *only* to those who can afford to pay for it. Food is also considered a public good that the government provides for some people regardless of their ability to pay for it. The government's food policy goals include *food security, food safety, promotion of American agriculture, and healthy food*.

During the Great Depression of the 1930s unemployment, poverty, and hunger were nationwide problems. President Franklin Delano Roosevelt captured the scope of the problem in his *Second Inaugural Address* (January 20, 1937):

> I see a great nation, upon a great continent, blessed with a great wealth of natural resources.... But here is the challenge to our democracy: In this nation I see tens of millions of its citizens—a substantial part of its whole population—who at this very moment are denied the greater part of... the necessities of life. I see millions of families trying to live on incomes so meager that the pall of family disaster hangs over them day by day. I see millions whose daily lives in city and on farm continue under conditions labeled indecent by a so-called polite society half a century ago. I see millions denied education, recreation, and the opportunity to better their lot and the lot of their children. I see millions lacking the means to buy the products of farm and factory and by their poverty denying work and productiveness to many other millions. *I see one-third of a nation ill-housed, ill-clad, ill-nourished.* [Emphasis added] It is not in despair that I paint you that picture. I paint it for you in hope because the Nation, seeing and understanding the injustice in it, proposes to paint it out....The test of our progress is not whether we add more to the abundance of those who have much; it is whether we provide enough for those who have too little.

Freedom from want includes freedom from hunger. Today, food security is provided by the food stamp program and the Supplemental Nutrition Assistance Program (SNAP), two social welfare programs that provide food support for low-income people.

The U.S. Department of Agriculture defines **food security** as access to an adequate and safe supply of food: "access by all people at all times to enough food for an active, healthy life—in U.S. households and communities." In 2008, 85 percent of U.S. households were food-secure throughout the entire year, and 14.6 percent of households were food insecure at least some time during that year, up from 11.1 percent in 2007. This is the highest recorded rate of food insecurity since 1995 when the first national food security survey was conducted.[2]

The government also has responsibility for ensuring a safe food supply. Food is more political today than in the past because today's consumers are much more dependent upon others to provide their food. Most people are dependent on others for their food: they are consumers of food rather than producers of food. And people are not getting their food from family, friends, or neighbors; they are getting it from national and international commerce. Consumer protection is one of the functions of government. Protecting food consumers, ensuring a safe food supply, is also a government function.

Unsafe, tainted, contaminated food, and outbreaks of E. coli, salmonella poisoning, and other food borne illnesses and deaths are public health issues. The Centers for Disease Control and Prevention reports on food borne illnesses in the U.S. illustrate why food safety is a political issue.

Centers for Disease Control and Prevention

"CDC Estimates of Food Borne Illness in the United States"
In 1999, 76 million ill, 325,000 hospitalized, and 5,000 deaths in the U.S. from food borne illnesses. In 2011, 48 million illnesses, 128,000 hospitalizations, and 3,000 deaths.
http://www.cdc.gov/foodborneburden/2011-foodborne-estimates.html

Food Safety News
http://www.foodsafetynews.com/2009/09/ten-of-the-most-meaningful-food-borne-illness-outbreaks-picked-out-of-so-many/

From a political science perspective, food is a public good in the sense that governments everywhere are responsible for insuring an adequate, affordable, and safe supply of food. Food is also made a political issue by events such as droughts, crop failures due to diseases, health threats from unsafe foods or food borne-illnesses, and high rates of inflation. A century ago, food consumed a large share of the typical American family's budget. In 1900, more than 40% of a family's income was spent on food.[3] But federal food policy has emphasized increasing farm production, which has resulted in cheap food. The result has been a dramatic reduction in the food share of the average American family's budget.

Today, the efficient production of an adequate food supply is not a serious problem for federal food policy. The new food issues are safety and nutrition and health.

15.12 | The Politics of Food

There is broad consensus that the federal government has a legitimate role in ensuring the safety of the food supply. But the government's role in promoting health and nutrition is much more controversial. The federal government does have a long history of promoting diet. One early government campaign promoted good diet as a patriotic contribution to the effort to win World War I.

Food and the War Effort
"Food Will Win the War: On the Homefront in WWI"
http://www.archives.gov/northeast/nyc/education/food-wwi.html

---

The Department of Agriculture also sponsored one of the earliest radio programs, "Aunt Sammy," (the domestic equivalent of Uncle Sam) as part of a government campaign to get farmwives to promote healthy diets.

> Think About It!
> "How Uncle Sam Helps Define America's Diet"
> National Public Radio
> http://www.npr.org/2011/06/07/136889407/how-uncle-sam-helps-define-americas-diet

15.2 | The Food Issue Network

The term **issue network** describes participation in the formulation of public policy. An issue network consists of the two main government participants (the congressional committees and executive departments/agencies with authority over a particular issue) and the various non-government participants (the interest groups who are interested in a particular issue). The **food issue network** consists of the House and Senate Agriculture Committees (and subcommittees), which are the primary congressional food policy makers; the Department of Agriculture (and the Food and Drug Administration); and interest groups. The following describes the traditional and modern food issue network.

15.21 | *The Traditional Food Issue Network*

The traditional food issue network consisted of the House and Senate agriculture committees, the Department of Agriculture, and agri-business interest groups that primarily represented farmers and ranchers (the food producers).

The Traditional Food Issue Network

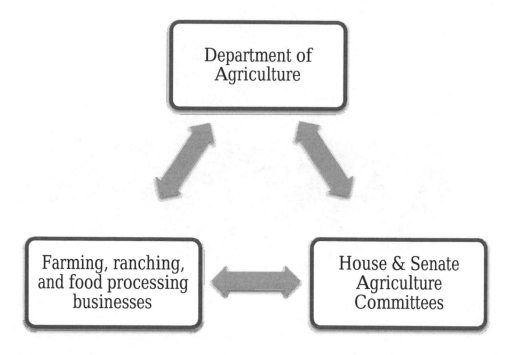

15.22 | *The Modern Food Issue Network*

But today another set of interest groups have worked their way into the food issue network. In the past, food producers and food processing companies were the main private sector participants in making food policy. Today, however, consumer groups, environmentalists, and public health advocates have joined the food issue network. They provide a different perspective on the goals of federal food policy.

The Modern Food Issue Network

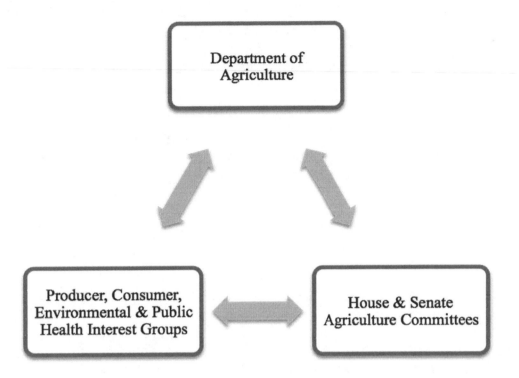

These new participants in the policy making process have made food policy more contentious because consumer, environmentalist, and public health groups have different interests than the food producers and processors. The following sections describe the three main types of participants in the modern food issue network

15.23 | *Congress: The House and Senate Agriculture Committees*

Congress makes food policy. The House of Representative Agriculture Committee (and subcommittees) and the Senate Agriculture, Nutrition and Forestry Committee (and subcommittees) have jurisdiction over bills, programs, and issues related to agriculture as well as supervision of the Department of Agriculture and other agencies with jurisdiction over food programs.

The following describes the agriculture committees and subcommittees in the 112th Congress. The House Agriculture Committee had six subcommittees, one of which was the Subcommittee on Nutrition and Horticulture which had jurisdiction over nutrition policy. The Senate Agriculture, Nutrition and Forestry Committee had five subcommittees, one of which was the Subcommittee on Nutrition, Specialty Crops, Food and Agricultural Research. Its legislative portfolio included provisions of the Food, Conservation and Energy Act of 2008; domestic and international nutrition and food assistance and hunger prevention; school and child nutrition programs; local and healthy food initiatives; food and agricultural research, education, economics and extension.

A letter from the ranking member of the Senate Agriculture Committee (Kansas Republican Senator Roberts) to the Secretary of Agriculture illustrates how the Senate Agriculture Committee interacts with the executive branch to advocate on behalf of agricultural interests. The October 3, 2012 letter entitled "Senator Roberts Concerned School Nutrition Programs Don't Meet Needs of Active Students" expressed concern that the Department of Agriculture was developing healthy food standards that provided insufficient calories for active students. In 2010 Congress passed the Healthy, Hunger-Free Kids Act. The Act required the Department of Agriculture's Food and Nutrition Service to revise rules for the National School Lunch Program and the School Breakfast Program to promote healthy food—in effect, to provide healthier school meals that included more vegetables and fruits and grains and fat-free or low-fat milk. Senator Roberts was concerned that the healthier food would increase student plate waste, increase costs, and not provide enough calories for active students.[4]

15.24 | *The Department of Agriculture*

The second government participant in the food issue network is the Department of Agriculture. In the U.S. and elsewhere one of the basic functions of government is to ensure that people have enough food to eat and that the food supply is safe. The origins of the federal government's food policy can be traced to President Lincoln's creation of an agricultural department in 1862. Lincoln called it "the people's department." Agriculture is sometimes called the nation's first industry; it was here before manufacturing. The department that Lincoln created eventually became one of the Cabinet agencies when the Department of Agriculture was created in 1889.

Historically, the United States Department of Agriculture (USDA) has functioned as a **clientele agency**. A clientele agency is an agency that is created to serve the needs or represent the interests of a specific group. The departments of Labor, Education, and Commerce are also clientele agencies that were created to represent labor, education, and business, respectively. The USDA was created to advocate for its major clientele— farmers and ranchers. In the 1920s, the USDA promoted industrial farming to increase production. The **Green Revolution** greatly increased agricultural production and in 1960 the USDA produced a video extolling the "Miracles from Agriculture" that made many of the amenities of modern life possible.

> The International Maize and Wheat Improvement Center (CIMMYT) played a pivotal role in the Green Revolution and continues to be a major research center working on increased productivity.
> http://www.cimmyt.org/

The Department of Agriculture's mission has been broadened beyond merely increasing production as federal food policy has expanded to include goals other than the promotion of agriculture. Today the USDA has the following areas of policy responsibility: promoting and marketing agricultural products at home and abroad; food safety and nutrition; conservation of natural resources; rural and community development; and providing job and housing assistance. However, the following short story about Pizza Politics reveals that the USDA is still a clientele agency that sees its mission as promoting American agricultural products. Domino's Pizza had falling sales.

A consumer survey of national pizza chains revealed that the Domino's pizzas tied for last in taste. In order to turn the sales trends around, Domino's worked with an organization called Dairy Management to develop a pizza with 40% more cheese. Dairy Management paid for a $12 million marketing campaign. The "Pizza Turnaround" television ads that were part of the Domino's marketing campaign.

The advertising campaign for the new cheesier pizza worked. It produced double-digit sales increases. This business case study is interesting but it would be irrelevant to the study of food policy except for the fact that Dairy Management is not a private industry business consultant. Dairy Management is an organization that was created by the USDA. Dairy Management worked with other restaurant companies to increase the amount of cheese that was on restaurant menus.[5] But the USDA also sponsors a healthy diet campaign that recommended *lowering* the amount of milk fats in the American diet! The cheese story illustrates how the USDA's dual mission—to promote American agriculture (in this instance, dairy products but in other instances beef or wheat or corn) and to promote healthy diets—sometimes conflict.

15.25 | *The Food and Drug Administration*

A third main government participant in the food issue network is the Food and Drug Administration (the FDA). The FDA is an independent regulatory commission but for the purposes of issue networks it is considered an executive agency because it implements legislation. Food safety was put on the federal government's agency in the early years of the 20th Century. In 1906 Congress passed the Pure Food and Drugs Act of 1906, which prohibited companies from interstate commerce in misbranded and adulterated foods, drinks and drugs. The 1906 Act was a response to two works that focused the public's attention on problems in the nation's food supply. Upton Sinclair published *The Jungle* in 1906, and a ten-part study by Harvey Washington Wiley on additives and chemicals in the nation's food supply. *The Jungle* was a novel that exposed the terrible conditions of the meatpacking industry. It focused on the plight of workers in meatpacking plants. Sinclair had gone undercover in meatpacking plants in Chicago and wanted to expose the American public to the problems faced by blue-collar workers. But the public's attention was captured by Sinclair's prose describing the unsanitary conditions in which their food was being handled in an industrial system that they did not associate with food. Sinclair wrote:

> [T]he meat would be shoveled into carts, and the man who did the shoveling would not trouble to lift out a rat even when he saw one—there were things that went into the sausage in comparison with which a poisoned rat was a tidbit. There was no place for the men to wash their hands before they ate their dinner, and so they made a practice of washing them in the water that was to be ladled into the sausage. There were the butt-ends of smoked meat, and the scraps of corned beef, and all the odds and ends of the waste of the plants, that would be dumped into old barrels in the cellar and left there. Under the system of rigid economy which the packers enforced, there were some jobs that it only paid to do once in a long time, and among these was the cleaning out of the waste barrels. Every spring they did it; and in the barrels would be dirt and rust and old nails and stale water—and cartload after cartload of it would be taken up and dumped into the hoppers with fresh meat, and sent out to the public's breakfast. *The Jungle*, Chapter 14, page 1.

A poster of the 1913 movie adaptation of Sinclair's novel

Congress created the Food and Drug Administration (the FDA) in 1930. The FDA is the primary federal regulatory agency with authority over food safety, although the Department of Agriculture also plays an important role in making federal food policy. The USDA promotes American agricultural production and sales abroad as well as ensures a safe food supply by inspecting food-processing plants. Today, the FDA has regulatory authority over about 25 cents of every dollar the consumer spends.

And of course significant portion of that dollar is spent on food consumed outside the home. The average person consumes about one-third of their calories on foods prepared outside the home.[6] As a result, the FDA has proposed new regulations that require labeling the calorie content of food served in restaurants and vending machines. The regulations would apply only to chain restaurants or vending machines companies with 20 or more locations as a concession to small businesses. The FDA's focus on food consumed outside the home reflects changes in patterns of consumption. But the FDA has not kept up with one change in where Americans get their food (and drugs). The U.S. now imports a larger share of its food. In the past, certain foods such as fruits and vegetables were only available seasonally. Today peaches and asparagus are available during the winter months in northern states because they are imported from other countries. But the FDA inspects only about 1% of imported food. Public concerns about the safety of the food supply have increased pressure to have the FDA expand its inspection of imported foods. The FDA has proposed placing more inspectors in the foreign countries from which we import food and drugs, rather than waiting until they enter the U.S., and it has opened an office in Beijing, China. But expanding the scope of the FDA's operations is controversial. It requires increasing the FDA's budget and increasing federal regulations. Addressing the food safety problem requires more than hiring more inspectors and doing more testing; it requires creating a regulatory system that works to provide food safety.

> **The Food Movement
> And
> Genetically Modified Organisms**
> In 1992 the FDA issued a rule that GMO were not materially different from other foods.
> http://www.councilforresponsiblegenetics.org/genewatch/Gene WatchPage.aspx?pageId=393

15.26 | *Interest Groups*

The third category of issue network participants is interest groups. Traditionally, these were groups that represented farming and ranching or food processing and distributing companies. Agribusinesses such as the Archer Daniels Midland Company have a vested interest in food policy and are important participants in the food network.

Today, however, a broad range of interest groups participate in the food issue network. Take, for example, consumer groups. Consumer groups represent individual consumers (i.e., people who buy food) and business consumers (e.g., companies such as The Coca-Cola Company, PepsiCo, Mars Incorporated, and The Hershey Company) that buy commodities such as sugar and corn syrup. Two groups that take opposing positions on food issues such as labeling the caloric and nutritional content of food, limiting the size of food portions, or taxing sodas are the Center for Science in the Public Interest and the Center for Consumer Freedom. The former organization generally plays offense: it is a consumer group that advocates for more government regulation of food. The latter organization generally plays defense: it is an industry group that opposes more government regulation of food. Public health advocates also generally support more government regulation to provide consumer information and to promote public health by reducing the consumption fat, salt, and sugar. The food industry worries about the general trend toward treating sugar or fat, for example, the way that tobacco and alcohol have been treated. Tobacco and alcohol have been subjected to "sin taxes." A sin tax is a tax on a vice such as smoking or drinking. The American Beverage Association, for instance, has mobilized industry opposition to treating sweetened beverages the way that tobacco and alcohol have been treated. The policy proposals to tax sugar or certain fats as harmful are based on the belief that consumption can be discouraged by taxing and regulating consumption.

15.3 | **The Farm Bill and the Food Aid Program**

The Farm Bill is a major component of the federal government's food policy. The Farm Bill, which is enacted every five years, is a nearly $300 billion dollar federal program. It was originally intended to promote food production, to promote marketing of U.S. food products abroad, and to keep food prices low. Crop subsidies are one of the primary ways that these goals were achieved. The USDA has commodity programs that subsidize growing wheat, corn, rice, cotton and a few other crops. The USDA also subsidized sugar prices and dairy prices, primarily milk price supports.

15.31 | *The Food Aid Program*

One component of the Farm Bill is the Food Aid Program. The Food Aid Program is a good example of a public policy that is both domestic policy and foreign policy. In 2007, the Food Aid Program was a $2 billion dollar program to provide food aid to other countries. The Food Aid Program began in 1954 as a way for the U.S. to dispose of surplus crops abroad. The Green Revolution, which began in the 1940s, greatly increased agricultural production. It was the result of the following developments:

- Biology. Scientific research produced more fertile and productive plants and animals.
- Chemistry. The chemical industry created more effective herbicides, pesticides, and fertilizers, which increased food production.
- Management. The industrial revolution transformed manufacturing before it reached agriculture, but eventually the agricultural sector changed from small family farms to large-scale corporate, agribusiness, or factory farming. The result was increased efficiency in growing, processing, and transporting foods.

The Green Revolution made American agriculture so productive that food policy had to address the problem of surplus, not scarcity or hunger. Food scarcity has not been the most important problem for food policy for decades. American agriculture produces far more food than can be consumed domestically. The economy of scale associated with factory farming made agriculture more efficient and more productive but it also contributed to the decline of the family farm. The "family farmer" is now analogous to the cowboy. Both are important symbols in American cultural heritage but they are no longer central figures in the economy. There are other critics of the Green Revolution. The Institute for Food and Development Policy, which is also known as Food First, advocates self-sufficiency and food sovereignty rather than dependence on international agribusiness companies.

15.32 | *Food Policy is both Domestic and Foreign Policy*

Domestic and foreign policy are often considered distinct areas of public policy. However, the food aid program is a good example of how domestic policy and foreign policy are linked. The food aid program includes provisions requiring 75% of the food aid be shipped in U.S. vessels, 25% of the food aid be shipped from Great Lakes ports, and mandating that the food aid be in the form of food (that is, American agricultural commodities such as dairy products, grain, or corn) not money. These requirements apply even when the food aid is a response to emergencies such as drought or disease. These requirements build domestic political support for the food aid program because American farmers, food processing companies, and transportation companies benefit from the program. The domestic political support is important because foreign aid is often welfare for other countries and therefore vulnerable during times of tight federal budgets and deficits. But the food aid program's requirements to buy American and ship American also create problems. One problem is that the high transportation costs of sending grain grown in the American Midwest (e.g., Kansas) to countries on the other side of the globe, and the time it takes to deliver food to where the food aid is needed, limit the effectiveness of the food aid program. A second problem is that federal corn subsidies keep the price of corn high and therefore reduce the amount of corn purchased for the food aid program. A third problem is that ethanol subsidies have resulted in corn being used for fuel rather than human or animal consumption. A Government Accounting Office (GAO) study found that it takes five months to get a new food aid to the country where it is needed. This means that the food aid may not be timely. In addition to timeliness, international food aid programs can also have a negative unintended consequence for local growers and producers. International aid can disrupt the local economy by displacing local producers when U.S. products flood the market in a country that receives foreign food aid because of a drought or other food supply problem. The food aid can solve an immediate problem but driving local companies out of business is an unintended consequence that has a negative long-term impact on a country's (or region's) ability to feed itself.

These problems of timeliness and impact on the local market have caused a new set of interest groups to participate in the creation of the food aid program in the Farm Bill. The new participants are lobbying government policy makers to pay more attention to nutrition, environmentalism, and international economic development as elements of the federal government's food policy. These new participants complicated federal food policy. The traditional food policy focused primarily on ensuring an adequate food supply in the U.S.[7] For example, CARE is a private international humanitarian organization that was created after WWII to alleviate poverty. It is one of the new participants in the food issue network that questions the effectiveness of the Food Aid Program's efforts to alleviate poverty in other countries.[8]

The United Nations Food Program and the World Bank are two international programs that provide emergency aid and economic development that is intended to help countries grow enough food to feed their own people. The United Nations Food Program provides food aid and The World Bank provides aid that will help countries achieve food self-sufficiency. In Africa, The World Bank programs have encouraged countries to eliminate fertilizer subsidies in favor of free market programs. One unintended consequence of The World Bank's program is a steep increase in fertilizer prices which can actually decrease food production. The United States Agency for International Development has also focused on promoting the private sector's role in providing fertilizer and seed, and considered government subsidies an impediment to the development of a private market in African countries such as Malawi, where famine has required extensive foreign food aid.[9] The U.S. and international aid organizations have a major impact on the way that government officials in other countries think about food policy because are associated with advanced technological and organizational skills that increase productivity.

15.33 | International Food Policy

The **Green Revolution** refers to the steep increase in agricultural production that began with wheat in Mexico in the 1940s. The Green Revolution contributed to economic development by making it possible for countries that were not able to produce enough food to feed their own people to produce enough food to feed their people or even surplus production to be sold abroad. Food security means producing enough food so that the government can assist during times of drought, conflict, or natural disasters in order to avert starvation. One standard way that governments achieve food security is to regulate food prices in order to ensure that producers were profitable so that they were able to stay in business. Some developing countries created food marketing boards which regulated the food industry. The boards managed the industry to stabilize commodity and food prices at levels that allowed businesses to be profitable while ensure that consumers had an affordable and adequate supply of food. The boards also bought commodities and stored them as insurance against a crop failure or inflation. These are examples of how the market model works.

15.34 | The Marketization of Food

Beginning in the 1980s, international aid agencies such as the World Bank and the IMF changed the goals of their programs. They strove to get countries to adopt food policies that reduced the government's role in achieving food security and increased reliance on market approaches. In effect, the international aid agencies urged countries to move away from the government model and toward the market model. This change in policy has been called the **marketization of food**.

The marketization of food is part of the broader trend toward privatization in other areas of domestic public policy. Privatization refers to the policy of returning government functions to the private sector or having services such as waste removal provided by private sector companies rather than government workers. The government model relies on regulations and subsidies to provide an adequate and safe food supply. In recent decades, the international aid community has begun to reconsider the government model which has relied on price supports; subsidies for the costs of fertilizer, herbicides, and pesticides, or high-yield crop seeds; and tariffs on imports. As economic development in general has promoted private sector activity, the international food aid community has considered the government model for food an unwise intervention in the marketplace. As a result, economic development policies have promoted market efficiency rather than government regulation.

The marketization of food meant that development aid encouraged countries to adopt policies that supported growing cash crops rather than food crops. Cash crops could be sold in the international or global marketplace. Food crops are grown primarily for domestic consumption. One result of international aid programs that emphasized marketization is that farmers grew crops like cocoa instead of staples such as maize, rice, or corn. Governments often encouraged international private investors to enter the marketplace in search of profits. Marketization and globalization are based on assumption that each country or region of the world should grow for the international marketplace what it can most efficiently produce, based on its distinctive climate or local soil. International food aid therefore emphasized economic development as measured by international trade in commodities rather than food self-sufficiency. The results are now evident in some unusual data. For instance, there has been a marked increase in the concentration of production of certain commodities. Fewer than five countries now account for around 90 percent of the corn exports and around five countries now account for around 80 percent of the world's rice exports. The increase in global efficiency has been accompanied by a global vulnerability to disruptions in trade or production. The increase in **private investment** has not entirely compensated for the **public disinvestment**. As a result, policy makers are rethinking the emphasis on market efficiency, and making food policy that encourages agricultural self-sufficiency as well as market efficiency. This will mean some government management of the agricultural sector of the economy. Food crises produce political crises (e.g., food riots) that governments are expected to respond to even if the politics does not. Some countries with rapidly growing populations and changes in patterns of food consumption are buying foreign land for growing crops to import.

> ### Think About It!
> ### How Many Earths Do We Need?
> The Global Footprint Network is an alliance of scientists who research the food supply necessary to sustain populations. The organization calculates, among other things, *how many earths* will be required to sustain human life at 1) current population levels and rates of consumption; and at 2) projected increases in population levels and consumption. The GFN measures consumption and waste at both individual level data and country level data.

15.4 | The Price of Food

Along with clothing and shelter, food is a basic commodity. It is one of the major items in the household budget. But the share of the average household budget that is consumed by food has steadily declined over the last half-century or so. See the following figure from U.S. Department of Agriculture data: [10]

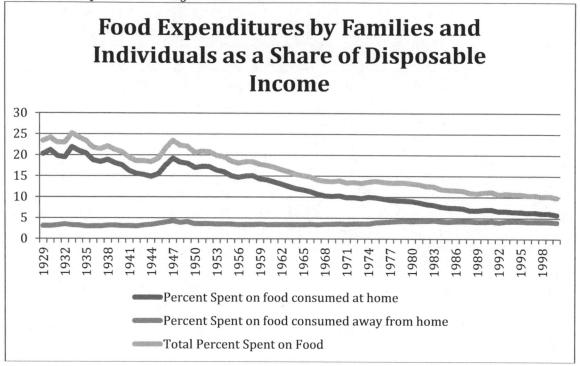

The decline in the food share of a household's disposable income explains why food security is not a high-profile issue in the U.S. However, a long-term change in food consumption patterns has made food more political: the increased share of food that is now consumed outside the home. In 1970, 26 percent of all food spending was on food away from home; by 2005, that share rose to 41 percent. A number of factors contributed to the trend of increased dining out:
- A larger share of women employed outside the home;
- More two-earner households;
- Higher incomes meant more disposable income;
- More affordable and convenient fast food outlets;
- Increased advertising and promotion by large foodservice chains; and
- The smaller size of U.S. households.

The continuation of these economic and demographic trends is expected to keep boosting the percentage of American income spent on eating outside the home. [11] Restaurants now account for almost half of the average household's food expenditures. As a result, food safety and nutrition are on the government's agenda. Consumers expect the government to inspect restaurants and food processing companies. And consumers are beginning to expect restaurants to provide consumers with more nutrition information about the items on the menu.

15.5 | Public Health Interest Groups and the Food Wars

The increase in rates of diabetes and obesity has prompted public health advocates lobby to add nutrition to the traditional emphases of federal food policy. Getting nutrition on the government's agenda has been an ongoing effort by individuals and organizations. Previously, such groups successfully lobbied the national government to make regulation of tobacco products a public issue after it was learned that nicotine was an addictive drug. Media campaigns play an important role in convincing government officials that they should act. The 2004 documentary *Super Size Me* (Directed by and starring Morgan Spurlock) called attention to the adverse health consequences of consuming fast food. http://freedocumentaries.org/film.php?id=98

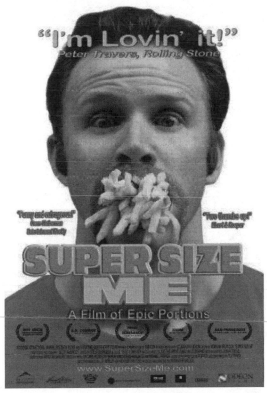

Interest groups representing the food industry, consumers, and health advocates have put food policy on the government's agenda by emphasizing two issues: food safety and public health. Food safety periodically becomes a high profile issue when outbreaks of E. coli, salmonella, botulism or some other food-related illnesses capture the public's attention. The demand for government action to ensure a safe food supply rises and falls with these episodic crises. Concerns about the health of the American population have also prompted calls for government action. The Centers for Disease Control and Prevention periodically conduct Health and Nutrition Examination Surveys.[12] The surveys show increased weight: In the early 1960s, 24 percent of American adults were overweight, defined as a body-mass index greater than 27. In 1980 the survey showed 33 percent were overweight. The weight increase presents an interesting research question: what caused the increase? The answer is essential to any policy solution. Explanations of the cause vary. Some natural scientists attribute the increased weight to biology: our brains have been developed to eat a great deal during times of plenty so that the body stores fat for lean times when the fat stores are consumed. Social scientists identify other causes. Economists blame public policies that make cheap food widely available.[13] The Green Revolution did make food cheaper relative to other goods and services that people purchase therefore people could consume more food—and chose to do so. Soft drinks, for example, are now part of daily calorie intake. Some public health advocates attribute the weight increase to addiction.

David Kessler is a former head of the Food and Drug Administration who advocated government regulation of nicotine as an addictive drug. Kessler maintains that the food industry has been reengineering food in ways that appeal to other kinds of human hunger.[14] The food industry has successfully used marketing that emphasizes "eatertainment" rather than nourishment. It produces fun products, interesting products, social products, products that are craved. Kessler calls the industry approach "conditioned hypereating." He compares the consumption of sweet and fatty foods with the conditioned response to gambling or substance abuse. McDonald's discovered that re-portioning (or super-sizing) was a very effective marketing strategy because the average consumer doesn't think in terms of calories, doesn't count calories, but rather thinks and counts in terms of the number of portions consumed. In fact, neither consumers nor food manufacturers seem to think in terms of nutrition. Most food marketing is not about nourishment—large food companies such as Pepsico, for instance, advertise the "aspirational" or lifestyle goals of consuming their product. The Pepsico Web site markets its brands as "bringing fun and refreshment to consumers for over 100 years." This is one reason why the comparison of the tobacco wars and the food wars is both appropriate and revealing.[15]

The role that large multi-national corporations play in providing food has caused some concern about their control over the food supply. After the Supreme Court ruled that life forms could be patented, companies began aggressively asserting property rights to, among other things, seeds. The documentary, _Food, Inc._, describes the role that the chemical company Monsanto has played in this movement. Monsanto now has property rights over 90% of the soybean seeds and asserts those rights in court to maintain control over the growing of soybeans.

Governments are resorting to some innovative and controversial public health approaches to regulating diet. One such approach is the use of zoning laws to limit the number of fast-food establishments. In July of 2008, the Los Angeles City Council adopted an ordinance that established a one-year moratorium on the building of new fast-food establishments in a 32-square –mile area of the city, including South Los Angeles which has around 900 restaurants (many of which are fast-food), and high rates of both adult obesity and diabetes. As more than two-thirds of American adults are fat, declaring war on junk food is politically risky; the government has to be careful about declaring war on junk food. Will the metaphorical war on junk food work like the war on drugs or the war on tobacco?

15.51 | _Is sugar the new nicotine?_

The following is based on an interview with New York City Mayor Michael Bloomberg about his portion control proposal to ban sweetened drinks in containers larger than 16 ounces.[16] Mayor Bloomberg has become famous (or infamous) for his proposals to require restaurants to provide nutrition labeling on menu items and to ban "supersized" soft drinks. A journalist asked Mayor Bloomberg about his "campaign against the sugar-industrial complex," the responsibilities of government and the responsibilities of individuals, and how he decides to pick his fights (priorities). Bloomberg replied that the government should not to ban goods; it should provide consumers with information and then let them make decisions about what to buy. He considered calorie counts and portion control two ways to provide such information about how much sugar is being consumed. Is eating like smoking? One person's weight does not hurt another person the way that one person's smoking hurts other people in the same area (second-hand smoke), but obesity does cost society which pays for health care. There is general agreement that government should prevent certain harms. Are sugary drinks like asbestos? The government would immediately pull people out of a building with an asbestos problem. The answer to the question, should the government regulate sugary drinks, is that it depends on the public-health issues. Bloomberg commented that obesity is an unusual public health problem because it is a disease that has gone from a rich person's disease to a poor person's disease: "For the first time in the history of the world, this year, more people will die from the effects of too much food than from starvation." He decided to make health an issue as mayor and for his foundation, Bloomberg Philanthropies, because he likes to tackle problems that others consider too political or too complex—guns, for instance. The portion-size question is interesting because of the correlation between the rise in obesity and the consumption of sugar. "Look, the beverage companies aren't stupid. Coca-Cola is run by a very smart guy; PepsiCo by a very smart woman. They see this train coming down the tracks at them. And that's why they're trying to get people to move over to Coke Zero or Diet Coke or Pepsi—Diet Pepsi—because down the road, the public *is* going to say "No *mas*. The cost of treating obesity is just out of control." McDonald's sued New York City when it first required the calorie now they are voluntarily providing them." The City is not proposing banning big drink it is proposing portion control: "All we're saying is that restaurants and theaters can't use cups greater than 16 ounces. So if you want to buy 32 ounces, you can buy 32 ounces, you just got to carry it back to your seat, or your table, in two cups." The public and the food industry initially opposed smoking bans. But now cities, states, and countries are creating smoke-free places.

15.6 | Environmentalism

American agriculture is extremely productive. The modern corporate, factory-farming model is very productive but it is also very energy and chemical intensive. The environmental movement has focused attention on the environmental costs of the industrial model of producing food. American agriculture requires a large amount of energy to produce crops such as corn and wheat and to produce commodities such as meat. Government crop subsidies increase food prices, increase food consumption, and increase environmental damage. The average American consumer eats 8 ounces of meat per day. About 30 percent of world's ice-free land is used directly or indirectly for livestock production, according to the United Nation's Food and Agriculture Organization. Livestock production generates 20 percent of world's greenhouse gases, which is more the greenhouse gases produced by a more familiar source of pollution: transportation. If Americans reduced meat consumption by 20 percent, the energy saved would be equivalent to their switching from a standard sedan (say a Toyota Camry) to a hybrid (say a Toyota Prius).[17]

15.7 | Final Food for Thought

The story of food's transformation from private decisions that individuals and families make to a major public policy issue illustrates how the U.S. system of politics and government works. Changes in economic conditions, patterns of consumption, the environment, or health can prompt individuals and organizations to put food on the government's agenda. These organizations then join the food issue network as participants in making food policy. These individual policy entrepreneurs and organizations are playing offense. Other individuals and organizations play defense and work to keep food policy off the government's agenda. The American Beverage Association and the National Restaurant Association generally oppose more government regulation of their industries. But government inspections that prevent food-borne illnesses can actually protect the food industry by ensuring a safe food supply. Nutrition is another issue. The initial opposition to menu labeling has softened as public opinion has supported it. Portion control is still opposed because it raises anew the central issue in the tobacco wars and the food wars (or the food fights): —the political debates about the proper size and scope of government as much as the proper size of soft drinks.

15.8 | Additional Resources

Earth Policy Institute: http://www.earth-policy.org/

Behavioral Economics and Getting Children to Eat Healthy:
http://www.npr.org/templates/story/story.php?storyId=130732347

Sinclair, Upton. 1906. *The Jungle.* Available at: http://www.gutenberg.org/ebooks/140

15.12 | In the Library

Finkelstein, Eric A. and *Fattening of America It Matters and What To* & Sons
Kessler, David. 2009. *Control of the* York: Rodale Books
Lindstrom, Martin. *About Why We Buy.*

KEY *TERMS*

Food security
Modern food policy
Clientele agency
Green Revolution
Marketization of food

Laurie Zuckerman. 2008. *The How The Economy Makes Us Fat, If Do About It.* New York: John Wiley

The End of Overeating: Taking Insatiable American Appetite. New

2008. *Buyology: Truth and Lies* London: Crown Business

[1] *National Federation of Independent Businesses v. Sebelius*, 567 U.S.___(2012).

[2] See "Food Security in the United States" at http://www.ers.usda.gov/Briefing/FoodSecurity/ .

[3] Atul Gawande, "Testing, Testing," *The New Yorker* (December 14, 2009), 34-41, at 34.

[4] http://www.ag.senate.gov/newsroom/press/release/senator-roberts-concerned-school-nutrition-programs_dont-meet-needs-of-active-students. Accessed November 19, 2012.

[5] Michael Moss, "While Warning About Fat, U.S. Pushes Cheese Sales," *The New York Times*, November 6, 2010. At http://www.nytimes.com/2010/11/07/us/07fat.html?ref=dominospizzainc

[6] http://www.fda.gov/

[7] http://www.npr.org/templates/story/story.php?storyId=16053196&sc=emaf

[8] See the CARE "White Paper on Food Aid Policy," (June 6, 20006). http://www.care.org/newsroom/publications/whitepapers/food_aid_whitepaper.pdf

[9] Celia W. Dugger, "Ending Famine, Simply by Ignoring the Experts," *The New York Times* (December 2, 2007: p.1,6.

[10] http://www.ers.usda.gov/Briefing/CPIFoodAndExpenditures/Data/Expenditures_tables/table7.htm

[11] http://www.ers.usda.gov/publications/AER829/ and http://www.ers.usda.gov/Briefing/DietQuality/FAFH.htm

[12] http://www.cdc.gov/nchs/nhanes.htm

[13] Finkelstein, Eric A. and Laurie Zuckerman. 2008. *The Fattening of America How The Economy Makes Us Fat, If It Matters and What To Do About It*. New York: John Wiley & Sons

[14] 2009. *The End of Overeating: Taking Control of the Insatiable American Appetite*. New York: Rodale Books.

[15] See Martin Lindstrom. 2008. *Buyology: Truth and Lies About Why We Buy*. London: Crown Business.

[16] http://www.theatlantic.com/magazine/archive/2012/11/the-bloomberg-way/309136/ Accessed November 23, 2012.

[17] Mark Bittman, "Rethinking the Meat-Guzzler," *The New York Times* (January 27, 2008, 1WK, 4WK).

CHAPTER 16: CRIME POLICY

16.0 | PUBLIC POLICY: CRIME

This textbook began with the question "Why do we have government?" One answer to the question is that governments are created to protect people from threats to their life, liberty, and property. Creating and maintaining public safety is one of the most important government functions. Crime prevention, investigation, prosecution, and punishment are basic responsibilities of governments everywhere. In the U.S., public opinion polls indicate that crime, along with the economy and national security, is usually mentioned as one of the most important problems facing the nation.

	% Mentioning
Economy in general	31
Unemployment/Jobs	22
Dissatisfaction with government/Congress/politicians; poor leadership; corruption; abuse of power	11
Immigration/Illegal aliens	7
Poor healthcare/hospitals; high cost of healthcare	7
Natural disaster response/relief	7
Federal budget deficit/Federal debt	6
Fuel/Oil prices	5
Wars/War (nonspecific)/Fear of war	4
Lack of money	3
Ethics/Moral/Religious/Family decline; dishonesty	3
Situation/War in Afghanistan	3
Education/Poor education/Access to education	3
Situation/War in Iraq	3

Source: Gallup. July 8-11, 2010. "What do you think is the most important problem facing this country today?

This chapter has three main purposes. First, it explains ideological thinking about crime. The crime control and due process models of justice are used to explain conservative and liberal views on the causes of crime and criminal justice policies that are intended to fight crime. Second, it introduces basic criminal law provisions in the Bill of Rights and, to a lesser extent, statutes. Third, it describes the main criminal justice officials (the police, the courts, and corrections) and the main criminal justice issue (the need to balance individual rights and government power). The main theme of this textbook is the power problem—the need to strike the right balance between granting government enough power to address the issues that the people expect government to solve and limiting government power enough to hold it accountable. The power problem is central to crime policy because the government's criminal justice powers include the power to take a person's life, liberty, and property—as long as the person is provided due process of law.

Americans, like people in other countries, expect government to provide safe homes, streets, subways, and parks. For most of the nation's history, these were almost exclusively the responsibility of state and local governments because the federal government dealt with national defense, foreign policy and interstate commerce. Today, however, all levels of government—local, state, national, and increasingly even international institutions—are involved with crime policy.

16.1 | THE POLITICS OF CRIME

An ideology is a set of beliefs and a program for acting on them. One of the beliefs is typically about crime. Crime policy is one of the issues that have consistently divided liberals and conservatives over the decades. Liberals and conservatives have differences of opinion on the causes of crime, the purposes of punishment, and the way criminal justice officials fight crimes. What causes crime? This is an important social science research question. There are two basic theories of the cause of crime. One theory is that crime is caused by human nature. The **human nature theory** assumes that the individual is the primary cause of crime and therefore the individual should be held responsible for their criminal acts. The human nature theory has two variants. One variant is the belief that some people are simply born bad—they are simply "bad seed" or have an evil nature. Another variant of the human nature theory is that human beings are rational actors who make a choice to commit a crime rather than to obey the law because they think they will gain from the illegal act. According to this variant, individuals calculate the costs and benefits of different courses of action and choose crime.

The **social theory** of crime assumes that social circumstances or cultural values cause people to commit crime. In effect, the causes of crime are social. Criminals are made not born: people are not born criminals they are made criminals by social circumstances such as poverty, violence, discrimination, neglect, bad upbringing, poor education, or other negative conditions or treatment.

Ideological beliefs about the causes of crime have a major impact on crime policy, particularly sentencing policies. The purposes of punishment include deterrence, incapacitation, retribution, and rehabilitation. The belief that criminals are evil justifies punishment policies that emphasize incapacitation and retribution. The belief that criminals are rational actors justifies policies that make the costs of  crime higher than the benefits. The belief crime is caused by poverty or discrimination justifies punishment policy that encourages rehabilitation. The American political culture of individualism creates support for punishment policies that hold individuals responsible for their actions, including crimes.

But the social theory of crime plays an interesting role in American popular culture, which includes memorable images of outlaws who are portrayed as people who were driven to their lives of crime by injustice. The social injustice (economic or political exploitation) transforms the victim into a Robin Hood figure who steals from the rich and powerful and gives to the poor and powerless. This is the mythology surrounding some of the notorious criminal figures in American history: Jesse James, Butch Cassidy and the Sundance Kid, Bonnie and Clyde (pictured), and even Al Capone. The enduring appeal of their criminal exploits is at least partly due to their images in popular culture as victims of social circumstances or outsiders who challenge a corrupt establishment.

In terms of the politics of crime, liberals generally support the social theory of crime. It has exposed liberals to the charge that they are *blame society firsters* who are

> "A conservative is a liberal who has been mugged.
> **A liberal is a conservative who has been arrested.**"
> **Tom Wolfe,** *Bonfire of the Vanities* (1987)

soft on crime. Conservatives generally support the human nature theory. The fact that they blame individuals for their criminal acts and support punishment rather than rehabilitation has resulted in the fact that conservatives are considered tough-on-crime.

16.12 | *Two Models of Justice: Crime Control and Due Process*

The difference between liberal and conservative thinking about crime policy can be understood by comparing two different models of how the criminal justice system should operate: the Due Process and Crime Control Models of Justice were developed by Herbert L. Packer.[1] According to the crime control model, the government's primary responsibility is crime control—the protection of the law-abiding citizenry is the highest priority and the protection of individual rights is an important but secondary responsibility. Advocates of the crime control model of justice believe that effective and efficient law enforcement is the key to protecting against crime. The due process model of justice emphasizes the importance of protecting individual rights by providing due process of law even at the cost of making the criminal justice system less efficient. The due process model is reflected in the sayings that a person is innocent until proven guilty and that it is better for 100 guilty to go free than one innocent person found guilty.

Crime control and rights protection are both values. The due process model emphasizes the protection of rights; the crime control model emphasizes effective crime fighting. When thinking about crime policy, it is important to remember that a person does not have to support EITHER the due process model OR the crime control model of justice. These are two models or sets of ideas that represent the extreme ends of a spectrum of ideas about crime. Members of the general public, government officials, and even judges are called conservative or liberal because they tend to be located at one or the other end of the scale. Liberals generally support using due process of law to check the power of police and prevent abuses of government power. Conservatives generally defend the power of police and prosecutors as key figures in the war on crime. Unless of course the liberal is a crime victim and the conservative has been arrested!

16.13 | *Punishment Policy: Incarceration*

Although incarceration (imprisonment) is not the only form of punishment, it is certainly the one that receives the most public attention. Trials capture the public's imagination. So do prisons. The rate of incarceration is one of the most common measures of sentencing policy. The following describes some changes in punishment policy over roughly the last century.

Table 16.1

RATE (PER 100,000 RESIDENTS) OF SENTENCED PRISONERS IN STATE AND FEDERAL INSTITUTIONS
[*Sourcebook of Criminal Justice Statistics, 1985*; and Bureau of Justice Statistics]

Year	Rate (per 100,000 Residents)
1925	79
1930	104
1935	113
1940	131
1945	98
1950	109
1955	112
1960	117
1965	108
1970	96
1975	111
1980	138
1985	201
1990	292
2000	481
2002	702
2005	737
2010	500

The above table shows the RATE of incarceration for various years. The total prison population on December 31, 2010 was 1,612,000. The 2010 RATE (500/100,000) is the first decline since 1972! The *federal* rate of imprisonment actually increased but the *state* rates have decreased.
http://www.ojp.gov/bjs/glance.htm#Corrections
http://www.usdoj.gov/02organizations/02_1.html
http://bjs.ojp.usdoj.gov/content/pub/ascii/p10.txt

What explains the dramatic change in the rates of imprisonment over time, particularly the increased rates of incarceration? And what is the likely cause of the recent decrease in state rates of incarceration beginning around 2010? These are some social science questions about imprisonment and sentencing policy.

Are these rates of incarceration high or low? One way to determine whether sentencing rates are high or low is to examine historical rates, look at trends, and to compare sentencing rates in the U.S. with other countries.
http://www.sentencingproject.org/template/page.cfm?id=107
http://www.sentencingproject.org/doc/publications/inc_comparative_intl.pdf

"We're Number One!" U.S. Inmate Count Dwarfs Rest of World
http://www.nytimes.com/2008/04/23/us/23prison.html?_r=1&scp=2&sq=rate+of+incarceration&st=nyt&oref=slogin

What causes a country's rate of incarceration? What explains a country's rate of incarceration? Why does the U.S. have such a high rate of incarceration? These are social science research questions. There is a causal relationship between crime rates One would expect there to be a causal relationship between crime rates and imprisonment. And one would expect that the increase in the rate of imprisonment to be caused by an increase in the crime rate, but the relationship is more complicated than simply changes in the rate of crime (increases or decreases) produces changes in the rate of incarceration (increases or decreases.

For the last several decades the crime rates have been stable or even declining while the rate of imprisonment continued to increase. Why? What other variables might explain rates of imprisonment? Do media stories about crime affect the popular perception of crime independent of actual crime rates? Does ideology (conservative thinking about crime) explain the continued rise? What about economics? What about privatization? Privatization is the policy of turning government functions over to the private sector.

When he left office, President Dwight Eisenhower warned the country about the creation of a military-industrial complex. The military-industrial complex is a term for the defense issue network among the congressional defense committees, the department of defense, and the aerospace and defense industries that have political and economic relationships that keep defense budgets high. Today, the high rate of incarceration has raised similar concerns about the creation of a *prison-industrial complex*. The term prison-industrial complex refers to the special interests that benefit from maintaining a large prison population. The complex includes private companies (a prison industry that benefits from prison building and prison service contracts); local government officials who view prisons as part of their economic development plans; and prison guard unions that lobby to protect prison jobs.

State and local governments see prisons as economic development policy. The building of for-profit prisons in communities such as Walnut Grove, Mississippi, or
http://www.npr.org/2011/03/25/134850972/town-relies-on-troubled-youth-prison-for-profits

states such as Louisiana where prisons are a growth industry, or http://www.nytimes.com/2000/03/16/us/privately-run-juvenile-prison-in-louisiana-is-attacked-for-abuse-of-6-inmates.html

Texas where privatization of prisons has created community dependence on for-profit prisons for jobs and taxes, a dependence that did not create problems as long as the rates of incarceration were increasing: http://www.npr.org/2011/03/28/134855801/private-prison-promises-leave-texas-towns-in-trouble

16.14 | *Civil Liberties and Criminal Justice*

The Bill of Rights includes provisions that protect against unreasonable search and seizure, self-incrimination, violations of due process, and cruel and unusual punishment. It also guarantees the right to trial by jury, the assistance of counsel, and the right to confront the accuser. Why do so many of the provisions of the Bill of Rights limit the government's criminal justice powers? Were the Founders soft on crime? Were the Founders trying to protect suspects and criminals? The answer to these questions is that the Founders were very concerned about the government criminal law powers. Their concerns were rooted in their political experiences. The government's criminal law powers are indeed worth thinking about because the government can take a person's property, liberty, and even life—as long as it provides due process before it does it. The Founders had lived through the period when the English King and colonial governors used criminal law powers for political purposes—to punish opponents or critics. The political use of criminal justice powers explains why the Fourth Amendment declared that individuals had a right to be free from unreasonable searches and seizures, why the Fifth Amendment guarantees due process of law and the right against self-incrimination, why the Sixth Amendment guarantees the right to a jury trial, and why the Eighth Amendment prohibits cruel and unusual punishment. The fact that these provisions of the Bill of Right are written in such general language means that criminal cases have been such an important part of the Supreme Court's docket.

16.15 | *The Fourth Amendment*

The meaning of the Fourth Amendment has changed over time. The Court originally interpreted the Fourth Amendment to places and things. The home and papers were given greater protection than other places and things. In *Olmstead v. U.S.* (1928) the Court ruled that the government did not have to get a search warrant before wire-tapping a suspect because a wiretap was not a physical search or an actual seizure. The Court considered wiretap technology something that enabled the government to listen to a telephone conversation without actually searching or seizing anything. Technology has greatly increased the government's power to gather information without ever physically seizing or searching anything. As a result, courts today interpret the Fourth Amendment more broadly. In Katz v. U.S. (1967) the Court held that wiretapping was a search and seizure that triggered the Fourth Amendment warrant protections.

16.16 | *What is a reasonable search and seizure?*

The Fourth Amendment provides constitutional protection against unreasonable search and seizure. But it does not define what an unreasonable search is—or what a reasonable search and seizure is. The Court's case law defines these provisions of the Fourth Amendment. The general rule is that a search is reasonable if a warrant is obtained from an independent magistrate (a judicial branch official). In order to obtain a search warrant, the police must convince the magistrate that there is probable cause that search of person or place will produce evidence of the criminal activity that they are investigating. This is the rule. There also is a long list of exceptions to the rule that a reasonable search requires a search warrant:

- **Consent**—an individual can knowingly give up the right to have a warrant.
- **Stop and frisk**—a stop is not really an arrest and a frisk is not really a search so a warrant is not required for a police officer to stop and frisk a person. (*Terry v. Ohio*)
- **Plain view**—if the police officer has a right to be where he or she is, then contraband and evidence can be seized without first getting a search warrant. The plain view doctrine also applies to concept of "open fields," which includes fields, buildings, garbage put out at the curb, and material seized using technology such as helicopters, drones, and even infrared technology when used to see or otherwise detect using thermal imaging marijuana grow houses.
- **Incident to a lawful arrest**—a police officer may search the area under immediate control of a person in order to ensure officer safety or to preserve evidence.
- **Hot pursuit**—a police officer in hot pursuit of a suspect does not have to stop the chase, get a search warrant, and then resume the pursuit.
- **Motor vehicles**—the mobility of motor vehicles presents special problems so there are many circumstances where warrant-less searches are allowed. Motor vehicles, telephones, cell phones, and computers are examples of how technological developments have changed reading of the Fourth Amendment's protection of persons, houses, papers and effects from unreasonable searches.
- **Drug testing**—the government has a compelling interest in public safety, therefore certain employees such as railway workers and customs officials can be required to submit to drug tests without warrants, probable cause, or individualized suspicion.
- **Schools**—schools are special institutions, therefore the standard for justifying the search of a student's locker or backpack is merely whether the search was reasonable rather than the higher standard of probable cause that the search will produce evidence of criminal activity.
- **Administrative searches**—Fourth Amendment rights are not as strong in settings other than criminal justice, such as enforcement of game laws by searching coolers or freezers, business regulation and inspection, food safety inspections of restaurants, immigration law enforcement, and enforcement of public housing rules.
- **National security**—Fourth Amendment protections are weaker than in other areas of law. The Foreign Intelligence Surveillance Act of 1978 created a special legislative court system, the foreign intelligence surveillance court (FISC), which

reviews government requests to gather intelligence without having to show probable cause. The USA PATRIOT ACT removed the "wall of separation" between intelligence gathering and criminal prosecution. The Federal Bureau of Investigation can issue National Security Letters demanding that individuals or companies produce requested information, and the National Security Agency has conducted secret intelligence surveillance.[2]

The general rule is that the Fourth Amendment requires a search warrant for a search and seizure to be constitutional. The large number of exceptions to the rule raises an interesting question. Is it still accurate to say that search warrants are required in order for a search to be constitutional? The rule is misleading. Would it be more accurate to say that there is a new rule: a warrant is not required for a search to be constitutional except under certain circumstances?

16.17 | *The Exclusionary Rule*

The Fourth Amendment declares a right to be free from unreasonable searches and seizures. But it does not provide a remedy for violations of that right. The Supreme Court has provided one (for violations of the Fourth Amendment or the 5th Amendment due process of law). The remedy is called the Exclusionary Rule. The Exclusionary Rule is a judge-created policy that evidence obtained illegally cannot be used in court to obtain a conviction. The Exclusionary Rule was first created and applied to federal courts in *Weeks v. U.S.* (1914). In *Mapp v. Ohio* (1961) the Warren Court applied the Exclusionary Rule to state courts.

Conservatives have consistently opposed the Exclusionary Rule for several reasons. First, the Exclusionary Rule is a legal policy that the Supreme Court created. As such, it is an example of judicial activism or legislating from the bench. Second, the Exclusionary Rule allows the guilty to go free on what conservatives consider legal technicalities such as the failure to get a search warrant or a warrant with a typographical error. The Exclusionary Rule does indeed sometimes allow a person to get away with murder. In those cases where a confession or a gun or a weapon is ruled inadmissible in court because the evidence was illegally obtained, a guilty person gets off on a legal technicality. Critics of the ER do not think that evidence should be given the "death penalty" merely because of the way it was obtained. Finally, conservatives oppose the Exclusionary Rule because they prefer giving police officers broad discretion to use their judgment to decide how best to go about doing their job. This difference between liberal and conservative views on how the criminal justice system should work is the reason for Tom Wolfe's quip in *The Bonfire of the Vanities,* the 1987 satirical novel about greed, race, and class in New York City, that a conservative is a liberal who was mugged (and want to get tough on crime), and a liberal is a conservative who was arrested (and quickly lawyers up). It also reflects the differences between the crime control and due process models of justice.

In fact, since the Warren Court the Court has become more conservative and significantly limited the ER by creating exceptions to the rule that illegally obtained evidence cannot be used. The exceptions include:

- **Grand jury**—illegally obtained can be presented to a grand jury.
- **Harmless error**—if the police made a harmless error the evidence can be used.
- **Civil court**—the ER does not apply to civil courts.
- **Good faith**—if the police made a good faith mistake the evidence can be used.
- **Independent source**—if the evidence could have bee obtained through another source, then it can be used.
- **Inevitable discovery**—if the evidence would have been discovered inevitably, it can be used.
- **Public safety**—if the police acted illegally, but to ensure public safety, the evidence can be used.
- **Preventive detention**—the ER does not apply to decisions about whether a person should be detained in order to prevent a criminal act.
- **Parole revocation**—the ER does not apply to decisions to revoke parole.
- **Prisoners**—the ER does not apply to disciplinary hearings for inmates.
- **Impeaching a witness**—illegally obtained evidence can be used to impeach a defendant's own testimony or that of an accomplice.
- **Physical evidence**? An emerging exception is for physical evidence (e.g., a gun a bullet or a knife) as distinct from testimonial evidence (e.g. a confession)?

The growing exceptions to the Exclusionary Rule raise the same question that has been raised about the rule that a search warrant is required for a search to be reasonable: Does the long and growing list of exceptions to the ER mean that the exceptions have now become the rule? Both examples do illustrate how changes occur in the reading of the U.S. Constitution's protections for civil liberties. The words in the Constitution may not change but their meaning does—and the changed legal meanings reflect political (ideological) changes.

16.18 | *The Fifth Amendment*

The Fifth Amendment includes a number of provisions that protect individual liberties: protection against self-incrimination, protection against double jeopardy, and a guarantee of due process of law:

"No person shall be held to answer for a capital, or otherwise infamous crime, unless on a presentment or indictment of a Grand Jury, except in cases arising in the land or naval forces, or in the Militia, when in actual service in time of War or public danger; nor shall any person be subject for the same offence to be twice put in jeopardy of life or limb; nor shall be compelled in any criminal case to be a witness against himself, nor be deprived of life, liberty, or property, without due process of law; nor shall private property be taken for public use, without just compensation."

Think about it! Conservatives think the Exclusionary Rule is an inappropriate remedy for violations of the Fourth Amendment. They recommend a tort law remedy: to sue the police for wrongful injury. Would this work?

Think about it!

Should police (or the military or the CIA) do whatever it takes to get information from a suspected criminal (or terrorist)?

The provision protecting against self-incrimination has ancient roots in the English tradition of common law. The right is central to one of the most important and familiar features of the U.S. legal system: the assumption that a person is innocent until proven guilty. The assumption of innocence places the burden of proof on the accuser (the government). The accused does not have to prove that they are not guilty as charged. The government must prove beyond a reasonable doubt that the accused did what they were accused of doing. Why place the burden of proof on the government? It would certainly be easier to obtain convictions if the accused had to prove they were innocent. The protection against self-incrimination can be traced to the reaction against religious investigations (inquisitions) that used torture in order to obtain confessions of sin. The story of John Lambert the heretic (1537) illustrates the revulsion against using torture to obtain confessions of sin (or otherwise):

> "No man ever suffered more diabolical cruelty at the stake than this evangelical martyr, he was rather roasted than burnt to death; if the fire became stronger, or if the flame reached higher than they chose, it was removed or damped. When his legs were burnt off, and his thighs were reduced to mere stumps in the fire, they pitched his broiling body on pikes, and lacerated his flesh with their halberds. But God was with him in the midst of the flame, and supported his spirit under the anguish of expiring nature. Almost exhausted, he lifted up his hands, such as the fire had left him, and with his last breath, cried out to the people, NONE BUT CHRIST! NONE BUT CHRIST! These memorable words, spoken at such a time, and under such peculiar circumstances, were calculated to make a deeper and more lasting impression on the minds of the spectators, than could have been effected by a volume written on the subject. At last his remains were beat down into the flames, while his triumphant soul 'mocked their short arm, and, quick as thought, escaped where tyrants vex not, and the weary rest.' "[3]

The religious justification for torturing a person was to ensure that sinners confessed before meeting their maker.

The use of the "third degree" by police officers in order to obtain confessions of crime was traditionally considered a politically and legally acceptable practice. However, in *Brown v. Mississippi* (1936) the Supreme Court held that torturing suspects was unconstitutional—in a case where the police torture appeared to have produced a tainted confession by a man who simply wanted the pain to stop. The Court ruled that due process of law prohibits trial by ordeal: "The rack and torture chamber may not be substituted for the witness stand."

The Fifth Amendment provision prohibiting a person from being "compelled to be a witness against himself" is not limited to forced confessions. The Supreme Court has broadened the scope of the Fifth Amendment so that suspects have a constitutional right to be informed of their constitutional rights prior to being questioned. This was the holding in the landmark case of *Miranda v. Arizona* (1966), which resulted in police officers reading suspects their Miranda Warnings. This decision is probably depicted in popular culture (television police shows and crime films) more than any other Court ruling[4]

> You have the right to remain silent. Anything you say can and will be used against you in a court of law. You have the right to speak to an attorney. If you cannot afford an attorney, one will be appointed for you. Do you understand these rights as they have been read to you?
> - Typical Miranda Warning

16.19 | *The Sixth Amendment*

The Sixth Amendment includes several provisions that provide rights in the criminal justice system.

> "In all criminal prosecutions, the accused shall enjoy the right to a speedy and public trial, by an impartial jury of the State and district wherein the crime shall have been committed, which district shall have been previously ascertained by law, and to be informed of the nature and cause of the accusation; to be confronted with the witnesses against him; to have compulsory process for obtaining witnesses in his favor, and to have the Assistance of Counsel for his defence."

The traditional reading of the Sixth Amendment right to the assistance of counsel was that a defendant had the right to pay for a lawyer if the defendant could afford one, but the state had no obligation to provide a defendant with a lawyer. However, in the 1930s, beginning with *Powell v. Alabama* (1932), the Court began to require states to provide defendants with lawyers in capital punishment cases involving special circumstances. The special circumstances included cases where there was evidence of racial hostility. Over time, number of special circumstances expanded to include cases involving very young offenders, poverty, illiteracy or a lack of education. The modern understanding of the right to the existence of counsel is that the right applies in all cases where an individual could lose his or her liberty.

16.2 | The Criminal Justice System

The criminal justice is the system of policies and institutions that are used to maintain public order, deter crime, investigate crimes, prosecute and try the accused, and punish individuals who have been convicted of crimes. Criminal justice was traditionally the responsibility of state and local governments. Beginning in the 1930s, the federal government began to make crime a national issue. The U.S. department of Justice and then the federal courts were concerned about corruption in state and local criminal justice systems, the emergence of organized crime that crossed local and state jurisdictions, and racial discrimination in law enforcement. The Warren Court's criminal justice rulings resulted in federal judicial supervision of state criminal justice policies. The liberal rulings expanded the rights of suspects and prisoners. Then, beginning in the 1960s, the media called an increase in crime a crime wave. Crime was transformed from a

Think about it! Is Chris Rock right about the Second Amendment and bullet control? http://www.youtube.com/watch?v=OuX-nFmL0II

local/state issue into a national political issue—but for different reasons. Liberals wanted the national spotlight focused on the social causes of crime. Conservatives wanted crime control. The national political debate was shaped by conservatives who blamed liberals and judges for expanding rights in ways that made it harder for police to fight crime. The result was further "federalization" of crime, but now it was for getting tough on crime rather than providing more federal protection of the rights of suspects and prisoners in the states. The 1967 President's Commission on Law Enforcement and Administration of Justice was charged by President Johnson to develop a plan that would allow us to "banish crime."

The Commission's Report, "The Challenge of Crime in a Free Society," made more than 200 recommendations as part of a comprehensive approach toward preventing and fighting crime. Some of the recommendations were included in a major new federal law, the Omnibus Crime Control and Safe Streets Act of 1968. This Act established the Law Enforcement Assistance Administration (LEAA), which provided federal grants for research on criminology, including the study of the social aspects of crime. By the 1970s, there were 729 academic programs in criminology and criminal justice in the United States. Over time, scholars of criminal justice began to include criminology, sociology, psychology and other disciplines to provide a more comprehensive view of the causes of crime and the organization and operation of the criminal justice system.

The Omnibus Act recommended that the criminal justice system be made more effective by improving coordination among the three main components of the criminal justice system: police, courts, and corrections. The politics of the 1968 Omnibus Crime Control Act are very interesting. It was passed in spring of 1968 by a Democratic Congress that was worried that Democrats were going to do badly in the upcoming fall elections because they were increasing seen as soft on crime and a time when the public was becoming much more worried about street crime than police brutality. Republicans sensed the public fear of crime and took tough on crime positions while portraying Democrats as soft on crime. Republican Richard Nixon's presidential campaign used getting tough on crime rhetoric and when he took office he began implementing crime control policies.

Two criminal justice issues that divide the ideological right and left are gun control and capital punishment. Guns are an important part of American political culture therefore debates about the wisdom and the legality of using gun control to increase public safety are often heated. Liberals generally support gun control as crime control. Conservatives generally oppose gun control as crime control. The debates are partly about effectiveness: the question whether gun control affects rates of crime and levels of public safety. The debates are also about rights. The Second Amendment guarantees the right to keep and bear arms. For a seriously funny alternative to gun control as a way to reduce violence listen to comedian Chris Rock's routine recommending bullet control rather than gun control. Can the constitutional problems with gun control be avoided because the Second Amendment mentions the right "to keep and bear arms" but says nothing about the right to keep and use bullets?

16.3 | Criminal Law

Law is a system of rules that are backed by sanctions for not complying with them. Sanctions mean that compliance is not voluntary. The U.S. legal system is divided into two forms of law: civil law and criminal law. **Civil laws** are generally the rules that govern interactions between individuals or organizations. Civil law is sometimes called private law because it does not usually involve the government. Business contracts, for example, are typically private law. **Criminal laws** are the system of rules that 1) define what behaviors are considered illegal and therefore criminal; 2) the legal procedures used to investigate, prosecute, and try those who are accused of crimes; and 3) the punishments (i.e., the sentences) that are considered appropriate for convicted offenders. Criminal law is public law for two reasons. First, crimes are considered harmful to both the individual victim and society in general: crimes are offenses against the public order. Second, the government prosecutes and punishes offenders.

The primary purposes of criminal law are to protect individuals from being harmed by others and to punish those who commit crimes. All countries have criminal laws. The oldest known codified law is the <u>Code of Hammurabi</u>, which was established around 1760 BC in ancient Mesopotamia. Historically, criminal law was private law in the sense that individuals and groups provided their own protection and punished offenders rather than relying on government to do so. The development of professional criminal justice officials (including police, prosecutors, and judges) and a system of codified laws (to replace common law), have diminished the layperson's role in delivering justice. However, in recent years vigilantism (individuals or organizations taking the law back into their own hands) and the gun rights movement have expanded the layperson's role.

16.4 | The Criminal Justice System

The criminal justice system consists of three main parts: (1) the police (sometimes called law enforcement; (2) the courts; and (3) corrections (jails and prisons). The police (including police officers and sheriffs), judges, and corrections officials (including guards and wardens) are all part of the criminal justice system. Another important set of criminal justice officials are prosecutors, who can be considered part of the policing or law enforcement function.

16.41 | *The Police*

A police officer is the criminal justice official that the typical person is most likely to have contact with. Police officers are in the community patrolling neighborhoods, streets, and areas where people congregate. The police are also the first criminal justice officials that an offender will have contact with because it is the police who investigate crimes and make arrests. The primary functions of the police are to prevent and investigate violations of criminal laws and to maintain public order. Police officers are empowered to use force and other forms of legal coercion and legal means to effect public and social order. The word police is from the Latin *politia* ("civil administration"), which itself derives from the Ancient Greek word for *polis* ("city"). The London Metropolitan Police established in 1829 by Sir Robert Peel is considered the first modern police force. It promoted the police role in preventing and deterring urban crime and disorder rather than the tradition reactive role of investigating crimes that had already been committed. In the United States, police departments were first established in Boston in 1838 and New York City in 1844. Early police departments were not held in very high regard because they had reputations for being incompetent, corrupt, and political.

In the 1990s, the New York City Police Department developed CompStat (**Compu**ter**Stat**istics) an information-based system for tracking and mapping crime patterns and trends. CompStat is also a tool for holding police departments accountable for dealing with crime. It has been replicated in police departments across the United States and around the world, and is an example of computer information systems are applied to organizations related to policing. The **Federal Bureau of Investigation** is the pre-eminent law enforcement agency in the U.S. It is responsible for investigating interstate crimes and crimes violating federal laws. Although the FBI is the most prominent police organization, it accounts for only a small portion of policing activity in the U.S. Most policing activities such as order maintenance and services such as crowd control or security are actually provided by a broad range of state and local organizations (e.g., state highway patrols; county sheriffs; city police; and school police).

16.42 | *The Courts: Criminal Trials*

The courts are examined in a separate chapter so this section provides a brief description of criminal trials. A trial is, in its simplest terms, a fact-finding process. In the U.S., the primary function of a trial court is dispute resolution. In the criminal justice system, the primary figures are the judge, the jury, the prosecutor, and the defense attorney. The courtroom work group also includes magistrates (who may perform some of the preliminary or ministerial functions of a trial), probation or parole officers, and other professionals who provide relevant information about a defendant or convicted offender. In the past, judges did not have to be lawyers. Justices of the peace were elected members of the community similar to other local leaders. Today, however, a judge in a criminal case is a lawyer. The jury, however, consists of lay people. The U.S. uses this combination of professional and lay people more than most countries, which have decreased their reliance on lay juries. It is a reminder of the close relationship between politics and law in the U.S. administration of justice.

The U.S. legal system is an **adversarial system**. An adversarial system is one where each of the two parties, the adversaries, presents its side of the case and challenges the other side's version of the facts and understanding of the law during a trial or a hearing. A neutral third party—a judge, a panel of judges (some appeals courts hear cases with panels of judges), or a jury—decides the case. The case should be decided in favor of the party who offers the most sound and compelling arguments based on the law as applied to the facts of the case.

Albert Ellery Berg, *The Universal Self-Instructor* (New York: Thomas Kelly, Publisher, 1883) 25.

The adversarial process allows each side to present its case to the judge or jury. The judge or jury is the neutral third party. Having a neutral party settle a dispute between two disputants is one of the oldest and most basic elements of justice—the belief that no one should be a judge of his or her own cause. Justice requires having a neutral third party deciding which side wins the case. In criminal justice, this means that a judge or jury determines whether a person is guilty or not guilty. In some American states, the jury verdict must be a unanimous decision; in others a majority or supermajority vote is enough to obtain a conviction. The prosecutor or district attorney is the government lawyer who brings charges against the person, persons or corporate entity accused of a crime. The prosecutor explains to the court, including the jury if it is a jury trial, what crime was committed and the evidence used to prove the charge. In the U.S. legal system, prosecutors have a great deal of discretion. They can decide whether to charge an individual with a crime, what charge to file, when to go to trial and what kinds of cases to prosecute, and what penalties to ask for upon conviction. For these reasons, prosecutors are extremely important figures in the criminal justice system. They are not merely bureaucrats who follow orders or implement the law. Prosecutorial discretion makes prosecutors powerful figures.

A defense attorney counsels the accused on the legal process, advises of the likely outcomes, and recommends legal strategies. The accused, not the lawyer, has the right to make final decisions on the most important aspects of their legal strategy, including whether to accept a plea bargain offer or go to trial, and whether to take the stand and testify at the trial. The defense attorney has a duty to represent the interests of the client, raise procedural and evidentiary issues, and hold the prosecution to its burden of proving guilt beyond a reasonable doubt. Defense counsel may challenge evidence presented by the prosecution or present exculpatory evidence and argue on behalf of their client. At trial, the defense attorney typically offers a rebuttal to the prosecutor's accusations.

The Sixth Amendment right to the assistance of counsel was originally understood to mean only that a person had a right to a lawyer if they could afford to pay for one, a right that was gradually expanded during the 20th Century. The right to a lawyer was first expanded to cases where a person could receive the death penalty (capital cases). Then the right was expanded to all cases where there were special circumstances such as very young defendants, uneducated defendants, or evidence of racial hostility. Then the right was expanded to all felony trials. And then it was further expanded to all serious cases. In the U.S. today, an accused person is entitled to a government-paid defense attorney, a public defender, if he or she cannot afford an attorney and the charge is so serious that a conviction could result in loss of life or liberty. These changes occurred primarily because judges came to consider the assistance of counsel an essential element of the administration of justice.

The vast majority of cases are settled by plea bargains, not trials. **Plea-bargaining** is when the accused pleads guilty in exchange for a reduction in the number of charges or the sentence. Ideally, a plea bargain is a deal that benefits both the prosecutor and the defense. The prosecutor saves time and money, avoids the risk of losing the case, and may include a requirement that the defendant cooperate with the police by testifying against others. The defendant typically gets a reduction in the number of charges, the severity of the charge offenses, a reduced sentence, and avoids the risk of a more serious loss of liberty or even life. Plea bargains settle over 90% of cases. Many nations do not permit the use of plea-bargaining because it can coerce innocent people to plead guilty in an attempt to avoid harsh punishment. Plea-bargaining is also controversial because it creates the public impression that criminals are getting much less punishment than they deserve. Because a plea bargain usually involves getting a sentence that is substantially less than the maximum penalty for an offense, the public tend to think of plea bargaining as evidence that the system is not as tough on crime as it might be.

Have you ever been called for jury duty? What did you think of the voir dire questioning of the jury pool?

16.43 | Barriers to Justice

There are a number of ways that the criminal justice system can produce unjust outcomes. The police can coerce confessions or make honest makes. Prosecutors may hide exculpatory evidence. Defense counsel can be inadequate. The judge or jury can acquit a guilty person or convict an innocent person. Or a person can be found guilty of a crime that is more or less severe than the one they actually committed. These mistakes can be intentional (misconduct) or unintentional. Bias presents an interesting case. Bias can undermine decision-making in any setting whether civil or criminal justice, employment, education, or health-care. Individuals can be biased for or against someone or something. A cognitive bias is the tendency to make systematic errors that are based on cognitive factors (what someone believes to be true) rather than the factual evidence. Cognitive biases are a common attribute of human thought, and often drastically skew the reliability of anecdotal and legal evidence. Biases can lead to discrimination. Prejudice on the part of the police, prosecutors, judges, or jurors can undermine the legitimacy and credibility of the legal process.

A **prejudice** is a prejudgment, an assumption or belief that is made about someone or something without knowledge of the facts. Prejudice is commonly thought of a preconceived judgment toward a people or a person because of race, class, gender, ethnicity, age, disability, religion, or political beliefs. A prejudice can be a positive prejudice (a favorable predisposition) or a negative prejudice (an unfavorable predisposition). Cognitive prejudice refers to what someone believes to be true. Affective Prejudice refers to what people like and dislike (e.g., attitudes toward members of a particular class, race, ethnicity, national origin, or creed). Behavioral prejudice refers to beliefs about how people are inclined to behave. Prejudices are an extremely important issue during the selection of juries. The jury selection process includes lengthy questions about individual backgrounds and attitudes in order to get a better sense of what prejudices might be indicated. If you have ever been called for jury duty you know how important discovering attitudes and biases is in the *voir dire* process of questioning the jury pool.

Racism is a combination of racial prejudice and discrimination. It involves pre-judging a person based on their race or ethnicity. It attributes to individuals characteristics associated with members of a group. Trials are fact-finding processes that use elaborate rules of evidence partly to minimize the impacts of bias.

One additional source of problems in the criminal justice system is inequality of resources. Legal representation is expensive. The lack of adequate financial or other resources puts a person at a significant disadvantage at all stages of the criminal justice process, not just the trial. The states are required to provide public defenders for those who cannot afford legal counsel, but the state systems vary a great deal and public defenders are not paid well in some states. This is particularly troubling in death penalty cases. This is why capital punishment is jokingly explained by the quip, "If you don't have the capital, you get the punishment."

16.44 | Corrections

After conviction, an offender is turned over to correctional authorities for incarceration in a detention facility (for juveniles), a jail (for shorter terms, usually less than one year), or a prison. The types and purposes of punishment have changed over the years. In early civilizations, the primary forms of punishment were exile, execution, or other forms of corporal (bodily) punishment such as dismemberment (e.g., amputating the hand of a thief) or branding. Traditional societies also relied extensively on informal methods of social control. Laws are a formal method of social control that may be supplemented by other, informal methods of social control, such as religion, professional rules and ethics, or cultural mores and customs. Punishment can also be formal or informal. Shame and shunning were ways to censure individuals whose behavior the community considered inappropriate. The Puritan stocks and the scarlet letter are examples of traditional methods of informal social control. Today, however, prisons and jails are the most important methods of punishment. Formal methods of social control—prosecution for violating the law—have replaced informal methods of social control and punishment. Monetary fines are one of the oldest forms of punishment and they are still used today. These fines may be paid to the state or to the victims as a form of reparation. Probation

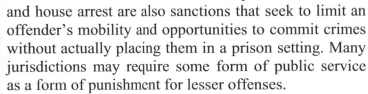

and house arrest are also sanctions that seek to limit an offender's mobility and opportunities to commit crimes without actually placing them in a prison setting. Many jurisdictions may require some form of public service as a form of punishment for lesser offenses.

Correctional reform in the United States was first initiated by William Penn in the latter part of the 17th century.[5] Pennsylvania's criminal code was revised to forbid torture and other forms of cruel punishment. Quakers were among the principal advocates of penal reform. They advocated replacing corporal punishment with institutions where criminals could be rehabilitated or made penitent. Hence the idealistic name penitentiary.

The purposes of punishment have also changed over time. The Quaker movement is commonly credited with establishing the idea that prisons should be used to reform or rehabilitate criminals. Punishment serves four purposes: incapacitation (removing offenders from the general population; deterrence (sending a message that crime does not pay); rehabilitation (reforming offenders); and retribution ("payback"). Many societies consider punishment a form of retribution, and any harm or discomfort the prisoner suffers is just "payback" for the harm they caused their victims. A third purpose is rehabilitation or reform. One aspect of the shift from liberalism to conservatism has been the shift from liberal thinking about crime to conservative thinking about crime. Beginning in the 1970s, sentencing policy moved away from rehabilitation and toward incapacitation, deterrence, and retribution. This policy change has resulted in the U.S. having the highest incarceration rate in the world. The economic and social costs of maintaining such a large prison population has prompted new efforts to find out who really needs to be imprisoned. Can science be used to better predict who will commit crimes or who is really a psychopath?

Think about it! Do humans have a three ice-cream scoop brain? Lister to Jon Hamilton's story "From Primitive Parts, A Highly Evolved Brain," http://www.npr.org/templates/story/story.php?storyId=129027124

Think about it! Can we develop a test to predict who is a psychopath? If so, should we use it to prevent crime? Listen to "Can a Test Really Tell Who's a Psychpath?"http://www.npr.org/2011/05/26/136619689/can-a-test-really-tell-whos-a-psychopath

16.47 | *Capital Punishment*

Capital punishment is probably the most controversial punishment issue. Once widely used in the U.S., it is now limited to capital crimes.[6] Concerns about wrongful convictions, inadequate legal representation, arbitrary or discriminatory application of the death penalty, and a general sense that execution is no longer consistent with the values of civilized societies, have reduced the use of the death penalty. However, efforts to declare it unconstitutional because it violates due process of law or is cruel and unusual punishment have been unsuccessful.

One of the current legal and political issues questions about the death penalty is who should be eligible to be sentenced to death. Should mentally handicapped individuals be eligible for the death penalty? At what point does a low IQ score make a person ineligible for the death penalty? Should minors be eligible for the death penalty? Determining the age at which children become culpable for their behavior is a controversial question. It raises political, moral, and increasingly even scientific questions. Recent advances in brain science have greatly increased the understanding of brain development and the relationship between brain development and behavior, including the kinds of youthful risk-taking behavior that include crime. Brain research has discovered that humans have a rather primitive brain, primitive in the sense that the human brain developed from a jellyfish foundation (which is characterized by primitive neural networks), then added a serpent's brain (which is characterized by simple threat response), and then added the mammal brain (the ape brain).

What does this have to do with crime policy? Brain science research has had an impact on thinking about punishment. The Supreme Court Justices tend to be empirical decision makers in the sense that they rely on evidence-based argument for or against a law. When considering the constitutionality of a law that limits television or radio broadcasts of offensive or indecent material, the Justices consider the empirical evidence of the government's interest in regulating programming. What is the evidence of harm? What percentage of the audience are children during the hours from 10:00 p.m. to 6:00 a.m.? The Justices will also take empirical evidence into consideration when deciding cases involving challenges to laws that make minors eligible for the death penalty. What does the latest brain development research say about the brains of adolescents? Should adolescents be held accountable for their violent actions in the same way that an adult is, and be tried as adults?

In recent years the Supreme Court has struggled with the issue of punishing minors. Once the Court ruled that it was unconstitutional to execute minors it had to decide when someone was too young to execute. This required drawing age lines. Could a person who committed a crime at 17, 16, 15, or 8 years of age be sentenced to death? In *Eddings v. Oklahoma* (1982), the Court set aside the death sentence of a 16 year old.[7] In *Stanford v. Kentucky* (1989) the Court rejected the argument that executing a person who was older than 15 but younger than 18 when they committed the crime violated the 8th and 14th Amendments.[8] In *Thompson v. Oklahoma* (1988), the Court ruled that it was unconstitutional to execute a person who was under age 16, and then in *Roper v. Simmons* (2005) the Court ruled that a person who was under age 18 could not be executed.

16.5 | Resources

One of the most valuable sources of information about crime and the federal criminal justice system is the U.S. Department of Justice (DOJ). One of the DOJ agencies that gathers and reports criminal and civil justice statistics is the Bureau of Justice Statistics. The BJS data on crime rates and rates of incarceration and prison populations provide information about a broad range of subjects including public opinion.[9] The BJS reports include the prison population, rates of imprisonment, and changes in rates of imprisonment. The BJS reports also provide information about capital punishment (i.e., "Death Penalty"). The high rate of incarceration during the years of getting tough on crime has made the U.S. the country with the highest rate of imprisonment in the world. The heavy reliance on imprisonment as punishment is a public policy issue because it is expensive to maintain prisons and because there are questions about its effectiveness.[10]

16.6 | The States

As sovereign entities in a federal system of government, the states have substantial responsibility for crime policy. Each state can create its own criminal laws and criminal justice system. As a result, crime policies vary widely. The rate of incarceration varies dramatically from state to state and region to region. The Southern states have the highest rates of incarceration. The map below indicates the number of state prison inmates per 100,000 residents

Incarceration Rates, 2006

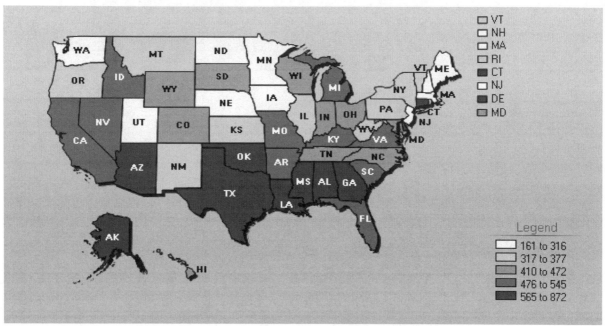

Number of State Prison Inmates per 100,000 State Residents[11]

16.7 | Internet Sources

The Code of Hammurabi. 1760 BC. http://www.wsu.edu/~dee/MESO/CODE.HTM

The U.S. Department of Justice gathers and reports criminal and civil justice statistics. The Bureau of Justice Statistics data on crime rates and rates of incarceration and prison populations provides important information about criminal justice policies: http://www.ojp.usdoj.gov/bjs/

Bureau of Justice Statistics. http://bjs.ojp.usdoj.gov/

The Florida Office of the Attorney provides information about crime in Florida at http://myfloridalegal.com/.

The Florida Department of Corrections also provides information about prisons in Florida at http://www.dc.state.fl.us/.

Information about Florida's Death Row (who is on death row, or what a death row cell looks like), is available at:

> **TERMS**
>
> The Crime Control and Due Process Models of Justice
> Civil law
> Criminal law
> Federal Bureau of Investigation
> Federalizing Crime
> Rates of Incarceration
> Adversarial system
> Plea bargaining
> Prejudice
> Legal Discrimination

http://www.dc.state.fl.us/oth/deathrow/index.html

---

[1] Packer explained the two models in *The Limits of the Criminal Sanction* (Stanford: Stanford University Press, 1968).

[2] On the Foreign Intelligence Surveillance Act Courts, see
http://judgepedia.org/index.php/United_States_Foreign_Intelligence_Surveillance_Court
http://www.fas.org/irp/agency/doj/fisa/. For information about FBI National Security Letters see
http://www.u-s-history.com/pages/h1205.html Domestic military operations also raise questions of constitutional protections. See http://www.aclu.org/safefree/torture/34745res20030314.html

[3] http://www.apuritansmind.com/Reformation/MemoirsReformers/MemoirsJohnLambert.htm

[4] http://www.oyez.org/cases/1960-1969/1965/1965_759
http://www.pbs.org/wnet/supremecourt/rights/landmark_miranda.html
http://www.pbs.org/wnet/supremecourt/rights/landmark_miranda.html
[5] http://www.quaker.org/wmpenn.html
[6] See *Kennedy v. Louisiana* (2008) at http://www.law.cornell.edu/supct/html/07-343.ZO.html
[7] http://www.law.cornell.edu/supct/html/historics/USSC_CR_0455_0104_ZO.html
[8] http://www.law.cornell.edu/supct/html/historics/USSC_CR_0492_0361_ZS.html
[9] See http://www.ojp.usdoj.gov/bjs/
[10] http://www.pewcenteronthestates.org/report_detail.aspx?id=35904
[11] http://www.pewcenteronthestates.org/ttw/trends_map_data_table.aspx?trendID=11&assessmentID=24

CHAPTER 17: GLOBAL AFFAIRS

17.0 | Global Affairs: Foreign Policy, National Security, and War Powers

How did the U.S., which was founded as a republic that was opposed to empires, become an empire? When did the U.S. become the world policeman? How did the president become the leader of the free world? Is the Caribbean Sea "an American lake" where the U.S. is largely free to do what it wants? What will the world be like in the year 2030? These are some of the questions that are examined in this chapter on global affairs, an area of public policy that presents special challenges for holding government power politically or legally accountable.

The term global affairs includes foreign policy—the federal government's plans to advance national interests in dealing with other nations; national security—policies and actions to protect against domestic and foreign threats to the U.S. government or the territorial integrity of the U.S.; and war powers—the use of military force. Like domestic policy, global affairs involve politics. However, there are two important differences between the politics of domestic affairs and global affairs. One of the differences concerns the fact that the political system of accountability does not operate in global affairs the way it operates in domestic affairs; the other difference concerns the legitimacy of projecting government power abroad.

The power problem in global affairs is *accountability*. Global affairs present special challenges for the political system's mechanisms to hold government officials politically and legally accountable for their use of power. The accountability problem has been a recurring theme in debates about foreign affairs from the founding of the republic to the war on terror.

- The Constitutional Convention. The delegates to the constitutional convention in 1787 extensively debated how to hold the government accountable on matters related to war powers and external (foreign) affairs.
- The early years of the republic. The debate about accountability continued during the early years of the republic when the U.S. was a new nation that was surrounded by imperial powers that were ambitious to expand their sphere of influence and Native Americans that sometimes opposed American expansion westward.
- Becoming a world power. Accountability was an issue in the latter part of the 19th Century when the U.S. developed into an economic and military power and used that power to acquire territory and exert influence beyond the nation's original borders.
- Acting as the world's policeman. In the early years of the 20th Century accountability was an issue when the U.S. assumed the role of world policeman and leader of the free world in the early years of the 20th Century.
- The Cold War. During the Cold War, the emphasis on secrecy and emergency powers in the global fight against communism weakened the ordinary methods of holding government (particularly executive officials) accountable for the use of power in national security affairs.
- The War on Terror. Congress delegated the president broad power to make and implement counterterrorism policy. Holding presidential power politically or legally accountable has remained one of the most important and controversial issues in the debates about counterterrorism policy.

Legitimacy is an important concept in political science. It is a normative term that refers to the belief that something is appropriate, legal, right, or just. A legitimate government, law, or public policy is one that is accepted as appropriate. A democratic government is the legitimate authority to govern domestically. But what gives a government—even a democracy—the right to project power abroad? This is a political question that has been asked from the founding of the republic to contemporary debates about U.S. involvement with global affairs.

This chapter examines accountability and legitimacy by discussing four main questions about global affairs policy.

- Should the U.S. be involved in global affairs?
- What should global affairs policy be?
- How is American power projected abroad?
- Who should make global affairs policy?

The first question is **whether** the U.S. should be involved in global affairs or stay out of external matters and concentrate on domestic affairs. This is basically the question of engagement or isolation. The second question is substantive: once the decision has been made to get involved with global affairs, what should public policy be concerning international drug cartels, international trade, global warming, the Middle East, or the strength of the dollar? Elements of the policy making process (or stages) apply here—although there are some differences between domestic and foreign policy. The third question about global affairs is **how** should the U.S. project American power? Should the U.S. use *hard* power—that is, military force—or *soft* power—that is, economic power and political influence including diplomacy—in order to achieve its objectives? The fourth question is **who** should make policy. The question, who should make foreign affairs policy, is primarily the struggle between congress and the president (and to a lesser extent the courts) over control of global affairs. The institutional conflict between congress and the president is one of the things that make the politics of global affairs distinctive and different from domestic affairs. There are some non-governmental actors who participate in the foreign affairs issue networks but interest groups play a smaller role than they do in domestic affairs. The fourth question is about the system of checks and balances. The system of checks and balances is much weaker in global affairs than domestic affairs, which is another reason why the politics and governance of global affairs is distinctive. The weaker checks and balances present special accountability problems particularly for holding presidents legally accountable for the way they use power. Two aspects of presidential power over foreign affairs create accountability problems. The first is the **Sole Organ Doctrine**. The Sole Organ Doctrine holds that the president is the sole organ of the nation in its dealings with other countries. To paraphrase President George W. Bush, "I am the decider." By this he meant that congress and the courts were NOT the deciders. The second aspect of presidential power that creates special accountability problems is **executive discretion**. Executive discretion is an executive official's freedom of choice to decide upon a course of action. Executive discretion is exemplified by war powers statutes, national security statutes, or other statutes that delegate the president power to do whatever the president thinks is necessary. The chapter includes prominent examples of statutes that give the president broad discretion to act in domestic and national security affairs. Executive discretion is one of the distinguishing features of global affairs policy.

> But I am the decider, and I decide what is best."
>
> President George W. Bush

17.1 | The Weak System of Checks and Balances in Global Affairs

There are several ways that the politics and government of global affairs are different than domestic affairs. **First**, global affairs typically involve different kinds of conflicts. Domestic conflicts typically involve economic or values choices; global affairs conflicts typically involve national interests or security. **Second**, global affairs have historically involved a different set of government and non-government actors than those that are typically involved with domestic affairs. State and local governments and the set of interest groups that participate in domestic policy making are not as prominent in global affairs. **Third**, the system of checks and balances does not work in global affairs the way it works in domestic affairs. In domestic affairs, policy choices are typically between competing **economic** interests (e.g., business versus labor),

partisan conflict (e.g., Republicans versus Democrats), **ideological** conflict (e.g., conservative versus liberal views on the size and role of government), or **institutional** conflicts between Congress, the president, the Supreme Court, or between the national and state governments. The Madisonian system of checks and balances that was intended to prevent government abuse of power includes the separation of powers, federalism, public opinion, and (today) partisanship. But these checks and balances do not operate in global affairs the way they operate in domestic affairs.

17.11 | *Partisanship*

Party politics has become part of the system of checks and balances: the party IN power is supposed to be held accountable by the party OUT of power. But party politics does not work in global affairs the way it works in domestic affairs. For example, there is an old saying that politics stops at the water's edge. This saying describes the belief that it is appropriate to **play politics** in domestic policy but not foreign policy. The belief that politics should stop at the water's edge reflects the desire to put aside party politics or other political differences so that the U.S. can present a united front in its dealings with other countries. The belief that politics should stop at the water's edge is the basis for appeals to create bipartisan foreign policy. The appeal for bipartisanship in foreign affairs is based on the assumption that partisan conflict and competition are appropriate for domestic politics but not foreign affairs.

17.12 | *Separation of Powers*

The separation of powers among the three branches of government is different in domestic and global affairs. In global affairs, the president is the most powerful actor. Congress generally follows the president's lead. The Supreme Court has a tradition of judicial restraint in global affairs—it generally stays out of disputes involving global affairs. Furthermore, in cases where individuals, companies, or Congress have challenged presidential actions, the Supreme Court has ruled that the president has primary, and perhaps exclusive, responsibility for the conduct of global affairs. In *U.S. v. Curtiss-Wright Export Corporation* (1936) a company in the business of selling weapons, the Curtiss-Wright Export Corporation, challenged the president's power to declare an arms embargo prohibiting the sale of arms to two South American countries that were fighting over a disputed border region. President Franklin Roosevelt declared the arms embargo because he thought it would aid the American foreign policy goal of bringing peace to the region. The Supreme Court upheld the president's power using the **Sole Organ** doctrine. The Sole Organ doctrine, which was first stated by Representative John Marshall, is that the Constitution makes the president the "sole organ" of the nation in its dealings with other nations. The Court's ruling strengthened subsequent presidential claims that the president, not Congress or the courts, has the power to conduct foreign policy. There are differences of opinion about the scope of the Sole Organ doctrine. Congress and the Supreme Court do challenge presidential actions, but both Congress and the Supreme Court have agreed that the president has broad powers in the area of global affairs and they generally defer to the president's determination of what policies are appropriate. The president can limit partisan or other challenges to foreign affairs policies, particularly those related to national security, by portraying critics or political opponents as un-American, unpatriotic, or even a threat to national security. Presidents play the Commander-in-Chief card to limit political opposition.

17.13 | *Federalism*

Federalism is the geographic division of powers between the national and state governments. Federalism does not operate as a very important check on presidential power in global affairs because global affairs are predominantly, and on some matters exclusively, national rather than state government powers. The <u>Supremacy Clause</u> provides that federal laws (the Constitution, statutes, and treaties) shall be "the supreme law of the land" and states are required to recognize federal laws. According to the **preemption doctrine**, federal policies trump state policies where they conflict. The states can pass laws in policy areas where the federal government also legislates (e.g., education, crime, the environment). But federal law preempts state laws that conflict with federal law. Immigration policy is one of the areas where state and federal laws sometimes conflict because states bordering Mexico, for example, have special interests in immigration issues. As the number of illegal immigrants has increased in some states, and the number of immigrants in general has increased in some states, voters in those states have enacted laws that clash with federal laws—or reflect a different view of how to enforce existing immigration laws, or present different views on eligibility for public services such as education, health care, and social welfare.

17.14 | *Public Opinion*

In democratic systems, public opinion is considered a vital essential check on government power. But there are three reasons why public opinion is often a weak check on government power in global affairs. **First**, the public is not as well informed about foreign affairs as it is about domestic affairs. The typical voter pays much closer attention to domestic issues such as the condition of the schools, the economy, and the roads than matters of foreign affairs. **Second**, the public is more dependent on the federal government for information about global affairs. A person may know a great deal about the condition of the local roads that they drive regularly because they have personal experience with driving them. A person may know a great deal about whether their neighborhood is safe and whether their local schools are good. But the average person is dependent on the government for information about most of the issues related to global affairs. This information dependency gives the government a freer hand to act independent of public opinion or even to create public opinion. **Third**, the typical public reaction to an international crisis, emergency, or foreign threat is to *rally around the flag*. This phrase describes the increase in patriotic support for the government that typically occurs in the wake of a foreign threat, attack, or crisis. The rally effect certainly occurred after the terrorist attacks of 9/11 when presidential approval ratings increased dramatically. The president, as the government official most closely identified with global affairs, can expect increased public support in the immediate aftermath of a foreign crisis that touches on national security. However, public support will decline if a crisis continues, a hostage rescue or military action fails, or a war lingers on for a long period of time.

17.2 | Two Traditions: Isolation or Engagement?

There are two competing views of U.S. global affairs policy: **isolationism** and **engagement**. These two views describe what U.S. global affairs policy is and, to a certain extent, what global affairs policy should be. The isolationist view is that the U.S. should maintain its tradition of staying out of foreign affairs or at least minimizing its engagement. Isolationists advocate inward looking politics where the government focuses on domestic or internal affairs rather than outward looking politics where the government focuses on foreign or external affairs. The isolationist tradition in American politics can be traced to three causes. First, the country was founded as a republic that was born of a revolution fought against the imperial tradition of global engagement practiced by the European powers, primarily the British, French, and Spanish empires. The second reason is geography. The U.S. was a young nation that was separated from the intrigues of European power politics by two great oceans, the Atlantic and the Pacific, which enabled it to minimize interactions with other countries. The third reason is ideological. The ideological argument for isolationism is that the U.S. has rejected activist or engaged foreign policy because it has an "anti-statist ideology" that includes a rejection of centralized government power.[1]

Engagement refers to the argument that the U.S. has a political tradition of active engagement in global affairs and that this engagement is appropriate policy. Supporters of engagement describe the U.S. history of involvement with other nations from the earliest days of the republic. They maintain that the U.S. has strategically used its economic, military, and political power to advance its interests abroad. The view presented in this chapter is that the U.S. has elements of both isolation and engagement. The engagement in global affairs has historically been controversial because the anti-statist ideology—sometimes expressed by liberals and sometimes expressed by conservatives—opposes national government activism abroad. But American politics also includes very prominent examples of engagement in global affairs.

17.21 | *Isolation*

American politics has from the founding included debates about whether to be involved with global affairs and how any involvement should occur. One of the most famous expressions of isolationist policy is President George Washington's *Farewell Address*. This famous *Address*, which was delivered as Washington was preparing to leave office in 1796, is remembered today primarily for the father of the country advising the young republic's future leaders to stay out of foreign affairs and international intrigues—particularly the European politics that produced seemingly endless wars. Washington did indeed advise the country's leaders to avoid entangling alliances. But Washington did not advise isolation. He did not urge the nation's leaders to look inward not outward. His advice was more nuanced. Washington advised having **commercial** (or business) relations with other nations but not political relations:

> "History and experience prove that foreign influence is one of the most baneful foes of republican government…. The great rule of conduct for us in regard to foreign nations is, in extending our commercial relations to have with them as little *political* connection as possible."

He though that avoiding political connections was the best way for the young republic to keep out of the European politics that had a long history of complicated political entanglements that resulted in many and long wars. Washington urged the country's future leaders to be skeptical of

Think about it!
Was Washington right to warn the nation's leaders to stay out of foreign affairs?

"entangling" U.S. peace and prosperity with the European tradition of the politics of intrigue and avarice. When political connections with other countries were necessary, he recommended "temporary alliances" for those emergencies and warned the nation's leaders to "steer clear of permanent alliances with any portion of the foreign world." He also worried about the U.S. joining an alliance with another country because he believed that "a small or weak" country that attached itself to a "great and powerful nation dooms the former to be the satellite of the latter."

Washington's *Farewell Address* was not limited to giving advice about how the country could avoid war, while not becoming subservient to great powers, and still pursue the national interest. He also spoke about the importance of remaining true to the nation's founding values while pursuing national self-interest. He specifically mentioned values such as observing good faith and justice towards all nations, promoting peace and harmony with all nations, avoiding "inveterate antipathies" against some nations and "passionate attachments" to others, and advocating trade with all nations. Washington and other leading members of the Federalist Party, most notably Alexander Hamilton, wanted the U.S. to develop as a "commercial republic." But Hamilton disagreed with those who believed that commercial republics were the key to a peaceful world because commercial republics would not engage in armed conflict with other countries because they would be interested in trade rather than imperial power or national glory. In *Federalist Number 6*, for example, Hamilton argued that it was naïve idealism or "utopian" to think that commercial enterprises would replace war.

Isolationists also opposed U.S. participation in WWI and initially opposed U.S. fighting in WWII. One of the most famous advocates of isolationism was Charles Lindbergh. Lindbergh was a national hero whose strong statements urging the U.S. to stay out of WWII permanently damaged his reputation. His 1941 <u>Address to the America First Committee</u> is a strong statement of isolationism.

17.22 | *Engagement*

The political tradition of engagement also has roots in early American politics. The active engagement tradition is evident in early 19th Century thought and action. The Monroe Doctrine (1823) declared that the entire Western Hemisphere was within the U.S. sphere of influence and any attempts by European imperial powers to colonize countries or to interfere with political developments within the region—at a time when Latin American countries were experiencing independence movements from the Spanish Empire—would be considered justification for American military action. The doctrine of **Manifest Destiny** and the idea of **American Exceptionalism** also provided political and religious justifications for territorial expansion. Manifest Destiny is the belief that the United States was destined to expand its sphere of influence over the western territories of North America and even beyond the region. Manifest Destiny provided the political justification for westward expansion to settle the American frontier. It provided a justification for fighting Indian Wars to remove Native Americans from their traditional lands. It also provided a justification for territorial expansion by buying vast tracts of land through agreements such as the Louisiana Purchase in 1803, which almost doubled the geographic size of the nation. The nation's territory also expanded in 1819 when Spain ceded the territory of Florida and in 1845 when the U.S. annexed Texas.

The Louisiana Purchase greatly increased the geographic size of the U.S.
http://www.nps.gov/archive/jeff/lewisclark2/circa1804/herita ge/louisianapurchase/louisianapurchase.htm

Manifest Destiny also justified military expansion by fighting the Mexican-American War (1846-1848) and Spanish-American War (1898). When the U.S. won the Mexican-American War in 1848 it acquired the vast territories that comprise California, Arizona, and New Mexico. The U.S. bought Alaska from the Russian Empire in 1867 and annexed the Republic of Hawaii in 1898. The U.S. victory over Spain in the Spanish-American War gave the U.S. possession of the former Spanish colonies of the Philippines and Puerto Rico and control over Cuba. The Spanish-American War was politically controversial in the U.S. because it involved an offensive use of American military power abroad. Critics of the War argued that it transformed the U.S. from a republic into an empire. The U.S. was a young republic that had successfully fought a revolutionary war against Great Britain, a great imperial power. In fact, the U.S. Declaration of Independence and Revolutionary War served as models for other nations to assert their national independence from other imperial powers that ruled over other people. William Graham Sumner (1840-1910) was an American academic whose essay entitled "The Conquest of the U.S. By Spain" (1899) argued that the U.S. won the Spanish-American War but paid a high price for its military victory: the U.S. won the war but lost its status as a republic because it acquired colonies and became an imperial power.[2]

American Exceptionalism is the belief that the U.S. is a special country, that its creation and rise to superpower status are indications that the U.S. is a great country that is destined to play a unique role in world politics, and that it has a responsibility to use its power. Exceptionalism has played a very important role in the nation's global affairs, particularly in providing a justification for the legitimacy of the U.S. using its political, military, and economic power to project American influence abroad. American Exceptionalism continues to play an important role in American political discourse, presidential campaign rhetoric, and public policy.

The U.S. role in world politics has changed a great deal since the country was founded. The U.S. plays a much **greater** role and a very **different** role in international affairs. The conventional wisdom is that the Founders opposed U.S. involvement in foreign affairs, particularly getting involved with the intrigue of European power politics. While they were indeed wary of foreign affairs, they did not advise isolation rather than engagement. Reading two major sources of the Founders' thinking—the debates at the constitutional convention of 1787 and the *Federalist Papers*—paints a more complicated picture. The convention delegates thought a great deal about how a young republic should deal with other nations and extensively debated foreign affairs. They knew that a successful republican government must be strong enough to provide national security from foreign threats. The Founders were not isolationists— at least not in the sense that they wanted the U.S. to be a republic that only looked inward and was only concerned about domestic affairs. They were aware of world politics. They understood that the Revolutionary War was not **merely** about the U.S, that the Revolutionary War for independence was part of a broader, even global conflict that involved the U.S. and the global powers of the day: England, France, Spain, and the Netherlands.

In fact, the Founders realized that the U.S. was likely to be unable to remain unaffected by politics outside the country even if it wanted to remain isolated. Therefore they supported the creation of a **commercial republic**. A commercial republic was one that was actively involved with other countries (particularly the European power) but primarily by commercial dealings.

The engagement was international trade rather than the use of military force. The belief that the U.S. should be engaged in international trade made political sense. The U.S. was a struggling young nation. It faced economic difficulties. Sectional differences between the north, the sound and the frontier raised questions about national unity. The young republic did not have a substantial military, and it was surrounded by territories controlled by Indian Tribes and three expansionist imperial powers (France, England, and Spain). The Founders were acutely aware of foreign threats to their existence.

17.3 | Foreign Policy

Foreign policy is defined as the set of goals and public policies that a country establishes for its interactions with other nations and, to a lesser extent, non-state actors. Foreign policies are designed to promote national interests, national security, ideology, political values, and economic prosperity. The tools of foreign policy include economic, political, social, diplomatic, technological, and military resources.

As U.S. economic and military power increased during the latter part of the 19th century, the U.S. became an increasingly important player on the global stage. This aspect of American political development marked an important, long-term shift in U.S. foreign policy that included territorial expansion, more active involvement in foreign affairs, and more engagement in international relations. In the early years of the 20th Century, U.S. foreign policy was shaped primarily by growing international trade, concerns about immigration, participation in World War I, and claims of a national right to intervene in Caribbean and Central American politics.

The U.S. role on the global stage continued to increase after WWII with American efforts to avoid another global conflict by bringing order to the anarchistic world of international relations. International relations were "anarchistic" in the sense that each country pursued its national interest using power politics, whereby might makes right and justice is merely the national interest of the stronger nation, and relying on military force as the primary way to settle the disputes that inevitably arose. The U.S. interest in playing a role in world peace did not begin with the WWII era. It has older roots. President Woodrow Wilson had ambitious, idealistic plans to use American power to make the world safe for democracy. One component of this plan was the creation of a League of Nations. However, the Wilson administration was unable to convince Congress to support the League of Nations. The U.S. never joined the League of Nations partly because of the political tradition emphasizing unilateral action rather than joining international organization and the preservative of U.S. sovereignty.

In the years preceding WWII, the United States was involved with foreign trade, but otherwise its foreign policy in the 1920s and 1930s tended to be isolationist. As a result, when Germany and Japan built up their military in the 1930s and used military force against their neighbors, the Roosevelt administration had to overcome strong public resistance to joining international efforts to confront the threats presented by these new totalitarian regimes. The U.S. did provide military aid to Great Britain in its fight against Germany (e.g., though the Lend-Lease Program) and then entered the war and lead allied war efforts against Germany, Japan, and Italy. The contribution of U.S. industrial production as the American economy was converted from peacetime production to wartime production was a major factor in winning the war. Until WWII, the U.S. would mobilize the military for war and then demobilize the military after the war. After WWII, the U.S. returned to a peacetime economy and industrial production but kept some of the most important government institutions that were responsible for national security and military readiness. The U.S. kept a standing peacetime army for the first time in its history. And the federal government kept the institutions that were created to ensure national defense and national security. Therefore one legacy of WWII is the **warfare state**. The term warfare state refers to the permanent national security and defense institutions, including the <u>Department of Defense</u>, the <u>Central Intelligence Agency</u>, and <u>the National Security Agency</u>. One result of the Great Depression was the creation of a social welfare state. One result of WWII was the creation of a warfare state.

During the middle years of the 20th Century, American foreign policy was dominated by World War II and the Cold War. The post-WWII era of U.S. economic prosperity contributed to the expansion of American influence abroad and extended engagement in global affairs. The end of the **hot** war did not mean the end of conflict. The U.S. adopted the Cold War policy of **containment** to limit the Soviet expansion of its influence over regions of the world. Containment was a multi-faceted policy that was intended to counter Soviet influence in countries or regions where the Soviets were extending their influence. Containment included the use of American economic, military, and political power.

- Economic power. This included using foreign aid and other types of economic or development assistance as instruments of foreign policy.
- Political influence. This included diplomacy, treaties (such as the North Atlantic Treaty Organization or NATO), and other international agreements such as executive orders as instruments of foreign policy.
- Military power. This included overt military actions, covert operations, and even proxy wars. A proxy war is a war that is militarily supported by one country but found by another usually smaller country.

In a famous *Farewell Address* delivered January 17, 1961, President Eisenhower warned of the dangers presented by the national security establishment. He advised the American public and government officials to "guard against the acquisition of unwarranted influence...by the military-industrial complex."[3]

The dissolution of the Soviet Union in 1989 meant that the U.S.'s main adversary during the long Cold War period was no longer an immediate military threat. As a result, American foreign policy shifted away from the military and toward international trade, human rights, and diplomacy as ways to achieve foreign policy goals. This change from military power to international relations as the central element of foreign policy continued until the terrorist attacks of 9/11.

17.31 | *The Modern Conservative Era*

In foreign policy, the modern conservative era began in the latter 1960s and early 1970s as a reaction against liberalism. Conservatives blamed liberals and liberalism for making the U.S. economically vulnerable and militarily weak. They specifically blamed liberals for the following problems:

- Going soft on communism. Conservatives thought that American foreign policy was no longer sufficiently anti-communist, that the American emphasis on peace and diplomacy reflected efforts to appeasement the Soviet Union that were similar to British efforts to appease Hitler's Germany prior to WWII.

- The loss of the <u>War in Vietnam</u>. The loss of the war, punctuated by media images of the chaotic withdrawal of the remaining Americans when Saigon fell in 1975, raised questions about both the *effectiveness* of American military power and the *willingness* to use military power in the national interest. Conservatives blamed liberals for the loss of national confidence in American power, a condition that conservatives called the "Vietnam Syndrome."

- Energy dependency. In the 1970s, two oil embargoes by <u>The Organization of the Petroleum Exporting Countries</u> (OPEC) exposed how vulnerable the American economy (and lifestyle) was because of dependence on foreign oil.

- The Soviet invasion of Afghanistan. The Soviet Union invaded Afghanistan in December 1979. The perception that the U.S. could do little about the invasion or similar aggressive actions by the United States' main Cold War adversary contributed to a sense of American military weakness or decline.

- The Iran Hostages. In 1979, Americans were taken hostage in Iran as part of a revolution against the Shah of Iran, an authoritarian ruler who had been an ally of the U.S. in the Middle East. The hostage-taking, and a failed hostage rescue mission, reinforced the perception of American weakness.

In order to counteract these real and perceived weaknesses, conservatives (and Republican presidents) advocated a buildup of the American military and a restoration of the American sense of a duty to act with a national purpose on the world stage. Richard Nixon's *Address to the Bohemian Society* in July 1967 explains the intellectual foundations of President Nixon's foreign policy goals and those of Republican Presidents Reagan, George H.W. Bush, and George W. Bush. This *Address* is significant because it shows that already in the mid 1960s conservative political leaders were describing communism as a failed and failing ideology; giving American military superiority credit for the years of peace following World War II (which came to be called *Pax Americana*); encouraging a military buildup based on the conservative idea of "Peace Through Strength;" and advocating the use of American economic power as an instrument of foreign policy to counter Soviet influence across the globe.[4] In fact, many of the ideas in Nixon's 1967 *Address* informed President Reagan's foreign policy in the 1980s.

Ronald Reagan won the 1980 presidential election at least partly because he campaigned on the promise of rebuilding the national spirit and the military to fight Soviet communism. After the fall of the Soviet Union, conservatives advocated American acceptance of its responsibility as the sole remaining superpower. In *The Case for Goliath: How America Acts as the World's Government In the Twenty-First Century* (2006), Michael Mandelbaum argued that the U.S. had become a de facto world government because of its status as the sole remaining military and economic superpower. The U.S. offered military security in regions of the world through alliances such as NATO, the promotion and regulation of international trade through economic treaties as the General Agreements on Tariff and Trade (which is now the World Trade Organization), financial stability through the maintenance of a solid dollar as a global currency, and support for legal recourse for the violation of human rights.

17.32 | *New Foreign Policy Issues: Trade*

The end of the Cold War in 1991 began a period where American foreign policy shifted away from the East-West conflict between two military superpowers (the U.S. and the Soviet Union). Post-Cold War foreign policy emphasized economic issues: the promotion of trade; economic development; and global economic competition. Economic competition has focused on China, India, and Brazil, who have emerged as major economic competitors particularly in manufacturing. China is also a Communist country therefore its rapid economic development and emergence as an economic competitor has raised concerns about whether it will present a military and political threat to the U.S. The economic results of China's public policy strategy to promote rapid economic growth and development are already apparent. China now has the world's second largest economy (as measured by Gross Domestic Product) having surpassed Japan. The close relationship between economics and politics has historically raised questions about how a nation plans to use its power, and the political consequences of China's emergence as a world economic power are certainly a part of American political debates about China.

The emergence of these new international economic competitors has prompted debates about what public policies the U.S. should adopt to ensure that the U.S. remains competitive in the global marketplace. The Conference Board is a "global business membership and research association" that describes itself as working to advance the public interest by providing the world's leading organizations with practical knowledge to improve their performance and to better serve society. Like many other business organizations, the Conference Board promotes public policies that encourage economic growth. It believes that the current low rates of economic growth in the U.S. have two main causes. The first is **demographics**. The U.S., like other developed countries, has an aging population. An aging population means an increased percentage of elderly people. Elderly people require more medical care and other social services and they are less likely to be working—therefore they are more likely to be consumers of services rather than producers. The Conference Board believes that the second cause of low economic growth is **educational**: stagnant educational attainment is blamed for stagnant economic growth rates. The Conference Board recommends changing immigration policy to solve the demographic problem of an aging population—specifically, changing immigration policies to allow more high-skilled workers into the country. Business interest groups generally support immigration policy as a partial solution to the problem of stagnant educational attainment or a mismatch between employer needs and employee skill sets.

Should the U.S. grant more temporary work visas for certain skilled foreign workers in order to meet the demand for high tech workers? The H-1B Visa Program was designed to do so. But now employers are using the program for a different purpose. Listen to "Older Tech Workers Oppose Overhauling H-1B Visas."

> **Think About It!**
> Is immigration the solution to the problem of low economic growth?
> **Act on It!**
> Contact a government official (in the U.S. or another country), a business leader, or an interest group or political party official to see what they think about immigration policy.

17.33 | *New Foreign Policy Issues: Globalization*

Think about it!
See the British Broadcasting Corporation's "Meet China's Booming Middle Class" Aired July 2012
http://www.bbc.co.uk/news/business-18901437

Globalization is a broad term two meanings. It refers to **the process** whereby governments, economies, cultures, and societies are becoming more and more interconnected and interdependent. It also refers to **the results** or impacts of these processes. The process of globalization began with the promotion of international trade, primarily international business, but it has extended far beyond trade to include issues such as human rights, environmental policy, sustainable development, and even good governance.[5] Globalization is one of the factors that diminish the differences between domestic affairs and global affairs.

Globalization makes the people of one country more connected with the people of other countries. It also makes people more interdependent. This is ironic because Americans do not know very much about the people, politics, geography, and economics of other countries compared to what people of other countries know about the U.S. One reason why people in other countries know more about the U.S. than American know about them is the U.S. media do not provide much coverage of politics in other countries compared to other countries' media coverage of U.S. politics. Read a newspaper or magazine, watch a television news program, or go to your favorite Web site to see how much news coverage is state/local, national, and international.

Think About It!
What do people in other countries think about U.S. presidential elections?
Public Radio International's *The World* provides "Foreign Views on the American Presidency and the Election," (November 5, 2012).
http://www.theworld.org/

Act on it!
Write a letter to the editor of one of the major newspapers of the world to see whether it gets published.

17.34 | *New Foreign Policy Issues: Religion*

Human rights issues are one of the foreign policy. In recent years, freedom of religion has become one of the human rights issues that foreign policy makers have addressed. As a result, the Department of State's Office of International Religious Freedom now provides information about the status of freedom of religion in various countries that can be used as a benchmark for assessing freedom of religion as one component of how free a political system is.

17.4 | Instruments of Foreign and Defense Policy

Treaties and executive agreements are the two major forms of official agreements with other countries. The major difference between treaties and executive agreements is that executive agreements are less formal than treaties and they are not subject to the constitutional requirement of ratification by a two-thirds vote of the Senate.

17.41 | *Treaties*

Treaties are formal written agreements between two or more countries. The Treaty Clause of the Constitution (Article II, Section 2) provides that the President "shall have Power, by and with the Advice and Consent of the Senate, to make Treaties, provided two thirds of the Senators present concur...." This means that the president or his advisors negotiate a treaty with another country or countries, but the Senate must ratify it in order to take effect. There are at least four reasons why the Senate might reject a treat. First, senators might oppose the **substance** of the treaty. A proposed treaty can be opposed on policy grounds and voted against the same way that proposed legislation is voted against. Second, senators might have a principled objection to treaties in the tradition of heeding President Washington's advice to beware entangling alliances with other countries. President Wilson proposed the Treaty of Versailles after World War I but the Senate rejected it primarily because the **isolationist tradition** made Senators wary of U.S. participation in permanent international organizations.

   Sovereignty and **federalism** are the third and fourth reasons why Senators, state government officials, and the general public are wary of treaties. The term sovereignty means the supreme and independent government authority. The idea of national sovereignty and the commitment to preserving U.S. national sovereignty is very strong in the U.S., much stronger than in many European countries for instance. Treaties can obligate U.S. government officials to comply with international law or treaty obligations, thereby weakening U.S. national sovereignty defined as the power to act independently. Therefore defenders of U.S. national sovereignty, organizations such as Sovereignty International, Inc., alert Americans to the threats presented by treaties, executive agreements, and the general trend toward global governance. National sovereignty is one of the reasons for political opposition to the United Nations, opposition to putting U.S. troops under UN control, and even opposition to treaties that strengthen human rights or the rights of children—two issues that might seem on their face to be non-controversial. Figure 17-1 below describes three levels of sovereignty (state, national, and supranational). American political development includes the change from the founding era when the states were considered the primary level of government to the modern era when the national government has assumed greater powers. This change has been controversial and remains one of the reasons for opposition to "big" government. Efforts to create supranational governing authorities are even more controversial because they would mark a shift toward locating sovereignty outside the U.S. political and government system.

Figure 17.1: Three Levels of Sovereignty

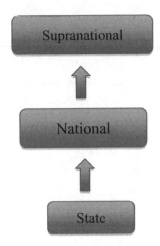

Think About It!
Do globalization and international relations threaten U.S. national sovereignty?
http://sovereignty.net/

The fourth reason why Americans are wary of treaties is federalism. In most nations, treaties supersede domestic law: the treaty trumps domestic law where there is a conflict between the two kinds of law. In the U.S., federalism complicates the legal status of treaties. Treaties are considered federal laws. But their effects on state laws are complicated because of the divisions of power between the national and state governments.

The Constitution's Supremacy Clause provides that federal law trumps state law where the state law conflicts with federal law. Treaties (and executive agreements) have the same legal status as federal laws. State government officials may be even more opposed to treaties that limit state criminal justice policies—for instance, prohibiting the execution of minors or requiring the state to notify consular officials when a non-citizen has been arrested in the state—than federal laws.

Exactly where treaties fit into the U.S. legal system is further complicated by three factors. First, Congress can modify treaties, reinterpret treaty obligations, and even repeal treaties even if doing so constitutes a violation of international law. Second, the president can unilaterally reinterpret provisions of treaties—as President Carter did with the Panama Canal Treaty. Three, the Supreme Court has ruled that it has the authority to declare a treaty unconstitutional just as it has the authority to declare a statute unconstitutional (but it has never done so).

The legal status of treaties is provided for in the Vienna Convention on the Law of Treaties. The State Department has taken the position that the Vienna Convention represents established law (but note the three complicating factors mentioned above). One of the responsibilities of the State Department is to report on treaties.[6] The following are major treaties:

- The North Atlantic Treaty (1949) established the North Atlantic Treaty Organization (NATO). NATO was the major international treaty organization during the Cold War era. The Treaty created the major alliance between the Western powers that confronted the Soviet Union.
- The World Trade Organization (WTO) is one of the international bodies that promotes and regulates international trade with the goal of *liberalizing* international trade—that is, minimizing trade barriers. The WTO's emphasis on trade reflects the post-Cold War shift toward trade rather than national security.
- The North American Free Trade Agreement (NAFTA) is an example of the foreign policy emphasis on promoting free trade in regions of the world.

17.42 | *Executive Agreements*

An executive agreement is a formal document that is negotiated between the president and the head of another government (typically the prime minister). As such, executive agreements are not permanent agreements because they do not necessarily bind subsequent presidents the way that treaties do. An executive agreement does not have to be ratified by the senate. For this reason, over time presidents have relied less on treaties and more on executive agreements and the number of treaties has decreased and the number of executive agreements has increased. The Constitution does not mention executive agreements. But in a 1937 case, U.S. v. Belmont, the Supreme Court recognized the constitutionality of executive agreements, the president's power to enter into executive agreements, and determined that executive agreements have the same legal status as treaties. In fact, the Court's unanimous ruling stated that the federal government's "external powers" could be exercised without regard to state laws. The president's power to enter into executive agreements is now part of the American political and legal tradition.

17.5 | The Actors: Institutions and Organizations

Government and non-government actors participate in the Global Affairs policy-making process, particularly foreign policy. The following describes some of the major participants in the global affairs issue network, their roles, and their goals.

17.51 | *Congress*

Article I of the Constitution vests all legislative power in Congress. The Constitution also grants Congress specific powers. The Constitution grants Congress the power to declare war and it requires treaties, which are negotiated by the president, to be ratified by the Senate. Congress also has the power of the purse. This is relevant to global affairs because it means that Congress enacts the civilian budget for the State Department, which is one of the main foreign policy actors, and the military budget for the Department of Defense. Congress uses its power of the purse, its budget authority, to influence foreign and national security policy.

The House and the Senate have committees with jurisdiction over various areas of foreign policy. The Senate Foreign Relations Committee website describes the committee history, members, hearings, and legislation. The committee plays an important role in shaping foreign policy as well as legislative oversight of the government agencies responsible for implementing foreign policy. After the Republican takeover of the House of Representatives in the 2010 mid-term elections, Representative Ileana Ros-Lehtinen (R-Florida) was selected as Chair of the Foreign Affairs Committee. The Committee's Website candidly acknowledged that the president, not Congress, takes the lead in foreign policy. According to the History of the Committee, the executive branch "does take the lead on nearly every aspect of foreign policy, [but] congressional committees use the power of the purse" to exert influence over the president's policies.[7] In the 113th Congress, the House Foreign Affairs Committee website (accessed February 2, 2013) described its jurisdiction as being "responsible for oversight and legislation" related to a broad range of policy responsibilities, including oversight and legislation relating to foreign assistance; the Peace Corps; national security developments affecting foreign policy; strategic planning and agreements; war powers, treaties, executive agreements, and the deployment and use of United States Armed Forces; peacekeeping, peace enforcement, and enforcement of United Nations or other international sanctions; arms control and disarmament issues; activities and policies of the State, Commerce and Defense Departments and other agencies related to the Arms Export Control Act, and the Foreign Assistance; international law; promotion of democracy; international law enforcement issues, including narcotics control programs and activities; Broadcasting Board of Governors; embassy security; international broadcasting; public diplomacy, including international communication, information policy, international education, and cultural programs; and other matters.

17.52 | *The President*

In a parliamentary system, foreign policy is the responsibility of the head of government—usually the prime minister and the foreign minister, who is a political appointee of the prime minister. In the U.S., the president and the secretary of state, a presidential appointee, are the primary actors responsible for making and managing foreign policy. The president's importance in conducting foreign policy is reflected in the fact that the president's name is often attached to the administration's foreign policy: the Monroe Doctrine; the Truman Doctrine; the Kennedy Doctrine; the Nixon Doctrine; the Reagan Doctrine; the Bush Doctrine; and the Obama Doctrine. A president's doctrine typically announces the major outlines of an administration's policy. The Monroe Doctrine announced that the U.S. considered the Caribbean within its sphere of influence and opposed European intervention. The Truman Doctrine announced the administration's Cold War policy: stopping Soviet expansion; supporting free people who were resisting subjugation; and negotiating regional defense treaties (the Rio Pact of 1947—Latin America; NATO in 1949); ANZUS with Australia and New Zealand; and SEATO with Southeast Asia). The Truman Doctrine greatly expanded the role of the U.S. as the world's policeman. A president's doctrine also announces the administration's policy concerning the use of military force, particularly whether its approach to resolving international conflicts and pursuing national interest will rely on hard power (the military) or soft power (diplomacy). A president's doctrine is sometimes a reaction to the predecessor's doctrine if the predecessor was of a different political party. For example, the Bush Doctrine under Republican President George

W. Bush emphasized unilateral military action to advance national interests and the Obama Doctrine under Democratic President Barack Obama emphasized multilateral action.

The secretary of state is the functional equivalent of the **foreign minister** in a country with a parliamentary system of government. The secretary of state conducts diplomacy, state-to-state policy discussions, and certain interactions with the government officials of other countries. The secretary of state and ambassadors are nominated by the president and confirmed by the Senate. Congress also has power to regulate commerce with foreign nations.

It is ironic that the president is today the dominant foreign affairs actor because most presidents come to office with little or no experience with global politics. A president's political experience is usually limited to domestic politics. A president may have served as the governor of a state (usually one of the larger, more influential states), a senator (again, usually from one of the large, more influential states), or served as vice-president. This means that most presidents get on-the-job training when it comes to global affairs. But presidents typically come to office with high public expectations about serving as the leader of the free world, acting on the global stage by flying around on Air Force One, or perhaps acting as the Commander-in-Chief deploying the U.S. military. Congress also has high expectations for the president's foreign policy agenda.

Congress has greatly increased presidential power over global affairs by statutorily delegating broad legislative power to the president. With the possible exception of the War Powers Resolution of 1973, the following are examples of congressional delegations of legislative power to the president on matters of national security, war powers, and emergency powers. They all illustrate the problem of holding presidents legally accountable for the use of power because they give the president the power to do whatever the president thinks is necessary. This is such a vague standard that it not an effective way to hold power accountable.

- Hostage Rescue Act (1868). This Act authorized the president to take "all actions necessary and proper, not amounting to war, to secure the release of hostages."
- The Gulf of Tonkin Resolution (1964). "WHEREAS, the communist regime in Vietnam....have repeatedly attacked U.S. vessels lawfully present in international waters...." RESOLVED, That the Congress approves the determination of the President "to take all necessary measures to repel any armed attack against the forces of the United States and to prevent further aggression."
- The First War Powers Act of 1941. This Act delegated broad powers to the president to organize and wage war.
- The War Powers Resolution of 1973. In order to ensure collective judgment when committing troops to hostilities or situations where hostilities are imminent, the president shall consult with Congress, report to Congress, and shall seek authorization to maintain commitments beyond specified time periods.
- International Economic Emergency Powers Act (1977). This Act authorizes the President to declare a national emergency and order embargoes, trade sanctions, asset seizures.
- Public Law 105-235 (SJR54-Trent Lott) January 27, 1998. WHEREAS, Operation Desert Storm ended January 28, 1991, and United Nations Security council Resolution 686 (providing for UNSCOM nuclear inspectors) and 687 (providing for economic sanctions until weapons of mass destruction were disclosed, destroyed, and Iraq pledged to not use such weapons) were still in force; (Followed by 27 more whereases) RESOLVED, that Iraq is in "material and unacceptable breach of its international obligations," and

therefore the president is urged to take appropriate action, in accordance with the U.S. Constitution and relevant laws of the U.S., to bring Iraq into compliance with its international obligations.

- Authorization for Use of Military Force Against Terrorists. (Public Law 107-40, Enacted September 18, 2001.) The Act authorized the President "to use all necessary and appropriate force against those nations, organizations, or persons he determines planned, authorized, committed, or aided the terrorist attacks that occurred on September 11, 2001, or harbored such organizations or persons, in order to prevent any future acts of international terrorism against the United States by such nations, organizations or persons."

- Authorization for Use of Military Force Against Iraq Resolution. (Public Law 107-243, Enacted October 16, 2002.) This resolution began "WHEREAS, Iraq remains in material and unacceptable breach of its international obligations, [Followed by a list of 22 "whereases" listing among others the invasion of Kuwait, violations of UN cease fire terms of disarmament, weapons inspections, weapons of mass destruction, threat to the national security of the United States, 9/11 attacks and terrorists known to use Iraq, UN Sec. Council Res. 678 authorizing use of force to enforce UN Resolutions] and resolved that "The President is authorized to use the Armed Forces of the United States as he determines to be necessary and appropriate" in order to (1) defend the national security of the United States and (2) "enforce all relevant United Nations Security Council resolutions regarding Iraq."

17.53 | *The State Department*

The Secretary of State is the head of the Department of State. The State Department is the main executive branch agency responsible for developing and implementing foreign policy under the president's direction. The following is the State Department's mission statement from the November 2010 Agency Financial Report: "Advance freedom for the benefit of the American people and the international community by helping to build and sustain a more democratic, secure, and prosperous world composed of well-governed states that respond to the needs of their people, reduce widespread poverty, and act responsibly within the international system."[8] This mission statement reveals the State Department's broad mission. It includes promoting democracy, security, and prosperity abroad.

The State Department and the Central Intelligence Agency's *The World Factbook* provide a great deal of useful information about government and politics in other countries. For information about a country and descriptions of U.S. relations with that country see the Additional Resources section at the end of this chapter which includes links to the Department of State "Countries and Regions." One way to develop a better understanding of politics and government in the U.S. is to compare the U.S. with other countries. The Library of Congress' Country Studies Website provides a great deal of information about the countries of the world.

17.54 | *The Department of Defense*

The Department of Defense (DOD) plays a central role in providing for national security. The Department of Defense is an executive department. The Secretary of Defense is a political appointee who is usually a member of the President's **inner cabinet**—the small number of heads of the executive departments who lead the most important agencies: State; Defense; Treasury; and Justice). The Pentagon is the building where much of the DOD policy making and business operations are headquartered. DOD publications describe a broad range of defense matters.

The U.S. spends a great deal of money on national defense. The military budget is large as measured in absolute dollar amounts or when compared with defense spending in other countries. The Global Studies website provides a report on comparative data on worldwide military spending. The end of the Cold War was expected to bring a "peace dividend," a government saving from reduced defense spending. But then the War on Terrorism began with wars in Afghanistan and Iraq. Even with reductions of military forces in those two countries cutting defense spending is hard for some of the same reasons that cutting government spending in general is hard. Defense contractors, members of Congress, and the Department of Defense have vested interests in maintaining or increasing spending. Military contracts are distributed across states and congressional districts.

> Think about it! Why is it so hard to cut defense spending?
>
> http://www.npr.org/2012/07/23/157243328/defense-cuts-how-do-you-buy-1-8-submarines

17.55 | *The National Security Agency*

The NSA is located within the Department of Defense, Office of the Undersecretary of Defense for Intelligence. The NSA is such a secret agency that its letters are sometimes said to refer to No Such Agency. The NSA's core missions "are to protect U.S. national security systems and to produce foreign signals intelligence information. The Information Assurance mission confronts the formidable challenge of preventing foreign adversaries from gaining access to sensitive or classified national security information. The Signals Intelligence mission collects, processes, and disseminates intelligence information from foreign signals for intelligence and counterintelligence purposes and to support military operations. This Agency also enables Network Warfare operations to defeat terrorists and their organizations at home and abroad, consistent with U.S. laws and the protection of privacy and civil liberties." The NSA is responsible for collecting and analyzing foreign communications and foreign signals intelligence as well as protecting U.S. government communications and information systems. Locating the NSA within the Department of Defense gives you a sense of the complexities of the DOD and NSA.

17.56 | *The Central Intelligence Agency*

The CIA's website provides information about its history, organization, and mission. Its mission statement describes the CIA as "the nation's first line of defense." It carries out its mission by:

- "Collecting information that reveals the plans, intentions and capabilities of our adversaries and provides the basis for decision and action.
- Producing timely analysis that provides insight, warning and opportunity to the President and decision makers charged with protecting and advancing America's interests."

17.57 | *The Department of Homeland Security*

The DHS was created in 2003 after the terrorist attacks of 9/11 to better coordinate anti-terrorist activities. The DHS is a huge, complicated organization that performs varied functions. It can be considered an umbrella organization because it has responsibility for such a broad range of functions that are related to homeland security ranging from transportation to immigration to telecommunications policy. The Transportation Security Agency was created after 9/11. In 2003 it was moved from the Department of Transportation to the Department of Homeland Security to highlight its role in protecting national security. The TSA is responsible for ensuring freedom of movement of individuals and commerce.

One national security policy that the average American sees (and sometimes feels!) is airport screening of passengers. The passenger screening policy that is being implemented by the Transportation Security Administration is based on a strategy that involves searching for bombs rather than bombers. Passengers and luggage are searched to find dangerous materials (bombs, weapons, and items that could be used for terrorism). The alternative strategy is to search for bombers, to look for individuals who are likely to be threatening or dangerous, to screen passengers than luggage. One reason why the U.S. focuses on searching for bombs rather than bombers is because looking for individuals is controversial. It requires data gathering about people and making assumptions about who is likely to be a threat and who is not. Government data banks raise concerns about big government monitoring people. The government does maintain a **No Fly** list. Furthermore, a TSA decision to search individuals based on their physical appearance, their religion, their dress, their nationality, or their travel or educational patterns, is profiling.

The DHS is also responsible for certain aspects of immigration policy: maintaining border security, providing immigration services, and enforcing immigration laws. The USA Patriot Act and other counter-terrorism policies have substantially increased the size and scope of government power, thereby raising familiar questions about maintaining "that delicate balance" between individual freedom and government power.

17.58 | *Non-governmental Organizations (NGOs)*

Government officials are not the only individuals and organizations that are active in the politics of global affairs. There is a large and growing body of non-governmental actors that lobby in the area of global affairs policy. The interest groups are varied, with organizations advocating on behalf of economic, ideological, ethnic and national identity, religious, and other issue-based interests or causes.

The Foreign Policy Association (FPA) is a non-profit organization that was founded in 1918 to foster public knowledge of and interest in the world by providing publications, programs, and forums. The Foreign Policy Association's website describes its mission as serving "as a catalyst for developing awareness, understanding of, and providing informed opinions on global issues" and "encourage[ing] citizens to participate in the foreign policy process." One of the FPA's outreach efforts is the Great Decisions Global Affairs Education Program. Great Decisions is composed of the annual Briefing Book, Great Decisions TV, the National Opinion Ballot Report, discussion groups across the country and the Great Decisions Online newsletter. Great Decisions has become the largest nonpartisan public education program on international affairs in the world. It has published a Citizen's Guide to U.S. Foreign Policy and founded the World Affairs Council of Washington, D.C. See

Think tanks and public policy organizations such as the Council on Foreign Relations are also influential in the policy making process. They produce studies of various issues, they provide policy experts who testify at congressional committee hearings, and they lobby for and against specific policies and issues. These organizations are also influential because their members are recruited for government positions. When a new administration comes into office, it recruits government officials from these organizations: Republican presidents tend to recruit government officials from organizations with Republican or conservative leanings while Democratic presidents tend to recruit government officials from organizations with Democratic or liberal leanings. Think tanks and public policy organizations also provide places for policy experts to work while they, their party, or their ideas are out of government.

The Council on Foreign Relations (CFR) was established in 1921. The CFR website describes the CFR as "an independent, nonpartisan membership organization, think tank, and publisher" that serves as a resource for its members, government officials, business executives, journalists, educators and students, and civic and religious leaders.

Economic interest groups are also active lobbyists in formulating foreign policy. Business organizations such as the Chamber of Commerce and the National Association of Manufacturers, as well as labor organizations such as the AFL-CIO, lobby on behalf of international trade, commerce, and labor issues. In fact, globalization and the importance of international trade as an aspect of foreign policy have expanded the political arena in the sense that economic interest groups lobby for or against public policies in both the domestic and foreign policy arenas. Interest group politics now extends beyond the territorial boundaries of the U.S.

A broad range of business interests have a major stake in foreign and national security policies. For example, the federal government does not manufacture military weapons or other equipment. The federal government buys military equipment from private sector companies. Consequently, the aerospace and defense industry has a big financial stake in the defense budget, the National Aeronautics and Space Administration's (NASA) budget, and other federal programs. For instance, the decision to scuttle the shuttle program has had major impacts on the aerospace industry and the communities surrounding the manufacturing and launching sites. In fact, privatization has increased the private sector's stake in the defense budget (as well as the budgets of other federal agencies). The U.S. military has privatized a broad range of services. It now relies on private sector companies to provide services that were once provided by members of the military. The Army and Air Force Exchange Services, which the government created to provide merchandise and services to members of the military, strives to provide American troops and their dependents with a "taste of home" wherever they are stationed across the globe. These tastes include familiar fast food franchises and other amenities. The military now contracts with food service companies to provide food that was once provided by army cooks in mess halls.

Privatization is not limited to support services such as food or amenities. Most of the contractors are unarmed service providers, but the military signs logistics contracts with companies that provide armed security guards for the military and civilian support personnel. Of the more than 70,000 private sector civilians that were working in Iraq in 2011 on military contracts to provide necessities and amenities for troops in Iraq and Afghanistan, a great majority are service sector workers. Many of these employees are "third-country nationals," workers hired by foreign companies to work under service sector contracts for the military. The extensive reliance on privatization—relying on private sector to provide public services—presents new accountability problems. The U.S. military is responsible for its own actions. The U.S.

government negotiates Status of Forces Agreements (SOFA) with countries where the military is deployed. The SOFA agreements typically include provisions that describe which country's court system will be used to try individuals who commit crimes. Who is responsible for poor or unsafe working conditions when the military contracts with private sector companies that use subcontractors or employers that are not even American? Who is legally accountable when military contractors commit crimes while employed for the U.S. military? Blackwater, Inc. (which is now called Xe) was a U.S. company that received large government contracts to provide security services in Iraq and Afghanistan. The CEO of Blackwater described his company's mission as doing for the national security apparatus what FedEx did to the postal service.[9] When Blackwater employees were accused of criminal acts including rape, torture, and murder, the murky legal accountability presented serious problems that were highlighted during congressional hearings.

Think about it!
Should the U.S. hire private "soldiers"? See "Private Warriors"
http://www.pbs.org/wgbh/pages/frontline/shows/warriors/

17.6 | War (and Emergency) Powers

The need to get the power problem right by striking the right balance between granting and limiting power is especially important for war and national emergencies. A successful constitution is one that strikes "that delicate balance" between granting government enough power to be effective while also limiting power enough so that government officials can be held accountable. The Founders gave a great deal of thought to war powers. They sought to give the national government enough power to protect the country from foreign invasion. The delegates at the Constitutional Convention of 1787 extensively debated issues related to foreign affairs, national security, and war powers. National security was an important political issue during the constitutional convention and in the early years of the republic because the U.S. was a young republic, and a militarily weak nation that was surrounded by ambitious imperial powers: The Spanish Empire, The British Empire, and the French Empire. The debates during the constitutional convention of 1787 reflect the concerns about whether a monarch-like president was needed to protect the country's national security, or whether a republic was strong enough to protect it. The Founders worried about giving the new national government too many war powers. They were especially concerned about the creation of a new executive official, the president. The creation of the presidency was controversial because it was seen as a step away from a republic and toward monarchy, the form of government that the Revolutionary War was fought against. Furthermore, the colonial experiences that inspired the Declaration of Independence and the Revolutionary War included monarchs who used war powers for their personal or national glory. The first American form of government, the Articles of Confederation, did not have an executive figure because not having an executive was considered the best way to avoid the problem of imperial ambition.

The delegates to the Constitutional Convention in 1787 debated whether to create a presidency and what to do about war powers. A majority thought that the lack of an executive was one of the major flaws in the Articles of Confederation and, after extensive debate, the delegates decided to create a presidency. Some of the worries about war powers were eased by the decision to divide control over war powers. The Constitution provided that Congress declares war and the president as Commander-in-Chief wages war.

17.61 | *Divided Control of War Powers*

The war powers are divided between Congress and the president. Congress was delegated the power to declare war and the power to raise and support armies. The president was made the Commander-in-Chief of the armed forces: the president waged war as the "top general." This division of control over war powers is usually described by saying that Congress makes war (decides whether to go to war) and the president wages war (as the Commander in Chief). During the colonial era, the Founders experienced the offensive use of war powers by imperial powers. The British, French, and Spanish imperial model of government included using military power to expand the empire. The colonists' experience with offensive imperial power caused the delegates to the Constitutional Convention in 1787 to be concerned about war powers. They decided to give the new national government defensive war powers so that it could effectively defend the young republic against foreign invasion. But they nevertheless worried about war powers.

In "Political Observations" (April 20 1795), James Madison described war as the "germ" that presented the greatest threat to liberty and republican government:

"Of all the enemies of true liberty, war is, perhaps, the most to be dreaded, because it comprises and develops the germ of every other. War is the parent of armies; from these proceed debts and taxes; and armies, and debts, and taxes are the known instruments for bringing the many under the domination of the few. In war, too, the discretionary power of the Executive is extended; its influence in dealing out offices, honors and emoluments is multiplied; and all the means of seducing the minds, are added to those of subduing the force, of the people. The same malignant aspect in republicanism may be traced in the inequality of fortunes, and the opportunities of fraud, growing out of a state of war, and in the degeneracy of manner and of morals, engendered in both.

No nation can preserve its freedom in the midst of continual warfare.
War is in fact the true nurse of executive aggrandizement. In war, a physical force is to be created; and it is the executive will, which is to direct it. In war, the public treasuries are to be unlocked; and it is the executive hand which is to dispense them. In war, the honors and emoluments of office are to be multiplied; and it is the executive patronage under which they are to be enjoyed; and it is the executive brow they are to encircle.

The strongest passions and most dangerous weaknesses of the human breast; ambition, avarice, vanity, the honorable or venal love of fame, are all in conspiracy against the desire and duty of peace.
Letters and Other Writings of James Madison , Volume IV, page 491.

These are extremely strong words warning the country about the dangers that the war powers presented to republican government! Madison acknowledged that the decision to increase security by granting the government power to repel foreign invasions also increased insecurity by exposing the nation to the risk that the war powers would be used internally to threaten republican government. Is this **germ theory** of war powers accurate? As the U.S. became an economic and military power, it did use its powers to extend American influence abroad. Two notable 19th Century examples of this use of U.S. military power are the Mexican-American War and the Spanish-American War. World Wars I and II were fought primarily for reasons other than extended American power abroad, but one consequence of WWII was a greater awareness of how the U.S. could use its economic, political, and military power abroad to prevent war. This was once of the policies underlying the Cold War foreign policy. As a result military force was not limited to defensive actions but also included offensive actions. This was an important shift in thinking about national security and foreign policy. President George W. Bush declared that his administration was adopting the doctrine of preventive war, which is the use of military force for policy wars or using military force as an instrument of foreign policy. President George W. Bush's September 2002 National Security Strategy announced elements of what was unofficially called the Bush Doctrine, the set of principles that guided the Bush Administration's foreign policy. The Bush Doctrine had two main principles. First, it announced that the U.S. would unilaterally withdrawal from treaties dealing with arms control and global warming. Second, it emphasized that the U.S. would take unilateral military action to protect national security interests: the U.S. would act alone to use military force and it would take **preventive** military action. The Bush Doctrine of preventive military force was controversial because it declared that as a matter of policy the U.S. would not wait to use military force defensively—it would use military force preemptively in order to prevent threats to national security interests. According to the National Security Strategy document,

"The gravest danger our Nation faces lies at the crossroads of radicalism and technology. Our enemies have openly declared that they are seeking weapons of mass destruction.... The United States will not allow these efforts to succeed. We will build defenses against ballistic missiles and other means of delivery. We will cooperate with other nations to deny, contain, and curtail our enemies' efforts to acquire dangerous technologies. And, as a matter of common sense and self-defense, America will act against such emerging threats before they are fully formed. We cannot defend America and our friends by hoping for the best. So we must be prepared to defeat our enemies' plans, using the best intelligence and proceeding with deliberation. History will judge harshly those who saw this coming danger but failed to act. In the new world we have entered, the only path to peace and security is the path of action."[10]

17.62 | *Wars*

The U.S. has declared war against another country only five times:

- War of 1812 (1812-1814). The U.S. declared war against Britain. The war ended with the Treaty of Ghent in 1814.
- Mexican-American War (1846-1848). The U.S. declared war against Mexico in 1846. The war ended with the Treaty of Guadalupe Hidalgo in 1848.
- Spanish-American War (1898). The U.S. declared war against Spain in 1898. The war ended with the Treaty of Paris 1898.

- World War I (1914-1918). The U.S. declared war against Germany and Austro-Hungarian Empire 1917. The war ended in 1918.
- World War II (1939-1945). The U.S. declared war against Japan in December 1941 and the global war was fought against Japan, Germany, and Italy (The Axis Powers). The war ended in 1945.

But the U.S. has taken many more military actions than these four officially declared wars. Some of the undeclared wars, ongoing military conflicts, and military actions were approved by Congress (e.g., congressional resolutions authorizing the use of military force) or international bodies such as the United Nations. These military actions include the following:

- The Quasi-War with France (1798-1800)
- The Indian Wars
- The Civil War (1861-65)
- The Russian Civil War (1918)
- The Korean War (1950-1953)
- The Vietnam War (1961-1975)
- The Gulf War or Operation Desert Storm (1991-1994)
- Afghanistan War 2001—)
- Iraq War (2003—)

Two of the most prominent military conflicts (that is, undeclared wars) are the Korean War and the Vietnam War. The Vietnam War was an especially controversial war. It has had a profound and lasting impact on American politics. Long after the war was over, political debates about foreign affairs, national security, and war powers still reference Vietnam. Supporters and opponents of the Vietnam War, and supporters and opponents of contemporary military action, still refer to the war to justify their positions for or against war. The critics of military action (e.g., in Afghanistan or Iraq or Iran) appeal for "No more Vietnams." This slogan is usually meant to remind the public and government officials that the decision to use military force as an instrument of foreign policy is fraught with risks. On the other hand, those who support the use of American military power abroad urge the nation to recover from "The Vietnam Syndrome." They use the term Vietnam Syndrome to describe a condition where the nation is so worried about the use of military power that it is afraid to use U.S. military power to accomplish foreign policy objectives. The modern conservative movement's support for building up the military and the use of military force during the Republican presidencies of Ronald Reagan, George H.W. Bush, and George W. Bush, was intended to recover from the Vietnam Syndrome.

17.63 | *The War of 1812*

The War of 1812 was fought against Great Britain, Canadian colonists loyal to Britain, and Native Americans allied with the British. The U.S. declared war against Great Britain for several reasons. First, the U.S. wanted to expand its national borders into the Northwest Territory, which included areas under British control. Second, trade restrictions during Great Britain's war with France limited U.S. commerce. Third, the British had impressed (that is, forced into service) American merchant sailors into the British Royal Navy. And fourth, British support for Indian tribes conflicted with U.S. policy of westward expansion into frontier areas. During the years when Great Britain was at war with France, its imperial adversary, Great Britain was preoccupied and did not actively resist American expansion. But when Napoleon was defeated in 1814 the British sent armed forces to North America. They captured and burned Washington, D.C. in the summer of 1814. However, in the fall and winter U.S. forces defeated British forces in New York and New Orleans. The battle of New Orleans created a renewed sense of American patriotism. The defense of Baltimore inspired the U.S. national anthem, The Star-Spangled Banner. The sense of national pride in fighting and winning another war against Great Britain, an imperial power, produced what historians called The Era of Good Feelings. The label was attached to the period from around 1816 to 1824 (the presidency of James Monroe) when partisan politics and domestic political conflict was subdued compared to the preceding era.

What a person thinks about a war depends upon which side they were on. Americans have a very different perspective on the War of 1812 than Canadians. Southerners have a different perspective on the Civil War than Northerners. The Vietnamese have a very different view of the War in Viet Nam, which they call "The American War," than Americans.

> Think About It!
> Teaching the War of 1812 Different in U.S., Canada"
> http://www.npr.org/2012/06/18/155308632/teaching-the-war-of-1812-different-in-u-s-canada

17.64 | The Mexican-American and Spanish-American Wars

These two 19th Century wars are considered together here because they were declared for basically the same purpose: territorial expansion and global influence. The Mexican-American War was fought to expand the territory of the U.S. over the North American continent as part of the belief in Manifest Destiny and westward expansion to settle frontier areas. The Spanish-American War was fought during an era of American politics included debates about how to project the American economic, political, and military power and influence abroad. The Spanish-American War was controversial because it resulted in the U.S. acquiring territories abroad, which opponents believed transformed the U.S. from a republic, which had fought the Revolutionary War against imperial power, into an imperial power. The following image is a poster from the 1900 presidential campaign. It describes the Spanish-American War of 1898 as one that was fought for political ideals (using military power in the service of humanity) rather than for projecting American imperial power abroad.

17.65 | *The Cold War*

The Cold War was the period of almost continuous conflict between western democracies and communist countries from the end of World War II in 1945 until 1991 with the fall of the Soviet Union. It was called a Cold War because it was primarily a period of non-shooting conflict as opposed to a hot war or shooting war. The Cold War began in 1946 or 1947. In 1946 Winston Churchill delivered his famous "Sinews of Peace" Speech at Westminster College in Fulton, Missouri, in 1946. Churchill described an Iron Curtain descending across Eastern Europe all along the countries that bordered the Soviet Union. The Iron Curtain delineated the boundaries between the western, democratic, or "free world" and the communist world. The Iron Curtain was a powerful metaphor that Churchill intended to alert the West, which had just fought a long and bloody war against Germany, Japan, and Italy, to mobilize against the new threat that the west faced from its former ally during World War II: the Soviet Union.

Then in 1947 the U.S. directly intervened in a civil war in Greece in order to prevent Greece from falling into the Soviet sphere of influence. And in 1948 the U.S. implemented the

Marshall Plan (The European Recovery Program) to rebuild Europe in order to stop Soviet expansion.

> Cold War Time Lines
> http://www.history-timelines.org.uk/events-timelines/03-cold-war-timeline.htm
> http://www.archives.gov/exhibits/featured_documents/marshall_plan/

The Cold War was a period of political, economic, and military, conflict and competition between the East and the West. The conflict sometimes included proxy wars. A proxy war is when two major powers (such as the U.S. and the Soviet Union) use third parties (other countries or even non-state actors such as freedom fighters, revolutionaries, insurgents, or even terrorists) to fight for them against their major adversary. During the Cold War, the U.S. and the Soviet Union sponsored proxy wars in Angola, Afghanistan, and Latin America. The Korean and Vietnam Wars were also part of the Cold War confrontation between East and West. The U.S. and its western allies including Great Britain, France, and Western Germany confronted the Soviet Union and its satellite states (e.g., East Germany; Poland; Hungary). The Cold War competition included the space race (the first to launch a satellite; the first to put a man on the moon) and even Olympic competition.

The terms East and West are not primarily geographic terms. They refer to two different political, economic and social systems. The Western world consisted of the United States and its allies. Although U.S. and Soviet military forces never directly fought one another, conflict was expressed and organized through military coalitions, conventional force deployments, providing financial and military support for allies, espionage, propaganda, a conventional and nuclear arms race, and technological competitions such as the Space Race. Nation-states relied heavily on the two superpowers and other aligned nations to assist their national security. This relationship was referred to as collective security, a term popularized after World War I. Since the breakup of the Soviet Union, the end of the Cold War, and the rise of terrorism, U.S. national security policy is no longer framed as a bi-polar world of the two superpowers. The Cold War finally ended with the collapse of the Soviet Union in 1991.

The Cold War has had profound and lasting effects on American government and politics. The American public believed that life in a nuclear age meant living with an enemy, the Soviet Union, which was poised to launch a nuclear attack against the United States and its western allies. This belief changed the way the American government worked. The American public supported a federal government that was prepared to take decisive **preventive** or **defensive** action to protect national security. As a result, the power of the federal government, particularly the power of the president, increased. During the Cold War, power flowed from the states to the national government, which had primary responsibility for national security; and it flowed from congress to the president because Congress is an institution that was designed for representation and deliberation, not for decisive action in the nuclear age. As Alexander Hamilton put it, the presidency was designed to provide an executive official who could act "with dispatch" or speed in times of emergency.

One way to get a sense of the political climate of the Cold War times is to watch some of videos that were produced by the government to educate the public about the threat of nuclear war and how to protect themselves from it. The "Duck and Cover" videos were intended to teach children how to protect themselves in case of a nuclear attack by ducking and covering themselves with whatever was available. In a classroom, students would duck and cover under a desk. The government also took videos of nuclear tests. Declassified videos show nuclear tests that were conducted in the 1950s in a Nevada valley that was sardonically called the valley where the giant mushrooms grow. President Truman created the Nevada Test Site in 1950 to provide a continental nuclear test site which was cheaper than the existing Pacific test sites. Two of the videos are *Operation Plumbbob* and *Let's Face It*:

- The U.S. Atomic Energy Commission presents *Operation Plumbbob*, the Department of Energy Video #0800022 "Military Effects Study." *Operation Plumbbob* consisted of around 30 nuclear test explosions to measure the impacts of nuclear explosions on buildings, animals, plant life, soil and air contamination—and people, including the people who witnessed the explosions.
- The Federal Civil Defense Administration presents *Let's Face It*, U.S. Nuclear Test Film #55.

The Nevada Test Site can now be visited by tourists who want to walk through "Doom Town" and see where more than 100 atomic tests were conducted. One Atomic Tourist Web site reassures potential visitors with the following statement: "Radiation badges are no longer necessary when visiting."

> The Cold War
> http://www.youtube.com/watch?v=HpYCplyBknI

17.66 | *The War on Terror*

The war on terror is a politically and legally distinctive war. First, it is not an armed conflict between countries—it is a conflict between the U.S. and terrorist organizations (principally al Qaeda) and the individuals and organizations that support it. In international law, a war is a state of armed conflict between two or more nations: it is an armed international conflict. Second, Congress did not declare war on al Qaeda. On September 14, 2001 Congress passed a joint resolution, The Authorization for the Use of Military Force (AUMF), which authorized the president to use all necessary and appropriate armed force "against those responsible for the recent [9/11 terrorist] attacks launched against the United States." The AUMF gave the president power to go to war. The AUMF is an example of how Congress has delegated to the president power to do whatever the president thinks is necessary and appropriate to protect national security. It is difficult to hold a government official legally accountable for their use of power when they have such a broad grant of discretionary authority to act.

The third reason why the war on terror is distinctive is that it is a war without a battlefield. It is a global conflict that is not limited to a geographic "theater of war" or actual battlefield. The war on terror does include actual battlefield theaters of war: Iraq and Afghanistan, for instance. But the U.S. government describes the war on terror as a global conflict that is fought within the U.S. and within other countries, and it describes the war on terror as a conflict that requires a broad range of assets: military force, economics, intelligence, and surveillance. And it is a war that requires protecting infra-structure from attacks, protecting the financial system from cyber-attacks, and a broad range of counterterrorism policies.

Finally, the war on terror is distinctive in that it is a war with no apparent end. In conventional warfare, one side usually wins and the war is declared over. The war on terror does not seem to provide any such benchmarks for determining victory.

The war on terror has focused attention on political violence. Political violence is the use of violence to achieve a political goal. Political violence has historically been one of the most controversial issues in politics whether it is domestic affairs, global affairs, or national security policy. The use of military force has been controversial throughout American history. The terrorist attacks on 9/11 renewed the focus on terrorism as a distinctive use of political violence. Political violence, that is violence that is intended to achieve a political objective, is not considered inappropriate in American political culture. On the contrary, political violence has been an important part of some of the nation's most important developments: the nation was founded as the result of a Revolutionary War; the union was preserved as a result of the Civil War; the westward expansion of the country and the settling of the frontier is mythologized; and the U.S. has used military force (violence) to expand its territories and extend its sphere of influence globally. Terrorism is a kind of political violence. Not all political violence is terrorism. Terrorism is general considered the inappropriate or illegal use of political violence. The central problem with defining terrorism is that it is extremely difficult to clearly and objectively differentiate between acts of political violence that are considered legitimate and those acts of political violence that are considered illegitimate. The saying, "One person's freedom fighter is another's terrorist," captures the difficulty providing an objective definition of terrorism. Pacifists who consider all use of violence or force illegitimate have the clearest position. By contrast, those who consider political violence appropriate for certain purposes or causes face the challenge of explaining the legitimate and illegitimate reasons for using violence. This challenge is made difficult by the subjectivity trap. There are two ways to fall into the subjectivity trap: defining causes that you support as legitimate and those you oppose as illegitimate; and concluding that the ends justify the means (if the end is legitimate then the means are legitimate).

17.67 | *The Wars in Iraq and Afghanistan*

The wars in Iraq and Afghanistan are unconventional wars. A conventional war is one that is fought between the uniformed military of two or more countries (or nation-states). Unconventional conflicts are fights against insurgents—individuals and organizations rather than government forces. The combatants may not be in uniform, may not be part of a formal military chain of command, they may not carry arms openly, and they may be intermingled with the general population. There may also not be a battlefield, an actual geographic place where the fighting takes place. The fighting occurs in the cities and rural areas where the people live and work and try to go about their daily lives during the fighting. In an unconventional war, it is often difficult to identify the enemy, whose physical appearance may be identical to civilians who are not the enemy. Civilian casualties are often one of the high costs of such unconventional warfare. The problem of killing innocent civilians is especially troubling in unconventional, asymmetrical warfare.

Symmetrical warfare is warfare where the combatants have roughly equal military might, have similar kinds of power, and use similar weapons. **Asymmetrical warfare** is warfare where one side has a great deal more military power than the other. As a result of the great differences in military power, the two sides in asymmetrical warfare are likely to use very different weaponry. Iraq and Afghanistan are examples of asymmetrical warfare. The U.S. has vastly greater economic, military, and technological power than Iraq and Afghanistan. As a result, the U.S. and its opponents use very different weapons. The U.S. uses its military and technological advantage to wage high technology warfare that relies on sophisticated weapons systems including missiles, airplane bombers, and unmanned drones that are controlled by personnel who can be stationed half-way around the world from the actual battlefield. But other great powers have not had a great deal of military success in fighting in Afghanistan. With the collapse of the Soviet Union and the end of the Cold War, the U.S. was the sole remaining military superpower. U.S. military hegemony meant that any military conflicts that the U.S. engaged in were going to be asymmetrical warfare where the enemy relied on weapons and strategies very different from the strengths of the U.S. military. The counter-insurgencies the U.S. faced in Iraq and Afghanistan are examples of asymmetrical warfare that frustrated military superpowers in the past and frustrated the U.S. military. In Afghanistan, for instance, counter-insurgencies made it very difficult for the British and Soviets, two military superpowers, to *get out* of the country after invading it and finding some initial success.

> Think about it!
> Is it easier for a military power to enter a country than it is to exit? Listen to the National Public Radio Broadcast, "For Invaders A Well-Worn Path Out of Afghanistan," (December 6, 2010) http://www.npr.org/2010/12/06/131788189/for-invaders-a-well-worn-path-out-of-afghanistan

The U.S. military had a hard time adapting to the fighting in Iraq. The Iraq war began with the U.S. conducting a "blitzkrieg" attack. The U.S. military quickly overwhelmed Iraqi defenses but then it faced ongoing resistance and conflict that required it to militarily occupy Iraq. U.S. political officials and military leaders were reluctant to acknowledge this aspect of the fighting. In fact, the Joint Chiefs of Staff refused to call the ongoing conflict an insurgency because the word insurgency evoked memories of the U.S. being bogged down in Vietnam. In fact, the military was not prepared to fight such a conflict. The U.S. Army is a large bureaucratic organization. The Army field manual assumed that the battles it would be fighting would be large scale "set pieces" where the armies of the countries at war would engage one another on a battlefield. This conventional wisdom left the U.S. military unprepared for the ongoing conflict that it faced in Iraq and Afghanistan. A small band of high-ranking young officers with military experience fighting unconventional wars in Vietnam and elsewhere realized that the Army had to change in order to be prepared to fight insurgencies. One of these "insurgents" was David Petraeus. In *The Insurgents: David Petraeus and the Plot to Change the Army Way of War* (2012), Fred Kaplan describes how this "cabal" of "insurgents" forced the Army to change.

One challenge in unconventional warfare is minimizing the risks of civilian casualties, which are sometimes euphemistically called "collateral damage." Civilian casualties are a serious problem because in unconventional warfare against insurgencies "the people are the prize." Successful wars against insurgencies usually require paying some attention to "winning the hearts and minds of the people" so that they will not support insurgents. This goal is frustrated when innocent civilians become casualties of warfare. One of the ways that the U.S. military has adapted to the problem of identifying the enemy in Iraq and Afghanistan (and more broadly as part of counterterrorism policy) is to use sophisticated information systems in addition to sophisticated weapons technology. The military is using social network analysis to identify insurgents who are a threat that lives and works among the general population, which is not a threat. Terrorist groups such as al Qaeda and insurgencies are organized as networks: individuals or groups that work together. This helps identify the insurgents rather than the civilian population. The military now uses social network analysis to attack the network of insurgents rather than merely to target individual insurgents who might plant a roadside bomb or other Improvised Explosive Device.

> Think about it! How does the military use social network analysis to attack the network of insurgents rather than just targeting individual insurgents?
> Listen to the NPR report, "U.S. 'Connects the Dots' to Catch Roadside Bombers:"
> http://www.npr.org/2010/12/03/131755378/u-s-connects-the-dots-to-catch-roadside-bombers

In conventional warfare the objective may be to overwhelm the enemy by destroying its military resources and undermining the popular support for continued fighting. In counterinsurgency warfare, the goal is different. Jingoist slogans such as "Bomb them back to the stone ages" or "Nuke them all and let God sort them out" are morally, politically, and militarily problematic in conflicts where one goal is getting the people on your side. Counterinsurgency is militarily complicated because "The people are the prize in a counterinsurgency operation."[11] The U.S. use of drones—that is, unmanned aerial vehicles or UAVs—for "targeted killings" presents serious political, legal, and moral questions.

- Is "targeted killing" a euphemism for assassination?
- Who decides whom to target, to put on a kill list?
- What legal checks limit the use of drones?
- What will happen when other nations or organizations develop or obtain the technology to use drones against the U.S. or its allies?

> Think About it!
> The following PBS program examines Targeted Killings:
> http://www.pbs.org/newshour/rundown/2013/01/targeted-killings.html

The Association for Unmanned Vehicle Systems International is an organization whose mission includes supporting and advocating for unmanned systems and the robotics industry. The Association has been closely aligned with military uses of the technology but it now actively supports expansion into law enforcement and even the private sector markets for unmanned vehicles.

17.68 | *The "Air" Wars: Developing a media war plan as a force multiplier*

The term **air power** usually refers to missiles, bombers, jet fighters, helicopters, and now drones (unmanned aerial vehicles). The U.S. Air Force is the primary branch of the military that fights air wars and strives to maintain control over the skies. Today, the term *air war* includes another entirely different kind of air power: the media. The U.S. strategy for winning the war in Iraq included the development of a media war plan as a force multiplier. The media war plan included elaborate efforts to get the media to provide the public with the military's views of the conflict, particularly video images of American military technology. The air power in this case included embedding reporters with troops. The goal of the media war plan was to develop and maintain public support for the war effort.[12]

17.69 | *Types of Military Action*

Table 17.69 below describes three types of military action. The defensive use of military force is the least controversial and the Constitution specifically provided for it in the Constitution. The use of military power to preempt an imminent attack is also not very controversial and the courts have recognized that the government can act before an armed enemy that is poised to attack actually attacks. The third type of military action is the most controversial politically and legally. A preventive war is a policy war: the government simply decides to use military force. The War in Afghanistan was a defensive war fought against a country that enabled a terrorist organization to attack the U.S. The War in Iraq was a preventive war. The Bush administration decided to use military force to obtain regime change in Iraq. In fact, the buildup to the War in Iraq is a good example of how the government can control or even create public opinion on matters of national security. The government's false claims that Saddam Hussein had contacts with al Qaeda and possessed weapons of mass destruction (WMDs) created public support for the invasion of Iraq.

Think About It!
Can the government create public opinion about global affairs?
http://www.youtube.com/watch?v=qxhIkzTg14M

Table 17.69: TYPES OF MILITARY ACTION

DEFENSIVE	PREEMPTIVE	PREVENTIVE
Enumerated Powers: Article I, section 8 provides that "The Congress shall have Power...To declare War...; ...suppress Insurrections and repel Invasions." Article II grants the president power as Commander-in-Chief ***Implied Powers***: The government, particularly the president, has the implied power to use military force for rescue missions (such as the Mayaguez and Iranian Hostage rescue missions).	***Case Law***: Supreme Court rulings allow the government to respond to a "clear and present danger," a legal doctrine. The logic of conspiracy also means that the government does not have to wait until an armed enemy that is poised to attack actually attacks.	***Policy Wars***: The decision to use military force as an instrument of foreign policy.

17.7 | National Security

The term **national security** refers to a country's use of economic, political, and military power and influence to maintain its territorial integrity and political institutions. The concept of national security can be traced to the creation of nation-states, when armies were used to maintain domestic order and provide protection from foreign attacks. People create governments and form nation-states to provide for the defense of individuals and their civilization. These are basic government functions: "The most elementary function of the nation-state is the defense of the life of its citizens and of their civilization." A government that is unable to defend these values "must yield, either through peaceful transformation or violent destruction," to one that is capable of defending them.[13]   Each nation develops and implements its national security policy as an attribute of national sovereignty.

17.71 | *Elements of national security*

In his classic book, *Politics Among Nations* (1948), Hans Morgenthau—a leading figure in international relations theory, politics, and law—described national security policy to include the following elements:

- **Diplomacy**. Diplomacy is the practice of negotiating agreements between two or more nations. Diplomacy is used to build alliances and isolate threats. Professional diplomats usually conduct diplomatic relations as representatives of their nation on matters related to war and peace, trade, economics, culture, the environment, and human rights. U.S. diplomats negotiate the terms of international treaties and executive agreements prior to their endorsement by the president and, if a treaty, ratification by the Senate.

- **Emergency Preparedness**. Protecting national security includes protecting communication systems, transportation, public health systems, and the economy from attacks. The increased reliance on electronic communications in these sectors has highlighted the importance of protecting them from cyberattacks.
- **Economic power**. Nations use their economic power to reward allies by creating favorable trade and foreign aid agreements, to build international support by such favorable treatment, and to punish threats by, for example, promoting trade sanctions or even embargoes.
- **Military force**. Nations use military force or the threat of military force to meet threats to national security interests and to prevent nations or organizations from presenting threats.
- **Domestic Legislation.** Laws that target individuals or organizations that support violence or terrorism, for example. The State Department maintains a list of terrorist nations and laws such as the PATRIOT Act give the government power to prosecute individuals or organizations that provide material aid to such groups.
- **Surveillance**. Nations use surveillance, spying, and covert operations for national security purposes. The U.S. uses its intelligence agencies to respond to threats and to prevent them. The Central Intelligence Agency, the National Security Administration, and the Defense Intelligence Agency are federal agencies that are responsible for providing surveillance related to national security (as opposed to ordinary criminal activity). The Cold War and the War on Terror have blurred some of the traditional lines between domestic surveillance and foreign surveillance.
- The FBI is used to protect the country from internal threats to national security or public order.

17.72 | *U.S. National Security*

During the Cold War era, U.S. national security relied heavily on military force or the threat of military force. National security became an official guiding principle of U.S. foreign policy with the enactment of the **National Security Act of 1947**. The Act created

- The National Military Establishment (which became the Department of Defense when the Act was amended in 1949);
- A Department of the Air Force from the existing Army Air Force;
- Separate military branches that were subordinated to the Secretary of Defense, which was a new cabinet level position;
- The National Security Council. The National Security Council was created to coordinate national security policy in the executive branch. The NSC is the president's main forum for considering national security and foreign policy issues.
- The Central Intelligence Agency. The CIA was the nation's first peacetime intelligence agency.
- The National Security Agency. The National Security Agency was so secretive that the letters NSA were humorously said to mean No Such Agency. The NSA Web site describes it as the home of the government's "code makers and code breakers."

For most of the 20th Century, national security was defined primarily in terms of military power. National security required having a military that was strong enough to protect the country from foreign attacks or threats. For example, WWII was armed conflict between nation-states: the U.S. and its allies fought against countries (Germany, Japan, and Italy) that had invaded other countries. The Cold War included armed conflict between nation-states, but it also involved non-state actors or non-state actors that were supported by nation-states. Today, non-state actors such as terrorist organizations or international drug cartels are considered greater threats to U.S. national security than military attacks by another country. Since the end of the Cold War the concept of national security has been broadened to include economic security, technology, natural resources, and even environmental conditions.

In the 21st Century, national security is being defined more broadly to include resources other than military power that are vital to a country's national security. The U.S. Department of State acknowledges this broader definition of national security. During the Obama administration the Department of State's mission statement committed the department to advancing freedom by building a more democratic, secure and prosperous world where government addressed the needs of the people—including poverty. (Website accessed January 28, 2013)

The interest groups that advocate for national security policies also recognize this broader definition of national security. For example, the Center for New American Security defines natural security to include natural resources. The concept of national security was broadened to include more than military power beginning with recognition of the importance of petroleum. The world's economies are dependent on fossil fuels: oil, coal and natural gas. American dependence on imported oil is one of the main reasons why the U.S. has been so involved with the Middle East. The region's abundance of oil has played a role in American foreign and defense policy. The American economy's dependence on foreign oil has made petroleum an important factor in maintaining U.S. military strength. Energy independence is a goal with economic, military, and national security benefits. However, oil is not the only natural resource that is considered vital to national security.

17.73 | Food and Water

Governments are responsible for providing an adequate and safe food supply. Population growth and hunger are related issues that can become national security issues. The U.S. has a strategic oil reserve that is used to prevent disruptions in the energy supply. China, the world's most populous country, has a strategic pork reserve that it uses to prevent food scarcity from becoming a national security issue.

> **Think About It!**
> A Strategic Pork Reserve?
> "Food for 9 Billion: Satisfying China's Growing Demand for Meat"
> http://www.pbs.org/newshour/bb/world/july-dec12/china_11-13.html

Water is also a vital resource for human and other life. Access to an adequate and safe supply of fresh water is considered a component of a nation's security in a world where there is increased competition for this valuable and increasingly scarce resource. A United Nations Report "Water Scarcity" states that almost 20% of the world's population now lives in areas of physical scarcity. It provides information about and prospects for "water for life" in a world where (to quote Samuel Coleridge, Rime of the Ancient Mariner) there is "Water, water everywhere, nor any drop to drink." As nations compete for access to water, water will become a more important component of a nation's national security.

> Glenn Beck's Blaze TV presents a short discussion of "War for Water."
>
> http://www.video.theblaze.com/media/video.jsp?content_id=20256131

Every four years the National Security Council compiles a Global Trends Report that describes and analyzes developments that are likely to affect national security. The National Security Council is comprised of 17 U.S. government intelligence agencies. The 2012 Report describes 2030 as "a radically transformed world." Asian countries will surpass the U.S. and Europe. The good news is that compared to 2012, there will be less poverty, more democracy, more individual rights, and increased health. The bad news is that the world of 2030 is likely to include much more fighting over natural resources, particularly food and water.

> Think About It!
> What will the world be like in 2030?
> http://www.npr.org/2012/12/10/166895624/the-world-in-2030-asia-rises-the-west-declines

17.74 | *Non-fuel minerals*

Non-fuel minerals are also important for advanced economies where rare and precious minerals used in the manufacturing and high-tech economies of the world. Non-fuel minerals are essential to manufacture of aircraft and computers and automobiles. In the information age, cell phones require tantalum, liquid crystal displays require indium, and other familiar products that are part of everyday modern life require platinum group metals. Rare earth minerals with properties such as conductivity, luminescence, and strength are very valuable for high-tech economies. Organizations such as the Center for New American Security, which identifies national security as increasingly dependent on a secure supply of natural resources, lobby for a broader perspective on national security, one that includes energy, minerals, water, land, climate change, and even biodiversity.

17.75 | *Immigration*

Immigration has a special place in American politics. The U.S. proudly proclaims that it is a nation of immigrants. The Statue of Liberty famously welcomes immigrants seeking opportunities for a better life. Immigration is one part of the American dream of individuals and families working hard for a better life for themselves and their children. But immigration has also been very controversial from the early decades of the 19th Century until today. Immigration first became controversial during periods of increased immigration especially from non-Anglo regions of the world—particularly eastern Europe and Asia. The debates about immigration have historically been about the quantity (the number of immigrants to allow into the country) and the quality (what kinds of immigrants are desirable and what kinds are undesirable) of immigrants. One government document, The Dillingham Commission Report on Immigration, ranked immigrant groups, which influenced immigration policy for decades.

Historically, congress had plenary power to determine immigration policy. Immigrants did not have rights, therefore immigration policy, including decisions to deport immigrants, were entirely political decisions. However, the various civil rights revolutions during the latter half of the 20th Century extended rights to more and more groups. Immigrant rights groups advocated for providing certain legal protections for immigrants. The American Civil Liberties Union's Immigrants' Rights Project, the National Network For Immigrant and Refugee Rights, and other organizations work to provide immigrants and refugees rights. The general trend toward extending rights to immigrants was reversed by three events.

- The War on Terror. The first and most significant event has been the war on terror following the 9/11 attacks. The threat of terrorism made immigration and control of the nation's borders—border security—central elements of national security policy. This mean that the normal politics surrounding immigration policy, including questions about how much due process immigrants were entitled to, was overshadowed by national security (or national insecurity) policy: national security trumped interests in protecting immigrants.
- Patriotism. The patriotic fervor that swept the country in the aftermath of the terrorist attacks on 9/11 also created a sense that the U.S. needed to better protect its national identity by limiting the number and kinds of people who were coming to the country legally and illegally. Concerns about protecting national identity have periodically shaped public debate about immigration policy. Patriotism or the preservation of a distinctive American identity is sometimes expressed as opposition to immigration.
- The Great Recession. The third event was the Great Recession and the lingering economic downturn that followed it. Economics affects politics. Economic hard times once again increased the sense that immigrants, particularly illegal immigrants, were taking scarce jobs from citizens, depressing wages, and consuming government benefits such as education, health care, and social welfare without paying a fair share of taxes.

The failure to prevent the terrorist attacks on 9/11 was blamed in part on failure to maintain border security. As a result, the federal government was reorganized in order to provide more control over information about immigration. The Department of Homeland Security includes the Customs and Immigration Services Agency (CIS). The CIS uneasily combines the provision of services for immigrants and the function of enforcing immigration laws. In the U.S. system of federalism, immigration is the responsibility of the federal government, not the states. But the American political experience includes people turning to *whatever* level of government they think will address a problem that they think the government needs to solve. Recently, voters in several states have concluded that state action is necessary to control the borders and enforce immigration laws because the federal government does not seem willing or able to effectively maintain control of national borders or enforce immigration laws by deporting illegal immigrants. These are the policy reasons that state legislatures make when they enact anti-immigration measures. Arizona is a border state whose government officials worry about illegal immigration and inadequate control over the Mexican border. The Arizona Legislature passed the Legal Arizona Worker's Act which required state employers to check the immigration status of employees and provided for revocation of the business license of state companies that employed undocumented workers. The U.S. Chamber of Commerce challenged the law. The Chamber of Commerce argued that the federal government has complete power over immigration policy, and that under the **preemption doctrine**, a state law that conflicts with a valid federal law is unconstitutional under the Supremacy Clause of the Constitution. In Chamber of Commerce of the U.S. v. Whiting (2011), the Supreme Court upheld the state law on the grounds that the state law requiring employers to check the immigration status did not conflict with the federal law. The Arizona legislature also passed SB1070, which made it a crime to be in the state illegally and required Arizona law enforcement officials to question individuals whom they detained about, among other things, their immigration status. In Arizona v. U.S. (2012) the Court struck down three provisions of the law and upheld one.

17.8 | Comparative Politics and International Relations

17.81 | *Comparative Politics*

Comparative politics is a field of political science that relies heavily on the comparative method of studying government and politics. Comparative politics is one of the oldest fields in the study of politics. Aristotle compared the different forms of government to determine the best form of government. Today, comparativists are generally divided into one of two categories: area-specialists (e.g., Africa, Latin American, Asia, or the Middle East) or scholars who apply social science methods to the study of different political systems by comparing similar systems or comparing different systems. Comparative politics is often considered the study of non-U.S. government and politics, but the comparative method is also used to study American politics (e.g., comparative state politics). One way to increase understanding of U.S. government and politics is to compare it with government and politics in other countries. Some important comparative works include Giovanni Sartori's 1976 study of party systems, Gabriel Almond and Sidney Verba's 1963 study of civil culture, and Samuel Huntington's 1968 study of developing countries. Today, global organizations describe and analyze issues such as freedom, economic development, good government, and corruption from a comparative perspective. Transparency International provides information about corruption, including corruption by country. It defines corruption as the "abuse of entrusted power for private gain." It examines corruption related to topics such as access to information, education, humanitarian aid, and intergovernmental bodies. The organization's goal is to work toward government, politics, business, and civil society that is free of corruption.

Think about it!
When comparing countries, would a different kind of map, a non-geographic map, be useful?
http://www.theworld.org/2012/11/frank-jacobs-and-his-strange-maps/

17.82 | *International Relations*

International relations (or international studies) is the study of relations between countries. International relations involves the study of organizations, law, and issues including national security, economic development, crime (drug, terrorism, trafficking), environmental sustainability, social welfare, and human rights. International relations examines nation-states or countries but it is not limited to governments. International relations is also the study the behavior of intergovernmental organizations such as the United Nations and the Organization of American States; non-governmental organizations; and multinational corporations. In fact, international non-governmental organizations and businesses have become very important participants in international relations. Interpol, the International Criminal Police Organization, is an international intergovernmental organization whose mission is to "Connect Police for a Safer World." The development of national and international organized criminal enterprises prompted the development of international policing efforts. With 190 countries as members, Interpol is one of the largest intergovernmental organizations. Its organizational structure includes a president, and executive committee, and a General Assembly which meets annually to discuss coordination of policing.

Historically, international law was the body of rules and principles that governing nations and their dealings with individuals of other nations. This is ***public international law*** because it deals with government bodies. International law, which included *jus gentium* (the law of nations) and *jus inter gentes* (the agreements between nations), was the body of rules of conduct that are generally accepted as binding or controlling. International law is based on the consent of the parties that are subject to it. The United Nations is the major public international law organization. Its main judicial body is the International Court of Justice. Over time, international law has extended its scope to include non-government actors. This is **private international law**—the body of rules and principles that govern individuals and non-governmental organizations. International law is a growing body of law that has been developing piecemeal—that is, it has developed area by area or domain by domain. Trade law, intellectual property and contract law, human rights law, criminal justice law, and environmental law have been developed largely independently of one another, based on the interests and consent of the parties, rather than as a comprehensive strategy for coordinated legal development enacted by a single authoritative source. In terms of modern American foreign policy, "internationalists" are advocates of U.S. engagement in global affairs.

There are two general theories of international relations: realism and idealism. One element of a political ideology is a belief about human nature as good or bad, self-interested or public-minded. Ideological assumptions about individual behavior are also applied to thinking about the behavior of nations (which are, after all, organizations of individuals). Realism and idealism are based on different assumptions about the behavior of nations.

Realism is the theory that international relations can be best explained by the fact that nations are rational actors that primarily pursue their self-interest. Realists assume that human beings are by nature self-interested and competitive rather than benevolent and cooperative, and this self-interested individual behavior also characterizes nation-states. Accordingly, a nation's paramount self-interest is national security—survival in a Hobbesian world where nations, like individuals, pursue their self-interest without being constrained by national or international government. Realist believe that other goals and values such as democracy, equality, peace, human rights, and justice may be important but they are *secondary* to the primary goal of national self-interest. Human rights and justice are recognized when they happen to coincide with national interest, but when they conflict with national interest, the pursuit of national interest trumps these other political values.

Realists assume that the natural state of international relations is anarchy. Anarchy is a condition where governments (or individuals) are able to pursue their own interests without legal restrictions. Without a governing body or set of rules to limit the actions of nations, countries exploit power advantages over one another to achieve their national interest. Realism is therefore associated with power politics. Power politics is the belief that (national) might makes right. In other words, there is no objective understanding of justice because justice is merely whatever the stronger power (e.g., the winner of a war) says it is.

Two famous political theorists whose views reflect realist assumptions about human and national behavior are the Italian political philosopher Niccolo Machiavelli (1469-1527) and the English political philosopher Thomas Hobbes (1588-1679). In *The Prince*, Machiavelli argued that a political leader had to use power politics in order to accomplish the two main goals that he though all good leaders should strive for: maintaining the state (or nation) and achieving great things. Machiavelli defined **power politics** to include deception, manipulation of other actors, and the use of force—whatever means were necessary to accomplish their goals. In *Leviathan* (1651), Hobbes argued that strong government was necessary to create and maintain good order because individuals were by nature self-interested and had to be controlled. Both Machiavelli and Hobbes are considered realists in the sense that they believed that good strong leadership required a willingness to do what was effective rather than what was morally or legally right.

*Think about it! Do you think that **nations** act the way people act?*

Idealism is the theory that international relations can be organized and conducted according to values other than, and perhaps even higher than, national self-interest alone. These values or higher ideals include justice, human rights, and the rule of law. In international relations, idealists believe that the behavior of nations can include actions that are motivated by political values other than national interest. In contrast to realists, idealists believe that the self-interested nature of individuals and governments can be tempered or limited by the introduction of morality, values, and law into international relations. President Woodrow Wilson (1913-1921) is perhaps the American political official who is most strongly identified with idealism. Indeed, in International Relations idealism is sometimes referred to as Wilsonian Idealism. After the end of WWI, Wilson worked to create what he called a "Just Peace." He believed a just peace could be creating by developing an international system where individual nations were able to put aside their narrow self-interest and power politics to work for international peace and cooperation. At the Paris Peace Conference in 1919, Wilson advocated for a treaty, The Treaty of Versailles, which would commit nations to his peace plans and create the League of Nations. However, the U.S. Senate failed to ratify the Treaty in part because of the fear that U.S. national sovereignty would be compromised by legal requirements to comply with decisions of the League of Nations.

This concern about preserving U.S. sovereignty can still be heard today by critics of the United Nations, generally, and by opponents of specific treaties such as the Law of the Seas Treaty (the LOST) which was negotiated during the United Nations Law of the Sea Conference from 1973-1982. The U.S. Senate has not ratified the LOST. There are two main reasons for opposition to the treaty. First, opponents are concerned that the treaty's environmental policies, which are intended to promote sustainability of marine resources and environments, would require increased government regulation of business and commercial activities. This concern is understandable because the Law of the Seas Treaty marks a change from the historical view that under the law of *mare liberum* each nation was free to use resources in international waters as they saw fit, to a legal regime that regulated international waters to conserve resources and achieve sustainability. Second, opponents of the LOST worry that it would further erode U.S. sovereignty by requiring the United States to enforce laws that were developed to represent interests other than those of U.S. interests. Government regulation and national sovereignty are two issues of special interest to conservatives. Consequently, conservative organizations such as the Heritage Foundation and the National Center for Policy Research, and libertarian organizations such as the Cato Institute, opposed ratification of the Treaty.

> The Senate's Role in the Ratification of Treaties
> http://www.senate.gov/artandhistory/history/common/briefi
> ng/Treaties.htm

The political debate about how the U.S. should use its power, whether the U.S. global affairs policy should be idealist or realist, is not merely theoretical argument. The debate has a profound impact on foreign relations. During the Cold War, the debate about idealism or realism was framed as the question whether the U.S. could even win the war against communism while adhering to democratic values and the rule of law. The "hawks" leaned toward realism (i.e., fighting the way the enemy fought; doing whatever was necessary to win) and the "doves" leaned toward idealism (i.e., playing by the rules of limited warfare). The war on terror revived this debate. The realists in the Bush administration argued that the existing legal rules governing the criminal justice system and the laws of war were inadequate for the war on terror. As a result, the administration authorized the use of enhanced interrogation and special military commissions. Idealists considered enhanced interrogation, such as waterboarding, a euphemism for torture which was prohibited by domestic and international law. Idealists also defended the use of the existing legal systems for trying individuals suspected of terrorism.

> **Think about it!**
> Watch the video of the congressional investigation of the use of "coercive management techniques" for perspectives on the debate about torture, harsh interrogation, or enhanced interrogation: http://video.pbs.org/video/1629461216

17.9 | Additional Resources

Almond, Gabriel, and Sidney Verba. 1963. The Civic Culture. Princeton: Princeton University Press.

Huntington, Samuel. 1968. Political Order in Changing Societies. : New Haven, CT: Yale University Press.

Madison, James. "Political Observations." In *Letters and Other Writings of James Madison.* [Philadelphia, Pennsylvania: J.B. Lippincott and Co., 1865]. Volume IV: 491-2. http://www.archive.org/stream/lettersotherwrit04madi/lettersotherwrit04madi_djvu.txt

Mandelbaum, Michael. 2006. The Case for Goliath: How America Acts as the World's Government In the Twenty-First Century (2006),

Sartori, Giovanni. 1976. Parties and Party Systems. Cambridge: Cambridge University Press.

17.91 | *Additional Resources*

The U.S. Department of State Country and Foreign Policy Information

The United Kingdom: https://www.gov.uk/
U.S. relations with the United Kingdom: http://www.state.gov/p/eur/ci/uk/
Canada: http://www.canada.gc.ca/home.html
U.S. relations with Canada: http://www.state.gov/r/pa/ei/bgn/2089.htm
Mexico: http://en.presidencia.gob.mx/
U.S. relations with Mexico: http://www.state.gov/r/pa/ei/bgn/35749.htm
Israel: http://www.gov.il/firstgov/english
U.S. relations with Israel: http://www.state.gov/r/pa/ei/bgn/3581.htm
Germany:
http://www.bundesregierung.de/Webs/Breg/EN/Homepage/_node.html
U.S. relations with Germany: http://www.state.gov/r/pa/ei/bgn/3997.htm
Brazil: http://www.brasil.gov.br/?set_language=en
U.S. relations with Brazil: http://www.state.gov/r/pa/ei/bgn/35640.htm
Japan: http://www.mofa.go.jp/j_info/japan/government/index.html
China: http://english.gov.cn/
U.S. relations with China: http://www.state.gov/r/pa/ei/bgn/18902.htm
Saudi Arabia:
http://www.saudi.gov.sa/wps/portal/yesserRoot/home/!ut/p/b1/04_Sj9CPykssy0xPL
MnMz0vMAfGjzOfd3Z2dgjTNJAz8zUMMDTxNzZ2NHU0NDd29DfWDjU_T0_1z
yc1P1C7ldFQFV9YhO/dl4/d5/L2dBISEyZ0FBIS9nQSEh/
U.S. relations with Saudi Arabia:
http://www.state.gov/j/drl/rls/hrrpt/2005/61698.htm

[1] Theodore J. Lowi and Benjamin Ginsberg. 1996. *American Government*. Fourth Edition (New York: W. W. Norton & Company): 689.

[2] Sumner's anti-imperialist, anti-war essay defending republican government is available at http://praxeology.net/WGS-CUS.htm

[3] Eisenhower's *Farewell Address* is available at: http://www.americanrhetoric.com/speeches/dwightdeisenhowerfarewell.html

[4] Nixon's *Address* is available at http://www.state.gov/r/pa/ho/frus/nixon/i/20700.htm

[5] For an educational perspective on how to present globalization see http://www.cotf.edu/earthinfo/remotesens/remotesens.html

[6] http://www.state.gov/g/drl/hr/treaties/

[7] http://foreignaffairs.house.gov/about.asp?sec=documents. Accessed May 15, 2011.

[8] http://www.state.gov/s/d/rm/index.htm Accessed December 22, 2010.

[9] Quoted in http://www.pbs.org/moyers/journal/10192007/blackwater.html

[10] See http://www.globalsecurity.org/military/library/policy/national/nss-020920.htm

[11] Quoting Colonel Peter Masoor in "Army Focus on Counterinsurgency Debated Within," By Guy Raz, *National Public Radio*, May 6, 2008. Accessed May 10, 2008. www.npr.org

[12] See http://www.gwu.edu/%7Ensarchiv/NSAEBB/NSAEBB219/index.htm. Accessed May 15, 2011.

[13] Hans J. Morgenthau. 1960. *The Purpose of American Politics* (New York: Knopf):169-170.

Bill of Rights

Congress of the United States,

begun and held at the City of New York, on
Wednesday, the fourth of March, one thousand seven hundred and eighty nine.

The Conventions of a number of the States having, at the time of their adopting the Constitution, expressed a desire, in order to prevent misconstruction or abuse of its powers, that further declaratory and restrictive clauses should be added: And as extending the ground of public confidence in the Government, will best insure the beneficent ends of its institution:

Resolved, by the SENATE and HOUSE of REPRESENTATIVES of the UNITED STATES of AMERICA in Congress assembled, two thirds of both Houses concurring, That the following Articles be proposed to the Legislatures of the several States, as Amendments to the Constitution of the United States; all, or any of which articles, when ratified by three fourths of the said Legislatures, to be valid to all intents and purposes, as part of the said Constitution, viz.

Articles in addition to, and Amendment of the Constitution of the United States of America, proposed by Congress, and ratified by the Legislatures of the several States, pursuant to the fifth Article of the Original Constitution.

Article the first ...... After the first enumeration required by the first Article of the Constitution, there shall be one Representative for every thirty thousand, until the number shall amount to one hundred, after which, the proportion shall be so regulated by Congress, that there shall be not less than one hundred Representatives, nor less than one Representative for every forty thousand persons, until the number of Representatives shall amount to two hundred, after which, the proportion shall be so regulated by Congress, that there shall not be less than two hundred Representatives, nor more than one Representative for every fifty thousand persons.   [Not Ratified]

Article the second .... No law, varying the compensation for the services of the Senators and Representatives, shall take effect, until an election of Representatives shall have intervened.   [Not Ratified]

Article the third .... Congress shall make no law respecting an establishment of religion, or prohibiting the free exercise thereof; or abridging the freedom of speech, or of the press; or the right of the people peaceably to assemble, and to petition the Government for a redress of grievances.

Article the fourth ..... A well regulated Militia, being necessary to the security of a free State, the right of the people to keep and bear Arms, shall not be infringed.

Article the fifth .... No Soldier shall, in time of peace, be quartered in any house, without the consent of the owner, nor in time of war, but in a manner to be prescribed by law.

18.0 | Civil Liberties and Civil Rights: Freedom and Equality

This chapter continues the examination of the need to strike the right balance between granting and limiting government power by examining civil liberties and civil rights. Civil liberties and civil rights are directly related to government power. Debates about them are debates about where to strike the balance between individual freedom and government power to limit it. The main purpose of the chapter is to

- Define the terms civil liberties and civil rights. Although *civil liberties* and *civil rights* are commonly used to refer to the same thing—**individual rights**—there are three important differences between them. They have different legal sources (constitutional versus statutory), they serve different purposes (freedom versus equality), and they have different relationships with government power (grants versus limits).
- Describe the development of specific rights and liberties; and
- Explain why freedom and equality are often so controversial despite widespread public support for these two political values.

18.1 | Defining Terms

18.12 | *Civil Liberties*

In the U.S., civil liberties are **constitutional** guarantees that protect individual **freedom** from government power. This is the negative (as opposed to the positive) concept of individual liberty. Civil liberties are stated negatively. For instance, the Constitution does not give an individual the right to freedom of expression or equal protection of the laws. The First Amendment prohibits Congress from limiting freedom of expression and the 14th Amendment prohibits a state government from denying equal protection of the laws. The main source of civil liberties is the Bill of Rights—the first ten amendments to the Constitution—but some civil liberties are provided in the body of the Constitution (e.g. the writ of habeas corpus), the 13th, 14th, and 15th Amendments, and the 19th Amendment (which prohibits denying the right to vote "on account of sex"). The Bill of Rights include freedom of expression (religion, speech, press, and association); the right to keep and bear arms; protection against unreasonable search and seizure; guarantees of due process of law; the right to a trial by jury and the assistance of counsel; protection against cruel and unusual punishment; and the right to privacy. The civil liberties provisions that apply to criminal justice are examined in the chapter on criminal justice.

Civil liberties cases are conflicts between individual freedom and government power. They are typically conflicts between an individual (or an organization) who claims a right to do something—such as burn a flag as a political protest, demonstrate at a funeral, obtain an abortion, view sexually explicit material on the Internet, carry a handgun or make unlimited campaign contributions—and the government which claims the power to limit that right. As part of the judiciary's dispute resolution function, courts serve as a neutral third party to settle these civil liberties disputes between individuals and the government. This is an important function in constitutional democracies such as the U.S. because civil liberties are the individual or minority rights that limit the power of the majority. The burden of proof is on the government. If the government "substantially burdens" a fundamental freedom, the government must demonstrate that it has a compelling interest in limiting the freedom *and* that it has no less restrictive means to achieve it.

18.13 | *Civil Rights*

Civil rights are legal claims that are generally provided in **statutory** law (legislation) rather than the Constitution. They typically are claims to **equal treatment** rather than freedom. And they are legal claims that can be made against other individuals or organizations—not just against the government. Civil rights legislation prohibits racial, ethnic, religious, and gender-based discrimination in voting, education, employment, housing, public accommodations, and other settings. Civil rights movements in the 19th and 20th centuries promoted egalitarianism for racial and ethnic and national minorities, prisoners, juveniles, women, the elderly, the handicapped, aliens, and gays and lesbians. Civil liberties generally promote freedom by limiting government power. Civil rights typically promote equality by using government power to limit individual freedom to discriminate.

18.14 | *Uncivil Liberties: Disturbing the Peace (of Mind)*

Fewer political actions cause a bigger political stir than when people actually use their civil liberties. The American political experience includes a history of strong-willed people standing up for their political and religious beliefs despite the threat of community hostility or government sanction. Some of these people were noble individuals standing for political principles; others were ignoble individuals who were merely taking advantage of constitutional rights. In either case their actions created a political stir. The following is a short list of some of the individuals whose convictions made them part of the American story of civil liberties.

- William Penn preaching on the streets of London and taking a stand for freedom of religion against the charge of unlawful assembly.
- Charles Schenck, the Secretary of the Socialist Party, distributing leaflets that opposed U.S. participation in WWI, which he called a capitalist enterprise to exploit workers, and compared the military draft with slavery.
- Walter Barnette objecting to a school board policy that required school children to recite the pledge of allegiance.
- Gregory Lee Johnson burning an American Flag during the 1984 Republican Party convention.
- Fred Phelps picketing at the funerals of veterans to express his belief that the veteran's death was God's punishment for American toleration of homosexuality.
- Xavier Alvarez lying about being a decorated military veteran and then claiming that he could not be prosecuted for violating the Stolen Valor Act of 2005 because the First Amendment prohibits Congress from passing laws that limit freedom of speech.

These are all examples of civil liberties cases where an individual challenges government power to limit freedom of expression. The London trial of <u>William Penn</u> is part of the American story of religious freedom because a jury refused to convict him despite the fact that he was guilty of unlawful assembly. <u>Charles Schenck</u> was less fortunate. The Supreme Court upheld his conviction during WWI on the grounds that Congress can prohibit speech that presents a "clear and present danger" that it will cause evils—in this instance, refusal to comply with a military draft law—that Congress has power to prevent.

A WWII era case, <u>West Virginia State Board of Education v. Barnette</u> (1943), had a different outcome. During the national wave of patriotism during World War II, the West Virginia Board of Education adopted a policy that required all students in public schools to salute the flag as part of daily school activities. Walter Barnette, a Jehovah's Witness, argued that the requirement violated his child's freedom of religion. The Supreme Court agreed. When Gregory Johnson burned an American flag as a protest outside the Dallas, Texas City Hall in 1984 he was convicted of violating a Texas law prohibiting desecration of the flag and fined $2,000. He appealed his conviction arguing that the First Amendment protects expressive actions such as flag burning. <u>The Supreme Court agreed</u>. The ruling was not popular with the general public or many government officials. A constitutional amendment was proposed to ban flag burning but the amendment was never adopted.

Fred Phelps continued this tradition of intentionally using freedom of expression to disturb the peace of mind in a particularly uncivil way. For more than two decades members of the Westboro Baptist Church picketed military funerals as a way to express their belief that God is punishing the United States for tolerating homosexuality. The picketing also condemned the Catholic Church for sex scandals involving its clergy. On March 10, 2006 the church's founder, Fred Phelps, and six parishioners who are relatives of Phelps picketed the funeral of Marine Lance Corporal Matthew Snyder at a Catholic Church in Maryland. Corporal Snyder was killed in Iraq in the line of duty. The picketing took place on public land about 1,000 feet from the church where the funeral was held, in accordance with rules established by local police. For about 30 minutes prior to the funeral, the picketers displayed signs that stated "Thank God for Dead Soldiers," "Fags Doom Nations," "America is Doomed," "Priests Rape Boys," and "You're Going to Hell." Matthew Snyder's father saw the tops of the picketers' signs on the way to the funeral, but he did not learn what was written on them until he watched that evening's news broadcast. He sued Phelps and his daughters. A jury awarded Snyder more than a million dollars in compensatory and punitive damages. Phelps appealed. The jury award was overturned on the grounds that Phelps' actions were protected by the First Amendment freedom of expression because they were comments on matters of public affairs and were not provably false. Snyder then took the case all the way to the U.S. Supreme Court, which ruled in Phelps's favor in the case of *Snyder v. Phelps*.

Mr. Alvarez was a member of a water district board who in speeches falsely claimed to be a retired marine who received the Congressional Medal of Honor. Criminal defendants have two defense strategies. They can challenge the facts ("I did not do what the government says I did!") or they can challenge the law ("The law used to prosecute me is unconstitutional!"). Mr. Alvarez admitted the facts but argued that the Stolen Valor

Act was unconstitutional. The Supreme Court agreed that the First Amendment protects lying. Justice Kennedy's opinion for the Court in <u>U.S. v. Alvarez</u> (2012) begins:

> "Lying was his habit. Xavier Alvarez…lied when he said that he played hockey for the Detroit Red Wings and that he once married a starlet from Mexico. But when he lied in announcing he held the Congressional Medal of Honor, respondent ventured onto new ground; for that lie violates a federal criminal statute, the Stolen Valor Act of 2005. 18 U. S. C. §704."

So Mr. Alvarez, a person whom a Supreme Court justice described as a habitual liar, is now one of the ignoble individuals whose actions are now part of the American story of civil liberties. The general public and government officials often react to court rulings that protect hateful and bigoted speech, flag burning, anti-war demonstrations, or even lying, with disappointment, disbelief, profound disagreement, or disgust. The reaction reflects disapproval of the individual's behavior and the courts for reading the Constitution to protect such behavior.

18.2 | The First Amendment

The First Amendment guarantees freedom of expression: freedom of religion, freedom of speech, freedom of the press, and freedom to assemble and petition the government to redress grievances. Freedom of expression is today universally recognized as an essential condition for democracy and self-government. The political importance of freedom of expression is reflected in the fact that it is listed as the first of the Bill of Rights freedoms and the fact that all 50 state constitutions also guarantee freedom of expression. The following sections of this chapter describe freedom of religion and freedom of speech. Freedom of the press is examined in a chapter on the media.

18.21 | *Freedom of Religion: the Two Religion Clauses*

The First Amendment has two religion clauses: the **Establish Clause** and the **Free Exercise Clause**: "Congress shall make no law…respecting the establishment of religion or prohibiting the free exercise thereof." But the public, judges, and other government officials do not read the First Amendment to mean there can be *no* laws limiting freedom of religion. <u>Freedom of religion</u> is more complicated than the absolutist language of the First Amendment suggests.

Freedom House is an organization that compares freedom of expression in different countries. Check out the rankings of nations: http://www.freedomhouse.org/

18.22 | *Freedom of Religion: the Establishment Clause*

Let's start the explanation with the first freedom of religion issue: the Establishment Clause. There are two interpretations of the Establishment Clause: the Wall of Separation and Accommodation. The **Wall of Separation** reading holds that the government cannot establish a religion as the official religion of the country, establish religious belief (as opposed to atheism or agnosticism) as the official position of the country, or support or oppose a particular denomination or religion in general. The Wall is a metaphor for the separation of church and state (government). The **Accommodation** reading is that the government can "accommodate" or support religious belief as long as an official religion is not declared. The Accommodation reading allows fairly extensive government support for religion (school prayer, school aid, tax credits for tuition) and public displays of religious symbols and items (e.g., the Ten Commandments, crèches, crosses and crucifixes, and other religious icons). These two readings of the First Amendment Establishment Clause have fairly consistently divided political conservatives and political liberals as well as legal conservatives and legal liberals. Liberals tend to be secularists who advocate for the Wall of Separation while conservatives tend to be religionists who advocate for more government support for religion and moral values.

The colonists explicitly believed that government and politics had explicitly religious purposes. Their founding documents such as the Mayflower Compact described government as responsible for making people morally good (as defined by the tenets of an established church) and politics as a community's efforts to make people morally good (by legislating morality). During the colonial era people came to the new world for, among other reasons, religious freedom. Colonial governments established official churches and used laws for religious purposes including church attendance and punishing blasphemy. The ratification of the Bill of Rights changed the relationship between church and state. But studying religion and American politics reveals ongoing debates about the nature of the relationship between religion and government, debates that have been renewed by the increased religiosity in American politics over the past several decades. In fact, one dimension of the culture wars is the fight over the relationship between church and state.

The Supreme Court developed the **Lemon Test** to help guide decisions about when government support for religion violates the Establishment Clause. Lemon v. Kurtzman (1971) presented a claim that Pennsylvania and Rhode Island laws providing public support for teacher salaries, textbooks, and other instructional materials in non-public (primarily Catholic) schools violated the Establishment Clause. Chief Justice Burger upheld the laws and explained the three-pronged test to be used in such cases—a test that came to be called the Lemon Test. First, the law must have a *secular legislative purpose* (in this case, the state aid helped educate children). Second, the law must *neither help nor hurt religion*. Third, the law must *not foster excessive government entanglement* with religion. The Lemon Test is still used today. However, political conservatives are critical of the Lemon Test for being too separationist, and they advocate the Accommodation reading of the Establishment Clause. The conservative justices on the Supreme Court share this view and it possible that the Court will eliminate the Lemon Test or change its application to allow Accommodation on matters of religion and government, church and state.

Although the Establishment Clause and the Free Exercise Clause are two separate provisions of the First Amendment, they are related in the sense that government support for one religion or denomination can limit the free exercise of individuals who belong to religions other than the one or ones supported by the government.

18.23 | *Freedom of Religion: the Free Exercise Clause*

Despite the absolutist language, the First Amendment has never been understood by the American public, government officials, or the courts to mean that there could be no limits on freedom of religion. The Free Exercise Clause has always been understood to mean that government can limit free exercise of religion. This apparently unusual reading of the Clause can be traced to the Supreme Court's ruling in the landmark 19th Century case _Reynolds v. U.S._ (1879).

The case arose from a law passed by Congress to prohibit the Mormon Church's practice of bigamy. The law, the Anti-Bigamy Act, made bigamy a federal offense. George Reynolds was prosecuted in the federal district court for the Territory of Utah with bigamy in violation of the Act: "Every person having a husband or wife living, who marries another, whether married or single, in a Territory, or other place over which the United States have exclusive jurisdiction, is guilty of bigamy, and shall be punished by a fine of not more than $500, and by imprisonment for a term of not more than five years." Reynolds was a Mormon who argued that church doctrine required male Mormons to practice polygamy. He asked the trial court "to instruct the jury that if they found from the evidence that he was married...in pursuance of and in conformity with what he believed at the time to be a religious duty," then the jury verdict must be "not guilty."

The Supreme Court acknowledged that Reynolds sincerely believed that this duty was of "divine origin" and that male members of the Church who did not practice polygamy would be punished by "damnation in the life to come." The Court noted that the First Amendment expressly prohibited Congress from passing a law restricting the free exercise of religion. However, it also noted that the government has always been allowed to regulate certain aspects of religious freedom. Some of the colonies and states established churches and punished certain religious beliefs and practices. In 1784 Virginia considered a bill to provide state support for "for teachers of the Christian religion." James Madison wrote _Memorial and Remonstrance_ in opposition to the bill. Not only was the bill to provide for teachers of Christianity defeated, the Virginia Assembly passed Thomas Jefferson's bill "establishing religious freedom." The act described government efforts to restrain ideas because of their supposed "ill tendency" as a threat to religious liberty. Jefferson maintained that government power should be limited to "overt acts against peace and good order," that it should not have any power "in the field of opinion." According to Jefferson, beliefs are the business of the Church and actions are the business of the government. This principle separating religious beliefs and political opinions from religious and political actions remains an important principle limiting the scope of government power. A little more than a year after the passage of this Virginia statute, the members of the constitutional convention drafted the Constitution. Jefferson was disappointed that the new Constitution did not specifically guarantee freedom of religion but he supported ratification because he believed the Constitution could be improved by an amendment specifically limiting government power to restrict religious freedom. The first session of the first Congress did so by proposing the First Amendment.

In _Reynolds_, the Court quoted Jefferson's belief that religion is a private matter "solely between man and his god." Accordingly, a person is accountable only to God "for his faith or his worship." The legislative powers of government "reach actions only, and not opinions... " This distinction between faith and actions remains one of the most important rules for determining the limits of government power. According to Jefferson, the First Amendment meant that "the whole American people" declared that Congress could make no law respecting an establishment of religion or prohibiting the free exercise thereof," thereby building a wall of separation between church and state. The Reynolds Court considered Jefferson's view "an authoritative declaration of the scope and effect" of the First Amendment: "Congress was deprived of all legislative power over mere opinion, but was left free to reach actions which were in violation of social duties or subversive of good order."

The Court then explained why polygamy was not protected by the First Amendment, why Congress could make a law prohibited polygamy: "Polygamy has always been odious among the northern and western nations of Europe, and, until the establishment of the Mormon Church, was almost exclusively a feature of the life of Asiatic and of African people. At common law, the second marriage was always void…, and from the earliest history of England polygamy has been treated as an ofence against society."

Reynolds created two legal principles that are still used today to decide civil liberties cases. The first principle is that the First Amendment does not guarantee absolute freedom of religion. It guarantees absolute freedom of belief but it allows government to restrict religious practice. This distinction between religious belief and practice also applies to political expression: the government cannot restrict political ideas but it can restrict political actions. The second principle established in *Reynolds* is that government has the power to limit certain kinds of religious practices that were considered morally or socially unacceptable. Many state constitutions, for example, guarantee freedom of religion but only to those religious practices that are consistent with good moral order. The belief that state governments could prohibit certain morally or socially unacceptable practices is relevant to current debates about state laws that have traditionally defined marriage as between one man and one woman.

Think About it!

Should the First Amendment be read to prohibit *any* law that limits the free exercise of religion? Snake handling? See the CNN video of snake handlers in Tennessee at http://www.youtube.com/watch?v=cwBVcsWYJd8

18.24 | *Free Exercise Today*

As noted in the chapter on the courts, the modern Supreme Court's role as a protector of civil liberties can be traced to the constitutional revolution of 1937 when the Court announced in the famous Footnote Four in *United States v. Carolene Products Company* that laws aimed at particular religious, national, or racial minorities had a weaker presumption of constitutionality. According to the Court, "prejudice against discrete and insular minorities" (including religious minorities) may be a special condition which cannot be remedied through the majoritarian political process therefore the legal remedy, going to court to enforce constitutional rights, must be more readily available.

The Court first began reading the First Amendment to protect the free exercise of religion in the 1940s. In *Cantwell v. Connecticut* (1940), the Court ruled that the Free Exercise Clause of the First Amendment applied to the state governments, not just Congress or the federal government. This ruling signaled the Court's willingness to review state laws that historically restricted religious beliefs and practices that were considered unpopular, politically unacceptable, or immoral.

The Supreme Court has issued some very controversial rulings in both Establish Clause and Free Exercise cases. The decision declaring that organized school prayer in public schools was unconstitutional was particularly controversial. One issue that the Court has been very wary of becoming involved with is defining what beliefs systems constitute a religion. The definition of religion is important because there are many important legal benefits, including tax benefits that come with an organization being officially recognized as a religion. A related question is whether an individual's personal ethical or moral beliefs should be treated as the equivalent of a religion for the purposes of the First Amendment. One material benefit for an organization that is officially recognized as a religion is tax-exempt status. The legal benefit for an individual whose personal beliefs are recognized as religious beliefs, or the equivalent of religious beliefs include religious exemption from compulsory military service (the draft), religious exemptions from certain workplace rules, and religious exemptions from state drug laws for sacramental drug usage (e.g., peyote; marijuana; communion wine).

Three examples of government defining or officially recognizing religions are the "I am" movement, the Department of Veteran's Affairs policy on cemetery headstones, and the Internal Revenue Service rulings on the Church of Scientology.

Guy Ballard was a follower of the "I Am" movement. He solicited money from people for faith healing. The government accused Ballard's organization of being a business enterprise that was engaged in fraud while claiming to be a legitimate religious enterprise. Ballard maintained that his organization was a legitimate religious enterprise and took his case to the U.S. Supreme Court. The Court's reluctance to define what is and what is not a religion, and its reluctance to allow the government to define what is and what is not a religion, is evident in the 1944 case *U.S. v. Ballard*, 322 U.S. 78 (1944). The Court advised the government to be very reluctant to define what was and was not a legitimate religious activity, and to allow very broad claims of religious activity.[1]

Since 1944, the Court has broadened the definition of religion by accepting broad claims that beliefs were consistent with the concept of religion. The Court held that an individual could claim that personal "spiritual" beliefs or reasons of conscience (conscientious objector status) were legitimate reasons for religious exemption from the military draft. The claim to exemption from the military draft was not limited to identifiable religious doctrines.

There are many benefits that come with being an officially recognized religion. Must the government recognize witchcraft or humanism as religions? The Department of Veteran's Affairs had a policy to allow military families to choose any of 38 authorized images of religion that the Department would engrave on the headstones of veterans. The Department created a list of authorized headstone symbols. It included symbols for Christianity, Buddhism, Islam, Judaism, Sufism Reoriented, Eckiankar, and Seicho-No-Ie (Japanese), but not the Wiccan pentacle—a five-pointed star in a circle. The widows of two Wiccan combat veterans (approximately 1,800 active-duty service members identify themselves as Wiccan) sued the government claiming the policy that did not allow their religion's symbol on headstones violated the First Amendment. The court rulings have directed the Department of Veteran's Affairs to allow the Wiccan symbol because the government should not have the power to define a legitimate or acceptable or officially recognized religion. In 2007, the Department finally agreed to allow the Wiccan pentacle to be engraved on veterans' headstones.[2]

The Church of Scientology engaged in a three decade-long political and legal battle to get the government (specifically, the Internal Revenue Service) to recognize Scientology and related organizations as a church. The government's initial denial of tax-exempt status was challenged in court. In 1993 the IRS finally recognized Scientology as a religious organization and granted it tax-exempt status as a 501(c)(3) religious or charitable organization for the purposes of the tax code.

18.25 | *Content Neutrality*

The court rulings striking down a Department of Veteran's Administration policy that allowed some religious symbols to be engraved on headstones but excluded others was based on a well-established legal principle: content neutrality. **Content Neutrality** is the principle that the government is supposed to be neutral toward political and religious beliefs. Government is not supposed to take sides in political debates by supporting some ideas but not others, or opposing some ideas but not others. Content neutrality applies broadly to freedom of expression both political and religious. It means that the government should not favor one religion over others, religious belief over non-belief, one ideology over others, or one political party over others. In effect, content neutrality means that government is not supposed to discriminate for or against ideas. If the government regulates religion, for example, the regulations should be content neutral. If the Internal Revenue Service grants religious organizations tax-exempt status, content neutrality prohibits the IRS from granting the status to some religious organizations but not others. The Department of Veterans' Affairs might be able to deny all religious symbols on headstones, but the principle of content neutrality prohibited it from singling out the Wiccan symbol for exclusion. State laws that provide tax credits or vouchers for costs associated with sending children to religious schools cannot be limited to Christian schools, for example, without violating the idea of content neutrality. Content neutrality means that the government should not take sides in debates about religious or political ideas.

Of course, the government frequently and inevitably takes sides in debates about the relationship between religion and government and politics. The relationship between church and state was once very close. Most states once had Sunday closing laws which required most businesses to close on Sunday. These laws either established Sunday as the day for religious worship or merely designated Sunday as the day of rest. Today, Sunday closing laws (or laws limiting hours or the sale of certain products such as alcohol) are allowed for secular reasons, but not for religious purposes. But regardless of the reason, Sunday closing laws burden religious believers whose Sabbath did not fall on Sunday because observant sabbatarians would have to keep their businesses closed two days a week. State and local laws can recognize Christmas as an official holiday, and even put up public displays such as crèches (nativity scenes), but that is primarily because Christmas is treated as a holiday season rather than a religious season.

State and local governments once required bible reading or organized school prayer in public schools. Legal challenges to such laws promoting religion in public schools have resulted in court rulings that they violate either the Establishment Clause or

Free Exercise Clause of the First Amendment. These rulings weakened the relationship between church and state. The Supreme Court has upheld state laws that prohibit religious practices such as snake handling, and laws that require vaccinations even though an individual's religious beliefs forbid vaccinations. These laws are upheld if they serve a secular purpose (e.g., protecting public health) but struck down if they are intended to show public disapproval of a particular religious belief or practice.

States can also pass laws that are intended to discourage drug use even if they restrict freedom of religion. In *Employment Division of Oregon v. Smith* (1990) the Court upheld an Oregon law that was intended to discourage illegal drug use by denying unemployment benefits to workers who were fired drug use. Native Americans who were fired for sacramental drug use argued that the denial of unemployment benefits was unconstitutional because it restricted their freedom of religion. The Court ruled that it was reasonable for a state to pass such a law to discourage illegal drug usage, and that there was no evidence that the generally applicable law was passed to discriminate against Native Americans. Advocates of religious freedom were very critical of the ruling because the Court said that it would use the **reasonableness test** to determine whether a generally applicable law that substantially burdened freedom of religion was constitutional. Prior to this ruling, the Court used the **strict scrutiny test**, which required the government to have a compelling reason for burdening freedom of religion. Religion advocates saw the reasonableness standard as weakening constitutional protection of free exercise of religion. They lobbied Congress to pass The Religious Freedom Restoration Act of 1993 which by statute restored the strict scrutiny test.

A church in Boerne, Texas used the Religious Freedom Restoration Act to challenge the city's zoning laws that limited the church's building expansion. Zoning laws can prohibit churches in residential neighborhoods or limit remodeling and building expansion. The church was located in an historic district of Boerne, Texas. The city rejected the church's building expansion plan and the church went to court claiming the zoning restriction was a violation of freedom of religion. In *Boerne v. Flores* (1997) the Supreme Court held that the Religious Freedom Restoration Act was unconstitutional because the Court, not the Congress, determines how to interpret the First Amendment. As a result, the courts still use the reasonableness test when determining whether a generally applicable law, a law that is intended to serve a legitimate public purpose rather than targeting specific unpopular religious practices, can limit freedom of religion. However, Congress then passed the Religious Land Use and Institutionalized Persons Act of 2000 to provide stronger protection for freedom of religion. Advocates of greater protection for religious freedom and greater government support for religion challenge the secularist and Wall of Separation understanding of the relationship between church and state as part of the "war on religion."

Think about it!

Should religious individuals, churches, and religious organizations be given religious exemptions from laws?

Is there currently a war on religion or a war on Christianity?

18.3 | Freedom of Speech

Freedom of speech is essential for democracy. Some of the same legal rules that the Court uses to decide freedom of religion cases apply to freedom of speech. The first rule is that <u>freedom of speech</u> is not absolute: the government can restrict freedom of speech. The second rule is that the legal principle for determining whether the government can restrict freedom of speech is *the distinction between thought and action*. This distinction in analogous to the distinction between religious belief, which government cannot restrict, and religious action, which the government can restrict. The government cannot restrict political thought but it can restrict political action. Political actions are subject to what are called *time, place, and manner* restrictions: freedom of speech does not mean that people can say whatever they want (e.g., certain provocative words such as hate speech can be limited), however they want (use of bullhorns can be limited as can public demonstrations), wherever they want (speech on private property or in certain public places such as residential neighborhoods or special places such as airports can be limited), and whenever you want (you can make a good point but maybe not at 4:00 in the morning). Despite these limits, there is a presumption of freedom of speech—which means that the government bears the burden of proof to show the need to restrict a fundamental freedom such as freedom of expression. In a capitalist country such as the U.S., where the idea of a free market of goods and services has great appeal, the idea of a free marketplace of ideas also has strong appeal. The assumption is that government intervention in the political marketplace should be limited—that individuals should have freedom of choice of goods, services, and ideas.

Each of the 50 state constitutions provides for freedom of expression. Virtually all of the constitutions in the countries of the world provide for freedom of expression. Comparing state constitutions and national constitutions can increase understanding of the First Amendment to the U.S. Constitution and the different approaches to guaranteeing freedom of expression.

Choose one or two states, or one or two countries, and compare how their constitutions provide for freedom of expression. Search state government web sites, national government web sites or sites that provide national constitutions such as http://www.constitution.org/cons/natlcons.htm

---

Think About it!
Is the U.S. a Christian Nation? And what does that mean?
http://www.npr.org/2012/08/08/157754542/the-most-influential-evangelist-youve-never-heard-of

18.4 | The Second Amendment

Gun rights are an important part of American political culture. The Second Amendment declares, "A well regulated Militia being necessary to the security of a free State, the right to keep and bear Arms shall not be infringed." There are two readings of this Amendment: an individual rights reading and a federalism reading. For 70 years the Supreme Court read the Second Amendment as a provision of the Constitution that was intended to protect state militias from the federal government. This is the federalism reading of the Second Amendment. It holds that the Second Amendment was included in the Bill of Rights to protect the states from the federal government. The new Constitution reduced the powers of the states and greatly increased the power of the federal government by among other things, giving Congress the power to create a military. The Second Amendment protected state militias by preventing the federal government from abolishing state militias. This federalism reading of the Second Amendment is a "state's rights" reading.

Then in a 2008 case, District of Columbia v. Heller, the Court ruled 5-4 that the Second Amendment guaranteed an individual right to keep and bear arms. Justice Scalia's opinion for the majority described the right as a fundamental right that had two basic purposes. The first purpose is self-defense. This anti-crime purpose is a reminder that the government does not have a monopoly on the use of force. Individuals have the right to keep and bear arms to fight crime. The second purpose is even more explicitly political. Individuals have the right to arm themselves to fight against government tyranny. The *Heller* ruling declared an individual right and acknowledged that it was not an absolute right, that some gun control measures were constitutional. But it did not say what kinds of gun control laws were constitutional. That is being left up to future cases using the same analysis that the courts apply to other fundamental rights. The government has the burden of proof to demonstrate that the limits on individual freedom are necessary. The *Heller* ruling also did not say whether the Second Amendment applied to the states (and local governments). In McDonald v. Chicago the Court ruled that it did. So now individuals can use the Second Amendment to challenge state and local gun laws. The Court's changed reading of the Second Amendment is one chapter in the story of how the law changes in a conservative era of American politics. The liberal activist Warren Court had a different agenda than the conservative activist Roberts Court.

> **Think About it!**
> Does the Second Amendment give individuals or groups of individuals a constitutional right to armed rebellion against the government? Read about the Stono Slave Rebellion in South Carolina in 1739.
> http://www.pbs.org/wgbh/aia/part1/1p284.html

18.5 | Civil Rights

Civil liberties are constitutional protections for individual freedom. Civil rights are statutory laws that promote equality. Liberty and equality are democratic values but the relative emphasis on each value varies from country to country and over time.

Democratic systems generally value individual freedom more than equality. Socialistic systems value equality more than freedom. In the U.S., equality is today a much more important value than it was when the nation was founded.

Equality *is* one of the political values extolled in the Declaration of Independence, which asserts human equality in especially memorable language:

> "We hold these truths to be self-evident, that all men are created equal, that they are endowed by their Creator with certain unalienable Rights, that among these are Life, Liberty and the pursuit of Happiness."

But the Declaration of Independence is not a governing document (the Constitution is the government document) or a legal document (it does not create any legally enforceable rights claims). Equality is not one of the political values embodied in the Constitution. The Constitution recognized slavery and did not recognize gender equality. Early statutes also recognized slavery. The Northwest Ordinance of 1787 prohibited slavery in parts of the country (western territories north of the Ohio River) but also provided that fugitive slaves could be "lawfully reclaimed." The Missouri Compromise of 1820 prohibited slavery in territories north of the parallel 36.5 degrees north of the equator. And the Fugitive Slave Law of 1793 authorized federal judges to recognize a slave owner's property rights claim to fugitive slaves.

18.51 | *Making Equality an American Value*

Equality only became an important political and legal value in the latter half of the 19th Century with the rhetoric of Abraham Lincoln, the three Civil War Amendments, and federal civil rights legislation enacted under the authority of the 14th Amendment. The Civil War Amendments were passed to guarantee the rights of newly freed slaves by limiting the power of states to discrimination on the basis of race. The 13th Amendment prohibited slavery. The Fourteenth Amendment prohibited states from making or enforcing any law that shall "deprive any person of life, liberty, or property, without due process of law; nor deny to any person within its jurisdiction the equal protection of the laws." The Fifteenth Amendment prohibited states from denying the right to vote on account of "race, color, or previous condition of servitude." Section 5 of the Fourteenth Amendment gave Congress the power to enforce "by appropriate legislation" the provisions of the Amendment.

These three Civil War Amendments became the constitutional foundation for civil rights legislation. Congress passed the Civil Rights Act of 1866 to guarantee "citizens, of every race and color…the same right, in every State and Territory…to make and enforce contracts, to sue, be parties, and give evidence, to inherit, purchase, lease, sell, hold, and convey real and personal property…" and enjoy other benefits of the laws. Congress passed the Civil Rights Act of 1875, which made it a federal offense for owners or operators of any public accommodations (including hotels, transportation, and places of amusement) to deny the enjoyment of those accommodations on account of race or religion. Innkeepers, theater owners, and a railroad company challenged the law as exceeding government power because it regulated private businesses. The Supreme Court agreed in *The Civil Rights Cases* (1883). The ruling greatly limited Congress's power to

> "The law, in its majestic equality, forbids the rich as well as the poor to sleep under bridges, to beg in the streets, and to steal bread."
>
> **Anatole France**,
> *The Red Lily, 1894,*
> *chapter 7*

use the 14th Amendment as authority for laws promoting racial equality. As a result, matters of racial equality were left to state laws until the 1930s and 1940s. In *Brown v. Mississippi* (1936), the Supreme Court abandoned its traditional hands-off policy toward state criminal justice amid growing federal concern about racial discrimination. In *Brown* the Court unanimously held that police torture of a black suspect in order to compel a confession, questioning that was euphemistically called ***the third degree***, violated due process of law. The subsequent federal court rulings in cases involving racial administration of criminal justice were part of the broader civil rights movement in other areas of public policy.

The Civil Rights Act of 1964 and the Voting Rights Act of 1965 are major landmarks in the civil rights movement. The <u>Civil Rights Act of 1964</u> expanded the federal government's power to act to eliminate a broad range of discriminatory actions. Congress passed the Act to "enforce the constitutional right to vote, to confer jurisdiction upon the district courts of the United States to provide injunctive relief against discrimination in public accommodations, to authorize the Attorney General to institute suits to protect constitutional rights in public facilities and public education, to extend the Commission on Civil Rights, to prevent discrimination in federally assisted programs, to establish a Commission on Equal Employment Opportunity, and for other purposes." The <u>Voting Rights Act of 1965</u> expanded the federal government's power to remedy a specific type of racial discrimination, racial discrimination in voting, that directly affected how the democratic process worked. Section 2 of the 1965 Act provided that "No voting qualification or prerequisite to voting, or standard, practice, or procedure shall be imposed or applied by any State or political subdivision to deny or abridge the right of any citizen of the United States to vote on account of race or color."

18.52 | *Does Equality Mean Treating Everyone the Same*?

Each of the various civil liberties and rights movements that made equality a more important political value prompted debates about the meaning of equality. It turns out that equality is more complicated that it initially seems, and defining it is harder than one might expect. Equality does *not* mean treating everyone the same. This chapter began with a famous 1894 quote of the French author, Anatole France, who sarcastically praised a law that prohibited anyone, rich and poor alike, to sleep under the bridges of Paris as egalitarian. On its face, the law treated everyone equally—but of course not everyone needs to sleep under bridges. Almost all laws create categories of individuals and actions, and treat them differently. State driver's license laws treat people different based on age: very young people and sometimes very old people are treated different than middle-aged people. Food stamp programs and Medicaid are means-tested programs: they limit benefits to individuals below certain income levels. Income tax rates vary according to income levels. Laws typically limit the rights of felons to vote, possess firearms, or hold certain kinds of jobs. Some government benefits are limited to veterans while others are limited to married people. Social security is an age and income based program. Medicaid is a program that provides benefits for the poor.

Equality is a political value with social, economic, political, and legal dimensions. The Equal Protection of the Laws is generally understood to require states to provide legal equality to all persons within their jurisdiction. Legal equality means equal standing before the law, but not social or economic equality. Equality does not mean that everyone must be treated the same. Laws create classifications that treat individuals different. In one sense, then, legislation discriminates by treating individuals and actions differently. This definition of discrimination or treating people different is not what is commonly understood as discrimination. Discrimination is usually used to mean prejudice or bias against individuals or groups based on inappropriate or invalid reasons. This is the pejorative meaning of discrimination. Discrimination also has a positive meaning whereby "to discriminate" means the ability to see or make fine distinctions among individuals, objects, values, or actions. It refers to making valid distinctions or differences between individuals.

18.53 | *Expanding federal civil rights law: the constitutional revolution of 1937*

As noted in the chapter on the judiciary, 1937 is an important date in U.S. constitutional history because the Court changed from protecting business from government regulation to protecting political liberties. During the latter part of the 19th Century and into the 1930s, the Supreme Court had struck down many federal and state laws that regulated business and economic activity because the Court saw its role as protecting business from government regulation. During the Great Depression, for example, the Court struck down some of the most important provisions of the Roosevelt Administration's New Deal legislation. The result was a constitutional conflict between the president, and the Court. President Roosevelt used his "bully pulpit" to take to the radio airwaves to blame the Court for not being a team player. Roosevelt's famous March 9, 1937 Fireside scolded the Court for not being part of the three-horse team that had to pull together if the country were to get out of the Great Depression.[3] Roosevelt also took action against the Court. He proposed a court-packing plan to increase the size of the Court to a maximum of fifteen Justices, with the additional six Justices expected to support the President's views on government power to regulate the economy because the President would nominate them. Against the background of these political pressures, the Court changed its rulings on the government's economic regulatory power. In late 1936, Justice Roberts, who had been voting with a conservative bloc of Justices who struck down the New Deal laws, changed sides and began to vote with the liberal bloc that upheld New Deal economic regulatory legislation. This was the constitutional revolution of 1937. Retirements eventually gave President Roosevelt the opportunity to change the ideological balance on the Court, and he appointed eight Justices during his terms in office. As a result, the Court changed its role from one that protected economic liberties from government regulation to one that protected political liberties. And one of the Court's special concerns was racial discrimination

18.54 | *Racial Classifications*

Dred Scott v. Sanford (1857) is a landmark Supreme Court case that is famous, or infamous, for its ruling limiting an individual slave's constitutional rights and Congress's power to limit slavery. Scott was a slave whose owner took him to Illinois and an area of the Louisiana Territory that prohibited slavery. Scott filed a lawsuit claiming that his residence in areas that prohibited slavery made him a free man. The Supreme Court ruled that Scott, as a slave, was not a citizen and could not go to court to claim that he was free. It also ruled the Missouri Compromise of 1820, which prohibited slavery in certain states, unconstitutional. The *Dred Scott* ruling made it clear that slavery was not likely to be resolved politically, and that a civil war was likely.[4]

The three constitutional amendments that were passed after the Civil War were intended to prohibit state action that discriminated against Blacks. Congress also passed civil rights statutes to promote racial equality. But in *The Civil Rights Cases* (1883), the Court greatly limited the federal government's power to regulate racial discrimination.[5] And in *Plessy v. Ferguson* (1896) the Court held that states could by law require racial segregation as long as the law did not treat one race better than another. This was the famous **Separate but Equal Doctrine** that allowed states to have racial segregation as a matter of public policy for schools, public accommodations, and other services and facilities. Justice Harlan's dissenting opinion in *Plessy* used memorable language to argue that racial segregation was unconstitutional: "Our Constitution is colorblind, and neither knows nor tolerates classes among citizens."[6] But the majority on the Court held that states could discriminate between blacks and whites, by requiring segregation, as long as the separation of the races did not include treating them unequally.

18.55 | *The Story of School Desegregation*

The story of school desegregation is a classic story of political litigation. Political litigation is the use of litigation to change public policy. Organizations such as the National Association for the Advancement of Colored People used the legal arena (courts) to get what they could not get in the political arena: desegregation of public schools. The state political systems that created racial segregation in public schools continued to support segregation despite political efforts advocating desegregation. As a result, advocates of desegregation went to the federal courts arguing that segregation violated the 14th Amendment's equal protection of the laws. The legal strategy worked. The Supreme Court began chipping away at the **Separate but Equal** doctrine. In *Missouri ex rel. Gaines v. Canada* (1938) the Court struck down a Missouri law that denied Blacks admission to the state's law school, but provided money for Blacks to attend out-of-state law schools. Then in 1950 (*Sweatt v. Painter*) the Court struck down a Texas law that created a separate law school for Blacks as a way to avoid having to admit a Black man to the University of Texas Law School. And on the same day that the Court decided, the Court decided *McLaurin v. Oklahoma State Regents* (1950) McLaurin was a Black man who was admitted to the University of Oklahoma's School of Education graduate school, but a state law required that he be segregated from other doctoral students: separate seating in the classroom; designated cafeteria table; separate library table. The Court ruled that this violated the equal protection of the laws because the treatment was separate but unequal. In these three cases the Court struck down the state segregated education policies because they did not provide separate but equal educational opportunities. The NAACP and other advocates of desegregation continued to target the separate but equal doctrine. Finally, in the landmark case of *Brown v. Board of Education* *of Topeka, Kansas* (1954), the Court ruled that de jure segregation in public schools, segregation by law, was unconstitutional. The separate but equal doctrine was itself unconstitutional.[7]

The *Brown* ruling was extremely controversial. Critics of Chief Justice Earl Warren put up "Save Our Republic: Impeach Earl Warren" highway billboards because Warren presided over a Court that issued a broad range of controversial rulings. It integrated public schools, and its school prayer rulings "kicked God out of" public schools. The backlash against these rulings included government officials who asserted states' rights to oppose expanded federal power over race relations. One classic statement of federalism-based states' rights opposition to *Brown v. Board* is the 1956 Southern Manifesto. Strong opposition to the *Brown* ruling prompted the Florida Legislature to pass an Interposition Resolution in 1957. Interposition is a Civil War-era doctrine that asserts that a state, as a sovereign entity in the U.S. system of federalism, has the power to "interpose" itself between the people of the state and the federal government whenever the state believes the federal action is unconstitutional. Interposition is a doctrine that gives states power to protect the people from unwarranted federal action.

At the time of the *Brown* ruling, William H. Rehnquist, who went on to become an Associate Justice and then Chief Justice of the Supreme Court, served as a law clerk to Justice Jackson. Rehnquist wrote a controversial *Memorandum* to Justice Jackson which concluded that the **Separate but Equal Doctrine** was still good law and should be upheld.[8] Rehnquist's understanding of the legislative history of the intentions of the Framers of the 14th Amendment may be accurate. And requiring racial segregation while treating the races equally, for example by requiring that blacks and whites sit in alternate rows rather than requiring blacks to sit in the back of the bus, may technically meet the "equal protection of the laws" standard. However, the history of separation was inequality. And the argument that the Constitution allows racial apartheid as long as the races are treated equally is no longer considered politically acceptable.

The *Brown* ruling did not order the immediate desegregation of public schools. The Court stated that the segregated school systems had to be dismantled "With all deliberate speed." Some states took advantage of this ambiguous phrase to choose deliberation rather than speed.[9] Beginning in the latter 1960s, after more than a decade of little or no action to dismantle the system of segregated public schools, courts began to order actions to integrate public schools. These actions included court-ordered busing, judicial drawing of school attendance zones, racial quotas, and affirmative action programs.

18.56 | *School busing*

Court rulings that ordered busing to dismantle segregated schools were always controversial, but court-ordered busing was especially controversial when it was used to remedy *de facto* racial segregation. *Brown* ruled *de jure* segregation unconstitutional. *De jure* segregation is segregation "by law." *De jure* segregation includes segregation that results from any government policy or official actions (such as drawing school attendance boundaries to produce racially segregated schools). *De facto* segregation is segregation that results "by fact." *De facto* segregation results from private actions such as housing patterns where people of one race or ethnicity or class decide to live with others of the same racial or ethnic or economic background and that just happens to result in segregation. As the country became more conservative during the latter 1970s and 1980s, public opposition to school busing and other race-based remedies for segregated schools increased. And in an interesting twist, conservatives turned to Justice Harlan's 19th Century ideal of a color blind Constitution, which he used to argue that state laws requiring racial segregation were unconstitutional, to argue that affirmative action policies, which take race into consideration when making school admissions decisions or employment decisions, are unconstitutional. Critics of affirmative action also oppose the recognition of group rights rather than individual rights. Indeed, the conservatives on the Rehnquist and Roberts Courts have been very skeptical of affirmative action and closely scrutinize affirmative action policies to determine whether they violate equal protection of the laws.[10]

> **Think About It!**
> Should college students have rights? The Foundation for Individual Rights in Education (FIRE) defends individual rights in higher education:
> http://thefire.org/

18.6 | Civil Rights: Employment

The civil rights movements also targeted employment discrimination. Efforts to expand equal opportunity in employment focused on personnel policies related to hiring, firing, and promotion; equal pay for equal work; and awarding business contracts to minority companies. One strategy was to use affirmative action to remedy past discriminatory practices and promote equality. The use of affirmative action to produce a more diverse work force, one that reflected the racial composition of the community was very controversial. Critics called the affirmative action use of racial or gender quotas or targets in employment settings reverse discrimination. As public support for using equal rights laws to promote greater equality in the workplace decreased, the courts limited the use of affirmative action policies particularly race-based policies.

The civil rights movement to end racial discrimination had one unintended negative consequence. Efforts to end racial segregation unintentionally contributed to the breakup of black economic communities that had developed in segregated areas. The end of *de jure* racial segregation meant that members of the black community were able to live in other neighborhoods and buy goods and services outside of the black business community. This is one of the reasons for the decline in the number of black-owned businesses since desegregation. For an interesting story about one black family's efforts to "Buy Black" for a year, see "One Family's Effort to Buy Black For a Year."

"One Family's Effort to Buy Black For a Year,"
PBS Newshour (June 19, 2012)
http://www.pbs.org/newshour/bb/business/jan-june12/makingsense_06-19.html

18.6 | Gender

Historically, government officials and private sector individuals (such as employers) were free to treat people differently based on gender. The Supreme Court did not examine gender-based legislative classifications until the 1970s. Prior to that time period, the Court did not consider laws that treated women different than men a violation of the Fourteenth Amendment. Gender discrimination was presumed to be constitutional. Laws that treated the "second" sex or the "weaker" sex different than the "first sex" or the "stronger" sex were presumed to reflect natural differences, social values, or public policy preferences. The policy preference for treating women and men differently was considered a matter of politics, not law, a question that was appropriate for the elected representatives of the people rather than the legal judgments of courts.

As a result, states historically used their policy making powers to pass laws that treated men and women different for purposes of voting, employment, education, social welfare benefits, jury duty, and other purposes. Some of these laws were **paternalistic** in the sense that they were intended to protect women. A good example of such a paternalistic law is the Oregon law that limited the hours that women could work in factories. The law was challenged in court but the Supreme Court upheld the law in _Muller v. Oregon_ (1908). Justice Brewer's opinion for the majority reflected the widely accepted belief that it was reasonable for a state legislature to think that women's physical constitution and the social role assigned to women in raising children might merit special protection in the workplace:

> "….That woman's physical structure and the performance of maternal functions place her at a disadvantage in the struggle for subsistence is obvious. This is especially true when the burdens of motherhood are upon her. Even when they are not, by abundant testimony of the medical fraternity, continuance for a long time on her feet at work, repeating this from day to day, tends to injurious effects upon the body, and, as healthy mothers are essential to vigorous offspring, the physical wellbeing of woman becomes an object of public interest and care in order to preserve the strength and vigor of the race. …[H]istory discloses the fact that woman has always been dependent upon man. He established his control at the outset by superior physical strength, and this control in various forms, with diminishing intensity, has continued to the present. As minors, though not to the same extent, she has been looked upon in the courts as needing especial care that her rights may be preserved…." [There are individual exceptions but women are generally not equal to men and are therefore properly placed in a class to be protected by legislation]. "It is impossible to close one's eyes to the fact that she still looks to her brother, and depends upon him. Even though all restrictions on political, personal, and contractual rights were taken away, and she stood, so far as statutes are concerned, upon an absolutely equal plane with him, it would still be true that she is so constituted that she will rest upon and look to him for protection; that her physical structure and a proper discharge of her maternal functions—having in view not merely her own health, but the

wellbeing of the race—justify legislation to protect her from the greed, as well as the passion, of man. The limitations which this statute places upon her contractual powers, upon her right to agree with her employer as to the time she shall labor, are not imposed solely for her benefit, but also largely for the benefit of all."

It is interesting to note that Justice Brewer described gender protective laws as benefiting women **and** society as a whole. This *gender difference rationale* reflected the conventional wisdom of the day and provided the justification for a broad range of public policies that treated women different than men. For instance, states prohibited women from serving on juries.[11] Equality does not mean treating everyone the same—but it does require having good reasons for treating people different. The black civil rights movement provided inspiration and energy for the women's rights movement. Gender discrimination was put on the government's agenda by the women's rights movement. The women's rights movement challenged traditional assumptions about how public policy could treat women different than men, lobbied for statutory laws that prohibited gender discrimination, advocated for an equal rights amendment to the U.S. Constitution, and adopted a legal strategy of political litigation that filed lawsuits that were intended to change public policy toward women.

In 1963 Congress amended the Fair Labor Standards Act to require equal pay for

> The 40th Anniversary of the 1972 Title IX Amendments marked an occasion to assess its impact on educational opportunity. One aspect of the changes is discussed in the National Public Radio report, "40 Years On, Title IX Still Shapes Female Athletes."
> *http://www.npr.org/2012/06/22/155529815/40-years-on-title-ix-still-shapes-female-athletes*

equal work. The Civil Rights Act of 1964 prohibited gender discrimination by employers and labor unions. Title VII of the Civil Rights Act of 1964 prohibits sexual harassment in the workplace. In 1972, the Civil Rights Act was amended to require in Title IX that all programs or activities, including educational institutions, provide equal athletic facilities and opportunities for women. Title IX had a major impact on women's opportunities. Compare the experience of Kathrine Switzer, who in 1967 was the first women to run in the Boston Marathon with women's opportunities 40 years after Title IX.

The women's movement also worked for passage of an Equal Rights Amendment. Congress proposed the ERA in 1972 but it was never ratified by the required three-quarters of the states. Only 35 of the required 38 states ratified the ERA.[12] The political litigation strategy was been successful. Court rulings limited gender discrimination. Women's rights advocates argued that courts should treat gender more like race when considering the enforcement of anti-discrimination laws. Doing so would make gender discrimination more like racial discrimination: a suspect classification. The Court did hold that the Fourteenth Amendment's equal protection clause applied to women, but it

Think about it! Are single-sex schools wise/constitutional?
http://www.npr.org/2011/10/25/141692830/are-single-sex-classrooms-better-for-kids

never accepted the argument that gender discrimination was analogous to racial discrimination. Unlike race-based legislative classifications, which are considered suspect classifications that trigger strict scrutiny, the Court has never considered gender classifications **suspect classifications** that trigger strict scrutiny.[13] But courts do closely scrutinize laws that treated people different based on gender, and fewer gender classifications are now considered constitutional. For example, in *U.S. v. Virginia* (1996) the Court ruled that it was unconstitutional for Virginia to create a separate female military institute as a remedy for a court-ordered finding that the state's male Virginia Military Institute violated the equal protection clause of the Fourteenth Amendment.

One interesting twist in the debates about racial and gender segregation in education is the recent emphasis on the quality of the education rather than racial or gender integration. Are single-sex schools wise (that is good educational policy)? Are they legal?

Gender equality is also an issue in the political and legal debates over abortion policy. The impact on women of state laws prohibiting abortion was a central issue in the decision to adopt a legal strategy to challenge abortion laws, a decision that resulted in the Roe v. Wade (1973) ruling that the right to privacy included the decision whether to continue or terminate a pregnancy.

Think About It! Act on It!
Can an individual make a difference by deciding to act on something they believe in? Listen to Sarah Weddington's story.
http://www.bbc.co.uk/programmes/p0133chj

18.7 | Other Legislative classifications

18.71 | *Alienage, Citizenship, and Personhood*

Most of the civil liberties provisions refer to "people" or "persons." The Fifth Amendment provides that no "person" shall be deprived of due process of law. The 14th Amendment prohibits states from denying "to any person" within its jurisdiction the equal protection of the laws. However, these constitutional provisions do not mean that citizens and non-citizens have the same constitutional rights. There are important differences between the rights of citizens and non-citizens because citizenship is a legal status that is relevant in many areas of law. Aliens do not have the same rights as citizens when aliens are entering the United States or when challenging the decision to be deported. Early in the nation's history, federal legislation targeted aliens, both alien enemies and alien friends. The Alien and Sedition Acts of 1798 are examples of early federal laws that not only treated aliens different than citizens but subjected aliens to harsh treatment. The Alien Act provided that in time of war or a threat against the territorial integrity of the U.S., the president could arrest and deport as "enemy aliens" any males 14 years or older who are citizens or residents of the "hostile" country.

For most of the 20th Century, immigration matters were entirely political in the sense that Congress had plenary power to determine immigration policy. However, as equality became a more important political value in American politics and as the various civil rights movements increased expectations of equality for more and more individuals in more and more settings, political and legal developments expanded the legal protections afforded aliens. In a 1971 case, _Graham v. Richardson_, the Court held that **alienage** was a suspect classification, and that an Arizona law that limited welfare benefits to citizens and created residency requirements for aliens violated the 14th Amendment provision that prohibited a state from denying to any person within its jurisdiction the equal protection of the laws. And in a 1982 case, _Plyler v. Doe_, the Court ruled that Texas could not deny public education to undocumented aliens.

But states were not required to treat aliens and non-residents the same as citizens who were residents of the state. A state can charge out-of-state individuals higher college tuition rates and higher fishing and hunting license fees for example. And states can require that individuals who hold certain public sector jobs (including teachers and police officers) be citizens. And states can restrict certain government benefits to citizens. In an interesting 2001 case dealing with a federal citizenship law that was based on both alienage and gender classification, the Court explained that the government had a valid legislative purpose when imposing different requirements for a child to become a citizen depending upon whether the citizen parent is the mother or the father. The law made it easier for a child to become a citizen if the mother was the citizen parent than if the father was the citizen parent. So public policy can make a distinction between a citizen mother and a citizen father. This is an example of how equality, and equal protection of the laws, does not mean treating everyone the same.[14]

18.72 | *Economic Classifications*

Public policies can also treat people different based on income without violating the equal protection of the laws. Public policies that provide government benefits (social security or Medicaid or food stamps) based on income create economic classifications. Tax policies may also treat people different based on income. Progressive income tax laws treat individuals different based on their income, with lower tax rates for lower income levels and higher rates for higher income levels. The history of the federal income tax shows how this occurs. In 1861, Congress passed an income tax law that established a flat 3% tax on incomes over $800. Since then, income tax law has incorporated graduated rates and even progressive tax rates. Inheritance taxes also typically treat estates different based on the size of the estate. For revealing insights into the political rhetoric of debates over estate taxes, read or listen to "How We Got from Estate Tax to 'Death Tax.'"

Most states have public school funding policies that rely heavily on property taxes. The result is large disparities in the amount of money available to school districts. School districts in rich communities have much more money than school districts in poor communities. Does this violate the 14th Amendment equal protection of the laws? The

San Antonio Independent School District filed a lawsuit on behalf of its poorer students arguing that Texas' property tax violated the equal protection of the laws. The Supreme Court disagreed, holding that the 14th Amendment does not require exactly equal funding of districts, that some funding disparities are legal. Most states do transfer some money from wealthier communities to poorer communities in order to reduce funding disparities. These Robin Hood policies of taking from the rich and giving to the poor are generally supported by liberals more than conservatives.

18.8 | Ways of Looking at Rights

18.81 | *"Conservative Rights" in a Conservative Era*

The story of civil rights is usually told as the story of liberals who used political litigation to achieve greater equality. In this conservative era in American politics, conservative civil rights and civil liberties movements advocate for *conservative* rights: the right to life (to define an unborn child or fetus as a person); property rights; gun rights; and religious rights. Like liberal public interest groups before them, conservative public interest groups adopted political and legal strategies to achieve their public policy goals. They used political litigation to challenge campaign finance regulations, zoning laws, and gun control laws. Some of these efforts have been very successful. The Roberts Court ruled that the Second Amendment does guarantee an individual right to keep and bear arms, defined campaign contributions as First Amendment freedom of expression, and weakened the distinction between economic and political liberties that conservatives believed relegated economic liberties to second-class status.

Think about it! Do you prefer the Florida and California Constitutional provisions for freedom of religion or the First Amendment to the U.S. Constitution?

18.82 | *Civil Liberties in State Constitutions*

In the U.S. system of federalism, civil rights and liberties are provided for in both state and federal law. The 50 state constitutions were modeled on the U.S. Constitution therefore some of the language and the rights in state constitutions resembles the provisions of the Bill of Rights. Article I of The Florida State Constitution, "Declaration of Rights," provides for civil liberties including freedom of religion, speech, press, and the right of privacy. However, the Florida Constitution provision for freedom of expression is very different than the First Amendment to the U.S. Constitution. And the California State Constitution is a very lengthy document: Article I "Declaration of Rights" provides a much more specific, detailed, and lengthy description of civil liberties than the U.S. Constitution's Bill of Rights.

18.9 | Internet Resources

An Overview of Civil Rights: http://topics.law.cornell.edu/wex/Civil_rights

The Freedom Riders: http://video.pbs.org/video/1930441944

Photographs of the Civil Rights Movement in Florida:
http://www.floridamemory.com/OnlineClassroom/PhotoAlbum/civil_rights.cfm

[1] http://religiousfreedom.lib.virginia.edu/court/us_v_ball.html

[2] See "Use of Wiccan Symbol on Veterans' Headstones Is Approved,"
http://www.nytimes.com/2007/04/24/washington/24wiccan.html

[3] Frankin D. Roosevelt's March 9, 1937 "Fireside Chat,"
http://www.presidency.ucsb.edu/ws/index.php?pid=15381#axzz1NlGuPlqw

[4] For additional information about Dred Scott, see http://www.pbs.org/wgbh/aia/part4/4p2932.html
http://www.oyez.org/cases/1851-1900/1856/1856_0

[5] http://www.law.cornell.edu/supct/html/historics/USSC_CR_0109_0003_ZS.html
http://www.oyez.org/cases/1851-1900/1882/1882_2

[6] See http://www.oyez.org/cases/1851-1900/1895/1895_210/
http://www.law.cornell.edu/supct/html/historics/USSC_CR_0163_0537_ZS.html

[7] The Missouri case is available at:
http://en.wikipedia.org/wiki/Missouri_ex_rel._Gaines_v._Canada
http://supreme.justia.com/us/305/337/case.html
The Texas case is available at:
http://www.oyez.org/cases/1940-1949/1949/1949_44
The Oklahoma case is available at:
http://www.law.cornell.edu/supct/html/historics/USSC_CR_0339_0637_ZS.html
The Kansas case is available at:
http://www.oyez.org/cases/1950-1959/1952/1952_1/

[8] http://www.nytimes.com/2005/09/11/weekinreview/11lipt.html
http://www.gpoaccess.gov/congress/senate/judiciary/sh99-1067/324-325.pdf

[9] http://americanhistory.si.edu/brown/history/6-legacy/deliberate-speed.html

[10] For recent rulings see *Gratz v. Bollinger* (2003)
http://www.oyez.org/cases/2000-2009/2002/2002_02_516; *Grutter v. Bollinger* (2003)
http://www.oyez.org/cases/2000-2009/2002/2002_02_241; *Meredith v. Jefferson County Board of Education* (2007); and recent rulings from Kentucky and Seattle, Washington
http://www.oyez.org/cases/2000-2009/2006/2006_05_915

[11] In *Hoyt v. Florida* (1961) the Court unanimously concluded that the equal protection clause did not prohibit the State of Florida from excluding women from jury duty. See
http://www.law.cornell.edu/supct/html/historics/USSC_CR_0368_0057_ZS.html

[12] http://www.equalrightsamendment.org/
http://www.law.umkc.edu/faculty/projects/ftrials/conlaw/nineteentham.htm

[13] See *Reed v. Reed* (1971). One of the lawyers who represented Sally Reed is Ruth Bader Ginsburg, who later became a Supreme Court Justice. Her personal employment experience, and her professional legal experience representing women in court, may explain her voting record as a Justice who is sympathetic to claims of gender discrimination in the workplace.
http://www.law.cornell.edu/supct/html/historics/USSC_CR_0404_0071_ZO.html
http://law.jrank.org/pages/13163/Reed-v-Reed.html

[14] *Nyugen v. Immigration and Naturalization Service* http://www.oyez.org/cases/2000-2009/2000/2000_99_2071